A Review of the Events of 1979

The 1980 World Book Year Book

World Book–Childcraft International, Inc.
A subsidiary of The Scott & Fetzer Company

Chicago London Paris Sydney Tokyo Toronto

Staff

Editorial Director
William H. Nault

Editorial Staff
Executive Editor
Wayne Wille

Managing Editor
Paul C. Tullier

Chief Copy Editor
Joseph P. Spohn

Senior Editors
Patricia Dragisic
Marsha F. Goldsmith
Beverly Merz
Jay Myers
Edward G. Nash

Copy Editor
Irene B. Keller

Senior Index Editor
Marilyn Boerding

Chief Statistical Editor
Robert Gauron

Editorial Assistant
Madelyn Krzak

**Executive Editor,
The World Book Encyclopedia**
A. Richard Harmet

Art Staff
Executive Art Director
William Dobias

Art Director
Roberta Dimmer

Senior Artists
Joe W. Gound
Stanley A. Schrero

Artist
Edmond Fenech

Senior Designer
Bernard Arendt

Photography Director
Fred C. Eckhardt, Jr.

Photographer
Stephen Hale

Photo Editing Director
Ann Eriksen

Senior Photographs Editors
Karen Koblik
John S. Marshall
Carol A. Parden
Paul Quirico
Jo Anne M. Ticzkus

Research and Services
Head, Editorial Research
Jo Ann McDonald

Senior Researcher
Robert Hamm

Head, Research Library
Indrani Embar

Head, Cartographic Services
H. George Stoll

Product Production
Executive Director
Philip B. Hall

Director of Manufacturing
Joseph C. LaCount

Director of Pre-Press
J. J. Stack

Manager, Composition
John Babrick

Product Managers
Sandra Grebenar
Barbara Podczerwinski

Manager, Film Separations
Alfred J. Mozdzen

Assistant Manager, Film Separations
Barbara J. McDonald

Manager, Research and Development
Henry Koval

Preface

The 1979 meeting of the YEAR BOOK Board of Editors was very different from the preceding 17 annual sessions. When the board met in New York City late in the year, long-familiar faces were missing, new ones were there, and the goal was to produce one major interpretative article for the Year in Focus section. The result is the thought-provoking article "How Much Freedom? How Much Control?" that begins on page 24. Like the Focus section in previous editions of THE YEAR BOOK, the article analyzes some of the major events and trends of the year. But the analysis is now in the form of a group discussion by the board members, rather than individual articles as in the past. The new approach does away with the previous restrictions of category and space, and the reader is—in effect—sitting in on the discussion, getting a variety of opinions on the subjects, seeing how events interrelate, and gaining insights into some of the important issues of the day.

In addition to the new format, there are two new members on the board. They are James J. Kilpatrick and Carl T. Rowan, widely syndicated newspaper columnists who also are frequent guests on television discussion programs. These two authoritative journalists joined three long-time board members—Harrison Brown, Lawrence A. Cremin, and Sylvia Porter—for the Focus discussion. We miss our four friends who have retired from the board—Alistair Cooke, John Holmes, James Reston, and Red Smith—but we are sure you will agree that the new members carry on the fine Focus tradition they helped to establish.   WAYNE WILLE

James J. Kilpatrick, left, and Carl T. Rowan join the YEAR BOOK Board of Editors in the Focus discussion of inflation, energy, and leadership.

Contents

A tear-out page of cross-reference tabs for insertion in THE WORLD BOOK ENCYCLOPEDIA appears after page 16.

Contributors

Contributors not listed on these pages are members of THE WORLD BOOK YEAR BOOK editorial staff.

Adachi, Ken, M.A.; Literary Editor, *The Toronto Star.* [LITERATURE, CANADIAN]

Adams, T. W., Ph.D.; Director General, Tecno Asesores, S.A. [CUBA; MEXICO]

Alexander, George, B.S.J.; Science Writer, *Los Angeles Times.* [Special Report: DO YOU MAKE CAGE CALLS, DOCTOR?]

Alexiou, Arthur G., M.S.; E.E.; Associate Director, Office of Sea Grant. [OCEAN]

Anderson, Leo S., B.A.; Editor, *Telephony Magazine.* [COMMUNICATIONS]

Anderson, Virginia E., B.A.; M.S.W.; Free-Lance Writer. [COMMUNITY ORGANIZATIONS; HANDICAPPED; NATIONAL PTA (NATIONAL CONGRESS OF PARENTS AND TEACHERS); SOCIAL SECURITY WELFARE; YOUTH ORGANIZATIONS]

Antonini, Gustavo A., B.S., M.A., Ph.D.; Professor of Latin American Studies and Geography, Director of Professional Training, Association of Caribbean Universities and Research Institutes, Kingston, Jamaica. [WORLD BOOK SUPPLEMENT: DOMINICA; ROSEAU]

Araujo, Paul E., Ph.D.; Assistant Professor of Human Nutrition, University of Florida. [NUTRITION]

Asimov, Isaac, B.S., M.A., Ph.D.; Author; Professor of Biochemistry, Boston University School of Medicine. [Special Report: CALL IT SF OR SCI-FI, IT'S BIG!]

Banovetz, James M., Ph.D.; Chairman, Department of Political Science, Northern Illinois University. [CITY; City Articles; HOUSING]

Barabba, Vincent P., M.B.A.; Director, U.S. Bureau of the Census. [CENSUS]

Barber, Margaret, B.A.; M.L.S.; Director, Public Information Office, American Library Association. [AMERICAN LIBRARY ASSOCIATION]

Beaumont, Lynn, Member, Tourism Advisory Board, New School for Social Research. [TRAVEL]

Beckwith, David C., J.D.; Managing Editor, *Legal Times of Washington.* [COURTS AND LAWS; CRIME; PRISON; SUPREME COURT]

Benson, Barbara N., A.B., M.S., Ph.D.; Assistant Professor, Biology, Cedar Crest College. [BOTANY; ZOOLOGY]

Berkwitt, George J., B.S.J.; Chief Editor, *Industrial Distribution Magazine.* [MANUFACTURING]

Bornstein, Leon, B.A., M.A.; Labor Economist, U.S. Dept. of Labor [LABOR]

Boyum, Joy Gould, Ph.D.; Professor of English, New York University. [MOTION PICTURES]

Bradsher, Henry S., A.B., B.J.; Foreign Affairs Writer, *Washington Star.* [Asian Country Articles]

Brown, Kenneth, Editor, *United Kingdom Press Gazette* [EUROPE and European Country Articles]

Cain, Charles C., III, B.A.; Automotive Editor, Associated Press. [AUTOMOBILE]

Carlson, Eric D., Ph.D.; Senior Astronomer, Adler Planetarium. [ASTRONOMY]

Clark, Phil, B.A.; Free-Lance Garden and Botanical Writer. [GARDENING]

Cook, Robert C., former President, Population Reference Bureau. [POPULATION]

Cromie, William J., B.S.; Executive Director, Council for the Advancement of Science Writing. [SPACE EXPLORATION; Special Report: UNLOCKING THE SECRETS OF THE SEVEN SEAS]

Csida, June Bundy, former Radio-TV Editor, *Billboard* Magazine. [RADIO; TELEVISION]

Cuscaden, Rob, Editor, *Home Improvement Contractor Magazine.* [ARCHITECTURE]

Cviic, Chris, B.A., B.Sc.; Editorial Staff, *The Economist.* [Eastern European Country Articles]

Dale, Edwin L., Jr., B.A.; Writer, Business Analyst. [INTERNATIONAL TRADE AND FINANCE]

Deffeyes, Kenneth S., M.S.E., Ph.D.; Professor of Geology, Princeton University. [GEOLOGY]

DeFrank, Thomas J., B.A.; M.A.; White House Correspondent, *Newsweek.* [ARMED FORCES]

Delaune, Lynn de Grummond, M.A.; Assistant Professor, College of William and Mary; Author. [LITERATURE FOR CHILDREN]

Derickson, Ralph Wayne, Public Information Associate, Council of State Governments. [STATE GOVERNMENT]

Dernberger, Robert F., B.A., M.A., Ph.D.; Professor of Economics, University of Michigan. [WORLD BOOK SUPPLEMENT: CHINA]

Dewald, William G., Ph.D.; Professor of Economics, Ohio State University. [Finance Articles]

Diamond, Norma, Ph.D.; Professor of Anthropology, University of Michigan. [WORLD BOOK SUPPLEMENT: CHINA]

Dixon, Gloria Ricks, B.A.; Director of Public Affairs/Education, Magazine Publishers Association. [MAGAZINE]

Dodson, Peter, B.Sc., M.Sc., Ph.D.; Assistant Professor of Anatomy, School of Veterinary Medicine, University of Pennsylvania. [WORLD BOOK SUPPLEMENT: DINOSAUR]

Eaton, William J., B.S.J., M.S.J.; Washington Correspondent, *Los Angeles Times.* [U.S. Political Articles]

Edwards, Richard, Ph.D.; Professor of Chinese Art, University of Michigan. [WORLD BOOK SUPPLEMENT: CHINA]

Esseks, John D., Ph.D.; Associate Professor of Political Science, Northern Illinois University. [AFRICA and African Country Articles]

Farr, David M. L., D.Phil.; Professor of History and Director, Paterson Centre for International Programs, Carleton University, Ottawa. [CANADA and Canadian Province Articles; DEATHS OF NOTABLE PERSONS (Close-Up); SCHREYER, EDWARD RICHARD]

Feather, Leonard, Author, Broadcaster, Composer. [MUSIC, POPULAR; RECORDINGS]

Feuerwerker, Albert, A.B., Ph.D.; Director, Center for Chinese Studies, and Professor of History, University of Michigan. [WORLD BOOK SUPPLEMENT: CHINA]

French, Charles E., Ph.D.; Study Director, President's Reorganization Project. [FARM AND FARMING]

Gayn, Mark, B.S.; Member, Editorial Board, *The Toronto Star;* Author. [ASIA and Asian Country Articles]

Goldner, Nancy, B.A.; Critic, *Dance News, The Nation and Christian Science Monitor* [DANCING]

Goldstein, Jane, B.A.; Publicity Director, Santa Anita Park. [HORSE RACING]

Goy, Robert W., Ph.D.; Director, Wisconsin Regional Primate Research Center, Professor of Psychology, University of Wisconsin. [PSYCHOLOGY]

Graham, Jarlath J., B.A.; Director of Editorial Development, *Advertising Age.* [ADVERTISING]

Griffin, Alice, Ph.D.; Professor of English, Lehman College, City University of New York. [THEATER]

Gwynne, Peter, M.A.; Science Editor, *Newsweek.* [ENERGY (Close-Up)]

Hales, Dianne Rafalik, B.A., M.S.; Editor/Writer. [HEALTH AND DISEASE; HOSPITAL; MEDICINE; MENTAL HEALTH; PUBLIC HEALTH]

Hechinger, Fred M., B.A. Vice-President, *The New York Times* Company Foundation, Inc. [EDUCATION]

Jacobi, Peter P., B.S.J., M.S.J.; Professor, Medill School of Journalism, Northwestern University. [MUSIC, CLASSICAL]

Jessup, Mary E., B.A.; former News Editor. *Civil Engineering* Magazine. [BUILDING AND CONSTRUCTION; DRUGS; STEEL]

Joseph, Lou, B.A.; Manager, Media Relations, American Dental Association. [DENTISTRY]

Kaiman, Arnold G., M.A., D.D.; Rabbi, Congregation Kol Ami. [JEWS AND JUDAISM]

Karr, Albert R., M.S.; Reporter, *The Wall Street Journal.* [TRANSPORTATION and Transportation Articles]

Kind, Joshua B., Ph.D.; Associate Professor of Art History, Northern Illinois University; Author, *Rouault;* Contributing Editor, *New Art Examiner.* [VISUAL ARTS]

Kisor, Henry, B.A., M.S.J.; Book Editor, *Chicago Sun-Times.* [LITERATURE]

Kitchen, Paul, B.A., B.L.S.; Executive Director, Canadian Library Association. [CANADIAN LIBRARY ASSOCIATION]

Koenig, Louis W., Ph.D., L.H.D.; Professor of Government, New York University; Author, *Bryan: A Political Biography of William Jennings Bryan.* [CIVIL RIGHTS]

Langdon, Robert, Executive Officer, Pacific Manuscripts Bureau, Australian National University, [PACIFIC ISLANDS; WORLD BOOK SUPPLEMENT: FUNAFUTI; SOLOMON ISLANDS; TUVALU]

Levy, Emanuel, B.A., Editor, *Insurance Advocate.* [INSURANCE]

Lewis, Ralph H., M.A.; Volunteer, Division of Museum Services, National Park Service. [MUSEUMS]

Litsky, Frank, B.S.; Assistant Sports Editor, *The New York Times.* [Sports Articles]

Livingston, Kathryn, B.A., Senior Editor, *Town and Country.* [FASHION]

Maki, John M., Ph.D.; Professor of Political Science, University of Massachusetts. [JAPAN]

Martin, Everett G., A.B.; Latin American Correspondent. *The Wall Street Journal.* [LATIN AMERICA and Latin American Country Articles]

Marty, Martin E., Ph.D.; Fairfax M. Cone Distinguished Service Professor, University of Chicago. [PROTESTANTISM; RELIGION; RELIGION (Close-Up)]

Mather, Ian, M.A.; Defense and Diplomatic Correspondent, *The Observer* (London). [GREAT BRITAIN; GREAT BRITAIN (Close-Up); IRELAND; NORTHERN IRELAND]

Mathews, Thomas G.; B.A., M.A., Ph.D.; Research Professor, Institute of Caribbean Studies, University of Puerto Rico. [WORLD BOOK SUPPLEMENT: SAINT LUCIA]

Miller, J.D.B., M.Ec.; Professor of International Relations, Australian National University [AUSTRALIA]

Miller, Julie Ann, Ph.D.; Life Sciences Editor, *Science News.* [BIOCHEMISTRY; BIOLOGY]

Mullen, Frances A., Ph.D.; Secretary General, International Council of Psychologists, Inc. [CHILD WELFARE]

Munro, Donald J., A.B.; Ph.D.; Professor of Philosophy, University of Michigan. [WORLD BOOK SUPPLEMENT: CHINA]

Murphey, Rhoads, A.B., M.A., Ph.D.; Professor of Geography, University of Michigan. [WORLD BOOK SUPPLEMENT: CHINA]

Murray, G.E., M.A.; Poetry Columnist; Free-Lance Writer. [POETRY]

Nelson, Larry L., Ph.D.; President, Snyder Associates, Inc. [FARM AND FARMING]

Newman, Andrew L., M.A.; Information Officer, U.S. Department of the Interior. [CONSERVATION; ENVIRONMENT; FISHING; FISHING INDUSTRY; FOREST AND FOREST PRODUCTS; HUNTING; INDIAN, AMERICAN; WATER]

Oatis, William N., United Nations Correspondent, The Associated Press. [UNITED NATIONS]

Offenheiser, Marilyn J., B.S.; Free-Lance Writer. [ELECTRONICS]

O'Leary, Theodore M., B.A.; Special Correspondent, *Sports Illustrated* Magazine. [BRIDGE, CONTRACT; CAT; CHESS; COIN COLLECTING; DOG; GAMES, MODELS, AND TOYS; HOBBIES; STAMP COLLECTING]

Parke, Jo Anne, B.A.; Author; Journalist. [Special Report: THE CULT QUESTION: NO EASY ANSWERS]

Pawelek, Richard, B.A.; Managing Editor, *Senior Scholastic* Magazine. [Special Report: HOW POLLSTERS TAKE THE PULSE OF POLITICS]

Pearl, Edward W., Meteorologist, Geophysical Research and Development Corporation. [WEATHER]

Plog, Fred, Ph.D.; Professor of Anthropology, Arizona State University. [ANTHROPOLOGY; ARCHAEOLOGY]

Poli, Kenneth, Editor, *Popular Photography.* [PHOTOGRAPHY]

Price, Frederick C., B.S., Ch.E.; Free-Lance Writer. [CHEMICAL INDUSTRY]

Rabb, George B., Ph.D.; Director, Chicago Zoological Park. [ZOOS AND AQUARIUMS]

Rocheleau, Dianne E., Research Scholar in Caribbean Geography, University of Florida. [WORLD BOOK SUPPLEMENT: DOMINICA; ROSEAU]

Rowse, Arthur E., I.A., M.B.A.; President, Consumer News, Inc. [CONSUMER AFFAIRS]

Schmemann, Alexander, S.T.D., D.D., LL.D., Th.D.; Dean, St. Vladimir's Orthodox Theological Seminary, New York. [EASTERN ORTHODOX CHURCHES]

Shand, David, A., B.C.A., B.C.M.; Senior Lecturer, Australian National University. [NEW ZEALAND]

Shaw, Robert James, B.S., B.A.; former Editor, *Library Technology Reports,* American Library Association. [LIBRARY]

Shearer, Warren W., Ph.D., J.D.; former Chairman, Department of Economics, Wabash College. [ECONOMICS]

Sheerin, John B., C.S.P., A.B., M.A., LL.D., J.D.; General Consultor, American Bishops' Secretariat for Catholic-Jewish Relations. [ROMAN CATHOLIC CHURCH]

Skalka, Patricia, B.A.; Free-Lance Writer. [Special Report: HELP AND HOPE FROM HYPNOSIS]

Spencer, William, Ph.D.; Professor of Middle East History, Florida State University; Author, *Land and People of Algeria.* [MIDDLE EAST and Middle Eastern Country Articles; North Africa Country Articles]

Stockwell, Foster P., B.A.; Free-Lance Writer. [NOBEL PRIZES; SAFETY; SCIENCE AND RESEARCH]

Stoner, Carroll, B.A.; Associate Feature Editor, *Chicago Sun-Times.* [Special Report: THE CULT QUESTION: NO EASY ANSWERS]

Summers, Larry V., Ph.D.; Agricultural Economist, U.S. Department of Agriculture. [FOOD]

Thompson, Carol L., M.A.; Editor, *Current History* Magazine. [U.S. Government Articles]

Thompson, Ida, Ph.D.; Assistant Professor, Department of Geological and Geophysical Sciences, Princeton University. [PALEONTOLOGY]

Tiegel, Eliot, B.A.; Managing Editor, *Billboard Magazine.* [MUSIC, POPULAR RECORDINGS]

Ting, William Pang-yu, Ph.D.; Assistant Professor of Political Science, University of Michigan. [WORLD BOOK SUPPLEMENT: CHINA]

Verbit, Lawrence, Ph.D.; Professor of Chemistry, State University of New York. [CHEMISTRY]

White, Thomas O., Ph.D.; Lecturer in Physics, Cambridge University, Cambridge, England. [PHYSICS]

Woods, Michael, B.S.; Science Editor, *The Toledo Blade.* [COAL; ENERGY; MINES AND MINING; PETROLEUM AND GAS]

Chronology

1975
1976
1977
1978
1979

A month-by-month listing highlights some of
the significant events of 1979.

See November 4, page 20.

Jan. 6

Jan. 12

January

	1	2	3	4	5	6
7	8	9	10	11	12	13
14	15	16	17	18	19	20
21	22	23	24	25	26	27
28	29	30	31			

1 **United States formally opens** diplomatic relations with the People's Republic of China and ends its ties with Taiwan's Chinese Nationalist government.
China adopts Pinyin phonetic alphabet. In the new system, Peking becomes Beijing, and Teng Hsiao-p'ing becomes Deng Xiaoping.

4 **Shah Mohammad Reza Pahlavi** appoints Shahpour Bakhtiar prime minister of Iran.

6 **The new U.S.-China relationship** will not harm détente with Russia, say leaders of France, Great Britain, the United States, and West Germany, meeting in Guadeloupe.

7-8 **Phnom Penh falls** to Cambodian rebels and Vietnamese troops, who name Heng Samrin president, replacing Communist Party Secretary and Prime Minister Pol Pot.

8 **John W. Gacy, Jr., is indicted** for seven murders. Police eventually dig up 29 bodies buried under his home in a Chicago suburb and recover four more from nearby rivers.

10 **West German steelworkers** approve new contract and end 44-day strike.

World's highest inflation rate in 1978 was Argentina's 169.8 per cent, the National Statistics Institute reports.

11 **"Overwhelming evidence"** links cigarette smoking to cancer, heart and lung disease, and other illnesses, says the U.S. surgeon general in a 1,200-page report.

12 **Record blizzard** strikes the U.S. Midwest, killing more than 100 persons.
Bella S. Abzug is fired by President Jimmy Carter as co-chairman of his National Advisory Committee on Women.

16 **Shah Mohammad Reza Pahlavi leaves Iran** on "vacation."

17 **Greenland voters approve home rule.**

21 **The Pittsburgh Steelers** defeat the Dallas Cowboys, 35-31, in football's Super Bowl.

22 **New York City enters** the public credit market for the first time since 1975, selling $125 million in short-term notes.
A $29-billion deficit is proposed in President Carter's "lean and austere" 1980 budget.

23 **State of the Union message** by President Carter outlines a "new foundation" for controlling inflation and armaments.

24 **John B. Connally announces his candidacy** for the 1980 Republican presidential nomination.

25 **Major Canadian confederation changes** are recommended by the Task Force on Canadian Unity.

27 **Pope John Paul II** opens a bishops' conference in Mexico City, Mexico, on his first papal trip abroad.

29 **British truckdrivers end strike,** accept a 20.75 per cent pay increase.

Feb. 1

Feb. 5

Feb. 5

February

				1	2	3
4	5	6	7	8	9	10
11	12	13	14	15	16	17
18	19	20	21	22	23	24
25	26	27	28			

1 **Ayatollah Ruhollah Khomeini returns** to Iran after 15 years in exile, calls the government "illegal."
Patricia Hearst is released from prison under a presidential executive-clemency order.

5 **Three thousand farmers** march on Washington, D.C., to demand higher price supports.
Teng Hsaio-p'ing (Deng Xiaoping), China's deputy premier, ends a nine-day official visit to the U.S., the first by a Chinese Communist leader. His trip included a tour of a Ford Motor Company plant (pictured above).

6 **Carter assures Thailand** that the U.S. is committed to the integrity of its borders.
Floods kill 700 persons and leave 350,000 homeless in Brazil after 42 days of rain.

7 **Algeria elects** Chadli Bendjedid president.

10 **Pakistan's president institutes** the law of Islam.

11 **Iran's Prime Minister Bakhtiar is ousted.** Mehdi Bazargan, selected six days earlier by Ruhollah Khomeini, succeeds him.

Tanzanian forces and Ugandan exiles invade Uganda, according to President Idi Amin of Uganda.

14 **U.S. Ambassador** to Afghanistan Adolph Dubs is abducted and killed by Muslim extremists.
Mexico's president criticizes U.S. petroleum and immigration policies during President Carter's visit to Mexico City.
Three Cuban exiles are convicted in Washington, D.C., of the 1976 murder of former Chilean ambassador Orlando Letelier.

17 **China invades Vietnam.**

18 **Russia warns China** to stop its Vietnam invasion "before it is too late."

18-19 **Blizzard dumps** 20 inches (51 centimeters) of snow on Baltimore, leading to heavy looting.

20 **Ice clogs the Great Lakes** for the first time in recorded history, says the U.S. Coast Guard.

21 **The National Organization for Women** may boycott conventions in states that have not ratified the Equal Rights Amendment, a U.S. district court declares.
Volcano erupts in Java, killing 175 persons.

27 **New Orleans police strike** dims Mardi Gras celebration as festivities move to the suburbs.
Chicago Mayor Michael A. Bilandic loses to Jane M. Byrne in the Democratic primary election.

28 **Ugandan rebels** and Tanzanian troops advance on Kampala, the capital of Uganda.
U.S. television viewing is declining, according to a *Washington Post* survey.

March 26

March

				1	2	3
4	5	6	7	8	9	10
11	12	13	14	15	16	17
18	19	20	21	22	23	24
25	26	27	28	29	30	31

1 **Spain's ruling party wins** parliamentary elections.
 Wales home-rule bill loses. The vote on a similar bill in Scotland is favorable, but voter turnout is too low for approval.

2 **A 5 per cent decrease in 1979 oil demand** is agreed upon by the United States and 19 other industrial countries.

5 *Voyager 1* comes within 172,000 miles (278,000 kilometers) of Jupiter and sends back spectacular photographs.
 China announces troop withdrawals from Vietnam.

6 **Vietnam agrees** to allow citizens to emigrate to countries that will accept them.

8 **France suspends reorganization** of its steel industry after violent protests by workers fearing layoffs.

8-12 **Thousands of Iranian women protest** against government restriction of their rights.

8-13 **Egypt and Israel accept** President Carter's compromise proposals, paving the way for a peace treaty.

9 **A federal judge restrains** *Progressive* magazine from publishing an article about the workings of the hydrogen bomb.

13 **Nuclear Regulatory Commission closes** five nuclear power plants on the East Coast because of questionable protection against earthquakes.
 The European Monetary System takes effect among Common Market countries.

16 **Chad civil war ends** as the government agrees to a coalition with Muslim rebels.

20 **New Italian government** is formed with Giulio Andreotti as prime minister, but it falls 11 days later in a no-confidence vote.

26 **Egypt and Israel sign a treaty** in Washington, D.C., ending nearly 31 years of war.

27 **Oil price is raised** 9 per cent by the Organization of Petroleum Exporting Countries (OPEC).

28 **Great Britain's government falls** after losing a vote of confidence.
 Accident at Three Mile Island nuclear reactor in Pennsylvania arouses fears of major loss of lfe.

30 **Ireland ends its currency's link** with the British pound.

30-31 **Iranians vote** in favor of a Muslim republic.

31 **Economic boycott of Egypt** is approved by ministers of 18 Arab League countries and the Palestine Liberation Organization (PLO).

April 3

April 16

April 9

April 24

April

1	2	3	4	5	6	7
8	9	10	11	12	13	14
15	16	17	18	19	20	21
22	23	24	25	26	27	28
29	30					

3 **Jane M. Byrne is elected** mayor of Chicago with 82.5 per cent of the vote, the highest since 1901.

4 **Greece agrees to join** the European Community (EC or Common Market) on Jan. 1, 1981.
Pakistan hangs former Prime Minister Zulfikar Ali Bhutto for conspiracy in a 1974 murder.

5 **Carter orders gradual decontrol** of domestic oil prices and proposes tax on windfall profits.

6 **U.S. withdraws aid** from Pakistan because it is secretly building a uranium-enrichment plant that can produce atomic bomb material.

7 **Iran executes** former Prime Minister Amir Abbas Hoveyda for "crimes against the nation."

9 *Deer Hunter,* a film about the Vietnam War, wins Oscar as the best picture. Awards for best actress and best actor go to Jane Fonda and Jon Voight.
Three Mile Island "crisis is over," says the federal official investigating the accident.

10 **U.S. and Taiwan** establish unofficial relations.

Ten-day U.S. Teamsters truck strike and lockout ends.

11 **Ugandan capital falls** to rebels and Tanzanians, who install Yusufu K. Lule as head of government.

12 **International tariff agreement** is initialed after 5½ years of negotiations, but developing countries maintain that industrialized nations did not make promised concessions.

13 **Boston University faculty strike** ends after nine days, the first such action against a major U.S. university.

16 **Bill Rodgers wins** second straight Boston Marathon in 2 hours 9 minutes 27 seconds. Joan Benoit leads the women, in 2:35.15.

18 **Journalists sued for libel** must answer questions about their "state of mind" when they prepared allegedly libelous material, the Supreme Court rules.
Lebanese Christian militia group secedes, declares a strip of land 6 miles (10 kilometers) wide along the Israeli border independent.

24 **Rhodesia elects Abel T. Muzorewa** its first black prime minister. His party wins 51 of 100 seats in parliament.
Robert S. Strauss is named U.S. ambassador-at-large for talks on Palestinian autonomy.

26 **Smoking is declining** among 12- to 18-year-olds, reports Secretary of Health, Education, and Welfare Joseph A. Califano, Jr.

27 **United States exchanges two Russian spies** for five Russian dissidents.

CANADA

May 22

May 3

May 25

May

		1	2	3	4	5
6	7	8	9	10	11	12
13	14	15	16	17	18	19
20	21	22	23	24	25	26
27	28	29	30	31		

2 **Great Britain reaches a wage settlement** with unions representing about 600,000 civil-service workers.

3 **Margaret Thatcher becomes** prime minister of Great Britain, the first woman to hold the post.

6 **About 65,000 persons demonstrate** against nuclear power in Washington, D.C.
Bruno Kreisky wins a record fourth term as Austria's chancellor.
China cuts back its economic development program.

9 **California starts rationing** gasoline on an odd-even license-plate plan.
Italy mobilizes its army to curb terrorism.

10 **Carter's standby gasoline-rationing plan** is rejected by the House of Representatives.

14 **Suits for sex bias** against educational institutions that receive federal funds get go-ahead from Supreme Court.

15 **U.S. Senate** says it wants economic sanctions against Rhodesia ended.

15-16 **International meeting** in Jakarta, Indonesia, discusses Indochinese refugee problem.

18 **Jury awards $10.5 million** in damages to the estate of Karen Silkwood, a laboratory technician contaminated by radiation while working at a Kerr-McGee plutonium plant.

19 **Greek and Turkish Cypriots agree** to discuss reunification for the first time since 1977.
Jordan rejects Israel's offer to negotiate a peace treaty.

20 **Swiss voters approve** tight controls on the nuclear industry and reject a value-added tax.

21 **Montreal Canadiens win** the Stanley Cup for the fourth straight year, defeating the New York Rangers.

22 **Joseph Clark** becomes Canada's youngest prime minister as Progressive Conservative Party ends Pierre Elliott Trudeau's 11-year tenure.

23 **Karl Carstens,** a former Nazi, is elected president of West Germany.
El Salvador's minister of education is assassinated. The government suspends constitutional rights.

25 **DC-10 jet crashes** in Chicago, killing all 272 persons aboard and two on the ground in America's worst air disaster.
Florida electrocutes John A. Spenkelink, the first execution in the United States since 1977.
Israel begins withdrawal from the Sinai Peninsula.

31 **Rhodesia gets black-majority rule** and changes its name to Zimbabwe Rhodesia.

June 18

June 3

June

					1	2
3	4	5	6	7	8	9
10	11	12	13	14	15	16
17	18	19	20	21	22	23
24	25	26	27	28	29	30

2-10   **Pope John Paul II visits** his native Poland in the first papal journey to a Communist country.

3   **Oil well blows out** off Mexico's Yucatán Peninsula and creates a giant oil slick.

3-4   **Communists suffer major losses** in Italian elections for the first time in 30 years.

4   **Frederick William Kwasi Akuffo** is ousted as Ghana's head of state.

Balthazar Johannes Vorster resigns as South Africa's president after an official report charges him with covering up a secret government fund scandal.

5   **Veterans' job preference** in public-service employment is upheld by the U.S. Supreme Court.

6   **All U.S. DC-10s** are grounded because of the May 25 crash in Chicago.

Nicaraguan state of siege is declared as President Anastasio Somoza Debayle acts against general strike and guerrilla fighting.

7   **Carlos da Mota Pinto resigns** as Portugal's prime minister following a censure motion protesting his 1979 budget proposal.

7-10   **European Parliament** is chosen by citizens of EC countries in the first direct elections to an international body.

13   **Sioux Nation is awarded** $105 million to compensate for the confiscation of the Black Hills of South Dakota in 1877.

16   **Ghana executes** former head of state Ignatius Kutu Acheampong for fostering corruption.

18   **Salt II** arms-limitation treaty is signed in Vienna, Austria, by President Carter and Russia's Chairman Leonid I. Brezhnev.

20   **House of Representatives** holds a closed session for the first time since 1830, to hear a statement about Panama's alleged part in the Nicaraguan rebellion.

Godfrey L. Binaisa replaces President Yusufu Lule in Uganda after a no-confidence vote in the country's temporary parliament.

21   **Quebec sovereignty** referendum is set for the spring of 1980.

22   **Jeremy Thorpe,** a former leader of Great Britain's Liberal Party, is acquitted of conspiracy to murder.

26   **Ghana executes** former heads of state Akuffo and Akwasi A. Afrifa for using their positions to accumulate personal wealth.

27   **Employers and unions may use quotas** to help women and minority workers get jobs, the U.S. Supreme Court decides. Brian F. Weber, a white, had challenged a training program that favored blacks.

28   **OPEC increases oil prices** by 24 per cent to a minimum of $18 and a maximum of $23.50 per barrel.

Number of Indochinese refugees admitted to the United States is increased from 7,000 to 14,000 per month.

July 17

July 19 and 20

July 17

July

1	2	3	4	5	6	7
8	9	10	11	12	13	14
15	16	17	18	19	20	21
22	23	24	25	26	27	28
29	30	31				

2   **Russia increases prices** of luxury items up to 50 per cent.

6-7   **Martina Navratilova and Bjorn Borg repeat** as Wimbledon tennis title winners.

6-8   **PLO leader Yasir Arafat** meets Austria's Chancellor Bruno Kreisky in Vienna in his first reception by a Western European head of government.

10   **Carter orders that temperatures** of commercial and public buildings be held no lower than 78°F.(25.5°C) in summer to save energy.

11   **U.S. space station** *Skylab* **falls** to earth in the Indian Ocean and Australia, but no injuries result.

13   **Flight ban is lifted on DC-10s.**

15   **President Carter proposes** a $140-billion energy program in a nationally broadcast speech after 10 days of conferences with national leaders, energy authorities, and ordinary citizens.

17   **Simone Veil** of France is elected president of the European Parliament.

Anastasio Somoza Debayle resigns as president of Nicaragua. Sandinista rebels seize Managua, the capital, two days later.

Carter appoints Hamilton Jordan chief of the White House staff and asks all Cabinet members for their resignations.

19-20   **Carter shakes up Cabinet.** Deputy Attorney General Benjamin R. Civiletti replaces Attorney General Griffin B. Bell; Deputy Secretary of Defense Charles W. Duncan, Jr., replaces Energy Secretary James R. Schlesinger; Patricia Roberts Harris, secretary of housing and urban development (pictured above), replaces Joseph A. Califano, Jr., as secretary of health, education, and welfare; Navy Secretary W. Graham Claytor temporarily replaces Transportation Secretary Brock Adams; and Federal Reserve Chairman G. William Miller replaces Treasury Secretary W. Michael Blumenthal.

24   **President Richard M. Nixon's** tapes are made available to the public at 11 listening centers.

27   **Carter nominates** Moon Landrieu as secretary of housing and urban development and Neil E. Goldschmidt as secretary of transportation.

28   **Charan Singh** becomes India's prime minister. Morarji Desai resigned on July 15 after more than 100 members of parliament left his Janata Party.

31   **House of Representatives** censures Charles C. Diggs, Jr. (D., Mich.), who had been convicted of taking kickbacks from his staff.

Chrysler Corporation posts a record loss of $207.1 million in the second quarter of 1979, seeks federal aid.

Here are your
1980 YEAR BOOK
Cross-Reference Tabs

For insertion in your WORLD BOOK

Each year, THE WORLD BOOK YEAR BOOK adds a valuable dimension to your WORLD BOOK set. The Cross-Reference Tab System is designed especially to help youngsters and parents alike *link* THE YEAR BOOK's new and revised WORLD BOOK articles, its Special Reports, and its Close-Ups to the related WORLD BOOK articles they update.

How to Use These Tabs

First, remove this page from THE YEAR BOOK. Begin with the first Tab, "CHICAGO."

Then, turn to the *C* or *C-Ch Volume* of your WORLD BOOK set and find the page of the "Chicago" article. Moisten the gummed Tab and affix it to that page.

For the New Article on "DOMINICA," mount the Tab in the *D Volume* where the article should appear in its alphabetical sequence.

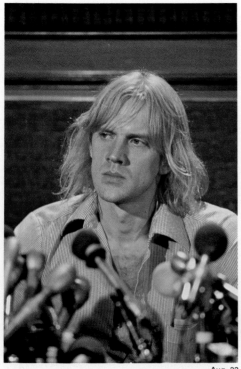

Aug. 28

Aug. 15

Aug. 23

<table>
</table>

August

			1	2	3	4
5	6	7	8	9	10	11
12	13	14	15	16	17	18
19	20	21	22	23	24	25
26	27	28	29	30	31	

1   **Romania demands** that foreign travelers pay for gasoline in Western currencies.
Russia's wheat-purchase allowance is raised by 2 million metric tons (2.2 million short tons) by the U.S. Department of Agriculture.

1-7   **Commonwealth nations agree** on constitutional proposals for Zimbabwe Rhodesia.

2   **Nuclear Regulatory Commission** says the Three Mile Island accident was preventable.

3   **Equatorial Guinea's President** Macias Nguema Biyogo Negue Ndong is overthrown by a junta led by Theodore Nguema Menzogo.

5   **Francesco Cossiga is sworn in** as Italy's prime minister, heading a three-party coalition.

6   **Bolivia's Congress elects** Walter Guevara Arze provisional president.

11   **At least 5,000 persons die** in Morvi, India, after a dam bursts.

12   **Forests burn** on 171,000 acres (69,000 hectares) in California, Idaho, Montana, Oregon, and Wyoming.

11-12   **Japan approves** a seven-year economic plan that calls for 5.7 per cent growth per year.

15   **Andrew Young resigns** as U.S. ambassador to the UN during controversy over his unauthorized meeting with a PLO representative.

16   **U.S. banks raise** prime lending rate to 12 per cent, the highest since 1974.

19   **Russian cosmonauts** Vladimir Lyakhov and Valery Ryumin land after spending 175 days in space, breaking the record of 139 days set by another Soviet cosmonaut team in 1978.

20   **Charan Singh resigns** as India's prime minister because of impending loss of a confidence vote, but stays on as caretaker.

21   **Southern Christian Leadership Conference** leaders meet PLO representatives and express support for Palestinian self-determination.

23   **Russian ballet dancer** Alexander Godunov defects to the United States during a tour. U.S. officials delay his wife's departure from New York City until they determine on August 27 that she wishes to return to Russia.

27   **IRA kills Earl Mountbatten** of Burma, British World War II hero, and three others by placing a bomb on his boat.

28   **Flow of Vietnamese "boat people"** resumes after a two-week lull, the U.S. Navy reports.
Physicists announce that recent experiments may prove the existence of the *gluon,* a fundamental particle of matter.

31   **Donald F. McHenry** succeeds Andrew Young as U.S. ambassador to the UN.
U.S. intelligence reports that Russia has a combat unit in Cuba.

Sept. 7

Sept. 5

Sept. 9

September

						1
2	3	4	5	6	7	8
9	10	11	12	13	14	15
16	17	18	19	20	21	22
23	24	25	26	27	28	29
30						

1 **Unmanned *Pioneer 11*** flies past Saturn and beams back information about that planet and two newly discovered rings.

5 **Earl Mountbatten of Burma** is buried.

6 **Carter commutes sentences** of four Puerto Rican terrorists who had been imprisoned since the 1950s.

7 **Hurricane David** ends an eight-day rampage through the Caribbean Sea and the U.S. Eastern Seaboard, leaving 1,100 persons dead.

8 **Amtrak announces a record gain** of 25 per cent in June ridership.

9 **Sixth summit of nonaligned nations** ends in Havana, Cuba, with a final statement more favorable toward Russia than the United States.

10 **Angola's President** Agostinho Neto dies in Moscow after cancer surgery. José Eduardo dos Santos succeeds him the next day.

12 **Hurricane Frederic strikes** the U.S. Gulf Coast, sending 500,000 persons inland.

13 **South Africa declares** the black homeland of Venda independent, but no other nation recognizes it.

16 **Hafizullah Amin replaces** Afghanistan's Revolutionary Council President and Prime Minister Noor Mohammad Taraki.

17 **Great Britain complains** about its heavy contributions to the European Community after that body approves a 1980 draft budget.

18 **Russian skaters** Oleg Protopopov and Ludmila Belousova defect to Switzerland.

20 **Central African Empire's Bokassa I** is overthrown. David Dacko succeeds him as president of the Central African Republic.

21 **France and Great Britain agree** to stop producing *Concorde* supersonic airliners.

23 **More than 200,000 demonstrate** against nuclear power in New York City.

24 **European Monetary System revalues** West Germany's Deutsche mark upward against the other currencies.

25 ***The Montreal Star,*** a daily newspaper, stops publishing after 111 years because it lost too much circulation during a strike.

26 **Carter signs energy bill** that exempts the Tellico Dam project from the Endangered Species Act. The U.S. Supreme Court had blocked completion of the dam because it would endanger the snail darter, a small fish.

Thailand assures international officials that it will allow Cambodian refugees to remain on its soil while they are being resettled.

29 **China's Cultural Revolution** of the 1960s is called a "catastrophe" by Communist Party Senior Deputy Chairman Yeh Chien-ying (Ye Jianying).

Oct. 7

Oct. 17

October

	1	2	3	4	5	6
7	8	9	10	11	12	13
14	15	16	17	18	19	20
21	22	23	24	25	26	27
28	29	30	31			

6 **U.S. Federal Reserve Board** announces tight control of money supply to dampen inflation. **Russia may withdraw about 20,000 troops** and 1,000 tanks from East Germany, Brezhnev announces.

7 **Pope John Paul II** ends his tour of Ireland and the United States. Visit includes New York City motorcade on October 2, pictured above. **Japan's Prime Minister** Masayoshi Ohira retains power in local elections.

9 **Thorbjorn Falldin** becomes Sweden's prime minister after September elections upset Ola Ullsten's government.

10 **U.S. Senate denounces** Senator Herman E. Talmadge (D., Ga.) for "reprehensible" conduct in handling his finances.

14 **Russia questions nuclear power's** safety in a Communist Party magazine article. **Mexico installs** a huge cone to capture oil escaping from a well that blew out off the Yucatán Peninsula in June.

15 **Military junta overthrows** El Salvador's President Carlos Humberto Romero.

16 **Pakistan's President** Zia-ul-Haq postpones national elections scheduled for November 17. **Special Counsel** Paul J. Curran declares that no money was diverted from the peanut business of President Carter's family to his 1976 presidential campaign treasury.

17 **Pittsburgh Pirates win** the World Series, defeating Baltimore, four games to three. **Carter signs a bill** creating a Department of Education. The Department of Health, Education, and Welfare will become the Department of Health and Human Services. **Nobel Peace Prize** is awarded to Mother Teresa of India, a Roman Catholic nun.

20 **John Tate wins** World Boxing Association heavyweight championship, defeating South African Gerrie Coetzee.

22-26 **U.S. oil industry reports** big profit increases for the third quarter.

25 **Spanish Basques** approve home rule.

26 **South Korea's President** Chung Hee Park is assassinated by the head of South Korean intelligence. The Cabinet names Prime Minister Kyu Ha Choi acting president.

27 **Great Britain grants independence** to St. Vincent and the Grenadines, a nation of Caribbean islands.

30 **France's Minister of Labor** Robert Boulin commits suicide because of suspicion and press accounts of his real estate dealings. **President Carter names Shirley Hufstedler** to head the new Department of Education. **A special commission** urges Carter to replace the NRC with an agency that would police the nuclear power industry.

Nov. 4

Nov. 19

November

			1	2	3	
4	5	6	7	8	9	10
11	12	13	14	15	16	17
18	19	20	21	22	23	24
25	26	27	28	29	30	

1   **Bolivian troops oust** Interim President Walter Guevara Arze, install Alberto Natusch Busch.

4   **Iranians seize U.S. Embassy,** take hostages, and demand that the United States return the ousted Shah Mohammad Reza Pahlavi, who is in a U.S. hospital.

6   **Mehdi Bazargan resigns** as Iran's prime minister. Ayatollah Khomeini orders the Revolutionary Council to run the government.
Masayoshi Ohira is re-elected prime minister of Japan by House of Representatives.

7   **Senator Edward M. Kennedy declares** that he is a Democratic presidential candidate.

8   **Governor Edmund G. Brown, Jr.,** of California says that he will seek the 1980 Democratic presidential nomination.

12   **Suleyman Demirel** becomes Turkey's prime minister, succeeding Bulent Ecevit.
United States suspends oil imports from Iran.

13   **London newspaper** *The Times* resumes publishing after labor problems cause an 11-month shut-down.

14   **Carter freezes** all Iranian assets in the U.S.

UN General Assembly demands that Vietnam withdraw its troops from Cambodia.

15   **Rebels accept transition plan** for temporary British rule in Zimbabwe Rhodesia.
Sir Anthony Blunt, former curator of Queen Elizabeth's art collection, admits publicly that he spied for Russia in the 1950s and 1960s. He confessed to the government in 1964.

16   **American Airlines pays** a record $500,000 fine for improperly maintaining DC-10s.
Bolivia's Congress elects Lydia Gueiler Tejada as interim president, succeeding Alberto Natusch.Busch, who agreed to step down.
Philip M. Klutznick is named secretary of commerce, succeeding Juanita M. Kreps, who resigned in October for personal reasons.

19   **Lane Kirkland is elected** president of the American Federation of Labor and Congress of Industrial Organizations (AFL-CIO); succeeding George Meany (pictured above), who retires.

19-20 **Iran releases** 13 of the U.S. hostages — eight blacks and five women.

20   **Fundamentalist Muslims seize** the Great Mosque in Mecca, Saudi Arabia, but government troops recapture it.

21   **Mob burns U.S. Embassy** in Pakistan.

25   **Israel turns over** Sinai oil fields to Egypt under terms of treaty signed in March in Washington, D.C.

26   **International Olympic Committee** declares both China and Taiwan eligible for the 1980 games.

28   **Air New Zealand DC-10 airliner** crashes in Antarctica, killing all 257 persons aboard.

29   **Mexico announces** that it will not readmit the shah of Iran.

Dec. 4

December

						1
2	3	4	5	6	7	8
9	10	11	12	13	14	15
16	17	18	19	20	21	22
23	24	25	26	27	28	29
30	31					

2   **The shah of Iran is moved** to Lackland Air Force Base hospital near San Antonio, Tex.
A mob sets fire to the U.S. Embassy in Tripoli, Libya, but the staff escapes.

3   **Iranian voters ratify** a Constitution that makes Khomeini leader for life.

4   **UN Security Council demands** unanimously that Iran release the U.S. hostages.
President Jimmy Carter announces that he will seek a second term.
Crowd crushes 11 people to death while rushing to get unreserved seats at a rock concert in Cincinnati, Ohio.

11   **Charles Haughey succeeds** Jack Lynch as Ireland's prime minister.
President Carter leads Senator Kennedy for the first time in nearly two years in a nationwide Gallup Poll of Democrats.

12   **Western Europe bases** for U.S. medium-range nuclear missiles are approved by the North Atlantic Treaty Organization.
Zimbabwe Rhodesia reverts temporarily to its former status as the British colony of Rhodesia

as Governor Lord Soames takes control. Great Britain lifts economic sanctions imposed against Rhodesia in 1965.

13   **Canada's government falls** on a vote of confidence.

15   **The shah of Iran moves to Panama.**
International Court of Justice orders Iran to release U.S. hostages.

17   **Cease-fire plan** is accepted by Rhodesian Patriotic Front guerrillas.

18   **The Vatican forbids** Swiss theologian Hans Küng to continue teaching as a Catholic theologian.

19   **Industrial nations face** double-digit inflation in 1980, the Organization for Economic Cooperation and Development warns.

20   **OPEC ends meeting** in Caracas, Venezuela, without setting 1980 oil price, but its members charge from $24 to $30 per barrel.
Court order ends Chicago's first transit strike since 1922 after four days.
Senate and House agree on a framework for a $227.3-billion windfall-profits tax on the oil industry.

24   **Rain and blizzards** batter California, Oregon, and Washington, leaving more than 400,000 Californians without electricity.

25   **United States asks** the UN Security Council for economic sanctions against Iran.

26   **Price of gold** tops $500 per troy ounce (31 grams) for first time.

27   **Afghanistan government** falls in a coup d'état aided by massive intervention of Russian troops.

The Year
in Focus

The meaning of some of the important events
and trends of 1979 is discussed by the members
of THE YEAR BOOK Board of Editors:

Harrison Brown, Director, the
East-West Resource Systems Institute, the
East-West Center, Honolulu, Hawaii.
Lawrence A. Cremin, President, Teachers
College, Columbia University.
James J. Kilpatrick, columnist for the
Universal Press Syndicate.
Sylvia Porter, columnist for the
Field Newspaper Syndicate; author of *Sylvia
Porter's New Money Book for the 80s*.
Carl T. Rowan, columnist for the Field
Newspaper Syndicate.

Left to right: Rowan, Brown, Porter, Kilpatrick, Cremin.

Lawrence A. Cremin   Sylvia Porter   Harrison Brown   Carl T. Rowan

How Much Freedom? How Much Control?

In solving the problems of the 1980s, we must seek the right balance between a free and a controlled society

When the YEAR BOOK Board of Editors met at Teachers College, Columbia University, in New York City in mid-November 1979, they discussed three of the most significant issues of the year–rampant inflation, the problem of leadership, and the energy situation. But running through the discussion, regardless of the specific issue being talked about, was the question–How much freedom and how much control? It is a fundamental question for American society, and for other democracies. This Focus discussion is both a look back at 1979 and a part of the ongoing search for answers to the question. Joining the discussion were William H. Nault, editorial director of World Book-Childcraft International, Incorporated, and Wayne Wille, executive editor of THE WORLD BOOK YEAR BOOK.

James J. Kilpatrick

William H. Nault

Wayne Wille

William H. Nault: Sylvia, when the YEAR BOOK Board of Editors met 10 years ago, at the end of the 1960s, you said that 1969 would go down in modern economic history as the year in which we in the United States "finally looked squarely at the tortuous question of a runaway inflation psychology and the destructively rapid price-wage spiral" and discovered that we didn't have the answers. Well, it is now the end of the 1970s, and we are still in the midst of the worst, most prolonged stretch of inflation this country has ever known.

Sylvia Porter: I want to start by saying that the spotty recession of 1979 is turning almost certainly into what will be a deepening recession in 1980. And the basic reason will be that the psychology of inflation–the self-fulfilling prophecy that inflation is becoming permanent–which was so rampant throughout the 1970s, reached an intolerable level in 1979. Millions of people adopted the philosophy of "buy now, because tomorrow it will cost more; borrow to the hilt, because tomorrow you will pay it back in dollars that will be worth less; do not save, because saving is no longer a virtue, it is a waste." That psychology of inflation will doom this country and this society unless it can be ended. Because of that psychology, and because of the basic causes of the inflation itself, the inflation rate accelerated into double digits long before any of us anticipated. I don't know anyone who believed that the end of 1979 would see the inflation rate up over 13 per cent, where it is now.

Take the practical approach?

James J. Kilpatrick: But as a practical matter, is there anything wrong with the arithmetic of the approach you are condemning? Setting philosophy to one side, setting morality to one side, Sylvia, if you were advising a child or grandchild how to dispose of his own income today, simply as a practical matter wouldn't he be wise to borrow in order to pay back with cheaper dollars in the future?

Porter: He would be wise, if I went along with the implication of your question, Jack.

Kilpatrick: You mean, that inflation will continue.

Porter: Yes. Your question implies that we are not going to get it under control, and my answer is that we *will*. We are going to get it under control at the price of a slump of unpredictable depth, breadth, and duration. That is the price being forced upon us by the Federal Reserve Board's new, deliberately engineered policy of forcing a slump by tightening the money supply. But we will get it under control.

Carl T. Rowan: One of the big questions is whether there were things government could have done to get it under control *without* a slump.

Porter: Without any question there were. It never should have occurred. When the Carter Administration came in in January 1977, that was when the real war on inflation should have been declared. The country was just waiting to be called to sacrifice, to do something that would help revive a stable dollar. The country was waiting for that. Instead, we got mush.

Rowan: Mike Blumenthal [former Secretary of the Treasury W. Michael Blumenthal] says that they were handcuffed by schizophrenia. That President Carter had some natural constituencies in the Democratic Party–like blacks, for example–who said, "Don't fight inflation by throwing me out of work," and that, therefore, the Administration couldn't take a strong stand against inflation because it was worried about alienating some of the groups that put Carter in office in the 1976 election.

Porter: If that is the philosophy, inflation will never be brought under control. As a result of the early failure to do anything to bring the money supply back to tolerable levels, we have fueled the engine of inflation beyond any reasonable range. Dollars have been cranked out by federal budget deficits, by loans of considerable doubt to the developing nations, and the supply of dollars wallowing around in Europe is the most dangerous of all of the developments that we have permitted to happen to us abroad. So now we are forced to take the most cruel corrective measures. You are right, Carl–it means unemployment, and it means the first people to go will be those who are most dispensable. In a lot of cases, that will be the untrained, the disadvantaged. It will be "last in, first out"–and that was the black, and that was the woman, and they will be among the first persons to be unemployed.

Kilpatrick: I would like to go back to something you said a moment ago, Sylvia, to inject a little reality into your sentimental comment when you said that the country was waiting to be called to sacrifice. Two or three examples come to mind: The 55-mile-an-hour speed limit, for one, a modest measure, is violated wholesale all over the country. There is absolute disdain for the 55-mile-an-hour limit. The President tried to get us to lower our thermostats. The federal judges– those examplars of public morality and responsibility–refused to abide by the President's request when it came to heating their own courtrooms. I have yet to see any evidence of this willingness to sacrifice. What absolute evidence do you have that it is out there? Any?

The will was there in 1977

Porter: I would say that it was there, but that it has disappeared because of the disenchantment, if not disgust, with those who have been leading this country for the past three years. But in January 1977, something could have been done, and we would have reduced the extent to which the psychology of inflation has gripped the nation, the extent to which inflation itself has accelerated. That was the time to do it. I think we could have achieved it then. Certainly a tighter money policy than was the policy until Paul A. Volcker took over at the Federal Reserve Board in 1979 would have been in order.

Kilpatrick: But if there was this willingness to sacrifice that you perceived in 1977, it was not perceived by the United States Congress, because the deficits in fiscal 1977, 1978, and 1979 have been mountainous. They finally got the deficit for this current fiscal year down to something in the neighborhood of $30 billion. And the cumulative deficits over this period have, in my own judgment, been the primary —if not the only—cause of this 13-plus per cent inflation that is the cruel affliction on our body politic. The country didn't do anything.

Porter: I don't disagree with you about what the attitude is now, because I think that it has been permitted to continue and to develop. But I perceive a swing toward the kind of conservatism where a balanced budget is now almost a darling of living-room conversation.

Rowan: Sylvia, you thought the Carter Administration should have gone to a tight money policy?

Porter: Long before the policy-makers finally did, in October 1979.

Rowan: And you wanted something at least close to balanced budgets, and you figured they could have cut out the deficits?

Porter: Yes.

Rowan: Let me say this, to go back to this business of the mood of the American public, and the shift to conservatism you see. As I went around the country in 1979, I didn't see anybody willing to ask for less for himself. I didn't find any teachers who didn't want more money appropriated for education. The farmers wanted more. The unions wanted more. Everybody wanted more for medical-care systems, and so forth. I say that the mood of this country is not really to spend less when you get down to the nitty-gritty of who is willing to give up his program.

Lawrence A. Cremin: This comes back to the leadership that the President did not exert when he had the opportunity. We may want to talk later about the quality of leadership the country needs, but as far as I am concerned, a President who really wants to lead needs to be doing certain things by way of teaching as President. He has a very important role in his political addresses to the people and to Congress of detailing the situation. I think one of the problems with inflation is that there is not a widespread public understanding of what causes it or of what is needed to control it. I think if people had a firm sense of what was needed to control inflation, if the President had pressed the legislation that he presented to Congress but did not press, if he had used his authority with the Treasury Department to insist on certain actions, and if he had put teaching together with all this political activity, there might have been less of a sense of skepticism and cynicism on the part of the public. Instead, the public saw the inconsistencies in the kind of leadership he was providing.

Harrison Brown: I must say that I agree completely about the unwillingness at the present time of the American people to sacrifice, and yet, when you look back, they have been willing to sacrifice. What is the difference today? How was it that in World War II, when we were barely getting out of the Great Depression, we saw real wages double during a five-year period? We saw rationing of almost every necessity of life, and we accepted it? Today, our politicians say it must be voluntary, on an individual, self-sacrificing basis, and I wonder if that is possible. Why were we able to do it then? Was it the common well-perceived goal of winning the war that carried us through that

Porter: "The era of John Maynard Keynes [*below, left*] is dead dead dead.... A tighter money policy than was the policy until Paul A. Volcker [*left*] took over at the Federal Reserve Board in 1979 would have been in order."

difficult period? Or was it that we were able to tolerate government controls? And if they worked then, why wouldn't they work now?

Rowan: When you lay on controls in a way that you make people believe the suffering is going to be shared reasonably equally, then you get a sense of patriotism coming to the fore. But you will never get it voluntarily in the America that exists today.

Kilpatrick: Harrison and Carl have raised a fundamental question about American society, and that has to do with drawing the line between a free society—a voluntary one—on the one hand, or a controlled society on the other. Surely controls work, at least temporarily. You cite the example of the controls on rent, on housing, on jobs, wages, prices, interest, and dividends, all through the war period. They worked, but at what cost? At the cost of a great deal of freedom in terms of what we could do with our money and what we could do with our lives. We had a relatively controlled society because of the war, and it worked in terms of the end purpose—winning World War II. Right now, as Carl says, we are facing that same question in a time of peace: Will a voluntary society work?

Rowan: It's a good question—how to get people to do it; will a voluntary society work? Take the petroleum situation as an example. How do you curb America's appetite for oil—we're the great energy glutton of all time, and we are increasingly dependent on imported oil. Can we do it voluntarily, or do we have to lay on rationing?

Kilpatrick: You said we could not do it voluntarily, that we have to have rationing.

Rowan: I'm afraid that is the case. I would rather not have it, but I would rather have rationing than have this country's economy virtually destroyed because we retained this terrible dependence on foreign oil.

Nault: Carl just talked about the possibility of our economy being destroyed, and Sylvia said earlier that if inflation is not brought under control it could mean doom for our society. Why, Sylvia?

Porter: We are reaching a point in this country where we are in real trouble, at a crossroads. We cannot survive as a relatively free private enterprise system with inflation running at a double-digit rate. If inflation runs at 10 per cent, it takes only seven years for prices to double. At today's 13 per cent rate, prices double in about 5½ years. Now, if you have to live with that kind of runaway inflation, you cannot plan for your children's education or anything called a decent retirement, not for anything.

Cremin: Sylvia's "destruction of society" is a metaphor for the fact that, with continued high inflation, values come into play that we have traditionally found contemptible. The values that the United States has traditionally stood for go under, and other values surface, the ones that enable you to survive in this kind of economy. Society goes on, but things that used to be seen as vices become virtues. It comes back to this matter of practicality that Jack was talking about and that enables you to survive. The virtue of thrift goes out, and the vice of spending comes in. The virtue of thinking for the future goes

Porter: "At today's 13 per cent inflation, you cannot plan for anything— your children's education or a decent retirement."

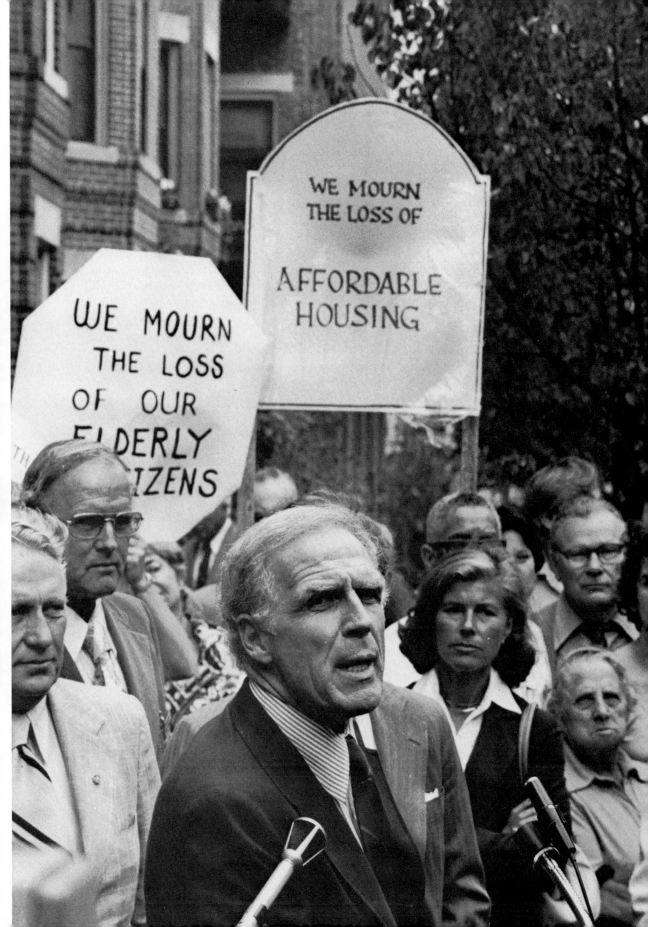

out, and the vice of living for today, because you don't know about the future, becomes the thing that enables you to survive.

Porter: Yes. Society goes on, but in a different form. That is what I meant when I said we are destroying society.

Wayne Wille: Sylvia, you said before that we can get inflation under control. Can you tell us how?

Porter: Well, for one thing, I have never seen so much support for a balanced budget, and that is a key requirement. It may mean that people will have to give up certain social programs. It may mean that they will have to accept higher taxes. Because you balance the budget only by spending less or raising taxes—those are the only two ways to do it. Unfortunately, a slump like the one ahead will lower the government's revenue, so the achieving of a balanced budget will be harder than ever; these are not uncomplicated questions. The balanced budget has to be, however, the beginning of the solution. Another thing that will help is a little longer-term—it will take a few more years to have a major effect—and that is the fact that our population mix is changing. Skilled workers are coming onto the market in increasing numbers. The skilled worker is a more productive worker, and that means that this will help increase productivity—which is the second key answer to inflation.

Wille: But hasn't there been a fall-off in the rate of growth of productivity—and how does that influence inflation?

Porter: All right—productivity is the amount of output that a worker accomplishes per hour. When that rate goes up, the company employing the worker can increase the worker's wages, increase the company's profits, and still maintain stable prices. Let us put it in terms of widgets. Let's say that you, Wayne, turn out 10 widgets per hour, and I pay you $1. If suddenly you turn out 15 widgets per hour, I could pay you $1.50, and I could still make the same amount of profit without raising the price of the widget. But let's say that you turn out only 10½ widgets per hour, and I want to maintain my profit. If I give you that $1.50, then I have to increase my prices to maintain the profit—and that adds up to inflation. So the rate of increase in productivity is a key factor in controlling inflation. For years, this country led the world in increasing the rate of productivity. But it has been declining in recent years, and now our rate of increase is only about 1 per cent—far behind such countries as Japan and West Germany.

Kilpatrick: One of the factors involved in increasing productivity is the availability of capital to develop the new tools that would add to the productivity of the individual worker. And so long as we have policies in the federal government that tend to discourage capital investment, we are going to continue to see the rate of productivity go down.

Cremin: Jack, what are some of the governmental policies that discourage investment?

Kilpatrick: Some of the environmental regulations that have been imposed upon industry. The electric power industry, for example—the scrubbers they have been required to install to reduce air pollution. That is a fine thing for the environment, but it diverts capital

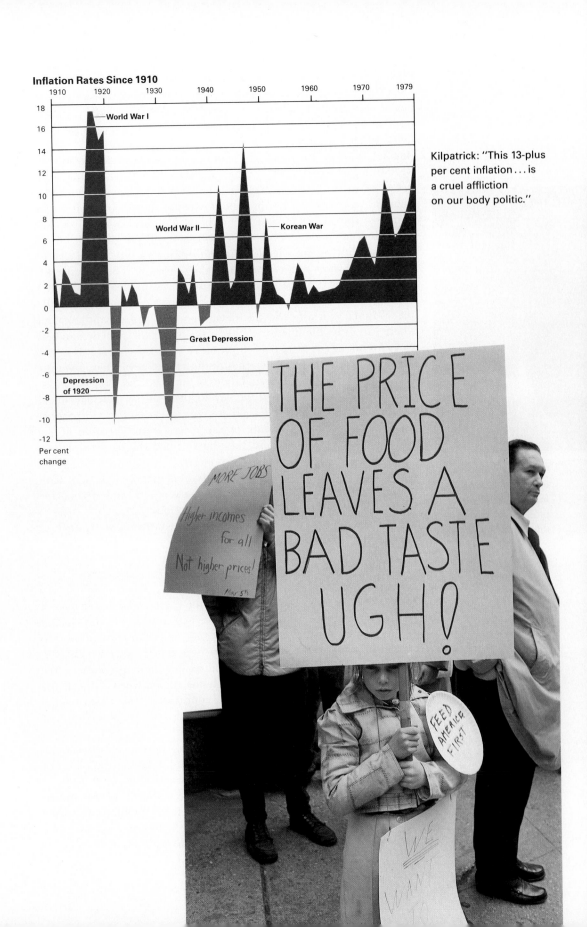

Inflation Rates Since 1910

World War I

World War II — Korean War

Great Depression

Depression of 1920 —

Per cent change

Kilpatrick: "This 13-plus per cent inflation...is a cruel affliction on our body politic."

MORE JOBS

Higher incomes for all Not higher prices!

May 5th

THE PRICE OF FOOD LEAVES A BAD TASTE UGH!

FEED AMERICA FIRST

WE WANT TO

that would otherwise be invested in the actual output of goods. And all of the governmental regulations having to do with occupational health and safety—I have yet to see any evidence that would persuade me that these regulations have contributed one iota to the productivity of our work force. I don't think they have.

Rowan: Here we are again, at the old issue of what kind of society do we want. The schizophrenia that engulfs us Americans on this issue shows up in the position black groups often find themselves in. For example, say they are arguing about whether the government ought to impose restrictions on a steel mill because somebody says it is polluting the air—and somebody else says that will put the mill out of business. And you get a leader of a black group saying, "Wait a minute, who are most of the workers in the steel mill? They are blacks, mostly unskilled." So he says, "Okay, so you want clean air, but if I starve to death because I can't get a job, I won't be around to breathe any of that clean air." So this debate goes on and on and on, and where you draw the line as to what is the best of all these demands of society is one of the most ticklish problems we face.

Kilpatrick: Well, we have seen that in the area of new drugs. Over the past 20 years, the excess of regulations of the Food and Drug Administration has virtually stopped the development of the pharmaceutical industry in the United States. There is no great increase in productivity there, or in the profits of the drug houses, because of the bureaucratic regulations, and they have stifled the development of new drugs.

Rowan: Yet you look at some of the disasters that we have had with the few drugs that didn't get properly supervised, and you do see the need for some controls and some supervision.

Kilpatrick: How much freedom, how much control? I come back to the question I have been asking all morning.

Moving in the right direction

Porter: But the bright part of it—and the reason why I still have a deep residue of optimism in the way we will come out of this—is that we are moving toward incentives not only to encourage, but also to make it impossible *not* to build new plants and new equipment and to modernize some of the steel mills to make them more productive. We are moving toward deregulation of some of the worst rules of the Occupational Safety and Health Administration and toward some easing of overly strict environmental controls. We are moving in the direction of increasing our rate of productivity.

Kilpatrick: We don't know as we are having our conversation today what is going to happen to the windfall-profits tax on the oil companies. And that will be an indicator of whether you are right or wrong, Sylvia, on the incentives that will be left to the energy industry, how much will be taken away from them in potential capital for distribution to poor people in terms of heating oil or whatever. The petroleum industry needs all the capital it can get if it is to develop the

Porter: "We are moving in the direction of increasing the rate of productivity of our industries and services."

energy that will be our lifeline for the decade of the 1980s. Yet at least now, in mid-November, there seems a good deal of disposition in the Carter Administration and in parts of Congress to take most of this potential capital away from the private sector and put it back into the public sector. That is not a development that I find encouraging.

Rowan: That is because a great many people in the Carter Administration and Congress have some doubts that the oil companies are going to plow all of this windfall money back into energy-producing enterprises. And also, a great many people feel that you have to do something about this issue of "eat or heat," the problem faced by a great many people this winter who cannot pay food prices and higher heating oil prices at the same time. So here we are again at the business of balancing the needs of society, and where Congress is going to come out in terms of how you do that, I don't know.

Old solutions and new needs

Cremin: One of the things we are finding at the end of the 1970s is that solutions we once thought would be solutions for all time are not, in fact, solutions for all time. I work in a university, and sometimes if you change your mind in a university you are seen as a foolish person who has no consistency, who doesn't know what his point of view is. Yet, if anything is needed in facing this situation at the beginning of the 1980s, it is a rethinking of positions that some of us came to in the '60s and '70s that we thought would be good for all time. Those positions may have been good then, but they need to be balanced against new needs.

Porter: One thing we have certainly come to a conclusion about throughout the world is that the era of John Maynard Keynes is dead, dead, dead. Keynes was very well attuned to the 1930s, because his theory of spend and spend, lend and lend, and pull yourself out by using public money to do all sorts of things, make government intervention acceptable, was good policy for curing a depression. But that theory is no longer applicable to the problems of the 1980s. We cannot blame what has happened to the world on following Keynes, but I would say we followed him far, far too long.

Nault: There appears to be agreement here about certain things that must be done to help curb inflation. Could you look into your crystal balls for a moment and indicate how hopeful you are that these things might come to pass?

Brown: I think that if there is any one thing that has emerged from this discussion, it is the precariousness of our democratic system, our so-called freedoms. We are faced with a desperate need to make decisions on a relatively short time scale. Yet, to cite an example, five or six years have elapsed since the great crisis of the Arab oil embargo, there has been a fourfold increase in the price of crude oil, and we have yet to develop what amounts to a full-fledged, well-rounded energy policy in the United States. Five years is a very long time when you consider the rate at which things are changing. I cite this with respect

Kilpatrick: "The petroleum industry needs all the capital it can get if it is to develop the energy that will be our lifeline for the decade of the '80s."

to energy, but I think the same thing applies to all of the major problems we have touched upon so far.

Kilpatrick: I would agree with that, but I am basically optimistic about the eternal verities we on the conservative side believe in. I believe in the free-market economy. If left largely alone—not wholly alone, but if it is left largely alone to do the job—it will do the job. One of the many problems is that in recent years we have introduced so many elements of governmental control into the market economy that the market economy is unable to function in its classic patterns. It can't do the job. We have reins on it, chains on it, various fetters on our economy, and yet I am hopeful that the conservative tendency in this country will manifest itself before long in a reduction of the controls, in an elimination of some of the needless regulations that seem to be stifling our economy. I am basically optimistic, and yet I have to face the realities, the political realities of a Congress that seems disposed to tax and tax and tax away the incentives that would permit us to develop new capital. We have to have a reversal of these trends. We have to have a turning back toward the idea of freedom, letting the business community make its own decisions.

Cremin: I, too, tend to be optimistic. I believe, as Harrison does, that the situation is quite precarious, but I believe also that the American people have never been better educated. They have never been more prepared to understand the issues that face them, and to work out decent and reasonable, just and equitable, sensible and workable solutions. I do think this calls for new kinds of leadership, a leadership of exemplars rather than people who say, "Don't do as I do; do as I

Cremin: "If anything is needed in facing this situation at the beginning of the 1980s, it is a rethinking of positions that some of us came to in the '60s and '70s that we thought would be good for all time."

say"; leadership of people who have the patience to teach and persuade; leadership of people who have the courage to recommend decisions, debate them, and then try to gather the political consensus to work them through. I believe in our classic faith that people who know the truth will apply its findings and remain free.

Rowan: Well, I have, I gather, a higher measure of pessimism than my colleagues here, because I see a considerable bit of evidence that Americans have really been spoiled a bit by a marvelously high standard of living, and I note that one of the most difficult things you can ask an individual to do is take a pay cut or reduce his living standard.

Porter: As I said, I am optimistic, because I believe that we will get inflation and the inflation psychology under control. I believe that we will reach the point of conservation of energy and of changing our uses of energy to the point where we can handle that problem, too.

Brown: Could I add to my statement? I am not an optimist. I am pessimistic, though I don't believe that the situation is hopeless. However, I feel that American democracy, American civilization, is in a more vulnerable situation today than at any time since the Civil War. And I don't believe that that is because of the Soviet Union, though that is a contributing factor. I think that it is because of the kinds of problems we have been talking about here—the energy problem, inflation, where we are going as a society, productivity.

The question of leadership

Rowan: "I really wonder if we aren't looking for the miracle man who doesn't exist."

Wille: I don't think we can talk about solving all these problems without exploring the question of leadership—or the lack of it. It's already been mentioned several times today, and we heard that word all throughout 1979 from potential presidential candidates.

Rowan: Yes. That was the big question on the political hustings in 1979—who has leadership? And I raise the real question of whether there is in existence the kind of person who can lead this country in a way that matches the dreams and desires of a great many people. For example, Harrison mentioned that five years of an energy crisis have gone by, but nothing happens. Congress can't seem to get off the dime. I know that Jimmy Carter is not the kind of leader people are looking for, because he couldn't push Congress to do what needed to be done. Neither could President Richard Nixon, by the way. But we have to take into account the fact that some of our institutions have changed, and Congress is one of them. There is no way today that Tip O'Neill [the speaker of the House of Representatives, Rep. Thomas P. O'Neill, Jr. (D., Mass.)] can run the House the way Sam Rayburn [Texas congressman, speaker of the House for 17 years] ran it. There is no sense of party loyalty today of the sort that existed in the past. You have new congressmen coming in who say, "I'm not going to let these jokers tell me what to do." Beyond that, I really wonder if we aren't looking for the miracle man who doesn't exist when we talk about looking for a leader who can bring all of those disparate elements together and make them do what ought to be done.

38

Wille: I saw a public opinion poll a few weeks ago in which people were asked what they felt were the most important factors in the upcoming presidential race, and "leadership" was by far the most important factor they listed. The second most important one was "integrity," and a very, very poor third was "policies." You got the impression that there was a hunger for leadership of any sort, without respect to where this leadership would take us.

Kilpatrick: I would hope we would have more integrity instead of a Hitler on a white horse, but I can only echo what Carl is saying; I think our difficulties in leadership are both personal and institutional. Personal in the case of Jimmy Carter. Look, after all, at his biography. He came to Washington, D.C., with total inexperience in Washington. He never had a constituency up on Capitol Hill. And he himself, I think, gravely mistook the attitude of the American people toward the presidency as such, so that Carter set out early in his Administration further to de-imperialize the presidency. We went through the long period in which he was banning the limousines, and going on the air in his sweater, and all that. It was a grave mistake on his part. It cost him at the outset the immense prestige, or the aura, of the presidency that could have made up for his lack of constituency.

It was a personal thing in Carter's case, but, as Carl says, this coincided with changes in leadership in Congress. In the revolution that struck the House a few years back, they got rid of the seniority system, for all practical purposes. They robbed the committee chairmen of the powers they used to exercise, stripped the speaker of some of his powers, and developed an attitude independent of the two-party system, which had been crumbling at a fast rate. Suddenly, there was no political leadership up there on the Hill. That is the situation we find ourselves in now. The President can ask, but it is like summoning spirits from the vasty deep. There is no way that Carter can get an answer, not from this Congress.

Cremin: "I do think this calls for a new kind of leadership, a leadership of exemplars rather than people who say, 'Don't do as I do; do as I say.'"

A demagogue for President?

Nault: Your comment about a man on a white horse, Jack, is a little scary, in terms of the kind of leadership we might get. That leader might be a charismatic individual who could very well pose a threat to the society that we talked about earlier. What are the chances that the mood of the people is such that a demagogue might become President?

Kilpatrick: The chances are, unhappily, very good. You take these public opinion polls, and you find that the people are like the prisoners who, after a while, get fond of their chains. There is a great mood in the people to have price and wage controls, to have a regimented society. It turns up in every poll that is made on it. There is a tremendous majority in the urban areas that would like to see rent controls imposed, but they won't learn from the disastrous history of these controls—what happened to their freedoms and their property.

Brown: Carl touched on certain institutional changes, but nobody has mentioned what I consider to be a very important change, and

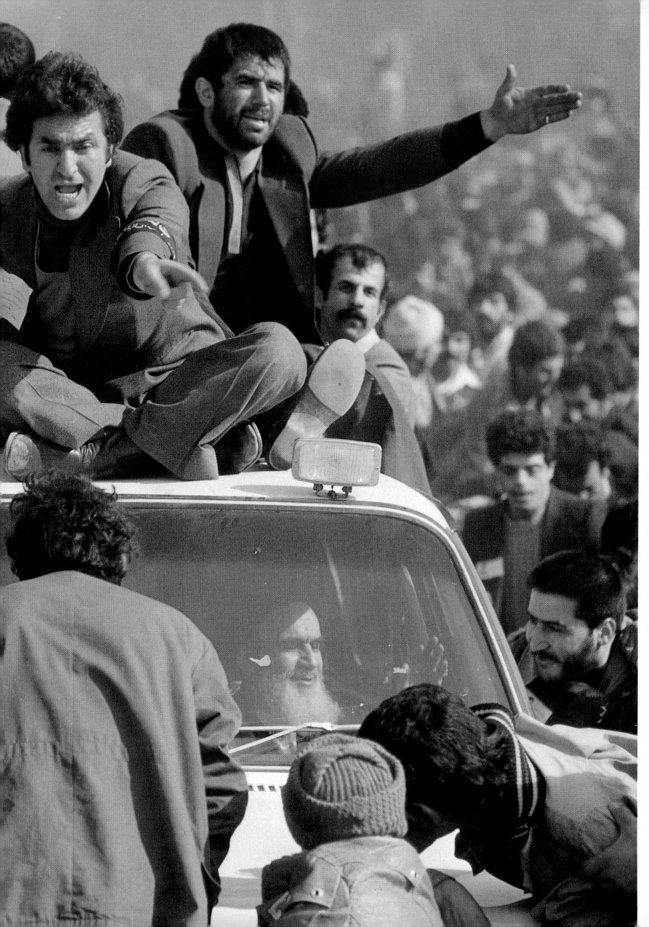

that is the emergence of very strong single-issue lobby groups that care only about getting their way on that one issue, without regard for any of the other important issues facing us. These have become so strong and have terrified so many members of Congress that one can raise the question—even with a very strong leader, what difference will it make? How can even a strong leader navigate his way through this morass of single-issue groups?

Rowan: Yes. We have that single-issue passion in a great many areas—abortion, gun control, and so on—and it does really complicate the political system in this country.

Kilpatrick: If I might expand for a moment on the matter that Carl brought up earlier, the two-party system. I think it is politically quite important to the specific-issue voting, also. Almost without realizing it, our political system has gone through a major change in the past 20 years. There was a time in this country when the two political parties had some meaning, and not merely in the political sense of grooming candidates for office and doing the usual political things—arranging the rally in the park, raising money, and so on. Political parties also performed welfare functions, social functions.

Now all of those functions that once were performed by the political parties, and gave them substance, are gone. Fund-raising has been taken over very largely by political action committees, so that a political party's most important purpose of raising money is gone. They no longer have the rallies in the park. Instead, a candidate goes on television and speaks to a hundred thousand people at a crack. He is removed from the political party process as such. There is very little left of party discipline. There is not much of patronage left; patronage has gone into civil service. So we are at a point now, as we enter the 1980s, where little remains of our two-party system except form. We cling stubbornly to the form—we organize the committees of Congress by majority and minority parties. But it is all form; there is very little substance left. Time after time, Speaker O'Neill will take the well of the House and plead with fellow Democrats to follow the leadership of their President, and a hundred of them at a time desert him.

There is no party system left that has any meaning. This, coupled with the special-interest voting, has led some political scientists to talk about the possibility of new forms of organization in Congress, new forms of coalition politics. It is conceivable that by 1990 we might have a reorganization in ideological terms—"liberals" and "conservatives." Certainly "Democrat" and "Republican" are labels that have ceased to have very much meaning.

Cremin: May I suggest that this is a problem throughout the society. It is a problem not unrelated to that question of freedom and control we were talking about before. The authority of the leader is nowhere near what it was 25 or 50 years ago. The authority of the union leader, the ability of the business leader to make decisions, the right of the university president to appoint faculty, to make budget decisions, is not what it was 20, 30, 40 years ago. The requirements for leadership have changed; you need to listen a great deal more, to consult many

Cremin: "I think we need to clarify the kind of leadership a democratic society needs, because the most charismatic leader in the world at the end of 1979 is the Ayatollah Khomeini."

more groups. If a university president wants to make an appointment or change a budgetary policy, he has to consult with faculty members and students and other interested groups.

Porter: Let's get back to the specific issue of leadership we are discussing—the lack of leadership in the United States at a time when the entire country is yearning for one person to whom it can look to go into the world and represent us and bring back some of the eminence and strength, some of the standards and importance we once had. What we are talking about is a leader who can go before Congress and can stir the emotions of the American people. You are raising all kinds of hobgoblins when you talk about a leader who will turn into a demagogue or, worse, a dictator. Let us for the moment put that fear aside and talk about what we really are yearning for. I know that what I want in that White House is someone I can respect. I want to see someone in that seat in the Oval Office who carries with him the eminence of his office. When I see him sitting next to those flags, I want to feel a sense of awe. I want that sense of feeling that I am in the presence of a leader, and I don't feel that we have had that for years.

Rowan: The question is whether the people we see at the end of 1979 represent the kind of leadership you are talking about. Perhaps we subject our potential leaders now to such close scrutiny and demand so much that the kind of person you are talking about has long ago said, "I don't need the hassle. I don't need to go through this business of telling them every dollar I own, every piece of stock I own, where I went Wednesday night, August 13th." Have we driven the best talent out of the business of running for President of the United States?

Rowan: "Five years of
an energy problem have
gone by, but nothing
happens. Congress can't
seem to get off the dime."

Cremin: We should not put aside the question of the person on the white horse, because that, alas, is what many people mean by leadership. I think what we need to do is clarify the particular kind of leadership a democratic society needs. Bear in mind that the single most charismatic leader in the world at the end of 1979 – the one who gave charismatic leadership to the revolution in Iran – is the Ayatollah Ruhollah Khomeini.

Kilpatrick: There are lessons in that, surely, and this was the point I was trying to make earlier. Our apprehension is that in the slump that we foresee in the United States, the leader who will come along who will command the respect and the following will be a leader who will take us into more controls, less freedom – and not in the direction that Sylvia is praying for, the direction of greater freedom and greater cooperation and better attitudes toward work and more incentives. This is where leadership should be headed. But will it? Where do we find a leader? Is Carl right? Have they all gone back into private enterprise and the academies, making themselves unavailable for political life?

Brown: Carl has raised a very important point. The changes that have taken place in the past couple of decades make it extremely difficult for a person – no matter how honorable the intentions, no matter how dedicated – to run for President. How many of us in this room would subject ourselves to the kind of questioning and so forth that they get, the prying into their lives?

Rowan: I spent four and a half years in government, and I can say categorically that there is no way they could get me back, because of the financial sacrifices, the time away from your family, the loss of any privacy whatsoever. All these things militate against a really outstanding person going into a top-level job in the U.S. government these days. I think that is one of the things we have to worry about.

A leadership check list

Wille: If we could develop a list of attributes of the kind of leader we say we need, what would be included? Integrity? Eloquence?

Kilpatrick: Inspirational qualities.

Porter: Knowledge. I want the leader of this country to be a person with a grasp of politics, a grasp of economics, a grasp of social welfare.

Cremin: Sylvia, may I add something to that – the kinds of broad knowledge we associate with a gifted journalist. One of my arguments against some of my colleagues in the university world is their unwillingness to pay attention to the needs of students for a broad general education, along with whatever particular technical and specialized education that they receive. The fact is that anybody who is going to lead in any area of life, but especially in politics and the presidency, needs a broad general basic knowledge and sympathy of the sort that our schools are too infrequently equipped to give these days.

Kilpatrick: I think all of us would agree that there are men and women in the United States who have the characteristics and the capacities

Kilpatrick: "There are men and women who have the characteristics needed for leadership. The question is – will they make themselves available for public service through the political process?"

needed for leadership. The question, as Carl says, is—will they make themselves available for public service through the political process? That is a very serious question we have before us.

Nault: And the answer to that question?

Kilpatrick: The answer is no, at least tentatively no. We are in bad trouble and don't know how to get out of it.

Rowan: Another question is, do our political systems permit that kind of individual to get on the inside where he will be permitted to take the levers of power?

Kilpatrick: No, because we say nominations must be won; they are not going to be bestowed. We demand that our candidates get out there on the hustings and fight it out through a year or two of the most arduous and expensive campaigning. It is a bloodying process, Carl. Those who can stay in the chase the longest without collapsing are those who wind up at the national conventions.

Modify the system?

Brown: Perhaps we ought to think more about modifying the system than about asking for a great leader. Are there ways and means by which the system itself can be modified in order to make it more effective in solving these horrendous problems, without needing the charismatic leader who inspires everyone and pushes this through and that through?

Kilpatrick: Are you thinking of actual structural changes, such as going to a parliamentary system of amending the Constitution?

Cremin: "Anybody who is going to lead in any area of life, but especially in politics and the presidency, needs a broad general basic knowledge and sympathy of a sort that our schools are not really equipped to give."

Brown: I am not thinking of things that dramatic. I am thinking of making rules changes to lessen the impact of the single-issue lobbies. Making changes in campaign financing to free congressmen to vote their conscience as distinct from voting the wishes of a very few people in their constituency.

Kilpatrick: That is one of the troubles in Congress these days. We have far too many congressmen voting as independents with no regard to the party line. You can't find a party line. There are plenty of leaders up on the Hill; the problem is there aren't enough followers.

Cremin: This problem of individuality versus party discipline, a sense of individual versus community need, is one that has been characteristically American in its power. Every society fights it out, but we have fought it out philosophically since the days of Ralph Waldo Emerson, with his proclamations that every individual has his own view, is a church of one, is a polity of one. I think we find ourselves in the historic circumstance where the liberation movements of the 1960s moved us very much in the direction of individualism. What I hear in our discussion today is a sense that we seem to share with many people I have talked to around the country—of the need for a readjustment back to the direction of community, of "public concern," a readjustment for the balance of individualism and community.

Now, community in one sense means control, but if it is a voluntary community it means seeing that I as an individual am inevitably

Brown: "The Three Mile Island incident was unfortunate... but out of it may well emerge the basis for the development of a substantial nuclear power industry in this country."

wrapped up in the public, and if the public doesn't fare well, I don't fare well. And I think we *will* be seeing in the 1980s a readjustment back toward public concerns, public needs, community needs, possibly the willingness to submit to controls rather than "I drive as I please, I sell as I please, I set my thermostat as I please," and so on. And again, it is going to take wise leadership to help us toward a better reconciliation through persuasion rather than coercion.

Kilpatrick: How much freedom and how much control?

Cremin: That is right. It's a theme that has cropped up persistently through our discussion, the theme of the late 1970s and early '80s.

Nault: The question of energy has come up several times; how it affects the other topics we talked about today—inflation, the leadership crisis. One of the problems is that people don't seem to be certain about what the energy problem *is*, let alone how to solve it.

Brown: First of all, the world as a whole has become highly dependent on petroleum as a fuel, in part because it has been less expensive than other forms of fuel. Unfortunately, the sources of petroleum are not very equitably distributed. They exist in pockets and are scattered in various parts of the world, but there is nothing comparable to what exists in the Middle East. As the demand for petroleum increases, the price goes up, and this clearly has an effect on inflation. And with inflation rampant in the West, the petroleum-exporting countries find that oil under the ground is more valuable than oil on top of the ground. They are limited as to how rapidly they can spend money for imports, and, as a result, production is likely to decrease with time. But at the same time, demand for oil goes up, and when this happens, the price of the oil goes up even more. So, more inflation.

Now, most of the exporting countries are countries that are not very stable politically. Some of that instability transcends logic, as we have seen in Iran, so we are in an extremely vulnerable position. It seems to me that the grave danger facing us lies in the threat of a cutoff of our supply of petroleum. That is a substantial threat. The only way out is to diversify our sources of energy, to develop our coal to the maximum, to develop synthetic fuels, solar heating, and nuclear power.

Wille: But at the same time we see the possibility of our oil being cut off, we hear people say coal is too dirty, nuclear is too dangerous.

Brown: Well, there are problems no matter what route you take. All of them have higher prices attached, all of them have environmental problems attached, and all of them have biological risks in varying degrees. You have to balance what you are willing to pay with the risks you are willing to take.

Kilpatrick: You also have to balance our political differences in forming an energy policy. If he is renominated, Carter's chief political problem in winning re-election in 1980 will be to hold on to the South. This was the basis of his support in 1976. If he cannot again carry Texas and Louisiana, he is in very deep trouble, and an energy policy is of enormous importance in those two oil-producing states. Then, you have different considerations in New England. We would be naive not to agree that these considerations will enter into an energy policy.

Brown: It behooves us, regardless of such differences, to achieve a real measure of energy independence as quickly as possible. This is not going to be easy, and I think the most important single element of it is a recognition that we have been spoiled by inexpensive energy, and that we are going to have to pay a lot more for our energy.

But, once you get up to the level of paying $2 for a gallon of gasoline, then a whole range of competitive fuels that presently are too expensive becomes economical. With gas that expensive, synthetic fuels made from coal or from oil shale will be competitive. Now, the problem is—and here we come to the question of free enterprise—that the amounts of capital required to build the synthetic fuel plants are enormous, and no company really has the wherewithal at present.

Rowan: That is where the windfall-profits tax that Jack doesn't like may come in, because it can produce a fund large enough for us to do some things that private enterprise is not going to do.

Kilpatrick: Yes, but the risk you take, among other risks, Carl, is that the same wonderful people who gave us Amtrak and the Postal Service will set up the synthetic fuel operation—fiasco!

Rowan: But the simple fact is, it is not going to be done unless government does it. And either you want to get out from under this dependency on foreign oil or you don't.

Brown: Yes, the capital investment will be enormous, and the government will have to expedite it in some way. There are many ways one can go about doing that—some you would approve of, Jack, and some not. I don't think the capital is going to emerge from what you call the free play of the market place. It will require government incentives.

Kilpatrick: That could be a part of the free market place. It always has been. Historically, the tax structure has been a major factor in the creation of incentives. You either tax, or you forgive a tax, or you adjust a tax, and this is your incentive toward capital investment. So I have no objection on earth to the use of the tax structure to provide incentives for the needed capital formation.

Cremin: Your point—voluntary?

Kilpatrick: Yes, don't get government into doing it. Certainly I think it is better to rely on a voluntary approach, spurred by governmental tax incentives, than it is to put the government itself into the ownership and operation of synthetic fuel plants. I don't want the U.S. government in the business of producing energy. It is a fatal policy.

Cremin: I would like to raise again the theme that has been in our discussion all day, the theme of individualism versus community. I would make the point that the use of energy in America is connected with the ways in which we use our resources, and what we are talking about now is a new policy of conservation, where the use of the resources at our disposal is seen as not solely an individual matter, but also as something that has to do with the kind of society we live in. The point was made earlier, "Why should I turn off the lights if I know Jones isn't turning off his lights?" Once again, there has to be enough of a community feeling so that Jones and I both feel that we are giving something up for our common good.

Nault: Could we examine the nuclear power question? There has been opposition to it all along, of course, but the incident at Three Mile Island certainly dramatized both the possible dangers of nuclear energy and the pressures to eliminate nuclear as an energy source.

Brown: I'm aware of its dangers, of course. But dangers are relative things. And when we look at our needs over the next couple of decades, I don't see any way in which the industrial democracies—Western Europe, Japan, the United States, Canada, and so on—are going to get through all of this without making use of nuclear power for the generation of substantial amounts of electricity. I happen to be convinced that this can be done relatively danger-free. I think that some of our industries have played fast and loose with the business. They haven't devoted adequate attention to safety, and we may have to modify substantially our approaches to the whole problem of training, licensing, and so forth. But this is a mode of generating electricity that is very close to being as safe as any other method.

Kilpatrick: We kill about 110 coal miners a year, don't we?

Nault: Given all this, what are the chances that we will get an effective energy policy?

Kilpatrick: I think the chances may have improved appreciably with the crisis in Iran. This has called to our attention the volatility of the Middle East situation and the risks of losing our foreign supplies of oil. I think we are likely to get a fairly coherent package of bills before Congress very soon. It might not satisfy me, or Carl, but it will be the first thing approaching a package since April 1977, when President Carter went to the Hill and proposed an energy program in his "moral equivalent of war" speech.

Nault: So developing crises will motivate its development?

Kilpatrick: That is the way it always is. We never move until we are galvanized.

Nault: At any rate, I detect a little more optimism on this topic than on the previous ones. There seems to be a feeling that we can develop an effective policy of energy development and conservation.

Rowan: It may be easier to find more energy than to find the leader we were looking for.

Nault: And on that concise summing-up, Carl, I think we will end the discussion. I want to thank you for gathering with us and discussing these key issues of 1979—indeed, the key issues of the years ahead as our society continues to grapple with the question that kept arising today: How much freedom and how much control?

For further reading:

Numerous articles in THE WORLD BOOK ENCYCLOPEDIA provide valuable background information on some of the matters discussed in this FOCUS article. These articles include BUDGET (Government Budgets); CONGRESS OF THE UNITED STATES; ENERGY SUPPLY; FEDERAL RESERVE SYSTEM; FREE ENTERPRISE SYSTEM; INFLATION AND DEFLATION; KEYNES, JOHN MAYNARD; LOBBYING; MONEY (Money and the National Economy); and POLITICAL PARTY.

Special
Reports

1974
1976
1977
1978
1979

Seven articles give special treatment to subjects of current importance and lasting interest.

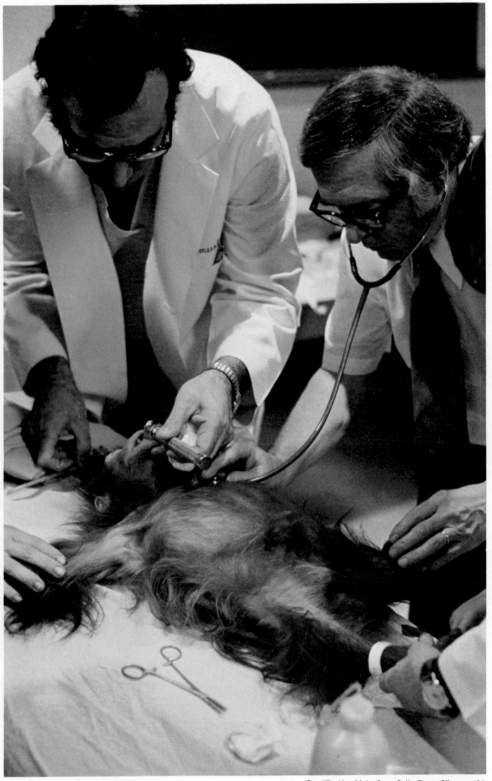

See "Do You Make Cage Calls, Doctor?" page 104.

Call it SF or Sci-Fi, It's Big!

By Isaac Asimov

Science fiction has become a major literary form and a popular subject for filmmakers

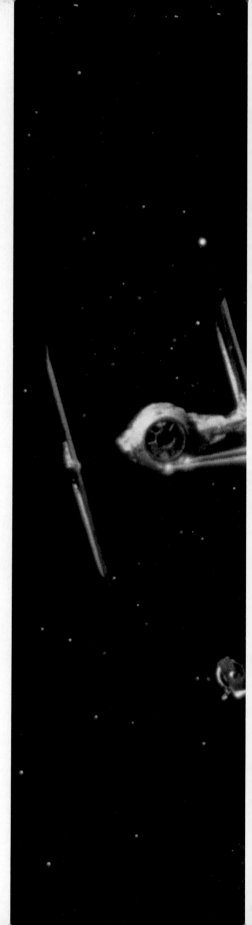

When I began to write science fiction, more than 40 years ago, there were just three science fiction magazines. Only one, *Astounding Stories*, was any good. It paid a penny a word, which meant that a writer could earn about $50 for a short story and $600 for a novel-length, three-part serial. A story would be available for a month or so and then disappear forever, except for the odd copy stored in the attic of a magazine collector. Science fiction readers were few in number, though intensely loyal.

And now? Science fiction is a highly respectable form of literature–some say it is the only form thriving today. Science fiction films are extremely popular and highly profitable. So are the toys, games, and other items that capitalize on the new popularity of science fiction.

A *Trip to the Moon* (1902), one of the earliest science fiction films, shows the moon as angry after being hit by a rocket, *above.* The idea of space explorers on the moon, a reality in 1969, was considered daring when the film *Destination Moon, right,* was released in 1950.

The author:
Isaac Asimov is the author of more than 200 books; many are science fiction and nonfiction.

Omni, a slick, expensive magazine, features several science fiction stories in every issue. Science fiction novels appear in hardback by the dozens each year and in paperback in even greater numbers. Go to any paperback bookstore and you will find rack upon rack of science fiction titles. Science fiction book clubs flourish, and there are bookstores devoted to this specialty. Some science fiction writers can get advances of more than $100,000 for a new novel.

What happened? Reality changed, along with people's perceptions of reality. When I began writing science fiction, the subjects that interested science fiction writers seemed laughable to most "sensible" people. Our stories dealt with such topics as television, robots, intelligent machines, space flight, atomic bombs, and overpopulation.

The first clear indication that the people who wrote and read science fiction lived in the real world and everyone else lived in a fantasy came during World War II when, on Aug. 6, 1945, the United States dropped an atomic bomb on Hiroshima, Japan.

Now everyone did not suddenly begin to read science fiction after Hiroshima. But, once and for all, science fiction stopped looking like nonsense. It could no longer be laughed at. In fact, it was more advanced than most people had realized. Science fiction stories had dealt with a number of "imaginary" situations that have since become stark reality–including the bomb itself, the superpowers' nuclear stalemate, peaceful uses of nuclear fission, and nuclear radiation dangers. And, of course, other fictional "fantasies" also came true–such as the V-2

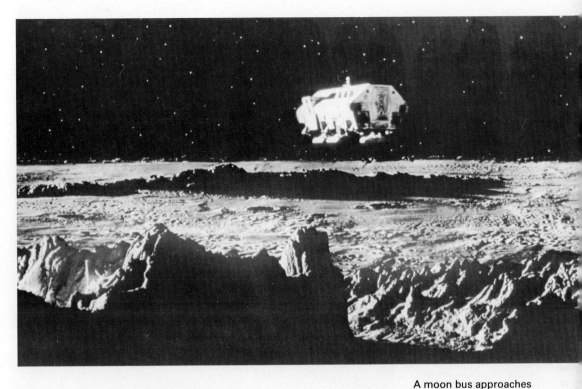

A moon bus approaches the lunar surface for a landing in one of the best science fiction films ever made, *2001: A Space Odyssey* (1968).

long-range missile, a rocket-powered weapon developed in Germany during World War II that traveled faster than the speed of sound.

The new appeal of science fiction quickly became apparent. Less than a year after the horror of Hiroshima, such tradition-minded houses as Crown Publications and Random House published large and elaborate hard-cover anthologies of science fiction. In 1949, Doubleday and Company initiated a special line of hard-cover science fiction novels. There was a major boom in science fiction magazines in the early 1950s, and dozens of new periodicals appeared.

Although science fiction grew popular quickly, it still had to earn respectability. This did not happen overnight.

Early modern science fiction—stories written in the 1800s by such eminent authors as Jules Verne and H. G. Wells—was generally well written. It included thoughtful tales about the hopes, possibilities, and dangers of scientific advances. Verne's contributions included *A Journey to the Center of the Earth* (1864) and *From the Earth to the Moon* (1865). Wells's books included *The Time Machine* (1895), *The War of the Worlds* (1898), and *The Shape of Things To Come* (1933). Many such works are considered classics of literature, as well as science fiction classics.

Magazine science fiction, however, began as a pulp-fiction phenomenon in 1926. Pulp magazines, printed on cheap, rough-edged paper made from wood pulp and left unglazed, were produced by the dozen in those days. Pulps came in all categories, including love stories, detective and Western yarns, war stories, jungle adventures, and

Exploring the universe
in a spaceship is one
enduring theme in
science fiction films.
These ships, *clockwise
from top left,* appeared
in *When Worlds Collide*
(1951), *Destination
Moon* (1950), *The Time
Travelers* (1964), the
Russian film *Voyage to
a Prehistoric Planet*
(1964), and *Master of
the World* (1961).

In an unusual twist, an atomic submarine and its crew explore inside the human body in *Fantastic Voyage* (1966), *left.* The interior of the "Death Star" in *Star Wars* (1977) is so vast that it dwarfs a large spacecraft parked inside, *below.*

sports stories. They featured such popular superheroes as the Shadow and Doc Savage.

The pulps paid their writers little, but they offered a seemingly endless market for stories that didn't have to be sophisticated or polished. Scores of young people, fired with the ambition to write, got their chance to be published in pulp magazines. Science fiction magazines were perhaps the least successful part of the pulp magazine phenomenon, and they did not stay part of it.

Credit for raising the level of science fiction writing must go to John W. Campbell, Jr., who in 1937 became editor of *Astounding Stories.* Campbell was one of the best-known writers of the early 1930s, so he knew pulp writing and wanted something better.

Campbell changed the name of the magazine to *Astounding Science Fiction* and sought out writers who knew science and engineering and understood what makes scientists tick. He found such writers, then

Robots have long been film favorites. Famous mechanical characters have included Maria the Robot, *above,* from the film *Metropolis* (1926); Robbie the Robot, *top center,* from *The Forbidden Planet* (1956); and a drone robot, *top right,* communicating with actor Bruce Dern in *Silent Running* (1972).

Children of all ages love the robots, *left,* from *Star Wars* (1977)—R2-D2 (right) and C-3PO. Actor Yul Brynner plays a lifelike robot with a problem, *above left,* in *Westworld* (1973). The chrome police robots, *above right,* from *THX 1138* (1970) are sinister.

bullied and coaxed them into writing stories that dealt with plausible advances in technology and what such advances might mean to society. The stable of writers he developed dominated the field for decades, and their names still ring bells today—Robert A. Heinlein, Arthur C. Clarke, Lester del Rey, Theodore Sturgeon, A. E. van Vogt, Hal Clement, and even Isaac Asimov.

While Campbell was finding and editing good writers, other changes were taking place in science fiction magazines. Comic books came along in the late 1930s and began drawing off younger readers of the pulps. The trend accelerated until the pulp magazines had virtually vanished by the late 1940s. But science fiction magazines survived because they had changed and graduated from the field—as had one or two mystery magazines.

Throughout the 1950s, magazine science fiction—with Campbell and his writers in the lead—probed scientific gadgetry. Sometimes they were not far ahead of the scientists; many technical advances were made during this period. The nuclear bomb became far more dreadful with the development of the hydrogen bomb in the 1950s. The invention of the transistor in 1947 eventually made possible all sorts of compact electronic devices, from pocket-sized radios to desk-top computers—the "intelligent machines" described in science fiction. Jet planes and television were other science fiction fantasies that soon came true.

Then Russia launched *Sputnik 1*, the first earth satellite, on Oct. 4, 1957, and scientists began to work toward the goal of putting human beings in orbit—and even of reaching the moon. How science fictional could you get?

The Campbell style of science fiction eventually changed, of course, for several reasons. Science fiction that stayed close to the nuts and bolts of scientific advances read too much like the science columns of *The New York Times* and seemed a bit dull.

Then, too, many people were becoming disillusioned with some of the directions taken by science. The nuclear bomb was an ever more frightening threat, and—to many—scientists seemed more and more like mercenaries in the service of the military establishment. So Campbell's essentially optimistic view of scientific advance was at odds with popular feeling. At that time, also, freedom of expression was increasing. Sex and vulgar language became more acceptable in print, and Campbell's puritanical editing seemed dated.

Most important, the rapid growth of television in the 1950s affected the entire world of printed fiction. Many people stopped reading popular fiction of any kind, preferring to watch television fiction, including Westerns, crime shows, and situation comedies.

All magazine fiction, except for science fiction, dwindled in popularity. Fewer fiction books of every variety, except science fiction, were published. For young people filled with the urge to write, the main market was now science fiction.

Audiences love to hate "little green men" or "bug-eyed monsters" like these fearsome Morlocks from *The Time Machine* (1960).

What a change that introduced! In previous years, the only writers who tried science fiction were fanatically devoted to the field, excited by science and technology, and writing about it by choice. From 1960 on, many of the new authors wrote science fiction because of a shortage of other outlets for their work. Many were not interested in science; others—like Harlan Ellison and Robert Silverberg—seemed almost antagonistic to science.

As a result, a revolution in science fiction began in the 1960s that was as important as Campbell's earlier revolution. Most of these "new wave" stories were about ordinary people affected by science, not about science and scientists. In many cases, the science was far in the background, scarcely noted. New wave writing was experimental in writing style, content, and structure, and much of it used sex and violence freely.

The new wave roused violent passions, both for and against, among science fiction readers. Its more extreme form did not succeed, but the new wave was generally a good thing. It broke the mold that was beginning to fit too tightly around science fiction and made for freer expression. This helped even those writers who continued to produce "hard science fiction," the variety that stresses technology and the physical sciences—writers like Ben Bova, a science writer and the author of *Millennium* (1975), and Larry Niven, who wrote *Ringworld* (1969) and *Protector* (1973).

An interesting side effect of the new wave was that it brought writers from other countries to the fore. Earlier, of course, there had been a strong European component in science fiction. After all, Verne was

French, and Wells was English. Then, in 1926, Hugo Gernsback, an immigrant from Luxembourg, founded *Amazing Stories,* the first American science fiction magazine, and the early issues featured reprints of European science fiction. However, most of the new writers that came forward for about 30 years were American, so the United States dominated the field. Magazines published in other nations were not usually successful, and those that survived did so largely by reprinting American science fiction.

American readers tended to view the field as purely American. When the World Science Fiction Convention became an annual affair in the late 1930s, it was taken for granted that the meetings would be held in North American cities. And yet the field was never as American as some thought. Of the so-called big three writers, only Robert Heinlein is a native-born American; Arthur C. Clarke is an Englishman, and I was born in the Soviet Union.

But the new wave began in Great Britain. British writers were less enamored of technology than Americans and were also closer to the forefront of the new experiments in style. The English writer Brian W. Aldiss, author of *Barefoot in the Head* (1969), was one of the leaders of the new wave with his emphasis on ecological crises and his highly imaginative writing style.

Bizarre creatures populate the universe of *Battlestar Galactica,* a television series in the 1970s and a motion picture in 1979.

Soon, science fiction was an international phenomenon. Shortly after World War II, there was some evidence that the Russians viewed science fiction as a form of Western propaganda. This idea soon faded. Science fiction has flourished in the Soviet Union, and much American science fiction has been translated into Russian. Science fiction writers from Eastern Europe became popular in the West; Stanislaw Lem of Poland, author of *Solaris* (1961) and *The Investigation* (1976), is a notable example.

The American-sponsored World Science Fiction Conventions began to be held in cities on other continents—London and Melbourne, Australia, for example. In 1970, the convention was held for the first time in a non-English-speaking city—Heidelberg, West Germany.

The new wave brought another change, as women became more influential. Men dominated science fiction through the 1950s. Most of the editors, writers, and readers were men, and most were young. If women appeared in the stories at all, they were passive characters whose function was to complicate the plot—to give the male heroes someone to win or to rescue. Even the few women who wrote science fiction in the early days tended to write in this fashion—notably Catherine L. Moore, who wrote "Shambleau" (1933), and Leigh Brackett, author of "Martian Quest" (1940).

With the new wave, however, style and content changes—as well as the growing lack of alternate forms of fiction—encouraged more women to begin reading and writing science fiction. This, in turn, led to a broadening and deepening of the manner in which women were portrayed in the stories.

In 1970, Ursula K. LeGuin won the coveted Hugo award for the best science fiction novel of the year, *The Left Hand of Darkness* (1969). Anne I. McCaffrey has written such phenomenally successful science fiction fantasies as *The Ship Who Sang* (1970). Militant feminists such as Joanna Russ, author of *The Female Man* (1975), have used science fiction as a medium for advancing their views.

The broadening of science fiction meant also that it was approaching the "mainstream" novels—those written for the well-educated public generally—in style and content. Also, mainstream novelists began incorporating science fiction themes into their novels. Thus, Michael Crichton's novel *Andromeda Strain* (1969), a tale about a satellite that jumped orbit and spread deadly germs on earth, made the best-seller lists.

Science fiction writers found their books becoming popular with the general public and—in some cases—used in schools. Courses in science fiction were offered in many high schools and colleges in the United States. Such books as Heinlein's *Stranger in a Strange Land* (1961), Frank Herbert's *Dune* (1965), Clarke's *Childhood's End* (1953), and my own *Foundation* trilogy (1951, 1952, and 1953) are widely read in classes.

Some fiction writers have become international celebrities and speakers in great demand. Others are routinely sought out by the

Special effects, which add spice to science fiction films, often begin with the building of a model—like the ship being built here for *Battlestar Galactica*.

The *Battlestar* television crew photographs a spaceship. A pylon that holds the ship is wrapped in blue cloth that will not show on the completed film.

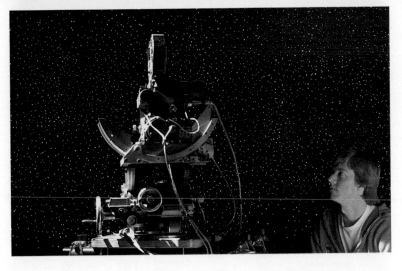

An electronic camera photographs the universe as imagined in special effects. The universe is depicted by pinholes in a black velvet cloth under special lighting.

Heroes and villains—
male and female—are a
staple of science fiction
films. In *Flash Gordon*
(1935), *above,* Flash
(actor Buster Crabbe)
holds his fiancée, Dale
(Jean Rogers), to protect
her from the cloaked
villain Ming the
Merciless (Charles
Middleton). In *Things
to Come* (1936), *right,*
Raymond Massey is the
good guy, opposing
Ralph Richardson,
far right. As a hero
from outer space in *The
Day the Earth Stood
Still* (1951), *bottom,*
Klaatu (Michael Rennie)
shows his spacecraft to
Helen (Patricia Neal).

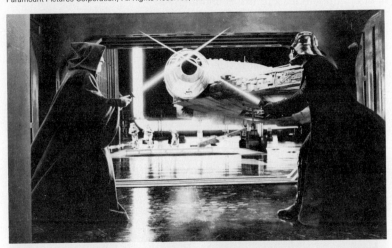

The *Star Trek* film (1979), *above,* brings back the heroes of the television series, including William Shatner as Captain Jim Kirk (seated, center) and Leonard Nimoy as Mr. Spock (standing, second from left). In *Star Wars* (1977), *left,* the masked Darth Vader duels with Obi-Wan Kenobi (Alec Guinness), a Jedi knight upholding "the force." Luke Skywalker (Mark Hamill), *bottom left,* fights for justice in *Star Wars* and its 1980 sequel, *The Empire Strikes Back.* Princess Leia Organa (Carrie Fisher), *bottom right,* also fights for justice.

media for their views on almost any conceivable topic. Ray Bradbury, the one great science fiction writer of the 1940s who was not a Campbell discovery, was probably the first of these celebrities—his books include *Martian Chronicles* (1950), *Illustrated Man* (1951), and *Fahrenheit 451* (1953). Clarke was profiled in *The New Yorker* magazine in 1969 by Jeremy Bernstein and praised for his "profoundly poetic feeling for the strange and only partly understood objects—stars, moons, planets, asteroids—that populate our universe."

It probably would not occur to scientists today to apologize for their interest in science fiction. Astronomer Carl Sagan, a professor at Cornell University in Ithaca, N.Y., wrote an article published in the May 28, 1978, issue of *The New York Times Magazine* praising science fiction for its "thoughtful pursuit of alternative futures." In that article, he also noted, "Many scientists deeply involved in the exploration of the solar system (myself among them) were first turned in that direction by science fiction."

But all this represents only the science fiction that appears in print. Of overwhelming importance to many more people is the visual science fiction that appears in motion pictures and on television. Visual science fiction is, in my opinion, quite different from printed science fiction, and the reasons are economic.

A science fiction hard-cover novel can make money if it sells in the thousands; a magazine, in the tens of thousands; and a paperback, in the hundreds of thousands. But film or television science fiction can be profitable only if it attracts tens of millions of viewers, because production costs are so high.

Thus, many science fiction films have been low-budget productions that require little in the way of acting or writing. Such quickie films

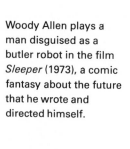

Woody Allen plays a man disguised as a butler robot in the film *Sleeper* (1973), a comic fantasy about the future that he wrote and directed himself.

are at about the level of comic books. But since they are seen by many more people than read science fiction, the quality—or lack of it—of those films has lent a deceiving air of imbecility to the whole field.

There were some honorable exceptions to this rule, such as the film made of Wells's novel *The Shape of Things to Come*, released in 1936. Heinlein worked on the script for *Destination: Moon* (1950), but the levels of cinematography and acting were low.

The real breakthrough in visual science fiction came in 1966, with the television series "Star Trek," a brainchild of science fiction writer and producer Eugene Roddenberry. The series presented realistic characters interacting warmly and facing problems of lasting importance. However, the tales of the starship *Enterprise* on its tour of the Galaxy did not win an enormous audience and, as the first season waned, it became clear that "Star Trek" would not be renewed. But then the unexpected occurred. The dedicated viewers of "Star Trek" bombarded the television network with unprecedented protests, and astonished network executives decided to continue the adventures of Captain James Kirk, Mr. Spock, Dr. Leonard McCoy, and company.

"Star Trek" was finally discontinued in 1969, after three seasons and 78 episodes. But it was not forgotten. Instead, enthusiasm grew and was fed by reruns. Ten years after the program was dropped, it had more fans than it had during the series' lifetime. Fans calling themselves "Trekkies" flocked by the tens of thousands to "Star Trek" conventions, in a number of cities. Many of them were too young to have seen the original episodes.

In motion pictures, a turning point came in 1968 with *2001: A Space Odyssey*, which Clarke helped write. This realistic portrayal of space travel attracted a big audience and was the first science fiction movie to become a runaway hit.

Why is it, though, that so many watch "Star Trek" and *2001: A Space Odyssey* when so few—by comparison—read science fiction? Nor is there an enormous crossover. Only a handful of the tens of millions introduced to visual science fiction begin to read science fiction.

Clearly, visual science fiction offers something printed science fiction does not—"special effects." Technical skills are used to simulate intergalactic battles, alien beings, and superhuman abilities that come with such circumstances as zero gravity.

Today's emphasis on special effects makes visual science fiction almost a different species from the printed variety. The difference is even reflected in their nicknames. Printed science fiction has long been referred to as "SF" by its devotees. Hollywood people use the term "sci-fi"—a term that SF readers detest.

Special effects hit the big time in terms of profits with the motion picture *Star Wars*, directed by George Lucas and released in 1977. In content, this film was very much like the Flash Gordon serials of the 1930s. However, excellent cinematography, along with the film's good humor and inspired use of a pair of robots called R2-D2 and C-3P0,

Visions of future cities
have long occupied
science fiction
filmmakers, as in *Just
Imagine* (1930), *above;*
Things To Come (1936),
above right; and the
more recent *Logan's
Run* (1976), *right.*

resulted in enormous popularity and unprecedented profits. (A sequel, called *The Empire Strikes Back,* was scheduled for release in 1980.) Special effects were also the key to the popularity of director Steven Spielberg's film *Close Encounters of the Third Kind,* which also was released in 1977.

A host of *Star Wars* imitations appeared. As usual, the imitations were not as good as the original. Most chose the elements they saw as money-makers—particularly the special effects—and did not understand the importance of the cleverness and good humor.

What about the future of science fiction? What themes will it deal with? This is impossible to predict exactly, of course, but one can make intelligent guesses. Science fiction tends to reflect the times in which the writer lives. Therefore, as the world's population continues to rise and as more and more resources are used up, there is bound to be a tone of deepening pessimism. There is bound to be an increase in doomsday themes—stories dealing with survival after a nuclear war, or after a complete breakdown of government. There will probably be many stories dealing with the problems of space colonization, and with encounters between human and alien intelligences. And stories involving conflicts between human beings and intelligent machines will increase.

None of these themes are new. There is no such thing as a completely new plot; the restless human mind has in one way or another thought of almost everything thinkable.

With time, however, science fiction writers will have the chance to sharpen their themes. For example, authors have been writing about robots for decades, but few have considered in detail the power source that keeps robots going. Imagine a future society that depends heavily on robots. Could an energy crisis force human beings to keep some robots and dismantle others? If so, which would they choose?

And much has been written about teaching machines. But the real thing will soon be on us full force, with the advent of communications satellites, sophisticated laser beams, optical fibers, and computerized libraries. How will society change when computerized teaching machines are used everywhere? Will human teachers continue to share in the teaching? Will children lose touch with one another?

Or, for that matter, will disillusionment with science and technology grow, turning science fiction readers to fantasy? I hope not, for that would be a dangerous sign of society's decay.

For further reading:

Ash, Brian (editor). *The Visual Encyclopedia of Science Fiction.* Harmony Books, 1977.

Carter, Paul A. *The Creation of Tomorrow: Fifty Years of Magazine Science Fiction.* Columbia University Press, 1977.

Gunn, James. *Alternate Worlds: The Illustrated History of Science Fiction.* Prentice-Hall, 1975.

Holdstock, Robert (editor). *The Encyclopedia of Science Fiction.* Mayflower Books, 1978.

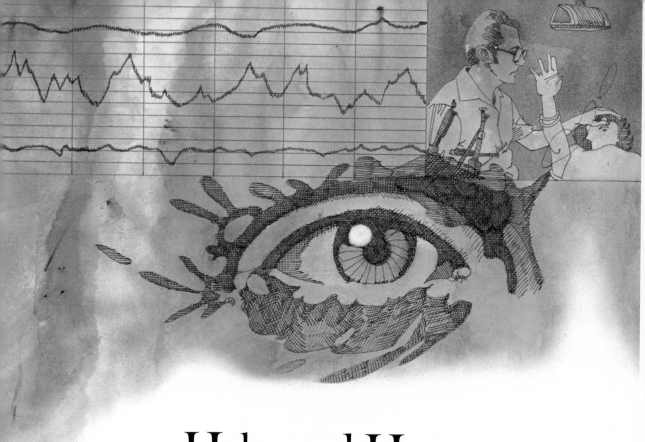

Help and Hope from Hypnosis

By Patricia Skalka

Once viewed mostly as a novelty, hypnosis is growing in use in medicine, police work, and athletics

I sat in a comfortable chair, eyes closed, with my arms extended in front of me and my fingers loosely curled into my palms. I was told that each hand held a plastic bucket, the kind children use at the beach. As suggested, the buckets soon began to feel heavy, and my arms began to waver and drop. I was told that my arms were being controlled by ropes that were tied to my wrists and attached to pulleys on the ceiling. The ropes allowed my left arm to drop while my right arm rose. Then, I was told that the ropes were no longer tied to my wrists. My arms stopped moving. Next, an imaginary shovelful of sand was added to the left bucket, and my left arm was pulled slowly down-

G. Courtmann

 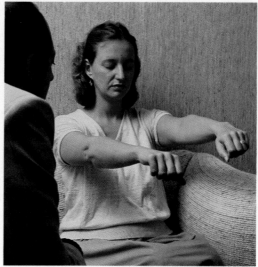

ward. When my left hand touched my lap, the elbow bent, and my
arm dropped limply to my side, sending a wave of relaxation through
my body. My right arm was lowered in the same way, and another
relaxing wave coursed through me.

Next, I was told to imagine that a big, red balloon filled with helium was tied to my wrist. I felt my hand being tugged upward until I
was told that the string had been cut and the balloon had floated to
the ceiling. I was told to open my eyes and look for the balloon. I
could see it only faintly, but the texture of the ceiling looked different
–blanked out–where I imagined the balloon to be.

I shut my eyes then and a voice said, "On the count of three, you
will open your eyes." I did. "On the count of five, you will become
fully awake and aware of your surroundings." I did.

I had just been hypnotized. I had volunteered for the session in
order to get firsthand experience as background for this article.

The session left me feeling very comfortable, but it had been quite
different from what I had expected. The room was not dark, and there
was no swinging pendulum, no mysterious person bidding me to look
into his eyes. Instead, I sat in a sunlit office on a warm afternoon, and
the hypnotist, psychiatrist Bennett G. Braun, sat to my right out of my
line of vision. I had not even been asleep. I remembered everything
that happened during the entire session and could recall all of it. Only
my sense of time had been distorted. The session had lasted seven
minutes, and I guessed later that it had been only two minutes long.

I had experienced an altered state of consciousness. "We all experience these all the time," explained Braun, who is vice-president of the
American Society of Clinical Hypnosis (ASCH) in Des Plaines, Ill.
"When you get lost in a book, when you're so distracted that you don't
hear the conversation around you, even when you daydream, you're

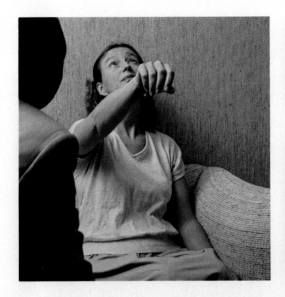

in an altered state." Hypnosis is a homing in, a focusing of attention on the voice of the hypnotist and what he suggests. The power of suggestion is intense, and a subject, like me, can be made to see a red balloon where none exists.

I have no special talent that makes me easy to hypnotize. In fact, experts say that almost everyone can be hypnotized to some extent, though fewer than 20 per cent can go into a deep trance. Children are good subjects, as are adults who have strong imaginations and the ability to become engrossed in work or hobbies.

For years, entertainers used hypnosis to get people to perform unusual acts—to crow like chickens, or to shrink in terror from nonexistent storms, for example. Many people viewed hypnotism as an amusing novelty, but some saw it as dangerous tampering with the mind. Few believed that it could be used to do anything worthwhile. In recent years, however, hypnosis has been used widely in medicine and criminal investigation. And its use is growing.

The number of health professionals who regularly use hypnosis as a therapeutic tool is increasing steadily. Psychologist Melvin A. Gravitz, president of ASCH, estimates that between 40,000 and 50,000 physical, mental, and dental health experts in the United States, 7 to 9 per cent of the total, have been trained in *hypnotherapy*—the medical use of hypnotism—and 2,000 to 3,000 more are being trained each year.

The American Psychological Association's (APA) Division of Psychological Hypnosis found in a 1978 survey that more than 40 per cent of the graduate departments of clinical psychology, 35 per cent of the medical schools, and 30 per cent of the dental schools in the United States offer courses in hypnosis, twice as many as in 1974.

The Law Enforcement Hypnosis Institute (LEHI) in Los Angeles has taught investigative hypnotism to 600 law-enforcement officers in

Austrian physician Franz Mesmer, *this page, right,* thought hypnosis could influence magnetic fluids that he said regulated health. At Mesmeric séances in the late 1700s, *above,* subjects sat around tables with bottles of the fluids. Such objects as crystals, watches, and jeweled glass were used to hypnotize subjects. By the late 1800s, some persons thought hypnosis had magic powers, *opposite page, top.* But serious study of it was also well underway, *opposite page, bottom.*

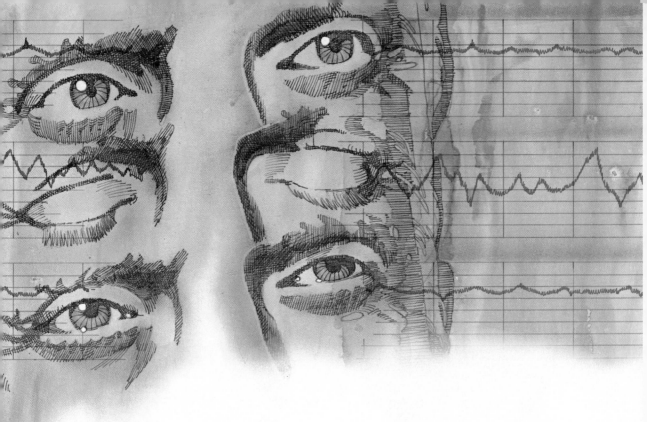

A hypnotized person's brain gives off short, rapid electric waves, *bottom,* like those of a fully awake person, *top,* rather than the long, slow waves that occur during most of a normal night's sleep, *middle.*

the United States since it was established in 1976 by psychologist Martin Reiser, director of behavioral science services for the Los Angeles Police Department (LAPD). Reiser estimates that 200 local, city, and state police departments, including some in Arizona, Colorado, Florida, Georgia, Illinois, Kansas, Michigan, New Jersey, New York, Oregon, Texas, and Washington, now use hypnotism in their investigative work. In addition, both the Central Intelligence Agency and the Federal Bureau of Investigation have agents trained in *forensic hypnosis,* which deals with legal and criminal applications.

Hypnotism was probably first used in medicine. Priests in ancient Egypt and Greece are believed to have used it to cure people and to impress them with their power. Then in 1778, an Austrian physician, Franz Anton Mesmer, introduced it to the Western world. At that time, some scholars believed that the sun and stars gave off a magnetic fluid that was essential to human health. An imbalance of this fluid was thought to cause illness. Mesmer claimed that he could manipulate this magnetic fluid and cure the sick. He treated his patients by seating them in large open tubs, hypnotizing them, and then waving magnetic wands over their bodies to correct their fluid imbalances. However, a special investigating committee of outstanding scientists determined in 1784 that there was no such thing as a magnetic fluid. Mesmer and his techniques were discredited. But in the 1840s, Englishman James Braid experimented with Mesmer's methods. Braid did not believe in magnetic fluid. He believed that people changed profoundly during mesmerization, but that the change was psychological, not physical–in the mind rather than the body. He coined the term *hypnosis*–from Greek words meaning *to put to sleep*–to describe the trance. Modern science, however, does not support the view that the trance is like sleep. "The brain waves of a sleeping person are not the same as the brain waves of a hypnotized person," says Gravitz. In fact, a hypnotized subject exhibits no measurable physiological difference from a normal, conscious person.

Interest in hypnotism has fluctuated since Mesmer's time. Until about 50 years ago, most Americans considered hypnosis so much hocus-pocus. Then in the 1930s, the noted psychologist Clark L. Hull conducted the first modern scientific experiments to study the powers of hypnosis, and doctors working in clinics in the United States and in Europe began using the technique with patients. The public began to take hypnosis seriously in the mid-1940s when doctors used it successfully to treat members of the military in World War II for combat fatigue and neurosis. The most recent surge in interest, which began in the late 1950s, changed the status of hypnosis dramatically. The American Medical Association studied hypnotism for two years, and recognized it in 1958 as a legitimate healing tool. At that time, the United States had only one organization for medical professionals interested in hypnosis—the Society for Clinical and Experimental Hypnosis, founded in 1949 in Liverpool, N.Y. The ASCH was established in 1957, and the APA Division of Psychological Hypnosis was organized in 1970. About 5,000 doctors, dentists, psychiatrists, and psychologists belong to these groups.

The upsurge of interest in hypnotherapy is not limited to the United States. Work has been going on in Russia and other East European countries for many years, and there are medical hypnosis organizations in Argentina, Australia, Brazil, Canada, Great Britain, Israel, Italy, Japan, Mexico, the Netherlands, Spain, and West Germany.

"Hypnosis is being accepted because it works," says Braun. "It is not a cure-all, but it is an effective therapy to be used along with other more traditional kinds of treatment."

For example, dentists use hypnosis to help patients ease their anxiety and fear, control excessive bleeding, overcome such habits as thumb-sucking, and reduce pain that sometimes goes along with injections. Some patients have teeth extracted and, in rare cases, undergo root-canal work, with hypnosis as the sole anesthetic agent.

I n the laboratory, about 1 in 5 patients can screen out pain almost completely with hypnotic suggestion," says Clorinda Margolis, associate professor of psychiatry and human behavior at Thomas Jefferson University Medical College in Philadelphia. In the clinical setting, with persons actually being treated for some ailment, the same percentage can screen out pain completely and an additional number can substantially reduce their pain experience. "They might cut down their anxiety or be able to say, 'The pain is still there but it's not interfering with my life the way it was before,' " says Margolis.

Some psychiatrists and psychologists use hypnotism to help people overcome such phobias as fear of flying or fear of high places. They

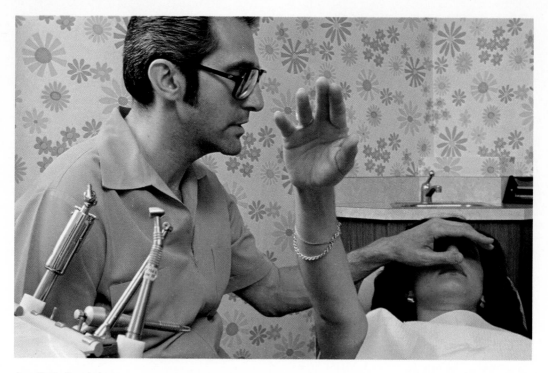

A patient signals her dentist that she is going into a deep trance. Many dentists use hypnosis to calm patients and ease pain.

may also use it in psychotherapy as a short cut to identifying the deeply rooted causes of a patient's emotional problem.

Hypnotism helps some people fight off asthma attacks and migraine headaches. It can help hemophiliacs reduce or eliminate blood loss, and it has been used to treat ulcers, epilepsy, high blood pressure, insomnia, and obesity. Heavy cigarette smokers have successfully shed their habit through hypnosis, women have given birth using hypnosis instead of painkilling drugs, and some children have been cured of bed-wetting.

Some hypnotherapists use a technique called visualization. Just as I visualized myself holding two plastic buckets, the hypnotized hemophiliac can be taught to envision a tourniquet near a wound. And just as the imaginary buckets weighed down my arms, the hemophiliac's imaginary tourniquet can shut off the supply of blood to the wound.

Many persons suffering from intense pain undergo hypnosis at hospitals to lessen their agony. Hypnotherapy was introduced in 1972 at the Walter Reed Army Medical Center's Pain Clinic in Washington, D.C., and more than half of the patients there now are treated with hypnosis. Some learn to transfer pain from a large area such as a leg to a small area such as a fingertip so that the suffering seems less overwhelming. Other patients learn to minimize or ignore their pain.

Persons suffering from severe arthritis, for example, can be convinced under hypnosis that their affected limbs are being bathed in a comfortable, soothing whirlpool. A victim of persistent back pain can imagine being suspended in a soft, painless environment. Even burn victims can be helped. Hypnosis is used at a number of treatment centers to help such patients through the painful process of cutting away dead tissue. One man was hypnotized into thinking he was on a hunting trip. He imagined that the stings and pain of the treatment came from walking through brambles and thorny undergrowth.

But pain treatment does not end at the hospital or clinic exit. Most hypnotherapists also teach patients to hypnotize themselves. Most people cannot do this immediately, mainly because they cannot tell when they are in a trance. Therapists may schedule special sessions to help patients or may provide trance-inducing tapes or phonograph records for patients to play at home.

Once patients learn the technique, however, they can literally take it with them. The man who suffers recurrent headaches can hypnotize himself into a painless state when he feels the pressure begin to mount. The asthmatic can stave off an attack by mentally relaxing the chest and bronchial area. The woman who gulps tranquilizers to calm her nerves can imagine her way into the same relaxed state without drugs.

Even more spectacular is the use of hypnosis as an anesthetic. Visualization distracts the patient from the medical problem. For example, Braun anesthetized an expectant mother for a Caesarean delivery by having her concentrate on an imaginary wall picture he helped her visualize through hypnosis. Other hypnotherapists have anesthetized patients for amputations, appendectomies, hysterectomies, tonsillectomies, abdominal surgery, and even brain surgery. Hypnotism spares the patient from the negative side effects that often follow the use of chemical anesthetics and may accelerate recovery.

The newest and most controversial medical use of hypnosis is in treating cancer patients. Psychologist Bernauer W. Newton and his staff at the Newton Center for Clinical Hypnosis in Los Angeles began working with cancer victims in 1975. In the beginning, patients came only on their own, but now Newton is getting referrals from several physicians. The Newton Center uses hypnotism to ease pain and other symptoms associated with both cancer and such traditional treatment methods as chemotherapy, to improve the patient's emotional state, and, says Newton, to teach the body to fight the disease.

Hypnotism also became a popular law-enforcement tool in the 1970s. The LAPD became the first major U.S. police force to use hypnosis as a memory aid. Investigators asked Staff Psychologist Martin Reiser, who later founded the LEHI, for help with a murder case because they believed that a witness knew more than she could tell them under routine questioning. Reiser hypnotized the witness, who then recalled details she could not otherwise remember.

Word of Reiser's success spread quickly through the department, and he soon received more requests to use hypnosis in difficult cases. He received so many requests, in fact, that he asked the LAPD in 1974 to allow a panel of hypnosis experts to teach investigative hypnosis techniques to experienced detectives. The department agreed, and Reiser began a one-year, three-stage demonstration program in 1975 with 11 police lieutenants and two captains participating. An outside consultant attended every hypnosis session during the first phase; consultants were on call but not necessarily present for phase-two sessions; and the detectives worked on their own most of the time after about eight months, in phase three.

The detectives used hypnosis in about 70 cases during the program and gathered more information than was otherwise available in 50 of those cases. The LAPD adopted hypnosis as an investigative tool in June 1976, and won the $10,000 Police Science Award in 1977 for "pioneer work in developing hypnosis as a crime-fighting technique."

"We work only with volunteer witnesses and victims," Reiser explained. "We use hypnosis as a tool to get more information that will allow investigators to go out and do more investigating and hopefully corroborate the information and get additional evidence. Our records show hypnosis helped elicit additional information in 80.2 per cent of the cases in which it was used. We've encountered no negative emotional aftereffect, and, in fact, 19 per cent of the people who were hypnotized said they felt they had derived significant emotional benefit from having undergone hypnosis."

Still, there is criticism of such police work. The American Civil Liberties Union and some forensic psychiatrists warn that there is danger of accidentally leading a subject to a desired response, of contaminating or misshaping a memory, and of feeding facts that will influence testimony. Therefore, the hypnotists must form questions carefully. For example, a detective should not question a witness about an individual fleeing the scene of a crime by asking, "Did you see a man come out of the door?" The cooperative witness who really saw a woman climbing out through a window might "remember" seeing a man coming out of the door and go on to describe him. There is even some question about whether testimony obtained under hypnosis is admissible in court. Critics say that all such information must be checked and corroborated. In addition, they argue that police should thoroughly explain the procedure to potential subjects before asking for permission to hypnotize them. They also contend that impartial observers should tape and monitor hypnosis sessions.

More debate centers on the training. "This is a very controversial issue of ethics," says Gravitz of ASCH. "I'm on the side of those who say this: Anyone who uses hypnosis for whatever purpose must first be very thoroughly trained in human behavior and then can learn hypnosis as another technique."

Hypnosis is most useful in crimes that cause great emotional stress on witnesses and victims, such as murder and rape. Many people react to such stress by unconsciously erasing the memories of the crimes. Hypnotists try to bring back such memories without causing undue additional trauma.

Patients at stop-smoking clinic raise their hands to show the therapist, Joe Walsh, *above,* how deep their trance has become. Walsh then makes suggestions designed to help them stop or cut down on their smoking.

This technique has been used with spectacular success in a number of recent instances. The bus driver in the 1976 Chowchilla, Calif., kidnapping of 26 children, for example, was able to recall the kidnappers' license number only under hypnosis. In 1978, a 15-year-old female hitchhiker was raped, had her arms cut off, and was left wandering along a California highway. Under hypnosis, she supplied information that led to the arrest and conviction of her assailant. Hypnotism also was used with at least one witness in the 1979 murder trial of Theodore R. Bundy, convicted of killing two students at Florida State University in Tallahassee.

Just as hypnotism works in the hospital and police station, so too does it work on the playing field. Many athletes have used it to conquer pain, increase their motivation, and sharpen their concentration. Outfielder Paul Blair supplied a dramatic example of the value of hypnotism in sports in 1973. Then with the Baltimore Orioles, Blair had seen his batting performance suffer for three years after he was *beaned*–hit on the head with a pitched ball. After psychiatrist Jacob H. Conn hypnotized him, Blair went on what he calls the "hottest streak I've ever been on in my career." His batting average went from .218 to .325, he finished the season at .281, and he was selected for the 1973 American League all-star team. Conn, who has treated many athletes –including pitchers, skeetshooters, and golfers–points out that Blair was a good athlete all along. If you're not good at a sport to begin with, he explains, hypnosis won't help.

Conn taught Blair to relax and then to imagine seeing himself play ball as he did before he was beaned. Blair learned to take a mental journey as far back as his boyhood baseball competition, to convince himself that he had the ability to play well and to avoid reinjury.

Hypnotists use visualization to guide other athletes through mental "practice" of their sports. "It's been shown experimentally that a person who is hypnotized and then imagines shooting a pistol at a target, playing basketball, skeetshooting, playing golf, or whatever, will definitely improve his performance on the field," says Conn. "What we're saying is that athletic performance depends to a great extent on remembering what to do and how it feels to do it, and on being confident in what we are doing. That is why mental 'practicing' can improve the player's score, increase his performance level above what he achieves from routine practice, and could be used as a supplement to that practice."

Although individual players have used it, no major athletic team has yet officially employed hypnosis on a large scale. And despite warnings that Russia is using hypnotism to improve its athletes' performances in the 1980 Olympic Games, the U.S. Olympic Committee (USOC) has no plan for a hypnosis program.

Psychologist Robert Singer of the USOC Sports Medicine Council says that the reported use of hypnosis among Russian athletes is "not a matter of great concern. Better athletes have a highly developed ability to concentrate. They have the ability to energize whatever needs to be energized to achieve just the correct psychological and physiological state just prior to an event. We've been trying to help people learn to identify their states and put themselves into more appropriate states, but not in a formal setting of hypnosis."

Whatat are the limits of hypnosis? Can hypnotized people be made to do something they would not do normally? Most experts say no, but some, including Gravitz, say this is possible. He also believes there is some evidence that people can be hypnotized either without realizing it or against their will. "In most instances, however, people can be assured that with hypnosis they are in charge of the situation," he explains. "They can resist the hypnosis, and will not necessarily answer all questions they're asked or do all they're told to do." Nor does hypnosis produce amnesia, though the hypnotist can suggest that the subject forget an entire session.

Hypnosis does not function as a lie detector. Subjects can distort the truth while hypnotized. Reiser once hypnotized a prison inmate who claimed to have overheard and then forgotten information about the murder of a policeman. "It developed later that what the man wanted was a day out of prison and some good food. Everything he'd told us under hypnosis was all dreamed up," Reiser says.

"With hypnosis we are not able to do anything the subject cannot basically do," Gravitz explains. "For example, I cannot use hypnosis to help somebody run a mile in two minutes. It is physiologically

impossible to run that fast, though the person *will* run faster than he normally would."

Gravitz and other experts warn against the indiscriminate use of hypnosis. "There is definite danger in being hypnotized by an unqualified person," he says. "Anyone who uses hypnosis should first be very thoroughly grounded in psychology, in human behavior, in knowledge of the unconscious forces that determine behavior, in knowledge of what to do if an emergency develops. Even something as mundane as quitting smoking or losing weight can pose a risk to the patient's psychological structure, and the hypnotist had better be prepared to deal with the whole person rather than just with their smoking or eating.

"Always ask to see the credentials of a person or clinic advertising hypnosis for any purpose," cautions Braun. "If you have any questions, call a local hospital or university psychiatry department."

Braun warns against participating in stage-show hypnosis or volunteering to be the subject of a cocktail-party hypnotist. "You don't want just anyone tampering with your mind," he warns.

Self-hypnosis helps some athletes reach the proper mental and physical states before they compete, though it cannot transform a poor athlete into a good one.

Psychologist Martin Reiser of the Los Angeles Police Department (left) questions a hypnotized witness, who furnishes details that enable police artist Fernando Ponce to sketch a picture of a suspect.

Braun recalls an incident that occurred when he was demonstrating hypnosis to a group of health-care professionals. He asked for a subject from the audience, someone not undergoing psychotherapy, and a woman volunteered. He hypnotized her and she soon began to panic. She had age-regressed, without any suggestion from Braun, to the time of her mother's death and was re-experiencing the trauma of that period. "This could have been a critical experience," explains Braun. "As the person doing the hypnosis, I had to know how to deal with this dangerous situation."

In another instance, several medical students were practicing hypnosis on one another. "One student could not bring his subject out of trance," says Braun, "and I had to intervene." These and other problems can develop with hypnosis, whether the hypnotist is a stage performer, a weight-reduction instructor, or a trained medical specialist. According to the experts, it is vital that the person conducting the session know what to do when such a problem arises. And they argue that only extensive knowledge and experience in the behavioral sciences provides the necessary expertise.

Even self-hypnosis can be dangerous for some people, particularly those who often have severe problems in dealing with others in normal social activities. Most of us have occasional minor problems of this kind, and they are nothing to worry about. But everyday experiences make some people so unhappy that they would retreat into a world of their own thoughts if they could learn how to do it. Teaching such people self-hypnosis could cause severe emotional damage if they used it to withdraw further and further from ordinary reality.

Improper hypnosis can also pose grave danger to an individual who handles deep inner conflict by focusing mental anguish on a *depressive equivalent* – such as a physical pain or a specific habit such as smoking or drinking heavily. The mind creates the depressive equivalent to think about and avoids thinking about the conflict. For example, a person who otherwise would be extremely depressed may instead suffer from a back pain formed by the mind. An uninformed hypnotist who cured the pain without treating the emotional problem that caused it might endanger the patient's mental health. The patient, now exposed to the conflict, might solve the new problem by creating a new depressive equivalent – a limp, for example. But if the patient could not do this, then the old turmoil could return in full force.

Disaster of a different kind may await an athlete who is guided by a careless hypnotist in an effort to improve performance. A distance runner who is trained to ignore fatigue may suffer harmful physical exhaustion. A baseball pitcher who is taught to improve concentration may become so intent on performance that he ignores normal danger signs and exposes himself to injury – for example, by failing to report the sudden onset of shoulder pains.

These dangers are so serious that medical practitioners favor a ban on hypnosis except as a therapeutic tool subject to licensing and other regulation. Health-care professionals with the required knowledge of psychology and hypnosis would be allowed to use hypnotherapy only as part of their regular work. For example, a dentist would be allowed to use hypnosis to anesthetize patients while working on their teeth. Some medical experts also would like to limit forensic hypnosis to psychologists and psychiatrists. Others caution that only practitioners trained in behavioral sciences and sports medicine should be allowed to hypnotize athletes.

Oregon passed a strict law governing hypnosis in 1973, but it is the only state to have done so. There, only persons licensed in the healing arts may practice hypnosis. Elsewhere, literally anyone can hang up a sign and claim to be an expert.

Braun likens hypnosis to a scalpel. "Anyone can be taught to use one," he explains, "but you wouldn't want anybody but a trained surgeon actually using a scalpel on you."

For further reading:

Block, Eugene B. *Hypnosis: A New Tool in Crime Detection*. David McKay, 1976.
Crasilneck, Harold B. and Hall, James A. *Clinical Hypnosis: Principles and Applications*. Grune, 1975.
Kroger, William S. *Clinical and Experimental Hypnosis in Medicine, Dentistry, and Psychology*. Lippincott, 1977.
Marcuse, F. L. *Hypnosis: Fact and Fiction*. Penguin, 1959.

The Riches of Jupiter's Realm

By Marsha F. Goldsmith

**Voyagers 1 and 2 traversed oceans of
space for an awesome close-up view of
the remarkable Jovian planetary system**

Picture postcards sent back to Earth by some cosmic Columbus
might carry remarkable color photographs like the ones on these
pages. Their electronically transmitted message would surely say,
"Having wonder-filled time–wish you were here."

In fact, these stunning pictures were sent back by recent travelers to
distant parts of the solar system. The unmanned *Voyager 1* and *Voyager
2* spacecraft approached Jupiter in the spring and summer of 1979 and
returned astonishingly detailed photographs that gave astronomers
data they could have bettered only by being there. Thousands of vivid
images, which scientists will continue to study for years, give amazingly clear details of the beauty and complexity of the planet and its
14 moons, or satellites.

First, there was Jupiter itself. Scientists had learned much about the
planet since the Italian astronomer Galileo studied it in 1610 with the
telescope he invented. They knew that it was a rapidly spinning ball of
molten hydrogen and helium more than 11 times the size of Earth and
318 times as massive, about 400 million miles (650 million kilometers)
from us in space. They had seen its Great Red Spot, a massive, stormy
area large enough to contain several Earths, amid dense, swirling
clouds. But they still had many questions about the giant planet and

A collage of king and minions in their relative positions puts
the moon Io (upper left) nearest the planet Jupiter (upper right),
then Europa (center), Ganymede, and Callisto (bottom).

its moons. When the National Aeronautics and Space Administration's (NASA) *Voyager 1* probe passed within 170,000 miles (272,000 kilometers) of Jupiter's surface on March 5, those questions began to be answered.

More than 100 scientists, including astronomers, physicists, and geologists from many nations, worked together at the California Institute of Technology's Jet Propulsion Laboratory (JPL) in Pasadena, Calif., analyzing and interpreting the *Voyager* transmissions. Astronomer Bradford A. Smith of the University of Arizona in Tucson, leader of the imaging science team that interpreted the photographs, described the "enormous" excitement as scenes of previously unimagined wonders appeared on imaging screens.

The author:
Marsha F. Goldsmith
is a senior editor for
THE WORLD BOOK YEAR
BOOK and SCIENCE YEAR.

The Great Red Spot was only a blot on Jupiter's face in this 1973 *Pioneer 10* photo, *above.* But when *Voyager 1* was 3 million miles (5 million kilometers) from Jupiter on March 1, 1979, its photos, *opposite,* clearly showed the spot (upper right) in all its turbulence. Familiar features like the large white oval (middle right) stood out anew.

One feature scientists knew nothing about before is Jupiter's ring. A single 11-minute time exposure, taken as the probe crossed the planet's equatorial plane, revealed the ring's presence. Other photographs showed the scientists that Jupiter has strong auroras, similar to the Earth's northern and southern lights.

But the most spectacular surprises came as *Voyager 1* investigated Jupiter's four largest moons, the so-called Galilean satellites. Io, Europa, Ganymede, and Callisto turned out to be uniquely different from one another and unlike any other heavenly body. Volcanoes are active on Io, making that craterless orb the only place in the solar system besides Earth where such internal upheaval is known. Surface features of the other satellites also were novel. Their variety made

Text continues on page 97

Special color processing enhances cloud structure details in Jupiter's naturally colorful atmosphere. Distinct zones are (top) the North Equatorial Belt, containing a large dark, long-lived structure; (middle) the Equatorial Zone, a plumy area whose northern, bluish tips may be warmer; and (bottom) wild white clouds west of the Great Red Spot.

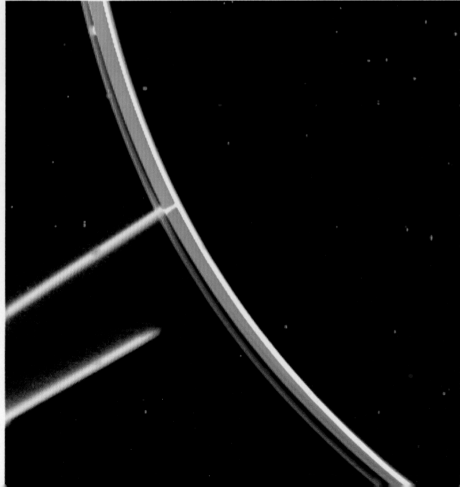

Sulfurous Io, the size of
Earth's moon, shines
like a bright copper
penny against a seething
Jovian surface, *above.*
A color composite of
time exposures, *left,*
shot in Jupiter's shadow,
makes its ring system
appear as two faint
lines at left of the
planet's luminous edge.

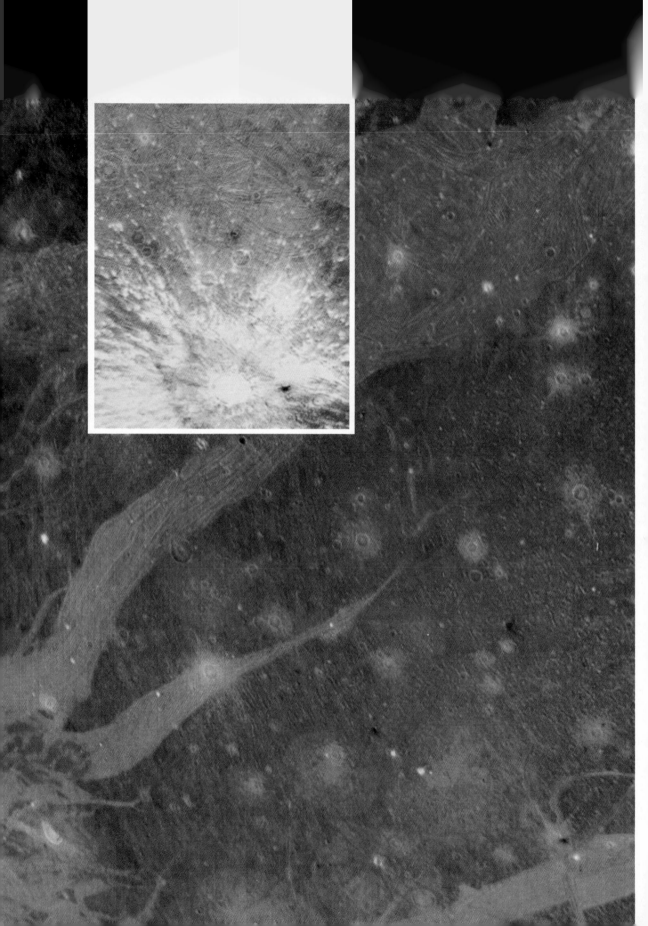

Fresher material ejected from craters on ice-encrusted Ganymede, *opposite page, inset,* shines brightly against the ancient, heavily cratered dark areas that cover most of that moon's surface. Broad, lightly grooved regions may be fault zones. Meteorite impact craters pockmarking icy Callisto, *above,* may date from its formation.

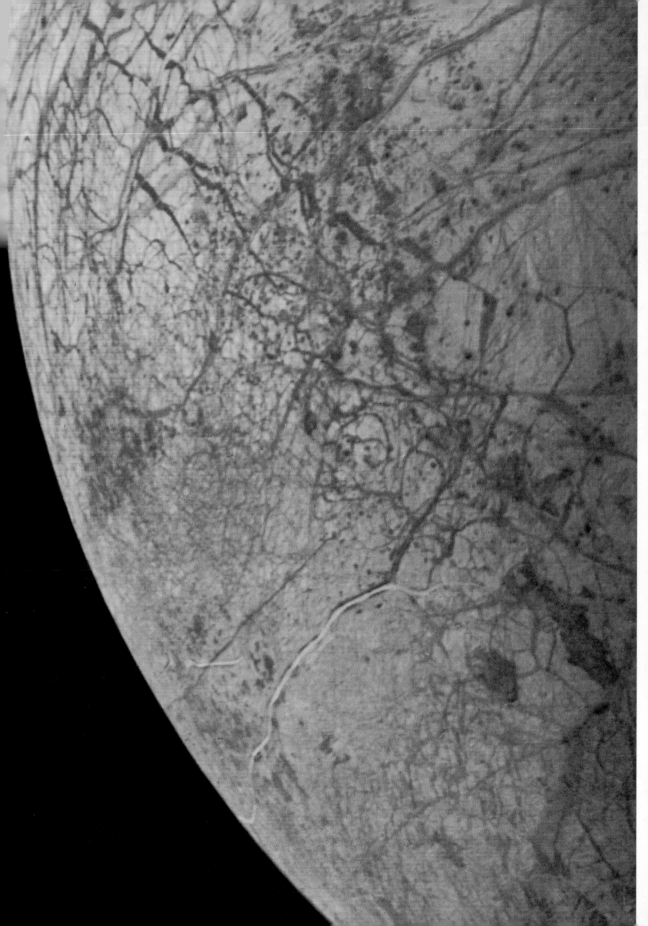

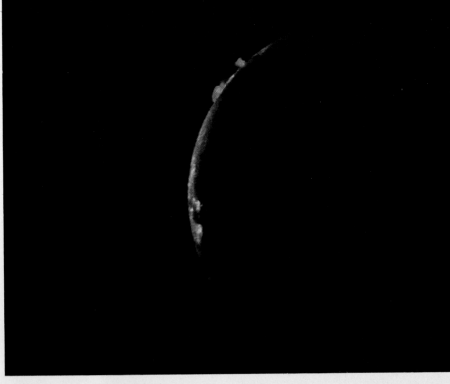

Volcanic plumes on Io, *left, Voyager 1*'s biggest surprise, confirmed that the densest moon's ruddy surface results from lavish sulfur deposits. Scientists see further evidence of volcanism in the dark spot, *below,* surrounded by irregular radiations that are most likely eruptions of lava.

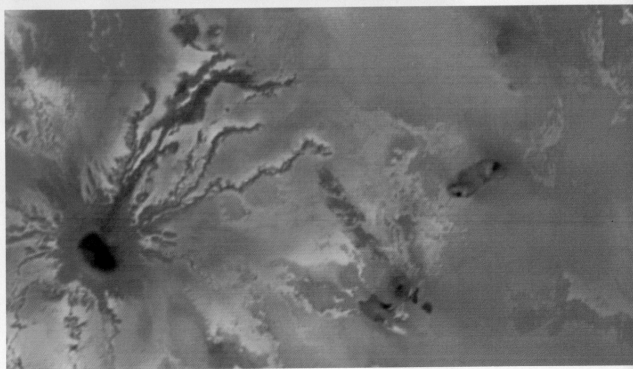

Opposite page: Complex crack patterns on dense, rocky Europa's flat, almost craterless surface, suggest that fractures on the brightest Galilean satellite were filled from below with ejected darker material. Europa probably has a silicate rock core covered by a water-ice glacier.

Eruption-scarred Io is dressed in a mantle of debris befitting an ever-changing ball of fire and brimstone. Its surface bears hellish signs of every type of volcanism that occurs on Earth.

Laurence Soderblom, an imaging specialist from the U.S. Geological Survey in Flagstaff, Ariz., exclaim, "There ain't no such thing as a boring Galilean satellite." He added that *Voyager 1* revealed so many new facts about the Jovian world that "we'd have been surprised if we *weren't* surprised" by the extraordinary discoveries.

The splendid *Voyager 1* mission findings were followed by even more intriguing information from *Voyager 2*. That probe came within 400,000 miles (640,000 kilometers) of Jupiter on July 9, and returned pictures that clearly showed changes in the Jovian atmosphere that had occurred since *Voyager 1*'s visit. *Voyager 2*'s varied perspectives on the ring system and on the large moons suggested new questions even as the old ones were answered. Physicist Edward C. Stone of JPL, chief project scientist, summed up the observers' reactions: "We obviously had expected certain things," he said, "but what we found when we went and made a measurement is that not only is it different, which is interesting, but in fact it's different in a way that's telling us something we hadn't understood before."

Scientists will have another chance to satisfy their curiosity about the riches of Jupiter's realm when NASA launches its *Galileo* mission in 1982. Meanwhile, the original probes move on. *Voyager 1* should reach Saturn late in 1980, and *Voyager 2* is scheduled to fly by Uranus in 1986. Far-seeing scientists using far-out technology will continue their search for something new under the Sun.

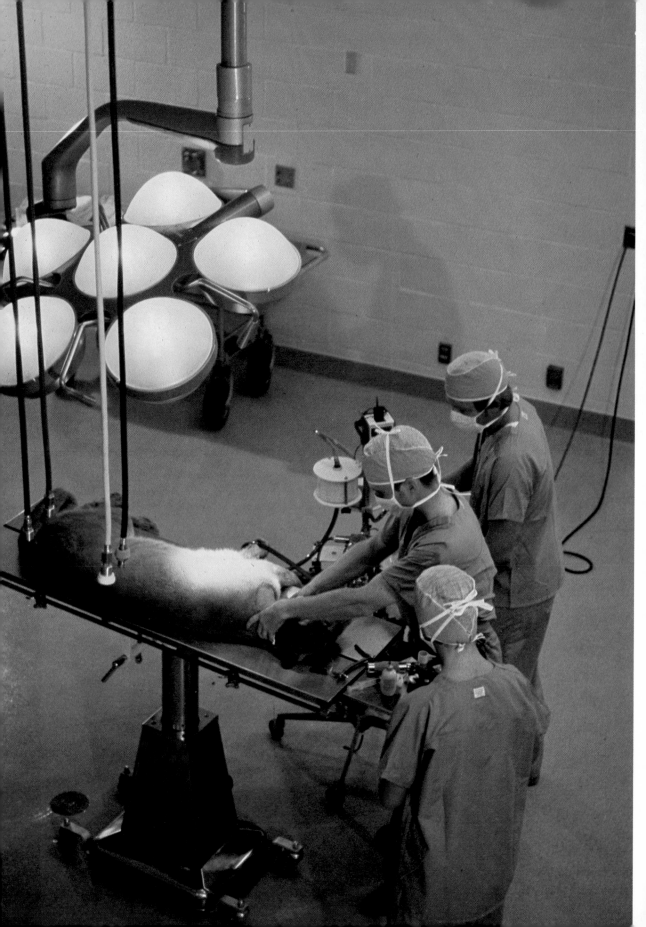

Do You Make Cage Calls, Doctor?

By George Alexander

**Wild animals are difficult patients, but today's
dedicated zoo veterinarians treat their ills with new
tools and drugs—and old-fashioned love and care**

The baby baboon, not much bigger than a house cat, lay motionless on its side in the Intensive Care Unit cage at the San Diego Zoo. Bandages were wrapped securely around its abdomen, its lower jaw was wired, and a tube dripped a saline solution into a vein. Every now and then, the tiny animal shuddered in its sleep.

"She unfortunately happened to run between two fighting adults," said Phillip T. Robinson, the 35-year-old director of veterinary services for the San Diego Zoo, as he opened the glass door of the cage and put his stethoscope to the baboon's chest. "It was a bad fight, involving the dominant male. This little female got in the way and he eviscerated [disemboweled] her. He also broke her jaw."

Rushed to the zoo hospital—one of the newest and finest facilities of its type—the little baboon, less than a year old, was operated on by Jane E. Meier, an associate veterinarian. Meier carefully sewed up every rip she could find in the animal's intestines and then gently placed them back inside the abdominal cavity in an operation that lasted three hours. She also wired the baboon's lower jaw together. "We did everything we could," Meier said later, as she munched a sandwich and stared wistfully at her unconscious little patient. "We'll just have to wait and see if she makes it through the day."

Robinson and Meier are, in a way, perfect examples of what is happening in the field of zoo veterinary medicine today. They are young, well-trained, and skilled medical practitioners, totally dedicated to the care of exotic animals. But in another way, they are unusual—they have jobs. Many are called to this interesting and challenging profession, but only a few—a very few—are chosen.

Indeed, there are more astronauts today than zoo veterinarians. There are now about 45 doctors of veterinary medicine working full time in United States zoos, and fewer than 100 worldwide, according to Mitchell Bush, 38, chief of the Office of Animal Health at the National Zoological Park in Washington, D.C. While that is roughly four times as many zoo veterinarians as there were in 1969, it does not imply a booming job market. Lester E. Fisher, director of Chicago's Lincoln Park Zoo, described the 1970s as a period of great growth for both the practice and the practitioners of zoo medicine. The practice is still growing, but now, in an era of tight public budgets, the opportunities for practitioners have slowed drastically.

As recently as 20 years ago, most zoos called in local veterinarians, usually those with practices built around cows, horses, and household pets, to treat an ailing cheetah or water buffalo. These pinch-hitting veterinarians, as Robinson pointed out, "often looked to the exotic animal's domesticated counterpart for an approach to the problem, because of anatomical similarities. Take digestion, for example. The vet could make some informed inferences about an ailing lion or antelope based upon what he already knew about the digestive tracts of the domestic cat or cow."

Inference, however, was still a long way from factual information about the wild animal's physiology, and factual information was very hard to come by. If the sick animal was a truly dangerous creature, such as a lion or a rhinoceros, the veterinarian either tried to lure it into a *squeeze box*—a cage with sides that can be moved in against the animal to immobilize it—or waited until it was so weakened by its illness that it offered no resistance. For less dangerous animals, such as certain species of gazelle, zoo workers might use a lasso or a net.

"There just wasn't any good way to get hold of a sick animal prior to the early 1960s, either to diagnose it or to treat it," said Bush. "Human anesthetic drugs weren't of much help to the veterinarian because they had to be administered intravenously. And in order to get the drug into an animal's veins, you had to have your hands on it, and that meant you had to capture it somehow. So you were right back where you started from. Yes, there were paralyzing drugs that you could load in a dart gun and shoot the animal with, immobilizing it, but they didn't anesthetize it. And you were presented with the very real risk of [the animal slipping into] respiratory arrest."

But when several new tranquilizing and anesthetizing drugs were introduced, and improved ways of injecting them into everything from bears to elephants were developed, zoo medicine began to make dramatic advances in the care of captive wild creatures. "No longer were veterinarians doing what we used to call 'over-the-fence' diagnoses,"

The author:
George Alexander is a
science writer for
The Los Angeles Times.

Until fairly recently, most zoos kept wild animals in cages, *left*. The latest trend, however, is to allow the animals to roam freely in natural surroundings while the human visitors are confined to tour buses or trains, as at San Diego's Wild Animal Park, *below*.

Robinson said. "With these new drugs, we were able to get right to the animal at the onset of its illness."

Drugs such as etorphine, ketamine, and xylazine proved to be potent and fast-acting on animals, either tranquilizing or anesthetizing them. Moreover, these drugs had the advantage of working intramuscularly. They did not have to be injected directly into an ailing animal's bloodstream to be effective. They could simply be shot into a shoulder or a haunch – targets considerably easier to hit than a vein.

Getting these new drugs into an ailing animal was also made easier. New developments included improved dart guns with smaller, lighter-weight projectile syringes; pole syringes (basically a long stick tipped with a hypodermic needle); and that old stand-by of jungle tribes, the blowgun.

At many zoos, the blowgun is the preferred means of injecting an animal. "It's quiet and doesn't startle the animal like a gun does," San Diego's Robinson explained, as he picked up a plastic pipe and slipped a dummy syringe casing into it. "And with the trend toward more natural exhibit areas, instead of the old-fashioned cages, it's sometimes hard to get at a sick animal without alarming the others. The quietness of the blowgun allows you to inject one animal without stirring up the others. Now then, see that chart on the far wall? Pick out one of the big letters along the bottom." I did, and, with one explosive puff of breath, he hit it squarely with the casing.

Robinson recalled how he "darted" Bob, one of the San Diego Zoo's orang-utans. A keeper reported that the primate had a runny nose and seemed to be snuffling, but was otherwise in good shape. "I ordered his rations to be doctored with antibiotics, figuring Bob had a cold," the young veterinarian said, "and his condition improved. But when we stopped giving him the antibiotics, he quickly got decidedly worse. He was stumbling and had difficulty standing up. So I got out the blowgun, put a syringe in it, went out, and darted him."

When zoo personnel tranquilized Bob and got him into the hospital, Robinson examined him and discovered that the orang-utan had a badly decayed tooth. Indeed, the infection had spread from the abscessed molar into one of the animal's sinuses and from there into his inner ear, which explained the stumbling and loss of balance. "We treated him with massive doses of antibiotics until we could get the infection under control," said Robinson, "and then our dental consultant [a local dentist who helps out at the zoo] came in and did a root canal [excavating the decayed tissue in the tooth and replacing it with filling]. Bob's just fine now."

Bush also endorses the blowgun for restraining a sick or injured animal. "It allows us to pick up on a problem, like a bone fracture, soon after it occurs," he said, "before its effects become irreversible."

As unlikely as it might seem, bone fractures are almost as common in zoos as they are on ski slopes. Broken limbs often occur when zoo workers try to move animals from one area to another, or when they try to capture one for some reason, such as the examination of a newborn animal.

"Most of the fractures we see here are among the excitable herd animals, like deer or antelope," Bush said. "These are animals whose primary response to any sign of predation or danger in their natural habitat is a great burst of speed to get away." He explained that frequently something will startle a herd and all the animals will dash off suddenly, with one of them being trampled or tripping and snapping a foreleg.

Bush recalled one particularly frustrating case involving a newborn Père David's deer. Bush and a keeper were trying to capture the fawn to give it a postnatal physical examination. But their attempt to grab the fawn set off the rest of the herd, and some of the deer stepped on the delicate baby in their frantic rush to escape, breaking a bone. Bush caught the newborn deer, rushed it to the hospital, and set the fracture and applied a splint.

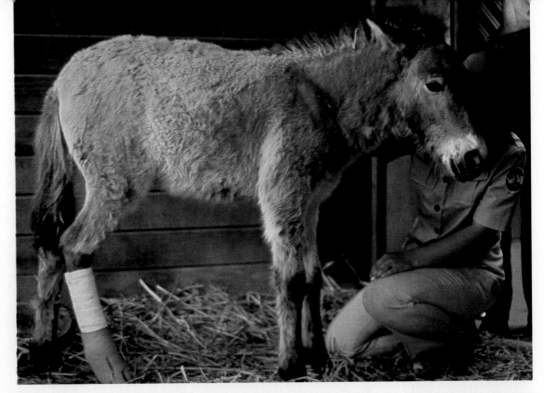

Everything appeared to be going well until Bush set out to capture the fawn two weeks later to remove the splint. The little deer panicked and bolted–breaking another bone, this time a toe bone. "Fortunately," said Bush, "the first fracture had healed by then. So we splinted the new fracture." Zoo personnel later removed the second splint without any further injury to the animal.

Bush's experience points up a major problem for zoo veterinarians– their animal patients tend to resist every effort to make them well again. A human with a fractured arm or leg normally cooperates with the physician, either by remaining in bed during the recovery period or by using crutches or slings and avoiding stress on the fracture. But an animal is almost invariably uncooperative. Either it will try to continue functioning with the broken bone, compounding the break, or, once fitted with a cast or splint, it will immediately attempt to use the injured limb as if nothing had ever happened to it.

Recognizing that wild animals are not likely to change their natural traits, zoo veterinarians have looked for surgical techniques that enable them to treat an animal's injury, while at the same time allowing the animal to regain some use of that part of its body. One such technique is *bone plating*.

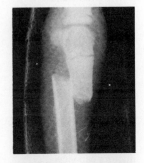

Originally developed in Switzerland more than 20 years ago for skiers suffering bad fractures, bone plating involves attaching a stainless steel brace to a broken bone. Much like the reinforcing brace a carpenter nails across a cracked beam, the plate transfers the load of the animal's weight around the fracture. The plate is secured by a number of stainless steel screws sunk into healthy, solid bone above and below the fracture. The injured limb is also usually wrapped in a

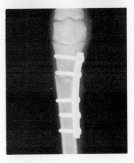

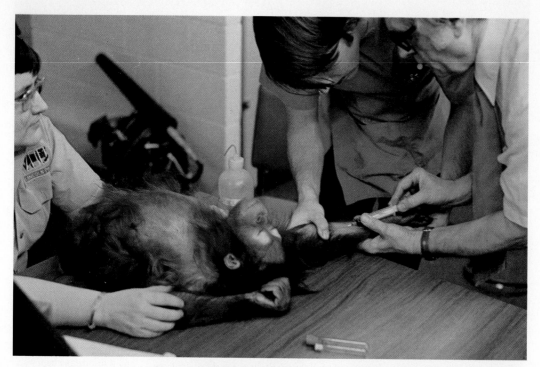

Erich's Eye Operation
Erich, an orang-utan at
Chicago's Lincoln Park
Zoo, has a cataract
removed at the University
of Illinois Hospital. The
veterinarians and eye
doctors follow the same
procedures as on humans,
from the anesthesia,
above, and examination,
right, to the removal of
the cataract, *opposite
page, center,* and the
postoperative care,
opposite page, bottom.
Reporters and other
doctors can view
Erich's operation on
closed-circuit TV,
opposite page, top.

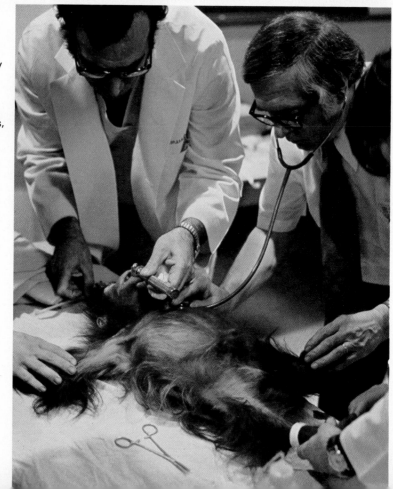

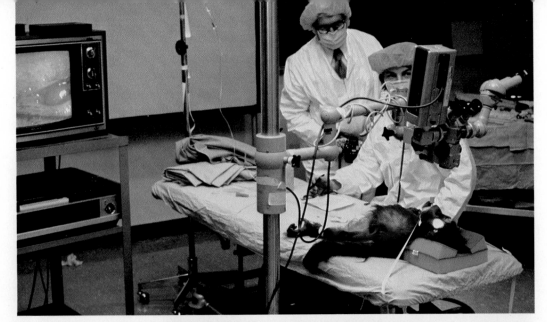

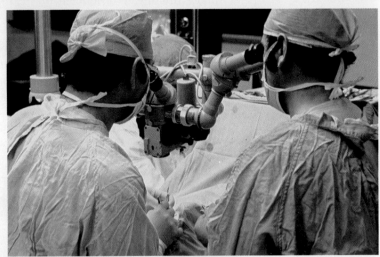

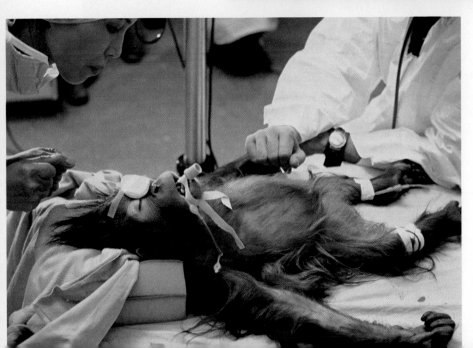

lightweight fiberglass cast. This bone plating technique has been used successfully on such different animals as a Przewalski's horse and a Komodo dragon at the San Diego Zoo and a Siberian tiger at Brookfield Zoo near Chicago.

Of course, many fractures can be set right by conventional orthopedic casts. But even here, as Bush noted, consideration must be given to the animal's nature. "A lot of animals will try to remove a cast with their teeth," he said, "especially if it is heavy or restricts an important function, like grasping." A siamang gibbon at the National Zoo once chewed off several plaster casts protecting its broken forearm before the veterinarians noticed that the casts they put on extended down over the animal's hand and prevented it from using its fingers. When a new cast short enough to leave the gibbon's hand free was placed on the reset bone, the animal tolerated it, and the broken bone healed in about eight weeks.

Almost any disease or ailment that can happen to a human can happen to a zoo animal. Yes, animals get tuberculosis, pneumonia, diabetes, arthritis, even cancer.

At San Diego, Robinson and Meier have treated several different species, including an Asian elephant and an Indian rock python, for various kinds of tumors. The female elephant, a circus performer, was appearing in San Diego when a nonmalignant genital tumor about as big as a melon began to bleed. The circus called in Robinson, and, after examining the animal, he suggested that the tumor be cut away.

Working under the circus "big tent," Robinson and Meier sedated

Infected inner pulp is removed from a jaguar's upper canine tooth in root canal dental work at the Gladys Porter Zoo in Brownsville, Tex. Dental problems are common in zoo animals.

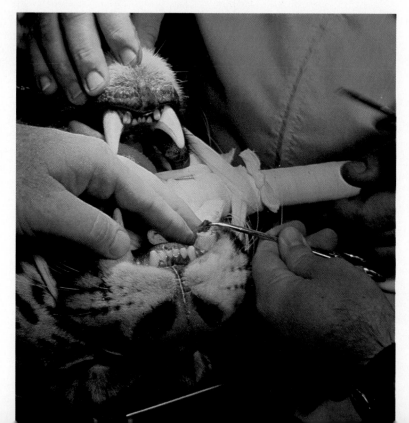

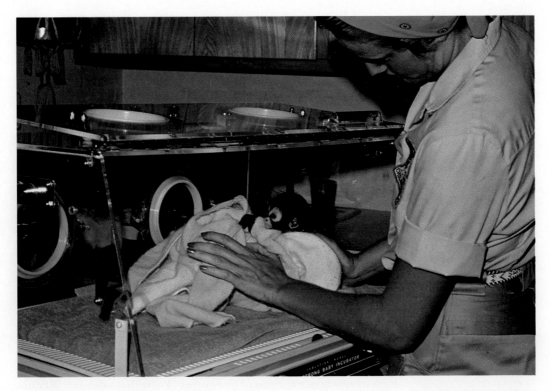

An infant spider monkey is placed in an incubator by a zoo attendant. Many animals born in zoos must be separated from their mothers after birth for reasons of health or safety.

the elephant and injected the area round the base of the tumor, where they planned to cut, with a painkilling drug. Before they could operate, however, they had to devise a tourniquet to stop the bleeding at the incision – there was nothing in the zoo's equipment large enough to cope with a mass nearly 7 inches (18 centimeters) in diameter.

They improvised, splitting a wooden dowel about the size of a broom handle down the middle and placing the halves on opposite sides of the tumor's base. Then they slipped two hose clamps – the kind used on automobile radiator-hose connections – over the ends of the dowel pieces. Tightened with a screwdriver, the wooden pieces were pressed together securely enough to form a very effective tourniquet. The veterinarians then removed the tumor, which weighed more than 7 pounds (3.2 kilograms), and sewed up the incision. The elephant recovered nicely.

The python had a different kind of tumor, and the treatment was not as successful. The snake – 8 feet (2.4 meters) long – had a sore mouth, and the San Diego keepers thought at first it might be suffering from mouth rot, a fairly common disease among captive snakes. When the big snake was brought to the zoo hospital, however, Robinson discovered that it actually had a malignant tumor in its mouth the size of a ping-pong ball.

The tumor was removed surgically, but it grew back within just a few weeks. The San Diego staff then decided to irradiate the tumor with cobalt-60, a radioactive element used to treat many human cancers. The tumor shrank and disappeared completely about six months after the first irradiation. But then the snake became very lethargic, refused to eat, and died a month later. An autopsy disclosed that similar malignant growths had spread to the snake's liver and gastrointestinal tract.

Autopsies are very important procedures that benefit the living, Bush explained as he showed a visitor around the cavernous building at the National Zoo where hundreds of such operations are carried out every year. "We autopsy every animal that dies here," he said, "from mice to rhinos. We even did an elephant a few years ago." Knowing the cause of death for an animal often enables veterinarians to take swift action to protect other animals, if the death was caused by an infectious agent or a controllable poison.

Many zoos now have clinical pathology laboratories where such studies as blood and urine analyses, pregnancy tests, and fecal examinations are carried out. "You just have to have a pathology lab today," Bush said, "if you're going to keep as many of your animals as possible in good health."

For example, members of San Diego's pathology department noticed several years ago that many of the birds they autopsied showed signs of severe malnutrition. The keepers knew that adequate quantities of food were provided daily to the inhabitants of the Rain Forest, the big exhibit cage where many of the malnourished birds had been housed, so they began monitoring the feeding process more closely. They discovered that some of the more aggressive birds were claiming the feeding stations as their exclusive territories, driving off other birds and preventing them from eating properly. The solution was simplicity itself—add more feeding stations and place them at different heights throughout the structure. When this was done, the number of birds dying of malnutrition dropped sharply.

Sometimes, however, the solution of one problem gives rise to another. "Because of advances in medicine, good management, and nutrition," said Frank Wright, 30, veterinarian-in-charge at Brookfield Zoo, "a lot of our animals are living a long time. And some are starting to get a little senile. They're pretty healthy, but they do have their cranky episodes."

"It's difficult to believe," interjected George B. Rabb, the director of Brookfield, "but our Lion House is a geriatric ward." The elderly cats that live there may not look like candidates for rocking chairs on the porch of an old folks' home, Rabb added, but they are candidates for most of the old-age ailments that humans are prone to.

"Half of the lions have had cataract operations," said Wright. "We have a 14-year-old female Bengal tiger who has had six or eight eye operations over the last six years. And we have a male tiger that has a touch of spinal arthritis." Wright said that the arthritic tiger is given doses of thyroid extract in its food to ease its discomfort. "No one knows why it helps animals with spinal arthritis," he said, "but it does."

For that matter, there are more unknowns than knowns when it comes to exotic animals. "What's normal for a lot of these animals simply has not been established," Robinson said. And trying to determine just what is normal, while at the same time coping with abnormal situations, places a heavy load on the small medical staffs at these zoos.

"The great crush of animals here and at Wild Animal Park [an 1,800-acre (728-hectare) reserve some 30 miles (48 kilometers) north of the main San Diego Zoo] greatly reduces the veterinarians' time to do research," said pathologist Kurt Benirschke, director of research at the San Diego institution. Still, the effort is made. "Every clinical incident is a research opportunity," said Bush, as he looked in on two bull snakes, in separate glass tanks, that seemed tangled in a maze of wires. Catheters—very fine tubes—had been surgically slipped into each snake's body and carefully pushed deeper until one end rested inside the snake's heart. In this way, National Zoo researchers could draw off small

A zoo doctor has a large and varied practice. He makes daily rounds, checking former patients and examining new arrivals. Constant attention to the animals' present health can prevent many problems.

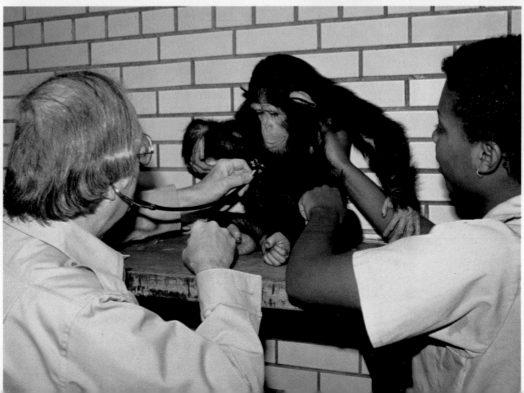

Special foods and privacy are important for many animals. A cobra, which usually eats only live prey, devours a sausage treated to smell like a snake, *above*. Gardener clips eucalyptus leaves, *above right,* to feed to finicky koala bears. A koala and her newborn cub are isolated in a breeding center while she rears the cub, but visitors can watch them via television, *right*.

amounts of oxygenated blood to identify and measure gases, such as oxygen and nitrogen. Periodically, the snakes also received varying amounts of different anesthetics so that the veterinarians might learn how reptiles respond to these drugs. Such information will come in handy when Bush or his associates have to care for an ailing snake.

The information will be stored in a computer as an essential part of the National Zoo's health-care system. Both research and clinical data, the latter obtained from treating sick animals, are encoded and will be placed in the computer. "In addition," said Bush, "every new acquisition that we receive is X-rayed, has blood samples drawn from it, is given an electrocardiogram, and has its blood pressure measured and its teeth examined. Essentially, it's a '1,000-mile checkup.'"

The National Zoo's computerized information system is still in the early stages of development. When completed, it will consist of medical records on each animal in the zoo's collection, along with research data gathered by the zoo and other institutions. Other zoos, such as Chicago's Lincoln Park and San Diego, are either installing or considering the installation of comparable computer systems.

Looking years ahead, Bush sees a network of interconnected computer systems through which zoos and other organizations, such as veterinary schools of medicine, will pool their knowledge. Internation-

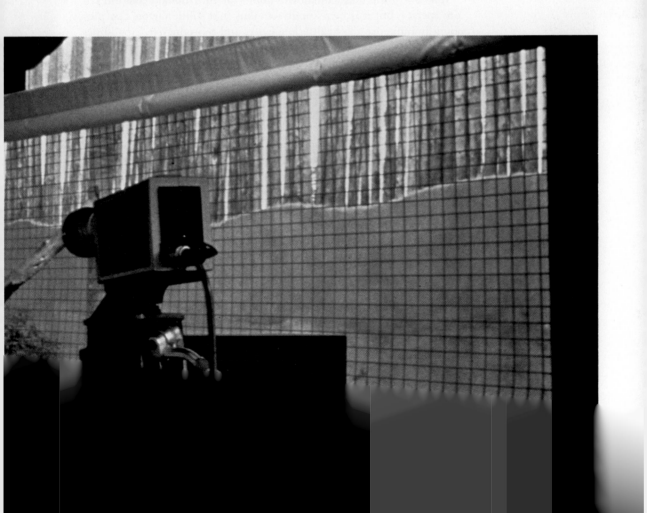

ally, too, such institutions might be able to share their particular strengths. Brookfield's Wright feels, for example, that European zoos are ahead of their U.S. counterparts in pharmacology, especially in restraint drugs. Bush credits European zoos with greater depth in clinical medicine, but says that American zoos have more sophisticated surgical and diagnostic techniques.

In San Diego, where a great deal of research is done, Benirschke—who also holds a position at the University of California, San Diego, School of Medicine—is presently carrying out a study of cholesterol levels in the blood of lowland gorillas. Zoo officials have been concerned about their gorillas' diets ever since Trib, an adult male, suffered an epileptic seizure in 1978.

Tests recorded the level of cholesterol in Trib's blood, but researchers could not say whether it was high, average, or low for gorillas. The animal's diet was reviewed, and chicken-egg supplement, which he had been receiving, was crossed off the list. More leafy roughage was added to his rations because gorillas, said Benirschke, eat a lot of leaves in the wild. An antiseizure drug was also slipped into his food. Trib has had no further epileptic seizures, and his cholesterol level is about 40 per cent lower than it was in 1978, though the veterinarians still don't know if Trib's level is high or low for a lowland gorilla.

There are still many unknowns about the nutritional needs of various species, but it is increasingly obvious that subtle factors can profoundly influence the health, longevity, and reproductive capabilities of animals in captivity. The National Zoo has a full-time nutritionist, and other zoos call upon local specialists for assistance when an animal seems to have a dietary problem.

To date, much of the research done in zoological nutrition has been characterized by luck—stumbling onto something. Someone discovered several years ago, for example, that adding small amounts of vitamin E and the chemical element selenium to animals' diets reduced the incidence of *white muscle disease,* a calcium mineralization of muscle tissue that strikes many newborn animals. So much calcium is deposited in the animal's muscle that it looks white when autopsied.

No one is quite sure why or how vitamin E and selenium work against this disease, but as Bush said, "All of our birds and mammals now get it in their rations, and it has cut down significantly the death rate of newborns from this disease." Fisher of the Lincoln Park Zoo said that vitamin D_3 has been found to be vital to the health of such small South American primates as marmosets.

One of the most exciting and challenging parts of zoo medicine today is reproduction, or breeding. Zoos are fast becoming the final sanctuary for some species, and the men and women who care for these animals recognize that their continuation may well depend upon successful breeding programs in captivity.

"You can't always put a male and female together and expect them to produce young," said Bush. "We're working closely now with scien-

The computers of ISIS, the International Species Inventory System, keep records on more than 40,000 zoo animals in the United States.

tists at several institutions on artificial insemination. We inseminated two white tigers in June 1979 and plan to inseminate a cheetah soon."

Why inseminate, instead of letting nature take its course? "There are a lot of good reasons to do it artificially," Bush answered. "With the tigers, it was a matter of the females not mixing well with the male. We weren't at all confident that they'd mate if we isolated them. With the cheetah, it was a matter of nonavailability of a male. The zoo down in Brownsville [Texas] does have a male, however, and we got the semen from them. It's cheaper to fly a vial of semen up here [to Washington] than it is to fly the animal." Bush said that if these artificially inseminated cats become pregnant and bear healthy young, the zoo may try to inseminate its giant pandas—gifts from the People's Republic of China—sometime in 1980 or 1981. The Chinese have already artificially impregnated a giant panda in one of their own zoos. Two cubs were born in September 1978, and one survived.

The technique has great potential, Bush believes. "If we're successful," he explained, "it could mean that someday we would capture wild males, sedate them for a short spell, and collect semen. We then could use that semen to impregnate captive females in our zoos. That way, we wouldn't have to worry about inbreeding." He quickly added that artificial insemination will always be only an occasional and useful adjunct to natural breeding, not the main technique. "The thing is, we want to develop the technique of artificial insemination so that we'll have it when we need it—for those times when the male refuses to

Yuanjing, the first giant panda ever to be successfully produced by artificial insemination, rests quietly in its mother's arms at the Peking Zoo in China.

mate with the female and maybe even tries to kill her when they are brought together, or when the male and female are located in widely separated zoos and it is simply impossible to transport him to her every time the female comes into heat. You can't count on mating taking place at those times and, even if you could, you still couldn't count on a successful pregnancy."

At some veterinary schools, including the University of California at Davis, Michigan State University, and the University of Missouri, students may take "core" packages of courses dealing with exotic animals. For example, Davis veterinary students can take a block of six elective courses dealing with such topics as restraint pharmacology; exotic animal physiology; and fish, bird, and mammal diseases. At any one time, there are perhaps a dozen graduate and undergraduate students taking the zoo-medicine electives. A handful of zoos, such as New York City's Bronx Zoo, San Diego, National, Sacramento, and St. Louis, have intern programs where a newly graduated veterinarian receives practical training in treating animals, just as newly graduated physicians do in hospitals.

At the end of the internship, the young veterinarian hopes to land a staff position with a zoo somewhere, and, so far, the production of these specialists has pretty closely matched available positions. "But," said Lincoln Park Zoo's Fisher, cautioning would-be zoo veterinarians about the realities of this profession, "the number of job opportunities is limited, and the turnover rate is low." Robinson and Meier said that a good employment year will yield one or two jobs for zoo veterinarians, but that it is not at all unusual for a year to pass with no jobs opening up in the field.

Jane Meier talked about her career in zoo medicine as she worked on Patrick, a 450-pound (200-kilogram) Himalayan bear. The bear had demolished a wood bench in its cage several weeks before. In the process, it also did considerable damage to two claws on its front left paw. The claws became so infected that they had to be amputated, along with a small portion of the paw.

The anesthetized bear, draped over the operating table like a lumpy bearskin rug, offered no resistance as Meier cut away the old bandage, cleansed the healing wound, and rebandaged the paw. When she was a little girl, she recalled as she nonchalantly washed the bear's paw, her parents took her to "just about every zoo in the world," and she loved it. As far back as she can remember, she had always wanted to work with exotic animals in a zoo. After graduating from Purdue University's School of Veterinary Medicine in West Lafayette, Ind., she got her chance when the San Diego Zoo offered her a position as assistant veterinarian. She loved her work, she said, and she was fond of the animals, especially Patrick, "a very nice bear, for bears."

The wounded paw now dressed, hospital technicians wheeled Patrick back to a holding cage until the effects of the tranquilizing drugs wore off. Meier was stripping off her surgical gloves and cleaning up the corner of the operating room where she had worked on Patrick, when someone hurried in to report that the baby baboon—the little female injured earlier that day—had taken a turn for the worse.

Meier and Terry Willingham, an animal technician who had assisted at the baboon's operation, hurried down the corridor to the Intensive Care Unit. Willingham got there first. She opened the cage and knelt down beside the little animal. The baboon showed no outward signs of life.

Still, the young woman clung to some hope. She gently rolled back the baboon's eyelids and tapped its pupils with her fingertips. There was no response. She pressed her ear against the animal's chest, listening for a heartbeat, but heard none.

"What?" she said in mock indignation. "Die? How dare you! After all we've done for you!" It was futile. She dropped her head on her forearm for the briefest of moments in sadness, affection, and loss.

For further reading:

Campbell, Sheldon. *Lifeboats to Ararat*. Times Books, 1978.
Durrell, Gerald. *A Zoo in My Luggage*. Penguin Books, 1976. *The Stationary Ark*. Simon and Schuster, 1977.
Herriot, James. *All Creatures Great and Small*. St. Martin's Press, 1972.
Zoonooz, published monthly by The Zoological Society of San Diego, Inc., Balboa Park, San Diego, Calif. 92112.

How Pollsters Take the Pulse of Politics

By Richard Pawelek

It's important to understand the workings of public opinion polls, which take on added significance in a presidential election year

What percentage of Democrats from the Far West would vote for Senator Howard Baker for President of the United States if the 1980 election were held tomorrow? How many voters aged 18 to 30 would go for former California Governor Ronald Reagan? How many–if any–registered Republicans who voted for Richard M. Nixon in 1972 would support California Governor Edmund G. Brown, Jr.?

As Election Day–Tuesday, Nov. 4, 1980–draws near, voters in the United States are being bombarded by a flood of public opinion polls designed to answer these questions and many others. More than a year before the election, the evening television news and the morning newspaper were busily reporting polls showing how voters rated President Jimmy Carter and a variety of Democratic and Republican hopefuls.

But political polls, visible as they are, represent only the tip of the iceberg. The social science and statistical techniques used in polling and its related field, marketing research, affect virtually every area of our lives today. Pollsters make studies that are used to determine whether we will accept the Susan B. Anthony dollar coin, which television programs we watch or might watch, whether we would buy a car named Amaryllis, how we feel about having a neighbor with a different racial or ethnic background, and how regularly we go to church. Business and government leaders use many of the answers that pollsters get to make key decisions.

As polls become more and more influential, it is important for us to understand them. How can a national poll be accurate if only 1,200 to 1,500 persons are questioned? How do pollsters choose the people to be polled? A poster hanging in the offices of veteran pollster George H. Gallup, Sr., humorously illustrates that concern: "Gallup didn't ask *me* either."

Political commentators have raised another interesting question: Can polls create a bandwagon effect for a candidate? When they show that candidate Smith is ahead of candidate Jones, do voters switch to Smith because they want to vote for a winner? On the other hand, a poor showing in the polls can alert losing candidates to the reality of their situation and spur them on to try harder or to change tactics.

The bandwagon effect can also work against an officeholder or candidate. For example, polls during much of 1979 showed low public support for President Carter's performance in office. Some commentators suggested that the gloomy reports might further erode support for the President. Senator Robert Dole of Kansas, a candidate for the Republican nomination for the presidency, conceded that "to a small extent, the popularity polls do add to the creation of a negative atmosphere" regarding Carter. Dole added, however, that "the polls to a large degree reflect the American public's feeling that President Carter has not done an effective job."

Patricia Y. Bario, deputy press secretary for the White House, said, "There is no denying that the constant repetition of polls saying that the President is not popular and not doing a fantastic job or whatever does create some sort of a negative attitude and, perhaps, a sense of unrest at the time they are going on." But she added, "The only poll that counts, of course, is the one taken on the first Tuesday after the first Monday in November 1980."

Commentators have also wondered whether officeholders rely too much on poll results. Members of Congress would be reluctant to admit that they cast their votes on the basis of what was popular, rather than on the basis of their conscience. Nor would governors be likely to say that they planned their state programs on the basis of what the public seemed to want at a given moment—as captured in a poll. But some officeholders may be tempted to count heads instead of exerting leadership in critical situations.

With all facets of polling in mind, the voter or student of politics may ask who is policing the pollsters. No legal sanctions exist. However, pollsters formed the National Council on Public Polls (NCPP), a professional association based in Washington, D. .C., and devoted to maintaining high standards on a voluntary basis, in 1968. The council's president, Albert H. Cantril, said his group had 18 members in 1979, including the American Institute of Public Opinion, which publishes the Gallup Poll; Louis Harris and Associates, Incorporated; The Roper Organization; and the Columbia Broadcasting System-New York Times Poll.

To maintain their reputations as objective pollsters, Gallup and Harris do not accept polling assignments from candidates or parties, though both have separate divisions engaged in marketing research for

The author:
Richard Pawelek is managing editor of *Senior Scholastic Magazine,* a national publication for students.

1948 Election

	30	40	50 Percentage
Harry S. Truman			
Gallup estimate		44.5%	
Roper estimate	37.1%		
Crossley estimate		45%	
Actual popular vote		49.6%	
Thomas E. Dewey			
Gallup estimate		49.5%	
Roper estimate		52.2%	
Crossley estimate		50.1%	
Actual popular vote		45.1%	

Three major pollsters surveying the 1948 presidential election, *left,* failed to measure accurately the support for Harry S. Truman, shown above holding a copy of a newspaper that went out on a limb.

commercial clients. But many other polling firms, including some NCPP members, conduct private polls for individual candidates.

Private polls conducted for political candidates are big business. Herbert E. Alexander, director of the Citizens' Research Foundation at the University of Southern California in Los Angeles, estimates that 1,000 to 1,500 such polls will be commissioned for the 1980 election candidates. Although exact figures are not available, Alexander said the total cost of these private polls might be "in the area of $12 million to $15 million."

How do private polls taken for candidates differ from the "objective" polls taken by Gallup and Harris that we see in the newspapers? All pollsters use the same statistical methods. But in constructing a poll, there are a number of key points at which the pollsters decide what and whom to ask. So a candidate's staff could conceivably limit polling to areas known to have voted for that candidate in the past. In an election year especially, Cantril stresses the importance of finding out who took the poll being cited and who paid for it.

It is also vital to determine if what you are reading or hearing refers to an actual poll, or to a more casual survey. The term *public opinion poll* refers to a carefully designed set of questions that are put to a selected number of people who, taken together, are called the *sample.* Statisticians determine how many people the sample should contain to be representative of a larger group whose opinions the pollster wants to measure. This larger group–all registered voters in the United States, for a presidential poll–is called the *sample universe.*

As a registered voter, you may receive a questionnaire from your alderman, assemblyman, representative, or senator. Such questionnaires usually list 15 to 20 questions and carry the request: "Here are some issues that may be coming up for a vote soon. Please take a few moments to check the appropriate boxes indicating what you, my valued constituent, think about these issues." This type of survey, though praiseworthy, is not a poll. Nor is a survey taken by a newspaper reporter who questions three or four people on their immediate reactions to a news event and reports a summary of their comments in your morning newspaper.

A public opinion poll always involves a formal and methodical process based on the laws of statistics, no matter who commissions it. But some basic decisions about the poll are based on human judgment. Usually the poll editor makes those decisions.

The first step in taking a poll is to decide the goal (survey objective). If the poll editor wants to find out who the voters favor before the

Pollsters Hit the Mark in Recent Presidential Votes
Such organizations as the Gallup Poll and Louis Harris and Associates make their final surveys of public support for each candidate just before presidential elections. In the last four such elections, *right,* the Gallup and Harris findings almost matched the popular vote actually received by the major candidates.

1964 Election

		30	40	50	60 Percentage
Lyndon B. Johnson	Actual popular vote				61.1%
	Gallup estimate				64%
	Harris estimate				64%
Barry M. Goldwater	Actual popular vote	38.5%			
	Gallup estimate	36%			
	Harris estimate	36%			

1968 Election*

		30	40	50	60 Percentage
Richard M. Nixon	Actual popular vote		43.4%		
	Gallup estimate		42%		
	Harris estimate	40%			
Hubert H. Humphrey	Actual popular vote		42.7%		
	Gallup estimate	40%			
	Harris estimate	43%			

*George C. Wallace, a third-party candidate, got 10 per cent of the popular vote. Gallup estimated 13 per cent; and Harris, 14 per cent.

Tennessee primary election in May 1980, the questions should deal only with candidates entered in that primary. And, of course, the sample should be drawn from Tennessee voters only.

Writing the questions is the next big step. Pollsters know from experience that they can get completely different answers by phrasing a question in several ways. Reputable pollsters make sure that the questions are neutral—that is, the questions do not call forth a predetermined, desired response. As an extreme example, compare your own response to these two questions: "Should hard-working taxpayers continue to pour out huge sums of money to support those who refuse to work?" versus "Do Americans of good conscience have a responsibility to aid their less fortunate neighbors?"

Another key point is whether the question presumes some knowledge on the part of the person answering. For example, the Gallup Poll in 1979 sought to measure what the voters thought about the Strategic Arms Limitation Talks agreement (SALT II) negotiated between the United States and Russia. But perhaps the person being polled had not heard of SALT II. So the Gallup Poll editor included a question to find out if the person polled had heard or read about

1972 Election

		30	40	50	60	Percentage
Richard M. Nixon	Actual popular vote				60.7%	
	Gallup estimate				61%	
	Harris estimate				61%	
George S. McGovern	Actual popular vote	37.5%				
	Gallup estimate	35%				
	Harris estimate		39%			

1976 Election

		30	40	50	60	Percentage
Jimmy Carter	Actual popular vote			50.1%		
	Gallup estimate		46%			
	Harris estimate		46%			
Gerald R. Ford	Actual popular vote		48%			
	Gallup estimate		47%			
	Harris estimate		45%			

The Poll-Taking Process: Pinpointing the Fors, Againsts, and Undecideds

1. As a key executive, chairman George H. Gallup, Sr., of the American Institute of Public Opinion makes policy based on his 40 years of experience.

2. Poll editor James Shriver selects the candidates to be included in a political poll. He also writes the questions, phrasing them neutrally.

3. To ensure that the sample will represent all Americans, poll workers include in it a mix of people by geographic area, sex, race, and religion.

4. The subject, key element in a poll, answers questions in her home. Research has shown that personal interviewing is highly effective.

5. Pollsters sometimes question their survey subjects by telephone. Such interviews are faster and cheaper than face-to-face meetings.

6. When questionnaires are completed, office workers code the responses—the first step in the complex data processing that goes into a poll.

7. A keypunch operator makes cards for the coded entries, one for each item in the questionnaire, so that the data can be processed by computers.

8. A computer operator puts the data cards into a high-speed sorting machine, which groups them according to such factors as age, sex, and race.

9. The computer operator prepares the computer to process the data. The computer "chews up" thousands of facts to produce the poll statistics.

10. A service writer or programmer checks the computer's tabulations to be sure that the master program established for the poll is valid.

11. Once the statistics have been formed into a poll story, the story is reproduced—as by this complex copier—for client publications.

12. Before the poll story appears in print, an editor for a client checks to make sure that it explains fully just how the polling was done.

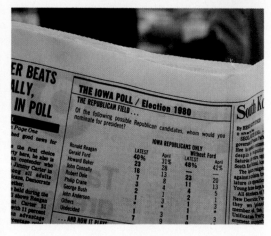

THE IOWA POLL / Election 1980
THE REPUBLICAN FIELD . . .
Of the following possible Republican candidates, whom would you nominate for president?

IOWA REPUBLICANS ONLY

	LATEST	April	Without Ford LATEST	April
Ronald Reagan	40%	31%	48%	42%
Gerald Ford				
Howard Baker	23	28	23	20
John Connally	16	13	23	20
Robert Dole	7	8	11	13
Philip Crane	3	4	4	5
George Bush	2	1	2	1
John Anderson	1	3	1	3
Others	*	3	1	*
Undecided	7	9	6	3

Patrick H. Caddell, *top* (second from right), talks with White House staffers about polls he takes for the Democratic National Committee. Television networks take polls, too; Harry Reasoner, *above* (left), and Walter Cronkite (right), discuss a poll in 1978. Some newspapers, like the *Des Moines* (Iowa) *Register,* conduct their own local political polls, *above right.*

SALT II, and another asking the person to name a plus or minus of the treaty. Only those who indicated some knowledge of SALT II were then asked if they approved it.

Poll questions come in two main types. For a *closed question,* each person interviewed is handed a list of possible answers—such as a list of presidential candidates or a list of issues—and is asked to select one or more or to rank them according to interest. The *open question,* on the other hand, asks people to answer in their own words. As an example, consider a poll that attempts to find out which national issues are of concern to Americans. The poll editor can write a closed question with a list of issues to be ranked—for example, inflation, energy policy, education, busing, relations with China, and the diplomatic crisis in Iran. Or the poll editor can write an open question, asking each person something like this: "In your opinion, what is the most important national issue confronting the United States today?"

The major pollsters that monitor elections—Gallup, Harris, some television networks, and some major newspapers—must exercise fine judgment in deciding which candidates to include in a poll and which questions to ask. For example, Carter was virtually unknown nationally in early 1975, yet he won the Democratic nomination and was elected President in 1976. The poll editor must decide whether it is fair to include an unknown hopeful in a popularity poll with known vote-getters, or whether it is fair not to.

Once the questions are set, the size of the sample must be decided. The Gallup Poll is usually based on 1,500 persons, though Gallup includes up to 3,000 in its final election-year polls. The Roper Organization usually polls 2,000 persons, and the Iowa Poll interviews about 600 Iowa residents. These numbers seem small. But the major polls have come close to the percentage of the popular vote received by the winner in all recent presidential elections.

Perhaps the most publicized error made by pollsters in calling a presidential election was made in 1948. In that year, all the major pollsters selected Republican Thomas E. Dewey over Democrat Harry S. Truman as the probable winner. But Truman won with more than 24 million popular votes to Dewey's 21.9 million. Another dark day came in 1936, in the early days of polling. A *Literary Digest* magazine poll picked Alfred M. Landon, the Republican candidate, to win the 1936 presidential race, but President Franklin D. Roosevelt, a Democrat, won re-election that year. The *Digest* poll was mailed to 10 million persons, and 2 million of them replied. But these random replies had included too many people who owned automobiles and telephones—signs of wealth in those Great Depression times and, usually, indications of Republican Party preference. But statistical techniques have been improved since then, and pollsters carefully include all major social and economic groups in their sample.

In making up the sample, most major pollsters now use *probability sampling*, or random sampling. Probability, a branch of mathematics, is the study of odds—the chances that an event will occur or the number of times it will occur. If you flip a coin, you know that your chances of winning a toss are 1 in 2, because the coin has two sides and you are tossing it once. But the odds change if you agree to go for 2 out of 3 flips. Mathematicians have devised formulas for gauging probability in such situations.

The A. C. Nielsen Company uses another example to explain how its random selection of American families creates a sample that represents all U.S. television viewers. Suppose that you have 100,000 beads mixed together in a washtub—30,000 are red, and 70,000 are white. You know the total number, but not the breakdown by color. If you scoop out 1,000 beads at random, the mathematical odds are 20 to 1 that there will be 270 to 330 red beads in the 1,000, and the remainder will be white. In 20 out of 21 tries, you will have 27 to 33 per cent red beads in your sample group.

If you scoop out 1,000 beads in groups of 10, you get a clearer picture of the breakdown between red and white. You can mark down the number of red and white beads in each group of 10 and use the numbers to plot a graph that statisticians call a *frequency curve*. The curve will be bell-shaped, and about 70 per cent of the groups of 10 will contain 2, 3, or 4 red beads. Only rarely will all 10 beads be either red or white, so the "tails" of the curve are tiny in comparison to the main curve of the bell.

Pollsters use a mathematical formula based on such a bell-shaped curve to determine the probability of error for a sample of a given size. For example, the results of a television presidential preference poll in which 1,200 persons were interviewed were said to be "subject to a sampling error of up to 3 per cent." The poll stated that 56 per cent supported candidate X.

The poll's statistician used a formula to determine the sample's *standard error*—a unit of measurement that helps determine how much the result obtained from the sample deviates from the result that would have been obtained from polling the entire population. Using this standard error, the statistician determined—with 95 per cent certainty—that candidate X's support fell between 53.18 and 58.12 per cent; that is about 3 percentage points on each side of the 56 per cent support that was reported by the poll "subject to a sampling error of up to 3 per cent." Even allowing for the maximum polling error, candidate X was still the clear favorite.

Would it reduce the chances of error to interview 1,800 persons instead of 1,200? Not much. To double the accuracy represented in 1,200 interviews, the laws of mathematics indicate that pollsters would have to use four times as many cases, or 4,800 persons. This is because square roots are involved. The Gallup organization uses a table of possible error for samples of different sizes. From their calculations, they know there is a 3 per cent margin of error for their usual sample of 1,500 persons. For 400 persons, the margin of error would rise to 6 per cent. To reduce the margin of error to 2 per cent, the pollsters would need to include interviews with 3,000 persons. So economics generally dictates a sample of about 1,500 persons.

If you want to take a poll yourself or check the standard error for a poll that you see published, you can use the same formula used by the statistician who determined candidate X's support. Suppose you interview 600 students to find out who they support for student-council president and find that 420, or 70 per cent, support Jane Black. All the other candidates together receive the support of 30 per cent of those polled. This formula applies:

$$\sigma = \sqrt{\frac{p \times q}{n}}$$

where σ is the standard error; p equals 0.70 (the percentage supporting Jane Black); and q equals 0.30 (those supporting all other candidates, or 1.00 minus p). The n stands for the total number polled, or 600. In this instance, the standard error will be about 0.0187. You then multiply this answer by 1.96 to obtain the standard level of confidence of 95 per cent. The ultimate answer is that your poll results will be correct within a margin of error of 0.0367, which is 3.67 per cent. It would therefore be safe to say that between 66.33 and 73.67 per cent of the students preferred Jane Black at the time the poll of the students was taken.

After the size of the sample has been determined, pollsters select the sample by geographic location, to ensure that all areas are represented. The number of sampling points—the places where interviewing is done—must be determined. For example, Gallup uses 360 sampling points to get 1,500 interviews. In a national political poll, Cantril explains, the pollsters divide the country into regions, usually seven or eight. Within each region, they maintain a list of counties, which they ultimately break down by street or other small unit. They also classify these divisions by population density, so that the sample includes people from sparsely populated rural areas as well as from cities and towns. The pollsters use random selection to pick out counties and then streets that will be sampled. For example, they may take every ninth street in every 10th county, starting with the third county.

Interviewers visit their prospective subjects in the evening or on weekends, when more people are likely to be at home. Some pollsters use telephone interviews, and studies are being conducted to see if telephoning yields accurate and complete results.

Statisticians check to see that the random process has reached people in all the various groups, covering such factors as sex, age, race, and income. The interviewer has taken data on these factors.

While these tested statistical methods are available, the public has no guarantee that pollsters use them in each and every poll. The NCPP urges the media to publish all background facts about any poll they report, and it suggests a check list that is valuable for the public, too. The NCPP check list asks: Who sponsored the poll? When was the interviewing done—is the poll up to date? How were the interviews obtained? How were the questions worded? Who was surveyed? How big was the sample?

Polls perform a valuable function in reflecting how the public thinks on a given issue at a given time. But public opinion is always in flux. Daniel Yankelovich, president of the polling firm Yankelovich, Skelly, and White, writing in *The New York Times* in October 1979, said that a poll is like "an attitudinal 'snapshot' of the public in the act of making up its mind." In a busy election year, wise voters must judge what is pictured by any particular poll.

For further reading:

Berelson, Bernard, and Janowitz, Morris. *Reader in Public Opinion and Communication.* Free Press, 1966.

Gallup, George H., and Rae, Saul F. *Pulse of Democracy: The Public Opinion Poll and How It Works.* Greenwood, 1968.

Oskamp, Stuart. *Attitudes and Opinions.* Prentice-Hall, 1977.

Roll, Charles W., Jr., and Cantril, Albert H. *Polls: Their Use and Misuse in Politics.* Basic Books, 1972.

Unlocking the Secrets of the Seven Seas

By William J. Cromie

Scientists of many countries cooperated to examine the world's oceans in the largest, longest scientific expedition in history

I looked down in time to see the shark rushing at my feet. It was only a small shark, but it aroused fear out of all proportion to its size. The lagoon water was waist deep, and my companion was too far away to help. I kicked furiously at the pointed snout. "This only works on television," I thought, and waited for the searing pain. But when the cloud of fine coral sand drifted away, the shark was gone and my feet were still intact. I moved them as fast as possible to catch up with geophysicist Martin Vitousek of the University of Hawaii.

After I regained my composure, we squished through the coconut palms in our mildewed sneakers to the windward side of Fanning Island. One of the small atolls that make up the Line Islands, Fanning lies near the equator in the central Pacific

Ocean. It is one of the most isolated places on earth. The two of us clambered to the top of a ridge of coral fragments torn from the offshore reef and piled up by strong waves that had traveled halfway across the Pacific Ocean from South America. Red-footed gannets protested our presence with raucous screams, and curious frigate birds paused to watch us repair instruments that measure winds and water temperature. Thermometers showed that this part of the central Pacific was cooler than normal in August 1978. For the Line Islanders, there would be little wind and rain to bring down coconuts and make them easy to harvest. For Vitousek and his colleagues, the cooler ocean water was a clue to how cold and wet the next winter would be in the United States and Canada.

In the following weeks, we journeyed to Palmyra Island and Christmas Island in a 35-year-old tugboat and a 16-year-old Piper Aztec plane. Our work included checking tide gauges, one link in the process of forecasting a natural event that periodically ruins the world's most productive fishery. By studying sea level changes in August in the middle of the Pacific, we could tell Peruvian fishermen how good or bad their anchovy catch would be six months later. In this way, natural events in the central Pacific provided a dramatic demonstration that the world's weather and food supply—indeed, its whole future—is inextricably tied to the ocean.

Ｈow this works is a global puzzle. While Vitousek and I labored on one piece of it, scientists all over the world were working on others. We were all part of the largest, longest, scientific expedition in history—the International Decade of Ocean Exploration (IDOE), which began in 1970 and by 1979 involved researchers from 36 countries. "The IDOE has revolutionized the way we think about the oceans," says oceanographer Feenan D. Jennings of Texas A & M University in College Station, who headed the United States program from 1970 to 1978. "And since oceans cover more than 70 per cent of this planet, the IDOE also has revolutionized what we know about earth's climate, its resources, and what it will be like in the next century."

Oceanographers, envious of the time and money spent on space exploration, began a campaign in the mid-1960s to convince the Congress of the United States that, in the words of engineer Willard Bascom, "the ocean's bottom is as important as the moon's behind." Congress was persuaded, and in 1970 the IDOE was launched, with the National Science Foundation given responsibility for the program in the United States.

Ships began going to sea in 1971 to check the health of the oceans. They crisscrossed the Atlantic and Pacific oceans, the Gulf of Mexico, and the Caribbean Sea. Scientists from Canada, Great Britain, the United States, and West Germany analyzed water and air samples for metals, oil-based pollutants, and such chemicals as polychlorinated biphenyls (PCB's). This yearlong effort—the Pollutant Baseline Study—provided a reference point so that future measurements could reveal

The author:
William J. Cromie was a merchant marine officer and oceanographer. He is now executive director of the Council for the Advancement of Science Writing.

whether pollutants are building up to a dangerous level. While some conservationists claim that pollutants are destroying the oceans, scientists who have been measuring sea contaminants for years disagree. "The oceans are not dying," insists marine chemist Robert A. Duce of the University of Rhode Island in Kingston. "No evidence exists that man's activities have raised pollutants in ocean waters away from coastal areas to a dangerous level."

This does not mean that the ocean is free of pollution problems, however, particularly in coastal areas. According to an IDOE report, "*hot spots* [highly polluted areas] such as those adjacent to river mouths, sewer outfalls, and dumping grounds are increasing in extent. Like their counterparts in cities, these 'marine slums' are indicative of an unhealthy situation in need of change."

If pollution or food shortages occur in certain areas, worldwide problems may result. Although the oceans provide 300 times more living space than all land and freshwater areas combined, more than half the world's seafood catch comes from only 1 per cent of the oceans. In half a dozen areas, cold nutrient-laden waters upwell, or rise, from the depths and fertilize amazingly productive gardens of plants and animals. Such areas exist off the West Coast of the United States, off northwest Africa, off the "horn" of Africa's east coast and south of the Arabian Peninsula, off Western Australia, and off the west coast of South America. Paradoxically, many of the 1.5 billion people in the world who suffer from malnutrition live near these teeming sources of protein. IDOE scientists therefore designed a project called

Fanning Island residents gather data at one of the few weather stations located in the equatorial regions. A technician, *below left,* checks the operation of a radar set that tracks weather balloons. A Micronesian woman, *below,* reads a tide gauge for data on changes in sea level.

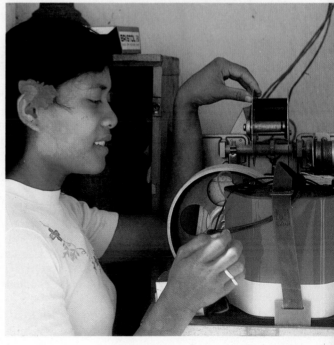

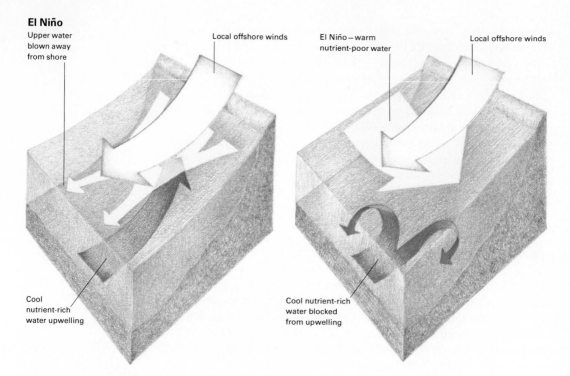

El Niño

Upper water blown away from shore

Local offshore winds

El Niño—warm nutrient-poor water

Local offshore winds

Cool nutrient-rich water upwelling

Cool nutrient-rich water blocked from upwelling

North and south of the equator, offshore winds blow surface water out to sea and cool water rich in nutrients rises to the top along South America's coast. Fish thrive on the nutrients. But equatorial winds can blow so hard that surface water piles up on the opposite shore of the Pacific. As the winds ease, that warm water sloshes back as El Niño, covering the deep, nutrient-rich water and reducing the fish yield.

Coastal Upwelling Ecosystem Analysis (CUEA) to learn what makes these areas so fertile, how to protect them from overfishing, and how to forecast their productivity from year to year.

Much of the CUEA work has centered on the west coast of South America, the world's most productive fishery. In past years, 1 of every 5 tons of fish came from the waters off Peru, where upwelling nutrients sustained huge populations of one-cell microscopic plants called diatoms. A single quart (0.95 liter) of water collected off Callao, Peru, in the spring may contain more than 1 million diatoms. Vast legions of silver, finger-length anchovies graze these liquid pastures, eating their fill and then filling the nets of fishermen. Different from the Mediterranean variety that adds flavor to pizza and antipasto, most of these anchovies go into making fish oil to fatten chickens and beef cattle.

Biologist Richard T. Barber of Duke University in Durham, N.C., describes the winds that power these protein factories: "Away from the equator, off Oregon and West Africa, local winds control upwelling. Blowing offshore, they push coastal water seaward, and deep water wells up to fill the space. In the equatorial regions, on the other hand, upwelling is almost totally independent of local winds. Off South America, it depends on large-scale forces that involve the entire Pacific equatorial region. This natural system runs near capacity to produce a maximum amount of fish. It is so fine-tuned that almost any change is bad."

One change comes from time to time and causes a disastrous drop in productivity that is felt throughout the world. A current of warm, nutrient-poor water flows east along the equator, then south along the South American coast. It covers the deeper fertile water like a stagnant blanket. Coastal people call this current *El Niño* (The Child) because it arrives during the Christmas season—late spring-early summer in the Southern Hemisphere. But El Niño brings no joy, because it involves upwelling of water from the barren layer rather than from the rich waters below it. El Niño greatly reduces the diatom population. Without diatoms, anchovies cannot survive and—without anchovies—tuna, bonito, sea birds, and fishermen cannot survive. Fish and birds die, and the guano industry, based on fertilizer made from bird droppings, slumps. The price of chickens and beef in U.S. supermarkets soars because they must be raised on more costly feeds.

Before the IDOE, scientists blamed El Niño on a slackening of the southeast trade winds that blow seaward from South America. However, Klaus Wyrtki, head of the Department of Oceanography at the University of Hawaii in Hilo, studied weather records and concluded by 1974 that the trade winds often blow stronger during the years that precede a visit by El Niño. He installed tide gauges on islands all over the Pacific. Gauges on the western side of the ocean showed an in-

When El Niño stays away, Peru's fishermen process huge anchovy catches at sea in a floating fishmeal factory.

crease in sea level after the wind grew stronger. This meant that the surface of the Pacific sloped upward from South America westward to Samoa and New Zealand. It was obvious to Wyrtki that the winds pile up water against the shores of New Zealand and Southeast Asia. "When the trade winds relax," he explains, "the water sloshes back, flowing along the equator, then flows southward as El Niño."

This flow can be traced by changes in tide-gauge readings on islands in the Pacific. Six months before El Niño hits the South American coast, it announces its coming with a rise in the ocean level off the Line Islands. Another investigator, meteorologist William H. Quinn of Oregon State University in Corvallis, found that air pressure changes associated with the wind shifts also herald the approach of El Niño about six months in advance. Both signs indicated that the devastating El Niño would come again in 1975.

Oceanographers loaded their ships and headed for South America. In February, instruments lowered from the University of Hawaii research ship *Moana Wave* detected a mass of warm, barren, low-salinity water off Peru. There was no doubt about it–for the first time in its long ages of occurrence, oceanographers had successfully predicted the coming of El Niño.

The El Niño study showed that ocean and air are locked in an intimate embrace; one cannot move without affecting the other. IDOE researchers found that this holds as true in the North Pacific as in the equatorial region. Abnormal temperatures, such as Vitousek and I found off the Line Islands, are tied to huge pools of cold and warm water off California. These pools, which are a few degrees colder or warmer than the surrounding sea, change the course of westerly winds blowing over the Pacific and influence how cold and wet the winter will be in North America. For example, oceanographers found a pool of abnormally warm water centered about 1,000 miles (1,600 kilometers) off California in late 1978. About 1,200 miles (1,900 kilometers) across, 1,000 feet (330 meters) deep, and as much as 3°F. (1.7°C) warmer than normal, this heat source deflected to the north those winds that normally bring weather to the United States and Canada. In place of the diverted winds, cold air swept down from the Arctic, making the winter of 1978-1979 in North America one of the coldest and snowiest on record. Similar conditions accounted for the previous two frigid winters.

Meteorologist Jerome Namias of the Scripps Institution of Oceanography in La Jolla, Calif., predicted each of these severe winters on the preceding December 1. He based his forecasts on what he calls the ocean's "memory." Warm summer winds and plenty of sunshine produce ocean pools warmer than the surrounding water, and cold summer winds and clouds create colder pools, Namias believes. "The ocean has a greater persistence than air," he explains. "It holds the heat and the cold much longer. This creates a memory for the atmosphere that feeds back conditions from a previous season and produces

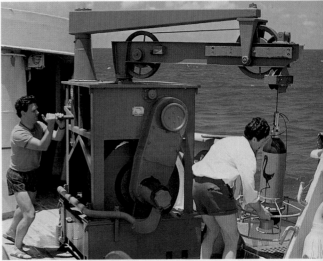

anomalous [uncommon] weather." Although his theories have not been widely accepted, other scientists have been forced to agree that the ocean plays a much greater role in weather and climate than anyone thought possible before the IDOE.

Scientists in the past theorized that winds and storms played the major role in carrying heat from the equatorial regions to the temperate and polar zones. Most of the sun's heat falls on the earth's midsection, and it must be redistributed to prevent equatorial regions from becoming unbearably hot and temperate regions from becoming as cold as Siberia. Satellites provided a way to test this theory. Measurements made from space revealed that more heat reaches the polar regions than can be carried there by winds or can come directly from the sun. According to the satellite data, the oceans must move as much heat as the air does, thus playing an equal role in keeping the climate of North America and Europe temperate. "This was an unexpected finding," says oceanographer Warren S. Wooster of the University of Washington in Seattle. "It left us with the problem of figuring out how the ocean does it. This is not just an academic question. Long-term changes in heat transport change climate; shorter-term, small-scale variations make up what we call weather."

It was obvious that much of this heat is carried by ocean currents. Great rivers in the sea, such as the Gulf Stream, move warm water on the western side of the Atlantic, Pacific, and Indian oceans toward the poles. In addition, oceanographers thought that heat moved toward the North and South poles in broad, sluggish flows through the central parts of the oceans. British oceanographer John Swallow tried to measure this flow through the deep Atlantic in 1959. He designed floats that sank to a predetermined depth and then drifted along, beeping radio signals by which he tracked them. Swallow was startled to find that the floats 2 miles (3.2 kilometers) below the surface zipped along at more than 2 miles an hour, up to 100 times faster than predicted. The floats seemed to be caught in a rotating column of water moving through the ocean just as a storm moves through the air. Swallow decided that he had found an underwater storm, or *eddy*, 120 miles (190 kilometers) in diameter and 2 miles deep.

Swallow lacked the technology to prove his theory. But 14 years later, IDOE researchers, using newly developed instruments, found an underwater storm 120 miles (190 kilometers) wide in the North Atlantic. In March 1973, after more than two years of discussion, the scientists agreed on a place where the storms were likely to occur. They selected an area 360 miles (580 kilometers) in diameter between Florida and Bermuda, and deployed a network of instruments in one of

When an oil well in the Gulf of Mexico blew out, the results showed up on Texas beaches. Tar from such oil spills threatens to foul coasts throughout the world.

the largest oceangoing expeditions ever undertaken. The joint U.S.-British expedition involved six ships, two airplanes, numerous shore stations, and an international team of 50 scientists.

The scientists manned their stations for four months. Never had a patch of ocean been so closely monitored for so long. In July 1973, oceanographer Henry M. Stommel of the Woods Hole Oceanographic Institution in Massachusetts announced the results. "We *did* catch an eddy," he told the jubilant scientists. "By good fortune, one was centered in the area where we placed the instruments. Others appeared nearer the edges of our network. For the first time, we have seen a developing undersea weather system."

To study these systems in more detail, Canada, France, Great Britain, Russia, the United States, and West Germany joined forces. The Canadian researchers investigated complex water movements under and around the Gulf Stream off the east coast of North America. British, French, and West German oceanographers set out networks of instruments in the northeastern Atlantic. Soviet scientists, who had studied deep-water circulation in the Pacific Ocean and the Arabian Sea, joined their U.S. counterparts to monitor parts of the North Atlantic. American and Soviet researchers explored the same and adjacent areas, using compatible standards and instruments so that measurements could be used by both groups. Workers on Soviet vessels radioed data to the U.S. National Weather Service, which made charts of ocean circulation and sent them to U.S. and Soviet ships.

These and other IDOE expeditions uncovered eddies in all the oceans. The eddies ranged from 30 to 200 miles (50 to 320 kilometers) across and moved at a rate of about 1 mile (1.6 kilometers) per day. The studies also revealed that in addition to their impact on weather and climate, eddies distribute pollutants and distort sound signals used for underwater navigation and detection.

Oceans not only influence changes in climate; they keep a record of such changes that stretches back millions of years. Thick layers of sediment that carpet parts of the sea floor serve as a natural encyclopedia in which events of the past are recorded. The pages are layers of brown, red, and gray mud and clay. Billions of tiny shells and skeletons, the remains of microscopic plants and animals that lived in the oceans in the past, spell out the story of changing climate. Temperature dictated where various kinds of organisms lived and caused such adaptations as changes in the thickness and shape of their shells. As these creatures died and sank, this information was preserved in chronological order—the youngest fossils in the upper layers, older ones at increasing depth. Researchers on an IDOE project called Climate: Long Range Investigation, Mapping and Prediction (CLIMAP) studied the sea-floor encyclopedia and learned the cause of ice ages, the last of which ended about 10,000 years ago.

Scientists from Colombia, Denmark, Great Britain, Israel, the Netherlands, Norway, and West Germany joined United States scien-

Sophisticated cameras and sensing equipment on the submarine *Alvin, above,* recorded the facts about marine life on the ocean floor at the Galapagos Rift while scientists inside the vessel gazed in awe at the colorful assortment of fish, crabs, and tube worms, *above right,* that live near vents from which warm water rises.

tists working on this program. British geophysicist Nicholas J. Schackleton discovered a way to determine how much snow fell in prehistoric times by analyzing oxygen in the shells of long-dead sea creatures. This and other research showed that the average air temperature during the last Ice Age was only 5°F. (2.8°C) cooler than it is now. Furthermore, the change from the cozy warmth of the present to a frigid ice age can occur in less than 3,000 years. It occurs, CLIMAP scientists concluded, when the gravitational pull of the other planets changes the shape of the earth's orbit around the sun and the *precession,* or wobble, of the earth's axis.

When the IDOE began, no one knew precisely what natural materials the oceans contain, or what happens to man-made materials that are dumped there. To find out, IDOE officials launched the Geochemical Ocean Sections Study (GEOSECS), history's largest chemical experiment. This effort yielded the first inventory of what is in the vast water world. The program was carried out by U.S. investigators from 14 universities and geochemists from Belgium, Canada, France, Great Britain, India, Japan, and West Germany. United States ships crisscrossed the Atlantic, Pacific, and Indian oceans from 1972 to 1978, carefully sampling 144 million square miles (370 million square kilometers) of water averaging 12,500 feet (3,750 meters) deep. Researchers took as many as 66 samples at each of the more than 300 locations, and performed about 50 tests on each sample.

"The most important discovery we made is that water in the deep parts of all the oceans circulates much more rapidly than we thought," notes Woods Hole geochemist Derek W. Spencer. "Before IDOE, we believed that deep water in the North Atlantic reached the venerable age of 500, 600, or even 800 years before cold water sinking in the Arctic replaced it. Now we know that parts of the deep Atlantic are flushed out in 200, 150, or fewer years. Water in the bottom of the Caribbean Sea and in the deep parts of South Asian seas is renewed in 50 years. Eddies undoubtedly play a role in flushing out these basins."

"This knowledge has an immediate impact on what we know about the dispersion of pollutants and disposal of nuclear waste in the ocean," adds geochemist Wallace S. Broecker of Lamont-Doherty Geological Observatory in Palisades, N.Y. "Plans to dump radioactive material on the deep ocean bottom were based on the idea that it would be undisturbed for a thousand years. Now we know that nuclear waste from leaking containers could come back to the surface in a few hundred years—before it decayed to a harmless substance."

IDOE is the most recent worldwide ocean exploration effort. The earliest was the 3½-year voyage of H.M.S. *Challenger*, which left England in 1872. British scientists aboard that ship dredged up strange black lumps, or nodules, from various areas on the ocean bottom, especially in the Pacific. Surveys since that time have revealed many areas where such nodules occur. They are composed mainly of manganese and iron, but many of them also contain valuable metals, such as cobalt, copper, and nickel. "The distribution of metal-rich nodules depends on the production of microscopic plants and animals at the surface," explains marine geologist G. Ross Heath of Oregon State University. "These organisms concentrate metals in their bodies and transport them to the sea floor when they die. Exactly how the nodules form remains unknown, but once we determine what factors control their formation and growth we should be able to predict where they will be found." Several international corporations are developing machinery to dredge up this treasure trove.

Much of the manganese in the ocean comes from a worldwide system of cracks, or rifts, that split the earth's crust into about 20 huge sections or plates. These rifts occur mainly on the ocean bottom, and they mark areas where molten material and mineral-rich water rise from the earth's interior. The water, rocks, and sediments here may contain concentrations of iron, zinc, copper, lead, manganese, and even silver and gold. In fact, marine geologists believe that all metal deposits on earth originate in this way.

Why, then, are most of them found in mountainous land regions far from the sea floor? The geologists have developed a mind-stretching scenario known as the *geostill theory* to answer this question. According to this theory, seawater flows into the cracks in the ocean floor, becomes heated, and dissolves metals out of the semisolid material pushing up from below. As the floor cracks open and spreads apart, the water gushes up through vents in the form of mineral-rich hot springs. The crust continues to open up, and molten material rises into the gap. Along with the metals, it solidifies into a new strip of sea floor. This new material pushes apart the huge plates that make up the continents and ocean floor. These slowly drift away from each other at speeds of a few inches a year. Over a million years, for example, the distance between Europe and North America may increase 30 miles (50 kilometers). At the same time, the Atlantic Ocean widens as a new section of similar size is added to its bottom.

The Geostill Theory
Molten material full of metals pushes up from earth's interior, breaks through a rift, then spills out and forms a new piece of ocean crust. This metal-rich strip spreads as the crustal plates drift apart by inches each year. Eons later, the strip reaches a trench and is forced under an oncoming plate. The resulting intense heat and pressure scrape the metals free, and they are pushed up onto the land by volcanic action.

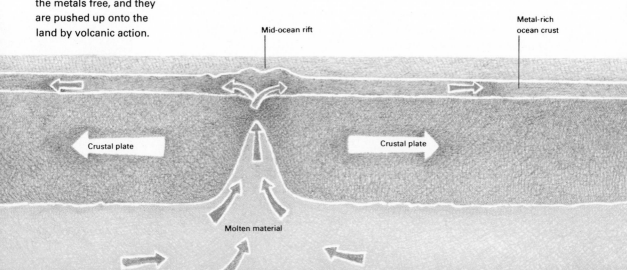

Mid-ocean rift

Metal-rich ocean crust

Crustal plate

Crustal plate

Molten material

As the sea floor spreads, metals created in the rifts move outward from them. After moving for millions of years, the lodes reach other rifts where the ocean floor is being pushed under a continent instead of moving with it. Pressure and heat melt and break off the edge of the sinking crustal plate, and metals in the plate rise up onto the land through volcanoes. Volcanism, along with plate movements that squeeze sea-bottom sediments up into mountains, concentrates the metals into minable deposits. The geologists believe that the lodes of copper, gold, iron, lead, and zinc in the Andes Mountains of South America originated in this way.

IDOE researchers found impressive evidence to support the geostill theory. During a 1974 expedition called the French-American Mid-Ocean Undersea Study (FAMOUS), French and U.S. submarines descended 9,000 feet (2,700 meters) into the Mid-Atlantic Rift Valley, which splits the floor of the Atlantic Ocean. The northern part of the rift, where the dives took place, separates two major crustal plates. One—called the North American plate—includes North America and the western half of the North Atlantic, and the other—the Eurasian plate—holds Asia, Europe, and the eastern half of the North Atlantic. The rift continues into the South Atlantic, where it separates South America and Africa. It lies in a valley between two high, steep, under-sea mountains. The floor of this valley, says Woods Hole aquanaut-geophysicist James R. Heirtzler, "looked like a place where a giant has walked around crushing things. It's horrendous, extremely busy with earthquakes and volcanic eruptions." In this convulsive chasm, Heirtzler and others took photographs, collected samples, and made measurements showing that the formation of the earth is a continuing process. "Many scientists had the idea that new crust formed in gigantic pieces," says Heath. "Now it appears that small, intermittently active volcanoes add strips of lava less than a mile or two in extent over hundreds of years."

In 1977, 1978, and 1979, aquanauts dived into rifts where the earth is being destroyed. Along the coast of Central America and South

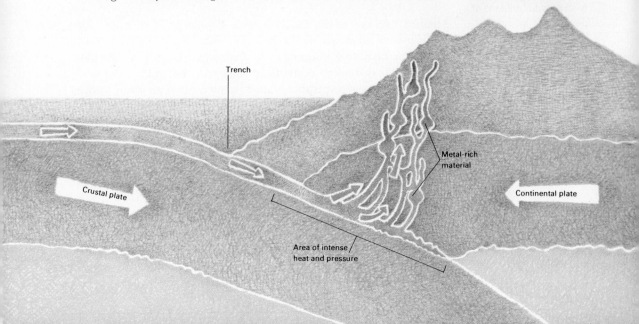

Volcanic mountain chain

Trench

Metal-rich material

Crustal plate

Continental plate

Area of intense heat and pressure

Fish are an important food item for millions of people throughout the world. This Tokyo fish market sells 7 million metric tons (6.3 million short tons) of marine products each year.

America, sections of the Pacific Ocean floor are forced under the continents as spreading in the Atlantic pushes the continents westward. The dives took place near the Galapagos Islands off Ecuador and near Mexico, south of the Baja California peninsula.

The Galapagos expedition found numerous vents from which plumes of hot water rise like chimneys venting the infernal regions. Geologists spotted multicolored deposits of copper, manganese, and nickel surrounding the vents at depths of 9,000 feet (2,700 meters).

Scientist-aquanauts John B. Corliss of Oregon State University and Robert D. Ballard of Woods Hole went down in the submarine *Alvin* in March 1977 to get a close look at the Galapagos rift. "One second we were moving over a black rocky desert lit only by *Alvin*'s strobe lights," Ballard recalls. "Then there was a sharp increase in temperature, and we could hardly believe our eyes. There were hundreds of large white clams and brown mussels. We saw orange and white crabs scurrying all over. No one ever suspected, much less saw, such an accumulation of life on the deep ocean floor. It was incredible."

On other dives, the inner space explorers discovered redheaded worms 8.5 feet (2.6 meters) long living in vertical tubes attached to the lava. Fish swam among the worm tubes, and a purple octopus hunted orange crabs. The scientists also saw red sea cucumbers and grey eels through *Alvin*'s portholes. Scientists christened another area the "Dandelion Patch" because it harbored a creature resembling a fluffy pink dandelion gone to seed. It turned out to be a rare, sedentary relative of the Portuguese man-of-war jellyfish. Biologists identified what looked like spaghetti draped over the edges of cracks in the lava as long, thin acorn worms.

"It's like finding life on another planet," says Spencer. "This is one of the most exciting discoveries of the century." It was exciting, but puzzling. How do all these creatures survive in a submerged desert of lava where the sun never shines? No life on earth was known to survive without the energy of sunlight. The solution to the mystery came from a rotten-egg odor given off by water samples collected by the submarines. Hydrogen sulfide gas produces this pungent smell. Exotic types of bacteria use sulfur in this compound the way plants use sunlight for photosynthesis. The sulfur becomes an energy source that powers the conversion of carbon dioxide to edible carbon in the bodies of the bacteria. Microscopic plants and animals munch on the bacteria and, in turn, make a meal for tube worms and spaghetti worms, clams and mussels. The latter provide sustenance for crabs, eels, fish, and octopuses. "For the first time, we've discovered a chain of life based on energy from the earth instead of energy from the sun," Corliss explains. "This provides new insight into the origin and evolution of life. We now know that life can originate and develop in areas of sulfurous hot springs on earth or, perhaps, on other planets."

The impressive catalog of discoveries and knowledge that flowed from 10 years of international cooperation has changed the science of oceanography and altered the popular and scientific picture of the 70 per cent of earth covered by water. Oceanographer Ned Ostenso, deputy assistant administrator for the National Oceanic and Atmospheric Administration, sums up the results: "IDOE produced a fantastic body of information upon which all future decisions about the oceans will be based." Since these decisions involve weather, environmental quality, food, metals, and fuel, they will affect the lives of everyone living on the "Water Planet."

For further reading:

Cromie, William J. *Secrets of the Seas*. Reader's Digest Association, 1972.
Heintze, Carl. *The Bottom of the Sea and Beyond*. Thomas Nelson, Inc., 1975.
Imbrie, John and Katherine P. *Ice Ages: Solving the Mystery*. Ridley Enslow Publishers, 1978.
Van Andel, Tjeerd. *Tales of an Old Ocean: Exploring the Deep Sea World of the Geologist and Oceanographer*. W. W. Norton and Co., Inc., 1978.

The Cult Question: No Easy Answers

By Carroll Stoner and Jo Anne Parke

Questions about today's religious cults abound: What is their lure? What do they do to their members? What should society do about them?

They appear to have little in common. Some dress in orange robes and sport a lone braid dangling from a shaven head; others wear conservative business suits and conventional haircuts. Some forage through garbage cans for food; others regularly enjoy lavish, multi-course feasts. Some show contempt for traditional moral and sexual standards; others are almost prudish in their behavior. But regardless of their appearance or life style, these people share a common bond – they are all members of extremist religious cults.

We first became aware of these cults in 1975 when we were researching a magazine article on the effects of raising children in homes that practice no religion. While involved in that research, we began to see signs of another – and far more disturbing – religious phenomenon that was affecting thousands of American families. Friends and colleagues told us about young people they knew, many from nominally religious middle-class families, who believed they had found salvation in religions that were in no way part of the mainstream of Christianity or Judaism. These young people had joined unorthodox groups led by men with a mystic popular appeal. It seemed that almost everyone had a story to tell about someone—a relative, neighbor, or friend whose life had been touched by some new and bizarre form of religion. Most of these stories were related with a sense of great concern: Will these cult members be forever alienated from society? Are their leaders misdirecting young Americans? Are they usurping the talent and productivity of youth for destructive ends?

We decided to examine the despondency of the parents, the dreams of their children, and the motives of the cult leaders. We wanted to find out what makes young people ripe for membership in such cults and how they and their families can deal with the problem. If these new religions were as bad as their critics claimed, we wanted to be able to show people how to avoid getting "hooked."

During our two-year study we went to cult rallies and festivals. We visited cult recruiting centers, studied their literature, and stood on street corners with their fund-raising teams. We interviewed hundreds of current and former cult members and their families. We lived with cult members. We talked to clergymen and psychiatrists. We attended congressional hearings on the cults.

As we became immersed in this project, we were struck by the fact that the United States was going through a sort of religious revolution. By the early 1970s, many middle-class Americans were either leaving the mainstream churches and temples or transforming them into instruments for social action. But as 1980 drew near, church membership was once again on the upswing. Interestingly enough, this new growth was concentrated in radical fundamentalist movements within Judaism, Protestantism, and Roman Catholicism. Charismatic prayer meetings attracted thousands of Catholics. Pentecostal revivals became commonplace as "born again" Protestant Christians discovered *proselytizing* (seeking converts) and *witnessing* (asserting their beliefs). Hasidic Jews took to prayer vans and street corners to urge their brethren to practice their religion more intensely.

And in a nearly parallel reaction, cults began to surface outside the umbrella of established religions. Each had a leader who claimed that his philosophy guaranteed salvation and satisfaction. Each leader gathered followers and remained the central figure in the group. Then, the pattern shows, the self-styled messiah began to tell of divine revelations or claimed that he possessed special powers. Each of the 12 cults we studied began in much this way.

A cult's doctrine is based on the leader's revelations, and it takes the place of, or supplements, traditional religious doctrine or Scripture. The cult leader claims absolute authority over the members, and many live in regal splendor while their subjects live in poverty.

All cults seem to promise a system in which a convert may work to save the world and humanity, but none seem to put forth any actual

The authors:
Carroll Stoner, the associate feature editor of the *Chicago Sun-Times,* and free-lance writer Jo Anne Parke are co-authors of *All Gods Children,* a study of religious cults.

Illustrations by Gary Soszynski

programs. Instead, the daily work of the cult members is demeaning and makes little use of their intelligence, training, or education. Members may be required to sell, beg, or even engage in sex to raise funds for the cult leader.

Each cult is an exclusive social system. Members must cut themselves off from their jobs, schools, friends, and families. They are taught that they are "superior" to persons outside the group.

Finally, each cult seems to practice some form of mind control over the members, especially during recruitment and indoctrination. They encourage repetitive recitations and teach new members to suppress all "negative" thoughts. Some require members to take part in rituals that may prove to be physically as well as emotionally dangerous. For example, two members of a cult in the Northwest died after sniffing industrial solvent as part of a ceremony.

The cult makes members dependent on its authority and discourages individual action and thought. In short, while mainstream religions, for the most part, try to help members function better in the world, cults work in many ways to isolate their members.

Although many typical cult practices are questionable, most are not illegal. However, the combination of total trust and the willingness to unquestioningly follow a single leader can have dangerous implications. Nowhere was this more evident than in the mass suicide and murder of the People's Temple cult members in Jonestown, Guyana, in November 1978. Members were willing to follow a "higher law" as interpreted by their leader, Jim Jones, and more than 900 died as a result. The Jonestown massacre prompted closer investigations into other cults, their practices, and the men who lead them.

Each group must be judged individually, of course. The Unification Church led by Sun Myung Moon puts a much greater emphasis on evangelism than do most Christian sects. The *Moonies* (followers of Moon) believe that their own personal salvation depends on recruiting at least three new cult members. They live in communal centers. The men wear conservative slacks and shirts. The women wear modest skirts and blouses or dresses.

The Moonies spend nearly all of their waking hours either raising funds or recruiting. They sell peanuts, candy, or costume jewelry made in a factory in France that is owned by the Unification Church. They suggest that they are raising funds for missionary work or to help young people, but will not mention their affiliation with Moon unless pressed. In reality, the Unification Church has used these funds to finance extensive real estate holdings and fishing fleets as well as Moon's personal yacht and 25-room mansion in Tarrytown, N.Y.

Members of the Center for Krishna Consciousness, unlike the Moonies, invite attention as they chant on street corners. They present a marked contrast to the Moonies in appearance. Krishnas of both sexes wear saffron robes with sandals or sneakers. The men have shaved heads or wear a single braid of hair.

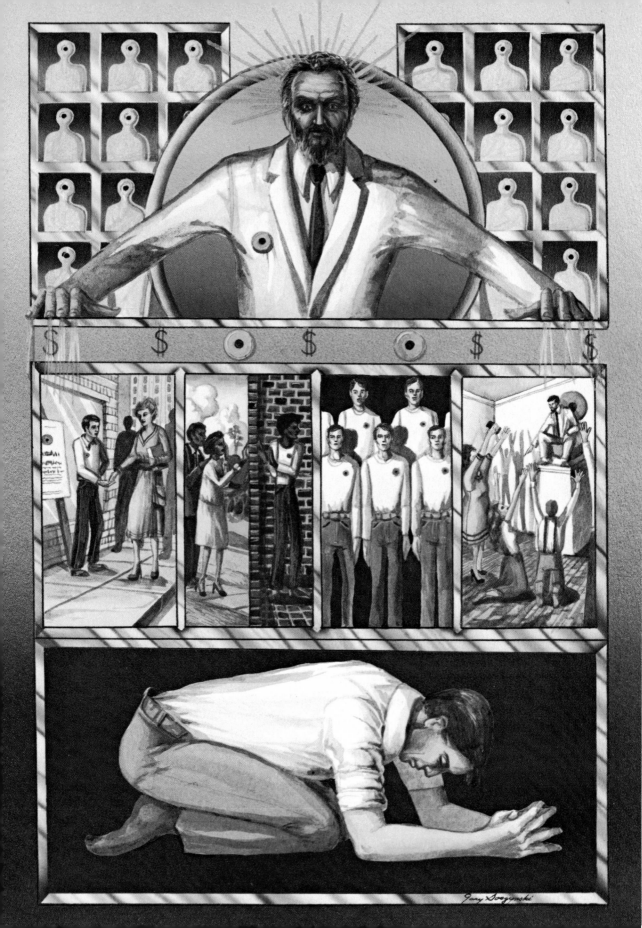

Krishnas follow the teachings of Swami A. C. Bhaktivedanta Prabhupada, a Hindu monk who died in 1977 at the age of 82. Most of the Krishnas live communally in large houses in metropolitan areas. They have sexual relations only within marriage and then only to have children. The Krishnas are vegetarians and hold weekly multi-course "feasts" for members and potential converts.

The fund-raising Krishnas are out by 10 A.M. daily selling Krishna Consciousness propaganda on busy streets and in airports. Although they are persistent and successful fund-raisers, most of their reported wealth goes to support the members of the group itself, and is invested in real estate in the United States.

The Moonies and the Krishnas are two of the most visible and easily identifiable of the new cults. Both say that they work within the laws and limits of society, though there are allegations that they break the law. Other cults seem to break the law deliberately, however. The Children of God say that they have been mandated by their leader, David Berg, to do so. Their activities are directed by Berg in pamphlets that encourage various illegal sexual activities. Other groups, such as the Church of Armageddon, have abused their members' children and have explained the harsh and severe physical punishment by saying that the devil must be driven out of those who misbehave. There is evidence that members of this cult use drugs regularly as part of their rituals and are poorly fed. Former members say that they were encouraged to search through garbage cans outside restaurants and grocery stores for food.

> Cult members abandon their old lives to concentrate on serving the leader. They give up their personal identity and isolate themselves from family and friends, devoting their days to raising funds for the cult.

All the cult members we have met strongly assert that they are willing members of their new religions. But most former members say they did not understand how they were converted or the principles of the cult that converted them. In many cases, cult evangelists hide the fact that they belong to an extremist group. Some former members say they were not told of the group's real purposes for weeks after their conversion. And many of these members were subjected to systematic ego destruction, by methods similar to those used on U.S. prisoners of war in North Korea and China during the Korean War.

Robert J. Lifton, author of *Thought Reform and the Psychology of Totalism: A Study of Brainwashing in China* (1961), a classic text on the subject, identifies several conditions present in this type of ego destruction. We found that in recruiting and indoctrinating new members, cults usually use one or more of the practices Lifton listed.

The cult totally controls each recruit's surroundings by eliminating or monitoring all communication with the outside world, severely limiting sleep, changing the recruit's diet, and supervising all conversations. These are the easiest ways to disorient an individual.

The cult convinces the potential convert of its higher purpose and of the need to conform to its goals. It instills strong feelings of guilt and shame and convinces each individual of his or her own need to reform. Group confessions are also used to strengthen the group's bonds and the recruits' sense of separation from the outside world. The cult makes each new member feel insignificant compared with the group, its work, and its doctrine, and classifies everything that a person has learned earlier as unacceptable.

Finally, the cult draws a sharp line between those who will be saved —members of their group—and all others. This is the last step in establishing the "we and they" attitude that helps set the cult members apart from the rest of society.

Whether we approve of their practices or not, most cult members are idealistic. Many are searching for a purpose in life and a strong sense of community. It is not surprising that cult promises appeal strongly to them.

We attended workshops operated by various cults so that we could observe how they convert people, and found that the cult begins by administering a heavy dose of love and approval to the recruit. This outpouring of love—along with all the conditions that lead to disorientation, such as keeping recruits involved in constant group activity and depriving them of sleep—leads to a high emotional pitch and a feeling of euphoria.

As the individual's mind becomes more open to suggestion, recruiters make cult life look safe and attractive. "Parent or family problems? None of those here," they say. "Financial worries, sex-related anxieties, or worries about relationships with friends?" they ask. And then they claim that they have answers to all those problems. Since almost everyone faces some of these problems at some time, there are many periods when a person might be particularly vulnerable. To someone who is feeling great social or family pressure, life in a group where all decisions are made can seem appealing.

When the recruit's mind has been opened to suggestion, the group begins to introduce new beliefs. Little by little, the manipulated recruit accepts theories and practices that would have been highly unacceptable under other circumstances.

During this stage the cults preach acceptance of all they teach: "Skepticism is negativism. Think positively. Trust us and accept our belief system little by little and when you see the whole picture, then you may question." We heard that advice again and again. And so, forbidden to question, in a communal setting of total love and acceptance, new cult members are born.

Mariellen Howe was one of the many cult members we talked to who became a member in much this way. She had been traveling across the country with three friends when they stopped in Berkeley, Calif., for a few days. "A girl and guy came up to us on a street near the University of California campus and started talking," recalls Mariellen. "They came on so strong, I wanted to tell them to cool it, but they invited us to dinner. It was a free meal, so we went.

"At dinner, everyone in the room was talking about the group's farm in the mountain valley north of San Francisco. They invited us

When worries about family, school, work, sex, money, drugs, and other pressures of the "real world" build up, life in a cult, where all decisions are made for members, can often seem very appealing.

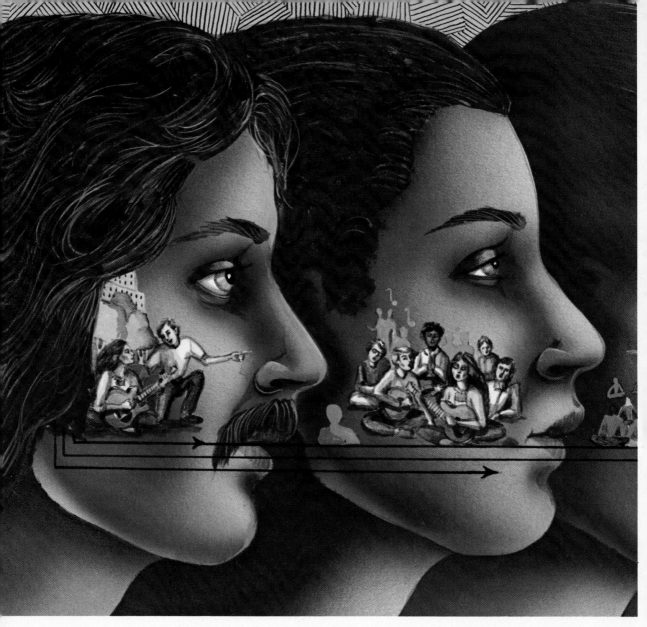

A dinner invitation can lead to cult indoctrination, as the "guest" is smothered with affection and then is subjected to such brainwashing techniques as lack of sleep and marathon lectures.

there for the weekend, and two of us decided to go. We got on their bus after dinner, and, after a four-hour ride, we came to the farm. We were hustled into a trailer where we spread out our sleeping bags and quickly fell asleep.

"After what seemed like only two hours, a girl with a guitar came into the trailer and began to sing. I tried to ignore the racket and go back to sleep until I realized that I was the only one who wasn't up and singing. I got up and joined in.

"After a cold breakfast and some group singing, the first lecture started. It was given by one of those superserious guys who tells bad jokes to prove how hip he is—not my type at all. But I felt guilty for judging him and tried hard to like him. He talked about some of the

things I had been thinking about—caring for others and things like that. After the lecture we exercised to keep our minds alert.

"The lecture after lunch was given by a really neat-looking guy. His talk was kind of vague, but it seemed to deal with skepticism. He told us that skepticism is the result of partial information and that we had to share our experiences with each other to learn the truth. Afterward, we talked about our insecurities and feelings of guilt. I mentioned not knowing what I wanted to do with my education and how I was tired of playing sexual games with guys I knew. The group leader told us how important it was to live pure, good lives.

"When the lecture was over, I tried to talk to my friend, but I couldn't find her. Instead, I talked to another girl in the group about how the group financed its work. When she told me about selling candy and peanuts, I said, 'You're not Moonies, are you?' She looked shocked and answered, 'No.' I believed her. (By the time I found out they were members of a religious group, I was so involved with them that I didn't care that they had lied to me. As they explained, 'If we had told you the truth, you might not have listened,' and I knew they were right.)

"After dinner, there was more singing and another lecture. I tried to talk to my friend, but kept getting intercepted by other group members. I was tired anyway, so I gave up and went to bed.

"The next day brought more of the same—lectures, exercise, group discussions, and singing. That night, when the bus was ready to leave, I planned to go back to Berkeley. I was interested in what the group had been telling me, but I needed more time to think.

"About an hour before I was ready to go, the girl I had talked to earlier and a guy I had gotten to know took me aside and talked to me about my doubts. They said that I needed to give them a chance to clear them up. 'Maybe,' he said, 'we haven't loved you enough.' That did it. I really dug this guy, and there he was, talking to me about loving me."

Mariellen stayed, but only for a month. After a day's visit with her mother, who had flown to California to see her, she became convinced that what she was involved in was not right for her.

Mariellen has read a great deal about brainwashing since leaving the Moonies and has drawn a number of parallels to her experiences there. "Everything in my world was changed or altered in a very short period of time. The food was different. We didn't sleep much and we ran like crazy all day long. Everything was on such a high emotional plane, which is probably why I slept for a week when I first got home.

"Before I joined the Moonies I used to love to argue about issues, but I found that I couldn't argue with the Moonies because they would analyze my every word and then caution me about being negative. Their trust is absolute, and if I didn't understand it I should study the lessons harder and try to learn more. Everyone was so severely judgmental that I was afraid of them.

"Was I brainwashed? I just don't know. I definitely felt 'high' most of the time I was there, and I was doing things I didn't believe were right—like fund-raising and saying almost anything to get money for Moon. The thing that worries me most is not knowing for sure if I would have stayed if my mother hadn't come."

After months of observing the cults, we believe that, like Mariellen, anyone can be vulnerable to the appeals of these groups at one time or another. Three types of people seem to be especially susceptible, however. Young people who are in the midst of trying to establish their independence from family and peers and have not yet put down roots or established values that will carry them through life are especially vulnerable. The cults offer them a fully developed value system and life style, free for the asking. Those with emotional problems also find cult life attractive. Group life shelters them from the real world and its harsh realities. Cults are also beginning to attract the poor and members of racial-minority groups. As we saw in Jonestown, those who feel like outsiders in an affluent society may find it easier to follow a strong leader who promises to "take care of them" than struggle for a better standard of living within the mainstream.

While getting into a cult is easy, getting out can be difficult. Some cult members, however, leave on their own. They simply walk away from the restrictive lives led by the group.

The single most effective way to encourage voluntary leaving seems to involve maintaining close family ties with cult members. These families might say, "Although we don't approve of your membership in the group, we still love you and want you to stay in touch with us." Eventually, cult members may find that family ties are stronger than those binding them to the cult, and return home.

Kent Burtner, a Roman Catholic priest who has been active in campus ministry at the University of Oregon, has counseled cult members and their families for several years and has developed an understanding of their problems. Burtner advises parents of cult members to try to understand how their sons and daughters got involved by examining the problems and needs in their children's lives that made them vulnerable to cult indoctrination. He tells parents to be tolerant and neutral when communicating with their children and not to be negative. He advises parents to keep all the literature that members send home and gather all the information they can on the cult.

Burtner also tells parents to keep a diary to help them better understand their own feelings concerning their child's membership in a cult. This self-examination should help them decide what to do about their child's new life. He urges parents to get in touch with parents of other cult members. When they can see they are not alone, they lose some of the guilt of feeling they have failed their child.

Finally, Burtner advises parents to consider deprogramming, an option as controversial as the cults themselves. Each deprogramming story is different, but the techniques are similar. Deprogramming is a process in which people are forced to question their beliefs and to examine the process that led them to adopt a cult doctrine and its practices. It is a confrontation of opposing viewpoints, in many instances a forced one, in which the cult member is kidnapped from the cult and held behind locked doors while the deprogramming is done – a process that may last for days.

While some parents are convinced that deprogramming offers the only possible salvation for a cult member, others see it as "reverse brainwashing." They claim that holding people against their will and subjecting them to an emotional and intellectual battering is wrong, no matter who does it. The legality of deprogramming is still being debated in the courts.

A dinner invitation can lead to cult indoctrination, as the "guest" is smothered with affection and then is subjected to such brainwashing techniques as lack of sleep and marathon lectures.

there for the weekend, and two of us decided to go. We got on their bus after dinner, and, after a four-hour ride, we came to the farm. We were hustled into a trailer where we spread out our sleeping bags and quickly fell asleep.

"After what seemed like only two hours, a girl with a guitar came into the trailer and began to sing. I tried to ignore the racket and go back to sleep until I realized that I was the only one who wasn't up and singing. I got up and joined in.

"After a cold breakfast and some group singing, the first lecture started. It was given by one of those superserious guys who tells bad jokes to prove how hip he is—not my type at all. But I felt guilty for judging him and tried hard to like him. He talked about some of the

Dreams die hard, and many attempts to rescue cult members eventually fail. Even the individual who wants to leave the cult must go through a serious and often difficult readjustment to life. Former cult members need to understand just how they got into the cult.

A number of rehabilitation programs have been developed to help former cult members explore their reasons for joining and to guide them as they readjust to normal life. Such programs vary from a few hours of professional counseling to several weeks at live-in rehabilitation centers. Most clergymen, educators, and psychologists who have studied the problem agree that former cult members need some "decompression time" before they are ready to go to school or work.

In addition to the many questions that cult members and their families must answer, one very important question faces all of society. Should we regulate groups simply because they instill contempt for our laws and traditional values?

Religious cults that violate Internal Revenue Service regulations and immigration and naturalization laws can be prosecuted, and local laws can be applied without prejudice. For example, the City Council in Evanston, Ill., ordered local Hare Krishna leaders to comply with city statutes that require property upkeep, adequate off-street parking, and noise control.

But we must remember that laws designed specifically to keep "undesirable" groups out of "good" neighborhoods can also be applied to other groups. Consider the plight of the Mormons. Their barns and fields were systematically burned in the 1830s and 1840s until they were pushed westward into the territory of Utah. Jews have had trouble buying or renting space for synagogues and temples outside of big cities, and Roman Catholics and Protestants have suffered religious persecution at times.

We have learned from history that messianic movements are often passing phenomena, and we believe that the cult experience of the 1970s is no exception. Eventually, today's religious cults will either pass into oblivion or modify to become part of the mainstream.

But what of the thousands who are already unwitting subjects of these self-proclaimed prophets? Should young men and women searching for God, community, and a satisfying life spend important years of their lives selling peanuts on street corners and religious tracts in airports? Can society ignore the frustration of their parents? There are no easy answers.

Cult members with strong family ties may go back home voluntarily. Others have been "kidnapped" and "deprogrammed," practices that are being challenged in the courts as society tries to balance its responsibility to the individual and principles of religious freedom.

For further reading:

Edwards, Christopher. *Crazy for God*. Prentice-Hall, 1979.
Patrick, Ted with Dulak, Tom. *Let Our Children Go*. Ballantine Books, 1976.
Singer, Margaret T. "Coming Out of the Cults," *Psychology Today*, January 1979.
Stoner, Carroll and Parke, Jo Anne. *All Gods Children*. Penguin Books, 1979.
Wax, Judith. "Sharing a Son with Hare Krishna," *New York Times Magazine*, May 1, 1977.

A Year in Perspective

1874
1876
1877
1878
1879

THE YEAR BOOK casts a backward glance at the furors, fancies, and follies of yesteryear. The coincidences of history that are revealed offer substantial proof that the physical world may continually change, but human nature—with all its inventiveness, amiability, and even perversity—remains fairly constant, for better or worse, throughout the years.

See page 168.

Today's Worries, Yesterday's Woes

By Paul C. Tullier

Rising prices, static incomes, runaway taxes, and wasteful spending made 1879 a frustrating year for Congress, the President, and the public

When January 1 rolled around, the year ahead seemed to the typical American more a cause for concern than a reason for exuberance. The economy was in a downward cycle. Inflation was soaring. The purchasing power of the dollar at home was diminishing while its value abroad had fallen to an all-time low on France's money market, the Bourse. The United States, for the most part, feared a return to the financial panic of an earlier era that had been aggravated and prolonged by what some experts said was an oversupply of currency, both paper and metal. "History is repeating itself," warned August P. Belmont, a prominent financier of the day. "Paper money is now exchangeable for silver....To keep the silver interests happy and assure themselves a steady outflow of their metal, they have badgered our acquiescent government into printing more and more paper money with which to purchase it. This [oversupply of currency] has contaminated and debased our dollar to an extent which can only be corrected if the government ceases to feed its presses with paper."

Highlights of 1879 include, *clockwise from upper left:* women get to vote in Massachusetts; Belva Lockwood is admitted to practice before Supreme Court; former President Grant eyes running again; money glut causes inflation.

1879

RESUMPTION.

The government, confronted by this and other problems, was hindered in 1879 by an ongoing confrontation between the executive and the legislative branches. Congress complained that the President was abusing his veto power. Rutherford B. Hayes, America's 19th President, complained that Congress was chipping away at executive prerogatives. "Congress," explained his loyal secretary of the treasury, John Sherman, "is attempting to enact laws objectionable to the President by attaching them as 'riders' to necessary appropriations bills, thus violating constitutional guarantees of the equality of branches of government." A second cause of discord was the need to revise the nation's proliferating, often conflicting tax laws. "The chaotic confusion that exists in the tax laws is compounded by the want of a uniform system for collecting them," said the President, "and the inequalities victimize the middle-class citizens who are being made to bear the burdens of corporate capital and of the money kings." Congress expected the President to initiate new proposals to right the imbalance; the President looked to Congress to provide the initiative.

This indecisive leadership was irritating to an increasingly frustrated public, which placed part of the blame on an inept Civil Service. "The public servants appointed to high office are poorly qualified for their positions," wrote one journalist. "Qualified men are...refusing to accept appointments because of the low salaries being offered. Any man with a good education can easily command higher wages in real life than any offered by government bureaus." Higher salaries, he assumed, would ensure higher quality. Conversely, other critics argued that not only civil servants were overpaid, but also U.S. senators. "Never before in the history of the country," reported the newly formed Anti-Spending League of New York, "have members of the legislative and executive branches of government fallen so far below the measures of their duties and the height of their opportunity. Their tendency to drift without a rudder is exceeded only by their talents toward wastefulness."

The public was ever ready to provide not only examples of waste, but also ways by which it could be stopped. Cutting back unnecessary or overgenerous expenditures, it was suggested, was one way to curtail "the liberality shown by the government in its lavish treatment" of Civil War veterans. Senator John T. Morgan of Alabama agreed: "Totally disabled pensioners are paid $865 per annum," he said. "Another 701 get $600, and the remaining 34,890, including widows and children, receive $102. Is it for such squandering of public wealth that we are paying insufferably high taxes?" In an earlier speech on the Senate floor, Senator Morgan had referred to the 13 states that had once formed the Confederacy as the "Solid South," thereby adding a new political term to the American vocabulary.

In the North as well as the South, special groups were bringing pressure to bear on the federal government for action on a wide variety of interests, including the adoption of the metric system and "an

The author:
Paul C. Tullier is
Managing Editor of
THE WORLD BOOK
YEAR BOOK

end to the government's adherence to the old-fashioned and, in many respects, inconvenient system of weights and measures that now prevails." In Chicago, a group was seeking government subsidies for the arts. "Berlin, Stuttgart, Naples, Vienna, Copenhagen, Weimar, and Stockholm all have subsidized opera," said Theodore Thomas, the noted symphony orchestra conductor. "Why not the United States?" A Massachusetts-based branch of the American Society for the Prevention of Cruelty to Animals was pressing for action to stop the slaughter of "black fish [whales] which...so-called sportsmen allow to rot on the shore." In Iowa, a grass-roots movement was seeking legislation to curb the pricing policies of the gas companies. "They are rapacious and greedy," said one editorial. "Gas that costs 60 to 80 cents per 1,000 cubic feet is sold to customers at $2.50 and up to $3.50 per 1,000 cubic feet, according to locality. Their profits range from 212 per cent to 337 per cent. Where," the article demanded, "is the merchant, manufacturer, or banker audacious enough and so contemptuous of the public need that he would dare to realize such extortionate gains?"

So the United States sailed through troubled waters under the captaincy of a disgruntled President, a truculent congressional crew, and a quarrelsome electorate. Adding to the unease was the fact that 1879 was a pre-election year and at least half a dozen potential candidates were waiting in the wings. Some thought William Tecumseh Sherman would make a strong chief executive. In a speech at Michigan Military Academy, he had roused the audience to a fever pitch by declaring that "war is hell." But no name aroused such a mixture of enthusiasm and dislike as that of former President Ulysses S. Grant, who reportedly was contemplating another run for the presidency. His tour around the world, with glowing reports of his receptions by the crowned heads of Europe and Asia, had kept his name before the public. Only one unhappy episode marred the journey. In Ireland, where bitter controversy raged between Protestants and Roman Catholics, the Council of Cork had refused to receive Grant because he allegedly was anti-Catholic.

The ongoing religious crisis in Ireland contrasted sharply with the situation in Poland, where Roman Catholic Pope Leo XIII had ended a church-state confrontation by persuading the Russian-dominated government that priests were not fomenting anti-Russian sentiments. Papal *bulls* (announcements) could now be circulated in Poland.

From Venice–the Queen of the Mediterranean–came disturbing news. In May, a series of fierce storms accompanied by high tides had inundated St. Mark's Square and the principal streets leading to it. Travel on the canals had been suspended because the gondolas could not pass beneath the bridges. The ground floors of many palaces had been flooded, and their inlaid mosaics were severely damaged. An editorial in *Harper's Weekly* struck an ominous note: "Does Venice face death by water?" it asked.

Few readers responded, possibly because their attention was captured by reports of Russia's "extraordinary barbarity of repressive methods," toward Jews, against whom a massive *pogrom* (racial massacre) was launched in the summer. In August, the Russian government reaffirmed its right "to imprison for indefinite periods anyone suspected of conspiring against [it]." In September, it began expelling survivors of the pogroms after terrorists—allegedly Jewish—had set fire to the Kremlin. By December, thousands of these Jewish refugees were reported to have died in Romania, where the pro-Russian government, pending their expulsion, had imprisoned them in open stockades during one of the coldest winters in the Balkans.

Weather was a contributing factor to the unrest that was spreading through much of Europe in 1879. A summer drought the year before had resulted in serious crop failures throughout the continent—and only a large surplus of U.S. wheat (exported at higher prices than U.S. farmers had known for many years) helped avert widespread famine. Conversely, the winter had been so cold that the Seine River in Paris had frozen over. Great Britain had been unaffected by the drought, but it was devastated by the Arctic-style weather. Compounding Britain's widespread misery, coal miners in Wales had gone on strike in January for higher wages, thereby halting the production of heating fuels. In the spring, dockworkers had brought shipping to a standstill, and strikes against a proposed wage cut by employees of 18 engineering firms had paralyzed the nation's construction industry. In the sour mood that prevailed, even the royal family did not escape censure. One critic in the House of Commons denounced Queen Victoria for the extravagance involved in maintaining royal residences that rarely saw the reclusive monarch. Even some Canadians, loyal to the Crown though they might be, were not too happy with the appointment of the Marquis of Lorne as governor general of Canada. The marquis' consort, Princess Louise, was Victoria's daughter, and a cartoonist wickedly drew a caricature of the princess holding an empty purse. "Like Mother, like Daughter?" was the provocative caption beneath the cartoon. Americans, by way of contrast, could only view with awe the apparently unlimited financial resources of Chen Lan-Pin, China's first official ambassador to the United States, who had moved into his exotically furnished and jade-filled new embassy in Washington, D.C., in January.

The establishment of diplomatic relations with China was part of a new U.S. policy to enlarge its trade with the Orient. To overcome obvious language barriers, America's educational community acted. A professorship of Chinese language was established at Yale University in March; Ko-Kun-Hua, a bilingual Chinese scholar from Soochow, was engaged for three years at a salary of $1,800 per year.

Clockwise from upper left: Mastodon bones are found near Newburgh, N.Y.; Sarah Bernhardt plans a U.S. tour; St. Patrick's Cathedral is dedicated in New York City; free child-care centers become popular.

Harvard University and the University of California followed with similar courses. "It is," said Protestant minister Henry Ward Beecher, "the spirit of the pioneer invading the hitherto sacrosanct domain of scholarship, to the betterment of our educational institutions."

Innovations introduced at other educational institutions confirmed Beecher's enthusiasm, including a greatly enlarged department of zoology and geology at Princeton University. (A Princeton professor had been a key figure in the discovery, near Newburgh, N.Y., of a mastodon skeleton. It was "the largest and most perfect yet found," conceded the head of the Department of Zoology and Geology at rival Harvard.) The first permanent chair in pedagogy in a U.S. college was established at the University of Michigan in 1879. The course was listed as the Science and Art of Teaching. The University of Missouri on May 23 introduced the nation's first course in journalism. A state veterinary school was established in the spring at Iowa State College in Ames. It was the first four-year course in such a subject and the first veterinary school to require a high school diploma for entrance.

At Vanderbilt University, formerly known as Central University, ground was broken for a theological building that would cost an unheard-of $65,000. The university had changed its name soon after becoming the beneficiary of a $1-million gift from Cornelius Vanderbilt. He was firmly opposed to granting higher education to women and had barely been dissuaded from specifying that the university's student body be all male. The exclusion of women was condoned by many universities, however, because, according to one newspaper, "it was expected that females might faint from the strain [of higher education], or cause the lowering of academic standards for men." Coeducational systems did have an ardent supporter, however, in Professor Frederick Barnard of Columbia College in New York City. "The time will come," he said, "when every college will open its doors to women the same as men."

It was an observation that would take decades to come true. Yet there were already telltale signs that, male opposition notwithstanding, women were moving out of the shadow of prejudice. About 50 per cent of all elementary schoolteachers were women—hitherto a male-dominated profession. The University of Southern California, made possible by an endowment of land in 1879, reportedly planned to consider women for its faculty. And other doors were opening. In March, Belva Ann Lockwood of Washington, D.C., became the first woman lawyer permitted to practice before the Supreme Court of the United States. (For her first court appearance, Lockwood wore "a semimannish blue cloth sacque with brass buttons and a plain velveteen skirt.") In California, Mary Josephine Young was admitted to practice before the Supreme Court of California. She was, according

Clockwise from top: Joaquin Miller's play *Mexico* opens in New York City; crowd awaits arrival of first train at Las Vegas in territory of New Mexico; Thomas A. Edison works to create electric incandescent light.

to one account, "an industrious little bee who sips harmony from every experience in life." In the fall, about 1,000 women in Massachusetts cast ballots during municipal elections. Although it was only for the local school boards, it was the first time women had been permitted the vote in Massachusetts and as such was considered a great victory "for emancipated womanhood." But prejudice still existed. The Illinois legislature in May passed a labor law specifically prohibiting the employment of women in mines. In New York City, a woman demanding "equal rights" was arraigned on charges of being a witch.

Fortunately, women's voices were not excluded from the world of publishing. Ouida, the prolific English writer, was at work on her new novel, *Moths*. French novelist George Sand's *Deronda* had finally reached America in translation, and its involved plot found an avid readership. Harriet Beecher Stowe was "collating" a new collection of her short stories. But the most intriguing book published during the year was *Progress and Poverty: An Inquiry into the Cause of Industrial Depression and Increase of Want with Increase of Wealth* by a 40-year-old economist named Henry George, who insisted that his single-tax theory could solve the nation's economic ills.

In a lighter vein, Americans were buying such popular paperback reprints as *Housekeeping Made Easy: Or, American Practical Cookery; Hoyle's Games: Guide to all games of chance or skill*; and *Ten Nights in a Bar Room, and What I Saw There* by T. S. Arthur. Robert Louis Stevenson's new book, *Travels with a Donkey in the Cévennes*, was also popular, as was the author himself. In midyear, he journeyed from New York City to San Francisco on a train filled with illegal Chinese immigrants being deported. Stevenson sorrowed for the plight "of those whose forefathers watched the stars before mine had begun to keep pigs." America's poet Walt Whitman also journeyed westward in 1879 and reported from Colorado that he was amazed and pleased by "the grandeur of the mountains" as well as by the cowboys, whom he found "bright eyed as hawks and strangely interesting."

Neither Whitman nor Stevenson was mentioned in the *People's Encyclopedia*, a new "all encompassing, easily readable" reference work that also failed to recognize one of America's most popular writers, Joaquin Miller. *Mexico*, Miller's latest play, was a rousing success at New York City's Grand Opera House. Miller's popularity was rivaled only by Dion Boucicault's, whose *Rescued* was playing at Booth's Theatre. *Hearts of Oak*, by a 20-year-old San Franciscan named David Belasco, was enjoying a heartening success. The acclaim encouraged the playwright to head for New York City, where the gold, he said, "is easier to come by than in the West, where you have to dig for it." France's Sarah Bernhardt, who was being "feted and ovated" by London's "barristers, baronets, and beau monde" was anxious to gather her

Clockwise from upper left: New kind of life-saving buoy is used to rescue passengers from a grounded ship; Clara Barton speaks on behalf of the American Red Cross; bicycle races join baseball as a great U.S. sport.

share of American loot. In June, she began negotiating a contract for her first American tour. Only one stumbling block held up the negotiations: She insisted on being paid nightly—in gold.

Two of Bernhardt's admirers, William Gilbert and Arthur Sullivan, were already in the United States. Throughout the year, their operetta *H.M.S. Pinafore* had been New York City's biggest theatrical drawing card. It had reached a high point of sorts when it was performed on a real ship floating in a gigantic tank of water in Madison Square Garden. But *Pinafore* was fated to be displaced by an even more popular Gilbert and Sullivan work, *The Pirates of Penzance*, which opened on December 30 at the Fifth Avenue Theatre. For the occasion, composer Sullivan served as conductor and Gilbert cavorted onstage disguised as a member of the pirate crew.

Classical music lovers in New York City were treated, on February 8, to a performance of Peter Ilich Tchaikovsky's *Symphony No. 3 in D*— the first time one of his symphonies had been performed in the United States. In San Francisco's Baldwin Theatre, impresario Tom Maguire presented the West Coast première of Georges Bizet's "Carmen" with Marie Rose and Annie Louise Carey singing Carmen and Micaela respectively. Maguire lost $20,000 on the production. To report these and other events, a new theatrical weekly called the *New York Mirror* began publication. It was endorsed by no less a personage than Mrs. John Jacob Astor, whose blessing carried great weight in social circles. It was Mrs. Astor who was responsible for the social acceptance of the latest fad to hit the United States, thanks to Tiffany and Company— pins, charms, bracelets, and even walking-stick handles in the form of tiny gold or silver piglets. The less well-to-do could console themselves with brooches made from the last tree cut down in New York City's Bowery the year before to make way for a new elevated railroad.

Both the carriage trade and the hoi polloi in Boston, New York City, and Chicago were talking about a new kind of shopping emporium introduced by Frank W. Woolworth. After serving his apprenticeship as a clerk in the firm of Moore & Smith, Woolworth had joined with Moore to open a "five-ten" store in Utica, N.Y. It failed. But within six months he had opened a second store. This time he offered a wider selection of merchandise, and unabashedly called the operation a "five-and-ten-cent store." It was a resounding success, and new outlets soon multiplied. Woolworth, who kept a sharp eye on the dollar, was tempted to invest in a new device called "Ritty's Incorruptible Cashier." Its inventor, James Ritty, was a cafe-saloon proprietor in Dayton, Ohio, who had tired of having his bartenders dip into the open cash drawer for pocket money. To eliminate the thefts, Ritty devised a machine that not only registered the sale, but also controlled the opening and closing of the drawer.

Clockwise from top: Vacationers in Massachusetts slaughter "black fish"; Russian Jews fleeing pogroms are driven from Romania; ex-convicts learn trade at "re-entry" home; medium holds séance at Spiritualism meeting.

Ritty's invention was motivated primarily by self-interest. However, not all inventions in 1879 were so inspired. Some took a broader view of human needs. In Germany, the world's first commercial electric railway was installed by William and Werner von Siemens at the Berlin Exhibition of 1879. Work on a railroad tunnel under the Hudson River that would connect New York and New Jersey had resumed after a five-year delay caused by various injunctions and lawsuits. The Jouett-Hoff life-saving buoy, which could serve as a mooring for a ship-to-shore lifeline for stranded vessels, was patented in 1879. Out West, the new settlers celebrated the opening of the first railroad in the New Mexico Territory. Opening-day passengers to Las Vegas, where the line ended, predicted the town would become the most important center of population in the territory. The territory's governor was enthusiastic about the new link as well as his historical novel in progress, tentatively entitled *Ben-Hur, A Tale of the Christ*. His name was Lew Wallace.

The subject of the Wallace book was in keeping with another trend of the times. More and more Americans sought, in spiritual solace, a refuge from grinding economic pressures, a rebellious post-Civil War generation, and what many felt was a weakening of the nation's moral strength. Membership in the major religions remained fairly constant, but new avenues of faith were syphoning off those who found the traditional ones insufficient to cope with their needs. Cults were flourishing in forms as diverse as the needs of their followers, with Spiritualism by far the most popular. Almost every large city had its well-patronized *mediums* who supposedly interceded with the spirits of the dead on behalf of clients seeking guidance. Itinerant mediums traveled well-exploited "trade routes" within wagon or horseback reach of their base cities. No fees were collected, but "offerings" were accepted. Magnetism, self-expansionism, and self-compressionism were also popular escape routes for the more gullible.

In some medications, as in some beliefs, gullibility was the basic ingredient. There was Dr. Gounod's Sandaline, a "great remedy for all local and chronic complaints of whatever nature–no matter how long standing or deep seated." Floreline, a new liquid dentrifice with medicinal properties, was guaranteed to "prevent dyspepsia, whooping cough, and lung collapse" by "cleansing all decayed teeth of parasites and animaliculae." From Stuttgart, Germany, came word that one Hans Jager had made a "fresh investigation of the subject of the human nose." He announced that, according to his findings, "the human nose is the seat of the human soul, and that the workings of the latter are recorded on the surface of the former; also that use of certain volatilizing chemicals in the nostrils could alter specific traits of character as well as changes in temperament."

The curative powers of these medications–and the motives of their promoters–were questionable. But, in general, there was no denying the sincerity behind many an American's efforts to aid the less fortunate. "Waifs' Homes" were being established in the larger cities, such as New Orleans, to care for orphans, runaways, or abandoned children. The Society of Ethical Culture of New York City established a free kindergarten for the children of working mothers. Convicted criminals, too, were sharing in the wave of compassion, with facilities such as Michael Dunn's Home for Convicts being established in New York City and Father Kerrigan's Mission for Reformed Criminals in San Francisco.

One selfless example of human reaching out to human was provided by Mrs. James Bryant of Lowndes County, Alabama. Concerned over the suffering of yellow fever victims in Memphis, Tenn., where an epidemic was raging, Mrs. Bryant donated "her colossal fortune of natural black hair for the benefit of sufferers." Wigmakers were impressed. Clara Barton, known from Civil War days as the *Angel of the Battlefield*, addressed the Editorial Association of New Jersey in May and implored its members to help win American endorsement of the Red Cross. A Charity Workers Guild, founded to aid those in need, was active in the Archdiocese of New York where a new cathedral, St. Patrick's, was opened on May 25.

Americans were also finding time to enjoy athletic diversion. Archery was edging out lawn croquet as America's newest sports enthusiasm. There was scarcely a city or town without its group of archers. The first annual national meeting of the National Archery Association was held at White Stocking Park in Chicago in mid-August. About 70 men and 20 women from various cities competed for the honor of scoring the most bull's-eyes, and nearly 2,000 spectators were there to cheer them on. However, more than double that number attended the four-day World's Championship Bicycle Race, which was held in an oblong tent on Huntington Avenue in Boston in the fall. The sports novelty of the year was the Pedomotor, a pair of roller skates whose wooden wheels were equipped with an outer rim of India rubber. The Pedomotor's inventor, J. H. Hobbs of Philadelphia, claimed that the skates could travel noiselessly and at a top speed of 12 miles (19 kilometers) per hour.

Hobbs's do-it-yourself transportation was, in its own way, American inventiveness at its most individual. Another such individualist, George B. Selden, became the first American to apply for a patent on a carriage that would be powered by an internal-combustion engine— a forerunner of the gasoline automobile. And in Paris, A. M. Bailey invented an electric-spark pen that could produce engravings on copper or zinc—an invention that would ultimately lead to modern-day engraving. But it was on December 30 that Thomas A. Edison startled Americans with the first public exhibition of his newest inventions—an incandescent electric lamp and a current-distribution system to activate it. In a Biblical sense, Edison had shown that "out of the darkness there came light." It was a thought from which even the most depressed of Americans could take heart—in 1879 or any other year.

The Year
on File

1974
1976
1977
1978
1979

Contributors to THE WORLD BOOK YEAR BOOK report on the major developments of 1979. The contributors' names appear at the end of the articles they have written, and a complete roster of contributors, listing their professional affiliations and the articles they have written, is on pages 6 and 7.

Articles in this section are arranged alphabetically by subject matter. In most cases, the article titles are the same as those of the articles in THE WORLD BOOK ENCYCLOPEDIA that they update. The numerous cross references (in **bold type**) guide the reader to a subject or information that may be in some other article or that may appear under an alternative title. "See" and "See also" cross references appear within and at the end of articles to direct the reader to related information elsewhere in THE YEAR BOOK. "In WORLD BOOK, see" references point the reader to articles in the encyclopedia that provide background information to the year's events reported in THE YEAR BOOK.

See "Asia," page 195.

ADVERTISING

ADVERTISING. Despite the slowdown of the United States economy in 1979, particularly in the last six months, advertising volume rose for the fourth consecutive year. According to Robert J. Coen, senior vice-president of McCann-Erickson Worldwide, who conducts an annual study of ad volume for that agency, the 1979 volume was close to $49-billion, about 12 per cent higher than in 1978.

Advertising is not recession-proof, Coen pointed out, but it was bolstered in 1979, as it was expected to be in 1980, by special trends and projects. Coen cited such factors as the increase in working wives; the growth in the big-spending 25- to 44-year-old segment of the population; and the upcoming broadcast coverage of the 1980 Olympic Games and the presidential election campaigns.

Ad Growth was healthy throughout the world, with international agencies reporting to *Advertising Age* that 1979 gross income was up 21 per cent to $2.6 billion and billings up 22 per cent to $17 billion. Dentsu in Japan was again the largest agency in the world, with gross income of $321.4 million on billings of $2.2 billion. J. Walter Thompson Company in New York City retained its place as the second largest agency, with gross worldwide income of $221.5 million on billings of $1.5 billion.

China became the "new frontier" for U.S. advertisers, agencies, and media. Early in the year, the People's Republic threw open its doors to foreign advertising in virtually all media in that country. Ogilvy & Mather International in May became the first ad agency to place ads in China since 1949. N W Ayer ABH International, Young and Rubicam Incorporated, J. Walter Thompson, Compton Advertising Incorporated, and Doyle Dane Bernbach Incorporated were also planning some China ventures. Coca-Cola led the way among advertisers, just as its arch rival Pepsi-Cola had done earlier when it became the first U.S. soft drink to be sold in Russia.

Television Advertising was at the center of an important court decision handed down in October. MCA Incorporated and Walt Disney Productions had filed suit against the Sony Corporation, maintaining that Sony's Betamax videotape recording (VTR) machines deprive TV advertisers of the audiences they want when they want them, reducing the value of their TV advertising and televised shows. United States District Court Judge Warren J. Ferguson denied the plaintiffs' request that Sony and other VTR makers be ordered to stop the sales of and home use of their machines. In essence, the judge said that viewers would be exposed to the commercials when they initially recorded TV programs, so he did not believe that the advertiser would be cheated.

The biggest story on the regulatory front in 1979 was the Federal Trade Commission (FTC) activity concerning advertising aimed at children. FTC hearings got underway in San Francisco in January.

The cure for pollution is people. Working together.

Our streets and countryside have become dumping grounds for trash. But all across America, people are now recycling 8 million tons of it a year.

We create staggering amounts of garbage. But in Virginia Beach, they turned a mountain of garbage into a recreational hillside.

For a brochure showing how you can participate in dozens of projects like these, write **Keep America Beautiful, Inc.** 99 Park Avenue, New York, N.Y. 10016

A public-service advertisement aimed at reducing waste features examples of ways that people can control pollution and improve the environment.

At the opening session, representatives of consumer groups charged the cereal and toy industries with "deliberately deceiving and lying to children." Cereal and toy industry spokesmen questioned the FTC's authority to act on behalf of children. Critics of TV advertising to children called for a total ban on such advertising. But by the time the San Francisco hearings ended and hearings began in Washington in March, most observers felt that an outright ban on most TV ads aimed at children was unlikely.

Cigarette Advertisers suffered a setback when the FTC won an important court decision in January. A U.S. district court judge criticized the cigarette industry's legal tactics and ordered six cigarette manufacturers and 20 ad agencies to comply with FTC subpoenas, and turn over thousands of pages of marketing and advertising information to FTC investigators. The FTC issued the subpoenas in 1976. Cigarette company and agency lawyers are appealing the decision because they see the FTC's subpoenaing of this data as the beginning of an FTC attempt to further restrict cigarette advertising, or to ban such advertising completely.

The marketing success story of the year was Perrier water. This French import in the fancy bottles – and with a fancy price – became the darling of the American drinking, and nondrinking, set, and sales soared. Perrier's success led to a flood of competition and lots of advertising, from U.S.

brands of bottled water and many imports, such as Evian, Radenska, Apollinaris, and Ramlesa.

Account Changes. The two largest account switches in history took place in 1979. The largest was Chrysler Corporation's move of its $120-million to $150-million account from BBDO, Young and Rubicam, and Ross Roy Incorporated to Kenyon and Eckhardt Incorporated. The other large move was that of Miller Brewing Company, billing an estimated $80 million, from McCann Erickson to Backer and Spielvogel, a new agency formed by Bill Backer and Carl Spielvogel, two former top executives of McCann.

The shock of losing Chrysler was eased somewhat when Young and Rubicam was awarded the $63-million Lincoln-Mercury account that Kenyon and Eckhardt had resigned in order to accept the much larger Chrysler account. McCann Erickson recouped part of its loss by getting the $17-million Pabst beer account from Young and Rubicam.

Two major agency mergers took place in 1979. Young and Rubicam acquired Marsteller Incorporated, and the giant Interpublic Group of Companies acquired SSC&B Incorporated.

Daniel Starch, a pioneer in advertising research and founder of Daniel Starch and Staff, died on February 8 at age 95. *Jarlath J. Graham*

In WORLD BOOK, see ADVERTISING.

AFGHANISTAN. The growing revolt against the Russian-backed regime finally triggered an invasion by Soviet troops on Dec. 27, 1979, and a change of government. The revolt pitted Muslims and Afghan tribes against the Afghan army and its 4,000 Russian "advisers." The rebels saw their freedom, religion, and way of life threatened.

President Noor Mohammad Taraki resigned on September 16, citing poor health. He died soon after. His successor, Marxist Prime Minister Hafizullah Amin, who had purged intellectual and religious leaders and suppressed tribal customs, could not halt the rebellion. The Afghan army controlled the cities, but the poorly equipped rebels held the mountainous rural areas.

Thousands of Russian soldiers were in Kabul, the capital, when Amin was ousted and executed on December 27. His successor, pro-Russian Babrak Karmal, immediately asked for more Russian economic and military aid. As the year ended, it was estimated that up to 45,000 Russian troops were fighting in the Afghan countryside.

U.S. Ambassador Adolph Dubs was kidnapped in Kabul on February 14 by rebels demanding the release of religious leaders. Dubs was killed as police tried to rescue him. *Joseph P. Spohn*

See also ASIA (Facts in Brief Table). In WORLD BOOK, see AFGHANISTAN.

Rebel Muslim tribesmen, fighting against harsh government reforms, display a Russian-built army helicopter downed in Afghanistan.

AFRICA

Africa experienced both promising political changes and discouraging continuities during 1979. Military regimes gave way to elected civilian governments in Ghana and in the continent's most populous country, Nigeria. Repressive dictatorships were toppled in the Central African Republic, Equatorial Guinea, and Uganda; and Zimbabwe Rhodesia's leaders, both black and white, agreed to a cease-fire in that territory's seven-year-long civil war (see Close-Up).

However, agreement on a peaceful transition to independence still eluded Namibia (South West Africa). Civil wars persisted in Angola and Ethiopia, and Morocco continued to battle nationalist guerrillas for control of the former Spanish Sahara.

Military Rule Ended. After seven years of military rule under three separate regimes, an elected president and parliament took office in Ghana on September 24. Two factors – corruption in government and economic difficulties – had been blamed for the country's instability. The new civilian president, Hilla Limann, inherited a still-troubled economy, with Ghana's major export industry, cacao, in serious decline. However, further political corruption may have been discouraged by the June executions of three former heads of state and four high-from Muslims in the north, he did well in other parts of the country. However, his National Party failed to win a majority in either house of the federal legislature. See NIGERIA; SHAGARI, SHEHU.

Democracy was also tested in Kenya. Many observers feared that the country's system of competitive politics would disintegrate after the death in 1978 of Kenya's strong founding father, President Jomo Kenyatta. However, the parliamentary elections of November 8 went smoothly, and the voters turned unpopular government leaders out of office. Although only one political party, the Kenya African National Union (KANU), was legal in Kenya, up to eight KANU candidates contested each parliamentary seat. Seven members of the Cabinet, more than one-third of the total, failed to win re-election.

Dictators Ousted. Three harsh dictatorships fell during 1979. Uganda's President Idi Amin Dada was driven from office in April 1979. Amin, who gained power through a military coup in 1971, was deposed by an invasion force from neighboring Tanzania, aided by mutineers from his own army. The invaders consisted of Ugandan exiles opposed to his rule and regular Tanzanian troops, who shared the objective of destroying a government reputed to be the cruelest in Africa. Up to 300,000 Ugandans may have died from executions, beatings in prison, and other actions during Amin's regime. Amin was reported living in Libya. See UGANDA.

Equatorial Guinea's President Macias Nguema Biyogo Negue Ndong was deposed on August 3 by troops loyal to his nephew, Lieutenant Colonel Obiang Nguema Mbasogo. Macias Nguema, president since 1968, was arrested in a jungle hideout on August 18 and charged with genocide. Opponents said his government was responsible for the deaths of up to 50,000 Equatorial Guineans. He was found guilty and executed. See EQUATORIAL GUINEA.

The government of Emperor Bokassa I in the Central African Empire was overthrown on September 20 in a bloodless coup by supporters of former President David Dacko, whom Bokassa had ousted in 1966. Jean-Bedel Bokassa crowned himself emperor on Dec. 4, 1977, in ceremonies that cost his poverty-stricken country an estimated $10 million. In April 1979, schoolchildren in the capital city of Bangui staged protests against the mandatory purchase of school uniforms from a store allegedly owned by Bokassa's wife. He retaliated by arresting about 250 students between the ages of 6 and 16. About 100 students died in crowded prisons and witnesses accused Bokassa of personally killing 39 students.

French troops were airlifted into Bangui to support the new government. After unsuccessfully seeking asylum in France, Bokassa was allowed to enter the Ivory Coast on September 24. Following his removal, the country assumed its former name, the Central African Republic; Dacko became president.

Abel T. Muzorewa is sworn in as Zimbabwe Rhodesia's prime minister in June. In December, a British governor took over, pending new elections in 1980.

ranking military officers for misuse of public funds and offices. See GHANA.

On October 1, Nigeria gained its first civilian government since January 1966. The new president, Shehu Shagari, inherited an economy blessed with a strong oil industry. However, ethnic and regional rivalries that triggered two military coups d'état in 1966 and a bloody civil war from 1967 to 1970 continued to threaten Nigeria's political stability. While Shagari gathered most of his electoral support

Facts in Brief on African Political Units

Country	Population	Government	Monetary Unit*	Foreign Trade (million U.S. $)	
				Exports†	Imports†
Algeria	19,628,000	President Chadli Bendjedid; Prime Minister Mohamed Benahmed Abdelghani	dinar (3.8 = $1)	6,036	7,819
Angola	7,538,000	President José Eduardo dos Santos	kwanza (49.8 = $1)	1,227	625
Benin	3,557,000	President Mathieu Kerekou	franc (210 = $1)	31	246
Bophuthats-wana	1,719,000	President Lucas Mangope	rand (1 = $1.21)	no statistics available	
Botswana	804,000	President Sir Seretse M. Khama	pula (1 = $1.21)	194	288
Burundi	4,280,000	President Jean-Baptiste Bagaza	franc (90 = $1)	67	98
Cameroon	7,042,000	President Ahmadou Ahidjo; Prime Minister Paul Biya	franc (210 = $1)	705	784
Cape Verde	329,000	President Aristides Pereira; Prime Minister Pedro Pires	escudo (49.8 = $1)	1	32
Central African Republic	3,009,000	President David Dacko; Prime Minister Henri Maidou	franc (210 = $1)	82	63
Chad	4,473,000	President Goukouni Oueddei	franc (210 = $1)	63	116
Comoros	347,000	President Ahmed Abdallah; Prime Minister Salim Ben Ali	franc (210 = $1)	10	14
Congo	1,540,000	President Denis Sassou-Nguesso; Prime Minister Louis Sylvain-Goma	franc (210 = $1)	173	282
Djibouti	250,000	President Hassan Gouled Aptidon; Prime Minister Barkat Gourad Hamadou	franc 177.7 = $1)	20	74
Egypt	41,314,000	President Anwar al-Sadat; Vice-President Hosni Mobarak; Prime Minister Mustafa Khalil	pound (1 = $1.49)	1,737	6,727
Equatorial Guinea	338,000	President Obiang Nguema Mbasogo	ekuele (70.7 = $1)	36	20
Ethiopia	31,779,000	Provisional Military Government Chairman Mengistu Haile Mariam	birr (2.1 = $1)	307	455
Gabon	1,124,000	President Omar Bongo; Prime Minister Leon Mebiame	franc (210 = $1)	1,096	663
Gambia	596,000	President Sir Dawda Kairaba Jawara	dalasi (1.8 = $1)	44	103
Ghana	11,603,000	President Hilla Limann	new cedi (2.8 = $1)	811	862
Guinea	4,980,000	President Ahmed Sekou Toure; Prime Minister Lansana Beavogui	syli (19.1 = $1)	272	206
Guinea-Bissau	567,000	President Luis de Almeida Cabral; Commissioner Joao Bernardino Vieira	peso (33.8 = $1)	11	31
Ivory Coast	7,847,000	President Felix Houphouet-Boigny	franc (210 = $1)	2,155	1,752
Kenya	15,951,000	President Daniel T. arap Moi	shilling (7.3 = $1)	1,213	1,284
Lesotho	1,335,000	King Motlotlehi Moshoeshoe II; Prime Minister Leabua Jonathan	rand (1 = $1.21)	12	154
Liberia	1,825,000	President William R. Tolbert, Jr.	dollar (1 = $1)	486	464
Libya	3,002,000	Leader of the Revolution Muammar Muhammad al-Qadhaafi; General People's Congress Secretary General (Chief of State) Abd al-Ati al-Ubaydi; General People's Committee Secretary General (Prime Minister) Jadallah al-Talhi	dinar (1 = $3.38)	9,503	6,144
Madagascar	9,303,000	President Didier Ratsiraka; Prime Minister Desire Rakotoarijaona	franc (210 = $1)	275	285
Malawi	5,735,000	President H. Kamuzu Banda	kwacha (1 = $1.22)	174	339
Mali	6,872,000	President Moussa Traore	franc (420 = $1)	124	159
Mauritania	1,693,000	Military Committee for National Safety President Mohamed Mahmoud Ould Ahmed Louly; Prime Minister Mohamed Khouna Ould Haidalla	ouguiya (45.9 = $1)	121	184

Country	Population	Government	Monetary Unit*	Foreign Trade (million U.S. $)	
				Exports†	Imports†
Mauritius	942,000	Acting Governor General Dayendranath Burrenchobay; Prime Minister Sir Seewoosagur Ramgoolam	rupee (5.9 = $1)	313	488
Morocco	20,070,000	King Hassan II; Prime Minister Maati Bouabid	dirham (3.8 = $1)	1,508	2,970
Mozambique	10,343,000	President Samora Moises Machel	escudo (49.8 = $1)	129	278
Namibia (South West Africa)	1,027,000	Administrator-General Gerrit Viljoen	rand (1 = $1.21)	no statistics available	
Niger	5,259,000	Supreme Military Council President Seyni Kountche	franc (210 = $1)	134	127
Nigeria	72,031,000	President Shehu Shagari	naira (1 = $1.74)	10,557	11,913
Rwanda	4,753,000	President Juvenal Habyarimana	franc (92.8 = $1)	70	79
São Tomé and Príncipe	86,000	President Manuel Pino da Costa	dobra (34.8 = $1)	9	10
Senegal	5,791,000	President Leopold Sedar Senghor; Prime Minister Abdou Diouf	franc (210 = $1)	482	640
Seychelles	64,000	President France Albert Rene	rupee (5.9 = $1)	9	37
Sierra Leone	3,421,000	President Siaka Stevens	leone (1.1 = $1)	127	189
Somalia	3,614,000	President Mohamed Siad Barre	shilling (6.3 = $1)	85	167
South Africa	28,841,000	President Marais Viljoen; Prime Minister Pieter Willem Botha	rand (1 = $1.21)	7,182	7,193
Sudan	18,509,000	President & Prime Minister Gaafar Muhammed Nimeiri	pound (1 = $2.50)	489	1,124
Swaziland	553,000	King Sobhuza II; Prime Minister Prince Mabandla	lilangeni (1 = $1.21)	191	200
Tanzania	17,420,000	President Julius K. Nyerere; Prime Minister Edward Moringe Sokoine	shilling (8.2 = $1)	470	1,150
Togo	2,530,000	President Gnassingbe Eyadema	franc (210 = $1)	159	284
Transkei	5,916,000	President Kaiser Matanzima	rand (1 = $1.21)	no statistics available	
Tunisia	6,828,000	President Habib Bourguiba; Prime Minister Hedi Nouira	dinar (1 = $2.50)	1,090	2,119
Uganda	13,599,000	President Godfrey Lukogwa Binaisa	shilling (7.5 = $1)	568	190
Upper Volta	6,918,000	President Aboubakar Sangoule Lamizana; Prime Minister Joseph Conombo	franc (210 = $1)	55	209
Venda	320,000	President Patrick Mphephu	rand (1 = $1.21)	no statistics available	
Zaire	28,622,000	President Mobutu Sese Seko; Prime Minister Bo-Boliko Kokonga	zaire (1.5 = $1)	925	588
Zambia	5,896,000	President Kenneth D. Kaunda; Prime Minister Daniel Lisulo	kwacha (1 = $1.29)	898	680
Zimbabwe Rhodesia	7,493,000	Governor Lord Christopher Soames	dollar (1 = $1.50)	650	541

*Exchange rates as of Dec. 1, 1979. †Latest available data.

Rhodesian Peace Plans. Civil war had persisted in Rhodesia since 1972, with black nationalist guerrillas fighting a white-dominated government. However, Bishop Abel T. Muzorewa became the country's first black prime minister on June 1, 1979, heading a biracial black-majority government. The important black Patriotic Front, led by Joshua Nkomo and Robert Mugabe, rejected Muzorewa's government as too protective of white interests, particularly in land ownership. With a force of about 15,000 guerrillas inside the country, the front continued its attacks on the government.

Great Britain organized a peace conference on Zimbabwe Rhodesia that began in London on September 10. Britain, represented at the conference by Foreign Secretary Lord Carrington, maintained that the country was still legally a British colony because its white minority government had unilaterally declared independence in 1965.

British Prime Minister Margaret R. Thatcher was pressured by members of her ruling Conservative Party to recognize Muzorewa's government and lift the trade ban and other economic sanctions that Britain had imposed on Rhodesia after the 1965 break. However, Thatcher wanted to end the civil war first.

President Jimmy Carter was also under political pressure to support Muzorewa and end sanctions that the United States government had legislated against Rhodesia. Both houses of the Congress of the United States passed legislation in August requiring Carter to lift the sanctions by November 15 or declare why it was in the national interest to continue them. Carter said on November 14 that he would not end the sanctions at that time.

The London peace conference brought Muzorewa, Nkomo, and Mugabe together with Ian D. Smith, white former prime minister of Rhodesia. They agreed on November 15 to a new constitution and the replacement of Muzorewa's government with a British governor and about 300 other British administrators, who would prepare the country for new elections and a transfer of power.

Hard negotiations continued after November 15 to find agreement on the conditions for a cease-fire. The seven-year war had cost more than 20,000 lives and bred intense suspicions among black factions and fueled animosities between blacks and whites.

The British governor, Lord Soames, was installed on December 13, and the nation once again became the British colony of Rhodesia until new elections could be held. Great Britain lifted its economic sanctions on December 13, and President Carter lifted the U.S. sanctions on December 16. Then, on December 21, the Patriotic Front leaders signed an agreement in London calling for a cease-fire and elections in 1980 that could bring international recognition for an independent Zimbabwe. See ZIMBABWE RHODESIA.

Other Negotiations. Chad's civil war, which erupted in 1965 pitting the Muslim north against largely Christian political forces in the south, gave some promise of ending in 1979. Eleven Chadian political factions met in Lagos, Nigeria, on August 20 and 21 and agreed on a cease-fire and the establishment of a new government with a northerner as president and a southerner as vice-president.

Peace negotiations to end Namibia's guerrilla war stalled over conditions for a cease-fire and elections leading to black-majority rule. Namibia has been under South African rule since 1920, and black nationalists of the South West Africa People's Organization (SWAPO) began to rebel in 1966.

South Africa objected to any cease-fire plan permitting SWAPO guerrillas to infiltrate Namibia from bases in neighboring Angola. In October 1979, Great Britain and four other Western powers sought to meet South Africa's objections by proposing a demilitarized zone on either side of the Namibia-Angola border, with United Nations (UN) forces policing the zone and UN supervision of subsequent elections. A peace conference was convened in mid-November in Geneva, Switzerland, to discuss these proposals. See NAMIBIA.

Guerrilla Warfare also continued in Ethiopia. Despite substantial Russian and Cuban military assistance, Ethiopia's central government could not suppress secessionist guerrillas fighting in three regions – Eritrea and Tigre provinces in the north and Ogaden in the southeast. The Somali-speaking Ogaden secessionists had sought to join neighboring Somalia since 1960. Continuing warfare drove thousands of the region's inhabitants to seek refuge in Somalia. By year's end, more than 300,000 refugees were living in Somalia. See ETHIOPIA.

Angola had, since its independence in 1975, been plagued by a civil war in which the guerrilla forces of the National Union for the Total Liberation of Angola (UNITA) fought the central government. UNITA guerrillas operated in Angola's eastern and southern regions during 1979, cutting off transportation on major roads and the key east-west Benguela Railway, creating serious food shortages in the capital city, Luanda. An estimated 20,000 Cuban troops were stationed in Angola, most of them battling the UNITA rebellion.

Angola's president since 1975, Agostinho Neto, died on September 10 in Moscow while undergoing treatment for cancer. The central committee of the ruling Popular Movement for the Liberation of Angola named José Eduardo dos Santos, Neto's Russian-educated planning minister, as his successor. UNITA expressed a willingness to negotiate with Dos Santos, but only if Cuban troops withdrew.

Western Sahara was yet another African war zone in 1979. Following the end of Spanish rule there in 1976, King Hassan II of Morocco claimed the territory's northern two-thirds as part of his king-

A Century Of Struggle

On May 29, 1979 – a balmy, sunlit day – Abel T. Muzorewa, a Methodist bishop, was sworn in as the first black prime minister of Zimbabwe Rhodesia. Symbolically, the ceremony was held on the spacious grounds of a palatial Dutch colonial mansion that was once the official residence of the governors appointed by the British monarch. The ceremony ended nearly 100 years of bitter, often bloody struggle over who – the white minority or the black majority – would rule.

It was a struggle born when Zambezia, a region named after the great river flowing through its center, came under British influence. The man who brought that influence to bear was Cecil J. Rhodes, the financier, statesman, and empire builder for whom the colony was named by the British. Firmly in control of neighboring South Africa through his British South Africa Company, Rhodes acquired Rhodesia for personal gain and also to add another colonial jewel to the British Crown. There was untold copper wealth to be had there; tin, zinc, gold, and cobalt abounded. Labor was plentiful and cheap.

Rhodes was a master at exploitation. In 1888, he was granted mineral rights in the copper-rich Matabele region by its chief, Lobengulu. On Sept. 12, 1890, Rhodes dispatched a band of pioneers to Matabele, where they built a fort and established a settlement. White rule had begun; black African uprisings against it were ruthlessly crushed.

Ian D. Smith

The whites ruled for three decades, largely free of the controls Britain exercised over its other African holdings, and they expanded their operations throughout the territory. Nor did their rule diminish greatly when Rhodes's British South Africa Company ceded authority over the territory to the Crown in 1923. London divided the colony into Northern Rhodesia and Southern Rhodesia, with the Zambezi River dividing them. The change meant little to Africans, even though Southern Rhodesia became a self-governing British colony.

However, the winds of change began to sweep across colonial Africa

Abel T. Muzorewa

after World War II. The "dark continent" had seen the light of freedom, and it liked what it saw. Germany's colonial empire in Africa had been dissolved after World War I. Now it was Belgium's turn to relinquish its African holdings. France followed and, ultimately, so did Britain. For most of the British African colonies, the transition to independence was swift and fairly easy. But Rhodesia proved a harder nut to crack, particularly because of white resistance to change. Northern Rhodesia became independent Zambia in 1964, but Southern Rhodesia, still a self-governing British colony, remained a problem.

At issue was the degree of power to be given Southern Rhodesia's black majority. Blacks outnumbered whites by more than 20 to 1 – about 6.8 million blacks to fewer than 250,000 whites in 1979.

On Nov. 11, 1965, with negotiations deadlocked, Rhodesia's Prime Minister Ian D. Smith rejected British insistence on black-majority rule and unilaterally declared Rhodesia independent. There followed a decade of fruitless negotiations, international sanctions endorsed by the United Nations, and an upsurge in black nationalist guerrilla terrorism. In 1975, and again in 1976, Smith and black leaders met, but failed to agree.

In March 1978, the white-minority government and three black leaders agreed to establish a biracial government to lead the way to black-majority rule. A constitution was drafted. Elections were held in April 1979, and Muzorewa's predominantly black government was installed. But the two leading guerrilla groups, Joshua Nkomo's Zimbabwe African People's Union and Robert Mugabe's Zimbabwe African National Union, had boycotted the election, and violence continued. After more negotiations, in London, a peace agreement was finally signed on December 21. It returned to the blacks that measure of self-rule they had been deprived of nearly 100 years earlier. With new elections scheduled for early in 1980, they could finally see independence on the horizon.   Paul C. Tullier

See also ZIMBABWE RHODESIA.

Tanzanian soldiers advance on Jinja, Uganda's second largest city, in
April in the invasion that routed President Idi Amin and his forces.

dom. Mauritania took the southern third. Western Saharan nationalists opposed these annexations. Organizing the Polisario Front guerrilla movement with military aid from Algeria and Libya, they waged war against both Mauritania and Morocco. Mauritania's government agreed in August to withdraw from the territory and to recognize the Polisario's Saharan Arab Democratic Republic.

On August 14, however, Hassan claimed Mauritania's former share – the area called Tiris el-Gharbia – as a new province of Morocco. At year's end, Hassan had about 40,000 troops committed to the war against Polisario, whose forces were estimated to be between 10,000 and 15,000.

Hassan embarrassed the Carter Administration by asking for military assistance for the war in Western Sahara. Carter preferred neutrality, but Morocco was an old and reliable friend of the United States in North Africa. The United States finally agreed on October 22 to provide counterinsurgency weapons, including armed reconnaissance planes and helicopter gunships.

The Organization of African Unity (OAU) held its 16th annual summit conference in Monrovia, Liberia, in July. The conference called on all nations to reject Bishop Muzorewa's Zimbabwe Rhodesian government and to recognize, instead, the Patriotic Front, led by Joshua Nkomo and Robert Mugabe, as the legitimate representatives of the Zimbabwe peo-

ple. Another resolution proposed a referendum in which the people of Western Sahara would choose between independence or continued association with Morocco and Mauritania. Morocco walked out of the conference to protest this proposal. The resolution obtained the necessary two-thirds majority by a single vote.

The European Community (EC or Common Market) signed a new agreement for economic cooperation in November with 37 African nations and 20 other developing countries in the Caribbean and Pacific Ocean regions. The five-year agreement, the Lome II Convention, was to go into effect on March 1, 1980, and was to provide a more liberal entry of exports into EC markets, $6 billion in economic aid from EC countries, and a special fund to cushion certain mining industries in the developing countries against severe market declines.

President Joachim Yhombi-Opango of the Congo was ousted on February 8. The ruling Congolese Workers' Party on March 31 named Colonel Denis Sassou-Nguesso to succeed him.   John D. Esseks

In WORLD BOOK, see AFRICA.
AGRICULTURE. See FARM AND FARMING.
AIR FORCE. See ARMED FORCES.
AIR POLLUTION. See ENVIRONMENT.
AIRPORT. See AVIATION.
ALABAMA. See STATE GOVERNMENT.
ALASKA. See STATE GOVERNMENT.

ALBANIA opened itself slightly to the outside world in 1979, but continued its hard-line Stalinist course at home. Italy's Foreign Trade Minister Rinaldo Ossola visited Tiranë in January to sign a 1979 trade agreement, becoming the first Italian Cabinet minister to visit Albania since it passed from Italian control in 1943. Albania indicated in February that it was interested in resuming diplomatic relations with West Germany. In August, that country replied through its embassy in Yugoslavia that it was interested, too, but that there must be no preconditions. Albania had insisted previously that West Germany pay $4.5 billion in reparations for loss of life and destruction that occurred when Germany occupied Albania in 1943 and 1944 during World War II.

Albania established informal contacts with Great Britain, also through Yugoslavia, concerning $16-million in Albanian gold that Great Britain has held since World War II. In September, Albania said that it would send students to Austria, France, Italy, and Sweden for the first time since World War II. Albania's trade with Yugoslavia increased from $34-million in 1978 to $53.6 million in 1979.

Albania attacked China's normalization of relations with the United States in January and China's invasion of Vietnam in February, but received the Chinese ambassador in Tiranë in April.   Chris Cviic

See also EUROPE (Facts in Brief Table). In WORLD BOOK, see ALBANIA.

ALBERTA voters gave the Progressive Conservative administration of Premier Peter Lougheed an impressive 74 of 79 seats in the Legislative Assembly in a provincial election on March 14, 1979. The combined opposition strength was cut by one, leaving only four Social Credit members and one New Democratic Party representative to stand against the governing party.

Lougheed's government used its treasury, swollen by oil and natural gas royalties, to offer substantial financial bonuses to Albertans. It announced on February 1 that $1 billion of the budget surplus would be distributed to municipalities, virtually wiping out their debts. The move was expected to reduce property taxes by 10 to 20 per cent.

The Alberta Heritage Savings Trust Fund, a public endowment that had been allocated 30 per cent of the province's oil and gas royalties, was expected to grow to $6.2 billion by the end of the 1979-1980 fiscal year. The fund was loaned on short-term investments within Alberta and to other provinces.

Lougheed named a new 29-member cabinet, the largest in any Canadian province. He lost an experienced member on September 24 when Hugh M. Horner, deputy premier and economic development minister, was named to serve as federal grain transport coordinator.   David M.L. Farr

See also CANADA. In WORLD BOOK, see ALBERTA.

ALGERIA. A new era began with the election on Feb. 7, 1979, of Colonel Chadli Bendjedid as president of the republic (see BENDJEDID, CHADLI). He succeeded Houari Boumediene, who died in December 1978. The new president had been commander of the Oran military region since 1969 and served as defense minister during Boumediene's last illness. His election represented a compromise between "moderate" and "radical" factions of the ruling National Liberation Front (FLN).

The New President lost no time in launching Algeria on a different course, though he worked within the framework of Boumediene's political policies. His Cabinet included 14 first-time ministers. He also appointed Algeria's first prime minister, Mohamed Benahmed Abdelghani. Boumediene and his predecessor had held the office themselves.

The FLN policymaking role was enlarged. The Cabinet was made responsible to a 17-member FLN Political Committee that was to apply the Algerian National Charter and draft national development plans. Another change made the FLN secretary-general the automatic choice for president. At the same time, the National Assembly, Algeria's main legislative body, amended the 1976 Constitution to limit the presidential term to five years and to establish rules of succession. The new government also made a number of social changes involving

With a portrait of the country's late leader, Houari Boumediene, in the background, Colonel Chadli Bendjedid becomes Algeria's president.

taxes, wages, and housing to ease the effects of inflation.

Prisoners Freed. Another sign of the new era was the release of political prisoners and opponents of Boumediene. Ferhat Abbas and Benyoussef ben Khedda, two of the last surviving leaders of the War of Independence, were pardoned in April. On July 4, former President Ahmed Ben Bella, under house arrest since 1965, was also released.

Algeria celebrated the 25th anniversary of its war of revolution against France on November 1. A three-hour parade in Algiers displayed Algeria's modern, well-equipped armed forces.

Higher oil prices and the growing demand for Algerian natural gas continued to spur economic growth. Sonatrach, the state oil and gas organization, sold 120 billion cubic feet (3.4 billion cubic meters) of gas to the Netherlands and West Germany in March, after the United States Department of Energy refused to raise the ceiling placed on gas imports by U.S. companies. On June 19, a 1,533-mile (2,468-kilometer) gas pipeline that stretches across Tunisia and then under the Mediterranean Sea to Italy began carrying Algerian gas directly to European consumers.   William Spencer

See also AFRICA (Facts in Brief Table). In WORLD BOOK, see ALGERIA.

AMERICAN LEGION. See COMMUNITY ORGANIZATIONS.

AMERICAN LIBRARY ASSOCIATION (ALA). More than 10,600 librarians, publishers, and friends of libraries met in Dallas for the ALA's 98th annual conference in June 1979. Isaac Bashevis Singer, winner of the 1978 Nobel Prize for Literature; economist John Kenneth Galbraith; and educator Francis Keppel participated in special programs on the theme "The Library in American Society." The program included a special celebration of the Freedom to Read Foundation's 10th anniversary. Attorney Robert M. O'Neil and author Jessica Mitford addressed the conference on the subject of the First Amendment during the next 10 years. Thomas J. Galvin, dean of the Graduate School of Library and Information Sciences at the University of Pittsburgh, took office as ALA president.

International Cooperation was evident during 1979 in a library "first," a seminar sponsored by the ALA, the International Communications Agency (ICA), and the United States Library of Congress. Seven Russian librarians met with their American counterparts to hear a presentation of papers on aspects of Russian libraries. The participants made plans to hold a return seminar in Moscow, perhaps as soon as 1980.

The ALA devoted major attention to preparing for the White House Conference on Library and Information Services that was held in November. The Gallup Organization conducted a survey on

"Book Reading and Library Usage; a Study of Habits and Perceptions." According to the survey, more than half of all adult Americans used their public library in the previous year.

Friends of Libraries USA was created in 1979 to encourage the formation of Friends of Library groups across the United States. It is estimated that there are already more than 500,000 members in 2,000 groups.

National Awards. The Committee on the Status of Women in Librarianship received the 1979 Bailey K. Howard-World Book Encyclopedia-ALA Goals Award to finance a demographic profile of the women members of ALA. The Office for Library Personnel Resources Minimum Qualifications Task Force won the 1979 J. Morris Jones-World Book Encyclopedia-ALA Goals Award to fund a study of the ramifications of the Master of Library Science requirement in relation to equal opportunity laws.

Ellen Raskin, the author of *The Westing Game,* won the 1979 Newbery Medal for the most distinguished contribution to American literature for children. Paul Goble, illustrator and author of *The Girl Who Loved Wild Horses,* won the 1979 Caldecott Medal for the most distinguished American picture book for children.   Margaret Barber

See also CANADIAN LIBRARY ASSOCIATION (CLA); LIBRARY; LITERATURE FOR CHILDREN. In WORLD BOOK, see AMERICAN LIBRARY ASSN.

ANDERSON, JOHN B. (1922-   ), a congressman from Illinois since 1961, became a candidate for the 1980 Republican presidential nomination on June 8, 1979. Although as chairman of the House Republican Conference he is the third-ranking Republican in the House of Representatives, Anderson was little known outside of Washington, D.C., and his home state when he entered the race.

John Bayard Anderson was born in Rockford, Ill., on Feb. 15, 1922. He graduated from the University of Illinois in 1942 and received a law degree from that university in 1946. He earned a Master of Law degree from Harvard University in 1949. He returned to Rockford to practice law before joining the United States Foreign Service in 1952. He served with that agency in West Berlin, West Germany, until 1955, when he resumed his law practice.

Anderson was elected to Congress in 1960. Initially a staunch conservative, he has become an advocate of such traditionally liberal causes as civil rights and environmental protection.

He married Keke Machakos in 1953. The Andersons have five children.   Beverly Merz

ANDORRA. See EUROPE.

ANGOLA. See AFRICA.

ANGUILLA. See WEST INDIES.

ANIMAL. See CAT; CONSERVATION; DOG; ZOOLOGY; ZOOS AND AQUARIUMS. See also WORLD BOOK Supplement section, DINOSAUR.

ANTHROPOLOGY

ANTHROPOLOGY. A number of discoveries in 1979 promised to alter greatly some theories of the ancestry of human beings and apes. Anthropologist Russell L. Ciochon of the University of North Carolina in Charlotte, and paleontologist Donald E. Savage of the University of California, Berkeley, in May discussed the results of research they conducted with Burmese scientists in the Pondaung Hills near Mandalay, Burma. They recovered the remains of two primates, each a new genus, *Pondaungia* and *Amphipithecus,* which lived in the area 40 million years ago. The earliest primates previously known lived in Egypt about 10 million years ago.

As reconstructed from fossil fragments, both primates weighed about 30 pounds (14 kilograms) and had characteristics similar to such simple primates as lemurs, but also like monkeys and apes. Existing evolutionary theories generally hold that monkeys evolved from the early primates, and then apes evolved from monkeys. These new results suggest that both had a common ancestor in the distant past.

New Hominid Species. Physical anthropologists Donald C. Johanson of the Cleveland Museum of Natural History and Timothy D. White of the University of California, Berkeley, in January summarized evidence for a new hominid species they call *Australopithecus afarensis.* The fossils they described were recovered in independent projects in Ethiopia and Tanzania. They studied 350 fossil fragments, representing the remains of at least 57 different individuals. At one location, they found the fossils of 13 individuals killed by a natural catastrophe, possibly a flash flood.

Johanson and White came to the conclusion that the legs of this hominid were those of an animal that walked on two feet in a fully erect fashion. But the jaws, teeth, and skull appeared to be those of a chimplike animal. The creatures lived between 3 and 3.8 million years ago and were between 3.5 and 4 feet (105 and 120 centimeters) tall.

While the claims of Johanson and White immediately aroused controversy, many anthropologists were convinced by the evidence. Their discovery is important for two reasons. The animal apparently lived earlier than other forms of *Australopithecus* and humans—indicating that *Homo sapiens* was not a descendant of the later *Australopithecus* species, as had been thought. Also, there is no evidence that *A. afarensis* was a toolmaker. Many anthropologists had reasoned that hominids began walking upright on two feet to free their hands so they could make and use tools. It now seems likely that food sharing and other activities of a close family life may have been the cause of walking on two feet.

Ancient Footprints. Mary N. Leakey and geologist Richard L. Hay of the University of California,

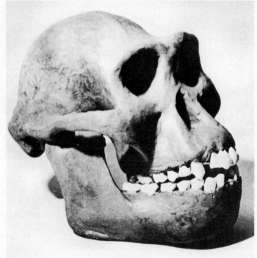

Physical anthropologist Donald C. Johanson, *left,* and a colleague reconstructed a skull from African fossils to represent *Australopithecus afarensis,* a proposed new species of hominid.

187

AQUARIUM

Berkeley, clarified Leakey's 1978 discovery of footprints at least 3.6 million years old. The footprints were made by at least two individuals walking in parallel lines for a distance of about 75 feet (23 meters). While it cannot be shown conclusively that the individuals were walking together, this appears to have been the case.

Another set of footprints was described in November 1979 by Glynn L. Isaac of the University of California, Berkeley, and anthropologist Richard Leakey of the Kenya National Museum. Found in northern Kenya, these footprints were apparently left by *Homo erectus,* a direct ancestor of modern man, about 1.5 million years ago.

Early Diet. The foods eaten by early ancestors of man have long been a subject of great controversy among anthropologists. In an effort to resolve at least some of the issues, Alan Walker of Johns Hopkins University in Baltimore examined scratches on the teeth of human fossils under a microscope. Walker's analysis indicated that hominids prior to *Homo erectus* were basically plant eaters, though they may have occasionally eaten meat. He says *Homo erectus* was the first *omnivore* (eating both plants and animals).   Fred Plog

In WORLD BOOK, see ANTHROPOLOGY; PREHISTORIC MAN.

AQUARIUM. See ZOOS AND AQUARIUMS.

ARCHAEOLOGY. Two studies shed new light in 1979 on the prehistory of the Nile River Valley cultures in early Egypt. Despite extensive knowledge of the very advanced civilization that eventually grew up in the area, archaeologists have known little about earlier peoples in the area.

Archaeologists Keith C. Seele and Bruce Williams of the University of Chicago announced in March the preliminary results of their analysis of materials from 33 tombs in the Qustul cemetery near the Egypt-Sudan border. This cemetery was excavated about 15 years ago as part of efforts to salvage the remains of sites that were being flooded by Lake Nasser, behind the Aswan Dam. Seele and Williams noted that scientists originally thought the inhabitants of the area had been organized in small tribes, some led by a chief. But the rich array of pottery, jewelry, and other artifacts found suggested to them that the tombs were of high-status individuals, probably kings. The decorations on one incense burner, for example, showed a palace, a king on a throne, and the falcon god Horus. The materials date to about 3300 B.C. When researchers decipher hieroglyphs on some of the artifacts, they may get further clues about this early society – which may have been a formally organized state.

Early Farming. Anthropologist Fred Wendorf of Southern Methodist University, Dallas, and an in-

ternational team of scientists in September described the results of their excavations at Wadi Kubbaniya, also in the Aswan area of Egypt. Previous research had shown that between 12,000 and 14,500 years ago, local people had used sickles and grinding tools in their quest for food. However, there was no clear evidence of whether they were harvesting wild or domesticated resources.

The sites excavated by the Wendorf team, radiocarbon-dated to between 17,000 and 18,300 years ago, yielded evidence of carbonized barley. The size and condition of the barley grains suggest that it was domesticated, not wild. This is evidence of organized farming – as opposed to random gathering of crops – 10,000 years earlier than that found elsewhere in the Middle East. Moreover, other evidence of early farming has been recovered from sites in mountainous or marginal environments, not the areas that later became the breadbasket of the Fertile Crescent, parts of what are now Syria and Iraq. Thus, these findings will require substantial revision of theories as to how and why farming started and its impact on social organization.

Early Life in Syria. Archaeologist Paolo Matthiae of the University of Rome had announced in 1976 that his excavations at Ebla, in Syria, revealed the existence of a major civilization in an area previously thought to be a barren wasteland inhabited only by nomadic herders. The translation of some of the 15,000 clay tablets recovered from the site were made public in 1979. The translations, done by Giovanni Pettinato of the same university and a team of experts working with him, revealed a rich variety of information: political documents, expense accounts, inventories, and even dictionaries – one of which is a list of 3,000 words. Pettinato first deciphered "Eblaite," the cuneiform language of the tablets, which is the oldest known Semitic language and is related to Sumerian.

The Ebla tablets are proving to be far richer than those recovered from other Middle Eastern sites. From them, scientists have learned that Ebla once had 30,000 people, including about 11,700 civil servants. About 260,000 people lived in the territory controlled by the Eblaites, which was ruled by a king elected for seven years. International conferences of scholars were held in the city, and the tablets include records of professors from other nations who came to teach in the schools.

Of particular interest are the names of residents similar to biblical figures – for example, Abraham and Esau. This discovery has caused considerable controversy because it strongly suggests an early link between Israel and Syria. The present Syrian government, vehemently anti-Israeli, has stated that there can be no connection between early cultures in Syria and Israel.   Fred Plog

See also ANTHROPOLOGY. In WORLD BOOK, see ARCHAEOLOGY.

ARCHITECTURE. The American Institute of Architects (AIA) zeroed in on the theme "A Celebration of Design" at its annual meeting held in Kansas City, Mo., from June 3 to 7, 1979. In sharp contrast to recent annual meetings, the Missouri convention concentrated on design rather than the business side of architecture.

Keynote speakers Norris K. Smith, professor of art history at Washington University in St. Louis, and Pietro Belluschi, who designed the Juilliard School of Music at the Lincoln Center for the Performing Arts in New York City, chastised architects for seeking visual pleasure at the expense of social goals. Both men urged them to concentrate on time-honored values and pay less heed to image and fashion.

AIA Awards. I. M. Pei received the AIA Gold Medal, which honors a lifetime of design accomplishments. In his acceptance speech, Pei warned delegates against the division of architectural expertise. "There seems to be the world of practice and the world of ideas, each in alienation from the other," Pei said. "The schism that exists between the two confuses and divides the profession. Ideas and practice are complementary. I reject the notion that they require two different kinds of architects. They belong together in one world of architecture."

The AIA Architectural Firm Award went to Geddes Brecher Qualls Cunningham of Philadelphia and Princeton, N.J. The principals invited the entire office staff to share the stage with them in receiving the award. The AIA's annual award for a significant building designed at least 25 years ago went to Louis Kahn's pioneering Yale University Art Gallery.

Contractor Role. The decision made at the 1978 convention to change the AIA code of ethics to permit members to engage in "design-build" practice, enabling them to handle construction and contracting as well as design, was subject to a three-year monitoring period. The monitoring task force reported that while 60 per cent of member firms support the concept, most exhibited little interest in it and barely 10 per cent indicated they had experience in operating a design-build practice.

Arena Collapse. The roof of the five-year-old R. Crosby Kemper Jr. Memorial Arena in Kansas City collapsed during a violent rainstorm on June 4, only hours after AIA delegates had toured the architectural showcase. The $12.2-million facility was designed by Helmut Jahn of C. F. Murphy Associates, Chicago, and won an AIA design award in 1976. Consultant James L. Stratta of Menlo Park, Calif., announced in August that the roof's collapse was triggered by the failure of high-strength bolts that gave way when an estimated 640 short tons (576 metric tons) of rain water flooded the roof.

New Buildings. Ground was broken in downtown New Orleans on August 1 for the 21-story Chevron

The John F. Kennedy Library in Boston, dedicated in October, is I. M. Pei's dramatic showcase for the papers and memorabilia of the former President.

Plaza Building, described as one of the most energy-efficient structures currently under construction. The precast reinforced-concrete building was designed by architects Stanley Muller & Associates with a heating, ventilating, and air-conditioning system designed to consume one-third less energy than systems in structures of comparable size.

Construction began in midsummer on a 44-story apartment tower over New York City's Museum of Modern Art. The tower's 275 luxury condominium units will rest on an eight-story addition to the museum. Cesar Pelli, dean of the Yale University School of Architecture, is design adviser for both the tower, which was designed by Edward Durell Stone Associates, and the museum extension, designed by the New York City office of Gruen Associates.

Work on Denver's tallest and largest skyscraper began on July 30. Designed by Hellmuth, Obata & Kassabaum of St. Louis, the 42-story, $93-million structure will contain 1.1 million square feet (100,000 square meters) and will house a 622-room Marriott Hotel on the first 19 floors, topped by 23 floors of offices.

New Johnson Plans. Famed architect Philip C. Johnson, who stirred up controversy in 1978 with his plans for the baroque-modern American Telephone & Telegraph Company's headquarters in New York City, unveiled plans on April 26 for the PPG Industries headquarters complex in Pittsburgh. The complex will cost more than $100 million and will contain 1 million square feet (90,000 square meters) of space in a 40-story tower and up to 600,000 square feet (54,000 square meters) in five lower associated buildings. The centerpiece tower will be a Gothic-style structure clad in reflective glass. Pointed arches at the corners and turrets decorating the roofline will provide the building with an appearance much like London's Houses of Parliament.

Johnson's ability to incite controversy was cited when he was awarded the first annual Pritzker Architecture Prize of $100,000. Sponsored by the Hyatt Foundation, it is the largest monetary award in the field of architecture and honors "outstanding creative endeavors." Jay A. Pritzker, president of the foundation, termed the 72-year-old Johnson "dean of American architects" and said that Johnson was "doing more than anyone in the world to keep modern architecture lively and unpredictable."

The Long-Anticipated "Transformations in Modern Architecture" show at the Museum of Modern Art in New York City during March and April featured photographs of some 400 buildings by more than 300 architects. A pictorial review of design over the past 20 years, it traced the paths modern architecture has taken in its transition from the steel-and-glass ethic that prevailed in 1959 to today's eclecticism.   Rob Cuscaden

In WORLD BOOK, see ARCHITECTURE.

ARGENTINA. The ruling military junta came under intense international pressure in 1979. At least 6,000 persons had disappeared over a three-year period after allegedly being apprehended by police during an ongoing campaign against left wing subversives. Various investigative groups, including the Inter-American Commission on Human Rights of the Organization of American States (OAS), were concerned with their whereabouts.

Beginning on September 6, the commission conducted two weeks of hearings in several Argentine cities. According to a report in *The New York Times,* the commission found "overwhelming evidence of methodical killing and torture of prisoners in the country at the same time that it saw evidence of recent efforts by the military regime to reduce human rights violations." In a preliminary report to the OAS General Assembly in La Paz, Bolivia, in late October, the commission cited four specific cases involving persons who had disappeared under mysterious circumstances as evidence of human rights violations. Argentina was condemned, along with Chile, Uruguay, and Paraguay, by an assembly vote of 19 to 2 on October 29.

The Pope's Appeal. Although Argentine newspapers did not report the assembly's action, they gave full coverage to Pope John Paul II's appeal on October 28 to Argentina and Chile to "make good on their promises to clarify the situation of those in prison." Prior to the OAS commission's arrival, General Albano Harguindiguy, the minister of interior, had stated that 1,438 political prisoners were still being detained of the 5,018 that the government had held in May 1977. This did not include 1,500 who had been tried and sentenced by military courts or who were awaiting trial.

To ease the legal problems created for the families of persons who had disappeared, the government issued a decree on August 24 declaring that all persons missing in the past five years could be presumed to be dead so that their estates could be settled. Then, on September 25, the regime released Jacobo Timerman, a leading figure in Argentina's substantial Jewish community and publisher of the daily newspaper, *La Opinión,* who had been held since 1977 on the suspicion that he had aided antigovernment terrorist groups. Most of that time he had been held under house arrest, though he was never charged. Two days after his release, Timerman arrived in Tel Aviv-Yafo, Israel.

The military, in defending its position, argued that its forces were engaged in a "dirty war" that had been started by the terrorists. Earlier in the year, General Roberto Viola had declared that "like all wars, this one has left tremendous wounds that only time can heal. There are the dead, the wounded, the jailed, and those who are absent forever. Don't ask for explanations where there are none." And although arrests of suspects and attacks by terrorists

continued in 1979, they were down sharply from previous years.

The Economy. Argentina continued to record one of the world's highest inflation rates. In September, it was reported that the cost of living had increased 11.5 per cent during the preceding month, bringing inflation for the 12-month period ending in August up to 171.1 per cent. Soaring inflation had been a carryover from the regime headed by President María Estela (Isabel) Martínez de Perón, the widow of former dictator Juan Perón. Critics of the military junta said it had failed to take such strong measures as cutting back on government spending in order to hold prices down. The military maintained that spending had remained high to avoid plunging the country into a recession that might in turn create political unrest and high unemployment. Nevertheless, a 24-hour general strike was called on April 27 to protest the military government's ban on union activities and its inability to control inflation. A split within the labor movement and a government drive against labor leaders apparently undermined the strike. With the exception of two rail lines in Buenos Aires, most businesses in major cities operated normally.   Everett G. Martin

See also LATIN AMERICA (Facts in Brief Table). In WORLD BOOK, see ARGENTINA.

ARIZONA. See STATE GOVERNMENT.
ARKANSAS. See STATE GOVERNMENT.

ARMED FORCES. After seven years of negotiations, the United States and Russia reached agreement in 1979 on a new Strategic Arms Limitation Treaty (SALT II). The new treaty is the first to limit the two nuclear powers to the same maximum number of strategic weapons. Signed by U.S. President Jimmy Carter and Supreme Soviet Presidium Chairman Leonid I. Brezhnev in Vienna, Austria, on June 18, the SALT II agreement expanded a 1972 accord and a 1974 interim agreement. Under its provisions, both countries are limited to 2,250 strategic missiles or bombers by the end of 1981. Under that ceiling, a maximum of 1,320 missiles or bombers may be armed with multiple warheads or cruise missiles, and only 820 of these can be land-based intercontinental ballistic missiles (ICBM's).

Both sides are allowed to deploy one new strategic missile but are restricted on the number and range of cruise missiles. Russia also agreed not to increase the production rate of the Backfire bomber.

Carter hailed the treaty as a major step toward reducing the threat of nuclear war, but critics charged the agreement allowed Russia to gain strategic superiority over U.S. nuclear forces. The U.S. Senate Foreign Relations Committee approved the agreement on November 9 by a 9-6 vote, but further consideration of the treaty was halted near year's end after Russia moved large numbers of troops into Afghanistan. See AFGHANISTAN.

Cuban Qualms. The spirit of détente was strained when U.S. intelligence confirmed on August 31 the existence of a Russian combat brigade in Cuba. Amid congressional demands for withdrawal of the 2,000 to 3,000 Russian troops and their tanks, Administration officials termed the brigade a serious threat to ratification of the SALT treaty. Russian officials insisted the troops were in Cuba in a training capacity and had been on the island since 1962.

After a month of futile negotiations, Carter announced several military countermeasures on October 1, including increased surveillance of Cuba, expanded military maneuvers in the Caribbean, and the establishment of a permanent joint military task force at Key West, Fla.

Russian Gesture. Less than a week later, Brezhnev announced in East Berlin that Russia would withdraw up to 20,000 troops and 1,000 tanks from East Germany and would reduce the number of Russian medium-range nuclear missiles aimed at Western Europe if the North Atlantic Treaty Organization (NATO) reversed its plan to deploy several hundred more U.S. nuclear weapons in Europe. Although Carter and NATO rejected the offer, the action was seen by defense analysts as an attempt to improve prospects for passage of the SALT treaty. On December 5, the Russians began withdrawing a 6th Armored Division unit from East Germany.

Strategic Developments. Despite the SALT II treaty, both superpowers continued work on new strategic weapons. The United States proceeded with full-scale development of the *Trident* submarine-launched ICBM and the air-launched cruise missile. To counter the increasing vulnerability of land-based Minuteman missiles, Carter ordered full production of the M-X mobile ICBM in June and approved an underground basing system, probably to be located in Utah and Nevada, for the 95-short-ton (86-metric-ton), 10-warhead missile on September 7. Under the "race-track" concept selected by Carter, giant transport vehicles would shuttle 200 M-X missiles among 4,600 shelters. Carter said this system would protect the M-X from a Russian attack, while still complying with the terms of SALT II. The M-X system would be operational in 1989 at a cost of $33 billion.

Military Strength. The United States trimmed its military forces slightly again in 1979. On September 30, troop strength stood at 2,027,246, the lowest level since 1962. More than 456,000 troops were stationed overseas, including 239,000 in West Germany and West Berlin, 46,000 in Japan and Okinawa, 39,000 in South Korea, 14,000 in the Philippines, and 48,000 at sea. The withdrawal of the remaining U.S. combat troops from South Korea was halted until at least 1981 after a policy reassessment concluded that

President Jimmy Carter and Chairman Leonid Brezhnev of Russia exchange SALT II treaty documents after signing ceremonies in Vienna, Austria.

North Korea's military strength was greater than originally thought.

The U.S. Department of Defense announced on March 29 that it planned to close or restructure operations at 157 installations for an estimated annual savings of $264 million.

Defense Budget. President Carter submitted a Department of Defense budget request to Congress for fiscal year 1980 (Oct. 1, 1979, to Sept. 30, 1980) on January 22. It asked for $122.7 billion, $10.8-billion more than the previous year's request.

The budget supported a military establishment of 16 Army and 3 Marine divisions, 26 Air Force tactical wings, 17 Navy and Marine air wings, 17 strategic airlift squadrons, and a Navy fleet of 530 vessels. Strategic forces remained constant at 450 Minuteman II and 550 Minuteman III missiles, 54 Titan II missiles, and 656 Polaris-Poseidon submarine-launched missiles. An estimated $10.8-billion was allocated for strategic forces, $50 billion for general purpose forces, $11.8 billion for research and development, and $9.1 billion for military intelligence and communications. The Navy was scheduled to receive $38.8 billion; the Air Force, $34.2 billion; and the Army, $29.6 billion.

The Navy asked for $2.4 billion for the *Trident* nuclear submarine and ballistic missile, $1.62 billion for a conventionally powered aircraft carrier, $1.26 billion for six guided missile frigates, $1.04-billion for the F-18 Hornet carrier-based jet fighter, and $666.1 million for the F-14 Tomcat jet fighter.

The Air Force requested $1.7 billion for 175 F-16 jet fighters, $989.5 million for 60 F-15 Eagle jet fighters, $903.9 million for 144 A-10 close-support jet fighters, $675.4 million for the M-X strategic missile, $549.5 million for cruise missiles, and $397.2-million for modernizing the B-52 bomber force.

The Army asked for $711.3 million for 352 XM-1 main battle tanks and $223.4 million for 251 M-60 tanks, $569.4 million for 155 SAM-D (Patriot) air-defense missiles, $308.2 million for 410 Roland missiles, and $176.2 million for an attack helicopter.

The Carter Administration asked Congress for a $4.7-billion increase in the fiscal 1980 military budget on September 11. The amended spending request was designed to maintain a 3 per cent rise in defense spending after inflation and to satisfy some senators who threatened to hold the SALT II treaty hostage unless the Administration agreed to significant increases in defense spending. Despite the new budget request, Carter was pressured to increase the Pentagon budget by even larger amounts, and Administration officials disclosed in November that the fiscal 1981 defense budget would rise to about $145-billion, with major increases for shipbuilding, conventional weapons, and strategic airlift craft.

Personnel Developments. The volunteer army continued to fall short of its recruiting goals, prompting several members of the Joint Chiefs of

The firing tube of the M-X intercontinental missile punches up through earth and concrete over its underground shelter to allow missile launching.

Staff to urge Congress – unsuccessfully – to reinstitute the military draft. With even more severe shortages in the reserve forces, the Army opened a previously limited test of enlistment bonuses and incentives to all the reserve components in March. But, faced with runaway personnel costs, the Pentagon also proposed a radical change in the military compensation system that would reduce pension costs by several billion dollars by the year 2000.

Command Changes. General Alexander M. Haig, Jr., supreme commander of Allied forces in Europe, retired on July 1. He was replaced by General Bernard W. Rogers, who was succeeded as Army chief of staff by General Edward C. Meyer. General Louis H. Wilson retired as commandant of the Marine Corps and was replaced by General Robert H. Barrow. Colonel Frank E. Petersen, Jr., the first black Marine aviator, became the first black Marine general on April 27. Secretary of the Air Force John C. Stetson resigned in May and was succeeded by Undersecretary Hans M. Mark. W. Graham Claytor was appointed deputy secretary of defense in August and was succeeded as secretary of the Navy by Edward Hidalgo.   Thomas M. DeFrank

In WORLD BOOK, see DISARMAMENT and articles on the service branches.

ARMY. See ARMED FORCES.

ART. See ARCHITECTURE; DANCING; LITERATURE; MUSIC, CLASSICAL; POETRY; VISUAL ARTS.

ASIA

Asia presented a landscape of distress in 1979. From Afghanistan to the China-Vietnam border, Asian troops met in combat and ravaged occupied countries. Hundreds of thousands of starving and frightened people rolled like tidal waves across borders in search of food and refuge (see Close-Up). The last United States troops had left Vietnam four years earlier, but their departure had not brought the peace and plenty that many had anticipated. Instead of the U.S. armies, rival Communist forces were now doing the fighting. From South Korea to Afghanistan, political leaders died violently, but their passing rarely benefited their people. And on the whole, democracy yielded ground in 1979.

Two Invasions. Russia and Vietnam had signed a mutual aid treaty on Nov. 3, 1978, in a Kremlin ceremony in Moscow. It soon became apparent that the pact was a prearranged prelude to the invasion of Cambodia by massive Vietnamese forces. By mid-January 1979, the Vietnamese had installed a puppet regime in Phnom Penh, Cambodia's capital, and Vietnamese troops fanned out across the country in search of guerrilla forces supporting the ousted pro-China regime of Pol Pot.

Vietnam anticipated China's retaliation, and actively prepared for it. It heavily fortified its border with China and also stepped up its drive against the ethnic Chinese living in Vietnam. China's armies crossed Vietnam's border on February 17. In the month that followed, the attackers inflicted heavy losses on Vietnam's border towns, but at a high cost to their own armed forces and economy. The Chinese withdrew in mid-March, and "peace" negotiations soon began. But by year-end, the two sides were still accusing each other of truce violations.

In addition, Thailand claimed its territory had been shelled by Vietnamese troops in Cambodia, and strengthened its border forces. In occupied Laos, Vietnamese troops pushed north toward the Chinese border. And civil war in Afghanistan between the Russian-backed Communist regime and tribal guerrillas drove tens of thousands of refugees into Pakistan, especially after Russian troops entered Afghanistan on December 27.

Broader Impact. The drama in Vietnam, which had broad repercussions, represented a major expansion of Soviet influence, and the conversion of Indochina into a new Chinese-Russian battleground. Thailand protested in vain against Russian air transports carrying arms to Vietnam through its air space. Similarly, Japan watched in dismay the passage of Russian warships and aircraft south, toward Vietnam. Once the Vietnam War ended, the vast Cam Ranh Bay naval facility built by the United States became in effect a Russian base. In this way, the Chinese-Vietnamese war produced a deep southward extension of Soviet power.

Military developments produced a chill in the Association of Southeast Asian Nations (ASEAN) countries – Thailand, Malaysia, Singapore, Indonesia, and the Philippines – as well as in Japan. Vietnam's intrusion into Cambodia and Laos was seen in part as a realization of Hanoi's old dreams of conquering Indochina. But many saw Vietnam as Moscow's proxy in Asia, as Cuba was in Africa.

Redrawn Map. The war between China and Vietnam therefore represented a radical change in the strategic map of East and Southeast Asia. Despite reverses in Vietnam, the United States had remained a power in the region. But in 1979, China and Russia assumed ever more significant roles. This produced new fears – and a new surge of armament. All around the rim of Asia, nations expanded their armies, bought sophisticated new weapons in other countries, and enlarged their own armament industries. According to Western intelligence reports, Pakistan was secretly building facilities to produce nuclear bombs. India, which exploded a test nuclear device in May 1974, indicated that it would make atomic weapons if Pakistan did.

China continued to develop its nuclear warheads and intermediate and intercontinental missiles. Japanese space scientists who were allowed a rare look at the Chinese installations reported in October that the Chinese had developed a three-stage rocket with a missile range of about 4,000 miles (6,400 kilometers), far enough to reach major Russian industrial centers. The Japanese described China's space technology as "far more advanced than is generally thought." China also negotiated with Western European countries for the purchase of weapons.

Japan also steadily improved and expanded its defenses, despite the renunciation of "land, sea, and air forces, as well as other war potential" in the nation's Constitution. Its 1979 military budget was already the sixth largest in the world, and opinion polls showed wide public acceptance of rearmament. Relations between Japan and Russia cooled. Moscow rejected Tokyo's repeated protests against the fortification of four Kuril islands occupied by Russia in the closing days of World War II.

The Giants' Feud. Try as they might to avoid involvement in the struggle between China and Russia, the smaller Asian nations found themselves increasingly caught up in it. Vietnam, Cambodia, and Laos seemed to be Moscow's clients. The ASEAN countries, on the other hand, began to see China as a bulwark against an expansive Vietnam.

A refugee, one of the "boat people," sees safety ahead as he scrambles on board a U.S. Navy ship after a perilous voyage through the Pacific.

Facts in Brief on the Asian Countries

Country	Population	Government	Monetary Unit*	Foreign Trade (million U.S. $) Exports†	Imports†
Afghanistan	21,859,000	Revolutionary Council President & Prime Minister Babrak Karmal	afghani (43.5 = $1)	313	491
Australia	14,480,000	Governor General Sir Zelman Cowen; Prime Minister John Malcolm Fraser	dollar (1 = $1.10)	14,382	15,749
Bangladesh	92,181,000	President Ziaur Rahman; Prime Minister Azizur Rahman	taka (15.7 = $1)	576	1,294
Bhutan	1,311,000	King Jigme Singye Wangchuck	Indian rupee	1	2
Burma	34,938,000	President U Ne Win; Prime Minister U Maung Maung Kha	kyat (6.5 = $1)	243	389
Cambodia (Kampuchea)	8,540,000	People's Revolutionary Council head Heng Samrin	riel (1,650 = $1)	10	101
China	893,873,000	Communist Party Chairman & Premier Hua Kuo-Feng (Hua Guofeng)	yuan (1.5 = $1)	8,100	7,200
India	662,958,000	President Neelam Sanjeeva Reddy; Prime Minister Charan Singh	rupee (8.1 = $1)	6,415	7,405
Indonesia	154,340,000	President Suharto; Vice-President Adam Malik	rupiah (625 = $1)	11,643	6,690
Iran	38,071,000	Ayatollah Ruhollah Khomeini	rial (71.5 = $1)	22,721	14,968
Japan	118,747,000	Emperor Hirohito; Prime Minister Masayoshi Ohira	yen (249.5 = $1)	97,501	78,731
Korea, North	19,312,000	President Kim Il-song; Premier Yi Chong-ok	won (1.4 = $1)	655	777
Korea, South	40,457,000	President Kyu Ha Choi; Prime Minister Hyon Hwack Shin	won (475 = $1)	12,713	15,074
Laos	3,691,000	President Souphanouvong; Prime Minister Kayson Phomvihan	kip (200 = $1)	9	55
Malaysia	13,790,000	Paramount Ruler Ahmad Shah Ibni Almarhom Sultan Abu Bakar; Prime Minister Datuk Hussein Onn	ringgit (2.2 = $1)	8,058	6,508
Maldives	148,000	President Maumoon Abdul Gayoom	rupee (8.5 = $1)	3	10
Mongolia	1,689,000	People's Revolutionary Party First Secretary & Presidium Chairman Yumjaagin Tsedenbal; Council of Ministers Chairman Jambyn Batmonh	tughrik (2.9 = $1)	83	112
Nepal	14,372,000	King Birendra Bir Bikram Shah Dev; Prime Minister Surya Bahadur Thapa	rupee (12 = $1)	82	206
New Zealand	3,361,000	Governor General Sir Keith J. Holyoake; Prime Minister Robert D. Muldoon	dollar (1 = $1.03)	3,752	3,500
Pakistan	81,451,000	President & Chief Martial Law Administrator Zia-ul-Haq	rupee (9.9 = $1)	1,468	3,191
Papua New Guinea	3,132,000	Governor General Sir Tore Lokoloko; Prime Minister Michael Thomas Somare	kina (1 = $1.41)	779	675
Philippines	50,119,000	President Ferdinand E. Marcos	peso (7.4 = $1)	3,425	5,143
Russia	269,306,000	Communist Party General Secretary & Supreme Soviet Presidium Chairman Leonid Ilich Brezhnev; Council of Ministers Chairman Aleksey Nikolayevich Kosygin	ruble (1 = $1.55)	52,176	50,546
Singapore	2,427,000	President Benjamin Henry Sheares; Prime Minister Lee Kuan Yew	dollar (2.2 = $1)	10,134	13,049
Sri Lanka	15,568,000	President Junius Richard Jayewardene; Prime Minister R. Premadasa	rupee (15.6 = $1)	847	928
Taiwan	17,696,000	President Chiang Ching-kuo; Premier Sun Yun-hsuan	new Taiwan dollar (35.7 = $1)	12,682	11,051
Thailand	48,711,000	King Bhumibol Adulyadej; Prime Minister Kriangsak Chamanan	baht (20 = $1)	4,093	5,360
Vietnam	54,763,000	President Ton Duc Thang; Prime Minister Pham Van Dong	dong (2.2 = $1)	300	900

*Exchange rates as of Dec. 1, 1979. †Latest available data.

In response to the Russian march into Afghanistan, the United States in January 1980 hinted at closer collaboration with China. Russia, in turn, denounced the "American-Chinese-Japanese axis." The "axis" did not exist, but Moscow's growing strength and muscle-flexing produced a community of anxiety among the three countries.

Political Instability helped to deepen the continent's uneasiness. The murder in October of South Korea's heavy-handed President Chung Hee Park by his own intelligence chief led to a power struggle among that nation's generals in December. In Pakistan, President Zia-ul-Haq permitted the execution of former Prime Minister Zulfikar Ali Bhutto in April. Another striking manifestation of Pakistan's instability was the burning of the U.S. Embassy by a mob in November. In neighboring India, the ruling Janata coalition fell apart as predicted, and Indira Gandhi won a sweeping victory in the January 1980 election. She had never repented her harsh emergency rule from 1975 to 1977, and many Indians feared that her return to power would signify a new erosion of democracy.

The Russian invasion of Afghanistan only underscored this general instability. Uneasy about the situation, the United States initiated steps to resume aid to Pakistan, which shares a border with Afghanistan. The United States also speeded up arms deliveries to Thailand and Malaysia.

Economic Uncertainty could be blamed for some of the political turmoil. Early in the year, the grain prospects for most of Asia looked promising, with good weather, better seed, and wider irrigation producing large rice surpluses in many countries. India's bins were full. The Philippines for the first time had a sizable surplus for sale abroad.

But food prospects turned bleak in late summer. The worst drought in generations destroyed much of India's grain harvest and produced near-famine conditions in several states. China enjoyed a record harvest. But Laos and Vietnam had indifferent crops again, and war-ravaged Cambodia went hungry.

The grain problem was compounded by trouble with oil. Such oil exporters as Indonesia and China benefited hugely from soaring oil prices (see PETRO-LEUM AND GAS). Others, such as India and the Philippines, found some offshore oil and were frantically looking for more. Still, the region's daily output was only 8 per cent of the 1979 world total, and less than half of Saudi Arabia's production. As a result, the year's three massive oil-price boosts nearly doubled Asia's oil-import bill and proved to be disastrous. In most nations, the high price of oil fed inflation and slowed economic growth.

Atomic Energy. In the industrialized Asian countries, including India, Japan, South Korea, and Taiwan, the uncertain and increasingly costly oil supply led to heavy emphasis on nuclear power. The accident at the Three Mile Island nuclear power

Chinese troops advance on the city of Cao Bang shortly after invading Vietnam on February 17. The border fighting lasted about one month.

plant near Harrisburg, Pa., in March produced some anxiety and debate. But faced with a choice between possible nuclear catastrophe and their need for energy, Asian nations pushed their fears of disaster to the back of their minds. Predictably, the nuclear power program was especially ambitious in Japan, which is short of other fuels and intent on keeping up its high growth rate. About 11 per cent of Japan's 1979 electric supply, 12.6 million kilowatts, came from 20 atomic reactors.

Birth Control. Despite a declining birth rate in some Asian countries, the continent remained, by and large, a ticking population time bomb. Of the large countries, China made the greatest progress in limiting population. China began an intensive drive for just one child per family. An official announced in August that two children would be tolerated, but, under a system of restraints and incentives, families that had a third child born after 1979 would be penalized. Despite the campaign, the official *People's Daily* newspaper complained in December that China's birth rate was still too high.

The situation was much worse in Bangladesh, India, Indonesia, and Pakistan, where booming birth rates put an unbearable strain on housing, schools, the job market, medical facilities, and food supplies. See POPULATION.   Mark Gayn

See also the various Asian country articles. In WORLD BOOK, see ASIA.

Asia's Starving Homeless

Seldom has the collective heart of humanity been so moved as by the tragedy of Indochina's refugees. They were Vietnam's "boat people," forced from their homes by a harsh government. They were Cambodians fleeing from harsh rule, war, famine, and disease. They were Laotians pushed from their homeland by war.

No one knows just how many Indochina refugees were adrift in 1979. Some estimates of the boat people run as high as 500,000. There were perhaps 250,000 Laotian refugees in Thailand, and in December a United States official estimated that close to 1 million Cambodian refugees waited for help in camps in Thailand.

Nor can it ever be known how many died trying to reach a haven. Many boat people died at sea, the victims of pirates, the stormy seas, or the cruel politics of some "free world" governments. Australian sources estimated that about 200,000 Vietnamese died at sea.

The boat people's tragedy began in March 1978, when Vietnam nationalized most of the 30,000 private companies in Cholon, the Chinatown of Ho Chi Minh City (formerly Saigon), and other mainly ethnic Chinese areas. Yesterday's shopkeepers and clerks were assigned to move to "new economic zones," a glamorized term for patches of jungle to be settled.

A means of escape was provided, however. If paid at least $3,000 in gold per person, government-designated "organizers" would locate small boats or ships, with crews, in which the ethnic Chinese could flee the country. Correctly anticipating war with China, Vietnam wanted to rid itself of its Chinese population and, in a bitterly ironic situation, made them pay for the privilege of being ejected from their country.

Once en route, the refugees were hard-pressed to find new homes. In fact, they became pawns in elaborate international negotiations, with allies and enemy countries pressuring one another about the refugees.

Neighboring Asian countries, most of them poor and underdeveloped themselves, took in thousands of refugees per month in the beginning, but they soon turned hostile. The masses

Refugees

of refugees were unwanted. In March, for example, Malaysia's navy towed back to open waters an overcrowded boat carrying Vietnamese refugees who were trying to land in Malaysia. The boat capsized and 104 persons drowned.

In June, Malaysia threatened to expel the 75,000 Vietnamese refugees already encamped within its borders and fire "on sight" on new refugees approaching its shores. After an international outcry, Malaysia withdrew its threat to kill.

For four days in June, Cambodians fleeing into Thailand were forced back across the border. Thus, 30,000 persons faced almost certain death. This practice, too, was stopped only after pressure from the United Nations (UN) High Commissioner for Refugees and concerned countries.

Members of the Association of Southeast Asian Nations (ASEAN) — Indonesia, Malaysia, the Philippines, Singapore, and Thailand — announced in June that they would take "firm and effective measures to prevent further inflow" of refugees. They also called on other countries to provide more aid, rather than simply supplying moral indignation.

After this chilling ASEAN announcement, 65 countries gathered for a UN-sponsored conference on refugees in Geneva, Switzerland, on July 20 and 21. They pledged more than $190 million in aid and offered asylum to about 260,000 persons. Many of these refugees were to go to the United States, and Canada pledged to take in 50,000.

Food, medical aid, and other supplies for at least 2 million persons in Thailand remained an urgent problem. Rosalynn Carter, the wife of President Jimmy Carter, visited refugee camps in Thailand in November "to express the profound concern of all Americans for the suffering" of the refugees. Following her visit, President Carter committed about $69 million to UN and Red Cross relief efforts. But relief efforts, like the placement of refugees, were bogged down by politics — while nearly a million desperate refugees, many of them starving, waited in camps. And the tragedy continued.   Patricia Dragisic

ASTRONOMY. A peculiar star in the Milky Way Galaxy called SS 433 posed a mystery for astronomers in 1979. The object had earlier been found to be a radio and X-ray source, but new spectra showed that it is apparently shooting out beams of very hot hydrogen and helium gas. The ejected particles move away from SS 433 in opposite directions at speeds of at least 50,000 kilometers (31,000 miles) per second. From Earth, our viewing angle of the beams makes it impossible to measure their full speed, estimated at about 75,000 kilometers (45,000 miles) per second – or about one-fourth the speed of light. The speeds of the two beams vary in a cycle of about 164 days. Such ejection speeds are completely unprecedented, exceeding by several times the ejection speeds in supernova explosions. Although astronomers do not understand the source of its beams, SS 433 may possibly be a neutron star, emitting the particles while *precessing* (changing orientation) in its 164-day cycle.

Jupiter Discoveries. Two fly-by missions to Jupiter sent back color photographs with unprecedented details of the giant planet's cloud deck and the surfaces of its four largest moons. The National Aeronautics and Space Administration's (NASA) *Voyager 1* spacecraft passed within 278,000 kilometers (172,000 miles) of Jupiter on March 5, and *Voyager 2* gained more data from a distance of 640,000 kilometers (400,000 miles) on July 9.

The probes revealed lightning and auroral displays on Jupiter's night side, but among the most surprising discoveries was a ring of very fine matter around Jupiter about 6,400 kilometers (4,000 miles) wide and about 30 kilometers (19 miles) thick. The ring's outer edge extends 56,000 kilometers (35,000 miles) above Jupiter's cloud deck. Just beyond the ring, Jupiter's 14th moon was discovered orbiting the planet every 7 hours 8 minutes at a speed of 108,000 kilometers (67,000 miles) per hour, making it the fastest-moving satellite in the solar system.

Close-up photographs of Io, the innermost of Jupiter's four largest moons, revealed a gold-orange surface covered with lava flows and black volcanic *calderas* (craters). Nine volcanoes were erupting at the time of the first fly-by, and seven of these were still erupting during the second fly-by. Astronomers believe that most of Io's interior is molten, and its crust may be only a few kilometers thick. Its heating may be caused by internal friction, because Jupiter's immense, changing tidal pull deforms Io's shape as the moon moves along its elliptical orbit.

Europa, the second large moon out from Jupiter, proved to be a yellowish-white expanse of ultraflat ice plains marked with dark shallow valleys and bright low ridges. Ganymede is the third satellite out and largest of Jupiter's moons. Ganymede's surface is a complex of ancient, dark, cratered lowlands with vast expanses of lighter ice ridges, which may have been produced by interior expansion. Callisto, the

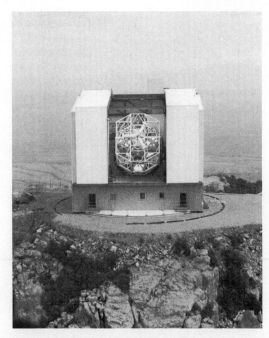

Dedication in May of the unique Multiple Mirror Telescope Observatory on Arizona's Mount Hopkins opens a new eye on the sky for optical astronomers.

outermost of the group, has an ancient surface saturated with craters. In the Special Reports section, see The Riches of Jupiter's Realm.

New Data on Saturn. NASA's *Pioneer 11* spacecraft reached its long-awaited rendezvous with Saturn on September 1. It left Earth 6½ years earlier, on April 6, 1973, and flew by Jupiter on Dec. 2, 1974. As *Pioneer 11* approached Saturn from the north side of the rings, the sun was shining on the south side of the rings. Never seen before, this pattern of light shining through the ring system, instead of reflecting from it, is almost like a photographic negative of the familiar view. Judging from their rate of cooling in Saturn's shadow, the water-ice particles forming the ring system are small, from 1 to 3 centimeters (about 0.5 inch to 1 inch), in diameter. The three major rings – called A, B, and C – show an easily visible dark lane called the Cassini division between the outer A ring and the bright B ring. French astronomers in 1943 claimed to have seen a smaller division between the B ring and the very faint inner C ring, and the *Pioneer 11* fly-by confirmed the existence of this second division. The probe also discovered a faint new ring 8,000 kilometers (5,000 miles) wide, just outside the A ring. The space between the new ring and the A ring is 2,100 kilometers (1,300 miles) wide and has been tentatively called the Pioneer division; the ring itself is called the F ring. Before the fly-by, Earth-based observers had detected what they thought were a D ring inside the C ring and an E ring outside the A ring, but the *Pioneer* spacecraft saw neither of these. *Pioneer 11* detected a G ring far outside the main ring system, between the orbits of the Saturn moons Rhea and Titan, according to NASA. At least one, and probably several, small moons were detected near the outer edge of the rings.

A New Vision of Venus. Data from the December 1978 United States and Russian space missions to Venus gave a dramatic new view of the planet's atmosphere. NASA's *Pioneer* Venus mission included one orbiter, four probes that descended through the atmosphere to hard landings, and the probes' "bus," which sampled the upper atmosphere before burning up. Two Soviet spacecraft, *Venera 11* and *Venera 12,* soft-landed on the planet's surface but took no photographs.

The *Pioneer* probes revealed a high atmospheric haze, probably made of sulfuric acid droplets. Within the haze are three zones of clouds made up of three sizes of particles of unknown composition. They may be sulfuric acid droplets plus contaminants. Clouds are lower over both poles, and above the north pole downflowing air apparently drives the clouds low enough to evaporate them in the heat of lower altitudes, creating a wide "hole" in the cloud deck.

From about 12 kilometers (20 miles) altitude to the surface, the atmosphere is clear of particles but so thick that the ground would not be visible from higher than 6 kilometers (4 miles). Daylight at the surface is similar to an overcast day on Earth, except that sunlight at this depth in the thick air is a murky red color. Ground temperatures registered about 450°C (850°F.), and the air pressure is 90 times that on the Earth, comparable to water pressure 900 meters (3,000 feet) below our ocean surface. The atmosphere consists of 95.5 to 97.5 per cent carbon dioxide and 2.5 to 4.5 per cent nitrogen, with traces of water vapor and a dozen other molecules.

United States probes detected a strange glow on the night side of Venus, but scientists cannot yet explain what causes it. The Russian landers detected very rapid lightning bursts, and possibly thunder. The surface of Venus, as revealed by radar from the orbiter, seems more like Mars than like Earth. It has continent-sized plateaus, vast basins, mountain ranges, volcanic peaks, and huge impact craters.

Mars. The *Viking 2* lander photographed a thin frost layer as winter came again to Mars's northern hemisphere. *Viking 1* and *2* landers are now carrying out a longer-range survey mission that will continue through 1990. The *Viking 1* lander transmits to Earth once a week. The *Viking 2* orbiter, in Mars orbit, shut down on July 24, 1978, and the *Viking 1* orbiter was expected to cease operations early in 1980.   Eric D. Carlson

See also SPACE EXPLORATION. In WORLD BOOK, see ASTRONOMY; articles on the planets.

AUSTRALIA. The Liberal-National Country Party coalition government headed by Prime Minister John Malcolm Fraser faced few political challenges in 1979, though there were foretastes of difficulties to come. The Cabinet remained intact until September, in spite of the five-day resignation of Finance Minister Eric Robinson in February. Ian Sinclair, minister for primary industries, deputy leader of the National Country Party, and leader of the House of Representatives, resigned on September 26. Sinclair quit after the New South Wales state government published a report by special investigator Michael Finnane that accused Sinclair of forgery and misappropriation of funds in connection with family companies. Charges were later filed against Sinclair.

State Politics showed varying tendencies in general elections in three states. Victoria voters returned the Liberal government headed by Rupert Hamer to office on May 5, but with a reduced majority of only one seat in the Legislative Assembly. Tasmania's Labor government under Douglas Lowe was returned with an increased majority in a special July 28 election called to highlight what the state government called the federal government's bad financial treatment of Tasmania.

South Australia voters produced a political upset on September 15. The popular Labor premier, Donald A. Dunstan, had retired on February 15 for health reasons, and his successor, James D. Corcoran, held the September election hoping for a personal mandate. However, a 10 per cent swing to the opposition gave Liberal David Tonkin a victory.

There was no state election in Queensland, but the National Country and Liberal parties disagreed over whether they should put forward a joint ticket at the 1980 Senate elections as they had done in the past. Each party decided to run its own ticket. The National Party seemed likely to slate Flo Bjelke-Petersen, the popular wife of the premier.

Domestic Policy. Uranium mining continued to be an important political issue. The congress of the Australian Council of Trade Unions (ACTU) voted on September 14 to continue its uranium mining and export ban despite the fact that some union members worked in the mines. ACTU President Bob Hawke spoke strongly against the policy, but he was defeated. Soon afterward, Hawke sought and won nomination for the safe Victoria Labor seat of Wills in the federal Parliament. It was generally expected that Hawke would challenge party leader Bill Hayden after the 1980 federal elections if Hayden did not become prime minister by then.

A new Federal Police Force was created on October 19 when the former Commonwealth Police merged with the Australian Capital Territory Police. Sir Colin Woods, chief inspector of constabulary for England and Wales, became commissioner of the new force, which was expected to concentrate on antiterrorist activity. Also in October, the federal

Parliament passed a bill to provide a new charter of operation for the Australian Security Intelligence Organization.

Foreign Policy was largely concerned with economics. Attention focused on the need for greater foreign investment in minerals and more markets for Australian products. Reduced air fares between Australia and Great Britain brought disagreement with members of the Association of Southeast Asian Nations (ASEAN). The ASEAN countries feared that arrangements between Qantas Airways Limited and British Airways would squeeze out their national airlines and harm their tourist industries.

After years of negotiation, Australia and the European Community (EC or Common Market) announced an agreement on May 29 to allow more Australian foods to be shipped into the EC countries.

The flow of refugees from Indochina caused Australians much concern as exhausted "boat people" arrived in northern ports. The government agreed in July to accept an increased number of refugees from camps in Southeast Asia until a total of 14,000 was reached in 1979. On October 2, the acting minister for foreign affairs announced an increase of $2.2 million in aid to Cambodia.

A special committee's report on Australia's relations with the Third World, released on September 18, symbolized the government's interest in the problems of underdeveloped countries. The report came after Prime Minister Fraser spoke out in favor of the Common Fund for stabilizing commodity prices. It also followed Fraser's active part in the Commonwealth heads of government meeting in Lusaka, Zambia, in August, when agreement was reached about proposals for Zimbabwe Rhodesia.

The Economy continued to worry the government and the public. The inflation rate increased during the year, and the unemployment rate increased unexpectedly in the quarter ending in September. However, there were compensations. The Bureau of Agricultural Economics forecast on April 26 that farmers, especially those producing meat, grain, and wool, would earn almost twice as much as in 1978. A record wheat harvest was expected.

During the financial year 1978-1979, Australia recorded the largest inflow of private capital since 1971-1972. There were major investment plans that combined local and foreign capital. Among them were a decision by General Motors-Holden in February to build an engine plant at Fisherman's Bend in Victoria and schemes for new and expanded aluminum smelters at Newcastle, New South Wales; Gladstone, Queensland; and Geelong, Victoria, at a cost of $1.47 million. Plans were also underway to mine uranium at Yeelirrie in Western Australia and Roxby Downs in South Australia. Discovery of a vast iron ore deposit in the Pilbara region of Western Australia was announced in February.

Bicentennial Planning. The 200th anniversary of European settlement in Australia will be celebrated in 1988. Among the projects underway is a massive effort by historians to describe changes in Australian life since 1788. A new Parliament House on Capital Hill in Canberra is scheduled to open as part of the bicentennial celebration. An architectural competition for the design of the building was announced in April, and the five finalists were announced in October. Construction is expected to begin in 1983. Canberra will also be the site of a new national museum, which will join the Australian War Memorial, National Library, and National Art Gallery there. Minister for Home Affairs Robert Ellicott said in September that the museum would have three main themes: aboriginal history, the interaction of human beings and their environment, and the history of European civilization in Australia.

Sports-loving Australians were intrigued when the principal horse-racing clubs announced on March 9 that women jockeys would compete against men. The Australian Cricket Board and Kerry Packer's World Series Cricket (WSC) agreed on May 30 to end their dispute, which had led to the banning of some players from official Test cricket, thus allowing WSC players to return to normal cricket.   J.D.B. Miller

See also ASIA (Facts in Brief Table). In WORLD BOOK, see AUSTRALIA.

A large piece of debris from the space station *Skylab* that fell on Australia in July is inspected by Australian and U.S. scientists in Perth.

AUSTRIA. Bruno Kreisky, chancellor since 1970, scored his biggest electoral victory on May 6, 1979, when his Socialist Party gained two parliamentary seats for a total of 95. Josef Taus, whose conservative People's Party lost three of its 80 seats, decided not to seek re-election as opposition leader. The Freedom Party gained one seat and now has 11. More than 90 per cent of the 5.2 million eligible voters cast ballots.

The Socialists campaigned under the slogan "Kreisky – Austria needs him," and pointed out that his leadership had provided an annual growth rate of close to 4 per cent between 1970 and 1978 with almost full employment and a reasonable rise in personal income. Kreisky, 68, declared on July 19 that he would serve out his four-year term.

Arafat Visits. Yasir Arafat, leader of the Palestine Liberation Organization (PLO), visited Kreisky and former West German Chancellor Willy Brandt in Vienna in July at a meeting of the Socialist International, the organization of Western Socialist parties. Kreisky greeted Arafat at the airport in the way a visiting head of state is received, the first Western leader to receive Arafat formally. Kreisky claimed that he was acting as vice-president of the Socialist International. In protest against the talks, Israel withdrew its ambassador to Austria, but Kreisky said on July 9 that "it would be absolutely ridiculous to think the PLO is out to destroy Israel."

Austria's Chancellor Bruno Kreisky votes in May parliamentary elections that increase the strength of his ruling Socialist Party.

No Visa. Travelers between Austria and Hungary were allowed to cross the 200-mile (320-kilometer) border without visas beginning on January 1, in the first such agreement between a European Communist country and a non-Communist neighbor. Czechoslovakia and East Germany had pressured Hungary into tightening its border surveillance in 1978, because they were concerned about their citizens escaping to the West. Kreisky visited Czechoslovakia in January, but failed to arrange a similar agreement. Czechoslovakia's Prime Minister Lubomir Strougal said his country could not "go the Hungarian way" because conditions were different. For instance, Hungary's prices are adjusted to world markets, but Czechoslovakia's prices are much higher than those in Austria. However, Kreisky initiated trade talks that might lead to $240 million in contracts for Austria.

Parliament unanimously approved a bill on February 27 giving manual workers the same severance-pay scale that white-collar employees have had since 1921. Employers will phase in the scale over five years.

Inflation was running at 3.5 per cent, Europe's lowest, toward the end of 1979. However, the government refused to ease credit in an effort to cut the $38-million trade deficit.   Kenneth Brown

See also EUROPE (Facts in Brief Table). In WORLD BOOK, see AUSTRIA.

AUTOMOBILE. The United States automobile industry ran into a host of problems in 1979, with Chrysler Corporation's monetary woes standing out as the industry's number-one headache. Inflation, recalls, fuel shortages, and competition from import cars were among the factors that caused U.S. auto production to drop to an estimated 8,412,000 for the year, down 8.3 per cent from the 9,170,743 built in 1978. The output marked a four-year low, the deepest cut since the recession of 1974-1975.

United States sales were estimated at about 10.6 million cars, including 2.3 million imports, and 3.5 million trucks. General Motors Corporation (GM) Board Chairman Thomas A. Murphy and other industry officials predicted 1980 car and truck sales would virtually duplicate those of 1979.

Companies Cut Back. Sales nose-dived at the end of the year. October sales were down 17 per cent from year-earlier figures. During the first 10 days of November, the news was even worse; new-car sales plummeted 26 per cent. The pattern continued in December, and automakers expected a similar drop in that month.

As a result, auto manufacturers planned to close some plants and make personnel cuts. The Ford Motor Company and Chrysler closed a total of nine auto-assembly plants for a week in October. Layoffs were common. GM dropped some 5,750 employees permanently in October, and Chrysler and Ford

Rows of autos fill Holloder Stadium in Rochester, N.Y., as Chrysler-Plymouth and Dodge dealers hold a special sale to reduce their auto inventories.

provide aid for Chrysler. The Senate plan included $1.5 billion in federal loan guarantees; $525 million in wage concessions by union workers; $150 million in omitted pay hikes for executives; and a new $175-million stock issue by Chrysler. The House plan was similar, but slightly smaller. Congress finally passed a compromise package on December 21. It made possible about $3.5 billion in aid – $1.5-billion in federal loan guarantees, with the rest from private sources and UAW wage concessions.

In the midst of efforts to find a solution to Chrysler's problems and keep the auto firm afloat, Chairman John J. Riccardo resigned on September 17. He was replaced by Lee A. Iacocca, who moved up from the presidency. J. Paul Bergmoser was named president. Both Bergmoser and Iacocca are former Ford executives.

Chrysler was not the only firm in trouble. According to the *Wall Street Journal* of November 15, an internal memo forecast a $1-billion loss for Ford on its North American operations in 1979. Its overseas operations remained in good shape, however.

Late in the year, Ford agreed to turn over other confidential memos to the prosecutor of an unprecedented reckless homicide charge brought against the company in Indiana. The case stems from the deaths of three teen-age girls in the crash of a 1973 Ford Pinto in 1978. The prosecution charges the company with reckless design and production of the car.

Henry Ford II, grandson of the original Henry Ford, relinquished the post of chief executive officer in October, turning the job over to Philip Caldwell. It marked the first time since the days of automotive pioneer Henry Ford that a Ford was not in the top job at the Ford Motor Company.

Henry Ford II, who held the job for 34 years, said he would continue to serve as chairman of the company's finance committee and would be "a roving elder statesman for the auto company."

Union Settlement. The UAW made sizable gains at the bargaining table in 1979 as they got new three-year contracts from GM in September and Ford in October. The UAW won a 3 per cent annual wage hike over three years, increased pensions for retirees, and increased cost-of-living allowances. The UAW continued what its president, Douglas Fraser, said was a move toward the "inevitable four-day workweek," as it upped its total of paid personal holidays to 26 in the third year of the contract. Total wages and benefits for GM and Ford production workers rose to $13.75 per hour in the first year of the contract, $15 in the second, and $20 in the third.

In the new contract agreed to with Chrysler in October, the UAW agreed to defer a 3 per cent per year wage increase for six months during the first contract year; four months in the second year; and two months in the third year. The UAW also agreed to wait until December 1980 for an addition to the

temporarily idled more than 33,000 persons. On November 12, Ford and GM laid off 30,000 more workers, bringing the total for the industry to 120,000 unemployed.

To spur sales, Chrysler offered $400, then $300 rebates to buyers on almost all of its models, except for its fast-selling subcompacts. In November, GM offered discounts to dealers of $100 to $400 per car.

Chrysler in Trouble. The financial problems of the Chrysler Corporation were abundant and large. Virtually everyone from President Jimmy Carter and the Congress of the United States to the United Auto Workers (UAW) union was involved in efforts to save America's number-three auto company – ranking behind GM and Ford – from bankruptcy.

Chrysler stunned the auto world by announcing a $207-million loss for the second quarter of 1979 and a projected $1-billion deficit for the year. The company pushed for financial aid from the federal government and for an easing of emissions standards that would cost Chrysler an estimated $600 million.

Several suggestions were put forth for financial aid to Chrysler, and there was considerable support for a plan that would provide $1.5 billion in federal loan guarantees, on the condition that the auto firm could raise a similar amount from other sources.

A Chrysler Bailout. The House of Representatives and the U.S. Senate approved bailout packages on December 18 and 19, respectively, that would

cost-of-living allowance and accepted a freeze on sickness and accident benefits until the third year. Chrysler workers would get no additional personal days off in 1979 but would get a total of 20 by 1981, leaving them six days behind GM and Ford workers. The UAW also agreed to defer $200 million in company payments to the union's pension fund. The UAW agreed to the congressional Chrysler aid plan in December, which required it to forgo some $462.5-million of an estimated $1.3 billion in wage gains between 1980 and 1982.

Smaller Engines. The auto industry continued to cut its output of V-8 engines. In the 1969 model year, 75 per cent of cars sold in the United States were powered with V-8s. By 1979 that had dropped to 48 per cent.

Japanese sources said Datsun and Toyota are working on two versions of the Wankel rotary engine. Introduction of the engines was set for 1983. Meanwhile, in West Germany, West Germany-Audi-NSU shelved a twin-rotor Wankel project.

GM, which got the jump on the rest of the U.S. auto industry in reducing the size of its cars, brought out a series of front-wheel-drive compacts in early 1979 – the "X cars" – and claimed they represented increased fuel efficiency at a time when the price of gasoline was climbing.   Charles C. Cain III

See also CONSUMER AFFAIRS. In WORLD BOOK, see AUTOMOBILE.

Donnie Allison, right, and Cale Yarborough crash during the last lap of the Daytona 500. Then, with Bobby Allison, they staged a fistfight.

AUTOMOBILE RACING. The cars that race in the Indianapolis 500 were involved in more 1979 combat off the track than on. A rebellion of car owners split the United States Auto Club (USAC), which sanctioned the Indianapolis 500 and other races for Indy-type cars. The dissidents, who included most of the affluent owners and drivers, formed Championship Auto Racing Teams (CART). USAC and CART conducted separate series, though drivers from both competed on May 27 in the $1,271,954 Indianapolis 500, the richest auto race in history. CART wanted a larger voice in USAC, and it opposed USAC's plan to limit engine power so that $10,000 stock-block engines could race alongside $35,000 Cosworths and Fords.

USAC President Dick King said, "Cheaper racing doesn't mean lower-quality racing. You don't need engines with 800 horsepower and speeds of 200 miles per hour to put on a good auto race."

A.J. Foyt of Houston, the career driving leader in Indy-type cars, criticized the people who run USAC. But he returned to USAC, saying that most of CART's original goals had been realized.

The Indianapolis 500 was threatened first by the USAC-CART battle, then by almost daily changes in rules that resulted in a starting field of 35 cars rather than 33. CART cars won four of the first five places (Foyt finished second). Rich Mears of Bakersfield, Calif., won in a Penske-Cosworth, a ground-effect car that channeled air beneath the chassis to create suction and thus helped in cornering the car.

Bobby Unser of Albuquerque, N.Mex.; Mears; and Mario Andretti of Nazareth, Pa., drove Penske-Cosworths to the first three places in that order in the $294,000 California 500 on September 2 at Ontario, Calif. Mears won the CART season point series and Foyt the USAC title.

NASCAR Series. The highlight of the National Association for Stock Car Auto Racing's (NASCAR) Grand National series of 31 races was the $595,000 Daytona 500. The 125,000 spectators at Daytona Beach, Fla., saw a startling finish to the February 18 race.

Second-place Cale Yarborough of Timmonsville, S.C., tried to pass Donnie Allison of Hueytown, Ala., also in an Oldsmobile, on the inside on the final turn. Allison moved down to cut Yarborough off. Yarborough went off the track, then back on, bumped Allison, bounced off, and rammed him. Both cars hit the outside wall and spun down onto the grass. Seconds later, there was a fistfight involving those two drivers and Bobby Allison, Donnie's brother, who was also in the race.

Meanwhile, Richard Petty of Randleman, N.C., in an Oldsmobile in third place, breezed by and won Daytona for a record sixth time. It was the first victory in 46 races for Petty. He was driving at Daytona against doctor's orders after ulcer surgery.

Yarborough and the two Allisons were fined $6,000 each, and Donnie Allison and Yarborough were placed on probation for six months by NASCAR.

Darrell Waltrip of Franklin, Tenn., won seven races; Petty and Bobby Allison, five each; and Yarborough, four. Petty won his seventh season point title, barely defeating Waltrip, but Waltrip led in earnings with $465,870 to Petty's $430,650.

Jody Scheckter of South Africa won the world drivers' championship, Ferrari's third in five years in the series for Formula One cars. Scheckter won three of the 15 races and finished in the top six a dozen times. Gilles Villeneuve of Berthierville, Canada, in a Ferrari, won both Grand Prix races in the United States. Alan Jones of Australia drove a Saudi-Williams to victory in the Canadian Grand Prix.

Land Speed Mark. The world land speed record was raised unofficially to 739.666 miles (1,186.0849 kilometers) per hour on December 17 at Edwards Air Force Base, California. Hollywood stuntman Stan Barrett drove a 48,000-horsepower rocket car with 6,000 pounds (2,721 kilograms) of added thrust from the engine of a Sidewinder missile.

This was the first record under a year-old International Motorcycle Federation rule that records could be established in one run rather than in two runs in opposite directions. Because the rocket car had three wheels, it was technically a motorcycle.   Frank Litsky

In WORLD BOOK, see AUTOMOBILE RACING.

AVIATION companies in the United States reported decreased profits in 1979 because of fuel price hikes and a slowdown in passenger-traffic gains late in the year. The worst airline disaster in United States history occurred on May 25, when an American Airlines DC-10 crashed shortly after take-off in Chicago, killing 274 persons.

Domestic-airline passenger traffic through October was up 12.5 per cent from the first 10 months of 1978, air freight was up 0.4 per cent, domestic air freight edged up 0.5 per cent, and international air freight was up 0.2 per cent. The International Air Transport Association (IATA) estimated that scheduled airlines carried 16.8 per cent more paying passengers on North Atlantic routes in the first eight months of 1979, but cargo fell 18.1 per cent, compared with the same period in 1978. International traffic carried by U.S. airlines increased 16.7 per cent through October. But George W. James, the industry's chief economist, estimated in November that U.S. scheduled carriers' 1979 profits would fall to $600 million, down 50 per cent from 1978.

The Civil Aeronautics Board (CAB) faced protests from other countries and their airlines over its mid-1978 proposal to end IATA's fare-setting agreements. So the CAB on December 5 barred only U.S. airlines from participating in certain pacts. The CAB curbed operations of airlines from Canada, France, Ireland, and Peru, because they had im-

posed flight or fare restrictions on U.S. carriers. Some of these disputes were later resolved. The CAB in September approved the first direct U.S.-China air service in 30 years – three charter flights by Pan American World Airways (PanAm) and three by the Civil Aviation Administration of China.

Fare, Flight Changes. Tight fuel supplies caused a flurry of flight cutbacks on international routes. PanAm said on October 25 that it would abandon some routes, drop all charter service, and forego a plan to expand services 10 per cent in 1980.

The CAB acted selectively on proposed fare boosts for international routes. It favored increases in first-class and discount fares, but frowned on many increases in the basic economy fare. The CAB approved higher fares for routes serving nations that signed liberal bilateral aviation agreements with the United States, but rejected those involving other countries. The CAB backed many fare increases for PanAm and Trans World Airlines (TWA), but said that increases in IATA agreements were noncompetitive and too sweeping. The board rejected IATA-pact fare increases of 7 per cent for May 1 and 9 per cent for September 1. IATA members tried again in October, proposing a 5 per cent fare hike to take effect in January 1980.

Airline Deregulation got into full swing under a 1978 law. The CAB granted routes freely, generally giving carriers any authority they sought. Most airlines used the new rights sparingly. They switched service from some low-volume markets to more profitable routes, but airline service generally expanded. Commuter airlines took up the slack in many communities abandoned by larger carriers, but some cities lost service.

Some flights were canceled when fuel supplies grew tight in the spring. Fuel costs soared, and traffic growth slowed later in the year, so airlines started trimming flights.

Airlines continued to offer discount fares, but basic-fare cutting was limited, and climbing fuel costs forced coach fares up more than 30 per cent in 1979. The CAB allowed basic-fare increases of 4 per cent on May 15, 7.3 per cent in July, 4.3 per cent in August, 9.5 per cent in September, and 3.7 per cent on November 1. On January 12, American, Capitol International Airways, PanAm, and World Airways received permission to offer one-way fares on flights between the East and West coasts for as little as $100 plus tax. World Airways offered the fare on April 11, and United offered it on May 28 as a way to attract customers that were lost during a 55-day strike that ended on May 24. American and TWA matched United immediately. A long strike halted World Airways service on August 3, and the other carriers raised the fare in August. Capitol and PanAm offered the $100 one-way fare in September.

United also announced a discount plan on May 24. United gave its passengers coupons that they

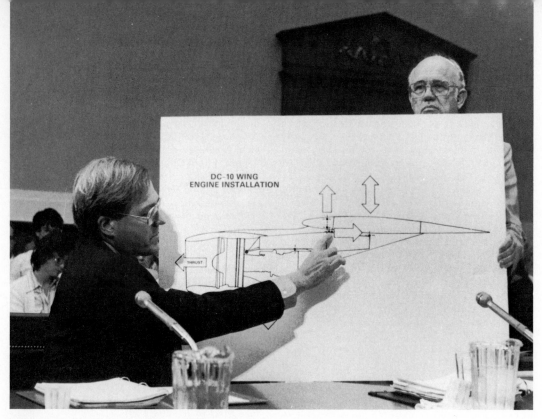

Administrator Langhorne Bond of the Federal Aviation Administration
explains a wing drawing during a House inquiry into the DC-10's safety.

could redeem for half-fare tickets on other flights in
the second half of the year. American matched the
plan, and a sizable market in buying and selling
half-fare coupons developed.

The Merger Movement that began in 1978
began to jell in 1979. The CAB approved a merger of
Southern Airways into North Central Airlines on
May 16, forming Republic Airlines. On July 10, the
board tentatively approved PanAm's proposal to
buy National Airlines, and a competing bid by
Texas International Airlines to gain control of National against National's wishes. On September 27,
the CAB rejected an Eastern Air Lines bid to take
over National. PanAm won the battle, buying Texas
International's holding of National stock and increasing its ownership to 61.8 per cent by October
18. The CAB approved the merger on October 29;
President Jimmy Carter approved it in December.

But the CAB on July 21 rejected a proposed
merger of Continental Air Lines and Western Airlines, because it threatened to reduce competition.
Texas International indicated in September that it
wanted to buy out TWA, but TWA's parent company, Trans World Corporation, opposed the idea.
Seaboard World Airlines, a cargo airline that had
fought a take-over attempt by Tiger International,
Incorporated, agreed on July 18 to a proposed
merger with Tiger's air-cargo subsidiary, Flying
Tiger Line Incorporated.

Air Safety. The May 25 DC-10 crash in Chicago
caused a sharp increase in the number of airline
deaths in the United States. The National Transportation Safety Board, a federal agency, tentatively
reported that airline crashes in the United States
killed 279 persons in 1979, compared with a total of
160 in 1978.

The Federal Aviation Administration (FAA) suspended the DC-10's certification on June 6, because
the investigation of the May 25 crash in Chicago
indicated that the planes might develop problems
similar to those that caused the crash. The ban
affected domestic flights and flights of foreign-
owned DC-10s to and from the United States. The
FAA investigated the plane's design and maintenance, then lifted the grounding on July 13. The
FAA blamed the crash on a crack in the DC-10's
engine-mount assembly. The crash occurred when
the engine and assembly came off the aircraft and
severed control and stall-warning lines. The FAA
said that an American Airlines maintenance procedure caused the crack, and moved to tighten its
surveillance of maintenance work. The procedure
deviated from a recommendation by McDonnell-
Douglas Corporation, the manufacturer. The FAA
also said it might require McDonnell-Douglas to
redesign the assembly. Albert R. Karr

See also TRANSPORTATION. In WORLD BOOK, see
AVIATION.

206

AWARDS AND PRIZES presented in 1979 included the following:

Arts Awards

Academy of Motion Picture Arts and Sciences. *"Oscar" Awards: Best Picture, The Deer Hunter. Best Actor,* Jon Voight, *Coming Home. Best Actress,* Jane Fonda, *Coming Home. Best Supporting Actor,* Christopher Walken, *The Deer Hunter. Best Supporting Actress,* Maggie Smith, *California Suite. Best Director,* Michael Cimino, *The Deer Hunter. Best Original Screenplay, Coming Home,* story by Nancy Dowd; screenplay by Waldo Salt, Robert C. Jones. *Best Cinematography, Days of Heaven,* Nestor Almendros. *Best Film Editing, The Deer Hunter,* Peter Zinner. *Best Original Music Score, Midnight Express,* Giorgio Moroder. *Best Feature Documentary, Scared Straight,* Arnold Shapiro, producer. *Best Visual Effects, Superman,* Warner Brothers. *Jean Hersholt Humanitarian Award,* Leo Jaffe, chairman of the board, Columbia Pictures. *Special Awards,* Walter Lantz, animator; King Vidor, director; Sir Laurence Olivier, actor; and the film department of the Museum of Modern Art, New York City.

American Academy and Institute of Arts and Letters. *Goddard Lieberson Fellowships.* Gerald Levinson, assistant professor of composition and theory, Swarthmore College, Swarthmore, Pa., and Bruce MacCombie, assistant professor of music, Yale University School of Music, New Haven, Conn. *Awards,* Vivian Fine, Paul Chihara, Morton Subotnick, and Robert Starer. *Charles Ives Scholarships,* Susan Blaustein, Robert Beaser, Marilyn Bliss, David Goodman, Carl Brenner, and Tobias Picker.

American Institute of Architects. *Gold Medal,* for his life's work, I. M. Pei. *Architectural Firm Award,* Geddes, Brecher, Qualls, Cunningham, of Philadelphia, Pa., and Princeton, N. J. *Medal,* for his influence on the architectural profession, Barry Commoner, professor of environmental science, Washington University, St. Louis, Mo. *Medal,* for his book, *Experiencing Architecture,* to Danish architect and town planner Steen Eiler Rasmussen. *Medal,* for arts or crafts related to architecture, to Bulgarian artist Christo. *Medal,* for accomplishments demonstrating the integration of several disciplines related to architecture, to the Bedford-Stuyvesant Restoration Corporation, Brooklyn, N.Y. *Design Award,* for a significant building at least 25 years old, to the Yale University Art Gallery in New Haven, Conn., which was designed by the late Louis I. Kahn.

Antoinette Perry (Tony) Awards. *Drama: Best Play, The Elephant Man,* by Bernard Pomerance. *Best Actor,* Tom Conti in *Whose Life Is It Anyway? Best Actress* (tie), Constance Cummings in *Wings,* Carole Shelley in *The Elephant Man. Best Director,* Jack Hofsiss, for *The Elephant Man. Musical: Best Musical, Sweeney Todd. Best Actor,* Len Cariou, *Sweeney Todd. Best Actress,* Angela Lansbury, *Sweeney Todd. Best Choreography,* Michael Bennett and Bob Avian, for *Ballroom. Best Book,* Hugh Wheeler for *Sweeney Todd. Best Score,* Stephen Sondheim for *Sweeney Todd. Best Director,* Harold Prince for *Sweeney Todd. Special Tony Awards,* Henry Fonda, Walter Diehl, Eugene O'Neill Theatre Center, American Conservatory Theatre. *Lawrence Langner Award,* Richard Rodgers.

Cannes International Film Festival. *Golden Palm Grand Prize* (tie), *Apocalypse Now,* United States; *The Tin Drum,* West Germany. *Best Actor,* Jack Lemmon in *The China Syndrome. Best Actress,* Sally Field in *Norma Rae. Best Director,* Terrence Malick for *Days of Heaven.*

Capezio Foundation. *Capezio Dance Award,* Alvin Ailey, choreographer, teacher, and founder of the Alvin Ailey American Dance Theater, as a "humanist who has interpreted the black heritage as a powerful and unusual expression common to all."

John F. Kennedy Center for the Performing Arts. *Honors,* "to build more enthusiasm for the performing arts and to bring the public's attention to the artist's true place in society," Aaron Copland, composer; Henry Fonda, actor; Ella Fitzgerald, singer; Martha Graham, dancer and choreographer; Tennessee Williams, playwright.

National Academy of Recording Arts and Sciences. *Grammy Awards: Record of the Year,* "Just the Way You Are," Billy Joel. *Album of the Year,* "Saturday Night Fever," Bee Gees. *Song of the Year,* "Just the Way You Are," Billy Joel. *Best New Group of the Year,* A Taste of Honey. *Best Jazz Vocal Performance,* "All Fly Home," Al Jarreau. *Best Jazz Performance, Solo,* "Montreux '77 – Oscar Peterson," Oscar Peterson. *Group,* "Friends," Chick Corea. *Big Band,* "Live in Munich," Thad Jones and Mel Lewis. *Best Pop Vocal Performance, Female,* "You Needed Me," Anne Murray. *Male,* "Copacabana," Barry Manilow. *Duo Group, or Chorus,* "Saturday Night Fever," Bee Gees. *Best Pop Instrumental Performance,* "Children of Sanchez," Chuck Mangione. *Best Rhythm and Blues Vocal Performance, Female,* "Last Dance," Donna Summer. *Male,* "On Broadway," George Benson. *Duo, Group, or Chorus,* "All and All," Earth, Wind, and Fire. *Instrumental,* "Runnin'," Earth, Wind, and Fire. *Best Country Vocal Performance, Female,* "Here You Come Again," Dolly Parton. *Male,* "Georgia on My Mind," Willie Nelson. *Duo or Group,* "Mamas Don't Let Your Babies Grow Up To Be Cowboys," Waylon Jennings and Willie Nelson. *Instrumental,* "One O'Clock Jump," Asleep at the Wheel. *Best Country Song,* "The Gambler," Don Schlitz. *Best Gospel Performance, Contemporary or Inspirational,* "What A Friend," Larry Hart. *Traditional,* "Refreshing," Happy Goodman Family. *Best Ethnic or Traditional Recording,* "I'm Ready," Muddy Waters. *Best Latin Recording,* "Homenaje a Beny Moro," Tito Puente. *Best Recording for Children,* "The Muppet Show," Muppets. *Best Comedy Recording,* "A Wild and Crazy Guy," Steve Martin. *Best Cast Show Album,* "Ain't Misbehavin'," Thomas (Fats) Waller and others, composers. *Album of the Year, Classical,* "Brahms: Concerto for Violin in D Major," Itzhak Perlman and the Chicago Symphony Orchestra, conducted by Carlo Maria Giulini. *Best Classical Orchestra Performance,* Beethoven: *Nine Symphonies,* Berlin Philharmonic, conducted by Herbert Von Karajan. *Best Opera Recording,* Lehar: *The Merry Widow,* Beverly Sills, New York City Opera and Chorus, conducted by Julius Rudel. *Best Classical Choral Performance,* Beethoven: *Missa Solemnis,* Chicago Symphony Orchestra and Chorus, Sir Georg Solti conducting; Margaret Hillis, choral director. *Best Chamber Music Performance,* Beethoven: *Sonatas for Violin and Piano,* Itzhak Perlman and Vladimir Ashkenazy. *Best Classical Performance by Soloist with Orchestra,* Rachmaninoff: *Concerto No. 3,* Vladimir Horowitz, Pianist, the Philadelphia Orchestra, conducted by Eugene Ormandy. *Best Classical Performance by a Soloist Without Orchestra,* "The Horowitz Concerts 1977/78," Vladimir Horowitz, pianist. *Best Classical Vocal Performance,* "Hits From Lincoln Center," Luciano Pavarotti.

National Academy of Television Arts and Sciences. *Emmy Awards: Best Comedy Series,* "Taxi." *Lead Actress, Comedy Series,* Ruth Gordon, in *The Sugar Mama* segment of "Taxi." *Lead Actor, Comedy Series,* Carroll O'Connor in "All in the Family." *Best Drama Series,* "Lou Grant." *Lead Actress, Drama Series,* Mariette Hartley in "The Incredible Hulk." *Lead Actor, Drama Series,* Ron Liebman in "Kaz." *Best Limited Series or Special,* "Roots, The Next Generations." *Best Actor in a Limited Series or Special,* Peter Strauss in *The Jericho Mile. Best Actress,* Bette Davis, in *Strangers: The Story of a Mother and Daughter. Outstanding Drama Special, Friendly Fire. Outstanding Information Program, Scared Straight. Special Achievement Award, Who Are the Debolts and Where*

Did They Get 19 Kids? **Outstanding Children's Program,** *Christmas Eve on Sesame Street.* **Outstanding Classical Program in the Performing Arts,** *Balanchine: TV Great Performance.*

New York Drama Critics Circle Awards. Best Play, *The Elephant Man* by Bernard Pomerance. **Best Musical,** *Sweeney Todd,* score by Stephen Sondheim and book by Hugh Wheeler.

Journalism Awards

American Association for the Advancement of Science (AAAS) *Science Writing Awards:* **For science writing in newspapers with over 100,000 daily circulation,** Christine A. Duerr, University of Rhode Island Marine Advisory Service, for "Bay Life," an article published in *Rhode Islander,* the Sunday magazine of the *Providence* (R.I.) *Journal-Bulletin;* **for science writing in newspapers with under 100,000 circulation,** Mike Lenehan, *Chicago Reader,* for "The Essence of Beeing," an article on beekeeping; **for science writing in general circulation magazines,** Frederic Golden, *Time,* for "Those Baffling Black Holes."

American Society of Magazine Editors. *National Magazine Awards:* **Specialized Journalism,** *National Journal.* **Essays and Criticism,** *Life.* **Fiction,** *The Atlantic Monthly.* **Public Service,** *New West.* **Reporting,** *Texas Monthly.* **Service to the Individual,** *American Journal of Nursing.* **Visual Excellence,** *Audubon.*

Long Island University. *George Polk Memorial Awards,* Richard S. Salant, retiring president of CBS News, for his lifetime achievement in gathering news. **News Photography,** Eddie Adams, the Associated Press, for coverage of the Rhodesian civil war. **Foreign Reporting,** John F. Burns, John Darnton, and Michael T. Kaufman, *The New York Times,* for their reports on Africa. **National Reporting,** Ronald Kessler, *The Washington Post,* for articles on corruption in the General Services Administration. **Local Reporting,** *The Dallas Times Herald,* for reporting on the deaths of Mexican Americans at the hands of Texas law-enforcement officers. **Regional Reporting,** *Southern Exposure,* the quarterly of the Institute for Southern Studies, for articles on Southern culture and politics. **Public Service Reporting,** Jane Shoemaker, Thomas Ferrick, Jr., and William Ecenbarger of *The Philadelphia Inquirer,* for reporting on corruption in the Pennsylvania legislature. **Education Reporting,** *The Chronicle of Higher Education,* for coverage of college and university administrative affairs. **Television Reporting,** Don Harris and Robert Brown, NBC News, for their courageous coverage of events at Jonestown, Guyana (awarded posthumously—both men were murdered in Guyana). **Film Documentary,** Golden West Television Productions, for *Scared Straight,* about a crime-prevention program operated by state prisoners at Rahway, N.J.

The Newspaper Guild. *Heywood Broun Award,* Paul Magnusson and Susan Watson, *The Detroit Free Press,* for a 10-part series on the abuse of retarded children at Michigan's Plymouth Center for retarded children. The series, plus some 100 other stories written by the two reporters, led to firings, indictments, and a massive overhaul of Plymouth Center.

The Society of Professional Journalists, Sigma Delta Chi. *Newspaper Awards:* **General Reporting,** Pamela Zekman, Zay N. Smith, James R. Frost, and Eugene Pesek, *The Chicago Sun-Times,* for their series "The Mirage," in which they reported on the corruption tavernkeepers must deal with in Chicago. The series resulted in more than 30 indictments of state and city inspectors. **Editorial Writing,** Philip R. Goldsmith, *The Philadelphia Inquirer,* for a series of editorials on Pennsylvania's Supreme Court. **Washington Correspondence,** Joseph Albright, Cox Newspapers, for articles on lax security at nuclear and chemical weapons installations in the United States. **Foreign Correspond-**

ence, Charles A. Krause, *The Washington Post,* for his coverage of the Jonestown, Guyana, massacre. **News Photography,** Norman Y. Lono, *The Philadelphia Daily News,* for coverage of a seven-hour shootout between Philadelphia police and members of MOVE, a counterculture group, in which one policeman was killed and seven others were wounded. **Editorial Cartooning,** James Mark Borgman, *The Cincinnati Enquirer,* for a political cartoon, "Bite A Bullet For Inflation." **Public Service in Newspaper Journalism,** *The Chicago Sun-Times,* for "The Abortion Profiteers," a series that exposed negligence and illegal medical treatment in Chicago's legal abortion clinics. **Magazine Awards: Reporting,** Tony Green, *Philadelphia* magazine, for "Hiding Out," a study of the United States Department of Justice's Witness Protection Program, which is designed to help informants in criminal cases establish new identities. **Public Service in Magazine Journalism,** *New West,* Beverly Hills, Calif., for "Hell On Wheels," by Moira Johnston, an article that played a major role in forcing the recall of more than 13 million Firestone 500 radial tires. **Radio Journalism, Reporting,** WGST Newsradio 92, Atlanta, Ga., for coverage of the shooting of *Hustler* magazine publisher Larry Flynt. **Public Service in Radio Journalism,** KXL Radio, Portland, Ore., for more than 20 investigative reports on aviation safety, particularly in the Portland area. **Editorializing on Radio,** KYW Newsradio, Philadelphia, for editorials urging listeners to write to President Carter to protest the dismissal of U.S. Attorney David M. Marston. **Television Journalism, Reporting,** Steve Howell and John Britton, KCST-TV, San Diego, for their coverage of the mid-air collision on Sept. 25, 1978, between a small private plane and a Pacific Southwest Airlines jet, in which 144 persons were killed. **Public Service in Television Journalism,** WCCO-TV, Minneapolis, Minn., for "A Death in The Family," a series that studied the impact of television on the American family. **Editorializing on Television,** Peter Kohler, WCBS-TV, New York City, for "The Revolving Door," a series on aid for discharged mental patients. **Research in Journalism,** John Hohenberg, University of Tennessee, Knoxville, for *A Crisis For The American Press,* a book that deals with the current state of the news media. **Distinguished Teaching in Journalism,** Floyd G. Arpan, professor of journalism, Indiana University, Bloomington, Ind.

Literature Awards

Academy of American Poets. *Lamont Poetry Selection Award,* Frederick Seidel, for his book *Sunrise.* *Walt Whitman Award,* David Bottoms, for his first book of poetry, *Shooting Rats at the Bibb County Dump.* *Academy Fellowships,* Josephine Miles, author of *To All Appearances: Poems New and Selected,* and May Swenson, author of *New and Selected Things Taking Place.*

American Academy and National Institute of Arts and Letters. *Gold Medal for Poetry,* Archibald MacLeish. *Award for Distinguished Service to the Arts,* Lloyd Goodrich, director of the Whitney Museum in New York City.

American Library Association (ALA). *Bailey K. Howard—World Book Encyclopedia—ALA Goals Award,* to the Committee on the Status of Women in Librarianship of the ALA. *Allie Beth Martin Award,* for "an extraordinary range and depth of knowledge about books and other library material," Harriet E. Bard, Morrisson-Reeves Library, Richmond, Ind. *Joseph W. Lippincott Award,* Helen Hugenor Lyman, professor emeritus, University of Wisconsin, Madison. *Melvil Dewey Medal,* Russell E. Bidlack, Dean, School of Library Science, University of Michigan, Ann Arbor. *Newbery Medal,* for the most distinguished contribution to children's literature, Ellen Raskin for *The Westing Game.* *Caldecott Medal,* for the most distinguished American picture book for children, Paul Goble for *The Girl Who Loved Wild Horses.*

Association of American Publishers. National Book Awards: Biography, Arthur M. Schlesinger, Jr., for *Robert Kennedy and His Times.* **Contemporary Thought,** Peter Matthiessen, for *The Snow Leopard.* **Fiction,** Tim O'Brien, for *Going After Cacciato.* **History,** Richard Beale Davis, for *Intellectual Life in the Colonial South, 1585-1763.* **Poetry,** James Merrill, for *Mirabell: Books of Numbers.* **Children's Literature,** Katherine Paterson, for *The Great Gilly Hopkins.* **Translation,** Clayton Eshleman and Jose Rubia Barcia, for their translation from the Spanish of Cesar Vallejo's *The Complete Posthumous Poetry.*

Canadian Library Association. Howard V. Phalin– World Book Graduate Scholarship in Library Science, Richard Hopkins, Calgary, Alta. **The Book of The Year for Children Award,** Kevin Major for *Hold Fast.* **Amelia Francis Howard-Gibbon Illustrator's Award,** Ann Blades for *A Salmon for Simon.*

Governor General's Literary Awards (Canada), Alice Munro for *Who Do You Think You Are?* Patrick Lane for *Poems New and Selected.* Roger Caron for *Go Boy!* François-Marc Gagnon for *Paul-Emile Borduas.* Jacques Poulinx for *Les grandes marées.* Gilbert Langevin for *Mon refuge est un volcan.*

Pulitzer Prizes

Journalism. Public Service, *The Point Reyes* (Calif.) *Light,* for articles on Synanon, a California-based drug-rehabilitation program said to have become an authoritarian cult. **General Local Reporting,** *The San Diego Evening Tribune,* for its coverage of the collision of an airliner and a private plane over San Diego on Sept. 25, 1978. **Special Local Reporting,** Gilbert M. Gaul and Elliot G. Jaspin, *The Pottsville* (Pa.) *Republican,* for a yearlong investigation into the collapse of the Blue Coal Corporation, engineered by a group with ties to organized crime. **National Reporting,** James Risser, *The Des Moines* (Ia.) *Register,* for a seven-part series on pollution caused by farmers. **International Reporting,** Richard Ben Cramer, *The Philadelphia Inquirer,* for reporting about the effects of war on individuals in the Middle East. **Editorial Writing,** Edwin M. Yoder, editorial-page editor of the *Washington Star,* for a broad range of topics. **Spot News Photography,** Thomas J. Kelly III, the *Pottstown* (Pa.) *Mercury,* for a series of photographs of a man who held his family hostage, then killed his grandmother and pregnant wife. **Feature Photography,** the 16-member photographic staff of *The Boston Herald American* for 16 pages of photographs of the New England snowstorm that caused 54 deaths in February 1978. **Editorial Cartooning,** Herbert L. Block (Herblock), *The Washington Post,* for his lifework. **Distinguished Commentary,** Russell Baker, *The New York Times,* for his humorous columns on politics and society. **Distinguished Criticism,** Paul Gapp, *The Chicago Tribune,* for his architectural criticism. **Feature Writing,** Jon D. Franklin, *The Baltimore Evening Sun,* for a two-part feature about a brain operation.

Letters. Biography, Leonard Baker, for *Days of Sorrow and Pain: Leo Baeck and the Berlin Jews.* **Drama,** Sam Shepard, for *Buried Child.* **Fiction,** John Cheever, for *The Stories of John Cheever.* **General Nonfiction,** Edward O. Wilson, for *On Human Nature.* **History,** Don E. Fehrenbacher, for *The Dred Scott Case.* **Music,** Joseph Schwantner, for *Aftertones of Infinity.* **Poetry,** Robert Penn Warren, for *Now and Then: Poems 1976-1978.*

Science and Technology Awards

American Association for the Advancement of Science (AAAS). AAAS Socio-Psychological Prize, Murray Melbin, professor of sociology, Boston University. **AAAS-Newcomb Cleveland Prize,** Eric J. Knudsen, Masakazu Konishi, and John D. Pettigrew, division of biology, California Institute of Technology, Pasadena.

American Chemical Society, Priestley Medal, Glenn T. Seaborg, professor of chemistry, University of California, Berkeley. **Adams Award,** Melvin S. Newman, professor of chemistry, Ohio State University, Columbus.

American Geophysical Union. William Bowie Medal, Frank Press, director, Office of Science and Technology. **Maurice Ewing Medal,** Wallace S. Broecker, director, Geochemistry Laboratory, Lamont-Doherty Geological Observatory, Columbia University. **John Adams Fleming Medal,** Syun-Ichi Akasofu, professor of geophysics, University of Alaska. **Walter H. Bucher Medal,** Edward Irving, Department of Energy, Mines, and Resources, Canada.

American Institute of Physics. John T. Tate International Medal for Distinguished Service, Abdus Salam, professor of physics, London University, and director, Trieste Centre for Theoretical Physics. **Tom W. Bonner Prize for Nuclear Physics,** Willy Haeberli, University of Wisconsin, and Roy Middleton, University of Pennsylvania. **Leo Szilard Award for Physics in the Public Interest,** F. Sherwood Rowland, University of California, Irvine. **Dannie Heineman Prize for Mathematical Physics,** Gerard 't Hooft, University of Utrecht, the Netherlands.

American Physical Society. Davisson-Germer Prize in Atomic or Surface Physics, Joel A. Appelbaum and Donald R. Hamann, Bell Laboratories, Murray Hill, N.J. **Irving Langmuir Prize in Chemical Physics,** Donald S. McClure, Princeton University. **Oliver E. Buckley Solid-State Physics Prize,** Marvin L. Cohen, University of California, Berkeley.

Columbia University. Louisa Gross Horwitz Prize, Walter Gilbert, professor of molecular biology, Harvard University, Cambridge, Mass., and Frederick Sanger, Medical Research Council Laboratory of Molecular Biology, Great Britain.

The Franklin Institute. Franklin Medal, Elias J. Corey, professor of chemistry, Harvard University, Cambridge, Mass. **Walton Clark Medal,** Paul N. (Red) Adair, president, Red Adair Company, Incorporated, Houston. **Frank N. Brown Medal,** Henry J. Degenkolb, president, H. J. Degenkolb & Associates, consulting engineers, San Francisco.

Gairdner Foundation. Gairdner International Awards, for outstanding contributions to medical science, Sydney Brenner, MRC Laboratory of Molecular Biology, Cambridge, England; Jean-Pierre Changeux, Institut Pasteur, Paris; Donald S. Fredrickson, National Institutes of Health, Bethesda, Md.; Samuel O. Freedman and Phil Gold, McGill University, Montreal, Canada; Edwin G. Krebs, University of Washington, Seattle; James A. Miller and Elizabeth C. Miller, University of Wisconsin Medical School, Madison; Lars Terenius, University of Uppsala, Sweden.

Geological Society of America. Penrose Medal, J. Harlen Bretz, professor emeritus of geology, University of Chicago, for his pioneering work on the channelled scablands of Washington state. **Arthur L. Day Medal,** Walter M. Elsasser, Department of Earth and Planetary Sciences, Johns Hopkins University, Baltimore.

Albert and Mary Lasker Foundation. Albert Lasker Medical Research Award, Walter Gilbert, Harvard University; Frederick Sanger, Medical Research Council, Great Britain; and Roger W. Sperry, California Institute of Technology, Pasadena, Calif. **Special Public Service Award,** Sir John Wilson, president of the International Agency for the Prevention of Blindness.

Mount Sinai School of Medicine. Lita Annenberg Hazen Award, for outstanding achievement in clinical research, Jesse Roth, chief, diabetes branch, National Institute of Arthritis, Metabolism, and Digestive Diseases.

Edward G. Nash

BAHRAIN. See MIDDLE EAST.

BAKER, HOWARD HENRY, JR. (1925–),
United States senator from Tennessee and minority
leader of the Senate, declared his candidacy in
November 1979 for the 1980 Republican presidential nomination. Baker first gained national attention in 1973 as ranking Republican and vice-
chairman of the Senate committee that conducted
the Watergate hearings. He was forthright and
persistent in investigating the White House staff of
President Richard M. Nixon, also a Republican.

Baker was born on Nov. 15, 1925, in Huntsville,
Tenn., to a family steeped in politics. His father, an
attorney, served seven terms in the U.S. House of
Representatives. After studying at Tulane University of Louisiana and the University of the South, in
Sewanee, Tenn., Baker served in the U.S. Navy from
1943 to 1946. In 1949, he received a law degree from
the University of Tennessee.

Before his election to the Senate in 1966, Baker
was a senior partner in a Knoxville, Tenn., law firm.
He was elected Senate minority leader in 1977. A
critic of the Administration of President Jimmy
Carter, Baker took issue with SALT II, the strategic
arms limitation treaty negotiated in 1979.

Baker married Joy Dirksen in 1951. Her father,
the late Senator Everett M. Dirksen (R., Ill.), served
as Senate minority leader from 1959 to 1969. The
Bakers have two children.   Patricia Dragisic

BALLET. See Dancing.

BANGLADESH enjoyed political stability in 1979
for the first time in its troubled eight-year history.
President Ziaur Rahman, the ruling general known
as Zia, announced on January 5 that he would
release nearly all political prisoners, and promised
that the next Cabinet would be responsible to Parliament. The February 18 parliamentary election was
peaceful, but only 40 per cent of the voters showed
up at the polls. The Bangladesh Nationalist Party,
formed in September 1978 from five parties supporting Zia, won 207 of the 300 seats in the new chamber
and an additional 30 seats reserved for women.

The once-powerful Awami League of President
Sheik Mujibur Rahman, assassinated in 1975, became splintered and won only 40 seats. In April, Zia
announced the end of martial law and promised that
this would lead to "civilian democratic rule." While
Zia refused to make Bangladesh a Muslim state, the
Constitution was revised to bring the country closer
to the Muslim family.

A Sick Economy remained Zia's main preoccupation. There were some bright spots. Foreign aid
exceeded $1 billion for the first time. Exports rose.

However, a prolonged drought caused the loss of 1
million metric tons (1.1 million short tons) of rice,
endangered the jute crop, and sharply cut power
generation. This meant that foodgrain imports
would have to be nearly doubled to 3 million metric
tons (3.3 million short tons), out of the country's

annual consumption of around 14 million metric
tons (15 million short tons). Arab oil price boosts in
March and June dealt another blow; the cost of
imported grain and oil was likely to exceed the
country's total export earnings.

The Landless. But underlying these seasonal woes
were the fundamental problems. The population,
now at 92 million, continued to grow at the rate of
2.5 to 3 per cent, with nearly half the population
under the age of 15. The government pressed for
family planning, but budgeted only $44 million for
it. Coupled with this was the fact that half the
peasants own less than one-fifth of an acre (0.08
hectare) of land, and hunger is widespread.

The deep-rooted rural misery was compounded
by Hindu-Muslim riots in India's neighboring West
Bengal state in June. With the number of dead
reported at 28, but probably much higher, thousands of Muslims fled across the border into Bangladesh. In this, as in other moments of tension in
1979, Bangladesh and India worked in
collaboration – not often seen in the past. A formal
sign of that cooperation was a series of agreements
between Zia and India's Prime Minister Morarji
Desai, announced on April 18. The agreements dealt
with border disputes and trade between the two
neighbors.   Mark Gayn

See also Asia (Facts in Brief Table). In World
Book, see Bangladesh.

BANKS AND BANKING. Inflation raged at about
a 13 per cent annual rate in the United States and a
10 per cent rate in Canada in 1979. Interest rates rose
to unprecedented levels to compensate lenders for
the rapidly depreciating value of dollars. Because a
dollar's buying power is halved in 5½ years at a 13
per cent inflation rate, depositors in banks and thrift
institutions – such as credit unions and savings and
loan associations – that are subject to the Federal
Reserve System's interest rate maximum of about 5
per cent faced losing half the buying power of their
savings in seven years. As more and more depositors
came to realize the brutal impact of inflation on their
net worth, they began to withdraw money from
accounts subject to ceiling rates and to reinvest in
higher-yielding alternatives. They also borrowed
more on credit lines available on credit cards and
insurance policies, or wherever else interest was
contractually set at rates that had become bargains,
considering a 13 per cent inflation rate.

Interest Rates. Wealthy investors could turn to
three-month U.S. Treasury bills with annual yields
of more than 12 per cent as of October 1979. The
minimum denomination was $10,000. Comparable
maturities of large-denomination certificates of deposit issued by banks yielded 13 per cent if issued in
the United States or 14 per cent in the Eurodollar
market. Even small savers were able to blunt the
thrust of inflation by turning to a variety of new

credit instruments created as a way to get around the interest ceilings. For example, banks and thrift institutions struggled to hold onto funds by issuing large certificates of deposit and money market certificates, recently introduced instruments that paid an interest return tied to the U.S. Treasury bill rate.

Because of the success of money market certificates, savings and loan institutions (S&L's) were better able to supply funds to finance purchases of houses and apartments, including condominiums, than they were during 1974's tight-money episode. Nevertheless, by the last quarter of 1979, S&L's experienced substantial net outflows of funds, mortgage rates were pushed to record levels of 12 per cent and up, and the housing industry again experienced a decline that was expected to bring housing starts down by at least 25 per cent.

The money market mutual fund was another anti-inflation phenomenon. Issued by mutual fund companies, the money market mutual fund was invested in short-term, highly liquid securities. Yields to investors often were more than double those on deposits subject to interest ceilings, and funds could generally be withdrawn by check, usually in amounts of at least $250. Nearly $40 billion was invested in money market mutual funds by October, triple the level at the beginning of the year and about one-third the amount of transactions balances held in currency and demand deposits with commercial banks.

Interest on Checking Accounts. Depository institutions devised three ways to pay interest on checking accounts in 1979. Payment of interest on checking accounts had been prohibited from the 1930s until a regulation by the Federal Deposit Insurance Corporation in 1978 made it legal. *Repurchase Agreements* (RP's) enable large depositors to buy a security from a bank with the bank agreeing to repurchase the security the next day at a price set to yield the depositor an interest return. *Automatic Transfer Savings* (ATS) accounts are savings accounts paying 5 per cent interest that can be transferred automatically to cover checking account deficits. *Negotiable Orders of Withdrawal* (NOW) accounts at S&L's and banks, and *share drafts* at credit unions, are comparable accounts that pay interest and can be used to make money payments.

High interest rates made noninterest-bearing currency and checking accounts costly compared with the alternatives, and the ratio of money to total spending fell to only 16 per cent – down from 22 per cent 10 years earlier. Because the buying power of a dollar bill had fallen by half from 1969 to 1979, it was perhaps timely that a U.S. government study proposed eliminating the half-dollar coin.

Inflation and high interest rates were a worldwide phenomenon in 1979, though perhaps not so pronounced in Japan and in major European industrial countries as in the United States. A general decline

"See your raise and raise you back."

in the value of money during the previous decade made commodities and real estate attractive holdings. While prices on most items almost doubled in the decade, gold, which was valued at over $500 per troy ounce (31 grams) and silver, at about $33 per ounce in 1979, were up more than tenfold. Neither gold nor silver served as a means of payment any longer; they became commodities held for industrial uses and as speculation on continued price increases. Even the lowly penny, 95 per cent copper and 5 per cent zinc, would, at the 1979 rate of inflation, be worth more as metal than money by the end of 1982. House values, another inflation hedge, increased about 10 per cent annually through the 1970s. This was somewhat more than the 7 per cent annual increase in the general level of prices, but still more attractive than holding currency that was depreciating at a 7 per cent annual rate or common stocks that, on the average, did not even keep their dollar value over the decade.

The source of the inflation and high interest rate problem was the creation of an excessive supply of money and credit, largely stimulated by unusually large federal government deficits in the 1970s. These deficits were financed in three main ways. First, sales of interest-bearing federal securities to banks and to the public tended to increase interest rates directly. Second, sales of federal securities to Federal Reserve Banks, which they paid for by issuing currency and bank reserves, increased the demand for goods and services and increased inflation. Third, sales of securities to foreign governments and central banks, which tended to finance balance-of-payments deficits in U.S. trade and long-term investments, had the effect of importing U.S. inflation into those countries.

Inflation rates in Europe, Japan, and North America in the 1960s were generally well below 5 per cent per year. In fact, they were less than 3 per cent in Canada and the United States. In the 1970s, inflation rates more than doubled in almost every developed country and were linked strongly to the start of inflation in the United States. An additional factor, though minor by comparison, was the sharply rising cost of petroleum. That it was not the major inflationary factor is indicated by the fact that inflation rates in Japan and West Germany were well below those in the United States and Canada in the 1970s, even though those countries imported almost all of their oil, whereas Canada, on balance, imported none and the United States imported less than half the oil it required.

Volcker and the Fed. In July, United States President Jimmy Carter named G. William Miller as secretary of the Treasury and chose Paul A. Volcker to replace Miller as chairman of the Federal Reserve Board (see VOLCKER, PAUL A.). After years of rapid

increases in money, inflation, and interest rates, the Federal Reserve in October took a variety of actions designed to fight inflation rather than contribute to it. It increased the discount rate on loans to member banks from 11 per cent to a record 12 per cent and imposed required reserves on managed liabilities of banks that had previously not been subject to requirements. Most important, the Federal Open Market Committee's operating procedures were changed to control member-bank reserves and money directly, rather than indirectly through control of interest rates, as had been done previously.

Because interest rates had not been allowed to increase early in the business boom, the old policy had resulted in the Federal Reserve pumping money into the economy, thereby contributing to inflation and causing interest rates to rise late in the boom to such inordinately high levels. As a consequence of the new procedures – long advocated by critics of the Federal Reserve – the daily range of federal funds rates increased from about 1 to 5 per cent, but the monetary growth rate, which was more than 10 per cent in the second and third quarters of 1979, was cut back so substantially that financial forecasters generally expected the slow growth in 1979 to be transformed into a recession. William G. Dewald

See also ECONOMICS; The Year in Focus section. In WORLD BOOK, see BANKS AND BANKING.

BARBADOS. See WEST INDIES.

BARRY, MARION S., JR. (1936–), a Democrat, was sworn in as mayor of the District of Columbia on Jan. 2, 1979. He was elected on Nov. 7, 1978, after defeating Mayor Walter E. Washington in the primary on September 12. Barry was the first militant black leader of the 1960s civil rights movement to become mayor of a major city.

Barry was born in Itta Bena, Miss., on March 6, 1936, and grew up in Memphis, Tenn. He graduated from LeMoyne-Owen College in Memphis in 1958 and earned a master's degree in chemistry at Fisk University in Nashville, Tenn., in 1960. Barry helped to organize the Student Nonviolent Coordinating Committee (SNCC) while a graduate student at the University of Tennessee in Nashville in 1960. He became SNCC's first national chairman in 1960 and was a part-time organizer until 1964.

Barry moved to Washington, D.C., in 1965 to direct the SNCC office there, but his interests soon turned to broader issues. In 1966, he headed the Free D.C. movement, which advocated home rule for the district, then under federal control. Barry helped found a group in 1967 that provided jobs for young, underprivileged blacks. He was elected in 1970 to a panel that dealt with police-community relations and was president of the school board from 1971 to 1974, when he was elected council member at-large for the District of Columbia. Barry married Effi Slaughter in 1978. Jay Myers

An armed bandit caught by a security-system camera tries to escape after robbing a New York City bank. An epidemic of bank holdups occurred in 1979.

BASEBALL. Major-league baseball underwent broad changes in 1979. All four 1978 division winners were upended. There were close pennant races in three of the four divisions, all involving teams that had seldom been contenders. In the end, the Pittsburgh Pirates won the World Series by defeating the Baltimore Orioles, 4 games to 3. The Pirates became only the fourth team to win the series after trailing by 3 games to 1. They limited the Orioles to two runs and 17 hits over the last three games.

Regular-season attendance of 43,548,450 broke the record for the fourth straight year. Overall attendance climbed 7 per cent from 1978 and 46 per cent from 1975. Eight teams bettered 2 million attendance at home, and 15 exceeded 1.5 million.

The Pirates and Cincinnati Reds won the National League division titles, the sixth for each in the 1970s. The Pirates beat the surprising Montreal Expos by two games in the East on the last day of the season. The Reds finished 1½ games ahead of the surprising Houston Astros in the West. The Los Angeles Dodgers, 1977 and 1978 league champions, were last at midseason, and finished 11½ games behind the Reds. The Philadelphia Phillies, defending champions in the East, finished 14 games behind.

The Pirates, managed by Chuck Tanner, combined the slugging of first baseman Willie Stargell and outfielder Dave Parker, the hitting of Tim Foli

at shortstop and Bill Madlock at third base, the speed of center fielder Omar Moreno (77 stolen bases), and the relief pitching of Kent Tekulve (94 games), Enrique Romo (84), and Grant Jackson (72).

The Reds played the season without manager Sparky Anderson and third baseman Pete Rose. Anderson was fired unexpectedly after the Reds lost the two previous division titles to the Dodgers. Rose, bitter because the Reds refused to make an acceptable salary offer, became a free agent after 16 years with Cincinnati and signed with the Phillies. Ray Knight replaced him and played well. Outfielder George Foster, catcher Johnny Bench, shortstop Dave Concepcion, and pitcher Tom Seaver had their usual good seasons.

The three-of-five-game play-off ended quickly. The Pirates beat the Reds in three straight games, 5-2 (in 11 innings), 3-2 (in 10 innings), and 7-1.

The Orioles scored 102 victories, the most in the majors, and won by eight games in the American League East. In the American League West, the California Angels beat the 1978 champion Kansas City Royals by three games, the Texas Rangers by five, and the Minnesota Twins by six.

The Orioles' division title was their sixth in Earl Weaver's 11 full years as manager. Jim Palmer spent two months on the disabled list with an injured right elbow, but lefthander Mike Flanagan took up the

Billy Martin's second term as Yankee manager was brief. Summoned to revive the club in June, he was fired in October after a barroom fight.

pitching slack with 23 victories, the major-league high. Outfielder Ken Singleton and first baseman Eddie Murray were the Orioles' key hitters.

The Angels' title was their first. In their previous 18 seasons, they had finished an average of 23$\frac{1}{2}$ games behind. This time, managed by Jim Fregosi, they overcame injuries that cost them pitcher Frank Tanana and their new first baseman, Rod Carew, for much of the season. Nolan Ryan struck out 223 batters in 222 innings, and outfielders Don Baylor and Dan Ford, catcher Brian Downing, and second baseman Bobby Grich provided the hitting.

The Orioles took the pennant play-off in four games. They won the first two games, 6-3 (in 10 innings) and 9-8; the Angels won the third, 4-3; and the Orioles won the fourth, 8-0.

The World Series was played from October 10 to 17, often in rain and cold. The weather tempo was set in the first game. The Orioles won, 5-4, with five runs in the first inning off Bruce Kison, whose pitching fingers were stiff from the cold. Second baseman Phil Garner of the Pirates, his hands numb, fumbled a potential double-play grounder that would have ended the inning without a run.

The Pirates won the second game, 3-2, and the Orioles took the next two, 8-4 and 9-6. So the Pirates had to win three straight games to win the series. They won them – 7-1, 4-0, and 4-1.

The 38-year-old Stargell was voted Most Valuable Player of the series. In addition to being the Pirates' inspirational leader, he was their slugging leader. In the final game, he made four hits, including a two-run home run. Overall, he batted .400, and his 12 hits included three home runs and four doubles and drove in seven runs. Garner collected 12 hits; Moreno, 11; and Parker and Foli, 10 each as the Pirates batted .323.

The New York Yankees, World Series champions the two previous years, endured a season of turmoil and tragedy. They were never in their division race and finished 13$\frac{1}{2}$ games behind the Orioles.

The problems started in April when their star relief pitcher, Rich Gossage, and reserve catcher Cliff Johnson fought in the shower. Gossage suffered a torn ligament in his right (pitching) thumb and was sidelined for three months. Johnson was traded to the Cleveland Indians.

With the team languishing, Manager Bob Lemon was replaced in June by his fiery predecessor, Billy Martin. In August, Thurman Munson, the catcher and captain, was killed in the crash of the twin-engine jet plane he owned and piloted. In October, when Martin tried to cover up details of a barroom fight, he was fired and replaced by Dick Howser.

Individual Stars. Outfielder Lou Brock of the St. Louis Cardinals and first baseman Carl Yastrzemski

Final Standings in Major League Baseball

American League

Eastern Division	W.	L.	Pct.	GB.
Baltimore	102	57	.642	
Milwaukee	95	66	.590	8
Boston	91	69	.569	11$\frac{1}{2}$
New York	89	71	.556	13$\frac{1}{2}$
Detroit	85	76	.528	18
Cleveland	81	80	.503	22
Toronto	53	109	.327	50$\frac{1}{2}$
Western Division				
California	88	74	.543	
Kansas City	85	77	.525	3
Texas	83	79	.512	5
Minnesota	82	80	.506	6
Chicago	73	87	.456	14
Seattle	67	95	.414	21
Oakland	54	108	.333	34

Offensive Leaders

Batting Average—Fred Lynn, Boston	.333
Runs—Don Baylor, California	120
Home Runs—Gorman Thomas, Milwaukee	45
Runs Batted In—Don Baylor, California	139
Hits—George Brett, Kansas City	212
Stolen Bases—Willie Wilson, Kansas City	83

Leading Pitchers

Games Won—Mike Flanagan, Baltimore	23
Win Average—Mike Caldwell, Milwaukee (16-6)	
(162 or more innings)	.727
Earned-Run Average—Ron Guidry, New York	2.78
Strikeouts—Nolan Ryan, California	223
Saves—Mike Marshall, Minnesota	32

Awards

*Most Valuable Player—Don Baylor, California
*Cy Young—Mike Flanagan, Baltimore
*Rookie of the Year—John Castino, Minnesota; Alfredo Griffin, Toronto (tie)
†Manager of the Year—Earl Weaver, Baltimore

National League

Eastern Division	W.	L.	Pct.	GB.
Pittsburgh	98	64	.605	
Montreal	95	65	.594	2
St. Louis	86	76	.531	12
Philadelphia	84	78	.519	14
Chicago	80	82	.494	18
New York	63	99	.389	35
Western Division				
Cincinnati	90	71	.559	
Houston	89	73	.549	1$\frac{1}{2}$
Los Angeles	79	83	.488	11$\frac{1}{2}$
San Francisco	71	91	.438	19$\frac{1}{2}$
San Diego	68	93	.422	22
Atlanta	66	94	.413	23$\frac{1}{2}$

Offensive Leaders

Batting Average—Keith Hernandez, St. Louis	.344
Runs—Keith Hernandez, St. Louis	116
Home Runs—Dave Kingman, Chicago	48
Runs Batted In—Dave Winfield, San Diego	118
Hits—Garry Templeton, St. Louis	211
Stolen Bases—Omar Moreno, Pittsburgh	77

Leading Pitchers

Games Won—Joe Niekro, Houston; Phil Niekro, Atlanta	21
Win Average—Tom Seaver, Cincinnati (16-6)	
(162 or more innings)	.727
Earned-Run Average—J. Rodney Richard, Houston	2.71
Strikeouts—J. Rodney Richard, Houston	313
Saves—Bruce Sutter, Chicago	37

Awards

*Most Valuable Player—Keith Hernandez, St. Louis; Willie Stargell, Pittsburgh (tie)
*Cy Young—Bruce Sutter, Chicago
*Rookie of the Year—Rick Sutcliffe, Los Angeles

*Selected by Baseball Writers Association of America.
† Selected by *The Sporting News.*

of the Boston Red Sox, both 40 years old, became the 14th and 15th players in history to reach 3,000 hits. Rose set a major-league record of 10 seasons with at least 200 hits a season.

The Niekro brothers – 34-year-old Joe (21-11) of Houston and 40-year-old Phil (21-20) of the Atlanta Braves – led National League pitchers in victories. J. Rodney Richard of Houston led them in strikeouts (313) and earned-run average (2.71).

Hall of Fame. Willie Mays, for 22 years an electrifying center fielder, was elected to the Baseball Hall of Fame in Cooperstown, N.Y., in his first year of eligibility. Duke Snider and Enos Slaughter, both outfielders, were next in the balloting and fell just short of election. The Veterans Committee selected the late Hack Wilson, a slugging outfielder, and the late Warren Giles, an executive for 50 years. Less than four months after his induction, Mays was forced to resign as good-will ambassador for the New York Mets because he signed a public-relations contract with an Atlantic City, N.J., gambling enterprise.

Major-League Umpires refused to sign individual contracts before the season. They were replaced by amateur and minor-league umpires until they settled their dispute on May 18. Their new overall agreement provided higher wages and benefits and time off during the season.   Frank Litsky

In WORLD BOOK, see BASEBALL; MAYS, WILLIE.

BASKETBALL. The Seattle SuperSonics won their first National Basketball Association (NBA) championship in 1979, and Michigan State University won its first National Collegiate Athletic Association (NCAA) basketball title. In addition, a women's professional league made its debut, and a United States team won the women's world amateur championship for the first time since 1967.

NBA Problems. Perhaps the year's most interesting situation was the series of problems faced by the NBA. Attendance was down 1.1 per cent. More significantly, the 22 NBA teams were playing to only 60 per cent of capacity as against 80 per cent in the National Hockey League, which had a similar number of games, and 93 per cent in the National Football League, which had a shorter schedule. Television ratings for the CBS Sunday "Game of the Week" dropped significantly. One reason was local oversaturation of weeknight cable telecasts.

Another reason for flagging interest, though NBA officials publicly denied it, might have been racial. Almost three-fourths of the league's players were black and three-quarters of the spectators were white. As Seattle forward Paul Silas, president of the players association and a black, said:

"It is a fact that white people in general look disfavorably upon blacks who are making astronomical amounts of money if it appears they are not working hard for that money. Our players have

Larry Bird of Indiana State wins a rebound from Michigan State's Greg Kelser, but Michigan State won, 75-64, on March 26 to take the NCAA title.

Eastern Conference

Atlantic Division	W.	L.	Pct.
Washington	54	28	.659
Philadelphia	47	35	.573
New Jersey	37	45	.451
New York	31	51	.378
Boston	29	53	.354

Central Division			
San Antonio	48	34	.585
Houston	47	35	.573
Atlanta	46	36	.561
Cleveland	30	52	.366
Detroit	30	52	.366
New Orleans	26	56	.317

Western Conference

Midwest Division	W.	L.	Pct.
Kansas City	48	34	.585
Denver	47	35	.573
Indiana	38	44	.463
Milwaukee	38	44	.463
Chicago	31	51	.378

Pacific Division			
Seattle	52	30	.634
Phoenix	50	32	.610
Los Angeles	47	35	.573
Portland	45	37	.549
San Diego	43	39	.524
Golden State	38	44	.463

Leading Scorers	G.	FG.	FT.	Pts.	Avg.
Gervin, San Antonio	80	947	471	2,365	29.6
Free, San Diego	78	795	654	2,244	28.8
M. Johnson, Milwaukee	77	820	332	1,972	25.6
Malone, Houston	82	716	599	2,031	24.8
McAdoo, New York-Boston	60	596	295	1,487	24.8

Women's Professional Basketball League

Eastern Division	W.	L.	Pct.
Houston	26	8	.765
New York	19	15	.559
Dayton	12	22	.353
New Jersey	9	25	.265

Midwest Division			
Chicago	21	13	.618
Iowa	21	13	.618
Minnesota	17	17	.500
Milwaukee	11	23	.324

College Champions

Conference	School
Atlantic Coast	Duke-North Carolina (tie-regular season)
	North Carolina (ACC tournament)
Big Eight	Oklahoma
Big Sky	Weber State
Big Ten	Michigan State-Iowa-Purdue (tie)
Eastern 8	Villanova (regular season)
	Rutgers (E-8 tournament)
Ivy League	Pennsylvania
Mid-American	Central Michigan-Toledo (tie-regular season)
	Toledo (MAC play-off)
Missouri Valley	Indiana State
Ohio Valley	Eastern Kentucky
Pacific Ten	UCLA
Southeastern	Louisiana State (regular season)
	Tennessee (SEC tournament)
Southwest	Arkansas-Texas (tie-regular season)
	Arkansas (SWC tournament)
Sun Belt	South Alabama (regular season)
	Jacksonville (SBC tournament)
West Coast Athletic	San Francisco
Western Athletic	Brigham Young

College Tournament Champions

NCAA Division I	Michigan State
NCAA Division II	North Alabama
NCAA Division III	North Park (Chicago)
NAIA	Drury
NIT	Indiana
AIAW (Women)	Old Dominion

become so good that it appears they're doing things too easily, that they don't have the intensity they once had."

Salaries were indeed astronomical, averaging $148,000. The Houston Rockets gave a new three-year contract to their center, Moses Malone, and the San Diego Clippers signed Portland Trail Blazers center Bill Walton, a free agent, for seven years, each receiving close to $1 million a year. Larry Bird of Indiana State and Earvin (Magic) Johnson of Michigan State, the outstanding college players, signed multiyear pro contracts, each for about $600,000 per year. See BIRD, LARRY; JOHNSON, EARVIN.

There were more problems. When any two teams involved could not decide on compensation for the signing of a free agent, the decision was left to Commissioner Larry O'Brien. In 1978, when 7-foot 1-inch (216-centimeter) Marvin Webster of Seattle signed with the New York Knickerbockers, O'Brien awarded Seattle Lonnie Shelton, a number-one draft choice, and $450,000. The Knicks and the players association protested that the compensation was excessive, and a federal judge upheld them in September 1979. O'Brien's compensation award for Walton—forward Kermit Washington, center Kevin Kunnert, guard Randy Smith, two number-one draft choices, and $350,000—made about a week before the Webster ruling, faced similar peril.

The Pro Season. Defending champion Washington, San Antonio, Kansas City, and Seattle won the 1978–1979 division titles and joined eight wild-card teams in the play-offs. Seattle, which lost to the Washington Bullets in the 1978 finals, won the title this time, beating the Los Angeles Lakers in five games, the Phoenix Suns in seven, and Washington in five. Dennis Johnson and Gus Williams scored 256 of Seattle's 505 points in the finals.

George Gervin of San Antonio repeated as scoring champion, averaging 29.6 points per game. Malone was fifth in scoring (24.8) and first in rebounding (17.6 per game) and set an all-time record of 587 offensive rebounds in one season.

The College Season. Of the 248 major-college teams in NCAA Division I, only Indiana State and Alcorn State of Mississippi finished the regular season undefeated, and they lost in post-season tournaments. Indiana State was ranked number-one nationally and was favored in the NCAA tourney.

Indiana State reached the final, though it barely got by De Paul, 76-74, in the semifinals. Michigan State gained the final by beating Lamar by 31 points, Louisiana State by 16, Notre Dame by 12, and Pennsylvania by 34. Michigan State won the final, 75-64, on March 26 in Salt Lake City, Utah. The loss was Indiana State's first in 34 games.

Lawrence Butler of Idaho State became national scoring champion, averaging 30.1 points per game. Bird was second in scoring with 28.9 and fourth in rebounds with 14.9. Bird and Johnson, a sophomore, made most all-America teams along with Bill Cartwright of San Francisco, David Greenwood of University of California, Los Angeles (UCLA), and Sidney Moncrief of Arkansas.

Women. The Women's Professional Basketball League played its first season with eight teams and enrolled six more for the 1979-1980 season. Original franchises cost $50,000. Every team lost money, averaging about $260,000. Salaries averaged from $5,000 to $15,000 – the highest was $25,000. The Chicago Hustle had the best attendance, averaging 3,105 in a 5,000-seat arena. The Houston Angels won the title by beating the Iowa Cornets in the play-off finals, 3 games to 2.

The United States amateurs defeated Canada, 77-61, for the world championship on May 13 in Seoul, South Korea. The U.S. lost only to South Korea in the opening game of the seven-team round-robin finals.

Carol Blazejowski of Fairview, N.J., scored 25 points and Nancy Lieberman of Far Rockaway, N.Y., scored 13 for the U.S. in the world final. On March 25 in Greensboro, N.C., Lieberman helped Old Dominion University beat Louisiana Tech, 76-65, in the final of the Association for Intercollegiate Athletics for Women championships. She also received the Wade Trophy as woman college player of the year.   Frank Litsky

In WORLD BOOK, see BASKETBALL.

A stage in Brussels, Belgium, exploded in August as a British band was about to play. The Irish Republican Army was believed to be responsible.

BELGIUM. Wilfried Martens, leader of the Flemish Social Christian Party, formed a five-party coalition government on April 2, 1979. His action ended the political stalemate that followed the December 1978 general elections. The coalition replaced Paul vanden Boeynants' caretaker administration and included five of the six members of the coalition government of Leo Tindemans, which fell in October 1978. Martens' first task was to reform the Constitution to end rivalries between Dutch-speaking Flemings in the north and French-speaking Walloons in the south. The crisis had eased when the various parties saw that new elections would be necessary if a new government was not formed soon.

Inflation Surge. The government forecast that the inflation rate would rise from 1979's 4.5 per cent to 6 per cent in 1980 and that the gross national product's real growth would drop from 3 per cent in 1979 to 2.5 per cent in 1980. It feared that rising inflation could hamper exports, so it proposed a budget cut of $7.4 billion in state borrowing, less spending on social services, higher taxes on automobiles and gasoline, and a levy on roads. The Belgian franc fell to its lowest allowable limit in the European Monetary System (EMS) in June. See ECONOMICS; EUROPE.

Trade unions and employers shelved plans for a 36-hour workweek and discussed a proposal for a 38-hour week by the end of 1980. The government would compensate employers for lost production time under this plan, and it would help create jobs by giving bonuses to companies that hired the unemployed.

Other Troubles. Brussels faced bankruptcy in the first week of June when the city could not pay its employees. The city had used up anticipated revenues for 1979 and 1980, but it raised emergency funds for hardship cases. Martens ended the crisis by arranging interim financing and guaranteeing future funding.

Eurosystem Hospitalier, the leading company in a $1.2-billion hospital construction project in Saudi Arabia, went bankrupt in July because it paid excessive payoffs to get the hospital contract. The government ordered Societé Generale, the country's largest holding company and partial owner of the bankrupt company, to pay about $135 million to save the project or face loss of export guarantees for its other businesses.

On April 7, Mayor Fernand Hubin decided to close a nuclear power station in Huy because he thought it was unsafe, but the national government reversed his decision. Atomic energy provides 25 per cent of Belgium's electricity.   Kenneth Brown

See also EUROPE (Facts in Brief Table). In WORLD BOOK, see BELGIUM.

BELIZE. See LATIN AMERICA.

BENDJEDID, CHADLI (1929-), was elected president of Algeria on Feb. 7, 1979, replacing his long-time friend Houari Boumediene, who died in December 1978. An army colonel, Bendjedid was a compromise candidate of the only political party and was put forward by the army. He pledged to continue Boumediene's socialist policies.

Bendjedid was born into a peasant family on April 14, 1929, at Bouteldja in eastern Algeria. He was educated in Annaba and began working for Algerian independence from France as a youth. He joined the National Liberation Front in 1954 and the National Liberation Army in 1955.

In 1962, Bendjedid joined the general staff and began working with Boumediene. He commanded the Northern Military Zone in 1962 when Algeria gained its independence. He played an active role in the "Revolutionary Readjustment," the coup d'état in which Boumediene wrested control of the government from President Ben Bella in 1965, and became a member of the Council of the Revolution. In 1969 he was promoted to colonel and given command of the Second Military Region, in Oran. Although he strongly supported Boumediene's policies and programs, Bendjedid appears to have remained a middle-of-the-roader in Algerian politics. He is married and has four children.   Edward G. Nash

BENIN. See AFRICA.

BHUTAN. See ASIA.

BINAISA, GODFREY L. (1920-), a former attorney general, became president of Uganda on June 21, 1979, after Yusufu K. Lule was forced out of office by the legislature's vote of no confidence. Lule had presided over the provisional government that was installed on April 13 after President Idi Amin Dada fled before invading Ugandan exiles and Tanzanian troops. See AFRICA; UGANDA.

Binaisa was born in Kampala on May 30, 1920. He graduated from Uganda's Makerere University and earned a law degree from King's College in London. Although he was admitted to the British bar in 1956, Binaisa returned to Uganda to practice law. After Uganda became independent in 1962, Prime Minister Apollo Milton Obote named Binaisa attorney general. He resigned that post in 1967 and returned to private practice.

In the late 1960s and early 1970s, Binaisa represented Israeli business concerns in suits against the Ugandan government. His activities aroused the wrath of Amin, who had overthrown Obote in 1971. Threatened with arrest and execution, Binaisa fled to Great Britain in 1973. He emigrated to New York City in 1977, where he founded the Uganda Freedom Union, one of many exile organizations that banded together to seize power from Amin. He was a trial lawyer with a Manhattan law firm until he returned to Uganda in May 1979. Binaisa and his wife, Irene, have seven children.   Beverly Merz

BIOCHEMISTRY. Research teams from Genentech Incorporated in South San Francisco, Calif., and the University of California in San Francisco announced almost at the same time in July 1979 that they had independently produced human growth hormone in the laboratory, using bacteria cells. This is the first time that scientists have been able to use recombinant DNA techniques to produce a medically useful material that is not available in adequate amounts from other sources.

To get recombinant DNA, biochemists break a chain or ring of deoxyribonucleic acid (DNA), which carries genetic information. They then insert genetic material from a different source and insert the resultant hybrid DNA molecule into a cell like the one from which it came. The recombinant DNA, including the inserted genetic message, is passed on when the cell reproduces. The value of altering an organism's heredity with recombinant DNA has been controversial, so advocates of the so-called gene-splicing technique were happy to point to human growth hormone as an example of favorable medical news about recombinant DNA.

The growth hormone is used in treating pituitary dwarfism, a rare hereditary condition that affects at least 10,000 children in the United States. The hormone may also help to promote healing of burns. Because no animal growth hormone will work in humans, only limited amounts of the hormone from cadaver pituitaries have been available for research.

The two laboratories used different variations on the basic recombinant technique to engineer bacteria to produce human growth hormone. The Genentech group chemically synthesized a portion of the growth hormone gene and copied the remainder from the natural human gene. The synthetic portion included a "start" signal for the bacterial system. Genentech is the research company that used recombinant DNA to make the first bacteria-produced human insulin in 1978. The University of California research team linked the natural growth hormone gene to a bacterial gene, which has built-in control segments. For development of large-scale growth hormone production, the Genentech researchers signed a contract with a Swedish drug firm, and the university scientists agreed to work with a United States drug company.

Gene-Splicing Safety. Researchers at the National Institutes of Health (NIH) maximum-safety facility at Fort Detrick, Maryland, completed initial experiments designed to assess the likelihood that recombinant DNA experiments might accidentally create a cancer epidemic. NIH scientists Malcolm Martin and Wallace Rowe announced reassuring results for those experiments in March. Genes from viruses that cause tumors in mice were combined with bacterial DNA, and bacteria harboring that recombinant DNA were fed or injected into susceptible mice. No viral infections of the mice resulted,

Shawn Shawn's parents were a male gibbon and a female siamang. Atlanta zoo biologists were surprised that these two species were able to mate.

synthesis acts differently in mitochondrial protein synthesis and inserts the amino acid tryptophan. Also, the signal that normally specifies the amino acid leucine is used in yeast mitochondria to specify another amino acid – threonine. Tzagoloff said the mitochondrial version of the genetic code is probably a simplified form of the familiar code.

Biochemistry in Context. An analytical tool long used by chemists to identify compounds in pure solutions was modified by biochemists to trace the complex, coordinated chemistry of living cells. Robert G. Shulman of Bell Laboratories in Murray Hill, N.J., reported in April that he had used nuclear magnetic resonance (NMR) spectroscopy to observe major metabolic cycles of the cell and how cell biochemistry changes in response to hormones. Other scientists used the technique to study muscle contraction, muscle deficiencies in various diseases, and the synthesis of complicated cell products.

In NMR spectroscopy, instruments chart the radio wave energy absorbed by a sample in a magnetic field. Because atoms vary in magnetic properties, molecules absorb different amounts of energy of various frequencies, and the resulting profile identifies chemical components present. Using that profile, scientists can follow the changes in molecules within a cell without disturbing its functioning.   Julie Ann Miller

In WORLD BOOK, see BIOCHEMISTRY; CELL.

demonstrating that the tumor-causing genes did not escape from the bacteria and infect the mice. Martin and Rowe concluded that most research using recombinant DNA was safe as long as the standard enfeebled bacteria *Escherichia coli* K12 were used.

The NIH Advisory Committee on Recombinant DNA Research in September proposed a major relaxation of its guidelines. About 85 per cent of the experiments originally covered would be exempted from most of the rules. However, experiments currently prohibited would not be affected.

Genetic-Code Exception. The first exception to the "universal" genetic code was discovered in 1979. Previously, all genes analyzed in bacteria, plants, and animals were found to follow the same coding rules – a three-nucleotide sequence in the genetic material specified the same amino acid in protein synthesis or a "terminate protein" signal. The exceptional case is a common structure inside cells – the mitochondrion, the cellular powerhouse that contains some genetic material separate from that of the surrounding cell.

Bart Barrell and Fred Sanger of the Medical Research Council in Cambridge, England, and Giuseppe Macino and Alexander Tzagoloff of Columbia University in New York City announced in August that they had found code variations in yeast and human placental mitochondria. One nucleotide sequence that is a termination signal in cell protein

BIOLOGY. Researchers made major advances in experimental manipulation of animal embryos in 1979. Karl Illmensee of the University of Geneva in Switzerland reported in July that he had performed the first successful nucleus transplant. He transferred the nucleus of a mouse embryo cell into an egg cell and removed the egg's original genetic material. When the remodeled egg was implanted in a mouse foster mother, she gave birth to a normal mouse pup. Illmensee has not yet tried to transplant a nucleus from an adult cell into an egg. Such a feat would be the first scientifically documented case of mammalian *cloning* (creation of an exact duplicate by asexual means).

In another experiment, Pierre Soupart of Vanderbilt University, Nashville, Tenn., created an embryo with two mothers and no father. He used a standard cell-fusion technique to combine two unfertilized mouse eggs and allowed the new cell to grow in a laboratory dish. The double-egg cell divided as if it were a fertilized egg and eventually reached an apparently normal 64-cell blastocyst stage. Soupart said that if such embryos could be transferred routinely to foster mothers, farmers could produce female animals exclusively.

Biological Compasses. Scientists discovered that bacteria and pigeons carry lodestone compasses, as the ancient mariners did. Tiny magnets had been detected in the abdomens of honeybees in 1978.

Chains of microscopic magnets were found in 1979 in several species of mud-dwelling bacteria that usually swim northward, which is downward in their habitat. Richard B. Frankel of the Massachusetts Institute of Technology, Richard P. Blakemore of the University of New Hampshire, and Ralph S. Wolfe of the University of Illinois, Urbana, reported in March that they had analyzed one type of "magnetotactic" bacterium that can grow under laboratory conditions. They found that each bacterium contained a chain of about 22 cubic crystals of magnetite — an iron oxide also called lodestone. The researchers showed that the magnets help the bacteria to orient or adjust themselves in the earth's magnetic field.

Pigeons, which have a far more complex life style than bacteria, also appear to depend on a magnetic sense. Charles Walcott of State University of New York at Stony Brook and James L. Gould and J. L. Kirschvink of Princeton University reported that pigeons have magnetite particles located near the skull in a piece of tissue that also contains nerve fibers and connective tissue. Physiological and behavioral experiments were needed to determine whether those magnets are actually used in navigation.

Acoustic Microscope. Sound, like light, is now a powerful tool for examining cellular structures. Calvin F. Quate and Randy N. Johnston of Stanford University developed an acoustic microscope that produces dramatic images, depicting structures as small as 0.2 micron in diameter. A micron is one-millionth of a meter. The researchers reported in July that the instrument sends high-frequency sound waves into a sample, which partially absorbs them.

A New Theory proposes that life originated in salt-water droplets swirling above the earth before the oceans formed, rather than in the ancient seas. The idea called forth excitement, although not unanimous agreement, at a meeting sponsored by the National Aeronautics and Space Administration in August. The major break with accepted thinking came from microbial geneticist Carl R. Woese of the University of Illinois, who had proposed in 1977 that methane-producing bacteria are a third form of life, in addition to plants and animals, and probably the most primitive form. Woese's new theory proposes that water droplets are the forerunner of cell shape. He suggests that the first organisms did not absorb all their nutrients from the environment, but synthesized organic molecules using energy from sunlight, as do modern plants. Thus, the production of methane, often found near swamps, was the first metabolism. Research at the University of Texas by Allen J. Bard and Harald Reiche seemed to support Woese's theory. In those experiments, "semiconductor" particles of titanium dioxide and platinum in solution with water, ammonia, and methane captured sunlight and produced amino acids. Julie Ann Miller

In WORLD BOOK, see BIOLOGY.

BIRD, LARRY (1956–), became the most publicized college basketball player in the United States in 1979. Bird led Indiana State University, Terre Haute, to the finals of the National Collegiate Athletic Association tournament in March, where the Sycamores lost to Michigan State University, 75-64, Indiana State's only loss in 34 games. In June 1979, Bird agreed to play with the Boston Celtics of the National Basketball Association for a reported $3.25 million for five years. See BASKETBALL.

Bird was born in French Lick, Ind., on Dec. 7, 1956, and became an all-state high school basketball star at Springs Valley High School. He enrolled at Indiana University in 1974, but left there after a few weeks. In 1975, he enrolled at Indiana State. He soon attracted nationwide attention.

During his college career, Bird scored 2,850 points, an average of 30.3 per game. In 94 college games, he scored 40 or more points in a game 15 times; 30 or more, 49 times; 20 or more, 87 times; and less than 20, seven times. He was held to less than 10 points only once — by Bradley University of Peoria, Ill., in February 1979.

Bird was an all-America selection in both 1978 and 1979, and he was named the top male college player in 1979. He stands 6 feet 9½ inches (207 centimeters) tall and weighs 225 pounds (102 kilograms). Joseph P. Spohn

BIRTHS. See CENSUS; POPULATION.

BISHOP, MAURICE RUPERT (1944–), became prime minister of Grenada on March 25, 1979, after a March 13 coup inspired by his New Jewel Movement (NJM) overthrew Sir Eric M. Gairy and the Grenada United Labour Party. Bishop also assumed the offices of minister for foreign affairs, national security, home affairs, information, and culture.

Bishop was born on May 29, 1944, in St. George's, Grenada. He attended Wesley Hall School, St. George's Primary School, and the Presentation Brothers College there. Bishop then received a law degree from the University of London in 1966.

In England, Bishop became president of the West Indian Students Society. He also established the Assembly of Youth After Truth, a group of young people concerned with Grenadian issues.

Bishop returned to Grenada in 1970. In 1972, he helped form the Master Assembly for the People, which merged with the Joint Endeavor for Wealth, Education, and Liberation (JEWEL) movement in 1973 to form the NJM, a "black power" party.

In 1976, Bishop became leader of the opposition in the Grenada House of Representatives. Since 1977, he has been regional director of the Caribbean Human Rights and Legal Aid Corporation.

Bishop is married to the former Angela Redhead. They have two children. Marsha F. Goldsmith

BLINDNESS. See HANDICAPPED.

BOATING. England's Fastnet race, one of the most famous in yachting, produced the worst disaster in the history of yacht racing in August 1979. On August 13 and 14, winds up to 70 miles (113 kilometers) per hour and waves as high as 30 feet (9 meters) ravaged the fleet in the Irish Sea off the southwest coast of England. Eighteen yachtsmen, including two Americans, died, and 24 yachts valued at $4.5 million sank or were abandoned.

The biennial race attracted yachts 30 to 70 feet (9 to 21 meters) long, and only 90 of the 306 starters finished the 605 miles (974 kilometers). In a rescue effort costing $752,500, the Royal Navy saved 136 yachtsmen, including 75 by helicopter.

"Too many people took risks who should have known better," said Tom McLaughlin, a San Diego sailmaker who took part in the race. "Many small boats put to sea and sailed in conditions they knew to be dangerous. The people I respect are the ones who quit the race."

Turner Wins. Among the skippers in the Fastnet race were former British Prime Minister Edward Heath and Ted Turner, owner of the Atlanta Braves baseball team and Atlanta Hawks basketball team. Heath was badly bruised when he was thrown across the cabin, where he was navigating. Turner won the race in his 61-foot (19-meter) sloop, *Tenacious.*

On June 19, Turner and *Tenacious* won the 475-mile (765-kilometer) race from Annapolis, Md., to Newport, R.I. In January and February, Turner and *Tenacious* took fourth place overall in the Southern Ocean Racing Conference (SORC) series of six races in Florida and the Bahamas. The SORC champion was *Williwaw*, a 46-foot (14-meter) aluminum sloop owned by Seymore Sinnett of Plainfield, N.J., and sailed by Dennis Conner of San Diego. In the four SORC series from 1976 to 1979, Conner finished first twice and second twice.

Turner won the most recent America's Cup defense, in 1977, with the sloop *Courageous,* and he was preparing *Courageous* for the next defense, in 1980. A major rival for the right to represent the United States as defender appeared to be *Freedom,* a new yacht to be sailed by Conner.

In Powerboating, 56-year-old Betty Cook of Newport Beach, Calif., the world offshore champion in 1977 and United States champion in 1978, won the national championship series and world title again. She alternated two 38-foot (11-meter) boats named *Kaama* – an English-built tunnel hull and an American-built Scarab. They were powered by twin 625-horsepower MerCruiser engines.

Bill Muncey of La Mesa, Calif., 50, won the national unlimited-hydroplane series for the seventh time and its major race, the Gold Cup, for the eighth time. His boat, *Atlas Van Lines,* was powered by a Rolls-Royce 12-cylinder supercharged airplane engine.   Frank Litsky

In WORLD BOOK, see BOATING; SAILING.

BOLIVIA. A two-year effort to return to civilian government after 12 years of military rule ended in yet another military coup d'état on Nov. 1, 1979. In nationwide elections held on July 1, Hernan Siles Zuazo, a leftist who headed a coalition known as the Democratic Popular Unity, received 36 per cent of the more than 1.8 million votes cast. Second place went to Victor Paz Estenssoro, head of the center-left Revolutionary Nationalist Movement. Both men are former presidents. Since neither captured 50 per cent of the popular vote, the Constitution required that the newly elected congress of 27 senators and 117 deputies choose between the two.

Although Siles had the highest popular vote, Paz's party had more members in congress. The resulting stalemate forced the president, General David Padilla Arancibia, commander in chief of the armed forces, to postpone the ceremonial handing over of power to the civilians, scheduled for August 6. On that day, however, the congress settled on Walter Guevara Arze, president of the senate, as a compromise president pending new presidential elections in May 1980. Guevara survived one coup attempt in October, but failed to survive a second carried out on November 1 by Colonel Alberto Natusch Busch. Natusch claimed the Guevara government was controlled by Communists.

The Natusch Coup met with widespread popular resistance. Students rioted in La Paz and other cities, and the labor unions staged a general strike. General Padilla was forced into hiding after failing to persuade Natusch to return power to the civilians.

For several days, civilians clashed with army tanks in La Paz. At one point, Natusch ordered air force planes to strafe demonstrators in the capital. The Bolivian Human Rights Commission claimed that 600 persons were killed, wounded, or missing. On November 16, Natusch agreed to turn the government over to Lydia Gueiler Tejada, president of the House of Deputies, until the May 1980 elections.

The Economy. The coup focused attention on Bolivia's serious economic problems. The treasury had no foreign-exchange reserves, and the trade balance was in deficit by some $200 million. Foreign debt under the military had risen to $3 billion, and there was little possibility that Bolivia would be able to come up with the $300 million in service charges due before the end of the year. However, the U.S., which had cut off $56 million in aid to Bolivia to protest the Natusch coup, restored it when Gueiler took over. She announced that her first priority would be to renegotiate the debt.   Everett G. Martin

See also LATIN AMERICA (Facts in Brief Table). In WORLD BOOK, see BOLIVIA.

BOND. See STOCKS AND BONDS.

BOOKS. See CANADIAN LITERATURE; LITERATURE; LITERATURE FOR CHILDREN; POETRY; PUBLISHING.

BOPHUTHATSWANA. See AFRICA.

BOTANY. Biologist James D. Lawrey of George Mason University, Fairfax, Va., and botanist Mason E. Hale, Jr., of the Smithsonian Institution in Washington, D.C., reported in April 1979 that significant amounts of automobile exhaust halt the growth of young lichen plants. But once the plants reach a mature stage, they can survive and grow despite the pollution. The researchers studied the species *Pseudoparmelia baltimorensis* on two islands in the Potomac River in Maryland. Lichens consist of both algal and fungal organisms that coexist and cannot exist separately. These plants are often used to measure environmental quality because they are long-lived and tolerate a wide range of stresses, both natural and manufactured. A major interstate highway runs through one of the islands used in the study, while the other is relatively free from exhaust.

The larger, more mature *thalli* (plant bodies) grew at about the same rate on both islands. However, the smaller, younger plants – less than 0.1 square millimeter (0.0016 square inch) – on the island subjected to automobile exhaust showed a major drop in growth rate. Young lichens on the less polluted island showed no reduction in growth rate and grew almost three times larger than the young plants on the polluted island.

Because lead is readily measured, the researchers determined concentrations of lead in the lichens.

They reported that lead concentrations were significantly higher in lichens on the polluted island, but pointed out that the difference in the size of the plants may be caused by any of the pollutants in automobile exhaust.

Polar Bears are white, and this makes sense for camouflage purposes in their natural snow-covered environment. However, three polar bears in the San Diego Zoo turned green in 1978, and scientists were puzzled. They expected to find tiny algae plants clinging to the bears' hair, but did not. Phycologist Ralph A. Lewin of the Scripps Institution of Oceanography and zoologist Philip T. Robinson of the San Diego Zoo reported in March 1979 that they had solved the mystery; they found algae inside the bears' hairs.

The algae in the hairs were of a previously unknown type. Testing indicated that the new form of algae is a member of the phylum *Cyanophyta*, or the blue-green algae. The algae apparently entered through *lateral* (crosswise) ducts leading from the outside of the hair to the hollow area inside. Lewin and Robinson theorized that the algae may have eaten parts of the keratin surface of the hairs, thus creating the lateral ducts. But incubating hairs with a pure culture of the algae showed no evidence of keratin digestion.   Barbara N. Benson

In WORLD BOOK, see ALGAE; BOTANY; LICHEN.

BOTSWANA. See AFRICA.

BOWLING. The professional bowling tour for men continued to grow in the United States in 1979, with more prize money and more television exposure. As usual, the stars included Mark Roth of North Arlington, N.J., and Earl Anthony of Kent, Wash.

Roth led in tournament earnings and scoring average from 1977 to 1979, and Anthony dominated the mid-1970s. From February to October 1979, the 28-year-old Roth captured six tournaments – in Florissant, Mo.; Overland Park, Kans.; San Jose, Calif.; Portland, Ore.; Greenwood, Ind.; and Fairview Park, Ohio. He earned $124,517.

Anthony won a tournament in Garden City, N.Y., and consistently finished among the leaders. He was the runner-up in the two most prestigious tournaments – the $125,000 United States Open in April in Windsor Locks, Conn., and the $100,000 Professional Bowlers Association (PBA) championship in June in Las Vegas, Nev. Joe Berardi of Pearl River, N.Y., won the Open, and 19-year-old Mike Aulby of Indianapolis took the PBA title – the first tour victory for each.

The PBA Tour consisted of 34 tournaments with purses totaling almost $3.75 million, the highest ever. The richest competition was the $150,000 Tournament of Champions in April in Akron, Ohio. George Pappas of Charlotte, N.C., won.

The PBA tour was televised nationally for the 18th straight year, a longevity record for sports surpassed

A cube-shaped watermelon was developed by a Tokyo designer, not by a botanist. He started the plant in a plastic box to get the shape.

only by college football. The winter tournaments were shown by the American Broadcasting Companies, the summer tour by CBS Inc., and the autumn competition by the new Entertainment and Sports Programming Network, which serviced cable television in 43 states.

Nineteen-year-old John Johns enjoyed an astonishing season in Canton, Ohio. Bowling for the first time in a league sanctioned by the American Bowling Congress (ABC), he averaged 240.09 pins for 99 games, the highest average in the ABC's 83 years.

Anthony was named to the men's all-America team for the eighth time. Also on the team were Roth, Pappas, Marshall Holman of Medford, Ore., and Larry Laub of Santa Rosa, Calif.

The Women's Tour. The Women's Professional Bowlers Association conducted a more modest tour, with fewer tournaments and less prize money. The most glamorous competition was the Women's International Bowling Congress (WIBC) Queens tournament, held in May during the WIBC championships in Tucson, Ariz. Donna Adamek, 22, of Monrovia, Calif., won in a field of 401.

The women's all-America team chosen by the *Bowlers Journal* consisted of Adamek; Pat Costello of Union City, Calif.; Vesma Grinfelds of San Francisco; Betty Morris of Stockton, Calif.; and Virginia Norton of South Gate, Calif.   Frank Litsky

In WORLD BOOK, see BOWLING.

World Champion Boxers			
Division	Champion	Country	Year Won
Heavyweight	†Larry Holmes	U.S.A.	1978
	*John Tate	U.S.A.	1979
Light-heavyweight	*Marvin Johnson	U.S.A.	1979
	†Matthew Saad Muhammad	U.S.A.	1979
Middleweight	†*Vito Antuofermo	U.S.A.	1979
Junior-middleweight	*Ayud Kalule	Uganda	1979
	†Maurice Hope	England	1979
Welterweight	*José Cuevas	Mexico	1976
	†Ray Leonard	U.S.A.	1979
Junior-welterweight	*Antonio Cervantes	Colombia	1977
	†Kim Sang-Hyun	South Korea	1978
Lightweight	†Jim Watt	Scotland	1979
	*Ernesto Espana	Venezuela	1979
Junior-lightweight	*Samuel Serrano	Puerto Rico	1976
	†Alexis Arguello	Nicaragua	1978
Featherweight	†Danny Lopez	U.S.A.	1976
	*Eusebio Pedroza	Panama	1978
Junior-featherweight	†Wilfred Gomez	Puerto Rico	1977
	*Ricardo Cardona	Colombia	1978
Bantamweight	*Jorge Lujan	Panama	1977
	†Lupe Pintor	Mexico	1979
Flyweight	*Luis Ibarra	Panama	1979
	†Park Chan Hee	South Korea	1979
Junior-flyweight	*Yoko Gushiken	Japan	1976
	†Kim Sung Jun	South Korea	1978

†Recognized by World Boxing Council
*Recognized by World Boxing Association

BOXING. Since 1964, Muhammad Ali of Los Angeles was either world heavyweight champion or about to become the champion again. In 1979, at age 37 and badly overweight at 250 pounds (113 kilograms), Ali retired.

He had retired in 1975, 1976, and 1978, only to fight again, and he had become the first to win the heavyweight title three times. But this time, he sent a letter of resignation to the World Boxing Association (WBA), seemingly ending a career marked by controversy, turmoil, and incredible popularity.

With Ali's departure, the WBA crowned John Tate of Knoxville, Tenn., as his successor. The World Boxing Council (WBC) recognized Larry Holmes of Easton, Pa. Both were unbeaten as pros.

Holmes and Tate. Holmes knocked out three challengers during the year—Osvaldo Ocasio of Puerto Rico in seven rounds on March 23 in Las Vegas, Nev.; Mike Weaver of Las Vegas in 12 rounds on June 22 in New York City; and Earnie Shavers of Warren, Ohio, in 11 rounds on September 28 in Las Vegas. Despite his virtuosity, Holmes did not approach Ali as a television attraction or public favorite.

To find a new champion, the WBA conducted an elimination tournament among Tate, former champion Leon Spinks of St. Louis, and Gerrie Coetzee and Kallie Knoetze of South Africa. Tate stopped Knoetze in eight rounds on June 2 in Mmabatho,

Bophuthatswana, and Coetzee stopped Spinks in one round on June 24 in Monte Carlo, Monaco. Then Tate won a decision over Coetzee for the title on October 20 in Pretoria, South Africa.

Other Champions. The world champion with the longest continuous reign was Roberto Duran of Panama, lightweight king since 1972. Duran gave up the title in 1979; he had been struggling to make the 135-pound (60-kilogram) limit. Duran immediately began fighting as a welterweight, where the limit is 147 pounds (67 kilograms).

Unbeaten Wilfred Benitez of Puerto Rico won the WBC welterweight title by outpointing Carlos Palomino of Huntington Beach, Calif., on January 14 in San Juan, Puerto Rico. But he lost the title on November 30 to Sugar Ray Leonard of Palmer Park, Md., on a 15th-round knockout in Las Vegas, Nev. Light-heavyweight champions kept busy. Victor Galindez of Argentina regained his WBA title by stopping Mike Rossman of Turnersville, N.J., in 10 rounds on April 14 in New Orleans. Matthew Saad Muhammad (Matthew Franklin) of Philadelphia stopped Marvin Johnson of Indianapolis, Ind., in eight rounds on April 22 in Indianapolis. Then Johnson knocked out Galindez in 11 on November 30 in New Orleans.   Frank Litsky

In WORLD BOOK, see ALI, MUHAMMAD; BOXING.
BOY SCOUTS. See YOUTH ORGANIZATIONS.
BOYS' CLUBS. See YOUTH ORGANIZATIONS.

Rock-hurling protesters, in support of a strike by bank workers demanding higher pay, shatter windows of a bank in São Paulo, Brazil, in September.

BRAZIL. General Joao Baptista de Oliveira Figueiredo took over as president for a six-year term on March 15, 1979. He vowed to continue the process begun by his predecessor, Ernesto Geisel, of gradually returning the country to democratic government.

An important step in the process had been concluded in 1978 when a government decree was allowed to expire that had permitted the president to shut down Congress, overrule the courts, dismiss elected officials, or deprive citizens of their political rights. A further step was taken on August 28 when Figueiredo proclaimed a general amnesty for all those who had been dismissed, stripped of their rights, or exiled for political crimes. Only those who had been condemned for terrorism, bank robbery, kidnapping, and assault were excluded from the amnesty.

The Economy. Politics could not match the problems that gripped the economy, however. Crop failures, rising world oil prices, and climbing interest rates on Brazil's $49-billion foreign debt combined to form a bleak picture. Exports fell $2 billion behind imports, and oil import costs rose from $4.5 billion in 1978 to nearly $7 billion, even as the country was forced to borrow to pay the $4.6 billion due on its debt payments. Since 70 per cent of Brazil's debt had floating interest rates, the tight money policy instituted by the United States Federal Reserve Bank

alone cost Brazil $1 billion in higher interest. The inflation rate, 40 per cent in 1978 and targeted for 36 per cent in 1979, soared to nearly 80 per cent.

On August 10, Mario Henrique Simonsen, minister of planning and the official in charge of the economy, resigned abruptly. He was replaced by Minister of Agriculture Antonio Delfim Netto, who had directed the economy during the early 1970s. Netto pledged to curb inflationary government spending and boost exports, particularly of agricultural products, by 30 per cent in 1980.

Labor Unions, freed of most government restraints, struck for higher wages throughout the year. More than 160,000 metallurgical and auto workers in São Paulo went on strike on March 13, paralyzing the nation's auto industry. They demanded a 77 per cent increase, considerably more than the 44 per cent limit the government had set, and rejected a subsequent government offer of 63 per cent because it did not compensate them for time lost during the strike. After 10 days, troops occupied the union's offices and stripped its officers of power. The workers were ordered back to work without resolving the issues.

Some 40,000 construction workers fared better in Belo Horizonte when they struck on July 29, demanding 110 per cent wage increases. The strike was declared illegal after they rejected an employers' offer of 78 per cent increases. However, the local labor tribunal declared on August 3 that the strike was legal, and it doubled the workers' wages to end the walkout. Clashes with police during the strike left one person dead and 50 injured.

Protest Price Hikes. Nationwide civilian protests and temporary stoppages by taxi drivers in Rio de Janeiro and São Paulo greeted a 58 per cent increase in gasoline prices that raised them to $2.60 per gallon (3.8 liters) for regular grade. The taxi drivers were granted fare increases of up to 50 per cent, but they struck again demanding subsidized gasoline and lower fares because of a sharp drop in passengers they experienced.

The Brazilian delegate to a United Nations energy meeting in Montreal, Canada, declared on November 29 that "50 per cent of Brazil's export earnings is spent on petroleum and the other 50 per cent goes toward paying our foreign debt. We must stop this situation." By 1990, he claimed, all vehicles in the country would be burning alcohol made from sugar cane as the result of a $10.4-billion program to build 228 alcohol distilleries throughout the country and increase acreage planted in sugar cane. However, oil experts indicated that the effort, if successful, would meet only 15 per cent of the country's petroleum needs.   Everett G. Martin

See also LATIN AMERICA (Facts in Brief Table). In WORLD BOOK, see BRAZIL.

BRIDGE. See BUILDING AND CONSTRUCTION.

BRIDGE, CONTRACT. In a final match marked by alternating bursts of scoring, the United States won the world team championship in Rio de Janeiro, Brazil, in October 1979. The victory margin over Italy was only five points, smallest in tournament history. Members of the winning team were Eddie Kantar and Bill Eisenberg of Los Angeles, Paul Soloway of Seattle, and Bob Goldman, Mike Passell, and Malcolm Brachman of Dallas.

At the American Contract Bridge League (ACBL) spring championships in March in Norfolk, Va., the Harold A. Vanderbilt knockout team championship was won by Eddie Wold of Houston; Mark Lair of Canyon, Tex.; Cliff Russell of Miami, Fla.; Richard Freeman and Lou Bluhm of Atlanta, Ga.; and Tom Sanders of Nashville, Tenn.

The Spingold knockout team title was won in August in Las Vegas, Nev., by the Aces: Bob Wolff and Bob Hamman of Dallas; Ira Rubin of Paramus, N.J.; and Fred Hamilton of North Hollywood, Calif. The Spingold event was the largest in bridge history, attracting 18,515 tables of players, 107 more than the 1978 summer nationals.

The ACBL expelled two players, Steve Sion of Margate, Fla., and Allan Cokin of Pompano Beach, Fla., in July for "prearranged improper communication" at a grand national team play-off in Atlanta in June.   Theodore M. O'Leary

In WORLD BOOK, see BRIDGE, CONTRACT.

BRITISH COLUMBIA voters returned the free-enterprise Social Credit government of Premier William R. Bennett to power again on May 10, 1979. Bennett's party, in office since 1975, won 31 seats in the 57-seat legislature. The socialist New Democratic Party, under former Premier David Barrett, won 26 seats, a gain of eight, and an unprecedented 46 per cent of the vote. It gained at the expense of the Liberals and Conservatives, who were eliminated from the legislature for the first time.

A popular Social Credit measure was the offering of five free shares in the British Columbia Resources Investment Corporation to every resident of the province. A government-owned holding company, the corporation operates pulp mills, sawmills, and pipelines and holds oil and gas rights. Residents were offered 15 million shares, and 87 per cent of the population applied for the certificates. In August, the shares began to be traded on stock exchanges, where demand for them was strong.

William A.C. Bennett, Premier Bennett's father and premier of British Columbia from 1952 to 1972, died on February 23. Prime Minister Joe Clark promised on September 21 to transfer federal control of offshore oil and mineral rights to the province. His action satisfied a long-sought objective of British Columbians.   David M.L. Farr

See also CANADA. In WORLD BOOK, see BRITISH COLUMBIA.

BROWN, EDMUND GERALD (JERRY), JR. (1938-   ), governor of California, became a candidate in November 1979 for the 1980 Democratic presidential nomination. In 1976, Brown won primary elections in California, Maryland, and Nevada in his unsuccessful campaign for the nomination.

Since his election as governor in 1975, Brown has been a newsworthy and controversial public figure. Critics have sometimes labeled him a political opportunist. He made a ringing conservative endorsement of Proposition 13, to cut state and local authority to tax, but only after it was passed by California voters in 1978. Then in 1979, he joined liberals and radicals in denouncing nuclear power.

Brown was born on April 7, 1938, in San Francisco. His father, Edmund G. (Pat) Brown, a lawyer, served as governor of California from 1959 to 1967. Jerry Brown entered a Jesuit seminary in 1956, but he left in 1960 before completing studies for the priesthood. He received a bachelor's degree in classics from the University of California, Berkeley, in 1961, and a law degree from Yale University, New Haven, Conn., in 1964.

In 1966, Brown began practicing law in Los Angeles. As California's secretary of state from 1970 to 1974, he reformed its campaign practices law.

Brown is unmarried. His social life and Spartan style of living have attracted much attention in the media.   Patricia Dragisic

BUILDING AND CONSTRUCTION. New and widespread interest in solar construction, spurred by the shortage of conventional heating fuels, keynoted construction in the United States in 1979. Financial incentives for research and development proliferated, most of them in the form of income and property tax breaks. California, the acknowledged leader in solar development, had projects totaling some $175 million underway. Throughout the country, even in the cold Northeast, some 40,000 units were under construction.

Codes and Specifications. A group of five major national building-code organizations headed by the Council of American Building Officials prepared a tentative model solar-construction code in April 1979. Industry representatives and building-code officials throughout the United States contributed to the project, which covers requirements for performance and installation of solar system components.

The National Bureau of Standards (NBS) reported in 1979 that it had developed a system for evaluating the fire safety of hospitals and health-care facilities. The NBS believes the new system can significantly reduce the cost of meeting accepted fire-safety standards. The system, which permits the comparison of 13 construction factors that affect fire safety, is an alternative to the widely used Life Safety Code of the National Fire Protection Association.

Spending for Construction in the United States rose 7 per cent in 1979 to an estimated $221.5 billion. Spending for housing units, exclusive of mobile homes, reached an estimated $98.5 billion, up from the $92 billion spent in 1978. Spurred by high costs of new construction and more than $1.6 billion a year in federal subsidies, the rehabilitation market was booming. *Engineering News-Record*'s annual construction cost index for 20 major cities in the United States rose 6 per cent.

Construction unemployment dipped to 8.5 per cent in July, compared with the July 1978 rate of 9.5 per cent. Although the government's suggested wage-price guideline program and open-shop gains helped keep wage demands down, settlements in the late spring and summer pushed building trades wages considerably higher. Hourly wage rates for laborers across the United States averaged $11.10 in the month of September.

New Techniques. Work began in August on an innovative 44-story apartment tower over the Museum of Modern Art in New York City. The structure, planned for completion in 1981, will be one of the city's tallest cast-in-place concrete-frame buildings. With its base resting above the eastern half of an eight-story addition to the museum, also part of the project, the glass-clad tower – 100 feet (30 meters) square – will feature up to 275 luxury condominium apartments. The structural system will consist of cast-in-place concrete columns of varying thickness spaced at irregular intervals on each floor to permit varying apartment layouts. A series of steel transfer girders just above the top floor of the museum extension will pick up the tower column heads. The museum extension, also clad with a glass curtain wall, will double the existing gallery space.

Plans were announced in May for transforming 36 grain silos into a 260-room luxury hotel, a final project in the renovation of a Quaker Oats Company factory in Akron, Ohio. The hotel, to be run by the Hilton Hotel Corporation, will be part of a complex that already includes offices, restaurants, and retail shops. Each of Quaker Square Hilton's circular rooms will occupy an entire floor in the renovated silos and will be 40 per cent larger than conventional accommodations. The concrete silos, which were built in 1932, are arranged in three rows that form an "L" pattern. The lobby and the hotel's convention and banquet facilities will be housed in a single-story structure to be built at one end of the hotel complex.

Bridges and Dams. The Jacksonville (Fla.) Transportation Authority called for bids in October on a cable-stayed bridge with a main span of 1,300 feet (395 meters) to cross the St. Johns River. The contract, estimated at from $65 million to $80-million, covers only the principal three-span river crossing, part of a planned 13-mile (21-kilometer) $150-million Dame Point Expressway.

A giant dam being built in northern China's Hupeh Province will control the waters of the Luanho River and produce electricity for Tientsin.

In a unique rebuilding project, the center section of the Grant Bridge over the Ohio River at Portsmouth, Ohio, is removed for cable repair.

The Oregon Department of Transportation awarded the prime contract in May for the largest and longest concrete box-girder bridge to be built in the United States. The north-channel portion of the Interstate 205 Columbia River crossing between Washington and Oregon will be erected in a joint venture headed by S. J. Groves & Sons Company of Minneapolis, Minn., at a cost of $71.6 million. The 2,770-foot (840-meter) crossing will consist of a pair of structures with roadways 60 feet (18 meters) wide and spans ranging up to 600 feet (180 meters) long.

After five years' work, Russian engineers completed drawings and specifications early in June for the Rogun rock-filled dam in the Soviet Republic of Tadzhikstan. At 1,098 feet (335 meters), this structure in a mountainous area of Central Asia bordering Afghanistan and China will be the highest dam in the world. Plans call for placing more than 91 million cubic yards (70 million cubic meters) of material in a narrow hard-rock canyon on the Vakhsh River. Early work has begun in an area about 40 miles (64 kilometers) upstream from the nearly completed 980-foot (300-meter) high earth-fill Nurek Dam, the world's highest.

Chinese planners enlisted the advice of Japanese engineers on their planned $30-billion dam-construction program. The project calls for the building of four large dams and hydroelectric power stations with an estimated capacity of 32,000 mega-

watts. Two of the dams will be built at Lungmen and Taliushu on the Huang Ho and two at San-hsia and Hsiang-chia-pa on the Yangtze River. First-stage construction of the gravity concrete Ko-chou-pa Dam, the first to be built on the main stream of the Yangtze, was nearing completion in 1979.

Tunnels. One of the world's longest vehicular tunnels, the Enayama Tunnel on the Chuo Expressway in central Japan, was opened to traffic early in January. The 5.3-mile (8.5-kilometer) tunnel, under construction since July 1966, cost $373 million.

After a six-month dispute with federal highway authorities, Baltimore officials agreed to go along with federal insistence on a steel tubular design for a Baltimore Harbor tunnel, instead of the rectangular, reinforced-concrete underwater tunnel they had planned. The steel tunnel will carry an eight-lane extension of Interstate 95 under the harbor between Fort McHenry and Canton, Md. It is scheduled to be completed in 1982.

Rapid Transit. The Metropolitan Atlanta (Ga.) Rapid Transit Authority opened the first line of the city's new rapid transit system, a 6.7-mile (10.8-kilometer) subway link, in July. The system will include 53 miles (95 kilometers) of rail line, including subway, at-grade, and elevated lines and 8 miles (13 kilometers) of busways.   Mary E. Jessup

In WORLD BOOK, see BRIDGE; BUILDING CONSTRUCTION; DAM; TUNNEL.

BULGARIA remained preoccupied with economic questions in 1979 but also managed to play an active diplomatic role in the Balkans and beyond. West German Chancellor Helmut Schmidt visited Bulgaria in May to discuss economics, particularly Bulgaria's trade deficit with West Germany, $207-million at the end of 1978. State Council Chairman Todor Zhivkov went to Greece in April to discuss industrial cooperation and, during a July visit to Turkey, signed agreements on visas and on automobile transportation between the two countries. Zhivkov signed treaties of friendship and cooperation with Vietnam, Laos, and Cambodia in September and October.

Yugoslavia's President Josip Broz Tito criticized Bulgaria on April 17 for denying the legitimacy of the Yugoslav Republic of Macedonia. Zhivkov repeated in an April 27 speech that Bulgaria claimed no Yugoslav territory and recognized the Republic of Macedonia within Yugoslavia. Senior Bulgarian Communist Party Politburo member Pencho Kubadinski visited Yugoslavia for an inconclusive foreign policy discussion.

Bulgaria normalized its relations with the Roman Catholic Church in May by allowing it to set up a Diocese of Sofia under Bishop Bogdan Dobranov and to appoint Samuel Dijoundrine, a parish priest, as bishop of Nikopol.

Russia's Supreme Soviet Presidium Chairman Leonid I. Brezhnev visited in January, in the wake of 1978 visits to Yugoslavia and Romania by China's Premier Hua Kuo-feng (Hua Guofeng in the Pinyin alphabet adopted by China on January 1).

New Faces. Three persons joined the Politburo in July – Peko Takov, deputy chairman of state council since 1975; Zhivkov's daughter, Lyudmila Zhivkova, minister of culture since 1975; and Todor Bozhinov, secretary of the central committee since 1978. Bulgaria closed its ministry of agriculture in April and passed its activities to the new National Agro-Industrial Union, whose Chairman Vasil Tsanov received the rank of minister. Zhivkov told the new department in April that the old ministry was too large and too bureaucratic.

Business and Prices. Industrial production in the first six months of 1979 was 6.7 per cent higher than in the first half of 1978, and foreign trade grew 16 per cent. On May 21, the government decreed an odd-even license-plate plan for private automobiles to use the roads and raised the gasoline price by 50 per cent to $4.25 per gallon (3.8 liters). On November 12, Bulgaria doubled bread prices and increased the prices of milk and other dairy products, sugar, rice, beans, and oil by 35 per cent; wine and liquor by 45 per cent; and building materials by 40 per cent. The prices of coal, electricity, and telephone service also went up.   Chris Cviic

See also EUROPE (Facts in Brief Table). In WORLD BOOK, see BULGARIA; MACEDONIA.

BURMA. War with Communist and tribal forces dragged on in 1979. Also, the black market remained an essential part of the economy, with the shelves of state stores nearly bare. It was estimated that smugglers – taking gems, tea, and rice into Thailand and bringing back essentials – accounted for $300 million of Burma's foreign trade.

The nation continued to be governed by the military, led by President U Ne Win, a general. Foreign economists agreed that the army was doing a poor job. Corruption and breaches of human rights went on undiminished. A foreign correspondent reported that "many" of the 10,000 convict laborers working on a new highway apparently were political prisoners.

Civil War. Huge areas, especially along the borders with the People's Republic of China and Thailand, were controlled by insurgents. The strongest force, more than 10,000 armed men, was directed by the Burmese Communist Party (BCP). China has long armed and trained the BCP, but its aid declined in 1979.

Elsewhere, the Burmese army was fighting smaller forces of the Shan, Kachin, and Karen hill tribes, which wanted autonomy. These forces financed their activities by smuggling drugs. The tribes control the Golden Triangle, the mountainous area where the borders of Burma, Thailand, and Laos meet. As much as two-thirds of the worldwide illegal opium supply may originate in the Golden Triangle.

Slide Ended? An International Monetary Fund report suggested that Burma's years of stagnation may be ending. Under World Bank pressure, the state had doubled the low prices it was paying farmers for rice. Also, the workers were offered incentives for increasing production. After a long decline, the rice output began to rise, and it ultimately exceeded 10 million metric tons (11 million short tons) in 1978-1979, giving promise of renewed large exports.

After years of rejecting foreign aid, Burma began to seek such assistance. In 1979, foreign credits totaled about $300 million, mostly from Western nations that also agreed to extend $350 million in long-range assistance.

Nonaligned Split. Foreign Minister Myint Maung told the United Nations General Assembly on September 28 that Burma, disappointed with the results of the nonaligned nations summit meeting in Cuba, was leaving the nonaligned nations movement. Burma had called for a statement of "inviolable principles" of nonalignment, but the issue was ignored and the meeting ended on a pro-Russian theme.   Mark Gayn

See also ASIA (Facts in Brief Table). In WORLD BOOK, see BURMA.

BURUNDI. See AFRICA.

BUS. See TRANSIT; TRANSPORTATION.

BUSH, GEORGE H. W. (1924-   ), became a candidate for the Republican presidential nomination on May 1, 1979. Bush cited his experience in the party, his record in foreign and domestic affairs, and his business background as president and chairman of an oil-drilling company.

Bush was born on June 12, 1924, in Milton, Mass., the son of a Republican senator. He served as a U.S. Navy pilot in World War II and then entered Yale University in New Haven, Conn. He graduated in 1948 with a B.A. degree in economics and entered the oil business. In 1954, he founded a drilling company in Texas.

Bush moved to Houston in 1959 and soon became active in Republican politics there. He was elected chairman of the Harris County Republican organization there in 1963. He ran unsuccessfully for the U.S. Senate in 1964 and 1970, but was elected to the U.S. House of Representatives in 1966 and 1968.

Bush was named representative to the United Nations in 1971, chairman of the Republican National Committee in 1973, and envoy to the People's Republic of China in 1974. He directed the Central Intelligence Agency from January 1976 until January 1977.

Bush married Barbara Pierce in 1945. They have four sons and a daughter.   Jay Myers

BUSINESS. See ECONOMICS; LABOR; MANUFACTURING.

BYRNE, JANE M. (1934-   ), was elected mayor of Chicago on April 3, 1979, the first woman to gain that office. She won by the largest majority in the city's history, with 82 per cent of the vote. But her most astounding victory came in February, when she defeated the powerful Chicago Democratic Party machine and Mayor Michael A. Bilandic in the primary. See CHICAGO; ELECTIONS (Close-Up).

Byrne was born on May 24, 1934, in Chicago, the second of the six children of Edward and Katherine M. Burke. She received a B.A. degree in 1955 from Barat College of the Sacred Heart in nearby Lake Forest, Ill., and did graduate work in education at the University of Illinois, Chicago Circle.

Byrne entered politics in 1960 as secretary-treasurer for the Chicago campaign headquarters of presidential candidate John F. Kennedy. In 1963, Mayor Richard J. Daley named her to a post in the city's Anti-Poverty program, and in 1968 she became the first commissioner of the city Department of Consumer Sales, Weights, and Measures. She held that post until her dismissal in March 1977 by Bilandic, who became mayor after Daley died in December 1976.

She married William P. Byrne in 1956. They had one daughter, Kathy. A U.S. Marine Corps pilot, William Byrne was killed in a plane crash in 1959. Jane Byrne married Jay McMullen, a Chicago newspaperman, in 1978.   Edward G. Nash

CABINET, UNITED STATES. President Jimmy Carter undertook a massive reorganization of his Cabinet on July 17, 1979, when he asked for the resignations of all of the department secretaries. By July 24, he had accepted the resignations of five Cabinet members—Joseph A. Califano, Jr., secretary of health, education, and welfare (HEW); W. Michael Blumenthal, secretary of the Treasury; Griffin B. Bell, attorney general; James R. Schlesinger, secretary of energy; and Brock Adams, secretary of transportation. Bell and Blumenthal had planned to leave office, but the others were, in effect, fired.

New Department Heads. President Carter appointed Deputy Attorney General Benjamin R. Civiletti to succeed Bell. Patricia Roberts Harris, secretary of housing and urban development (HUD), became HEW secretary; and Moon Landrieu, former mayor of New Orleans, replaced Harris as HUD secretary. Other new Cabinet members installed were Neil E. Goldschmidt, former mayor of Portland, Ore., as secretary of transportation; Charles W. Duncan, Jr., former deputy defense secretary, as secretary of energy; and G. William Miller, chairman of the Federal Reserve System, as secretary of the Treasury.

The Cabinet was again disrupted on October 3 by the resignation of Juanita M. Kreps, secretary of commerce, who cited personal reasons for leaving

Patricia Roberts Harris, former secretary of housing and urban development, became secretary of health, education, and welfare on August 3.

her post. President Carter on November 15 named Philip M. Klutznick, a Chicago businessman, to replace her.

New Department. President Carter on October 17 signed a bill creating a Cabinet-level Department of Education. The new department will be built around the Office of Education, formerly part of HEW, with an initial budget of about $14 billion and a staff of more than 17,000 persons. The department will also administer schools for overseas dependents now operated by the Department of Defense, the Department of Agriculture graduate school, certain science programs run by the National Science Foundation, college nursing loans administered by HUD, and migrant-worker education programs handled by the Department of Labor.

Shirley M. Hufstedler, judge of the U.S. Ninth Circuit Court of Appeals, was appointed by Carter on October 30 to head the new department when it becomes effective early in 1980. At that time, HEW will be renamed the Department of Health and Human Services. Beverly Merz

See also CIVILETTI, BENJAMIN R.; DUNCAN, CHARLES W.; GOLDSCHMIDT, NEIL E.; HUFSTEDLER, SHIRLEY M.; KLUTZNICK, PHILIP M.; LANDRIEU, MOON. In WORLD BOOK, see CABINET; HEALTH, EDUCATION, AND WELFARE, DEPARTMENT OF (HEW).

CALIFORNIA. See LOS ANGELES; STATE GOV'T.

Vietnamese troops and Cambodian rebels take over the Royal Palace in Phnom Penh, Cambodia's capital, in January.

CAMBODIA suffered the agonies of war again in 1979, and the brutality of contending armies brought greater suffering to the civilian population. The conflict disrupted agriculture, causing widespread famine. United Nations (UN) Secretary-General Kurt Waldheim said in October that perhaps half the population had been killed, and that at least 2.5 million persons were in danger of death.

Vietnamese troops and Cambodian guerrillas captured Phnom Penh, the Cambodian capital, on January 7. The next day, the Kampuchean (Cambodian) United Front for National Salvation announced that Prime Minister Pol Pot's government of Democratic Kampuchea had been overthrown. The front created on Dec. 3, 1978, under Vietnamese auspices, formed the People's Revolutionary Council of Kampuchea to run the country. It was headed by Heng Samrin, identified as a former provincial official in Pol Pot's regime.

Cambodia's former leader, Prince Norodom Sihanouk, was released by Pol Pot from three years' house arrest on January 5 and flown to Peking (Beijing in the phonetic Pinyin alphabet China adopted on January 1). Sihanouk denounced both the barbarity of Pol Pot's rule and Vietnam's "flagrant aggression." He asked the UN not to recognize the Heng Samrin regime. The UN General Assembly voted 71-35 on September 21 to continue to recognize Pol Pot's right to Cambodia's UN seat.

Guerrilla War. After losing the capital, Pol Pot disappeared into the countryside to lead his Khmer Rouge guerrilla forces in scattered fighting. Vietnamese troops pushed Khmer Rouge forces against the border of Thailand in May and June and again in October after the rainy season. Thai sources said that minimal aid from China was reaching the guerrillas, who were desperately short of food and medicine.

A court in Phnom Penh tried Pol Pot and a deputy in absentia and sentenced Pol Pot to death on August 19 for the deaths of more than 3 million persons. The regime said that he had "massacred" former officials and soldiers of the Lon Nol administration, overthrown in 1975.

Help for Starving. The Heng Samrin regime blamed Pol Pot for creating the conditions that caused widespread famine, but made no mention of the continuing warfare as a cause. Initially, the Heng Samrin regime resisted relief efforts. The UN Children's Fund and the International Committee of the Red Cross delivered food, medicine, and other supplies, but distribution was poor. United States officials estimated that thousands were dying monthly late in 1979. Henry S. Bradsher

See also ASIA (Facts in Brief Table). In WORLD BOOK, see CAMBODIA.

CAMEROON. See AFRICA.

CAMP FIRE GIRLS. See YOUTH ORGANIZATIONS.

CANADA

Canada saw the defeat of the Liberal government headed by Pierre Elliott Trudeau on May 22, 1979, its replacement by a minority Progressive Conservative (PC) administration led by Charles Joseph (Joe) Clark, and the defeat of that administration on December 13 after only a little more than six months in office. These dramatic events plunged the country into a winter election, scheduled for Feb. 18, 1980.

The federal elections in May administered a severe check to the dominance of the Liberal Party and to Trudeau's personal fortunes. The 59-year-old Trudeau, in power for 11 years, campaigned on the claim that he and his government could best maintain the country's unity, but the message failed to move English-speaking Canadians. His defeat came not so much from a rival as from the impression that he headed a government that was exhausted and no longer capable of providing leadership. On November 21, Trudeau announced his resignation as Liberal Party leader, but December's events led to uncertainty as to who would lead the Liberals in the February 1980 election. The party caucus, meeting for 10 hours on December 14, formally asked Trudeau to reconsider and stay on as leader. He agreed to do so. See TRUDEAU, PIERRE ELLIOTT.

The Canadian electorate voted against Trudeau and his colleagues in 1979 to bring into office a man 20 years Trudeau's junior. Clark, national PC leader since 1976, and his party won 136 seats in the 282-seat House of Commons, 6 seats short of an absolute majority. The Liberals captured 114 seats, down from the 141 they had taken in 1974.

Clark and the Conservatives offered the image of a fresh and resourceful team to cope with the country's difficulties. The emphasis on "team" was deliberate. Clark advocated an approach he called "consensus politics," emphasizing cooperation among the national and provincial governments to achieve common goals. He urged a return to restraint in government programs and spending, claiming that swollen federal expenditures contributed to inflation. He asserted that government corporations, such as the petroleum company Petro-Canada, should be returned to private ownership.

Clark also said that the federal government's bias toward Ontario and Quebec must be corrected to give the Western provinces a larger voice in national decisions. The Conservatives promised tax cuts and advocated the United States practice of allowing mortgage interest and real estate taxes to be deducted from taxable income.

Victorious Progressive Conservative leader Joe Clark and his wife greet backers after the party's May 22 election win makes him prime minister.

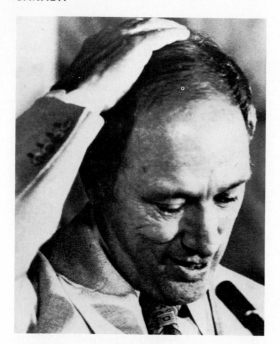

Outgoing Prime Minister Pierre Elliott Trudeau gives a pensive speech in Ottawa after the May 22 election defeat of his Liberal Party.

The Conservatives' march to power was heralded by a succession of provincial victories. One after another, the provinces turned Liberal governments out of office: Manitoba in 1977, Nova Scotia in 1978, and the last Liberal provincial government, Prince Edward Island, just a few weeks before the May 22 general election. The Liberals' national election defeat meant that, for the first time since confederation in 1867, there was not a sitting Liberal government in Canada. There were seven Conservative administrations in the provinces and a Social Credit (SC) government in British Columbia that was conservative in all but name. The New Democratic Party (NDP) ruled in Saskatchewan. The Parti Québécois government held sole power in Quebec.

Clark's Cabinet. Clark appointed 29 ministers, fewer than the largest Trudeau Cabinet of 33, but he gave some of them double portfolios. Clark planned to keep some vacancies for additional Quebec representatives. He tried to attract Quebecers from outside Parliament into his Cabinet, but failed to persuade anyone of stature to accept appointment. Clark had to fall back on the two Conservative members of Parliament from Quebec and two Quebec senators who served in the John Diefenbaker Cabinet before 1963. Every province and the Yukon Territory were represented in the Cabinet, with the majority of seats going to Ontario, which got 12, and the West with eight.

Clark made several significant appointments. The post of finance minister went to John Crosbie, 48, a Newfoundland Liberal cabinet minister before leaving the party over policy differences. Flora MacDonald, 53, became the first woman to serve as secretary of state for external affairs. A popular party figure from Cape Breton, Nova Scotia, she ran for its leadership in 1976. Walter Baker, 48, a solid constituency politician from Ottawa who was close to Clark, became House leader and minister of national revenue; Sinclair Stevens, 52, a Toronto businessman and the chief advocate of reducing government spending, was appointed president of the Treasury Board. Robert René de Cotret, 35, an economist and former head of the private Conference Board in Canada, became minister of economic development and trade. Although defeated in his Commons seat, De Cotret was appointed by Clark to the Senate in order to allow him to enter the Cabinet. David Crombie, 43, who had served three terms as mayor of Toronto, was named minister of national health and welfare. Clark also arranged that a smaller, 12-minister group would form an inner cabinet, responsible for coordinating policies and making rapid decisions.

Parliament. Although the Conservatives did not have a majority in the 282-seat House of Commons, on most issues they could count on the votes of the five Social Credit Party members. Two vacancies occurred shortly after the new House was elected – one caused by former Prime Minister John G. Diefenbaker's death on August 16 and the other by Donald Jamieson's decision to become leader of the Liberal Party in Newfoundland. By-elections held on November 19 did not change party standings in the House of Commons.

Prime Minister Clark's Speech from the Throne opened the 31st Parliament on October 9. It dealt mainly with government methods rather than with Canada's problems. Although it contained no reference to international affairs and no mention of the Quebec referendum on separation scheduled for June 1980, Clark later made it clear he opposed separation. The new government stated its intention of improving federal-provincial relations and promised a more open administration – its first piece of legislation was Canada's first freedom-of-information bill. The Clark administration's economic strategy aimed at reducing the burden of government; relying more on individual enterprise; helping people to build up a stake in Canada; promoting the welfare of all regions in the country; and striving for energy self-sufficiency by 1990.

Conservative hopes of an active session of legislation were dashed on December 13 when Finance Minister Crosbie presented his first budget. It was a tough one, designed to battle inflation, reduce energy consumption, and stimulate the private sector. An immediate excise tax of 18 cents per gallon (3.8 liters)

Man from Canada's Prairies

Canada lost a commanding political personality with the death of former Prime Minister John G. Diefenbaker in Ottawa, Ont., on Aug. 16, 1979. The first prime minister to come from neither wholly British nor French stock, Diefenbaker headed the federal government from 1957 to 1963.

He brought the Progressive Conservative Party to power after 22 years of Liberal rule by exploiting the fading appeal of his opponents and by presenting policies for a dynamic Canada. In 1958 he spelled out his program, emphasizing Canada's need to preserve its economic independence and develop the resources of its northland. Canadians responded enthusiastically, giving Diefenbaker the largest electoral majority ever gained by a Canadian political leader – 208 of the 265 seats in the House of Commons.

Although he was born of German and Scottish ancestry in 1895 in Ontario, Diefenbaker was always identified with the Canadian prairies. There his family settled as homesteaders, and there he was educated and practiced law in small farming communities. He made his name as a courtroom lawyer, one who was always ready to take on a case involving the defense of civil rights. He failed five times in attempts to win public office, but in 1940 he was elected Conservative member for Lake Centre in central Saskatchewan. Thereafter, he never looked back. He held his seat through 12 consecutive elections and gained the party leadership a year before he led it to power.

Diefenbaker's record in office was uneven. He sponsored a Bill of Rights that embodied his longheld convictions on the need for equality before the law, but the measure was easily amendable and proved to have little impact. He brought in ambitious social programs and regional development plans. Lake Diefenbaker, 125 miles (190 kilometers) long, which was formed by damming the South Saskatchewan River, represented one of his most constructive plans. He spoke often of what he called the "northern vision," translated into roads and railways to open up Canada's northern resources.

Although he was a forceful campaigner, Diefenbaker proved to be indecisive as a prime minister. His government was in serious disarray by the early 1960s, and it fell from power over the controversial issue of arming Canadian forces with nuclear weapons. Diefenbaker's personal commitment to disarmament conflicted with what many people considered to be Canada's obligations as a member of the North Atlantic Treaty Organization and the North American Air Defense Command. This dilemma was resolved when his government was defeated in the election of April 1963. For the next 16 years, Diefenbaker served as an unrelenting critic of Liberal Party Prime Ministers Lester B. Pearson and Pierre Elliott Trudeau, and his slashing oratory made him a dangerous opponent. He died as he had lived for almost 40 years – as a sitting member of the House of Commons.

Diefenbaker's dedication to a few basic loyalties gave him his great hold on the Canadian people. He believed in the freedom of the individual under the law, and cherished the institutions that symbolized this ideal – the monarchy, Parliament, the courts, the British North America Act, and the Royal Canadian Mounted Police. He spoke for people who felt excluded from the political process and made them feel that he cared about their welfare. He exhibited a fierce patriotism that was firmly rooted in the West and its values.

By the end of his 83 years, Diefenbaker had become a folk hero. He was an old-fashioned politician, rhetorical and mischievous, his eyes flashing and his jowls shaking as he stormed through political life. His vanity was monumental, and he could be ruthless and vindictive. Yet there was a unique quality about Diefenbaker that commanded attention; he could not be ignored. Prime Minister Joe Clark, also a Conservative, said on hearing of Diefenbaker's death that "the chief" was a man of passion who did not "tiptoe through the public life of Canada." Rather, he strode through it, one of the last colorful and heroic survivors of Canada's pioneer past.

David M. L. Farr

John G. Diefenbaker
(1895–1979)

on gasoline, a new federal tax to take half the revenues of an oil price increase above $2 per barrel, and a surtax on corporation income tax were included in the budget. Government spending was to be held to an increase of 10 per cent a year, with the aim of reducing the federal deficit from $11.2 billion in 1979-1980 to $9 billion in 1983-1984.

The Liberals and the NDP made it plain that they were unhappy with the budget and threatened no-confidence motions at the first opportunity. Their chance came on the evening of December 13 when they rallied 139 votes (112 Liberals and 27 NDP), exceeding the 133 cast by government members. Three members of Clark's party were unavoidably absent, but more serious was the withdrawal of

support by the five SC members because of their refusal to accept the gasoline tax increase.

The defeat of a key expression of government policy, such as a budget, inevitably leads to the resignation of the government under the parliamentary system. Clark went immediately to Governor General Edward R. Schreyer to ask for a dissolution of the House of Commons. Schreyer granted the request, and the February 1980 election was then scheduled.

Canada's Economy responded, without the customary time lag, to the United States slump in 1979. The real gross national product began to decline in the second quarter for the first time since mid-1976. Labor income per worker, adjusted for inflation, was down and production slackened in some of the major exporting industries, such as aluminum, pulp and paper, and motor vehicles. The merchandise trade surplus was not expected to compare favorably with 1978's record value of $3.5 billion. The forecast surplus for 1979 was $2 billion, which — with the $9-billion shortfall on services — would leave a current deficit of $7 billion. Capital investment was high during 1979, leading to a larger growth in imports than in exports.

Although recession appeared to be on the horizon, inflation remained Canada's major economic problem. Toward the close of the year it showed signs of accelerating. After moderate rises during the summer, the consumer price index gained almost a full point in September, leading to a 9.6 per cent increase over the previous 12 months. Rises in nonfood prices were the chief cause, especially a July increase in the wellhead price of crude oil, the effects of which spread rapidly through the economy.

The steady rise in United States interest rates created difficulties for Canadian policymakers, who were obliged to keep Canadian rates higher to attract foreign capital. There were a number of increases in the bank rate, which reached 14 per cent by October 25. The latest increase moved the rate to a point almost double the 8.5 per cent figure of April 1978. The high cost of borrowing was certain to restrain loan and money supply growth, a prime objective of the Bank of Canada. The Canadian dollar hovered around 84 to 86 cents (U.S.) in 1979.

U.S. Relations. The "fish war" between Canada and the United States ended with an interim agreement in January 1979 to settle maritime differences. Treaties signed on March 29 granted reciprocal fishing access to coastal waters to Canadian and U.S. fishermen, with an international commission established to set maximum catches for major fish species. A second agreement would submit to international arbitration the disputed maritime boundary over the waters and continental shelf in the Gulf of Maine. At the end of 1979, the treaties were still awaiting approval by the U.S. Senate.

Another dispute broke out late in August when

Federal Spending in Canada
Estimated Budget for Fiscal 1980*

	Billions of Dollars
Health and welfare	18.033
Public debt	8.350
Economic development and support	5.539
Defense	5.337
Transportation and communications	2.999
Fiscal transfer payments to provinces	2.797
General government services	2.245
Education assistance	1.865
Internal overhead expenses	1.572
Foreign affairs	1.030
Culture and recreation	1.001
Total	50.768

*April 1, 1979, to March 31, 1980

Spending Since 1974

Billions of dollars

Fiscal Year

Source: Treasury Board of Canada

albacore tuna unexpectedly moved into Canada's 200-nautical-mile fishing zone off the Pacific coast. Eight U.S. fishing boats pursued the tuna, and the Canadians seized them. In retaliation, the United States banned tuna imports from Canada. Since the 1979 season was almost over, the two countries agreed in September to try to reconcile their positions for 1980.

Another source of disagreement between the two countries was the location of oil pipeline routes. At issue was a route for Alaskan oil to the Midwestern United States. Canada preferred two mainly overland connections, one paralleling the gas pipeline to be built along the Alaska Highway through the Yukon and the other using ships between Valdez and Skagway in the Alaska Panhandle and then connecting with the Alaska Highway pipeline. United States Secretary of Energy James R. Schlesinger and Secretary of the Interior Cecil D. Andrus favored a third possibility – the all-United States Northern Tier pipeline. This $1.6-billion project called for shipping Alaskan oil along the British Columbia coast in tankers to a port in Washington state. From there, the oil would move to the Midwest through a U.S. pipeline.

Andrus favored the Northern Tier project because he believed it would be easier to raise private financing for that pipeline. British Columbians opposed the Northern Tier, however. They believed that tanker traffic along their rugged coast would involve the risk of damaging oil spills. Recommendations were to go to President Jimmy Carter for a decision by December 6. Prime Minister Clark and President Carter were expected to discuss the subject on Carter's first official visit to Canada on November 9 and 10, but Carter postponed his visit because of the crisis that resulted when Iran seized hostages in the U.S. Embassy in Teheran.

Meanwhile, the 4,800-mile (7,700-kilometer) Alaska gas pipeline was already two years behind its projected 1983 completion date. Financing problems were one cause of the delay. Another was the slow progress of approval for the project through U.S. regulatory agencies. Preparations for the Canadian portion of the line were almost a year ahead of those in the United States.

Acid rain emerged as a new Canada-United States problem in 1979. Coal-fired power plants and industries on both sides of the border discharge smoke containing sulfur and nitrogen oxides that fall as rain on lakes, forests, and fields in eastern North America. As many as 50,000 lakes in Canada and New England may be damaged by this toxic precipitation over the next 20 years. Canadian and U.S. environment officials discussed the danger in August. Canada promised to make its emission control standards as strict as those in the United States, but pointed out that the United States produced seven times as much air pollution as Canada and that the

The Ministry of Canada*
In order of precedence

Joe Clark, prime minister

Jacques Flynn, minister of justice and attorney general of Canada, and leader of the government in the Senate

Martial Asselin, minister of state for the Canadian International Development Agency

Walter Baker, president of the queen's privy council for Canada and minister of national revenue

Flora MacDonald, secretary of state for external affairs

James McGrath, minister of fisheries and oceans

Erik Nielsen, minister of public works

Allan Lawrence, solicitor general of Canada and minister of consumer and corporate affairs

John Crosbie, minister of finance

David MacDonald, secretary of state of Canada and minister of communications

Lincoln Alexander, minister of labor

Roch LaSalle, minister of supply and services

Donald Mazankowski, minister of transport

Elmer MacKay, minister of regional economic expansion

Jake Epp, minister of Indian affairs and northern development

John Fraser, postmaster general and minister of the environment

William Jarvis, minister of state for federal-provincial relations

Allan McKinnon, minister of national defense and minister of veterans affairs

Sinclair Stevens, president of the Treasury Board

John Wise, minister of agriculture

Ronald Atkey, minister of employment and immigration

Ramon Hnatyshyn, minister of energy, mines and resources and minister of state for science and technology

David Crombie, minister of national health and welfare

Robert René de Cotret, minister of economic development and trade

Heward Grafftey, minister of state for social programs

Perrin Beatty, minister of state for the Treasury Board

Robert Howie, minister of state for transport

Steven Paproski, minister of state for fitness and amateur sport and minister of state for multiculturalism

Ronald Huntington, minister of state for small business and industry

Michael Wilson, minister of state for international trade

*As of Dec. 31, 1979.

Premiers of Canadian Provinces

Province	Premier
Alberta	Peter Lougheed
British Columbia	William R. Bennett
Manitoba	Sterling R. Lyon
New Brunswick	Richard B. Hatfield
Newfoundland	Brian Peckford
Nova Scotia	John Buchanan
Ontario	William G. Davis
Prince Edward Island	Angus MacLean
Quebec	René Lévesque
Saskatchewan	Allan Blakeney

Commissioners of Territories

Northwest Territories	John H. Parker
Yukon Territory	Douglas Bell, Administrator

Canada and Provinces Population Estimates
(in thousands)

	1977	1978	1979
Alberta	1,896.4	1,952.1	2,008.9
British Columbia	2,493.7	2,530.1	2,566.9
Manitoba	1,029.1	1,032.8	1,030.5
New Brunswick	687.1	694.9	701.0
Newfoundland	564.0	569.0	574.0
Northwest Territories	43.3	43.6	43.2
Nova Scotia	835.0	841.0	846.9
Ontario	8,355.0	8,444.9	8,499.8
Prince Edward Island	120.2	122.0	122.8
Quebec	6,275.8	6,283.0	6,298.8
Saskatchewan	937.0	947.5	957.1
Yukon	21.1	21.7	21.6
Canada	23,257.6	23,482.6	23,671.5

Metropolitan Population Estimates
(in thousands)

	June 1, 1977	June 1, 1978
Toronto	2,832.6	2,856.5
Montreal	2,823.8	2,823.0
Vancouver	1,168.1	1,173.3
Ottawa-Hull	709.2	726.4
Winnipeg	584.9	589.1
Edmonton	568.7	581.4
Quebec	549.0	554.5
Hamilton	532.9	536.3
Calgary	487.9	504.9
St. Catherines-Niagara	303.8	306.0
Kitchener	276.0	280.1
London	272.1	274.1
Halifax	269.7	271.2
Windsor	246.9	246.3
Victoria	219.7	222.5
Regina	156.2	160.0
Sudbury	155.9	155.0
St. John's	145.3	146.5
Oshawa	137.1	139.3
Saskatoon	136.9	139.2
Chicoutimi-Jonquiere	129.4	129.7
Thunder Bay	119.9	120.7
St. John	115.3	117.2

prevailing winds move the acid rain clouds northward. Although both countries want a comprehensive bilateral regulatory treaty, President Carter's desire to replace energy-generating oil with coal complicated the negotiation of an agreement.

Foreign Affairs. Soon after taking office, Prime Minister Clark was forced to turn his attention to international diplomacy. The Tokyo summit conference of the seven leading industrialized nations, held on June 28 and 29, gave Clark his first chance to meet with world leaders. He played a watching role, occasionally intervening to suggest compromise between positions held by the United States and European nations. With the other heads of government, he pledged reductions in petroleum consump-

tion. He announced that the annual average increase for Canada between 1979 and 1985 would be held to 1 per cent, a lower figure than that proposed by the National Energy Board.

Clark flew to Africa to attend the 39-nation Commonwealth Heads of Government Conference in Lusaka, Zambia, from August 1 to 7. Discussion of the future of Zimbabwe Rhodesia dominated the meetings, and Clark worked behind the scenes to promote consensus. On the way to Zambia, Clark visited Cameroon. He spent two days in Tanzania as the guest of President Julius K. Nyerere.

The most controversial international issue during the new government's first months was Clark's election promise to move the Canadian Embassy in Israel from Tel Aviv-Yafo to Jerusalem. The outraged Arab states threatened an economic boycott of Canada if the embassy were moved. Some contracts in Arab countries were canceled while others were threatened. Clark sent Robert L. Stanfield, the previous head of the Conservative Party, to the Middle East, and he reported that Canada would not retain credibility if the embassy were moved. On October 29, Clark said, "We do not intend to move the embassy in Israel."

Industrial contracts were also affected by the Argentine government's decision not to buy a second CANDU nuclear reactor for generating electricity from Atomic Energy of Canada Limited. Although Canada's rigorous "full-scope" safeguards on the export of nuclear materials and technology may have influenced the Argentinean decision, problems experienced in building the earlier Canadian reactor in Argentina were a more likely reason.

Canada showed a practical concern for human rights by agreeing in July to take as many as 50,000 Indochinese refugees (3,000 per month) during the remainder of 1979 and in 1980. The plan, announced on July 18, involved sponsorship by private groups, with the federal government matching their efforts. At the July 20 conference in Geneva, Switzerland, on the plight of the "boat people," Secretary of State for External Affairs MacDonald strongly criticized Vietnam for its "flagrant and outrageous" invasions of personal rights. She appeared before the United Nations General Assembly on September 25 and appealed for the establishment of an undersecretary-general with power to bring about effective human rights action.

Facts in Brief: Population: 23,671,500. Government: Governor General Edward Richard Schreyer; Prime Minister Joe Clark. Monetary unit: Canadian dollar. Foreign trade: exports, $46,065,000,000; imports, $43,434,000,000.   David M. L. Farr

See also Canadian provinces articles; CANADIAN LIBRARY ASSOCIATION (CLA); CANADIAN LITERATURE; CLARK, CHARLES JOSEPH (JOE); SCHREYER, EDWARD RICHARD. In WORLD BOOK, see CANADA; CANADA, GOVERNMENT OF.

CANADIAN LIBRARY ASSOCIATION (CLA) won a major victory on Feb. 8, 1979, when Pierre De Bané, federal minister of supply and services, reversed an earlier decision to cut from 586 to 302 the number of libraries that received free copies of federal publications. Canada's Cabinet had prompted the earlier decision by cutting in half the federal Publishing Centre's budget for free distribution. CLA, the Canadian Association of University Teachers, the Association of Universities and Colleges of Canada, and other organizations protested the cut. They sent letters to members of Parliament and briefs to Publishing Centre officials, pointing out the key role that libraries play in giving government information to the public. In addition, the opposition raised the issue in the House of Commons.

The CLA resolved at its annual meeting in Ottawa on June 17 to urge the federal government to establish an adequate program for the visually and physically handicapped at the National Library. That library had decided to eliminate its fledgling liaison office for handicapped people because of doubts about getting enough money to develop an adequate program. An April 1979 brief to the federal Commission of Enquiry on Educational Leave and Productivity covered paid educational leave for library personnel and the role of libraries in supporting persons on educational leave.

Project: Progress. CLA commissioned a Toronto consulting firm in June to undertake Project: Progress, a $110,000 study on the future of public libraries. The firm will gather data from all Canadian public library service points and make recommendations on public library objectives, the political environment, interlibrary cooperation, and personnel use by June 30, 1980. Money for the project came from public libraries and private grants.

CLA raised $16,000, including cash from four provincial associations, for an intellectual-freedom defense fund. Several provincial associations endorsed CLA's statement that libraries have a basic responsibility to maintain intellectual freedom.

Awards. CLA presented its new Outstanding Service to Librarianship Award in June to Jack E. Brown, professor of library science at McGill University in Montreal and former director of the Canada Institute for Scientific and Technical Information in Ottawa. CLA awarded the Howard V. Phalin-World Book Graduate Scholarship in Library Science to Richard Hopkins of Calgary, Alta.; the H. W. Wilson Education Foundation Scholarship to Karen Wiandt of Waterloo, Ont.; and the Elizabeth Dafoe Scholarship to Donald Meakins of Vancouver, B.C. The Book of the Year for Children Award went to Kevin Major for *Hold Fast* (Clarke Irwin); and the Amelia Frances Howard-Gibbon Illustrator's Award went to Ann Blades for *A Salmon for Simon* (Douglas and McIntyre).   Paul Kitchen

In WORLD BOOK, see CANADIAN LIBRARY ASSN.

CANADIAN LITERATURE produced a rich crop of fiction in 1979, but Margaret Trudeau's memoir, *Beyond Reason,* captured the widest national interest and provoked the most reaction. The book was especially popular because it was published shortly before her estranged husband, Pierre Elliott Trudeau, was defeated as prime minister (see CANADA). It was not notable for its literary qualities, but its intimate revelations of the author's anxieties and self-admitted inadequacies guaranteed best-selling status. The election campaign also inspired *Points of Departure,* an urbane and vivid account by Dalton Camp, and Clive Cocking's *Following the Leaders,* a study of how reporters interpreted the events.

Fiction. Margaret Atwood's fourth novel, *Life Before Man,* was typically brilliant in allusion and style in its account of a man caught between two women. Brian Moore, who has twice won the Governor General's Award, contributed his 12th novel, *The Mangan Inheritance,* a chronicle of a failed poet drifting through Montreal, New York City, and Ireland. Hugh Hood's *Reservoir Ravine* was the third novel in his ambitious 12-volume social and philosophical series about life in Canada between the 1930s and the year 2000. Jack Hodgins' *The Resurrection of Joseph Bourne,* a stylish dark comedy of life on Vancouver Island, once again demonstrated that the author is among Canada's major writers.

Satiric novels of interest were Max Braithwaite's *The Commodore's Barge Is Alongside,* which mocked the pretensions of Canada's navy; and William Weintraub's *The Underdogs,* which examined the plight of the English in a future Republic of Quebec. Other noteworthy novels include *Dolphin's Wake* by Peter Such, *The Sweet Second Summer of Kitty Malone* by Matt Cohen, *Random Descent* by Katherine Govier, and *Lunar Attractions* by Clark Blaise. The best collection of short stories was Mavis Gallant's *From the Fifteenth District.*

The trend toward commercial thrillers continued to accelerate. William Deverell's *Needles,* about the Vancouver heroin trade, won the second annual $50,000 Seal Books first-novel competition. Christopher Hyde's *The Wave* and Richard Rohmer's *Balls!* spun variations on the disaster theme, but only David Gurr's *Troika,* a spy story in the traditional mold, was distinguished by literary skill.

English translations of novels by Quebec writers provided insights into French-Canadian modes of life and thought. These included Marie-Claire Blais's *Nights in the Underground,* Hubert Aquin's *Hamlet's Twin,* Gabrielle Roy's *Children of My Heart,* and Diane Giguere's *Wings in the Wind.*

Biography. Perceptive accounts of influential political figures included *C. D. Howe* by Toronto historians Robert Bothwell and William Kilbourn, which analyzed the controversial Liberal Party Cabinet minister's contributions to Canada's industrial development. Allan Hustak's *Peter Lougheed* traced that Alberta premier's meteoric rise to power. Maggie Siggins' *Bassett* was an account of the career of John Bassett, a controversial Toronto television tycoon, newspaper publisher, and former football team owner. Anthony Mardiros made a valuable contribution to political history with *William Irvine,* about the Prairie radical who helped found Canada's Socialist Party.

The best of the memoirs was novelist Farley Mowat's account of his World War II experiences with the Canadian Army in Italy. Raymond Massey, the Toronto-born actor, published the second volume of his memoirs, *A Hundred Different Lives,* a plodding but useful account of his stage and film career in Toronto, London, and Hollywood. A poet's discerning eye illuminated Douglas LePan's *Bright Glass of Memory,* a memoir of the literary and diplomatic career that brought him into contact with such diverse figures as economist John Maynard Keynes and poet T. S. Eliot. In *My Quebec,* that province's Premier René Lévesque discussed English-French relationships and the possibility of his province separating from the rest of Canada.

Three works examined the life and work of an eccentric West Coast painter and visionary – *Emily Carr: The Untold Story* by Edythe Hembroff-Scheicher, *Emily Carr* by Maria Tippett, and *The Art of Emily Carr* by Doris Shadbolt. Two other influential painters, Cornelius Krieghoff and Norval Morrisseau, were examined: *Krieghoff* by J. Russell Harper; and *The Art of Norval Morrisseau* by Lister Sinclair and Jack Pollock.

History did not have a vintage year, but Doug Fetherling's *Gold Diggers of 1929* gave a lively journalistic account of how the Great Depression affected Canada. And Betty Kennedy's *Hurricane Hazel* provided a vivid oral history of the 1954 storm that claimed the lives of 81 persons in Ontario. Popular Prairie historian James Gray took up the theme of immigrant settlement and expansion in the 1930s in his entertaining *Boom Time,* and man-of-letters George Woodcock explored Canada's social and cultural history in *The Canadians.*

Poetry. The best of the collections was Michael Ondaatje's *There's a Trick with a Knife I'm Learning to Do,* powerful poems gathered from some 17 years of accomplished writing that range over such subjects as love, violence, jazz, nature, family, and travel. Susan Musgrave, perhaps the most gifted of Canada's younger poets, produced *A Man to Marry, A Man to Bury,* an unnerving collection filled with images of death and mutilation. But although poetry flourished across the country, new collections by such major poets as Dennis Lee, Irving Layton, Robert Kroetsch, George Bowering, and Earle Birney neither broke new ground nor diminished their reputations. The most curious publishing event was the almost simultaneous release by different publishers of two anthologies featuring poems by most of Canada's major poets. These were *The Long Poem Anthology,* edited by Ondaatje, nine poems usually omitted by anthologists because of their length; and *To Say the Least,* edited by P. K. Page, 200 poems under 12 lines by 102 poets.

Governor General's Literary Awards for books published in 1978 went to Alice Munro for *Who Do You Think You Are?* (English fiction); Patrick Lane for *Poems: New and Selected* (English poetry); Roger Caron for *Go Boy!* (English nonfiction); François-Marc Gagnon for *Paul-Emile Borduas* (French nonfiction); Jacques Poulin for *Les grandes marées* (French fiction); and Gilbert Langevin for *Mon refuge est un volcan* (French poetry).

The Sir John A. Macdonald Prize for the historical work that made the most significant contribution to understanding the Canadian past went to Michael Bliss for *A Canadian Millionaire: The Life and Business Times of Sir Joseph Flavelle.* Michael Bullock won the Canada Council Translation Prize for his English translation of *Stories of Late Night Drinkers,* a collection of stories by Michel Tremblay, and Gilles Hénault won for his French translation of *Without a Parachute,* a novel written by David Fennario. Sondra Gotlieb won the Stephen Leacock Memorial Award for humor for her novel *True Confections.* Ken Adachi

In WORLD BOOK, see CANADIAN LITERATURE.

CAPE VERDE. See AFRICA.

CARRINGTON, LORD (1919-   ), was named foreign secretary of Great Britain on May 5, 1979, by newly elected Prime Minister Margaret Thatcher. The appointment capped a distinguished career that began when the Sixth Baron Carrington took his hereditary seat in the House of Lords in 1946.

Peter Alexander Rupert Carington (the title is spelled with two *r*'s, the surname with one) was born on June 6, 1919, in London. He attended Eton and Sandhurst, the British military college, then served with the Grenadier Guards in World War II.

Prime Minister Winston Churchill named Carington joint parliamentary secretary to the Ministry of Agriculture and fisheries in 1951. Three years later he held a similar position in the Ministry of Defense.

From 1956 to 1959, Carington was ambassador to Australia. Prime Minister Harold Macmillan made him a privy councillor and First Lord of the Admiralty in October 1959.

Carington became Conservative Party leader in the House of Lords in 1963, and handled foreign office assignments as minister without portfolio. From 1970 to 1974, he served as Prime Minister Edward Heath's secretary of state for defense, then led the Opposition until the 1979 elections.

Carington is married to the former Iona McClean. Marsha F. Goldsmith

See also GREAT BRITAIN; ZIMBABWE RHODESIA.

CARTER, JAMES EARL, JR. (1924-   ), 39th President of the United States, endured his most discouraging year and faced his worst international crisis to date in the White House in 1979. He wrangled with Congress over his badly mauled energy program; made unprecedented changes in his Cabinet in an attempt to revive and unify his Administration; and criticized American apathy and what he perceived as "malaise" in American society. Struggling with inflation and energy problems, he declared his candidacy for the 1980 Democratic presidential nomination on December 4, facing a strong challenge from Massachusetts Senator Edward M. Kennedy. But Carter's toughest problem flared in Iran when, on November 4, fanatic Iranian students seized at least 50 American hostages at the United States Embassy in Teheran and demanded that the United States return the ailing, exiled Shah Mohammad Reza Pahlavi to Iran (see IRAN; MIDDLE EAST).

Jimmy Carter was perceived by many as weak and vacillating, unable to prod Congress into approving his energy program, to direct his Cabinet, to assert political leadership, to force the release of the hostages in Iran, or to boost his record-low rating in public-opinion polls. Nonetheless, dealing with crisis after crisis, Jimmy Carter revealed himself as a patient, honest, and peace-loving leader and doubled his approval rating in the polls.

Carter Finances. In accordance with the law, President Carter reported in May that, as of Jan. 1, 1979, his net assets totaled $1,005,910. The President's 1978 income totaled $254,029, including more than $20,000 in royalties from his autobiography, *Why Not the Best?* The President and his wife, Rosalynn, reportedly paid more than $91,000 in federal taxes on their 1978 income. In addition to the disclosure of their income and assets, the Carters also listed gifts they received in 1978 from 68 donors.

The Federal Election Commission (FEC), on investigating the financing of the President's 1976 primary campaign, reported on April 2 that it had discovered no major violations, but it ordered the campaign committee to repay $5,872 to the government for inadequately documented campaign expenses and imposed a $1,950 fine for illegal bank-deposit practices. On June 4, the FEC asked the Carter presidential campaign committee to repay about $50,000 in federal tax funds out of the $21.8-million given to the committee for the 1976 campaign. Special Counsel Paul J. Curran, appointed by the Department of Justice, reported on October 16 that his investigation into $9.8 million in loans made by the National Bank of Georgia to the Carter family's peanut business cleared the President and his brother, Billy.

Family Holidays. President and Mrs. Carter and their daughter, Amy, cruised for a week in August on the Mississippi River on the stern-wheeler *Delta Queen,* followed by a retinue of Secret Service men and reporters. Along the 660-mile (1,060-kilometer) trip, the President stopped to greet crowds and to urge Americans to support his energy program.

Carter took part in a 6.2-mile (10-kilometer) race on September 15 in Catoctin Mountain National Park. One of 980 runners, the President dropped out near the 4-mile (6-kilometer) point suffering from heat exhaustion, but he recovered quickly.

The First Lady, Rosalynn Carter, took an increasingly active role in her husband's official life in 1979, keeping regular office hours. The President's almost constant companion, she lunched with him, sat in on Cabinet meetings, and helped edit his speeches.

Rosalynn Carter testified on February 7 before the Senate Resource Committee's subcommittee on health and scientific research, urging strong support for federal funds for mental health programs and facilities. She addressed the World Health Organization in Geneva, Switzerland, in May and headed the United States delegation to the inauguration of Ecuador's President Jaime Roldos Aguilera on August 10. In November, Rosalynn Carter visited Cambodian and Laotian refugee camps in Thailand. When she returned, she urged increased food and medical aid for the refugees.   Carol L. Thompson

See also PRESIDENT of the UNITED STATES. In WORLD BOOK, see CARTER, JAMES EARL, JR.

President Jimmy Carter and his wife, Rosalynn, relax on the deck of the *Delta Queen* during a vacation excursion down the Mississippi River in August.

CAT. Buddy, a yellow kitten owned by the Arnold Davidson family of Clarkston, Wash., made national headlines in August 1979 when he "came back from the dead." Buddy appeared to have been fatally injured in an accident, and the Davidsons buried him in their backyard. Five days later, 8-year-old Barbette Davidson heard a weak "meow." She and her sister Kelly, 12, ran to the gravesite and unearthed a hungry, thirsty, and wobbly kitten.

Veterinarian Richard Nelson of Washington State University explained, "It's possible for such a resurrection if the cat was in a comatose state in which its breathing and metabolic processes were severely reduced . . . like a bear in hibernation."

Melissa, a white longhair, received the 1979 National Cat Hero award from the Friskies Cat Council for preventing an armed robbery. Melissa's hisses distracted a knife-wielding holdup man in a Denver book and record shop, allowing store owner Diane Wakabayshi to run next door for help.

The Cat Fanciers' Association selected Gr. Ch. Clare-Way Cheers, a black-and-white Persian owned by Clare V. Johnson of San Jose, Calif., as Best Cat of the Year. Best Kitten was Gr. Ch. Kyina Patience of Oakway, a tortoiseshell Persian owned by Anne and Amanda Bright and Judy Sturm of Oakville, Ontario, Canada.   Theodore M. O'Leary

In WORLD BOOK, see CAT.

Mac, part-Persian and a former stray, leaps through flames at Animal Actors' ranch in California. Mac's bag of tricks also includes tightrope walking.

CAULKINS, TRACY (1962-   ), an American swimmer, won the James E. Sullivan Memorial Award in February 1979. The award is presented each year by the Amateur Athletic Union (AAU) to the U.S. amateur athlete judged to be the most outstanding on the basis of character and achievements the previous year. The youngest athlete to win the award, she became 16 on Jan. 11, 1979.

As a 15-year-old Nashville, Tenn., ninth-grader, Caulkins led the U.S. women's swimming team to a stunning victory in August 1978 in the Third World swimming championships in West Berlin, winning five gold medals. During that year, she also won seven gold medals in the AAU national short-course championships, seven in the AAU national long-course championships, four in the U.S.-Russia short-course meet, four in an international meet, and six of 12 individual races in the Seventeen Meet of Champions. She also won four gold and two silver medals in the 1979 Pan American Games.

Caulkins started swimming when she was 8 years old. By the time she was 11, she was setting age-group records. She suffered a hairline fracture of the right ankle late in 1977, but resumed swimming three weeks later wearing a waterproof cast. The cast limited the use of her legs and forced her to use her arms more. When the cast was removed two months later, the added arm strength had greatly improved her performance.   Joseph P. Spohn

CENSUS. The United States Bureau of the Census prepared in 1979 for the 1980 Decennial Census of Population and Housing—the 20th such survey since 1790. The federal government's single largest peacetime undertaking, the census will collect information on some 222 million persons in more than 80 million households.

The 1980 census will be taken chiefly by mail. Every household is to receive a census form before April 1. About 80 per cent of U.S. households are to get a basic short form, and the rest are to receive a longer form with more detailed questions about housing and socioeconomic characteristics. Census takers will call on only about 15 per cent of U.S. households, most of them in small towns and rural areas, to check the forms.

Black and Latino leaders expressed concern that their groups would be undercounted in the census. The Census Bureau estimated that 1 in 7 Latinos and 1 in 14 blacks were missed in the 1970 census, compared with 1 in 50 whites. Such undercounting is a serious problem because census figures are used to determine the allocation of up to $60 billion in federal funds for education, job-training, and other social programs. The figures are also used to reapportion congressional representation and to redistrict state legislatures and other bodies. Vincent P. Barabba, who replaced Manuel D. Plotkin as census director on June 1, said that changes in questionnaires and in census procedures should help to correct the undercounting problem.

The U.S. Population on Jan. 1, 1979, including the armed forces overseas, was estimated at 219.5 million. This represented an increase of 1.7 million in 1978 – the result of 3.3 million births, 1.9 million deaths, and 343,000 added by net immigration.

There were 24.8 million blacks in the United States, 11.6 per cent of the total population, in March 1978. The majority of blacks were urban – 75 per cent resided in metropolitan areas and about 50 per cent lived in central city areas.

The U.S. population also included about 12 million Latinos. About 7.2 million persons in this group were of Mexican origin; 1.8 million were Puerto Rican; 700,000 were Cuban; and 2.4 million were of other Spanish origin.

The U.S. birth rate dropped in 1978 to 15.2 per 1,000 persons from 15.3 in 1977. The average number of children at the 1978 rate is about 1.8 per woman, well below the 2.1 children per woman required for natural replacement of the population.

Divorce Rate Up. In March 1978, there were an estimated 90 divorced persons for every 1,000 married persons in intact marriages in the United States. This ratio was a 91 per cent increase over the 1970 level of 47 divorced persons per 1,000 persons in intact marriages, and a 157 per cent increase over the 1960 level of 35 per 1,000.

A whopping 40 per cent of the estimated 14.8 million U.S. population growth from 1970 to 1978 occurred in California (up 2.3 million), Texas (up 1.8 million), and Florida (up 1.8 million). The West was the fastest growing region, with especially rapid growth in the Mountain States. The West increased by 15.1 per cent between 1970 and 1975, adding an estimated 5.3 million persons. Although the West grew fastest, the South posted the largest total gain, 7.8 million.

The U.S. Labor Force averaged 100 million persons, or 63 per cent of the civilian noninstitutional population over 16 years of age in 1978. Since 1970, the civilian labor force has grown by 21 per cent, compared with an increase of 16 per cent in the population. The total number of women in the 1978 labor force was 42 million.

Median family income for whites was $16,740 in 1977, an increase of 1 per cent in real dollars from the 1976 median. The 1977 median income for black families ($9,560) and for Latino families ($11,420) showed no significant change in real terms from the previous year. However, the real median for whites was 5 per cent higher in 1977 than in 1970. No statistically significant difference was found between the real median income in 1977 and 1970 for black and Latino families.   Vincent P. Barabba

In WORLD BOOK, see CENSUS; POPULATION.

CENTRAL AFRICAN EMPIRE. See AFRICA.

CEYLON. See SRI LANKA.

CHAD was in turmoil for much of 1979 as warring factions struggled for control. Thousands were killed in the capital, N'Djamena, and the government changed hands three times.

Chad's 14-year-old civil war between Arab Muslim guerrillas from the north and government troops, composed principally of blacks from the south, flared up in February and March, with President F. Malloum Ngakoutou Bey-Ndi in control of government forces and Prime Minister Hissene Habre backed by guerrillas. Malloum fled the country on March 23, and a provisional government headed by guerrilla leader Goukouni Oueddei took over. That government was replaced by a 29-member government headed by figurehead President Lol Mohamat Choua, on April 24.

Although both governments had been formed under Nigerian mediation, Nigeria joined with five neighboring countries, including Libya, on May 27 to demand Lol's resignation and the formation of a broader-based government. On June 25, Libya sent about 2,500 troops to support anti-Lol guerrillas operating in northern Chad.

Chadian political factions met in Lagos, Nigeria, on August 20 and agreed to a new government with Oueddei as president and Abdelkadar Kamougue, a southerner, as vice-president.   John D. Esseks

See also AFRICA (Facts in Brief Table). In WORLD BOOK, see CHAD.

CHEMICAL INDUSTRY sales in the United States in the first half of 1979 were outstanding, but the general economic slowdown took its toll in the second half of the year. Rising interest rates threatened to dry up the housing market, affecting companies that supply construction materials.

Spending for new plants, expansions, and environmental equipment totaled $8.1 billion, according to the McGraw-Hill Publications Company's Department of Economics – an increase of about 11 per cent over 1978, but about 4 per cent less than industry executives estimated at the beginning of the year. Capital spending for chemicals and such allied products as drugs, paint, and soap was up 12 per cent to $9.7 billion. Overseas capital spending of U.S. companies climbed 18.5 per cent to $3.2 billion.

How's Business? About 75 per cent of chemical manufacturers showed sales gains of at least 10 per cent for the first half of the year and more than half were up more than 20 per cent. Demand for plastics continued unabated, permitting price increases that covered rapidly escalating raw-materials costs. Synthetic fiber shipments remained fairly high.

Concern over high inventories intensified during the last half of the year when business gradually slowed down. Housing starts, automobile production, and retail sales were down, but chemical sales held up fairly well. Shipments for the first seven months were valued at $85.7 billion, up 14.6 per cent

241

from the first seven months of 1978, but inventories were up only 6.7 per cent. When demand appeared to slacken, some observers asked where all the chemicals were going. To the export markets, said many. Exports of chemicals and allied products were valued at $9.5 billion, a 37.8 per cent jump. The experts admitted that techniques used to determine inventory left much room for error.

Benzene Battle. The chemical industry and the U.S. Department of Labor's Occupational Safety and Health Administration (OSHA) continued their court fight over a standard that would lower the permissible workplace exposure to benzene to 1 part per million (ppm) from 10 ppm. The Fifth Circuit Court of Appeals in New Orleans vacated the standard in October 1978, but the U.S. Department of Justice asked the Supreme Court of the United States to review the decision because the appeals court in New Orleans contradicted decisions of three other appeals courts. The Supreme Court accepted the case among 79 that it would hear between October 1979 and June 1980. This is a landmark case because it will affect how federal health and safety regulations are applied, the amount of scientific data needed for enforcement, and the role of the regulators.

Health and Safety. The problem of building a chemical plant in a city that does not meet national air-pollution standards was eased in January to help bolster urban development. Now, a new plant can be built if pollution from other sources is reduced so that total emissions are lower. Previously, no new pollution source, however small, was allowed, even with offsetting reductions. The criteria for building plants in so-called clean-air areas were also eased after the District of Columbia Court of Appeals ruled in September that the intent of the Clean Air Act was to regulate plants having the "potential to emit" 100 short tons (91 metric tons) or more per year of any regulated air pollutant after pollution controls were installed. The U.S. Environmental Protection Agency (EPA) had been interpreting the act to regulate plants that had the potential before they installed controls.

EPA issued final regulations curtailing the manufacture, processing, and use of toxic polychlorinated biphenyls (PCB's) in April. The regulations permit capacitors and transformers that use PCB's for internal cooling to remain in operation for the life of the machinery in which they are used, but forbid manufacturing new equipment that uses PCB's.

The government ban on nonessential uses of fluorocarbons became effective on April 16, when the Food and Drug Administration began to prohibit shipment across state lines of such products as hair sprays and deodorants that are propelled by those chemicals. Most such spray-on products now use hydrocarbon propellants.　　　Frederick C. Price

In WORLD BOOK, see CHEMICAL INDUSTRY.

CHEMISTRY. Chemists working at the Louis Pasteur University in Strasbourg, France, announced in 1979 that they had discovered two new ways to split water by means of solar energy. One of these reactions produced hydrogen, while the other one liberated oxygen.

Jean-Marie Lehn, Michèle Kirch, and Jean-Pierre Sauvage produced hydrogen in March by allowing sunlight to fall on a water solution containing $Ru(bipyridine)_3^{+2}$, a photosensitizer that absorbed light and initiated the reaction; a rhenium ion, $Rh(bipyridine)_3^{+3}$, which played an intermediate role in the reaction by storing electrons temporarily; an organic compound, triethanolamine, which donated electrons to hydrogen atoms, freeing them; and a platinum catalyst that made the reaction proceed rapidly.

Lehn, Sauvage, and Raymond Ziessel reported in July a sunlight-catalyzed reaction that generated oxygen from water. The water solution contained $Ru(bipyridine)_3^{+2}$, a cobalt ion such as $Co(NH_3)_5CI^{+2}$, and ruthenium oxide. Sunlight striking the $Ru(bipyridine)_3^{+2}$ ion raised it to an electronically excited high energy state so that it contributed an electron to the cobalt ion. The $Ru(bipyridine)_3^{+3}$ ion, catalyzed by the ruthenium oxide, in turn picked up an electron from a water molecule, becoming $Ru(bipyridine)_3^{+2}$ again and producing oxygen.

The next step will be to find a way to combine the two reactions to generate hydrogen and oxygen simultaneously. A cheaper, more efficient system might become a practical source of hydrogen fuel and oxygen.

Multibridged Cyclophanes. Chemists Virgil Boekelheide, Y. Sekine, and M. Brown of the University of Oregon in Eugene reported in June that they had synthesized superphane, a molecule made up of two *benzene rings* (molecules that have six carbon atoms arranged in a hexagon) connected by two-carbon bridges at all 12 of their carbon atoms. Superphane resembles a pair of six-legged spiders connected through their legs with the two benzene rings as the spider bodies. Two carbon atoms form the "joints" of each leg.

The synthesis took 11 steps, but the key was a new reaction, coupling *substituted benzocyclobutenes* (benzene rings that have four of their six carbon atoms bonded to carbon atoms outside the ring) at 650°C (1200°F.) to prepare *multibridged cyclophanes* (pairs of "six-legged spiders" that have some of their "legs" joined). The chemists synthesized 0.4 per cent of the benzocyclobutene into superphane.

Some of this molecule's atoms are *strained* (pulled out of the positions that they occupied in the simpler molecules), so superphane helps chemists test theories of strain and bonding. Researchers also use the molecule to study what happens when benzene rings are put so close to each other.

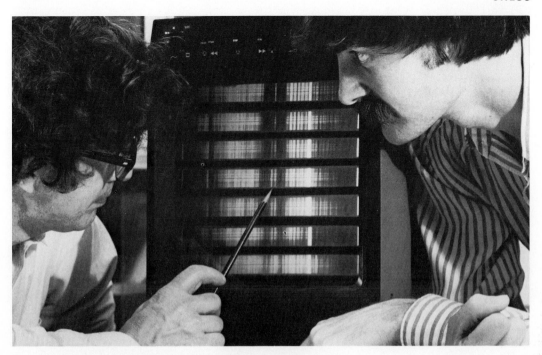

IBM researchers Peter Sorokin, left, and Donald Bethune examine pictures of a chemical reaction taken by their new high-speed laser technique.

Primordial Chemistry. Chemists at the University of Texas in Austin reported in May that they had discovered new clues to the origin of life on earth. They formed amino acids from ammonia and methane in conditions similar to the terrestrial atmosphere of about 2 billion years ago.

Allen J. Bard and Harald Reiche shone visible light into water containing a solution of ammonia or ammonium chloride and a platinized titanium dioxide catalyst while a stream of methane gas bubbled slowly through the solution. After 66 hours, a mixture formed that contained the amino acids glycine, alanine, serine, aspartic acid, and glutamic acid. Amino acids are the principal building blocks of proteins, so these results may be similar to early stages of chemical evolution.

Nobel and Priestley Prizes. British-born Herbert C. Brown, 67, of Purdue University in West Lafayette, Ind., won half of the 1979 Nobel Prize for Chemistry for applying boron compounds to organic synthesis, and Georg Wittig, 82, of Heidelberg University in West Germany won the other half for similar work with phosphorous compounds (see NOBEL PRIZES). Milton Harris, 73, of Washington, D.C., former vice-president and research director of the Gillette Company in Boston, won the 1980 Priestley Medal of the American Chemical Society, the highest award in U.S. chemistry.   Lawrence Verbit

In WORLD BOOK, see BENZENE; CHEMISTRY.

CHESS. World champion Anatoly Karpov and former world champion Mikhail Tal, both of Russia, tied for first place in the richest tournament in chess history, the Man and His World Challenge Cup, played in April and May 1979 in Montreal, Canada. Lajos Portisch of Hungary finished third. The $110,-000 prize was surpassed only by purses for head-to-head championship matches. Lubomir Kavalek of Washington, D.C., winner of the 1978 United States Open chess championship, originated the idea of the Challenge Cup as a small gathering of some of the world's best players, with the players handling organizational details. Other participants included Kavalek and former world champion Boris Spassky.

Eight Left. Three U.S. players took part in interzonal competition for the right to challenge Karpov for the world championship in 1981. James Tarjan of Berkeley, Calif., and Edmar Mednis of Woodside, N.Y., competed in Riga, Russia, and Leonid Shamkovich of Flushing, N.Y., competed in Rio de Janeiro, Brazil. No U.S. player qualified for the next round, the 1980 candidates matches. Tal won in Riga and Lev Polucaevsky of Russia was runner-up. Two Hungarians, Zoltan Ribli and Andras Adorzan, tied for third, and Adorzan was awarded third on tie-breaking points.

The Rio de Janeiro interzonal finished in a three-way tie for first place among Robert Hübner of West Germany, Portisch, and former world champion

Jane M. Byrne raises her arms in victory after narrowly defeating Chicago
Mayor Michael A. Bilandic in the Democratic primary on February 27.

Tigran Petrosian of Russia. Joining the six winners from Riga and Rio de Janeiro in the candidates matches will be the two participants in the match that decided who played Karpov for the world championship in 1978 – Viktor Korchnoi, a Russian defector living in Switzerland, and Spassky.

Other Tournaments. The Louis Statham Masters Plus Tournament, played in March and April in Lone Pine, Calif., finished in a four-way tie among Vlastimil Hort of Czechoslovakia, Swetozar Gligornic of Yugoslavia, Vladimir Liberzon of Israel, and Florin Gheorghiu of Romania.

In the seventh annual World Open in July in Philadelphia, six players tied for first place with scores of 8-2 – Anthony Miles of Great Britain; Walter Browne, Arthur B. Bisguier, Bernard Zuckerman, and John Fedorowicz of the United States; and Haukur Angantysson of Iceland. Each won $1,686. Gheorghiu won the 1979 U.S. Open chess championship, played in August in Chicago, and Bisguier was runner-up.

Rachel Crotto of New York City won the United States Women's Chess Championship, played from July 8 to 23 in Los Angeles. She scored $10^{1/2}$ points to $8^{1/2}$ for runner-up Ruth Haring of Alexandria, Va. Winner of the U.S. Junior Chess Championship, held from June 17 to 26 in Hollywood, Calif., was Yasser Seirawan of Seattle.　　　Theodore M. O'Leary

In WORLD BOOK, see CHESS; HOBBY.

CHICAGO. Jane M. Byrne on April 3, 1979, became the first woman to be elected mayor of Chicago. Byrne, a Democrat and former commissioner of consumer affairs, received 82.5 per cent of the vote in a landslide victory over Republican Wallace D. Johnson. But her biggest victory came on February 27, when she narrowly defeated incumbent Michael A. Bilandic in the mayoral primary. That victory was aided by a record total snowfall of 89.7 inches (228 centimeters) and Bilandic's failure to keep city streets clear and public transportation moving. See BYRNE, JANE M.; ELECTIONS (Close-Up).

Education Problems. The Department of Health, Education, and Welfare (HEW) asked the Department of Justice to seek a court-ordered desegregation program for Chicago's public schools on October 29. HEW had rejected the city's voluntary desegregation plan on September 26 and substituted a proposal requiring busing for 55 per cent of the system's students, but the school board rejected it.

Superintendent of Schools Joseph P. Hannon and school board President John D. Carey resigned in late November amid disclosures that school administrators had issued misleading financial statements. Investigations revealed that the school board owed $44 million in payroll deductions that had not been forwarded to the proper agencies, and that its overall deficit was about $500 million. The school board failed to meet its payroll on December 21.

Transit Plans. A $2.4-billion mass-transportation program, including plans to extend rapid-transit service to O'Hare International Airport, was announced on October 2. The proposal came after Chicago and the state of Illinois scrapped plans to build a controversial cross-town expressway, freeing $2 billion earmarked for that project.

The Regional Transportation Authority was authorized by the Illinois state legislature on September 19 to levy a 1 per cent sales tax in the six-county Chicago area. The tax went into effect on November 1, raising the total Chicago sales tax to 6 per cent.

City Management. Mayor Byrne's $1.4-billion 1980 budget, approved on December 27, represented only a 1 per cent increase in city spending from 1979. It included a provision to repay $36.6 million of the city's $103-million deficit, and pared expenses by eliminating almost 1,500 city jobs. The budget also included a sewer tax and increased utility taxes.

Federal Judge Nicholas J. Bua ruled on September 24 that the patronage system for hiring city and county workers was unconstitutional. Mayor Byrne and Cook County Board President George M. Dunne said they would appeal the decision.

A December 20 court order ended a four-day transit-workers strike that had seriously affected some 400,000 commuters. James M. Banovetz

See also CITY. In WORLD BOOK, see CHICAGO.

CHILD WELFARE received special emphasis in many parts of the world during 1979, which was designated the International Year of the Child (IYC) by the United Nations. Many conferences on children's problems were held, and some innovative programs were begun. However, in the United States, the official impact did not extend much beyond speeches and discussions. Although Congress established a national commission for IYC, minimal resources in both power and money limited its role of encouraging and coordinating the efforts of others.

Retrenchment. Continuing economic constriction and inflation and increased spending for defense and energy research claimed federal, state, and private funds that might have gone for children's services. Despite President Jimmy Carter's avowed support of the family, he and many members of Congress resisted requests for new or increased spending on child welfare. And because of inflation, the budget appropriations set for many continuing programs will probably pay for fewer services. There also appeared to be a lack of interest in the subject – the 1980 White House Conference on Children and Youth was moved to 1981; its Conference on Families will be replaced by regional meetings.

Child Abuse continued to arouse public concern. Prevention and treatment plans in 1979 focused on

A rare sight: Children testify at a U.S. Senate Labor Subcommittee on Child and Human Development hearing on May 1, Save the Children Day.

broader targets, such as intrafamily violence caused by adults or other children, adolescent problems, and the plight of children in institutions.

When adolescents began to receive more attention as targets of abuse, such problems as incest (sex between close relatives) had to be faced more openly. The National Center on Child Abuse and Neglect in 1979 funded five new programs to study and treat incest victims and offenders. In Los Angeles, as in many other cities, the Police Department's Juvenile Division increased its efforts to combat the problem. Police officials reported that "sexual abuse and exploitation of juveniles involves virtually all geographic areas and segments of society in Los Angeles." A *Los Angeles Times* article called the situation "a national epidemic of incest."

Early Childhood Projects. The General Accounting Office, the U.S. government's watchdog agency charged with evaluating the cost-effectiveness of federally funded projects, published a review in 1979 of research findings on compensatory programs for underprivileged children. The agency concluded that Head Start and other early-childhood projects resulted in substantial developmental gains for the children involved in them.

Long-term studies by psychologist Irving Lazar of Cornell University and by the Department of Health, Education, and Welfare provided new evidence that some of the earliest programs have had lasting benefits. The programs were especially successful when they focused on helping parents interact with their children as well as on aiding the children directly. Psychologist J. McVicker Hunt reported, after conducting research in Teheran, Iran, and Mount Carmel, Ill., that dramatic improvement occurred when certain patterns of stimulation were offered to infants. As the underprivileged infants he studied grew older, they exceeded several of the norms for middle-class American children.

Foster Care. Agencies that arrange foster care for children who cannot be cared for at home came under increasing criticism in 1979. Investigators charged that the agencies kept children in foster homes too long, moved them about too frequently, and did not work hard enough to return children to their own homes or to remove barriers to permanent adoption. The U.S. National Commission for Children in Need of Parents reported in April that the U.S. foster-care system was an "unconscionable failure" that harmed many of the 500,000 children it served. The commission saw as major problems the reluctance of courts to terminate parents' rights and free children for adoption, and the prohibition against using federal funds for adoption subsidies for hard-to-place children.   Frances A. Mullen

See also MENTAL HEALTH. In WORLD BOOK, see CHILD WELFARE.

CHILDREN'S BOOKS. See LITERATURE FOR CHILDREN.

CHILE. Relations between Chile and the United States reached a low point in 1979. On October 1, the Chilean Supreme Court refused a U.S. request to extradite three military officers indicted by a U.S. grand jury for planning the assassination of Orlando Letelier in Washington, D.C., in 1976.

Letelier was a former Chilean foreign minister under deposed Marxist President Salvador Allende Gossens. He had been working in the United States to discredit the junta that replaced Allende. Michael Townley, an American who had worked for Chile's secret police, confessed to planting in Letelier's car the bomb that killed him and an associate, Ronni Moffitt.

Townley's testimony led to the conviction on February 14 of his three U.S. accomplices. Two received life sentences and one eight years for spying. Townley was sentenced on May 11 to a maximum of 10 years in prison.

Also implicated by Townley's testimony was General Manuel Contreras Sepulveda, head of Chile's secret police in 1973, as well as two of his aides, Lieutenant Colonel Pedro Espinoza Brava and Captain Armando Fernandez Larios. In an unprecedented move, the U.S. Department of Justice attempted to extradite the three officials, but Chile's Supreme Court upheld an earlier ruling denying the request on grounds that Townley's evidence was not admissible under Chilean law.

The U.S. Reacts. On November 29, U.S. President Jimmy Carter acted in retaliation for what he called the "condonement of an act of international terrorism." It was announced that the United States would reduce its embassy and military staffs in Santiago, cut off military credits, and no longer finance or guarantee loans for projects submitted either to the U.S. Export-Import Bank or the Overseas Private Investment Corporation.

Outright violations of human rights all but ceased in 1979, and the press was allowed much more freedom, though on June 26 the opposition newsweekly *Hoy* was banned from publishing for two months. However, in an address on September 11 marking six years of military rule, President Augusto Pinochet Ugarte rejected growing demands for political normalization.

The Economy. Under the guidance of a civilian economic team that stressed free enterprise, the economy continued to recover, and the gross national product registered a gain of 8 per cent, one of the highest in Latin America. Unemployment, which totaled 15 per cent in the Santiago region, continued to be a problem, and economists said it would not improve until Chile had met the heavy payments of its international debt due in 1979 and 1980, after which it could obtain more foreign credit for such projects as low-cost housing.   Everett G. Martin

See also LATIN AMERICA (Facts in Brief Table). In WORLD BOOK, see CHILE.

The first shipment of "Tastes Good, Tastes Happy," a beverage Westerners call Coca-Cola, is loaded at Hong Kong in January for transport to China.

CHINA, PEOPLE'S REPUBLIC OF. The 30th anniversary of the People's Republic on Oct. 1, 1979, saw just one demonstration in Peking (Beijing in the phonetic Pinyin alphabet China adopted on January 1 [see Close-Up]). About 200 young people marched up the Boulevard of Eternal Tranquility with posters and chants. But, instead of hailing the national day, they were chanting, "We demand political democracy. We demand artistic freedom." The march, organized by four underground magazines, was to protest the police closing of an unofficial art exhibition.

Two days earlier, at a meeting of 11,000 senior officials gathered to celebrate the national day, China's Defense Minister Yeh Chien-ying (Ye Jianying) delivered a 20,000-word assessment of the government's three decades. He conceded that the first 17 years were worthy but described the Cultural Revolution of 1966 to 1976 as a "calamity" that plunged the country into "bloodbaths and terror." Most important, he departed from the praise usually bestowed on the late Communist Party Chairman Mao Tse-tung (Mao Zedong). "Leaders are not gods," he said, "they're not infallible and, therefore, they should not be deified."

Season of Unrest. The unauthorized march and the candid speech were symptoms of general uneasiness. In 30 years, the people have enjoyed a small measure of civil freedoms only during brief thaws.

The most recent one began late in 1978 and reached a climax in January and February at the Democracy Wall, where posters appeared criticizing party policies. China's leaders then decided that free speech was getting out of hand. Wei Ching-chang (Wei Jingsheng), a leading activist of the "Peking Spring," arrested in March, was sentenced in October to 15 years in prison on the questionable charge of "military espionage." The official attitude to human rights was summed up by Communist Party Chairman Hua Kuo-feng (Hua Guofeng): "We cannot use democracy to disrupt social order."

Deputy Premier Teng Hsiao-p'ing (Deng Xiaoping), the real power in Peking, delivered a speech on March 16 ordering a halt to "excessive democracy" and forbidding close contacts with Westerners. Beginning in April in Peking and Shanghai, stern provincial decrees put restraints on the latest thaw.

Mounting Grievances. During the summer, thousands of people – including students shipped to the countryside, unhappy peasants, and demobilized soldiers unable to regain the jobs they held before being drafted – descended on Peking to ask the government for economic assistance.

Poor and often hungry, they slept under bridges or in doorways. In August, about 400 such persons demonstrated in front of the Chungnanhai, the crimson-walled quarter where the leaders live and

Speaking of Zhongguo...

Have you ever dreamed of taking a slow boat to Zhongguo or making a religious pilgrimage to Xizang? These place names may sound obscure or unreal, but they refer to well-known places. Zhongguo is China, and Xizang is Tibet.

Place names like Xizang and personal names like Deng Xiaoping — deputy premier of the People's Republic of China — are examples of the Pinyin system for transcribing Chinese into English or any language that uses the Roman alphabet. Before Pinyin, Deng Xiaoping was Teng Hsiao-p'ing. That was before Jan. 1, 1979.

The State Council of China now insists that all information originating in China and using the Roman alphabet must use Pinyin. So the official New China News Agency uses Pinyin in all its news releases. China has asked all other governments and news media to use the system, so that names will be standardized worldwide. The United Nations and the United States Department of State agreed to use Pinyin, as did *The New York Times* and most newspapers in the English-speaking world.

Almost every organization makes one or more exceptions, however. For example, most continue to use the word *China* rather than *Zhongguo*. And many prefer to use *Peking* for China's capital, rather than the Pinyin *Beijing*.

Such familiar names as Peking and Mao Tse-tung were transcriptions in the Wade-Giles system, which is now giving way to Pinyin. Wade-Giles had been widely used since it was developed in the 1800s by British diplomat Sir Thomas Wade and refined about 1900 by British linguist Herbert A. Giles.

The Chinese language does not have an alphabet. Instead, the written Chinese language consists of characters that look like sketches to the Western eye. Each character represents an object, an idea, or a sound. For example, one character stands for the word *sun*, and another represents a sound. It is relatively easy to transcribe a common noun like *man* from Chinese into English, but proper names — those of people, places, or things — have always required a system of common agreement.

China's government says that Pinyin is superior because it most closely approximates the sounds used in the Chinese language. In fact, the word *Pinyin* means *transcription*. The Chinese government hopes that Pinyin will help standardize pronunciations within China, too, where there are many regional dialects.

To approximate the sounds of spoken Chinese, Pinyin uses many q's, x's, and z's. But the sounds these letters represent are not necessarily the sounds English speakers are used to. For example, the letter x is pronounced as "sh" rather than as "eks."

At first, Pinyin evoked a wave of humor. A letter to the editor complained about a newspaper's use of Pinyin, "Xurely you zhest." A *Wall Street Journal* headline joked, "In Beijing, Xiamen and All China, People Are Minding Their X's and Q's."

But Pinyin is no laughing matter to those librarians, book publishers, and mapmakers who have a substantial backlog of materials and information using another transcription system. The cost of switching to Pinyin will be enormous for publishers of atlases and owners of card catalogs with thousands of names on file.

China has made available a list of its political leaders, and of course any name that appears in Chinese news dispatches from now on will be in Pinyin. But place names remain a big problem. By September 1979, China had released only about 18,000 place names in Pinyin. The U.S. Board on Geographic Names (BGN), which standardizes place names, has about 100,000 Chinese place names on file. A few, such as Harbin, are the same in Wade-Giles and Pinyin, but most are different. China has promised to supply the other names.

The Library of Congress decided tentatively to change to Pinyin in its comprehensive catalog of books and other materials, but a final decision was delayed until 1980, placing in limbo materials that arrive in the meantime. The British Library has already switched. And the Pinyin bandwagon to Guangzhou (Canton) rolls on.

Patricia Dragisic

©1979 Arnie Levin

work. Hundreds of persons from the provinces also demonstrated in the capital in September, demanding the right to move back there. They had been relocated to the provinces by the government during the Cultural Revolution.

Some of this unrest was fueled by massive unemployment. One official put the number of jobless at 20 million, but this was probably a huge underestimate. One person in 11 was out of work in Peking early in the year. And in June, the National People's Congress was told that about 7.5 million new jobs would have to be found each year for young people entering the labor force. The official newspaper *People's Daily* also estimated that from 1979 to 1984, jobs would have to be provided annually for 3 million high school graduates.

To cope with this dangerous new problem, the government ordered local governments to create jobs, either by banding the young in service cooperatives or by make-work projects in parks and streets.

Forward Steps. But the regime headed by Teng and Hua made some reforms. The People's Republic adopted its first criminal code in July, to become effective on Jan. 1, 1980. Thousands of people persecuted by the "Gang of Four" in the early 1970s were "rehabilitated," and many were restored to their previous positions. Unlike Mao, who distrusted alien ideas, the new rulers opened the gates to Western and Japanese ideas, arts, technological know-how, and visitors. For example, Charlie Chaplin's films were seen in 1979 in every major city, along with other long-banned Hollywood movies. Western tales and novels were translated, and sold out within hours. The classics of Western music were again heard in China. And, at the hours when radio stations broadcast English lessons, life seemed to come to a halt across China. Despite the restraints on civil rights, the people felt freer than at any time in more than 20 years.

Painful "Readjustment." The decision to give the top priority to the Four Modernizations— agriculture, industry, national defense, and science and technology — had been made by the new regime in 1977. But in late 1978, the leaders realized that China was in no position to pay for all that its trade missions had ordered from Europe, Japan, and the United States. Thus, in May 1979, the government ordered a painful "readjustment," which really meant belt-tightening. Trade officials again went abroad, but this time to cancel or sharply reduce the deals made in 1978.

Priorities were reordered. Instead of emphasizing heavy industry, the leaders now gave top priority to agriculture, which employs 4 of every 5 workers. Next came the manufacture of consumer goods, which would provide the greatest number of jobs, and exports for hard currency. Third on the list came transport and energy; some newly completed plants stood idle for months for lack of electric power. Last

on the high-priority list came some steel mills and 13 major fertilizer plants.

Hua said in June that the belt-tightening would last until 1982, and this meant that the ambitious goals set for 1985 would not be met. But China bought $3 billion worth of industrial technology and equipment in 1979, more than double the figure for 1978. Imports and exports both increased. World bankers regarded the nation as an excellent risk, and, by fall, commercial credit to China had reached $26 billion. The harvest of 305 million metric tons (336 million short tons) of grain was a near record.

China took vigorous steps to control its growing population, which according to some sources totaled 893.8 million. Financial and educational incentives were introduced to limit the number of children per family – preferably to one child, but not more than two. Beginning in March 1980, the salaries of workers who have a third child were to be cut by 10 per cent.

"Defensive Attack." To Peking, the signing of the Russian-Vietnamese treaty on Nov. 3, 1978, was a reminder of Moscow's growing influence in Indochina – something that China was determined to prevent. Beginning in 1978 also, Chinese intelligence kept reporting Vietnam's preparations for invading Cambodia, which was then aligned diplomatically with Peking.

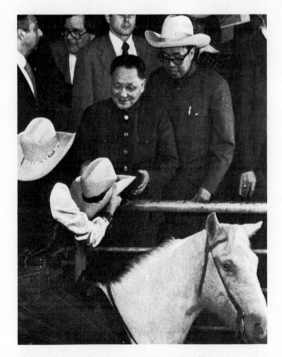

China's Deputy Premier Teng Hsiao-p'ing (Deng Xiaoping in the Pinyin transcription system) gets a cowboy hat during a February visit to Texas.

On February 17, an estimated 250,000 Chinese troops attacked Vietnamese border settlements in mountain passes defended mainly by paramilitary forces. There were threatening Russian words and moves, but the Chinese limited their advance to a frontier strip 20 to 25 miles (32 to 40 kilometers) deep. Russia did not enter the war.

The costs of the month-long war were high to both countries. In May, Peking reported its casualties at 20,000 killed and wounded, and Vietnam's at 50,000. United States sources estimated that this meant 5,000 Chinese troops were killed. The "peace" talks dragged on through the rest of the year, with a continual exchange of charges and skirmishes.

Looking Outward. China and the United States established full diplomatic relations on January 1. As part of Peking's increasingly outward-looking policies, China was turning to the West and Japan for help in becoming a powerful industrial and military nation by the year 2000. Teng visited the United States for nine days beginning January 28. In Washington, D.C., he met with President Jimmy Carter, congressional leaders, and business executives. He also visited Atlanta, Ga.; Houston; and Seattle. On the way home, Teng visited Tokyo on February 6 and 7 to meet with Japanese leaders. And Premier Hua toured Western Europe in October. Steadily, the policies of the United States and China came closer together.

The Enemy. At times, relations between Peking and Moscow came dangerously close to a breaking point. China and Russia agreed in July to resume talks on normalizing relations. There was little progress, however, when talks started in October. And both nations continued to pursue their struggle on the political battlefronts of the world. In their travels, Chinese leaders tried to persuade the United States, Japan, and Western Europe to resist Russian "hegemony," Peking's term for expansionism.

Dangers Ahead. All through the year, Teng continued to solidify his hold on the Communist Party and the government. Old comrades who had been victimized by Mao during the Cultural Revolution were reinstalled in command of the economy. Twelve persons purged by Mao were named to the Communist Party's Central Committee in September, and some regained seats on the ruling Politburo, where Teng's allies now held a 3 to 1 edge over the radicals who survived the post-Mao purges. Teng had also begun to groom political heirs, to avoid the kind of internal warfare that marked Mao's last years. But, the press said millions feared a struggle for power when the old leaders die. Mark Gayn

See also ASIA (Facts in Brief Table). In WORLD BOOK, see CHINA.

CHRONOLOGY. See pages 8 through 21.

CHURCHES. See EASTERN ORTHODOX CHURCHES; JEWS AND JUDAISM; PROTESTANTISM; RELIGION; ROMAN CATHOLIC CHURCH.

CITY. The financial plight of many United States cities grew steadily worse in 1979 as urban areas continued to suffer high levels of inflation and unemployment. The June 1978 passage of California's Proposition 13, which cut property taxes there by 57 per cent, aroused a tax-cutting fervor that left cities generally unable to pass tax increases. Moreover, existing tax bases continued to shrink as urban populations declined and state and federal governments failed to provide increased grants to the cities.

As double-digit inflation ate into their revenues, cities were forced to cut spending. New York City's balanced-budget program called for the elimination of up to 24,000 municipal jobs by 1982. Chicago's 1980 budget specified at least 1,000 fewer jobs. In Cleveland, similar economy measures did not prevent the city from sinking deeper into default. It defaulted on $3.3 million in city notes on August 31, following a December 1978 default of $14 million. See CHICAGO; NEW YORK CITY.

The Urban Policy announced in 1978 by President Jimmy Carter made little headway in overcoming the cities' deep-seated problems. Although designed to increase federal aid and provide incentives for investment in the cities, it was severely crippled when the 95th Congress failed to provide funding for most of the programs. The 96th Congress approved one element of Carter's program on May 2, however, when it authorized $200 million in aid during fiscal 1979 to 1,230 cities and counties that had unemployment rates of at least 6.5 per cent during the period from April to September 1978.

The Carter Administration restated its commitment to the cities on February 6 when it announced, in conjunction with the Federal National Mortgage Association, that an additional $500 million would be made available for residential loans in older urban areas. Under this program, the loans carry an interest rate of 6.8 to 10 per cent.

In a congressional hearing in May, the General Accounting Office (GAO) reported that the National Urban Development Action Grant (UDAG) program had authorized $400 million annually in grants to stimulate investment by local governments and private corporations since it was established in 1977. The GAO reported that, in the sample areas it had studied, government grants of $80 million had generated private expenditures of $382 million. The report also stated that two-thirds of the grants went to older cities in 18 Northeastern and Midwestern states. Opponents of the program criticized this regional bias as well as UDAG's tendency to support such commercial ventures as hotels.

Many cities had to deal with the expiration of another federal measure, the Comprehensive Employment and Training Act (CETA). About 100,000 public service workers completed this federally financed job-training program. CETA workers in some cities, such as Philadelphia and Miami, Fla., were given job extensions by the Department of Labor, but workers in other cities were dismissed on October 1.

Municipal Strikes continued to plague cities, many of which were either unwilling or unable to meet demands for increased benefits and wages. New Orleans was one of the hardest hit. A 16-day strike of about 1,100 police officers forced the cancellation of many Mardi Gras activities and cost millions in tourist dollars. The strike ended on March 4 when officers returned to work without union approval.

Transit strikes stranded commuters in Los Angeles and Cleveland in August. Bus service to 1.2 million Los Angeles residents was interrupted when 5,000 drivers and 1,700 clerks and maintenance workers staged a three-day walkout. In Cleveland, 2,000 bus drivers and mechanics held a three-day wildcat strike. Chicago transit workers struck on December 17 for four days. Public workers also walked off the job in Indianapolis; Woodbridge, N.J.; Santa Monica, Calif.; Pittsburgh; and Toledo, Ohio.

Teachers' strikes interrupted classes in several cities in March. An eight-week school strike in St. Louis ended on March 12, but only after private industry provided $600,000 to help meet salary demands. More than half of the District of Columbia's 6,200 teachers struck for 23 days, and Baton Rouge, La., endured a 15-day strike.

Former New Orleans Mayor Moon Landrieu, an advocate of federal aid to the cities, became the secretary of housing and urban development on September 24.

The new school year was delayed by strikes in cities in 14 states. Detroit; San Francisco; Indianapolis; and Spokane, Wash., endured major walkouts in the fall, and the teachers' strike that broke out in Cleveland on October 16 had not been settled by year-end.

School Integration was a prominent issue in many cities as they struggled to map out plans that would comply with federal guidelines. Milwaukee settled a 14-year school desegregation case on May 4 by agreeing to raise the number of students in integrated schools to 80 per cent of the total enrollment. St. Louis avoided school busing when U.S. District Judge James Meredith ruled on April 12 that the city's racially unbalanced schools had resulted from racial distribution of the population rather than from school board policies.

Busing programs aimed at desegregating the schools went into effect in Cleveland and Columbus, Ohio, in September. Cleveland's plan, the result of six years of court deliberations, called for the busing of about 9,500 students in 1979. In Columbus, court-ordered busing involved an estimated 50,000 students. New or expanded busing programs also went into operation in Pittsburgh; Shreveport, La.; Tucson, Ariz.; San Diego; and Wichita, Kans.

The Department of Health, Education, and Welfare (HEW) rejected Chicago's latest school desegregation plan on September 26 and on December 13 the U.S. Department of Justice asked the attorney general to sue the city. According to HEW analysts, the plan failed to accomplish the maximum practical amount of desegregation.

Population Trends. According to a report released in January by the Department of Housing and Urban Development (HUD), more than twice as many people moved from central cities to suburbs as from suburbs to cities during the period from 1975 to 1978. HUD concluded that the movement of the middle class into the cities accounted for no more than a "tiny fraction" of the nation's urban population. During that time, Chicago lost an average of 12,000 middle-class families per year, and New York City lost 37,000. Among the nation's 10 largest cities, only those in the "sun belt" – Houston, San Diego, and San Antonio – registered population gains during the 1970s.

A report prepared by Richard P. Nathan of the Brookings Institution in Washington, D.C., and issued by the National Tax Association in January, asserted that certain conditions may reverse this trend in the future. Nathan cited an increase in the number of childless households, higher commuting costs, reduced urban crime rates, and restoration projects in the inner cities as factors likely to attract middle-class suburbanites back to the cities.

International population trends also projected a bleak outlook for cities in developing nations. Projections issued by the International Bank for Recon-

50 Largest Cities in the United States

Rank	City	Population (a)	Per cent change in population since 1970 census	Mayor or City Manager (b)
1.	New York	7,297,787	− 7.6	Edward I. Koch (D, 12/81)
2.	Chicago	3,062,881	− 9.1	Jane M. Byrne (D, 4/83)
3.	Los Angeles	2,761,222	− 1.8	Tom Bradley (NP, 6/81)
4.	Philadelphia	1,778,345	− 8.8	William J. Green (D, 12/83)
5.	Houston	1,544,960	+17.9	Jim McConn (NP, 1/82)
6.	Detroit	1,289,910	−14.8	Coleman A. Young (D, 1/82)
7.	Dallas	844,528	− 0.6	*George R. Schrader (1973)
8.	Baltimore	804,304	−11.2	William Donald Schaefer (D, 12/83)
9.	San Diego	799,725	+14.7	*Ray Blair (1978)
10.	San Antonio	793,374	+12.0	*Thomas E. Huebner (1977)
11.	Honolulu	717,852	+13.9	Frank F. Fasi (D, 1/81)
12.	Indianapolis	704,556	− 3.5	William Hudnut (R, 12/83)
13.	Washington, D.C.	684,891	− 9.5	Marion S. Barry, Jr. (D, 1/83)
14.	Phoenix	684,516	+16.2	*Marvin A. Andrews (1976)
15.	Memphis	668,443	+ 1.7	Wyeth Chandler (I, 12/83)
16.	San Francisco	655,072	− 8.5	Dianne Feinstein (NP, 1/84)
17.	Milwaukee	653,417	− 8.9	Henry W. Maier (D, 4/80)
18.	Boston	618,493	− 3.5	Kevin H. White (D, 12/83)
19.	Cleveland	609,187	−18.9	George V. Voinovich (D, 11/81)
20.	San Jose	583,402	+26.5	*Ted Tedesco (1973)
21.	New Orleans	561,266	− 5.4	Ernest N. Morial (D, 4/82)
22.	Columbus, O.	532,339	− 1.4	Tom Moody (R, 12/83)
23.	Jacksonville, Fla.	527,777	+ 4.7	Jake Godbold (D, 5/83)
24.	St. Louis	517,671	−16.8	James Conway (D, 4/81)
25.	Seattle	488,928	− 7.9	Charles Royer (NP, 1/82)
26.	Denver	475,098	− 7.7	William H. McNichols, Jr. (D, 1/83)
27.	Kansas City, Mo.	458,573	− 9.6	*Robert A. Kipp (1974)
28.	Pittsburgh	442,139	−15.0	Richard S. Caliguiri (D, 1/82)
29.	Nashville-Davidson	428,957	+ 0.7	Richard H. Fulton (D, 9/83)
30.	Atlanta	416,715	−15.8	Maynard Jackson (D, 1/82)
31.	Cincinnati	403,363	−11.1	*William V. Donaldson (1975)
32.	El Paso	395,419	+22.7	Thomas D. Westfall (NP, 5/81)
33.	Buffalo	390,065	−15.7	James D. Griffin (D, 12/81)
34.	Portland, Ore.	383,904	+ 0.4	Connie McCready (D, 12/80)
35.	Oklahoma City	371,802	+ 1.0	*James J. Cook (1976)
36.	Fort Worth	367,993	− 6.5	*Robert L. Herchert (1978)
37.	Omaha	365,711	+ 2.0	Al Veys (NP, 5/81)
38.	Minneapolis	360,269	−17.1	Donald M. Fraser (D, 1/82)
39.	Toledo	358,677	− 6.4	*Walter C. Kane (1977)
40.	Miami	346,716	+ 3.5	*Joseph R. Grassie (1976)
41.	Long Beach	336,697	− 6.8	*John E. Dever (1977)
42.	Tulsa	334,365	+ 1.2	James M. Inhofe (R, 5/80)
43.	Oakland	332,385	− 8.1	*David A. Self (1978)
44.	Newark	324,138	−15.1	Kenneth A. Gibson (D, 7/82)
45.	Austin	323,250	+24.9	*Dan H. Davidson (1972)
46.	Louisville	322,870	−10.7	William Stansbury (D, 11/81)
47.	Baton Rouge	308,178	+13.7	W. W. Dumas (D, 12/80)
48.	Tucson	301,152	−12.6	*Joel D. Valdez (1974)
49.	Charlotte	295,685	+ 2.9	*David A. Burkhalter (1971)
50.	Albuquerque	291,187	+19.5	David Rusk (D, 11/81)

Sources:
(a) 1977 estimates (U.S. Bureau of the Census).
(b) *Asterisk before name denotes city manager (as of September 1978, *Municipal Year Book, 1979,* International City Management Association); all others are mayors (as of June 1978, National League of Cities). Dates are those of expiration of term for mayors and dates of appointment for city managers.
D—Democrat; R—Republican; NP—Nonpartisan; I—Independent.

Average cost of living (family of 4) (c)	Unemployment rate (d)	Revenue (e)	Gross debt outstanding (e)	Per capita income (f)	Sales tax rate (g)
$21,587	9.5	$15,922,707	$14,881,027	$8,105	8%
18,794	5.5	1,459,821	1,351,558	8,522	5-6%
17,722	5.5	1,950,819	2,659,347	8,429	6%
19,416	7.0	1,303,829	1,565,024	7,436	6%
17,114	3.1	493,171	788,783	8,247	5%
19,145	7.5	1,061,015	683,743	8,535	4%
16,714	3.4	355,917	465,353	7,704	5%
18,699	6.2	1,151,766	498,477	7,155	5%
17,707	6.2	291,303	130,655	7,070	6%
n/a	5.5	467,179	570,374	6,007	5%
23,099	5.8	306,183	241,866	7,950	4%
18,193	5.3	310,649	283,522	7,563	4%
20,105	4.3	1,672,950	1,510,866	9,306	5%
n/a	4.8	266,375	397,227	7,174	4%
n/a	6.4	626,190	746,210	6,465	6%
19,427	6.1	945,149	624,232	9,260	6%
20,025	3.5	310,778	256,003	7,908	4%
22,117	6.4	863,725	555,303	7,590	5%
18,987	4.5	340,487	434,105	8,315	4$^1/_2$%
n/a	4.7	210,781	138,009	8,632	5$^3/_4$%
n/a	6.5	270,157	259,155	6,801	6%
n/a	4.3	187,339	317,799	6,798	4%
n/a	5.8	422,190	526,571	6,536	4%
17,897	5.8	327,490	163,000	7,524	4$^1/_8$%
18,671	6.4	363,330	491,600	8,457	5.425%
18,565	4.0	403,645	396,301	8,050	6%
18,262	4.2	282,989	318,473	7,883	3$^5/_8$%
18,008	5.7	167,312	137,772	7,487	6%
16,627	4.7	453,406	411,216	6,647	6%
16,897	4.5	252,796	587,913	7,352	4%
18,354	4.6	515,347	243,369	7,272	4$^1/_2$%
n/a	7.4	90,126	62,435	5,071	5%
19,517	7.5	417,575	269,852	6,980	7%
n/a	5.3	155,059	54,222	7,875	—
n/a	3.1	179,419	385,014	6,932	4%
n/a	3.4	135,653	184,059	7,704	5%
n/a	5.5	121,324	117,048	6,986	4$^1/_2$%
19,389	3.1	202,567	205,200	8,021	4%
n/a	6.9	129,952	140,184	7,312	4$^1/_2$%
n/a	6.0	118,363	117,517	7,755	4%
n/a	5.5	205,203	128,443	8,429	6%
n/a	3.0	138,319	242,543	7,383	4%
n/a	6.1	197,021	167,986	9,260	6%
n/a	6.3	378,696	164,308	8,632	5%
16,211	3.0	230,392	423,421	6,212	5%
n/a	5.4	195,521	347,524	7,300	5%
16,806	6.5	123,029	264,742	6,649	6%
n/a	3.9	120,849	164,644	6,317	4%
n/a	3.9	115,034	165,154	7,050	4%
n/a	6.3	117,257	140,491	6,592	4%

(c) Estimates for autumn, 1978, for Standard Metropolitan Statistical Areas (U.S. Bureau of Labor Statistics). n/a—not available.
(d) September 1979 preliminary (U.S. Bureau of Labor Statistics).
(e) 1976–77 figures in thousands (U.S. Bureau of the Census).
(f) 1977 figures for Standard Metropolitan Statistical Areas (U.S. Bureau of Economic Analysis).
(g) Includes state, county, and city sales and use taxes (Commerce Clearing House, Inc.).

struction and Development in August indicate that cities and towns in less-developed countries will have to cope with 1 billion more residents in the year 2000 than they had in 1975. The report predicted that 600 million of these city dwellers will be living in "absolute poverty."

Urban Neighborhoods were more organized, vocal, and influential than ever before in 1979. The President's National Commission on Neighborhoods presented the results of a 15-month study to Congress on March 15. The report detailed over 200 recommendations representing "a major new direction for America's neighborhoods." It urged the federal government to outlaw insurance *redlining* (denying coverage to applicants in certain neighborhoods); work toward full employment; and provide income tax and property tax incentives for neighborhood reinvestment. The commission also recommended that state and local governments adapt building codes to encourage housing rehabilitation, channel human services through neighborhood organizations, and encourage neighborhood representatives to attend city meetings and take part in neighborhood projects.

The National Association of Neighborhoods held 47 conventions in 1979, and a total of 10,000 delegates developed grass-roots neighborhood platforms. Proposals put forth in these platforms were combined in a single platform at the association convention in Louisville, Ky., in November. The composite platform contained planks on housing and community development; energy, environment, and transportation; jobs and economic development; social services and crime; and neighborhood government.

Mayoral Elections were held in many cities in 1979, and voters in most cities appeared to be satisfied with the present administration. Among the victorious incumbents in 1979 were Democrats William H. McNichols, Jr., of Denver; William D. Schaefer of Baltimore; Richard G. Hatcher of Gary, Ind.; Kevin H. White of Boston; and Ted L. Wilson of Salt Lake City, Utah; and Republicans William H. Hudnut of Indianapolis and Lila Cockrell of San Antonio.

There were notable exceptions to this trend, however. In Chicago, Jane M. Byrne defeated Michael A. Bilandic in the February 27 Democratic primary and was elected mayor on April 3 (see ELECTIONS [Close-Up]). Dennis J. Kucinich, the controversial mayor of Cleveland, was defeated by Republican George V. Voinovich on November 6. Democrat Richard Arrington became the first black elected mayor of Birmingham, Ala., on October 30.

In other mayoral contests, William J. Green was elected in Philadelphia; Donald M. Fraser in Minneapolis, Minn.; and Dianne Feinstein in San Francisco. See ELECTIONS.   James M. Banovetz

In WORLD BOOK, see CITY and articles on cities.

CIVIL RIGHTS. A report issued by the United States Department of State on Feb. 10, 1979, indicated "an increased awareness of human rights conditions around the world." Several countries increased citizens' political rights during the year.

In Spain, President Adolfo Suarez Gonzalez formed the first constitutional government since 1936 after his party won a plurality in national elections on March 1. Nigeria elected Shehu Shagari, its first civilian leader in 13 years, in a five-stage election in July and August (see SHAGARI, SHEHU).

Unfortunately, gains in civil liberties in some nations were accompanied by reduced freedoms in others. The Inter-American Human Rights Commission reported on September 15 that it had overwhelming evidence that prisoners were being methodically killed and tortured in Argentina. On September 25, Argentina expelled publisher Jacobo Timerman, who had been held without formal charges for 29 months. Timerman fled to Israel.

The United States Department of State, in a report made public on February 8, accused Israel of abusing the rights of Arabs in the occupied West Bank and Gaza Strip. The State Department called for the release of more than 100 political prisoners following President Jimmy Carter's state visit to South Korea in July.

Brian Weber, who was passed over in favor of black candidates for a job-training program, sued but lost his case in a Supreme Court ruling in June.

Trials and executions of those who displeased the regime of Ayatollah Ruhollah Khomeini were commonplace in Iran throughout the year, and opposition newspapers were shut down in August.

Black Rights. Vernon E. Jordan, Jr., president of the National Urban League, characterized 1979 as "a year of crisis for America's black people" on January 17. Jordan cited the high unemployment rate among black youths as the single most serious problem and urged the adoption of a national goal of full employment to avoid pending "disaster" for blacks. Leaders of the National Association for the Advancement of Colored People on May 18 emphatically reaffirmed their support of nuclear energy as "less costly to consumers than many alternatives."

Several black leaders became deeply engrossed in Middle East problems and moved to establish ties with Palestinians following the resignation of Andrew J. Young, Jr., on August 15 as U.S. ambassador to the United Nations. Young resigned after admitting that he had held an unauthorized meeting with a representative of the Palestine Liberation Organization (PLO) (see UNITED NATIONS). Joseph E. Lowery, president of the Southern Christian Leadership Conference (SCLC), met with Zehdi Labib Terzi, the PLO observer at the United Nations on August 20, and declared that the SCLC unconditionally supported "the human rights of all Palestinians, including the right of self-determination in regard to their own homeland." Lowery urged the PLO and Israel to negotiate. Jesse L. Jackson, head of Operation PUSH, journeyed to the Middle East in September, met with PLO leader Yasir Arafat, and called for Israel-PLO talks.

Black leaders were by no means unanimous in their support of the PLO, however. Some, concerned with the growing rift between blacks and Jews, made public appeals for reconciliation. In October, Jordan severely criticized black leaders who had been meeting with the PLO, stressing the interdependence of blacks and Jews in the United States. Historically, Jews have been among the largest contributors to black civil rights causes.

School busing was prominent in judicial and political deliberations in 1979. The Supreme Court of the United States on July 1 upheld federal orders that Dayton and Columbus, Ohio, use busing to diminish racial segregation. On September 25, the Department of Health, Education, and Welfare (HEW) rejected a school desegregation plan submitted by Chicago school officials on the grounds that it failed to accomplish the maximum practical amount of desegregation. On October 29, HEW turned the Chicago case over to the Department of Justice, which asked the attorney general in December to sue the Chicago Board of Education. The U.S. House of Representatives on July 24 defeated a proposed constitutional amendment banning the use of busing to desegregate public schools.

Court Decisions. In a landmark decision, *United Steelworkers of America v. Weber,* the Supreme Court ruled on June 27 that private employers can legally give special preference to black workers to eliminate "manifest racial imbalance" in traditionally white-only jobs. A federal district court dismissed on May 15 a suit brought by Sears, Roebuck & Company challenging federal equal-employment programs.

Women's changing status was further defined by two Supreme Court decisions. The court ruled on March 5 that state laws requiring husbands, but not wives, to pay alimony violated the equal protection clause of the U.S. Constitution. On June 25, it ruled unconstitutional a Social Security Act provision allowing benefits to families of unemployed fathers but denying the same benefits to families left equally needy by a mother's joblessness.

The Supreme Court made several important civil liberties rulings affecting police procedures. It declared on March 27 that police cannot constitutionally stop motorists to inspect their drivers' licenses without reason to believe that they are violating the law. The court relaxed curbs on illegally seized evidence when it ruled on June 25 that evidence taken from a suspect during a legal arrest is admissible even if the law under which the arrest was made is meanwhile declared unconstitutional. Also, the court ruled on June 20 that police do not need a search warrant before installing a device to record the numbers dialed from a particular telephone.

One of the year's major civil liberties controversies centered around the publication of a magazine article that, the Department of Justice contended, described "how a hydrogen bomb works." On March 9, Milwaukee Federal District Judge Robert W. Warren had prohibited publication of the article in *The Progressive,* a magazine of political commentary based in Madison, Wis. While the case was being reviewed, a similar article was published in *The Madison Press Connection,* a Wisconsin newspaper, on September 16. The Justice Department moved to dismiss the case on September 17, and the controversial article was published in October.

The Supreme Court ruled on April 18 that when defending their work against libel suits by public figures, journalists can be required to disclose the opinions they held while preparing the material and their reasons for making the particular news judgments. In *Gannett Company v. DePasquale,* the Supreme Court ruled on July 2 that the public and the press have no constitutional right to attend pretrial criminal hearings. The ruling permits trial judges to close their courtrooms during such hearings if they believe the rights of the accused would be violated by publicity. Critics feared it could be invoked to close full-scale trials.   Louis W. Koenig

See also articles on individual countries; COURTS AND LAWS; SUPREME COURT OF THE UNITED STATES. In WORLD BOOK, see CIVIL RIGHTS.

CIVILETTI, BENJAMIN RICHARD (1935-   ), was sworn in as United States attorney general on Aug. 16, 1979. He succeeded Griffin B. Bell, who resigned on July 19. See CABINET, UNITED STATES.

Civiletti joined the Department of Justice in 1977 as head of the Criminal Division. He was then sworn in as deputy attorney general on May 16, 1978, supervising such agencies as the Federal Bureau of Investigation, the Drug Enforcement Administration, and the Criminal Division. As deputy attorney general, he became involved in several major controversies, including the investigation of T. Bertram Lance, former director of the Office of Management and Budget. As attorney general, Civiletti is expected to continue Bell's efforts to toughen law enforcement against white-collar crime and police brutality, improve the administration of justice, and prevent political interference in Justice Department operations.

Civiletti was born on July 17, 1935, in Peekskill, N.Y. He earned a B.A. degree at Johns Hopkins University in Baltimore in 1957, and a law degree in 1961 from the University of Maryland School of Law in College Park. Civiletti was assistant U.S. attorney in Maryland from 1962 to 1964. He then joined a law firm in Baltimore. He was a member of the Maryland State Legislature's Task Force on Crime in 1975 and 1976. Civiletti and his wife, Gaile, have three children.   Madelyn Krzak

CLARK, CHARLES JOSEPH (JOE) (1939-   ), became prime minister of Canada on June 4, 1979. The youngest person and the first Western Canadian to head the country, Clark resigned on December 14, the day after his government was defeated in a vote in Parliament on his proposed budget. See CANADA.

Clark was born on June 5, 1939, in High River, Alta., where his family had published the weekly *High River Times* since 1905. He attended local public schools and earned a B.A. in history from the University of Alberta in 1960. He received an M.A. in political science there in 1972, and his law degree from the University of New Brunswick in 1976.

Starting early in the political arena, Clark served as president of the Progressive Conservative Student Federation from 1962 to 1965. From 1965 to 1967, he took an active part in the Progressive Conservative Party's (PCP) provincial organization in Alberta, developing new campaign strategies that led to Peter Lougheed's election as a member of the Alberta parliament in 1967 and as premier in 1971.

On Oct. 30, 1972, Clark was elected to the federal House of Commons from Alberta's Rocky Mountain district. He won re-election in 1974 and solidified his position in 1976 when the PCP national convention elected him party leader.

Maureen Anne McTeer, a lawyer, married Clark in 1973.   Marsha F. Goldsmith

CLOTHING. See FASHION.

COAL. The long-term prospects of the United States coal industry brightened on July 15, 1979, when President Jimmy Carter announced a new energy program that committed America to increased use of coal in conventional electric power plants and in a new generation of synthetic-fuels plants (see ENERGY). The commitment sent waves of optimism cascading through the nation's coal fields, where production was at least 100 million short tons (91 million metric tons) below capacity. Carter's November cutoff of Iranian oil imports after a mob of students, with government support, seized the U.S. Embassy in Teheran, further spurred interest in domestic coal resources.

Coal production reached 632 million short tons (575 million metric tons) by November, up from 519 million short tons (472 million metric tons) during the same period in 1978. Consumption during the second quarter of 1979 was 8 per cent higher than during the second quarter of 1978.

The New Energy Program would compel electric utilities that now burn oil to switch to coal, thus decreasing the electric-utility industry's consumption of oil — now about 1.6 million barrels per day — by 50 per cent by 1990. The Carter energy program also called for the construction of plants that convert coal into *synfuels* (synthetic liquid fuels) and gas similar to natural gas. With existing technology, it takes 1 short ton of coal to produce about 3 barrels of liquid fuel or about 15,000 cubic feet (425 cubic meters) of gas. A full-scale synthetic-fuels industry would increase coal consumption by hundreds of millions of tons per year.

Coal Rights. Secretary of the Interior Cecil D. Andrus announced in June that the federal government would resume leasing the rights to coal on federal lands in 1981 and 1982. The leasing program had been held up since 1971 by a variety of problems.

The initial plan would release about 1.5 billion short tons (9.7 million metric tons) of coal for mining. Environmental impact statements would be required from the mining companies. Ultimately, some 200 billion short tons (181 billion metric tons) may be available for production. About 60 per cent of all the coal in the western United States is in federally controlled land.

Environmentalists Worry. Environmentalists and some scientists expressed concern that increased coal use would worsen ecological problems related to coal combustion. Two of the major problems cited were "acid rain," caused by industrial pollutants harmful to wildlife, and the build-up of carbon dioxide in the earth's atmosphere, which may affect climate.

The U.S. Department of Energy (DOE) agreed early in 1979 to help fund construction of a series of industrial boilers that demonstrate *fluidized-bed combustion*, a clean method for burning coal. In fluidized-bed combustion, sulfur dioxide – a troublesome air pollutant – is removed during the combustion process, rather than being released into the atmosphere.

More on Synfuels. West Germany and the United States signed a major agreement in October to cooperate in building and operating a coal-to-liquid-fuel demonstration plant near Morgantown, W. Va. The West German government and several West German industrial firms will pay 25 per cent of the cost, estimated at $700 million. The plant will convert 6,000 short tons (5,400 metric tons) of high-sulfur coal into a variety of synthetic fuels – equivalent to about 20,000 barrels of oil per day.

In South Africa, the government approved a $2-billion expansion of its SASOL-2 plant, which will produce oil from coal. SASOL-1 is the world's only full-scale coal-to-oil plant. SASOL-2 will go into production in 1980, and a third plant will be operational in 1982. The SASOL plants, named for the state-owned South African Coal, Oil, & Gas Corporation, use the same basic process that permitted Germany to obtain 35 per cent of its oil from coal during World War II. Great Britain, preparing for the exhaustion of its North Sea oil fields early in the next century, decided to build two coal-conversion plants.   Michael Woods

See also MINES AND MINING. In WORLD BOOK, see COAL.

Chicagoan Walter Perschke buys a Brasher's doubloon for $430,000 in July. It has a sunrise on the face, *bottom left,* and an eagle on the back, *bottom right.*

COIN COLLECTING. Prices paid for rare coins soared to unprecedented heights in 1979, partly because of spectacular increases in the gold and silver markets. As their values increased, coins became attractive to investors as well as collectors.

Record Coin Sale. At an auction held in Bridgeton, Mo., on July 26 and 27, Walter Perschke, a Chicago coin dealer, paid $430,000 for a 1787 Brasher's doubloon owned by the Capital Coin & Stamp Company, Incorporated. It was the highest price ever paid for a coin at a public auction.

The Brasher's doubloon is believed to have been one of the first gold coins minted in America and is one of seven such specimens known to exist. It was privately minted by Ephraim Brasher, a goldsmith and silversmith in New York City.

At an auction held in New York City on June 21 and 22, an ultrahigh-relief United States 1907 $20 gold piece, designed by sculptor Augustus Saint-Gaudens, sold for $225,000 to an anonymous bidder. The coin features Miss Liberty on one face and a flying eagle on the other.

New Coins. The Franklin Mint, a private company, announced on May 30 that it was minting three new gold pieces whose price would be based on the market price of gold plus a premium. The coins carry the same design but have different weights: 1 troy ounce (31.1 grams); 0.5 troy ounce (15.6 grams); and 0.25 troy ounce (7.8 grams). They feature Benjamin Franklin on the face and an eagle on the reverse.

The Canadian Treasury began to sell a 1-troy-ounce gold coin – the Maple Leaf – on September 6. The coin bears the image of Queen Elizabeth II of Great Britain on one side and the maple leaf, Canada's national symbol, on the other.

These coins were designed to compete with the highly successful South African Krugerrand, which has become the world's best-selling gold coin. Since 1970, more than 22 million Krugerrands have been sold. Figures released in June indicated that sales of Krugerrands in 1978 exceeded 6 million – more than twice the number sold in 1977. On December 31, Krugerrands reached a price of more than $560 each. The coins contain 1 troy ounce of 91.66 per cent pure gold.

An 11-sided U.S. dollar coin, made mostly of copper and nickel and bearing a portrait of suffragist leader Susan B. Anthony, went into circulation on July 21. It is the first U.S. coin featuring the likeness of an actual woman, rather than the symbolic Miss Liberty.

The General Services Administration (GSA) announced in August it would hold a public sale in 1980 of the nearly 1 million silver dollars that remain of the 3 million such coins produced by the Carson City mint from 1879 to 1891.   Theodore M. O'Leary

In WORLD BOOK, see COIN COLLECTING; GOLD.

COLOMBIA. President Julio Cesar Turbay Ayala suspended a number of constitutional guarantees on Jan. 9, 1979, to facilitate a military drive against a wave of left wing terrorist attacks. The military was allowed to make arrests without warrants on charges of "threatening the public order." Military courts assumed judicial power previously exercised only by penal courts.

A Guerrilla Raid on January 1 touched off the military crackdown. Guerrillas raided the main military arsenal north of Bogotá, and about 4,000 firearms and a large amount of ammunition were stolen. A communiqué issued on January 1 by Carlos Toledo Plata, a former member of the Chamber of Deputies who was thought to be in Costa Rica, claimed that the M-19 guerrilla group was responsible for the raid. M-19 was described as a "Castroite" group operating with the aid of Cuban and other foreign advisers.

By January 22, the defense ministry claimed that 90 per cent of the weapons had been recovered. M-19 communiqués claimed, however, that the group still had 7,000 weapons stolen in raids on several arsenals during the previous year. In April, the military announced that its crackdown on the M-19 group was completed with the arrest of 714 persons. A military trial for 219 of them began in Bogotá on November 23.

Armed Clashes. An even larger group, the Armed Revolutionary Forces of Colombia (FARC) fought several battles with the army in rural areas of Cundinamarca department. FARC, by an agreement with another Castroite group – the National Liberation Army (ELN) – operated in the countryside while the ELN operated in the cities. FARC was led by Manuel Marulanda Velez, a member of the central committee of the pro-Russian Colombian Communist Party. A fourth guerrilla group following Maoist ideology, the Popular Liberation Army (EPL), claimed credit for the May 1 bombing of the residence of the U.S. Embassy Marine guards; one marine and two women were injured.

The FARC, M-19, and the EPL announced the unification of their forces in June. Official sources interpreted this as an indication that the terrorists were feeling the pressure of the military crackdown. However, members of the Colombian Congress expressed fear that President Turbay was giving too much power to the armed forces in its campaign against terrorists, and there were charges that torture was being used against captives.

The armed forces were also in charge of the Turbay government's efforts to stem marijuana smuggling in the northern coastal area near the cities of Santa Marta and Ríohacha. Everett G. Martin

See also LATIN AMERICA (Facts in Brief Table). In WORLD BOOK, see COLOMBIA.

COLORADO. See STATE GOVERNMENT.

COMMON MARKET. See EUROPE.

COMMUNICATIONS was the keynote at Telecom 79, a giant exhibition and symposium held in Geneva, Switzerland, in September 1979. Telecom is staged once every four years by the International Telecommunication Union (ITU), the United Nations agency that guides and coordinates worldwide telecommunications.

Top telecommunications administrators and executives from virtually every nation were in Geneva to study the latest technology and to exchange views on policy matters affecting the operation of communications systems. They focused their attention on three major areas – the necessity for a continuing transfer of technological information, so that developing nations may enjoy the benefits of up-to-date communications systems; the ongoing merger of computer and communication technology, from which new media and new types of communications are developing; and the need for integration of the worldwide telecommunications network.

Technological Advances continued throughout the year. Viewdata, an electronic communications system developed by the British Post Office that went into operation as Prestel in Great Britain in 1978, was scheduled to be tested in Canada in 1980. The system supplies users with information by connecting television receivers with a central data bank via telephone lines. Canadian users will be able to call up any of 100,000 pages of such listings as news bulletins, airline schedules, stock market quotations, and entertainment information. Exclusive rights to market the Viewdata system in the United States, as well as in Canada, were obtained in June 1979 by the General Telephone & Electronics Corporation. No date has been set for a U.S. test program.

The first all-digital telephone system is being built in Denmark and is scheduled for completion in 1982. The system will convert a caller's voice into numerically evaluated segments then transmit it in digital form to a digital switch, which sends the signal to the person called. The recipient's digital telephone translates the signals back into the voice of the caller. The system produces higher-fidelity transmission than the old analogue systems in which the signals followed the wavy line configurations of the human voice. It also uses simpler hardware.

Legislative Efforts to enact a new set of U.S. communications rules bogged down in midyear when a comprehensive bill that had been introduced in the House of Representatives in March was abandoned by its sponsors after several months of hearings. The bill would have encouraged competition wherever feasible in the telephone industry – a government-sanctioned monopoly since the Communications Act of 1934 established the Federal Communications Commission (FCC).

Representative Lionel Van Deerlin (D., Calif.), chairman of the House Communications Subcommittee and principal sponsor of the bill, said the

A portable terminal that clips onto an ordinary telephone has a keyboard and displays three lines of 12 letters to allow the deaf to make calls.

COMMUNITY ORGANIZATIONS. Jerome H. Holland, former educator and United States ambassador to Sweden, was appointed chairman of the American National Red Cross by President Jimmy Carter on April 1, 1979. The Red Cross and Baxter Travenol Laboratories, Incorporated, announced on March 15 that they had agreed to build and jointly operate a human blood plasma facility in North Carolina. The new unit will process plasma for use in therapeutic care.

The Salvation Army. Commissioner Ernest W. Holz was appointed national commander of Salvation Army operations in the United States on February 16. Emphasizing the army's unique combination of religion and social work, the new commander said, "We recognized from the very beginning that you can't preach to a man with an empty stomach."

The Young Men's Christian Association (YMCA). Registered YMCA participants in the U.S. reached a total of 9.8 million persons in 1979. Women and girls again registered the greatest growth and now make up 41 per cent of the membership. Family memberships also continued to grow. Major national efforts included values education, family programs, and physical fitness and cardiovascular programs.

The Young Women's Christian Association (YWCA) had more than 2.5 million 1979 members in the United States, women and girls of diverse backgrounds from 49 states in 5,000 locations. The YWCA carried out programs in health, juvenile justice, sex and age discrimination, and affirmative action.

Service Organizations. Kiwanis International reported its 1979 membership at more than 300,000 in 7,500 clubs in 69 nations. Mark A. Smith, Jr., an Atlanta, Ga., businessman, was elected president in June, and announced a program called "Rightstart . . . Hand in Hand with Youth." It is aimed at supplementing the family's role in helping youths.

Lions International elected Lloyd Morgan of Lower Hutt, New Zealand, president in June. He called for a program of international peace, service, and understanding. Membership stood at 1.27 million in 32,909 clubs throughout the world.

Rotary International celebrated its 75th anniversary in 1979 with more than 850,000 members in more than 18,250 clubs. The clubs, in 152 countries and geographical regions, are supporting a Health, Hunger, and Humanity (3-H) Program. The first 3-H project, started in 1979, is a five-year immunization program for 6 million Philippine children.

Veterans Organizations. Max Cleland, chief of the Veterans Administration (VA), announced on May 28 that new studies by the U.S. Air Force and the Department of Health, Education, and Welfare would supplement a VA inquiry on the long-term effects of exposure to "Agent Orange," a herbicide containing the poison dioxin. United States planes

hearings had established agreement among his colleagues on several points, and they were ready to rewrite the Communications Act of 1934 to reflect their findings. The points of agreement centered on the desirability of deregulating communications wherever possible.

The FCC took a step toward encouraging competition when it voted unanimously on January 25 to end Western Union Corporation's 36-year monopoly over domestic telegram service. The FCC authorized Graphnet Systems, Incorporated, a subsidiary of Graphic Scanning Corporation of Englewood, N.J., to enter competition with Western Union by granting it the right to deliver inbound international cable messages to United States customers. Western Union realized about $66 million in revenues in 1978 from its telegram monopoly.

The FCC granted permission on August 1 to a group of American companies to build a seventh transatlantic cable. The giant American Telephone & Telegraph Company is among those involved in the project, which will be undertaken jointly with European communications agencies. The new cable is expected to cost nearly $200 million and to be ready for use in 1983. It will provide 4,200 two-way voice-grade circuits between Tuckerton, N.J., and Land's End, England.   Leo S. Anderson

In WORLD BOOK, see COMMUNICATIONS; TELE-PHONE.

sprayed nearly 2 million acres (800,000 hectares) of Vietnam jungle with Agent Orange between 1962 and 1970, trying to destroy Vietcong food and cover. The VA action came in response to complaints from hundreds of veterans who had filed claims alleging physical damage from exposure to the herbicide.

The Supreme Court of the United States ruled on June 5 that a state could hire veterans in preference to nonveterans without unconstitutionally discriminating against women. By a vote of 7 to 2, the justices upheld a Massachusetts law that gives job preference to any veteran who passes the civil service test.

Early in May, a group of veterans organized the Vietnam Veterans of America, headed by Robert O. Muller, a former Marine lieutenant crippled in that war. The group charged that the government neglected the health, employment, education, and psychological needs of Vietnam-era troops.

The American Legion and the Veterans of Foreign Wars both opposed the new Strategic Arms Limitation Treaty (SALT II). The veterans groups argued that it would place the United States in a militarily inferior position to Russia, and lobbied in Congress for changes in the treaty. Virginia E. Anderson

In WORLD BOOK, see articles on the various community organizations.

COMOROS. See AFRICA.

CONGO (BRAZZAVILLE). See AFRICA.

CONGO (KINSHASA). See ZAIRE.

Senator Herman E. Talmadge (D., Ga.), center, faces financial misconduct charges by aide Daniel Minchew, right, and is denounced by the Senate.

CONGRESS OF THE UNITED STATES. The first session of the 96th Congress of the United States convened on Jan. 15, 1979, with sizable Democratic majorities in both houses. In his televised State of the Union message to Congress on January 23, President Jimmy Carter asked Congress and the people to "build a new and firmer foundation for the future – for a sound economy . . . more effective government . . . and a stable peace." Two days later, the President sent a more detailed, 23,000-word, 50-page, written State of the Union message to Capitol Hill.

But despite the Democratic majorities in Congress, most of the President's program was blocked in one house or the other during the year. Throughout the first session, Congress was an argumentative, independent, and voter-conscious body. Responding to special-interest lobbies, it balked at passing the President's energy package, a pared-down budget, enabling legislation for the Panama Canal Treaty, and the Strategic Arms Limitation Treaty (SALT II). The first session recessed five times – in April, August, September, October, and November – and may have passed less major legislation than any other Congress in the 1970s.

Congressional Leaders. Vice-President Walter F. Mondale served in his constitutional role as president of the Senate. West Virginia's Robert C. Byrd was majority leader. Alan Cranston of Califor-

nia was majority whip, and Warren G. Magnuson of Washington was president pro tem. Howard H. Baker, Jr., of Tennessee was re-elected minority leader, and Theodore F. Stevens of Alaska was minority whip.

Thomas P. (Tip) O'Neill, Jr., of Massachusetts was re-elected speaker of the House; James C. Wright, Jr., of Texas was majority leader, with John Brademas of Indiana as majority whip. Arizona's John J. Rhodes was minority leader and Illinois' Robert H. Michel, minority whip.

The Budget. On January 22, the President sent Congress "a lean and austere budget" for fiscal 1980, beginning Oct. 1, 1979. His budget called for spending $531.6 billion, taking in $502.6 billion in revenue, with a consequent deficit of $29 billion. In order to keep down the deficit and bring the federal budget more nearly into balance, the President proposed cuts in some social services, health care, aid to cities, energy spending, and environmental projects. Military spending was to rise 3 per cent after an adjustment for inflation, to $122.7 billion.

Congress countered with its own budget proposal in May, which projected a deficit of $23 billion – $6-billion less than that proposed by the Administration. However, fiscal 1980 began without any budget, the first time this had happened since the congressional budget process was inaugurated five years earlier. Despite efforts to hold down federal

Members of the United States Senate

The Senate of the second session of the 96th Congress consisted of 58 Democrats, 41 Republicans, and 1 Independent when it convened in January 1980. Senators shown starting their term in 1979 were elected for the first time in the Nov. 7, 1978, elections (Senators Donald W. Stewart of Alabama and David F. Durenberger of Minnesota were elected on November 7 but were sworn into office on November 9 because they replaced senators who had been appointed to serve only until the election). Those shown ending their current terms in 1985 were re-elected to the Senate in the same balloting. The second date in each listing shows when the term of a previously elected senator expires. For organizational purposes, the one Independent will line up with Democrats.

State	Term	State	Term	State	Term
Alabama		**Louisiana**		**Ohio**	
Donald W. Stewart, D.	1978—1981	Russell B. Long, D.	1948—1981	John H. Glenn, D.	1975—1981
Howell T. Heflin, D.	1979—1985	J. Bennett Johnston, Jr., D.	1972—1985	Howard M. Metzenbaum, D.	1977—1983
Alaska		**Maine**		**Oklahoma**	
Theodore F. Stevens, R.	1968—1985	Edmund S. Muskie, D.	1959—1983	Henry L. Bellmon, R.	1969—1981
Mike Gravel, D.	1969—1981	William S. Cohen, R.	1979—1985	David L. Boren, D.	1979—1985
Arizona		**Maryland**		**Oregon**	
Barry Goldwater, R.	1969—1981	Charles McC. Mathias, Jr., R.	1969—1981	Mark O. Hatfield, R.	1967—1985
Dennis DeConcini, D.	1977—1983	Paul S. Sarbanes, D.	1977—1983	Robert W. Packwood, R.	1969—1981
Arkansas		**Massachusetts**		**Pennsylvania**	
Dale Bumpers, D.	1975—1981	Edward M. Kennedy, D.	1962—1983	Richard S. Schweiker, R.	1969—1981
David H. Pryor, D.	1979—1985	Paul E. Tsongas, D.	1979—1985	H. John Heinz III, R.	1977—1983
California		**Michigan**		**Rhode Island**	
Alan Cranston, D.	1969—1981	Donald W. Riegle, Jr., D.	1977—1983	Claiborne Pell, D.	1961—1985
S. I. Hayakawa, R.	1977—1983	Carl M. Levin, D.	1979—1985	John H. Chafee, R.	1977—1983
Colorado		**Minnesota**		**South Carolina**	
Gary Hart, D.	1975—1981	David F. Durenberger, R.	1978—1983	Strom Thurmond, R.	1956—1985
William L. Armstrong, R.	1979—1985	Rudolph E. Boschwitz, R.	1979—1985	Ernest F. Hollings, D.	1966—1981
Connecticut		**Mississippi**		**South Dakota**	
Abraham A. Ribicoff, D.	1963—1981	John C. Stennis, D.	1947—1983	George S. McGovern, D.	1963—1981
Lowell P. Weicker, Jr., R.	1971—1983	Thad Cochran, R.	1979—1985	Larry Pressler, R.	1979—1985
Delaware		**Missouri**		**Tennessee**	
William V. Roth, Jr., R.	1971—1983	Thomas F. Eagleton, D.	1968—1981	Howard H. Baker, Jr., R.	1967—1985
Joseph R. Biden, Jr., D.	1973—1985	John C. Danforth, R.	1977—1983	James R. Sasser, D.	1977—1983
Florida		**Montana**		**Texas**	
Lawton Chiles, D.	1971—1983	John Melcher, D.	1977—1983	John G. Tower, R.	1961—1985
Richard B. Stone, D.	1975—1981	Max Baucus, D.	1979—1985	Lloyd M. Bentsen, D.	1971—1983
Georgia		**Nebraska**		**Utah**	
Herman E. Talmadge, D.	1957—1981	Edward Zorinsky, D.	1977—1983	Edwin Jacob Garn, R.	1975—1981
Sam Nunn, D.	1972—1985	J. James Exon, D.	1979—1985	Orrin G. Hatch, R.	1977—1983
Hawaii		**Nevada**		**Vermont**	
Daniel K. Inouye, D.	1963—1981	Howard W. Cannon, D.	1959—1983	Robert T. Stafford, R.	1971—1983
Spark M. Matsunaga, D.	1977—1983	Paul Laxalt, R.	1975—1981	Patrick J. Leahy, D.	1975—1981
Idaho		**New Hampshire**		**Virginia**	
Frank Church, D.	1957—1981	John A. Durkin, D.	1975—1981	Harry F. Byrd, Jr., Ind.	1965—1983
James A. McClure, R.	1973—1985	Gordon J. Humphrey, R.	1979—1985	John W. Warner, R.	1979—1985
Illinois		**New Jersey**		**Washington**	
Charles H. Percy, R.	1967—1985	Harrison A. Williams, Jr., D.	1959—1983	Warren G. Magnuson, D.	1944—1981
Adlai E. Stevenson III, D.	1970—1981	Bill Bradley, D.	1979—1985	Henry M. Jackson, D.	1953—1983
Indiana		**New Mexico**		**West Virginia**	
Birch Bayh, D.	1963—1981	Pete V. Domenici, R.	1973—1985	Jennings Randolph, D.	1958—1985
Richard G. Lugar, R.	1977—1983	Harrison H. Schmitt, R.	1977—1983	Robert C. Byrd, D.	1959—1983
Iowa		**New York**		**Wisconsin**	
John C. Culver, D.	1975—1981	Jacob K. Javits, R.	1957—1981	William Proxmire, D.	1957—1983
Roger W. Jepsen, R.	1979—1985	Daniel P. Moynihan, D.	1977—1983	Gaylord Nelson, D.	1963—1981
Kansas		**North Carolina**		**Wyoming**	
Robert J. Dole, R.	1969—1981	Jesse A. Helms, R.	1973—1985	Malcolm Wallop, R.	1977—1983
Nancy Landon Kassebaum, R.	1979—1985	Robert Morgan, D.	1975—1981	Alan K. Simpson, R.	1979—1985
Kentucky		**North Dakota**			
Walter Huddleston, D.	1973—1985	Milton R. Young, R.	1945—1981		
Wendell H. Ford, D.	1975—1981	Quentin N. Burdick, D.	1960—1983		

Members of the United States House

The House of Representatives of the second session of the 96th Congress consisted of 275 Democrats and 159 Republicans (not including representatives from the District of Columbia, Guam, Puerto Rico, and the Virgin Islands) with 1 seat vacant when it convened in January 1980, compared with 276 Democrats and 157 Republicans, with 2 seats vacant, when the first session convened. This table shows congressional district, legislator, and party affiliation. Asterisk (*) denotes those who served in the 95th Congress; dagger (†) denotes "at large."

Alabama
1. Jack Edwards, R.*
2. William L. Dickinson, R.*
3. William Nichols, D.*
4. Tom Bevill, D.*
5. Ronnie G. Flippo, D.*
6. John H. Buchanan, Jr., R.*
7. Richard C. Shelby, D.

Alaska
† Don Young, R.*

Arizona
1. John J. Rhodes, R.*
2. Morris K. Udall, D.*
3. Bob Stump, D.*
4. Eldon Rudd, R.*

Arkansas
1. Bill Alexander, D.*
2. Edwin R. Bethune, Jr., R.
3. J. P. Hammerschmidt, R.*
4. Beryl Anthony, Jr., D.

California
1. Harold T. Johnson, D.*
2. Don H. Clausen, R.*
3. Robert Matsui, D.
4. Vic Fazio, D.
5. John L. Burton, D.*
6. Phillip Burton, D.*
7. George Miller, D.*
8. Ronald V. Dellums, D.*
9. Fortney H. Stark, D.*
10. Don Edwards, D.*
11. Bill Royer, R.
12. Paul N. McCloskey, Jr., R.*
13. Norman Y. Mineta, D.*
14. Norman Shumway, R.
15. Tony Coelho, D.
16. Leon E. Panetta, D.*
17. Charles Pashayan, Jr., R.
18. William M. Thomas, R.
19. Robert J. Lagomarsino, R.*
20. Barry M. Goldwater, Jr., R.*
21. James C. Corman, D.*
22. Carlos J. Moorhead, R.*
23. Anthony C. Beilenson, D.*
24. Henry A. Waxman, D.*
25. Edward R. Roybal, D.*
26. John H. Rousselot, R.*
27. Robert K. Dornan, R.*
28. Julian C. Dixon, D.
29. Augustus F. Hawkins, D.*
30. George E. Danielson, D.*
31. Charles H. Wilson, D.*
32. Glenn M. Anderson, D.*
33. Wayne Grisham, R.
34. Dan Lungren, R.
35. Jim Lloyd, D.*
36. George E. Brown, Jr., D.*
37. Jerry Lewis, R.
38. Jerry M. Patterson, D.*
39. William E. Dannemeyer, R.
40. Robert E. Badham, R.*
41. Bob Wilson, R.*
42. Lionel Van Deerlin, D.*
43. Clair W. Burgener, R.*

Colorado
1. Patricia Schroeder, D.*
2. Timothy E. Wirth, D.*
3. Ray Kogovsek, D.
4. James P. Johnson, R.*
5. Ken Kramer, R.

Connecticut
1. William R. Cotter, D.*
2. Christopher J. Dodd, D.*
3. Robert N. Giaimo, D.*
4. Stewart B. McKinney, R.*
5. William Ratchford, D.
6. Anthony J. Moffett, D.*

Delaware
† Thomas B. Evans, Jr., R.*

Florida
1. Earl Hutto, D.
2. Don Fuqua, D.*
3. Charles E. Bennett, D.*
4. William V. Chappell, Jr., D.*
5. Richard Kelly, R.*
6. C. W. Young, R.*
7. Sam M. Gibbons, D.*
8. Andy Ireland, D.*
9. Bill Nelson, D.
10. L. A. Bafalis, R.*
11. Dan Mica, D.
12. Edward J. Stack, D.
13. William Lehman, D.*
14. Claude D. Pepper, D.*
15. Dante B. Fascell, D.*

Georgia
1. Ronald Ginn, D.*
2. Dawson Mathis, D.*
3. Jack T. Brinkley, D.*
4. Elliott H. Levitas, D.*
5. Wyche Fowler, Jr., D.*
6. Newton L. Gingrich, R.
7. Lawrence P. McDonald, D.*
8. Billy Lee Evans, D.*
9. Ed Jenkins, D.*
10. Doug Barnard, D.*

Hawaii
1. Cecil Heftel, D.*
2. Daniel K. Akaka, D.*

Idaho
1. Steven D. Symms, R.*
2. George Hansen, R.*

Illinois
1. Bennett Stewart, D.
2. Morgan F. Murphy, D.*
3. Martin A. Russo, D.*
4. Edward J. Derwinski, R.*
5. John G. Fary, D.*
6. Henry J. Hyde, R.*
7. Cardiss Collins, D.*
8. Dan Rostenkowski, D.*
9. Sidney R. Yates, D.*
10. Vacant

11. Frank Annunzio, D.*
12. Philip M. Crane, R.*
13. Robert McClory, R.*
14. John N. Erlenborn, R.*
15. Tom Corcoran, R.*
16. John B. Anderson, R.*
17. George M. O'Brien, R.*
18. Robert H. Michel, R.*
19. Thomas F. Railsback, R.*
20. Paul Findley, R.*
21. Edward R. Madigan, R.*
22. Daniel Crane, R.
23. Charles Melvin Price, D.*
24. Paul Simon, D.*

Indiana
1. Adam Benjamin, Jr., D.*
2. Floyd J. Fithian, D.*
3. John Brademas, D.*
4. J. Danforth Quayle, R.*
5. Elwood H. Hillis, R.*
6. David W. Evans, D.*
7. John T. Myers, R.*
8. H. Joel Deckard, R.
9. Lee H. Hamilton, D.*
10. Philip R. Sharp, D.*
11. Andrew Jacobs, Jr., D.*

Iowa
1. James Leach, R.*
2. Thomas J. Tauke, R.
3. Charles E. Grassley, R.*
4. Neal Smith, D.*
5. Tom Harkin, D.*
6. Berkley Bedell, D.*

Kansas
1. Keith G. Sebelius, R.*
2. James E. Jeffries, R.
3. Larry Winn, Jr., R.*
4. Dan Glickman, D.*
5. Robert Whittaker, R.

Kentucky
1. Carroll Hubbard, Jr., D.*
2. William H. Natcher, D.*
3. Romano L. Mazzoli, D.*
4. Marion Gene Snyder, R.*
5. Tim Lee Carter, R.*
6. Larry Hopkins, R.
7. Carl D. Perkins, D.*

Louisiana
1. Robert L. Livingston, R.*
2. Lindy Boggs, D.*
3. David C. Treen, R.*
4. Claude Leach, D.
5. Jerry Huckaby, D.*
6. W. Henson Moore, R.*
7. John B. Breaux, D.*
8. Gillis W. Long, D.*

Maine
1. David F. Emery, R.*
2. Olympia Snowe, R.

Maryland
1. Robert E. Bauman, R.*
2. Clarence D. Long, D.*

3. Barbara A. Mikulski, D.*
4. Marjorie S. Holt, R.*
5. Gladys N. Spellman, D.*
6. Beverly Butcher Byron, D.
7. Parren J. Mitchell, D.*
8. Michael Barnes, D.

Massachusetts
1. Silvio O. Conte, R.*
2. Edward P. Boland, D.*
3. Joseph D. Early, D.*
4. Robert F. Drinan, D.*
5. James Shannon, D.
6. Nicholas Mavroules, D.
7. Edward J. Markey, D.*
8. Thomas P. O'Neill, Jr., D.*
9. John J. Moakley, D.*
10. Margaret M. Heckler, R.*
11. Brian Donnelly, D.
12. Gerry E. Studds, D.*

Michigan
1. John Conyers, Jr., D.*
2. Carl D. Pursell, R.*
3. Howard Wolpe, D.
4. David Stockman, R.*
5. Harold S. Sawyer, R.*
6. Bob Carr, D.*
7. Dale E. Kildee, D.*
8. Bob Traxler, D.*
9. Guy Vander Jagt, R.*
10. Donald Albosta, D.
11. Robert Davis, R.
12. David E. Bonior, D.*
13. Charles C. Diggs, Jr., D.*
14. Lucien N. Nedzi, D.*
15. William D. Ford, D.*
16. John D. Dingell, D.*
17. William M. Brodhead, D.*
18. James J. Blanchard, D.*
19. William S. Broomfield, R.*

Minnesota
1. Arlen Erdahl, R.
2. Thomas M. Hagedorn, R.*
3. Bill Frenzel, R.*
4. Bruce F. Vento, D.*
5. Martin Sabo, D.
6. Richard Nolan, D.*
7. Arlan Stangeland, R.*
8. James L. Oberstar, D.*

Mississippi
1. Jamie L. Whitten, D.*
2. David R. Bowen, D.*
3. G. V. Montgomery, D.*
4. Jon Hinson, R.
5. Trent Lott, R.*

Missouri
1. William L. Clay, D.*
2. Robert A. Young, D.*
3. Richard A. Gephardt, D.*
4. Ike Skelton, D.*
5. Richard Bolling, D.*
6. E. Thomas Coleman, R.*
7. Gene Taylor, R.*

8. Richard H. Ichord, D.*
9. Harold L. Volkmer, D.*
10. Bill D. Burlison, D.*

Montana
1. Pat Williams, D.
2. Ron Marlenee, R.*

Nebraska
1. Douglas Bereuter, R.
2. John J. Cavanaugh, D.*
3. Virginia Smith, R.*

Nevada
†James Santini, D.*

New Hampshire
1. Norman E. D'Amours, D.*
2. James C. Cleveland, R.*

New Jersey
1. James J. Florio, D.*
2. William J. Hughes, D.*
3. James J. Howard, D.*
4. Frank Thompson, Jr., D.*
5. Millicent Fenwick, R.*
6. Edwin B. Forsythe, R.*
7. Andrew Maguire, D.*
8. Robert A. Roe, D.*
9. Harold C. Hollenbeck, R.*
10. Peter W. Rodino, Jr., D.*
11. Joseph G. Minish, D.*
12. Matthew J. Rinaldo, R.*
13. James A. Courter, R.
14. Frank J. Guarini, D.
15. Edward J. Patten, D.*

New Mexico
1. Manuel Lujan, Jr., R.*
2. Harold Runnels, D.*

New York
1. William Carney, R.
2. Thomas J. Downey, D.*
3. Jerome A. Ambro, Jr., D.*
4. Norman F. Lent, R.*
5. John W. Wydler, R.*
6. Lester L. Wolff, D.*
7. Joseph P. Addabbo, D.*
8. Benjamin S. Rosenthal, D.*
9. Geraldine A. Ferraro, D.
10. Mario Biaggi, D.*
11. James H. Scheuer, D.*
12. Shirley Chisholm, D.*
13. Stephen J. Solarz, D.*
14. Frederick W. Richmond, D.*
15. Leo C. Zeferetti, D.*
16. Elizabeth Holtzman, D.*
17. John M. Murphy, D.*
18. S. William Green, R.*
19. Charles B. Rangel, D.*
20. Ted Weiss, D.*
21. Robert Garcia, D.*
22. Jonathan B. Bingham, D.*
23. Peter A. Peyser, D.
24. Richard L. Ottinger, D.*
25. Hamilton Fish, Jr., R.*

26. Benjamin A. Gilman, R.*
27. Matthew F. McHugh, D.*
28. Samuel S. Stratton, D.*
29. Gerald Solomon, R.
30. Robert C. McEwen, R.*
31. Donald J. Mitchell, R.*
32. James M. Hanley, D.*
33. Gary Lee, R.
34. Frank Horton, R.*
35. Barber B. Conable, Jr., R.*
36. John J. LaFalce, D.*
37. Henry J. Nowak, D.*
38. Jack F. Kemp, R.*
39. Stanley N. Lundine, D.*

North Carolina
1. Walter B. Jones, D.*
2. L. H. Fountain, D.*
3. Charles Whitley, D.*
4. Ike F. Andrews, D.*
5. Stephen L. Neal, D.*
6. L. Richardson Preyer, D.*
7. Charles Rose, D.*
8. W. G. Hefner, D.*
9. James G. Martin, R.*
10. James T. Broyhill, R.*
11. Lamar Gudger, D.*

North Dakota
†Mark Andrews, R.*

Ohio
1. Willis D. Gradison, Jr., R.*
2. Thomas A. Luken, D.*
3. Tony P. Hall, D.
4. Tennyson Guyer, R.*
5. Delbert L. Latta, R.*
6. William H. Harsha, R.*
7. Clarence J. Brown, R.*
8. Thomas N. Kindness, R.*
9. Thomas L. Ashley, D.*
10. Clarence E. Miller, R.*
11. J. William Stanton, R.*
12. Samuel L. Devine, R.*
13. Donald J. Pease, D.*
14. John F. Seiberling, D.*
15. Chalmers P. Wylie, R.*
16. Ralph S. Regula, R.*
17. John M. Ashbrook, R.*
18. Douglas Applegate, D.*
19. Lyle Williams, R.
20. Mary Rose Oakar, D.*
21. Louis Stokes, D.*
22. Charles A. Vanik, D.*
23. Ronald M. Mottl, D.*

Oklahoma
1. James R. Jones, D.*
2. Michael L. Synar, D.
3. Wes Watkins, D.*
4. Tom Steed, D.*
5. Mickey Edwards, R.*
6. Glenn English, D.*

Oregon
1. Les AuCoin, D.*
2. Al Ullman, D.*
3. Robert B. Duncan, D.*
4. James Weaver, D.*

Pennsylvania
1. Michael Myers, D.*
2. William H. Gray III, D.
3. Raymond F. Lederer, D.*
4. Charles F. Dougherty, R.
5. Richard T. Schulze, R.*
6. Gus Yatron, D.*
7. Robert W. Edgar, D.*
8. Peter H. Kostmayer, D.*
9. E. G. Shuster, R.*
10. Joseph M. McDade, R.*
11. Daniel J. Flood, D.*
12. John P. Murtha, D.*
13. Lawrence Coughlin, R.*
14. William S. Moorhead, D.*
15. Donald L. Ritter, R.
16. Robert S. Walker, R.*
17. Allen E. Ertel, D.*
18. Doug Walgren, D.*
19. William F. Goodling, R.*
20. Joseph M. Gaydos, D.*
21. Donald A. Bailey, D.
22. Austin J. Murphy, D.*
23. William F. Clinger, Jr., R.
24. Marc L. Marks, R.*
25. Eugene Atkinson, D.

Rhode Island
1. Fernand J. St. Germain, D.*
2. Edward P. Beard, D.*

South Carolina
1. Mendel J. Davis, D.*
2. Floyd D. Spence, R.*
3. Butler C. Derrick, Jr., D.*
4. Carroll A. Campbell, Jr., R.
5. Kenneth L. Holland, D.*
6. John W. Jenrette, Jr., D.*

South Dakota
1. Thomas A. Daschle, D.
2. James Abdnor, R.*

Tennessee
1. James H. Quillen, R.*
2. John J. Duncan, R.*
3. Marilyn Lloyd Bouquard, D.*
4. Albert Gore, Jr., D.*
5. William H. Boner, D.
6. Robin L. Beard, Jr., R.*
7. Ed Jones, D.*
8. Harold E. Ford, D.*

Texas
1. Sam B. Hall, Jr., D.*
2. Charles Wilson, D.*
3. James M. Collins, R.*
4. Ray Roberts, D.*
5. James Mattox, D.
6. Phil Gramm, D.
7. Bill Archer, R.*
8. Bob Eckhardt, D.*
9. Jack Brooks, D.*
10. J. J. Pickle, D.*
11. Marvin Leath, D.
12. James C. Wright, Jr., D.*
13. Jack Hightower, D.*
14. Joe Wyatt, Jr., D.
15. Eligio de la Garza, D.*
16. Richard C. White, D.*
17. Charles Stenholm, D.

18. Mickey Leland, D.
19. Kent Hance, D.
20. Henry B. Gonzalez, D.*
21. Thomas G. Loeffler, R.
22. Ronald E. Paul, R.
23. Abraham Kazen, Jr., D.*
24. Martin Frost, D.

Utah
1. K. Gunn McKay, D.*
2. Dan Marriott, R.*

Vermont
† James M. Jeffords, R.*

Virginia
1. Paul S. Trible, Jr., R.*
2. G. William Whitehurst, R.*
3. David E. Satterfield III, D.*
4. Robert W. Daniel, Jr., R.*
5. W. C. Daniel, D.*
6. M. Caldwell Butler, R.*
7. J. Kenneth Robinson, R.*
8. Herbert E. Harris, D.*
9. William C. Wampler, R.*
10. Joseph L. Fisher, D.*

Washington
1. Joel Pritchard, R.*
2. Allan B. Swift, D.
3. Don Bonker, D.*
4. Mike McCormack, D.*
5. Thomas S. Foley, D.*
6. Norm Dicks, D.*
7. Michael E. Lowry, D.

West Virginia
1. Robert H. Mollohan, D.*
2. Harley O. Staggers, D.*
3. John M. Slack, D.*
4. Nick J. Rahall, D.*

Wisconsin
1. Les Aspin, D.*
2. Robert W. Kastenmeier, D.*
3. Alvin J. Baldus, D.*
4. Clement J. Zablocki, D.*
5. Henry S. Reuss, D.*
6. Thomas E. Petri, R.
7. David R. Obey, D.*
8. Toby Roth, R.
9. F. James Sensenbrenner, Jr., R.

Wyoming
† Richard B. Cheney, R.

Nonvoting Representatives
District of Columbia
Walter E. Fauntroy, D.*

Guam
Antonio Won Pat, D.*

Puerto Rico
Baltasar Corrada, D.*

Virgin Islands
Melvin H. Evans, R.

A technician monitors the first gavel-to-gavel television coverage
of House of Representatives proceedings, which began on February 22.

spending, the final 1980 budget adopted in November called for a total outlay of $547.6 billion.

The federal debt ceiling, which for years has been raised by a series of congressional enactments, dropped from $798 billion to the permanent ceiling, $400 billion, on April 1. The lower ceiling meant that the federal government had exceeded its credit limit and could not borrow funds to pay bills or finance new debts. After warnings from the Department of the Treasury that "default was certain" without a new law, the House approved a temporary ceiling of $830 billion on April 2. The Senate had approved the debt limit on March 27.

The House approved by voice vote on October 9 a compromise money-authorization bill to finance the federal agencies until November 20. Members of Congress received a 5.5 per cent increase in salary, according to the terms of the legislation, which passed in the Senate by a vote of 44 to 42 on October 12. The bill also limited the use of federal funds for abortions — an increasingly controversial issue — to cases of rape or incest or when the pregnancy endangers the life of the mother.

Congress completed action on an emergency appropriation bill for fiscal 1980 on November 16, and the anti-abortion amendment was again included. Federal departments were to operate on their fiscal 1979 budgets until a regular fiscal 1980 appropriation bill was passed.

Foreign Policy. The House held a secret session for the first time in 149 years in June to discuss legislation that would make the Panama Canal Treaty, which was ratified by the Senate in 1978, effective. The Senate approved the enabling legislation on September 25 and the House voted 232 to 188 on September 26 to approve a version of the bill worked out by a House-Senate conference committee. The treaty went into effect on October 1.

The SALT II treaty signed with Russia on June 18 was approved by the Senate Foreign Relations Committee on November 9, but a Senate vote on SALT II was not scheduled in 1979.

House and Senate votes on March 28 and March 29, respectively, overwhelmingly approved legislation allowing the United States to maintain "unofficial" relations with Taiwan. But the Senate rebuked the President on June 6, voting 59 to 35 to approve a resolution criticizing the President's plan to terminate the U.S. mutual-defense treaty with Taiwan in December 1979 without asking for Senate approval.

On May 15, the Senate adopted a resolution asking President Carter to lift the sanctions against Rhodesia within two weeks of the installation of a black president in Zimbabwe Rhodesia. The resolution was not binding on the President. However, a Senate amendment to the $40.1-billion defense appropriation bill, which authorized spending of $670 million for the development of a new mobile missile system, ordered the President to lift the sanctions by November 15 unless he notified Congress that this action was contrary to the interests of the United States. President Carter signed the bill on August 15. The President notified Congress on November 14 that he would lift the sanctions as soon as a provisional British governor was installed in Rhodesia. Carter lifted the sanctions on December 16 (see ZIMBABWE RHODESIA). The President signed a $4.4-billion security assistance bill on October 29, including a grant to Turkey of $50 million.

Trade and Energy. The House voted 395 to 7 on July 11 to approve the Trade Liberalization Act, making effective the pact signed by 99 nations in Geneva, Switzerland, in April. The Senate approved the legislation on July 23, 90 to 4, and the President signed it on July 26.

Although the establishment of a comprehensive energy policy was a priority for Congress and President Carter, most of the President's energy plan was mired in the 96th Congress. Legislation setting temperature controls in public and commercial buildings to conserve energy was approved by the Senate on May 2 and the House on May 10. Buildings could not be heated to more than 65°F. (18°C) in winter, nor cooled to less than 78°F. (26°C) in summer. On the same day, the House voted 246 to 159 to reject President Carter's request for a stand-by gasoline-rationing plan, despite Senate approval on May 9. The vote was a surprising defeat for the Administration and a measure of the pressure against the energy program. The Senate approved a compromise version on October 17, and, on October 23, the House finally voted 301 to 112 to approve stand-by rationing. The new law gave the President authority to set up a stand-by gasoline-rationing plan to become effective within 30 days after the President decides that there is a gasoline shortage. However, at that time, both houses of Congress in joint session could reject the plan.

Federal funds to help needy families pay their home heating bills were made available when the President signed legislation to that effect on November 27. Meanwhile, Congress considered establishing an Energy Mobilization Board to speed government approval of the construction of synthetic fuel plants and conservation projects. The House and Senate approved their own versions of the board, and the measure was in conference at year-end.

On November 9, both houses of Congress approved their own versions of the President's request for $19 billion for synthetic fuel development, plus funds for solar energy research. The act containing these provisions was in conference at year-end.

A key section of the energy program – the windfall-profits tax on oil to force the oil companies to share the profits made after fuel oil prices were decontrolled – was bogged down in congressional debate. The President proposed the tax in April. The House passed its version in June; the Senate passed another version on December 17. A conference committee agreed on a $227.3-billion tax on December 20, but delayed apportioning the tax until 1980.

Conservation. The President signed the $10.8-billion energy and water development appropriations bill of 1980 on September 26. The act specifically exempted the $115-million Tellico Dam project from the provisions of the Endangered Species Act, allowing work on the dam to be completed despite protests that it endangers the survival of the tiny snail darter fish. See CONSERVATION.

On October 17, President Carter signed legislation establishing a new Cabinet-level Department of Education. Most offices dealing with education in the Department of Health, Education, and Welfare were transferred to the new department. See CABINET, UNITED STATES; EDUCATION.

The President proposed a $1.5-billion loan-guarantee plan on November 1 to aid the ailing Chrysler Corporation, with a provision for matching funds. The House and Senate approved a compromise plan on December 21. See AUTOMOBILE.

Senate Rules. In February, the Senate voted 78 to 16 to limit cloture debate to 100 hours. On March 8, in a voice vote, the Senate postponed for four years enforcement of its rule limiting a senator's outside earnings to 15 per cent of his salary or $8,625. Under existing rules, senators can earn up to $25,000 annually to supplement their salaries. The Senate reaffirmed this decision in a March 28 roll-call vote.

Committee Hearings. The Senate Committee on Foreign Relations opened preliminary hearings on the SALT II treaty on July 9, began consideration of the treaty itself on October 15, and voted 9 to 6 on November 9 to send the treaty to the full Senate. The Senate Select Committee on Intelligence reported on October 5 that SALT II would "enhance the ability of the United States to monitor Russian weapons."

In its final report on July 17, the House Assassinations Committee concluded that a conspiracy was "likely" in the assassinations of President John F. Kennedy and civil rights leader Martin Luther King, Jr. The committee also said that earlier investigators had not explored the possible involvement of organized crime in the Kennedy killing or of a right wing business group in King's murder.

The Senate Subcommittee on Energy, Nuclear Proliferation, and Federal Services heard testimony on the March accident at the Three Mile Island nuclear power plant near Harrisburg, Pa., and on nuclear weapons. On October 2, Department of Energy officials told the subcommittee that at least eight "highly sensitive" documents on nuclear weapons had been mistakenly declassified. On May 17, the Senate granted subpoena power to the President's commission on the accident at Three Mile Island in its investigation (see ENERGY).

Senator Howard H. Baker (R., Tenn.) chats with Secretary of State Cyrus R. Vance and Secretary of Defense Harold Brown before SALT II hearings in July.

Scandals and Improprieties. The trial of Representative Daniel J. Flood (D., Pa.) on criminal charges of bribery and conspiracy was declared a mistrial on February 3. Flood's retrial, scheduled for June, was postponed because of illness. On June 7, the House Committee on Standards of Official Conduct (Ethics Committee) voted to file charges against Flood on 25 counts of violating House rules. Flood said in November that he would resign from the House for health reasons effective Jan. 31, 1980.

The committee also conducted hearings on alleged violations of House rules by Representative Charles C. Diggs, Jr. (D., Mich.), who was convicted and sentenced in 1978 to three years in prison for mail fraud and filing false payroll vouchers. On July 31, the House voted 414 to 0 to censure Diggs.

On October 11, the Senate voted 81 to 15 with 4 abstentions to follow committee recommendations and "denounce" Senator Herman Talmadge (D., Ga.) for financial mismanagement of his Senate expense account and political contributions. After a 10-month investigation, the Senate Select Committee on Ethics concluded on March 20 that former Senator Edward W. Brooke (R., Mass.) committed only minor violations of congressional conduct regulations.   Carol L. Thompson

See also PRESIDENT OF THE UNITED STATES; UNITED STATES, GOVERNMENT OF THE. In WORLD BOOK, see CONGRESS OF THE UNITED STATES.

CONNALLY, JOHN BOWDEN (1917-   ), announced his candidacy for the 1980 Republican presidential nomination on Jan. 24, 1979. A longtime Democrat, he joined the Republicans in 1973.

Connally was born on Feb. 27, 1917, in Floresville, Tex. He received a law degree from the University of Texas in 1941. He then joined the U.S. Navy and saw action in the Pacific during World War II.

After the war, Connally returned to Texas, where he threw his considerable energies into law, business, and politics. He was successful in all three.

At the same time, he became an active supporter of Lyndon Baines Johnson, managing several of Johnson's campaigns for Congress. In 1961, President John F. Kennedy appointed Connally secretary of the Navy. In 1963, he was elected governor of Texas. On November 22 of that year, he narrowly escaped death when he was wounded during the Kennedy assassination in Dallas. He served as governor until 1969.

In 1971, Connally was appointed secretary of the treasury by President Richard M. Nixon, and in 1973, a presidential adviser. During the Watergate scandal, he was accused of accepting $10,000 from milk producers for his support of higher milk subsidies. A federal grand jury dismissed the charges.

Connally married Idanell Brill in 1940. They have three children.   Edward G. Nash

CONNECTICUT. See STATE GOVERNMENT.

CONSERVATION. The United States House of Representatives on May 16, 1979, approved by a 268-157 vote a bill that set aside more than 125 million acres (50 million hectares) of federal land in Alaska for parks, wildlife refuges, and forests. Environmental groups supported the bill, calling it the greatest conservation decision in U.S. history. President Jimmy Carter called it his Administration's highest environmental priority.

The two Alaska senators, Theodore F. Stevens and Mike Gravel, fought the bill bitterly. Stevens attempted to negotiate a compromise as he had in 1978, but Gravel threatened to filibuster.

On October 30, the Senate Energy and Natural Resources Committee approved, 17-1, an Alaska lands bill that an environmental coalition called "unacceptable." The Alaska Coalition objected to provisions that would allow oil exploration in the Arctic Wildlife Range, encourage heavy logging in southeast Alaska, and permit mining of molybdenum in the Misty Fjords National Monument. Gravel said that he would attempt to filibuster the bill, but it did not come up for final action.

The Alaska senators and Alaska's Governor Jay S. Hammond joined in an admittedly futile request on September 13 that Congress overturn President Carter's 1978 decision to set aside 56 million acres (23 million hectares) of Alaska's lands as national monuments. Stevens conceded that there was no chance to change the 1906 law under which Carter created 17 monuments in Alaska.

Secretary of the Interior Cecil D. Andrus testified on September 13 that if Congress did not enact the Alaska lands bill he would again protect Alaska's scenic lands administratively. Andrus withdrew 110 million acres (45 million hectares) of federal land from development for three years in 1978.

The Senate approved on November 20 a bill that would designate 2.2 million acres (0.89 million hectares) in Idaho as wilderness. On November 26, the Senate passed legislation that would set aside 506,000 acres (205,000 hectares) in Oregon as wilderness areas and 134,000 acres (54,300 hectares) as a conservation area.

Sagebrush Rebellion. Many elected officials from the Western States joined on September 6 to map strategy for a major assault on federal ownership of millions of acres of land in 12 states. At a meeting of the Western Council of State Governments in Reno, Nev., Senator Orrin G. Hatch (R., Utah) likened the so-called Sagebrush Rebellion to a "second American Revolution." The rebellion began in Nevada on July 13 when Governor Robert F. List signed legislation that challenged federal control of 63 per cent of that state's lands. The measure declared state sovereignty over nearly 50 million acres (20 million hectares).

At issue is federal ownership of about 750 million acres (300 million hectares) in the West and in Alaska. A condition for admission to the Union was that the Western States must renounce "all right and title" to the federal lands left within their boundaries. But rebellion leaders claim that the Western States were blackmailed into acceding. They hope to take legal action that will lead to a decision by the Supreme Court of the United States that the provision violates the constitutional requirement calling for all states to enter the Union on an equal footing.

Hatch introduced legislation on August 3 to transfer to state ownership lands managed by the U.S. Bureau of Land Management and the U.S. Forest Service. Representative Morris K. Udall (D., Ariz.) said on September 5 that the Sagebrush Rebellion had little or no chance in Congress.

M-X Missile. President Carter on September 7 approved a plan to house the new M-X mobile missiles in clusters of underground shelters in Utah and Nevada. Each missile would be wheeled continually around a "race track" that served a cluster of underground shelters, each equipped to launch missiles. An enemy would be less capable of hitting the mobile missiles and therefore less capable of destroying the U.S. ability to launch mobile missiles (see ARMED FORCES). Environmentalists pointed out that the 4,600 shelters and 200 race tracks might require 24,000 square miles (62,000 square kilometers) of land, which would be removed from such other uses as grazing and wilderness preservation.

Surface Mining. Environmentalists fought for a decade for 1977 landmark legislation that would control the ravages of strip mining. They may face another long struggle in the courts and Congress because coal-mine operators, backed by the United Mine Workers union, have challenged federal regulations that would carry out the 1977 act. These opponents say that the regulations add tremendously to mining costs. A preliminary injunction in Virginia blocked enforcement for six months. The court order was overturned on August 10, but Virginia coal operators said that they would institute further court actions challenging the power the act gives the federal government to regulate the use of private land.

By a vote of 68 to 26, the Senate approved a bill on September 11 that would virtually repeal the Department of the Interior's tough strip-mining regulations. The bill would permit the states to require compliance only with the standards specifically set out by law. Interior Secretary Andrus said that if similar legislation passed the House, he would recommend a presidential veto.

Whales Win. Conservationists hailed actions of the International Whaling Commission (IWC) at its annual meeting in London in July as a major victory in their long battle to end killing of whales. The IWC voted 18 to 2 for a worldwide moratorium on whaling by factory ships, protecting all but the

Conservationists tow a balloon replica to protest whale killing
during an International Whaling Commission meeting in London.

relatively populous Minke whale. The moratorium
will protect sperm whales, which have been heavily
harvested since other great whales, such as blue and
humpback, were hunted nearly to extinction. Almost 10,000 sperm whales were killed in 1978.

Japan and Russia, which use factory ships to
process whales killed by smaller hunting ships, will
be affected the most by the ban. Their delegates
complained they were being discriminated against
by nonwhaling nations. The IWC banned all whale
hunting for the next decade in the Indian Ocean, the
Arabian and Red seas, and the Persian Gulf.

Snail Darter Loses. Environmentalists won some
battles in their fight to save the tiny snail darter, an
endangered species of perch, from possible extinction, but finally lost the war. One of the 1970s'
biggest conservation controversies ended on September 25 when President Carter signed legislation
that forces completion of Tellico Dam on the Little
Tennessee River, the home of the tiny snail darter.

Congress attached a rider to the $10.8-billion
public-works appropriations bill exempting the dam
from any laws that might hinder its completion. On
September 24, a group of 45 environmental and
consumer organizations urged the President to veto
the bill, and the President said he signed the legislation "with regret."

Spokesmen for environmental groups angrily
warned at a news conference on September 26 that

Carter might lose their support in the 1980 political
campaign. Elizabeth Kaplan of Friends of the Earth
said the President's failure to veto the Tellico project
was "the straw that broke the camel's back" and
charged that Carter had "abandoned his environmental commitment."

Federal agencies began moving the remaining
snail darters from the Little Tennessee River to the
nearby Holston River on October 2. Some snail
darters transplanted to the Hiwassee River in southeastern Tennessee in 1975 are reproducing, but
federal experts said that the chances of long-term
survival of the transplanted snail darter populations
are not good.

National Parks. Fears of gas shortages and rising
fuel prices reduced tourism in many of the National
Park System's western units. A dramatic exception
to the general decline in park visits was the Golden
Gate National Recreation Area in San Francisco,
which registered more than a 50 per cent increase.

On August 14, the National Park Service banned
searches for nuclear fuels in the national parks. The
service also opposed proposals to lease geothermal
areas in the Targhee National Forest adjoining
Yellowstone National Park because of fears that
even test drilling might threaten the park's geysers,
including Old Faithful.   Andrew L. Newman

See also ENVIRONMENT; FOREST AND FOREST
PRODUCTS. In WORLD BOOK, see CONSERVATION.

CONSTITUTION OF THE UNITED STATES. A movement to amend the Constitution to require a balanced federal budget gained momentum in 1979. Thirty of the 34 states needed had passed resolutions calling for a constitutional convention to draft such an amendment. The Constitution specifies that any amendment drafted by convention or passed by Congress must then be adopted by three-fourths of the states – or 38 states – to become law.

Two amendments previously passed by Congress made little progress toward ratification in 1979. The Equal Rights Amendment (ERA), which would prohibit discrimination on the basis of sex, failed to gain the approval of any additional state legislatures, remaining three states short of ratification. An amendment to secure voting representation in Congress for District of Columbia residents had been ratified by seven states, but rejected by 10, at year-end.

Congress killed two proposed amendments during the year. One, defeated in the Senate on July 10, would have substituted the direct popular election of the President for the electoral college system. The House of Representatives on July 24 voted down one that would have prohibited busing to achieve school integration.   Beverly Merz

In WORLD BOOK, see CONSTITUTION OF THE UNITED STATES; ELECTORAL COLLEGE.

CONSUMER PROTECTION. To consumers' dismay, inflation picked up speed in the United States in 1979. The government's Consumer Price Index increased from 12 per cent to a 13.2 per cent adjusted annual rate from March to September, dashing the Carter Administration's goals of keeping the increase to 10.6 per cent for the year.

Prices for the necessities of life – housing, food, energy, and medical care – rose more than twice as fast as other items during the first nine months, according to the National Center for Economic Alternatives in Washington, D.C. The four items account for about 66 per cent of the household budget for 80 per cent of U.S. families.

Energy prices rose faster than all others. The average price of gasoline reached 99.8 cents a gallon (3.8 liters) in September, up 31.3 cents from January levels. And the average cost of home heating oil hit 84.9 cents per gallon in September, an increase of 30.3 cents from the first of the year. Heating oil prices ranged from a low of 77.1 cents in Baltimore to a high of 91.4 cents in Buffalo, N.Y., according to the Bureau of Labor Statistics.

Credit became a critical problem for many people because of record interest levels and the drying up of loan funds in many institutions. Prime interest rates reached a record 15.75 per cent in November, after the Federal Reserve System's Board of Governors

Bruce Ratner, New York City's consumer affairs commissioner, solicits testimony on rising food prices from consumers and industry spokesmen.

jacked up rates and clamped new restrictions on bank reserves. Many people switched from savings accounts to investments with higher yields, leaving banks with less money to lend.

With prices rising faster than wages, consumer buying power – take-home pay adjusted for inflation – dropped 4.4 per cent during the 12 months ending in September.

Safety Hazards also became an increasing concern in 1979. An accident in March at the Three Mile Island nuclear plant near Harrisburg, Pa., the worst in the industry's history, suddenly brought home the hazards of nuclear energy to millions of Americans. A series of investigations led to a virtual moratorium on approval of new plants by the Nuclear Regulatory Commission and even higher fuel prices for many consumers, as some utilities switched to coal and others faced huge renovation costs. See ENERGY (Close-Up); ENVIRONMENT.

The public became concerned about the dangers of asbestos in consumer products after a television investigative reporter, working with the Environmental Defense Fund, revealed that about 100 models of hand-held hairdriers contained asbestos, a known cancer-causing agent. Acting on an April request from the Consumer Product Safety Commission, manufacturers recalled about 12 million hairdriers for repair.

Consumer Issues were debated in Congress, but few new laws were passed. One of the most discussed was the President's overall energy package, which contained proposals for increasing the tax breaks set up a year earlier for homeowners and businesses who install more efficient heating and cooling systems and increase insulation.

Americans gained some important new rights from a bankruptcy law that became effective on October 1. A complete revision of 40-year-old federal laws, the legislation gives individuals a much better chance of obtaining at least partial refunds from bankrupt parties than did previous rules. Title 11 of the law gives priority over all other unsecured creditors to people who have made deposits for undelivered merchandise or services.

The law also increased the number of individual possessions exempt from seizure in bankruptcy actions, including up to $7,500 equity in a home, $1,200 in a car, and $200 each for household goods, furnishings, and clothing. The law allows states to reject these exemptions for residents, however.

FTC Under Fire. One of the most controversial issues before Congress was whether to impose new restraints on federal agencies that regulate the marketplace, notably the Federal Trade Commission (FTC). Sensitive to prodding from lobbyists, legislators offered numerous proposals to cut back on FTC rules and regulations.

In September, the Senate passed by voice vote an unprecedented measure to give courts greater power to overturn government regulations. In effect, the amendment to the Federal Courts Improvements Act of 1979 would order courts to assume no longer that rules issued by agencies are valid. After hearing weeks of critical testimony, Senator Wendell H. Ford (D., Ky.), chairman of the Senate Consumer Subcommittee, proposed legislation to slash the FTC's subpoena power, cut its funds, block several pending business rules, and subject the agency to semiannual oversight hearings.

The House showed even more hostility toward the FTC, the government's principal consumer-protection agency. On November 27, the House voted, 321–63, to allow either branch of Congress to reject any final FTC rule within 90 days.

More or Less? These actions came in the face of numerous polls showing a strong public sentiment for more, rather than less, regulation over product hazards and unfair marketplace practices. An informal survey of newspaper readers initiated by Congressman James H. Scheuer (D., N.Y.) found that when asked, "How much government regulation do you think is necessary to protect consumers?" 69 per cent of those responding answered: "More than we now have."

New FTC regulations continued to flow, however. Final rules required marketers of franchises to disclose full financial details to potential investors. And associations of doctors and dentists were prohibited from restricting advertising by members.

Montgomery Ward and Company agreed on May 29 to pay $175,000 to settle an FTC complaint about its credit practices. The FTC charged that the company failed to give accurate reasons for denying credit to applicants. Also, the FTC prohibited the use of postal ZIP codes in scrutinizing credit applicants. Consumerists hailed that decision as prohibiting discrimination against low-income consumers in so-called redlined areas.

Tire Grading. A U.S. Department of Transportation rule requiring the grading of automobile tires went into effect on April 1 after vigorous opposition by the rubber industry. Manufacturers began grading bias-ply tires either A, B, or C for traction and temperature resistance, and on a numerical scale for tread wear based on 100 as standard. For example, a tire with a tread-wear grading of 150 should last half again as long as a tire graded 100. Grading of bias-belted tires began on September 1. Radials were to be graded beginning on April 1, 1980.

Small Savers have seen their annual interest eaten up by inflation for several years. They finally got some relief from the Federal Reserve Board and other agencies, largely because of pressures applied by the Gray Panthers, an activist group of older persons. As of July 1, commercial banks could raise their interest rates – for the first time since 1973 – to 5.25 per cent for small savings accounts. Savings and loan institutions could pay 5.5 per cent. Savings banks were authorized to offer new four-year certificates with an interest rate tied to that for U.S. Treasury certificates – about 9 per cent. Also, penalties were softened for early withdrawal of funds from long-term accounts.

Court Actions. The Supreme Court of the United States ruled unanimously in June that individual consumers may sue a business for triple damages in a price-fixing case. The suit, brought by a Minnesota woman against five hearing-aid manufacturers, accused them of conspiring to set prices. The June decision appeared to go beyond a 1977 high court ruling that a state could not sue a brick company on behalf of individual consumers as a group.

United States District Court Judge John J. Sirica ruled in March that the Public Citizen Health Research Group – a consumer group founded by activist Ralph Nader – had no standing to sue the U. S. government on behalf of the general public. The decision was later reversed on appeal.

The number of companies with consumer-affairs executives continued to increase. As the drive to reduce government regulations began to bear fruit, business firms appeared to be increasingly willing to demonstrate their concern for good customer relations. Arthur E. Rowse

In WORLD BOOK, see CONSUMER PROTECTION.

COSTA RICA. See LATIN AMERICA.

COURTS AND LAWS. The legal profession experienced relative tranquility throughout the world in 1979. Although the death penalty was returned to the United States criminal justice system in force during the year, it reappeared without strenuous protest or opposition. Internationally, the United Nations (UN) Law of the Sea Conference bogged down without reaching an accord on seabed mining rights (see OCEAN).

The UN's International Court of Justice at The Hague, the Netherlands, on December 10 heard urgent charges lodged by the United States over seizure of American hostages in Iran (see IRAN). Citing "the inviolability of diplomatic envoys and embassies," the court ruled unanimously on December 15 that Iran should release the hostages immediately. Iran ignored the ruling.

The European Court of Human Rights ruled on April 26, in an 11 to 9 vote, that a 1972 British court injunction violated the freedom of expression provisions of the European Convention on Human Rights. The court had prevented *The Sunday Times* of London from publishing an article on the drug thalidomide on the grounds that publicity would prejudice the outcome of a lawsuit against the drug manufacturer filed by parents of deformed children.

Amnesty International's annual report on February 1 cited human rights violations in 110 countries

A defense attorney uses special visual aids in his final argument in the televised trial of William Waddill in Santa Ana, Calif., in May.

in 1978. The United States was cited for inhuman conditions in some prisons, and for allegedly framing such political activists as the Wilmington 10 in North Carolina on criminal charges.

Extradition Refused. Chile's Supreme Court refused on May 14 to extradite three Chilean army officers, including General Manuel Contreras Sepulveda, former chief of the secret police, who had been indicted in the United States for the 1976 murder of former Chilean Ambassador Orlando Letelier and an aide in Washington, D.C. In February, a U.S. district court sentenced two Cuban exiles to life terms for their role in the slayings. An American, Michael V. Townley, was sentenced on May 11 to a minimum of 40 months in prison for the murders after he cooperated with authorities.

Involuntary Capital Punishment was reintroduced in the United States on May 25 when Florida electrocuted John A. Spenkelink, 30, for the 1973 motel murder of a fellow drifter. The execution was only the second since 1967. Gary Gilmore was shot by a firing squad in Utah in January 1977, after he refused to pursue court appeals. The Supreme Court of the United States gave the green light for resumption of capital punishment in 1976, but death penalty opponents had hoped to forestall executions indefinitely by claiming that their infrequency made the penalty cruel and unusual punishment, and therefore unconstitutional. Jesse W. Bishop, 46, was executed in Nevada on Oct. 22, 1979, and some 550 others awaited execution in 28 states.

Press and Law. The American Bar Association (ABA) was caught in a dispute between Chief Justice Warren E. Burger and electronic journalists at its midwinter meeting in Atlanta, Ga., in February. Burger refused to be filmed and walked out of one scheduled appearance in an attempt to pressure television crews to leave. The ABA announced later that its future meetings would be open to press coverage and that Burger would have to abide by those rules if he attended.

With bar opposition breaking down slowly, several states increased experimentation with televised court proceedings during 1979. One of the year's most celebrated trials, involving accused murderer Theodore R. Bundy, was televised on public stations in a number of cities, over Bundy's objections. He was convicted in Miami in July of murdering two young women attending college in Tallahassee in 1978 and sentenced to death in the electric chair.

Press groups fought a rearguard action, however, against a July 2 Supreme Court decision limiting access to courtrooms. A survey published by the Reporters Committee for Freedom of the Press on November 2 revealed that attempts were made to close off hearings or trials in 81 criminal cases throughout the United States during the four months following the decision, and that judges ordered at least some closure in 48 of those cases.

Other Trials. Heirs of Karen Silkwood, a laboratory technician contaminated by radiation in an Oklahoma plutonium plant and later killed in a 1974 auto accident, were awarded a $10.5-million judgment against the Kerr-McGee Corporation, her former employers, by a federal jury in Oklahoma on May 18.

A jury in Portland, Ore., awarded $2 million to Julie C. Titchbourne on August 15. A former member of the Church of Scientology, she accused the cult of defrauding her on its promise to give her a better life. Five Scientologists were sentenced to prison terms of four or five years in December, after they were convicted of conspiring to obstruct justice and to obtain government documents pertaining to the cult.

One of the decade's most perplexing crimes was apparently resolved in August when a jury convicted physician Jeffrey R. MacDonald of the 1970 slayings of his wife and two children in North Carolina. MacDonald, a U.S. Army doctor at the time, had claimed that intruders had committed the crimes.

Stanley Mark Rifkin, a computer consultant who had pleaded guilty to two counts of wire fraud in connection with the computer theft of $10.2 million from a Los Angeles bank in 1978, was sentenced to eight years in prison in March.   David C. Beckwith

See also CRIME; SUPREME COURT OF THE UNITED STATES. In WORLD BOOK, see COURT; LAW.

CRANE, PHILIP MILLER (1930-   ), an Illinois congressman, campaigned throughout 1979 for the 1980 Republican presidential nomination. By announcing his candidacy early and waging an incessant campaign, Crane hoped to duplicate Jimmy Carter's rise from relative obscurity to the presidency. See REPUBLICAN PARTY.

Crane was born in Chicago on Nov. 3, 1930. His father, George W. Crane, is a physician and psychologist who has written a syndicated newspaper advice column, "The Worry Clinic," since 1935. A brother, Daniel, also is an Illinois congressman.

Crane grew up in Hillsboro, Ind., and graduated from Hilldale College in Michigan. After serving in the United States Army, he returned to college, earning a master's degree and a doctorate in history from Indiana University. He taught history at Indiana from 1960 to 1963 and was assistant professor of history at Bradley University in Peoria, Ill., from 1963 to 1969.

A conservative who advocates reduced government intervention and greater individual self-reliance, Crane campaigned for Republican presidential candidates Barry M. Goldwater in 1964 and Ronald W. Reagan in 1968. He was elected to the House of Representatives in 1969.

Crane married Arlene Catherine Johnson in 1959. They have eight children. The Cranes have homes in McLean, Va., and Mount Prospect, Ill. Beverly Merz

CRIME. International terrorism continued unabated during 1979. Ireland was hit particularly hard. On August 27, Earl Mountbatten of Burma, a British naval hero and cousin of Queen Elizabeth II, and three others were killed after a bomb exploded on their boat off County Sligo, Ireland; 18 British soldiers died because of an ambush the same day near Belfast, Northern Ireland. The Irish Republican Army claimed responsibility.

More Skyjackings. Aircraft hijacking continued in 1979, but without bloodshed. A former Cuban air force officer took over a plane flying from New York City to Fort Lauderdale, Fla., on June 11 and ordered the pilot to fly to Havana, Cuba, in the first successful skyjacking from the United States to that country since 1972. The 205 passengers and crew were returned to Miami, Fla., the following day. Serbian nationalist Nikola Kavaja hijacked a New York City-to-Chicago flight on June 20, and eventually landed in Ireland, where he surrendered.

Three deserters from the Spanish Foreign Legion took over a DC-9 in the Canary Islands on August 4. Refused permission to land in Morocco, they finally touched down in Switzerland, where they were arrested. Three Lebanese religious protestors took over an Alitalia DC-8 near Beirut, Lebanon, on September 8 and flew to Rome and Teheran, Iran, before surrendering to authorities.

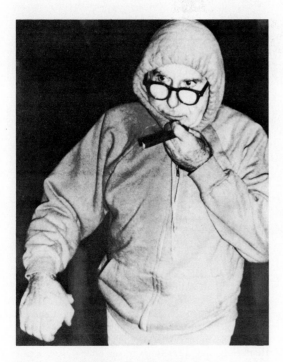

Carmine Galante, a New York City crime figure who left prison on bail in March pending a parole hearing, was killed by three men in July.

Stolen Art. International police noted a worldwide increase in art thefts. A Greek marble head worth at least $150,000 was stolen from New York City's Metropolitan Museum of Art on February 9, the first major theft in the museum's history. It was recovered, damaged, on February 14. Thieves broke into a Roman Catholic convent in Rome on June 3 and took eight Flemish paintings worth $1.2 million, including one by Peter Paul Rubens.

Bank Robberies increased dramatically in the United States in 1979. One Federal Bureau of Investigation (FBI) official forecast at midyear that there would be 6,000 bank robberies in 1979, up 13 per cent from 1978. New York City banks were particularly hard hit – 10 robberies on August 21 alone, including $2 million taken from an armored truck at a Chase Manhattan Bank branch.

The federal government continued its stepped-up campaign against white-collar crime, including political corruption and computer fraud. A study released on March 8 showed about 1,500 incidents of white-collar crime in the 582 largest U.S. corporations over a two-year period. The study noted that corporate officials were criminally prosecuted in fewer than 1 per cent of the cases.

Crime in the United States resumed an upward surge during 1979 after leveling off for two years. Violent crime – murder, robbery, forcible rape, and aggravated assault – increased 13 per cent during the first nine months of 1979, compared with the same period in 1978. More-numerous property crimes – burglary, larceny-theft, and motor vehicle theft – increased 9 per cent.

Crimes of Violence. Three FBI agents were slain in two incidents on August 9. An unemployed community services worker under investigation for misuse of public money shot two agents in their El Centro, Calif., office, then turned the gun on himself. The third agent was shot while hunting a fugitive in a Cleveland housing project, and a suspect was arrested on August 16. Prior to these shootings, only 23 agents had been killed since the FBI started as the Bureau of Investigation in 1908.

The most spectacular murder of 1979 was the gangland-style execution of Carmine (Lilo) Galante at an Italian restaurant in Brooklyn during the lunch hour on July 12. Three masked intruders shot Galante, his bodyguard, and the restaurant owner only months after Galante had completed 13 years in prison for narcotics and parole violations and had been released on bail. Federal authorities said Galante still headed a New York City crime family.

John Wayne Gacy was scheduled to go on trial in Cook County, Illinois, in January 1980, in one of the worst mass murder cases in U.S. history. Gacy is charged with the deaths of 33 young men. The bodies of most of them were found under his house in a Chicago suburban area.   David C. Beckwith

In WORLD BOOK, see CRIME; TERRORISM.

Cuban President Fidel Castro stresses a need for more aid to developing nations during speech to the United Nations General Assembly in October.

CUBA. The United States government announced on Aug. 31, 1979, that there was a 2,000- to 3,000-member Russian combat brigade stationed in Cuba. Both Cuba and the Soviet Union claimed that the troops were there solely for training purposes and were not in violation of a 1962 agreement banning the Russians from using the island for any offensive measures. In an address to the American people on October 1, President Jimmy Carter said Russian troops in Cuba were "no reason to return to the Cold War" of the 1950s. He said that a far greater danger to U.S. security was "the breakdown of a common effort to preserve the peace and ultimate threat of a nuclear war." President Carter thus chose to defuse the controversy and not link it to the more important issue of ratification by the U.S. Senate of the U.S.-Russian Strategic Arms Limitation Treaty (SALT II). See CONGRESS OF THE UNITED STATES.

However, the President authorized an intensification of U.S. intelligence-gathering activities over Cuba and the improvement of U.S. capabilities to respond to military threats in the Caribbean. He also secured a pledge from Moscow that Russian troops would not threaten Western Hemisphere nations. The expansion of a Russian submarine base at Cienfuegos was not a cause for alarm, according to the U.S. Department of State.

During the year, an estimated 40,000 Cuban troops were reportedly assisting pro-Marxist forces in Africa, particularly in Angola and Ethiopia. Closer to home, Cuba lent active support to the revolution in Nicaragua. It also aided leftist elements in El Salvador and Guatemala, and stationed 450 "advisers" in Jamaica. These military adventures were one reason the U.S. chose not to lift the economic embargo it had imposed on Cuba in 1960.

Other Developments. For one week beginning on September 3, Cuba played host to delegates from 92 countries attending the sixth summit conference of nonaligned nations. President Fidel Castro Ruz upset some of the Third World delegates when he admitted to being a "friend of Russia," but he nonetheless strongly championed the nonaligned cause when he addressed the United Nations General Assembly in New York City on October 12. In that speech, he urged the world's rich nations to give $300 billion over 10 years to help the poor.

In December 1978, Castro had promised to release about 3,600 political prisoners in 1979 as "a gesture to the Cuban-American community." By November, he had almost fulfilled his promise. Half of those released went to the United States under a special parole program. Castro also encouraged Cuban Americans to return to the island as tourists, and thousands took advantage of his offer.   T. W. Adams

See also LATIN AMERICA (Facts in Brief Table). In WORLD BOOK, see CUBA.

CYPRUS. See EUROPE.

CZECHOSLOVAKIA struggled with an energy shortage and other economic problems during 1979. Heavy snow and ice disrupted industry and transportation in January and cost the country $600-million. Prime Minister Lubomir Strougal revealed in March that Czechoslovakia would have to import an extra 273,000 metric tons (300,000 short tons) of crude oil from members of the Organization of Petroleum Exporting Countries (OPEC) during the year and would have to cut imports from the hard-currency Western nations. Czechoslovakia agreed in April to invest about $375 million in equipment—mainly trucks and reactors—for a $2.3-billion Russian nuclear power station in the Ukraine. Russia agreed in turn to give Czechoslovakia regular supplies of electricity until the year 2003. Strougal announced on September 5 that, after 1980, the country would have to buy its extra crude oil from OPEC members, rather than from Russia.

More Business. Industrial production increased 2.6 per cent in the first half of 1979, compared with the first half of 1978. Foreign trade went up 7.3 per cent in the first six months of the year, with exports up 8.1 per cent and imports 6.4 per cent higher. Exports to West Germany, Czechoslovakia's main Western trading partner, increased 10 per cent and imports from it rose 9 per cent. But the 1979 grain harvest was 9 million metric tons (9.9 million short tons), 2 million metric tons (2.2 million short tons) less than the target. On July 21, the price of gasoline went up 50 per cent to $2.65 per gallon (3.8 liters), and the prices of gas, coal, coke, fuel oil, electricity, central heating, children's clothing, and postal and telephone services increased 50 to 100 per cent.

Dissidents. Czechoslovakia continued to crack down on dissidents. The government sentenced Jaroslav Sabata, spokesman for the Charter 77 dissident movement, to nine months imprisonment on January 11 for insulting a policeman. At the end of April, it arrested 10 members of the Committee for the Defense of the Unjustly Persecuted, a Charter 77 offshoot. Six of those arrested, including playwright Vaclav Havel, were sentenced to prison terms ranging up to five years on October 23. Czechoslovakia arrested four Roman Catholic priests and two laymen in September. On October 4, the government prevented Pavel Kohout, a writer and leader of Charter 77, from returning from Austria, where he had been on a year's visa since October 1978, and deprived him of his citizenship for publishing an "anti-Socialist" book in West Germany and for associating with Czechoslovak émigrés. Chris Cviic

See also EUROPE (Facts in Brief Table). In WORLD BOOK, see CZECHOSLOVAKIA.

DAM. See BUILDING AND CONSTRUCTION.

Czechoslovakia built an extensive park on rock and dirt piles left over from a mine on the edge of the Bohemian city of Most.

DANCING

European dance companies visiting the United States in 1979 supplied substantial, and sometimes controversial, novelty. A small touring group from the Royal Danish Ballet introduced Americans to a wide sampling of the work of August Bournonville, a Danish choreographer of the 1800s. His ballets are rarely performed outside Denmark, but in June and July, to mark the centenary of his death, the Danish soloists toured Los Angeles; San Francisco; New York City; Hartford, Conn.; Minneapolis, Minn.; and Ambler, Pa. The dancers offered excerpts from full-length ballets that delighted audiences eager to learn about a relatively obscure but charming style.

Exponents of contemporary European ballet also received much attention. Jiri Kylian, a 32-year-old Czech whose ballets comprised almost the entire repertory of The Hague's Nederlands Dance Theater, won sensational acclaim. The troupe's July 9 to 21 visit to the New York City Center became a marathon of artistic discovery. Several critics, however, noted that while Kylian's style was advanced by European standards, it was more visually imposing than choreographically interesting.

Other Visitors. Similar comments applied to the work of French choreographer Maurice Béjart and his Ballet of the 20th Century, which appeared on Broadway from March 6 to 25. The repertory featured Béjart's reworkings of such classics as *Petrouchka* and *Le Spectre de la Rose.* While his modernizations were most noteworthy for the controversy they provoked, only his ballet called *Life* – a vehicle for the great French dancer Jean Babilée, who had not danced in the United States for some 20 years – was deemed worthy of the occasion.

The visit of Great Britain's Royal Ballet suggested that classics need not be reinterpreted to be viable. Opening a six-week tour on June 26 at Wolf Trap Farm Park in Virginia, the company showed that cohesive ensemble dancing and intelligent staging of *Swan Lake* and *The Sleeping Beauty* could revitalize these staples.

Dancing Defectors. Russia's Bolshoi Ballet, which played the New York State Theater for the month of August followed by engagements in Chicago and Los Angeles, brought a repertory controversial in that it was all choreographed by Uri Grigorovich. However, defections by three soloists overshadowed discussions about Grigorovich's caliber as artist and director. Alexander Godunov defected on August 23, while the fate of his wife, Ludmila Vlasova, was played out via diplomatic channels at Kennedy International Airport in New York City. Her plane was delayed for three days, while U.S. officials made certain that she was leaving of her own free will. Then, on September 16, Leonid and Valentina Kozlov left the company in Los Angeles and were granted asylum just before the Bolshoi was due to return to Moscow.

The Kozlovs made their debut as defectors on October 12 with the Ballet Galaxie in New Orleans. Godunov joined American Ballet Theater (ABT) for its December season at Kennedy Center for the Performing Arts in Washington, D.C. But when that engagement was cancelled due to a labor dispute, he asked to be released from his contract, and did not dance in the U.S. again in 1979. Throughout this political *pas de trois,* balletomanes concentrated on the question of Grigorovich's future. It was unclear what effect the defections might have on his career.

Baryshnikov Moves. An earlier Russian defector, Mikhail Baryshnikov, continued to make headlines. It was announced in June that he would take over the artistic reins of ABT as of Sept. 1, 1980, when Lucia Chase will resign as director of the company she co-founded in 1940. The announcement was surprising, both because Baryshnikov, at 31, is young for such a demanding administrative post, and because his heralded tenure with the New York City Ballet would end after only 15 months. The dancer announced in October that injuries, including tendinitis, made it dangerous for him to dance for the time being.

The companies involved in Baryshnikov's changing affiliations were busy in 1979. The New York City Ballet toured extensively – to upstate New York in March, Chicago in April, the Kennedy Center for two engagements, and to London for three weeks in September. With artistic director George Balanchine suffering from a heart ailment, new works were given by Jerome Robbins and Peter Martins. Both Martins' *Guiardino de Scarlatti,* premièred on July 13 in Saratoga Springs, N.Y., and Robbins' *The Four Seasons,* premièred on January 18 during the company's winter run at the New York State Theater, gave convincing evidence of company strength.

Although ABT continued to rely on guest stars to draw audiences, there were indications that management was trying to develop principal performers from within the ranks. For the first time, several young dancers were cast in leading roles in ABT's gallery of classics. There was only one world première, Glen Tetley's *Contredances,* which featured Anthony Dowell and Natalia Makarova at the opening in Los Angeles on January 22.

Other American Companies. The Feld Ballet appeared in Chicago and throughout Texas and the South, and concluded with a European debut in Paris on November 27. But Eliot Feld created only

Profiles, a new ballet by choreographer Paul Taylor, is the sixth of his works to be premièred at the American Dance Festival in Durham, N.C.

Russian defectors Valentina Kozlova and her husband Leonid Kozlov dance on October 20 in Brooklyn, N.Y., *right*. Alexander Godunov, also a former Bolshoi Ballet star, rehearses, *above*.

one new work, *Papillon*. Perhaps the most distinguished new American work was by Twyla Tharp. *Baker's Dozen,* first danced on February 25 at the Brooklyn Academy of Music, continued Tharp's fruitful association with jazz and boasted a new clarity of form and an even sharper wit than she showed in the past. Merce Cunningham, America's foremost choreographer, premièred a minor piece called *Roadrunners* at the American Dance Festival in Durham, N.C., on July 19. The festival also commissioned other new dances by Paul Taylor and Laura Dean.

The New Talent Search is never-ending, and 1979 saw two novel variations on the theme. The Boston Ballet sponsored the first annual International Choreographers' Competition, which culminated in a showcase presentation of seven winners on January 27. The overall winner of the $5,000 Boston Ballet Award was Constantin Patsalas, a soloist with the National Ballet of Canada. The first U.S.A. International Ballet Competition was held in Jackson, Miss., from June 18 to 29. Top medals were won by two male dancers, 23-year-old Ludomir Kafka of Czechoslovakia and 17-year-old Koenraad Onzia of Belgium. Among the 64 dancers from 14 countries who took part was a delegation from the Peking Dance Conservatory and the National Dance Company of China. They held a lecture-show of Chinese dances.   Nancy Goldner

In WORLD BOOK, see BALLET; DANCING.

DEATHS OF NOTABLE PERSONS in 1979 included those listed below. An asterisk (*) indicates the person is the subject of a biography in THE WORLD BOOK ENCYCLOPEDIA. Those listed were Americans unless otherwise indicated.

Acheampong, Ignatius K. (1931-June 16), Ghana's head of state from 1972 to 1978.

Ager, Milton (1893-May 6), composer of hundreds of popular songs including "Ain't She Sweet?", written for his daughter – journalist Shana Alexander.

Allbritton, Louise (1920-Feb. 16), actress who played in *Pittsburgh* (1943) with John Wayne and Marlene Dietrich.

Anderson, Charles (Chic) (1931-March 24), radio and television announcer who called 16 Kentucky Derby races since 1960.

Angoff, Charles (1902-May 3), Russian-born writer, editor of *American Mercury* magazine from 1925 to 1936. He wrote a series of autobiographical novels on Jewish-American life.

Arzner, Dorothy (1897-Oct. 1), Hollywood's only woman film director in the 1930s and 1940s. Her films included *Get Your Man* (1927), starring Clara Bow.

Bartlett, Dewey F. (1919-March 1), governor of Oklahoma from 1967 to 1971 and Republican U.S. senator from 1972 to 1979.

Barzani, Mustafa (1904-March 1), leader of Kurdish resistance in Iran from 1960 to 1975.

Beltrán, Pedro G. (1897-Feb. 16), prime minister of Peru from 1959 to 1961.

Benét, Laura (1884-Feb. 17), poet and novelist whose books included *The Hidden Valley* (1938).

*****Bennett, William A. C.** (1900-Feb. 23), premier of British Columbia, Canada, from 1952 to 1972.

Berndt, Walter (1899-Aug. 13), cartoonist whose comic strip "Smitty" appeared in hundreds of newspapers for more than 50 years.

Bernstein, Theodore M. (1904-June 27), the ultimate copy editor and authority on English usage with *The New York Times* for 46 years. His many books included *The Careful Writer* (1965).

*****Bhutto, Zulfikar Ali** (1928-April 4), political leader of Pakistan from 1971 to 1977.

Bishop, Elizabeth (1911-Oct. 6), poet whose elegant evocations of the natural world in *North and South* and *A Cold Spring* won a Pulitzer Prize in 1956.

Blondell, Joan (1906-Dec. 25), Hollywood film actress who played the brassy but good-hearted heroine in dozens of comedies and musicals.

Bolton, Guy (1884-Sept. 5), British writer who collaborated with Jerome Kern on such early Broadway musicals as *Leave It to Jane* (1917).

Bourget, Maurice (1907-March 29), speaker of Canada's Senate from 1963 to 1966.

Breckinridge, John B. (1913-July 29), Democratic congressman from Kentucky from 1973 to 1978.

Brent, George (1904-May 26), actor, best known for such early films as *Jezebel* (1938) and *Dark Victory* (1939).

Brodie, Sir Israel (1895-Feb. 13), chief rabbi of Great Britain from 1948 to 1965.

Buchanan, Edgar (1903-April 14), actor who appeared in 100 motion pictures and played Uncle Joe in the TV series "Petticoat Junction." He was a former dentist and head of oral surgery at Eugene Hospital in Oregon.

Cain, Harry P. (1906-March 3), Republican senator from Washington from 1946 to 1952.

Capehart, Homer E. (1897-Sept. 3), Republican senator from Indiana from 1944 to 1962.

*****Capp, Al (Alfred Gerald Caplin)** (1909-Nov. 5), cartoonist who created the comic strip *Li'l Abner*, which appeared in U.S. newspapers from 1934 to 1977.

Carroll, John (1907-April 24), actor who starred in swashbuckling Zorro movies.

Cassidy, Ted (1933-Jan. 16), actor who played the lumbering servant, Lurch, in the TV comedy series "The Addams Family."

Cavanaugh, John J. (1899-Dec. 28), president of Notre Dame University from 1946 to 1952.

*****Chain, Sir Ernst B.** (1906-Aug. 12), British biochemist who shared the 1945 Nobel Prize for Physiology or Medicine as a co-discoverer of penicillin's healing properties.

Chaliapin, Boris (1904-May 18), Russian-born portrait artist who created some 400 covers for *Time* magazine.

Chapman, Ceil (1912-July 13), designer of glamorous party dresses in the 1940s and 1950s.

Chapple, Charles C. (1903-March 23), pediatrician who invented an incubator that revolutionized the care of premature infants in the mid-1930s.

Cochran, Colonel Philip G. (1910-Aug. 25), pilot who led the First Air Commando Force in Burma in World War II. He was the model for Flip Corkin of the *Terry and the Pirates* comic strip.

Conrad, Max (1903-April 3), record-breaking pioneer aviator who logged more than 50,000 hours of flight time.

Costello, Dolores (1905-March 1), actress who starred in the silent film *The Sea Beast* (1926) and played the mother in *Little Lord Fauntleroy* (1936).

Coughlin, Charles E. (1891-Oct. 27), Roman Catholic "radio priest" of the 1930s whose virulent Fascist sermons were eventually silenced by the church hierarchy and the federal government.

Cousteau, Philippe (1940-June 28), photographer and diver who filmed his father's award-winning TV series "The Undersea World of Jacques Cousteau."

Creavy, Tom (1911-March 3), who won the 1931 Professional Golfers' Association championship.

Crockett, James U. (1915-June 13), horticulturist and host of public television's "Crockett's Victory Garden."

Dalgliesh, Alice (1893-June 11), author of such children's books as *Little Wooden Farmer* and *The Courage of Sarah Noble*.

Dehnert, Henry (Dutch) (1898-April 20), Hall of Fame basketball player who developed the pivot play.

*****Diaz Ordaz, Gustavo** (1911-July 15), president of Mexico from 1964 to 1970.

*****Diefenbaker, John G.** (1895-Aug. 16), Conservative prime minister of Canada from 1957 to 1963 and a colorful figure in politics. See CANADA (Close-Up).

Donald, Peter (1918-April 30), English-born actor, best known as the storyteller on the radio and TV show "Can You Top This?"

Douglas, Aaron (1899-Feb. 2), "father of black American art," who founded and chaired the Fisk University Art Department in Nashville, Tenn.

Dubs, Adolph (1920-Feb. 14), U.S. ambassador to Afghanistan, who was killed after being kidnapped by terrorists.

Easter, Luscious (Luke) (1915-March 29), former Cleveland Indian first baseman and one of the first blacks to break into major-league baseball.

Eaton, Cyrus S. (1883-May 9), Canadian-born millionaire industrialist and banker who advocated friendly relations between Russia and America during the Cold War in the 1950s.

Eisenhower, Mamie Doud (1896-Nov. 1), widow of President Dwight D. Eisenhower. The two were married in 1916 when Eisenhower was an Army lieutenant.

*****Empie, Paul C.** (1909-Sept. 1), clergyman, a national and international leader of the Lutheran Church, and president of Lutheran World Relief.

*****Farrell, James T.** (1904-Aug. 22), novelist, best known for his 1930s Studs Lonigan novels.

*****Fiedler, Arthur** (1894-July 10), conductor of the Boston Pops Orchestra for 50 years. See MUSIC, CLASSICAL (Close-Up).

Fields, Dame Gracie (1898-Sept. 27), British music-hall singer and comedian whose bouncy personality and

Great Britain's Prince Charles, standing at the pulpit, reads the lesson
at the September 5 funeral of Lord Louis Mountbatten in Westminster Abbey.

broad Lancashire accent made her a hit in such songs as "The Greatest Aspidistra in the World."

Flatt, Lester (1914-May 11), singer and guitarist who, with Earl Scruggs, formed and led the well-known Foggy Mountain Boys bluegrass band.

Fleischer, Dave (1895-June 25), film animator who, with his brother Max, created the cartoon characters Popeye the Sailor and Betty Boop.

Focke, Heinrich (1890-Feb. 25), German aviation engineer who developed the first successful helicopter in 1937.

Foran, Dick (John Nicholas) (1910-Aug. 10), singing actor in some 200 Westerns.

*****Forssmann, Werner** (1904-June 1), German surgeon and urologist who shared the 1956 Nobel Prize for Physiology or Medicine for his work in using the catheter to study the heart.

Gabor, Dennis (1900-Feb. 9), Hungarian-born British physicist who won the 1971 Nobel Prize for Physics for his development of holography.

Galento, Two-Ton Tony (Dominick Anthony) (1910-July 22), brawling heavyweight boxer who knocked Joe Louis down in a losing bid for the championship in 1939.

Gargan, William D. (1905-Feb. 17), stage and screen actor who taught esophageal speech to cancer victims after his larynx was removed in 1960. He died of a heart attack.

Garner, Hugh (1913-June 30), Canadian writer, best known for *Cabbagetown*, a novel about the Toronto slums.

Gathings, E.C. (Took) (1903-May 2), Democratic congressman from Arkansas from 1939 to 1969.

Gehlen, Reinhard (1902-June 8), German chief of intelligence under Adolf Hitler. He also served as the first chief of intelligence in postwar West Germany from 1955 to 1968.

Geismar, Maxwell D. (1909-July 26), writer and literary critic whose work included *Writers in Crisis: The American Novel 1925-1940* (1942).

Giles, Warren (1896-Feb. 7), president of baseball's National League from 1951 to 1970.

Gordon, Mildred (1905-Feb. 3), writer, co-author with her husband, Gordon, of such popular books as *That Darn Cat*.

Gramatky, Hardie (1907-April 29), illustrator and author of the *Little Toot* series of children's books.

Granahan, Kathryn O. (1895-July 10), U.S. treasurer from 1963 to 1966. A Democrat, in 1956 she became the first woman ever to be elected to Congress from Pennsylvania.

Gross, Benjamin S. (1891-Aug. 13), radio and TV critic for the New York *Daily News* for 46 years.

Guggenheim, Peggy (1898-Dec. 23), influential collector and patron of modern art who nurtured the development of abstract expressionism.

Hack, Stanley C. (1909-Dec. 15), third baseman who played for the Chicago Cubs from 1932 to 1947 and later managed the Cubs and St. Louis Cardinals.

Haley, Jack (John Joseph) (1899-June 6), film actor who played the role of the Tin Woodman in *The Wizard of Oz*.

Hall, Leonard W. (1900-June 2), Republican national chairman from 1952 to 1957.

Halsman, Philippe (1906-June 25), Latvian-born celebrity photographer whose work graced 101 *Life* magazine covers.

Hardy, W. G. (1895-Oct. 31), Canadian novelist whose books include *Father Abraham*.

*****Harris, Roy** (1898-Oct. 1), composer of orchestral, choral, and chamber music. His best-known works are *Symphony No. 3* and *An American Overture*, based on "When Johnny Comes Marching Home."

Hartnell, Sir Norman B. (1901-June 8), British dress designer who made Queen Elizabeth's wedding and coronation gowns.

Hathaway, Donny (1945-Jan. 13), Grammy-winning singer and composer of such hit songs as "You've Got A Friend."

Hayward, Max (1924-March 18), a leading British translator of contemporary Russian writers. The son of an itinerant worker, Hayward taught himself Russian.

Hodge, Al (1912-March 19), actor who played Captain Video in TV's first science fiction series from 1948 to 1956.

*****Hilton, Conrad N.** (1887-Jan. 3), founder of the Hilton Hotel Corporation.

Hoveyda, Amir Abbas (1919-April 7), premier of Iran from 1965 to 1975.

Hunt, Pee Wee (Walter) (1907-June 22), trombonist whose *Twelfth Street Rag* was the largest-selling record in ragtime history.

Hutton, Barbara (1912-May 11), Woolworth heiress whose ill health and other misfortunes earned her the name of "poor little rich girl." Her seven husbands included actor Cary Grant.

Hutton, Jim (1934-June 2), actor, best known for his role as Ellery Queen in the 1975 TV series.

Jones, Preston (1936-Sept. 19), actor and playwright known for his recent work, *A Texas Trilogy*.

Kadar, Jan (1918-June 1), Czechoslovak-born director of such films as *The Shop on Main Street*, winner of a 1965 Academy Award Oscar.

Kelly, Emmett (1898-March 28), circus clown whose bedraggled Weary Willie delighted audiences for some 50 years.

Kenton, Stan (1912-Aug. 25), jazz musician and leader of one of the most controversial big jazz bands.

Kilian, Victor (1891-March 11), actor who played the Fernwood Flasher in the 1976 TV series "Mary Hartman, Mary Hartman."

Kinney, Richard (1923-Feb. 19), president of Hadley School for the Blind in Winnetka, Ill. He was the third deaf and blind person to graduate from a U.S. college.

Laire, Judson (1902-July 5), actor who played Papa in the 1950s TV series "I Remember Mama."

Larsen, Roy E. (1899-Sept. 9), first publisher of *Life* magazine and creator of *The March of Time*.

Lawrence, Marjorie (1907-Jan. 13), Australian-born soprano whose career was curtailed by polio in 1941.

Leonetti, Tommy (1929-Sept. 15), singer on the television series "Your Hit Parade" in 1957 and 1958.

Little, Lou (1893-May 28), football coach at Columbia University from 1930 to 1956.

*****Liu Shao-chi** (1900?-reported Jan. 29), chairman of the People's Republic of China from 1959 to 1968. His death was previously reported in 1974.

*****Lynen, Feodor** (1911-Aug. 8), West German biochemist, co-winner of the 1964 Nobel Prize for Physiology or Medicine for his research on cholesterol and fatty acid metabolism.

Lyon, Ben (1901-March 22), actor in more than 70 films. He broadcast a popular radio show in the 1940s with his wife, Bebe Daniels.

Manion, Clarence E. (1896-July 28), lawyer who hosted the "Manion Forum" radio show from 1954 to 1979 and dean of the University of Notre Dame Law School from 1941 to 1952.

Marcuse, Herbert (1898-July 29), German-born philosopher and educator, a Marxist critic of Western society.

*****Massine, Léonide** (1896-March 16), Russian ballet dancer and one of the great choreographers with Sergei Diaghilev's Ballets Russes.

McCreary, Conn (1921-June 28), jockey who won 1,500 races in 21 years, including the Kentucky Derby in 1944 and 1951.

*****McDonald, David J.** (1902-Aug. 8), president of the United Steelworkers of America from 1952 to 1965.

*****McIntyre, James Francis Cardinal** (1886-July 16), dynamic Roman Catholic archbishop of Los Angeles from 1948 to 1970.

Merritt, H. Houston (1902-Jan. 9), pioneer neurologist, co-developer of Dilantin, a drug that controls epileptic seizures.

Miller, Don (1902-July 28), one of the legendary Four Horsemen of Notre Dame – a running back for the 1920s football team. He served as a U.S. Bankruptcy Court judge from 1965 to 1977.

Mingus, Charles (1922-Jan. 5), leading jazz musician, bandleader, and composer who elevated the bass into a solo melodic instrument.

Mitchell, Blue (Richard A.) (1930-May 21), jazz trumpet player whose albums included "Smooth as the Wind."

*****Monnet, Jean** (1888-Mar. 16), French statesman who played a leading role in formation of the European Economic Community (Common Market).

*****Monsarrat, Nicholas** (1910-Aug. 8), British writer best known for *The Cruel Sea* (1951), a novel about naval combat during World War II.

Morton, Rogers C. B. (1914-April 19), secretary of the interior from 1971 to 1975 and secretary of commerce from 1975 to 1976. He was Republican national chairman, 1969 to 1971, and served as congressman from Maryland.

*****Mountbatten, Louis (Earl Mountbatten of Burma)** (1900-Aug. 27), British naval leader, great-grandson of Queen Victoria. A daring and courageous military strategist, he became first sea lord of Great Britain in 1955 and admiral of the fleet in 1956.

Muir, Malcolm (1885-Jan. 30), publisher who rose from file clerk to chairman of the board of McGraw-Hill Publishing Company and became head of *Newsweek*.

Thurman Munson, Yankees catcher and captain.

Mary Pickford, once America's Sweetheart.

Zulfikar Ali Bhutto, once Pakistan's prime minister.

Al Capp, who created Dogpatch's Li'l Abner.

Munson, Thurman (1947-Aug. 2), New York Yankee catcher, the American League's Rookie of the Year in 1970 and Most Valuable Player in 1976.

Nagy, Ferenc (1903-June 12), prime minister of Hungary from 1946 until he was ousted by Communists in 1947.

Narayan, Jaya Pradesh (1902-Oct. 8), Indian leader and disciple of nonviolence.

*__Natta, Giulio__ (1903-May 2), Italian chemist who shared the 1963 Nobel Prize for Chemistry.

Neave, Airey M. S. (1916-March 30), British Conservative member of Parliament for 25 years, murdered by Irish Republican Army terrorists.

Nervi, Pier L. (1891-Jan. 9), Italian engineer and architect known for his imaginative use of reinforced concrete in huge sports arenas and stadiums.

Neto, Agostinho (1922-Sept. 10), president of Angola since 1975.

Newhouse, Samuel I. (1895-Aug. 29), publisher whose communications empire included 31 newspapers, 7 American magazines, and 5 radio stations.

Novaes, Guiomar (1893-March 7), Brazilian pianist, the "Paderewski of the Pampas." She was regarded as one of the great interpreters of Frédéric Chopin.

Oberon, Merle (1911-Nov. 23), Tasmanian-born actress noted for her exotic beauty. She starred in such films as *The Scarlet Pimpernel* (1935) and *Wuthering Heights* (1939).

Ohlin, Bertil (1899-Aug. 3), Swedish economist and politician, co-winner of the 1977 Nobel Prize for Economics for his work in international finance.

O'Malley, Walter F. (1903-Aug. 9), major-league baseball executive who moved the Brooklyn Dodgers to Los Angeles after the 1957 season.

Ottaviani, Alfredo Cardinal (1890-Aug. 3), Italian ecclesiastic, head of the Vatican's Holy Office under Pope Pius XII and Pope John XXIII.

*__Park, Chung Hee__ (1917-Oct. 26), president of South Korea since 1963.

Parsons, Talcott (1902-May 8), sociologist who developed the theory that all human societies, simple or complex, are organized in the same fundamental way.

Partridge, Eric H. (1894-June 1), New Zealand-born and Oxford-educated lexicographer. His books include *A Dictionary of Clichés* and *Usage and Abusage.*

*__Perelman, S. J. (Sidney Joseph)__ (1904-Oct. 17), celebrated writer and humorist whose books include *Chicken Inspector No. 23.* Much of his work appeared in *The New Yorker* magazine.

Petra, Sultan Yahya (1917-March 28), king of Malaysia since 1975.

*__Pickford, Mary__ (1893-May 29), "America's Sweetheart," star of such silent films as *Poor Little Rich Girl* and *Rebecca of Sunnybrook Farm.* She won an Oscar in 1929 for her first sound film, *Coquette.*

Pious, Minerva (1903-March 16), Russian-born actress who joyously mangled the English language as Mrs. Nussbaum on the Fred Allen radio show.

Rand, Sally (1904-Aug. 31), fan dancer whose ostrich feathers made her the hit of the 1933 Chicago World's Fair and launched a 30-year career.

*__Randolph, A. Philip__ (1889-May 16), long-time labor leader who played a leading role in the struggle for black rights from the 1920s to the 1960s. He founded the International Brotherhood of Sleeping Car Porters and became vice-president of the American Federation of Labor and Congress of Industrial Organizations (AFL-CIO) in 1957.

Reitsch, Hanna (1912-Aug. 31), German pilot and the first woman to be awarded the Iron Cross and fly a helicopter. She was a favorite of Adolf Hitler.

Ray, Nicholas (1911-June 16), director of such highly acclaimed films as *Rebel Without a Cause* and *King of Kings.*

Renoir, Jean (1894-Feb. 12), French-born film director, best known for *The Grand Illusion* (1937), an antiwar drama. He was the son of the renowned impressionist painter Pierre Auguste Renoir.

Rhys, Jean (1894-May 14), British writer who received acclaim for such books as *After Leaving Mr. Mackenzie* (1930) and *Wide Sargasso Sea* (1966).

Richards, Ivor A. (1893-Sept. 7), British linguist and critic who supported the adoption of an 850-word basic English. His influential works include *Principles of Literary Criticism* (1924) and *The Meaning of Meaning* (1923).

Riperton, Minnie (1947-July 12), singer whose hits included "Loving You."

Roach, Hattie K. (1871-April 14), the first white person born in Turner County, South Dakota. She left 120 direct descendants.

Robb, Inez (1901-April 4), journalist whose columns appeared in more than 140 newpapers.

*__Rockefeller, Nelson A.__ (1908-Jan. 26), Republican Vice-President of the United States from 1974 to 1977 and governor of New York from 1959 to 1973.

*__Rodgers, Richard__ (1902-Dec. 30), gifted composer of more than 1,000 popular songs and 43 musicals including *Oklahoma!, The King and I,* and *The Sound of Music.*

Rolf, Ida P. (1896-March 19), biochemist who developed "Rolfing," a tissue-manipulation technique said to promote more efficient body energy.

Rovere, Richard H. (1915-Nov. 23), writer and historian, noted for his penetrating commentaries on U.S. political life as a columnist for *The New Yorker* magazine.

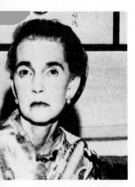

Barbara Hutton, the Woolworth heiress.

Nelson A. Rockefeller, former Vice-President.

Cyrus S. Eaton, a noted industrialist.

Archbishop Fulton J. Sheen, a noted Roman Catholic.

The Duke Loses His Last Fight

On May 23, 1979, the Congress of the United States voted to award him a special Gold Medal honoring his services to the nation. On May 26, his 72nd birthday, he received the award at the University of California Medical Center in Los Angeles. And on June 11, in the same hospital, his family near at hand, actor John Wayne died of cancer.

A sobbing Maureen O'Hara, who had co-starred with Wayne in several motion pictures, told a congressional subcommittee in May, "John Wayne is not just an actor. John Wayne is the United States of America."

Certainly, there has never been an actor more closely linked with the "American spirit" – with what many Americans thought their country was once, or could have been, or should have been.

His film character – which became the man himself – was tough, brave, dead honest, and ornery. He was kind to his horse, courteous to women, and never backed down from a fight. Maureen O'Hara was somehow right – whether he led a wagon train West, a cattle drive North, or a cavalry charge in any direction, he was America. And, in some 200 motion pictures over 50 years, he was the biggest box-office draw in history.

Wayne was born Marion Michael Morrison on May 26, 1907, in Winterset, Iowa. The Morrisons moved to California in 1913, and young Marion grew up in Glendale, near Los Angeles. He soon picked up the nickname Duke, the name of his pet Airedale terrier, and gained his first public notice playing football for Glendale High School. He played for the University of Southern California from 1925 to 1927.

He worked in Hollywood as a prop man for the Fox Film Corporation and played a few bit parts under John Ford's direction. His first big role was in a flop called *The Big Trail* in 1930. He soon became John Wayne and spent the next eight years making B and C Westerns.

Wayne's rise to stardom began with his role as the Ringo Kid in the John Ford masterpiece *Stagecoach* (1939). Action movies of all kinds followed – even a few comedies.

By the late 1940s, Wayne had fully developed his image and made some of his best films. He was nominated for an Academy Award for his role in *Sands of Iwo Jima* (1949). The Westerns he made in those years – such as *She Wore A Yellow Ribbon* and *Red River* (1948) – are considered classics. In 1952, he starred with O'Hara in *The Quiet Man*. Movie followed movie, some good, some bad, but always, unmistakably, Wayne's.

Wayne's political views became better known in the 1950s and 1960s. He was strongly conservative and a dedicated anti-Communist. His support of the Vietnam War brought him great attention – and strong criticism. Wayne starred in *The Green Berets*, a film that unabashedly supported the war. It appeared in theaters in 1968, a time of student riots and a President driven from office by public opposition to the war.

Still, he could charm his opponents. Invited to speak to the student body of Harvard University in 1974, he arrived in Harvard Yard in an armored personnel carrier and proceeded to delight and conquer his would-be Ivy League opponents.

Duke Wayne finally won an Oscar in 1970 for his role as Rooster Cogburn, a "one-eyed, fat old man" in *True Grit*. Though he played old men now, he kept the lumbering, yet delicate, gait, the slightly crooked grin, and the drawl. In his last movie, *The Shootist* (1976), he played an aging gunfighter dying of cancer.

John Wayne fought many real fights, too. His last, the longest, was with death. Cancer took a lung in 1964, and Wayne recovered. "I licked the big 'C,'" he said. Then there was open-heart surgery and a gallbladder operation in 1978.

His stomach was removed in January 1979, when a malignancy was discovered. Still he made a memorable appearance at the 1979 Academy of Motion Pictures Arts and Sciences annual awards ceremony in April. By May, the disease had spread, and he tried radiation treatments. He refused drugs because he wanted to be alert when his family visited. In the end, of course, he lost the fight – but he had fought well.

Edward G. Nash

John Wayne (1907-1979)

DEATHS OF NOTABLE PERSONS

Ryan, Elizabeth (1892-July 6), American tennis champion who won 19 Wimbledon tennis titles between 1919 and 1934.

Saltonstall, Leverett (1892-June 17), Republican governor of Massachusetts from 1939 to 1944 and a U.S. senator from 1944 to 1967.

Sawyer, Charles (1887-April 7), secretary of commerce from 1948 to 1953.

Schenken, Howard (1903-Feb. 20), a leading contract bridge player and the author of a syndicated column for more than 30 years.

Sheen, Archbishop Fulton J. (1895-Dec. 9), dynamic Roman Catholic priest whose 1950s television program titled "Life Is Worth Living" attracted up to 30 million viewers.

Simonov, Konstantin M. (1915-Aug. 28), Russian author and playwright, best known for *Days and Nights*, an epic story of the Battle of Stalingrad in World War II.

Skinner, Cornelia Otis (1901-July 9), actress and writer of such monodramas as "The Wives of Henry VIII." Her books included *Madame Sarah*, a biography of Sarah Bernhardt.

Smith, Charlie (1842?-Oct. 5), who claimed to be the oldest American. He said he was born in West Africa, sold into slavery in 1854, and freed in 1863.

Soo, Jack (1916-Jan 11), actor who played Nick Yemana, the coffee-making detective in the "Barney Miller" TV series.

Stafford, Jean (1915-March 26), writer and novelist whose *Collected Stories* (1969) won a Pulitzer Prize.

A. Philip Randolph, noted labor leader.

Mamie Eisenhower, widow of President Eisenhower.

Jean Monnet, a French statesman

Emmett Kelly, a circus clown for about 50 years.

Starch, Daniel (1883-Feb. 8), psychologist who developed market-research techniques in 1921 to determine the effectiveness of advertising.

Svoboda, Ludvík (1895-Sept. 20), president of Czechoslovakia from 1968 to 1975.

Taliaferro, Mabel (1887-Jan. 24), one of the first stars of silent films in 1911 and a veteran of more than 100 Broadway plays.

Taraki, Noor Mohammad (1919-Sept. (?)), president of Afghanistan from April 1978 to September 1979.

*****Tate, Allen** (1899-Feb. 9), poet and critic who defended Southern traditions. His most famous poem is "Ode to the Confederate Dead" (1930).

Tawes, J. Millard (1894-June 25), governor of Maryland from 1959 to 1967.

Teitelbaum, Joel (1887-Aug. 19), Romanian-born rabbi, spiritual leader of the Satmar Hasidic sect.

Tolstoy, Alexandra L. (Sasha) (1884-Sept. 26), last surviving child of Russian novelist Leo Tolstoy. She prepared the definitive edition of his works.

*****Tomonaga, Sin-itiro** (1906-July 8), Japanese physicist who won the 1965 Nobel Prize for Physics.

Tugwell, Rexford Guy (1891-July 21), one of the original members of President Franklin D. Roosevelt's New Deal "brain trust," who became governor of Puerto Rico and chancellor of the University of Puerto Rico.

Van Slyke, Helen (1919-July 3), best-selling novelist of such blockbusters as *A Necessary Woman*. She wrote her first book after she was 50 years old.

Vance, Vivian (1912-Aug. 17), actress, longtime co-star of the "I Love Lucy" television series.

Velasco Ibarra, José M. (1893-March 30), president of Ecuador five times between 1934 and 1968. He was forced into exile several times during his turbulent career.

Villot, Jean Cardinal (1905-March 9), French ecclesiastic who served three popes as Vatican secretary of state.

Waltari, Mika (1908-Aug. 26), Finnish writer, best known for his worldwide best-selling novel *The Egyptian*.

Ward, Richard (1915-July 1), gravel-voiced actor whose many roles included Grandpa Evans in the TV series "Good Times."

*****Wayne, John (Marion Michael Morrison)** (1907-June 11), Oscar-winning star of more than 200 films over 50 years. He epitomized the "good guy" – the tough, strong hero of the American West. See Close-Up.

Werner, Alfred (1911-July 14), Austrian-born art critic and author of many biographies.

Weyland, General Otto P. (1902-Sept. 2), who headed the air support for General George S. Patton's Third Army in World War II and served as commander of the Far East Air Forces during the Korean War.

Wilding, Michael (1912-July 7), British stage and screen actor, a former husband of Elizabeth Taylor.

Williams, T. Harry (1909-July 6), historian, an authority on the Civil War. His many books include the Pulitzer Prizewinning *Huey P. Long* (1970).

Wilson, Kenneth L. (Tug) (1897-Feb. 1), former president of the United States Olympic Committee and commissioner of the Big Ten Conference.

Woodcock, George (1904-Oct. 30), British union leader, head of the powerful Trades Union Congress from 1960 to 1969.

Woodward, Robert B. (1917-July 8), organic chemist who won the 1965 Nobel Prize for Chemistry for his contributions to organic synthesis.

*****Wright, John J. Cardinal** (1909-Aug. 10), head of the Vatican Congregation of the Clergy, the highest-ranking American in the Roman Catholic Church.

Zanuck, Darryl F. (1902-Dec. 22), who was the last of the flamboyant movie moguls. He produced the first full-length sound film, *The Jazz Singer* (1927), starring Al Jolson.

Irene B. Keller

DELAWARE. See STATE GOVERNMENT.

284

DEMOCRATIC PARTY was torn once again in 1979 by intraparty strife as an incumbent Democratic President faced a strong challenge to his re-election from fellow Democrats. With public opinion polls showing President Jimmy Carter's approval rating near a historic low point, Senator Edward M. Kennedy (D., Mass.) and California Governor Edmund G. Brown, Jr., announced on November 7 and 8, respectively, that they would seek their party's presidential nomination in 1980. Carter, vowing a fight to the finish, formally announced his candidacy for a second term on December 4.

Kennedy, the youngest of three brothers to try for the White House, began the year by saying that he expected to support Carter's re-election. But as the President's ratings plummeted in the polls Kennedy seemed to waver. Draft-Kennedy movements sprang up across the nation, and a Gallup public opinion poll released in April indicated that Democrats favored Kennedy over Carter 2-to-1.

Carter Fights Back. After considerable work, Carter's political strategists mustered endorsements from 21 Democratic governors meeting at Louisville, Ky., on July 8. Four abstained and seven others, including Brown, did not attend the session.

Long gasoline lines, along with rising prices and high interest rates, continued to hurt Carter's standing throughout the summer. An ABC-TV News poll released on July 9 showed that Carter's positive rating was 25 per cent, the lowest rating for a President in history.

Florida Vote. Before Kennedy formally declared his candidacy, however, he tested his strength against Carter in a statewide Democratic caucus in Florida on October 13, in which 879 delegates were chosen to attend the state convention on November 18. The Kennedy backers set a goal of winning a majority of the 879, but Carter won 522 to 269 for Kennedy, even defeating a pro-Kennedy slate of delegates in the Miami area where Kennedy was favored.

Carter began to suffer a series of defections in October, however. Former Senator Dick Clark of Iowa announced on October 30 that he was resigning as Carter's coordinator for refugee affairs to join the Kennedy campaign. Senator George S. McGovern of South Dakota, the 1972 Democratic presidential candidate, and Maine Governor Joseph E. Brennan endorsed Kennedy on October 19. Chicago Mayor Jane M. Byrne, who had previously voiced lukewarm support for Carter, joined the Kennedy camp on October 30, declaring that Carter's candidacy would be a "disaster" in Chicago.

Carter appointed veteran Democratic politician Robert S. Strauss to run his re-election drive. Strauss replaced Tim E. Kraft, a former White House aide who had himself replaced Evan Dobelle, former Republican mayor of Pittsfield, Mass., and protocol chief of the Department of State.

Massachusetts Senator Edward M. Kennedy in 1979 became President Carter's leading challenger for the 1980 Democratic presidential nomination.

Hats in the Ring. Kennedy made his formal declaration of candidacy on November 7 in Boston's historic Faneuil Hall with a strong attack on Carter's leadership.

The next day, in Washington, D.C., Brown entered the contest, picturing himself as an underdog with only a 4 per cent rating in the polls. "My principles are simple – protect the earth, serve the people, and explore the universe," Brown said. He had defeated Carter in several late primaries in 1976.

Carter, alarmed by the challenges, began mobilizing his own support. About 500 prominent Democrats attended a dinner in Washington to show their support for the President in October.

A December 7 public-opinion poll of Democrats showed Carter leading Kennedy for the first time. Forty eight per cent of those polled favored Carter; 40 per cent, Kennedy.

Kennedy, Carter, and Brown planned to debate in Iowa in January 1980, but Carter bowed out, citing the tense state of world affairs.

The Democratic National Committee decided to return to New York City for its 1980 convention. The meeting will open on August 11.

Election Results. While the presidential maneuvering got most of the public's attention, Democrats won two governors' races and retained mayoralties in most major cities in 1979. Democrat John Y. Brown, Jr., easily defeated former Republican Governor Louie B. Nunn in Kentucky on November 6. In Mississippi, former Lieutenant Governor William F. Winter, a Democrat, defeated Republican candidate Gil Carmichael.

Cleveland's maverick Democrat Dennis J. Kucinich was ousted by Republican Lieutenant Governor George V. Voinovich after Cleveland twice defaulted on bond payments during Kucinich's term. The Democrats lost control of city hall in Kansas City, Mo., for the first time since the 1920s. Republican Richard L. Berkley was elected mayor on March 27, defeating black Democratic candidate Bruce R. Watkins in the predominantly Democratic city. Democrat Jane Byrne became Chicago's first woman mayor after successfully challenging the political machine created by the late Mayor Richard J. Daley (see CHICAGO; ELECTIONS [Close-Up]).

Democrats lost two special congressional races. In Wisconsin, Democrat Gary M. R. Goyke lost to Republican Thomas Petri for the seat held by the late William A. Steiger, a Republican. In California, Democrat Joe Holsinger lost to Republican William H. Royer for the seat held by the late Leo J. Ryan, a Democrat. William J. Eaton

See also BROWN, EDMUND G., JR.; BYRNE, JANE M.; CABINET, UNITED STATES; CARTER, JAMES EARL, JR.; KENNEDY, EDWARD M.; PRESIDENT OF THE UNITED STATES. In WORLD BOOK, see DEMOCRATIC PARTY.

Greenlanders celebrate after a January 17 referendum that approved home rule, ending Danish control of most of the island's affairs.

DENMARK. Prime Minister Anker Henrik Jorgensen resigned on Sept. 28, 1979, in a dispute with his coalition partners, the Liberals, over how to cut $528-million from the budget. But he formed a new government after his Social Democratic Party won 69 seats, a gain of four, in the *Folketing* (parliament) in elections on October 23. The Liberals, Conservatives, Center Democrats, and Christian People's Party gained only three seats for a total of 55.

Liberal Party members of the coalition government had wanted big cuts in federal spending as well as wage and price controls. Under pressure from labor unions, the Social Democrats refused to cut welfare payments or defer wage hikes. The coalition had survived an earlier crisis on March 22 when Jorgensen forced a wage settlement through the Folketing by threatening to call elections. The settlement gave public employees a smaller pay increase than a previous agreement had given workers in the private sector. Jorgensen called for the settlement after a government mediator ordered two 14-day delays in planned strikes and lockouts. The pact was expected to increase the average wage by 9 per cent in 1979 and 6 per cent in 1980.

Economic Plan. On November 5, Jorgensen froze wages and prices, halted mortgage loans to individuals, barred pension funds and insurance companies from making private loans, and banned conversion of rental apartments built before 1966 to cooperative ownership. Jorgensen said that the freeze was the first of a series of economic adjustments that would eliminate the balance of payments deficit. Denmark's 1979 deficit was $5 billion, 25 per cent of its gross national product. Denmark devalued the krone 5 per cent against the other currencies of the European Monetary System on November 29. See EUROPE.

Denmark was one of the few members of the International Energy Agency to heed that agency's call to cut oil consumption by 5 per cent. Temperatures in public buildings had a top limit of 20°C (68°F.) Speed limits were cut, and the gasoline tax was increased 20 per cent.

Greenland Home Rule. Greenland voters approved a home-rule measure in a referendum on January 17 and elected a *Landsting* (parliament) on April 4. The moderate socialist Siumut Party, led by Jonathan Motzfeldt, won 12 of the 21 seats. Motzfeldt became prime minister on May 1, when Denmark's Queen Margrethe II granted home rule to Greenland in a ceremony in its capital, Godthåb.

Denmark retained control of defense and foreign relations, but trade, taxation, and control of the fishing industry will be turned over to Greenland by 1982. Greenland may leave the European Community (Common Market) if it wishes. Kenneth Brown

See also EUROPE (Facts in Brief Table). In WORLD BOOK, see DENMARK; GREENLAND.

DENTISTRY. The Federal Trade Commission (FTC) on April 27, 1979, provisionally accepted a proposed settlement in its two-year-old suit against the American Dental Association (ADA) involving, among other things, prohibitions on advertising by dentists. Under the terms of the tentative settlement, the ADA agreed not to restrict or declare unethical truthful advertising by dentists. Because the legal issues closely parallel those in the earlier FTC suit against the American Medical Association (AMA), the ADA agreed to tie the outcome of its case to the AMA's case.

In October, the FTC was upheld against the AMA, which announced that it would appeal the decision. Settlement of that appeal may take years.

Other Advertising. ADA officials testified in January before the Federal Communications Commission on television advertising aimed at children that features highly sugared foods. Noting that many of these products contain more than 50 per cent sugar, the ADA spokesmen cautioned that sugared snack foods pose a potential risk to a child's dental health. They recommended the control of all misleading and deceptive advertising intended for children and that all children's TV programs include positive messages on good nutrition and dental hygiene.

Dentists can help identify and report child abuse cases, Reidar F. Sognnaes, a dental researcher at the University of California, Los Angeles, suggested in March. Dentists can be a first line of defense for the estimated 2 million children per year who are neglected, battered, or killed in the United States by disturbed parents, babysitters, and other persons.

Dentists should look for loose and dislodged teeth, broken and discolored teeth, gag marks around the mouth, bruises around the cheeks, and swollen or lacerated lips, Sognnaes said. He emphasized that dentists are morally and legally bound to report suspected cases to the proper authorities.

Tranquilizing Patients. According to Raymond Dionne of the National Institute of Dental Research in Washington, D.C., patients anesthetized with 10 or 20 milligrams of the tranquilizing drug Valium have no recollection of the discomfort associated with the drilling, filling, or extraction of teeth or even with complicated oral surgery such as the removal of impacted wisdom teeth and parts of the jawbone. Dionne reported in March that 6 per cent of the patients anesthetized intravenously with Valium in experiments did not remember the experience and had no sensation of anxiety or pain. Local anesthetics were also used to relieve discomfort in the mouth. See Drugs.

The number of Americans covered by prepaid dental-care plans stood at over 60 million in 1979, compared with 12 million in 1965.   Lou Joseph

In World Book, see DENTISTRY; TEETH.

U.S. Dental Plan Participation Growth

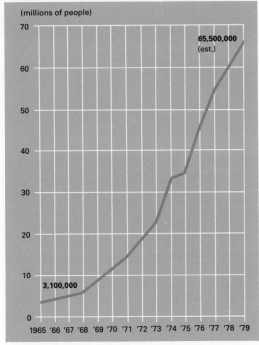

(millions of people)

65,500,000 (est.)

3,100,000

1965 '66 '67 '68 '69 '70 '71 '72 '73 '74 '75 '76 '77 '78 '79

Source: American Dental Association

DETROIT. A cash shortage forced Wayne County, which incorporates Detroit and some of its suburbs, to hand 5,100 of its 5,300 employees layoff notices on Oct. 31, 1979. The notice set November 11 as the termination date for the employees, who had received their paychecks in mid-October. However, the date was postponed several times as revenues trickled in to keep the county government operating.

Wayne County's cash-flow problem stemmed from a budget deficit of about $19 million for the 1979 fiscal year. The county had operated with budget deficits for three years, borrowing against future tax revenues. However, the Michigan Municipal Finance Commission refused to allow the county to continue the practice until the county commissioners presented an acceptable plan to eliminate the deficit. The commissioners responded with a budget for fiscal 1980 of $289 million – a $70-million reduction from the previous year. The budget was approved on November 29.

The county's financial picture had been murky for some time. Michigan state accountants concluded an eight-month study of its finances in August, reporting that the books were "unauditable" because of inadequate record keeping.

Strikes and Settlements. Approximately 3,800 county workers defied a court order and walked off their jobs on February 7 in a contract dispute. The strike, which affected the sewage department, medi-

287

Detroit Mayor Coleman A. Young holds a picture of himself on an elephant to symbolize his city's selection to host the 1980 Republican convention.

cal examiner's and clerk's offices, several courts, and the county jail, ended on February 10.

Detroit's 12,000 teachers walked out on September 10, closing the city's 300 public schools until a tentative contract agreement was reached on September 27. Teachers voted on October 5 to accept that settlement, which provided a three-year contract that granted a 7 per cent wage increase in the first year and an annual increase of 9 per cent thereafter.

Economic Boost. A report by a New York City consulting firm released in March said that the Renaissance Center, Detroit's $337-million complex of shops, restaurants, offices, and a hotel, had injected as much as $1 billion into the city's economy since it opened in 1977. The Republican National Committee announced on January 23 that it had selected Detroit as the site of its 1980 national convention.

The United States Court of Appeals for the Sixth Circuit ruled on October 12 that the Detroit Police Department's policy of promoting blacks ahead of whites did not constitute "reverse discrimination." The court ruled that discrimination against whites must be judged differently than discrimination against blacks.   James M. Banovetz

See also CITY. In WORLD BOOK, see DETROIT; MICHIGAN.

DICTIONARY. See DICTIONARY SUPPLEMENT.
DISARMAMENT. See ARMED FORCES.

DISASTERS. Severe weather claimed many lives in 1979. Hundreds perished in winter storms in the Midwestern and Northeastern United States, and hurricane David, which swept through the Caribbean and along the Atlantic Coast of the United States, killed at least 1,300 persons in August.

An air tragedy took 274 lives when a DC-10 lost an engine shortly after take-off from O'Hare International Airport in Chicago on May 25. As a result of this disaster, all U.S. DC-10s were grounded while the engine mounts were inspected. See AVIATION.

Disasters that resulted in 10 or more deaths in 1979 included the following:

Aircraft Crashes
March 14 – Doha, Qatar. A Jordanian Boeing 727 crashed in a thunderstorm, killing 45 persons.
March 14 – Peking, China. A Chinese Trident jet on a military training flight crashed into a factory, killing 44 persons.
March 17 – Moscow. Ninety persons were killed when a Russian TU-104 jetliner crashed shortly after take-off from Moscow airport.
March 29 – Quebec, Canada. A Quebecair F-27 turboprop crashed shortly after take-off on a commuter flight to Montreal, killing 17 of the 24 persons on board.
May 25 – Chicago. An American Airlines DC-10 crashed shortly after take-off from O'Hare International Airport, killing the 272 persons on board and two on the ground. It was the worst civil air disaster in U.S. history involving one plane.
May 27 – Off Senegal. Twelve persons, including Prime Minister Ahmed Ould Bouceif of Mauritania, were killed when a Mauritanian Army plane plunged into the Atlantic Ocean during a sandstorm.
May 30 – Maine. A Downeast Airlines commuter plane crashed in heavy fog on an approach to Owls Head airport, killing 17 of the 18 persons on board.
July 11 – Indonesia. All 61 persons on board died when an Indonesian airliner crashed into Mount Sibayak.
Aug. 11 – Ukraine, U.S.S.R. Two Russian airliners collided in mid-air, killing 173 persons.
Oct. 31 – Mexico City. A Western Airlines DC-10 originating in Los Angeles crashed on landing at the airport, killing 74 persons. Preliminary reports blamed poor visibility.
Nov. 26 – Near Jidda, Saudi Arabia. A Pakistani jet crashed in the Hejaz Mountains, killing at least 156 persons returning from a religious pilgrimage to the Muslim shrine at Mecca, Saudi Arabia.
Nov. 28 – Antarctica. An Air New Zealand DC-10 crashed into Mount Erebus, a volcano, killing all 257 persons on board. It was history's fourth worst aviation disaster.
Dec. 23 – Ankara, Turkey. A Turkish Airways Fokker VFW F-28 crashed on approach to the Ankara airport, killling 39 of the 43 persons on-board.
Bus and Truck Crashes
Jan. 11 – Canal Zone, Panama. Sixteen U.S. soldiers died when a U.S. Army truck crashed through a bridge guardrail and plunged down a canal bank.
Feb. 11 – Assam, India. At least 15 persons died when a bus plunged into a pond.
March 14 – Greece. A bus and a gasoline tanker truck collided near the Yugoslav border, and 30 persons were burned to death.
March 27 – Kiambu, Kenya. A truck and a minibustaxi collided, killing 11 persons.
March 30 – Southern India. A bus crash near Quilou in southern India killed 34 persons and injured more than 100 others.

April 10 – **Benavente, Spain.** Fifty of the 60 persons on board died when a school bus plunged into a river near Benavente.

April 13 – **Bangkok, Thailand.** A bus and a rice truck collided head-on, killing 22 persons.

April 17 – **Eastern Brazil.** A bus carrying sugar-refinery workers plunged into the Paraíba do Sul River, killing at least 15 persons.

April 23 – **Crofton, Md.** Ten teen-agers were killed, eight instantly, when the pickup truck they were riding in crashed into a tree.

June 2 – **Thailand.** A gasoline truck smashed into a bus on a mountain road and exploded, killing 52 persons.

June 9 – **Quebec Province, Canada.** At least 11 persons were killed when a chartered bus veered off the Trans-Canada Highway and crashed into a concrete support during a rainstorm. The bus was returning 49 senior citizens from an outing.

June 20 – **Recife, Brazil.** About 40 persons were killed when a truck smashed into a line of vehicles, including a bus, stopped by highway repairs.

Aug. 15 – **Near Belgrade, Yugoslavia.** A bus collided with a truck and plunged into a ravine, killing 14 persons.

Aug. 18 – **Great Rift Valley, Kenya.** At least 44 persons were killed and dozens were injured when a bus and several trucks collided.

Aug. 24 – **Northern Thailand.** A truck and a tour bus collided head-on, killing 17 persons and injuring nine others.

Aug. 25 – **Central Romania.** Sixteen persons were killed when a train hit a bus at an unguarded crossing.

Oct. 20 – **Cairo, Egypt.** About 30 persons were killed when a bus and a train collided at a grade crossing.

Oct. 20 – **Near Tarbes, France.** A bus carrying Spanish pilgrims home from a visit to the Lourdes shrine stalled on railroad tracks and was hit by a train; 21 persons were killed in the collision.

Dec. 20 – **Isabela Province, Philippines.** A bus plunged into a river, killing at least 50 persons.

Earthquakes

Jan. 16 – **Eastern Iran.** About 200 persons were killed in a quake estimated at 6.7 to 7.5 on the Richter scale. No Richter measurement was available because local geologists were out celebrating the departure of Shah Mohammad Reza Pahlavi when the quake occurred.

Feb. 16 – **Southern Peru.** An earthquake rocked the southern part of the country, including Arequipa, killing at least 13 persons.

April 15 – **Yugoslavia-Albania border.** A major earthquake measuring 7.2 on the Richter scale and with more than 400 aftershocks hit the coastal area, killing 129 persons.

May 30 – **Indonesia.** At least 20 persons died in an earthquake on the island of Lombok.

Nov. 14 – **Northeastern Iran.** An earthquake measuring 6.7 on the Richter scale hit the area near Meshed, killing about 500 persons.

Nov. 23 – **Colombia.** An earthquake measuring 6.4 on the Richter scale hit a sparsely populated area on the Pacific coast, killing about 60 persons and destroying about 1,000 buildings.

Dec. 12 – **Colombia-Ecuador Border.** An earthquake measuring 7.7 to 8.1 on the Richter scale killed nearly 400 persons, mostly in Colombia, and leveled several villages.

Dec. 18 – **Bali, Indonesia.** An earthquake measuring 6.1 on the Richter scale hit the island of Bali, killing 25 persons and injuring 200.

Explosions and Fires

Jan. 8 – **Bantry Bay, Ireland.** An explosion and fire in a French oil tanker killed about 50 persons.

Authorities examine a jet engine that fell off a DC-10 just before it crashed on take-off at Chicago on May 25. The crash killed 274 persons.

A concrete dam on the Machu River in India, built in 1978, collapsed August 11 and flooded the nearby village of Morvi. At least 5,000 persons died.

eight states. Chicago was hit hard by subzero temperatures, and a near-record snowfall of more than 27 inches (69 centimeters) halted most activity for more than a week.

Jan. 20-21 – Eastern United States. At least 17 persons died in storm-related accidents, as snow and flooding rains pounded the East Coast.

Feb. 15 – Northern Europe. A blizzard killed at least 19 persons, including fishermen who drowned when their boats went down in the icy North Sea.

Feb. 18-19 – Eastern United States. A snowstorm caused at least 13 deaths in several states. The District of Columbia was virtually paralyzed by a snowfall of 18.75 inches (47.5 centimeters) in 24 hours.

March 30 – Fiji. More than 50 persons were reported dead after four days of severe storms. At least 21 of the victims were killed in a cyclone on the island of Oxo on March 27.

April 10 – Oklahoma-Texas border. Tornadoes hit several towns, killing at least 60 persons and injuring more than 800. At least 44 persons died in Wichita Falls, Tex. National Guard troops were called out in Wichita Falls and Lawton, Okla., to aid in the search for survivors and to prevent looting.

April 18 – Philippines. A typhoon killed at least 12 persons, left hundreds homeless, and caused property damage estimated at $3.5 million.

May 14 – Southeast India. At least 600 persons died as a result of a hurricane and flooding on the southeast coast. About 1 million persons were left homeless by the storm.

Aug. 15 – Southern Bangladesh. A cyclone killed at least 50 persons, including many who drowned when about 40 fishing boats sank in the Bay of Bengal.

Aug. 25-26 – South Korea. At least 43 persons died and 20,000 were left homeless in two days of flooding and landslides caused by a typhoon on the coast.

Jan. 23 – Virrat, Finland. A flash fire in the wooden wing of a nursing home killed 26 persons.

Feb. 15 – Warsaw, Poland. A mysterious explosion in a crowded bank killed about 50 persons and injured more than 100.

March 16 – Sandnassjon, Norway. Eleven persons died in a nursing-home fire.

March 29 – Manila, Philippines. A fire in a discothèque and massage parlor killed 15 persons.

April 2 – Farmington, Mo. A fire in a retirement home killed 25 persons, some of whom were state mental patients.

July 12 – Saragossa, Spain. An explosion in the kitchen of a luxury hotel started a fire that took at least 71 lives. It was the worst hotel fire in Spain's history.

July 13 – Taipei, Taiwan. A chemical explosion and fire in a residential district killed at least 15 persons and injured more than 60.

Aug. 15 – Near Ciudad Real, Spain. A series of forest fires that raged for eight days killed 26 persons.

Sept. 28 – Vienna, Austria. A fire during the night killed at least 25 tourists in a hotel.

Floods

Feb. 6 – Southeast Brazil. More than 700 persons died and 350,000 were homeless after 42 days of torrential rain. The state of Minas Gerais was hit hardest.

June 14 – Jamaica. At least 32 persons died in two days of flooding caused by heavy rains. Many of the deaths occurred in farm areas on the western part of the island. About 14 feet (4 meters) of water was reported in the tourist town of Montego Bay.

June 30 – Southwestern Japan. Twenty-two persons died in five days of severe flooding that was caused by heavy rains.

Hurricanes, Tornadoes, and Other Storms

January – Midwestern United States. A severe blizzard that started on January 12 killed at least 100 persons in

Wichita Falls, Tex., is the community hardest hit by a series of tornadoes that struck the Oklahoma-Texas border on April 10, killing at least 60 persons.

Aug. 29-Sept. 6 – Caribbean and Eastern United States. Hurricane David killed more than 1,300 persons and left 100,000 homeless. The storm moved through several countries in the Caribbean, then struck Florida and the Eastern Seaboard of the United States. The Dominican Republic was hardest hit.

Sept. 12 – U.S. Gulf Coast. Hurricane Frederic struck Florida, Alabama, and Mississippi, killing 13 persons and injuring at least 4,711. Insurance companies termed it the most expensive U.S. hurricane in history (see INSURANCE).

Mine Disasters

Feb. 24 – Glace Bay, Nova Scotia. Ten persons were killed by an explosion in a coal mine.

April 14 – Chungsun, South Korea. An explosion in a coal mine killed 26 persons.

Shipwrecks

June 24 – Off Rome. A French freighter and an Italian tanker collided in the Tyrrhenian Sea, killing 14 persons.

Aug. 13-14 – Off England. In the world's worst yachting disaster, winds of up to 70 mph (113 kph) whipped up mountainous seas that sank boats and killed 18 sailors. The yachts were competing in the Fastnet yacht race in the English Channel and the Irish Sea. See BOATING.

Train Wrecks

Jan. 4 – Turkey. An eastbound train en route from Ankara to Istanbul collided head-on with a westbound train during a blizzard, killing at least 56 persons.

Jan. 9 – Turkey. A passenger train rammed into another passenger train that was stopped on a blocked track. Thirty persons were killed and nearly 100 injured.

Jan. 19 – Mexico City, Mexico. A freight train hit a crowded bus, killing 17 bus passengers and injuring 35.

Jan. 27 – Bangladesh. A speeding passenger train jumped the tracks and plunged into a canal, killing at least 70 persons and injuring about 200.

April 22 – Near Karachi, Pakistan. A locomotive rammed a stopped passenger train, killing 44 persons.

July 10 – Near Naples, Italy. At least 13 persons were killed and 60 injured when two trains collided head-on.

Sept. 13 – Near Belgrade, Yugoslavia. At least 50 persons were killed and 100 injured when a freight train rammed the rear of an express passenger train.

Dec. 3 – Southern India. An express train en route to Bangalore jumped the tracks, killing at least 25.

Other Disasters

Feb. 21 – Indonesia. At least 175 persons were killed and 1,000 injured when a volcano erupted on the island of Java.

March 12 – Northern India. At least 230 persons died in snowstorms and avalanches in Himalayan mountain villages in Himachal Pradesh state.

April 30 – Sumatra, Indonesia. At least 82 persons were killed by a landslide on the slopes of Merapi volcano.

July 1 – Multan, Pakistan. A three-day heat wave during which temperatures rose to 117°F. (47°C) killed 40 persons.

July 18 – Lomblen Island, Indonesia. A powerful wave more than 6 feet (1.8 meters) high caused by a landslide on nearby Mount Werung hit the island, killing 539 persons. Authorities said that 364 persons were swept out to sea.

Aug. 11 – Morvi, India. At least 5,000 persons were killed when a dam on the Machu River, built in 1978, collapsed.

Sept. 13 – Indonesia. Officials reported that 100 persons were killed by a tidal wave generated by earth tremors that hit Yapen Island.

Dec. 3 – Cincinnati, Ohio. Eleven persons were killed and about 20 injured in a crush of young people trying to enter a rock concert by The Who in the Riverfront Coliseum. Patricia Dragisic

DJIBOUTI. See AFRICA.

DOG. An Irish water spaniel, Ch. Oak Tree's Irishtocrat, familiarly known as Dugan, was named best-in-show at the Westminster Kennel Club show in New York City on Feb. 13, 1979. It was the first time in the show's 102-year history that an Irish water spaniel had taken top honors. After the show, Dugan's owner, Ann Snelling of Ottawa, Canada, informed handler W. J. Trainor of Oxford, Mass., that she was making him a co-owner of the spaniel. There were 3,154 dogs entered in the show.

Top honor at the International Kennel Club show held in Chicago on March 31 and April 1 went to Ch. Lou Gins Kiss Me Kate, a standard poodle owned by Terri Meyers and Jack and Paulann Phelan of Manhattan, Ill. The show drew 2,720 dogs.

According to figures released in March, more poodles were registered with the American Kennel Club (AKC) in 1978 than any other breed. Poodles have led in AKC registrations since 1960. Following them in order were Doberman pinschers, German shepherds, cocker spaniels, Labrador retrievers, beagles, golden retrievers, dachshunds, miniature schnauzers, and Irish setters. Total registrations were 980,299, compared with 1,013,650 in 1977. Some authorities attributed the drop to the higher costs of maintenance and increased restrictions against dogs in many areas. Theodore M. O'Leary

In WORLD BOOK, see DOG.

DOLE, ROBERT J. (1923-   ), United States senator from Kansas, announced on May 14, 1979, that he was a candidate for the Republican presidential nomination in 1980. He was the Republican candidate for Vice-President in 1976.

Apparently concerned because some commentators have termed him "negative" in the past, Dole stressed his "positive" record in the Senate since 1968. He also criticized the growth of the federal bureaucracy and pledged to "get back to building the nation."

Dole was born on July 22, 1923, in Russell, Kans. He earned two Purple Heart decorations for wounds received in Army combat in Italy in World War II that left him with a crippled right arm. Dole studied at the University of Kansas and the University of Arizona before earning his bachelor of arts degree and law degree in 1952 from Washburn University in Topeka. He was first elected to the Kansas legislature in 1951, while still in school.

After serving as Russell County prosecuting attorney, Dole was elected to the U.S. House of Representatives in 1960, and was Republican national chairman from 1971 to 1973. Dole married his second wife, Elizabeth Hanford, a federal trade commissioner, in 1975. Patricia Dragisic

DOMINICAN REPUBLIC. See LATIN AMERICA.

DRAMA. See THEATER.

DROUGHT. See WATER; WEATHER.

DRUGS. Hard drugs continued to be a major concern for United States health and law-enforcement authorities in 1979. A joint program with the government of Colombia, initiated and financed by the United States, resulted in the seizure of huge quantities of marijuana and hundreds of arrests at some 600 airstrips on Colombia's Atlantic Coast. But major marijuana shipments continued to pour into the United States, with New York City and Miami, Fla., the major markets. Colombian officials estimated that 10,000 farmers cultivated marijuana.

New York state legislators and Governor Hugh L. Carey formally agreed on legislation to modify the narcotics-control law drafted by Governor Nelson A. Rockefeller in 1973. The new bill, signed into law by Carey on July 7, softens or dismisses sentences for first offenders and stiffens them for repeat offenders. The new law also permits the re-sentencing of some of the 1,800 persons imprisoned under the old law.

Darvon and Valium. Joseph A. Califano, Jr., secretary of health, education, and welfare (HEW), announced in February that HEW would not ban propoxyphene, the main ingredient in the widely prescribed drug Darvon. In congressional testimony in November 1978, physician Sidney Wolfe, director of Ralph Nader's Health Research Group, had asked that HEW ban the sale of propoxyphene. Wolfe said that the drug kills almost as many people each year as heroin, methadone, and morphine combined. As a painkiller, however, he said, it is only about as effective as aspirin. Califano asked the Food and Drug Administration (FDA) to hold hearings on the advisability of increasing controls on the sale of Darvon.

Joseph A. Pursch, U.S. Navy psychiatrist and head of the Alcohol Rehabilitation Service at the Navy's Long Beach Regional Medical Center in California, told a Senate Subcommittee on Health on September 9 that Valium, one of the most widely used drugs in the United States, is addictive and that physicians should not prescribe it for everyday stress. More than 44 million Valium prescriptions were filled in 1978.

Laetrile Ban. The Supreme Court of the United States on June 18 unanimously upheld the federal government's authority to ban the interstate sale and distribution of laetrile, a substance purported to cure cancer. The decision reversed an appeals court ruling that terminally ill cancer patients be allowed access to the apricot-pit derivative. The Supreme Court's decision affirms federal authority to block the transportation of laetrile in interstate commerce, to seize the substance when federal agents find it, and to prosecute distributors. Despite the Supreme Court opinion, however, underground traffic in laetrile will probably continue. At least 20 states, including Illinois and New Jersey, have legalized the substance. An estimated 20,000 cancer patients got laetrile legally in 1979 through FDA-sanctioned

procedures, and about 80,000 others used black market supplies smuggled into the United States from Mexico and Europe.

Saccharin. Without debate, the House of Representatives voted on July 24 to delay a ban on the use of saccharin in diet foods and beverages for two additional years. The measure extends an 18-month moratorium, forestalling a ban proposed by the FDA in 1977, after studies had shown that saccharin could cause cancer in rats. Though it refused to ban saccharin, Congress ordered that diet foods and drinks containing the substance be labeled with a cancer warning.

DES Awards. A jury in the New York State Supreme Court awarded $500,000 damages in July to Joyce Bichler, whose mother took diethylstilbestrol (DES) while she was pregnant with her. Bichler developed vaginal and cervical cancer as a young adult. In another case involving DES, a federal district court jury in Chicago in August awarded $800,000 damages to cancer patient Ann Needham, whose mother had taken DES. See MEDICINE.

For the first time, a pharmacist was appointed commissioner of food and drugs – thus, head of the FDA. Jere E. Goyan, 49, dean of the School of Pharmacy, University of California, San Francisco, was appointed in November. He said he hopes to persuade "overmedicated" Americans to cut down on their use of drugs.   Mary E. Jessup

DUNCAN, CHARLES WILLIAM, JR. (1926-), was sworn in as United States secretary of energy on Aug. 24, 1979. He replaced James R. Schlesinger, who resigned on July 20, 1979. Duncan had served as deputy secretary of defense since 1977.

Duncan was born on Sept. 9, 1926, in Houston. During World War II, he served in the Army Air Corps. He earned a B.S. degree in chemical engineering from Rice University in Houston in 1947 and completed two years of graduate study in management at the University of Texas, then joined the Humble Oil and Refining Company as an unskilled worker.

Duncan joined the family-owned Duncan Food Company in 1948 and became president of the firm in 1958. He was elected to the Coca-Cola Company board of directors when Duncan Foods merged with Coca-Cola in 1964. He became president of Coca-Cola in 1971. He resigned in 1974 to work with an investment firm in Houston.

Duncan became deputy secretary of defense in 1977. In this post, he was responsible for Pentagon operations. He attracted congressional criticism for his decisions to relocate U.S. troops in the Panama Canal Zone and for closing Fort Dix in New Jersey.

Duncan is a Wyoming rancher who enjoys hunting and fishing. He married Thetis Anne Smith in 1957. They have two children.   Madelyn Krzak

EARTHQUAKE. See DISASTERS.

EASTERN ORTHODOX CHURCHES. Elias IV, the patriarch of Antioch, primate of the Orthodox Churches in Lebanon, Syria, and Iraq, died of a heart attack in Damascus, Syria, in June 1979. He visited the United States in 1977, becoming the first Orthodox patriarch to do so. On July 2, the Holy Synod of the Patriarchate of Antioch, meeting in Damascus, elected Metropolitan Ignatius Hazim of Latakia, Syria, as his successor. Born in Lebanon, he received his theological education at St. Sergius Theological Institute in Paris and, prior to his consecration as bishop, served as dean of the Patriarchal School of St. John of Damascus in Lebanon.

Patriarch Justin, head of the Orthodox Church of Romania, visited the United States in May. During his stay, he met with the heads of the various jurisdictions in America.

The plight of the Christian minority in Turkey grew worse in 1979, especially that of the Greek ecumenical patriarchate in Istanbul. Ecumenical Patriarch Demetrius charged that Turkish authorities had undertaken "illegal activities which surpass any undertaken by the Ottoman Empire" against the Orthodox Church in Turkey.

Patriarch Demetrius met with Pope John Paul II, leader of the world's Roman Catholics, in Turkey in November. The two pledged publicly to "hasten the day of full communion" between their churches.

Gleb Yakunin, an Orthodox priest and chairman of the Committee for the Defense of Religious Rights in Russia, was arrested on November 1 in Moscow. For several years, Yakunin has been a leading and vocal opponent of the oppression of religious rights in Eastern Europe.

In the United States. On February 23, the Monastic Community of New Skete in Cambridge, N.Y., was received into the Orthodox Church in America. The community started as a Roman Catholic Byzantine Rite monastery.

Georges Florovsky, an Orthodox priest and a leading theologian and scholar, died in Princeton, N.J., on August 11 at the age of 86. Born in Russia, he went into exile in 1920 and eventually became dean of St. Vladimir's Orthodox Theological Seminary in Crestwood, N.Y.

In June, the head of the Greek Orthodox Church in North and South America, Archbishop Iakovos, celebrated the 20th anniversary of his primacy. A reception was held in his honor at the White House.

Archimandrite Mark Forsberg was consecrated bishop for the Albanian diocese within the Orthodox Church in America on November 11. American born, Archimandrite Forsberg held several pastorates in the United States. Alexander Schmemann

See also RELIGION. In WORLD BOOK, see EASTERN ORTHODOX CHURCHES.

Archbishop Iakovos discusses preparations for the celebration of his 20th anniversary as leader of the Greek Orthodox Church in the Americas.

Alfred E. Kahn, chairman of the Council on Wage and Price Stability, puzzles over a question on inflation during congressional testimony.

ECONOMICS. Seldom since the early 1930s have economic affairs in the United States been so prominent in the headlines and in the minds of people as they were during 1979. Public opinion polls throughout the year listed inflation as the primary concern. Energy, which is really part of the same inflation problem, usually ran a close second.

When the year began, many experts predicted that 1979 would be marked by a recession. The major dispute seemed to be whether it would be sharp or mild. Confirmation of this prediction apparently appeared during the second quarter when the gross national product (GNP) showed a mild decline in real terms, corrected for price increases, but it rebounded in the third quarter and promised to produce an increase of about 1.7 per cent in the output of goods and services over that of 1978. This put the GNP at approximately $2.4 trillion, more than 9.5 per cent above 1978 before correction for increased prices.

High Employment continued throughout the year, rising from 95 million at the start to nearly 99 million in July and closing the year with about 98 million persons at work. Unemployment remained moderate at 6 per cent of the work force, despite the slowdown in economic growth. However, this 6 per cent represented about 6 million persons, and it included disproportionate numbers of teen-agers and blacks.

When unemployment figures are analyzed in depth, however, the picture is somewhat rosier. Less than half of those unemployed had actually lost a job. The balance consisted of people who had voluntarily left their jobs, those who were new entrants into the labor market, and those re-entering the labor market. Only about 500,000 of the 6 million unemployed persons had been out of work more than 26 weeks.

Inflation figures were more alarming than unemployment data. The Consumer Price Index rose steadily throughout the year and at year-end was about 13 per cent above the level at which it had closed in 1978. Although there was a popular tendency to put most of the blame for the increase on the 40 per cent rise in the cost of energy, prices increased in all sectors of the economy. The effect was that, though the hourly earnings of wage earners continued to grow in current dollars at a rate slightly in excess of 8 per cent, the net purchasing power of these dollars was down some 4 per cent.

Wage, Price Controls. Attempts by the Jimmy Carter Administration to hold down the rate of inflation through voluntary wage and price controls were a failure. The original guidelines from the Council on Wage and Price Stability called for limiting wage increases to 7 per cent per year, but it rapidly became apparent that organized labor would not accept such a limitation when inflation rates, both present and anticipated, were higher.

In the usual labor contract, 7 per cent compounded for three years would have resulted in a 22.5 per cent increase over the life of the contract, but exceptions were made quickly, and most contracts ended up with increases of 30 per cent or more in labor costs over three years (see LABOR). With productivity increases at current levels of 1 per cent or less per year, such contracts almost inevitably result in an underlying inflation rate of 7 to 10 per cent. Faced with this situation, the burden of fighting inflation shifted necessarily to monetary policies.

Interest Rates that fluctuate rapidly tend to be unsettling to financial markets, and high interest rates tend to have a serious impact on the housing industry and on costly durable goods, such as automobiles, for which people usually borrow a substantial portion of the price. Because of this, the Board of Governors of the Federal Reserve System (Fed) for years tended to set interest-rate "targets" calculated to stabilize the economy and permit the money supply to grow so that the targeted interest rates could be maintained. In 1979, however, the Fed discovered that maintaining stable interest rates, even at historically high levels, resulted in increases in the money supply that were well beyond its targets or expectations. This tendency reached its peak in September, when the money supply rose at an annual rate almost 11 per cent above that of March, more than double the desired rate of increase.

President Jimmy Carter meets at Camp David, Md., in July with economists, bankers, and union leaders to search for solutions to economic problems.

Probably for this reason, the Fed announced a basic change in policy on October 6 – one that some economists had long suggested – in stating that it would cease trying to stabilize interest rates and would focus its attention on controlling the money supply, allowing interest rates to move up or down as the demand for dollars fluctuated. As part of this move, the Fed increased the *discount rate,* the rate at which it would lend to member commercial banks, to the unprecedentedly high level of 12 per cent. It also increased reserve requirements on certain deposits at its member banks. The net result was a sharp increase in the *prime rate,* the rate of interest charged by major banks to their best customers, from 13.5 per cent in late September to 15.5 per cent in mid-November.

One effect of these high interest rates, if they continued long, would probably be a reduction in new housing construction and consumer durable purchases as consumers would find it too costly to meet the charges such interest rates impose. An early indication of this was the relatively poor demand for the 1980-model cars that were introduced in October. Lack of sales resulted in production cuts that brought planned output for November to 22 per cent below November 1978 (see AUTOMOBILE). Housing starts in October were 8 per cent below September, and the decline was expected to accelerate as the new Fed policy took effect (see HOUSING).

There was little indication that total employment would decline seriously, but unemployment seemed certain to worsen because the economy's growth rate is likely to be insufficient to absorb all would-be entrants into the labor market.

Ailing Auto Industry. Many people claimed that higher gasoline prices would not result in reduced oil imports, and they used that as an argument for resisting decontrol of gasoline prices. Yet there was substantial indirect evidence in automobile sales that American consumers were indeed reacting. For the first 10 months of the year, imported cars, which use substantially less gasoline than any except the smallest U.S. cars, increased their share of the market from 14.9 per cent in 1978 to 19.1 per cent in 1979. Not unexpectedly, most foreign makes also increased their actual sales at a time when sales of U.S.-made cars were dropping. Similarly, the smaller American cars were selling at a rate far ahead of their larger competitors.

Although the Chrysler Corporation's much-publicized difficulties were sometimes attributed to the greater impact of government regulation on that company than on its larger competitors, it seems likely that Chrysler's underlying difficulties rest in part in the fact that it produced relatively fewer small cars than did the other manufacturers.

The large decline in new car sales in October and November 1979 had added to Chrysler's problems.

"Morning, everybody—what's up?"

Even General Motors Corporation and the Ford Motor Company, the two much larger producers, showed third-quarter operating losses, and, at year-end, more than 100,000 auto workers were unemployed as a result of temporary or permanent plant closings. Total production of American cars during 1979 was down 8.3 per cent and reached only slightly more than 8.4 million units.

The Huge Chrysler Losses touched off a serious debate as to what, if anything, should be done to help the ailing giant, third largest automotive producer in the United States with about 12 per cent of the market. With losses of $1.5 billion projected for 1979 and probably that much more in 1980, financial experts questioned whether the company could avoid bankruptcy. Alarmists feared that the company might be forced to shut down completely, costing hundreds of thousands of jobs across the country among Chrysler workers and employees of suppliers.

To avert this possibility, Chrysler proposed a $1.5-billion government guarantee of Chrysler loans to enable the company to raise the money needed to redesign a more acceptable line of cars. This was finally proposed by the Carter Administration with the proviso that Chrysler should first raise an equal number of dollars without any government guarantee. There was serious question about the corporation's capacity to raise this amount. Bankers testified that they did not feel justified in advancing addi-

tional funds, given Chrysler's present prospects. Even if Chrysler were able to raise the money, the proposed government guarantee faced some rocky going in Congress.

Speculation was laid to rest on December 19 when the Senate voted 53-44 to approve the suggested $1.5 billion loan guarantee. The Senate package also included $525 million in wage concessions by United Auto Workers (UAW) members, $150 million in wage concessions by nonunion workers, and the issuing of $175 million worth of new stock by Chrysler. The House of Representatives passed a substantially similar bill on December 18, and the Congress approved a compromise measure on December 21 providing a $1.5 billion federal loan guarantee and calling also for private funds and wage concessions totaling $462.5 million by the UAW. The aid plan was considered a victory for the Carter Administration, the UAW, and Chrysler.

Agriculture, Business. Despite costs of production, which rose somewhat more rapidly than the prices farmers received, record crops seemed to assure farmers of record incomes of somewhat more than $31 billion in 1979. This was about 12 per cent above 1978 levels (see FARM AND FARMING).

Corporate profits vividly showed the effects of inflation. Before adjustment, they increased by somewhat more than 10 per cent to $227 billion, but after adjustments for inventory evaluation and capital consumption they were estimated at about $176-billion, up some 5 per cent. With inflation running at a double-digit clip, it was not surprising that the stock market performance disappointed investors. Measured by the Dow Jones average of 30 industrial stocks, the market was at about the same level at which it had closed in 1978. By the broader Standard & Poor's index and the New York Stock Exchange index, it was about 5 per cent higher.

Perhaps the most alarming fact about the inflation rate was that it moved much more rapidly in the United States than in the rest of the industrialized world, except for Italy and Great Britain, both weak spots in the international economy. The rate in West Germany and Japan was under 5 per cent.

Industrial Production growth rates in the more highly industrialized economies during 1979 were modest. Japan led the list with about 6 per cent, followed by West Germany and Italy at 4 per cent; France at 2.5 per cent; and the United States at 2 per cent. Britain brought up the rear with a modest 0.5 per cent. All these figures were corrected for the country's rate of inflation and represent real growth. Despite these unfavorable influences, United States exports grew more rapidly than imports, and it appeared that the balance of payments on current account would substantially reduce the 1978 deficit of almost $14 billion, probably to about $2 billion.

Non-Western Countries such as Russia make it difficult to obtain accurate data about their econom-

Selected Key U.S. Economic Indicators

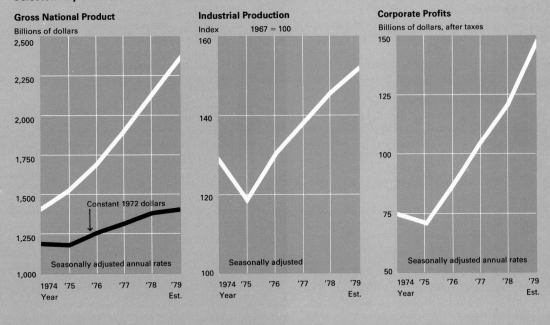

Gross National Product

Billions of dollars

2,500
2,250
2,000
1,750
1,500
1,250
1,000

Constant 1972 dollars ↓

Seasonally adjusted annual rates

1974 '75 '76 '77 '78 '79
Year   Est.

Industrial Production

Index   1967 = 100

160
140
120
100

Seasonally adjusted

1974 '75 '76 '77 '78 '79
Year   Est.

Corporate Profits

Billions of dollars, after taxes

150
125
100
75
50

Seasonally adjusted annual rates

1974 '75 '76 '77 '78 '79
Year   Est.

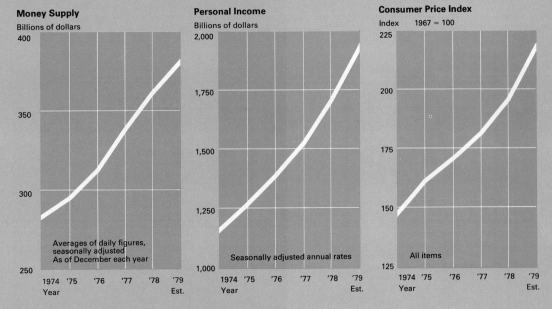

Money Supply

Billions of dollars

400
350
300
250

Averages of daily figures,
seasonally adjusted
As of December each year

1974 '75 '76 '77 '78 '79
Year   Est.

Personal Income

Billions of dollars

2,000
1,750
1,500
1,250
1,000

Seasonally adjusted annual rates

1974 '75 '76 '77 '78 '79
Year   Est.

Consumer Price Index

Index   1967 = 100

225
200
175
150
125

All items

1974 '75 '76 '77 '78 '79
Year   Est.

The most comprehensive measure of the nation's total output of goods and services is the *Gross National Product* (GNP). The GNP represents the dollar value in current prices of all goods and services plus the estimated value of certain imputed outputs, such as the rental value of owner-occupied dwellings. *Industrial Production* is a monthly measure of the physical output of manufacturing, mining, and utility industries. *Corporate Profits* are quarterly profit samplings from major industries.

Money Supply measures the total amount of money in the economy in coin, currency, and demand deposits. *Personal Income* is current income received by persons (including nonprofit institutions and private trust funds) before personal taxes. *Consumer Price Index* (CPI) is a monthly measure of changes in the prices of goods and services consumed by urban families and individuals. CPI includes selected goods and services. All 1979 figures are *Year Book* estimates.

ic conditions, but occasionally a glimpse of what the Russians are experiencing surfaces. One such glimpse occurred in November when *Pravda,* the Communist Party newspaper, ran a front-page editorial complaining of the failure of the Soviet oil and coal industries to meet the needs of their customers. This tended to confirm an earlier United States estimate that Russia would find it necessary to import oil by 1982. Russia vigorously denied this report, but the public airing of that country's energy problems in November appeared to soften that denial.

Pro and Con Keynes. Inflation problems and the inability of traditional remedies to deal with them touched off the first serious debate in almost 50 years about the appropriate direction of public policy. The Great Depression dominated the decade of the 1930s, and the ideas of British economist John Maynard Keynes came to dominate academic economic thinking and were readily incorporated into public policy. Keynes believed that it was possible to use government finance to regulate the economy in order to avoid periods of depression or inflation. In periods of high unemployment, the government's budget would run a deficit, thus providing more purchasing power and creating work. But during periods of high employment, government would run a surplus, thus reducing purchasing power and

preventing the economy from "overheating." The concept implies, but does not require, that the governmental budget be balanced over the business cycle. The basic tool is "demand management." Whatever the merits of the theoretical analysis, in practice there has been no tendency to balance the budget over the cycle, and President Jimmy Carter's promise of 1976 to have a balanced budget in four years is now seen as impossible to keep.

With double-digit inflation occurring and few indications that the rate can be reduced to the 1.5 to 3 per cent of the early 1960s, the theory has developed that the way to cut inflation is not by managing the demand for goods and services, but by focusing attention on the supply side of the demand-supply equation that determines the level of prices. According to this analysis, the best way to reduce inflation is to increase production and worker productivity. This could be accomplished by substantially reducing tax levels so that more money will be available for savings. These savings will in turn be invested in productive plant and equipment, which will then result in an increased output and flow of income. The most extreme form of this argument holds that if, for example, taxes were reduced by 10 per cent, there would be a sufficient increase in income, which would be taxed, to make up, or more than make up, the initial loss in revenues caused by the tax cut.

Leaders of seven nations take a break from solving monetary problems at economic summit sessions in Tokyo in June and relax at a Japanese dinner.

Figuring the Future. As the year ended, economists and analysts were busy discussing the prospects for the forthcoming year. There was substantial agreement that the first half of 1980 would see a recession, if indeed one had not already begun in the fourth quarter of 1979. But again, the experts differed widely as to whether this recession would be severe or mild. Apart from their differing interpretations of the underlying economic conditions, the problem was complicated by the fact that 1980 was an election year. If the decline in business activity were to be slight, without a significant increase in the unemployment rate and with inflation apparently slowing, then the recession would likely be mild. But if high interest rates brought a sudden and sharp slowdown with rising unemployment and little apparent effect on inflation, there would be pressure in two directions. First would come demands for employment-generating expenditures and then, despite all promises to the contrary, there would be a move toward mandatory wage and price controls. In short, economists in 1980 would be keeping one eye on the statistics of economic performance and the other on political dust storms from Washington, D.C.   Warren W. Shearer

See also INTERNATIONAL TRADE AND FINANCE; THE YEAR IN FOCUS section. In WORLD BOOK, see ECONOMICS; GROSS NATIONAL PRODUCT; NATIONAL INCOME.

A soldier in full battle gear maintains order as voters line up in April to vote in Ecuador's first free presidential election in 10 years.

ECUADOR. Jaime Roldos Aguilera was sworn in as president on Aug. 10, 1979. He was the first popularly elected president to take power after more than nine years of military rule. Roldos, the candidate of the left-of-center coalition Concentration of Popular Forces (CPF), easily captured 68 per cent of the votes in a two-man runoff election held on April 29. He defeated Sixto Duran Ballen Cordovez, the candidate of the conservative Social Christian Party.

The Roldos coalition also won 45 of the 69 seats in the new one-house Congress, which took office immediately after the inauguration. Simultaneously, the 18th Constitution in Ecuador's 149-year history went into effect.

In a preliminary, first-round election held in 1978, Roldos had been pictured as the puppet of Asaad Bucaram, to whom he is related by marriage. Bucaram, former mayor of Guayaquil and head of the CPF, was opposed by the military junta then ruling the country. Indeed, Roldos had campaigned in the first round under the slogan "Roldos in the Presidency, Bucaram in Power."

Break with Bucaram. But in the runoff campaign, he declared, "I am Jaime Roldos, and I will be the president and no one else." A break with Bucaram was inevitable; their ties created problems for Roldos' presidency. Bucaram's CPF, which he had founded, persistently blocked the Roldos administration's bills while passing measures that were unacceptable to it. On November 30, the 11 members of Roldos' Cabinet resigned in order to give him a free hand in his struggle for power with Bucaram. As one of his first moves, Roldos was expected to give several Cabinet seats to the Democratic Left Party, which held the second largest number of seats in the Congress, in exchange for legislative support.

The Roldos government faced serious financial challenges on assuming office. It faced a foreign debt of $4 billion and an inflation rate of 15 per cent. Export income depended largely on petroleum exports from fields in the Amazon Basin area that some experts predicted would be so depleted by 1985 that the country would have to begin importing oil.

Roldos Promised "firm and immediate" steps to expand oil exploration and indicated that foreign oil companies would be invited to help. He also pledged to fight corruption, improve health care, and redistribute rural land holdings in an effort to improve the lives of the poor, most of whom are Indians. As a gesture to Ecuador's large Indian population, he read a section of his inaugural speech in Quechua.

To underscore the United States pleasure at seeing a popularly elected president succeed a military dictatorship, President Jimmy Carter sent his wife, Rosalynn, and Secretary of State Cyrus R. Vance to represent him at the inauguration.   Everett G. Martin

See also LATIN AMERICA (Facts in Brief Table). In WORLD BOOK, see ECUADOR.

EDUCATION

EDUCATION in the United States faced two serious crises in 1979. It had to cope simultaneously with fiscal pressures created by a worsening taxpayers' revolt against government spending and with problems caused by declining enrollments. In many communities, excess classroom space led to heated discussion about school closings. Financial difficulties plagued education at all levels. Just as public schools, particularly in the big cities, had to reduce teaching staffs, an increasing number of colleges and universities began to cut their faculties.

New Education Department. After extensive debate, the U.S. Congress approved President Jimmy Carter's proposal, based on his 1976 campaign pledge, to create a separate, Cabinet-level Department of Education. Final action came on September 27 as the House approved a Senate-House compromise by a vote of 215 to 201, following a Senate vote of 69 to 22. On October 30, Carter named Shirley Mount Hufstedler, a federal judge in California, to head the new department (see HUFSTEDLER, SHIRLEY M.). The new department will have an initial budget of $14 billion and a staff of 18,000. The former Department of Health, Education, and Welfare (HEW) will become the Department of Health and Human Services.

In addition to HEW's Office of Education, the new department will include the Department of Defense's schools for overseas dependents, the Department of Agriculture's graduate school, the Department of Labor's education programs for migrants, several science education programs formerly run by the National Science Foundation, and college housing programs previously administered by the Department of Housing and Urban Development. Among the federal programs that will not be transferred to the new department are American Indian schools, which are administered by the Department of the Interior, and the preschool program Head Start, which remains with HEW's successor.

Total Enrollment in American schools and colleges declined for the seventh consecutive year, after almost three decades of constant growth. The National Center for Education Statistics reported that an estimated 58.4 million persons were expected to enroll in formal educational programs from kindergarten through graduate school in the 1979-1980 academic year. This would indicate a decline of nearly 5 per cent from the record high enrollment of 61.3 million reached in the fall of 1975 and a decline of more than 1 per cent from 1978's 59.1 million. Nevertheless, the number of Americans engaged directly in education was a substantial 62 million persons, including those who teach as well as those who learn – nearly 3 out of 10 of the U.S. population of 222.5 million.

White students are greeted by teachers and students of a predominantly black school in Cleveland on the first day of court-ordered busing.

Elementary grades enrolled 31.7 million children, with 27.9 million of them in public schools. This represented a decline of almost 2 per cent from the previous year's total of 32.2 million, a downward trend that began in 1970. At the same time, enrollment in nonpublic schools has held steady.

High schools were expected to enroll 15.3 million students, compared with 15.6 million in 1978, a drop of about 2 per cent. The number of students enrolled in public schools was expected to be 13.8 million.

Consolidation of the public school system continued in 1979. After World War II, there were more than 100,000 school districts. By 1979, the total was down to 16,200. However, in the past four years, there has been a reduction of only 500 districts, indicating that the proper balance appears to have been reached. Elementary and secondary education is offered by some 62,600 public elementary schools, 25,400 public secondary schools, 14,200 nonpublic elementary schools, and 3,800 nonpublic high schools. About 1 pupil in 10 is in a nonpublic school.

Office of Education estimates placed enrollment in higher education – colleges, universities, professional schools, and junior colleges – at a record 11.4 million, up about 100,000, or 1 per cent, from the previous year. Public colleges and universities, with an estimated 8.9 million, up from 8.8 million, continued to grow at a faster rate than private institutions, which gained only 25,000 students, less than half of 1978's modest increase.

The Graduates. The annual number of high school graduates had remained near 3.1 million for five years, but a small decrease of about 50,000 was expected for the class of 1980. Colleges and universities in 1979-1980 were expected to award some 950,000 bachelor's degrees, 330,000 master's, 33,000 doctorates, and 68,000 first professional degrees.

The Bureau of the Census reported that there were 99.9 million high school graduates in the United States in 1979. Nearly 20.6 million of these had also completed four or more years of college. The median number of school years completed by persons 25 years and over was 12.4. The comparable figure in 1949 was only nine years. In the last 30 years, the number of adults with less than five years of schooling decreased by nearly 50 per cent, from 8.6 million to 4.5 million.

The Teachers. There were an estimated 2.4 million elementary- and secondary-school teachers involved in classroom instruction in 1979, and 300,000 worked as superintendents, principals, and supervisors. In addition, there were 830,000 higher-education faculty members. The pupil-teacher ratio in public elementary and secondary schools has declined steadily in recent years, from 23.2 pupils per teacher in 1968 to 19.4 in the fall of 1978. Critics of the schools' effectiveness point out that more funds go to pay greater numbers of teachers while children's achievements decline, and say this is proof of

lower teacher productivity. As a result, several states have introduced competency tests for teachers.

The average salary of teachers rose to $14,244 in 1978 at all public school levels, and to $13,902 for elementary-school teachers, a gain of about 6.6 per cent over the previous year, but not sufficient to keep pace with inflation. Averages ranged from Arkansas' $10,400 to Alaska's $23,260.

Teachers' Unions. Competition continued between the two largest U.S. teacher organizations, the 1.8-million-member National Education Association (NEA) and the American Federation of Teachers (AFT), which has about 450,000 members. Their differences surfaced most dramatically over the issue of the creation of a separate Department of Education. The NEA, which had extracted the promise of such a reorganization from Carter, triumphed over the AFT, which had opposed it.

The 1979-1980 school year began with a slight increase in the number of teacher strikes. Work stoppages in September affected more than 865,000 students in 14 states. More than 45,000 teachers were on strike.

Education Expenditures at all levels for the 1979-1980 school year were estimated by the Office of Education at $161 billion, an increase of nearly $11 billion. Most of the increase was due to inflation. Higher education was expected to receive $58 billion, with the elementary and secondary schools' total set at almost $103 billion. Of the total expenditures, slightly more than $29 billion was slated for private schools, colleges, and universities.

State governments contributed slightly more than 36 per cent of the total educational cost; local governments, about 28 per cent; the federal government, between 10 and 11 per cent; and all other sources, just under 25 per cent. National educational expenditures remained constant at about 8 per cent of the gross national product.

Student Achievement remained under critical scrutiny. Scholastic Aptitude Test (SAT) scores of high school seniors fell slightly again in 1979, continuing a downward trend that began more than a decade ago. The average SAT verbal score dropped two points to 427, and the mathematics score dropped one point to 467. In 1969, the average verbal score was 463 and the math score, 493.

Another student evaluation indicated that the mathematics achievement of students in elementary and secondary schools declined in the 1970s. A report by the federally supported National Assessment of Educational Progress showed that the ability to use mathematical knowledge to solve problems had declined among 17-year-olds by four percentage points since 1973.

Public Attitudes toward the schools tended to be critical. In an annual survey of attitudes toward public schools, the Gallup Poll and the Charles F. Kettering Foundation reported that only 8 per cent

Retired Coca-Cola executive Robert W. Woodruff gave Georgia's Emory University $100 million, the largest educational gift in U.S. history.

of those polled gave the schools a grade of A on their overall performance, compared with 9 per cent in 1978 and 18 per cent in 1974, when the question was first asked. The number of respondents giving the schools an A or B – as opposed to C, D, Failing, or Don't Know – dropped from 36 to 34 per cent in 1979. Twenty-four per cent of the respondents cited lack of discipline as the "biggest problem" the schools confront.

Language Studies. The President's Commission on Foreign Language and International Studies concluded a 12-month evaluation of the two areas in November. It reported a "scandalous" neglect of foreign-language instruction at all school levels. The commission further warned that some of America's most crucial area- and language-study centers may collapse as a result of declining federal and educational foundation support. The 25-member body urged that $178 million in federal aid, in addition to greatly increased state, local, and private subsidies, be used to bolster these studies, calling them vital to national security in an increasingly interdependent world. The commission also urged the reintroduction of foreign-language requirements by schools and colleges and the financial support of student and scholarly exchanges – at least at 1969 levels.

A Truth in Testing law enacted by the New York state legislature – and regarded by its supporters as a model for federal legislation that is currently being debated – has set off new controversy over testing. The law requires compilers of standardized admissions tests to file the test questions and correct answers with the state education commissioner within 30 days after scores have been made public. Test publishers have charged that such procedures would substantially raise the cost of the tests and may make tests for limited numbers of people, such as admissions tests to specialized fields, too costly.

Biggest Gift. On November 8, Robert W. Woodruff, the retired chairman of the Coca-Cola Company, gave Emory University, in Atlanta, Ga., Coca-Cola stock worth $100 million. The gift is believed to be the largest single donation to an educational institution ever made, and makes Emory the richest private university in the South. With an endowment of $270 million, it ranks 11th nationally.

Segregation Case. On October 29, after months of fruitless negotiations, HEW formally asked the U.S. Department of Justice to sue the Board of Education of Chicago to force the integration of the city's schools. An April HEW report found a "racially discriminating dual school system" in Chicago, the worst of any large city in the North. Such a suit may prove to be the biggest legal battle over school segregation in U.S. history.

Illiteracy Fight. In a September report titled "Adult Literacy in the United States," the Ford Foundation sharply criticized existing U.S. programs against illiteracy. "Publicly proclaimed goals and actual achievements are far apart," the report claimed. "The public rhetoric of these programs is designed to secure legislation and funding from a Congress that knows little about its educationally and economically marginal constituents."

The foundation called for a network of neighborhood programs designed to increase literacy among the poor. Because many present programs are not relevant to the daily lives of the disadvantaged, new programs should be designed with the aid of the participants themselves, the foundation said.

Minimum Competency. A rigorous new set of competency standards that require students to prove their ability to do high school work before they receive a high school diploma has been enacted by New York state. New York, like 36 other states, has had some competency standards for several years. The new standards, which will begin with the high school graduating class of 1981, will be much more difficult.

Florida's competency program was delayed by a federal court order on July 13. Federal District Judge George C. Carr ruled that the equal protection clause of the 14th Amendment to the U.S. Constitution was sufficient reason to delay the new test until the 1982-1983 school year, to ensure that all students were properly prepared to take the test on an equal footing.   Fred M. Hechinger

In WORLD BOOK, see EDUCATION.

EGYPT. The peace treaty signed with Israel on March 26, 1979, ended a 30-year state of war between the two countries as Egypt became the first Arab nation to recognize the existence of Israel. The treaty capped 16 months of difficult, often-interrupted negotiations. It was signed by President Anwar al-Sadat and Israel's Prime Minister Menachem Begin in Washington, D.C., but the formal treaty documents were exchanged on April 25 at Umm Khisheib in the Sinai. Israel began its Sinai withdrawal on May 25, turning over the town of El Arish to Egypt. See MIDDLE EAST.

Egypt Alone. The treaty effectively isolated Egypt from the rest of the Arab world, as all Arab states except Sudan, Oman, and Somalia broke relations. On March 31, at a meeting in Baghdad, the Arab nations also suspended Egypt's membership in the Arab League and voted to move its headquarters from Cairo to Tunis, Tunisia. Egypt expected the anticipated loss of economic aid from the Arab oil-producing states to be made up by the United States, Japan, and West Germany.

Sadat moved vigorously to ensure domestic support for the treaty. Prior to the signing, it had been endorsed unanimously by the Cabinet, the People's Assembly, and the National Democratic Party (NDP). A national referendum on April 19 approved the treaty by a 99.95 per cent majority.

Sadat announced a reorganization of political life in April. Political parties were allowed, provided they were not based purely on religion or on Communist affiliation. A *Shoura* (consultative council) would be formed by election as an upper house of the Assembly, and the Assembly would be enlarged from 360 to 392 members. Elections were in June.

The Election Results, though marked more by voter apathy than enthusiastic support, were a solid victory for Sadat. Public criticism of the Israeli treaty was prohibited, and 330 seats went to NDP candidates against 29 for the major opposition Socialist Labor Party and 33 for independents.

With his opposition largely fragmented or muffled, Sadat's major problem was the need to bring economic stability to Egypt. Remittances from the 2 million Egyptians working in other Arab states increased $500 million to $4.5 billion and partially made up for the loss of Arab contributions. In March, Japan granted $145 million, including $7-million for a fish-processing complex on Lake Aswan; France gave $250 million toward the Cairo subway project; and the World Bank loaned $40-million for transportation projects. But the real hope was massive U.S. aid as a result of the treaty and open border with Israel.   William Spencer

See also MIDDLE EAST (Facts in Brief Table). In WORLD BOOK, see EGYPT.

Egypt's President Anwar al-Sadat waves to a welcoming crowd in the Sinai, after the first of a series of Israeli withdrawals from Egyptian territory.

ELECTIONS. If the off-year elections in the United States in 1979 made any significant statement, it was that voters in urban and Southern areas still seem to prefer Democrats. Democratic mayors were put into office in nearly all large cities, and although Republican hopes of capturing the governors' mansions in Kentucky and Mississippi were dashed, an upset victory gave the party the Louisiana governorship.

In Kentucky, millionaire Democrat John Y. Brown, Jr., easily defeated former Republican Governor Louie B. Nunn on November 6. Brown and his wife – Phyllis George, a television personality and former Miss America – ran a glamorous campaign by helicopter in Brown's first race for public office. Brown, who made a fortune with the Kentucky Fried Chicken fast-food business, had campaign help from Senator Edward M. Kennedy (D., Mass.). Nunn tried unsuccessfully to picture the Browns, who had married following recent divorces, as a "jet set" couple unacceptable to Kentuckians. After his defeat, Nunn said he would not run for office again.

In Mississippi, former Democratic Lieutenant Governor William F. Winter defeated Republican Gil Carmichael in an election notable because neither candidate tried to exploit racial fears and both sought black support. Although the national Republican Party sent funds and political specialists to Mississippi, and Carmichael, a well-known car dealer, was considered to have an excellent chance, Winter benefited from Mississippi's traditional Democratic leanings.

A surprise victory by Republican Representative David C. Treen on December 8 broke the Democratic Party's near stranglehold on the South. Defeating public service commissioner Louis Lambert, Treen became the first Republican to be elected governor of Louisiana since 1877. In 1972 he had become the first Republican elected to the U.S. House of Representatives from Louisiana in the present century.

The gubernatorial election was steeped in controversy from start to finish. In the nonpartisan primary on October 27, a shift in 4,800 votes between the first and final ballot counts transferred a berth in the runoff from Lieutenant Governor James E. Fitzmorris to Lambert. Charging vote theft, Fitzmorris threw his support to Treen.

Republican Treen took no chances in the runoff, using armed guards, state police, and volunteers to prevent vote tampering. The election was close, but a recount gave Treen a 9,871-vote victory.

City Contests. Mayor Dennis J. Kucinich of Cleveland, a Democrat, was defeated by Republican George V. Voinovich in a rare Republican city hall take-over. Kucinich, 33, contributed to his own downfall by alienating Democratic Party officials as well as the business establishment. Cleveland defaulted twice on bond payments while he was in office, and he narrowly survived a recall election in August 1978.

Racial issues may have been a factor in a Republican victory in the Kansas City, Mo., municipal election on March 27. Richard L. Berkley became the first Republican to win the city's mayoral race in more than 50 years. He defeated Democrat Bruce Watkins, a black.

In Chicago, Jane M. Byrne became the first woman mayor of her city on April 3. Byrne, a Democrat, successfully challenged the party's powerful political machine once controlled by the late Mayor Richard J. Daley, and narrowly defeated incumbent Mayor Michael A. Bilandic in a February 27 primary fight. She won 82.5 per cent of the vote in the April general election, the largest plurality since 1901. See Close-Up.

Former U.S. Representative William J. Green III, a Democrat, easily defeated Republican David W. Marston in Philadelphia on November 6. Marston received national attention in 1978 when he tried to block President Jimmy Carter's decision to replace him as U.S. attorney. Lucien Blackwell, a black candidate running as an Independent, got 20 per cent of the vote. Green succeeded Mayor Frank L. Rizzo, who was barred by law from seeking a third term.

Boston's Democratic Mayor Kevin H. White won an unprecedented fourth term, turning aside a challenge from his perennial rival, Democratic State Senator Joseph F. Timilty, who had opposed him in two previous mayoral elections.

Minneapolis voters also elected a Democratic mayor – former U.S. Representative Donald M. Fraser. Fraser won a 2-to-1 majority over his closest rival, former Republican Mayor Charles S. Stenvig. Former national chairman of the liberal Americans for Democratic Action, Fraser lost a 1978 primary race for the Minnesota Senate seat of the late Hubert H. Humphrey.

Runoff Results. In Memphis, black challenger W. Otis Higgs lost his bid to unseat incumbent Mayor Wyeth Chandler in a runoff election on November 15. Chandler won by about 14,000 votes – or less than half the margin of victory he accumulated in the race against Higgs in 1975.

In the November 4 San Francisco mayoral election, Mayor Dianne Feinstein was forced into a runoff against Supervisor Quentin Kopp. Feinstein, who became mayor after the murder of Mayor George Moscone in November 1978, led the field in the November election, but failed to get the required majority. She defeated Kopp in the runoff election on December 11.

Houston's Democratic Mayor Jim McConn defeated Democratic Councilman Louis Macey in a runoff election on November 20. McConn and Macey headed a field of four candidates that included former Commissioner of Immigration and Naturalization Service Leonel J. Castillo in the November 4 mayoral election.

Chicago's Machine Short-Circuits

The last of the United States big-city political machines suffered an unprecedented power failure on Feb. 27, 1979, in Chicago. The legendary Cook County Democratic Central Committee, which had produced every one of Chicago's mayors since 1931, failed to deliver a primary-election victory for Mayor Michael A. Bilandic. Ironically, Bilandic's defeat came at the hands of another machine product, former Consumer Affairs Commissioner Jane M. Byrne, a protégée of the late Mayor Richard J. Daley. See CHICAGO.

Byrne's victory was the culmination of a campaign that began almost a year earlier, shortly after Bilandic fired her for publicly accusing him of "greasing the way" for an unpopular increase in taxi fares. Few considered Byrne's candidacy a serious threat to Bilandic's re-election. She had no apparent bloc of support either outside or within the Democratic Party. She had a scant $125,000 to pit against Bilandic's $1-million campaign chest, and only a few campaign workers.

Byrne's greatest resource seemed to be an almost bottomless reserve of energy. Throughout the summer and fall of 1978, she took her campaign into Chicago's neighborhoods, visiting housing projects, grocery stores, and factory yards, and condemning the "cabal of evil men" at City Hall.

At first she had little impact. Year-end polls indicated that 63 per cent of those surveyed were satisfied with Bilandic's performance as mayor.

But the new year of 1979 brought an abrupt change in climate. A blizzard on January 13 and 14 dumped about 21 inches (53 centimeters) of snow on the city. Days of subzero temperatures followed, and the "city that works" stopped working.

Chicago's O'Hare International Airport was shut down for three consecutive days. Public schools closed for a week. Automobiles were buried in drifts on unplowed side streets, and even on major arteries traffic moved at a snail's pace. Elevated-train service was cut in half. Garbage collection virtually ceased. But snowbound Chicagoans saw Bilandic on television, assuring them that everything was all right.

Victory breakfast

Chicago's winter of discontent worked to Jane Byrne's advantage. She attacked Bilandic's inability to mobilize the city's snow-removal forces. She criticized him for awarding a $90,000 contract to a former City Hall friend to study the situation. The press began to pay attention.

Byrne capitalized on this new-found attention. She held frequent press conferences and appeared in TV newsrooms. She bought a new coat, changed her lipstick to soften her image, and hired a political strategist.

Throughout February, the weather continued to work in Byrne's favor. Temperatures remained below 20°F. (-7°C), too cold for salt to melt ice. Snowbound streets and impassable sidewalks plagued motorists and pedestrians alike, and uncollected garbage continued to pile up. Trains and buses, filled to overflowing with angry commuters, still ran up to an hour late. Neighbors fought over parking spaces; business losses climbed into the hundreds of millions of dollars; "cabin fever" reached epidemic proportions—and Chicagoans blamed Mayor Bilandic.

By election eve, Byrne and Bilandic were running neck and neck. And then election day dawned mild and clear—the kind of day favorable to the huge voter turnout an independent candidate needed to beat the machine. When that day ended, Chicago had produced the second largest primary election turnout in its history. And Jane Byrne had squeaked by Michael Bilandic by 15,000 votes.

Byrne had carried 29 of the city's 50 wards—and her support had come from the groups that were most inconvenienced during the winter. She took 14 of the 16 predominantly black wards and, pollsters estimated, two-thirds of the vote cast by low-income voters and voters under age 35.

With Bilandic out of the picture, the Cook County Democratic Central Committee regrouped behind Byrne. With party support augmenting her momentum, Byrne won the general election over Republican Wallace D. Johnson on April 3, 1979, by the largest margin ever recorded in a Chicago mayoral race to become the city's first woman mayor. Beverly Merz

Election victors include, *clockwise from lower left,* Democrat Richard Arrington, first black to become mayor of Birmingham, Ala., with his son; Democrat John Y. Brown, Jr., governor-elect of Kentucky; Democrat William J. Green, Philadelphia's mayor-elect; and George V. Voinovich, new Republican mayor of Cleveland, with the loser, Democrat Dennis Kucinich, at left.

Former police chief Biagio Di Lieto, a Democrat, was elected mayor of New Haven, Conn., after pledging war on street crime. Joel Skornicka was chosen mayor of Madison, Wis., in nonpartisan balloting on April 3. In other April elections, Democrats Jake Godbold and Thomas D. Westfall were elected mayors of Jacksonville, Fla., and El Paso, Tex., respectively.

Many incumbent mayors won re-election. Salt Lake City's Democratic Mayor Ted Wilson was returned to office in November despite a conservative drive to unseat him. Black Democratic Mayor Richard G. Hatcher easily won a fourth term in Gary, Ind. Other Democratic mayors re-elected were William Schaefer of Baltimore; Maurice Ferre of Miami, Fla.; William D. McNichols of Denver; Lila Cockrell of San Antonio, Tex.; Richard H. Fulton of Nashville, Tenn.; and Doug De Good of Toledo, Ohio. Three Republican mayors – Margaret Hance of Phoenix, Ariz.; Tom Moody of Columbus, Ohio; and William Hudnut of Indianapolis, Ind., were easily re-elected in November.

Republicans won two special congressional elections. In California, GOP candidate William H. Royer defeated Democrat Joe Holsinger to capture the seat left vacant by the death of Representative Leo J. Ryan, who was murdered in Jonestown, Guyana, while investigating a religious cult in November 1978. Wisconsin Republican Thomas E. Petri won a close race against Democrat Gary R. Goyke to replace the late Representative William A. Steiger (R., Wis.).

Ballot Issues. Voters also passed on a number of ballot issues. In California, where tax-cutting Proposition 13 was adopted overwhelmingly in June 1978, the voters on November 6 limited state spending by approving another amendment to the state constitution. The new measure forbids spending increases that go beyond the increases in the rate of inflation and the state's population. It was approved by 73 per cent of those voting.

Californians also adopted a constitutional amendment to limit busing in Los Angeles to achieve racial balance in public schools. Sixty-eight per cent of the voters approved this proposal, which essentially would not allow state courts to order additional busing beyond that which federal courts have already imposed in school desegregation cases.

There were mixed results on other issues. San Francisco voters rejected a rent-control proposal; a similar measure was approved in Baltimore. Maine voters opted to keep a law requiring deposits on bottled beverages; Ohio voters rejected the idea.

Voters in Dade County, Florida, on May 8 rejected an ordinance that would have banned cigarette smoking in many public places.   William J. Eaton

See also DEMOCRATIC PARTY; REPUBLICAN PARTY. In WORLD BOOK, see ELECTION.

ELECTRIC POWER. See ENERGY.

ELECTRONICS. Three production methods further developed in 1979 promised to reduce the size of electronic circuits even more. The amount of circuitry that a tiny electronic chip can hold continued to increase as the *line width* (width of the etched lines that make up the circuit elements) continued to shrink. Companies regularly produced chips with line widths of 2 to 3 micrometers (a micrometer is a millionth of a meter) in 1979, and prototype chips had lines of 1 to 2 micrometers. But ion-beam lithography and laser and pulsed-electron-beam *annealing* brought submicrometer chips within reach in 1979. Annealing is the process of re-forming damaged crystals by heating and cooling.

Some companies made experimental submicrometer chips by electron-beam and X-ray lithography. Both techniques resembled the traditional method of manufacture – directing light through a circuit mask onto a photosensitive wafer. First, the experimenters placed over the wafer a mask that contained the circuit pattern. Then, they directed the electron beam or X ray through the mask and a thin film, called the *resist,* on the wafer's surface. The beam caused chemical changes in the parts of the surface that the mask did not cover. Finally, etching removed these parts and left the circuit pattern on the surface. These techniques are limited in how narrow they can make lines. The electrons scatter in the resist, and the X rays are not sufficiently parallel. Ion beams, which have neither of these limitations, can produce wafers much more quickly.

Researchers at Hughes Research Laboratories in Malibu, Calif., began to build the first complete ion-beam system under a government contract, and others at the National Research and Resource Facility for Submicron Structures at Cornell University in Ithaca, N.Y., experimented with ion-beam lithography in 1979.

Wafer damage is inevitable in any production method. Correcting the damage caused by ion-beam lithography led to two new methods of annealing that are faster and more efficient than traditional thermal annealing, and cause less distortion.

A Laser Annealer. Quantronix Corporation in Smithtown, N.Y., produced the first commercial laser annealer. The annealer aims the laser at a specific part of the wafer, so that the laser beam recrystallizes the damaged area without affecting the rest of the wafer. Spire Corporation in Bedford, Mass., developed the pulsed-electron-beam annealer, which heats the wafer's entire surface, as does thermal annealing. But the electron pulse lasts less than one-millionth of a second and heats only the wafer's top layer to a high temperature. The rest of the wafer remains cool, reducing the risk of distortion in the entire chip.

Consumer Advances. After a few years spent mainly in improving existing technology, the industry came up with a few innovations. Lexicon Corpo-

EL SALVADOR

ration in Miami, Fla., was the first to offer a language-translating calculator. Its microcomputer stores 1,500 words or phrases of English and another language.

Japan's Matsushita Electric Industrial Company (Panasonic) developed a single-gun, single-beam color-television picture tube; conventional picture tubes use three guns. A 4.5-inch (11.4-centimeter) picture tube of this type needs only seven watts of electricity, so it can be battery-powered.

Matsushita also developed a pocket-size black-and-white TV by using liquid crystals instead of a picture tube. The crystals are arranged in an array 240 picture elements long by 240 wide, on an integrated circuit. The crystals produce the picture by changing "color" according to the currents in the circuit.

RCA Corporation celebrated 25 years of color TV by introducing a set that uses microcomputers. The set can be programmed to tune in certain channels at selected times for up to seven days. The audio system simulates stereophonic sound by dividing the audio signal in two and sending each signal to its own speaker.　　　　　　　　　　Marilyn J. Offenheiser

In WORLD BOOK, see ELECTRONICS.

EL SALVADOR. See LATIN AMERICA.

EMPLOYMENT. See ECONOMICS; EDUCATION; LABOR; SOCIAL SECURITY; WELFARE.

ENERGY. Gasoline shortages, steep price increases for all petroleum products, a November diplomatic crisis between the United States and oil-rich Iran, and concern about the safety of nuclear energy in 1979 created the strongest sense of urgency about energy in the United States since the Arab oil embargo of 1973-1974. Both President Jimmy Carter and Congress, spurred by the growing public outcry during the spring and summer, acted to reduce growing U.S. dependence on insecure foreign sources of oil. In a dramatic television address on July 15, Carter proposed a new program to reduce crude oil imports by 50 per cent by 1990.

The program called for the most massive peacetime commitment of money and resources in American history. It would span 10 years, cost an estimated $142 billion, and reduce oil imports by 8.5 million barrels per day (bpd) below the levels projected for 1990. "Never again will our nation's independence be hostage to foreign oil," Carter declared.

The President's Plan. The major provisions of the new energy program, which Carter asked Congress to enact, included:

■ Creation of an Energy Security Corporation similar to the synthetic rubber corporation that solved rubber shortages in World War II. The energy corporation would invest $88 billion to develop a synthetic-fuels industry capable of producing 2.5-

Nuclear Facilities — and Output

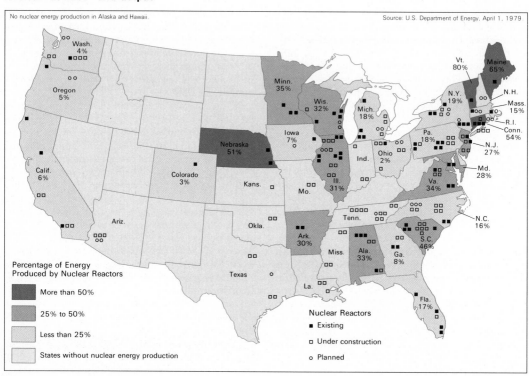

No nuclear energy production in Alaska and Hawaii.　　　　　　　　　Source: U.S. Department of Energy, April 1, 1979.

Wash. 4%　Oregon 5%　Minn. 35%　Wis. 32%　Mich. 18%　Vt. 80%　Maine 65%　N.H.　Mass. 15%　N.Y. 19%　R.I.　Conn. 54%　Iowa 7%　Pa. 18%　N.J. 27%　Nebraska 51%　Ind.　Ohio 2%　Md. 28%　Calif. 6%　Colorado 3%　Kans.　Ill. 31%　Mo.　Va. 34%　Ariz.　Okla.　Tenn.　N.C. 16%　Ark. 30%　Miss.　Ala. 33%　Ga. 8%　S.C. 46%　Texas　La.　Fla. 17%

Percentage of Energy Produced by Nuclear Reactors

- More than 50%
- 25% to 50%
- Less than 25%
- States without nuclear energy production

Nuclear Reactors

■ Existing
□ Under construction
○ Planned

Demonstrators protesting nuclear power are sprayed with water during an
October attempt to occupy the nuclear power plant at Seabrook, N.H.

million bpd of oil substitutes by 1990. The industry's
30 to 40 plants would manufacture synthetic-fuel
liquids and gases from coal, oil shale, peat, and even
agricultural crops. There also would be investments
to stimulate production of natural gas from geologic
formations that cannot be tapped with conventional
technology. About $83 billion in funding for the
corporation would come from a special tax on
"windfall" profits made by oil companies as a result
of federal decontrol of domestic oil prices.

■ Formation of an Energy Mobilization Board to
reduce environmental and other delays in the construction of non-nuclear energy projects.

■ Mandatory conversion of oil-fired boilers at electric power plants to coal.

■ Tax credits and other financial incentives to encourage development of heavy oil and unconventional natural gas.

■ Financial assistance to help poor families cope
with high energy prices.

In a move that did not require congressional
approval, Carter imposed an immediate import
ceiling on crude oil. Oil imports will be held to their
1977 level, which was a record high of about 8.6-
million bpd.

President Carter's energy proposals remained
mired in Senate-House conference committees.
Conferees finally agreed on December 20 on a
compromise windfall-profits oil tax that would raise

an estimated $227.3 billion over 10 years, but they
did not agree on how to split the burden among
segments of the industry. Also left in committee were
the President's modified $20-billion program for a
small-scale synthetic-fuels industry and a bill to
create an Energy Mobilization Board.

Petroleum Panic. The gasoline shortages that
preceded Carter's new energy program and rekin-
dled memories of the Arab oil embargo occurred as a
result of a January revolution that disrupted oil
exports from Iran. Normal Iranian production of 5
million to 6 million bpd – with 770,000 bpd going to
the United States – stopped completely for more
than two months. When oil production finally did
resume in March, it averaged only 3 million to 4
million bpd. By the end of March, oil industry stocks
in the United States were 70 million barrels below
normal levels. Worldwide, the oil shortfall reached
200 million barrels.

Gasoline shortages and panic buying appeared
first in California, then spread quickly to much of the
East and Midwest. On May 9, California imposed
an odd-even gasoline-sales system to control panic
buying. The system permitted vehicles with license
plates ending in an odd digit to buy gasoline only on
odd-numbered calendar dates, and those with an
even digit only on even days on the calendar.

In November, the U.S. barred further oil imports
from Iran after a mob in Iran seized the U.S.

Three Mile Island

It started quietly enough in the early hours of March 28, 1979, but rapidly mushroomed into the worst accident involving a commercial nuclear reactor. Nobody died, and probably no more than one person will die of radiation-induced cancer as a result of the accident at Three Mile Island in the Susquehanna River, near Harrisburg, Pa. But the incident terrified scientists, politicians, and the public, and stoked up a long-smoldering debate on the dangers of radiation.

The accident did not get as far as the ultimate nightmare of meltdown, in which a liquefied core of uranium drops through its shielding into the ground and spreads large amounts of radiation haphazardly across the countryside. But it showed the impotence of nuclear engineers as they tried to deal with a problem that they did not quite understand.

The crisis started shortly after 4 A.M., at the Metropolitan Edison Company's Nuclear Unit number 2, when maintenance workers inadvertently shut off the water supply carrying heat from the reactor to the turbine that generates electricity. Just as planned by the reactor's designers, the turbine shut down, and an auxiliary water pump started up, to keep cold water circulating around the heat-producing nuclear core.

Nuclear power plant

Unfortunately, the valve intended to release this fresh water supply had been set in a closed position for several days. As a result of this human error, the relief water could not reach the reactor core, and the temperature of the nuclear fuel rose rapidly, along with the pressure in the reactor vessel. However, the increasing pressure set in motion two other safety features — a special emergency valve that opened within seconds to admit the auxiliary water supply, and a system that shut down the reactor.

These two automatic actions caused both temperature and pressure to drop and the incident would have fizzled out if events had taken their normal course. But then a mechanical error occurred: The emergency safety valve did not close as it should have when its job was completed. Because the valve stayed open, the pressure continued to fall until

there was a danger that water inside the vessel might flash into steam, leaving the reactor core uncooled. The falling pressure activated yet another safety system. Pumps went into action, sending another supply of water into the reactor.

Only two minutes had elapsed since the incident started, but the train of events had already confused the plant operators in the control room. They had not recognized that the emergency relief valve had stuck at the open position. Their instruments seemed to indicate that water was completely flooding the reactor, a false indication. So another human error occurred. The operators overrode the automatic system that had correctly started the high-pressure water pumps. They reduced the pressure as much as possible, and deprived the core of cooling water. Even though the reactor had been shut down, atomic reactions inside it continued to produce heat. The reactor's temperature soared above 2000° F. (1100° C).

Some hours later, the experts pieced together what had really happened, and restarted the high-pressure water pumps. By 8 P.M., they had managed to bring the core's temperature down to about 280° F. (138° C). But the core had been damaged, water had ruptured an overflow system, and radioactive steam had escaped into the atmosphere.

Metropolitan Edison had issued a "general emergency" at the plant at 7:30 A.M. Forty-five minutes later, the federal Nuclear Regulatory Commission (NRC) dispatched experts to the scene. Their monitors picked up signs of radioactivity in the air around the site, caused by the vented steam.

The reactor eventually cooled, but the controversy did not. Antinuclear groups argued that the incident revealed the danger of a technology run by mistake-prone people. The nuclear industry could only respond that disaster — a meltdown — had been avoided.

A presidential commission, set up to study the accident, suggested new safety measures, better training of plant operators, better state and local plans for such emergencies, and a shake-up of the NRC.   Peter Gwynne

President Jimmy Carter inspects a new solar-powered hot-water heating system installed on the roof of the West Wing of the White House.

Embassy in Teheran and held U.S. citizens as hostages for the return of Shah Mohammad Reza Pahlavi. The ban's impact on the U.S. economy was unlikely to be felt until early 1980. See IRAN; PRESIDENT OF THE UNITED STATES.

Solar Sell. A special presidential message to Congress on June 20 set a national goal of using solar and other renewable energy sources to supply 20 per cent of all domestic energy needs by the year 2000. The President requested $1 billion for fiscal 1980 to finance tax credits for solar installations, research and development, and other activities. Other 1979 legislative proposals included bills to stimulate the use of *gasohol,* a mixture of 90 per cent gasoline and 10 per cent alcohol. The alcohol can be made from grain, coal, or other domestic resources.

Emergency temperature restrictions went into effect in July for about 5 million nonresidential buildings around the United States. Thermostat settings for air conditioning could be no lower than 78°F. (25.6°C), and no higher than 65°F. (18.3°C) degrees for heating. The restrictions were intended to save the equivalent of 200,000 to 400,000 barrels of oil per day.

Even as the government struggled to formulate a workable energy plan for the future, an accident on March 28 at the Three Mile Island nuclear power plant near Harrisburg, Pa., threw a monkey wrench into the plans of the nuclear energy industry. Subse-

quent investigations and administrative safety decisions closed several plants temporarily and brought new nuclear construction to a halt. See Close-Up.

Electric Highs. Despite all conservation efforts, U.S. consumption of electricity hit an all-time high on three separate occasions during 1979. Consumers used a record 48.6 billion kilowatt-hours (kwh) during the week ending on January 13. They broke that record with 49.2 billion kwh during the week ending on August 4, and set another record of 49.5 billion kwh for the week ending on August 11. However, total domestic consumption of electricity during the first half of 1979 was 7.9 per cent lower than the first half of 1978. Petroleum consumption decreased 0.7 per cent; natural gas consumption increased 3.4 per cent; and coal consumption was up 8.0 per cent. During the first seven months of 1979, Americans consumed 46.5 quadrillion British thermal units (B.T.U.'s) of all forms of energy, up from 45.7 quadrillion B.T.U.'s in 1978.

Cabinet Change. Growing criticism of U.S. Department of Energy (DOE) policies led to the resignation on July 20 of James R. Schlesinger, who had served as DOE secretary since the department's creation in 1977. Charles W. Duncan, Jr., deputy secretary of defense, was named new DOE secretary. See DUNCAN, CHARLES WILLIAM, JR.

New Energy Fixes. A major advance in storage-battery technology was announced on September 25

ENGINEERING

by General Motors Corporation (GM). The advance allows powerful zinc-nickel oxide batteries to be recharged repeatedly without deterioration, and brought GM closer to a firm decision to market a small electric automobile. Exxon Corporation announced on May 18 the development of a device for reducing the energy consumption of large electric industrial motors. The device, an alternating current synthesizer, allows electric motors to run at variable speeds. Existing alternating current electric motors operate constantly at maximum speed, even when they are under light loads. Exxon estimated that the synthesizer, if put into widespread use, could save the equivalent of 1 million barrels of oil per day by 1990.

Energy Developments Elsewhere. The executive commission of the European Community (Common Market) on June 13 proposed a $50-billion program to conserve energy and expand the use of coal and nuclear power. In July, Spain's government approved a 10-year National Energy Plan to reduce oil consumption to 50 per cent of total national energy consumption. Oil now accounts for 70 per cent of Spain's total energy use. At least 10 nuclear power plants and increased use of coal and natural gas will replace the oil.   Michael Woods

See also COAL; PETROLEUM AND GAS. In WORLD BOOK, see ENERGY; ENERGY SUPPLY.

ENGINEERING. See BUILDING & CONSTRUCTION.

ENVIRONMENT. Citizen environmental groups, which enthusiastically supported President Jimmy Carter in the 1976 election campaign, expressed increasing dismay in 1979 at what they regarded as the weakening of his commitment to environmental causes. The President began to lose significant environmental support on July 15 when he said in his energy address to the nation, "We will protect our environment. But when this nation critically needs a refinery or a pipeline, we will build it."

Environmentalists formed an "energy coalition" to oppose Carter's proposals for a massive crash program to develop a synthetic fuels industry and an Emergency Mobilization Board (EMB). They feared such a board could override environmental laws in the name of an energy crisis. The coalition said on September 26 that an EMB could undermine water rights, public health, and environmental quality. The environmental leaders cited four major issues on which they said the President had taken positions damaging to conservation interests: His signing of legislation forcing completion of the Tellico Dam in Tennessee, which had been delayed five years by a hallmark environmental battle to save the endangered snail darter; endorsement of U.S. Forest Service wilderness designations that opened up 36 million acres (14 million hectares) to lumbering; approval of increased timber cutting on government land; and his proposal to create the EMB.

To dramatize Denver's air pollution problem, Peter Calandruccio, right, operates an "oxygen oasis" downtown. A passer-by pays 25 cents for a sniff.

Three Mile Island. A major accident occurred at the Three Mile Island nuclear power plant near Harrisburg, Pa., on March 28 in which radiation was released (see ENERGY [Close-Up]). This led to demands by some environmental groups that the United States end its dependence on nuclear power. Shouting "No Nukes," a crowd of at least 65,000 protesters heard California Governor Edmund G. (Jerry) Brown, Jr., call reliance on nuclear power "a pathological addiction" at a rally in Washington, D.C., on May 6. More than 200,000 antinuclear protesters gathered in New York City on September 23 in the largest such demonstration in U.S. history.

Energy Conservation. Most environmental groups advocate conservation and solar energy development as solutions to U.S. energy problems. The Environmental Defense Fund said on August 29 that Americans could save 5 million barrels of oil daily by the late 1980s through a crash conservation program costing about one-third less than President Carter's $142-billion energy plan. While approving of conservation as part of the attack on energy shortages, industry sources said that development of new domestic supplies was also vital.

A hot debate continued on energy and other economic costs of environmental regulations. Industry sources attacked "regulatory overkill" and urged that the nation establish a better balance between energy and environmental objectives.

The Environmental Protection Agency (EPA) said on October 9 that federal programs to control pollution will cost government and business more than $360 billion between 1977 and 1986. The EPA also cited studies indicating that air pollution results in disease costing about $36 billion a year.

Air Pollution. Tough new federal standards limiting pollution from coal-fired power plants to be built in the future were issued on May 25 by EPA. Despite EPA's effort to balance competing energy and environmental concerns, the regulations – described as the most controversial and important ever issued by the agency – were challenged by both conservation and utility interests.

The new standard required the utility industry to cut air pollution from new coal-fired plants in half. Less stringent than the rules proposed in September 1978, the standards retained the current emissions ceiling of 1.2 pounds (0.5 kilogram) of sulfur per million British thermal units, but required plants to remove 70 to 90 per cent of the sulfur from emissions.

Environmentalists attacked the standard as a weak compromise. The Environmental Defense Fund charged the rules were developed under "raw political pressure" exerted by Senate Majority Leader Robert C. Byrd (D., W.Va.) on behalf of high-sulfur-coal interests. Utility spokesmen said scrubbers cannot operate efficiently enough to comply.

President Carter warned in his comprehensive environmental message to Congress on August 2 that efforts to improve the environment cannot be confined to U.S. national boundaries. Citing estimates that the world's forests are disappearing at alarming rates, he said forest losses in or near the tropics threaten severe environmental damage.

Acid Rain. Carter also noted the serious damage caused in many places by acid rain, precipitation carrying acidlike pollutants. He said that over the past 25 years, the acidity of rainfall has increased as much as 50-fold in parts of the eastern half of the United States. The President established a 10-year program for acid rain research.

The Canadian government met with U.S. environmental officials on August 10 to demand that the United States speed negotiation of an air pollution treaty to curb acid rain damage. John Fraser, Canada's environmental minister, said that a main cause of Canada's acid rain is sulfur dioxide carried over the border from industrial plants in the United States. The U.S. officials agreed, but said sulfur dioxide also comes from Canada, adding that it kills fish in at least 90 lakes in New York's Adirondack Mountains.

Mexican Oil Spill. A Mexican oil well in the Gulf of Mexico blew out on June 3 and caused the world's largest oil spill. The runaway Ixtoc I well in Campe-

The Ixtoc I oil well in Mexico's Bay of Campeche still burns in August after blowing out in June and causing the world's largest oil spill.

che Bay dumped more than 100 million gallons (380 million liters) of oil into the ocean before being brought partially under control on October 18. Oil from the spill hit Texas beaches in August and threatened marine environments before gulf currents shifted to the south on August 30.

Hazardous Wastes. Responding to a number of revelations about the dangers to public health posed by uncontrolled dumping of toxic chemicals, President Carter asked Congress on June 13 for legislation to help correct the problem. The White House called the proposal the most important environmental legislation to be proposed by the Administration in 1979. It would establish a $1.6-billion fund over a four-year period to clean up hazardous waste dumps and the effects of oil and chemical spills. Fees imposed on oil refineries and chemical manufacturers would produce about 80 per cent of the fund.

The EPA estimates that there are 33,000 to 50,000 dumpsites in the United States that may contain some hazardous wastes.

Hooker Chemical Company agreed on October 24 to spend at least $15 million to clean up a hazardous waste disposal site that has been leaking pesticide residue into an arm of Lake Michigan. Michigan authorities said the landmark settlement was the largest of its kind, but they had originally asked for $220 million.

New York state filed criminal charges against a Hooker division on August 31 for illegally dumping more than 1.5 million pounds (680,000 kilograms) of toxic wastes annually in the Bethpage, N.Y., municipal landfill. The U.S. Department of Justice filed suit on December 20 against Hooker asking more than $124 million in damages. The suit charged Hooker with dumping hazardous wastes in the Love Canal area of Niagara Falls, N.Y.

In the most widespread chemical contamination incident on record, federal investigators traced animal feed and agricultural products tainted with polychlorinated biphenyl (PCB) to at least 17 states in September. The contamination resulted when PCB leaked from a damaged transformer in a Billings, Mont., packing plant and became mixed with animal feed.

Manufacture of PCB was banned by the EPA in 1976, after it was reported to cause cancer in laboratory animals. The chemical is still found in many electrical transformers that are filled with oil containing PCB. Federal officials said the Billings incident demonstrated the multiplication effect when even a small amount of the banned chemical gets into the food chain.

Law of the Sea. The United Nations Conference on the Law of the Sea concluded its 1979 sessions on August 24 without agreeing on the long-sought treaty. See OCEAN.   Andrew L. Newman

See also CONSERVATION. In WORLD BOOK, see ENVIRONMENT; ENVIRONMENTAL POLLUTION.

EQUATORIAL GUINEA. President Macias Nguema Biyogo Negue Ndong, who headed one of Africa's most repressive governments for 11 years, was deposed on Aug. 3, 1979, in a military coup d'état led by Deputy Defense Minister Obiang Nguema Mbasogo. Macias Nguema had been president since the country became independent from Spain in 1968.

The deposed dictator fled to the jungle, where he was captured on August 18. With seven officials of his government, he was executed on September 29 after being convicted of mass murder, treason, and misuse of government funds.

Macias Nguema was thought to have been responsible for the deaths of as many as 50,000 Equatorial Guineans. During his rule, several thousand of his countrymen were imprisoned for political reasons, and thousands of others were forced to work on the country's cacao and coffee plantations. The new government, a military junta led by Mbasogo, released political prisoners and issued an invitation to return to an estimated 100,000 exiles – about one-third of Equatorial Guinea's population.

Mbasogo's immediate priorities were to rebuild the economy and repair foreign relations. Exports of the country's principal crop, cacao, dropped to 10 per cent of the 1968 level in 1979.   John D. Esseks

See also AFRICA (Facts in Brief Table). In WORLD BOOK, see EQUATORIAL GUINEA.

ETHIOPIA faced armed secessionist movements in three parts of the nation in 1979. Guerrillas struck in Eritrea, a northern province bordering on the Red Sea; Tigre province, south of Eritrea; and Ogaden in the southeast, bordering on Somalia.

The Eritrean separatist movement was strengthened by the merger on January 27 of two rival factions – the Eritrean Liberation Front and the Eritrean People's Liberation Front. They started joint military operations against government forces in June. The rebel forces held the towns of Nafka and Karora and much of the surrounding countryside, and resisted an attack by a government force of 50,000 mounted by Provisional Military Government Chairman Mengistu Haile Mariam.

Another secessionist force, the Tigre People's Liberation Front, captured five government garrison towns along Tigre's main north-south road in July. The Western Somali Liberation Front, seeking to unite Ogaden with Somalia instead of Ethiopia, claimed in April that its forces had ambushed and killed more than 200 government soldiers.

In early February, Mengistu launched a "National Revolutionary Development" campaign to revive the war-damaged economy. His government had received promises of long-term, low-interest loans from Communist countries.   John D. Esseks

See also AFRICA (Facts in Brief Table). In WORLD BOOK, see ETHIOPIA.

EUROPE

The first European Parliament elected by the citizens of member nations holds its first meeting in Strasbourg, France, on July 17.

Citizens of the nine European Community (EC or Common Market) countries elected the members of the European Parliament for the first time in June 1979. Two European countries also chose women prime ministers for the first time – Margaret R. Thatcher in Great Britain and Maria de Lurdes Pintassilgo in Portugal (see PORTUGAL; THATCHER, MARGARET R.). The EC established the European Monetary System (EMS) in March, after some delay, to stabilize member countries' currencies, and

struggled with problems of energy, nuclear safety, and unemployment in the steel industry.

Conservative Swing. The June parliamentary elections indicated a swing to the right throughout Europe, though the EC voter turnout was lighter than expected – just over 60 per cent of the electorate of 180 million. Conservatives won 60 of the 78 seats in England, Scotland, and Wales, and Christian Democrats matched their success in Belgium, Luxembourg, the Netherlands, and West Germany.

315

Centrist supporters of President Valéry Giscard d'Estaing won in France. The elections gave the Socialists the most members, 109. The Christian Democrats were next, with 107, followed by Liberals and Democrats with 40 each; European Progressive Democrats with 22; European Conservatives with 63; Communists and their allies with 46; and 23 members who were not attached to any party. The national governments had appointed members of the previous Parliaments.

Parliament's first task was to choose a president. Giscard d'Estaing sponsored France's Minister of Health Simone Veil, and she won on the second ballot with 192 votes to 138 for Italian Socialist Mario Zagari and 47 for Italian Communist Giorgi Amendola. See VEIL, SIMONE.

Budget Split. The EC member countries started the year with a squabble over a constitutional issue – Parliament's decision to increase the regional aid fund by $675 million. Denmark, France, and Great Britain pointed out that the increase was greater than Parliament was allowed to make and withheld part of their EC contributions. The Commission, the EC's ruling body, decided to take those three countries before the Court of Justice, the EC's supreme court. Great Britain's Prime Minister James Callaghan made the situation worse during his campaign for the British general election when he said that Britain's contribution to the EC was much too high. He said that Great Britain might cut its EC contributions after 1981 if the EC did not change its policies. Only Italy among other EC members supported Callaghan's view. Callaghan received support on March 27 when the Commission published the 1978 contributions. Great Britain had paid $1.5 billion and Italy $1.2 billion, compared with Germany's $537 million.

When the British Conservative Party took office in May, Chancellor of the Exchequer Sir Geoffrey Howe echoed Callaghan's criticism of the EC contributions. So leaders of the nine member nations instructed the Commission on June 21 to recommend reforms. The EC faced its worst crisis after a Dublin, Ireland, summit meeting in November. Thatcher warned that she was not afraid to "precipitate a crisis" when the EC leaders refused to cut most of Great Britain's projected $2 billion contribution to the 1980-1981 budget and offered her only a $729.3 million cut. But Thatcher agreed not to act until the next summit meeting in February.

Parliament plunged the EC into another crisis on December 13 by rejecting the 1980 budget. Until Parliament approves a budget, the EC must limit its monthly expenses in 1980 to one-twelfth of total spending for 1979.

Steel and Energy. The EC launched a cash-grant plan for Europe's hard-hit steelmakers on May 3 and began a program to slash overtime so that many of the 6.5 million unemployed persons throughout the EC could get jobs. Without such action, the Commission estimated that 15 million persons out of a labor force of 115 million would be unemployed by 1985. Europe's steelmakers laid off 100,000 workers between 1974 and 1978, and output fell 20 per cent.

Abrupt, heavy increases in the price of oil and the Iranian revolution, which stopped the flow of oil from that country, caused a continuing European oil crisis. The EC nations agreed on March 13 to cut 1979 oil consumption by 5 per cent to 500 million metric tons (550 million short tons) and to cut their oil imports to 50 per cent of the oil consumed by 1985, in line with an earlier decision by the International Energy Agency, representing the West's main oil-producing nations.

The EC would reduce its dependency on imports by conserving energy, by using coal instead of oil, and by using more nuclear power. The 24-nation Organization for Economic Cooperation and Development (OECD) reported on August 8 that consumer prices in Western countries rose by an annual rate of 11.8 per cent in the first half of 1979, mainly because of oil price hikes.

Nuclear Fears. The March 28 accident at the Three Mile Island nuclear power plant near Harrisburg, Pa., increased environmentalists' fear of such plants, so the European Commission set up a committee of experts on May 3 to report on European

European Parliament Members

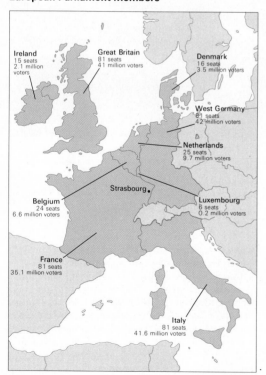

Ireland
15 seats
2.1 million voters

Great Britain
81 seats
41 million voters

Denmark
16 seats
3.5 million voters

West Germany
81 seats
42 million voters

Netherlands
25 seats
9.7 million voters

Strasbourg.

Belgium
24 seats
6.6 million voters

Luxembourg
6 seats
0.2 million voters

France
81 seats
35.1 million voters

Italy
81 seats
41.6 million voters

Facts in Brief on the European Countries

Country	Population	Government	Monetary Unit*	Foreign Trade (million U.S. $) Exports†	Imports†
Albania	2,868,000	Communist Party First Secretary Enver Hoxha; People's Assembly Presidium Chairman Haxhi Lleshi; Prime Minister Mehmet Shehu	lek (7 = $1)	149	248
Andorra	37,000	The bishop of Urgel, Spain, and the president of France	French franc & Spanish peseta	no statistics available	
Austria	7,574,000	President Rudolf Kirchschlaeger; Chancellor Bruno Kreisky	schilling (12.5 = $1)	12,205	16,013
Belgium	10,048,000	King Baudouin I; Prime Minister Wilfried Martens	franc (28.2 = $1)	44,300 (includes Luxembourg)	46,391
Bulgaria	8,995,000	Communist Party First Secretary & State Council Chairman Todor Zhivkov; Prime Minister Stanko Todorov	lev (1 = $1.13)	7,448	7,617
Czechoslovakia	15,340,000	Communist Party General Secretary & President Gustav Husak; Prime Minister Lubomir Strougal	koruna (10.4 = $1)	12,322	12,560
Denmark	5,155,000	Queen Margrethe II; Prime Minister Anker Henrik Jorgensen	krone (5.3 = $1)	11,886	14,810
Finland	4,803,000	President Urho Kekkonen; Prime Minister Mauno Koivisto	markka (3.7 = $1)	8,618	7,864
France	54,412,000	President Valéry Giscard d'Estaing; Prime Minister Raymond Barre	franc (4.1 = $1)	76,609	81,715
Germany, East	16,585,000	Communist Party Secretary General & State Council Chairman Erich Honecker; Prime Minister Willi Stoph	mark (1.8 = $1)	13,267	14,572
Germany, West	61,991,000	President Karl Carstens; Chancellor Helmut Schmidt	Deutsche mark (1.7 = $1)	142,090	120,668
Great Britain	56,326,000	Queen Elizabeth II; Prime Minister Margaret R. Thatcher	pound (1 = $2.19)	71,691	78,557
Greece	9,424,000	President Constantine Tsatsos; Prime Minister Constantine Karamanlis	drachma (37.4 = $1)	3,354	7,647
Hungary	10,767,000	Communist Party First Secretary Janos Kadar; President Pal Losonczi; Prime Minister Gyorgy Lazar	forint (20.3 = $1)	6,350	7,898
Iceland	232,000	President Kristjan Eldjarn; Acting Prime Minister Benedikt Grondal	krona (380 = $1)	641	674
Ireland	3,317,000	President Patrick J. Hillery; Prime Minister Charles J. Haughey	pound (1 = $2.14)	5,678	7,097
Italy	58,009,000	President Alessandro Pertini; Prime Minister Francesco Cossiga	lira (815.1 = $1)	56,055	56,446
Liechtenstein	26,000	Prince Franz Josef II; Prime Minister Hans Brunhart	Swiss franc	no statistics available	
Luxembourg	371,000	Grand Duke Jean; Prime Minister Pierre Werner	franc (28.2 = $1)	44,300 (includes Belgium)	46,391
Malta	335,000	President Anton Buttigieg; Prime Minister Dom Mintoff	pound (1 = $2.89)	355	593
Monaco	26,000	Prince Rainier III	French franc	no statistics available	
Netherlands	14,272,000	Queen Juliana; Prime Minister Andreas A. M. Van Agt	guilder (1.9 = $1)	50,280	53,812
Norway	4,124,000	King Olav V; Prime Minister Odvar Nordli	krone (4.9 = $1)	10,037	11,420
Poland	35,616,000	Communist Party First Secretary Edward Gierek; President Henryk Jablonski; Council of Ministers Chairman Piotr Jaroszewicz	zloty (30.6 = $1)	13,361	15,121
Portugal	9,904,000	President Antonio dos Santos Ramalho Eanes; Prime Minister Francisco Sá Carneiro	escudo (49.8 = $1)	2,355	5,174
Romania	22,317,000	Communist Party General Secretary & President Nicolae Ceausescu; Prime Minister Ilie Verdet	leu (4.5 = $1)	7,021	7,018
Russia	269,306,000	Communist Party General Secretary & Supreme Soviet Presidium Chairman Leonid Ilich Brezhnev; Council of Ministers Chairman Aleksey Nikolayevich Kosygin	ruble (1 = $1.55)	52,176	50,546
San Marino	21,000	2 captains regent appointed by Grand Council every 6 months	Italian lira	no statistics available	
Spain	37,580,000	King Juan Carlos I; President Adolfo Suarez Gonzalez	peseta (66.2 = $1)	13,115	18,708
Sweden	8,354,000	King Carl XVI Gustaf; Prime Minister Thorbjorn Falldin	krona (4.2 = $1)	21,560	20,123
Switzerland	6,448,000	President Georges-André Chevellaz	franc (1.6 = $1)	23,561	23,804
Turkey	45,794,000	President Fahri S. Koruturk; Prime Minister Suleyman Demirel	lira (47.1 = $1)	2,288	4,597
Yugoslavia	22,347,000	President Josip Broz Tito; Prime Minister Veselin Djuranovic	dinar (19.1 = $1)	5,659	9,987

*Exchange rates as of Dec. 1, 1979. †Latest available data.

317

reactor safety by the end of 1979. The OECD's nuclear energy agency forecast on July 2 that nuclear reactors would generate 34 per cent of the electricity used by developed nations by the year 2000, and that the use of oil would decrease from the present 19 per cent to 10 per cent. But OECD warned those nations to restore balance between oil supply and demand, or risk inflation that could bring on a recession as severe as that experienced in 1974 and 1975.

EMS Delayed. France blocked the start of the EMS, scheduled for Jan. 1, 1979, in a dispute over farm subsidies. France feared that the EMS would depress prices paid to French farmers, and demanded gradual phasing out of farm subsidies, the "green currency" system that costs the EC $2.2 billion per year. The EC compromised on agricultural compensation on March 12, and EMS began on March 13. Eight currencies – all those of the EC except the British pound – were fixed at the previous day's exchange rates. The EMS limited fluctuations in member countries' currency-exchange rates to 2.25 per cent, except for the more volatile Italian lira, which may fluctuate 6 per cent. The EC intends for the EMS to lead to a European Monetary Fund with a new currency, the European Currency Unit, in 1981.

The EMS's first effect was a sharp rise in the British pound until the Bank of England intervened. This intervention led Ireland to break the long-established equality of that currency and its own pound on March 30. Another early pressure on EMS was the Danish krone's rise above its permitted level. Great Britain's new Conservative government repeatedly postponed a decision on full EMS participation. Prime Minister Thatcher said she would await an EC review of EMS, due in late 1979, before deciding.

The EMS finance ministers raised the value of West Germany's Deutsche mark 5 per cent against Denmark's krone and 2 per cent against the other six currencies on September 24. In November, Denmark devalued the krone 5 per cent against the other EMS currencies because it had declined too much against the mark.

Farm Pricing Dispute. A dispute between France and West Germany over farm subsidies threatened the Commission's plans to freeze support prices for 1979 and 1980. France wanted the EC to discontinue monetary compensation amounts – subsidies and taxes that neutralize the effect that currency fluctuations have on farm prices. West Germany blocked the move because it would have cut West German farmers' incomes, and Great Britain demanded a total freeze on farm prices. The Commission advanced a compromise on March 7 that would have given British, French, and Italian farmers a 5 per cent increase but would have taxed overproduced milk progressively. But British Minister of Agricul-

ture John E. Silkin insisted that the EC freeze farm prices for four years to stop overproduction of milk, butter, and sugar. Great Britain capitulated on June 21 when EC farm ministers agreed to a 1.5 per cent average increase on all farm products except milk. The agreement was expected to increase dairy surpluses. Britain came off best with a 5 per cent devaluation of the "green pound," an artificial exchange that converts prices from European to national currency, but this caused a 3 per cent hike in food prices in Britain.

NATO Birthday. The 15-nation North Atlantic Treaty Organization (NATO) celebrated the treaty's 30th anniversary in 1979. United States Army General Alexander M. Haig, Jr., supreme commander of Allied forces in Europe, resigned on June 30 and was succeeded by U.S. Army General Bernard W. Rogers. Russia's nuclear build-up worried NATO leaders, so Western defense ministers agreed on April 24 to increase their own retaliatory force and to decide on new weapons by 1980. The growing threat of Russia's SS-20 medium-range missile, and the shorter-range SS-21, were likely to be matched by a long-range version of the U.S. Pershing 2 and ground-launched cruise missiles.

NATO defense ministers, meeting in Brussels, Belgium, agreed on May 15 to continue annual increases in defense spending well into the mid-1980s. Most NATO countries have agreed to raise defense spending by 3 per cent per year in constant dollars until 1985.

Russia's Supreme Soviet Presidium Chairman Leonid I. Brezhnev announced a troop and tank pullback on October 6 during a Berlin ceremony marking East Germany's 30th anniversary. Brezhnev said that Russia would withdraw up to 20,000 soldiers and 1,000 tanks from East Germany in the next 12 months and was ready to withdraw SS-20's from Eastern Europe. But he warned West Germany against deploying new U.S. missiles that could reach targets in Russia. Meeting in Brussels in December, NATO decided to place hundreds of U.S.-made Tomahawk nuclear missiles in Western Europe, beginning in 1983.

SALT Accord. U.S. President Jimmy Carter and Brezhnev signed the second Strategic Arms Limitation Treaty (SALT II) on June 18 in Vienna, Austria. The agreement, which runs until 1985 if ratified by the U.S. Senate, limits each side initially to 2,400 strategic weapons – missiles and long-range bombers – and 2,250 by the end of 1981. Neither side may introduce more than one type of intercontinental ballistic missile under the treaty (see ARMED FORCES). However, Soviet military intervention in Afghanistan in December hurt the treaty's chances.

Mountbatten Murdered. Irish Republican Army (IRA) terrorists killed Earl Mountbatten of Burma, a World War II hero and cousin of Great Britain's Queen Elizabeth II, his grandson, and another boy on August 27. The mother-in-law of Mountbatten's daughter died the next day. The IRA used a time bomb to blow up the Mountbatten fishing boat off County Sligo in Ireland. The terrorists also ambushed and killed 18 British soldiers in Northern Ireland on August 27.

Iceland's Ruling Coalition of Progressives, Marxists, and Social Democrats collapsed in October, and Social Democrat Benedikt Grondal took over as head of a caretaker government, succeeding Progressive Prime Minister Olafur Johannesson. National elections on December 4 failed to produce a majority party, so Grondal continued in office while the leading parties tried to form a new coalition.

COMECON Switch. The prime ministers of the Communist bloc's Council for Mutual Economic Assistance (COMECON), which also celebrated its 30th anniversary in 1979, signed an agreement on atomic power equipment in Moscow on June 29. The agreement paves the way for changing from oil to nuclear power from 1981 through 1990. Russia promised to increase deliveries of fuel and electric power to COMECON countries.   Kenneth Brown

See also the various European country articles. In WORLD BOOK, see EUROPE; EUROPEAN COMMUNITY; NORTH ATLANTIC TREATY ORGANIZATION (NATO).

EXPLOSION. See DISASTERS.

FARM AND FARMING. Agriculture in the United States enjoyed a second consecutive prosperous year in 1979. Records or near-records abounded – in total farm income, total production of all crops, agricultural exports, farm loans, foodgrain stocks, and fertilizer use.

Such a prosperous year for U.S. agriculture was not expected and came mainly because it was a disappointing year for world agriculture. Even though world grain production was near record levels, the decrease from 1978's total was the largest from one year to the next in recent times. Erratic weather sharply reduced agricultural production in eastern Europe, India, and Russia and adversely affected soybean, feed grain, and wheat harvests in the Southern Hemisphere.

Russian sunflower production was hit by bad weather for the second year in succession. South Korea had a shortfall in rice. Canada and Australia had grain transportation and handling problems. Developing countries generally had trouble meeting production goals. Even so, the demand for food increased throughout the world and, with production down in many countries, the bountiful U.S. production was much in demand.

Two Key Questions bothered U.S. agricultural experts at the end of the year: "How long will the good times last?" and "What problems lie ahead for

A caravan of farm tractors from the Southwest makes its way to Washington, D.C., to join others in a protest against low farm prices.

California consumers reaped some benefit from a June truckers' strike as merchants sought to unload the produce that they could not ship east.

agriculture?'' And potential problems did exist. United States consumer resistance to increased food prices raised the possibility that public support would dwindle for the high level of farm exports that boosted resultant farm prices as well as incomes. Also, the U.S. transportation system had serious bottlenecks in moving big harvests. Labor shutdowns occurred in the key Lake Superior ports of Duluth, Minn., and Superior, Wis., and on the Rock Island Line. Railroad inadequacies generally created problems, and there was a barge bottleneck at the Locks and Dam 26 near Alton, Ill., on the Mississippi River.

Conservationists were concerned about soil and water conditions. Secretary of Agriculture Bob Bergland spoke of this concern on November 1 when he urged farmers to plant only their best-protected lands to crops and save the rest for future generations. Other problems included the continued trend toward larger and larger farms and food processors, the increase in foreign ownership of U.S. farmland, a report questioning the legal powers of agricultural cooperatives, and the fact that in 1979 – for the first time – more of the consumer's dollar went to the food processing and distribution industries than to the farmers.

U.S. Farm Output set many new records in 1979. Crop output was 9 per cent above the previous high of 1978. Major crops that set new production records

included wheat, soybeans, corn, rice, citrus fruits, oilseeds, and peanuts. Soybeans were up 20 per cent to 2.2 billion bushels; corn up 7 per cent to 7.6 billion bushels; rice up 4 per cent to 140 million hundredweight (6.3 million metric tons); and peanuts up 1 per cent to 4 billion pounds (1.8 million metric tons). Substantial production increases were also recorded for cotton, up 34 per cent; grain sorghum, up 10 per cent; and wheat, up 18 per cent. Potato production fell 7 per cent, and tobacco production was down 20 per cent, the smallest crop since 1943.

The record U.S. crop output was achieved despite actual drops in acres planted in some crops, including corn and grain sorghum. Continually improving production practices plus favorable weather conditions resulted in record yields for corn at 109.2 bushels per acre (0.4 hectare), grain sorghum at 63.7 bushels per acre, and soybeans at 31.8 bushels per acre.

Livestock output in the United States was also high. Pork production increased 15 per cent, and broiler chickens were up 11 per cent. Beef production dropped 12 per cent primarily because farmers held cattle off the market as breeding stock to expand herds. The number of cattle on U.S. farms increased during 1979 after declining steadily since 1975.

Farm Prices continued the upward movement started in 1978 despite continuing increases in production. Overall, prices received by farmers were up 10 per cent in November 1979, compared with the previous November. Livestock prices rose 9 per cent, and crop prices went up 11 per cent. Livestock prices were up for all major items except hogs, which sold for $34.40 per hundredweight (45.4 kilograms) in November 1979, compared with $47.30 in November 1978. Selling prices were at or above 1978 levels for all major crops except soybeans, which dropped to $6.36 per bushel in November 1979 from $6.41 in November 1978.

Farm Labor. The farm work force was 3.9 million workers in October 1979, down 3 per cent. Family labor made up the majority of the farm-labor force, accounting for 64 per cent of all farmworkers. Wage rates for hired farm labor averaged $3.56 per hour, up 37 cents from 1978.

Agricultural Trade. The dollar value of both farm exports and imports increased 17 per cent, giving the United States an agricultural-trade surplus of $15.8-billion, the largest on record. Exports rose $4.7-billion to a record $32 billion, while imports reached $16.2 billion, up from $13.9 billion. Trade volume also grew, though less rapidly than dollar value due to rising prices. Export volume was at a record 137.5 million metric tons (151.5 million short tons), up 4 per·cent. Since 1971, U.S. farm export volume has doubled and dollar volume has quadrupled. Grain and feed exports accounted for $13.6 billion, up 16 per cent; oil seeds and products, primarily soybeans, were up 17 per cent to $8.7 billion; and livestock, dairy, and poultry products were up 28 per cent to $3.6 billion.

World Production. World grain production totaled 1.39 billion metric tons (1.53 billion short tons), down 4 per cent from the 1978 record.

A significant reduction in European and Russian crops more than offset the higher U.S. output. Bad weather reduced total grain output in Russia to 175 million metric tons (193 million short tons), down 26 per cent from 1978. The drop in world grain production resulted from a 9 per cent reduction in wheat and a 2 per cent decline in coarse grains. Rice production fell 3 per cent. World production gains were registered in soybeans, up 17 per cent; cotton, up 7 per cent; and coffee, up 3 per cent.

World meat production in 1979 was about equal to that in 1978. Beef production was down about 7 per cent, but increased pork and broiler production made up the difference.

U.S. Farm Finances improved in 1979, and total farm income was $32 billion, the second largest in history and more than 10 per cent above that of 1978. Total production costs jumped about 16 per cent in 1979 to $114 billion, but cash receipts also were up by 16 per cent to $129 billion.

The total value of farm assets stood at $950 billion, up 16 per cent from the year before and three times that in 1969. Farm real estate made up 75 per cent of that total. Farm debt outstanding at the end of 1979 was up 15 per cent, with farm real estate debt making up over 50 per cent of that.

Farmers' off-farm income exceeded last year's record $34.3 billion and contributed more than 50 per cent of the total farm family income.

Farm Policy was not a big issue in 1979. Bergland announced several policy decisions on wheat, feed grains, and credit in late March, but these were primarily adjustments and operating decisions determined by existing legislation. He said that those were "the only major changes that will be accepted for the 1979 program," and that position mainly set the tone for the year.

Congress on August 14 passed the International

Agricultural Statistics, 1979

World Crop Production
(million units)

Crop	Units	1978	1979	% U.S.
Corn	Metric tons	358.7	405.8	47.8
Wheat	Metric tons	438.8	400.6	14.4
Rice	Metric tons	386.0	373.2	1.7
Barley	Metric tons	178.6	161.5	4.8
Oats	Metric tons	48.8	44.6	17.3
Rye	Metric tons	26.3	21.6	3.0
Soybeans	Metric tons	80.9	94.4	63.8
Cotton	Bales**	59.8	63.8	22.5
Coffee	Bags***	76.8	79.3	0.3
Sugar (centrifugal)	Metric tons	91.3	87.7	5.8

**480 lbs. (217.7 kilograms) net
***132.276 lbs. (60 kilograms)

Output of Major U.S. Crops
(millions of bushels)

Crop	1962–1966*	1978	1979**
Corn	3,876	7,082	7,586
Sorghums	595	748	825
Oats	912	601	531
Wheat	1,229	1,799	2,114
Soybeans	769	1,870	2,236
Rice (a)	742	1,338	1,396
Potatoes (b)	275	365	348
Cotton (c)	140	109	145
Tobacco (d)	2,126	2,025	1,611

*Average; **Preliminary

(a) 100,000 cwt. (4.54 million kilograms)

(b) 1 million cwt. (45.4 million kilograms)

(c) 100,000 bales (50 million lbs.) (22.7 million kilograms)

(d) 1 million lbs. (454,000 kilograms)

U.S. Production of Animal Products
(millions of pounds)

	1957–59*	1978	1979**
Beef	13,704	23,936	20,822
Veal	1,240	611	413
Lamb & Mutton	711	309	281
Pork	10,957	13,164	15,184
Eggs (a)	5,475	5,596	5,751
Turkey	1,382	1,983	2,216
Total Milk (b)	123	122	122
Chicken (total)	4,880	10,850	11,929
Broilers	4,430	10,183	11,213

*Average; **Preliminary

(a) 1 million dozens

(b) Billions of lbs. (454 million kilograms)

Farmers plowed lettuce crops under in California's Salinas Valley when a truck strike and inadequate rail transport slowed their shipment to markets.

Development and Cooperation Act of 1979, which coordinated U.S. technical assistance to other countries. Speaking at the United Nation's 20th Food and Agriculture Organization (FAO) conference in Rome on November 13, Bergland announced that "U.S. bilateral assistance will emphasize those programs which increase food security in developing countries and make food supplies more available to the poor and nutritionally vulnerable." Such a commitment places the problem of developing and maintaining food reserves increasingly in the center of crop price and income policy.

The international trade negotiations conducted for six years under the auspices of the General Agreement on Tariffs and Trade (GATT) were completed in 1979. Delegates at the Rome FAO Conference echoed the U.S. disappointment that GATT had not achieved an international wheat or grain agreement. However, many GATT provisions affected U.S. agriculture, mainly by liberalizing trade. One provision established an International Agriculture Council as a forum for discussion of ongoing agricultural policy issues.

The European Community Council of Agricultural Ministers increased 1979-1980 farm commodity support prices 1.5 per cent for all commodities except milk. Recent annual support increases have averaged 6 per cent, but changes in currency conversion rates offset part of the difference.

Most other agricultural policy issues were unresolved at year's end. Policy bills still pending in Congress could affect meat imports, sugar, energy, natural disasters, natural resource management, and foreign ownership of U.S. land.

Farm Technology. Research on plants progressed in many countries. Calvin O. Qualset, an agronomy researcher at the University of California, Davis, and C. W. Wrigley of the Commonwealth Scientific and Industrial Research Organization's Wheat Research Unit in Sydney, Australia, demonstrated the use of *electrophoresis* (the analysis of molecular structures) to identify wheat varieties. C. R. Krause, a Department of Agriculture (USDA) plant pathologist at the Nursery Crops Research Laboratory in Delaware, Ohio, used an electron microscope to produce a three-dimensional image, magnified 200,000 times, on a television screen to identify elm varieties, and he is experimenting with other plants. The technique may improve plant-breeding techniques, worldwide plant-identification procedures, and grading techniques for use in international trade, as well as helping to protect plant breeders' legal rights.

Computer Marketing techniques for agricultural products also improved. By using computers, bids and offers from many buyers and sellers can be assembled and compared, eliminating the need for bringing buyers, sellers, and products to a physical market. More important than the savings, however, this technique will be a key to maintaining a competitive market in agriculture. A computerized cotton market called Telcot, developed by the Plains Cotton Cooperative Association in Lubbock, Tex., now links 150 cotton gins in two states with 40 buyers' offices.

Another computer is being used in a United States Department of Agriculture (USDA) pilot experiment to see if the system can be used to sell meat products, a market in which pricing has been highly controversial for a long time. Systems are being tested for the sale of live animals, eggs, and livestock products.

One important development in 1979 was the increased manufacture of gasohol, a mixture of gasoline and alcohol. The process converts everything from corn to manure to crop residues into usable energy. Both the techniques and the economics are controversial, but gasohol could provide a large farm market and a substantial source of energy. No fewer than 20 bills on gasohol were introduced in Congress during the year. USDA earmarked $6 million for gasohol research and $42.7-million in loan guarantees to build four pilot plants. Good consumer acceptance of gasohol was reported in several states.   Charles E. French and Larry L. Nelson

See also FOOD. In WORLD BOOK, see AGRICULTURE; FARM AND FARMING.

FARM MACHINERY. See MANUFACTURING.

FASHION grew up in 1979. The new assured attitude of a more dressed-up look was epitomized by the tailored suit, the pivotal garment of the year. Crisp and clean by day, soft and sensuous by night, the silhouette was uncompromisingly adult. It was a dramatic change from the casual air of sportswear, which had been a fashion mainstay throughout most of the 1970s. Trim, curve-conscious tailoring, with narrow waist and slimmer skirts, and such new details as peplums and defined shoulders, enabled women to create a look entirely different from the tossed-together, studied carelessness of past seasons.

With formality becoming important, basic sportswear components, such as blazers and pants or skirts, became more closely related even if they were not made of matching fabrics. They, too, resembled suits rather than separates. The trend started in 1978 with nostalgically derivative, almost comic, clothes referred to as the "Retro Look," that echoed such 1940s fashion themes as heavily padded shoulders. To complete the look, hats were seen on many previously bare heads, and even seamed stockings reappeared. But eccentric, campy individualism faded quickly. It evolved into an elegant style that prided itself on having the look of "power."

Fashion in 1979 was mainly the designers' response to the unprecedented upward movement of women in the work force. Increasingly, designers realized that their future customers would be working women rather than rich men's wives. Statistics presented the main clue. For the first time in United States history, some observers predicted that more women would be working outside the home in 1980 than in it. To the alert businessmen-designers, this fact pointed to a strong new market. They believed that women pursuing careers would be inclined to want to look up to date and to wear clothes that fit comfortably into the corporate world. The clothes would have to project an image of competence and self-confidence and, at the same time, femininity.

The Emerging Executive Woman had at least one tailored suit in her closet. The jacket was either short and shapely or long and lean. The somewhat straight skirt, slim over the hips, had a knee-length hemline or a front or side slit that put new emphasis on the legs. The enlarged shoulders on jackets were never angular, and exaggeratedly feminine accessories dispelled any implications of austerity or masculinity. Flirtatious hats and recklessly high heels added whimsy. Frivolously ruffled blouses, lace-collared shirts, sleek pullovers in handsome textures, or revealingly dipped camisoles were ready to emerge from under the tailored jackets.

After the suit, the novelty sweater was the most important ingredient. It was not for warmth alone, though thick, hand-knit styles were popularized by Perry Ellis, Geoffrey Beene, and Ralph Lauren. Beading, sequins, ribbon trims, and off-shoulder and asymmetric treatments were examples of the highly innovative ways angora, alpaca, cashmere, wool, and sparkling metallic yarns were knitted to emphasize the female form. Because these sweaters were so costly to buy, many women made their own.

Ultimate Color Combinations for 1979 were red and black, black and white, and white and red. The main color catalyst was a vivid purple with its related tones of plum, wine, magenta, fuchsia, and mauve. Gray – strong as steel, deep as charcoal, and soft as a dove – played a prominent role, as did earthy tones mixed in unexpected combinations.

Meltons and tweeds in bright shades expressed the new sophistication of fitted clothes. Redingotes and princess lines were seen, as well as three-quarter-length and seven-eighth-length jackets. Knits returned with slim, belted dresses. Luxurious evening pants, jewellike jackets, bare-armed petal dresses, and asymmetric evening gowns in rich silks and cut velvets with plenty of sparkling bugle beads took the new "mood" fashion to its zenith and allowed women to dazzle by night.

Menswear entered a new sensible era as designers combined strong statements of style with practical ideas and realistic basics. Traditional executive flannels and classic conservative, striped suits were restated with a clean, fad-free approach that stressed broader shoulders and slimmer lapels. The look was confident and versatile with a daring use of color touches and fabric textures initiated by Italy's Giorgio Armani, hailed as the most influential new menswear designer. More and more, business travel influenced a selection of expertly cut tissuelike wool suits that could take a man from city to city and climate to climate for sales calls and conferences. Unlined featherweight jackets in subtle blues, sea-greens, and heathery purples added spice.

Emphasis on physical fitness dictated trimmer waists, slimmer shaped suits, and narrowed-down shirt collars and ties. The rugged, Western look continued to be popular for men and women. Both sexes also turned to vests, parkas, and down-filled coats to provide warmth against the cold reality of petroleum-short country and city life.

The Coty Controversy. Halston and Calvin Klein, two designers who launched beauty products bearing their names in 1979, created a stir when they refused to accept the fashion world's equivalent of the Oscar, an award sponsored by the cosmetics firm of Coty, Incorporated. Nevertheless, the award ceremonies took place on September 27 at the Fashion Institute of Technology in New York City. Mary McFadden was inducted into the Hall of Fame. Winnie awards went to Perry Ellis for women's fashions and to Lee Wright for menswear. Alexander Julian won the Return Award for men's styles. Special awards were given to Barry Kieselstein-Cord for jewelry, to Conrad Bell for men's furs, and to Gil Truedsson for men's shoes.　　　Kathryn Livingston

In WORLD BOOK, see FASHION.

FINLAND. Voters swung to the right in general elections on March 18 and 19, 1979, and Conservatives gained 12 more parliamentary seats. Their total of 47 left them only 5 behind the Social Democrats, and well ahead of the Center Party with 36 and the Communists with 35. President Urho Kekkonen asked Conservative Harri Holkeri to form a government to replace the ruling coalition of Social Democrat Prime Minister Kalevi Sorsa, but he was unable to do so. Mauno Koivisto, a Social Democrat and governor of the Bank of Finland, then formed a coalition of Social Democrats, Centrists, and Communists that took office on May 26 and 27.

On January 9, the government, employers, and unions agreed to increase wages by 11.3 per cent. The government said that this agreement and the 1978 foreign trade surplus of $826 million would increase the nation's growth rate from 3.5 per cent in 1978 to 5 per cent in 1979 and cut unemployment from 8 per cent to 6 per cent.

Finland showed concern over tactical nuclear weapons being developed by the North Atlantic Treaty Organization and Warsaw Pact countries. Finland has a commitment to prevent attacks on Russia through its territory. Kenneth Brown

See also EUROPE (Facts in Brief Table). In WORLD BOOK, see FINLAND.

FIRE. See DISASTERS.

Finland's President Urho Kekkonen votes in March elections that toppled the ruling coalition of Social Democrat Prime Minister Kalevi Sorsa.

FISHING. The International Game Fish Association (IGFA), headquartered in Fort Lauderdale, Fla., in April 1979 announced angling rules for freshwater and saltwater all-tackle and line-class world records. A separate set of rules for saltwater fly fishing was also announced.

The association, which took over management of freshwater record-keeping from *Field and Stream* magazine in 1978, has undertaken a worldwide survey to solicit suggestions for updating rules and world-record requirements for freshwater, saltwater, and fly fishing in all-tackle, line-class, and tippet categories. The American Fishing Tackle Manufacturers Association, noting IGFA's "tremendous international credibility," endorsed IGFA as the official source for freshwater record-keeping.

More than 75 United States boats participated in Cuba's second annual Ernest Hemingway fishing tournament from May 16 to 20. IGFA President E.K. Henry called it "the largest and probably the best organized billfish tournament ever held in North and Central American waters."

New Records. Among the many new fishing records set in 1979 was a 61-pound 4-ounce (28-kilogram) cobia boated off Key West, Fla., in March to set a new 15-pound (7-kilogram) tippet-class world record. Angler Kenny Bittuer of Miami, Fla., fought the fish for almost an hour. The previous record was set in the same waters in 1971 for a 52-pound (24-kilogram) cobia.

Christian McMillan, 17, was the star of the 1979 Hawaiian International Billfish Tournament held in August at Kallua-Kona. McMillan landed two marlin weighing 462 and 506 pounds (210 and 230 kilograms) to win the event for the Nevada Gamefish Club.

Swordfish Catches by sports fishermen off Southern California were sporadic during the year. However, the Balboa Angling Club reported a "fantastic" early season for striped marlin. A catch of a 732½-pound (332-kilogram) bluefin tuna off Hatteras on June 14 shattered a 15-year-old North Carolina state record by more than 200 pounds (90 kilograms). The catch was made by Lyman B. Dickerson of Coral Gables, Fla., on 80-pound (36-kilogram) test line during the Hatteras Marlin Tournament in rough seas.

United States District Judge Noel P. Fox of Grand Rapids, Mich., ruled on May 8 that treaties of the 1800s guaranteed unrestricted fishing rights to the Bay Mills and Sault Ste. Marie Chippewa Indians.

More than 26 million fishermen paid over $158-million for fishing licenses in 1978. California, with more than 5 million resident fishermen purchasing licenses or permits, continued to be the largest Mecca for the sport. Michigan and Wisconsin attract the largest number of nonresident anglers to their waters during the year. Andrew L. Newman

In WORLD BOOK, see FISHING.

FISHING INDUSTRY. The United States and Canada signed an agreement on March 29, 1979, that was designed to end their "fishing war" in the prolific Georges Bank fishing area off Cape Cod. The two countries banned fishing in each other's waters in June 1978 when negotiations stalled on a comprehensive treaty setting maritime boundaries. The new treaty, still unratified at the end of 1979, provides for coordinated management of North Atlantic fish stocks. Failure to approve the agreement could cost U.S. fishermen $4.3 million in 1980 by keeping them out of Canadian waters.

Tuna, Salmon Troubles. A new "tuna war" broke out between the United States and Canada on August 26 when Canada seized eight U.S. fishing boats pursuing albacore tuna into the Canadian 200-nautical-mile zone. The Department of State notified Canada on August 31 that the United States does not accept Canada's jurisdiction over albacore tuna fishing because the species is migratory and is fair game anywhere beyond 12 nautical miles from shore. Canadian and U.S. officials announced on September 12 that the dispute could not be settled in the 1979 fishing season, but said they would work for mutually acceptable fishing arrangements for 1980.

Commercial fishermen in the Northwest have protested bitterly against restrictions imposed on their harvesting of salmon and steelhead ever since U.S. District Judge George H. Boldt of Tacoma, Wash., ruled in 1974 that Indians were entitled to half the fish that pass through the Puget Sound fishing grounds. On July 2, 1979, the fishermen and the states of Washington and Oregon lost an appeal to the Supreme Court of the United States, which upheld the Boldt decision by a vote of 6-3. When a federal judge, intending to ensure that Indian tribes could harvest their share of the depleted salmon run, ordered commercial fishing for salmon banned at sea from July 25 to August 4, commercial fishermen were irate. More than 100 commercial boats appeared off the coast on July 27, in what they called a "fake fish-in" to protest the restriction. See INDIAN, AMERICAN.

Record Catch. Despite their difficulties, U.S. commercial fishermen shattered all records for the amount and value of edible fish caught in 1978. They landed 6 billion pounds (2.7 billion kilograms) with a dockside value of $1.9 billion, breaking 1962's record. Compliance with the Fishery Conservation and Management Act of 1977, which required that conservation of depleted fish stocks be assured, concerned government officials. With more than 800 new vessels under construction for the U.S. fishing fleet, overfishing, even without the competition of other nations, was a possibility.   Andrew L. Newman

In WORLD BOOK, see FISHING INDUSTRY.

FLOOD. See DISASTERS.

FLORIDA. See STATE GOVERNMENT.

FLOWER. See GARDENING.

Canadian fisheries patrol vessel *Tanu,* center, seizes two U.S. boats for fishing inside the 200-nautical-mile zone off Vancouver Island.

FONDA, JANE (1937-   ), won the Academy of Motion Picture Arts and Sciences best actress award on April 9, 1979. She received the Oscar for her performance as the wife of a Vietnam War veteran in *Coming Home*. It was her second such Oscar; she won in 1971 for her role as a prostitute in *Klute*.

Jane Seymour Fonda was born on Dec. 21, 1937, in New York City. Her parents were actor Henry Fonda and Frances Seymour Brokaw. She lived in Brentwood, a suburb of Los Angeles, and in Greenwich, Conn. She attended Vassar College.

After studying at Actors Studio in New York City, Fonda played on Broadway in *There Was A Little Girl* in 1960 and made her movie debut about the same time in *Tall Story*. She has appeared in such films as *A Walk on the Wild Side* (1962), *They Shoot Horses, Don't They?* (1969), and *Julia* (1977).

In the 1960s and 1970s, Fonda became as famous for her political views as for her acting ability. Some accused her of treason when she visited North Vietnam in 1972 to talk to U.S. prisoners of war, inspect the damage caused by U.S. bombing, and make antiwar speeches. In 1979, the California legislature refused to ratify her appointment to the California Arts Council because of her politics.

Fonda married French film director Roger Vadim in 1965; they have a daughter. In 1973, Fonda married Tom Hayden, a political activist in the New Left of the 1960s.
                                    Edward G. Nash

FOOD. Grocery prices in the United States registered their second consecutive double-digit rise in 1979. Preliminary estimates by the U.S. Department of Agriculture indicated that prices for food eaten at home jumped 11 per cent, on top of the 10.5 per cent increase recorded for the previous year. Prices for food consumed away from home were also up 11 per cent after a 1978 increase of 9 per cent.

The farm value of domestic foods, a measure of the average price received by U.S. farmers for commodities contained in a typical market basket of food, rose 12 per cent. The farm-to-retail price spread, a measure of the costs and profits associated with processing and marketing these foods, also rose 12 per cent. A 6 per cent price increase for food products that do not originate on U.S. farms, such as chocolate, coffee, fish, and tea, softened the overall price rise at the grocery to its 11 per cent average.

The most rapid food price rise in 1979 occurred during the first quarter, led by large increases in farm commodity prices. Nearly all major food groups were involved, with meats and fresh produce rising the most. Tight supplies of beef, resulting from earlier reductions in the U.S. cattle herd, contributed most to the increase. Adverse winter weather and labor disputes also temporarily affected supplies of fresh produce and livestock products.

Retail food prices continued to rise during the spring. However, the rate of increase slowed in comparison with the rapid first-quarter pace, and the fundamental forces behind the increases changed. While prices for farm commodities began to subside, farm-to-retail price spreads increased more than enough to keep food bills rising.

Price Worries. President Jimmy Carter summoned food industry representatives to the White House on August 13 to discuss food price inflation. He noted that while farm prices had declined at a 17 per cent annual rate in April, May, and June, the farm-to-retail spread had increased at a 29 per cent rate. The President expressed concern about this rising farm-to-retail price spread and encouraged marketing firms to reflect the farm commodity price decreases quickly and fully in the price of food to consumers. The industry representatives contended that their industry remains highly competitive, that their costs for energy, labor, packaging material, and transportation were escalating rapidly, and that the time lag between the purchases of commodities from farmers and the sales of food to consumers distorts the monthly price spreads.

U.S. Food Supplies and consumption on a per capita basis presented a mixed picture in 1979. Beef and veal supplies were smaller, and per capita use dropped about 10 per cent from a year earlier. However, larger supplies of pork, chicken, and turkey produced a small increase in total meat and

Per Capita U.S. Food Consumption, 1978–1979		
	1978	**1979**
	Pounds (Kilograms)	
Milk and cream	285.9 (129.7)	284.2 (128.9)
Potatoes	122.9 (55.7)	123.0 (55.8)
Wheat flour (in all products)	114.0 (51.7)	112.0 (50.8)
Fresh vegetables	93.3 (42.3)	97.2 (44.1)
Sugar	93.1 (42.2)	91.6 (41.5)
Fresh fruits	81.6 (37.0)	80.5 (36.5)
Beef	88.9 (40.3)	79.9 (36.2)
Pork	56.5 (25.6)	64.8 (29.4)
Canned vegetables	54.1 (24.5)	55.0 (24.9)
Chicken	47.7 (21.6)	51.8 (23.5)
Eggs	35.2 (16.0)	35.8 (16.2)
Canned fruits	19.0 (8.6)	18.0 (8.2)
Cheese	17.3 (7.8)	17.9 (8.1)
Ice cream	17.8 (8.1)	17.7 (8.0)
Fish	13.4 (6.1)	13.4 (6.1)
Frozen fruits and fruit juices	11.3 (5.1)	11.8 (5.4)
Margarine	11.4 (5.2)	11.6 (5.3)
Frozen vegetables	10.8 (4.9)	11.1 (5.0)
Turkey	9.4 (4.3)	10.2 (4.6)
Coffee	7.9 (3.6)	7.8 (3.5)
Butter	4.5 (2.0)	4.5 (2.0)
Veal	2.5 (1.1)	1.6 (0.8)
Lamb and mutton	1.4 (0.6)	1.4 (0.6)
Tea	0.7 (0.3)	0.7 (0.3)

Source: U.S. Department of Agriculture.

"Sugar Snap," a new pea with an edible pod billed as the "greatest new vegetable" in a century, appeared in many home gardens in 1979.

ing eligibility rules for students, and eliminating food-stamp frauds from the program.

Tightening eligibility requirements had the effect of excluding some participants from the program. However, the combination of rising food prices, an economic slowdown, and the elimination of the purchase requirement resulted in large increases in total participation and in program costs. Preliminary data for the second quarter of 1979 indicated that nearly 18.4 million persons participated in the Food Stamp Program, up 2.5 million from the same period in 1978. Stamps worth some $1.7 billion were distributed during the second quarter of 1979, compared with $1.3 billion a year earlier. See WELFARE.

Food Regulations. The artificial sweetener question remained unsettled. Saccharin continued to be available for use in foods and beverages. The House of Representatives voted on July 24 to extend the moratorium preventing the U.S. Food and Drug Administration (FDA) from banning saccharin to June 30, 1981. Although the Senate had not acted, FDA indicated it would not ban saccharin while Congress was evaluating it. And, while cyclamates continued to be banned, the FDA also indicated hearings will be reopened to consider some specific questions about the safety of cyclamates that were not studied in earlier deliberations. Larry V. Summers

See also FARM AND FARMING. In WORLD BOOK, see FOOD; FOOD SUPPLY.

poultry consumption. Despite harsh winter weather, harvest labor strife in California, and transportation difficulties associated with a national truckers' strike, more fresh vegetables reached the market than in 1978, with a moderate increase in per capita use. Consumption of most major foods changed little.

World Food Supplies also provided a mixed scene. Owing to very large 1978 harvests, carry-over stocks of cereal grains, excluding stocks held in Russia and China, were up 8 per cent. This was the fourth consecutive year of world grain stock accumulation. Most of the increase was held in the exporting countries, such as Canada and the United States.

World food production prospects for 1979 were much less favorable. According to midyear forecasts by the United Nation's Food and Agricultural Organization, world wheat and coarse grain production was expected to be down about 6 per cent. Although further increases were expected for most other food products, only a small overall rise in world food production was foreseen in 1979 against a backdrop of continued growth in world population.

Food Stamps. Major changes went into effect in the U.S. Food Stamp Program in 1979. Beginning in January, eligible households no longer had to purchase additional food stamps in order to receive their allotment of "bonus" or free stamps. Other changes included lowering income-eligibility limits, tighten-

FOOTBALL. The Pittsburgh Steelers, who won the Super Bowl game in January 1979, dominated the National Football League's (NFL) season the following autumn and won the 1980 Super Bowl. The University of Alabama assured itself of the unofficial national college championship by winning the Sugar Bowl game on New Year's Day 1980.

Each of the NFL's 28 teams played a 16-game regular season, with the six division winners and four wild-card teams advancing to the play-offs. The Steelers and the San Diego Chargers, both in the dominant American Football Conference (AFC), posted the best regular-season records, each winning 12 games and losing four. Next, at 11-5, were the Houston Oilers, Dallas Cowboys, and Philadelphia Eagles. At 10-6 were the Miami Dolphins, Denver Broncos, Tampa Bay Buccaneers, Chicago Bears, and Washington Redskins.

Nine of those 10 teams qualified for the play-offs, and Washington missed out only after a 35-34 loss to Dallas in its final game. The other play-off team was the Los Angeles Rams, which won the National Football Conference (NFC) Western Division title despite a 9-7 record and became the first NFL team to win seven straight division titles.

The Play-Offs. Houston was the surprise team of the AFC play-offs. It upset Denver, 13-7, on December 23 in the wild-card game, despite groin injuries that knocked the three best Houston offensive threats – quarterback Dan Pastorini, running back Earl Campbell, and wide receiver Ken Burrough – out of the game. On December 29, with those three players sidelined, Houston upset San Diego, 17-14, as Vern Perry intercepted four Charger passes.

Pittsburgh routed Miami, 34-14, on December 30, scoring touchdowns on its first three possessions. That set up an AFC championship game on Jan. 6, 1980, at Pittsburgh, and the Steelers won it from Houston, 27-13, as Terry Bradshaw threw two touchdown passes. Pastorini and Campbell played for Houston, but the Steelers shut them down and held Campbell to 15 yards in 17 carries.

In the NFC wild-card game on December 23, Philadelphia rallied for a 27-17 victory over Chicago on Ron Jaworski's three touchdown passes. On December 29, Tampa Bay upset Philadelphia 24-17, as Ricky Bell ran 38 times, a play-off record, for 142 yards. The next day, Los Angeles upset Dallas, 21-19, on three touchdown passes by Vince Ferragamo, who had finished the season at quarterback for the injured Pat Haden. The Rams controlled the passing of Roger Staubach by using seven defensive backs in pass situations.

On Jan. 6, 1980, Los Angeles and Tampa Bay, two teams with better defenses than offenses, met at Tampa, Fla., for the NFL title. Los Angeles won, 9-0, on three field goals by Frank Corral. The Rams held Tampa Bay to seven first downs and advanced to the Super Bowl against Pittsburgh on January 20

Standings in National Football Conference

Eastern Division

	W.	L.	T.	Pct.
Dallas	11	5	0	.688
Philadelphia	11	5	0	.688
Washington	10	6	0	.625
New York Giants	6	10	0	.375
St. Louis	5	11	0	.313

Central Division

	W.	L.	T.	Pct.
Tampa Bay	10	6	0	.625
Chicago	10	6	0	.625
Minnesota	7	9	0	.438
Green Bay	5	11	0	.313
Detroit	2	14	0	.125

Western Division

	W.	L.	T.	Pct.
Los Angeles	9	7	0	.563
New Orleans	8	8	0	.500
Atlanta	6	10	0	.375
San Francisco	2	14	0	.125

National Conference Individual Statistics

Scoring

	TDs.	E.P.	F.G.	Pts.
Moseley, Washington	0	39	25	114
Franklin, Philadelphia	0	36	23	105
Septien, Dallas	0	40	19	97
Payton, Chicago	16	0	0	96

Passing

	Att.	Comp.	Pct.	Yds.	TDs.
Staubach, Dallas	461	267	57.9	3,586	27
Theismann, Washington	395	233	59.0	2,797	20
Jaworski, Philadelphia	374	190	50.8	2,669	18
Manning, New Orleans	420	252	60.0	3,169	15

Receiving

	No. Caught	Total Yds.	Avg. Gain	TDs.
Rashad, Minnesota	80	1,156	14.5	9
Francis, Atlanta	74	1,013	13.7	8
Young, Minnesota	72	519	7.2	4
Chandler, New Orleans	65	1,069	16.4	6

Rushing

	Att.	Yds.	Avg. Gain	TDs.
Payton, Chicago	369	1,610	4.4	14
Anderson, St. Louis	331	1,605	4.8	8
Montgomery, Philadelphia	338	1,512	4.5	9
Bell, Tampa Bay	283	1,263	4.5	7

Punting

	No.	Yds.	Avg.	Longest
Jennings, N.Y. Giants	104	4,445	42.7	72
D. White, Dallas	76	3,168	41.7	73
Partridge, New Orleans	57	2,330	40.9	61
Beverly, Green Bay	69	2,785	40.4	65

Punt Returns

	No.	Yds.	Avg.	TDs.
Sciarra, Philadelphia	16	182	11.4	0
Schubert, Chicago	25	238	9.5	1
Henry, Philadelphia	35	320	9.1	0
Hardeman, Washington	24	207	8.6	0

Standings in American Football Conference

Eastern Division

	W.	L.	T.	Pct.
Miami	10	6	0	.625
New England	9	7	0	.563
New York Jets	8	8	0	.500
Buffalo	7	9	0	.438
Baltimore	5	11	0	.313

Central Division

	W.	L.	T.	Pct.
Pittsburgh	12	4	0	.750
Houston	11	5	0	.688
Cleveland	9	7	0	.563
Cincinnati	4	12	0	.250

Western Division

	W.	L.	T.	Pct.
San Diego	12	4	0	.750
Denver	10	6	0	.625
Oakland	9	7	0	.563
Seattle	9	7	0	.563
Kansas City	7	9	0	.438

American Conference Individual Statistics

Scoring

	TDs.	E.P.	F.G.	Pts.
Smith, New England	0	46	23	115
Campbell, Houston	19	0	0	114
Bahr, Pittsburgh	0	50	18	104
Fritsch, Houston	0	41	21	104

Passing

	Att.	Comp.	Pct.	Yds.	TDs.
Fouts, San Diego	530	332	62.6	4,082	24
Stabler, Oakland	498	304	61.0	3,615	26
Anderson, Cincinnati	339	189	55.8	2,340	16
Zorn, Seattle	505	285	56.4	3,661	20

Receiving

	No. Caught	Total Yds.	Avg. Gain	TDs.
Washington, Baltimore	82	750	9.1	3
Joiner, San Diego	72	1,008	14.0	4
Stallworth, Pittsburgh	70	1,183	16.9	8
Largent, Seattle	66	1,237	18.7	9

Rushing

	Att.	Yds.	Avg. Gain	TDs.
Campbell, Houston	368	1,697	4.6	19
M. Pruitt, Cleveland	265	1,294	4.9	9
Harris, Pittsburgh	267	1,186	4.4	11
Gaines, N.Y. Jets	186	905	4.9	0

Punting

	No.	Yds.	Avg.	Longest
Grupp, Kansas City	89	3,883	43.6	74
Guy, Oakland	69	2,939	42.6	71
McInally, Cincinnati	89	3,678	41.3	61
Evans, Cleveland	69	2,844	41.2	59

Punt Returns

	No.	Yds.	Avg.	TDs.
Nathan, Miami	28	306	10.9	1
Smith, Kansas City	58	612	10.6	2
D. Hall, Cleveland	29	295	10.2	0
Upchurch, Denver	30	304	10.1	0

Tailback Charles White of Southern California, leading rusher in the nation, won the 1979 Heisman Trophy as college football's best player.

in Pasadena, Calif. Despite the defeat, the season was a success for Tampa Bay, which in 1976 and 1977 lost the first 26 games in its history.

The Rams surprised heavily favored Pittsburgh in the Super Bowl and led 19-17 with 12 minutes left to play. But Bradshaw threw long touchdown passes to Lynn Swann and John Stallworth, and the Steelers won their fourth Super Bowl, 31-19.

New Trends. Two major rule changes, made in 1978 to help the passing game, bore fruit in 1979. One change allowed the defense to bump a potential pass receiver only once, and then within five yards of the line of scrimmage. The other allowed offensive linemen more leeway in using their hands to block pass rushers.

As a result, scoring increased in 1979 by almost one touchdown per game. Scoring passes increased dramatically. Eleven quarterbacks passed for more than 3,000 yards for the season; only five reached that level in 1978.

The 37-year-old Staubach won his second straight NFL passing title, which is decided on a complex formula. San Diego, the most potent passing team, used the pass in all situations everywhere on the field. Dan Fouts, its quarterback, passed for 300 yards in each of four consecutive games, and his season total of 4,082 yards broke the NFL record. Joe Namath of the New York Jets set the previous record of 4,007 yards in 1967 in a 14-game season.

Campbell of Houston, with 1,697 yards, gained his second rushing title in his two years in the league. Walter Payton of Chicago was second with 1,610 and led the NFC for the fourth straight year. Ottis Anderson of the St. Louis Cardinals was third with 1,605, a rookie record. Pittsburgh led in total offense (391.1 yards per game) and scoring (26 points per game) and was second to Tampa in total defense.

The Rams started the year amid controversy because they planned to move from Los Angeles to Anaheim, 35 miles (56 kilometers) to the south, after the season. In April, Carroll Rosenbloom, the team's 72-year-old owner, drowned while swimming, and 70 per cent ownership of the team passed to his second wife, Georgia. After a power struggle with Steve Rosenbloom, her 34-year-old stepson, Georgia fired him as operating head of the Rams. After the season, Steve joined the New Orleans Saints as executive vice-president and general manager.

The Canadian Football League (CFL) scored a coup when the Montreal Alouettes signed Tom Cousineau, the first choice in the NFL draft. The Buffalo Bills had picked the Ohio State all-America linebacker and offered him $1.2 million over five years, including bonus and performance clauses. The Alouettes won, paying $1 million, including a $250,000 signing bonus, over three years.

The Edmonton Eskimos (12-2-2) and Montreal (11-4-1) won the conference titles and met in the

Grey Cup championship game on November 25 in Montreal, Que. Edmonton, which beat Montreal for the title the year before, won again, 17-9, on long touchdown passes by Tom Wilkinson and Warren Moon. Wilkinson was named to his all-conference team and Moon, his substitute, led the league with 20 touchdown passes. David Green of Montreal led the league in rushing with 1,678 yards and won the Schenley Award as the league's outstanding player.

Hall of Fame. John Unitas, former Baltimore Colts quarterback, and Dick Butkus, Chicago linebacker, were elected to the Pro Football Hall of Fame in Canton, Ohio, in their first year of eligibility. Offensive tackle Ron Mix of San Diego and punter Yale Lary of the Detroit Lions were also chosen.

The College Champion, as usual, was decided in polls, not games. There were several candidates.

When the regular season ended, Alabama, Ohio State, Florida State, Brigham Young, and McNeese State of Louisiana had 11-0 records. Southern California and Central Michigan had 10 victories, no losses, and one tie. Oklahoma, Nebraska, Arkansas, Houston, and Pittsburgh were 10-1; Yale, 8-1.

The final regular-season poll of the Associated Press (AP) board of writers and broadcasters placed Ohio State first, Alabama second, Southern California third, Florida State fourth, and Oklahoma fifth. The United Press International (UPI) board of coaches ranked Alabama first, Southern California second, Ohio State third, Florida State fourth, and Oklahoma fifth.

Alabama, one of the few remaining teams with a wishbone offense, ranked fourth nationally in rushing and first in scoring defense. Southern California was big, fast, and deep, and tailback Charles White, winner of the Heisman Trophy as the nation's outstanding college player, ranked first nationally in rushing with 180.3 yards per game. Ohio State, with Earle Bruce replacing the ousted Woody Hayes as coach, installed a strong passing game.

In the postseason bowl games, four of the five unbeaten and untied teams lost. Only Alabama survived, outplaying Arkansas, 24-9, in the Sugar Bowl in New Orleans. Southern California beat Ohio State, 17-16, in the Rose Bowl at Pasadena on White's touchdown in the last two minutes. Oklahoma overran Florida State, 24-7, in the Orange Bowl at Miami, and Houston upset Nebraska, 17-14, in the Cotton Bowl at Dallas on a tipped touchdown pass with 12 seconds remaining.

The next day, the final AP and UPI polls had the same first five. Alabama was named national champion, with Southern California second, Oklahoma third, Ohio State fourth, and Houston fifth.

Scandals. Arizona State University fired Frank Kush as coach on October 13, midway through his 22nd season. In a $1.1-million damage suit, Kevin Rutledge had charged that Kush punched him in the face the year before after Rutledge had made a poor punt, then harassed him until he gave up his athletic scholarship. Athletic Director Fred Miller of Arizona State fired Kush, saying that Kush had tried to cover up the incident by pressuring players and assistant coaches to lie.

Arizona State was involved in another scandal. The Pacific 10 Conference ordered the team to forfeit its five football victories because it had used eight ineligible players. The eight had received credit for a summer extension course, though none had attended classes or taken the final examination. Similar cases involved football and basketball players at New Mexico, Utah, San Jose State, Oregon, and Oregon State.

Frank Litsky

In WORLD BOOK, see FOOTBALL.

1979 College Conference Champions

Conference	School
Atlantic Coast	North Carolina State
Big Eight	Oklahoma
Big Sky	Montana State (Boise State ineligible for title)
Big Ten	Ohio State
Ivy League	Yale
Mid-American	Central Michigan
Missouri Valley	West Texas State
Ohio Valley	Murray State
Pacific Ten	Southern California
Southeastern	Alabama
Southern	Tennessee (Chattanooga)
Southwest	Arkansas-Houston (tie)
Southwestern	Grambling
Western Athletic	Brigham Young
Yankee	Boston U.-Massachusetts (tie)

The Bowl Games

Bowl	Winner	Loser
Bluebonnet	Purdue 27	Tennessee 22
Blue-Gray	Blue 22	Gray 13
Cotton	Houston 17	Nebraska 14
Fiesta	Pittsburgh 16	Arizona 10
Garden State	Temple 28	California 17
Gator	North Carolina 17	Michigan 15
Hall of Fame	Missouri 24	South Carolina 14
Holiday	Indiana 38	Brigham Young 37
Independence	Syracuse 31	McNeese State 7
Liberty	Penn State 9	Tulane 6
Orange	Oklahoma 24	Florida State 7
Peach	Baylor 24	Clemson 18
Rose	Southern California 17	Ohio State 16
Shrine	West 20	East 10
Sugar	Alabama 24	Arkansas 9
Sun	Washington 14	Texas 7
Tangerine	Louisiana State 34	Wake Forest 10

All-America Team (as picked by UPI)

Offense

Wide receiver —Ken Margerum, Stanford
Tight end—Junior Miller, Nebraska
Tackles—Greg Kolenda, Arkansas; Tim Foley, Notre Dame
Guards—Brad Budde, Southern California; Ken Fritz, Ohio State
Center—Jim Richter, North Carolina State
Quarterback—Marc Wilson, Brigham Young
Running backs—Billy Sims, Oklahoma; Charles White, Southern California; Vagas Ferguson, Notre Dame
Punter-kicker—Dale Castro, Maryland

Defense

Ends—Hugh Green, Pittsburgh; Jim Stuckey, Clemson
Tackles—Bruce Clark, Penn State; Steve McMichael, Texas
Middle guard—Ron Simmons, Florida State
Linebackers—George Cumby, Oklahoma; Ron Simpkins, Michigan; Dennis Johnson, Southern California
Defensive backs—Johnnie Johnson, Texas; Roland James, Tennessee; Ken Easley, UCLA
Punter—Jim Miller, Mississippi

FORD, GERALD RUDOLPH (1913-   ), the 38th President of the United States and titular head of the Republican Party, announced on Oct. 19, 1979, that he had made "a firm decision not to become an active candidate" for the presidency in 1980. Ford indicated that he would be available for the nomination only if the 1980 Republican National Convention became hopelessly deadlocked – a possibility he described as "very remote" – and he urged his supporters to work for other candidates.

To some, Ford's statement indicated a change in attitude toward the presidential race. In an April television interview, he stated that he "would not duck the responsibility" of becoming the Republican presidential nominee if the party failed to agree on another candidate, adding, "I learned a long time ago in politics, never say 'never.'"

Ford made a weeklong, four-state, speaking tour in late September. In a speech to the U.S. Army War College in Carlisle, Pa., he attacked President Jimmy Carter's economic policy as a "disaster" and urged defeat of the Strategic Arms Limitation Treaty (SALT II) unless military spending increased.

Memoirs and Memorabilia. *A Time to Heal,* Ford's memoir of his days in the White House, was published in June by Harper & Row and the Reader's Digest Press. Excerpts from the book were published in May in the *Reader's Digest.* In the book, Ford discussed his controversial pardon of Richard M. Nixon and the events before and after Nixon's resignation.

In June, Ford laid the cornerstone of the Gerald Ford Presidential Library at the University of Michigan in Ann Arbor. At the time, $8.4 million had been raised for the building, which will house 14 million documents – including the Nixon pardon, photographs, and film of Ford's presidency.

Business and Family. The former President and his wife, Betty, toured the Middle East for two weeks in January, visiting Egypt's President Anwar al-Sadat in Aswan. Ford also met with Mohammad Reza Pahlavi, the deposed shah of Iran, in Egypt.

Ford continued to add to his property holdings during the year. He bought for about $300,000 a 1-acre (0.4-hectare) homesite in Beaver Creek, Colo., near Vail, where the Ford family usually skis, in September. He also announced that he would become part owner of two radio stations.

Ford's daughter, Susan, was married to U.S. Secret Service agent Charles F. Vance on February 10 in Palm Desert, Calif. On April 22, the Fords welcomed their first grandchild, Sarah Joyce Ford, daughter of their oldest son, Michael, and his wife, Gayle.   Carol L. Thompson

See REPUBLICAN PARTY. In WORLD BOOK, see FORD, GERALD RUDOLPH.

Former President Ford gets a red-carpet welcome from President Anwar al-Sadat upon Ford's arrival in Aswan, Egypt, in January.

FOREST AND FOREST PRODUCTS. Forest fires blackened more than 171,000 acres (69,000 hectares) of timberland in five Western states in August 1979. California, Idaho, Montana, Oregon, and Wyoming were hit by the fires.

More than 150,000 acres (60,000 hectares) of Idaho forestlands were destroyed by the most devastating fires in the state's history. Some 2,000 fire fighters from other states helped to battle the blazes. Heavy rain on August 12 helped bring all but the 65,000-acre (26,000-hectare) Mortar Creek fire under control after two weeks.

Governor John V. Evans of Idaho criticized the United States Forest Service on August 8 for waiting too long before sending in fire fighters. His comment brought into focus the Forest Service's controversial policy of allowing some fires in remote wilderness areas to burn unimpeded. The "natural burn" theory is advocated by many conservationists. The Idaho fires demonstrated that this policy is unsound, critics charged, especially where there are no roads for fire-fighting equipment and personnel.

Presidential Decision. President Jimmy Carter asked the United States Congress on April 16 to add 15.4 million acres (6.2 million hectares) of roadless areas in national forests to the national wilderness system. He asked that 36 million acres (14.5 million hectares) that had been studied for inclusion in the wilderness system be opened to timber cutting and mining, and that 10.6 million acres (4 million hectares) be set aside for further study.

The President's decision came after eight years of controversy during which environmentalists disagreed strongly with the forest industry over how much of the roadless area in the national forest system should be designated as wilderness.

"We're relieved that there was not a substantial move for more wilderness," said Eugene Bergoffen of the National Forest Products Association. He added that a ban on timber cutting in the 15.4 million acres (6.2 million hectares) set aside for wilderness could force a 10 per cent reduction in future federal timber sales. William A. Turnage of the Wilderness Society described Carter's action as "among the most negative decisions in the history of public land management and one which threatens to negate the Administration's impressive environmental record."

Under timber industry pressure, Carter on June 11 announced a new policy designed to increase timber harvesting in the national forests by 1 to 3 billion board feet (2 to 7 million cubic meters) within the next two years.   Andrew L. Newman

In WORLD BOOK, see FOREST; FOREST PRODUCTS; FORESTRY.

FOUR-H CLUBS. See YOUTH ORGANIZATIONS.

Forest fires raged out of control through the West in August after an unusually hot, rainless summer left brush and timber as dry as tinder.

FRANCE. Socialists, Communists, Gaullists, and trade unions criticized Prime Minister Raymond Barre in 1979 for restraining wage hikes but not controlling inflation and unemployment. Even his own party supporters complained that his three-year economic stabilization plan was too austere. Barre proclaimed in July that the plan, which was nearly complete, was the only cure. No matter how bitter the medicine, he said, it must be swallowed. But he gave the flagging economy a $1-billion boost on August 29 in new aid for public works and housing, and increased social security payments.

The Council of Ministers (cabinet) approved a 1980 budget of $124.9 billion, an increase of 14.3 per cent, on September 5. The budget included $21-billion for defense – a 13.5 per cent increase – and a $7.3-billion deficit that would be financed through borrowing. The National Assembly rejected the revenue proposals on October 24, damaging the ruling coalition of Giscardians and Gaullists.

Scandal and Suicide. Minister of Labor Robert Boulin, who was under investigation for Riviera real estate deals, committed suicide on October 30. He left letters that accused a blackmailer, the judge in charge of the investigation, the justice minister, and the press of driving him to suicide. President Valéry Giscard d'Estaing said that the press "must be severely condemned by public opinion," but the leftist newspaper *Libération* said that the press was "the scapegoat of a system that is obsessed with acting in secrecy."

Steel Reorganization. The steel industry was $171 billion in debt at the end of 1978 and its productivity was low, so the government planned to cut 21,000 from the 154,000 work force, close some plants, and appoint new managers. But the plan caused labor unrest. Striking steelworkers blocked northern roads and railways, including the main highway from Paris to Brussels, Belgium, in the steel town of Denain, on February 22.

Union leaders hoped that a protest march in Paris on March 23 would pressure the government and employers into relaxing their stand on excess labor, but it turned into a riot that left 30 persons injured, including several policemen. At least 60,000 persons demonstrated, but most of the violence and vandalism occurred on the edges of the crowd. The unrest continued until July 24, when the main steel companies agreed to stop laying off extra workers. Instead, they would let 12,000 workers retire early, retrain 4,000 workers, and pay about $12,000 to workers who left voluntarily, in addition to the regular compensation for being laid off. The two largest steel producers, Usinor-Chatillon and Sacilor-Sollac, promised the government that they would be making a profit by 1981.

Wage Restraint. Barre said on January 4 that two years of wage restraints had not been enough. Continuing them to cut unemployment and limit

Thousands of steelworkers from all over France demonstrated in Paris in March against a government plan to lay off 21,000 workers.

inflation would be, he said, "the last essential act in the process of economic recovery." He gradually fulfilled a promise made before the 1978 general election to scrap price controls. The liberated goods included bread, which had been subject to government control since the French Revolution in 1789. Nevertheless, inflation held steady at 9.7 per cent early in the year.

The government on April 4 approved a $1.3-billion plan to stimulate investment by granting tax relief and low-interest loans to businesses that raised their investments in 1979, 1980, and possibly 1981. This plan followed the advice of the Organization for Economic Cooperation and Development to meet the 1979 growth target of 3.7 per cent.

Oil Crisis. Barre announced measures on June 20 to reduce oil imports, including less use of domestic heating oil, lower temperatures for office buildings, and stricter enforcement of highway speed limits. Barre's objective was to keep France within the commitment of the European Community (Common Market) to reduce annual oil consumption by 5 per cent. Giscard d'Estaing said in a nationwide broadcast that he wanted to maintain the average citizen's buying power by careful economic management and directing industry into less energy-intensive sectors. Oil price hikes were expected to cost France an extra $4.4 billion in 1979.

Leftist Gains. The Socialist and Communist parties gained in March elections for 1,847 seats in the councils of 48 of the 96 metropolitan departments that make up the country. They won control of eight councils as the Socialists gained 156 seats for a total of 544, and the Communists added 41 seats for a total of 244. But the left remained as disordered as the right. On May 15, French Communist leader Georges Marchais withstood a challenge at the party's 23rd Congress from hard-liners who wanted to abandon Eurocommunist cooperation with the government and the Socialists in favor of orthodox Communist opposition under Russian leadership.

Foreign Affairs. Giscard d'Estaing signed a 10-year economic agreement with Supreme Soviet Presidium Chairman Leonid I. Brezhnev in Moscow in April. France stopped all aid, except food, health, and education assistance, to the Central African Empire, a former French colony, on August 17. The action followed a legal commission report that 100 schoolchildren had been massacred in the capital, Bangui, in April, with the approval of Emperor Bokassa I. France had given the country $25 million in nonmilitary aid annually. Bokassa was deposed on September 20.   Kenneth Brown

See also EUROPE (Facts in Brief Table). In WORLD BOOK, see FRANCE.

FUTURE FARMERS OF AMERICA (FFA). See YOUTH ORGANIZATIONS.

GABON. See AFRICA.

GAMBIA. See AFRICA.

GAMES, MODELS, AND TOYS. Information released in March 1979 indicated that toys based on the motion picture *Star Wars* had become the biggest sellers in toy industry history. More than 25 million *Star Wars* figures and more than 5 million vehicles were sold since 1977.

Kenner Products, which is licensed to manufacture and market the toys, said 25 of its 80 new toys related to *Star Wars*. With sequels to the original motion picture scheduled to appear every two years, Kenner expected continuing sales. See Special Reports section, CALL IT SF OR SCI-FI, IT'S BIG!

Electronic Games played on home television sets and on independent consoles continued to have wide appeal. Estimates released early in 1979 indicated that sales of electronic console games and toys exceeded $60 million during the 1978 Christmas season.

Complex fantasy and role-playing games replaced some of the less sophisticated games of the past. One of the most popular, Dungeons and Dragons, could be played on various levels – some versions requiring electronic calculators, others only a pen and a set of dice. The object of the game, developed by TSR Hobbies, Inc., of Lake Geneva, Wis., was not to win or lose but to learn from past mistakes. Another product, *Creative Growth Games* by Eugene Raudsepp and George P. Hough, Jr., is

A father and son coasting down a New York City street were among the hundreds of thousands of Americans to enjoy a roller-skating revival in 1979.

actually a book of 75 games involving such activities as word association, writing captions, and completing pictures.

Barbie's Birthday. The Mattel Company's Barbie doll observed her 20th anniversary in 1979. More than 112 million Barbie, Ken, and other associated dolls have been sold, about half of which were various Barbie models. The newest of the 1,315 versions of the doll is a kissing Barbie.

Vintage Barbie dolls are also becoming increasingly popular with collectors. A mint copy of the original brought $501.59 in a national mail auction.

Interest in Roller Skating surged in 1979, accompanied by a sharp decline in skateboarding. The number of skateboard parks in use in the United States dwindled from 200 in 1977 to about 70 in 1979, and one manufacturer reported that skateboard sales were off 80 per cent. The major factor in the rebirth of interest in roller skating was the development of a new skate with low-friction polyurethane wheels attached to comfortable jogging shoes. Because these skates made it possible for skaters to attain much higher speeds, they also increased the danger of accidents. Medical authorities estimated during the year that more than 100,000 persons would be treated for rollerskating injuries in 1979.   Theodore M. O'Leary

In WORLD BOOK, see DOLL; GAME; MODEL MAKING; ROLLER SKATING; TOY.

GARDENING. The popularity of indoor plants and outdoor gardens, which increased steadily through most of the 1970s, appeared to level off in the United States in 1979. At the same time, the inflation-triggered expansion of vegetable-gardening also stabilized.

A new horticultural awareness led to increased sales of flowering and fruiting plants that are more difficult to grow, and many enthusiasts began collecting specialized plants. As a result, new plant societies sprang up, including the Hoya Society International, which publishes a quarterly magazine, *The Hoya,* devoted to the waxplant, and the Peperomia Society, which publishes *The Peperomia Gazette,* a quarterly dealing with that large and diverse group of plants.

Nostalgia contributed to the renewed popularity of some indoor flowering plants. It brought back such nearly forgotten old favorites as the trailing blue-flowered Italian bellflower (*Campanula isophylla*) and *Oxalis rubra,* which produces masses of pink bell-shaped flowers above shamrocklike leaves. The zeal for flowers led growers to develop a miniature cyclamen, "Beautiful Helena," that is easier to bring to flower year after year than the larger form. Its blooms are salmon-pink, white, or red. Many outdoor annual and short-lived perennial flowering plants, such as Browallia and black-eyed Susan vine (*Thunbergia alata*), were marketed for indoor hanging baskets. Unfortunately, many were sold without the warning that they need special care after heavy flowering.

White Fly, a pest affecting tomatoes, herbs, and other fragrant-leaved plants, is difficult to control. Entomologists Ralph E. Webb and Floyd F. Smith, of the U.S. Department of Agriculture's Science and Education Administration in Beltsville, Md., used sticky yellow boards to solve the problem in 1979. They found that the flying white flies apparently were distracted by the yellow color and then trapped by sticky motor oil they had smeared on the boards.

New Plants. All-America Selections included six bronze medals for ornamental plants in 1979. "Marigold Queen Sophia" produces flatter flowers than most French marigolds. It reaches 12 inches (30 centimeters) in height and bears light- to deep-copper double blooms. "Nicotiana Nicki-Red" bears true red flowers clustered on stems usually less than 24 inches (61 centimeters) tall. "Orange Prince" pansies yield round, slightly ruffled 3-inch (8-centimeter) blooms. They are yellow, deepening to apricot around a blackish center. "Gold Sun" zinnias bear 5-inch (13-centimeter) yellow flowers with old-fashioned flat petals on 30-inch (76-centimeter) plants, while "Zinnia Peter Pan" offers yellow blooms of twisted petals on plants half as tall as "Gold Sun." The ornamental pepper "Holiday Cheer," like the All-America pansy, should be started indoors. It produces marble-sized, round peppers that turn from yellow-green to purple-splashed to scarlet, on 9-inch (23-centimeter) plants.

"Kohlrabi Grand Duke" won the lone silver medal for 1979. Ready for eating in 45 to 50 days after planting, "Grand Duke" produces bulblike swollen stems, the edible part of this member of the cabbage tribe. Five bronze medals were given for vegetables. "Cucumber Saladin" is distinguished for its sweet skin, which makes it excellent for use in salads as well as for pickling. "Sugar Snap" peas were selected for their edible pods. "Dutch Treat," a sweet pepper, yields cone-shaped, yellow-green turning red fruits – good for slicing into salad. Two winter squash varieties were among the winners: "Early Butternut" with yellow, bell-shaped, orange-fleshed fruit and "Sweet Mama" – a round flat-bottomed green squash.

All three 1980 All-America rose selection winners were produced by William Warriner, director of plant research for the Jackson & Perkins Company in Medford, Ore. "Love," a lightly fragrant grandiflora, is red with white petal reverses; "Honor," a white hybrid tea rose, blossoms through the season; and "Cherish," very high centered for a floribunda, is shrimp-pink.   Phil Clark

In WORLD BOOK, see FLOWER; GARDENING; PLANT.

GAS AND GASOLINE. See ENERGY; PETROLEUM AND GAS.

GEOLOGY. Using techniques for finding oil perfected in earlier years, geologists in 1979 developed new theories about how the Appalachian Mountains were formed. Geologist Fred A. Cook of Cornell University, Ithaca, N.Y., reported in June that the earth's crust from eastern Tennessee to eastern Georgia showed an unexpected thin layer of rocks below the top layer of rock chunks and pieces of ocean floor thrown up in faulting.

According to the plate tectonics theory, the earth's crust is divided into about 20 giant plates, and almost all faulting, folding, quaking, and volcanic activity occurs along the boundaries between those plates. In the Appalachians, a boundary had been discovered and mapped even before the theory of plate tectonics was developed – the Brevard Zone, named for the town of Brevard, N.C. The rocks on one side of the Brevard Zone showed no resemblance to those on the other side, even those of the same age. Because the zone was roughly in the middle of the Appalachian Mountains and ran parallel to the trend of the Appalachians, many geologists accepted it as the "seam" joining two previously separated continents.

The Research. For three years, scientists at a group of United States universities have been doing research in the area, using *reflection seismology,* a technique developed for finding oil. Researchers make a sound wave at the surface – for example, by dropping a large weight – and record the echoes as that sound wave is reflected back from the rock layers beneath. By moving the sound source along the ground surface, geophysicists develop a profile of the underlying earth.

About 3.6 to 6 miles (6 to 10 kilometers) below the earth's surface in the Brevard Zone, the profile showed a thin layer of unbroken rock that apparently had never been faulted or disturbed. Scientists were divided on how to reconcile this evidence with the traditional plate tectonic theory on how the Appalachians were formed.

A modified plate tectonics theory that would fit the new data had been proposed several years earlier by geologist E. Ronald Oxburgh, now of Cambridge University, England. From his work in the Alps, Oxburgh stated that a collision of continents would not necessarily result in a simple vertical zone of crushed rock between the continents. Instead, a piece or flake from one continent might be driven up over the mass of the other. Applying Oxburgh's theory to the Appalachians, the Brevard Zone could be a boundary within a flake.

An Earthquake registering 6.4 on the Richter scale hit the Imperial Valley in California on October 15 – the strongest quake on the mainland United States since 1971. Seismic instruments provided few warnings of the quake.   Kenneth S. Deffeyes

In WORLD BOOK, see EARTH; GEOLOGY.

GEORGIA. See STATE GOVERNMENT.

GERMANY, EAST. Communist Party Secretary General Erich Honecker on May 1, 1979, ordered a review of all investments planned for 1979 and 1980 because the country – celebrating its 30th anniversary – was far behind its 1979 industrial growth target of 5.5 per cent. Growth was particularly sluggish in the chemical, metallurgical, and textile industries. New laws that gave workers three to six more vacation days per year were a factor in the reduced production. Honecker said that unauthorized investments in factory vacation camps and sports facilities had drained too much money from the production of consumer goods, and he vowed to increase central control of economic management.

An unusually severe winter added to East Germany's troubles, cutting energy, crippling industrial production and transportation, and killing livestock. Open-pit mining of *lignite* (brown coal) came almost to a standstill.

Energy prices charged to industrial users increased up to 30 per cent on June 27, responding to growing Russian complaints that countries of the Communist bloc's Council for Mutual Economic Assistance were not doing enough to save energy. Subsidized rates for householders remained low.

Currency Decree. On April 5, the government gave the public 10 days to convert their West German Deutsche marks into coupons that they could use to buy Western goods at government-sponsored Intershops. State banks issued the coupons, which bore the owners' names and were not transferable. Long lines formed outside Intershops as people tried to spend their Deutsche marks before the deadline. East Germans had been using Deutsche marks to buy at Intershops and on the black market.

The Organization for Economic Cooperation and Development (OECD) said in March that East Germany owed OECD countries $7.7 billion, one-third of it to West German banks and other institutions.

Breach of Accord. East Germany abolished one of the last symbols of four-power authority in East Berlin on June 28 by changing the method of selecting the city's delegates to the national *Volkskammer* (parliament). The City Council formerly appointed the delegates, but now they are chosen in public elections. The three Western Allies regarded the move, which Russia approved, as the most serious breach of a 1971 agreement forbidding unilateral changes in Berlin's governments.

East Germany celebrated its 30th anniversary with a huge military parade along East Berlin's Karl Marx Allee on October 7. The Communist Party leaders of all Warsaw Pact nations except Romania attended. East Germany also marked the anniversary by freeing political prisoners.   Kenneth Brown

See also EUROPE (Facts in Brief Table). In WORLD BOOK, see GERMANY.

GERMANY, WEST

GERMANY, WEST. Nuclear power plants and nuclear weapons caused succeeding crises in 1979. Environmentalists had prevented work on more than half of the nuclear power stations under construction in West Germany by the end of February. Then, the March 28 accident at the Three Mile Island nuclear power plant near Harrisburg, Pa., prompted the West German government to order a comprehensive report on reactor safety on April 4. On May 7, Chancellor Helmut Schmidt called on the governments of nuclear nations to sponsor a safety conference.

The Lower Saxony state government dealt a major blow to the federal government on May 16 by banning construction of an integrated nuclear center at Gorleben. The center would have processed spent nuclear fuel, provided a permanent storage site for radioactive wastes, and manufactured fresh uranium and plutonium fuels. The federal and state governments agreed on September 30 to abandon plans for an integrated center and build separate operations at various sites.

After attending the Tokyo summit conference on the energy crisis, Schmidt said on July 4 that West Germany must increase coal production and use nuclear power carefully in the 1980s, and that consumers must exercise self-restraint. But he was reluctant to impose strict controls, such as lower highway speed limits.

Foreign Minister Hans-Dietrich Genscher began talks on August 14 with Foreign Minister Christoph van der Klaauw of the Netherlands about basing in Belgium, Luxembourg, and the Netherlands U.S.-supplied nuclear missiles that could strike Russia. West Germany did not want to be the only continental country with such missiles on its soil. The North Atlantic Treaty Organization agreed in December to station the missiles in Western Europe.

The Economy remained healthy despite higher fuel costs. Unemployment rose slightly during the first six months to 803,700, a drop of 13 per cent from June 1978. But rising prices for imports and declining export sales pulled down trade surpluses during the first eight months, and economists said that West Germany was heading for a trade deficit by 1980.

IFO, a research institute in Munich, on July 31 forecast higher unemployment and slower growth in 1980 but said that inflation, running at 4.6 per cent, would probably not rise much above 5 per cent. Tight money policies and less European and U.S. demand for West German products would push the 1980 growth rate down to between 2 and 2.5 per cent. On July 19, the Organization for Economic Cooperation and Development predicted a 3 per cent growth rate for the next 12 months. However, it said that rising import prices in 1979 would cut domestic real income and demand.

Wages Deal. Responsible union attitudes continued to promote West Germany's economic stability.

Two East German families show how they rode in their home-made hot-air balloon that floated through a September night sky to West Germany.

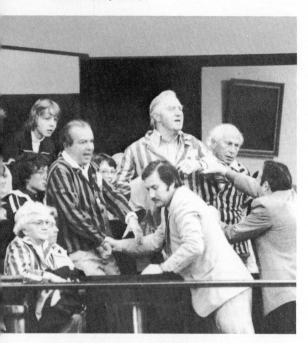

Protesters interrupt West German parliament during July debate on legislation making war criminals permanently liable to prosecution for murder.

Unions agreed on March 25 to pay increases for nearly 3 million workers. Public service employees accepted a 4 per cent pay increase plus a doubling of vacation money to $570. Chemical and print workers got similar raises. Workers won a major victory on March 2 when a federal court in Karlsruhe upheld the 1967 Workers' Participation Act, which gave employees of companies with more than 2,000 workers half the seats on company supervisory boards. Nine companies and 29 employers' associations argued that the act violated constitutional rights to private property, freedom of association, and freedom to conduct business.

New President. Karl Carstens, Christian Democrat speaker of the *Bundestag* (lower house of parliament), won a five-year term as president on May 23. He received 528 electoral college votes against 431 for Social Democrat Annemarie Renger, a former speaker. Carstens succeeded Walter Scheel, a member of the Free Democratic Party, the Social Democrats' partner in the federal government coalition. Carstens had been a member of the Nazi Party, but a West German tribunal ruled in 1948 that he had been a member in name only. Parliament voted in July to abolish the statute of limitations on murder so that persons accused of war crimes would be liable to prosecution the rest of their lives.   Kenneth Brown

See also EUROPE (Facts in Brief Table). In WORLD BOOK, see GERMANY.

GHANA. More than seven years of military rule ended on Sept. 24, 1979, when Hilla Limann, a former ambassador to Switzerland, was inaugurated as president of Ghana. Although his People's National Party won a majority of the seats in parliament in a June 16 election, Limann received only 35 per cent of the votes cast for president. However, he defeated Victor Owusu, candidate of the second largest parliamentary party, the Popular Front Party, in a July 9 runoff.

Limann headed the first civilian administration to govern Ghana since January 1972, when General Ignatius K. Acheampong deposed Kofi A. Busia in a bloodless coup d'état. Acheampong headed the country until July 1978, when another coup brought General Fred W. Akuffo to power. At that time, Akuffo pledged to return Ghana to civilian rule by July 1, 1979, scheduling parliamentary and presidential elections for June 1979. However, his government was overthrown on June 4 in a revolt led by junior army officers.

Ghana's third military government was headed by Flight Lieutenant Jerry Rawlings, who presided over a 15-member Armed Forces Revolutionary Council. Rawlings had led an unsuccessful coup attempt on May 15, 1979, and was rescued from prison during the June 4 uprising.

Public Executions. Rawlings' new government permitted elections to be held as scheduled but postponed the transfer of power until September, contending that it needed time to uproot corruption. In the course of Rawlings' anticorruption campaign, Acheampong and his aide, Lieutenant-General E. K. Utuka, were executed on June 16.

Two other former heads of state, Akuffo and Lieutenant General Akwasi A. Afrifa, and three senior military officers who had served in Akuffo's government were executed on June 26. A number of other officers were sentenced to long prison terms for alleged misappropriation of funds and profiteering.

Economic Problems. President Limann inherited an economy burdened with severe problems. The production of Ghana's main export commodity, cacao, had declined to a record low of 265,000 short tons (240,000 metric tons) in 1979 from approximately 500,000 short tons (450,000 metric tons) in the late 1960s. Lower export earnings contributed to a scarcity of foreign exchange.

During 1978 the consumer price index rose by more than 100 per cent, and preliminary data indicated a high rate of increase for 1979 also. During a two-week period that ended on March 27, Ghanaians were ordered to exchange all currency in circulation for newly printed bills at the rate of 10 old for seven new.   John D. Esseks

See also AFRICA (Facts in Brief Table). In WORLD BOOK, see GHANA.

GIRL SCOUTS. See YOUTH ORGANIZATIONS.
GIRLS CLUBS. See YOUTH ORGANIZATIONS.

GOLDSCHMIDT, NEIL EDWARD (1940-   ), mayor of Portland, Ore., took office as United States secretary of transportation on Aug. 15, 1979, though he was not confirmed by Congress until September 21. Goldschmidt replaced Brock Adams. See CABINET, UNITED STATES; TRANSPORTATION.

Goldschmidt was elected to the Portland City Council in 1970 and became mayor in 1973. In 1974, Mayor Goldschmidt killed plans for an inner-city freeway and used the money originally intended for that project to improve city streets and build a commuter-bus system. He also supported a downtown mall for Portland, which limited auto traffic to allow better bus service. Because of the effectiveness of Portland's mass-transit system, Goldschmidt was expected to promote mass transportation throughout the country as secretary of transportation.

Goldschmidt was born in Eugene, Ore., on June 16, 1940, the son of an accountant. He earned a B.A. degree in political science from the University of Oregon, Eugene, in 1963, and received his law degree at the University of California's School of Law in Berkeley in 1967.

After graduation, Goldschmidt worked as a legal aid lawyer in Portland, handling job discrimination problems, and served on a commission to improve local government.

Goldschmidt and his wife, Margaret, have two children.   Madelyn Krzak

GOLF. Tom Watson and Nancy Lopez won more tournaments and more money than any rivals on the 1979 professional tours, just as they had done a year earlier. The major men's tournaments were won by Hale Irwin and Frank (Fuzzy) Zoeller of the United States, Severiano Ballesteros of Spain, and David Graham of Australia. The key women's tournaments went to Donna Caponi Young and Jerilyn Britz.

The Professional Golfers' Association (PGA) tour ran from January to October. Its 45 tournaments paid gross purses of $12.6 million, up from 1978's record of $10.3 million.

The 29-year-old Watson, from Kansas City, was consistent. He played 20 tournaments, with 5 victories, 4 second places, and 14 finishes in the top 10. His victories came in the Heritage Classic at Hilton Head Island, S.C., and the Tournament of Champions at Rancho La Costa, Calif., in April; the Byron Nelson Classic at Dallas and the Memorial tournament at Dublin, Ohio, in May; and the Hall of Fame Classic at Pinehurst, N.C., in August.

Watson's earnings of $462,636 set a one-year record and made him the first golfer since Jack Nicklaus (1971-1973) to lead in earnings three straight years. Larry Nelson was second with $281,-022, a record for a tour rookie.

Men's Tournaments. In the Masters, the year's first major tournament, Watson, Zoeller, and Ed Sneed tied for first on April 15 at Augusta, Ga., with 72-hole scores of 280. Zoeller won the play-off with a birdie on the second extra hole. Sneed, who started the final round with a five-stroke lead, lost a chance to win by bogeying the 16th, 17th, and 18th holes.

Irwin won the U.S. Open on June 17 at Toledo, Ohio, with a 284. Jerry Pate and Gary Player tied for second at 286. On a dogleg hole, Lon Hinkle took a shortcut through an adjoining fairway and made a birdie 4. The next day, a newly installed 25-foot (8-meter) spruce tree blocking the shortcut, Hinkle defied the barrier and birdied the hole again. The 22-year-old Ballesteros, who dominated the European tour, won the British Open on July 20 at St. Anne's, England, with a 283 and a three-stroke victory over Jack Nicklaus and Ben Crenshaw.

Graham's birdie on the third extra hole beat Crenshaw in a play-off for the PGA championship on August 5 in Birmingham, Mich. Graham finished with a 65 for 272 despite a double-bogey 6 on the 18th hole. Rex Caldwell was two strokes behind.

Lou Graham (no relation to David) replaced his putter and 1962 irons in July, and won three tournaments in the next three months. The tour also produced first-time winners in John Fought, Nelson, Bob Byman, George Burns, Ed Fiori, Wayne Levi, Mark McCumber, Calvin Peete, Jack Renner, Curtis Strange, Howard Twitty, and D. A. Weibring.

For the first time since he turned professional in

Fuzzy Zoeller, right, and his caddy, center, salute his winning shot in Masters tournament play-off while loser Ed Sneed, left, looks on glumly.

1961, Nicklaus, now 39, failed to win a tournament or finish among the four leading money winners. He by-passed most tournaments in favor of business and family priorities. He watched his two teen-age sons play 12 of their 13 high-school football games and 24 of their 27 basketball games. See NICKLAUS, JACK.

LPGA Tour. The 22-year-old Lopez, who won nine tournaments and a record $189,813 in 1978, won nine tournaments and a record $197,488 this time. Her victories came in Rancho Park, Calif., and Las Vegas, Nev., in March; Hilton Head Island, S.C., and Clifton, N.J., in May; New Rochelle, N.Y., and Hershey, Pa., in June; Sunningdale, England, in August; and Portland, Ore., and Dallas in September.

The Ladies Professional Golf Association (LPGA) tour comprised 38 tournaments worth $4.4 million, both records. Jane Blalock and Amy Alcott won four tournaments each and JoAnne Carner, Sally Little, and Sandra Post won three each.

Post captured the richest tournament, the $250,-000 Colgate-Dinah Shore Winner's Circle, in April at Palm Springs, Calif. The unheralded Britz finished second to Young in the women's United States Open in June at Kings Island, Ohio, then won the LPGA championship in July at Fairfield, Conn., for her first professional victory.   Frank Litsky

In WORLD BOOK, see GOLF.

GOVERNORS, U.S. See STATE GOVERNMENT.

GREAT BRITAIN. "Mr. Speaker, now that the House of Commons has declared itself we shall take our case to the country. Tomorrow I shall propose to Her Majesty that Parliament be dissolved."

With these words on March 28, 1979, Prime Minister James Callaghan set in motion an election campaign that ended in a stunning victory on May 3 for Margaret R. Thatcher's Conservative Party. Thatcher's appointment on May 4 as Great Britain's first woman prime minister opened a new era in British politics and promised a fundamental reversal of many of the outgoing Labour Party's policies. See Close-Up.

It was an election for which Thatcher had waited patiently as Callaghan's sagging government, deprived of its overall majority by by-election defeats, staggered from one near defeat to another in the House of Commons.

The issue that finally brought down the Callaghan government was *devolution* (limited home rule) for Scotland and Wales. The government had organized March 1 referendums on devolution in Scotland and Wales. In Wales, only 11.9 per cent of the electorate voted "yes" to devolution. But the result in Scotland placed the government in a quandary. Of those entitled to vote, 30.85 per cent said "yes," 30.78 per cent said "no," and the rest did not vote. This did not suffice. Opponents of devolution had succeeded in introducing into the bill that

set up separate assemblies for Scotland and Wales a clause stipulating that at least 40 per cent of the electorate must vote "yes" or the legislation would have to be repealed.

Desperately trying to save home rule for Scotland, Callaghan offered all-party talks. The strongly pro-devolution minority Scottish National Party (SNP) and Liberal Party were furious. They offered a motion condemning the government for failing to implement the "yes" vote. Thatcher sensed that this was the moment to move in for the kill. She introduced a "no confidence" motion, and the Callaghan government lost that vote on March 28 by a single vote, 311 to 310. It was the first such vote against a government in 55 years.

The Election Campaign that followed was dominated by the "winter of discontent" that Britain had just endured. The government had been trying to hold a 5 per cent guideline for wage increases, but chaos and disruption spread as union after union struck for higher wages. In addition to a particularly severe winter, the British public had to endure strikes by health service and local municipal workers, civil servants, oil tanker operators, truckdrivers, and railroad engineers. The government patched up an agreement with the Trades Union Congress on February 14, but it was too late. The Conservatives fought the election on the issue of trade union reform, and the voters – with memories of unburied dead and piles of uncollected garbage fresh in their minds – took revenge on Labour on May 3.

The Conservatives won 339 of the 635 seats, which gave them a comfortable majority over all other parties. Labour dropped from 306 to 269 seats, the Liberals from 14 to 11, and the SNP from 11 to 2. Among Labour notables who lost their seats were Education Secretary Shirley Williams and eight other ministers. Other casualties included former Liberal leader Jeremy Thorpe, then awaiting trial at the Old Bailey on charge of incitement and conspiracy to murder a homosexual former model, Norman Scott. Thorpe and three other defendants were acquitted on June 22 after a sensational 32-day trial.

Conservative Policy. The party announced it would encourage individual initiative and effort, and reduce the role of government. Chancellor of the Exchequer Sir Geoffrey Howe announced a switch from direct to indirect taxation in the first Conservative budget on June 12. He cut the basic rate of income tax from 33 per cent to 30 per cent, raised personal tax allowances, and reduced the highest level of tax from 83 per cent to 60 per cent.

In the last half of July, the Conservative ministers produced a stream of proposals to dismantle many of

Campaigning for prime minister, Margaret Thatcher meets divers working on the Thames Flood Barrier at Woolwich for the protection of Greater London.

Labour's state controls. Secretary for Industry Sir Keith Joseph announced on July 17 that *assisted areas* (parts of Britain where industry qualified for special government grants) would be reduced from 40 per cent of the country to 25 per cent, and the size of grants would be cut. Two days later, Sir Keith announced that the role of the National Enterprise Board, a government body set up by Labour to rescue and take over ailing private companies, would be reduced and its powers to buy shares restricted. The board would have to sell off many of its assets and would no longer automatically be able to rescue stricken companies. *Receivership* (bankruptcy) "would normally be the right course where the private sector could not provide a solution to a company's problem," said Sir Keith in an uncompromising reversal of Labour's policy of supporting "lame duck" companies to provide employment.

Government Spending Cuts were the cornerstone of the Thatcher government's strategy to reduce the national budget deficit and halt soaring inflation, and the government announced its program on November 1 in a white paper. Cuts that would significantly curtail Britain's welfare state services in the fiscal year starting April 1980 were outlined for education, health, housing, public transportation, social work, and government aid to local authorities. Foreign aid was to be reduced as part of an attempt to keep total expenditure close to the current level. But the government proposed increased spending for crime control and for defense. Military spending was to be increased by the full 3 per cent recommended by the North Atlantic Treaty Organization (NATO). Parents and students in many places would have to start paying for school meals, milk, and transportation. Patients of the National Health Service would be charged higher dental and prescription fees, and commuters would have to pay higher train fares.

Trade Changes. On October 23, Sir Geoffrey Howe announced that all exchange controls would be scrapped immediately, completing a process he had cautiously begun shortly after taking office. He announced amid cheers that for the first time since 1939, Britons would be free to buy and use foreign currency as they wished. They could now take as much foreign currency out of the country as they wished, and open bank accounts anywhere.

Sir Geoffrey said controls had outlived their usefulness because confidence in the British pound was being maintained by a government "determined to maintain the right monetary and fiscal policies." Former Chancellor of the Exchequer Denis Healey criticized the move as "reckless" and "doctrinaire."

The Labour Party, in the wake of its electoral defeat, began a bout of soul-searching that seemed

The amir of Bahrain, Isa bin Sulman Al Khalifa, greets Queen Elizabeth II as she leaves the royal yacht *Britannia* on her February tour of Arabia.

Iron Lady
At 10
Downing

"Politicians are either warriors or healers," wrote one of Margaret Thatcher's biographers recently. Thatcher, the 54-year-old politician who became Great Britain's first woman prime minister on May 4, 1979, is a warrior. Because she was not born into a privileged family like many of the ministers in her Cabinet, she had to work hard to reach the top. And once installed as prime minister, she demonstrated a determination to do things in her own way.

Margaret Thatcher's political ideas spring directly from her personal background. Her political education began at home, a flat above a grocer's shop in the small town of Grantham, England. The shopkeeper was her father, a Conservative Party stalwart who later became mayor of Grantham, 105 miles (170 kilometers) north of London. The new prime minister's political speeches are rich in references to the virtues of the good shopkeeper as a model to rescue Britain from its economic woes. She speaks of the need for the nation to live within its means, satisfy its customers, work hard, and be thrifty.

A brilliant student, she gained admission to Oxford University in open competition and received a degree in chemistry, an unusual subject for a woman in the 1940s. She is the first British prime minister to have a science degree. She also studied law and became an attorney in 1953, specializing in tax law. She met London businessman Denis Thatcher at the Dartford Conservative Club while unsuccessfully campaigning for Parliament. They were married in 1951 and have a son and a daughter.

Margaret Thatcher

Mrs. Thatcher's career is a triumph of grit and determination. Elected to the House of Commons in 1959 as member for the North London suburban constituency of Finchley, she quickly began to identify herself with Conservative middle-class householders, who felt that their standard of living was being eroded in comparison with the advances being made by unionized labor. In a country where how one speaks seems almost to transcend what one says, some political strategists thought that her south-of-England, middle-class accent would put off northern voters. But Thatcher's emphasis on reducing household mortgage interest rates and on cutting taxes proved appealing to voters throughout a debt-ridden nation.

Chosen by Prime Minister Edward Heath to be minister of education and science in his Conservative government in 1970, Margaret Thatcher gave the first real hint of the abrasive, robust brand of Toryism that was later to become her hallmark. To save money, she cut off the supply of free milk to schoolchildren. That earned her the nickname "Thatcher the Milk Snatcher" from political foes.

She took the biggest step toward 10 Downing Street – the prime minister's residence – in February 1975 when she triumphed over Heath, then the Tory leader, to become leader of the Conservative Party after a brilliant campaign among Conservative Members of Parliament. From that moment on, all she had to do was avoid making any major political blunders while James Callaghan's Labour government, deprived of an overall majority in the House of Commons, drifted toward defeat.

Thatcher is considered Great Britain's most conservative prime minister since World War II. She has turned her back on the middle-of-the-road consensus politics all recent governments, both Labour and Conservative, have practiced. Yet there is a distinctly radical air about her beliefs. She maintains that the growth of the corporate state has smothered individual effort in postwar Britain. Remove the dead hand of the state, she declares, and the natural genius of the British people will rescue the country from its economic difficulties. Moreover, she is convinced that many services provided by the all-embracing welfare state are no longer appropriate, and that people should be encouraged to fend for themselves more.

Thatcher's reputation for tough talking has followed her into the foreign arena. After she made a harsh anti-Soviet speech, the Russians described her as "The Iron Lady." That is an epithet to which Great Britain's pro-work, anti-welfare warrior raises no objection, and one that has caused her not the slightest harm. Ian Mather

likely to produce far-reaching changes in its constitution and in the way it formulated future policies. The left succeeded in winning enough votes at Labour's annual conference in October to push through two of three fundamental changes that would give more power to grass-roots party workers who lean to the left at the expense of Labour Party members of Parliament (MP's), the majority of whom are centrist. These changes provided that Labour MP's must present themselves before each election for renomination by their local party, and gave sole control over the election manifesto to the party's executive committee. A decision on a third proposal – that the party leader should be elected by the conference and not by Labour MP's as at present – was postponed.

Foreign Affairs also confronted the Thatcher government with early tough decisions. Foreign Secretary Lord Carrington brought all the parties at war in Zimbabwe Rhodesia to London in September for a peace conference. They signed a cease-fire agreement on December 21. Rhodesian elections were scheduled for early in 1980. See CARRINGTON, LORD; ZIMBABWE RHODESIA.

Britain's partners in the European Community (EC or Common Market) were reminded of Thatcher's tough "fighting her own corner" reputation. Thatcher announced that it was "intolerable" that Great Britain, sixth in per capita income among the nine EC members, should have to make the highest net contribution to the EC budget, mainly to subsidize European farmers. Unless EC heads of government started reform of the EC's Common Agricultural Policy at their meeting in Dublin, Ireland, at the end of November, she declared, Great Britain would refuse to pay its required share next year. But when no compromise could be worked out at that meeting, Thatcher relented temporarily and agreed to give other EC leaders "one last chance" to negotiate the matter at the next summit meeting to be held in Brussels, Belgium, in the spring of 1980.

The European Parliament, the legislative arm of the EC, had members elected by citizens of the member countries for the first time in June (see EUROPE). Conservatives won 60 of the 78 seats in England, Scotland, and Wales.

Earl Mountbatten of Burma, a cousin of Queen Elizabeth II, and one of Great Britain's most distinguished statesmen, was killed on August 27 when a bomb blew up his fishing boat off the Irish coast. On August 30, two suspected members of the outlawed Irish Republican Army (IRA) were charged with the murder of Mountbatten and three other persons killed in the explosion. In November, one was convicted and one acquitted. Also on August 27, a vacationing Englishman and 18 British soldiers died in an IRA ambush in Northern Ireland.   Ian Mather

See also EUROPE (Facts in Brief Table). In WORLD BOOK, see GREAT BRITAIN.

GREECE. Prime Minister Constantine Karamanlis signed an agreement on May 28, 1979, to bring Greece into the European Community (EC, or Common Market) on Jan. 1, 1981. Until that time, Greece has the right to be consulted on any EC decisions.

Wages Raised. An arbitration court raised minimum wages and salaries 15 per cent on February 15 after negotiations between unions and employers failed. The government introduced austerity measures to cut inflation on August 22, including credit controls, public spending cuts, higher interest rates, and curbs on pay hikes. Prices rose 11 per cent in the first six months of 1979, and the current-account deficit jumped 55 per cent from a year earlier to $1.4-billion. Oil price hikes added $300 million to Greece's oil bill, bringing it to $1.3 billion. The price of gasoline, already among the highest in the world, went up 18 per cent on April 13 and another 15.4 per cent in July. The government rationed gasoline for private cars, imposed speed limits, and allowed only half the cars on the roads on weekends.

Greece decided to build two lignite-fired power stations with a total capacity of 600 megawatts and planned to spend $1 billion for natural gas pipelines to Italy and Bulgaria to bring in gas from Algeria and Russia. Greece gets 70 per cent of its energy from imported oil.

A government attempt to change banking hours caused bank strikes that crippled business in July and August. The government tried unsuccessfully to end the strike in July by threatening the workers with jail sentences. The strikes ended after a court declared on August 16 that the employees' union would have to pay each banking group $30,000 for every day the strike continued. However, talks between the union and the Labor Ministry broke down in September.

Foreign Affairs. Karamanlis and Bulgaria's State Council Chairman Todor Zhivkov signed an agreement on April 30. The pact encourages cooperation among Balkan countries in transportation, energy, communications, and the environment.

United Nations Secretary-General Kurt Waldheim visited Cyprus in May to arrange talks between Greek Cypriot and Turkish Cypriot leaders on unifying the island. They had not negotiated for two years. The talks began on June 15, but ended after four sessions. The sticking points remained Turkish insistence on separate zones for the two nationalities and disagreements on security.   Kenneth Brown

See also EUROPE (Facts in Brief Table). In WORLD BOOK, see CYPRUS; EUROPEAN COMMUNITY; GREECE.

GRENADA. See LATIN AMERICA.
GUATEMALA. See LATIN AMERICA.
GUINEA. See AFRICA.
GUINEA-BISSAU. See AFRICA.
GUYANA. See LATIN AMERICA.
HAITI. See LATIN AMERICA.

HANDICAPPED. The Supreme Court of the United States ruled unanimously on June 11, 1979, that colleges are not required to accept handicapped students whose handicaps prevent them from meeting the requirements of a particular program. Nor are colleges required to provide "extensive modifications" or help so that a handicapped student may attend. The decision was the court's first ruling on the scope of the Rehabilitation Act of 1973, which forbids discrimination against the handicapped.

Frances B. Davis sued Southeastern Community College in Whiteville, N.C., for denying her admission to a federally funded program for training registered nurses. Davis, who is severely hard of hearing, has been employed as a licensed practical nurse since 1967 and is a skilled lip reader. A federal appeals court ordered the college to admit Davis. On appeal, the college presented evidence that while she was able to perform as a practical nurse, there was reasonable doubt about her capacity to perform as a registered nurse. Even with a hearing aid, she could not understand what people said unless she was in a position to read their lips. This might reduce her effectiveness in an operating room, the college said. They also said she could miss a weak call for help from a patient.

The lower court and the U.S. Department of Health, Education, and Welfare (HEW) contended that the college had to give Davis special help to get around these problems under the terms of the Rehabilitation Act. But the Supreme Court ruled that institutions need not lower their standards.

Enforcement Problems. In 1979, it appeared that Congress and the government departments were unable to redeem the promises made by HEW Secretary Joseph A. Califano, Jr., in April 1977, when he signed regulations spelling out a number of steps government would take to stop discrimination against the handicapped.

By October 1979, Congress had not appropriated the funds authorized by the Rehabilitation Act or by the Education for All Handicapped Children Act of 1975. State and local governments said they could not meet federal requirements without full federal funding. Problems seemed acute in two areas—transportation and education.

The Department of Transportation issued controversial proposals on April 3, 1979, requiring that new buses purchased with Urban Mass Transportation Funds must have wheelchair lifts; new rail systems must offer easy access to the elderly and handicapped; and airports must have telescoping ramps and offer special assistance for deaf and blind passengers. Local governments were allowed five to 30 years to modify equipment and increase access to existing rail, subway, and bus systems. In a change from earlier proposals, transit systems could opt to provide access to key stations only and could offer alternative transportation to the handicapped.

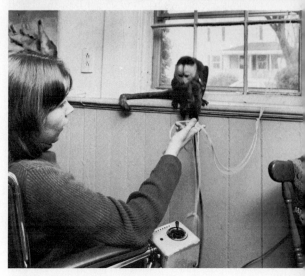

Linda Richards, paralyzed and confined to a wheelchair, has Tish, a capuchin monkey, trained for such tasks as fetching a shade cord.

Transit Officials around the country expressed alarm about the new regulations and had difficulty getting money from local governments to finance them. On the other hand, handicapped individuals complained that 30 years was too long to wait for changes in older systems and that alternative door-to-door transportation unfairly separated the handicapped from the mainstream of society.

In education, similar funding problems affected the Individualized Education Programs (IEP's) required by federal law. A separate IEP must be prepared for each of the nation's more than 3.5 million handicapped schoolchildren. Parents participate in the planning. HEW staff members found many instances in which school districts were not following federal regulations on IEP's.

The federal government allocated $564 million to help schools provide services to the handicapped in fiscal 1979, and the figure was set to rise to $804-million in 1980. But many educators said that the cost of educating the handicapped is so high that local districts cannot provide the services needed.

Jim Branotte of Preston, Calif., won the President's award for the Handicapped American of the Year. A triple-amputee Vietnam veteran, he owns and runs a ranch for the disabled. Virginia E. Anderson

In WORLD BOOK, see HANDICAPPED.

HARNESS RACING. See HORSE RACING.

HAWAII. See STATE GOVERNMENT.

HEALTH AND DISEASE. United States Surgeon General Julius B. Richmond in July 1979 called on Americans to launch a health "revolution" to prevent disease by changing their diet and habits. He said Americans could reduce the death rate in various age groups by 20 to 35 per cent by 1990 if they cut back their intake of alcohol, salt, sugar, and fats; exercised for 15 to 30 minutes three times a week; stopped smoking; wore seat belts in automobiles and obeyed speed limits; and underwent periodic medical screening and examination.

In taking this stand, Richmond and other officials of the Department of Health, Education, and Welfare (HEW) entered the controversy on the role of diet in disease. Earlier in the year, an international panel of heart specialists and nutritionists, sponsored by the American Health Foundation, had also proclaimed that the rate of coronary heart disease would decrease if Americans reduced their cholesterol levels by changing to a low-fat diet that included less meat. Other physicians challenged the linking of diet and heart disease.

War Against Cancer. In testimony in October to the Senate Subcommittee on Nutrition and Human Needs, Arthur Upton, director of the National Cancer Institute, for the first time linked diet with cancer and recommended that Americans eat a balanced, low-fat, high-fiber diet and cut down on meat and alcohol. Physicians at Boston's Beth Israel

The World Health Organization circulated a poster in 1979 offering a $1,000 reward for a prompt report of any active cases of smallpox.

Hospital reported in *The New England Journal of Medicine* in September that there may be genetic or inherited reasons for a higher incidence of cancer in some families. They found that 10 members in three generations of one family developed the same type of kidney cancer, and traced it to interchange of the genetic material in two chromosomes.

The *New England Journal* reported in February that long-term users of synthetic estrogen face a 10 to 30 per cent greater risk of endometrial cancer. Estrogen, a female hormone, is often used to relieve the symptoms of menopause.

On June 5, the National Institutes of Health announced new guidelines for breast cancer surgery, advocating the modified mastectomy – the removal of only the breast and lymph nodes – rather than the radical mastectomy, which also removes the chest wall. In September, physician Samuel Hellman of Harvard University told the National Conference on Breast Cancer meeting in New York City that the combination of a *lumpectomy* (removal of only the cancerous tumor) and radiation treatments may be as effective as a mastectomy. Several other researchers reported longer survival periods for breast cancer patients treated with cancer drugs. Scientists also reported that new techniques of *mammography* – taking images of the breast – have reduced the radiation dose and made radiation therapy safer for women under 50.

The Laetrile Controversy. A case involving another controversial cancer therapy – Laetrile – went before the Supreme Court of the United States in June. The court upheld the right of the Food and Drug Administration (FDA) to ban interstate distribution of the apricot pit derivative, even for terminally ill patients. However, the high court sent back two other issues to the district court for consideration – whether a patient's privacy rights are violated by the governmental restrictions on Laetrile and whether Laetrile, which was discovered before laws were passed requiring that drugs be proved effective, should be exempted from such laws. In January, a Massachusetts court ordered the parents of 3-year-old Chad Green to stop treating him with Laetrile for his leukemia. The family fled to Mexico to continue this unorthodox therapy. The boy died in Mexico in October.

The American Cancer Society reported in November that lung cancer in women continued to increase in 1979. For the first time, lung cancer became the second most fatal cancer for U.S. females – behind only breast cancer.

Joseph A. Califano, Jr., HEW secretary, also declared war on public health enemy number two – alcoholism – in May, and requested federal funds for rehabilitation, research, and education programs. The *Journal of the American Medical Association* reported on June 8 that investigators in Chile, Iceland, and Sweden have observed a recessive gene that may be responsible for alcoholism.

The first large-scale U.S. trials of a vaccine for a sexually transmitted disease, hepatitis B, were launched in April. Several clinics were to test the vaccine in 8,000 volunteers, many of whom are homosexual men, a high-risk group. An estimated 120,000 cases of hepatitis B occur each year. Meanwhile, the Center for Disease Control in Atlanta, Ga., announced that the venereal disease that occurs most frequently is nongonococcal urethritis.

Health Policy. Patricia R. Harris, secretary of Housing and Urban Development, changed Cabinet posts and replaced HEW Secretary Califano in July, ending the term of one of the most controversial HEW administrators (see CABINET, UNITED STATES). National health insurance resurfaced as a political issue, with both President Jimmy Carter and Senator Edward M. Kennedy (D., Mass.) outlining their plans. The President's national health plan, unveiled on June 12, is not comprehensive and it limits physician reimbursement. Kennedy introduced his plan, more comprehensive than Carter's, on May 14.

The federal government on February 6 stopped funding hysterectomies done primarily for the purpose of sterilization, under new Public Health Service sterilization rules. Dianne R. Hales

See also DRUGS; MEDICINE; PUBLIC HEALTH. In WORLD BOOK, see CANCER; HEALTH.

HEIDEN is the family name of two American speed skaters, brother and sister, who won world championships in 1979.

Beth Heiden (1959-   ), a civil engineering student at the University of Wisconsin, Madison, won the world overall title by taking all four races, at 500, 1,000, 1,500, and 3,000 meters. She also won the world overall junior title for women in 1978. She started as a figure skater, but she and her brother Eric entered races at a Madison speed-skating club, where Olympic speed-skating champion Diane Holum saw them racing. Holum became their coach and put them on a demanding physical-training program that combined hours of skating with bicycling, running, weight lifting, and other exercises. Beth stands 5 feet 2 inches (157 centimeters) tall and weighs 100 pounds (45 kilograms).

Eric Heiden (1958-   ), a premedical student at Wisconsin, was the first skater in history to win the world junior, sprints, and overall championships in the same year. He did this in 1977 and 1978. Over a three-year period, he won eight straight world championships – two in junior competition, three in overall races, and three in sprints. Eric Heiden stands 6 feet 2 inches (188 centimeters) tall and weighs about 165 pounds (75 kilograms). He has exceptionally thick, strong thighs that power his explosive racing start. Joseph P. Spohn

See also ICE SKATING.

HERRERA CAMPINS, LUIS (1925-   ), a Social Christian Party leader and journalist, took office as president of Venezuela on March 12, 1979, succeeding Carlos Andres Perez of the Democratic Action Party. The major issue in the December 1978 election was alleged waste and corruption in the government's handling of oil revenue.

Herrera was born on May 4, 1925, in Acarigua. He finished secondary school in Barquisimeto and went to Caracas to study at Central University. When the Social Christian Party was founded in 1946, he became director of its weekly publication. In 1952, when he was a law student, Herrera wrote an article opposing government censorship and tried to organize a university strike against military dictator Marcos Pérez Jiménez. The government imprisoned him for four months because of these acts and then deported him. Herrera went to Europe, where he helped found a publication opposing Pérez Jiménez. He received a law degree from Santiago de Compostela University in Spain.

Pérez Jiménez was overthrown in 1958, and Herrera returned to Venezuela. He was elected to the Chamber of Deputies in 1958, 1963, and 1968, and to the Senate in 1973.

Herrera and his wife have three sons and two daughters. Jay Myers

HIGHWAY. See BUILDING AND CONSTRUCTION; TRANSPORTATION.

HITCHCOCK, ALFRED JOSEPH (1899-), was awarded the American Film Institute's Life Achievement Award on March 8, 1979. The award commended Hitchcock's work as "having advanced the filmmaking art and having stood the test of time." He was also dubbed Knight Commander of the Order of the British Empire on December 31.

Born on Aug. 13, 1899, in London, Hitchcock attended St. Ignatius College and the University of London, where he studied electrical engineering. After working briefly as an electrical technician, he entered the motion-picture industry as a title artist in 1920. He worked as a film writer, production manager, and art director before directing his first film, *The Pleasure Garden,* in 1925.

Hitchcock moved to the United States in 1939, and his first American film, *Rebecca,* won an Academy Award for best picture of 1940. He received an Oscar nomination as best director of that film as well as for *Lifeboat* (1944), *Spellbound* (1946), and *Rear Window* (1954). Other notable Hitchcock films include *North by Northwest* (1959), *Psycho* (1960), and *Frenzy* (1972). He presented two television series that ran from 1955 to 1965.

A master of suspense, Hitchcock has delighted and terrified audiences with a mix of humor and horror. He assigns himself a brief walk-on role in each film.

Hitchcock married his assistant director, Alma Reville, in 1926. They have a daughter. Beverly Merz

Patrick Lindsay of Christie's prepares to auction a 1936 Mercedes 500K in Los Angeles in February. The car sold for $400,000—a record for vintage autos.

HOBBIES. "The craze for collectibles" drove prices for various collectors' items ever higher in 1979. Spurred partly by the declining value of currency and more conventional investments, buyers pushed the prices of everything from period furniture to whirligig toys and rare glass bowls to record highs.

Rare Glass. A Roman glass bowl believed to have been made in the Rhineland region of Germany about A.D. 300 was auctioned in London on June 4 for $1.04 million, the highest price recorded for a piece of glassware. The previous record, $150,000, was paid in 1978 for an Italian goblet.

The Eugene and Eleanor Gluck collection of lamps and other art objects by Louis Comfort Tiffany brought $1.1 million—a record for an art nouveau auction—in New York City on February 17. A spider web vase sold for $150,000—more than double the previous record price for such a vase; a wisteria lamp, mass-produced in its day, sold for $120,000—twice the previous high; and two flower containers set records of $19,000 and $17,000.

Period Furniture. A sale held in Monte Carlo, Monaco, on June 25 and 26 established a new sales record—$13 million—for a furniture auction. More than 900 persons attending the auction saw the previous record price of $585,500 for a single piece of furniture shattered four times. The highest price—$1.7 million—was paid for an ornate Louis XV corner cupboard decorated with an elaborate clock.

Other Records. An unidentified automobile collector, bidding by telephone from Monte Carlo, bought a 1936 Mercedes-Benz 500K roadster for $400,000 at a Los Angeles auction on February 25. Another Mercedes, a 1929 Model SS 38-250, sold for $320,000 at the same auction. Both prices topped the previous record of $235,000 for a car sold at auction.

J. Bradley Taylor, a Boston violin dealer, sold a 300-year-old violin made by master craftsman Antonio Stradivari to an anonymous buyer for about $400,000, a record price for a stringed instrument, in March. Only about 700 of the original 1,116 violins made by Stradivari still exist.

The sale of 195 lots of silver from the collection of Janiece Christner of Dallas in New York City on January 7 brought $766,730—a record for an American silver auction. A pair of Regency wine coolers that sold for $14,000 in 1971 went for $46,000. They were the work of Paul Storr, an English Regency silversmith. A silver service by Storr was sold for $533,598—a record for English silver—in London on March 21.

Folk-art collectors bid up prices for whirligigs, toys designed to spin in the wind. Record prices of $5,000 each were set in Boston for a flapping eagle and in New York City for a Revolutionary War toy soldier. Theodore M. O'Leary

See also COIN COLLECTING; STAMP COLLECTING. In WORLD BOOK, see HOBBY.

HOCKEY. The seven-year war between the established National Hockey League (NHL) and the upstart World Hockey Association (WHA) ended on March 30, 1979, when the NHL agreed to absorb four of the WHA's six surviving teams. The NHL accepted the New England Whalers, the Winnipeg Jets, the Edmonton Oilers, and the Quebec Nordiques. Each new team had to pay a $6-million franchise fee, the $24 million to be split by the NHL's 17 existing teams. In addition, the four new teams would pay a total of $6.35 million to the Birmingham Bulls and Cincinnati Stingers, the two WHA teams that would be dissolved.

Starting with the 1979-1980 season, the NHL employed new schedule and play-off formats. Each team played 80 games – two at home and two away – against every other team. The play-offs were to involve the four division winners and 12 wild-card teams.

The Merger Process. The new teams were not allowed to keep all their players. Instead, each could protect only two goalies and two skaters, with the other players available for a draft by the existing NHL teams. The new teams filled out their rosters with a draft from NHL teams, which were allowed to protect two goalies and 15 skaters.

The merger did not make everyone happy. Harold Ballard, president of the Toronto Maple Leafs of the NHL and a long-time merger foe, said, "I don't feel very good about this. They took 18 of my players

Standings in National Hockey League

Clarence Campbell Conference

Lester Patrick Division	W.	L.	T.	Points
New York Islanders	51	15	14	116
Philadelphia	40	25	15	95
New York Rangers	40	29	11	91
Atlanta	41	31	8	90

Conn Smythe Division				
Chicago	29	36	15	73
Vancouver	25	42	13	63
St. Louis	18	50	12	48
Colorado	15	53	12	42

Prince of Wales Conference

Charles F. Adams Division	W.	L.	T.	Points
Boston	43	23	14	100
Buffalo	36	28	16	88
Toronto	34	33	13	81
Minnesota	28	40	12	68

James Norris Division				
Montreal	52	17	11	115
Pittsburgh	36	31	13	85
Los Angeles	34	34	12	80
Washington	24	41	15	63
Detroit	23	41	16	62

Scoring Leaders	Games	Goals	Assists	Points
Bryan Trottier, N.Y. Islanders	76	47	87	134
Marcel Dionne, Los Angeles	80	59	71	130
Guy Lafleur, Montreal	80	52	77	129
Mike Bossy, N.Y. Islanders	80	69	57	126
Bob MacMillan, Atlanta	79	37	71	108
Guy Chouinard, Atlanta	80	50	57	107
Denis Potvin, N.Y. Islanders	73	31	70	101
Ernie Federko, St. Louis	74	31	64	95
Dave Taylor, Los Angeles	78	43	48	91
Clark Gillies, N.Y. Islanders	75	35	56	91

Leading Goalies	Games	Goals against	Avg.
Ken Dryden, Montreal	47	108	2.30
Michel Larocque, Montreal	34	94	2.84
Montreal Totals	80	204	2.55
Glenn Resch, N.Y. Islanders	43	106	2.50
Bill Smith, N.Y. Islanders	40	108	2.87
N.Y. Islanders Totals	80	214	2.68

Awards

Calder Trophy (best rookie)—Bobby Smith, Minnesota
Hart Trophy (most valuable player)—Bryan Trottier, N.Y. Islanders
Lady Byng Trophy (sportsmanship)—Bob MacMillan, Atlanta
Norris Trophy (best defenseman)—Denis Potvin, N.Y. Islanders
Art Ross Trophy (leading scorer)—Bryan Trottier, N.Y. Islanders
Conn Smythe Trophy (most valuable in Stanley Cup)—
  Bob Gainey, Montreal
Vezina Trophy (leading goalie)—Ken Dryden, Michel Larocque, Montreal

Standings in World Hockey Association

	W.	L.	T.	Points
Edmonton	48	30	2	98
Quebec	41	34	5	87
Winnipeg	39	35	6	84
New England	37	34	9	83
Cincinnati	33	41	6	72
Birmingham	32	42	6	70
*Indianapolis	5	18	2	12

*Team disbanded on Dec. 16, 1978

Scoring Leaders	Games	Goals	Assists	Points
Real Cloutier, Quebec	77	75	54	129
Robbie Ftorek, Cincinnati	80	39	77	116
Wayne Gretzky, Edmonton	80	46	64	110
Mark Howe, New England	77	42	65	107
Kent Nilsson, Winnipeg	78	39	68	107
Morris Lukowich, Winnipeg	80	65	34	99
Marc Tardif, Quebec	74	41	55	96
Andre Lacroix, New England	78	32	56	88
Peter Sullivan, Winnipeg	80	46	40	86
Terry Ruskowski, Winnipeg	75	20	66	86

Leading Goalies	Games	Goals against	Avg.
Dave Dryden, Edmonton	63	170	2.89
Ed Walsh, Edmonton	3	9	3.75
Ed Mio: Indianapolis	5	13	3.22
Edmonton	22	71	3.99
Hannu Kampurri, Edmonton	2	10	6.67
Edmonton Totals	80	260	3.23
Richard Brodeur, Quebec	42	126	3.11
Jim Corsi, Quebec	40	126	3.30
Louis Levasseur, Quebec	3	14	6.00
Quebec Totals	80	266	3.28
Michel Dion, Cincinnati	30	93	3.32
Mike Liut, Cincinnati	54	184	3.47
Cincinnati Totals	80	277	3.42

Awards

Gordie Howe Trophy (most valuable player)—Dave Dryden, Edmonton
Bill Hunter Trophy (scoring champion)—Real Cloutier, Quebec
Murphy Trophy (best defenseman)—Rick Ley, New England
Hatskin Trophy (best goaltender)—Dave Dryden, Edmonton
Kaplan Award (rookie of the year)—Wayne Gretzke, Edmonton
Deneau Trophy (sportsmanship)—Kent Nilsson, Winnipeg
Coach of the Year—John Brophy, Birmingham
AVCO Cup Play-Off Most Valuable Player—Rich Preston, Winnipeg

originally, and they cost me $6 million. You don't go to bed with people who do that to you."

The WHA gained instant credibility in 1972 by luring Bobby Hull from the Chicago Black Hawks of the NHL for $250,000 per year plus a $1-million signing bonus. While it made millionaires of other players, too, the WHA lost $50 million. It helped raise the NHL's average salary from $22,000 in 1972 to more than $100,000 in 1979. Almost 30 WHA franchises died or moved. The Ottawa Civics lasted one game; the New York Golden Blades, two weeks.

The Montreal Canadiens, as usual, won the 1979 Stanley Cup play-offs, though they did not dominate the NHL season as they did in winning the cup the three previous years. The regular-season division winners were the New York Islanders, Montreal, Boston Bruins, and Chicago Black Hawks. The Islanders had the best record (116 points to 115 for Montreal); the scoring champion (center Bryan Trottier with 134 points in 76 games); the top goal scorer (wing Mike Bossy with 69, the second-highest ever); and the top-scoring defenseman (Denis Potvin with 101 points, the second-highest ever).

Twelve of the 17 teams advanced to the play-offs. The New York Rangers, who had struggled for years, upset the Islanders, 4 games to 2, in the semifinals. Montreal beat Boston, 4 games to 3, in the semifinals and the Rangers, 4 games to 1, in the

finals. The Cup was the fifth in Scotty Bowman's eight years as Montreal coach, but because of disagreements with the front office, he quit to become general manager of the Buffalo Sabres.

Trottier won the Hart Trophy as the NHL's Most Valuable Player and the Art Ross Trophy as scoring champion; Potvin won the James Norris Trophy for defensemen; and Ken Dryden and Michel Larocque of Montreal, the Vezina Trophy for goaltending. Bob Gainey of Montreal won the Frank Selke Trophy as the best defensive forward and the Conn Smythe Trophy as Most Valuable Player in the play-offs; center Bobby Smith of the Minnesota North Stars, the Calder Trophy as Rookie of the Year; and Bob MacMillan of the Atlanta Flames, the Lady Byng Trophy for sportsmanship.

The WHA was reduced to six teams when the Indianapolis Racers dropped out in December 1978. Edmonton won the regular-season competition but lost to Winnipeg, 4 games to 2, in the play-off finals.

The Russian national team won the first Challenge Cup series from the NHL All-Stars. They met on February 8, 10, and 11 in New York City. The Russians lost the first game, 4-2, but won the last two, 5-4 and 6-0. Then they won their second straight world championship in an April tournament in Moscow.   Frank Litsky

In WORLD BOOK, see HOCKEY.

HONDURAS. See LATIN AMERICA.

HORSE RACING. Affirmed, the 1978 Horse of the Year, repeated his dominance as a 4-year-old in 1979, winning seven consecutive major stakes in the East and West. Affirmed earned $275,000 first money in the $500,000 Hollywood Gold Cup at Hollywood Park on June 24, and became the first thoroughbred to earn more than $2 million.

Hawksworth Farm's Spectacular Bid, champion of his age at 2, won the Kentucky Derby at Churchill Downs on May 5 and the Preakness at Pimlico on May 19, but his Triple Crown bid failed when he finished third to Coastal in the Belmont Stakes on June 9. After recovering from a punctured hoof he reportedly suffered on the morning of the Belmont Stakes, Spectacular Bid won the Marlboro Cup Handicap at Belmont Park on September 8.

Affirmed and Spectacular Bid met in the Jockey Club Gold Cup at Belmont on October 6 with Affirmed carrying 126 pounds (57 kilograms) and the 3-year-old carrying 121 pounds (55 kilograms) under weight-for-age conditions. Affirmed controlled the pace and won the $1\frac{1}{2}$-mile race by three-quarters of a length over Spectacular Bid. Coastal was third in the four-horse race.

New Records. Laffit Pincay, Jr., who rode Affirmed, set a new single-season earnings record for jockeys, passing the $8-million mark on December 9 with his 410th victory at Aqueduct. Lazaro Barrera topped his own $3,314,565 mark for trainers.

Montreal Canadiens captain Serge Savard carries the Stanley Cup around the ice after Montreal beat the New York Rangers in the finals in May.

Major Horse Races of 1979

Race	Winner	Value to Winner
Belmont Stakes	Coastal	$161,400
Canadian International Championship	Golden Act	120,000
Epsom Derby (England)	Troy	319,693
Grand National Steeplechase (England)	Rubstic	83,848
Irish Sweeps Derby	Troy	210,925
Jockey Club Gold Cup	Affirmed	225,000
Kentucky Derby	Spectacular Bid	228,650
King George VI & Queen Elizabeth Diamond Stakes (England)	Troy	217,258
Marlboro Cup Handicap	Spectacular Bid	180,000
Preakness	Spectacular Bid	165,300
Prix de l'Arc de Triomphe (France)	Three Troikas	290,640
Prix du Jockey-Club (France)	Top Ville	203,760
Santa Anita Handicap	Affirmed	192,800
Washington D.C. Int'l.	Bowl Game	120,000
Woodward Handicap	Affirmed	114,600

Major U.S. Harness Races of 1979

Race	Winner	Value to Winner
Cane Pace	Happy Motoring	$ 80,475
Hambletonian	Legend Hanover	150,000
Little Brown Jug	Hot Hitter	90,582
Meadowlands Pace	Sonsam	375,000
Roosevelt Int'l	Doublemint	100,000
Woodrow Wilson Pace	Niatross	431,375
Yonkers Trot	Chiola Hanover	118,883

The strong demand for thoroughbreds at auction resulted in increased prices at major sales. A son of Hoist the Flag sold for $1.6 million at Keeneland in Lexington, Ky., on July 24 for a new world record for a yearling.

Troy, a 3-year-old owned by Sir Michael Sobell, set an earnings record for horses trained in Great Britain, passing Alleged's $738,000. He won the Epsom Derby, King George VI and Queen Elizabeth Diamond Stakes, and Benson and Hedges Gold Cup in England, and the Irish Sweeps Derby. But he finished third in the Prix de l'Arc de Triomphe on October 7 at Longchamps in Paris, which was won by the filly Three Troikas.

Harness Racing. Abercrombie, a 4-year-old pacer, set a mile world record of 1 minute 53 seconds at the Meadowlands, N.J., on August 4. Sonsam won the Meadowlands Pace on July 19 to establish a mark of 1 minute 53²/₅ seconds for a 3-year-old.

The famous Hambletonian race, run at Du Quoin, Ill., since 1957, will be moved to a metropolitan setting at the Meadowlands in New Jersey by 1981, possibly as early as 1980.

Quarter Horse Racing. The $1.3-million All-American Futurity, the world's richest horse race, was won on September 3 by 2-year-old Pie in the Sky. He earned $437,500.   Jane Goldstein

In WORLD BOOK, see HARNESS RACING; HORSE RACING.

HOSPITAL. President Jimmy Carter on March 5, 1979, sent Congress a new bill to curb hospital costs. The bill, which Carter termed "one of the most critical anti-inflation measures," called for a 9.7 per cent "national voluntary limit" on cost increases for 1979, with mandatory controls to take effect on Jan. 1, 1980, if the limit were not met.

The bill was weaker than one proposed by the President in 1978, and it was further weakened in committee. But Congress was still not receptive. The American Hospital Association (AHA), American Medical Association (AMA), and Federation of American Hospitals (FAH) launched a vigorous and successful effort against the bill. The House passed a substitute bill in November that provided only voluntary controls.

The Voluntary Effort, launched by the AHA, AMA, and FAH in 1978 to cut hospital spending by 2 per cent, was succeeding, the groups claimed. The AHA said the program had kept the inflation rate below 11.6 per cent in 1979. In 1978, overall hospital costs rose 12.8 per cent, according to the AHA, down from a 15.6 per cent increase in 1977. But in six states that imposed mandatory controls in 1977, inflation was slowed to 10.4 per cent in 1978, compared with 15 per cent in other states.

According to figures released by the AHA and the federal government, hospitals receive 40 cents of every health dollar spent. The government also pays 55 per cent of the total U.S. hospital bill.

Most Cost-Cutting. In steps designed to curb hospital costs, the Blue Cross Association and the National Association of Blue Shield Plans, which represent state, local, and employer prepayment plans that insure a total of about 112 million persons in the United States, announced in February that they are asking member plans to stop paying for routine diagnostic tests for all patients admitted to hospitals. Such tests would be paid for by Blue Cross and Blue Shield only when specifically ordered by a physician. This might save as much as $200 million annually, an association spokesman said.

Blue Cross and Blue Shield also issued a list of 26 laboratory tests "considered outmoded, unnecessary, unreliable, or of no proven value." By refusing to reimburse for these procedures, they said they would save about $27 million.

In June, the Medical Policy Committee of Blue Shield of California, a trend-setting group whose recommendations have often been implemented nationally, recommended that more than 700 medical and surgical procedures be done on an outpatient or ambulatory basis. These included such common procedures as biopsies of breast lumps and hernia repairs. If such procedures do not require routine hospitalization, Blue Shield said some $1.6 billion in U.S. hospital charges might be saved. Dianne R. Hales

See also DRUGS; HEALTH AND DISEASE; MEDICINE. In WORLD BOOK, see HOSPITAL.

HOUSING. The United States housing industry bowed to recessionary forces during 1979, as rising home prices and record interest rates combined to produce a decline. New housing starts fell 12.1 per cent during the first six months of the year. The seasonally adjusted rate of 1.9 million annual housing starts for September, however, ran well ahead of the 1.6 million starts predicted by housing market analysts at the start of the year, but consistently below the 2-million level reached in 1978.

New home sales declined sharply after midyear, according to a report released on August 24 by Advance Mortgage Corporation. Mortgage bankers, meeting in Chicago on October 15, reported home-mortgage activity at a near standstill.

Mortgage Costs. Increased home-mortgage costs reflected both higher home prices and elevated interest rates. Chicago was hit hardest among the major cities with a 40 per cent decline in home sales during the first half of the year. The monthly mortgage payment in Chicago on an average new home bought with a 20 per cent down payment rose $120 per month, or 28 per cent, during the year ending in October 1979. The National Association of Realtors reported a 28 per cent increase nationwide on mortgages on existing homes bought with a 10 per cent down payment during the year ending in March 1979. Despite high payments, however,

home-mortgage delinquencies dropped to 0.6 per cent in June, the lowest rate ever recorded. The national average interest rate on new-home mortgages topped 11 per cent, a record high, in late September, and was expected to climb to more than 12 per cent by early 1980.

Home Selling Prices skyrocketed. The U.S. Department of Commerce reported on August 15 that the average price of a new single-family house had increased to $72,000 by midyear – up 158 per cent from $27,900 in 1969. The Federal Home Loan Bank Board reported on January 20 that an estimated 30 per cent of all first-time home buyers spend more than 33 per cent of their monthly income on housing. Robert H. McKinney, chairman of the board, predicted that the cost of such a home would reach $125,000 by 1988.

A report issued by the Urban Institute on May 12 indicated that the use of tax-exempt mortgage bonds, issued by state and local governments to provide home loans at lower interest rates, more than tripled in the preceding three years. The bonds were being issued at an annual rate of $13 billion during the first four months of 1979. The report noted that the bonds, originally designed to subsidize home purchases by low- and moderate-income families, tended to subsidize families in upper-income brackets instead. Congressman Henry S. Reuss (D., Wis.),

Clem Scalzitto, © 1979, The Kiplinger Washington Editors, Inc.
"I figure it's a good time to insulate."

chairman of the House Committee on Banking, Finance, and Urban Affairs, reported on April 8 that the bonds would cost the U.S. Treasury $340 million in lost revenue during fiscal 1980.

Housing for the Poor. According to reports released on April 11 by the U.S. Commission on Civil Rights and on July 22 by the Department of Housing and Urban Development (HUD), significant housing discrimination still exists more than a decade after legislation was passed to ban it. The HUD study noted that blacks seeking to buy homes were subjected to discriminatory treatment 33 per cent of the time in the North-Central states, 12 per cent of the time in the West, 11 per cent in the South, and 10 per cent in the Northeast. The Supreme Court of the United States ruled on April 17 that, under the Fair Housing Act of 1968, local governments have the right to sue real estate brokers who practice discrimination policies that block community integration.

HUD and the Federal National Mortgage Association announced a joint effort on February 6 to promote up to $1.4 billion in new private-development money for inner-city housing (see CITY). HUD also announced on March 31 that it was giving $5.2 million in grants to help counsel low- and moderate-income families in danger of losing federally subsidized homes.   James M. Banovetz

In WORLD BOOK, see HOUSE; HOUSING.

HOUSTON residents voted on Aug. 11, 1979, to restructure the City Council to provide better representation to the blacks and Hispanics who comprise about 40 per cent of the city's 1.7 million population. The new City Council has nine members elected from single-member districts and five elected at large. It replaced a council of eight members elected at large that included only one minority member, a black. In the November 6 general election, three blacks and one Hispanic won council seats.

Federal Action triggered the City Council change. Amendments to the Voting Rights Act of 1965 empower the United States Department of Justice to review proposed changes affecting voting in local areas. Federal courts postponed a tax-limitation referendum scheduled for April 7 while the Justice Department investigated the racial imbalance in the City Council, and the Justice Department on June 11 prohibited Houston's proposed annexation of 140,000 residents, most of them white, on the grounds that it would further dilute minority representation.

Although the August City Council alterations put Houston in compliance with the act, the city refused to reschedule the referendum, contending that state law prohibited charter changes more frequently than once every two years. Referendum supporters appealed the decision, but the appeal was rejected by Texas courts on November 15.

Other City Business. Mayor Jim McConn defeated Councilman Louis Macey in a runoff election on November 20. The two led a field of candidates in the November 6 election that included Leonel J. Castillo, former U.S. immigration commissioner.

The worst fire in recent Houston history destroyed or damaged about 1,000 units of the Woodward Square apartment complex and left 1,500 persons homeless on July 31. The City Council on August 2 passed an ordinance restricting the use of highly flammable wood shingles like those used to roof Woodward Square.

Police Affairs. Three former Houston police officers were sentenced to an additional day in jail on October 30 after a U.S. Court of Appeals ruled that their original one-year jail sentence was inadequate punishment for their conviction in connection with the 1977 drowning of a Mexican American prisoner. United States Attorney General Benjamin R. Civiletti said on August 19 that the U.S. would not file a police brutality suit against the city.

Former Houston Police Chief Carroll M. Lynn was sentenced to 12 years in prison and fined $10,000 on January 29 following his conviction for extortion.

Elmer Wayne Henley was convicted a second time on June 27 for six murders in the slayings of 26 young men in the Houston area. A similar 1974 conviction was thrown out in 1978.   James M. Banovetz

See also CITY. In WORLD BOOK, see HOUSTON.

HUFSTEDLER, SHIRLEY MOUNT (1925-   ), was approved by the U.S. Senate on Nov. 30, 1979, as the first secretary of the newly created United States Department of Education. The new agency formerly was part of the Department of Health, Education, and Welfare. See CABINET, UNITED STATES; EDUCATION.

Hufstedler was born in Denver, Colo., on Aug. 4, 1925. She earned her bachelor's degree in business administration at the University of New Mexico in 1945 after only 2½ years of study. In 1949, she received a bachelor of laws degree from Stanford University's law school.

Admitted to the California bar in 1950, Hufstedler practiced general civil law in Los Angeles from 1951 to 1961, then accepted an appointment as a Los Angeles County superior court judge. In 1966, she was promoted to the California Court of Appeals. Two years later, President Lyndon B. Johnson named her to the U.S. Ninth Circuit Court of Appeals. She was the second woman to be appointed to a federal appeals court, and when nominated as secretary of education, she was the highest-ranking woman judge in the United States.

Hufstedler is married to Seth Martin Hufstedler, an attorney. They have one son, Steven Mark. While Hufstedler's professional life has been devoted to law, she has always shown an intense concern over the quality of education in U.S. schools. Paul C. Tullier

HUNGARY expanded its economic relations with the West and took important steps to reform its economic system in 1979. István Huszár, deputy prime minister and Politburo member, visited the United States in July, becoming the highest-ranking Hungarian Communist to do so since World War II.

Sixty-six U.S. businessmen attended the Hungarian-American economic commission meeting in Budapest in October. West German Chancellor Helmut Schmidt visited Hungary in July, the highest-ranking Western politician to do so since World War II. Schmidt discussed economic relations during his visit. West Germany is Hungary's second most important trading partner (Russia is first). An earlier July visitor was Franz Josef Strauss, the minister president of Bavaria, a West German state, and the Christian Democrat candidate for chancellor of West Germany in the 1980 elections.

Relations with Romania improved after Romanian Prime Minister Ilie Verdet's July visit. But Hungary protested in August against a sudden Romanian demand that all foreign motorists pay for gasoline with hard currencies such as those of Western nations. In October, a Hungarian consulate opened in Transylvania, where most of Romania's 1.7 million people of Hungarian ancestry live.

Price Hikes. Hungary moved closer to aligning domestic prices with world prices in January by boosting the gasoline price 25 per cent and sharply increasing the prices of beer, cigarettes, newspapers, various foods, bicycles, washing machines, and building materials. On July 23, the government announced the biggest price increases in 30 years. Electricity went up 51 per cent; gasoline, 30 per cent; coal, 25 per cent; bread, 50 per cent; meat, 30 per cent; dairy products, 20 per cent; sugar, 23 per cent; paprika, 128 per cent; automobiles, 20 per cent, with the cash deposit for cars bought on credit raised to 50 per cent of the price; and building materials, 12 per cent. The government estimated that these increases would cause a 9 per cent jump in the official price index.

Industrial Production grew 2.5 per cent in 1979, compared with 1978, 1.5 per cent short of target. But the wheat harvest of 3.6 million metric tons (4 million short tons), was down 2 million metric tons (2.2 million short tons). Exports in the first half of 1979 were up 4.8 per cent, and imports rose 1.7 per cent. The total trade deficit was $1 billion.

A consortium of 52 U.S. banks loaned Hungary $400 million in June for export development. In October, a group of banks in Canada, Great Britain, Japan, and West Germany granted Hungary $250-million worth of credit in Eurodollars – U.S. dollars deposited in foreign banks. Chris Cviic

See also EUROPE (Facts in Brief Table). In WORLD BOOK, see HUNGARY.

HUNTING. Parts of 29 states in all four migratory waterfowl flyways were affected by steel shot regulations during the fall waterfowl hunting season in the United States in 1979. The U.S. Fish and Wildlife Service said that hunters are required to use steel shot in order to reduce the incidence of lead poisoning in waterfowl. An estimated 2 million waterfowl die of lead poisoning each year after eating spent lead shot, according to the service.

Claiming that steel pellets are inaccurate and too expensive, the Winchester-Western Company, the biggest manufacturer of lead pellets, and the National Rifle Association of America have continued to oppose the lead-shot ban.

Responding to pressure from some hunters, Congress approved a provision permitting states to decide whether or not to ban lead shot. Arizona, Arkansas, Idaho, Louisiana, Nevada, North Carolina, Oklahoma, and Utah elected not to enforce the lead-shot ban, and California, Iowa, Ohio, Oregon, and Washington decided to let the ban stand for only a few areas.

Some hunting groups fear that if the ban against toxic lead shot is not extended to all prime duck hunting areas, environmental groups may ask for a court injunction against the use of lead shot. Hunters using guns other than 12-gauge were permitted to hunt with lead shot during the year, but steel shot will be required in all gauges in the fall of 1980.

Fire fighters retreat from the flames at a gas well in Zsana, Hungary. An explosion started the fire, which took two weeks to extinguish.

Alaska Dispute. The National Park Service issued an urgent alert in August to sport hunters bound for Alaska to "ask before shooting." About 41 million acres (16 million hectares) of federal lands in Alaska were included in President Jimmy Carter's Dec. 1, 1978, proclamation that created 13 national monuments in which hunting is prohibited. The Real Alaska Coalition, a group of sportsmen opposed to the hunting ban, threatened to go hunting in these areas to protest the closures, and several hunters were arrested over the Labor Day weekend.

Members of the Alaska Guides Association claimed that the land set aside had placed 50 per cent of Alaska's Dall sheep and 70 to 80 per cent of its moose and caribou off limits. The Department of the Interior pointed out that the new monuments comprise only 11 per cent of the state's 375 million acres (152 million hectares), and that most of the area would be reopened to hunting when legislation setting aside land in Alaska for parks is passed by Congress (see CONSERVATION).

Wildlife Conservation Funds, tied up for 15 months by litigation, began to flow to the states in July after the Committee for Humane Legislation and Friends of Animals dropped their court challenge to the grant program. They had charged that administration of the program violated the National Environmental Policy Act.   Andrew L. Newman

In WORLD BOOK, see AMMUNITION; HUNTING.

HUSSEIN, SADDAM (1937-   ), an army general, became president of Iraq and chairman of the Revolutionary Command Council (RCC) on July 16, 1979, after Ahmad Hasan al-Bakr resigned because of ill health. Hussein had been vice-chairman of the RCC. Soon after the leadership change, a purge of government officials and Baath Party leaders was reported as Hussein consolidated his position. See IRAQ.

Saddam Hussein was born in 1937 in Tikrit, a small city about 100 miles (160 kilometers) north of Baghdad on the Tigris River. He attended secondary school in Baghdad and received a law degree in 1971 from al-Mustanseriyah University.

His political career began in 1959, when he participated in an attempted assassination of General Abdul Karim Kasim, then Iraq's premier. During the early 1960s, he worked with the underground leftist Baath Party, which overthrew Kasim in February 1963. After another coup in November of that year, Hussein spent two years in prison.

He escaped from prison in 1966. Since his conservative branch of the Baathists came to full power in July 1968, Hussein has played a prominent role in both party and government. He became deputy chairman of the RCC in 1969 and deputy secretary-general of the Baath Party in 1977.

Hussein is married and has two sons and three daughters.   Edward G. Nash

ICE SKATING. Eric Heiden of Madison, Wis., a 20-year-old premedical student at the University of Wisconsin, dominated men's speed skating in 1979 for the third consecutive year. His sister, Beth, a 19-year-old civil-engineering student at Wisconsin, was the world's outstanding woman skater. See HEIDEN.

There are three world championships in speed skating – overall, sprint, and junior. Eric won all three in 1977 and 1978. He swept the overall and sprint titles in 1979, but he was too old to compete again in the juniors.

In the overall championships on February 10 and 11 in Oslo, Norway, Heiden won all four races – 500, 1,500, 5,000, and 10,000 meters – and broke every meet record. The sprint championships on February 17 and 18 in Inzell, West Germany, consisted of two races at 500 meters and two at 1,000 meters. Heiden won all four and set a total point record of 151.430.

The Women's Championships were held February 3 and 4 at The Hague, the Netherlands (overall); February 17 and 18 at Inzell (sprint); and February 24 and 25 at Grenoble, France (junior). Beth Heiden swept the four races in the overall championships (500, 1,000, 1,500, and 3,000 meters) and the same four in the junior championships. She also won both 1,000-meter races in the sprint championships, but Leah Poulos Mueller of Milwaukee won both at 500

Tai Babilonia and Randy Gardner of California skate flawlessly to win the world championship in pairs figure skating in Vienna, Austria.

meters, and Mueller narrowly gained the title. Mueller retired in 1976 and started skating again only six weeks before the sprint championships.

In Figure Skating, Americans captured two world titles for the first time since David Jenkins and Carol Heiss won in 1959. Linda Fratianne of Northridge, Calif., won the women's singles and Tai Babilonia of Mission Hills, Calif., and Randy Gardner of Los Angeles won the pairs in the world championships in March in Vienna, Austria.

Fratianne, 18, a high school senior, regained the title she lost in 1978 to Anett Poetzsch of East Germany. Fratianne's once-bland style was gone, and her 4-minute free-skating routine earned scores of 5.7 and 5.8 (6.0 is perfect).

Babilonia, 18, and Gardner, 20, became the first Americans to win the world pairs in 29 years. Irina Rodnina and Alexander Zaitsev, the Russian husband-wife team that won this title six consecutive times, did not compete because their first child, a son, was born two weeks before the championships.

In the U.S. championships, held in Cincinnati from January 30 to February 4, Fratianne and Tickner won their third straight titles and Babilonia-Gardner their fourth straight.   Frank Litsky

In WORLD BOOK, see ICE SKATING.

ICELAND. See EUROPE.

IDAHO. See STATE GOVERNMENT.

ILLINOIS. See CHICAGO; STATE GOVERNMENT.

IMMIGRATION. Leonel J. Castillo resigned as commissioner of the U.S. Immigration and Naturalization Service (INS) on Aug. 10, 1979. Castillo, the first Mexican American to head the INS, cited "serious and glaring deficiencies" in United States immigration laws and called for *amnesty* (pardon) for illegal aliens who have been in the United States for years. President Jimmy Carter appointed INS Chief Counsel David Crosland acting commissioner.

Mexican Aliens once again presented the greatest problem for INS officials. About 400,000 Mexicans got visas for permanent U.S. residence in 1979, but about twice that number crossed the border illegally. More than half of the estimated 12 million illegal aliens in the United States are reported to have come from Mexico seeking jobs and higher wages, and in 1978, 93 per cent of the more than 1 million illegal aliens arrested came from Mexico.

During his February visit to Mexico, President Carter discussed the problem of illegal migration of Mexicans into the United States with Mexico's President Jose Lopez Portillo. The two agreed to "close consultation" on the issue. Carter appointed Theodore M. Hesburgh, president of the University of Notre Dame, to chair a select commission on immigration and refugee policy. Lopez Portillo agreed to cooperate in a joint study of the problem.

More than 1,000 demonstrators gathered along the Mexican border on February 12 to protest the

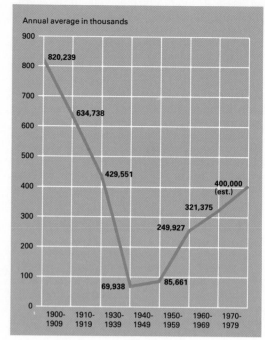

Immigrants Admitted to U.S.

Annual average in thousands

820,239
634,738
429,551
69,938
85,661
249,927
321,375
400,000 (est.)

| | 1900-1909 | 1910-1919 | 1930-1939 | 1940-1949 | 1950-1959 | 1960-1969 | 1970-1979 |

Source: U.S. Immigration and Naturalization Service

proposed construction of a border fence between El Paso, Tex., and Juárez, Mexico, and between San Ysidro, Calif., and Tijuana, Mexico. The U.S. Department of Justice announced on April 26 that for diplomatic reasons it had abandoned its plans for the proposed fence.

U.S. Policy Changes. President Carter urged Congress on March 8 to pass the Refugee Act of 1979. The proposed law would increase the normal flow of refugees from 17,400 to 50,000 per year and allow the President to exceed that quota when he felt it to be in the national interest. Carter announced on June 28 that the number of refugees from Indochina allowed to enter the United States each month would be raised from 7,000 to 14,000.

A U.S. Justice Department ruling in December ordered the INS to reinstate its ban of suspected homosexuals, which was lifted in August.

On November 13, the Department of Justice said that the estimated 200,000 Iranians in the United States should report to the INS by December 14 for a review of their status, or face deportation. The action, which came after Iranian students seized the U.S. Embassy in Iran, was declared unconstitutional on December 11. But an appeals court later upheld the government action. See IRAN.   William J. Eaton

In WORLD BOOK, see IMMIGRATION AND EMIGRATION.

INCOME TAX. See TAXATION.

INDIA. The ruling Janata Party collapsed on July 15, 1979, when Prime Minister Morarji Desai, 83, resigned. Desai quit on the eve of a no-confidence vote in parliament that he was certain to lose. The break had been expected almost from the day in March 1977 when the party was formed to defeat Indira Gandhi, who was then prime minister. Hastily put together, Janata was a loose coalition of groups held together only by their hatred of "that woman." This was not enough. By the time Desai resigned, the party had broken into rival groups and more than 100 Janata members of parliament, one-third of the group, had left the party.

Two rivals fought to inherit Desai's mantle and what remained of the party. One was Charan Singh, 77, finance minister and a leader of small landholders; the other, Jagjivan Ram, 71, defense minister and leader of the untouchables.

Gandhi's Return. Singh, whose intrigues were thought to have precipitated the crisis, formed a Cabinet on July 28 and 30. Like Desai's, it was a political crazy quilt, ranging from pro-Moscow Communists to Singh's own conservative peasant supporters. But the key to his survival was support by 71 members of Gandhi's Congress-I (for Indira) Party. Her price was clear. She wanted the government to drop all charges against her and her son, Sanjay, for excesses committed during the 18-month emergency rule she proclaimed on June 26, 1975. When Singh could not meet the price, his Cabinet fell on August 20.

Ram and the untouchables now demanded their chance to form a government, but President Neelam Sanjeeva Reddy, prodded by Gandhi, decided otherwise. On August 22, he ordered elections to be held; they were scheduled for January 1980.

If anyone benefited from the breakup of the Janata, it was Gandhi, who became a kingmaker. Impressionable politicians deserted other groups to join her camp. Observers agreed that one reason for her growing influence was Desai's failure to cope with the nation's economic woes. It was thought unlikely that she or her son would ever be brought to trial. Indeed, Gandhi counted on having the largest single bloc of seats in the next *Lok Sabha* (Lower House). She and the Congress-I Party scored a sweeping victory in the January 1980 balloting — which was marred by violent riots.

Severe Drought. After four excellent harvests in succession, India experienced its worst drought in 75 years. In nine of 22 states, tens of millions survived only with the help of soup kitchens and "food-for-work" programs. Before the monsoon season, the country expected a record-breaking harvest of 135 million metric tons (149 million short tons) of foodgrains. The drought might bring the harvest down closer to 120 million metric tons (132 million short tons). But, thanks to some 20 million kept in storage, no general famine was expected.

There were other problems. While the country's exports rose 20 per cent, the value of imports soared — because of two price boosts for Arab oil, expected to add about $1.2 billion to the trade deficit. Heavy hoarding of diesel oil and kerosene led to a booming black market. Profiteering also affected other items in short supply, including steel. The rate of inflation neared 20 per cent.

The Bomb. India has had the capacity to build an atomic bomb since its nuclear test in May 1974, but apparently has not done so. However, Pakistan's reported efforts to make nuclear weapons produced a demand in the Lok Sabha for India's own nuclear arsenal. Singh said in August that India would be forced to build an A-bomb if Pakistan did.

On August 10, India test-launched a ballistic missile with an 11-kilogram (24-pound) payload, in preparation for launching its first satellite. The mission failed.

Technology and Nature joined hands to produce disasters. Flood waters roared through the town of Morvi on August 11 after a dam collapsed and killed at least 5,000. Strikes by the underpaid police in June brought the army — and gunfire — in. At least 21 persons were killed in fighting between troops and strikers. In April, Hindu-Muslim clashes cost at least 110 lives.   Mark Gayn

See also ASIA (Facts in Brief Table). In WORLD BOOK, see INDIA.

INDIAN, AMERICAN. In the largest court settlement ever awarded American Indians, the United States Court of Claims on June 13, 1979, awarded the Sioux Nation $105 million for 7 million acres (2.8 million hectares) in the Black Hills of South Dakota. The sum includes a $17.5-million payment for the land and $87.5 million in interest accrued over 102 years. The land, awarded to the Sioux in an 1868 treaty, was seized by the U.S. government in 1877.

Sioux tribal leaders announced on October 1 that they would appeal this settlement and a 1978 settlement of $44 million for another 48 million acres (19 million hectares). They said the government should also return the western half of South Dakota and mineral rights to other former Indian lands west of the Mississippi River, in addition to the cash settlement.

Other Settlements. The Narragansett Indians of Rhode Island received 1,800 acres (730 hectares) in the first settlement of East Coast Indian lands claims under a bill approved by the Rhode Island Senate on May 4.

A tentative settlement of Cayuga Indian land claims in upstate New York was announced on August 20. The proposed settlement would establish a 6,481-acre (2,623-hectare) reservation for the tribe in the Finger Lakes area.

Hopes of settling the claims of Maine Indian tribes to 12.5 million acres (5 million hectares),

Jay Silverheels, who was Tonto in "The Lone Ranger" TV series, is overcome with emotion as his star is placed in the Hollywood Walk of Fame on July 19.

roughly two-thirds of Maine, were dimmed somewhat when the tribes announced on August 4 they wanted $17 million more than was offered in a 1978 proposal endorsed by President Jimmy Carter. The Indians' proposal called for $79 million to purchase 300,000 acres (120,000 hectares) of land and to establish school and job programs. The Maine Indian claims, as well as other Indian land claims in the East, are based on charges that the land was taken in violation of 1790 federal legislation that required congressional approval of land transactions with Indians.

The Energy Issue. Secretary of Energy Charles W. Duncan, Jr., met with leaders of the Council of Energy Resource Tribes (CERT), representing 25 tribes, on August 9 in Denver and pledged that Western tribes will be directly involved in the national energy picture. The meeting was held in response to a letter sent to President Carter by CERT chairman Peter MacDonald on July 24 to protest the omission of Indian leaders from Carter's conference on energy at Camp David, Maryland, in July.

CERT's member tribes are estimated to own up to half of the U.S. reserves of uranium, one-third of the low-sulfur coal in the West, and about 2 per cent of the U.S. oil and natural gas deposits. MacDonald announced that CERT would ask for up to $700-million in federal funds over the next decade to

develop Indian-owned energy resources. CERT officials maintain that with federal help, Indian lands could generate the equivalent of 2 to 4 million barrels of oil per day by 1990.

Fishing Rights. The Supreme Court of the United States, in a 6-3 ruling on July 2, confirmed in principle a lower court decision giving Indians in Washington the right to catch up to half of the state's annual run of salmon and steelhead. The Small Tribes Organization of western Washington called the decision a "historic victory."

Federal District Judge Noel P. Fox ruled on May 8 that the state of Michigan could not regulate Indian fishermen. The verdict upheld fishing rights granted to Bay Mills and Sault Ste. Marie Chippewa tribes in treaties signed with the United States government in 1836 and 1855.

The Nez Percé Indians and the federal government reached an agreement on June 7 settling a dispute over salmon fishing rights. The Indians, who have unlimited hunting and fishing rights in Idaho, agreed not to harvest the spring chinook spawning run from the Red River. Game officials sought to protect the salmon, which, because of a 1977 drought, were reduced to 10 per cent of their normal number. In return, the Indians were allotted 2,500 salmon from hatcheries.   Andrew L. Newman

In WORLD BOOK, see INDIAN, AMERICAN.

INDIANA. See STATE GOVERNMENT.

INDONESIA. The national drama in 1979 was played mostly on the economic stage. The government had devalued the country's monetary unit, the rupiah, 33.6 per cent in November 1978 in the hope of cutting down imports, putting new life into the export industries, and creating jobs.

The initial impact in early 1979 was severe. Despite a tax cut in March, as well as government appeals and threats, prices rose steeply, and there was some hoarding. The inflation rate topped 30 per cent. There were massive unrest and illegal strikes among the working class, hardest hit by the soaring prices. The domestic price of gasoline and fuel oil was increased 30 to 35 per cent on April 5, and the consumer was dealt another heavy blow – even though, for political reasons, the government left unchanged the subsidized price of kerosene for cooking.

Oil Income. In the hope of boosting sales, Indonesia raised the price of its crude oil only 2.58 per cent as of Jan. 1, 1979 – less than the 5 per cent rise agreed upon by other members of the Organization of Petroleum Exporting Countries (OPEC), of which Indonesia is the only Asian member. The OPEC nations voted additional price increases in March, June, and December. The price raises boosted Indonesia's oil receipts from $4.2 billion in 1978 to above $6.1 billion. Higher world prices for rubber, timber, tin, and coffee brought an additional $5.5 billion.

Thus, the grim outlook of January gave way in July to confidence and a miniboom.

The respite could only be brief, however. The population, estimated at 154 million, could reach 210 million by the year 2000. About 85 million of that total are crowded on the island of Java.

The government announced that it released 2,000 prisoners in October. Most had been jailed since an attempted coup d'état in 1965. Some sources estimated that about 4,000 persons remained interned.

Refugee Problem. The Association of Southeast Asian Nations (ASEAN) met in Kuta, Indonesia, in June to discuss a common strategy for dealing with the flow of refugees from Vietnam. The ASEAN foreign ministers, including the Indonesian delegate, concluded that they could no longer take in refugees, unless other countries accepted equal numbers. An Indonesian newspaper reported in July that the government had towed out to sea a wooden boat carrying about 800 refugees who had tried to land on the island of Bintan. See ASIA (Close-Up).

A Volcano erupted on Java on February 21, killing at least 175 persons and injuring 1,000. Evacuation efforts in the two villages near Mount Sinila crater were hindered by the heavy lava flow. Indonesia has 127 volcanoes that scientists term active, but Mount Sinila had been declared dormant. Mark Gayn

See also ASIA (Facts in Brief Table). In WORLD BOOK, see INDONESIA.

INSURANCE. Property and liability insurance underwriting in the United States went back into the red in 1979, ending a two-year profit cycle. At the close of 1978, when insurers recorded an underwriting gain of $1.25 billion, industry analysts predicted that inflationary pressures were about to overtake previous years' rate increases and bring a downward trend. They were correct. The first quarter of 1979 started poorly, with an underwriting loss in excess of $800 million. Some moderating factors improved the picture at the half-year mark so that the loss rose only to $974.9 million. Nevertheless, the underwriting loss for the full year was expected to reach $1.6 billion to $2 billion.

Ironically, the 1977 and 1978 profits played a significant role in the 1979 reverses. Insurance companies made less money for several reasons. State insurance commissioners, looking at the profit picture, rejected requests for rate increases on insurance for homes, automobiles, and workers' compensation. Also, overconfident insurers, eager to do even more business, wrote high-premium commercial policies at inadequate rates and willingly took on risks so hazardous they would previously have been unacceptable. Resulting losses ate into their profits.

Nature also delivered a blow in the form of the highest catastrophe losses in history. Reaching nearly $1.8 billion by mid-October, they were well above the previous record of $896.1 million for the full year

1965. Hurricane Frederic, which struck nine states on September 12 and 13, became the worst Gulf Coast storm on record for insurers. Its insured claims of more than $752.5 million exceeded the $715-million from Hurricane Betsy in 1965.

On the brighter side was the investment gain that grossed $4.3 billion by mid-1979 and was expected at least to double by year-end. For the first six months of 1978, the investment yield was only $1.2 billion. Written premiums were at $44.1 billion by midyear and were rising at a rate that indicated a year-end total near $85 billion. While this would exceed the $79.8 billion written in 1978, the 1979 rate of gain was about 10 percentage points below those of 1977 and 1978.

Holtzman Amendment. Insurance companies in Iowa, Minnesota, Missouri, New York, and Virginia lost the right to purchase riot reinsurance from the Federal Insurance Administration (FIA) on March 7, 1979, because those states refused to require that fire insurance rates for all purchasers be equalized. That requirement was mandated by the Holtzman Amendment, a measure regulating Free Access to Insurance Requirements (FAIR) plans. FAIR plans enable people with risks not acceptable to the ordinary market to purchase fire insurance, but they are generally charged higher rates. In an attempt to correct this rate inequity, Congress adopted an amendment introduced by Representative Elizabeth Holtzman (D., N.Y.) in October 1978 and set Jan. 31, 1979, as the deadline for compliance by 26 states and the District of Columbia, which had established the FAIR plans under a 1968 federal law. That law offered riot reinsurance to states adopting the plans. The Holtzman Amendment authorized the FIA to withdraw this coverage for noncompliance.

No-Fault Auto Insurance legislation was a dead issue in all 50 states in 1979, and the drive in Congress for a federal no-fault standards bill came to a virtual standstill. Nevada's no-fault statute became void at the end of 1979, reducing to 14 the number of states with no-fault coverage.

Fighting Fire. The American Insurance Association, a New York City-based trade group, made plans to inaugurate the Property Insurance Loss Register (PILR) on Jan. 1, 1980. PILR is a computer system designed to battle the nationwide increase in arson. According to Gerald Murphy, system manager, arson costs insurance companies more than $1.5 billion annually. Some 400 companies, which write nearly 90 per cent of the fire insurance in the United States, will contribute to the PILR data bank by reporting every claim in excess of $500. The computer will be programmed to designate property owners who hold more than one policy or who have had repeated fire losses. Emanuel Levy

In WORLD BOOK, see INSURANCE; NO-FAULT INSURANCE.

INTERNATIONAL TRADE AND FINANCE. A surge in world oil prices, the second major increase in five years, was the dominant event in the world economy in 1979. The rate of inflation worsened in nearly all countries, economic growth turned sluggish in the United States and elsewhere, and some nations faced renewed problems in paying the higher cost of imports.

Oil Up. Oil prices increased about 60 per cent, most of it coming as a result of a decision by the Organization of Petroleum Exporting Countries (OPEC) in June, which established a range of prices from $18 per barrel to a top of $23.50. By the fourth quarter of the year, several OPEC countries had announced further increases beyond the new ceiling, and there was the probability of another general increase in 1980. By comparison, the world oil price was about $3 per barrel in October 1973.

As in 1973-1974, when a Middle East war was the catalyst for the first explosion of international oil prices, the jump in 1979 was triggered by a political event – this time a revolution in Iran that deposed Shah Mohammad Reza Pahlavi and temporarily halted Iranian oil shipments to the world in late winter. In November, after Iranian students seized its embassy in Teheran, the U.S. banned oil imports from Iran, a move that further clouded the world petroleum situation (see IRAN). Actual shortages in the importing nations were not common, however, though there were gasoline lines in the United States for a brief period in the spring. More important was the steep price increase, which added some $75-billion to the annual bill of oil importing nations. See ENERGY; PETROLEUM AND GAS.

Gloomy Outlook. In his opening address at the annual meeting of the World Bank and International Monetary Fund (IMF) in Belgrade, Yugoslavia, in October, IMF Managing Director Jacques de Larosiere said bluntly, "The present world economic situation is gloomy." However, apart from the pains associated with worsening inflation, events in 1979 did not take on the dimensions of a crisis. World trade continued to grow, though probably by only 2 or 3 per cent.

In some countries, such as Japan and West Germany, economic expansion continued and unemployment remained low. In others, such as the United States and France, growth slowed or even halted, with some rise in unemployment, but there was no plunge into recession or depression. A more serious recession, particularly in the United States, was a distinct possibility for 1980.

Gold Rockets. A headline-catching feature was an upward burst in the price of gold, which hit more than $500 per troy ounce (31 grams), compared with less than $40 per ounce in 1969. This was more

President Jimmy Carter and special trade representative Robert S. Strauss joke after Carter signed into law a new 10-year international trade pact.

important psychologically than practically, because gold no longer serves a significant monetary purpose in the world. But the psychological impact aroused a fear among people in numerous countries that runaway inflation was likely. They bought gold in the hope that its rising price would keep them ahead of the ever-rising prices of other goods and services.

Money Floats. The world monetary system continued to operate under the system of "floating" currency exchange rates. Despite some ups and downs in the exchange rate of the U.S. dollar, the key world currency, and despite the surge in gold prices, foreign exchange markets on the whole functioned in orderly fashion. However, the dispute between the United States and Iran left the situation unsettled late in the year. The U.S. froze Iran's U.S. assets in mid-November. In retaliation, Iran began to insist on non-dollar payments for its oil and called upon other oil-producing countries to do the same. On November 23, the Iranian government appeared to repudiate much of its $15-billion foreign debt.

Eight of the nine nations of the European Community (Common Market) – all but Great Britain – established the European Monetary System (EMS) on March 13. The new system was a further step toward exchange-rate stability among the currencies of those countries (see EUROPE). The EMS was not perfect, however, because on September 24 the West German Deutsche mark had to be revalued upward and the Danish krone downward against the other currencies. The single most significant exchange-rate development of the year was the Japanese yen's decline of about 30 per cent against the dollar and other leading currencies, largely because Japan – with no oil of its own – was most severely affected by the increase in world oil prices. In November, the yen reached a two-year low against the U.S. dollar, before rising again.

Developing Problems. As in previous years, the problem of paying the much higher oil-import bill was more difficult for the less developed countries than for the industrial countries. De Larosiere noted at Belgrade that the industrial countries naturally "feel concern" about the domestic inflationary impact of the higher oil prices. But he added that the deterioration of their balance of payments as a group, estimated at about $30 billion in 1979, "does not generally impose serious problems of financing." In the United States, for example, the oil bill rose from less than $45 billion in 1978 to about $60 billion, but there were offsets in improved exports and increased receipts in nontrade items such as the income from foreign investments. For the poorer countries, however, the collective balance-of-payments deficit rose from $21 billion in 1977 to an estimated $45 billion in 1979 and a projected $50-billion or more in 1980, which will strain their ability to finance the gap by borrowing.

This problem was acute in only a few countries.

Turkey had the most serious crisis, with imports virtually suspended for a time because of lack of ability to pay (see TURKEY). There were continued strains in such nations as Peru and Zaire, but others, including Brazil, continued to borrow to meet their deficits. An unpublished IMF study warned that the number of countries in severe difficulty might rise from four or five to as many as 15.

Tokyo Round. A major accomplishment was the conclusion on April 12, after six years of negotiation, of a new international trade agreement that was dubbed the "Tokyo round" because the negotiations were launched in that city in 1973. Conducted under the auspices of the General Agreement on Tariffs and Trade, the pact reduced tariffs an average of 33 per cent, chiefly in the industrial countries. Nearly all the developing countries boycotted the signing. More important was the agreement on a new set of international codes to govern such trade-distorting devices as government subsidies, customs valuation, preference for local manufacturers in government procurement, and "dumping" of goods at less than the cost of production. After some adjustments, the Tokyo round agreement was overwhelmingly approved by the U.S. Congress in July. Edwin L. Dale, Jr.

See also ECONOMICS. In WORLD BOOK, see GENERAL AGREEMENT ON TARIFFS AND TRADE (GATT); GOLD; INTERNATIONAL TRADE.

IOWA. See STATE GOVERNMENT.

IRAN became the storm center of the Middle East in 1979 and designated an old ally, the United States, as the enemy. A yearlong popular revolution reached its goal on January 16, when Shah Mohammad Reza Pahlavi left the country with his family on a "vacation" that ended his 38-year rule.

The shah's exile odyssey took him first to Egypt, then Morocco, the Bahamas, and Mexico. Then, on October 22, he was allowed to enter the United States for medical treatment. Some 500 Iranians seized the U.S. Embassy in Teheran on November 4 and held Americans seized there as hostages. They vowed not to release them until the shah was returned to stand trial in Iran. The United States refused these demands, and the shah left the U.S. on December 15, settling temporarily on the Panamanian island of Contadora.

New Government. Behind him, the shah left a nation in turmoil. The Ayatollah Ruhollah Khomeini, chief religious leader of the Iranian Shiite Muslim sect and the shah's main political opponent, returned from 15 years in exile on February 1, to become the de facto head of state (see KHOMEINI, RUHOLLAH). Iran was declared an Islamic republic, and an "assembly of experts" began work rewriting the 1906 Constitution.

A national referendum in March, though challenged by various groups, approved the formation of an Islamic republic. The "experts" – by this time, all

The dark, brooding eyes of the Ayatollah Khomeini, focused on a world few other people could see, symbolized for many the revolution in Iran.

were religious leaders – completed the Constitution in December and it was approved by another national referendum. The Constitution provides for a *faqih* (trustee) to hold supreme power on behalf of the Shiite 12th *Imam* (guide) – who vanished 1,100 years ago and is expected by Shiites to return – as spiritual and temporal leader of the Iranian people.

Death and Chaos. However, the gulf between the real and ideal widened rapidly after Khomeini's return as the Iranian revolution took on more and more the coloration of the bloody French Revolution. A wave of executions, initially of agents of Savak (the shah's secret police) but later broadened to include military and business leaders and even some opponents of the shah, had claimed at least 600 victims by October. One prominent victim was former Prime Minister Amir Abbas Hoveyda, executed after a secret trial in April, though he was dismissed from office and arrested by the shah in 1977.

The Khomeini regime failed to form an effective governing coalition or reorganize the chaotic economy. After Shahpur Bakhtiar, the shah's last prime minister, left the country in February, Khomeini named a new Cabinet headed by moderate Mehdi Bazargan. But real authority rested with Khomeini's Revolutionary Council, a group of religious leaders and associates of Khomeini during his exile.

Ethnic Unrest. Another obstacle to stability was the emphasis placed by the Khomeini regime on Islamic purity and Shiite dominance in matters of law and custom. Ethnic minorities, notably the Sunni Muslim Arabs, the Kurds, and the Baluchis and Azeri Turks, pressed long-standing demands for greater autonomy. In May and June, the Arabs in the Khuzistan area in southwestern Iran clashed with army forces. The unrest in that area continued into the fall.

The Kurds were also on the move. In August, Kurdish guerrillas occupied Sanandaj, the provincial capital of Kurdistan, and Mahabad, where an abortive Kurdish Republic had been proclaimed in 1946. The Kurds surrounded Iranian army units in their barracks. The government ordered the bulk of the army into the rebellious province, supported by U.S.-made jet aircraft and tanks, and the two cities were reoccupied early in September after fierce fighting. A cease-fire followed, but fighting continued sporadically. On October 20, the Kurds retook Mahabad. In December, after the constitutional referendum, the Kurds became restive again.

Still another ethnic minority, the Azeri Turks of Azerbaijan, in northwestern Iran, clamored for some form of autonomy. The Azerbaijanis, led by Ayatollah Kazem Shariat-Madari, boycotted the December referendum and seized control of the provincial government in their largest city, Tabriz.

Hostages for the Shah. Assuming the United States supported the shah and was plotting his return, militants seized the U.S. Embassy in Tehe-ran on November 4 and held some 60 Americans hostage for his return. They accused him of repres-sion, misappropriation of funds, and embezzlement.

The U.S. refused to extradite the shah. Iran released 13 of the hostages – five women and eight blacks – on November 19 and 20. Despite its clear violation of diplomatic immunity under internation-al law, Iran refused to release the remaining hostag-es. It also ignored the United Nations (UN) Security Council and the International Court of Justice, which called for the release of the hostages. Most countries, including Arab nations, supported the U.S. but sympathized with Iran's burning desire to bring the shah to justice.

A solution to the stand-off was hampered by the resignations of the relatively moderate Bazargan and other officials, leaving the United States with no government to deal with except the intractable Khomeini. Two months after the seizure, it seemed that, short of military action or an Iranian response to UN Security Council resolutions, the stalemate would remain until the Iranian revolution sorted itself out.   William Spencer

See also INTERNATIONAL TRADE AND FINANCE; MIDDLE EAST (Facts in Brief Table); PRESIDENT OF THE UNITED STATES. In WORLD BOOK, see IRAN; ISLAM.

The United States Embassy compound in Teheran became a stronghold for Iranian militants when they seized it, and embassy personnel, in November.

IRAQ. Saddam Hussein, the secretary-general of the ruling Baath Party and chairman of the Revolu-tionary Command Council (RCC), succeeded Presi-dent Ahmad Hasan al-Bakr, who retired for health reasons on July 16, 1979. Within days, the new president moved against a "vile conspiracy" against his regime that involved several RCC members plus a number of senior military commanders. Some 250 persons were arrested and 21 executed as the Iraqi leader quickly asserted his authority over the coun-try. See HUSSEIN, SADDAM.

Ethnic and religious factors played a more impor-tant role in the conspiracy than political differences. Four of the five rebel leaders came from the Shiite Muslim population, a majority in Iraq but political-ly underrepresented and economically disadvan-taged. The government hinted that "external" forc-es supported the conspiracy, though no countries were named. Earlier, Bakr had agreed to a joint political command and a defense pact with Syria in a June meeting with Syrian president Hafiz al-Assad as the countries moved toward reconciliation.

The Kurds, another significant ethnic element in the population, also contributed to the general unrest. With the death of exiled Kurdish leader Mustafa Barzani in March, the struggle for Kurdish autonomy centered on two opposition groups, the Kurdish Democratic Party and the Patriotic Union of Kurdistan. Kurdish unrest in neighboring Iran spilled over into Iraq in May and June as Kurdish villagers resisting resettlement in flatland areas clashed violently with Iraqi Army units. The gov-ernment announced a $20-million special allocation for the "Autonomous Kurdish Region" that would include payment to 22,000 Kurdish families whose homes had been seized prior to resettlement.

Another barometer of internal difficulties was the Baath Party's relationship with the Iraq Communist Party (ICP). In January, the ICP boycotted the third congress of the coalition National Progressive Front (NPF), charging harassment of its members, and in March it quit the NPF entirely. On the ICP's 31st anniversary, 31 members were arrested for forming non-Baathist political cells and for political activity in the armed forces, both forbidden.

Strong Economy. The internal unrest had little effect on the country's hard-headed approach to economic development. Although relations with the United States remained frozen, Iraq spent $221-million on U.S. passenger jet aircraft and began sending its civil aviation personnel to Oklahoma's Spartan School of Aeronautics for training.

Discovery of a major new oil field near the Kuwait border was expected to double proven Iraqi oil reserves of 35 billion metric tons (38.6 million short tons), making the country equal to Iran as an oil producer.   William Spencer

See also MIDDLE EAST (Facts in Brief Table). In WORLD BOOK, see IRAQ.

IRELAND got a new prime minister on Dec. 7, 1979, when 54-year-old Charles Haughey was elected to replace Jack Lynch, who resigned. The ruling Fianna Fáil party chose Haughey, a hard-line Irish nationalist, by a vote of 44 to 38.

Earlier in the year, fresh hope followed dark despair as two contrasting events, occurring within weeks of each other, dominated the news. On August 27, Louis Mountbatten, Earl Mountbatten of Burma, a cousin of Queen Elizabeth II and one of Great Britain's most distinguished soldier-statesmen, was killed when a bomb blew up his fishing boat off the Irish coast. The explosion occurred in Donegal Bay off Mullaghmore, a village in County Sligo. Three other persons were killed, including Mountbatten's 14-year-old grandson, Nicholas, and three other family members were injured.

Lord Mountbatten was the supreme commander of the Allied forces in Southeast Asia in World War II, and Great Britain's last viceroy of India before that country gained its independence in 1947. Spokesmen for the Irish Republican Army (IRA) claimed responsibility for the attack. On August 30, two suspected members of the IRA were charged with the murders, and on November 23, Thomas McMahon was found guilty and sentenced to life imprisonment. Francis McGirl was acquitted.

Pope's Visit. The killing of Lord Mountbatten ended speculation that Pope John Paul II would visit Northern Ireland. But it did not deter the pope from visiting the Republic of Ireland, and on September 29 the pontiff arrived at Dublin airport.

The pope's three-day visit was remarkable. Two-thirds of Ireland's population of 3 million, together with many thousands of visitors from Northern Ireland, flocked to see him at open-air meetings. The formal purpose of his visit was to mark the climax of centenary celebrations at the Shrine of Knock in County Mayo, where the Virgin Mary is said to have appeared on Aug. 21, 1879, during a time of famine and repression. The pope issued an explicit condemnation of violence at Drogheda. He said: "It is Jesus Himself who said, 'All who take the sword will perish by the sword.' On my knees I beg you to turn away from the paths of violence."

The Economy. The Irish government cut the 150-year-old parity link between the Irish pound and the British pound sterling on March 30. It did so because Ireland had joined the European Monetary System (EMS) linking the nations of the European Community (EC or Common Market) in December 1978. That move obliged Ireland to keep fluctuation of the Irish pound within 2¼ per cent of the currency values of other EMS members. Great Britain had stayed out of the EMS.   Ian Mather

See also GREAT BRITAIN; NORTHERN IRELAND. In WORLD BOOK, see IRELAND; MOUNTBATTEN, LOUIS.

IRON AND STEEL. See STEEL INDUSTRY.

ISRAEL ended one era and started another with the signing of a peace treaty with Egypt on March 26, 1979. With the return of the Sinai town of Al Arish to Egyptian control on May 25, Israel had open borders with an Arab state for the first time in its 31-year history. The formal renunciation of war by both countries meant that Israel could savor the atmosphere of peace, despite the continued hostility of the rest of the Arab world.

Despite the general euphoria, there were many Israelis who felt that peace with Egypt might in the long run compromise the nation's security. Debate in the *Knesset* (parliament) over ratification of the treaty lasted three days, the longest on record over a single issue. The treaty was eventually approved by a 95 to 18 vote, but the opposition included many members of Prime Minister Menachem Begin's Likud Party. One member, Geula Cohen, resigned from the party to work against ratification.

West Bank Settlements. Disaffection of other supporters shook the Begin government. The heaviest blow was the resignation of Foreign Minister Moshe Dayan on October 21. Dayan quit because he disagreed with the government policy toward the Palestinians and the occupied territories of the West Bank and the Gaza Strip. However, the prime minister defeated all parliamentary challenges. The major divisive issue was the future of the Jewish

Members of the Knesset, Israel's parliament, congratulate Prime Minister Menachem Begin after he won a key vote to accept U.S. peace proposals.

settlements established on the West Bank by members of the ultranationalist Gush Emunim (Faithful Bloc) in defiance of the negotiations to prepare the area for transfer to an autonomous Palestinian authority. The Gush Emunim belief that the Holy Land was given by God to the Jewish people was shared by many Israeli leaders, including Begin himself. In April, the Cabinet lifted a ban on Israeli purchases of Arab land in the West Bank and approved new settlements if they were established on lands that had been taken over by the military and were justified on security grounds.

On December 26, during his first visit to the West Bank since April 1978, Begin vowed to keep the area under Israeli control. His remarks were intended to quiet the protests of the Israeli militants. Shortly before, the Knesset had rejected a bill aimed at annexation of the occupied territory.

Gush Emunim settlers began building a new West Bank settlement at Elon Moreh, near Nablus, in June. Arab farmers in the area protested, petitioning Israel's Supreme Court for redress. A demonstration by 40,000 members of the Peace Now movement, an Israeli group that advocated a ban on all such settlements, followed as Israeli public opinion turned against the settlers. In a landmark decision on October 22, the Supreme Court ruled Elon Moreh illegal and gave the settlers 30 days to move to another site on land not owned by Arabs. In a "last compromise" announced on November 19, near the end of the 30-day time limit, the government delayed departure of the Elon Moreh settlers, calling for a two-stage withdrawal from the area over a six-week period. The settlers won another five-week delay on December 30. The settlers were to move to Mount Kabir, an area with no privately owned Arab land. The plan was devised to avoid having to use Israeli troops to remove settlers.

Mayors Quit. Tension between the Israeli Palestinians and the government rose in November when the mayor of Nablus, Bassam al-Shaka, was arrested and threatened with deportation to Jordan on charges of supporting terrorism.

The arrest enraged the Palestinians, and, on November 13 and 14, all 25 mayors of the Arab towns in the occupied West Bank and the Gaza Strip resigned, leaving the areas without municipal leadership. The arrest also brought criticism of the government from other countries, notably the United States and Egypt, as well as from many Israelis. After weeks of talks and negotiations, the Israeli government reversed its order to deport Shaka and released him from prison on December 5. He returned to Nablus in triumph. The other mayors then withdrew their resignations.

An interest in minority rights also affected the Israeli Bedouin population. With the entire Sinai Peninsula scheduled for return to Egypt, Israel began building military bases to replace those given

Accompanied by his wife, Rosalynn, President Carter signs the register at the Yad Vashem memorial in Jerusalem during a visit to Israel.

up in the Sinai. But the expropriation of Bedouin-owned land for a road project resulted in another Supreme Court decision halting the work and citing the Government Land Authority for contempt.

Terrorism Down. There were fewer incidents of terrorism than in previous years, though a Palestinian raid on the Israeli coastal town of Nahariyya in April set off an Israeli invasion of southern Lebanon and Israeli air attacks as far north as Beirut. Friction between Israeli Jews and Israeli Arabs increased as the latter increasingly lined up with the Palestine Liberation Organization (PLO). In the West Bank, schools and the Arab Bir Zeit University were closed for most of the school year. Israel received considerable criticism for alleged mistreatment of Arab prisoners. A United States diplomat charged that beatings and torture of Palestinian prisoners were common practice in Israeli jails.

Coalition Shaken. Begin's fragile coalition was endangered on November 12 when a move to tighten Israel's relatively liberal abortion law was defeated in the Knesset. After the vote, the small, ultraconservative Agudat Israel Party threatened to withdraw its support of Begin, which would have cut his government majority to one vote.

Resubmitted to the Knesset on December 17, the amendment passed by a vote of 58 to 53. As a result, abortions will no longer be allowed in Israel for social and economic reasons. Essentially, the law

A smiling Moshe Dayan arrives at his home after
resigning as Israel's foreign minister in October
in a policy dispute involving the Palestinian issue.

affects the poor because expensive illegal abortions
are readily available and Israel has never prosecuted
a physician for performing such an operation.

Inflation Up. In the long run, Israel's future as a
viable nation depended more on the solution of
critical economic problems than on the handling of
Israeli-Arab or Israeli-Palestinian relations. Inflation rose from 48 per cent in 1978 to 80 per cent in
1979. During debate on the budget, approved by the
Knesset in July, opposition members walked out,
accusing the government of drafting a $14.8-billion
budget that was already inadequate to cover the
costs of inflation. Strikes in various sectors – the
largest being a strike of 40,000 civil servants in May
that shut down the country – added to the inflationary pressures. To make matters worse, the diamond
industry went into a worldwide recession, forcing a
one-month layoff of Israel's diamond workers. During October, Begin managed to survive several
confidence votes in the Knesset as well as the defection of Foreign Minister Dayan, mainly because
there was really no alternative to his regime.

Scientists found evidence that as much as 300
million to 2 billion barrels of oil may be lying
beneath Israel's Dead Sea valley. Such a find could
eventually make the country independent of foreign
sources of petroleum.   William Spencer

See also MIDDLE EAST (Facts in Brief Table). In
WORLD BOOK, see ISRAEL.

ITALY failed to solve its political crisis with a general
election in June 1979, and suffered through continuing terrorism, a shaky economy, and a bank scandal.
Prime Minister Giulio Andreotti's coalition of Christian Democrats, Republicans, and Social Democrats
resigned on January 31 because the Communists
threatened to withdraw their support. Republican
leader Ugo La Malfa tried to form a government,
but chances of avoiding a general election faded
with a final break between the Christian Democrats
and Communists on March 11. A new minority
government headed by Andreotti, sworn in on
March 21, lasted only 11 days. The Communists and
Socialists voted against it on March 31 and it fell on
April 2.

The election on June 3 and 4 solved nothing,
though the Communists lost ground for the first time
in 33 years. Their share of votes for the Chamber of
Deputies fell 4 per cent to 30.4 per cent. Andreotti's
effort to form still another government failed, as did
attempts by Socialist leader Bettino Craxi and
Filippo Pandolfi, a Christian Democrat.

New Prime Minister. Francesco Cossiga, a
Christian Democrat and former interior minister,
formed a government on August 5. He pledged to
continue the three-year economic recovery program
that Pandolfi drew up in 1978 and to reform police
and security forces so that they could deal more
effectively with terrorism. On September 24, the
police captured Prospero Gallinari, suspected as a
leader of the Red Brigades terrorist organization
and a key figure in the 1978 kidnapping and murder
of former Prime Minister Aldo Moro.

Shaky Economy. Italy's economic recovery,
which had been steady since 1976, faltered in 1979
because oil costs increased more than $3 billion.
Inflation, which had steadied to 11.5 per cent in
1978, rose to 15 per cent in September. Stalled wage
talks affecting 1.2 million metal and engineering
workers disrupted industry until a July 16 agreement
gave workers a 5.7 per cent pay hike, five more paid
vacation days in 1980, and an additional five paid
vacation days in 1981. Strikes at the end of the
summer stranded visitors on Italian islands and
disrupted rail services.

The Bank Affair. The Bank of Italy staff struck for
24 hours on March 26 because Deputy Director-
General Mario Sarcinelli and Governor Paolo Baffi
were charged in connection with low-interest loans
granted to the chemical group Societa Italiana
Resine. They denied all of the charges. A judge
suspended Sarcinelli on April 17, but Andreotti
restored him to his post on April 20 because the
bank's top management threatened to resign as a
group.   Kenneth Brown

See also EUROPE (Facts in Brief Table). In
WORLD BOOK, see ITALY.

IVORY COAST. See AFRICA.

JAMAICA. See WEST INDIES.

JAPAN

JAPAN. The conservative Liberal-Democratic Party (LDP) failed to win a majority in the general election for the House of Representatives on Oct. 7, 1979, contrary to the expectations of both the party and political analysts. Unpleasant weather kept the voter turnout at about 68 per cent, the second lowest turnout since World War II.

The LDP won only 248 of the 511 seats, 1 fewer than its total in the 1976 election, but it fashioned a shaky majority when 10 independent winners joined the party. Results for the other parties were: Socialists, 107 seats (down 16); the Komeito (Clean Government Party), 57 (up 1); Communists, 39 (up 20); Democratic Socialists, 35 (up 7); New Liberal Club, 4 (down 9); United Democratic Socialists, 2 (down 1); and Independents, 19 (down 1). Although the LDP lost a seat, it won 44.6 per cent of the popular vote, a gain of slightly under 3 percentage points, reversing a steady decline from the party's 60 per cent in 1963.

Prime Minister Masayoshi Ohira was "shocked" at the results. He had won the first round of voting for LDP president on Nov. 27, 1978, unexpectedly defeating former Prime Minister Takeo Fukuda. He was then designated prime minister by the National Diet. He was re-elected in November, despite a challenge from Fukuda after the 1979 election.

In this way, the government weathered the effects of a bribery scandal that rivaled the 1976 scandal involving former Prime Minister Kakuei Tanaka. Two officials of the Nissho-Iwai Company were indicted in April 1979 and two more in May for illegal payments to government officials to ensure the purchase of airplanes and other materiel from United States defense contractors. Mitsuhiro Shimada, an executive for Nissho-Iwai, committed suicide, allegedly because of the scandal.

Economic Affairs. Prior to the October election, Ohira had been attacked inside and outside his party for proposing tax hikes to deal with the country's economic problems. Wholesale prices had increased 20 per cent, and the energy crisis was worsened by two price increases by the Organization of Petroleum Exporting Countries (OPEC). In addition, the yen had declined in relation to the dollar, reaching a two-year low in November before rising again.

The rising cost of oil and the resulting increase in inflation continued to be Japan's most important economic problem. During most of the year, the inflation rate was kept at a low 4.2 per cent, but observers feared that rising wholesale prices would result in a sharp increase. The government remained optimistic that the economy would achieve a growth rate of slightly more than 6 per cent, the goal for the year and apparently the highest rate for any major industrial nation.

Japan recorded the highest foreign-trade surplus in its history, $20.6 billion for the fiscal year ending on March 31. Exports totaled $97 billion, a 16 per cent increase, and imports $76.4 billion, a gain of 21 per cent. Trade with the United States resulted in a huge surplus of about $11.5 billion for Japan, up from $9 billion the previous year. The U.S. dollar rose to a rate of about 222 yen to $1 on May 1, an increase of about 25 per cent over the 1978 low of 176 yen to $1, then fell again, then rose to about 250 at the end of November.

Heads of state of Canada, France, Great Britain, Italy, Japan, the United States, and West Germany met in Tokyo on June 28 and 29 for an economic summit conference on how to deal with their common problems. A principal agreement was to specify limits on oil imports for 1979 and 1980 and to agree generally to hold down imports through 1985. Japan agreed to a 1985 target of no more than 6.9 million barrels per day. The leaders also agreed to use more coal and nuclear power, the latter with guarantees of public safety. They also pledged to fight protectionism in world trade and to stabilize the foreign exchange market. In a statement on the Indochinese refugee "boat people," the leaders pledged increased support for their relief and resettlement by providing more funds and admitting more refugees. Also in June, Foreign Minister Sunao Sonoda announced that Japan would provide about half the total cost for the United Nations High Commissioner's refugees fund, pay half the cost of constructing a

Prime Minister Masayoshi Ohira was glum when his party failed to win Japan's general election on Oct. 7, 1979. But he was re-elected in November.

367

temporary refugee center on an Indonesian island, and gradually increase the number of immigrants to Japan. Japan had been criticized by many countries for failing to take in refugees; the country had permanently admitted only three persons by June.

Prime Minister Ohira began an official visit to the United States on April 30. He held talks with President Jimmy Carter on May 2, and the two leaders reaffirmed their desire to maintain close cooperation in economic and world affairs. Japan also pledged that it would intensify its efforts to reduce its trade surplus with the United States.

On October 2, Japan officially protested the build-up of Russian forces in the southern Kuril Islands off northern Japan. Tokyo charged that Russia has at least 10,000 troops there – up from about 2,000 in 1978 – along with antiaircraft missiles and attack helicopters. Russia rejected the protest. Japan claims the islands.

Relations with the People's Republic of China continued to be cordial. In September, China asked the government of Japan for a loan of about $5.5-billion for railway, port, and power projects.

Widespread mourning followed the death of Lan Lan, a female giant panda, on September 4. She was a gift to the Japanese people from the government of China in 1972. John M. Maki

See also ASIA (Facts in Brief Table). In WORLD BOOK, see JAPAN.

JEWS AND JUDAISM. The long search for peace in the Middle East produced new tensions between blacks and Jews in the United States in 1979. Andrew J. Young, Jr., U.S. ambassador to the United Nations (UN), resigned on August 15 amid controversy over his private negotiations with the Palestine Liberation Organization (PLO). Official U.S. policy forbids direct talks with the PLO. Young is a black minister with a background in the civil rights movement. See CIVIL RIGHTS.

Russian Jews. Russia issued 50,000 emigration permits to Jews in 1979. This increase of 20,000 can probably be attributed to Russia's desire to create a positive climate that would encourage the United States Senate to ratify the new Strategic Arms Limitation Talks (SALT II) treaty. Although many Russian Jews elected to go to Israel, the majority emigrated to the United States.

Also in the Soviet Union, five Jewish activists imprisoned in 1970 were freed on April 17. Convicted of trying to hijack an airplane in Leningrad in an attempt to escape from Russia, the five were freed 14 months before the end of their terms.

Mixed Marriages. The largest issue facing the American Jewish community in 1979 was probably intermarriage. Reports indicated that between 30 and 50 per cent of American Jews marry non-Jews. In 40 per cent of these mixed marriages, however, the non-Jewish partner converted to Judaism. A report from the American Jewish Committee's Department of Jewish Communal Affairs noted that the degree of Jewish identification in intermarried families depends heavily on the depth of knowledge and background in Judaism. And that degree of Jewish identity of the couple reflects the personal religious commitment of the Jewish partner.

Because of assimilation through intermarriage and lower birth rates, the number of Jews in America has declined. United States population figures indicated that there were 6 million Jews, about 2.5 per cent of the population, in 1979. But it was estimated that the Jewish community would represent less than 1 per cent of the U.S. population by the year 2079.

Rabbi Alexander M. Schindler, president of the Union of American Hebrew Congregations, proposed that information about Judaism should be actively offered to the unaffiliated and that conversion programs should be set up. Reaction ranged from enthusiasm to hostility. Traditionally, the major groups in Judaism – Orthodox, Conservative, Reform, and Reconstructionist – have frowned upon open *proselytizing* (attempts to win converts). Some rabbis cited the lack of Jewish education for children as the major cause of assimilation. Others pointed out that since World War II, attention has been shifted from the home and the local community to Israel, weakening interest in Jewish home life.

Rabbi Linda Joy Holtzman, the first woman to head a congregation in the United States, is fitted for a robe shortly after her appointment in August.

The Holocaust. President Jimmy Carter proclaimed April 28 and 29 as Days of Remembrance for victims of the Holocaust, the mass murder of Jews in Europe by Nazi Germany during World War II. A 34-member presidential commission on the Holocaust produced a report recommending that the U.S. establish a museum dealing with the Holocaust, to be attached to the Smithsonian Institution in Washington, D.C. The commission also recommended an annual weekend of remembrance.

"Holocaust," a four-part television dramatization of the Nazis' extermination of the Jews, was seen by an estimated 150 million persons worldwide. In West Germany, the showing of "Holocaust" provoked heated discussions over pending legislation that would prevent the statute of limitations from being applied to Nazi war crimes. West Germany's parliament on July 3 voted to abolish the statute of limitations for murder. The government had previously extended the statute from 1969 to 1979. Thus, West Germany ensured that war criminals can be prosecuted no matter when they are apprehended.

Linda Joy Holtzman, a Reconstructionist, became presiding rabbi of the congregation Beth Israel in Coatesville, Pa., on August 1. She is the first woman to lead a congregation, though other female rabbis have served as assistants. Arnold G. Kaiman

See also ISRAEL; MIDDLE EAST. In WORLD BOOK, see JEWS; JUDAISM.

JOHNSON, EARVIN (1959-   ), an all-America basketball star at Michigan State University, signed a contract in June 1979 to play professional basketball with the Los Angeles Lakers. Johnson reportedly agreed to a four-year contract at about $600,000 per year. The Lakers had first choice in the annual National Basketball Association (NBA) draft of college players. They chose Johnson, who forfeited two years of college eligibility in order to turn pro. See BASKETBALL.

Johnson was one of college basketball's best playmaking guards, an unusual position for a player who stands 6 feet 8 inches (209 centimeters) tall. His sensational ball-handling and passing ability earned him the nickname "Magic." During his two years at Michigan State, his great play and infectious enthusiasm helped to transform a lackluster team into champions. Michigan State won the Big Ten Conference title in Johnson's freshman year, then captured the Big Ten title and the national collegiate championship in his sophomore year. As a freshman, he averaged 17 points and 7.9 rebounds per game and had a total of 222 *assists* (passes to teammates who score). As a sophomore, he averaged 17.1 points and 7.3 rebounds per game and totaled 269 assists.

Johnson was born in Lansing, Mich., on Aug. 14, 1959. He was all-state three years and won all-America honors at Everett High School in Lansing before enrolling at Michigan State. Joseph P. Spohn

JORDAN became the first Arab state to break diplomatic relations with Egypt in 1979. The action came after the March 27 summit meeting of Arab League foreign ministers in Baghdad, Iraq, held to organize a united Arab front against Egypt for its peace negotiations with Israel (see MIDDLE EAST). The government of King Hussein I banned all Eygptian books, government documents, newspapers, and magazines. It also unilaterally annulled the Egyptian-Jordanian trade agreement that exempted Egyptian goods from customs duties, and imposed a 25 per cent duty on all such goods.

The Jordanian alignment with the Arab "rejection front" against Egypt produced no new initiatives other than a partial reconciliation with the Palestine Liberation Organization (PLO). PLO Chairman Yasir Arafat visited Amman on September 19, and a joint PLO-Jordanian committee was formed to channel Arab funds to West Bank guerrillas. Hussein agreed to release Palestinian detainees. He also relaxed travel restrictions for Jordanians visiting the West Bank and the Gaza Strip, and said they would be given Jordanian passports.

Student Clashes. Dissatisfaction with the lack of progress toward a return to parliamentary government, along with the deep-rooted antagonism between Jordanians and Palestinians living in Jordan, led to some unrest, particularly among students. In

Jordan's King Hussein is escorted by President Fidel Castro of Cuba as he arrives at a summit conference of nonaligned nations in Havana.

April, fights between the two groups at Jordan's two universities disrupted registration and caused the suspension of classes for several days. Police invaded the campuses to break up the rioting.

Earlier, Hussein named a 30-member Senate, headed by former Prime Minister Bahjat Talhouni, to serve as an advisory body to the Consultative National Assembly formed in 1978. In June, the king authorized the formation of political organizations "within the framework of the national charter." The charter itself remained to be drafted.

Economic Affairs. There were significant developments in the phosphate industry, Jordan's principal foreign-exchange earner and economic asset. Phosphate exports between January and April were 815,232 metric tons (898,640 short tons), a 43 per cent increase over the same period in 1978. This made Jordan the world's third largest phosphate producer after Morocco and the United States. In March, Britain loaned $20 million to the Jordanian Arab Potash Company to expand its Dead Sea potash-extraction project.   William Spencer

See also MIDDLE EAST (Facts in Brief Table). In WORLD BOOK, see JORDAN.

JUDAISM. See JEWS AND JUDAISM.

JUNIOR ACHIEVEMENT (JA). See YOUTH ORGANIZATIONS.

KAMPUCHEA. See CAMBODIA.

KANSAS. See STATE GOVERNMENT.

KENNEDY, EDWARD MOORE (TED) (1932-), declared his candidacy for the Democratic presidential nomination on Nov. 7, 1979, in a speech at Boston's historic Faneuil Hall. That action ended years of speculation about whether he would try for the presidency in 1980 or wait until 1984.

Several factors appeared to figure in Kennedy's planning. As senior senator from Massachusetts and chairman of the Senate Judiciary Committee, he enjoyed considerable power. His introduction of legislation dealing with such important issues as health insurance, crime prevention, and gun control gave voters something to think about besides the 1969 Chappaquiddick Island incident in which a female companion was drowned. The health of his wife, the former Virginia Joan Bennett, and of his 17-year-old son, Ted, Jr., was improving. Public opinion polls during much of the year showed that as many as three-fourths of Democratic voters favored his candidacy. Also important, Rose Kennedy, his mother, who had lost two sons to assassins' bullets, gave her consent to his running for the presidency.

Kennedy was born in Boston in 1932. He graduated from Harvard University and received his law degree in 1959 from the University of Virginia. He was elected to the Senate in 1962. He and his wife have three children.   Marsha F. Goldsmith

KENTUCKY. See STATE GOVERNMENT.

KENYA. See AFRICA.

KHOMEINI, RUHOLLAH (1900?-), returned to Iran after 15 years in exile on Feb. 1, 1979, less than two weeks after his archenemy, Shah Mohammad Reza Pahlavi, left the country. Khomeini, who is an *ayatollah* (Islamic religious leader), became the unofficial head of state in Iran, though he did not become a member of the government. After an April referendum, he declared Iran an Islamic Republic, governed by the laws of Islam. With summary executions and harsh social changes, the ayatollah and his supporters sought to remake Iran. In early December, after another national vote, he became the official ruler. See IRAN.

Khomeini was born in 1900 or 1901 in Khumain, a small city south of Teheran. His father, Sayed Mustafa Mussavi, also an ayatollah, was killed when Khomeini was very young, and the boy was raised by his mother and aunt. He received a religious education in Isfahan, Arak, and Qom in Iran.

He worked as a religious teacher in Isfahan and Qom, and by 1941 he had emerged as a foe of the throne. His growing reputation reached a peak during anti-shah riots in 1962 and 1963. He was arrested and imprisoned in 1963, after a violently anti-shah speech. In 1964, he was exiled to Iraq, where he continued his fight. Iraq expelled him in 1978, and he settled near Paris.

Khomeini's first wife died. His second is the daughter of a wealthy landholder.   Edward G. Nash

KIRKLAND, LANE (1922-), became president of the American Federation of Labor and Congress of Industrial Organizations (AFL-CIO) on Nov. 19, 1979, succeeding George Meany, who retired.

Joseph Lane Kirkland was born on March 12, 1922, in Camden, S.C., to Randolph W. and Louise Kirkland. In 1940, he enrolled in the U.S. Merchant Marine Academy in Kings Point, N.Y., from which he graduated in 1942. He received a bachelor's degree from the Georgetown University School of Foreign Service in Washington, D.C., in 1948.

Kirkland served as a Merchant Marine deck officer from 1941 to 1946. The following year, he became a nautical scientist in the Navy Department's Hydrographic Office. He joined the AFL research staff in 1948 and in 1953 became assistant director of the AFL-CIO's social security department, a post he held until 1958. From 1958 to 1960, he served as director of research and education in the International Union of Operating Engineers. Kirkland's long association with Meany began in 1961, when he became assistant to the AFL-CIO president. Since 1969, he had been secretary-treasurer.

Kirkland married Edith D. Hollyday in 1944. They had five daughters. In 1973, he married Irena Neumann, an Israeli citizen.   Edward G. Nash

In WORLD BOOK, see MEANY, GEORGE.

KIWANIS INTERNATIONAL. See COMMUNITY ORGANIZATIONS.

KLUTZNICK, PHILIP MORRIS (1907-   ), was named secretary of commerce by President Jimmy Carter on Nov. 16, 1979, succeeding Juanita M. Kreps, who resigned for personal reasons. A Chicago real estate developer and investor, Klutznick has served in every administration except Richard M. Nixon's since Franklin D. Roosevelt's years in the White House. See CABINET, UNITED STATES.

Born on July 9, 1907, in Kansas City, Mo., Klutznick attended the University of Kansas in 1924 and 1925 and the University of Nebraska from 1925 to 1926. He received a law degree from Creighton University in Omaha, Nebr., in 1929.

Klutznick's business career has centered primarily on real estate ventures. He has helped build a number of shopping centers and other developments, including Water Tower Place, a 74-story complex of department stores, shops, restaurants, condominiums, and a hotel on Chicago's prestigious North Michigan Avenue.

He was a member of the U.S. delegation to the United Nations (UN) in 1957, 1961, and 1962 and represented the United States, with the rank of ambassador, on the UN's Economic and Social Council from 1961 to 1963. He has been chairman of the board of governors of the World Jewish Congress since 1971.

On June 8, 1930, Klutznick married Ethel Riekes. They had five sons and one daughter. Edward G. Nash

KOREA, NORTH. United States intelligence sources in 1979 revised upward their estimates of the size of North Korea's army. The Department of Defense said that the country's army apparently consists of 41 divisions, rather than the 28 formerly estimated. Also, according to U.S. Congressman Les Aspin (D., Wis.), the number of North Korean troops stood at about 550,000 to 600,000 – rather than the 430,000 previously estimated. The revised figures would make North Korea's army the sixth largest in the world.

On January 25, North Korea responded to a proposal by South Korea's President Chung Hee Park for a meeting "at any time, at any place." Meetings were held at Panmunjom on February 17, March 7, and March 14, but they ended in deadlock.

In another move toward reunification, United Nations Secretary-General Kurt Waldheim visited North Korea in May and conferred with President Kim Il-song. Waldheim also visited South Korea. He had been invited for discussions by both nations.

Park and U.S. President Jimmy Carter proposed on July 1 that North Korea join them in reunification talks. North Korea rejected this, insisting it should deal only with the United States.

A North Korean ship was sunk on July 21 by South Korea. Henry S. Bradsher

See also ASIA (Facts in Brief Table); KOREA, SOUTH. In WORLD BOOK, see KOREA.

KOREA, SOUTH. President Chung Hee Park was assassinated on Oct. 26, 1979, by Jae Kyu Kim, head of the Korean Central Intelligence Agency (KCIA). Prime Minister Kyu Ha Choi became acting president immediately; in December, the 2,562-member National Conference for Unification elected him president. He immediately lifted the emergency decree that Park and his Democratic Republican Party (DRP) had used to suppress dissent. Also, he planned constitutional revisions that would permit direct popular election of the next president.

The murder followed rising political unrest. The DRP had won only 31.7 per cent of the popular vote in assembly elections held on Dec. 13, 1978, while the opposition New Democratic Party (NDP) got 32.8 per cent – but fewer seats. This result led to political agitation, as did Park's release of political opponent Dae Jung Kim from detention in December 1978.

Defying a ban on criticism of the Constitution, which Park revised in 1972 to strengthen his powers, Dae Jung Kim said on January 2 that the Constitution "was illegally adopted and its procedure is undemocratic." He supported the May 30 election of Young Sam Kim as NDP president. Young Sam Kim was vocal in his opposition to the regime, and a Seoul court removed him from his NDP post on September 8. He said on September 16 that the Park government was a "dictatorial regime" and that the United States should stop supporting Park. Reacting to this, all 159 pro-government Assembly members voted on October 4 to expel Young Sam Kim. All NDP members resigned in protest, and the United States recalled its ambassador. On October 16, demonstrations in Pusan supporting Young Sam Kim developed into the worst riot against the government since 1960, when violence led to Park's overthrow of President Syngman Rhee.

The KCIA under Jae Kyu Kim was officially responsible for preventing such outbreaks. Tensions grew between Jae Kyu Kim and Chi Chul Cha, Park's chief confidant and bodyguard, who believed Jae Kyu Kim was too soft on the opposition. Park and his aides met with Kim at dinner in a KCIA guesthouse to discuss the problem. Kim shot and killed both Park and Cha. Kim's aides killed four other presidential bodyguards.

Martial law was declared on October 27 under the army chief of staff, General Seung Wha Chung. Chung's command publicly blamed Jae Kyu Kim for the deaths and said Kim had wanted to become president. Chung and at least 15 other generals were arrested in December by troops commanded by Major General Too Hwan Chon, head of a military intelligence agency – raising doubts about the future of constitutional rule.

American Relations. Shortly after the assassinations, the United States repeated its determination to defend South Korea and warned North Korea not to interfere. The situation remained peaceful.

Jae Kyu Kim, South Korea's intelligence chief, re-enacts his shooting of President Chung Hee Park for police. The killing took place on October 26.

United States President Jimmy Carter had discussed the political situation with Park during a June visit to South Korea to inspect U.S. troops stationed there. Carter appealed to Park to match the nation's economic progress with human rights progress.

Carter had announced in February that his 1977 program for withdrawing U.S. ground forces from South Korea would be held up because of new intelligence reports showing that North Korea apparently had a larger army than previously thought (see KOREA, NORTH). Carter announced on July 20 that troop withdrawals would be halted until 1981, when the situation would be re-examined.

On an October visit to Seoul, U.S. Defense Secretary Harold Brown promised to increase U.S. artillery strength, provide more helicopters, and deploy a new squadron of ground-support aircraft in South Korea.

Economic Growth continued to exceed targets in 1979. The projected 1979 gross national product of $43.1 billion had already been exceeded in 1978, with a figure of $46 billion. At current prices, including inflation, per capita income reached $1,242. Industrial exports became increasingly sophisticated as South Korea moved away from simple products with high labor value.   Henry S. Bradsher

See also ASIA (Facts in Brief Table). In WORLD BOOK, see KOREA.

KUWAIT. See MIDDLE EAST.

LABOR. Double-digit inflation returned to bedevil the United States labor force in 1979. Although the jobless rate remained relatively low, rising prices had a severe impact on workers' take-home pay. However, higher interest rates and severe credit restrictions, enacted late in the year to dampen inflation, were expected to produce an economic slowdown with a significant rise in unemployment.

The Bureau of Labor Statistics (BLS) Consumer Price Index for all urban consumers (CPI-U) rose 12.6 per cent in the 12 months ending on Nov. 30, 1979, while the index for urban wage earners and clerical workers (CPI-W) increased 12.8 per cent in the same period. This compared unfavorably with an average CPI rise of 7.6 in 1978 and one of 6.5 per cent in 1977.

The nation's energy problems were reflected in housing prices, which rose 14.3 per cent due, in large part, to fuel cost increases and transportation costs, which increased 17.5 per cent, reflecting the large increases in gasoline prices. These and other dents in purchasing power were responsible for a 5.2 per cent decline in real average weekly earnings as a 7.8 per cent increase in average hourly earnings was offset by the 12.8 per cent rise in the CPI-W, and a 0.8 per cent decrease in average weekly hours.

A comparatively bright spot during most of 1979 was the jobless rate, which hovered between 5.6 and 6.0 per cent. Unemployment averaged 6 per cent in

1978 and 7 per cent in 1977. Total employment stood at 97.7 million in December, reflecting an increase of about 2.1 million over the prior December. Preliminary BLS estimates of major employment changes in 1979 are summarized below:

	1978	1979*
	(in thousands)	
Total labor force	102,537	104,743
Armed forces	2,117	2,086
Civilian labor force	100,420	102,657
Total employment	94,373	96,740
Unemployed	6,047	5,917
Unemployment rate	6.0%	5.7%
Change in real weekly earnings		
(Worker with 3 dependents—		
private nonfarm sector)	−0.1%	−4.3%†
Change in output per man-hour	0.8%	−1.2%‡

*January to September average, seasonally adjusted, except for armed forces data.
†For 12-month period ending Sept. 30, 1979.
‡Third quarter of 1979, compared with third quarter of 1978.

Fighting Inflation. President Jimmy Carter on September 28 announced a "national accord" with the American Federation of Labor and Congress of Industrial Organizations (AFL-CIO) in an effort to broaden the fight against inflation. Organized labor agreed to have six of its representatives sit on a new 15-member pay advisory committee. The labor representatives included new AFL-CIO President Lane Kirkland and the presidents of five unions— Frank Fitzsimmons of the International Brotherhood of Teamsters, Douglas A. Fraser of the United Auto Workers (UAW), Lloyd McBride of the United Steelworkers of America, William Wynn of the Food & Commercial Workers, and John Lyons of the Ironworkers. John T. Dunlop, who helped direct President Richard M. Nixon's anti-inflation effort, was named chairman.

The committee was established to advise the Council on Wage and Price Stability on formulating new guidelines for pay increases, previously set at 7 per cent. The new panel was also to advise the council on specific wage-guideline disputes. While the pay committee's role is advisory, council Chairman Alfred E. Kahn said he expects it to have a strong influence on policy matters.

The anti-inflation program suffered a blow on May 31 when federal District Judge D. Barrington Parker ruled that it was unlawful for the government to bar or withdraw contracts from companies violating the guidelines. He said that the use of sanctions constituted "a mandatory system of wage and price controls, unsupported by law," and was therefore beyond the President's authority. However, a federal appeals court ruled on June 22 that since the President is authorized by Congress to secure "economy" and "efficiency" in contracting, he is free to deny federal contracts to firms that violate the guidelines. The AFL-CIO appealed the reversal, but the Supreme Court of the United States refused to review the case.

Collective Bargaining. Major contract settlements through the first nine months of 1979 provided first-year wage adjustments of 7.5 per cent, virtually the same as the 7.6 per cent 1978 average. The preliminary BLS figures also showed that annual wage adjustments over the life of the agreements dropped to 6.1 per cent, compared with 6.4 per cent in 1978.

These figures appeared moderate in the face of double-digit inflation, but 58 per cent of the 2.6 million workers covered by these agreements were also covered by automatic cost-of-living adjustment (COLA) clauses. Where COLA clauses triggered pay raises during the first nine months, workers received an average increase of 5.8 per cent, which amounted to about half of the increase in the cost of living.

Workers' realization of the "protection" received under COLA influenced the size of settlements. Workers without COLA negotiated settlements that provided annual wage adjustments of 8.1 per cent averaged over the life of the agreements, while those with COLA protection were willing to settle for average 4.6 per cent a year raises, to be supplemented by COLA increases.

U.S. Wage and Price Increases

Negotiated pay raises vs. rising prices in a decade of inflation

—— First-year negotiated wage increase

—— Average rise in Consumer Price Index

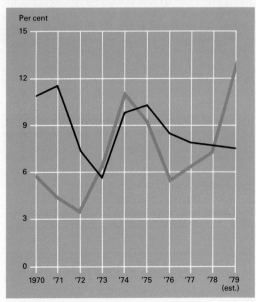

Source: Bureau of Labor Statistics

New Jersey state troopers form a protective line in front of the Statehouse in Trenton in July as some 19,000 state employees strike for higher pay.

Auto Settlements. The UAW and General Motors Corporation (GM) agreed upon a three-year contract on September 14. The pact provided 460,-000 UAW members with 3 per cent wage hikes in September 1979, 1980, and 1981. The improvement was partly offset by a provision specifying the withholding from COLA payments of a total of 14 cents an hour to help finance benefit improvements.

The UAW did not attain its goal of automatically linking pension adjustments to movements in the CPI. But the agreement provided retirees with a raise of $3.95 per month over the term for each year's service. Insurance improvements included liberalization of the eye- and dental-care programs. The union also moved closer to its goal of a four-day week, gaining a total of 26 paid personal holidays and 43 general paid holidays over the term of the new agreement.

The UAW reached a similar settlement for 190,-000 workers at Ford Motor Company, but negotiations with the financially ailing Chrysler Corporation made bigger news. The UAW and Chrysler — with 124,000 UAW members — agreed in October on a package that would cost Chrysler an estimated $203 million less than the GM and Ford packages. The congressional loan plan signed by President Carter in December required $462.5 million in concessions from union workers at Chrysler as one of the conditions for the loan guarantees.

Truck Strike. Teamsters began a 10-day tie-up of the trucking industry on April 1, after the expiration of a prior agreement with Trucking Management, Incorporated (TMI), an association of 500 trucking companies. Although the union struck only 73 selected TMI firms, all 500 companies responded with a nationwide lockout. The truck stoppage triggered lay-offs of about 500,000 workers in other industries.

The three-year settlement reached on April 10 provided a $1.50-per-hour wage increase over the term for local drivers and warehouse employees, and equivalent raises for distance drivers. Prior to the settlement, Teamsters reportedly earned $9.75 an hour, $12.65 including supplementary benefits. The COLA clause was changed to a semiannual, from an annual, basis, and the companies agreed to a $30-per-week raise over the term toward pension- and health- and welfare-fund payments. Although the negotiating parties assessed the wage increases at 30 per cent, or 10 per cent a year, Kahn insisted that, overall, the settlement fell within the 7 per cent-a-year guidelines.

Rubber Settlements. The United Rubber Workers (URW) and the "Big Four" rubber companies drew up new three-year contracts covering nearly 70,000 workers in 1979. The URW designated the settlement reached on June 15 with the B.F. Goodrich Company as the "pattern" for industry agreements. It was followed three days later by an agreement at Uniroyal, Incorporated, ending a month-long strike. Firestone Tire and Rubber Company followed the pattern in accordance with the "me too" agreement the company had signed in February, in which it agreed to withdraw from the industry's mutual-aid pact in case of a rubber industry strike and to accept the union's "designated industry settlement." In return, the URW agreed not to strike Firestone over economic issues. The pattern settlement was also accepted by the Goodyear Tire and Rubber Company on July 16.

The pacts provided hourly increases of 32 cents, retroactive to April 20, 1979, and of 20 cents in 1980 and 1981. Skilled trades workers got an additional 40-cent hourly increase. There was a provision for "advance" COLA payments of 20 cents the first year, and 15 cents the second and third years. The first 5 cents of some of the quarterly increases was to be withheld to offset the advances. Among other benefits was an increase in pension benefits of from $12.50 to $15 a month for each year's service.

New Petroleum Contracts were reached in January with the major refiners. The "pattern" was set by a two-year agreement between the Gulf Oil Corporation and the Oil, Chemical and Atomic International Union on January 11, providing a 73-cent-an-hour raise effective on Jan. 8, 1979, and a 5 per cent increase on Jan. 8, 1980. Gulf, which had also set the pattern in the 1975 and 1977 rounds, also agreed to boost its contributions to the medical insurance plan by $4.50 a month for single workers and $12 for families. Settlements at Standard Oil of Indiana; Texaco, Incorporated; Atlantic Richfield Company; Shell Oil Company; and other refiners covered 50,000 workers by the end of January.

Several unions resorted to strikes to gain a bargaining edge in 1979. Approximately 600 members of the American Federation of Grain Millers halted all shipments out of Duluth, Minn., and Superior, Wis., tying up about 10 per cent of the nation's grain shipments from July 6 until September 25. Two rail unions demanding pay gains won from other carriers staged a five-week walkout against the bankrupt Chicago, Rock Island, and Pacific Railroad that ended on October 4 after President Jimmy Carter appointed an emergency board to resolve outstanding issues. The International Association of Airline Mechanics grounded United Airlines for 55 days, before agreeing on May 25 to a three-year package that would raise mechanics' wages and benefits an estimated 35 per cent.

Leaders Depart. AFL-CIO chief George Meany, the architect of the AFL merger with the CIO in 1955 and president of the combined federation since its inception, retired in September. AFL-CIO Secretary-Treasurer Lane Kirkland, who had worked closely with Meany since 1948, was elected to a two-year term to succeed Meany as president on November 19. See KIRKLAND, LANE.

Retiring AFL-CIO President George Meany, right, talks with his successor, Lane Kirkland, before taking up the gavel for the last time in November.

Meany, who began his career as a plumber, served as an adviser to a succession of Presidents. However, he is most remembered in the labor movement as the man who held the 13.5-million-member federation together for almost a quarter of a century.

AFL-CIO policy under Meany's tenure was shaped by his staunch anticorruption and anti-Communist viewpoint, and was responsible for the departure of two major unions from the federation. The Teamsters Union was ousted for alleged ties to organized crime in 1957, while in 1968 the UAW was led out by its president, Walter P. Reuther, who objected to Meany's strong support of United States involvement in the Vietnam War. Although he did not publicly reveal why he stepped down, Meany had been slowed by a hip injury.

United Mine Workers (UMW) President Arnold R. Miller resigned on November 12 after his second heart attack in two years. He was succeeded by UMW Vice-President Samuel M. Church, Jr.

Other union presidents stepping down in 1979 included Matthew Guinan of the Transport Workers' Union, who was succeeded by William G. Lindner; President A. F. Grospiron of the Oil, Chemical, and Atomic Workers Union, succeeded by Bob Goss; Al H. Chesser of the United Transportation Union, succeeded by Frank A. Hardin; and William Sidell of the Carpenters' Union, succeeded by William Konyha.

Alice Peurala, elected president of United Steelworkers Local 65 in Chicago in April, became the
first woman to head a basic steel union local

Several labor leaders died in 1979. A. Philip
Randolph, who founded the Brotherhood of Sleeping Car Porters in 1925, died on May 16 at the age of
90. Randolph became the first black to serve as
vice-president of the AFL-CIO in 1957, and held the
office until his retirement in 1968. He was active in
the civil rights movement.

Jacob Potofsky died on August 5 after a long
illness. He was 85. He had retired as head of the
Amalgamated Clothing and Textile Workers
Union in 1972, after 58 years in the union.

David J. McDonald, who died on August 8 at the
age of 76, had been president of the United Steelworkers of America from 1952 to 1965. He had
served on the Steelworkers Organizing Committee
in the 1930s.

Merger. The Retail Clerks International Union
and the Amalgamated Meat Cutters and Butcher
Workmen merged on June 6 to create the 1.2-
million-member United Food and Commercial
Workers Union, the largest union within the AFL-
CIO. Union officials said the merger, the result of a
six-year effort, would provide improved collective
bargaining strength. William W. Wynn, who headed the Retail Clerks, was elected president, and
former Meat Cutters President Harry Pool became
the union's executive vice-president.   Leon Bornstein

See also AVIATION; CITY; ECONOMICS; RAIL-
ROAD. In WORLD BOOK, see LABOR; LABOR FORCE.

LANDRIEU, MOON (1930-   ), former mayor of
New Orleans, was sworn in as United States secretary of housing and urban development on Sept. 24,
1979. He succeeded Patricia Roberts Harris, who
became secretary of health, education, and welfare.
See CABINET, UNITED STATES.

Maurice Landrieu was born in New Orleans on
July 23, 1930. He graduated from Loyola University
in New Orleans in 1952 and received a law degree
from Loyola in 1954. After serving in the United
States Army until 1957, he established a law practice
in New Orleans in 1958.

In 1960, Landrieu was elected to the Louisiana
House of Representatives and served there until
1966. He became known as a champion of minority
rights by opposing legislation designed to block
Louisiana's compliance with desegregation orders.

He served in the New Orleans City Council from
1966 to 1970 and as mayor from 1970 to 1978. As
mayor, Landrieu was credited with opening the
city's government to blacks and with spearheading
the renovation of the city's historic French Market.
As chairman of the National Council of Mayors in
1975 he helped to formulate the federal revenue-
sharing program for cities.

Landrieu married Verna Satterlee in 1954. They
have nine children. Landrieu spent much of 1979
helping his daughter Mary win his old seat in the
Louisiana House of Representatives.   Beverly Merz

LANSBURY, ANGELA (1925-   ), a stage and
motion-picture actress, won the Antoinette Perry
(Tony) Award in 1979 for the best actress in a
musical for her role in the theater production of
Sweeney Todd, directed by Harold Prince, with
music and lyrics by Stephen Sondheim. In the part
of Mrs. Lovett, Lansbury baked meat pies filled with
human flesh. Critics said that only she could have
lent the desired light comic touch to such a role.

The 1979 award was Lansbury's third Tony for
best actress in a musical. She won her first Tony in
1967 for the title role in the long-running *Mame,* the
musical version of *Auntie Mame;* her second came in
1969 for her performance in *Dear World.*

Lansbury was born on Oct. 16, 1925, in London.
She enrolled in drama school in London in 1940 but
moved to the United States later that year.

She began a long career in Hollywood with her
role in *Gaslight* in 1944. She also appeared in
National Velvet, The Dark at the Top of the Stairs,
and *Death on the Nile.* Perhaps her most notable film
role was as a "heavy" in *The Manchurian Candidate.*

The critics loved her in *Hotel Paradiso* in 1957, her
Broadway debut, but the play flopped. Other Broad-
way shows in which she starred include *A Taste of
Honey, Something for Everyone,* and *Gypsy.*

Lansbury married Peter Shaw, her second husband, in 1949. They have two children, a girl and a
boy.   Patricia Dragisic

LAOS. Relief officials who toured the country in 1979 reported political arrests, economic scarcities, and growing economic stagnation. Each night, refugees swam across the Mekong River to Thailand. By March, Thai refugee camps held an estimated 250,000 Laotians. A report presented to the Association of Southeast Asian Nations in May said that about 6,000 Laotians were escaping into Thailand each month (see ASIA [Close-Up]). Citizens were routinely recruited to attend political seminars, and police continued to round up suspects for "re-education."

An estimated 10,000 to 15,000 soldiers, officials, and professionals were detained in camps in the jungle near the border with Vietnam and China. Those who were allowed to return home told tales of exhausting work, inadequate food, disease, and no medical help or drugs. Conditions were only a little better in the so-called seminar centers, which gave indoctrination to some soldiers, protesters, and people once employed by United States military forces or American businesses in Laos.

Stagnant Economy. After a drought in 1977 and floods in 1978, Laos had a fair rice crop. With the *kip,* Lao's monetary unit, officially depreciated to 200 kip to the $U.S.1 and about 1,600 kip to $U.S.1 in the black market and with essentials in short supply, the farmers kept most of the rice for their own use. They sold it in the black market, or smuggled it to Thailand. A United Nations report said that when farmers turned rice over to the state, it was in exchange for salt, sugar, and cloth. People in the cities and the troops – including the sizable Vietnamese garrison – ate the rice provided by foreign-aid agencies.

With a serious "brain drain" produced by the flight across the Mekong, an International Monetary Fund report said that government enterprises operated at only about 30 per cent of capacity.

Hanoi Dominant. With 30,000 to 40,000 Vietnamese troops garrisoned in the country, Laos became closely aligned with Hanoi, the Vietnamese-backed Heng Samrin regime in Cambodia, and Russia. The close relationship with Vietnam put the government of Prime Minister Kayson Phomvihan at odds with the People's Republic of China on several occasions. When Chinese troops crossed into Vietnam in March, Laos accused China of invading its borders at the same time. Laos said that China not only rejected an official protest on the troop movements on March 10, but also arrested the two Laotians who presented the protest. In addition, Laos said that China refused to withdraw its 3,000 construction workers in Laos.   Mark Gayn

See also ASIA (Facts in Brief Table); CAMBODIA; VIETNAM. In WORLD BOOK, see LAOS.

A billboard in Vientiane, Laos, reflecting an anti-American stance, shows citizens beating a United States Central Intelligence Agency spy.

LATIN AMERICA

The victory of the Sandinista National Liberation Front (FSLN) over Nicaragua's dictator, President Anastasio Somoza Debayle, in July was the most significant event of 1979 in terms of its implications for other countries in Latin America. It was a known fact that the FSLN had associations with Communist Cuba, the Palestine Liberation Organization, and several Latin American terrorist organizations, some of whose members fought alongside the Sandinistas. Their success aroused fears throughout the region that other Latin American terrorist groups, supported by Russia through its control of Cuba, might be emboldened to renewed action, even though such groups seemed to be in eclipse.

South American countries interpreted the Sandinista victory as a serious failure of United States policy. The military dictatorships tended to fault the Administration of U.S. President Jimmy Carter for not propping up Somoza, despite his regime's open corruption and lack of popular support. More moderate observers faulted the United States for not dropping Somoza sooner to pave the way for democratically inclined elements in Nicaragua to assume the government.

Sam Francis, a policy analyst for the Heritage Foundation in Washington, D.C., declared in an article that all but one of the 14 terrorist movements in Latin America are actively supported by the Soviet Union through Cuba. He noted that "progressive revolutionary organizations of Latin America," which included Argentine, Uruguayan, and other Latin American terrorist groups, met in Benghazi, Libya, on February 1. All had some type of Marxist-oriented ideology, Francis noted, and their "principal purpose . . . is the destruction of U.S. economic and political connections in Latin America," rather than the immediate takeover of specific countries – the unexpected success of the Sandinistas in Nicaragua notwithstanding.

More to Come. "In the future," Francis predicted, "Americans can expect that terrorism and guerrilla warfare will escalate in Latin America, that the United States and its businessmen and diplomats will be the targets . . . and both the Soviets and the Cubans will seek to destabilize and overthrow pro-American governments in Latin America in support of a long-term and well-planned campaign to reduce even further the U.S. political and economic influence in Latin America."

Constantine C. Menges, an associate of the Hudson Institute and an expert on the successful transi-

tion of Spain from a dictatorship to a working democracy, suggested in October that the Spanish experience could be applied to many Latin American countries. Brazil, Bolivia, and Peru were, for example, already in the process of reverting from dictatorships to democracy, and Chile, Argentina, and Uruguay were most likely to repeat the process in the near future. The key element, said Menges, is the support from other democracies.

The visit of Spain's President Adolfo Suarez Gonzalez to Brasília, Brazil's capital, on August 6 was seen as perhaps a step in this direction and was interpreted as a political endorsement of Brazil's step-by-step return to a democratic system by the man seen by many as largely responsible for Spain's

Cuba's President Fidel Castro, at rostrum of new
Convention Palace in Havana, addresses delegates
to September summit meeting of nonaligned nations.

successful transition. Latin American critics felt that
the United States, on the other hand, had focused
mainly on human rights violations without giving
adequate recognition to the fact that some governments guilty of brutal repression were reacting to a
genuine threat of terrorism. The U.S. Department
of State's response was to urge a rapid return to
democracy no matter what the cost. The chaos
plaguing Bolivia was the result of such a policy,
critics charged.

In a meeting with ambassadors of the Organization of American States (OAS) in Washington,
D.C., on May 10, U.S. National Security Adviser
Zbigniew Brzezinski went so far as to say that the
United States was no longer interested in Latin
America as a region. He explained that the current
U.S. policy of "globalism" toward Latin America
was the result of an emerging international climate
in which ideological problems such as the differences
between capitalism and communism, or democracy
and totalitarianism, had given way to an economic
order that had to accommodate the interests of 160
countries instead of 40.

"Liberation Theology." The third meeting of the
Latin American Episcopal Conference (CELAM) –

a Roman Catholic organization made up of bishops from the region – was held in Puebla, Mexico, from January 27 to February 13. At its conclusion, CELAM issued a document that called life in Latin America "a type of abomination" and claimed that not only was poverty worsening, but also there were countless instances of torture, kidnapping, exile, and other abuses of power by unnamed military governments. It urged priests and laymen alike to press for profound changes that would benefit the poor.

The document was seen as a victory for the progressive wing of the church, even though it stopped short of advocating church support of political parties and ideologies. Several church leaders took pains to explain that they were practicing the "theology of liberation" and were not at odds with the admonition Pope John Paul II issued to activist priests not to engage in overt political activity when he opened the meeting. "The pope was not talking about liberation but about liberation ideology,"

Facts in Brief on Latin American Political Units

Country	Population	Government	Monetary Unit*	Foreign Trade (million U.S. $) Exports†	Imports†
Argentina	27,776,000	President Jorge Rafael Videla	peso (1,560.5 = $1)	6,355	4,082
Bahamas	243,000	Acting Governor General Gerald C. Cash; Prime Minister Lynden O. Pindling	dollar (1 = $1)	1,989	3,053
Barbados	254,000	Governor General Sir Deighton Harcourt Lyle Ward; Prime Minister J. M. G. Adams	dollar (2 = $1)	132	314
Belize	163,000	Governor Peter Donovan McEntee; Premier George Price	dollar (2 = $1)	73	86
Bolivia	5,170,000	Interim President Lydia Gueiler Tejada	peso (25 = $1)	641	618
Brazil	126,497,000	President Joao Baptista de Oliveira Figueiredo	cruzeiro (31.9 = $1)	12,651	15,054
Chile	11,227,000	President Augusto Pinochet Ugarte	peso (39 = $1)	2,408	3,002
Colombia	27,548,000	President Julio Cesar Turbay Ayala	peso (43.4 = $1)	2,956	2,928
Costa Rica	2,230,000	President Rodrigo Carazo Odio	colón (8.6 = $1)	840	1,180
Cuba	10,120,000	President Fidel Castro Ruz	peso (1 = $1.39)	3,900	4,200
Dominica	79,000	Acting President Jenner Armour; Prime Minister J. Oliver Seraphin	dollar (2.7 = $1)	10	18
Dominican Republic	5,442,000	President Silvestre Antonio Guzman Fernandez	peso (1 = $1)	604	860
Ecuador	8,388,000	President Jaime Roldos Aguilera	sucre (27.2 = $1)	1,532	1,583
El Salvador	4,619,000	Junta leaders Adolfo Arnoldo Majano & Jaime Abdul Gutierrez	colón (2.5 = $1)	629	1,021
Grenada	98,000	Governor General Paul Godwin Scoon; Prime Minister Maurice Bishop	dollar (2.7 = $1)	17	32
Guatemala	7,014,000	President Fernando Romeo-Lucas Garcia	quetzal (1 = $1)	1,160	1,084
Guyana	841,000	President Raymond Arthur Chung; Prime Minister Forbes Burnham	dollar (2.6 = $1)	260	337
Haiti	4,974,000	President Jean-Claude Duvalier	gourde (5 = $1)	149	225
Honduras	3,173,000	Military Junta President Policarpo Paz Garcia	lempira (2 = $1)	597	693
Jamaica	2,192,000	Governor General Florizel Glasspole; Prime Minister Michael Norman Manley	dollar (1.8 = $1)	758	895
Mexico	71,524,000	President Jose Lopez Portillo	peso (22.9 = $1)	5,772	7,786
Nicaragua	2,253,000	5-member Government of National Reconstruction Junta	córdoba (10 = $1)	628	755
Panama	1,963,000	President Aristides Royo; National Guard Commander Omar Torrijos Herrera	balboa (1 = $1)	228	861
Paraguay	3,150,000	President Alfredo Stroessner	guaraní (126 = $1)	257	319
Peru	18,180,000	President Francisco Morales Bermudez Cerrutti; Prime Minister Pedro Richter Prada	sol (243 = $1)	1,433	1,614
Puerto Rico	3,602,000	Governor Carlos Romero Barcelo	US $	4,516	6,200
St. Lucia	115,000	Governor General Sir Allen Montgomery Lewis; Prime Minister Allan Fitzgerald Laurent Louisy	dollar (2.7 = $1)	17	14
St. Vincent and the Grenadines	128,000	Governor General Sir Sydney Gun-Munro; Prime Minister Milton Cato	dollar (2.7 = $1)	9	24
Surinam	484,000	President Johan H. E. Ferrier; Prime Minister Henck A. E. Arron	guilder (1.8 = $1)	230	266
Trinidad and Tobago	1,137,000	President Ellis Emmanuel Innocent Clarke; Prime Minister Eric E. Williams	dollar (2.4 = $1)	2,039	1,963
Uruguay	2,850,000	President Aparicio Mendez Manfredini	peso (8.4 = $1)	608	730
Venezuela	15,081,000	President Luis Herrera Campins	bolivar (4.3 = $1)	9,126	10,373

*Exchange rates as of Dec. 1, 1979. †Latest available data.

Anastasio Somoza Debayle, who resigned as president of strife-torn
Nicaragua in July, meets the press after fleeing to safety in Miami, Fla.

argued Bishop Leonidas Proano of Riobamba, Ecuador. "Liberation theology is a profoundly evangelistic, Christian concept. Christ came to earth to proclaim the good news to the poor. Christ was the liberator incarnate. We must continue to do the same thing." He said, "It is impossible to avoid politics, but we don't participate in political parties."

Regional Organization. The ninth General Assembly of the OAS met in La Paz, Bolivia, on October 22 to consider regional matters. The extensive agenda included reports on human rights violations, trade relations, and economic integration. Alejandro Orfila of Argentina was re-elected to a second term as secretary-general on October 24. Orfila's first term had been marked by criticism of his overlavish receptions and allegations that he was too involved, through business associations and personal relationships, with dictatorial regimes in Latin America.

The meeting's most controversial issue involved a proposal by Bolivia that the OAS back its demand to have Chile return territory taken from Bolivia during a war in 1879. The two countries nearly reached an agreement in 1976 under which Chile would cede a strip of territory to landlocked Bolivia, giving it access to the Pacific Ocean. However, Bolivia insisted that the negotiations be multilateral rather than bilateral. When Chile rejected that demand, diplomatic relations were severed. It was subsequently

agreed that negotiating procedures should be worked out with the aid of other OAS members.

During the meeting, a number of delegates said there was a need to reorganize the OAS so that it could play a more relevant role in helping solve regional problems faced by OAS members. However, no specific reorganization measures were proposed. There was also much discussion concerning bureaucratic problems, including arguments over the organization's $50-million budget, of which the United States provides 66 per cent.

Andean Group Activities. Members of the Andean Group of nations met in May in Cartagena, Colombia, the city where the organization was founded 10 years earlier. The group includes Bolivia, Colombia, Ecuador, Peru, and Venezuela. Chile had been a member, but dropped out because it wanted to adopt lower external tariffs than did other members.

The group was founded to create a regional common market that would be an integrated economic unit powerful enough to negotiate with the industrialized nations. The members wished to coordinate their economic development by allocating specific industrial operations to each nation.

Trade among the member countries increased from $100 million in 1969 to $900 million in 1979, but tension among the members still hampered the establishment of common development plans. No

Government troops, crouching behind a parked car, reload their automatic rifles during a May gun battle with demonstrators in El Salvador.

progress was made at the Cartagena meeting either toward adopting a common external tariff or in reducing tariff and nontariff barriers to trade within the group. A new effort was instituted, however, to adopt a program under which the metalworking industry would be divided among the members. The first metalworking plan, adopted in 1972, had not been implemented because of arguments between the members, a lack of investment capital, and confusion caused by the withdrawal of Chile and the admission of Venezuela in 1974. The new program represented an attempt to resolve the differences by assigning the manufacture of the 76 product groups, covering 323 items, to more than one member country.

The members were also authorized to negotiate with one another for the joint manufacture of items. Venezuela, Peru, and Bolivia, for example, agreed to the joint production of thermostats and drilling and mineral-crushing equipment. Colombia, Ecuador, Peru, and Venezuela also committed themselves to help Bolivia obtain financing and technology to establish a plant for making machine tools for metal-milling, radial, and threading machines; mechanical saws; and wire-drawing equipment.

Members also agreed that Venezuela would be the area's major steel producer. The Andean countries also decided to postpone until March 1980 a final decision on what basic automobile and truck

models each country would be assigned to make under the group's automobile agreement.

Regional Economics. The non-oil-producing countries in Latin America were experiencing severe difficulties in meeting the rising costs of imported oil. Many, already struggling to meet interest and amortization payments on their international debts, faced the added burden of borrowing to balance their international payments, which had soared after the quadrupling of oil prices in 1974. Their difficulties were further compounded by the new oil increases being prompted by the revolution in Iran.

The most prevalent trend was the intent by many countries to lower their external tariff barriers. It represented a challenge to the long-accepted theories of Argentine economist Raul Prebisch, who had influenced Latin American countries to erect high tariff barriers as a way to protect their fledgling industries, eliminate the need to buy imported goods, and provide more local jobs. Too often, however, the tariff barriers protected inefficient firms that monopolized their sector of industry and sold their goods at prices well above world levels. The tariffs also failed to solve the import problem because most of the countries had to import all of their raw materials. Latin American governments, trying to offset the monopolies by taking greater control of the economy, wound up paying the price of bureaucratic wastefulness.

Chile was the first Latin American country to challenge this approach by applying the so-called Chicago School theory of economics as taught by Nobel Prizewinning economist Milton Friedman, formerly a professor at the University of Chicago. Other countries with faltering economies were encouraged to emulate Chile by the International Monetary Fund (IMF).

The guiding principle behind the IMF's philosophy was that local industries, stripped of their tariff protection, would have to improve productivity and sell at competitive prices or else abandon that particular line of manufacturing. The country would thus end up with industries that were especially suited to its particular situation. In economic terms, this was known as using its "comparative advantage."

Tariff Adjustments. During the year, Chile completed its carefully staged lowering of tariffs, arriving at a level of 20 per cent for virtually all products except imported luxury cars that the government wanted to discourage its citizens from buying. In the process, Chile's electronics industry – among others – collapsed. But new exports of fruits and products utilizing the country's vast forest reserves were developing in their stead.   Everett G. Martin

See also articles on the various Latin American countries. In WORLD BOOK, see LATIN AMERICA and articles on the individual countries.

LAW. See CIVIL RIGHTS; COURTS AND LAWS; CRIME; SUPREME COURT OF THE UNITED STATES.

LEBANON. The resignation of Prime Minister Salim Ahmad al-Huss on May 16, 1979, after 2½ years in office highlighted the government's continued failure to achieve a reconciliation between the various feuding Christian and Muslim factions and impose authority over the entire country. The al-Huss government had been made up of nonpolitical bureaucrats, in the hope that they could bring about administrative efficiency without being subject to factional pressures. President Elias Sarkis continued al-Huss on an interim basis, and on July 16 al-Huss formed a new Cabinet of 12 ministers. Seven were former ministers and all were experienced politicians, indicating a new try for a political solution to Lebanese disunity.

Clans Clash. Unfortunately, the leaders of the major Lebanese factions continued their opposition to the government and to one another. On May 19, the first anniversary of the murder of Tony Frangie, son of former president and Maronite Christian chief Sleiman Frangie, Frangie supporters attempted to gun down Pierre Gemayel, head of the Christian Falange Party. The Falange-Frangie vendetta prompted a brief alignment of the Falange with former President Camille Chamoun's National Liberal Party, also a Maronite Christian faction. But their coalition collapsed in July.

Army Changes. The government also was largely unsuccessful in establishing a nonpolitical national army to carry out its authority. In March, the Chamber of Deputies, renamed the National Assembly in a unity gesture, passed a new defense law making the prime minister commander in chief of the army and setting up a Higher Military Council with equal representation of all factions.

Lebanese Army units replaced Saudi Arabian troops as they withdrew from the Arab peacekeeping force, and in June the army reoccupied several Beirut suburbs controlled by Christian militia since the start of the civil war in 1975. But an attempt in April to send army units to south Lebanon failed. Major Saad Haddad, head of the rebel Christian militia there, on April 18 unilaterally declared a 340-square-mile (900-square-kilometer) "Free Lebanon" along the Israeli border. Chamoun and other nongovernment leaders supported Haddad's action on the grounds that the main problem in Lebanon was the Palestinians, since their presence undermined national unity.

The bickering among Lebanon's leaders, the intermittent gun battles between factions, and the Israeli raids in retaliation for Palestinian attacks on Israel fell heaviest on the beleaguered Lebanese people. The national budget was $318 million in deficit. William Spencer

See also MIDDLE EAST (Facts in Brief Table). In WORLD BOOK, see LEBANON.

LESOTHO. See AFRICA.

LIBERIA. See AFRICA.

LIBRARY. Proposition 13, which severely limited property taxes in California after it was passed in 1978, continued to take its toll on the state's libraries in 1979. The director of the San Diego Public Library resigned rather than face another year of low library funding. Last-minute state aid — $623,000 — narrowly averted massive layoffs and library closings in the Los Angeles County Public Library System. In all, the California state legislature approved $11 million in emergency aid.

Similar problems occurred across the United States. At the Philadelphia Free Library, a $2-million budget cut eliminated 127 of the system's 779 jobs. The El Paso, Tex., public library saw its book budget cut in half, to $100,000. Library staff members there reportedly donated money to buy books.

Opposition to local property taxes as the major source of library support prompted several states to increase aid at the state level. Illinois increased its library aid $6 million to assist individual libraries as well as library systems. New York legislators approved a $3.7-million funding supplement for school and public libraries.

Many libraries, faced with frozen or reduced budgets, turned to volunteers to take up responsibilities that hard-pressed library staff could no longer handle. Alabama's Huntsville-Madison County Public Library used volunteers to manage the first

Budget cuts forced libraries in cities across the United States to shorten the number of hours they could stay open to serve the public.

branch library set up outside the city limits of Huntsville. In Maryland, volunteers operated three Baltimore County libraries.

National Library Act. A National Library Act introduced in Congress in June by Senators Jacob K. Javits (R., N.Y.) and Edward M. Kennedy (D., Mass.) proposed that a National Library Agency be created "to aid, augment, and support local and state library services." The agency would "not . . . exercise direct control over their operations or policies." The new agency would probably oversee federal library-aid programs and plan and coordinate a national library and information network, a system of federal libraries, and various forms of interlibrary cooperation. Other functions might include research programs, exchange programs with foreign libraries, and a national plan for the distribution of government publications. The agency might also help public libraries develop ways to issue information on government programs such as health and social security benefits.

Library Meetings. The Canadian Library Association's Annual Conference was held in Ottawa, Ont., from June 14 to 20. The 98th annual conference of the American Library Association was held in Dallas from June 23 to 29.   Robert J. Shaw

See also AMERICAN LIBRARY ASSOCIATION; CANADIAN LIBRARY ASSOCIATION. In WORLD BOOK, see LIBRARY.

LIBYA. Head of government Muammar Muhammad al-Qadhaafi's campaign to transform Libya into a true "peoples' democracy" proceeded without letup in 1979. At a special session of the General People's Congress on March 1, Qadhaafi resigned as that legislative body's secretary general. Declaring that "power should revert to the masses and the revolution should separate itself from administration of power," he dissolved the Revolution Command Council that had ruled since the 1969 revolution.

A 21-member General People's Committee was elected by the congress to implement legislative proposals that originate with smaller congresses representing various segments of the population. Although he held no official title, Qadhaafi was designated the director, symbol, and guide of the revolution and remained clearly in power.

Other Steps toward popular democracy as defined in Qadhaafi's *Green Book,* his handbook on the Libyan revolution, were the renaming of government ministries as secretariats. The head of each secretariat is to be elected by his own staff, thus becoming a member of the General People's Committee. The *Green Book* prohibits an appointed cabinet. A number of secretariats were eliminated in the reorganization, notably Interior, Trade, Youth and Sports, Food and Marine Wealth, and Dams. Also missing from the committee was a secretariat for Defense.

Part III of the *Green Book* was published in June. It deals with such social problems as education, the role of women, minorities, and the family.

Foreign Disasters. Qadhaafi's successes at home bore no resemblance to his handling of foreign affairs. In April, he sent a battalion of about 1,500 Libyan soldiers to help Uganda's President Idi Amin Dada repel an invasion by Tanzania and rebel Ugandans. About 400 Libyans were killed, and Libya later paid $40 million to ransom captured soldiers.

Libyan forces also intervened unsuccessfully in the civil war in Chad in April. However, the Chadian rebel faction that Qadhaafi had been supporting then united with other factions to drive the Libyans back to the border.

On December 2, the U.S. Embassy in Tripoli was stormed by rioters, protesting U.S. policies toward Iran. The Libyan government, after a strong U.S. protest, offered to restore the embassy. Awash with oil profits, the government on October 29 announced plans to build a 23-story building in New York City to house its United Nations and consular staffs.   William Spencer

See also AFRICA (Facts in Brief Table). In WORLD BOOK, see LIBYA.

LIECHTENSTEIN. See EUROPE.

LIONS INTERNATIONAL. See COMMUNITY ORGANIZATIONS.

LITERATURE. As if in response to the surprising upsurge of younger writers in the United States during the previous year, the major novelists produced a large body of distinguished work in 1979, an outpouring of first-class novels and short-story collections unmatched in the decade. It was one of American literature's most vigorous and memorable years since just after World War II.

Bernard Malamud began the parade with *Dubin's Lives,* an audacious and accomplished novel about a biographer's love affair with a young woman. Joseph Heller followed with *Good as Gold,* a scathing political novel notable for its author's return to the zany comic mode.

Philip Roth turned out *The Ghost Writer,* his best novel in years, and Kurt Vonnegut, after several self-indulgent novels, fulfilled his promise with *Jailbird,* a richly comic tale of a bureaucrat caught in the web of Watergate. William Styron's first novel in 12 years, *Sophie's Choice,* was a masterful epic of the Holocaust.

Wallace Stegner's 11th novel, *Recapitulation,* was a moving evocation of the American West. Stanley Elkin offered *The Living End,* a blasphemous and corrosively funny comic masterpiece. Mary McCarthy dipped into the thriller genre for *Cannibals and Missionaries,* a novel of international terrorism.

Norman Mailer carved a bright new jewel for his crown with *The Executioner's Song,* a fictional retell-

Aunt Erma's Cope Book, by columnist Erma Bombeck, tells people how to deal with the absurdities of today's world with great wit and good humor.

ing of the life of Gary Gilmore, the murderer executed in 1977 in Utah. The deeply affecting story was an astonishing display of stylistic versatility.

Even the year's disappointments – John Barth's monumental, almost unreadable *Letters,* Jerzy Kosinski's perverse *Passion Play,* Irwin Shaw's stilted *The Top of the Hill,* and James Baldwin's cranky *Just Above My Head* – suffered mostly in comparison with the authors' own best work.

First-rate short-story collections added to the considerable reputations of Donald Barthelme (*Great Days*), Isaac Bashevis Singer (*Old Love*), and John Updike (*Problems and Other Stories*).

Younger Writers held their own with short-fiction collections of exceptional merit. Ward Just's *Honor, Power, Riches, and the Love of Women,* Jim Harrison's *Legends of the Fall,* and John Casey's *Testimony and Demeanor* were examples.

Vigorous new novels also came from Alice Hoffman, Doris Grumbach, John Sayles, Phillip F. O'Connor, Elizabeth Hardwick, Alison Lurie, Scott Spencer, and Gilbert Sorrentino. One of the year's best first novels was Ron Hansen's *Desperadoes,* a juicy retelling of the legend of the Dalton Gang.

Two important posthumous collections were published – *The Uncollected Stories of William Faulkner,* edited by Joseph Blotner; and *The Price Was High,* the uncollected stories of F. Scott Fitzgerald, edited by Matthew J. Bruccoli. These collections

showed mostly the "commercial" side of both writers, but nevertheless were treasures for scholars.

It was also a good year for contributions from English-speaking writers in other countries. Nadine Gordimer's novel *Burger's Daughter* was a powerful plea for justice in South Africa. The Anglo-Indian novelist V. S. Naipaul strengthened his reputation as a fine stylist in the English language with *A Bend in the River,* a novel of trampled dreams in Africa.

Other important novels in English came from Len Deighton, John Wain, Kingsley Amis, William Golding, Muriel Spark, and Doris Lessing. V.S. Pritchett added to his laurels as Britain's best short-story writer with *On the Edge of the Cliff.*

From Poland came Stanislaw Lem's *A Perfect Vacuum,* 16 acidly comic reviews of nonexistent books. Russia contributed Vladimir Voinovich's hilarious collection of satires, *In Plain Russian.* Alexander Zinoviev's *The Yawning Heights,* smuggled out of Russia, was a scorching satire of Soviet society.

History, Politics, Public Affairs. The year's most interesting brouhaha revolved around Henry A. Kissinger's memoir, *White House Years.* Although his book was received favorably for the most part, Kissinger's version of events in Indochina was hotly disputed by journalist William Shawcross' *Kissinger, Nixon and the Destruction of Cambodia.* Almost as controversial was *The Brethren,* a revealing portrait of the Supreme Court by *Washington Post* reporters Bob Woodward and Scott Armstrong.

Journalists offered several other interesting histories. David Halberstam's *The Powers that Be* was a mildly exaggerated but immensely readable chronicle of the rise of *Time* magazine, the Columbia Broadcasting System, *The Washington Post,* and the Los Angeles *Times* to pre-eminence in journalism. Tom Wolfe's *The Right Stuff* celebrated the humanity of test pilots and astronauts.

Thomas Powers' *The Man Who Kept the Secrets,* ostensibly a biography of former Central Intelligence Agency chief Richard Helms, explored the disturbing relationship between the White House and America's intelligence services. The dubious links between several Presidents and a charismatic evangelist was sternly but sympathetically explored in Marshall Frady's *Billy Graham: A Parable of American Righteousness.*

Two important books on German history were published during the year. Gordon A. Craig offered the scrupulous *Germany 1866-1945;* and Telford Taylor, the massive and impartial *Munich: The Price of Peace.*

Ronald Fraser contributed *Blood of Spain,* a powerful oral history of the Spanish Civil War, written from interviews with its survivors. One of the most discussed books of the year was Elaine Pagels' stunning *Gnostic Gospels,* which re-evaluated the origins of Christianity as revealed in the Nag Hammadi scrolls found in Egypt in 1945 and dating from the A.D. 300s and 400s.

Several important books dealing with totalitarian repression came from abroad. Bernard-Henri Levy's *Barbarism with a Human Face* told how French political thinkers were rejecting Marxism. *Testimony: The Memoirs of Dmitri Shostakovich* purported to be the appalling story of the Russian musician's self-repression under Joseph Stalin. Russian officials denounced it as a fraud, though most Western experts accepted its authenticity.

Two other important oral histories came from abroad. Daniel Lang's *A Backward Look: Germans Remember* told how the German people deal with the memories of Nazism. Ronald Blythe's *The View in Winter*, a series of interviews with aged Britons, was a moving contribution to the literature on old age.

Biography and Autobiography. It was an undistinguished year for the genre. Few significant books were published, especially among literary biographies. Frederick R. Karl's *Joseph Conrad: The Three Lives* offered a new view of the novelist, and Leonard Schapiro's *Turgenev: His Life and Times* reassessed the first great Russian novelist to become known in the West. Herbert R. Lottman's *Albert Camus,* Stanley Olson's *Elinor Wylie: A Life Apart,* and Norman and Jeanne MacKenzie's *Dickens* were other important literary lives. Emir Rodriguez

Journalist Tom Wolfe's perceptive look at the U.S. astronauts, *The Right Stuff,* conveyed the excitement of the early years of the space age.

Monegal wrote *Jorge Luis Borges,* the first major biography of the Argentine author.

Among political biographies, lives of two U.S. Presidents won attention. David Burner's *Herbert Hoover: A Public Life* took a rigorous but sympathetic view. Edmund Morris' *The Rise of Theodore Roosevelt* ably explored its subject's early years.

Another interesting political biography was Peter Stansky's *Gladstone,* a life of the colossus of 19th-century British politics. Jean Monnet's *Memoirs* related the French statesman's contribution to the European Community (Common Market).

In the arts, Hans Moldenhauer and Rosaleen Moldenhauer turned out *Anton Von Webern,* a massive biography of the Austrian composer. Ernest Samuels' *Bernard Berenson* was the first major biography of the art historian, based on his papers.

The incredibly prolific Isaac Asimov's autobiography, *In Memory Yet Green,* was his 200th book. Editor-critic Geoffrey Wolff told the engaging story of his con-man father in *The Duke of Deception.* Lewis Mumford's *My Works and Days* was another volume of autobiographical fragments.

Three popular biographies won wide notice: Robert Conot's *A Streak of Luck,* a life of Thomas Alva Edison; Donald L. Barlett and James B. Steele's *Empire: The Life, Legend, and Madness of Howard Hughes;* and Shana Alexander's *Anyone's Daughter,* the story of the Patricia Hearst kidnapping.

For the centenary of Albert Einstein's birth, three important volumes were prepared: Helen Dukas and Banesh Hoffman's *Albert Einstein: The Human Side,* Nigel Calder's *Einstein's Universe,* and A.P. French's *Einstein: A Centenary Volume.*

Letters, Criticism and Essays. If significant biographies were few, the dearth was made up for by allied genres.

Several important volumes of literary letters were published. *The Habit of Being,* the witty and sophisticated letters of Flannery O'Connor, edited by Sally Fitzgerald, belied the common image of O'Connor as a Southern Gothic primitive. *The Nabokov-Wilson Letters,* edited by Simon Karlinsky, revealed much about the friendship and feuds of Vladimir Nabokov and Edmund Wilson — titans of literature.

From England came three significant volumes of correspondence. Morton N. Cohen selected *The Letters of Lewis Carroll.* The ongoing publication of *The Letters of Virginia Woolf* reached *Vol. IV (1929-1931).* And the first volume of the comprehensive *Letters of D. H. Lawrence (September, 1901-May, 1903)* were edited by James T. Boulton.

A highly important critical work was psychiatrist Robert Coles's generous and penetrating *Walker Percy: An American Search.* Richard Gilman's *Decadence: The Strange Life of an Epithet* argued brilliantly that there is no such thing as decadence. Leon Edel's *Bloomsbury: A House of Lions* explored that British group's contribution to literature.

Herbert Aptheker edited *The Correspondence of W. E. B. Du Bois, Vol. III (1944-1963),* which completed the first collection of any black American's letters.

Three collections of essays were published by important American thinkers: Bruno Bettelheim's *Surviving,* Adrienne Rich's feminist-oriented *On Lies, Secrets and Silence,* and Irving Howe's *Celebrations and Attacks: 30 Years of Literary and Cultural Community.*

Joan Didion, a master of the popular essay, offered a new collection, *The White Album.* Her husband, John Gregory Dunne, published his own, *Quintana and Friends.* Both took strongly individualistic and iconoclastic views of American life.

Paperbacks Gain. As inflation drove up costs of hard-cover books, paperbacks became more and more important to the American reader. Many readers chose to wait until hard-cover best sellers appeared in paperback before purchasing them.

Paperback publishers therefore paid everincreasing premiums for the rights to reprint hardcover books, and some even began to contract for books from authors, then sell them to hard-cover publishers for initial publication. All this gave paperback houses increasing power in the publishing world, and in 1980 they will be represented in the American Book Awards, which supplanted the National Book Awards in 1979.

Commercial fiction was the most sought-after genre in paperback rights auctions, which brought often-astronomical prices for books not yet published. Bantam Books paid $3.2 million for Judith Krantz's second novel, *Princess Daisy,* before its 1980 hard-cover publication.

Best Sellers. As 1979 began, the hard-cover best sellers were James Michener's *Chesapeake* and *Gnomes* by Wil Huygen and Rien Poortvliet. Bestselling paperbacks were *My Mother/Myself* by Nancy Friday and *The People's Almanac 2* by David Wallechinsky and Irving Wallace. At midyear, the hard-cover selections were Robert Ludlum's *The Matarese Circle* and *The Complete Scarsdale Medical Diet* by Herman Tarnower, M.D., and Samm Sinclair Baker. Paperbacks were led by Judith Krantz's novel *Scruples* and an exercise primer, *How to Flatten Your Stomach* by Jim Everroad.

As the year and the decade drew to a close, the hard-cover lists were led by Howard Fast's novel *The Establishment* and *Aunt Erma's Cope Book* by Erma Bombeck. Paperback sales were dominated by two novels, Mario Puzo's *Fools Die* and Kathleen E. Woodiwiss' *Ashes in the Wind.*   Henry Kisor

See also AWARDS AND PRIZES (Literature Awards); CANADIAN LITERATURE; LITERATURE FOR CHILDREN; POETRY. In WORLD BOOK, see LITERATURE.

LITERATURE, CANADIAN. See CANADIAN LIBRARY ASSOCIATION; CANADIAN LITERATURE.

LITERATURE FOR CHILDREN. Perhaps it was because it was the end of the decade, a natural time for looking back, but whatever the reason, 1979 was the year for reminiscence. Several works of fiction appeared that were based upon the author's childhood in the 1940s, and they evoked strongly the sense of what it was like to be a child in that particular time and in a particular place.

A concern for the welfare of animals also seemed to be a common thread in many books published in 1979. This theme appeared not only in a large number of informational books about animals, but also in several works of fiction. Fantasy and science fiction continued to be popular, and the number of these books appearing indicated the publishing response to that demand. Some outstanding books of 1979 were:

Picture Books

The Church Mice at Bay, by Graham Oakley (Atheneum). When the vicar goes away on a vacation, his position is filled by a young curate with ideas very different from those Sampson and the other mice are used to. The resultant excitement is conveyed with the verve and humor characteristic of this authorillustrator. Ages 5 and up.

A Sweetheart for Valentine, by Lorna Balian (Abingdon). Very original and delightful full-color illustrations show what happens when the village of St. Valentine adopts the young, but definitely not little, baby left on the steps of the village hall. Ages 4 to 8.

The Pigs' Wedding, by Helme Heine (Atheneum/McElderry). Delightful pictures filled with fat pigs show the unusual results when Porker decides to use his painting talent to help get everything ready for his wedding to Curlytail. Ages 4 to 8.

Chameleon was a Spy, story and pictures by Diane Redfield Massie (Crowell). Chameleon, because of his wonderful talent for blending in with his surroundings, becomes a spy for the Pleasant Pickle Company after a scientist steals its secret formula. Delightful illustrations add to the interest and excitement of his adventures. Ages 4 to 8.

Gator Pie, by Louise Mathews, illustrated by Jeni Bassett (Dodd). Charming little pictures of alligators with ribbons, derbies, or baseball caps add much to a short story of problems encountered in dividing a pie with a slight mathematical touch added. Ages 4 to 8.

The Garden of Abdul Gasazi, written and illustrated by Chris Van Allsburg (Houghton). A teacher of illustration at the Rhode Island School of Design, Van Allsburg has created a unique and beautiful picture book with powerful illustrations that convey a strong sense of place and atmosphere. Ages 5 to 8.

Mr. Jameson and Mr. Phillips, by Marjorie Weinman Sharmat, pictures by Bruce Degen (Harper). The title characters are two endearing animals who move from the city and its crowds to a deserted

Suddenly there was a flash of lightning, a crash and rumbling which shook the earth. The girl leapt to her feet in fright. Everything was awake. Horses were rearing up on their hind legs and snorting in terror. She grabbed a horse's mane and jumped on his back.

Paul Goble's *The Girl Who Loved Wild Horses* took the American Library Association's Caldecott Medal as the best illustrated children's book.

island, only to have the crowds follow. Their final solution to the problem seems perfect. Ages 4 to 8.

Everything About Easter Rabbits, by Wiltrud Roser, translated by Eva L. Mayer (Crowell). Written in a pseudo-serious style, this book tells about all the varieties of Easter rabbits and shows them at work. The full-color illustrations have originality and a nice touch of humor. Ages 4 to 8.

Martin by Himself, by Gloria Skurzynski, illustrated by Lynn Munsinger (Houghton). When Martin gets home from school, he remembers it is his mother's first day at work. But neither he nor his mother have anticipated the catastrophes that take place in this humorous account of his few hours alone. Ages 4 to 8.

Scarlet Monster Lives Here, an I Can Read Book by Marjorie Weinman Sharmat, illustrated by Dennis Kendrick (Harper). When Scarlet Monster moves into a new neighborhood, she prepares to welcome all her new neighbors and is very disappointed when no one comes. But it eventually turns out that she moved into just the right neighborhood after all. For beginning readers.

The Hungry Fox and the Foxy Duck, by Kathleen Leverich, illustrated by Paul Galdone (Parents'). A pleasant little story with a switch on the clever fox theme – here the duck outwits the fox and the early reader enjoys the action in the brightly colored pictures accompanying the easy text. Ages 4 to 8.

Argentaybee and the Boonie, by Catherine Hiller, illustrated by Cyndy Szekeres (Coward). Emily is very well-behaved – practically perfect – but her imaginary friends Argentaybee and the Boonie do all sorts of bad things. Delightful illustrations show an appealing little girl kitten and her friends engaged in a variety of activities. Ages 5 to 7.

The Story of an English Village, by John S. Goodall (Atheneum/McElderry). This book without words follows the changes in an English village from its beginnings to the present time, unfolding changing views inside and out as the beautiful water colors depict changes in fashions, customs, and transportation. All ages.

Animals

The Amazing Earthworm, by Lilo Hess (Scribner's). Excellent photographs and interesting, informative text tell about the life, structure, habits, and usefulness of this important creature. There is even information about how to raise worms as a hobby or business. Ages 8 to 12.

Spring Peepers are Calling, by Charlene W. Billings, illustrated by Susan Bonners (Dodd). This short but informative discussion of the peeper frog's appearance, development, habits, and habitat also has a section on keeping these tiny creatures as pets. Ages 7 to 10.

Possum Baby, by Berniece Freschet, illustrated by Jim Arnosky (Putnam). In attractive pictures and simple storylike text, this book gives an accurate account of the life of an opossum from birth until it is ready to be on its own. Ages 7 to 10.

Wild Babies, A Canyon Sketchbook, by Irene Brady (Houghton). Exquisite, accurate drawings make this book not only very interesting, but also beautiful. There are chapters on the bobcat, squirrel, bat, deer, hawk, and bear. Ages 10 and up.

Elephants on the Beach, by Irene Brady (Scribner's). The account, in sketches and notes, of the author's chance encounter with some elephant seals is interesting and gently informative. Ages 7 to 10.

People, Places, and Things

The Boy Who Dreamed of Rockets: How Robert H. Goddard Became the Father of the Space Age, by Robert Quackenbush (Parents'). A biography tells about the life of the inventor, who devoted himself to making his boyhood dream of sending a rocket into space come true. Large, full-color drawings add liveliness and interest. Ages 5 to 9.

The Armor Book, by Michael Berenstain (McKay). This short, interesting account of the history of armor has detailed illustrations that show the reader how armor evolved, how it was used, and how it was made, including pictures that show how a helmet was shaped and what tools an armorer used. Ages 7 to 10.

Glamorous Movie Stars of the Thirties Paper Dolls; Marilyn Monroe Paper Dolls; Rudolph Valentino Paper Dolls; all by Tom Tierney (Dover). These three collections would be of interest to two groups – children who wish to play with paper dolls and are fascinated by the lavish costumes of these well-known stars of the past; and people interested in costume design, because the clothes represented are authentic, and the name of the designer and the movie in which the garment was worn are given with each outfit. Ages 6 and up.

Model Buildings and How to Make Them, by Harvey Weiss (Crowell). The author goes from a simple cardboard construction to structures in wood, and ends with suggestions for building some quite elaborate model buildings and dollhouses. Black-and-white photographs and drawings add additional helpful information. Ages 10 and up.

Quick Wits and Nimble Fingers, by Bernice Wells Carlson, illustrated by Dolores Marie Rowland (Abingdon). This book includes 10 tales of tricksters from as many different countries and follows each with an introduction to one or two crafts typical of the land of origin or bearing some relation to the story. Ages 8 to 12.

Mr. Lincoln's Whiskers, by Burke Davis, illustrated by Douglas Gorsline (Coward). This accurate though fictionalized account of the correspondence with 11-year-old Grace Bedell that made Lincoln decide to grow a beard covers several incidents from his election to the presidency until his arrival in Washington, D.C. Ages 8 to 12.

A. J. Foyt, Racing Champion, by Bill Libby (Putnam). This biography of the "Babe Ruth of American car racing," while a little shaky on grammar at times, presents a lively picture of a tough, fiery competitor and gives detailed accounts of some of his big races. Ages 10 and up.

Baseball's Greatest All-Star Games, by Howard Liss (McKay). Rather than offering accounts of all the all-star games, the author has chosen 12 that were outstanding and presented them – with statistics and photographs – in a lively you-were-there style. Ages 10 and up.

Here Is Your Career: Airline Pilot, by Frank Stilley (Putnam). This excellent book for anyone thinking of flying as a profession has all the information needed – requirements, what a pilot does, and interviews with both men and women airline pilots. Ages 10 and up.

Fun With Monsters; Create Your Own Make-Up, Masks, and Props, by Richard Cummings (McKay). The book includes directions for making everything listed in the title, helpful informative drawings, sources of supply, and even "Sounds for Your Hair to Stand on End By." Ages 10 and up.

The Arabs, Their Heritage and Their Way of Life, by Rhoda Hoff (McKay). A fascinating collection of first-person accounts from the time of Muhammad to the present. Short selections give the reader a privileged glimpse of Arabian hospitality, of the finest Arabian horses, and of life in the women's quarters. Ages 12 and up.

Fiction

Dumb Old Casey Is a Fat Tree, by Barbara Bottner (Harper). Casey wanted to be a dancer in kindergarten, first grade, and second grade, but when she started taking ballet lessons she felt fat and awkward. The story of how she turns out to be the best tree in the recital is funny and realistic. Ages 6 to 9.

Help! I'm a Prisoner in the Library, by Eth Clifford, illustrated by George Hughes (Houghton). In this exciting and realistic adventure, two sisters find themselves locked in the library during a blizzard. When the power goes off and they hear a bump and a moan upstairs, it takes all their courage to investigate. Ages 7 to 10.

I Should Worry, I Should Care, by Miriam Chaikin, drawings by Richard Egielski (Harper). Molly and her family move to a new neighborhood and she is not sure she will ever be happy again. However, she soon finds friends and begins to enjoy life in this realistic picture of a Jewish family in Brooklyn about 1940. Ages 8 to 11.

Kitty in the Middle, by Judy Delton, illustrated by Charles Robinson (Houghton). Kitty, Margaret Mary who always does everything right, and Eileen who does everything in her own predictable way, enjoy one another in this often humorous semiautobiographical account of fourth-graders attending a Roman Catholic school in 1942. Ages 8 to 12.

The Newbery Medal, for "the most distinguished
contribution to American literature for children,"
went to a novel by Ellen Raskin, *The Westing Game.*

The Barkley Street Six-Pack, by Mary Francis
Shura, illustrated by Gene Sparkman (Dodd).
When Jane's best friend moves away, Jane has an
awful premonition that something terrible will happen, but she has no idea that the solution to a mystery
will change both her and her neighborhood. This
realistic story of a girl dominated by her best friend
presents a situation that many girls this age can
identify with. Ages 9 and up.

Good-bye, Chicken Little, by Betsy Byars (Harper).
When Jimmie's eccentric Uncle Pete announces that
he is going to walk across the ice-covered river,
Jimmie tries unsuccessfully to stop him. In the days
that follow the ensuing tragedy, Jimmie learns to
appreciate his unique family and comes to grips with
fears that have sometimes haunted him in the past.
Ages 10 and up.

Ghost Lane, by Jane Louise Curry (Atheneum/
McElderry). When his neighbor is robbed, 11-
year-old Richard decides to do some detective work
in the little English village where he is spending the
summer. The mystery deepens as boats stop at the
pier at night, shadowy figures walk down Ghost
Lane, and 6-year-old Noel disappears. Including a
visit to the opera, at Glyndebourne, the story takes
place in an interesting and realistically presented
setting. Ages 10 to 14.

The Famous Stanley Kidnapping Case, by Zilpha
Keatley Snyder (Atheneum). When the entire Stan-

ley family goes to Italy for a year, troublemaker Jane
suggests they might get kidnapped. A very real and
interesting family gives us a glimpse of some of the
usual, and unusual, things an American family
might encounter in Italy. Ages 10 to 14.

Thunder and Lightenings, by Jan Mark, illustrations by Jim Russell (Crowell). Winner of the Carnegie Medal in Great Britain, this story of a growing
friendship between two boys portrays characters one
feels are real people, interesting individuals that the
reader identifies with and cares about, as well as a
delightful quiet sense of humor. Ages 10 to 14.

Does Anybody Care About Lou Emma Miller? by
Alberta Wilson Constant (Crowell). Recreating life
in Gloriosa, Kans., in the early 1900s, this book
follows Lou Emma and her sister Maddy in their
involvement in the campaign of a woman mayor,
troubles with "the new girl in school," and some of
the eternal difficulties of growing up. A warm but
realistic family relationship adds depth and interest
to a satisfying book. Ages 10 to 14.

Presto, or The Adventures of a Turnspit Dog,
written and illustrated by Marilynne K. Roach
(Houghton). Presto, freed from his cruel turnspit
prison in which he works turning meat on a spit,
encounters many adventures in the London streets
before finding friends and a human of his own. This
lively and accurate picture of 18th-century London
shows many sides of the life of the times through the
eyes of its appealing canine hero. Ages 10 and up.

An Orphan for Nebraska, by Charlene Joy Talbot
(Atheneum). An immigrant whose mother dies on
the trip to America, Kevin finds himself alone in
New York City, sleeping in the streets and trying to
support himself as a newsboy. When winter comes,
he joins a group of orphans being resettled in the
West and begins a new and interesting life with a
small-town printer. The book gives a realistic picture of life in the late 1870s. Ages 10 to 14.

Go and Catch a Flying Fish, by Mary Stolz
(Harper). This book draws one into the breakup of a
marriage, seen through the eyes of the two older
children as their beautiful, often delightful, but
"free spirit" mother walks out on them, their 4-
year-old brother, and their father. The book evokes
the surroundings of southern Florida, and shows the
devastating effect their parents' actions have on the
three children. Ages 11 and up.

Fly Free, by Joan Phipson (Atheneum/
McElderry). Through an unusual event, quiet studi-
ous Wilfred and happy uncomplicated Johnny become friends and join forces to earn money for a
special trip by trapping animals. The money-
making project takes an ominous turn when Johnny
is caught in his own trap for a day and a night – an
experience that changes his whole attitude toward
catching animals. Ages 12 and up.

The Spellcoats, by Dianna Wynne Jones (Argo/
Atheneum). A mystical tale of the quest by Tanaqui,

the younger sister, and her brothers and sister, to find the spell that will loosen the Undying from their bonds before the Stealer of Souls can take over the land. The storyteller is the weaver of the Spellcoats, whose magic is necessary to destroy the evil power that is trying to gain control of the river around which their lives and their adventures revolve. Ages 12 and up.

Awards in 1979 included:

American Library Association Children's Service Division Awards: *The Newbery Medal* for "the most distinguished contribution to American literature for children" was awarded to Ellen Raskin for *The Westing Game;* the *Caldecott Medal* for "the most distinguished American picture book for children" went to Paul Goble for *The Girl Who Loved Wild Horses.* The *Mildred L. Batchelder Award* announced in 1979 cited Harcourt Brace Jovanovich for the 1978 publication *Rabbit Island,* written by Jörg Steiner, illustrated by Jörg Müller, and translated from the German by Ann Conrad Lammers. The winner of the National Book Award for Children's Literature was Katherine Paterson for *The Great Gilly Hopkins.*   Lynn de Grummond Delaune

See also CANADIAN LITERATURE; LITERATURE; POETRY. In WORLD BOOK, see LITERATURE FOR CHILDREN.

LIVESTOCK. See FARM AND FARMING.

LOS ANGELES-LONG BEACH. Transportation problems, triggered by the gas shortage and aggravated by a bus strike, plagued residents of the Los Angeles-Long Beach area during 1979. In response to requests from Los Angeles officials, California Governor Edmund G. Brown, Jr., signed emergency orders on May 8 establishing an odd-even gasoline rationing system.

As the gasoline crunch triggered a major energy-conservation effort, mass-transit ridership hit record levels, car pooling increased 15 per cent, and highway traffic declined. Amtrak broke all passenger records on its Los Angeles to San Diego trains in May, recording a 67 per cent increase in riders.

A strike by three transit unions shut down the Southern California Rapid Transit District on August 26. The walkout, which lasted until September 12, idled 2,600 buses and left 600,000 commuters without public transportation. The transit strike forced motorists back onto freeways and helped produce the worst smog in 24 years. In an unprecedented move, the Air Quality Management District in September issued "hazardous" air warnings.

Race Relations. The Los Angeles Board of Education voted on August 27 to seek court approval for its request to abandon its mandatory busing program, which involved 38,000 of the school district's 570,000 pupils. The California courts began hearing

A thick layer of smog, the worst in years, blankets the Los Angeles area in September, prompting officials to issue "hazardous air" warnings.

arguments on October 22 on a proposal for an all-voluntary desegregation plan.

United States immigration agents in October resumed a policy of raiding residential neighborhoods and local business districts in Los Angeles and southern California. Mayor Thomas Bradley wired the White House on November 4, seeking an end to the raids. They were discontinued in 1977 after complaints from the Latin American community.

Law Enforcement. The Los Angeles Police Commission, composed of five civilians, ruled in October that it must review all cases involving questionable shootings by police officers. The decision came in response to complaints over cases in which officers were accused of using unnecessary gunfire but were cleared by a departmental review board.

Chief of Police Daryl Gates reported on October 21 that, with the arraignment of Angelo Buono, Jr., the "Hillside Strangler" case was considered closed. Buono was charged with the murders of 10 women whose bodies were found on hillsides in the Los Angeles area between September 1977 and February 1978. Buono's cousin Kenneth Bianchi had admitted taking part in five of the slayings and implicated Buono. James M. Banovetz

See also CITY. In WORLD BOOK, see LONG BEACH; LOS ANGELES.

LOUISIANA. See STATE GOVERNMENT.

LUMBER. See FOREST AND FOREST PRODUCTS.

LUXEMBOURG. Pierre Werner, a Social Christian, became prime minister on June 19, 1979, leading a center-right coalition with the Liberals. Liberal Gaston Thorn had resigned the post on June 11, the day after his coalition with the Socialists lost its majority in parliamentary elections.

Thorn said during the campaign that his administration had avoided a recession, kept inflation down to 3.7 per cent, and held unemployment at 1 per cent. His Cabinet ministers said that the main issue was whether Luxembourg should be ruled by the Social Christians, a party with a large budget and control of the country's biggest newspaper.

On June 27, the government dropped plans to build a nuclear power plant at Remerschen. The plant was to be similar to the U.S. plant at Three Mile Island near Harrisburg, Pa., where an accident occurred on March 28. Instead, Luxembourg signed a deal on June 6 with Arbed SA, its biggest coal and steel corporation, for studies on a coal-fired power station. Arbed, Europe's fourth largest steel producer, began a five-year program to modernize its Luxembourg plants. The program would cut its work force from 20,800 to 16,500 and would cost $786.2 million. About $108.4 million of that would come from the government. Kenneth Brown

See also EUROPE (Facts in Brief Table). In WORLD BOOK, see LUXEMBOURG.

MADAGASCAR. See AFRICA.

MAGAZINE advertising revenues in the United States continued their upward trend in 1979, exceeding $2 billion for the second consecutive year, according to the Publishers' Information Bureau. The number of ad pages increased 5 per cent.

The Audit Bureau of Circulations in Chicago reported that the combined circulation of the leading 100 consumer and trade magazines totaled approximately 214 million for the first six months of 1979, down slightly from the same period in 1978.

Postal Rates for sending magazines by second-class mail increased about 22 per cent on July 6. Some publishers turned to private carriers, who were delivering approximately 1.3 million magazines each month by year-end.

Paper costs soared as publishers, faced with shortages of publication-grade paper, turned to more costly paper from foreign markets. In some cases, heavier paper added to delivery costs. As increases in publishing costs rose faster than the national inflation rate, many publishers tried to cut production costs by changing magazine size and paper stock and tried to minimize advertising rate increases by raising newsstand and subscription prices.

New Magazines. Among the estimated 275 to 300 new magazines launched in 1979, the most heavily advertised and expensively produced was *Geo*, a geography monthly. Published by Gruner & Jahr USA, Incorporated, with a $36 annual subscription price, *Geo* was expected to reach 75,000 subscribers. The American Association for the Advancement of Science introduced *Science 80*, a bimonthly.

Among the many new women's publications in 1979 were *Self*, a monthly dealing with emotional and physical fitness published by Condé Nast Publications, Incorporated, and *Enterprising Women*, published by Artemis Enterprises and directed at women who are self-employed or high-level corporate executives. *Holly Hobbie's Home Times*, a Charter Concepts, Incorporated, quarterly publication, was designed for women returning to "traditional female interests."

The first copies of the 134-page premier issue of *Inside Sports*, Newsweek, Incorporated's new monthly magazine, hit the newsstands on September 10. Publisher E. Daniel Capell said the magazine will concentrate on the big four spectator sports—baseball, football, hockey, and basketball.

Venture, "The Magazine for Entrepreneurs," a general business monthly publication that analyzes new enterprises and examines business opportunities, premièred in May. United Marine Publishing, Incorporated, introduced a monthly, *Inc.*, in April, directed at about 100,000 companies with sales volumes of between $1 million and $25 million.

Travel Illustrated, a monthly magazine with an anticipated circulation of 1.5 million, published its first issue in October. It was to be inserted into 11 major metropolitan Sunday newspapers and tar-

Readers survey the reborn *Look* magazine, which returned to the newsstands with great fanfare in February and died again quietly in August.

geted at suburban households with incomes above $25,000. *Rocky Mountain Magazine,* a 10-issues-a-year publication, premièred in April.

Major Business Ventures. *Esquire* magazine was purchased from the Associated Newspapers Group Limited of London by the 13-30 Corporation, a Knoxville, Tenn., publishing house, on April 29 after five months of negotiations. *Gentlemen's Quarterly* also changed hands in April when Condé Nast Publications, Incorporated, bought it from Esquire, Incorporated, for $9.2 million.

Look, a photo-essay magazine that ceased publication in 1971 after 34 years, returned to the newsstands in February. It underwent a series of editorial changes before dying again in August. Also discontinuing publication in 1979 were *American Girl, Viva,* and *New Times.*

The Progressive, a magazine of political commentary, was involved in one of the year's major controversies after a federal court ruling prohibited it from publishing an article in March that in part told how a hydrogen bomb works. After a newspaper published a similar article in September, the case against *The Progressive* was dismissed, and the article was published in October. See CIVIL RIGHTS; SCIENCE and RESEARCH.   Gloria Ricks Dixon

In WORLD BOOK, see MAGAZINE.
MAINE. See STATE GOVERNMENT.
MALAWI. See AFRICA.

MALAYSIA continued to be troubled in 1979 by racial tensions between the ruling Malays and the economically strong Chinese minority. The Chinese were perhaps most angered by the decision of Prime Minister Datuk Hussein Onn's government to block the creation of a new university for the Chinese. Discrimination also dominated the 20-year "new economic policy," at its midpoint in 1979, which was intended to benefit native Malays.

Amnesty International issued a report in August condemning Malaysia's violations of human rights. The report said that more than 1,000 persons were being held without trial.

Malaysia's human rights record was already blackened by its cold-blooded rejection of the "boat people." Thousands of refugees were towed back to sea in their flimsy crafts, and 104 drowned in one such incident in March. Others were beaten, robbed, and raped. Supposedly fortunate were those shipped to tragically overcrowded island "havens." Since most of the refugees were ethnic Chinese, some observers believed the refugee policy was part of the government's general anti-Chinese policy. See ASIA (Close-Up).   Mark Gayn

See also ASIA (Facts in Brief Table). In WORLD BOOK, see MALAYSIA.
MALDIVES. See ASIA.
MALI. See AFRICA.
MALTA. See EUROPE.

MANITOBA. Premier Sterling R. Lyon's Progressive Conservative administration, in office since October 1977, survived a stiff test in three by-elections on Oct. 16, 1979. The government faced criticism over positions taken during the year. Its determination to return publicly owned enterprises to the private sector proved controversial. At stake was the future of the government automobile-insurance monopoly, a seed company, and a bus manufacturer.

Two seats in the legislature were opened when their incumbents resigned to run in the May 22 federal election, and a third was vacated with the appointment of Manitoba's New Democratic Party leader, Edward R. Schreyer, as governor general. The results left the 57-seat assembly unchanged: Progressive Conservatives, 33; New Democratic Party, 23; Liberals, 1.

The legislature passed 58 bills during its session from February 15 to June 16. The most heated debate occurred over a proposal to eliminate an escalating mining royalty and a plan to put a five-year freeze on hydroelectric rates for individuals and most industries. The freeze would cost $31.3-million in the first year but would benefit the province. The budget, presented on May 15, estimated a deficit of $122.6 million.   David M. L. Farr

See also CANADA. In WORLD BOOK, see MANITOBA; PRAIRIE PROVINCES.

MANUFACTURING

MANUFACTURING. Double-digit inflation and the threat of a recession shadowed United States manufacturers throughout 1979. A surging first quarter followed by a sluggish second quarter brought cries of recession in the middle of the year. However, the third quarter rebounded vigorously and left economists, manufacturers, and consumers wondering where the recession went. But as the fourth quarter got underway, there were definite signs that all was not well with the economy.

Steadily increasing prices for gasoline and oil, caused by price increases from the Organization of Petroleum Exporting Countries (OPEC), and a scarcity of those same commodities caused American automobile manufacturers to cut production as cars piled up in dealer showrooms. With oil-base products reaching one new price high after another, inflation grew at an annual rate of about 13 per cent by October. Manufacturers cut back on production as consumers turned wary at the market place. Higher interest rates began to cut into capital expenditures and home building. By November, it seemed that a recession was imminent – or had already begun.

To buttress this view, the monthly survey by the National Association of Purchasing Management concluded that September's strong showing was achieved at the expense of October. The purchasing agents reported a "noticeable drop in new orders" and a decrease in production. This was confirmed by a drop of 4.2 per cent in new factory orders for durable goods in October after a solid rise of 5.4 per cent in September. The U.S. Department of Commerce said that the drop was due to a decline in the aerospace industry, which had an increase of 31 per cent in September.

Overall, October factory orders for durable goods fell by $3.2 billion to $74.8 billion. Durable-goods orders had begun to fall early in 1979, from $80-billion in February. In October, shipments at the rate of $75.6 billion outpaced new orders. Another unwelcome statistic was the 0.3 per cent decline in the backlog of unfilled orders, down $800 million to $260.1 billion. The decline was attributable completely to the hard-pressed transportation industry.

Industrial Production for October was held to a slim 0.1 per cent gain, following a rise of only 0.5 per cent in September, due to the auto-industry slump and strikes at heavy-equipment manufacturing plants. This meager two-month gain followed a drop of 0.8 per cent in August, when auto output was cut sharply because of falling sales. The industrial production index stood at 152.5 in October, or 52.5 per cent higher than the 1967 base-year figure of 100. It was up 1.9 per cent from October 1978.

The slump in new orders and the minute gains in industrial production were reflected in a drop in factory operations, which slipped to 85 per cent of capacity in October, down from 85.2 per cent in September, but slightly higher than August's 84.9 per cent level. The October rate was 2.1 percentage points lower than the March level, which was the highest since the 87.3 per cent rate of December 1973. For primary-processing industries, the rate was 87.4 per cent, compared with 87.7 per cent of capacity in October 1978.

Manufacturers were plagued by rising prices for materials and shortages of some basic materials and assemblies. Aluminum, copper, lead, steel (especially steel plates), silver, gold, gasoline and oil, paper and paper products, rubber, chemicals (especially solvents), and plastics cost more in October than they did in September. Products in short supply included castings, cobalt, molybdenum, integrated circuits, publication-grade paper, and heat-treated bars and tubing.

Capital Spending, which helped keep business stronger than most experts had expected, began to turn soft as the year ended. Total estimated expenditures for plant and equipment were put at $179-billion by the McGraw-Hill Publication Company's economics department, a 7 per cent rise in real investment. However, expenditures for 1980 were not expected to be as healthy. An expected rise to $196 billion would be offset by price increases for new plant and equipment, and the result would be little or no gain.

Chinese Deputy Premier Teng Hsiao-p'ing and his wife, guided by Henry Ford II, watch a Ford motor roll down the assembly line at the Hapeville, Ga., plant.

Worker Productivity in the United States rose at an annual rate of 1 per cent in the third quarter, after two consecutive quarters of sharp declines, the Department of Labor reported. Productivity declined at an annual rate of 2.2 and 3 per cent in the second and first quarters, respectively. Productivity measures the efficiency of both workers and labor-saving machinery, and a decline contributes to inflation by pushing up production costs and, ultimately, consumer prices. Between 1947 and 1967, United States productivity grew at an annual rate of 3.1 per cent, but the rate has been declining since then. Growth has slowed to an average 1.6 per cent a year, and in 1978 it grew at a rate of only 1.1 per cent. Many economists attribute the lagging growth rate to a sharp drop in investments by manufacturers for new labor-saving machinery.

Unemployment stood at 6 per cent in the United States in October, an increase from 5.8 per cent in September. The jobless rate was between 5.6 per cent and 6 per cent for a 14-month period. The number of workers employed in manufacturing was essentially unchanged from March, standing at a seasonally adjusted 21 million. During the 12 months ending in October 1979, manufacturing added only 325,000 workers, while service-producing industries grew by more than 2 million persons.

Gains won by labor in new contracts were a blow to President Jimmy Carter's fight against inflation. In 42 per cent of the settlements that did not contain cost-of-living adjustments (COLA), the first-year increase was 9.1 per cent, well above the Council on Wage and Price Stability guideline of 7 per cent. Contracts that included COLA clauses – 58 per cent compared with 37 per cent in 1978 – had an increase of only 6.1 per cent, but COLA produced an additional 5.8 per cent raise in wages, putting those contracts into the double-digit inflation range. See LABOR.

New Technology. The need to save energy and to produce energy-efficient machinery continued to be the wellspring for innovations and new technology. The General Motors Corporation (GM) unveiled a new electric power source for a small car – a zinc-nickel oxide battery that the company called a technological breakthrough. Although the battery was invented in 1895, GM claimed that its researchers had improved it so that its plates do not deteriorate and lose their capacity and power after relatively few recharges. The company said that the battery was at least twice as efficient as lead-acid batteries.

GM's battery-powered car would have a range of about 100 miles (160 kilometers) and a speed of up to 50 miles (80 kilometers) per hour, and the batteries would be rechargeable in eight hours. The battery pack, weighing 800 pounds (360 kilograms), would be replaced after 25,000 miles (40,000 kilometers). GM expects to put its electric car on the market in the mid-1980s, and said that electric vehicles could make up 10 per cent of auto production by 1990.

Refuse Energy Systems Company, in Saugus, Mass., became the first successful U.S. garbage-to-energy operation, turning a profit without government assistance. The company's $50-million facility burns 1,450 short tons (1,315 metric tons) of garbage per day, the equivalent of 67,000 gallons (254,000 liters) of oil. The system works efficiently. Trucks back into the plant and a giant crane scoops up the refuse, without presorting. The trash is then dropped onto a conveyor that feeds it into two giant furnaces. At 1650°F. (900°C) and under controlled pressures, almost everything burns. The heat fires boilers that produce steam, which goes to a General Electric Company plant across the Saugus River in Lynn, Mass. Magnets remove scrap iron from the ash. The system is an adaptation of a process used by Von Roll Limited of Zurich, Switzerland.

E. I. du Pont de Nemours & Company developed a nylon that is said to be the world's toughest engineering plastic. Zytel, the new material, has more than 10 times the impact strength of conventional nylon molding resins. It consists of a polyamide matrix and at least one polymer, both derived from petroleum. Before the development of Zytel, nylons and most other engineering resins had only modest impact strength when cut, scratched, or notched. The new tough resin does not permit cracks to spread and is said to resist heat and chemicals as well as impacts. Zytel is being used in the production of safety helmets, fire-extinguisher valves, and automobile and farm-equipment parts.

Machine Tool Orders in the United States, triggered by strong overseas and domestic demand from the auto and aerospace industries, rose 64 per cent in September over the 1978 level. The increase to $547.9 million from $334.7 million ran counter to trends in other industries, which began to feel the pinch of recession. September 1979 orders were up 29 per cent over August's $426.1 million, and brought the third quarter's rate to just 2 per cent below that of the second quarter. The order backlog grew 4.2 per cent to $4.9 billion. This represented 14 months of shipments at the September rate.

While machine tool executives did not expect to see orders continue at the September rate, neither did they think they would fall sharply. The industry's huge order backlog and extended delivery schedules tend to reduce the impact on orders of high interest rates and the likelihood of a worsening recession. For the first nine months of 1979, orders stood at $4.1 billion, compared to $3.1 billion for the same period in 1978.

The American Paper Institute reported that production of paper and paperboard was at a seasonally adjusted rate of 66 million short tons (59.4 million metric tons) per year for September, bringing the third quarter to a record 65.2 million short tons (58.7

million metric tons) per year, up slightly from the 64.9 million short tons (58.4 million metric tons) of the second quarter. With strong data for early October, the institute looked for continued strength through the final quarter and total production reaching 64.8 million short tons (58.1 million metric tons), some 5 per cent higher than in 1978.

The Rubber Industry had a disappointing year. The Rubber Manufacturers Association reported that for the first eight months, total new rubber produced was only 2.6 million short tons (2.4 million metric tons) compared with 2.5 million short tons (2.2 million metric tons) for the same period in 1978. A major reason for the flat performance was the serious decline in tire production, caused by gasoline shortages, declining auto sales, and labor troubles. August tire production stood at 13.9 million, with inventories at 40 million. In August 1978, production was 15.8 million, with inventories at 36.6 million. Total tire production for the first eight months was 118.6 million, compared with 120.9 million for the same period in 1978.   George J. Berkwitt

In WORLD BOOK, see MANUFACTURING.

MARINE CORPS, U.S. See ARMED FORCES.

MARYLAND. See STATE GOVERNMENT.

MASSACHUSETTS. See STATE GOVERNMENT.

MAURITANIA. See AFRICA.

MAURITIUS. See AFRICA.

MAYOR. See CITY.

McHENRY, DONALD F. (1936-   ), a career diplomat, was appointed chief United States delegate to the United Nations (UN) on Aug. 31, 1979. He succeeded Andrew Young, who resigned on August 15 amid controversy after a meeting with a representative of the Palestine Liberation Organization. Because both McHenry and Young are black, some observers viewed the appointment as an Administration move to regain the support of blacks alienated by the Young controversy. But President Jimmy Carter defended the appointment by citing McHenry's long experience in foreign affairs and his understanding of problems in southern Africa. See UNITED STATES, GOVERNMENT OF THE.

McHenry was born on Oct. 13, 1936, in St. Louis. He graduated from Illinois State University in Normal in 1957 and earned a master's degree at Southern Illinois University in Carbondale. From 1959 to 1962, McHenry taught English at Howard University in Washington, D.C. In 1963, he joined the Department of State. He became officer-in-charge of dependent-areas affairs in 1966, assistant to the secretary in 1968, and special assistant to the counselor in 1969. He joined the Carnegie Endowment for International Peace in New York City in 1973 and returned to government in 1977 as deputy representative to the UN Security Council.

McHenry married Mary Elizabeth Williamson in 1962. They have two daughters and a son. Jay Myers

MEDICINE. United States scientists who toured the People's Republic of China reported in January 1979 that Chinese physicians have developed a birth control pill for men that is 99.89 per cent effective. The Chinese said that several thousand men have used *gossypol*, a chemical extract of cottonseed oil that kills sperm cells, without serious side effects. Fertility usually returned within three months after a man stopped using the drug.

Swedish physicians reported in the August 4 issue of *Lancet*, a British medical journal, on their success with a nasal contraceptive, luteinizing-hormone releasing hormone (LRH), derived from a pituitary hormone. A daily sniff of LRH stopped ovulation in 25 of 27 women tested. Studies made in Quebec City, Canada, indicated that LRH is an effective contraceptive after intercourse. Researchers at the National Institutes of Health (NIH) in Bethesda, Md., hailed LRH as safer and more promising than the hormones used in conventional birth-control pills.

A report from the U.S. Center for Disease Control in Atlanta, Ga., in August implicated oral contraceptives as a cause of liver tumors in women over 27. The risk of cancer increased with length of use and higher hormone levels in certain pills.

Medroxyprogesterone acetate, or Depo-Provera, an injectable contraceptive effective for up to three months, is available in more than 60 countries. But the United States government, concerned over increased cancer risk in animal studies, formed a board of inquiry in July to look into approving the drug for U.S. use.

British gynecologist Patrick C. Steptoe and physiologist Robert G. Edwards, who made possible the conception and birth of Louise Brown, the first "test-tube" baby, in 1978, described their work to the American Fertility Society in February. The 1,200 physicians attending the meeting responded with a standing ovation. American research into test-tube fertilization, which had been halted in 1972, was given a green light by an ethics advisory board to the Department of Health, Education, and Welfare (HEW) after 11 public meetings.

Infant Care. Drugs and equipment used routinely during delivery and labor became the center of controversy in 1979. An NIH study of painkillers used during labor, obtained by the press in January, concluded that all these drugs are linked with lingering behavioral and motor problems in the infants delivered. The study, based on 3,528 infants, indicated that inhaled anesthetics pose greater problems than other types. A Food and Drug Administration (FDA) panel concluded there was no need for FDA regulation of such medications.

The use of electronic fetal monitors during labor became an issue for feminists as well as physicians. The American College of Obstetricians and Gynecologists and a special NIH task force endorsed monitoring for high-risk deliveries but not for nor-

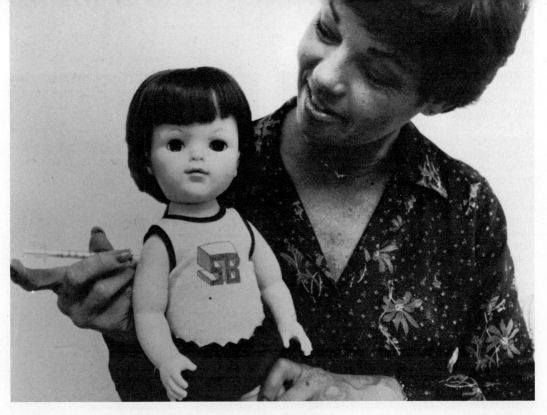

Diabetic Lory Needelman demonstrates Sugar Babe, a doll she designed to help other diabetics overcome fear of injecting themselves with insulin.

mal labor. Monitoring has been attacked as risky and costly, and opponents say it increases the incidence of *Caesarean sections* (abdominal deliveries).

Japanese physicians in April reported success in treating infants suffering from hyaline membrane disease, a respiratory distress syndrome that kills about 6,000 babies in Japan each year and about 10,000 in the United States. A mix of animal and synthetic solutions was injected directly into the trachea of critically ill babies. All survived.

Two daughters of women who took diethylstilbestrol (DES), a synthetic estrogen, to prevent miscarriages won settlements of $500,000 and $800,000 from pharmaceutical companies in separate court cases, establishing a patient's right to hold the pharmaceutical industry as a whole liable for a drug. Both young women had developed cancer of the reproductive tract. See Drugs.

As a group, DES daughters got fresh bad news in September. A project funded by the National Cancer Institute reported that more than two-thirds of DES daughters may have abnormalities of the reproductive tract that cause miscarriages, *ectopic pregnancies* (which occur outside the womb and endanger the lives of mother and baby), and premature labor.

Surgery. Using high-powered microscopes and delicate instruments to perform microsurgery, surgeons in 1979 rejoined severed limbs in several dramatic operations. A team of New York City surgeons on June 30 replanted the severed legs of a man hit by a subway train. Also in New York in June, the right hand of a 17-year-old music student, which had been amputated when she was pushed in front of a subway train, was successfully replanted. Surgeons estimated that 500 to 1,000 replantations, mainly of fingers and toes, are done each year worldwide, with 70 to 90 per cent survival rates for the rejoined appendages.

Using similar microsurgical techniques, University of Utah Medical Center surgeons in May separated 19-month-old Lisa and Elisa Hansen, Siamese twins who had been born with fused skulls and a common brain vessel. The 16½-hour operation was the first successful separation of twins sharing a major blood vessel in the brain.

University of Maryland surgeons on August 31 replaced the backbone of a 33-year-old woman in another historic operation. They fitted her with a metal prosthesis that bridged a gap from her ribcage to her pelvis caused when the removal of a tumor required the excision of several vertebrae. Now the patient can sit up and move around in a wheelchair.

A New York jury in May awarded $854,000 to a woman whose navel was placed off-center during plastic surgery on her abdomen. The judgment, which was against surgeon Howard Bellin, was later reduced to $200,000.

Discoveries. Researchers at the University of California in San Francisco, and at Genentech, Incorporated, a California firm, announced in July that they had used recombinant-DNA techniques to synthesize human growth hormone, which is used to treat children with certain forms of dwarfism (see BIOCHEMISTRY). Dermatologists at the National Cancer Institute in February announced the development of a powerful new acne treatment – a synthetic form of vitamin A called 13-cis-retinoic acid. In the initial study of 14 patients with severe, cystic acne, 13 went into complete, long-term remissions after several months on the oral medication. The 14th patient improved greatly.

Medical Practice. A National Academy of Sciences Institute of Medicine study released in April criticized the widespread prescribing and use of sleeping pills, taken by about 8 million Americans each year. The report stated that there is no proof such drugs are effective for periods of more than two weeks.

Unconventional Therapy. Eleven states had legalized clinical applications of marijuana for such diseases as cancer and glaucoma by June, but HEW Secretary Joseph A. Califano, Jr., said the drug should not be reclassified as a controlled drug with some medical uses. Dianne R. Hales

See also HEALTH AND DISEASE; PUBLIC HEALTH. In WORLD BOOK, see MARIJUANA; MEDICINE.

President Carter's wife, Rosalynn, urges more funds for mental health during testimony before a congressional subcommittee on February 7.

MENTAL HEALTH. The Supreme Court of the United States ruled on April 30, 1979, that patients cannot be committed to a mental institution against their will without "clear and convincing" evidence that they are both mentally ill and likely to be dangerous. The high court's historic decision thus imposed a higher standard of proof than "preponderance of the evidence," which had been used by some 20 states as the standard for involuntary commitment.

The Supreme Court ruled on June 20 that parents may have their children committed to a mental institution so long as a "neutral fact finder" – such as a physician – agrees that commitment is necessary. The child does not need a lawyer or an adversary hearing, the court said, because "the natural bonds of affection lead parents to act in the best interests of their children." Proponents of children's rights disagreed with the decision.

A New Jersey Superior Court judge ruled in July that Edward and Luanne Grady could have their mentally retarded daughter sterilized. Lee Ann Grady, 18, suffers from Down's syndrome. The parents had argued that if their daughter should become pregnant, there was no way to ensure care for her child after they – the parents – died.

Schizophrenia Research. Various research teams reported progress in 1979 in diagnosing and treating schizophrenia, one of the most severe forms of mental illness. Two Johns Hopkins University physicians reported in May that they have developed a simple blood test that uses a radioactive tracer to determine the levels of an antischizophrenia drug in the blood and to indicate how the body uses it.

British physicians reported in the medical journal *Lancet* in April that they had isolated "a viruslike agent" in the cerebrospinal fluid of 18 of 47 schizophrenics and in 8 of 11 patients with severe neurological diseases. Canadian and U.S. physicians reported that schizophrenics were helped by dialysis, a blood-cleansing technique. The largest controlled study of this approach began at the University of Louisville.

A West German psychiatrist reported more good news on schizophrenia at the Second World Congress for Biological Psychiatry in Barcelona, Spain. Of more than 750 patients studied for up to 30 years after diagnosis, one-fifth had fully recovered. Women were more likely to recover than men, as were those of both sexes who had high intelligence quotients and balanced personalities prior to their illness.

University of Michigan physicians in May reported yet another link between chemical imbalances and mental illness. They found that the growth hormone in the blood multiplies when a person with a phobia is exposed to the feared object or situation. The researchers could not explain the increase, but they found it occurred more frequently in women than in men.

Valium and Antidepressants. A U.S. Navy psychiatrist told a Senate subcommittee in September that the most widely prescribed drug in the United States, the tranquilizer Valium, is potentially addictive even in moderate doses. Antidepressant drugs proved effective in relieving chronic pain in a 16-month study at Henry Ford Hospital in Detroit. This indicates that emotions play a role in controlling pain in "pain-prone" individuals.

Electrical Implants in the brain, activated by the patient, also relieve pain, according to a report in January by researchers at the University of California, San Francisco, and the Salk Institute for Biological Studies, La Jolla. The researchers found that the electrodes increased the levels of beta endorphin, the body's own opiate, two to seven times over normal levels.

Americans between the ages of 15 and 24 killed themselves in 1978 at a rate three times higher than that of 25 years ago, a Harvard University psychiatrist told the American Academy of Pediatrics in October. Suicide was the third leading cause of death in young males and fourth in young females. Suicides also were reported to be rising among children between the ages of 6 and 10.   Dianne R. Hales

See also DRUGS. In WORLD BOOK, see MENTAL HEALTH.

MEXICO. State visits by two world leaders in 1979 underscored Mexico's growing importance as an oil-exporting country. United States President Jimmy Carter met with President Jose Lopez Portillo in February to review negotiations on the U.S. purchase of Mexico's natural gas and to ensure a continuing flow of petroleum. France's President Valéry Giscard d'Estaing visited in April to arrange a reciprocal agreement under which France would supply Mexico with a $240-million line of credit in exchange for assurances that France would be guaranteed 100,000 barrels per day (bpd) of oil beginning on Jan. 1, 1980.

Elections Held. In parliamentary elections held on July 1, the ruling Institutional Revolutionary Party (PRI) won 296 of the 400 seats in the enlarged Chamber of Deputies. The second largest bloc of 39 seats went to the National Action Party (PAN). Represented for the first time, the Mexican Communist Party (PCM) was third with 18 seats.

The government unveiled a 10-year development plan in March that projected an annual 10 per cent economic-growth rate and an end to unemployment by creating 600,000 new jobs by 1990. The plan also projected an increase in the inflation rate of only 1 percentage point per month, which some economists considered unrealistic. In June, the London *Financial Times* said Mexico's inflation in the first quarter of 1979 was at an annual rate of 20 per cent.

The 10-year plan also assumed that annual wage increases could be held to the current 12 per cent. But labor unions were unhappy with the 12 per cent ceiling because wages were obviously not keeping pace with prices. On April 24, some 23,000 employees of the state-controlled telephone company went on strike after the government refused to meet their demand for 25 per cent higher wages. Nine days later, a settlement was reached under which the workers were granted a 13.5 per cent increase that violated the government's anti-inflation guidelines, and forced large increases in the phone rates.

U.S.-Mexican Relations remained tense over the illegal immigration of Mexicans into the United States. An estimated 400,000 Mexicans with proper visas entered the U.S. in 1979, but an additional 800,000 allegedly entered the U.S. illegally. Mexico did not discourage this flow of undocumented workers into the United States. And although U.S. labor unions protested, claiming they took jobs away from U.S. workers, many farmers and textile manufacturers welcomed them as a source of cheap labor.

Relations with the United States were also strained by Mexico's refusal to allow the shah of Iran to re-enter the country in December after medical treatment in New York City. See IRAN.

Vegetable Controversy. The "tomato war" that began in September 1978 when Florida growers

President Jose Lopez Portillo, in light shirt, inspects Mexico's newest oil refinery facilities, which began operating at Cadereyta in October.

complained that $200 million of Mexican vegetables were being "dumped" on the U.S. market was resolved. On October 30, the U.S. Department of the Treasury tentatively found that the Mexican sales were not "at less than fair value." This favorable development in U.S.-Mexican relations came after Mexico had agreed to sell natural gas to the United States at a compromise price of $3.625 per 1,000 cubic feet (28 cubic meters).

Oil Spill. On June 3, a runaway oil well 50 miles (80 kilometers) off Yucatan's coast began gushing at a rate of up to 30,000 bpd. In five days the well created a slick 100 by 10 miles (160 by 16 kilometers) that reached the Texas shoreline before the well's outflow was partially contained in November.

President Lopez Portillo admitted "no responsibility" for the oil spill and refused to discuss anything related to liability. The U.S. Department of Justice decided on October 23 to file a $6-million damage suit to recover cleanup costs from Sedco, Incorporated, the United States company that drilled the well.

Pope John Paul II attended the Latin American Bishops' Conference in Mexico's fourth largest city, Puebla, in January. See RELIGION (Close-Up); ROMAN CATHOLIC CHURCH.   T. W. Adams

See also LATIN AMERICA (Facts in Brief Table). In WORLD BOOK, see MEXICO.

MICHIGAN. See DETROIT; STATE GOVERNMENT.

MIDDLE EAST. Muslim militants dominated regional affairs in 1979, a year in which Islam celebrated the 1,400th anniversary of its founding. (Muslims base the 1,400 years since A.D. 622, when Islam began, on a lunar calendar that is shorter than the solar year most Western countries use.) The Muslim militancy overshadowed extraordinary developments in the Arab-Israeli conflict. The heady mixture of religion and politics thrust a little-known 80-year-old Iranian religious leader, Ayatollah Ruhollah Khomeini, onto television screens and the front pages of newspapers around the world as his followers, acting in the name of Islam, overthrew Shah Mohammad Reza Pahlavi in a popular revolution in January. In November, they seized the United States Embassy in Teheran, holding a group of Americans they captured there hostage as the price of the shah's extradition for trial (see IRAN; KHOMEINI, RUHOLLAH.)

In neighboring Afghanistan, the Russian-backed Marxist governments of Revolutionary Council President and Prime Minister Noor Mohammad Taraki and his successor, Hafizullah Amin, were embroiled in conflict with Muslim tribesmen who opposed the presence of Russian military advisers. With Muslim opposition growing, Russian forces entered Afghanistan on December 27. President Amin was overthrown and executed. Pro-Moscow Babrak Karmal succeeded Amin. Fierce fighting

followed between Soviet troops and Muslim tribesmen, who feared the Russians threatened traditional Muslim values (see AFGHANISTAN). Even in the relatively secularized Arab countries, Muslim sectarianism, along with attempts by such supranationalistic organizations as the Muslim Brotherhood to reinstate religious law as the final authority, undermined national stability or limited the effectiveness of national leaders.

Peace in the Sinai. Although Khomeini held the headlines, what some saw as the major development in the region during the year concerned Egypt and Israel. The 30-year "state of war" that had divided the two nations was formally ended on March 26 when President Anwar al-Sadat of Egypt and Prime Minister Menachem Begin of Israel – with President Jimmy Carter as witness – signed a peace treaty in Washington, D.C. The treaty climaxed months of difficult negotiations that had followed Sadat's historic journey to Jerusalem in November 1977. With the exchange of formal treaty ratification documents on April 25, Egypt became the first Arab country to recognize Israel's existence as a nation.

Predictably, the rest of the Arab world exploded with fury following Egypt's break with the united Arab front against Israel. An Arab summit conference held in Baghdad, Iraq, on March 27 and 28 ended with resolutions that virtually isolated Egypt. All Arab states except Oman, Somalia, and Sudan broke diplomatic relations.

Egypt was expelled from membership in the Arab League and the various inter-Arab organizations. In May, Arab air space was closed to Egyptian planes. The Arab League transferred its headquarters to Tunis, Tunisia, from Cairo, Egypt, in March, and Tunisian Information Minister Chedli Klibi was elected as the first non-Egyptian secretary-general in its 34-year history.

Despite the political isolation of Egypt, the other Arab states applied economic sanctions ineffectively, and the United States, the World Bank, and European bankers took up the slack. In March, the United States committed $2 billion in military aid as part of a $5-billion package for Egypt and Israel that had been granted contingent on the signing of the peace treaty. With an estimated $3 billion in economic aid expected from foreign donors, the Egyptian economy would not be affected by the cutoff in Arab funds, though the peace treaty was unlikely to improve the economic outlook for the average Egyptian in the immediate future.

The Treaty was a complex document, with nine articles and three long annexes detailing Israeli withdrawal from the Sinai. Withdrawal would take place in stages over a three-year period. After that, the Egyptian-Israeli border would again be the pre-1948 boundary between Egypt and British-ruled Palestine. The first stage was completed on May 25 with the return of the coastal town of

Egyptian President Anwar al-Sadat, left, and Israeli Prime Minister Begin, right, sign a peace treaty as a pleased President Jimmy Carter looks on.

El-Arish on the Mediterranean Sea to Egyptian control. The Abu Darba Peninsula, on the Gulf of Suez, was returned in June, and Mount Sinai was handed back in November, two months ahead of schedule so Sadat could celebrate the anniversary of his 1977 Jerusalem journey there. The Egyptian leader pledged free access to the holy mount – which is sacred to Judaism, Christianity, and Islam.

In general, the Sinai disengagement process proceeded smoothly. One obstacle emerged in July, when the United Nations (UN) refused to renew the mandate for the UN Emergency Force stationed between Israeli and Egyptian forces. Russia had threatened to veto the renewal in the Security Council. A compromise agreement worked out in September by Begin and Sadat during the latter's official visit to Haifa, Israel, set up a truce force of joint Egyptian-Israeli patrols, UN personnel, and U.S. technicians to ensure treaty compliance.

The other provisions of the peace treaty bound both countries to renounce the use of force to settle their differences, establish diplomatic and consular exchanges, and open their borders. Israeli ships and Israeli-bound cargoes were given rights of passage through the Suez Canal.

Palestinian Question. Unmentioned in the treaty and still unresolved even in principle was the issue of Palestinian "rights" to statehood, which continued to impede progress toward an overall settlement.

Both Egypt and Israel were committed to adhere to UN Resolutions 242 and 338, which dealt with Israeli withdrawal from occupied territory and the rights of all sovereign states to peace, as well as the peace agreement reached at Camp David, Maryland, on Sept. 17, 1978, as the framework for a permanent Arab-Israeli settlement. Palestinian rights formed a key element in all three documents. But a divergence of views emerged between Israel and Egypt over the Palestinians' future.

Begin declared in an April speech to the *Knesset* (parliament) that Israel could envisage autonomy for the Palestinian Arabs but not for the *land*. The Cabinet then voted to permit purchase of Arab lands in the occupied West Bank, an action that sharply divided Israeli advocates of "Peace Now" from those who believe in the God-given right of Jews to all of Palestine. Members of the *Gush Emunim* (Faithful Bloc), supported by the two minority religious parties whose support is essential to the Begin coalition government, pressured the government into allowing additional Jewish settlements in the West Bank.

The Settlement Issue came to a head on June 3, when the Cabinet approved a Gush Emunim town at Elon Moreh, just outside the important West Bank Arab town of Nablus. The decision was justified by the Cabinet on the grounds that the settlement was necessary for Israel's security, and Israeli soldiers began helping the settlers move onto Arab property.

Arab riots and demonstrations protesting the action brought an Israeli crackdown, and the Palestinian Bir Zeit University, a center of Palestine Liberation Organization (PLO) support, was closed for the academic year.

Arab landowners sued to recover their property, and Israel's Supreme Court in October unexpectedly ruled in their favor. It said that Elon Moreh was not necessary to Israel's security and ordered the settlement vacated by November 23. But as the year ended, the settlers had not moved. On December 31, the government granted a second five-week delay.

West Bank Settlements. A further jolt to Palestinian prospects was the unveiling in November of a government master plan to triple Jewish settlements in the West Bank by 1983, the date set at Camp David for Palestinian autonomy. The plan envisaged a Jewish population increase from 14,000 to 60,000 by that time, grouped into five large towns spread over 19 "settlement points" to ensure an Israeli presence in the West Bank. The Cabinet split during discussions on the plan, and Foreign Minister Moshe Dayan resigned on October 21 in protest.

The Israeli government's uncompromising stance on the autonomy issue and the Jewish settlements provoked a much stronger reaction than in previous years from the Palestinian Arab community. Bassam al-Shaka, the Palestinian mayor of Nablus and a leading West Bank Palestinian political figure, was arrested in November for allegedly making state-

Facts in Brief on the Middle East Countries

Country	Population	Government	Monetary Unit*	Foreign Trade (million U.S. $) Exports†	Imports†
Bahrain	294,000	Amir Isa bin Sulman Al Khalifa; Prime Minister Khalifa bin Salman Al Khalifa	dinar (1 = $2.63)	1,891	2,044
Cyprus	662,000	President Spyros Kyprianou	pound (1 = $2.86)	344	753
Egypt	41,314,000	President Anwar al-Sadat; Vice President Hosni Mobarak; Prime Minister Mustafa Khalil	pound (1 = $1.43)	1,737	6,727
Iran	38,071,000	Ayatollah Ruhollah Khomeini	rial (71.5 = $1)	22,721	14,968
Iraq	13,494,000	President Saddam Hussein	dinar (1 = $3.40)	11,008	3,898
Israel	3,960,000	President Yitzhak Navon; Prime Minister Menachem Begin	pound (31.5 = $1)	3,716	5,582
Jordan	3,151,000	King Hussein I; Prime Minister Sharif Abdul Hamid Sharaf	dinar (1 = $3.36)	297	1,499
Kuwait	1,282,000	Emir Jaber al-Ahmad al-Jaber Al-Sabah; Crown Prince & Prime Minister Saad al-Abdullah al-Salem Al-Sabah	dinar (1 = $3.60)	10,543	4,295
Lebanon	2,658,000	President Elias Sarkis; Prime Minister Salim Ahmad al-Huss	pound (3.4 = $1)	497	1,224
Oman	894,000	Sultan Qaboos Bin Said	rial (1 = $2.89)	1,512	945
Qatar	173,000	Amir & Prime Minister Khalifa bin Hamad Al-Thani	riyal (3.7 = $1)	2,367	1,185
Saudi Arabia	8,361,000	King & Prime Minister Khalid ibn Abd al-Aziz Al-Saud	riyal (3.4 = $1)	37,935	22,852
Sudan	18,509,000	President & Prime Minister Gaafar Muhammed Nimeiri	pound (1 = $2.50)	489	1,124
Syria	8,649,000	President Hafiz al-Assad; Prime Minister Muhammad Ali al-Halabi	pound (4 = $1)	1,053	2,437
Turkey	45,794,000	President Fahri S. Koruturk; Prime Minister Suleyman Demirel	lira (47.1 = $1)	2,288	4,597
United Arab Emirates	964,000	President Zayid bin Sultan al-Nuhayan; Prime Minister Rashid bin Said al-Maktum	dirham (3.8 = $1)	9,049	4,892
Yemen (Aden)	1,961,000	Supreme People's Council Presidium Chairman Abd al-Fatah Ismail; Council of Ministers Chairman Ali Nasir Muhammad al-Hasani	dinar (1 = $2.90)	177	335
Yemen (Sana)	7,695,000	President Ali Abdallah Salih; Prime Minister Abdulaziz Abdul Ghani	rial (4.6 = $1)	19	730

*Exchange rates as of Dec. 1, 1979. †Latest available data.

ments in support of terrorism and was ordered expelled to Jordan. Defying the advice of PLO leaders, the Arab mayors of 25 other West Bank towns resigned in a body to protest the deportation order, which was stayed pending a court appeal. West Bank shopkeepers declared a brief general strike on November 12. Israel canceled the expulsion order and returned the mayor in early December. Nonetheless, one Palestinian merchant's comment that "Israel's democracy is a bad joke, and so is the Palestinian autonomy scheme" echoed the general sentiments of the Palestinians.

PLO Gains. Ironically, increased Palestinian disillusionment came at a time of growing respectability for the PLO and endorsement of Palestinian rights by many in the United States. In the months that followed the peace treaty, PLO guerrilla activity increased. A guerrilla raid on the Israeli coastal town of Nahariyya on April 22 caused several Israeli casualties. Israeli forces retaliated with air and artillery strikes at Palestinian bases in Lebanon.

This "hot pursuit" policy nearly escalated into full-scale war on June 27 when Syrian and Israeli jets fought an air battle over Lebanon. Syria lost five MIG-19 fighters and Israel lost no planes. Thereafter, Syria's preoccupation with internal matters and the PLO drive for international respectability reduced the tension.

The PLO issue – though it stopped short of accepting Israel's right to exist – won some new friends abroad. Austrian Chancellor Bruno Kreisky welcomed PLO Chairman Yasir Arafat to Vienna in July and endorsed a Palestinian homeland. A similar endorsement came from Spain, the first Western European country to extend an official invitation from its head of state to the PLO leader. Although the United States continued to hedge on the question of PLO recognition, American black leaders, Christian church groups, and UN Ambassador Andrew J. Young, Jr., separately endorsed the Palestinian cause and the PLO as the legitimate representative of the Palestinian people. Young resigned his post on August 15 after it became known that he had negotiated with the PLO observer at the UN in defiance of U.S. policy. Young defended his act by saying that a permanent peace in the region would never be achieved without PLO participation (see UNITED NATIONS).

Inter-Arab Conflicts took a back seat to the collective Arab will to deal harshly with Egypt. A brief border war between the rival Yemen (Sana) and Yemen (Aden) regimes broke out in March when the Aden regime supported a rebellion of North Yemeni tribesmen protesting alleged Saudi Arabian interference in their internal affairs. The Arab League arranged a cease-fire on March 29, after U.S. arms had been rushed to Yemen (Sana); the rebels promptly disappeared into the hills.

A well-armed force of some 200 men seized the

A mutilated photo of Shah Mohammad Reza Pahlavi lies in a Teheran trash can, symbolically closing out his 38 years as the absolute ruler of Iran.

Great Mosque in Mecca, Islam's holiest shrine, on November 20. In a two-week siege, Saudi Arabian troops killed or captured the intruders, reported to be members of a small tribe that had been at odds with the ruling Saudi family. See SAUDI ARABIA.

A more serious inter-Arab dispute developed in Western Sahara (the former Spanish Sahara), where the withdrawal of Mauritania left Morocco alone in the effort to crush the Algerian-backed Polisario, the guerrilla group fighting for the independence of the territory. Following Mauritania's defection, King Hassan II of Morocco unilaterally annexed the Mauritanian portion of Western Sahara in August as the province of Dakhla. But Moroccan troops could not defeat Polisario forces operating out of Algerian bases and suffered several military reverses in Moroccan territory.

The Algerian support of a Saharan Democratic Republic run by Polisario ran counter to Morocco's objective of developing the region and its vast phosphate reserves. With Hassan refusing to recognize Polisario or accept international mediation, and with Algeria equally adamant in its position, there was a possibility that the hot pursuit of the Saharans by Moroccan forces into Algerian territory would create another dangerous border situation. See MOROCCO.   William Spencer

In WORLD BOOK, see MIDDLE EAST and individual country articles.

MINING. A presidential commission working to develop a United States minerals policy warned in August 1979 that political instability in southern and central Africa threatened future supplies of four critical metals – platinum, chromium, manganese, and cobalt. These metals, used as catalysts in the petroleum and other industries, are also needed in the production of alloys, including the superalloys that are crucial in jet engines. The United States now imports 91 per cent of the platinum it needs, 92 per cent of its chromium, 98 per cent of its manganese, and virtually all of its cobalt.

However, the commission concluded that the United States and its allies must continue to rely upon these areas despite the political and social unrest. Russia, the only other supplier of chromium and platinum, might prove an even more unreliable source. Critics charged that the commission report failed to reconcile U.S. political policies that favor sanctions on some African suppliers of the metals and United States regulatory policies that discourage domestic production.

An April report by the General Accounting Office (GAO) also emphasized the need for a national materials policy to ensure adequate future supplies of critical raw materials. But GAO, which is Congress's investigative and auditing agency, concluded that President Jimmy Carter's Administration is not close to reaching a consensus on how to do this. A Bureau of Mines study found that domestic production of minerals and mineral-based commodities has slowed during the last 20 years, compared with world production rates. The study blamed such factors as the growing number of environmental and other regulations, and increasing energy costs.

Montana Platinum. Chevron Resources Company, a Standard Oil of California subsidiary, and Johns-Manville Corporation announced plans in June for a project that could reduce U.S. dependence on imported platinum. The two firms will explore 18,000 acres (7,300 hectares) in Montana that are believed to contain the largest platinum deposit in North America. Production potential is estimated at 300,000 troy ounces (9.3 million grams) per year. United States consumption is about 2.3 million troy ounces (71.5 million grams) annually. But the Montana deposit lies under a national forest, and stringent federal air-pollution and land-use regulations may jeopardize its development.

Open and Shut Cases. President Carter moved on April 16 to open 36 million acres (14.5 million hectares) of land in the national forest system to development by mining, petroleum, and timber companies. One month later, the House of Representatives voted to close 67 million acres (27 million hectares) of Alaska lands to development. The Alaska land is believed to be a potentially rich source of copper, silver, gold, zinc, and other minerals. The Department of the Interior acted in July to resume large-scale leasing of federal coal reserves in the West. Leasing was suspended in 1971 because of widespread activity by speculators.

In Other Countries. The Canadian government in August raised its estimates of proven uranium reserves by almost 6 per cent to 590,700 short tons (540,000 metric tons). Panarctic Oils Limited on May 15 announced a major natural gas find about 25 miles (40 kilometers) west of Lougheed Island in the Canadian Arctic. The field may contain up to 10 billion cubic feet (283 million cubic meters) of gas.

Miners in the rich Pilbara iron ore fields of Western Australia voted on August 3 to end a 70-day strike that reduced iron ore exports by 10 million short tons (9 million metric tons). The strike cost about $110 million in lost revenues and wages. The miners won a 20 per cent wage increase.

Peru's copper production fell about 75 per cent on March 13 when workers at the Cuajone and Toquepala mines and Ilo smelter struck for a 50 per cent wage increase. Workers began returning to their jobs by the end of the month, after union leaders were arrested. The strike helped to drive up international copper prices.   Michael Woods

See also COAL. In WORLD BOOK, see MINING.

MINNESOTA. See STATE GOVERNMENT.
MISSISSIPPI. See STATE GOVERNMENT.
MISSOURI. See STATE GOVERNMENT.
MONACO. See EUROPE.

MONDALE, WALTER FREDERICK (1928-   ), 42nd Vice-President of the United States and one of President Jimmy Carter's trusted advisers, traveled extensively on state business in 1979. Mondale made trips abroad to explain Carter Administration policies, strengthen old alliances, and cement good will between the United States and other nations.

Mondale made a three-day trip to Brazil and Venezuela in March to brief new presidents there on U.S. policies regarding the Strategic Arms Limitation Talks (SALT II) and the Middle East. He visited five Scandinavian nations and the Netherlands in April to reassure them of the U.S. commitment to their security. Mondale addressed the United Nations conference on refugees in Geneva, Switzerland, on July 21, outlining U.S. plans for aiding Indochina refugees (see ASIA).

Far Eastern Visit. The highlight of Mondale's year, however, was his trip to the Far East with his wife, Joan, and daughter, Eleanor, in August. In a week-long visit to the People's Republic of China, he conferred with Deputy Premier Teng Hsiao-p'ing (Deng Xiaoping in the phonetic Pinyin alphabet China adopted on January 1).

Mondale addressed 900 educators in Peking (Beijing) on August 27. In a televised speech he declared that a "strong and secure and modernizing China" was in the best interests of the United States, and promised U.S. technical and trade aid to China.

Vice-President Walter F. Mondale shops in an open-air market in Peking in August while making an official visit to China and the Far East.

Teng and Mondale signed a cultural exchange pact and a protocol on August 28 under which the United States would help China develop hydroelectric power, putting into effect an agreement signed by Teng and Carter on January 31 in Washington, D.C. At the close of his China visit, Mondale announced that Premier Hua Kuo-feng (Hua Guofeng) and Carter would exchange visits in 1980.

During his Far Eastern tour, Mondale also stopped in Hong Kong, where he met with officials of 12 relief organizations on September 2 to discuss problems of Indochinese refugees. He announced that, starting in October, the United States would admit 2,000 of the 67,000 Indochinese refugees temporarily sheltered in Hong Kong each month. The Vice-President conferred with Japan's Prime Minister Masayoshi Ohira in Tokyo on September 3. When he returned to Washington, he reported that Chinese-American relations were excellent.

Domestic Duties occupied much of Mondale's time in 1979. He addressed the National Association of Counties, the U.S. Conference of Mayors, and the National Governors' Association; and took part in the Camp David, Maryland, conference on energy policy.   Carol L. Thompson

In WORLD BOOK, see VICE-PRESIDENT OF THE UNITED STATES.

MONGOLIA. See ASIA.

MONTANA. See STATE GOVERNMENT.

MOROCCO. Failure to solve the guerrilla problem in the Western Sahara severely strained the Moroccan economy in 1979. Despite overwhelming superiority in numbers and equipment, the Moroccan army could not win a decisive victory over the Polisario guerrillas fighting for Saharan independence. Guerrilla units even briefly occupied the southern Moroccan town of Tantan in January and again in August. In the biggest military operation of the four-year-old war, 7,000 Moroccan soldiers, supported by 1,500 tanks and armored cars, moved against the Polisario guerrillas in November.

A cease-fire pact between Mauritania and the guerrillas in August left Morocco isolated among its neighbors. But despite these setbacks, Moroccan support for King Hassan II's Saharan policy held firm. The National Defense Council, formed in March to direct the guerrilla war, included leaders of all except the minor opposition parties.

Prime Minister Ahmed Osman resigned on March 22 after six years in office and was succeeded by former Justice Minister Maati Bouabid. The new prime minister's main problem was a wave of strikes that followed wage demands to meet galloping inflation caused by the Saharan war and escalating oil prices. The minimum wage was raised from 10 to 30 per cent in April.   William Spencer

See also AFRICA (Facts in Brief Table). In WORLD BOOK, see MOROCCO.

MOTION PICTURES. American film continued to dominate the world market in 1979, as it had throughout the decade. With production on the increase in the United States and on the decrease in other countries, and with American film displaying an ever increasing technical virtuosity and power, the trend seemed more pronounced than ever. Throughout the world, the leading box-office attractions were – with rare exception – made in the United States, with American films not only often proving more popular than domestic ones, but also, in the case of certain action-oriented films such as *The Concorde...Airport '79* and *Meteor*, proving much more successful abroad than at home.

At the same time, films from other countries showed some signs of renewed strength at the American box office. As has been the case traditionally, French films cornered the largest share of the market, followed by Italian films. Also traditionally, the top-grossing movies from both countries were noteworthy less for their artistry than for their sensational subject matter.

The two leading French imports, for example, were sex comedies: *La Cage Aux Folles* (*Birds of a Feather*), which garnered about $4 million at the U.S. box office and promised to be one of the most successful foreign-language films ever shown in the United States, and *Get Out Your Handkerchiefs,* a

wry, unsettling vision of male-female relations that grossed more than $3 million. The Italian imports were even more suggestive, with the box-office winners – Luchino Visconti's *The Innocent,* Marco Vicario's *Wifemistress,* and Luigi Comencini's *Till Marriage Do Us Part* – all focusing on infidelity and perversion. All three featured the voluptuous charms of Italian sex goddess Laura Antonelli. A notable exception to this run of suggestive films was the prizewinning Italian work *The Tree of the Wooden Clogs,* Ermanno Olmi's sensitive and deeply religious drama of peasant life.

West German Films made the greatest gains in the U.S. market, however. Widely acclaimed in the 1970s as the most artistically vital of the national cinemas, German films had nevertheless been unable to attract a following among U.S. audiences. But in 1979, several German films proved commercially viable, including *The Marriage of Maria Braun,* an allegorical vision of West Germany's recovery after World War II, directed by the prolific Rainer Werner Fassbinder; *Woyzeck,* Werner Herzog's adaptation of the Georg Büchner play; and *Nosferatu,* a retelling of the Dracula legend, also by Herzog.

The Box Office. Still, the film industry outside the United States had not completely regained the artistic vigor and impact it had in the late 1950s and early 1960s. Nor did these foreign imports represent

Actor Robert Duvall plays the mad Colonel Kilgore in Francis Ford Coppola's *Apocalypse Now.* Kilgore and his troops destroy entire villages in Vietnam.

anything but a small fraction of the total U.S. box-office gross, which in 1979 promised to reach an estimated $2.8 billion. This figure, a 5 per cent increase over the previous year's record-breaking totals, indicated that the American motion-picture industry was flourishing.

Yet, on closer examination, the picture turned out to be not so rosy after all. Adjusted for a 7.3 per cent increase in ticket prices, the year's total domestic gross reflected an actual decrease in admissions. Also, since 218 new movies had been released compared with 171 in 1978, there were, on an average, lower revenues per film. Moreover, production costs had skyrocketed, to as high as $40 million in some cases. According to the standard industry formula, such a film had to gross upward of $100 million just to recoup its investment.

Serious Themes. However, the motion-picture industry reaped profits of another kind, the fruits of experimentation. These included a marked increase in seriously intentioned films that dared to broach mature and even highly charged issues.

The American experience in Vietnam, for example, was the subject of Michael Cimino's widely acclaimed film *The Deer Hunter* (which opened in December 1978), winner of five Academy of Motion Picture Arts and Sciences "Oscar" Awards and the New York Film Critics' Circle Award for best picture. A celebration of courage and comradeship that followed the emotionally devastating adventures of three close friends, *The Deer Hunter* offered a vision of war as unsparing as it was controversial. Yet even the film's detractors admitted its extraordinary artistry, its emotional power, and the brilliance of its performances by Robert De Niro, Christopher Walken, and John Savage.

The Vietnam War was also the subject of the year's greatest disappointment — Francis Ford Coppola's long-awaited *Apocalypse Now,* starring Marlon Brando and Martin Sheen. More than three years in the making and produced at a cost of some $30 million, *Apocalypse Now* was an attempt at adapting "Heart of Darkness," Joseph Conrad's classic story set in a contemporary Vietnamese setting. Although it featured stunning cinematography and imposing scale, *Apocalypse Now* lacked coherence and was, generally, poorly received by critics.

The China Syndrome, directed by James Bridges and starring Jack Lemmon and Jane Fonda, also dealt with a serious subject — the hazards of nuclear power plants. By a terrifying coincidence, which greatly boosted its commercial success, the film opened in March, only days before a serious nuclear accident at the Three Mile Island nuclear power plant near Harrisburg, Pa.

Norma Rae, featuring an impressive performance by Sally Field in the title role, portrayed the inhuman conditions imposed on Southern textile workers

Cloth superstars Miss Piggy and Kermit the Frog starred in *The Muppet Movie,* a "road" picture in which the Muppet troupe conquers California.

and their efforts at unionization. *The Onion Field* and *And Justice for All* focused on the failures of the judicial system, though with greater success and effectiveness in the case of the former. *The Seduction of Joe Tynan,* starring and written by Alan Alda, explored the temptations and corruptions of political life.

Several films, as if in answer to a number of movies in recent years dealing with women and their emotional conflicts, examined similar problems from the male point of view. Blake Edwards' *10* was a comedy, but it explored seriously the problems of aging and changing sexual mores. Alan J. Pakula's *Starting Over,* starring Burt Reynolds and Jill Clayburgh, and Robert Benton's *Kramer vs. Kramer,* featuring Dustin Hoffman in his most acclaimed performance in years, both dealt with the devastating effects of divorce.

Another indication of the film industry's increasing earnestness lay in the most rapturously praised movie of the year — Woody Allen's *Manhattan,* an exploration of urban romance photographed in nostalgic black-and-white and accompanied by an equally nostalgic George Gershwin score. Although *Manhattan* contained humor, Allen pursued the essentially serious tone he had established in *Annie Hall.*

Even musicals had a serious side. Milos Forman attempted to add emotional depth to his screen

Star Trek—The Motion Picture features, from left, DeForest Kelley, William Shatner, Stephen Collins, and Leonard Nimoy in space adventures.

adaptation of the long-running Broadway play *Hair.* The year's show-business biography, *The Rose,* starring singer Bette Midler, detailed the last tragic days of a rock star, modeled on the life of the late Janis Joplin.

Other Films. The year was not without its trivia. Several exploitative horror films were released, including *Alien,* a futuristic tale about a space ship menaced by a deadly form of extraterrestrial life; *The Amityville Horror,* which told of a haunted house; *Prophecy,* dealing with monsters created by ecological carelessness; George A. Romero's *Dawn of the Dead,* a sequel to his classic *Night of the Living Dead;* and John Badham's adaptation of the Broadway play *Dracula,* starring Frank Langella. With the possible exception of *Alien,* all these movies were disappointing artistically and commercially.

Just as those horror films were prompted by the success of *The Exorcist* in 1974 and *The Omen* in 1976, another blockbuster — Sylvester Stallone's *Rocky* in 1977 — inspired a run of sports movies. These included *Rocky II,* a sequel; *The Main Event,* another boxing film, starring Barbra Streisand and Ryan O'Neal; *Players,* which focused on tennis; and *North Dallas Forty,* which dealt with an aging football player. *Rocky II* garnered big money, and *North Dallas Forty* reaped healthy profits and praise for actor Nick Nolte — but for the most part, the sports films were not well received.

Perhaps the most effective sports film was Peter Yates's *Breaking Away,* which really dealt with the problems of adolescence. The comedy centered on a Bloomington, Ind., youth with a passion for bicycle racing. Critically and commercially, *Breaking Away* was the sleeper of the year.

Very young filmgoers were treated to *The Muppet Movie,* featuring Jim Henson's Muppets. America's favorite nonhuman superstars Miss Piggy and Kermit the Frog were supported by a cast of human luminaries.

The year opened with a $40-million comic-book epic for youth, *Superman* (released late in 1978), and closed with a similar tale, *Star Trek — The Motion Picture.* Both relied on simplistic action and dazzling special effects. But, though the under-20 age group made up an even bigger part of the film audience than ever — up to 49 per cent of all admissions, as against 41 per cent in recent years — *Superman* was not a huge success (*Star Trek* at least opened strong). The message seemed clear — filmmakers were more interested in movies with substance, and so were audiences. Joy Gould Boyum

See also AWARDS AND PRIZES (Arts Awards); FONDA, JANE; HITCHCOCK, ALFRED; VOIGHT, JON. In the Special Reports section, see CALL IT SF OR SCI-FI, IT'S BIG! In WORLD BOOK, see MOTION PICTURE.

MOZAMBIQUE. See AFRICA.

MUSEUM. The Congress of the United States designated May 18, 1979, as National Museum Day. The observance coincided with the second International Museums Day, which is highlighted by special exhibitions and activities in museums around the world. Many museum exhibits in 1979 celebrated the United Nations International Year of the Child. The National Museums of Canada sent a children's exhibition, Ontario Science Centre's "Science Circus," on a nationwide tour. The Smithsonian Institution of Washington, D.C., organized an international symposium on museums and children.

Awards and Gifts. The Museum of Modern Art in New York City received an Oscar from the Academy of Motion Picture Arts and Sciences. The first such award made to a museum, it honored the institution's continuing work in film preservation and its treatment of film as an art medium. The annual Council of Europe Museum Prize went to the Bryggens Museum in Bergen, Norway, for preserving the cultural legacy of medieval merchants' associations.

A group of charitable foundations gave collections totaling 100,000 objects valued at $20 million to the Glenbow-Alberta Institute in Calgary, Canada. The foundations also offered the institute $2-million to help exhibit the collections. The Art Gallery of Ontario in Toronto, Canada, received 605 examples of Eskimo art.

Building Projects. In England, two new museums spanned 1,300 years of British history. A Concorde Museum building at Yeovil in Somerset, big enough to shelter Concorde 002, the British prototype of the supersonic airliner, was under construction. The Bede Monastery Museum opened at Jarrow. The museum, near Newcastle upon Tyne, displays materials and information on the Saxon and medieval history of the region where the Venerable Bede, an English historian and theologian who lived in the 600s and 700s, spent most of his life.

At Neah Bay, Wash., the Makah Indian tribe opened a museum exhibiting objects made and used by their ancestors. They had been buried by mud slides 500 years ago.

Special Exhibitions and Events. The Asian Art Museum of San Francisco and the Seattle Art Museum exhibited 345 art treasures from Korea representing 5,000 years of history. In Washington, D.C., the National Gallery of Art displayed "The Art of the Pacific Islands."

Inflationary pressures forced museums to seek increased government support in 1979. For example, the Department of Health, Education, and Welfare's Institute of Museum Services granted $7.4-million to U.S. museums mainly for operating costs, and the National Museums of Canada granted $3.5-million to 46 Canadian museums.   Ralph H. Lewis

See also VISUAL ARTS. In WORLD BOOK, see MUSEUM.

The Art Institute of Chicago celebrates its first hundred years. The museum is well known for its remarkable collection of French impressionist art.

MUSIC, CLASSICAL

The musical world tends to reflect what surrounds it. So it was not surprising that musicians and musical organizations concerned themselves in 1979 with financial matters – making ends meet – and with international politics.

Budgets were stretched more severely than ever as symphony orchestras and opera companies faced mounting deficits in an inflationary economy. The problem was made more difficult because potential donors themselves were burdened by the rising cost of living. To raise money, New York City's Metropolitan Opera sponsored a nationwide raffle in which a Gucci-designed Cadillac, a chinchilla coat, and other fancy items were offered as prizes. The Chicago Symphony went on the air once more for a weekend fund-raising radio marathon. The Seattle Opera presented Montserrat Caballé and Birgit Nilsson in concerts to benefit its sustaining fund.

The musicians, also trapped by the economic squeeze, sought better contracts. Stiffening resistance from beleaguered managements brought a series of strikes. Seattle Symphony musicians struck in February, and those at the Chicago and St. Louis symphonies in September. Orchestra members of the New York City Opera caused a shut-down in October when they rejected a contract offer.

International Politics. Russia's Ministry of Culture in September canceled a five-week fall tour of the United States by the Moscow State Symphony after the defections of three principal dancers touring the U.S. with the Bolshoi Ballet: Alexander Godunov and Leonid and Valentina Kozlov.

Music and politics threatened to be heatedly discussed following the publication in October of *Testimony,* said to be the smuggled memoirs of Russian composer Dimitri Shostakovich, who died in 1975. The memoirs describe his experiences under Stalinist repression in the 1930s, 1940s, and early 1950s and include some breast-beating on the composer's part for not having spoken out in opposition.

New and Different. In an effort to win audiences, various artists made use of classical music in a variety of nontraditional ways. For example, the renowned Italian motion-picture director Federico Fellini released *Orchestra Rehearsal,* a film in which he uses a symphony orchestra as a metaphor to express his thoughts about Fascism and tyranny. Director Joseph Losey filmed Wolfgang Amadeus Mozart's *Don Giovanni.* Not all the U.S. critics were won over by the film, but a sizable promotional campaign paved the way for national distribution.

Some Londoners frowned on the decision by classical guitarist John Williams to defect to rock music, taking along with him four other classical musicians to form a group called Sky. The musicians did not give up their heritage entirely, however, and mixed original rock compositions with "rocky" versions of such classics as the fugue from Johann Sebastian Bach's *Toccata and Fugue in D minor.*

Operas Premièred included Hans Henkeman's *Winter Cruise* (Netherlands Opera) and Siegfried Matthus' *Omphale* (Cologne, West Germany), both in January. *The Jealous Cellist and Other Acts of Misconduct,* a futuristic science-fiction opera by Eric Stokes (Minnesota Opera), and Ezra Laderman's *Galileo Galilei,* about the great Italian astronomer and his battles with conscience (Tri-Cities Opera in Binghamton, N.Y.), opened in February. Spring premières included Martin Kalmanoff's *The Harmfulness of Tobacco* (Manhattan Opera Singers, in March); John Harbison's *Full Moon in March* (Boston Music Viva, in April); *El Caballero Ledesma* by Eric Colón (Caracas, Venezuela, in May); and Stephen Paulus' *The Village Singer* (St. Louis, in June), about a church soloist living next door to the church who, when she hears she is about to be replaced, belts out music loud enough to drown out the competition. John Harbison had his second première of the year in August when *Winter's Tale* was given by the American Opera Project of the San Francisco Opera.

Soprano Beverly Sills, who took over as director of the New York City Opera in September following the resignation of Julius Rudel, participated in two world premières: Dominick Argento's *Miss Havisham's Fire,* drawn from Charles Dickens' novel *Great Expectations,* in New York City in March; and Gian Carlo Menotti's *La Loca,* based on the life of Juana of Castile, daughter of King Ferdinand and Queen Isabella of Spain, in San Diego in June.

Orchestral Works. Premières were offered by orchestras in Albany, N.Y. (Malcolm Arnold's *Eighth Symphony*); Baltimore (Leon Kirchner's *Metamorphosis*); Indianapolis (Anthony Newman's *Violin Concerto*); Minnesota (Jacob Gilboa's *Kathros Upsanterin*); New York City (Earl Kim's *Violin Concerto*); Philadelphia (Ulysses Kay's *Chariots*); Rochester, N.Y. (Erich Walter Sternberg's *Pacifica*); and Syracuse, N.Y. (Howard Boatwright's *First Symphony*). The National Symphony in Washington, D.C., added a *Flute Concerto* by Alan Hovhaness and a *Contrabassoon Concerto* by Gunther Schuller.

Some American Opera Companies took pride in offering full seasons consisting mainly of off-the-

In an imaginative new Met production of Wagner's *The Flying Dutchman,* Carol Neblett sings the role of Senta; Jose van Dam is the accursed Dutchman.

"Father" of The Pops

It has roaring cannons and tolling bells, long drumrolls and staccato bursts of trumpets – perfect music for the Fourth of July. And the 400,000 people who listened to it on Boston's Charles River Esplanade on America's Bicentennial celebration of the Fourth in 1976 loved it. They did not much care that Tchaikovsky's "1812" overture was composed to celebrate a Russian victory over a French army. Neither did the conductor, Arthur Fiedler of the Boston Pops. Conductor of the Pops from 1930 until his death at 84 in 1979, he had his own way of doing things.

Fiedler had an uncanny knack for gauging the American public's taste in concert music. His programs were light, but often innovative. He was the first to adapt the music of the Beatles to the symphony orchestra. In a single concert, he could balance Christmas carols, show tunes, and a Bach fugue. His sometimes frothy programming irritated some highbrow critics. "The classiest jukebox in the world," carped one. But Fiedler was a good conductor working with first-rate musicians.

Coupled with his programming and musical skills was a flair for showmanship that delighted his audiences. These gifts made him the best-known symphonic conductor in the United States, and by far the best selling on records. Fiedler and the Boston Pops sold more than 50 million records, and many of the jackets showed the maestro himself dressed as Santa Claus or Yankee Doodle Dandy.

Boston-born, Fiedler was bred to music. Both his grandfathers were violinists, and his father, two uncles, and a cousin all played with the Boston Symphony. Indeed, his family name in German means *fiddler*. Fiedler was born on Dec. 17, 1894, and lived in Boston until 1911. After his father retired, the family lived briefly in Austria, then moved to Berlin, where he studied at the Royal Academy of Music. Upon returning to the U.S. in 1915, he debuted with the Boston Symphony – as a violinist.

During his early years with the symphony, Fiedler played a number of instruments, including viola, piano, organ, and percussion. But his great ambition was to conduct. He formed a chamber orchestra, the Boston Sinfonietta, and in 1924 it rapidly gained a reputation for its skill and daring in playing little-known works.

The Boston Pops was already 45 years old when Fiedler became conductor in January 1930. But he dominated the Pops so completely during the decades that followed that it became almost impossible to think of the Pops without Arthur Fiedler. Although it remained a uniquely Boston institution, millions elsewhere came to know Fiedler and his orchestra through recordings and radio broadcasts. Later, millions of television viewers came to recognize the dapper, white-maned conductor with the snowy military mustache.

The man himself was a dynamo and, despite heart attacks and other ailments, remained active to the end. Besides his Pops performances and his recordings, he was a guest conductor in concert halls across the country. He dismissed those who criticized his concert fare as "culture vultures," saying, "I have trained myself to understand all kinds of music; I am not a horse with blinders on."

When he was nearly 50 years old, Fiedler gave up what he called "a very charming bachelorhood" to marry Ellen M. Bottomley, a Boston socialite some 20 years his junior. The couple had three children.

In 1969, Massachusetts proclaimed his 75th birthday as "Arthur Fiedler Day." Among the many gifts he received were a Dalmatian puppy from the Pops and a 1938 fire engine from his family. Both gifts were reminders of Fiedler's lifelong fascination with fires and fire fighting. Over the years, he had been made an honorary fire chief in about 350 cities worldwide.

Arthur Fiedler died of cardiac arrest on the morning of July 10, 1979, in his home in Brookline, Mass. That evening, assistant conductor Harry Ellis Dickson began the regular Pops concert with a change in program. He struck up a march long associated with Fiedler, John Philip Sousa's "Stars and Stripes Forever." As the orchestra played, Dickson left the podium. The Pops played the rousing march leaderless.   Edward G. Nash

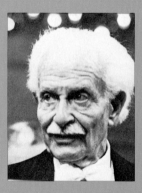

Arthur Fiedler (1894-1979)

beaten-track material. For instance, the Opera Theatre of St. Louis, which premièred *The Village Singer,* added Strauss's *Ariadne auf Naxos*; presented the U.S. première of Gustav Mahler's reconstruction of an old Carl Maria von Weber work, *The Three Pintos*; and then gave the traditionalists a break with Giuseppe Verdi's *La Traviata*. That Verdi work was on the San Francisco spring opera schedule; the rest of the season went to Musgrave's *Mary, Queen of Scots,* Jacques Offenbach's *La Perichole,* and Benjamin Britten's *Death in Venice.*

The U.S. première of Peter Schat's five-act, 17-scene *Houdini* in Aspen, Colo., required 30 soloists, circus performers, and dancers, and an orchestra that included steel drums. The first complete performance of Alban Berg's *Lulu* in the United States was staged in Santa Fe, N. Mex. Ottorino Respighi's *Lucrezia* had its U.S. debut at the Caramoor Festival in Katonah, N.Y., and Giacomo Meyerbeer's *Crusader in Egypt,* in New York City by the Sacred Music Society. The Boston Opera gave Sir Michael Tippett's *The Ice Break* its U.S. première.

Other unusual selections included Jules Massenet's *La Navarraise* (Tulsa, Okla.), his *Sappho* (Friends of French Opera in New York), and his *Cendrillon* (Washington, D.C.); the Kurt Weill-Bertolt Brecht *Rise and Fall of the City of Mahagonny* (New York City's Metropolitan); and Thomas Pasatieri's *Washington Square* (Augusta, Ga.).

Tours and Festivals. The Kirov Theatre of Leningrad, Russia, went to West Germany. The Dresden State Orchestra traveled to the United States, and the Vienna State Opera spent three much-heralded weeks at the Kennedy Center. The Boston Symphony went to China and the Cleveland Orchestra to Europe. The San Francisco Opera toured for the first time, traveling to the Philippines. For Chicago's Lyric Opera, an appearance at the Cervantes Festival in Mexico was another first, and the Baltimore Symphony also performed in Mexico.

The Houston Grand Opera and Chicago's Lyric Opera celebrated their 25th anniversaries; the Indianapolis Symphony, its 50th. The Dallas Symphony was 80 years old and the St. Louis Symphony, 100. It was 100 years of performances for the Geneva Grand Theatre in Switzerland and 200 for Mannheim's National Theatre in West Germany.

Festivals continued to be popular. They included both a Handel Festival and a celebration of "Paris: The Romantic Epoch" at the Kennedy Center; a Verdi Festival by the San Diego Opera; and Beethoven festivals in Seattle and Dallas, the latter including all of his symphonies, piano concertos, and major overtures, as well as the violin concerto.

Honors. Soprano Victoria de Los Angeles became the first recipient in 40 years of Spain's most prestigious cultural honor, the National Art Prize. Another soprano, Zinka Milanov, was similarly honored by her homeland, Yugoslavia. Australian soprano Joan

Music lovers throng the lobby of Civic Opera House on September 22 for opening night of the Lyric Opera of Chicago's 25th anniversary season.

Sutherland became a Dame Commander of the Order of the British Empire. Oxford University bestowed doctor of music degrees on West German baritone Dietrich Fischer-Dieskau and Austrian conductor Herbert von Karajan. Another conductor, Eugene Ormandy, in his 44th – and final – season with the Philadelphia Orchestra, received the Gold Baton of the American Symphony Orchestra League for "distinguished service to music."

Similar awards came from the National Opera Institute to the Santa Fe Opera for service to young artists; the Minnesota Opera for creation of new works; and the Seattle Opera for community service. Seattle's artistic director, Glynn Ross, was given West Germany's Order of Merit First Class, for championing Richard Wagner's *Ring* cycle. Lyric Opera's Carol Fox was cited by the Italian government for her service to opera. The Kennedy Center's Honors Awards included one for composer Aaron Copland. Tenor Luciano Pavarotti made the cover of *Time* magazine, and a five-room museum opened in Paris in memory of the late diva Maria Callas.

A New Luminary emerged in a series of U.S. debut concerts by Russian pianist Bella Davidovich, and critics and audiences responded enthusiastically to her playing. Another luminary, Arthur Fiedler, for 50 years conductor of the Boston Pops, died on July 10. See CLOSE-UP.   Peter P. Jacobi

In WORLD BOOK, see MUSIC.

MUSIC, POPULAR. The increasing popularity of the so-called new wave bands, both in Great Britain and the United States, was accompanied by a declining interest in disco music during 1979. The new wave groups and personalities, including Blondie, The Knack, the B-52s, Elvis Costello, Bram Tchaikovsky, and the Talking Heads, generally avoided the sleaziness and sensationalism that characterized punk rock.

As the audience for disco music began to drop off, disco clubs and radio stations began to incorporate rhythm and blues, new wave rock, and even country music into their programming. This new mix was often referred to simply as "dance music."

While most of those who disliked disco music simply boycotted it, a few responded more violently. For example, a riot broke out when Chicago rock disc jockey Steve Dahl held a disco-record-smashing ceremony at a Chicago White Sox-Detroit Tigers doubleheader in July. The White Sox had to forfeit the second game because the playing field was damaged by the antidisco demonstrators.

Top Artists. One of the most popular groups of the year was the British hard rock quartet Led Zeppelin. The release of "In Through The Out Door," the group's first new album in three years, led to a great surge of interest in all their previous releases. Within a short time Led Zeppelin had eight albums on the best-seller charts.

Although many "middle-of-the-road" (MOR) artists saw their records drop off the charts and the demand for their music fade, Herb Alpert, the trumpeter and bandleader, better known as the founder of A & M Records and the Tijuana Brass, achieved a surprise return. Alpert organized a new backup group to record a single record, "Rise," composed by his nephew, Randy Badazz, and Andy Armer. Its leap to the top of the charts prompted Alpert to record additional material and include "Rise" in an album.

Another MOR artist, Dionne Warwick, whose star had waned since the breakup of her partnership with the song-writing team of Burt Bacharach and Hal David, returned to the forefront with the help of another songwriter-producer, Barry Manilow. "I'll Never Love This Way Again," which Manilow wrote and produced, became her biggest hit single in years and was included in "Dionne," an album that *went gold* – that is, sold half a million copies.

Bob Dylan also successfully returned to the recording studios to produce the heavily spiritual "Slow Train Coming." His first studio-taped album released in more than a year, it soon topped the half-million sales mark. Dylan followed it up with a few of his rare appearances in concerts and on TV.

There was a growing tendency for pop superstars to minimize their personal appearances and time

them to coincide with the release of a record or movie. The Who toured the United States in December to promote their film, *Quadrophenia.* Eleven persons were trampled to death at the group's concert in Cincinnati on December 3 as thousands of fans attempted to get a limited number of general-admission seats.

Elton John's tour provided a happier contrast, however. In May, he became the first major international rock star to play in Russia, and his performances there drew a highly emotional response from popular music fans.

Soul and Country Music. Soul music, which enjoyed wide appeal among black audiences and is performed almost exclusively by black artists, maintained its strength. Michael Jackson, the Commodores, Ashford & Simpson, Funkadelic, and Earth, Wind & Fire retained and enlarged their followings.

The tendency for country music personalities to cross over to acceptance with pop and rock audiences continued. Such artists as Willie Nelson, Kenny Rogers, Dolly Parton, Crystal Gayle, and Waylon Jennings led the way.

In a ceremony at the White House on June 16, the Country Music Association presented President Jimmy Carter with an award commending his "enthusiasm" for the music. At its annual awards ceremony on October 8, the association named Willie Nelson entertainer of the year; Kenny Rogers, best male vocalist; Barbara Mandrell, best female vocalist; Charlie Daniels, best instrumentalist; and the Statler Brothers, best group.

Stage and Screen. Rock and country music stars invaded the motion-picture screen in unprecedented numbers in 1979. By October, at least nine country music films were in the planning stage or already in production. Several films involving rock musicians were released in 1979. Elvis Costello performed in *Americathon;* punk rock with the Ramones was featured in *Rock and Roll High School;* and The Who appeared in both *The Kids Are Alright,* based on a history of their career, and *Quadrophenia,* a film spin-off of their rock opera album.

A new rock opera, *Evita,* by Tim Rice and Andrew Lloyd Webber, who wrote *Jesus Christ Superstar,* came to the United States from London. After brief runs in Los Angeles and San Francisco in the spring it opened in New York City in September. *Grease,* the nostalgic rock-and-roll musical, with its 3,243rd performance on December 8, became the longest-running Broadway show in history.

Six "macho men," collectively known as the Village People, sang suggestive lyrics to a disco beat and generated a series of hit records in 1979.

Singer Kenny Rogers displays one of his trophies after the Academy of Country Music named him Entertainer of the Year and Top Male Vocalist.

The Jazz Scene. Jazz lost another major big-band leader with the death of Stan Kenton on August 25. His will stipulated that there would be no Kenton "ghost band" like the orchestras now using the names of Glenn Miller and Tommy Dorsey.

The Crusaders, once known as the Jazz Crusaders, scored multiple triumphs. The group reached the top of the jazz charts with the album "Street Life," and two of its founders, pianist Joe Sample and drummer Stix Hooper, scored with albums.

Singer Joni Mitchell attracted a broad audience, including many jazz fans, with "Mingus," an album dedicated to the great bassist and composer Charles Mingus, who died on January 5. Mitchell wrote lyrics to several of Mingus' compositions. Mitchell was among the participants when the Hollywood Bowl in Hollywood, Calif., drew big crowds for a two-night jazz festival presented by *Playboy* in June.

Two pianists also made a deep impression at jazz festivals during the year. JoAnne Brackeen, who formerly played with the Stan Getz Quartet, was featured at the second annual Women's Jazz Festival in Kansas City in March; and Tete Montoliu, a blind soloist from Barcelona, Spain, made his American jazz festival debut at Monterey, Calif., in September. Leonard Feather and Eliot Tiegel

See also AWARDS AND PRIZES; RECORDINGS. In WORLD BOOK, see JAZZ; POPULAR MUSIC; ROCK MUSIC.

MUZOREWA, ABEL TENDEKAYI (1925-   ), became the first black prime minister of Zimbabwe Rhodesia on May 29, 1979. His party, the United African National Council, won 67.3 per cent of the popular vote. He served until December, when a British colonial government took over until new elections in 1980. See ZIMBABWE RHODESIA.

Muzorewa was born on April 14, 1925, near an American Methodist settlement in eastern Rhodesia. His father was trained as a minister and teacher, but turned to farming to support his family. Muzorewa worked on the farm and attended a mission school nearby. After completing school, he wandered as a lay evangelist, preaching to tribes in the mountainous Mozambique border region.

On a scholarship, Muzorewa attended Methodist colleges in Fayette, Mo., and Nashville, Tenn., from 1958 to 1963. He was consecrated bishop of the 55,000-member Rhodesian wing of the United Methodist Church in 1968. Bishop Muzorewa campaigned successfully in 1971 and 1972 against the adoption of a constitution that would have given blacks only token representation in the government.

His ability to unite some black nationalist factions and to compromise with Rhodesia's ruling whites enabled Muzorewa to lead his party to victory. Although an unimpressive speaker, he dresses dramatically, often substituting vivid robes or stylishly tailored suits for his clerical collar. Beverly Merz

NAMIBIA. Administrator-General Marthinus T. Steyn ended the legal segregation of Namibia's hotels, restaurants, and residential neighborhoods in 1979. His action aroused anger among the territory's whites and led to Steyn's dismissal by South Africa on August 1. Namibia, or South West Africa, has been ruled by South Africa since 1920.

The guerrilla war between South African military forces and supporters of the South West Africa People's Organization (SWAPO) continued. South Africa said on May 8 that it would establish a Namibian assembly with limited legislative authority. SWAPO opposed this plan because the assembly appeared likely to be dominated by a white-led party, the Democratic Turnhalle Alliance (DTA). The DTA advocated a constitution that would divide political power among Namibia's main ethnic groups and give whites a veto over all major issues affecting whites.

Canada, France, Great Britain, the United States, and West Germany proposed a peace plan in October. The proposal called for a cease-fire in the guerrilla war, a demilitarized zone along both sides of Namibia's border with Angola (where SWAPO had bases), United Nations (UN) monitoring of the cease-fire, and UN-supervised elections leading to black-majority rule. John D. Esseks

See also AFRICA (Facts in Brief Table); SOUTH AFRICA. In WORLD BOOK, see SOUTH WEST AFRICA.

NETHERLANDS

NATIONAL PTA (NATIONAL CONGRESS OF PARENTS AND TEACHERS) continued in 1979 to give priority to preserving and strengthening public education. Under its new president, Virginia Sparling of Bellevue, Wash., the PTA continued its battle against offensive television programming; acted to focus national attention on the problems plaguing urban areas and city schools; increased public awareness of the need for comprehensive school-community health education; and launched a nutrition-education project related to school breakfast and lunch programs.

PTA members also studied such issues as corporal punishment and the effect of standardized and minimal-competency testing. The PTA's TV Project has influenced parents and television producers alike. PTA protests were believed to be responsible for a reduction in the amount of TV violence in 1979. The PTA released four *TV Program Review Guides,* which offer parents recommendations for family viewing, and was developing a curriculum in TV-viewing skills.   Virginia E. Anderson

In WORLD BOOK, see NATIONAL CONGRESS OF PARENTS AND TEACHERS; PARENT-TEACHER ORGANIZATIONS.

NAVY. See ARMED FORCES.

NEBRASKA. See STATE GOVERNMENT.

NEPAL. See ASIA.

NETHERLANDS. Prime Minister Andreas A.M. Van Agt drew criticism from unions and employers alike when he announced a 1980 budget of $66.8-billion on Sept. 18, 1979, though it included $1-billion to boost employment, strengthen industry, and save energy. Both spending and revenues would be 11 per cent higher than in 1979.

The government planned to increase tax revenue by adjusting tax brackets only partially to compensate for inflation. Lower-income workers would get tax cuts, but the unions questioned whether these cuts would be substantial enough to improve the workers' purchasing power. Employers said that the failure to cut government spending would confine most of the economic growth to the public sector, leaving too little to generate profits. Van Agt's Christian Democrat Party complained that the budget would not reduce unemployment in 1980. The Liberals, partners in the ruling coalition, said that it would not lift industry's tax and social security burdens.

Wage Demands. The Netherlands' largest trade union federation, FNV, demanded wage hikes early in 1979 to make up for price increases. FNV chairman Wim Kok said this would keep the average worker's real disposable income at $15,000 per year. Insurance employees dropped demands for a 35-hour week in April. Agreements reached in May

Dutch troops practice civilian-control techniques in the Netherlands before joining a United Nations detachment in Lebanon in October.

included payments for early retirement and extra vacation days.

Missile Bases. The government opposed a North Atlantic Treaty Organization (NATO) plan to install in Western Europe United States cruise missiles and Pershing 2 missiles that could hit targets in Russia. Van Agt traveled to Italy, Great Britain, the United States, and West Germany early in December to explain his country's position.

Gas Exports. The government began a 20-year program of annual 5 per cent reductions in gas production from the Groningen field in the North Sea. About half of Europe's natural gas originated from this source in 1977, providing 10 per cent of the nation's income. Peak production was 97 billion cubic meters (3.5 trillion cubic feet) in 1977. Production was cut to 90 billion cubic meters (3.2 trillion cubic feet) in 1979. The government agreed on April 5 to comply with European Community (Common Market) requests to cut oil consumption by 5 per cent. The country's only nuclear power station, which is located at Borssele, was shut down on April 19 and August 7 because of problems with the steam turbine's transmission system. Construction of three plants has stopped, pending a two-year public debate.   Kenneth Brown

See also EUROPE (Facts in Brief Table). In WORLD BOOK, see NETHERLANDS.

NEVADA. See STATE GOVERNMENT.

NEW BRUNSWICK. With strength in the legislature almost evenly divided between Conservatives and Liberals, the Conservative government chose a speaker from Liberal ranks on Feb. 1, 1979. Premier Richard B. Hatfield, with 30 Conservative seats in the 58-seat legislature, chose Robert McCready as speaker, thus reducing Liberal strength by one vote. A senate appointment in March further reduced Liberal voting power but the Liberals recaptured the seat in a November 5 by-election. McCready was expelled from the Liberal Party and given police protection for a time because feelings against him ran so high.

The legislature dealt with 86 bills during a session that ran from March 12 to June 14. Participation fees for hospital services were approved, making New Brunswick the seventh province to ask for this payment. The largest budget in the province's history was presented on March 29 by Finance Minister Fernand Dubé. It showed a deficit of $91.4 million.

A police strike left Bathurst without police protection for a week until a new contract was signed on July 11.   David M.L. Farr

See also CANADA. In WORLD BOOK, see NEW BRUNSWICK.

NEW HAMPSHIRE. See STATE GOVERNMENT.
NEW JERSEY. See STATE GOVERNMENT.
NEW MEXICO. See STATE GOVERNMENT.
NEW YORK. See NEW YORK CITY; STATE GOV'T.

NEW YORK CITY told the federal government in September 1979 that its comeback from near fiscal collapse in 1975 had left it in a better position to cope with a national economic recession. The report noted that "the first half of 1979 was favorable for the city government," and reported a general reserve surplus of $117 million.

The city demonstrated its improved fiscal health on January 22 when it re-entered the public credit market for the first time in four years, selling $125-million in short-term notes. The sale followed a qualified favorable credit rating given to the city on January 17 by Moody's Investors Service.

Administration Changes. Mayor Edward I. Koch announced a major streamlining of his administration on August 2, revealing that five of the city's seven deputy mayors would be leaving office by year-end. Their positions – those for policy, finance, intergovernmental affairs, administration, and criminal justice – would be eliminated. Koch created a new post – deputy mayor for operations.

Deputy Mayor for Human Services Haskell G. Ward, the highest ranking black in the Koch administration, resigned on August 20, reportedly after disagreeing with Koch's plan to close an East Harlem hospital as an economy measure. John G. de Roos resigned as senior executive officer of the New York City Transit Authority on June 22. He had

A New York City transit policeman waits with passengers on a platform as a campaign to fight subway crime goes into effect in March.

been criticized for opposing a lawsuit that had been filed against two manufacturers of defective subway equipment.

Strike Problems. New York City's 17 municipal hospitals survived their first strike on January 17 when interns and residents defied a court injunction and walked off the job for a day to protest planned cutbacks. New York City milk and dairy workers voted to accept a new contract on April 28, ending a nine-week strike.

An 88-day tugboat strike that idled the city's garbage barges caused litter to accumulate because street-cleaning crews were diverted to haul garbage to alternate dump sites. The problem was aggravated by a service-workers' strike from April 23 to May 1 that prevented the collection of garbage from thousands of apartment buildings. The tug strike was settled on June 27.

Subway Crime. To combat an increasing number of murders and other crimes in the subway system, Koch instituted a system of "saturation patrols" by transit police on March 17. However, he became dissatisfied with the system, put the transit patrol under the control of the New York City Police Department in September, then discontinued the program on December 31.   James M. Banovetz

See also CITY. In WORLD BOOK, see NEW YORK CITY.

NEW ZEALAND made a slow recovery from its economic recession in 1979. Real incomes grew at a faster rate, and prices for the country's important agricultural exports generally improved. However, balance-of-payments difficulties continued; partly because of reliance on imported petroleum. To reduce energy consumption, the government introduced no-driving days, restricted gasoline sales on weekends, rationed home-heating fuels, increased taxes on some fuels, and sharply increased electricity prices. It also moved to develop New Zealand's own energy resources by deciding to construct a multimillion-dollar methanol plant that would use offshore natural gas.

The Economy. While inflation fell to about 10 per cent annually, the rate was still higher than those of most of New Zealand's trading partners and seemed likely to increase in 1980. Government-backed increases in the 1979 rates for electricity, postal service, and rail freight added to the inflation spiral.

The government's deflationary policies were partly responsible for a significant increase in unemployment. About 4 per cent of the labor force was out of work, and some 40,000 persons emigrated to Australia in search of jobs.

The 1979 budget provided for new export incentives; lower income tax rates, particularly on middle-level incomes; higher sales taxes; and a

Prime Minister Robert D. Muldoon chats with British counterpart Margaret Thatcher about national and Commonwealth matters on a June visit to England.

reduction in the government's deficit before borrowing. Despite fairly tight controls on government spending in 1978, the deficit ballooned from an estimated $1 billion to $1.5 billion.

Politics. Prime Minister Robert D. Muldoon's conservative National Party continued in power after the triennial election in November 1978, though with a significantly reduced majority.

The new House of Representatives had 51 National members, 40 Labour, and 1 Social Credit, giving National an overall majority of 10 seats, compared with 23 in the previous Parliament. The moderate-left opposition Labour Party, led by former Prime Minister Wallace E. Rowling, made heavy gains and outpolled the National Party in popular votes in the South Island, where dissatisfaction with lack of regional development policies was strong. The Social Credit Party, led by B.E. Beetham and advocating monetary reforms, polled about 16 per cent of the total votes, reflecting widespread disenchantment with both major parties.

An Airline Disaster, the fourth worst in history, occurred on November 28 when an Air New Zealand DC-10 that was carrying 257 persons on a sightseeing flight from Christchurch to the Antarctic crashed with no survivors into Mt. Erebus in the McMurdo Sound.   David A. Shand

See also ASIA (Facts in Brief Table). In WORLD BOOK, see NEW ZEALAND.

NEWFOUNDLAND. The two major political parties changed leaders, and a new premier took office in 1979. Frank Moores, Conservative premier since 1972, announced his resignation on January 19, and the ruling Progressive Conservative Party on March 17 elected Brian Peckford, the 36-year-old minister of mines and energy in Moores's cabinet, leader.

Peckford became premier on March 26 and later called an election for June 18. Liberal leader William Rowe, who lost party support when he admitted leaking confidential police reports on an arson investigation, stepped down in July in favor of a new leader. The party executive then appointed Donald C. Jamieson to head the Liberals. The 58-year-old former minister of external affairs had just been re-elected to a federal seat. The Conservatives and Peckford won the June 18 province election easily, taking 33 of the legislature's 52 seats to the Liberals' 19. Peckford revamped his cabinet on July 3, bringing in two women ministers, Newfoundland's first.

Amid reports that Chevron Standard Limited had found promising traces of hydrocarbons while drilling on the Grand Banks, Peckford won an important concession from Prime Minister Joe Clark on September 5. Clark agreed to turn over federal control of offshore oil and mineral resources to the island province.   David M. L. Farr

See also CANADA. In WORLD BOOK, see NEWFOUNDLAND.

NEWSPAPER. *The Times* of London returned to the newsstands on Nov. 12, 1979, after an absence of almost a year. *The Times* and its companion, *The Sunday Times,* had been shut down on Nov. 30, 1978, in a labor dispute over the inauguration of computer typesetting, press-manning requirements, and wildcat strikes.

The dispute was resolved on October 21, a few hours short of the deadline set by the papers' owner, Lord Thomson of Fleet (Kenneth Roy Thomson), who had vowed to cease publishing if an agreement was not reached by 4 P.M. that day. Under the terms of the settlement, the Thomson organization agreed to defer the question of computer typesetting for 12 months, the unions agreed to a reduction in the number of press personnel, and both sides agreed on a new procedure for settling disputes.

An eight-month strike forced the 111-year-old *Montreal Star* to close its doors on September 25. F. P. Publications, Incorporated, the paper's owner, reported that the *Star* had lost $17.4 million – $7-million during the walkout of press personnel that ended in February and an additional $10.4 million due to a decline in circulation after it resumed publication.

Mergers, Changes, and Contracts. McClatchy Newspapers of Sacramento, Calif., purchased an 80 per cent interest in the *Anchorage Daily News,* Alaska's only morning newspaper, in January. The *News* became the chain's fifth newspaper and its first published outside California. *The St. Louis Post-Dispatch* and the *St. Louis Globe-Democrat* agreed to merge their business functions on April 16.

Two major papers instituted new editions in attempts to offset declining evening circulation. *The Boston Globe* replaced its morning and evening papers with a seven-edition all-day paper on February 5. *The Washington Star,* an afternoon newspaper acquired by Time, Incorporated, in 1978, inaugurated a morning edition on July 9.

The Washington Post and The Newspaper Guild, a union of editorial and clerical workers, signed a contract on July 30, ending a three-year contract lapse. The new agreement, effective through July 1982, gave *Post* reporters the highest minimum pay – $596 per week – of any United States newspaper under guild contract. Both parties pledged to allow the National Labor Relations Board to decide whether 160 jobs covered in the contract can be excluded from guild jurisdiction, as *The Post* insists.

Personnel Changes. Katherine Graham was succeeded as publisher of *The Washington Post* on January 10 by her son, Donald. She remained chairman and chief executive of the Washington Post Company. Robert C. Maynard became editor of *The Oakland Tribune* in September. He is the first black to direct editorial operations on a major U.S. daily newspaper.   Beverly Merz

In WORLD BOOK, see JOURNALISM; NEWSPAPER.

Junta members and officers of the Sandinista rebel movement make their first
public appearance after deposing Nicaragua's President Somoza in July.

NICARAGUA. President Anastasio Somoza Debayle resigned under pressure on July 17, 1979, thus ending a 42-year rule by the Somoza family. Somoza, accompanied by 45 top aides and family members, went into exile in Miami Beach, Fla.

Two days later, the Sandinista National Liberation Front guerrillas seized control of Managua, the capital. The take-over ended a seven-week-long civil war during which about 10,000 Nicaraguans were killed and nearly 500,000 left homeless.

A government was formed by a provisional military junta nominally headed by Sergio Ramírez Mercado and including Alfonso Robelo Callejas, Violeta Barrios de Chamorro, Moises Hassan Morales, and Daniel Ortega Saavedra. It announced plans to elect a 30-member legislative council by popular vote as soon as the country's political stability has been re-established and its economy has been revived.

Restrictions Eased. The junta promulgated a series of measures on August 9 easing curfew hours, lifting roadblocks, and granting permission for such public enterprises as movie theaters and restaurants to function "during normal night hours." On August 21, the junta issued a provisional 14-page, 52-article bill of rights that guaranteed a broad range of liberties, including "the right to freely and fully determine the political system and future economic, social, and cultural development." The bill also abolished the death penalty, set up strict guidelines for the administration of justice, and ruled against detention of any person without a court order "except in cases of flagrant crimes." Simultaneously, the junta announced that a council consisting of representatives from the country's major economic and social institutions would serve as a legislature until national elections could be held sometime in 1982.

Measures to speed the nation's economic recovery were announced by the junta in September. Nicaragua's monetary unit, the córdoba, was fixed at 10 units to the U.S. dollar in order to "eliminate the differences established by the Somoza regime between the purchase rate and the selling rate of foreign money."

Foreign Debts Repudiated. Ortega addressed the United Nations General Assembly in New York City on September 28, and announced that Nicaragua would be unable to repay $600 million in foreign loans granted to the Somoza regime. He said that the debt would have to be assumed by the international community. Financial experts believed, however, that Nicaragua's total foreign debt was closer to $1.6-billion. They contended that the $600-million figure represented only payments due in 1979 on the loans, most of them from private sources. Paul C. Tullier

See also LATIN AMERICA (Facts in Brief Table). In WORLD BOOK, see NICARAGUA.

NICKLAUS, JACK (1940-   ), one of the world's greatest golfers, was named the Athlete of the Decade for the period from 1969 to 1979 in May 1979. Nicklaus was named in a nationwide poll of 432 United States sports writers, editors, and broadcasters that was sponsored by the American Cancer Society.

Nicklaus has won 17 major championships and more than $3.4 million in prize money in a tournament golf career that began in the 1955 National Amateur tournament. He won the U.S. Amateur title in 1959 and 1961, then became a professional.

He became a star almost immediately. He beat Arnold Palmer in June 1962 in the United States Open, and a few months later he beat Palmer and Gary Player of South Africa in the first World Series of Golf. Nicklaus is the only golfer to win the famed Masters tournament five times. His success brought him wealth, and he heads a multimillion-dollar conglomerate, Golden Bear, Incorporated. The conglomerate has automobile dealerships, builds golf courses, and deals in real estate and merchandise.

Born on Jan. 21, 1940, in Columbus, Ohio, Nicklaus started playing golf when he was 10. He attended Ohio State University and became an outstanding collegiate golfer there. He played on the United States Walker Cup team in 1959. Nicklaus married Barbara Bash in 1960.   Joseph P. Spohn

NIGER. See AFRICA.

Pyramids of sacked groundnuts bear testimony to Nigeria's agricultural abundance. Some of it is stockpiled to avert future food shortages.

NIGERIA inaugurated its first civilian government in more than 13 years on Oct. 1, 1979. Power was transferred from the 23-member Supreme Military Council, headed by Lieutenant General Olusegun Obasanjo, to a national government composed of an elected president, Senate, and House of Representatives. On the same date, elected governors and legislators took office in Nigeria's 19 states.

Separate elections for each office took place on weekends from July 7 to August 11. The Federal Electoral Commission screened parties and candidates, and only five of the 52 parties that applied were permitted to enter candidates in the races. The commission also disqualified about 1,000 of nearly 9,000 candidates, most for nonpayment of taxes.

No party obtained a majority in either house of the national parliament. Most successful was the National Party of Nigeria (NPN), which won 38 per cent of the Senate seats and 37 per cent of those in the House of Representatives. Most of its support came from the Muslim northern region of Nigeria.

Shehu Shagari of the NPN was declared winner in the race for the presidency, an office with powers similar to those of the President of the United States (see SHAGARI, SHEHU). Shagari received about 5.7 million votes to the 4.9 million polled by his nearest rival, Chief Obafemi Awolowo of the United Party. However, there was a dispute over whether Shagari won the required 25 per cent of the vote in at least two-thirds of Nigeria's states. This condition, set by the military government's 1977 Election Decree to lessen the effect of regional and ethnic rivalries, was designed to prevent a candidate from winning with support from only one or two parts of the country.

Shagari received the required 25 per cent of the votes cast in 12 of the 19 states, but only 20 per cent in a 13th. However, the electoral commission ruled that this distribution of votes was sufficient.

An Oil Economy. The new civilian government inherited a relatively healthy economy. Inflation was down from 25 per cent in 1977 to an estimated 10 per cent in 1979. Nigeria's large oil production and high market prices boosted foreign-exchange reserves to about $4 billion.

Nigeria used its oil resources as a foreign-policy weapon. It warned Great Britain and the United States in May that it would retaliate if either nation extended diplomatic recognition to the government of President Abel T. Muzorewa in Zimbabwe Rhodesia (see ZIMBABWE RHODESIA). Nigeria is the second most important source – after Saudi Arabia – of imported oil for the United States. On July 31, Nigeria nationalized the British share in the Nigerian-Shell-British Petroleum Oil Company. Nigeria said British Petroleum had been supplying oil to white-ruled South Africa.   John D. Esseks

See also AFRICA (Facts in Brief Table). In WORLD BOOK, see NIGERIA.

NIXON, RICHARD MILHOUS (1913-   ), 37th President of the United States, prepared to move from San Clemente, Calif., to New York City in 1979 and to become more active in public life. However, continuing legal battles stemming from the conduct of his Administration shadowed his efforts to take up a new role as elder statesman.

Nixon returned to the White House on January 29 – the first time since his resignation on Aug. 9, 1974 – to attend a state dinner for China's Deputy Premier Teng Hsiao-p'ing (Deng Xiaoping in the phonetic Pinyin alphabet China adopted on January 1). Nixon met privately with Teng on January 31.

At the invitation of the Chinese government, Nixon and his wife, Pat, flew to Peking (Beijing) for a four-day visit during September. He was honored at a dinner hosted by Teng, and met with Prime Minister Hua Kuo-feng (Hua Guofeng), who called him an "old friend." This was Nixon's third trip to China – his second as a private citizen.

Legal Problems. The United States Court of Appeals for the District of Columbia on July 12 upheld a lower court ruling that "Presidents are scarcely immune from the judicial process." The ruling reinstated cases against Nixon, former Secretary of State Henry A. Kissinger, and others who had been charged with authorizing illegal wiretaps placed on the phones of former Kissinger aide Morton Halperin and *New York Times* correspondent Hedrick Smith.

Nixon received another legal setback on July 24 when U.S. District Court Judge Aubrey E. Robinson, Jr., approved plans for the public release of Nixon's White House tape recordings. Robinson also ruled that archivists could screen Nixon's recorded diaries to determine which thoughts were private and which could be made public.

Home and Family. The Nixons sold their San Clemente estate, La Casa Pacifica, early in 1979, reportedly for more than $2 million. After the sale, a "sense of Senate resolution," which does not have the force of law, asked Nixon to reimburse the U.S. government for about $60,000 of $764,000 in improvements made at taxpayers' expense for security reasons. Nixon paid $2,300 – the cost of erecting a flagpole that he wanted to keep – and asked that the government remove the other improvements within 60 days.

Nixon also made two attempts to buy an apartment in New York City in 1979. He withdrew both offers when tenants in the buildings objected that security measures associated with the Nixon tenancy would violate their privacy. In October, the Nixons bought a single-family town house instead.

The Nixons' first grandson, Christopher Nixon Cox, was born on March 14. He is the first child of Edward and Tricia Nixon Cox.   Carol L. Thompson

In WORLD BOOK, see NIXON, RICHARD MILHOUS.

Former President Richard M. Nixon shows off his first grandson, Christopher Nixon Cox, who was born to Edward and Tricia Nixon Cox on March 14.

NOBEL PRIZES in peace, literature, economics, and various sciences were awarded in 1979. Five of the 10 winners are Americans.

Peace Prize. Mother Teresa, 69, an Albanian Roman Catholic nun who has worked among the poor and sick of Calcutta, India, for more than 30 years, was named winner of the 1979 prize. She became the first person to win this prize for work involved with religion since civil rights leader Martin Luther King, Jr., a Baptist minister, was so honored in 1964. Born Agnes Ganxha Bojaxhiu, the daughter of a grocer, she went to India in 1928. At first she taught school in Calcutta, but in 1948 she decided to work among the poor of that city. In making the award, the Nobel committee said, "This year, the world has turned its attention to the plight of children and refugees, and these are precisely the categories for whom Mother Teresa has for many years worked so selflessly."

Literature Prize was given to Odysseus Elytis, 68, a Greek poet noted for his lyric verse and the way he uses myths and legends. Only one other Greek poet has received the award, George Seferis in 1963. Elytis became known as a poet in Greece during World War II, when he wrote poetry while aiding the underground resistance to the Italian Fascists in Albania. The Nobel committee praised Elytis especially for his *Axion Esti* (*Worthy It Is*), published in 1959 as part of a cycle of mythical poems.

Mother Teresa, an Albanian-born nun, won the 1979 Nobel Peace Prize for her more than 30 years' work with the poor and ailing of Calcutta, India.

Georg Wittig, a West German professor, shares his happiness with reporters on learning he is the co-winner of the 1979 Nobel Prize for Chemistry.

Economics Prize was awarded jointly to Theodore W. Schultz, 77, a professor at the University of Chicago, and Sir W. Arthur Lewis, 64, a British economist born in the West Indies and a professor at Princeton University. They were cited for "finding ways out of underdevelopment" and for "being deeply concerned about the need and poverty in the world." Lewis was the first black to receive a Nobel Prize in any category other than peace.

Chemistry Prize was shared by Herbert C. Brown, 67, of Purdue University in Indiana, and Georg Wittig, 82, of the University of Heidelberg in West Germany. Both men have devoted most of their careers to developing *reagents,* a group of substances capable of facilitating otherwise difficult chemical reactions. Their discoveries have made possible the mass production at reasonable cost of hundreds of important pharmaceuticals and industrial chemicals. Wittig based his work on compounds of phosphorus; Brown's was based primarily on compounds of boron.

Physics Prize was shared by Steven Weinberg, 46, and Sheldon L. Glashow, 46, both of Harvard University, and Abdus Salam, 53, a Pakistani physicist who works at universities in London and Trieste, Italy. They were honored for their complementary research on what physicists call the Weinberg-Salam Theory of Weak Interactions. The theory is regarded as a major step toward a unifying concept that links three fundamental forces of nature – electromagnetism, the strong interaction, and the weak interaction. Working separately, Weinberg and Salam developed a system of equations to make this link. Initial problems in applying the theory were numerous, but were overcome by Glashow's research on a type of fundamental particle known as the "charmed quark."

Physiology or Medicine Prize went to Allan M. Cormack, 55, a physicist at Tufts University in Medford, Mass., and Godfrey N. Hounsfield, 60, a British electronics engineer on the research staff of EMI, Limited, in Great Britain, for developing the computerized axial tomograph (CAT) scan, a new X-ray technique that gives doctors an astonishingly clear look into the living body. The CAT scan, which has been used to help diagnose ailments in millions of patients, allows technicians to take X-ray pictures with a rotating tube aided by a computer that reveals sections of the anatomy in more detail than is possible through other nonsurgical techniques. Cormack was born in South Africa but moved to the United States in 1956 and later became a naturalized citizen.   Foster Stockwell

In WORLD BOOK, see NOBEL PRIZES.

NORTH ATLANTIC TREATY ORGANIZATION (NATO). See EUROPE.

NORTH CAROLINA. See STATE GOVERNMENT.

NORTH DAKOTA. See STATE GOVERNMENT.

NORTHERN IRELAND experienced an even greater hardening of attitudes among extremists on both sides of the independence question in 1979. Protestants and Roman Catholics alike awaited a fresh political initiative promised by the Conservative government elected in May in Great Britain.

Airey Neave, the Conservative Party's spokesman on Northern Ireland, and a confidant of Prime Minister Margaret Thatcher, was killed on March 30 when a bomb exploded in his car outside the House of Commons in London. Then, on August 27, Lord Louis Mountbatten and three others were murdered in the Republic of Ireland, and 18 British soldiers were killed in Northern Ireland by a bomb hidden in a truck (see IRELAND). That attack marked the highest death toll in one incident for British troops in 10 years in Northern Ireland.

The INLA. Responsibility for Neave's murder was claimed by the Irish National Liberation Army (INLA), a shadowy new leftist guerrilla group that is thought to have about 100 members. INLA's stated objective is to create a Marxist united Ireland. Roy Mason, the British Labour Party's minister for Northern Ireland until May, said INLA and the Irish Republican Army (IRA) are rivals.

Pope John Paul II did not visit Northern Ireland, but made a plea for peace in an address at Drogheda in the republic. The IRA rejected the pope's peace plea, saying that "in all conscience. . . force is the only means of removing the evil of the British presence in Northern Ireland."

An ultra-Protestant group, the Ulster Freedom Fighters, which was banned in 1975, announced that it was resuming its armed campaign against the IRA, INLA, and prison personnel it accused of ill-treating "Loyalist" prisoners. A second Protestant group, thought to be the successors of the Red Hand Commando group that was banned in 1975, also said it was taking up arms again.

Diplomatic Decision. However, the pope's visit to Ireland and the Mountbatten murders did have some political effect. On October 5, Irish Foreign Minister Michael O'Kennedy and British Northern Ireland Minister Humphrey Atkins met in London. They agreed that British Army helicopters would be allowed to fly up to 6 miles (10 kilometers) into Irish territory in "hot pursuit" of terrorists fleeing Northern Ireland. However, the pilots would not be allowed to land, and would have to pass on information to the Royal Ulster Constabulary and the Irish police. Great Britain had argued for many years that the meandering border – 300 miles (480 kilometers) long – which is virtually impossible to guard, provided an escape route for IRA gunmen based in the republic. In return for the concessions, Britain agreed to discuss political development.   Ian Mather

See also GREAT BRITAIN; IRELAND. In WORLD BOOK, see NORTHERN IRELAND.

NORTHWEST TERRITORIES. The Territorial Council was increased from 15 to 22 elected members in 1979 in spite of opposition from the Territories' lone member of Parliament, Wally Firth. The bill was approved by a quick voice vote on March 8.

Elections for the council were held on October 1. Nine whites were elected, and the other councilors included *Inuit* (Eskimos) from the central and eastern Arctic and *Déné* (Athapaskan Indians) and *métis* (persons of mixed white and Indian descent) from the Mackenzie Valley. Although most councilors advocated greater powers for the Territorial Council, there were some differences. The Déné nation wished to replace the council with its own band councils. The eastern Arctic representatives wanted a geographic split of the Territories. Problems between native peoples and whites centered on the location and pace of resource development.

The last of a string of six airstrips for commercial development was completed in September at Spence Bay on Boothia Peninsula. The chain of airstrips stretches from the western shore of Hudson Bay to the northern end of Baffin Island. Land travel to the North was eased by the completion of the 403-mile (671-kilometer) Dempster Highway, connecting Dawson in the Yukon with Inuvik in the Mackenzie River Delta.   David M.L. Farr

See also CANADA. In WORLD BOOK, see NORTHWEST TERRITORIES.

NORWAY. Three countries bid for Norway's North Sea gas in 1979. France and West Germany offered to help finance a pipeline to carry the offshore gas to the continent, and Great Britain reopened the prospect of a Norwegian-British pipeline. But Norway delayed its decision until 1980, when drilling may confirm that substantial reserves exist. Proven reserves were 400 billion cubic meters (14.3 trillion cubic feet).

Meanwhile, Norway continued to explore the North Sea for petroleum with eight drilling rigs. Oil production increased by 25 per cent in 1979 to 44 million short tons (40 million metric tons), providing an income of $4.56 billion. Norway expected production at the new Statfjord field to build up in 1980, increasing the country's annual output to 66 million short tons (60 million metric tons) in 1981.

Aid for Industry. The Labor government on March 25 called for encouraging foreign businesses to establish industries in Norway and to place long-term orders for Norwegian goods in return for offshore oil concessions and long-term commitments to deliver oil. Petroleum production helped cut Norway's trade deficit for the first half of 1979 by one-third, to $408 million. But the economy was sluggish, with 1979 growth unlikely to exceed 1 per cent. Unemployment increased to 30,000, or 2 per cent of the labor force.

Wage Freeze. The government stood firm on a 15-month wage and price freeze that was to end on December 31. Prime Minister Odvar Nordli admitted that oil price hikes would make it difficult to keep the rate of inflation within the planned 4 per cent limit, but he kept the freeze on because he feared that some businesses might raise their prices unnecessarily if it were ended.

In October, the government presented a 1980 budget of $15.3 billion, up 13 per cent from 1979. It called for higher taxes on gasoline and electricity, higher postage, and rate hikes for public transportation, but lower taxes on stock trading.

Nuclear Issue Shelved. Ample supplies of cheap hydroelectric power from mountain rivers enabled Norway to postpone a decision on building nuclear power plants, at least until 1981. But conservationists continued to fight against plans for hydroelectric developments.

The Labor and Socialist parties, which control the national government, won only 40 per cent of the vote in local elections on September 17, a loss of 3 per cent. This was their poorest showing since the 1930s.

Small shareholders in Sweden blocked Norway's bid to buy part of AB Volvo, the Swedish automobile and truck company, in January. Opposition parties in Norway's *Storting* (parliament) had threatened to bring down the government if the deal went through.   Kenneth Brown

See also EUROPE (Facts in Brief Table). In WORLD BOOK, see NORWAY.

NOVA SCOTIA. Premier John Buchanan's Conservative government unveiled a $1.2-billion coal-development program in October 1979. It included the opening of three new mines and the expansion of existing ones. Plans were made to build two 300-megawatt coal-fired power stations on Cape Breton Island.

The Maritime Energy Corporation, a utility formed in 1978 to plan and construct large energy projects in the Atlantic area, moved ahead slowly because of a dispute over the Point Lepreau nuclear plant in New Brunswick.

The British oil tanker *Kurdistan* broke up in ice-filled waters off Cape Breton on March 15 and had to be towed to port.

The new Conservative government presented an austerity budget on April 6. Spending increases were limited to 4.6 per cent and higher taxes imposed on alcohol, tobacco, and other items. The deficit was projected at $17.6 million.

Good news came on September 14 when the new federal government agreed to transfer complete ownership of offshore resources to Nova Scotia and Newfoundland. The previous government had offered a division of the resources that would give 75 per cent to Nova Scotia and 25 per cent to the federal government.   David M. L. Farr

In WORLD BOOK, see NOVA SCOTIA.

NUCLEAR ENERGY. See ENERGY.

NUTRITION. The Food and Nutrition Board of the United States National Research Council released its ninth revision of the recommended dietary allowances (RDA's) in September 1979. The RDA's are considered the most authoritative measure of the average person's nutrient needs. They vary according to age and include special allowances for periods of pregnancy and *lactation* (breast feeding).

The 1979 revision included protein and energy needs (calories), as well as requirements for three of the four fat-soluble vitamins, six water-soluble vitamins, and six minerals. A new feature was a table listing the "Estimated Safe and Adequate Daily Dietary Intakes" of several vitamins and minerals for which the scientific evidence is not considered good enough to make an authoritative recommendation. Thus, some indication was given of the body's need for vitamin K, biotin, pantothenic acid, copper, manganese, fluoride, chromium, selenium, molybdenum, sodium, potassium, and chloride.

There were also several changes in the RDA's. These are the result of increased knowledge of human body functions and how diet and nutrients affect health. Since the Food and Nutrition Board researchers work on these nutrients, the conclusions published are considered the best available.

The energy requirements, for instance, show a drop, reflecting newer data concerning lowered exercise levels. This decrease in calorie requirements

eating more fiber, and avoiding excess calories and the resulting overweight. Upton indicated that evidence supporting these principles was not completely convincing, and critics of the dietary plan believe there are not enough data to justify them.

Obesity is a dietary problem that concerns many people in the United States. While researchers cannot agree on the problems directly associated with it, they acknowledge that it complicates existing problems. So American nutritionists received with great interest a 1979 report based upon data collected in the Health and Nutrition Examination Survey conducted by the National Center for Health Statistics.

Prepared by nutritionists Sidney Abraham and Clifford L. Johnson, the data indicated that about 30 per cent of American men between 20 and 74 years of age were more than 10 per cent above ideal body weight. About 14 per cent of the male population in these age groups were more than 20 per cent over ideal weight. Among women, 36 per cent were more than 10 per cent over ideal body weight; 24 per cent were 20 per cent over. The peak ages for overweight in men were between 35 and 44 years, when 40 per cent were more than 10 per cent overweight. Women were heaviest between the ages of 55 and 64, when 49 per cent weighed 10 per cent more than that considered desirable.   Paul E. Araujo

See also FOOD. In WORLD BOOK, see DIET; FOOD; NUTRITION.

Nutritionists Bonnie Liebman and Letitia Brewster, dressed as a broccoli plant and a tomato, tour the United States promoting better nutrition.

occurs predominantly in teen-age boys, though girls from 11 to 14 years old should consume fewer calories, too. A surprise is the recommendation that people in the 19- to 22-year-old group receive 7.5 micrograms of vitamin D per day and persons 23 years old and over receive 5 micrograms. These groups had had no RDA assignment for vitamin D.

Vitamin C. Among the nutrients for which the RDA was changed is ascorbic acid, or vitamin C. The RDA's were raised for every age group by 5 to 15 milligrams per day. The adult RDA, for instance, jumped from 45 to 60 milligrams. Vitamin B_6 requirements were increased by up to 30 per cent, and some B_{12} recommendations for infants and children were doubled.

The requirement for iodine was raised substantially for teen-agers and adults, and is now set at the same level for females and males. The board also recommended that 30 to 60 milligrams of supplemental iron per day be given in a pill to women for two or three months after childbirth.

Cancer and Diet. The debate about possible links between cancer and diet received the National Cancer Institute's attention. Arthur C. Upton, the institute's director until his resignation in December, announced "prudent interim principles" on October 2 for food-consumption patterns that would limit the risk of developing cancer. The major suggestions included consuming less fat and alcohol,

OCEAN. Scientists on the drilling ship *Glomar Challenger* found evidence in 1979 that tends to contradict previous ideas about the earth's surface. Some of the rigid plates that make up the earth's surface slide under other plates, and scientists thought that this sliding would gradually scrape away a certain amount of material. But the new evidence indicated that scraping, if it occurs at all, is not as orderly as they believed.

The researchers sampled rocks and sediment at the Middle America Trench off the Pacific Coast of Mexico and Central America, where the Cocos Plate is sliding eastward under the Caribbean Plate. They were surprised to find that only a few hundred meters of *accretion* (accumulated material) separated older mudstones on the trench floor from the Cocos Plate's crust. If scraping had occurred as they had thought, it would have deposited much more accretion. They concluded that most of the sediment and rock passed under the Caribbean Plate.

The scientists also discovered that the top layer of rocks from the trench's landward side resembles outcrops on land in Costa Rica and Panama, and rocks at the Tehuantepec Ridge off Mexico. This discovery suggests that the ancient North American continent extended farther south than previously thought and that the strait between the Caribbean Sea and the Pacific Ocean was narrower than scientists believed.

Giant sea worm, taken from the Galapagos Rift in the Pacific Ocean in February, is about 8.5 feet (2.6 meters) long, with no mouth or eyes.

Oil Well Blowout. Ixtoc I, a Mexican exploratory well in the Bay of Campeche, went out of control on June 3 and began spewing out 10,000 to 30,000 barrels of crude oil per day in perhaps the worst oil spill in history. The oil drifted 500 miles (800 kilometers) northwest to Texas. Workmen succeeded in partially capping the well on October 18, but an estimated 10,000 barrels per day was still escaping in mid-November (see ENVIRONMENT). The oil pressure and volume persuaded some experts to rate the oil discovery in the southern part of the Gulf of Mexico as a great find.

Down to Stay. More than 30 divers, scientists, and technicians studied the sunken ironclad vessel *Monitor* in August. The *Monitor*, which fought a historic battle during the Civil War, lies upside down in the sand under 210 feet (64 meters) of water 15 miles (24 kilometers) south of Cape Hatteras, off the North Carolina coast, where it sank in a storm in 1862. The expedition found that the ship was so fragile and deteriorated that it cannot be recovered.

Ocean Power. The first power plant that uses ocean heat to generate electricity was commissioned in Honolulu, Hawaii, on May 29 and floated to a location about 1.5 miles (2.4 kilometers) off Keahole Point on the island of Hawaii, where it began operating on August 3. The experimental plant, called Mini-OTEC (Ocean Thermal Energy Conversion) produces 50 kilowatts. Warm surface water

vaporizes liquid ammonia that drives a turbogenerator, which produces the electricity. Cold water pumped from 2,170 feet (660 meters) turns the ammonia back into a liquid for the next cycle.

The United Nations (UN) Law of the Sea Conference continued to grapple with the problem of deep-sea mining at sessions in Geneva, Switzerland, from March 19 to April 27, and in New York City from July 19 to August 24. The UN had proclaimed such resources to be the "common heritage of mankind" in 1969, but the U.S. Congress was considering legislation to allow mining pending an international agreement. Developing countries were determined to protect their interest in a proposed international seabed authority and viewed the U.S. stand as an attempt to pressure the conference into favoring U.S. miners. The United States and the People's Republic of China signed an agreement on May 8 in Peking (Beijing in the phonetic Pinyin alphabet China adopted on Jan. 1, 1979) to exchange marine data and to collaborate in various scientific studies.   Arthur G. Alexiou

See also GEOLOGY. In the Special Reports section, see UNLOCKING THE SECRETS OF THE SEVEN SEAS. In WORLD BOOK, see DEEP SEA DRILLING PROJECT; EARTH; OCEAN; TECTONICS.

OHIO. See STATE GOVERNMENT.

OKLAHOMA. See STATE GOVERNMENT.

OLD AGE. See SOCIAL SECURITY.

OLYMPIC GAMES. Preparations progressed in 1979 for staging the 1980 Winter Olympic Games in Lake Placid, N.Y., and the Summer Olympics in Moscow. Lake Placid tested its facilities with competition in most Winter Olympic sports, and Russia held its quadrennial Spartakiade multisport festival.

Lake Placid facilities generally were good, but there were other problems. The estimated total cost of the games had risen from between $25 million and $35 million in 1974 to $150 million, and the figure could reach $190 million. Most of the money would come from the federal and state governments.

Lake Placid lies in the Adirondack Mountains and is accessible mainly by narrow two-lane roads. Officials planned to keep cars out of the town during the Olympics, requiring spectators to park in lots on the outskirts and take shuttle buses to the competitions.

The Spartakiade. For the first time, Russia invited athletes from other lands. More than 2,300 from 80 nations joined 8,300 Russians in the competition in Moscow and other Russian cities from July 21 to August 5.

Russia trained a staff of 100,000 to handle its greatest tourist influx in history in 1980. It expected 300,000 foreign spectators – 20,000 Americans – plus 12,000 athletes, 7,400 journalists, 3,000 officials, 1,500 referees, and 300,000 Russian tourists.

The China Problem puzzled the International Olympic Committee (IOC). The People's Republic of China was readmitted to the IOC, but it insisted that Taiwan, which it regards as a province, be expelled. The IOC, reluctant to expel Taiwan, proposed that it should change its name, flag, and anthem for Olympic activities. China surprisingly agreed to this, but Taiwan sued the IOC on November 15 to prevent such a change.

Los Angeles Pact. The IOC finally reached agreement with Los Angeles on March 1 to stage the 1984 Summer Olympics. Los Angeles, determined to avoid a financial catastrophe similar to Montreal's in 1976, had rejected many of the liability terms demanded by the IOC. When the IOC threatened to take the 1984 Olympics elsewhere, the U.S. Olympic Committee (USOC) agreed to share administrative and financial responsibility with the Los Angeles organizers. The IOC accepted this unusual plan.

Television income was a key for the Los Angeles organizers, and they struck it rich. The American Broadcasting Companies Incorporated (ABC) paid $25 million for U.S. television rights to the 1976 Olympics, and the National Broadcasting Company $87 million for the 1980 rights. Los Angeles had hoped the 1984 rights would bring $125 million. Instead, ABC agreed in September to pay $225-million. Production costs were expected to send ABC's costs past $300 million.   Frank Litsky

In WORLD BOOK, see OLYMPIC GAMES.

OMAN. See MIDDLE EAST.

ONTARIO. The derailment of a Canadian Pacific train carrying toxic chemicals virtually emptied Mississauga, Canada's 10th largest city, on Nov. 12, 1979. More than 275,000 persons were evacuated for up to three days, and, though several explosions occurred, no one died.

Premier William G. Davis' Progressive Conservative government, holding only 58 of the 125 seats in the legislature, proceeded cautiously in 1979. The Liberals, with 34 seats, formed the official opposition. The New Democratic Party lost two seats through resignations, but won them back in by-elections on April 5 and held a total of 33.

The government made it plain in March that it would not agree to any large expenditures for new projects. It hoped to expand employment through increased business and technical education. Rent controls were renewed in June, and a 6 per cent ceiling on increases was also continued. The April budget raised many taxes, and health insurance premiums were increased.

The United States Nature Conservancy, a private conservation group, on March 24 gave Canada 5,683 acres (2,273 hectares) of marsh and uplands on Long Point in Lake Erie as a wildlife refuge. The area is on a bird migratory route.   David M. L. Farr

See also CANADA. In WORLD BOOK, see ONTARIO.

OPERA. See MUSIC, CLASSICAL.

OREGON. See STATE GOVERNMENT.

PACIFIC ISLANDS. The Sovereign Democratic Republic of Kiribati (pronounced Kiribas) became the Pacific's newest nation on July 12, 1979. The republic, a former British possession known as the Gilbert Islands, is made up of a number of small islands (mostly coral atolls) scattered over 2 million square miles (5 million square kilometers) on both sides of the equator northeast of Australia. The islands have a population of about 56,000.

Independence was achieved despite angry, last-ditch efforts by the people of Ocean Island (Banaba), who did not want their island included in the republic.

Kiribati began independence with a reserve fund of $67 million. The new republic signed a friendship treaty with the United States that provides for consultation on security and marine resources. The United States signed a similar treaty with Tuvalu and renounced its claims under the Guano Act of 1856 to several Tuvalu and Kiribati islands.

Great Britain moved closer to quitting the Pacific after Kiribati became independent. Only the New Hebrides, which Great Britain and France rule jointly, and tiny Pitcairn Island still fly the British flag. With the New Hebrides scheduled for independence in 1980, local and external pressure increased on France to grant independence to French Polynesia and to nickel-rich New Caledonia. But France resisted. Meanwhile, Australia announced that it would increase its aid to $84 million in Australian dollars ($U.S. 92 million) for the English-speaking island countries over the next three years.

Papua New Guinea, independent since 1975, faced a growing law-and-order crisis in 1979. In the urban areas, particularly Port Moresby, the capital, burglaries, robberies, vehicle thefts, and assaults and rapes occurred daily. A state of emergency was declared in the highlands in July because of continual tribal fighting, bandits on the highway from the coast, and massive destruction of houses, trade stores, coffee trees, and livestock. Violence and vandalism among university students, who demanded increased allowances, were other problems.

In the Cook Islands, former Prime Minister Sir Albert Henry was found guilty in August of having conspired to defraud the state of $337,000. Also convicted was Finbar B. Kenny, a United States citizen, whose New York City corporation had a contract to distribute postage stamps for the Cook Islands. Both were fined. According to court records, Kenny paid Henry $337,000, which Henry used to charter planes to fly 450 voters from New Zealand to the Cook Islands to vote for members of Henry's party in a March 1978 election.

Before the conspiracy case, a United States court fined Kenny's corporation $50,000 for criminal violation of the Foreign Corrupt Practices Act of 1977. Kenny agreed to make restitution of $337,000 to the Cook Islands government and to appear voluntarily

Costumed islanders welcome Great Britain's Princess Anne at ceremonies on
July 12 establishing the nation of Kiribati, formerly the Gilbert Islands.

at the conspiracy trial, provided no other charges were brought.

Greater Autonomy. Four island groups in the Caroline archipelago – Yap, Ponape, Truk, and Kosrae – began a new era of increased self-government on May 15 as the Federated States of Micronesia.

With Palau, the Northern Mariana Islands, and the Marshall Islands, which have opted for separate forms of autonomy, the new states make up the United Nations Trust Territory of the Pacific Islands. The United States has administered the islands since 1946.

Unusual Investment. Prime Minister Toalipi Lauti of Tuvalu, which has a population of 8,000, caused a stir in February when he flew to the United States and gave a check for more than $500,000 to Sidney Gross of Los Angeles. The check represented most of Tuvalu's ready cash. Lauti explained that Gross promised to pay 15 per cent interest on the money, which he would invest in his own business to help Tuvalu obtain a fishing fleet. Later, Tuvalu rejected a proposal by Gross to sell 500 Tuvaluan passports – and citizenship – for $60,000 each to raise revenue. Robert Langdon

In the WORLD BOOK SUPPLEMENT section, see SOLOMON ISLANDS; TUVALU. In WORLD BOOK, see PACIFIC ISLANDS.

PAINTING. See VISUAL ARTS.

PAKISTAN. A mob of Muslim fanatics stormed and burned the United States Embassy in Islamabad on Nov. 21, 1979, apparently because of false rumors that U.S. forces were involved in an attack on the Great Mosque of Mecca in Saudi Arabia (see SAUDI ARABIA). The embassy staff of about 90 retreated to a steel vault and remained there for six hours, waiting for rescue. Eventually, they escaped through a vent to the roof. Local police watched the riot from across the street, and Pakistan's army took six hours to arrive from its base in Rawalpindi, about 12 miles (19 kilometers) away.

Two U.S. guards were killed in the attack, along with two Pakistanis employed by the embassy and two rioters. In the following 24 hours, the United States evacuated 388 dependents and nonessential personnel.

President Zia-ul-Haq telephoned his "deep regret" to U.S. President Jimmy Carter and pledged to rebuild the gutted embassy – completed only six years previously, at a cost of about $21 million. But many U.S. questions about the long delay in Pakistani rescue efforts went unanswered.

"Islamic A-Bomb." Even before the violence in Islamabad, relations with the United States were strained by Pakistan's secret efforts to build an atomic bomb. According to Western intelligence agencies, Pakistan had been secretly buying components for a uranium-enrichment facility at Kahuta, which could produce weapons-grade uranium. The United States pressed Pakistan to abandon the project. On April 6, after Pakistan refused to allow international inspection of its facility, Washington cut off $45 million in aid proposed for 1980. But after Russia's military intervention in Afghanistan in December, Carter Administration officials said legislation would be introduced in Congress in January 1980 to allow the sending of military aid to Pakistan.

Bhutto's Death. On February 6, the Pakistani Supreme Court dismissed an appeal by former Prime Minister Zulfikar Ali Bhutto against a death sentence imposed by a lower court. Although the court suggested that Bhutto not be executed, and foreign governments pleaded for his life, Zia refused to grant clemency. Bhutto was hanged on April 4.

Zia announced on October 16 that the general election scheduled for November 17 would be indefinitely postponed. He also banned political parties and meetings, closed many newspapers, and authorized mass arrests and floggings. Zia said he was acting to ensure the nation's Islamic character and to maintain democracy. Zia had declared on February 10 that the law of Islam would rule Pakistan henceforth. See RELIGION.   Mark Gayn

See also ASIA (Facts in Brief Table). In WORLD BOOK, see ISLAM; PAKISTAN.

PALEONTOLOGY. A geologist reported in October 1979 that up to 96 per cent of all marine animal species died out at the end of the Permian Period, about 225 million years ago. Scientists have long known that the end of the Permian Period marked the most severe extinction event in the history of all life. But David M. Raup, chairman of geology at the Field Museum of Natural History in Chicago, used a statistical technique called rarefaction analysis to estimate just how thoroughgoing the extinction was.

It is not possible to count the number of species that existed before and after the Permian extinction because most animal species are never recovered as fossils. However, a family – which is made up of many species – has a much greater chance of being recovered. Raup found that only 52 per cent of all the families alive during the Permian Period survived the late Permian extinction. Using his knowledge of living families, he then estimated how many species the average fossil family might have had. Assuming that extinctions of species occurred at random, he calculated that 96 per cent of the various animal species would have to die out in order to reduce the number of families by 52 per cent.

Baby Dinosaurs. Dinosaurs were important newsmakers again in 1979. Vertebrate paleontologist John R. Horner of the Princeton University Natural History Museum in New Jersey led a field

Mourners in Rawalpindi, Pakistan, lament the death of former Prime Minister Zulfikar Ali Bhutto. His hanging on April 4 aroused violent protest.

A new head for the *Brontosaurus* skeleton at the Carnegie Museum of Natural History marks the correction of an 1879 error regarding the dinosaur.

A Heady Change. *Brontosaurus,* one of the best-known dinosaurs with its massive body and long neck and tail, has a new head. The Carnegie Museum of Natural History in Pittsburgh removed the old head from its *Brontosaurus* skeleton in October 1979 and replaced it with a skull that has a longer snout and longer, more delicate teeth. Paleontologists John S. McIntosh of Wesleyan University in Middletown, Conn., and David S. Berman, a curator at the Carnegie Museum, concluded after historical research that the old head really belonged to another dinosaur genus, *Camarasaurus.*

In 1879, Othniel Charles Marsh of the Yale Peabody Museum of Natural History in New Haven, Conn., found some bones that he thought belonged to a new genus of dinosaur. He was in a hurry to publish a description of the new dinosaur before a rival could do so, but he lacked a skull to go with the bones. Undeterred, Marsh used two skulls that he had found 4 miles (6 kilometers) and 400 miles (650 kilometers) away from the bones in his restoration and 1883 description of *Brontosaurus.* As early as 1915, another paleontologist suggested that the skulls were from *Camarasaurus.* But by that time, many paleontologists had a vested interest in retaining the original description.   Ida Thompson

In the WORLD BOOK SUPPLEMENT section, see DINOSAUR. In WORLD BOOK, see FOSSIL; PALEONTOLOGY.

party in search of juvenile dinosaurs in the Two Medicine Formation, a strata of rock dated to the late Cretaceous Period – about 70 million years ago – near Choteau, Mont.

Horner was returning to the area where he and his assistants found a nest of baby duckbilled dinosaur fossils in July 1978. During July and August 1979, they found more bones of juvenile dinosaurs, along with many eggs. Most of the bones and eggs were from plant-eating dinosaurs like the duckbilled babies. But two clusters of eggs were near the bones of *carnivorous* (meat-eating) juveniles, suggesting that the eggs were laid by carnivorous dinosaurs. If so, these are the first eggs from carnivorous dinosaurs ever recovered.

New Evidence that may bear on the extinction of the dinosaurs was announced in June 1979 by Walter Alvarez of the University of California, Berkeley. Scientists have long wondered why dinosaurs became extinct so suddenly, at the end of the Cretaceous Period. Alvarez found that the sediments on top of the Cretaceous fossils in Gubbio, Italy, which were deposited shortly after the dinosaurs died, contain about 25 times the expected amount of the element iridium. Alvarez theorizes that the iridium came from outer space, possibly from an extraterrestrial event that increased the amount of iridium drifting into the earth's atmosphere. The same event may have killed the dinosaurs, he says.

PAN AMERICAN GAMES. An incident involving Bobby Knight of Indiana University, coach of the victorious United States men's basketball team, overshadowed the competition in the 1979 Pan American Games in July. The quadrennial competition held in San Juan, Puerto Rico, attracted 4,400 athletes from 33 nations who competed in 25 sports.

After a dispute over who had the right to a practice court, the volatile Knight was arrested and jailed briefly on a charge of assaulting José Silva, a policeman. Knight later was found guilty, sentenced to six months in jail, and fined $500, though he said he would not return to Puerto Rico to go to jail. United States officials agreed with Knight that he was a victim of a miscarriage of justice.

The United States, as expected, dominated the competition. It won 126 gold, 92 silver, and 45 bronze medals for a record total of 263 medals. Cuba was second, with 65-49-32 – 146; and Canada third, with 24-44-67 – 135.

United States athletes won 28 of 29 gold medals in swimming, 25 of 39 in track and field, 14 of 20 in wrestling, 12 of 27 in shooting, 10 of 17 in roller skating, 6 of 30 in weight lifting, 4 of 11 in boxing, all 4 in archery and diving, 4 of 5 in tennis, all 3 in equestrian events, and 3 of 5 in yachting. Cuba was strong in weight lifting, winning 23 of 30 gold medals; men's gymnastics, all 8; fencing, 6 of 8; and boxing, 5 of 11.   Frank Litsky

PANAMA officially took control of the Panama Canal Zone on Oct. 1, 1979. The zone had been the exclusive enclave of United States personnel operating and defending the canal since 1903.

On the day control was transferred, thousands of Panamanians gathered at Ancon Hill, at the Pacific end of the canal, for a symbolic flag-raising ceremony. Later, a huge crowd gathered at Fort Amador, headquarters of the U.S. 193rd Infantry Brigade, which became a Panamanian base for the joint control of the canal's defenses on October 2. Huge crowds at Albrook Army Base heard speeches by President Aristides Royo, Mexico's President Jose Lopez Portillo, and U.S. Vice-President Walter F. Mondale.

Treaty Terms. The take-over was in accordance with Panama Canal treaties formally signed in Panama City on June 16, 1978, by U.S. President Jimmy Carter and Panama's then chief of government, Omar Torrijos Herrera. But certain areas of disagreement remained that required implementation by the U.S. Congress. A first version of proposed legislative implementation was voted down in the House of Representatives on September 20 but a second, compromise version was approved by the House on September 26 and signed by President Carter on September 27.

Added Provisions. Among the second version's provisions was one that required Panama to pay out of toll revenues about $100 million more of the cost of implementing the treaty. Another assured the U.S. Congress of an opportunity to review future property transfers. The bill also gave the U.S. President power to place the canal under U.S. military control if its security was threatened by foreign troops. The bill also authorized the expenditure of $467 million for the canal's operation until total control passes to Panama on Dec. 31, 1999.

On September 26, the Panama Canal Company imposed an immediate toll increase of 29.3 per cent. It would help sustain the annual payments to Panama called for by the treaties while the canal is still under the company's administration. Responsibilities for most public services were to be transferred to Panama over a 30-month transition period.

The U.S. House of Representatives held a closed-door hearing in June on alleged Panamanian involvement in an uprising in neighboring Nicaragua. President Anastasio Somoza Debayle of Nicaragua had denounced Panama on May 27, claiming that Panama was supplying guns, ammunition, and manpower to the Sandinista rebels who eventually ousted him (see NICARAGUA). Shah Mohammad Reza Pahlavi moved to Panama's Contadora Island on December 15 (see IRAN).   Paul C. Tullier

See also LATIN AMERICA (Facts in Brief Table). In WORLD BOOK, see PANAMA; PANAMA CANAL ZONE.

PAPUA NEW GUINEA. See ASIA; PACIFIC ISLANDS.

PARAGUAY. The downfall, in July 1979, of Nicaragua's dictator, President Anastasio Somoza Debayle, sent tremors of insecurity through the regime of President Alfredo Stroessner. According to a news report, members of the 66-year-old strongman's government feared that the United States would withdraw its support from Stroessner as it had from Somoza. Stroessner has ruled Paraguay for 25 years. See NICARAGUA.

One report cited a confidential memorandum circulated to army generals by Pastor Coronel, chief of the political police, accusing the U.S. Embassy, independent newspapers, and opposition political parties of preparing a "process of subversion" designed to "destabilize" the regime. "The embassy puts pressure on the regime over human rights to weaken our internal defenses," it said. "The press puts pressure on public opinion to generate a state of agitation. The opposition front exerts pressure on the international level to obtain sanctions against the government."

In June, the government closed two newspapers, *La Tribuna* and *Ultima Hora*, for 30 days. However, pressure from U.S. President Jimmy Carter on the human rights issue caused Stroessner to close the notorious detention camp at Emboscado and to set free hundreds of political prisoners held there. Only six political prisoners were reportedly still being held at year's end.

The Mengele Case. The Paraguayan government yielded further to international pressure during the year. Josef Mengele, a German war criminal accused of murdering 400,000 Jews at the Auschwitz concentration camp in Poland during World War II, had frequently been reported to be living in Paraguay. The government had persistently denied the charge even though documents found in 1970 indicated that Mengele had been granted Paraguayan citizenship. The government maintained it did not know his whereabouts, and even Simon Wiesenthal, a Nazi-hunter whose Documentation Center in Vienna, Austria, had traced Mengele to Paraguay, could not pinpoint his location.

The general belief was that Mengele was living in Paraguay's eastern region, where many German nationals had relocated after leaving Europe. Continuous pressure for his extradition by West Germany, seconded by United Nations Secretary-General Kurt Waldheim, eventually persuaded the Paraguayan government to strip Mengele of his citizenship on August 8. At year's end, however, he had still not been found.   Everett G. Martin

See also LATIN AMERICA (Facts in Brief Table). In WORLD BOOK, see PARAGUAY.

PARENTS AND TEACHERS, NATIONAL CONGRESS OF. See NATIONAL PTA (NATIONAL CONGRESS OF PARENTS AND TEACHERS).

PENNSYLVANIA. See PHILADELPHIA; STATE GOVERNMENT.

PERSONALITIES OF 1979 included the following:

Allen, Bryan, 26, of Bakersfield, Calif., found an albatross that brought good fortune instead of bad. The young cyclist pedaled the *Gossamer Albatross,* a human-powered plane, 22 miles (35 kilometers) across the English Channel on June 12 to win $205,000 and mark an aviation "first." The craft was designed by Paul MacCready, the 53-year-old California engineer whose human-powered aircraft, the *Gossamer Condor,* won the $95,000 Kremer Prize in 1977, with Allen as the pilot-engine. The 1977 exploit was the world's first controlled human-powered flight.

Brown, Louise, the first "test-tube baby," celebrated her first birthday on July 25 by plunging a foot into the layers of her chocolate birthday cake at her home in England. Her parents have written a book about her titled *Our Miracle Called Louise.*

Carson, Johnny, 54, star of "The Tonight Show" since 1962, was named Entertainer of the Year on May 6 at the 75th anniversary dinner of the Friars Club of New York City.

Queen Elizabeth, 79, queen mother of Great Britain, broke tradition and gained a new title on August 1. She was installed as the 160th Lord Warden and Admiral of the Cinque Ports in ceremonies at Dover, England. She is the first woman to hold the now-symbolic office in its 900-year history.

Fagan, Kevin, 22, is a college student, just like the cartoon character Drabble. The senior at Saddleback Community College in Mission Viejo, Calif., is also the creator of the comic strip *Drabble.* Its March debut in more than 100 newspapers made Fagan the youngest syndicated cartoonist in the United States.

Fields, Crystal, 11, does not throw "like a girl." She doesn't hit and run like one, either. The 5-foot (152-centimeter), 90-pound (41-kilogram) Little Leaguer is an all-star shortstop for the Cumberland (Md.) Phillies. On July 16, she became the first female to win the Pitch, Hit, and Run championship at the Little League All-Star Game in Seattle. She defeated seven 9- to 12-year-old boys in three categories: hitting for distance, speed in running a base path, and pitching at a target.

Goddard, Robert H., father of modern rocketry and space flight, for whom the Goddard Space Flight Center in Greenbelt, Md., is named, was inducted posthumously into the National Inventors Hall of Fame on February 11. The ceremony marked the dedication of that section of the United States Patent and Trademark Office in Arlington, Va. Also honored were Jay W. Forrester of Massachusetts Institute of Technology in Cambridge, a pioneer in computer development, and Charles J. Plank and Edward J. Rosinski of Mobil Oil Corporation's Research and Development Laboratory in

Ragtime composer Eubie Blake offers a piece of his 96th birthday cake to a cast member of the Broadway musical *Eubie* at a party on February 4.

Paulsboro, N.J., who invented new techniques for refining oil.

Godfrey, Arthur, 76, the "old redhead," celebrated a double 50th anniversary on August 18. Half a century earlier, he took to the air, both as an airplane pilot and a radio broadcaster, and he's been flying high in both fields ever since. Godfrey celebrated the event in a characteristic manner – he starred in a nostalgic 90-minute television special.

Gordon, Ron, 33, a high school economics teacher in Redwood City, Calif., went to bat for San Francisco Giants baseball fans and won praise from Council on Wage and Price Stability Chairman Alfred E. Kahn for his "heroic and unflagging campaign" against inflation. When the price of hot dogs at the Giants' Candlestick Park games rose from 75 cents to 80 cents, Gordon got hotter under the collar than ball-park mustard. He spent hundreds of hours proving that a concessionaire could make a good profit without raising prices, and finally won his point. Prices were rolled back and Gordon downed a couple of dogs – but no beer, which had risen from 85 cents to 90 cents and stayed there.

Harburg, E. Y. (Yip), 83, would rather be at his New York piano than in Philadelphia. Nevertheless, he accepted a commission to write a song about the city for the September 26 opening of Philadelphia's Fairmont Hotel. Harburg wrote the lyrics for *The Wizard of Oz* and such songs as "It's Only a Paper Moon" and "Brother, Can You Spare a Dime?" His new song should make Philadelphians forget that the Fairmont was once the Bellevue-Stratford – closed after the 1976 outbreak there of legionnaires' disease.

Hearst, Patty, 25, ensured herself of lifetime protection on April 1. Two months after she was released from prison, she married Bernard Shaw, 33, her former bodyguard, at Treasure Island Naval Base in San Francisco Bay. Her maid of honor was Trish Tobin, daughter of the owner of Hibernia Bank. Hearst was convicted of robbing the bank in 1974 while she was being held by the Symbionese Liberation Army.

Hooper, Marcus, 12, an English schoolboy, swam the English Channel on August 6, the youngest person to do so. His feat required 14 hours 39 minutes. A day earlier, another 12-year-old, Kevin Anderson of South Africa, swam the Channel in 12½ hours. But Kevin is three months older than Marcus. Making the crossing in 13 hours 7 minutes was Jim (Doc) Counsilman. On September 14, at the age of 58, Indiana University swimming coach Counsilman became the oldest person to swim the channel.

Lee, Robert Edward, 56, had a special day on February 21 – he legally became Roberto Eduardo León. And as a person with a Spanish surname, he became entitled to preferential promotion practices under federal law. He justified his action on the

Their faces tell the story: Katie Kerwin of Denver wins the National Spelling Bee on June 7; Julie Won of Harrisburg, Pa., is runner-up.

grounds that his maternal grandfather was of Spanish origin and said that, legally, anyone could change his or her name and enjoy the benefits of a law aimed at aiding minority groups to find employment. "My job with the county environmental protection agency is spotting loopholes, and I spotted one," Mr. Lee, or Señor León, explained.

Moore, Clayton, 64, the actor who portrayed the Lone Ranger for 30 years, was ordered by a California Superior Court in September to stop being "that masked man." The two companies that own the copyright to the character charged that Moore was too old to represent the Western hero, and that he was usurping their right to the Lone Ranger image by making public appearances wearing the black mask. Moore disagreed strongly, and gained widespread popular support. "For many Americans, the Lone Ranger is a hero," he said. "This country needs heroes, and there aren't many left." Sounding just like the masked rider of the plains, Moore intoned, "I've lived by the Lone Ranger creed for 30 years and I'm fighting now for fair play, justice, law and order."

Morton, John and Harriet, who live in Great Gidding, England, celebrated their 79th wedding anniversary on July 9. Morton, a farmer and Methodist preacher until his retirement in 1936, confided, "We have had a very happy married life." He is 103, and she is 101.

The Chicken, a cavorting creature embodied by San Diego radio personality Ted Giannoulas, adds to fans' enjoyment at many sports events.

kissing the blushing Vittoria Ianni, 22, and her new husband, Mario Maltese, 24. The pope also presented them with a leather-bound Bible, a picture of the Virgin Mary, and an undisclosed sum of money.

Raney, Michele Eileen, 27, a Los Angeles physician, gladly spent 1979 in a much colder climate. She was the first woman chosen to serve for a year as medical-facility director at the Amundsen-Scott South Pole scientific research station in Antarctica. Raney was responsible for the health and medical safety of 17 male scientists and their staff, and said she enjoyed working at the base, which is in darkness six months of the year, because "it offers a unique experience in the general practice of medicine."

Silverheels, Jay, 59, the Lone Ranger's faithful but stony-faced Indian companion, let his composure slip a bit on July 20. Overcome with emotion, he wept at ceremonies at which he became the first American Indian to have a star in his honor placed in the Hollywood Walk of Fame. Silverheels is the founder of the Indian Actors' Workshop.

Spiess, Gerry, 39, a saltwater sailor from White Bear Lake, Minn., set a record on July 24 for a solo transatlantic crossing in a small craft. He sailed the 10-foot (3-meter) *Yankee Girl* from Virginia Beach, Va., to Falmouth, England, in 54 days. Spiess's trite but true words on stepping ashore were, "Gee, I'm glad to be on land again."

Nelson, Willie, 46, well-known country music singer, hoisted a glass on May 15 with a well-known country music fan – President Jimmy Carter. The "glass" was a Steuben crystal bowl engraved with the thanks of the Country Music Association for Carter's support of their art. The President remarked to Nelson, "This is the first time I ever saw you with a glass in your hand without beer in it."

Nyad, Diana, 30, finally did it. On August 21, she completed the 60-mile (96-kilometer) swim from North Bimini Island, Bahamas, to Juno Beach, Fla., in 27 hours 38 minutes. "Everybody said it couldn't be done," exulted Nyad, the first person to win the battle against ocean currents, sharks, and jellyfish.

Oliveira, Elmar, 28, who in 1978 became the first American violinist to win a gold medal in the prestigious Tchaikovsky competition in Moscow, was honored as Man of the Year on March 18, 1979, by the Portuguese community of Newark, N.J., his home town. Oliveira shared the honor with his father, José, a Portuguese-born carpenter who made his son's first violin after reading *The Life and Work of Stradivarius.* The musician said he still plays his first instrument occasionally, even though he now owns a violin made in 1721 by the great Italian craftsman Antonio Stradivari himself.

Pope John Paul II, 59, the bishop of Rome, performed a wedding ceremony for two of his parishioners on February 25 and concluded it by

Clayton Moore, wearing sunglasses in place of his outlawed Lone Ranger mask, strikes a familiar pose at the New York Nostalgia Festival in September.

Stewart, Clarence, 2, a thoroughbred colt named after his trainer, is the first such horse to be registered as "white" by the Jockey Club. Not an albino because he has dark eyes, the colt is a genetic 187,500-to-1 shot. The human Clarence Stewart is also unusual – one of only half a dozen black trainers in thoroughbred racing.

Thornton, Stan, 17, a sharp-eyed young man from Esperance, Australia, was awarded $10,000 by the *San Francisco Examiner* on July 20 for turning in the first piece of the fallen *Skylab* space station. The National Aeronautics and Space Administration (NASA) laboratories in Huntsville, Ala., confirmed that the pieces of charred wood Thornton found in his backyard were indeed *Skylab* fragments.

Van DerZee, James, 92, known only as "the picture-taking man" in New York City's Harlem for 70 years, received overdue recognition in late February. Van DerZee was one of 17 elderly blacks honored by President Jimmy Carter for their achievement, and in March, an exhibition of his photographs – the richest pictorial record known of Harlem life – was held in New York City.

Von Hapsburg, Otto, 66, eldest son of the last Austro-Hungarian emperor, learned on June 11 that the democratic process works, too. He was elected as one of West Germany's representatives in the European Parliament, the advisory board of the European Community. Marsha F. Goldsmith

PERU. Civilian protests against austerity measures imposed by the military government occurred repeatedly throughout 1979. They arose from the government's decision, announced in January, to clamp down on wage increases.

On January 9, the Communist-led General Confederation of Peruvian Workers (CGTP) announced a general strike to protest a 40 per cent decline in workers' buying power. The government declared a state of emergency, suspended constitutional guarantees, and threatened to shoot anyone disturbing the peace. The Constituent Assembly, dominated by the centrist American Popular Revolutionary Action Party (APRA), joined the government in denouncing the strike. Because of government pressure, most workers refused to join the walkout, and the CGTP called it off in its second day.

School Strike. The military also declared a state of emergency in the copper-mining regions after several thousand miners and refinery workers struck on March 13. The miners returned to work on March 30.

Strikes also caused temporary stoppages in a variety of institutions, including the state-owned iron ore company, the justice department, and the banks. The most bitter conflict came during a four-month strike by 130,000 schoolteachers that began on June 4 and ended without a settlement on October 1 when the government began hiring re-

placements. More than three months of the school year had been lost.

The Economy. The austerity program, in its second year, had been forced on the government by the International Monetary Fund because overspending and heavy borrowing abroad had brought Peru close to bankruptcy. Although the government decreed several salary increases, they fell far short of compensating for the 60 per cent inflation rate. However, the restrictive economic policies, aided by higher world prices for copper, and the beginning of modest exports from new oil fields in the Amazon jungle, ended Peru's trade deficits and set the economy on the road to recovery. These improvements offered hope that the workers' plight might be eased in 1980.

On July 15, a constituent assembly charged with writing a new constitution voted to disband. It had handed its final draft to the military, but certain provisions such as the abolition of the death penalty and limitations of the powers of military courts were rejected by the government. Despite the assembly's action, the military leaders promised to go ahead with elections scheduled for July 28, 1980, that would return power to a civilian government and end almost 12 years of military rule. Everett G. Martin

See also LATIN AMERICA (Facts in Brief Table). In WORLD BOOK, see PERU.

PET. See CAT; DOG.

PETROLEUM AND GAS. President Jimmy Carter barred all petroleum imports from Iran on Nov. 12, 1979. The move was in response to Iran's seizure of the U.S. Embassy in Teheran, where Iranian students held U.S. citizens hostage.

Prior to the ban, the United States had been importing about 700,000 barrels of oil per day from Iran, about 4 per cent of domestic consumption. Experts felt that the loss would have little impact on the economy, other than some price rises. See IRAN; PRESIDENT OF THE UNITED STATES.

World oil prices increased dramatically during 1979, heightening inflation and worsening economic problems in the United States and other oil-consuming nations around the globe. Between January 1 and July 1, the Organization of Petroleum Exporting Countries (OPEC), the 13-nation oil cartel, raised crude oil prices by fully 60 per cent. OPEC ministers meeting in Geneva, Switzerland, on June 28 agreed to raise the world base price for oil to $18 per barrel, effective July 1. Individual OPEC members were given permission to add surcharges to bring prices to a maximum of $23.50 per barrel.

The July price increases were the largest since the 1973-1974 Arab oil embargo, and caused sharp increases in the price of gasoline, heating oil, diesel fuel, and other petroleum products. OPEC agreed to keep the new prices in effect through the rest of 1979, and the temporary price freeze added some stability

PETROLEUM AND GAS

Where the Oil Comes From

Imported Oil
Domestic Oil

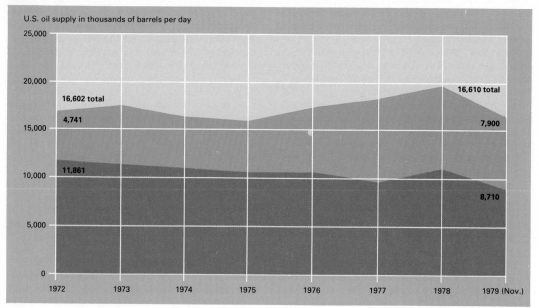

U.S. oil supply in thousands of barrels per day

25,000

20,000

16,602 total   16,610 total

4,741   7,900

15,000

11,861   8,710

10,000

5,000

0

1972   1973   1974   1975   1976   1977   1978   1979 (Nov.)

Source: U.S. Department of Energy

to world oil prices, which had fluctuated wildly early in the year when a revolution curtailed oil exports from Iran. In the United States, the price hikes and the temporary Iranian cutoff led to spot shortages with long lines and higher prices at the gas pump. As the cost of gasoline soared to over $1 per gallon (3.8 liters) in many parts of the country, some experts foresaw $2-per-gallon gas in the near future. See TRAVEL.

The OPEC price freeze lasted only until October 15, when Libya posted a new maximum price of $26.27 per barrel. Libya sells about 800,000 barrels per day to the United States. By early October, world oil prices were averaging about $20.80 per barrel, compared with $13.80 at the start of 1979.

Leaders of oil-importing nations reacted angrily to the OPEC action. President Carter, who was granted limited gas-rationing powers by Congress in October, predicted the higher price would increase inflation, unemployment, and recession. The increases helped boost America's 1979 bill for imported crude oil and refined petroleum products to an estimated $60 billion.

Planned Cutback. In the fall, OPEC nations began announcing cutbacks in future oil production, part of the cartel's long-term strategy to preserve income from their fixed petroleum resources for as long as possible. Saudi Arabia, which had raised production to 9.5 million barrels per day

(bpd) from their official 8.5-million-bpd ceiling in July in response to a request from President Carter, announced in October that its oil production would be reduced by 1 million bpd, effective Jan. 1, 1980. The Saudis changed their mind in November and decided to maintain 1979 production levels. However, OPEC could not agree on a new price structure in December and freed its member nations to set prices as high as they wish.

Imports and Production. United States crude oil imports averaged 6.2 million bpd by December, down from 7.2 million bpd during the same period in 1978, according to the American Petroleum Institute. Imports of refined petroleum products averaged 1.7 million bpd. Domestic crude oil production averaged 8.7 million bpd.

Despite Iran's production shortfall, world oil production reached a record during the first half of 1979, according to *Oil and Gas Journal*. Production was 5.8 per cent higher than 1978 and averaged 61.8 million bpd, compared with 58.7 million in 1978.

United States Crude Oil Prices also entered the early stages of what eventually will be their biggest rise in history. The increases originated in Carter's April 5 decision to permit the phased decontrol of domestic crude oil prices beginning on June 1. All domestic crude oil was expected to reach world price levels by late 1980. Prior to decontrol, the price of some domestic crude was as low as $6.30 per barrel.

Carter asked in April for a "windfall-profits" tax to take some of the oil companies' added profits after decontrol. Congress passed a $227.3-billion measure on December 21, and was to decide how to raise and spend the money in early 1980. Companies posted greatly increased third-quarter profits in October. Texaco, for example, was up 211 per cent; Mobil Oil Corporation, 131 per cent; and Exxon Corporation, 118 per cent.

In August, Carter removed all price controls on domestic heavy crude oil, a tarlike oil produced primarily in California. Oil-industry economists predicted that decontrol will raise gasoline prices 10 cents per gallon (3.8 liters). Decontrol is intended to give oil companies a greater financial incentive to increase exploration and production.

Bright Outlook for Gas. The Federal Energy Regulatory Commission (FERC) told Congress in June that residential customers and other high-priority users of natural gas will experience no shortages during the winters of 1979-1980 and 1980-1981, even if they are as severe as the recent record-cold winters. FERC's comprehensive study of future natural gas supplies was only one of several indicators of improved long-term prospects for the American gas industry. The respected Potential Gas Committee, for example, increased its estimates of U.S. potential reserves by 10 per cent.

The Carter Administration, which only two years earlier termed natural gas "a premium fuel in short supply" and discouraged industrial use, began urging industry in 1979 to convert from oil to natural gas. Energy Secretary James R. Schlesinger estimated that a "glut" of 1 trillion cubic feet (29 billion cubic meters) of gas existed early in 1979. He predicted an increase in domestic gas usage for the next 20 to 30 years. The American Gas Association estimated that at the current consumption rate of 20 trillion cubic feet (580 billion cubic meters) per year, U.S. conventional gas supplies will last 35 to 60 years. Local gas companies that for years had been unable to accept new industrial customers began providing hookups to large industrial users.

The gas industry said the bright new outlook is due primarily to changes in federal law that provide pricing incentives. Federal deregulation of some natural gas prices pumped more instrastate gas into interstate pipelines. In the past, natural gas was often kept in the state where it was produced to avoid price controls on gas pumped into interstate pipelines. The increased production is coming from conventional wells, and from previously uneconomical geologic formations. The number of completed gas wells drilled in the United States during the first nine months of 1979 increased 5.7 per cent, compared with the same period during 1978.

Ed Gamble in the *Nashville* (Tenn.) *Banner*

A poignant sign gives the bad news to drivers behind a van in a line at a California service station during spring's short-lived gas shortage.

Russian Oil. An unusually severe winter and heavy spring floods kept crude oil production in Russia well below the official goal of 11.9 million bpd during the first half of 1979. By June, production shortfalls forced the Soviet government to institute a strict conservation program to avoid heating-oil shortages during the upcoming winter. While Russian oil production foundered temporarily, natural gas production rose 10 per cent to 5.9 trillion cubic feet (167 billion cubic meters) by June. The official 1979 goal was 14.26 trillion cubic feet (404 billion cubic meters), up 9 per cent from 1978.

Mexican Boom. Mexico doubled its estimates of proven oil reserves to 45.8 billion barrels, and gas reserves to 70.3 trillion cubic feet (2 trillion cubic meters). Oil production was averaging 1.6 million bpd. Exports to the United States were expected to reach 550,000 bpd by December. After two years of negotiations, Mexico and the United States reached agreement on September 21 for sale of Mexican natural gas to American companies. Mexico will sell 300 million cubic feet (8.5 million cubic meters) per day beginning in January 1980 at a price of $3.625 per 1,000 cubic feet (28.3 cubic meters). The price was about 50 per cent higher than prevailing U.S. natural gas prices. The volume was less than originally hoped by U.S. officials. Michael Woods

See also ENERGY. In WORLD BOOK, see PETROLEUM; GAS (Fuel).

PHILADELPHIA. Democrat William J. Green, a six-term veteran of the U.S. House of Representatives, defeated Republican David W. Marston, a former U.S. attorney, in the mayoral election on Nov. 6, 1979. Green succeeds Frank L. Rizzo, who tried unsuccessfully to amend the city's charter in 1978 so he could seek a third consecutive term.

The U.S. Department of Justice filed a suit on August 13 charging the Philadelphia Police Department, the nation's fourth largest, with "across-the-board brutality" in the first federal suit to be brought against an entire police force rather than against individual officers. The complaint cited alleged incidents of police violence against suspects and prisoners without mentioning names or dates.

U.S. District Court Judge J. William Ditter, Jr., threw out a major portion of the suit on October 30, however, claiming that the U.S. attorney general did not have the right to bring such an all-encompassing suit and that such complaints should be filed by the victims of police brutality. He dismissed the remaining section on December 13, ruling that in failing to give specific details, the suit "set forth almost no factual arguments."

Environmental Agreements. The city settled two lingering water-pollution suits on May 30. In a settlement with the Environmental Protection Agency (EPA) and the state of Pennsylvania, it agreed to stop dumping sludge into the Atlantic Ocean by the end of 1980. The city also signed a consent decree resulting from two civil suits brought by the EPA in 1978 in which Philadelphia agreed to upgrade by 1983 three plants that dump treated sewage into the Delaware River.

Implementing the consent agreement is expected to cost about $692 million, but $519 million of that will be absorbed by the federal government. Its signing ended years of EPA accusations that Philadelphia had been stalling on complying with federal guidelines for waste water disposal.

Condo Ban. Mayor Rizzo signed a bill on September 27 calling for an 18-month delay on converting apartments into condominiums. The law, which was passed unanimously by the City Council, specifies that tenants be given a one-year written notice of intent to convert after the moratorium period ends.

The effectiveness of the new law was blunted by a rash of condo conversions that immediately preceded its signing. The law was also expected to be challenged in court.

Philadelphia's Bellevue-Stratford Hotel, registered as a national historic landmark, reopened on September 26 as the Fairmont Hotel after a $25-million restoration. The hotel closed in 1976, three months after the first known epidemic of legionnaires' disease broke out at an American Legion convention there. James M. Banovetz

See also CITY. In WORLD BOOK, see PHILADELPHIA.

PHILIPPINES. As the political, security, and economic problems facing the Philippines worsened in 1979, the Roman Catholic Church emerged as the focus of opposition to President Ferdinand E. Marcos. Jaime Cardinal Sin, archbishop of Manila, was the church's main spokesman, but hundreds of priests and nuns throughout the country opposed the effects of martial law and sought more economic justice.

Former Senator Benigno S. Aquino, Jr., Marcos' best-known political opponent, began his eighth year in prison. He wrote to Cardinal Sin on October 11, urging him and other church leaders to "speak out because you are the only acceptable and accepted principal educators of conscience." Aquino called on the cardinal to "provide the necessary leadership" for a nation whose politicians have "lost their credibility."

Marcos said on September 21, the seventh anniversary of the inception of martial law, that it should last at least another 18 months because of danger from Muslim and Communist rebellions and international economic problems. Economic growth slowed, partly because foreign investors began to lose confidence in the Philippines' future, and inflation rose above 20 per cent. Unequal distribution of income led to reports of malnutrition and other signs of poverty in many areas. Marcos conceded that there were major problems. He said he was disappointed by the return of "the same corruption, the same dishonesty, and the same self-centered selfishness" as before martial law.

Deputy Defense Minister Carmelo Barbero said on October 24 that 579 persons were under detention on charges of subversion, sedition, and rebellion. Guns were becoming common again, despite efforts to disarm the people, and the crime rate was rising toward the old level. Clergymen and others continued to charge human rights abuses by the armed forces, which denied them.

Marcos created a new Commission of Muslim Affairs in a Cabinet reshuffle on July 23. Rear Admiral Romula Espaldon, the commander of military forces fighting the Muslim rebellion, was named commissioner for two semiautonomous regional governments for Muslim areas. Created by a July 25 decree, they are in Mindanao and the Sulu Archipelago. But the long rebellion was becoming a nationalist independence struggle rather than just the effort of a group seeking autonomy within the Philippines. Meanwhile, the Communist New People's Army expanded its strength in scattered rural guerrilla bases.   Henry S. Bradsher

See also ASIA (Facts in Brief Table). In WORLD BOOK, see PHILIPPINES.

PHONOGRAPH. See RECORDINGS.

Philippines President Marcos, at right, smiles as his wife, Imelda, cuts a ribbon on February 16, symbolically ending U.S. control over Clark Air Base.

PHOTOGRAPHY. The revolution that began with the electronically automated Canon AE-1 35-millimeter (mm) single-lens-reflex (SLR) camera in 1976 continued to spread in 1979. Simple-to-use and relatively inexpensive versions of these cameras were offered by all major manufacturers. So popular did the 35-mm SLR become in 1979 that its sales were expected to increase by 20 per cent at a time when the prices of food, heating fuel, and gasoline were at record highs.

Already popular as add-on accessories for many cameras, motor winders – and rewinders in some cases – were in 1979 built into several new 110, 35-mm SLR, and 35-mm compact camera models for added convenience and fast handling.

In 1979, two pocket-sized SLR models using 110-cartridge film appeared on the market. The Pentax model offered interchangeable lenses, a motor winder, and an automatic flash unit designed specifically for the camera. Minolta introduced a 110 SLR model with noninterchangeable zoom lens going from normal to medium-telephoto focal lengths, and featuring aperture-preferred automatic exposure.

Increasingly popular with beginners and hobbyists were compact 35-mm cameras with noninterchangeable lenses and built-in flash. Some models even featured automatic focusing.

New Lenses showed several important developments. Both Nikon and Canon introduced lines of physically smaller, lighter lenses for their respective camera lines. Independent manufacturers also offered smaller, lighter, and more capable lenses. Fuji Company produced a 35-mm SLR camera and a line of lenses with a new bayonet-style lens mount that differed from their previous thread-mount models and from other bayonet mounts.

In general, a trend toward shorter-focal-length zoom lenses, many with close-focusing capability, appeared. The quality of zoom lenses continued to improve; many now rival the performance of fixed-focal-length lenses.

Darkroom Work and home processing continued to grow more popular. A survey of advanced hobbyists and professional photographers revealed a new demand for fiber-based enlarging paper that produces rich black tones. The paper has been disappearing from the market recently, replaced by resin-coated or plastic printing materials that process more quickly than the conventional papers.

Instant-film advances were few for the hobby photographer, but on December 3, Polaroid Corporation introduced a new instant color film that develops twice as fast as its SX-70 film and produces better color. The company also made its 20- by 24-inch-camera and film available to professional photographers for assignments and experiments.

Although a few new 8-mm movie cameras appeared, interest was relatively small. Eastman Kodak Company discontinued its line of sound-movie cameras for home use.

Videotape recorders and cameras, potential rivals of home-movie equipment, increased their sales. But no standard system has yet been adopted.

Another area of photography that continued to boom was print collecting. For example, two albums of landscapes by Carleton E. Watkins brought $100,000 and $98,000, respectively.

Rising Costs of manufacture caused camera makers to find less expensive production methods to keep prices down. The search for reduced costs led to the advanced cameras with electronic "brains" and fewer mechanical parts. But it also increased such practices as substituting plastic parts for what were formerly more durable metal ones.

While the popularity of 35-mm SLRs grew rapidly, little or no growth was shown by 110 pocket-sized and instant-film cameras.

Among those prominent in photography who died in 1979 were Katherine Burr Blodgett, who developed the antireflection coatings that make modern lenses possible; Philippe Halsman, portraitist; Wallace Kirkland, former *Life* magazine photographer; Ernst Leitz III, whose family-owned factory made the first Leica camera; Sheila Turner Seed, photographer, editor, and writer; and Paul S. Slade, news photographer.　　　　　　　　　　Kenneth Poli

In WORLD BOOK, see CAMERA; PHOTOGRAPHY.

PHYSICS. Experimental results brought physicists closer to understanding fundamental natural forces in 1979. Their studies of the behavior of matter ranged from the smallest elementary particles to some of the densest stars.

Squeezing Xenon. When solids are subjected to extreme pressures, their atomic arrangement may change, greatly altering their properties. For example, a solid that does not conduct electricity at atmospheric pressure may conduct it well at high pressures.

David A. Nelson, Jr., and Arthur L. Ruoff of Cornell University in Ithaca, N.Y., reported in February that xenon, a gas at room temperature, became a solid conductor when cooled to $-402°F$. ($-241°C$) and then compressed at 330,000 times atmospheric pressure. The scientists used a powerful press to squeeze a thin film of xenon between two tiny diamonds. A decrease in the film's electrical resistance indicated when the xenon became solid.

Gravity Waves? J. H. Taylor and L. A. Fowler of the University of Massachusetts at Amherst and P. M. McCulloch of the University of Tasmania announced new evidence for the existence of gravity waves in February. Modern theories of gravity state that accelerated matter loses energy as gravitational radiation – gravity waves. Gravity, however, is such a weak force that only bodies at least the size of stars undergoing enormous acceleration could produce

A Universal Man

"I am truly a 'lone traveler'," Albert Einstein once wrote, "and have never belonged to my country, my home, my friends, or even my immediate family with my whole heart." Einstein was indeed a "loner," a man who, through the sheer force of his intellectual achievements, won an impregnable position as the 20th century's pre-eminent scientist.

In 1979, the centennial year of his birth, commemorative stamps in his honor were issued in half a dozen countries. In March, 19 Nobel laureates gathered at the Institute for Advanced Study in Princeton, N.J. – Einstein's last academic home – to do him honor. Similar meetings followed in Switzerland and Israel.

The Smithsonian Institution in Washington, D.C., held a major exhibition on Einstein, and Paris' Beaubourg museum staged a similar event. New York City's Institute of Physics mounted an Einstein show that visited all 50 states in 1979. Television films featuring the man and his work were aired throughout the world.

United States and European publishers – plus two in China – brought out new works on Einstein, including special centennial editions of his "Autobiographical Notes." The ultimate tribute, perhaps, was a bronze statue of Einstein 12 feet (3.7 meters) high that was unveiled by the National Academy of Sciences on its Washington grounds in April.

The honors and tributes showered on Einstein celebrated the man and his world-changing theories that revolutionized scientific thought and opened the door to the atomic age. In all probability, Einstein would have looked with a bemused eye on some of the more florid tributes. But the cockles of this quaint professor's heart would have been warmed by the knowledge that everywhere in the world of science – his special world – men and women were still testing and proving the validity of his theories. His most famous equation, $E = mc^2$ (energy equals mass times the velocity of light squared), had provided the foundation stone in the development of atomic energy. The original paper rests in the Library of Congress in Washington, D. C.

Honors were nothing new to him. Einstein's company was sought by captains and kings. He accepted visiting professorships in England and the United States at one or another time in his life. He was lionized by the press, which quoted his every word. The newsreels delighted in having him on camera. Scientific symposiums took on new meaning when Einstein attended them. He became a supporter of dozens of causes, from Zionism to a League of Europeans and a World Government.

But at heart he remained a simple man, shrinking always from the adulation and almost idolatrous attention of the public. For relaxation, he frequently played the violin – rather badly, according to his more critical admirers. He cared nothing for appearances and it showed – in rumpled sweatshirts; sweaters that were unraveling at the sleeves; baggy trousers that never had known the luxury of a pressing; unruly hair that formed a disheveled mass around his huge forehead; disreputable-looking sandals that he invariably wore without socks. Visitors and students at Princeton looked on him with mingled awe and amusement as he shuffled down a street, on occasion concentrating on nothing more earthshaking than eating an ice cream cone.

Throughout his life, Einstein had great respect for a Supreme Being. He clung to a vision of an infallible, orderly creation. He argued heatedly with scientists who were developing the quantum theory of subatomic physics, in which chance and probability play major roles. "God does not play dice," he said.

When he died of a ruptured aortic aneurysm on April 18, 1955, his unfulfilled calculations on an ultimate principle that would unite the four major forces of nature – gravitation, electromagnetism, and the strong and weak nuclear forces – lay on a table beside his bed. "I believe in Spinoza's God," he once said, "who reveals Himself in the orderly harmony of what exists." It was exactly this quest for "orderly harmony" that Albert Einstein bequeathed – in a treasure-trove of ideas – to the scientists of the world.　　　　Paul C. Tullier

Albert Einstein

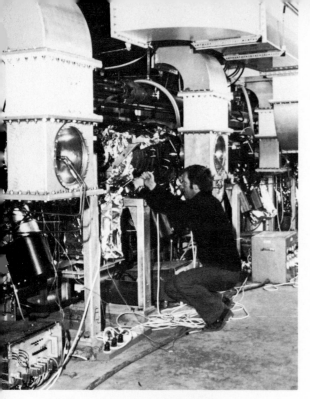

PETRA colliding-beam machine near Hamburg, West Germany, may have detected the gluon, a basic particle of matter, physicists said in September.

protons and neutrons. A key ingredient in the theories is the *gluon,* a hypothetical particle that carries forces between quarks just as the photon carries forces between electrically charged particles such as protons and electrons. The new evidence seems to show that gluons really exist. The experiments took place in the new PETRA storage ring at the DESY electron synchrotron laboratory near Hamburg, West Germany, in which beams of electrons and *positrons* (positive electrons) collide, then annihilate one another by changing to pure energy, and finally rematerialize as elementary particles. If the collision occurs at sufficiently high energy, two "jets" fly away from it. These jets are showers of particles, emitted as two quarks that materialize after the annihilation try to escape from each other. Researchers have never seen quarks as free particles.

But experimenters have seen a third jet after some collisions at the highest energies. This third jet is what the theories say to expect when a quark shakes off a gluon. The gluon makes its own jet of particles.

Furthermore, the equations that describe gluon emission closely resemble those describing how charged particles emit photons. Therefore, the gluon discovery makes physicists confident that they have taken another major step toward a unified theory that describes the behavior of gluons and photons.   Thomas O. White

In World Book, see Physics; Quark.

gravity waves that are strong enough to be detected. The scientists analyzed electromagnetic signals that the giant radio telescope at the Arecibo Observatory in Puerto Rico picked up from a *pulsar,* the tiny, extremely dense residue of a burned-out star that spins rapidly and emits pulses of electromagnetic radiation that correspond to its rotational velocity. This particular pulsar and another, initially unseen, star are orbiting around each other. The researchers analyzed the electromagnetic signals and calculated the duration of the pulsar's orbit. In addition, they calculated that the duration has decreased since the pulsar's discovery in 1975 by an amount consistent with the general theory of relativity. Their calculations thus seemed to show that gravity waves exist. But the calculations rest on the assumption that the companion star is small and dense, like the pulsar. In August, U.S. and Swiss astronomers observed a faint star, possibly the companion, that seems to be far less dense than had been assumed. If the faint star is the companion, then the pulsar's tidal interaction with its thin gases might account for all or most of the change in the pulsar's orbit. Gravity waves might not be necessary to explain the orbital change.

Elementary Glue. In September and October, several international groups of experimenters reported evidence that strongly supports current theories on the interaction of *quarks,* hypothetical constituents of some elementary particles, including

POETRY in the United States received important support in 1979 with the establishment of the National Poetry Series, designed to generate five new books of poems every year. More than $500,000 was provided for this program by James A. Michener and Edward J. Piszek; the Ford Foundation and Witter Bynner Foundation; and five publishers: Doubleday, E. P. Dutton, Harper & Row, Random House, and Holt, Rinehart & Winston.

The Nobel Prize for Literature was awarded to Greek poet Odysseus Elytis, whose works of "sensuality and light" portray man's struggles in a troubled world. Robert Penn Warren won his third Pulitzer Prize for *Now and Then: Poems 1976-1978,* which dealt with themes of love and the American landscape. James Merrill received his second National Book Award for *Mirabell: Books of Numbers,* a complex vision of the human soul. *The Poems of Stanley Kunitz: 1928-1978* profiled fearless self-explorations. Richard Hugo's *Selected Poems* celebrated blue-collar life. May Swenson's *New and Selected Things Taking Place* evoked the changing nature of contemporary existence. Swenson was cited by the Academy of American Poets for "distinguished poetic achievement."

W. S. Merwin won the 1979 Bollingen Prize "in recognition of his achievement in poetry over 25 years." Other milestones included Thom Gunn's *Selected Poems: 1950-1975;* Irving Feldman's *New* and *Selected Poems*; L. E. Sissman's *Hello, Darkness: Collected Poems* (published posthumously); and Edwin Honig's *Selected Poems: 1955-1976.*

Valuable New Collections were Ai's *Killing Floor,* historical lyrics that won the Lamont Poetry Prize in 1978, and Philip Levine's personal visions in *7 Years From Somewhere. American Journal* by Robert Hayden evoked black consciousness. Sandra McPherson's *Year of Our Birth* and Phillip Schultz's *Like Wings* examined interpersonal relationships. *Tenebrae* by British poet Geoffrey Hill focused on ecclesiastical values. Hayden Carruth's *Brothers, I Love You All* related simple truths of rural living.

Important work from new poets included the free-form lyricism of David Bottoms' *Shooting Rats at the Bibb County Dump* and Leslie Ullman's *Natural Histories,* the Yale Younger Poets selection. Alan Feldman's *The Happy Genius* was judged best small-press poetry book of the year.

Major Translations were Richard Howard's version of Roland Barthes' *A Lover's Discourse,* Jonathan Chaves' rendition of Yüän Hungtao's *Pilgrim of the Clouds,* and César Vallejo's *Complete Posthumous Poetry,* translated by Clayton Eshleman and José Rubia Barcia. Donald Hall's *Remembering Poets: Reminiscences and Opinions* was an outstanding biographical work. G. E. Murray

In WORLD BOOK, see POETRY.

POLAND moved toward a working relationship with the Roman Catholic Church and continued to tolerate dissent in 1979, but the economy deteriorated. The dominant political event was the visit of Pope John Paul II from June 2 to 10. It was the first papal visit to a Communist country and this pope's first visit to his homeland since his election in October 1978.

President Henryk Jablonski met the pope when he arrived in Warsaw, and Communist Party First Secretary Edward Gierek received him later in Warsaw's Belvedere Palace. The pope later visited Gniezno, Poland's ancient capital; the Jasna Gora monastery in Częstochowa; Oświęcim (Auschwitz), the site of a Nazi death camp during World War II; and Kraków, where he helped to celebrate the 900th anniversary of the martyrdom of Saint Stanislas, Poland's patron saint.

The Communist Party published guidelines for its February 1980 party congress in October, with conciliatory references to the Roman Catholic Church. Two pastoral letters by Polish bishops in September echoed the pope's insistence in his June speeches that the church should be accorded conditions under which it can fulfill its mission.

Dissident Activities continued. There were unofficial lectures as part of the so-called flying university held in private houses in Warsaw, Kraków, and

Worshipers display a big painting of Pope John Paul II at a Mass that the pope celebrated at Jasna Gora monastery in Częstochowa, Poland, in June.

other cities. A political party, the Confederation of Independent Poland, was founded in Warsaw on September 1, the anniversary of Germany's 1939 attack against Poland. In October, 11 dissidents held a weeklong hunger strike in a Warsaw church to support dissidents in Czechoslovakia.

Industrial Production increased more than 4 per cent in the first nine months of 1979, compared with the same 1978 period. Production for the home market was lower than planned, however, with the greatest shortfalls in timber, food, and light industry. The grain crop was 18.5 per cent or 4 million metric tons (4.4 million short tons) smaller than that of 1978. Foreign trade in the first six months of 1979 was up 6.9 per cent over the first half of 1978, with imports up 3.7 per cent and exports 10.7 per cent higher. But imports were 1.3 per cent short of target and exports only 1.1 per cent above target. Exports to Communist countries were 15.2 per cent higher and those to Western countries 3 per cent lower. A syndicate of Western banks organized a $500-million loan for Poland in February but, to obtain it, Poland had to provide an unprecedented amount of information about its economy.   Chris Cviic

See also EUROPE (Facts in Brief Table). In WORLD BOOK, see POLAND.

POLLUTION. See ENVIRONMENT.

POPULAR MUSIC. See MUSIC, POPULAR.

POPULATION. As of July 1, 1979, there were 4.4 billion persons in the world. The 1979 death rate of 12 per 1,000 population, combined with the birth rate of 31 per 1,000 population, gave the world an overall growth rate of 1.9 per cent. Demographers, estimating that the world's population was increasing at an annual rate of 84.3 million, said world population would double by the year 2017 if the present growth rate continues.

The highest annual growth rates were in the less developed countries of Asia, Africa, and Latin America. Africa led, with an annual birth rate of 46 per 1,000 population, a death rate of 19 per 1,000, and a growth rate of 2.9 per cent. Asia was second, with a birth rate of 34 per 1,000 population, a death rate of 12 per 1,000, and an annual growth rate of 2.1 per cent. Third was Latin America, where the birth rate was 36 per 1,000, the death rate was 9 per 1,000, and the annual growth rate was 2.5 per cent. In Oceania, which includes Australia and New Zealand, the birth rate was 22 per 1,0000, and the death rate was 9 per 1,000, for an annual growth rate of 1.3 per cent. Russia ranked fifth, with a birth rate of 18 per 1,000, a death rate of 9 per 1,000, and a growth rate of 0.9 per cent.

By contrast, the birth rate in Europe was 15 per 1,000, the death rate 11 per 1,000, and the growth rate 0.4 per cent. North America, including the

World Population in the Year 2000

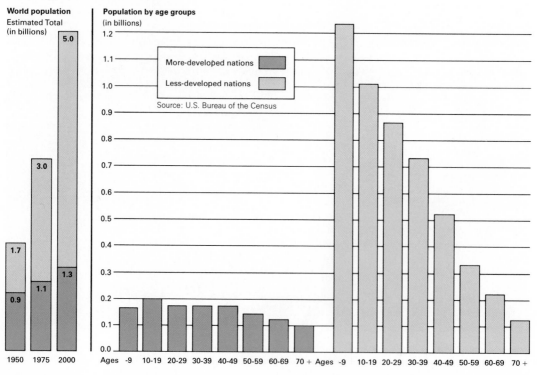

| World population Estimated Total (in billions) |
Population by age groups (in billions)

Source: U.S. Bureau of the Census

More-developed nations
Less-developed nations

1950   1975   2000

Ages -9 10-19 20-29 30-39 40-49 50-59 60-69 70 +   Ages -9 10-19 20-29 30-39 40-49 50-59 60-69 70 +

United States and Canada, recorded a birth rate of 15 per 1,000, a death rate of 8 per 1,000, and a growth rate of 0.9 per cent.

Continuing Concern for population growth and its effect on economics and resources was reflected in the number of special surveys or in-depth inquiries into the problem. The Environmental Fund, for example, added a new dimension to its annual report in 1979. With the cooperation of the United Nations (UN) International Labor Organization, the fund included in the report statistics relative to the labor force in most of the world's countries. According to the report, half of the population in most of the underdeveloped countries is teen-age or younger. Accordingly, the growth in the labor force in the 1980s is expected to be much more rapid than the growth of the population as a whole. The report indicated that some of the countries' problems are likely to become much worse.

The UN Fund for Population Activities published its annual State of World Population report in June. The report predicted that 90 per cent of the people born by the year 2000 will live in the Third World, where 20 per cent of the population already suffer from severe undernourishment; 30 per cent lack proper health care; 40 per cent have no jobs or are underemployed; and more than 50 per cent of those over 15 years of age are illiterate.   Robert C. Cook

In WORLD BOOK, see POPULATION.

Maria de Lurdes Pintassilgo is inaugurated as prime minister of caretaker government in Portugal in July, to serve until elections.

PORTUGAL ended a continuing government crisis on July 19, 1979, with the appointment of its first woman prime minister. Maria de Lurdes Pintassilgo, an industrial chemist and the country's ambassador to the United Nations Educational, Scientific, and Cultural Organization (UNESCO), was named to form a government to hold elections. The Democratic Alliance, a coalition of four center-right parties, won a general election on December 2 and local elections on December 16. The Alliance leader, Social Democrat Francisco Sá Carneiro, was appointed prime minister early in January 1980.

The nonparty government of Carlos da Mota Pinto had faced continuing battles with political factions and trade unions in the early months of 1979. A proposed 56 per cent tax on the traditional extra month's pay at Christmas 1978 particularly angered the left. Mota Pinto's government lost a vote on the budget issue on March 22. The Socialists and Communists introduced censure motions on June 4, and Mota Pinto resigned on June 7.

IMF Loan. Negotiations to renew Portugal's agreement with the International Monetary Fund (IMF) began on January 5 and dragged on for most of the year. Portugal and the IMF could not agree on how much Portugal should cut from its $920-million current account deficit and how it should stabilize its economy. Portugal wanted a stand-by credit of $50 million from the IMF, but a $300-million loan from a group of international banks on July 18 eased the country's financial situation.

In July, the Organization for Economic Cooperation and Development (OECD) criticized Portugal's inflation rate of 24 per cent, its unemployment rate of 8.5 per cent, its 1979 budget deficit of $2.6 billion, and its current account deficit. The OECD report urged continued limits on wage increases and "extreme caution" in policy changes because of unfavorable international conditions.

EC Negotiations. Portugal asked the European Community (EC or Common Market) Commission in Brussels, Belgium, to extend quotas on EC exports to Portugal and to continue import concessions for certain Portuguese products for five more years. The commission agreed on April 18 to revised trading terms, to start in January 1981 and continue through 1982. Pedro Pires Miranda, Portugal's chief of negotiations for membership in the EC, launched a nationwide campaign on May 3 to revive public interest in the EC. The commission asked Portugal to begin harmonizing its tax structure with that of member nations.

Portugal set aside $790 million in July to develop natural energy resources and mineral deposits. Oil imports were expected to increase 16 per cent to $88 million in 1979.   Kenneth Brown

See also EUROPE (Facts in Brief Table). In WORLD BOOK, see PORTUGAL.

POSTAL SERVICE, UNITED STATES, plagued with annual deficits for 34 years, reported a revenue surplus for the fiscal year ending on Oct. 1, 1979. Postmaster General William F. Bolger reported on November 27 that the surplus was more than $470-million because of a record volume of mail and higher postal rates. The Postal Service estimated total income at $17.9 billion, compared with estimated expenses of $17.5 billion for fiscal 1979. It was the first time it showed a profit since 1945.

The Postal Service moved a record 97 billion pieces of mail with 80,000 fewer employees than it had in 1971, when the semi-public agency replaced the United States Post Office Department. Bolger said that the surplus would allow the Postal Service to operate at present postal rates until at least 1981.

New Envelope Size. As part of its effort to speed mail processing through greater use of automated equipment, the Postal Service on July 15 introduced new standards for envelope sizes. According to the new rules, envelopes smaller than $3^1/2$ by 5 inches (89 by 127 millimeters) will be returned to the sender, and a surcharge of 7 cents will be placed on envelopes measuring more than $11^1/2$ by $6^1/8$ inches (292 by 156 millimeters). A Postal Service official explained that it is difficult for automated machinery to process extremely small or large envelopes.

The Postal Service also launched an experimental international electronic mail system called Intelpost in July. This service allowed customers in Washington, D.C., and New York City to use special service facilities located in such places as New York's World Trade Center to send electronic copies of documents to London by communications satellite. However, the plan ended abruptly on October 18 when the Federal Communications Commission denied permission to the Postal Service to beam messages across the Atlantic Ocean. It said the proposed service, which cost about $5 per page, was "inherently discriminatory" because it appealed almost solely to big-business users.

On October 24, the Postal Service relaxed its monopoly on letter mail delivery, adopting new rules that allow private firms to deliver mail classified as "extremely urgent." The postage fee for such mail must be double the first-class rate or $3, whichever is greater.

The Postal Service started a new service, Express Mail Metro, in 25 of the largest U.S. cities in April. The innovation guaranteed that letters and packages mailed before 10 A.M. to destinations in the same city would be received by 5 P.M. on the same day. Postage was set at $9 for the first pound (0.45 kilogram). But on April 30, Federal Judge Prentice Marshall in Chicago granted a restraining order to six private messenger companies that effectively blocked the new plan.   William J. Eaton

In WORLD BOOK, see POST OFFICE; POSTAL SERVICE, UNITED STATES.

PRESIDENT OF THE UNITED STATES Jimmy Carter faced the most difficult crisis of his presidency and revealed his talent for calm, patient leadership in November 1979. His long-debated and controversial decision to allow the exiled Shah Mohammad Reza Pahlavi of Iran to enter the United States for medical treatment led followers of the Ayatollah Ruhollah Khomeini to attack the United States Embassy in Teheran, Iran, on November 4 and take American hostages, demanding that the shah be returned to Iran. See IRAN.

The President acted with restraint in the weeks that followed, avoiding angry comments in an effort to save the lives of the hostages. Americans of every political persuasion supported the President as he stopped all U.S. purchases of Iranian oil, froze Iranian government assets in U.S. banks, and asked the U.S. Immigration and Naturalization Service to institute deportation proceedings against Iranian students living in the United States illegally.

When the U.S. Embassy in Islamabad, Pakistan, was attacked and burned on November 21, the President called on Pakistan to protect Embassy personnel. He also ordered most Department of State dependents and non-essential personnel in 11 Muslim countries to return to the United States and warned against travel in 14 Middle East nations.

In addition to the crisis in Iran, the President struggled with rising oil prices, an unstable dollar, Russian challenges in Cuba and Afghanistan, and a Senate hesitant to ratify the Strategic Arms Limitation Treaty (SALT II). Carter's effort to shift the U.S. role in the world away from that of policeman and to emphasize the new realities of power led some allies to doubt his commitment and some critics to fault him for a failure of will.

Foreign Policy Triumphs. Nonetheless, the President chalked up some striking foreign policy successes in his third year in office. President Carter traveled to the Middle East in March to work out final details of the Israeli-Egyptian peace treaty that he had helped to draft in 1978. He addressed the People's Assembly in Cairo, Egypt, on March 10, asking Palestinians to "join the negotiations on their future." Later that same day in Jerusalem, Israel, he noted that difficult issues regarding the Middle East peace must still be resolved.

The Egyptian Cabinet approved the peace treaty on March 15, and the Israeli *Knesset* (parliament) followed suit on March 22. In a historic moment on the White House lawn in Washington, D.C., Egypt's President Anwar al-Sadat and Israel's Prime Minister Menachem Begin signed the peace treaty on March 26, with President Carter adding his signature as a witness. On March 27, Begin and Sadat addressed a joint session of the U.S. Congress before they returned to the Middle East. See MIDDLE EAST.

President Carter enjoyed a partial victory with the signing of SALT II in Vienna, Austria, on June 18.

On a peace mission in March, President Carter phones Israeli Prime Minister Begin from Cairo while meeting with Egyptian President Sadat.

The President urged the nation to support ratification of the treaty to help stop the "uncontrolled and pointless nuclear arms race." However, opposition to the treaty was strong in the United States Senate and the disclosure on August 31 that Russia had stationed combat troops in Cuba stimulated further opposition to SALT II.

President Carter made a major policy address to the nation on October 1, urging support for SALT II despite the Cuban incident. Moving with restraint, he ordered American troops stationed in Key West, Fla., only 90 miles (140 kilometers) from Cuba, and asked Russia to withdraw its troops. But Russia insisted the unit was only a training unit. The treaty did not come to a vote in the Senate in 1979, and after Russia's military intervention in Afghanistan in December, Carter asked that a vote be postponed. See ARMED FORCES.

Carter responded to China's invasion of Vietnam on February 17 by demanding the immediate withdrawal of Vietnamese troops from Cambodia and of Chinese troops from Vietnam. On February 27, Secretary of the Treasury W. Michael Blumenthal delivered a note from President Carter to Chinese officials in Peking (Beijing in the phonetic Pinyin alphabet China adopted on January 1); Carter asked China to withdraw its troops from Vietnam "as quickly as possible." The incident underscored the role of the U.S. in Southeast Asia.

The President announced on March 9 that he was invoking the emergency provisions of the 1976 Arms Export Control Act that permitted him to by-pass Congress and approve the export of $390 million in arms to Yemen (Sana). Saudi Arabia bought the U.S. weapons to arm Yemen (Sana) against an invasion by Yemen (Aden).

An authorization bill signed by the President on August 15 ordered him to lift economic sanctions against Zimbabwe Rhodesia by November 15 unless he notified Congress that lifting the sanctions was not in the interest of the United States. The President notified Congress on November 14 that he was still unwilling to lift the sanctions. However, he lifted them on December 16, shortly after Lord Soames, a British parliamentary leader, was installed as transitional governor. See ZIMBABWE RHODESIA.

President Carter announced on June 28 that the United States would double the quota of refugees from Southeast Asia. Responding to accounts that the refugees were trying to escape by boat from Vietnam, the President on July 21 ordered U.S. Navy ships to pick up drifting "boat people" and take them to safety. As the plight of Cambodian refugees worsened, the President on October 24 pledged $70 million in food and medical relief for refugees in Cambodia and Thailand. See ASIA.

Travel Abroad. The President conferred with the heads of government of France, Great Britain, and

West Germany in Guadeloupe on January 5 and 6. The four leaders exchanged views on a wide range of topics and announced no real differences.

Carter went to Mexico City, Mexico, in February to discuss oil and the problem of illegal aliens with President Jose Lopez Portillo. The leaders signed pacts of cooperation in scientific development and in housing and agreed to open negotiations for the United States purchase of Mexican natural gas.

President Carter made a 12-day visit to Japan and South Korea in June. In South Korea, he and President Chung Hee Park discussed human rights, refugees, and security issues. As a result, the President on July 20 temporarily suspended the planned withdrawal of 32,000 American troops from South Korea, at least until 1981. In Japan, President Carter discussed mutual energy problems with Prime Minister Masayoshi Ohira. While he was in the Far East, the Organization of Petroleum Exporting Countries (OPEC) raised the price of crude oil a startling 24 per cent. Carter said that the OPEC action "will make a recession more likely."

Energy Programs. The President's 1977 energy program – his drive to make the United States independent of other nations for its energy needs, which he had termed the "moral equivalent of war" – faltered badly in 1979. In a nationally televised address on April 5, President Carter soberly outlined

Hamilton Jordan, White House chief of staff and one of the Carter Administration's most controversial figures, has a quiet briefing with the President.

another, more complicated and austere energy program, telling the American people that they would have to learn to use less energy and pay more for it because "the future of the country we love is at stake." His April plan included the gradual lifting of price controls on domestic oil, coupled with a "windfall-profits" tax on the oil companies that would finance the search for alternative sources of energy and help the nation's lowest-income families pay the rising fuel bills.

The President warned the nation on April 25 that gas shortages were imminent. He urged Congress to approve his stand-by gasoline-rationing plan, and revealed that he had told the Department of Energy to ensure that oil would be stockpiled for home-heating needs during the winter of 1979-1980.

A shortage of gasoline for cars and trucks developed suddenly in the spring, after the revolution in Iran cut off the flow of oil from that country to the United States. The President signed an executive order on May 29 allowing governors to regulate gasoline sales in their respective states. First asking for oil-company cooperation, and then castigating the oil companies, the President asked Americans to exercise voluntary restraint and urged them to pressure Congress to adopt his long-stalled energy program. Addressing the United Food and Commercial Workers International Union in Washington, D.C., on June 7, President Carter declared that "the greatest democratic system of government in the world is . . . being pulled apart by selfishness."

Canceling a scheduled energy speech on July 5, the President retired to Camp David, Maryland, to confer with Cabinet officials, senior advisers, state governors, and other prominent Americans. When the meetings at Camp David ended on July 11, the President remained in his mountain retreat to prepare a major energy address.

He unveiled his new energy program in a forceful speech from the White House on July 15. He proposed limiting oil imports to less than 8.5 million barrels per day (bpd); set a goal of cutting oil imports by 4.5 million bpd by 1990; set new goals for the development of synthetic fuel; proposed the formation of an Energy Mobilization Board to speed construction of energy projects; and again proposed the "windfall-profits" tax to increase aid to the nation's mass-transit systems and help the needy pay rising oil bills.

The following day, speaking in Detroit and Kansas City, Mo., the President spelled out the details of his new program. He called for a federal expenditure of $140 billion over the next 10 years to end U.S. dependence on foreign oil, and set 1979 import quotas at 8.2 million bpd. However, the 96th Congress passed parts of the President's energy program only after endless debate and avoided the key provision of the plan, the "windfall-profits" tax, until the end of the first session. See CONGRESS.

President Jimmy Carter and Teng Hsiao-p'ing, deputy premier of China, greet children who sang at a Washington, D.C., gala in Teng's honor in January.

The safety of the nuclear program was widely challenged after a frightening nuclear plant accident at the Metropolitan Edison Company's Three Mile Island plant near Harrisburg, Pa., on March 28. The President visited the plant on April 1 and appointed a commission to investigate the causes of the accident. On May 7, however, President Carter told a crowd of antinuclear power demonstrators in Washington, D.C., that it was "out of the question" to shut down all the nation's nuclear generating plants. The accident caused no fatalities, but it resulted in the temporary evacuation of thousands of people living near the plant and raised serious questions about the safety and environmental effects of nuclear power plants. See ENERGY.

Staff Shuffle. In an unprecedented move, the President asked for the resignations of 34 Cabinet and senior White House staff members on July 17. He accepted the resignations of five Cabinet officers, replacing them rapidly, often by reshuffling other Administration officials. At the same time, he reorganized his White House staff, making 34-year-old Hamilton Jordan chief of staff with far-reaching authority. Jordan's first official act was to distribute "evaluation forms" to Cabinet and senior White House officials, ordering them to evaluate hundreds of subordinates for their efficiency and loyalty to the administration. See CABINET, UNITED STATES.

The President described the reshuffle as "con-

structive" and declared that the new Administration would "now be better able to serve this country." In an attempt to "broaden his circle of advisers," Carter on July 25 named Hedley W. Donovan, former editor in chief of *Time* magazine, a senior presidential adviser. Lloyd N. Cutler, a well-known Washington lawyer, became the President's counsel on August 17, and in September, the President named Abelardo Lopez Valdez as White House chief of protocol.

Carter's firing of former New York Congresswoman Bella S. Abzug as co-chairman of his National Advisory Committee on Women on January 12 stirred up controversy, and 23 members of the committee resigned in protest. On May 9, he named Lynda Bird Johnson Robb, daughter of President Lyndon B. Johnson, to chair the committee.

New Commissions. As the inflation rate climbed, the President established a Pay Advisory Committee to advise him on the effectiveness of his voluntary wage-price guidelines. On October 16, the President named 17 members of the committee to serve under Chairman John Dunlop. Six members would represent the public; five, labor; and six, business interests. See LABOR.   Carol L. Thompson

See also CARTER, JAMES EARL, JR.; UNITED STATES, GOVERNMENT OF THE. In WORLD BOOK, see CARTER, JAMES EARL, JR.; PRESIDENT OF THE UNITED STATES.

PRINCE EDWARD ISLAND. Canada's smallest province elected a Progressive Conservative government on April 23, 1979, leaving the country without a single Liberal government in the provinces for the first time in more than 100 years. The Liberal defeat in national elections on May 22 confirmed the party's collapse. The Progressive Conservatives, led by J. Angus MacLean, won 21 of the 32 seats in Prince Edward Island's legislature. The Liberals took the remaining 11.

The election's main issue was nuclear power. The Conservatives opposed its import from a generating station being built in New Brunswick and stressed the value of preserving the province's rural economy based on the land and the sea.

The MacLean government was sworn in on May 3, and the premier appointed a nine-member cabinet. The July 10 budget forecast expenditures of $292.4 million against revenues of $267.1 million.

The new government differed with the province's physicians over their method of billing for services under Medicare. Thirty per cent of the 120 doctors in the province withdrew from the plan. There were fears that this action might violate a rule that federal contributions would be paid to provinces only if hospital and medical services were accessible to all of their citizens.   David M. L. Farr

See also CANADA. In WORLD BOOK, see PRINCE EDWARD ISLAND.

PRISON population in the United States topped 300,000 for the first time, according to a Law Enforcement Assistance Administration (LEAA) report released in June 1979. The inmate total in federal correctional institutions continued to decline because of federal authorities' new emphasis on white-collar crime, and the resulting transfer to state courts of car-theft and bank-robbery defendants. But mandatory sentencing and other factors expanded the state prison population even faster.

The LEAA conducted the first nationwide jail survey in 1979. It found that about 160,000 additional persons were in 3,493 county and municipal jails on a typical day.

Inmate Rights. Two important decisions by the Supreme Court of the United States affected prisoners' rights. The high court ruled 5 to 4 on May 29 that inmates are not entitled to full due process in state parole proceedings. States are basically free to administer their parole systems as they wish, the majority held. The court ruled, 6 to 3, on May 14 that prison officials may incarcerate pretrial detainees under harsh and strict conditions if "justified by compelling necessities of jail administration."

Prisoners won significant damage awards in two Virginia cases. The American Civil Liberties Union announced on March 17 that the U.S. Bureau of Prisons had paid $20,000 to settle a lawsuit brought by a male inmate who had been raped by other prisoners in the Petersburg, Va., federal penitentiary. And Virginia state officials agreed on January 5 to a $518,000 settlement, the largest such award in history, for a felon victimized by medical malpractice. The inmate had developed emotional problems and was given excessive drugs, then ignored. He developed severe skin problems and paralysis.

Clemency Scandal. On January 16, Governor Ray Blanton of Tennessee granted commutations or parole eligibilities to 52 convicts, including 23 serving long-term murder sentences. One of the convicted murderers was the son of a key political ally. Blanton cited court orders to reduce prison overcrowding. After learning that Blanton planned to grant 30 more clemencies, including 10 death-row commutations, Governor-elect Lamar Alexander took office on January 17, three days before his scheduled inauguration. On March 15, a federal grand jury indicted six persons, including five Blanton aides but not the former governor himself, for selling clemencies.

A federal judge placed the Alabama state prison system in receivership on February 2, citing unconstitutional conditions that amounted to "cruel and unusual punishment."   David C. Beckwith

In WORLD BOOK, see PRISON.

PRIZES. See AWARDS AND PRIZES; CANADIAN LIBRARY ASSOCIATION; CANADIAN LITERATURE; FASHION; NOBEL PRIZES.

PROTESTANTISM. The positive response to Pope John Paul II's visit to the United States in October 1979 demonstrated the hunger of Protestant church people for attention to the corporate life of the organized church, as well as for leadership in their own ranks (see RELIGION [Close-Up]). Two leadership changes during 1979 evoked varying responses in Protestantism. In September, the 65-million-member Anglican Communion, which includes The Episcopal Church in America, named Robert A. K. Runcie, 57, archbishop of Canterbury and leader of the Anglican Community. Runcie, a moderate, is known more for his diplomatic skills than for clearly stated theological positions. Observers noted that he would need those skills immediately to deal with controversies.

Although he is a moderate, Runcie had opposed the ordination of women in the Anglican priesthood "on principle and in practice." The ordination of women is a regular and popular act in Canada. Women have also been ordained in the more divided United States church. But the General Synod of the Church of England ruled in July that women may not act as priests in Great Britain, even if they have been ordained in North America. This decision was unpopular in Anglican circles outside Britain and was certain to be tested by women in Britain.

New Baptist Leader. More controversial was the choice of a leader by the majority of *messengers*

(delegates) in the Southern Baptist Convention, the largest Protestant group in the United States. At their annual meeting in Houston in June, the messengers chose Adrian P. Rogers of Memphis as president. He was the candidate of a determined and well-organized group of Baptists who stated their fears that the Southern Baptist Convention had been gradually compromising its conservative theological stand. These fears focused on the issue of the *inerrancy* (lack of error) of the Bible. Rogers' supporters charged that in many pulpits, and even in the group's seminaries, some clergy have taught that the Bible may not be completely accurate in all its geographical, historical, and scientific references. The conservatives insisted that only their own doctrine – that the original manuscripts of the Bible contained no errors of any sort – would ensure the strength of faith and survival of the church body.

Rogers' opponents claimed equally firm, if diverse, views of Biblical authority. But this more liberal group was not organized and failed to make its point to the messengers. After the meeting, the liberal group protested the aggressiveness of those supporting inerrancy. They also contended that several hundred votes had been cast by unregistered, and thus illegal, messengers; this charge was later confirmed in a nonpartisan investigation, but there were no moves to unseat Rogers.

Surrounded by his family, Robert A. K. Runcie discusses his designation in September as the new archbishop of Canterbury, leader of the Anglicans.

The convention did not give Rogers a clear order to "clean house" in the seminaries. He asserted that he would not sweep through the convention hunting heresy, though he would be watching those who deviated from his view of Biblical inerrancy.

Changing Congregations. The Baptists and all the smaller Protestant bodies directed much of their energy toward holding their own against the threats to organized religion. The threats sprang from the marked tendency of Americans, like their European counterparts before them, to make religion an ever more private affair. University of Colorado economist Kenneth E. Boulding spoke of a "decay of legitimacy" in such institutions as the government, the military establishment, and the business community. Many Americans seemed to feel that the institutional church was also experiencing such decay. Although the Protestant churches continued to hold the allegiance of millions of people, many others were making their search for faith a "private affair," putting together their own belief systems.

On this front, much attention was focused again on "the electronic church," the form of Protestantism propagated in radio broadcasts and, increasingly, on television. Many of these ministries were set up as huge congregations on which the microphone and camera "eavesdropped" for the sake of millions of viewers. The electronic ministries stressed conversion, healing, and an affirmative outlook on life that promised many blessings to followers. While the TV congregations encouraged the support of local churches, their own surveys showed that millions of Americans tuned into their programs but were not moved to take part in the organized church.

While many electronic church leaders were nonpolitical, some organized or supported conservative political agencies. During 1979, a group of conservatives formed Christian Voice, a lobby that purposely did not seek tax exemption so that it could engage in politics overtly. Announcing that it intended to work with the support of electronic evangelists, Christian Voice set as its goal the task of returning America to moral standards that it finds acceptable. In particular, the group will work against liberalizing laws relating to homosexuality, abortion, and pornography. Christian Voice leaders also announced that in 1980 they would work to defeat political candidates unacceptable to them. Several moderate Protestant leaders voiced opposition to this form of influencing the public order.

The Homosexual Issue, controversial in Protestantism for years, surfaced again in 1979. Loey Powell, a minister, announced from the pulpit that she is homosexual, as she led worship at the biennial meeting of the United Church of Christ in Indianapolis in June. The United Church voted to reaffirm its policy of handling decisions about ordination at the local level – a policy that has the effect of sanctioning the ordination of homosexuals, even though the denomination has taken no positive or direct stand that it will do so.

Ordination of homosexuals was also an issue at the Episcopal General Convention in Denver in September. The delegates had to decide whether that church, which had one of the more open attitudes on the matter, would ordain avowed and practicing homosexuals. While stating that it would continue its ministry in the homosexual community, the Episcopal majority voted not to ordain avowed homosexuals. A group of 21 bishops then affirmed that they would not be limited by the decision.

The Episcopal General Convention also voted final approval of a revised version of the *Book of Common Prayer*. But the convention made it possible for congregations that preferred to continue using the 1928 version to do so.

Mormons Expel Feminist. Sonia Johnson, 43, of Sterling, Va., was excommunicated from the Church of Jesus Christ of Latter-day Saints (Mormons) on December 5. The top leadership of the church, a group of three men, had taken an official stand against passage of the Equal Rights Amendment (ERA) to the U.S. Constitution. Johnson is head of a group called Mormons for ERA. Church leaders said that an individual Mormon has the right to support the ERA, but not to organize opposition to a stand taken by the church.

In Other Countries. Protestants focused their attention on the church in Russia. The release in April of Georgi P. Vins, 50, a Baptist who resisted the Communist regime, was a major event. For his resistance, he spent 15 years in Siberian prisons. Vins's group is a secessionist "Reform Baptist" assembly that is more militant about religious rights than is the mainline Baptist group in Russia. Vins was a disappointment to American Protestants who favor the church's political involvement, because he isolated religious rights from other human rights. Yet, even though his views were not acceptable to all, he called attention to the problems that people of many faiths face in hostile political climates.

The World Council of Churches (WCC), which was criticized for supporting the Patriotic Front guerrillas in Zimbabwe Rhodesia, sent another grant to the Front in September. The action displeased many American members of WCC-affiliated churches. Bishop Abel T. Muzorewa, then prime minister of Zimbabwe Rhodesia, is a Methodist with some support in the United States, so the differences in Protestant attitudes toward his nation caused tension among American Protestants. Some questioned whether Muzorewa had agreed to too much power for the white minority. However, Muzorewa's government was replaced in December by a temporary colonial governor, who would serve until elections early in 1980.   Martin E. Marty

See also RELIGION. In WORLD BOOK, see PROTESTANTISM and articles on Protestant denominations.

PSYCHOLOGY. Although psychologists have tried in recent years to establish links between human speech and ape communications, a 1979 study contended that the patterning of ape messages is not like human language. A team of psychologists headed by Herbert S. Terrace of Columbia University in New York City said in November that apes cannot combine words that they learn through sign language to make sentences, an essential feature of human language. The researchers used American Sign Language (ASL) – which was also used in the past to teach the female chimpanzee Washoe – to teach a male chimpanzee, Neam Chimpsky (Nim).

The investigators analyzed more than 19,000 of Nim's multiword signs, seeking patterns of grammar or *syntax* (sentence structure). Some evidence of syntax was found, but this was limited to Nim's two-word combinations. For example, he signed the phrases "more food" or "more drink" much more frequently than the opposite forms, such as "food more."

The Difference. Although Nim used some three-word combinations, the third word seemed only to be used for emphasis – for example, "eat Nim eat" or "drink me Nim." By contrast, children use a third word to add information – for example, "drink me juice." Nim's four-word signs – "drink Nim drink Nim," for instance – show the same pattern of repe-

University of Minnesota psychologists study the effects of environment on twin brothers separated as infants and raised by two different families.

tition for emphasis. But children use four-word phrases to elaborate meaning.

When Nim put together combinations that seemed more sophisticated, a close analysis of the videotapes made during his signing sessions showed that the human trainer had provided subtle, unconscious clues to elicit those combinations. The researchers linked this to what they term *anthropomorphism* (attributing human characteristics to animals) in some scientific literature about B. T. Gardner's and R. A. Gardner's work at the University of Nevada with Washoe. In an incident celebrated in the area of ape communications, Washoe had responded with the two-word combination "water bird" when her human companion pointed to a swan in a pond and asked, "What that?" Some researchers concluded from the incident that Washoe, lacking the word *swan* in her ASL vocabulary, had invented a two-word name for the strange animal. The Terrace team pointed out that Washoe might have been responding to the question by naming two objects, water and bird, both present in the area.

The Nim report concluded that learning of language by apes is very restricted. Apes readily learn isolated symbols, but probably no more readily than dogs and some other animals.

Life Without Adults. The well-known novel *Lord of the Flies* (1954) by William Golding explored the psychological consequences of a society made up of children living alone without adults. Golding's insights were given some reality by recent studies of monkeys carried out by Leonard Rosenblum and Edward H. Plimpton of the Department of Psychiatry at the Downstate Medical Center in New York. The researchers found that juvenile monkeys left together without adult supervision showed three to four times as much aggressiveness toward their peers as they did when adults were present. Apparently, it made little difference whether the adults present were their own mothers or other adult females. However, when juvenile monkeys were supervised by females other than their mothers, they showed unusual emotional distress.

Rosenblum and Plimpton concluded that adult monkeys clearly influence the emotional state of infants and juveniles, and that adults can inhibit or facilitate specific kinds of social responses among juveniles. How this happens is not clear. Presumably, the adults influence the nature of the social bonds that the juveniles form.

Toast of the Campus. Psychologist Alan Marlatt of the University of Washington, Seattle, opened a cocktail lounge on campus in June with a $43,000 government grant. Marlatt — who seeks to prevent alcoholism — found that nonalcoholic drinks produce the euphoria associated with alcohol, if the subjects think they are "drinking." Robert W. Goy

See also MENTAL HEALTH. In WORLD BOOK, see CHIMPANZEE; PSYCHOLOGY.

PUBLIC HEALTH. More than 90 per cent of United States schoolchildren were fully immunized against measles and such diseases as diphtheria, polio, typhoid, and whooping cough by September 1979. That achievement realized a goal set two years earlier by Joseph A. Califano, Jr., who was then secretary of health, education, and welfare (HEW).

The U.S. Center for Disease Control (CDC) in Atlanta, Ga., reported that measles cases declined about 50 per cent in the first six months of 1979, reaching an all-time low of 10,686 cases. This was a dramatic drop from the 1950s, when there were about 500,000 cases of measles and 500 deaths from it each year.

Unvaccinated teen-agers and young adults were particularly vulnerable. Up to 25 per cent of the measles cases reported in 1979 involved people between the ages of 15 and 20, the CDC reported.

Mumps also continued to decline, as it has since a vaccine was licensed in the late 1960s. In 1978, the incidence of mumps averaged 20 per cent lower than in the previous year.

Tuberculosis (TB) was a far more stubborn disease to eradicate. TB strikes about 3 million people around the world each year, including 29,000 Americans in 1978. American physicians noted at an international conference on TB in March that 3,000 persons had died of TB in the United States in 1977

A Lancaster, Pa., Amish family prepares for the polio vaccinations they have agreed to take because of confirmed polio cases in Amish colonies.

and that 21 states had reported increases in 1978.

Malaria also made a comeback in 1979. The World Health Organization reported that the disease remained *endemic* (occurring regularly) in tropical Africa and threatened to become endemic again in India, Southeast Asia, and Latin America.

An intensive immunization effort by the CDC was responsible for containing an outbreak of polio among members of the Amish religious community in Pennsylvania and other states. More than 15 cases were reported between January and June. CDC workers convinced the Amish that they were vulnerable to the highly contagious disease, and Amish colonies were vaccinated.

Other Developments. In October, the federal Office of Technology Assessment (OTA) criticized the government for permitting some vaccines to be sold without sufficient research into possible adverse side effects. The OTA also said the government failed to encourage vaccine research and depended too much on foreign pharmaceutical companies.

In a report released in April, the Population Crisis Committee noted that about 40 million illegal abortions are performed throughout the world each year and are a leading cause of death among women of childbearing age.

Dianne R. Hales

See also HEALTH AND DISEASE; MEDICINE. In WORLD BOOK, see PUBLIC HEALTH.

PUBLISHING mergers and acquisitions continued to spark controversy within the industry in the United States in 1979. In one of the biggest takeover attempts on record, the American Express Company made an initial offer of $830 million, or $34 per share of stock, for McGraw-Hill, Incorporated, one of the largest publishers in the United States, on January 9. McGraw-Hill's resistance to the offer triggered a series of lawsuits and countersuits in which American Express charged McGraw-Hill with obstruction and McGraw-Hill asked that American Express be barred from buying its stock. The controversy ended on March 1 with the expiration of American Express' final offer of $40 per share.

Other Mergers. The American Broadcasting Companies, Incorporated (ABC), ventured deeper into publishing in 1979. ABC bought a 51.6 per cent interest in the Chilton Company, a book and magazine publisher in Radnor, Pa., for about $26.6-million in April. It purchased McCall's Needlework and Crafts, Incorporated, publishers of handbooks for hobbyists, in May.

In a unique arrangement announced on February 12, William Morrow and Company and Bantam Books, Incorporated, formed Perigord Press for the simultaneous acquisition of hardback and paperback books. Marboro Book Stores, a chain of six New York City retail outlets of "remainders," announced

Visitors peruse volumes and browse through displays at the Moscow International Book Fair, which featured exhibits from more than 70 countries in September.

on October 22 the sale of its assets to Barnes & Noble, a 31-store retail chain.

Book Sales during the first six months of 1979 were "bleak," according to estimates released by the Association of American Publishers in July. Paperback sales, which declined for the first time since 1940, were down 10 to 15 per cent from the same period in 1978. Hard-cover general-interest books were down 15 per cent. The decline was attributed primarily to higher book prices.

In response, Bantam Books, Incorporated, the largest U.S. paperback publisher, announced in June that it would reduce the initial price of two of its leading entries in the 1979 market. It lowered the price of *The Far Pavilions* by M. M. Kaye from $3.50 to $2.95 and reduced *The Rich and the Beautiful* by Ruth Harris from $2.50 to $1.79.

Bantam pledged a record advance of $3.2 million in September for the paperback rights to *Princess Daisy* by Judith Krantz, and scheduled the paperback version for 1981 publication. United Artists paid a record $2.5 million in October for film rights to *Thy Neighbor's Wife,* a nonfiction book by Gay Talese about sexual practices in the United States, which was to be published by Doubleday & Company, Incorporated, early in 1980.　　Beverly Merz

See also CANADIAN LITERATURE; LITERATURE; MAGAZINE; NEWSPAPER; POETRY. In WORLD BOOK, see BOOKS; PUBLISHING.

PUERTO RICO. The sentences of four Puerto Rican nationalists, each of whom had served 25 years in prison in the United States, were commuted by President Jimmy Carter on Sept. 6, 1979. Three of them – Lolita Lebron, Rafael Cancel-Miranda, and Irving Flores Rodrigues – were imprisoned for an attack on the U.S. House of Representatives on March 1, 1954, in which five congressmen were wounded. The fourth, Oscar Collazo, was convicted of trying to kill President Harry S. Truman in 1950. The four, ardent supporters of independence for Puerto Rico, were welcomed to San Juan by a cheering crowd on September 12.

Many Puerto Ricans, including Governor Carlos Romero Barcelo, objected to the terrorists' release. They feared the four might precipitate renewed violence and agitate for an early plebiscite on Puerto Rico's status. The U.S. government, while acknowledging that the terrorists were "unrepentant," cited "humane considerations" for the decision to release them and said they did not pose a threat.

The Island's Future Status – as a continuing commonwealth, a state in the United States, or an independent nation – remained a major concern. On June 22, Governor Romero said a recent poll indicated that a plebiscite planned for 1981 would result in a strong vote for independence.

Vieques, a small island 9 miles (14 kilometers) off the coast of the main island used for military target practice and land-assault exercises by the U.S. Navy, became a point of confrontation between the Navy and Puerto Rican fishermen and their supporters early in the year. The fishermen insisted that the military activity endangered fishing and damaged delicate offshore reefs where the fish breed.

Protest Against Navy. On February 3, about 100 protestors eluded Navy guards on Vieques and occupied Caracas Beach for a sit-in protest that was eventually abandoned. On May 16, however, 12 fishermen attempting another sit-in were removed by Navy security forces. The Puerto Rican news media insisted that the Navy had used force in removing the trespassers as well as in photographing and fingerprinting them. The Navy denied it.

On December 4, terrorists ambushed a U.S. Navy bus that was transporting unarmed American personnel to a communication center outside San Juan. Two servicemen were killed and 10 other persons were wounded, two critically. Three Puerto Rican nationalist groups claimed responsibility for the attack, saying it was in retaliation for the death in a Florida prison of a Puerto Rican arrested in a protest on Vieques. The man was found hanged in his cell, but his death was ruled a suicide.　　Paul C. Tullier

See also LATIN AMERICA (Facts in Brief Table). In WORLD BOOK, see PUERTO RICO.

PULITZER PRIZES. See AWARDS AND PRIZES.

QATAR. See MIDDLE EAST.

QUEBEC. Premier René Lévesque, head of the separatist Parti Québécois (PQ) government, drew federal fire with his announcement on Nov. 1, 1979, that his province would hold a referendum on sovereignty-association with the rest of Canada in June 1980. In a press conference on November 2, Prime Minister Joe Clark said that Lévesque's plan for a sovereign Quebec linked economically with the rest of Canada was "absolutely unacceptable." Although a public opinion poll revealed in June 1979 that two-thirds of Quebec's citizens thought they should remain part of Canada, Clark said if there is heavy support for sovereignty in the French-speaking province, his government would show "by concrete gestures" its willingness to change the federal system to accommodate the aspirations of Quebec and other provinces.

Liberals Gain. The opposition Liberals won two provincial by-elections on April 30, boosting their standing to 26 seats. The PQ held 70. More important, Claude Ryan, the Liberals' passionate and articulate leader, entered Quebec's National Assembly for the first time. Friction within the PQ cabinet was revealed on September 21 when Minister of Industry and Commerce Rodrigue Tremblay resigned after criticizing PQ economic policies. On November 14, the Liberals won three more by-elections; two of them were in seats that were formerly held by the PQ.

The use of both French and English in air-traffic control systems in Quebec, a divisive issue in recent years, was settled quietly on August 21. The Clark government announced that bilingual air services would be established in Quebec.

Shocks were felt in Quebec's economy in 1979. *The Montreal Star,* for 110 years a major voice in Canadian journalism, closed in September following an eight-month strike and a costly seven-month circulation war with its English-language rival, the *Gazette.* Finance Minister Jacques Parizeau announced on September 24 that the government had made its final offer for the shares of Asbestos Corporation Limited, the Montreal-based subsidiary of General Dynamics Corporation, a U.S. firm. When the firm rejected the $42-a-share bid, Parizeau said the government would take over the company.

Power Project Starts. Lévesque pressed a button on October 27 to start the first four generators of the gigantic James Bay hydroelectric project. Begun in 1971, the scheme involved diverting four rivers into La Grande River on the east coast of Hudson Bay and building three enormous power stations. The first generators will produce 1,332 megawatts of power to meet the needs of Quebec and the northern United States.   David M.L. Farr

See also CANADA. In WORLD BOOK, see QUEBEC.

RACING. See AUTOMOBILE RACING; BOATING; HORSE RACING; SWIMMING; TRACK AND FIELD.

RADIO. Network radio in general, and music programs in particular, enjoyed a renaissance in the United States in 1979. More than 7.5 million adults were tuned to the FM network of the American Broadcasting Companies, Incorporated (ABC), on May 12 when ABC aired the first of its all-stereo live-music series "Supergroups in Concert." In addition to airing eight music specials during the year on its regular network, the National Broadcasting Company introduced The Source — a radio network aimed at young adults — in May.

Satellite Expansion. RKO Radio launched a new all-stereo network on October 1 that shared time on the Western Union *Westar 1* satellite with the Associated Press. The Mutual Broadcasting System announced its satellite expansion plan in 1979. It plans to have dish antennas receiving satellite signals in 200 communities by 1980.

The Federal Communications Commission on October 18 eliminated mandatory licensing of earth stations that receive but do not send signals. One network executive said that the deregulation should produce "the first major improvement in transmission quality in 54 years" by making satellite relay systems more accessible.

National Public Radio (NPR) started its new space-age network in 1979 and expected to have half of its stations connected to the new satellite system by January 1980. Although only one in five Americans had ever listened to NPR, it aired the richest and most innovative radio programming of 1979. Critically acclaimed NPR series during the year included "All Things Considered," a daily news magazine; "Earplay"; "Jazz Alive"; and "Shakespeare Festival" and "Masterpiece Radio Theatre," both produced by the British Broadcasting Corporation.

FM Audience Grows. For the first time in history, more people, an estimated 50.5 per cent of the listeners, tuned to FM stations rather than AM, according to a 1979 study. FM radio was not everyone's favorite, however. In November, the Recording Industry Association of America publicly deplored the growing practice of some FM outlets of playing record albums in their entirety without a commercial break, encouraging home taping of new releases.

At the beginning of the year, disco music was still radio's hottest new format. By fall, however, stations were discarding pure-disco formats in favor of "fusion-disco" — that is, disco-pop, disco-middle-of-the-road, disco-soul, and disco-rock music. Contemporary rock and "beautiful music" formats were still numbers one and two in popularity. There were more than 2,000 country music stations in 1979.

Representatives of 150 nations on December 6 signed a rule book governing global radio communications for the next 20 years.   June Bundy Csida

In WORLD BOOK, see RADIO.

RAILROAD companies in the United States gained financially in 1979. Business volume increased, and the government allowed the railroads to boost freight rates to compensate for higher fuel costs and other expenses. The industry and the Jimmy Carter Administration pushed for deregulation, but Congress resisted, largely because shippers opposed it.

The Association of American Railroads said U.S. railroads earned $476.1 million in the first nine months of 1979, compared with a $39.4-million loss in the same 1978 period. Operating revenues were $18.8 billion, up 18 per cent from a year earlier. Third-quarter profits were up $6.3 million from $29.6 million in the third quarter of 1978. Freight traffic had increased 5 per cent by late November. By October 15, the Interstate Commerce Commission (ICC) had approved cumulative rate increases of 14 per cent for 1979.

Deregulation Moves. The Carter Administration announced its deregulation proposal on March 23, but the industry pushed its own plan. Farm groups and some big corporation shippers fought provisions that would give the railroads more freedom to set rates. In November, the U.S. Senate Committee on Commerce, Science, and Transportation approved a modest regulatory-change measure that the railroads accepted. Meanwhile, the ICC expanded its deregulation efforts. It stopped controlling rates for fresh fruits and vegetables on May 28. On Septem-

Secretary of Transportation Brock Adams explains a proposal in January to cut 11,800 miles (19,000 kilometers) from Amtrak's passenger service.

ber 6, the ICC cited a study that showed that the railroads dominated the transportation market much less than experts had thought. The ICC said that, because of the study, it might allow the railroads to raise or lower rates more freely.

President Carter ordered striking Chicago, Rock Island, and Pacific Railroad workers back to their jobs on September 20, and on September 26 the ICC directed a group of 14 railroads to take over the operation of the bankrupt line. On October 26, a federal judge approved a request by the trustee of the bankrupt Chicago, Milwaukee, St. Paul & Pacific Railroad to stop service on 60 per cent of its track. But Congress prevented this cutback and provided funds to keep the system intact.

Consolidated Rail Corporation (Conrail) said that its 1979 loss would be smaller than its 1978 deficit of $385 million. Conrail made its first quarterly profit in the second quarter. But the federally financed road said it would need more than the $3.3-billion already authorized unless it was deregulated.

The National Railroad Passenger Corporation (Amtrak) survived an Administration plan to cut its track mileage by 43 per cent. Congress held the October cuts to six routes that represent 19 per cent of Amtrak mileage. The gasoline shortage stimulated ridership. Patronage was up 15.4 per cent in the first nine months of 1979.   Albert R. Karr

In WORLD BOOK, see RAILROAD.

REAGAN, RONALD (1911-   ), declared his candidacy for the 1980 Republican presidential nomination on Nov. 13, 1979. A former film star and two-term governor of California, Reagan, if elected, would become the oldest person to be inaugurated U.S. President. See REPUBLICAN PARTY.

Ronald Wilson Reagan was born in Tampico, Ill., on Feb. 6, 1911. He graduated from Eureka College in Illinois with letters in football, track, and swimming. He was a radio sports announcer in Des Moines, Iowa, during the 1930s.

Reagan played the part of a radio announcer in his first motion picture, *Love Is on the Air* (1937). He went on to play in more than 50 other films, notably *Kings Row* (1941) and *Storm Warning* (1950). During the 1940s and 1950s, Reagan served as president of the Screen Actors Guild and headed the Motion Picture Industry Council. From 1954 to 1965, he starred on television in "General Electric Theater" and "Death Valley Days."

An effective speaker and campaigner, Reagan was elected governor of California in 1966 on a conservative platform that advocated a reduction in government spending. He was re-elected in 1970. He campaigned unsuccessfully for the Republican presidential nomination in 1968 and 1976.

Reagan lives on a ranch in Malibu Hills, Calif., with his second wife, the former Nancy Davis. He has four children.   Beverly Merz

RECORDINGS

RECORDINGS. Record and tape sales in the United States nose-dived as much as 40 per cent in 1979. Companies raised album prices from $7.98 to $8.98, but profits decreased. The industry blamed the gasoline shortage, which decreased the amount of driving to record stores in shopping malls, a general reduction in spending, and consumers' use of blank tapes to record songs from radio. Several leading companies laid off hundreds of employees. Some firms changed their policy of giving full credit on unsold records that the stores returned.

Computer Aid. A new system called *digital recording* seemed likely to supersede the direct-to-disk method that had started to become popular. The digital system used computer technology to ensure high quality and a minimum of extraneous noise. CBS, Inc., planned a classical series in the new system, including Dimitri Shostakovich's *Fifth Symphony,* conducted by Leonard Bernstein in Tokyo, and Zubin Mehta conducting Igor Stravinsky's *Petroushka.* At least six major companies were committed to digital recording by the end of 1979.

The imminence of videodisks and video cassettes as products for general use was indicated when CBS formed a division in 1979 that planned to enter this market, thus becoming the first of the entertainment conglomerates to sell these products through a record company.

Singer Billy Joel won two Grammy Awards at the National Academy of Recording Arts and Sciences ceremony in February for "Just the Way You Are."

Conductor Frederick Fennell, right, listens to a playback of a recording session on digital-tape equipment invented by Thomas Stockham, left.

Awards. Singer and songwriter Billy Joel won Grammy Awards for best record and best song by recording his composition, "Just the Way You Are." The Bee Gees won the Grammy for best album for the sound track of the film *Saturday Night Fever*. A Taste of Honey was named best new group. Jazz winners included Al Jarreau as best singer, Oscar Peterson and Chick Corea as best instrumentalists, and Thad Jones-Mel Lewis in the big-band category. See Awards and Prizes.

Many record companies changed hands in 1979. MCA, Incorporated, bought ABC Records, Incorporated; EMI Limited bought United Artists Corporation with its various record labels; and Warner Communications, Incorporated, took over distribution for the increasingly important Editions of Contemporary Music (ECM), jazz specialists in Oslo, Norway.

Single record sales continued to drop, compared with album sales. Single records had accounted for about 9 per cent of record revenues in 1978. Cassette sales continued to gain in the tape field, accounting for 32 per cent of the sales, twice the 1970 percentage. Sales of eight-track cartridges slipped from almost 80 per cent of 1970 tape sales to 68 per cent in 1979.   Leonard Feather and Eliot Tiegel

See also Music, Classical; Music, Popular. In World Book, see Phonograph.

RED CROSS. See Community Organizations.

RELIGION. The world was confronted with an explosion of Islamic religious fervor in many Middle Eastern, African, and Asian nations in 1979. Many Westerners, accustomed to separation of church and state, were confounded.

Much of the ferment began in February with a revolution in Iran that ousted Shah Mohammad Reza Pahlavi and installed a government headed by Ayatollah Ruhollah Khomeini, a religious leader of the militant Shiite sect of Islam. Between February and May, he put to death at least 200 persons for crimes against Islam. With Khomeini's approval, Iranian students seized the United States Embassy in Teheran on November 4, and held more than 60 Americans as hostages. The students demanded that the United States deport the shah – in New York City for cancer treatment – to Iran for trial (see Iran; Khomeini, Ruhollah; Middle East).

Heavily armed members of another Muslim sect seized the Great Mosque at Mecca, Saudi Arabia, on November 20 and demanded that the Saudi government return to strict principles of Islam. The following day, a mob in Pakistan stormed and burned the U. S. Embassy in Islamabad, killing two U. S. marines, under the mistaken belief that the United States was involved in the attack on the Great Mosque at Mecca (see Pakistan; Saudi Arabia).

Religious scholars debated whether such violence was in the true spirit of Islam. But demonstrations, as

U.S. Church Membership Reported for Bodies with 150,000 or More Members

African Methodist Episcopal Church	1,970,000
African Methodist Episcopal Zion Church	1,093,001
American Baptist Association	1,500,000
American Baptist Churches in the U.S.A.	1,316,760
The American Lutheran Church	2,377,235
The Antiochian Orthodox Christian Archdiocese of North America	152,000
Armenian Church of America, Diocese of the (including Diocese of California)	326,500
Assemblies of God	1,293,394
Baptist Missionary Association of America	219,697
Christian and Missionary Alliance	158,218
Christian Church (Disciples of Christ)	1,231,817
Christian Churches and Churches of Christ	1,054,266
Christian Methodist Episcopal Church	466,718
Christian Reformed Church in North America	211,302
Church of God (Anderson, Ind.)	173,753
Church of God (Cleveland, Tenn.)	392,551
The Church of God in Christ	425,000
The Church of God in Christ, International	501,000
The Church of Jesus Christ of Latter-day Saints	2,592,000
Church of the Brethren	177,335
Church of the Nazarene	462,724
Churches of Christ	3,000,000
Conservative Baptist Association of America	300,000
The Episcopal Church	2,815,359
Free Will Baptists	216,831
General Association of Regular Baptist Churches	240,000
Greek Orthodox Archdiocese of North and South America	1,950,000
Jehovah's Witnesses	519,218
Jewish Congregations	5,775,935
Lutheran Church in America	2,942,002
The Lutheran Church-Missouri Synod	2,631,374
National Baptist Convention of America	2,668,799
National Baptist Convention, U.S.A., Inc.	5,500,000
National Primitive Baptist Convention, Inc.	250,000
Orthodox Church in America	1,000,000
Polish National Catholic Church of America	282,411
Presbyterian Church in the United States	862,416
Progressive National Baptist Convention, Inc.	521,692
Reformed Church in America	348,080
Reorganized Church of Jesus Christ of Latter Day Saints	185,636
The Roman Catholic Church	49,602,035
The Salvation Army	414,035
Seventh-day Adventists	535,705
Southern Baptist Convention	13,191,394
United Church of Christ	1,769,104
The United Methodist Church	9,731,779
United Pentecostal Church, International	450,000
The United Presbyterian Church in the U.S.A.	2,520,367
Wisconsin Evangelical Lutheran Synod	402,972

*Majority of figures are for the years 1978 and 1979.

Source: National Council of Churches, *Yearbook of American and Canadian Churches* for 1980.

461

The Pope
In America

John Paul II brought his papal pilgrimage to the United States for a week in October 1979, and was greeted by enthusiastic crowds at every stop. In New York City; Philadelphia; Des Moines, Iowa; Chicago; and Washington, D.C., people waited patiently for hours – sometimes in pouring rain – to see the pontiff or to participate when he celebrated Mass. And John Paul delighted them by his warm response. He often plunged into crowds to embrace a child or bestow a blessing. Thousands of non-Catholics joined the huge crowds, and millions of non-Catholics were in the television audience.

Thirty years earlier, some Protestants would certainly have sulked about so much attention being given to the leader of the world's Roman Catholics. They would probably have objected to the notice he received and the fact that he used public facilities for religious observances. But in 1979, following the Second Vatican Council (1962 to 1965) and years of the ecumenical movement designed to unite believers, if American Protestantism harbored any leftover anti-Catholicism, it was not apparent.

To avoid mere "papalmania" – the kind of uncritical passion that follows many celebrities and charismatic individuals – Protestants, Jews, and other non-Catholics took pains to spell out the serious reasons for their attention to the visitor. John Paul's tour was an event of humane and humanistic interest. The pontiff, who has chosen as his life theme "the dignity of the human person," consistently stressed human rights and attention to the poor. When this meant that he had to criticize the materialism of what he called a consumerist society, non-Catholics were ready to listen – if not fully ready to follow his injunctions. His words and even his manner of speaking called to mind many sacred concerns voiced in their own pulpits and press. When his passion for human dignity was extended also to fetal life, and when, in some cases, his policies – for example, against abortion – went against their own, they willingly listened to his pronouncements because of his overall positive concerns.

In addition, the papal visit endowed religion itself with a sense of meaning and value. Millions of Americans resent their image as mere materialists in much of the world. They see themselves as spiritually minded, also. When analysts describe the modern world as secular and godless, Americans look for opportunities to show that they are responsive to the call of the sacred and of God. Although they came for a variety of motives, those who gathered from Iowa's heartland to New York City's Harlem signaled their personal identification with religion.

The papal visit was also an endorsement of organized religion, which had declined during a decade of greater private religiosity. The pope's positive reception was not only a personal triumph, but also a mark of the enduring value of the church as a community. Protestants responded to this idea of community.

In some ways, it was easier for non-Catholics to react positively than for Catholics. After the pope was gone, Catholics knew they would have to analyze his words and actions to see how their concerns in the church might be affected. American Catholicism is a divided community that largely forgot its divisions during this morale-building occasion. But no papal visit could overcome these divisions. John Paul knows that popes today have no power to force, only to persuade. So he hoped to build up power for future persuasion.

Some thoughtful Protestants were especially sympathetic toward Catholics who would like to see women as priests and toward married Catholic men who are barred from the priesthood. The pope said in Philadelphia that the priesthood is permanent. "We do not return the gift once given," he said. He also reaffirmed the tradition of priestly celibacy and an all-male clergy. But for a few days in October, almost everyone was willing to suspend criticism of the positions he took. John Paul II seemed to embody human dignity, spirituality, and Christian faith, and his presence in our midst lifted our hearts in a time when many were hungry for spiritual affirmation.

Martin E. Marty

John Paul II

The Dalai Lama and Terence Cardinal Cooke (seated) celebrate an interfaith service in St. Patrick's Cathedral in New York City on September 5.

well as legal moves toward Muslim government, continued in such nations as Bangladesh, Egypt, Kuwait, and Turkey.

Dalai Lama's Visit. The Dalai Lama, leader of Tibetan Buddhism, visited the United States for seven weeks beginning in September – his first visit to the country. He represented the gentler voice of religion in a world deeply troubled recently by the connections between religion and violence.

In exile for 20 years from the Communist rule of his country, he dealt gingerly with the topic of a possible return to Tibet, speaking in timeless Buddhist style about his hope that he may someday return to his home. He spoke of love, compassion, and tolerance for others, rather than politics.

A highlight of his 22-city visit was an interfaith service held on September 5 in New York City's St. Patrick's Cathedral. Like many an Eastern religious leader, he declared that "all the world's major religions are basically the same." Terence Cardinal Cooke of New York said that he played host to the Dalai Lama not to support that idea but to show respect for one of the world's great holy men.

Another Non-Western holy man made news in 1979 when 84-year-old Acharya Vinoba Bhave announced he would fast to death if necessary to defend the Hindu principle that cows are sacred. His resolution highlighted a struggle between India's Hindus and local governments, some of them Communist, in

India, especially in West Bengal and Kerala states. Hindus consider cows to be sacred, while non-Hindus say cows should be killed for food.

India's Prime Minister Morarji Desai, himself a Hindu, persuaded Bhave to break his fast in April by sponsoring a constitutional amendment forbidding the killing of cows throughout India. But tensions remained.

The Growth of Cults. In the United States, interreligious tensions continued between the larger established churches and the small intense religious groups, which, some thought, misused their tax-exempt status and used questionable psychological means to gain and control members. A number of federal agencies, including the Internal Revenue Service, investigated the People's Temple, a California-based religious cult, in the wake of the mass suicide by temple members in Guyana in November 1978. Local governments also became involved with cults and the citizens who wanted to restrict them. For example, the Chicago City Council voted in October to restrict fund-raising by Hare Krishnas and members of other cults to a specific area at O'Hare International Airport. Martin E. Marty

See also EASTERN ORTHODOX CHURCHES; JEWS AND JUDAISM; PROTESTANTISM; ROMAN CATHOLIC CHURCH. In the Special Reports section, see THE CULT QUESTION: NO EASY ANSWERS. IN WORLD BOOK, see RELIGION and articles on religions.

REPUBLICAN PARTY members were aware of President Jimmy Carter's weakness in public opinion polls during much of 1979 and sensed the chance of a White House victory in 1980. Ten Republicans had entered the race for their party's presidential nomination by the end of 1979.

Former President Gerald R. Ford was one of the few who apparently chose not to run, declaring himself out of contention in October 1979. Ford left the impression, however, that he would be available if the 1980 Republican Party National Convention became deadlocked. See FORD, GERALD R.

The Contenders. Former California Governor Ronald Reagan, the choice of many conservatives, announced his candidacy on November 13 and claimed a front-runner's spot. But Reagan's age—68 at the time of his announcement—and his position at the far right of the political spectrum were seen as handicaps. See REAGAN, RONALD.

John B. Connally, former Democratic governor of Texas who switched to the Republican Party in 1973, announced his candidacy on January 24. Connally, who was secretary of the Treasury under President Richard M. Nixon, had strong business backing but failed to show as much strength as he had expected. See CONNALLY, JOHN B.

George H. W. Bush, former director of the Central Intelligence Agency and former U.S. ambassador to the United Nations, entered the race on May 1. The son of a senator and veteran of two terms in the House of Representatives, Bush had a strong field organization in the early testing states of New Hampshire and Iowa. See BUSH, GEORGE H. W.

Senator Howard H. Baker, Jr., of Tennessee, the Senate minority leader, announced his candidacy on November 1. Baker, who based his campaign largely on his opposition to the Strategic Arms Limitation Treaty (SALT II), suffered an early setback when he lost a straw poll at a Maine Republican dinner to Bush, even though Baker had the support of Maine's Senator William S. Cohen. See BAKER, HOWARD H.

Other Contenders were given less chance of success. Senator Robert J. Dole of Kansas, the party's vice-presidential nominee in 1976, announced his candidacy on May 14. Dole tried hard to overcome the "hatchet man" image he acquired in the 1976 campaign by displaying a highly developed sense of humor. See DOLE, ROBERT J.

Representative John B. Anderson of Illinois, as chairman of the House Republican Conference the third-ranking Republican in the House, declared his candidacy on June 8. A moderate by national standards, Anderson was viewed as a liberal inside Republican ranks.

Another Illinois Republican House member, Philip M. Crane, had announced in August 1978,

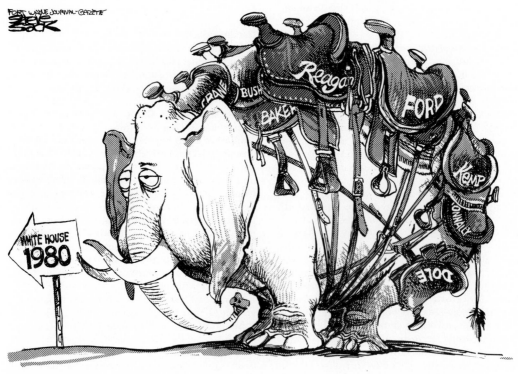

Steve Sack in the *Ft. Wayne Journal Gazette.*

the first in his party to do so. Crane, a hard-line conservative, had money problems and several staff shakeups that hurt his campaign. His chief fundraiser left Crane in August 1979 to work for Connally. However, Crane said he would remain in the running. See CRANE, PHILIP M.

Dark Horses. Three dark-horse candidates joined the presidential sweepstakes. The youngest GOP contender, freshman Senator Larry Pressler of South Dakota, 37, became a candidate for the presidency on September 25. Benjamin Hernandez, a Mexican American businessman from Los Angeles with no previous political experience, was also campaigning. And Harold E. Stassen, former governor of Minnesota, who has been in perennial pursuit of the presidency since 1948, also joined the race.

The Republicans decided to hold their 1980 nominating convention in Detroit, and scheduled it to open on July 14. Republican National Chairman William E. Brock III said the choice of Detroit as the site symbolized the party's interest in winning the votes of blacks and city dwellers, most of whom have voted for Democrats in the past. Detroit has a black-majority population.

Other Races. In state elections, Republicans lost two governors' races on November 6. In Kentucky, former Governor Louie B. Nunn lost to millionaire Democrat John Y. Brown, Jr. In Mississippi, GOP candidate Gil Carmichael lost to Democrat William F. Winter in a contest between two moderates on the race issue. However, the party claimed a significant victory in Louisiana on December 9, when Representative David C. Treen defeated Louis Lambert to become the first Republican governor of the state since 1877. Treen in 1972 had the distinction of becoming the first Republican to be elected to the U.S. House of Representatives from Louisiana in this century.

Republicans also prevailed in two special congressional elections on April 3. In California, Republican contender William H. Royer won the seat left vacant by the death of Democratic Congressman Leo J. Ryan. In Wisconsin, Republican Thomas E. Petri won a close race to fill the seat left vacant by the death of Representative William A. Steiger.

In March, Richard L. Berkley became the first Republican to be elected mayor of Kansas City, Mo., since the 1920s. He defeated a black Democratic candidate – Bruce R. Watkins. In Cleveland in November, Republican contender George V. Voinovich defeated Democrat Dennis J. Kucinich, who was mayor when Cleveland twice defaulted on bond payments and who survived a recall in 1978. See ELECTIONS. William J. Eaton

In WORLD BOOK, see REPUBLICAN PARTY.

RESEARCH. See SCIENCE AND RESEARCH.

RHODE ISLAND. See STATE GOVERNMENT.

RHODESIA. See ZIMBABWE RHODESIA.

ROADS. See TRANSPORTATION.

ROGERS, BERNARD W. (1921-   ), United States Army chief of staff since 1976, became head of U.S. forces in Europe and Supreme Allied Commander in Europe of the North Atlantic Treaty Organization (NATO) on July 1, 1979. President Jimmy Carter named Rogers, a four-star general, to succeed General Alexander M. Haig, Jr., who retired. Rogers' appointment as Supreme Allied Commander was approved by the 15 NATO nations.

Rogers was born on July 16, 1921, in Fairview, Kans. He received a B.S. degree from the U.S. Military Academy in 1943. A Rhodes scholar, he earned a B.A. degree in 1950 from Oxford University in England, studying philosophy, politics, and economics. During his three years at Oxford, he developed a reputation as an exceptionally literate "regular Army" officer. He also attended the Army War College from 1959 to 1960.

The much-decorated Rogers served as an infantry commander during the Korean War and as an assistant division commander in the Vietnam War. His other Army assignments included commandant of cadets at the U.S. Military Academy from 1967 to 1969 and chief legislative liaison for the Department of the Army from 1970 to 1972. He was promoted to the rank of general in 1974.

Rogers married Ann Ellen Jones in 1944. They have three children, including a son who is a captain in the Army. Patricia Dragisic

ROLDOS AGUILERA, JAIME (1940-   ), was elected president of Ecuador in a runoff election on April 29, 1979. Roldos, a member of the Concentration of Popular Forces Party, won 68 per cent of the vote to defeat conservative Sixto Duran Ballen Cordovez. His inauguration on Aug. 10, 1979, ended nine years of dictatorship.

Party leader Asaad Bucaram had expected to run in the first-round election in July 1978, but the military junta disqualified him, so Roldos ran instead. Early in the campaign, Roldos seemed to indicate that he would let Bucaram run the country, but he later developed his own following among the people. He promised improved education for the illiterate Indian population and favored a foreign policy that would support democracy and the aspirations of developing nations.

Roldos Aguilera was born on Nov. 5, 1940, in Guayaquil. He was valedictorian of his high school class in Guayaquil and had the highest grades in his class at the University of Guayaquil, where he earned a law degree. He taught at the high school and at two universities in Guayaquil, and held a post in the Ministry of Education. Roldos was elected to Congress in 1968 and 1970 and named to the Commission on Constitutional Reforms in 1977.

He married Bucaram's niece, attorney Marta Bucaram Ortiz, in 1962. They have two daughters and a son. Jay Myers

ROMAN CATHOLIC CHURCH

Pope John Paul II made a series of pilgrimages in 1979, including visits to Mexico, Poland, Ireland, the United States, and Turkey. Throughout his Western travels, the pope was greeted by huge, friendly crowds. See RELIGION (Close-Up).

In all the sermons and public addresses he delivered during his tours, the pope reaffirmed the church's traditional moral values and doctrines. In Puebla, Mexico, where he attended the Third General Assembly of Latin American Bishops in January, the pope rejected unequivocally the use of violence to counteract the armed violence of the region's political dictators. He re-emphasized that point later in a World Day of Peace Message in which he said, "Arms cannot be considered the right means for settling conflicts. . . . It is not permissible to kill in order to impose a solution."

He made a nine-day tour of five cities in Poland in June to commemorate the 900th anniversary of the martyrdom of Saint Stanislaus, Poland's patron saint. The pope stressed the fact that religious freedom was a "fundamental right," and he urged bishops to be forceful in the defense of church rights against government restrictions. During his tour, the pope visited the Auschwitz concentration camp complex, where he celebrated a Mass commemorating Jews slain during World War II.

John Paul II's visit to Poland was the first by a pope to a Communist country. On September 29, when he arrived for a five-city visit to Ireland, he again set a precedent by becoming the first pope to visit that country. During his stay there, he repeatedly urged an end to religious strife, a plea he reiterated on his departure for a seven-day visit in the United States, which began on October 1.

He was welcomed by throngs of American well-wishers in Boston; New York City, where he also addressed the United Nations General Assembly; Philadelphia; Des Moines, Iowa; Chicago; and Washington, D.C. The pope stressed world peace, human rights, and the need to narrow the gap between rich and poor. In Washington, D.C., his final stop, he was welcomed by President Jimmy Carter in a ceremony at the White House. It was the first time a pope was received in the Executive Mansion. The pope returned to Rome on October 7.

In his travels, the pope reaffirmed the church's traditional views on abortion, celibacy for priests, and the role of women in the church. Human rights, too, were frequently stressed in dialogues with various members of the Roman Catholic hierarchy.

Women's Rights. In March, Minnesota's seven Roman Catholic bishops issued a call for a more just role for women in church and society, declaring that, "We want women to know that we share their impatience as we ourselves struggle to come to terms with their rightful place in the church."

Pope John Paul II, however, spoke vigorously on several occasions against the ordination of women, and at a Mass he celebrated in the Shrine of the Immaculate Conception in Washington, D.C., on October 7, he again defined the role of women in the church. In a welcoming speech preceding the Mass,

John Paul II extends a benediction to the hundreds
of thousands of persons who attended the Mass
he celebrated in Chicago's Grant Park in October.

a nun had publicly dissented from the pope's view,
challenging him to respond to the voices of women.
Despite her plea, the pope remained committed to
his policy of nonordination for women.

Bishops' Meeting. The National Conference of
Catholic Bishops (NCCB) began its semiannual
meeting on November 14 in Washington, D.C.
Among its actions, it refused to accept motions
relating to allegedly sexist language in the liturgy of
the church. The NCCB also approved the details of a

letter in which the bishops declared racism a sin.

In an earlier meeting, the NCCB adopted a
program for the Roman Catholic community to use
in purchasing services and hiring employees. Bishop
Thomas C. Kelly, NCCB general secretary, advised:
"In the process of adopting an affirmative action
plan, the diocese is placing the community on notice
that it does not intend to discriminate in employment practices and that it will demonstrate this by
actively recruiting those who may be currently
underrepresented in the work force."

Labor Relations. The Supreme Court of the
United States ruled in March that teachers in
Catholic schools are not protected by the National
Labor Relations Act. Seven Catholic schools in

Chicago and northern Indiana had refused to recognize a union for their teachers. The high court supported the schools' contention that the First Amendment to the Constitution, which guarantees separation of church and state, rules out legal enforcement of the teachers' right to organize. However, many teachers held hopes that Roman Catholic Church leaders – in line with the pope's strong defense of human rights – would set up an agency to protect teachers' rights to organize.

Aiding Catholic Schools. The long-standing controversy over federal aid for nonpublic schools continued in 1979. During an interview at the White House with Roman Catholic editors and other members of the press in April, President Carter denied that he had gone back on campaign promises to give tax relief to parents of children in nonpublic schools. He claimed that it would be too expensive.

Other Developments. The ecumenical movement aiming for Christian unity made slow but steady progress during the year. Marriage, however, continued to be a stumbling block in Anglican-Roman Catholic relations – especially where divorce and remarriage were concerned. The Roman Catholic Church remained firmly opposed to divorce. Some ecumenists felt that a re-examination by Roman Catholics of Pope Leo XIII's decree of 1896 denying the validity of the Anglican priesthood might be a decisive step toward full communion.

The International Roman Catholic-Lutheran Commission published an "agreed statement" on the Eucharist in January identifying points of agreement and disagreement. The commission acknowledged that the Lutheran tradition affirms the Roman Catholic tradition, which holds that the bread and wine consecrated in the Eucharist become – by the power of the creative word – the body and blood of Christ.

Credentials Suspended. In December, the Vatican ordered liberal theologian Hans Kung, a priest, stripped of his teaching credentials for showing contempt of church document. Kung, a professor at the University of Tübingen in West Germany, had questioned the authority of Roman Catholic bishops and papal infallibility.

Church Finances. Pope John Paul II convened a rare "consultative" meeting of the College of Cardinals in the Vatican on November 5 – the first such consultation in at least 100 years, according to church officials. The discussions among the 123 cardinals reportedly focused on structural and administrative problems, including such matters as church finances and a reorganization of the Curia.

At the conclusion of the five-day meeting, the Vatican announced that the pope had promised to consider the proposals and advice offered by the cardinals. In its statement, the Vatican also pointed out that the income of the Holy See from its "real estate, movable assets, and institutional resources" was "not nearly enough to cover the expenses of the central government. . . ." It also stated that the Curia was operating with a budget deficit expected to reach $20.2 million by December 31, and, consequently, the cardinals had urged that the expenses of the Curia be "contained as much as possible." Proposals were also made to improve its organization and the functioning of unspecified agencies.

Year-End Journey. The pope traveled to Turkey on November 28 for a three-day meeting with Eastern Orthodox Church leaders in Ankara and Istanbul. The effort, he said, would further enhance chances of bringing about the unity of all Christians. Because of the tensions in the Middle East, the pope was heavily guarded during his stay.

Membership. According to the *Official Catholic Directory,* there were 58,430 priests in the United States in 1979, compared with 58,485 in 1978. The total Catholic population dropped to 49,602,035 in 1979 from 49,836,176 in 1978. The number of nuns decreased to 128,378 in 1979, from 129,391 in 1978. Catholic high school enrollment was 853,606 in 1979, down from 869,268 in 1978. The number of students enrolled in Catholic elementary schools was 2,379,816 in 1979, compared with 2,402,778 in 1978. There were 77,205 converts to Catholicism in 1979, down from 78,598 in 1978.   John B. Sheerin

In WORLD BOOK, see ROMAN CATHOLIC CHURCH.

ROMANIA pursued an active, independent foreign policy in 1979 and challenged Russia within the Eastern Europe bloc. Communist Party General Secretary and President Nicolae Ceausescu visited eight African countries in April, Spain in May, and Syria in August.

Romania broke ranks with the Russian bloc's Council for Mutual Economic Assistance (COMECON) in January by welcoming the decision by the European Community (Common Market) to authorize commercial and industrial negotiations with Romania. Also in January, Romania departed from Russia's policy by criticizing Vietnam's invasion of Cambodia. And when China attacked Vietnam in February, Romania appealed for the withdrawal of foreign troops from both Cambodia and Vietnam. Romania refused to sign a declaration condemning China at a July meeting of 10 Communist countries and Laos in East Berlin, East Germany. China sent a representative to Romania's Communist Party congress in November. He was the first Chinese representative to attend a foreign Communist congress since the mid-1960s.

Ceausescu said on August 12 that Romania had reached a spending limit, and called for cutting 10 to 15 per cent from the Warsaw Pact's military budget by 1985. He recommended using the money saved for economic and social purposes and for aiding developing countries.

Gas and Cars. Gasoline prices went up 40 per cent in January and 13 to 21 per cent in July. The government decreed on July 26 that all foreign motorists driving in Romania after August 1 would have to pay for gasoline with hard currencies, such as those of Western countries. Romania imports one-third of the oil that it consumes and needs hard currency to pay for it. Other COMECON countries protested the decree.

New Prime Minister. Major changes in the Communist Party and government took place in January, August, and October, and at the party congress. But the biggest change occurred in March when Ilie Verdet, secretary of the Communist Party Central Committee and head of the State Planning Committee, replaced Manea Manescu as prime minister.

The government tightened central control of agriculture in February to eliminate waste and improve local management. Romania signed a $325-million contract with British Aerospace in June to buy 80 BAC 1-11 commercial aircraft during the next 15 years. Chris Cviic

See also EUROPE (Facts in Brief Table). In WORLD BOOK, see ROMANIA.

ROTARY INTERNATIONAL. See COMMUNITY ORGANIZATIONS.

ROWING. See SPORTS.

RUBBER. See MANUFACTURING.

Newly freed Russian dissident Alexander Ginzburg talks with fellow exile Alexander Solzhenitsyn's wife, Natalya, in the United States in May.

RUSSIA completed the second round of its Strategic Arms Limitations Talks (SALT II) with the United States in 1979 while the aging Soviet leadership continued its drive to improve the economy. United States President Jimmy Carter and Supreme Soviet Presidium Chairman Leonid I. Brezhnev signed SALT II on June 18 in Vienna, Austria.

SALT II limits each country to no more than 2,400 strategic missiles or long-range bombers six months after the treaty takes effect and no more than 2,250 by the end of 1981. No more than 1,320 of these may be missiles with multiple warheads or bombers with cruise missiles. There may be no more than 1,200 land-based, sea-based, or air-to-surface ballistic missiles, and only 820 land-based intercontinental ballistic missiles with multiple warheads.

Russia must dismantle more than 100 bombers or strategic missiles to meet the initial 2,400 ceiling and must stop producing or deploying SS-16 strategic missiles. Both sides may build one new type of land-based ballistic missile.

Russia's Foreign Minister Andrei A. Gromyko warned SALT II critics in the United States on June 25 that new negotiations would be impossible if the treaty were not ratified as it stood. Prospects for ratification diminished on August 31 when the United States announced that U.S. intelligence had confirmed the presence of a Russian combat brigade in Cuba. But the Russian newspaper *Pravda* said in

September that the number and function of Russian military personnel in Cuba had not changed in 17 years. U.S. Senate debate on SALT II was to begin in early 1980. However, the debate was delayed and U.S. relations worsened after Russian troops entered Afghanistan on December 27 and fought rebelling anti-Communist Muslim and Afghan tribes.

Brezhnev announced in a major speech in East Berlin on October 6 that Russia intended to withdraw up to 20,000 men and 1,000 tanks from East Germany within the next 12 months. He also offered to reduce the number of medium-range missiles in western Russia if the North Atlantic Treaty Organization (NATO) would drop plans to modernize its medium-range nuclear weapons aimed at Russia. In December, Russia began to withdraw a unit of the Sixth Armed Division from East Germany.

Relations with China worsened in January when Russia backed Vietnam's occupation of Cambodia and in February when Russia strongly criticized China's retaliatory invasion of Vietnam. Russian ships began to deliver military supplies to Haiphong, Vietnam, on February 22, while Russian transport aircraft delivered other supplies. On March 2, Brezhnev called China "the most serious threat to peace in the whole world." But China and Russia exchanged four messages between April and June, indicating a possible thaw. China responded in June to a Soviet memorandum suggesting that deputy foreign ministers discuss normalized relations. A Chinese delegation arrived in Moscow on September 23 for consultations, but the talks failed to produce an agenda for formal negotiations.

Russia welcomed the end of Shah Mohammad Reza Pahlavi's rule in Iran in January and swiftly recognized the provisional government formed on February 5. But Russia repeatedly criticized Iran later in the year for allegedly supporting tribesmen opposed to Afghanistan's pro-Soviet government. On December 4, Russia joined the other members of the United Nations Security Council in demanding Iran release U.S. hostages it seized in November.

Russia continued to encourage Arab opposition to the March 1979 peace treaty between Egypt and Israel. Syria's President Hafiz al-Assad, who opposed the treaty, received a promise of Soviet military aid in Moscow in October.

Brezhnev's Health continued to dominate Western interest in Russia. Brezhnev visited Bulgaria in January, officially for rest and recuperation, but probably to discuss Balkan politics. Brezhnev conferred with Warsaw Pact leaders in the Crimea in July and August and attended East Germany's 30th anniversary celebration in East Berlin in October. Speculation grew when he made no public appearance for three weeks, but he surfaced on October 24 in Moscow.

Dissidents and Defectors. In January, the government prevented a public presentation of a literary collection called *Metropole* that contained many censored works. Russia's writers' union suspended two of *Metropole*'s original six editors, Viktor Yerofeev and Yevgeny Popov, in May. A number of Western books were withheld from exhibits at Russia's second international book fair in Moscow in September.

On April 27, in New York City, Russia exchanged five Russian dissidents detained or sentenced to jail as opponents of the government for two Russian citizens convicted of spying in the United States. The five dissidents were Jewish activists Eduard Kuznetsov and Mark Dymshits, Baptist pastor Georgi Vins, Ukrainian nationalist Valentin Moroz, and Alexander Ginzburg, a former administrator of a fund that helped Russian civil rights activists.

Alexander Godunov, a principal dancer of the Bolshoi Ballet, defected while on tour in the United States on August 23. His wife, dancer Ludmila Vlasova, elected to return to Russia alone after talking to U.S. officials at Kennedy International Airport in New York City. Leonid and Valentina Kozlov, also of the Bolshoi, defected on September 17. Figure-skating champions Oleg Protopopov and Ludmila Belousova asked for political asylum in Switzerland on September 18. Soviet authorities

Leonid I. Brezhnev, bottom row, right, is re-elected in April to Russia's top government post, chairman of the Supreme Soviet Presidium.

then canceled the Moscow State Symphony Orchestra's tour of the United States on September 27. The action spurred conjecture that Russia feared further defections, but Soviet authorities blamed a dispute with the booking company.

Slow Growth. Russia estimated in November that its 1979 national income would be up only 2 per cent from 1978. This gain would be the lowest since World War II. The current five-year economic plan called for 4.3 per cent growth. Russia estimated that its industrial production would be up 3.6 per cent, compared with a target of 5.7 per cent.

The government reported on October 30 that a Japanese firm working with Russia had discovered "promising" oil and gas fields off Sakhalin island north of Japan and that commercial production was possible by 1985. Oil production increased only 2 per cent in the first nine months, compared with an 8 per cent average annual growth in the past. On March 28, Russia signed an agreement with other countries of the Council for Mutual Economic Assistance (COMECON) to finance jointly a $2.3-billion nuclear power station in Khmelnitsky in the Ukraine. Council of Ministers Chairman Aleksey N. Kosygin announced in June that Russia would increase fuel and energy deliveries to its COMECON partners by 20 per cent during the period from 1981 through 1985.

Foreign Trade in the first half of 1979 amounted to $17 billion, 13 per cent higher than it was in the first half of 1978. Exports to non-Communist countries increased 19 per cent to $7.2 billion, and imports from the West rose 9.4 per cent to $9.8-billion. The trade deficit with the West decreased from $3.1 billion to $2.6 billion.

A severe winter followed by a spring drought and floods led to forecasts of the poorest grain harvest in four years, about 179 million metric tons (197 million short tons). The United States in October authorized extra grain sales to Russia, and Western experts predicted that Russia would buy 25 million metric tons (27.5 million short tons) of grain in the year ending Sept. 30, 1980. On Jan. 4, 1980, however, President Carter announced he was cutting shipments to 8 million metric tons (8.8 million short tons) because of Russia's military intervention in Afghanistan.

The October issue of the Communist Party magazine *Kommunist* proposed building future nuclear power plants in the northern part of Russia, which is sparsely populated, with plenty of wasteland. Prices of carpets and jewelry containing precious metals went up by 50 per cent on July 1. Car prices rose 18 per cent; imported furniture, 30 per cent; Russian-made furniture, 10 per cent; beer, 45 per cent; and restaurant meals, 25 to 45 per cent. Chris Cviic

See also EUROPE (Facts in Brief Table). In WORLD BOOK, see RUSSIA.

RWANDA. See AFRICA.

SAFETY. A judge in Karlsruhe, West Germany, ruled in March 1979 that motorists may not claim complete insurance coverage if they are injured in auto accidents while not wearing seat belts. Reversing a decision handed down from the same court in 1970, the judge said that drivers who fail to use such belts, required by West German law, "bear some of the responsibility" for their own injuries, even if the driver did not cause the accident.

The judge further ruled that the ordinance requiring motorists to use seat belts does not violate constitutional rights. He said "the fear that a motorist may not be able to free himself in time in the case of fire or accidents involving plunging into water no longer is applicable for the sensible motorist."

U.S. Accidental Deaths and Death Rates

	1978†		1979†	
	Number	**Rate††**	**Number**	**Rate††**
Motor Vehicle	32,720	23.6	32,880	23.4
Work	8,700	6.0	9,000	6.1
Home	15,400	10.5	15,100	10.2
Public	14,900	9.9	15,000	9.9
Total*	68,700	47.9	68,800	47.5

†For 8-month period up to August 31.

††Deaths per 100,000 population.

*The total does not equal the sum of the four classes because *Motor Vehicle* includes some deaths also included in *Work* and *Home*.

Source: National Safety Council estimates.

Highway Speed. United States National Highway Traffic Safety Administrator Joan Claybrook said in July that most U.S. insurance companies support the national speed limit of 55 miles (89 kilometers) per hour through advertising programs. "Insurance companies have two coinciding objectives – to save lives and reduce insurance costs," Claybrook said. "Therefore, 55 is important to them." Government studies show that Americans' life expectancy improved by 1.7 years from 1972 to 1976, an increase greater than that for the previous 10 years. Insurance companies say the speed limit is a leading cause of greater life expectancy.

A federal court of appeals in February affirmed the validity of the Traffic Safety Administration's tire-grading regulation, which began for bias-ply tires on April 1 and for bias-belted tires on September 1. The court ruled against eight tire companies that had entered a complaint about the reliability of the agency's measurements for grading tire wear. The manufacturers had also objected to the exclusion of radial tires from the regulations. However, the safety agency announced that radials would be added to the grading system on April 1, 1980.

Motorcycles and Skateboards. The Traffic Safety Administration released a report in January showing a significant increase in deaths due to head injuries among motorcycle riders in states that have repealed laws requiring motorcyclists to wear hel-

Illuminated road signs—powered by fiber-optic conductors—were planned for Great Britain's turnpikes. The lights can be seen in any weather.

SASKATCHEWAN. The leader of the official opposition Progressive Conservative Party, Dick Collver, resigned his post on May 29, 1979, because of what he termed unjustified personal attacks on his integrity and conduct. Collver had led the party since 1973 from political oblivion to a standing of 17 seats in the 61-seat legislature. Premier Allan Blakeney's New Democratic Party held the remaining 44 seats. A by-election held on October 19 did not change these standings.

New human rights legislation was enacted in the Blakeney government's third term, which began on February 22. It prohibited discrimination on the basis of age, marital status, or physical handicap as well as race and sex. In spite of a deficit of $49.3-million, the government claimed that Saskatchewan's per capita debt was the second lowest in Canada. Only Alberta's was lower.

Regina, the province's capital, was battered on August 18 by fierce winds that did great damage.

Construction of a $170-million coal-fired power station at Poplar River on the United States border was approved by Saskatchewan on November 14 without waiting for an expected report on possible changes in the area's air and water quality. Another plant, to open in May 1980, worried Montana residents because of possible damage from sulfur emissions.   David M. L. Farr

In WORLD BOOK, see SASKATCHEWAN.

SAUDI ARABIA raised its oil production from 8.5 million barrels a day to 9.5 million barrels in July 1979 at the request of U.S. President Jimmy Carter. Although they had planned to return to previous levels on Jan. 1, 1980, the Saudis announced on November 12 that they would continue their stepped-up output to "protect the well-being of the world economy."

Saudi Arabia joined the majority of Arab states by breaking diplomatic relations with Egypt on April 23 after Egypt established a separate peace with Israel in March. The Saudi government held off from imposing economic sanctions against Egypt, though it did agree to liquidate the Cairo-based Arab Industrial Organization, an inter-Arab arms-manufacturing organization financed largely by Saudi capital. The action dealt a severe blow to the $1.4-billion complex of small- and medium-sized industries near Cairo that supply most of the Egyptian Army's weapons and military spare parts.

Sacrilege at the Mosque. A heavily armed force of about 200 Muslim fanatics seized the Great Mosque of Mecca on November 20, and proclaimed their leader, Mohammed Abdullah al-'Utaibah, to be the *Mahdi* (messiah) of Islam. The Saudi government responded quickly, cutting off all communication with the outside world and storming the mosque with helicopters and crack National Guard troops. The fight lasted almost a week as the Saudis

mets. In Colorado, Kansas, and South Dakota, three states that repealed such laws in 1976, deaths associated with motorcycle accidents have doubled, according to the agency. Only 21 states now have laws requiring helmets.

The U.S. Consumer Product Safety Commission on June 21 turned down a petition asking for a ban on the use of skateboards. The government, in rejecting the petition brought by a consumer group, said that skateboard injuries result from the way the boards are used rather than the way manufacturers build them, and that skateboard accidents have been declining. The agency reported that 87,000 persons needed treatment in hospital emergency rooms in 1978 because of skateboard mishaps, a drop from the 140,000 skateboard accidents reported in 1977.

The Consumer Product Safety Commission ruled on January 25 that all power lawn mowers must be fitted with devices that shut off the blades within three seconds after the operator releases the handle and that the blades must be shielded from the operator. The regulation will go into effect on Jan. 1, 1982.   Foster Stockwell

In WORLD BOOK, see SAFETY.

SAILING. See BOATING.

SALVATION ARMY. See COMMUNITY ORGANIZATIONS.

SAN MARINO. See EUROPE.

SÃO TOMÉ AND PRÍNCIPE. See AFRICA.

Saudi Arabian Foreign Minister Saud al-Faisal greets U.S. National Security Adviser Zbigniew Brzezinski, who visited Riyadh in March.

SCHREYER, EDWARD RICHARD (1935-   ), was sworn in as Canada's·22nd governor general on Jan. 22, 1979, succeeding Jules Léger. For the first time, declared Prime Minister Pierre Elliott Trudeau, "the meaning of Canada will be expressed in a viceregal voice tinged with a truly Western accent."

Born on a prairie farm in Beausejour, Manitoba, Schreyer is a third-generation Canadian from a family of German origin. A graduate of the University of Manitoba, Schreyer taught there from 1962 to 1965. He was also a member of the Manitoba legislature for the New Democratic Party from 1958 to 1965. He served in the Canadian House of Commons from 1965 to 1969. He led his party to victory in his native province in 1969, and was premier of Manitoba until 1977. In 1978, when he was appointed governor general, he was an opposition member of the Manitoba legislature.

At a time when divisive feelings ran high between French-speaking Canadians and those of British origin, Schreyer's appointment brought into the highest office in the land a person unallied with either faction and passionately committed to the preservation of Canada's unity. To emphasize Canada's "internationalism of ancestry," Schreyer used five languages – English, French, German, Polish, and Ukrainian – in his installation address. Edward and Lilly Schreyer have four children. David M. L. Farr

See also CANADA.

SCIENCE AND RESEARCH. Nuclear power issues related to safety and national security were matters of heated public debate in the United States and throughout the world in 1979. One of the events that precipitated this debate was an accident at the Three Mile Island nuclear power facility near Harrisburg, Pa., on March 28. It caused widespread alarm around the world and led to demands for the closing of all nuclear power plants and demonstrations protesting the construction of any new power plants.

The Three Mile Island accident released some radiation into the atmosphere around the plant. President Jimmy Carter named an 11-member presidential commission to investigate the incident and make recommendations for future control and prevention of such accidents. He appointed John G. Kemeny, president of Dartmouth College, to head the commission, which said in October that basic changes must be made in nuclear reactor construction, operation, and regulation.

The federal government's Advisory Committee on Reactor Safety, composed of 14 leading reactor-safety experts, in April recommended improved systems to ensure better monitoring of temperatures within all reactors and other safety measures. The Nuclear Regulatory Commission re-evaluated its nuclear safety rules and admitted that its procedures before the accident had been inadequate. See ENERGY (Close-Up).

successfully fought their way through the sprawling mosque–which houses the Kaaba, Islam's most sacred shrine, thought to have been built by Abraham and later cleansed of idols by Muhammad in the A.D. 600s. Although the assault was thought to have been made by members of the 'Utaibah, a small group of nomadic Saudis, rumors of U.S. and Israeli involvement swept the Islamic world and triggered riots and demonstrations, including the burning of the U.S. Embassy in Islamabad, Pakistan. See PAKISTAN; RELIGION.

Peace Between the Yemens. Saudi Arabia was the principal mediator in the border conflict between Yemen (Aden) and Yemen (Sana) that broke out in February. A four-point Saudi peace proposal was accepted by both Yemens, and a cease-fire went into effect in March. The government's general policy of noninterference in the internal affairs of other Arab states was demonstrated in March when the Saudi contingent of the Arab peacekeeping force in Lebanon returned home.

To encourage foreign investment and attract skilled labor, the government in February extended the tax-exempt status for foreign companies to 10 years; a 25 per cent Saudi ownership was sufficient to qualify a firm for exemption.   William Spencer

See also MIDDLE EAST (Facts in Brief Table). In WORLD BOOK, see SAUDI ARABIA.

SCHOOL. See CIVIL RIGHTS; EDUCATION.

H-Bomb Article. The U.S. Department of Justice announced on September 17 that it was dropping its efforts to prevent the publication of an article in *The Progressive* magazine that included material on the making of a hydrogen bomb. The government had obtained a court order in Milwaukee in March, barring the magazine from publishing Howard Morland's article on the grounds that publication of the article would endanger national security.

The Senate's Governmental Affairs Subcommittee held sessions in September to investigate how allegedly "sensitive" data pertaining to the design of thermonuclear weapons ended up in the public domain and subsequently in Morland's article. At the hearing, the General Accounting Office (GAO) said that in the course of routine reviewing of secret documents to see if they should be declassified, at least 100 documents were "erroneously declassified."

The GAO explained that the Atomic Energy Commission undertook, from 1971 to 1976, to declassify documents as quickly as possible from inactive files for better access by the general public and the scientific community. Almost 2.8 million documents were reviewed, and close to 1.5 million were declassified, some in near-marathon sessions. The magazine's publishers cited the use of at least 22 of these declassified documents – obtained at the public library of the Los Alamos Scientific Laboratory in New Mexico – in their appeal of the government ban on the H-bomb article.

Science Budget. Allocations for basic research were boosted 9 per cent in the budget submitted by President Jimmy Carter to Congress in January for fiscal 1980 (Oct. 1, 1979, to Sept. 30, 1980). With inflation expected to run at about 7 per cent, the budget represented a real growth of about 2 per cent. Carter requested about $30.6 billion for research and development.

The U.S. Department of Defense, the Department of Energy, and the National Aeronautics and Space Administration received the largest increases in research and development funds. The National Science Foundation was allocated more than $1-billion, with the major increases going to basic research in chemistry, environmental biology, and the earth sciences.

Tellico Dam. In a decision that angered many scientists, President Carter signed a bill in September to authorize completion of the $116-million Tellico Dam in Tennessee. The project had been stopped by court order in 1977, under the Endangered Species Act of 1973, because it threatened the snail darter, a fish on the endangered species list.

Supporters of the dam were elated by the President's action. They had been trying to win an exemption from the law ever since the court decision. They maintained that the fish is not threatened by the dam and that it has been successfully transplanted to a nearby river. They also maintained that the dam would provide electricity for thousands of homes in a time of national energy shortages.

Following Carter's decision, archaeologists said they were preparing to go to court under the 1974 Archaeological Conservation Act, which provides protection for prehistoric sites endangered by any construction project licensed or funded by the federal government. The archaeologists said that the area that would be inundated by the waters of the Little Tennessee River, if the dam is completed, contains many important unexcavated sites.

Flight. A spidery, 55-pound (25-kilogram) craft named the *Gossamer Albatross* was flown across the English Channel on June 12. The pilot, Bryan Allen, thus became the first human being to fly – not just glide or float – across that body of water under his own power. The pilot, a noted bicycle racer, pedaled to drive the vehicle's propeller. The 22-mile (35-kilometer) journey from the English cliffs of Dover to a point about 15 miles (24 kilometers) south of Calais, France, took a little under three hours. The vehicle was designed by California engineer Paul MacCready. Foster Stockwell

See also the various science articles. In WORLD BOOK, see RESEARCH; SCIENCE.

SCOTLAND. See GREAT BRITAIN.

SCULPTURE. See VISUAL ARTS.

SENEGAL. See AFRICA.

SEYCHELLES. See AFRICA.

SHAGARI, SHEHU (1925-   ), was elected president of Nigeria in August 1979, the country's first civilian ruler in 13 years. He faced the enormous task of uniting a land known for its deep ethnic and regional divisions. Even before taking office in October, he had to fight a legal challenge to his election by opposition leader Obafemi Awolowo. See NIGERIA.

Shagari was born in 1925 in the village of Shagari, Nigeria, which was founded by his grandfather. He attended Kaduna College in Nigeria from 1941 to 1944 and Teacher Training College in Zaria, Nigeria, from 1944 to 1945. He began teaching in 1945 and later studied education in Great Britain.

He was elected to parliament in 1954. As a protégé of Prime Minister Abubakar Tafawa Balewa, he held several Cabinet posts from 1960 until a military coup d'état in 1966. These posts included minister of economic affairs, minister of internal affairs, and minister of works.

He escaped execution during the 1966 coup and went back to his village. General Yakubu Gowon appointed Shagari federal commissioner of economic development in 1970, then made him commissioner for finance in 1971. For three years before his election as president, Shagari served as chairman of an automobile company.

Shagari published a volume of verse in 1947. He is married and the father of five. Patricia Dragisic

The *Liu Lin Hai* arrives at Seattle in April, becoming the first ship from the People's Republic of China to dock at a United States port.

SHIP AND SHIPPING. Demand for vessels continued to decline in 1979. Lloyd's Register of Shipping reported that 1,877 merchant ships were under construction throughout the world on June 30, off 7 per cent from a year earlier. Orders, including ships being built, dropped from 3,210 to 2,976. Tonnage of vessels on order fell to 25.4 million gross tons, down 17 per cent.

But fewer oil tankers were deactivated because of low demand, and world rates for tanker rent rebounded sharply from depressed levels. Shipping rates climbed because of higher fuel costs.

United States shipbuilders held orders of about $12.2 billion. The Maritime Administration said commercial-ship orders were valued at $3.1 billion on September 1, down from $3.2 billion a year earlier. Some 50 ships were scheduled for completion by 1982, unchanged from Sept. 1, 1978. Contracts awarded in 1979 included orders totaling $427.9-million for Bethlehem Steel Corporation, $272 million for Ogden Corporation's Avondale Shipyards, and $239 million for National Steel & Shipbuilding Company. The Shipbuilders Council of America estimated that U.S. Navy orders amounted to $9.1-billion at the end of 1979, off 9 per cent.

Cargo Sharing. At a May meeting of the United Nations Conference on Trade and Development in Manila, the Philippines, wealthier ship-owning nations agreed to ratify a 1974 treaty that would give developing countries and their trading partners each 40 per cent of the ocean trade serving the developing countries. The agreement would benefit the shipping lines of developing countries by giving them much more business. When nations whose liners together carry 25 per cent of world tonnage ratify the treaty, it will become law.

On June 8, a federal judge fined seven shipping lines, including four U.S. companies, and 13 executives $6.1 million for illegal rate fixing.

China Trade. The U.S. government said on February 23 that the Lykes Brothers Steamship Company, a U.S. firm, and China Ocean Shipping Company, a Chinese carrier, had negotiated an agreement to ship cargo between Seattle and Shanghai. A Lykes Brothers ship took on cargo in Shanghai on March 17, marking the first time that the two countries had opened their ports to each other since 1949. Other U.S. carriers negotiated for such routes, and a U.S. Lines, Incorporated, ship picked up Chinese cargo in May. In October, the Maritime Commission approved an agreement between Lykes and China Ocean for regularly scheduled liner service.   Albert R. Karr

See also TRANSPORTATION. In WORLD BOOK, see SHIP.

SHOOTING. See HUNTING; SPORTS.
SIERRA LEONE. See AFRICA.
SIKKIM. See ASIA.

Slalom star Ingemar Stenmark of Sweden sweeps the slalom races, but fails to win his fourth World Cup after competition rules are changed.

SILLS, BEVERLY (1929-　　　), one of the greatest operatic sopranos of the mid-1900s, became director of the New York City Opera on July 1, 1979. Sills had announced in 1978 that she would end her singing career in 1980. She succeeded conductor Julius Rudel as director. Before taking the position, she announced a three-year campaign to raise $12-million for the opera company.

Belle Silverman was born in New York City on May 25, 1929. She began her career at the age of 3, as a star of a weekly New York City radio show. She left nine years later to continue her regular schooling and to study voice, piano, French, and Italian. She graduated from the Professional Children's School in New York City in 1945.

Sills made her operatic debut in Philadelphia in 1946 and sang with touring companies in 1950 and 1951. She joined the New York City Opera in 1955, eventually becoming the greatest box-office attraction in its history. Critics praised her blend of singing and acting, as, for example, Cleopatra in George Frideric Handel's *Julius Caesar* in 1966 and in the title role of Jules Massenet's *Manon* in 1969. She made her Metropolitan Opera debut in 1975 in Gioacchino Rossini's *Siege of Corinth*.

Sills married Peter B. Greenough in 1956. They have two children.　　　　　　　　　　　　Jay Myers

SINGAPORE. See ASIA.

SKATING. See HOCKEY; ICE SKATING.

SKIING. Peter Luescher of Switzerland won the 1979 World Cup overall title for men because skiing officials found a way to stop Ingemar Stenmark of Sweden. They changed the rules.

Stenmark became champion the three previous years by dominating the special slalom and giant slalom. He had never skied a downhill race and did not even own downhill skis. He said downhill skiing required different training and would hurt his slalom performance.

World Cup officials preferred the title to be held by an all-around skier. So they amended the rules to reduce the number of points a skier could receive in each category—special slalom, giant slalom, and downhill—and added four combined events.

The World Cup Races ran from December 1978 to March 1979 in Europe, the United States, and Japan. They embraced 35 competitions for men and 27 for women. In the Nations Cup standing, which combined men's and women's points, Austria finished first; Switzerland, second; Italy, third; the United States, fourth; and Canada, 11th.

The 23-year-old Luescher totaled 186 points as the first Swiss to win an overall title since the World Cup competition began in 1967. Leonhard Stock of Austria was second with 163; Phil Mahre of White Pass, Wash., third with 155; Stenmark, fifth with 150. Steve Mahre, Phil's twin, finished 10th. Ken Read of Calgary, Canada, was 22nd, the highest finish by a Canadian skier. Phil Mahre was second until he broke an ankle and missed the last six races.

Annemarie Proell Moser of Austria won her sixth women's title in nine years by overcoming defending champion Hanni Wenzel of Liechtenstein in the last race, 243 points to 240. Cindy Nelson of Lutsen, Minn., was fourth.

A Nordic World Cup was held from December to March in Europe and the United States, with nine individual races and two relays for men and a similar program for women. Oddvar Braa of Norway won the men's title, and Galina Kulakova led a 1-2-3-4 Russian sweep among the women. The highest American finisher was Alison Owen-Spencer of Anchorage, Alaska, seventh among the women. She also won two of the three U.S. individual titles.

The United States unveiled a world-class jumper in Jim Denney of Duluth, Minn. He placed eighth at Garmisch-Partenkirchen, West Germany, on January 2, the highest American finish in Europe in years. On February 10, he took third in the first competition on the 90-meter hill built at Lake Placid, N.Y., for the 1980 Winter Olympic Games.

André Arnold of Austria and Toril Forland of Norway were professional champions for the second straight year. Arnold won 10 of the 22 men's races and $82,788. Forland had five firsts and three seconds in the eight women's races.   Frank Litsky

In WORLD BOOK, see SKIING.

Bob Lenarduzzi of Vancouver brushes Tampa Bay's Wes McLeod away during Soccer Bowl championship game on September 8. Vancouver won it, 2-1.

SOCCER. Professional soccer continued to grow in the United States in 1979, and not only outdoors. One major indoor league played in the 1978-1979 season, and two started the 1979-1980 season.

Outdoors, the 24-team North American Soccer League (NASL) strengthened itself for its 13th season. Well-financed groups bought the Washington, Toronto, and Oakland teams, and Oakland was moved to Edmonton, Canada. Lucrative contracts lured such outstanding foreign stars as Johan Cruyff of the Netherlands to Los Angeles, Johan Neeskens of the Netherlands to the Cosmos, and Gerd Muller of West Germany and Cubillas of Peru to Fort Lauderdale, Fla.

Vancouver Wins. Each team played 30 games from March to August, with 16 teams advancing to the play-offs. The Cosmos, champions for two years, had the best regular-season record – 24 victories against 6 defeats. The Vancouver Whitecaps (20-10) were fourth best. Vancouver won the championship by defeating the Tampa Bay Rowdies, 2-1, on September 8 at East Rutherford, N.J.

Of the NASL players, the 45 per cent from the United States and Canada averaged $12,000 in salary and the 55 per cent from other countries averaged $20,000. The players union called a strike on April 14. Almost three-fourths of the players had indicated they would support a strike, but only one-fourth struck. The strike ended on April 18.

The American Soccer League expanded to 11 teams by adding franchises in Columbus, Ohio; Las Vegas, Nev.; and Pennsylvania, which played in Allentown. The California Sunshine, which had the best regular-season record (22-3-3), lost to the Sacramento Gold in the Western Division play-off finals. Sacramento then beat the Columbus Magic, 1-0, for the championship.

The Major Indoor Soccer League of six teams played its first season from December 1978 to March 1979. The six-man teams played in hockey arenas, with wider goals and continuous action. Scoring averaged 12 goals per game. The New York Arrows won the championship. Most Valuable Player in the play-offs was Shep Messing, the Arrows' goalie and the league's highest-paid player at $50,000 a year. Every team lost money, but the average attendance of 4,442 encouraged many people.

In Europe, Nottingham Forest of England won the European Champions Cup with a 1-0 victory over Malmo of Sweden. Barcelona of Spain beat Fortuna Dusseldorf of West Germany, 4-3, to win the European Cup Winners Cup. Borussia Münchengladbach of West Germany scored a 1-0 triumph over Red Star of Belgrade, Yugoslavia, for the UEFA Cup. In England, Liverpool won the first division, and Arsenal won the Football Association Cup.   Frank Litsky

In WORLD BOOK, see SOCCER.

SOCIAL SECURITY. President Jimmy Carter in January 1979 proposed cutting some Social Security benefits as part of his austere federal budget for fiscal 1980. The Social Security system has been caught in a squeeze, with a slowly growing work force paying the bills for a rapidly growing number of pensioners. Stanford G. Ross, commissioner of Social Security, stated in July that a long era of expansion of programs and rising benefits has ended and that the 1980s must be "a decade of reform" in which Congress mandates "painful adjustments."

President Carter hoped to save $600 million in 1980 and $3 billion a year by 1984. He proposed ending the $255 lump-sum death payment paid to families of beneficiaries; ending benefits for dependent children when the youngest child reaches 16 (rather than 18); phasing out college student benefits; closing out minimum benefit payments (which currently do not fall below $122 per month); and tightening disability benefits. None of the changes would affect recipients now receiving benefits.

The Proposals met with sharp criticism from labor unions, welfare activists, and senior-citizen groups. Some 100 organizations joined in a Nationwide Coalition to Protect Social Security.

Congress acted on only one of the President's proposals, the revamping of disability programs. The number of people receiving Social Security disability benefits has escalated from 700,000 in 1965 to about 4.8 million in 1979. On September 6, the House of Representatives approved a measure that would prevent disabled workers from receiving a benefit exceeding 80 per cent of the normal pay they received before becoming disabled. This would affect only those placed on the rolls after Jan. 1, 1980. The bill provided strong incentives for the disabled to try to return to work by liberalizing medical benefits. The bill would save $1.2 billion by 1984.

Other Developments. Current Social Security benefits were raised 9.9 per cent on July 1, in a cost-of-living adjustment. Alaska's state employees voted to withdraw from Social Security on Jan. 1, 1980, and establish their own retirement program – making it the first state to withdraw its workers; state workers in six states had never joined.

The Supreme Court of the United States on June 25 ruled unconstitutional a provision of the Social Security Act that provided benefits to families with unemployed fathers but denied them to families with mothers out of work. The Social Security Administration said that as of Jan. 1, 1980, people age 65 to 71 can earn up to $5,000 per year without losing any benefits, an increase of $500 a year. For people under 65, the permissible earning level was increased from $3,480 to $3,720. Commissioner Ross in November announced his resignation.   Virginia E. Anderson

In WORLD BOOK, see SOCIAL SECURITY.
SOCIAL WELFARE. See WELFARE.
SOMALIA. See AFRICA.

SOUTH AFRICA. President Balthazar Johannes Vorster resigned on June 4, 1979, after a government commission accused him of covering up a scandal while he was prime minister. Marais Viljoen was named to succeed him in the ceremonial post.

A commission of inquiry accused Vorster, who served as prime minister from 1966 to 1978, of helping to cover up misappropriations from a secret fund for pro-government propaganda. The commission found that the Department of Information had secretly funded propaganda efforts in South Africa and abroad, and had tried unsuccessfully to purchase the *Washington* (D.C.) *Star.* The commission rejected Vorster's claim that he was ignorant of the use of public funds for these activities.

Journalists called the scandal "Muldergate," after Cornelius P. Mulder, who was information minister at the time of the secret program. Former Information Secretary Eschel M. Rhoodie, who directed the program, was tried for fraud, convicted, and sentenced on October 8 to six years in prison. Mulder was dismissed from the government.

Race Issues. South Africa's white government agreed on May 2 to permit blacks to form labor unions and to have the right to strike. However, mixed unions of white and black workers were still forbidden, and many black workers were excluded from union rights.

Chairman Hennie van der Valt of the Commission of Inquiry into Consolidation of Homelands recommended on September 19 that the land area assigned to homelands for black population groups be expanded to make them more viable economically. A 1936 law allocated only 13 per cent of the country's land to the homelands, though blacks who would populate the homelands comprise about 70 per cent of South Africa's population. The white government plans that all the homelands will eventually become sovereign states. Venda became the third such state when it gained political independence on September 13 (see VENDA).

Nuclear Tests? A United States *Vela* satellite detected an explosion with characteristics of a nuclear blast that occurred somewhere between southern Africa and the Antarctic on September 22. South Africa's government, suspected because it conducts an advanced highly secret nuclear research program, denied any knowledge of an explosion.

On March 4, Iran broke diplomatic relations with South Africa and banned further Iranian oil shipments. South Africa had relied on Iran for nearly 90 per cent of its oil imports.   John D. Esseks

See also AFRICA (Facts in Brief Table). In WORLD BOOK, see SOUTH AFRICA.
SOUTH AMERICA. See LATIN AMERICA and articles on Latin American countries.
SOUTH CAROLINA. See STATE GOVERNMENT.
SOUTH DAKOTA. See STATE GOVERNMENT.
SOUTH WEST AFRICA. See NAMIBIA.

SPACE EXPLORATION. Unmanned planetary probes from the United States discovered new moons and rings around Saturn and Jupiter in 1979, while Russian cosmonauts continued to break space-endurance records. Rocket-engine problems kept U.S. astronauts grounded, and the *Skylab* space station fell from orbit.

Pioneer 11, launched in April 1973, completed a 3-billion-kilometer (2-billion-mile) journey to Saturn on September 1, when it flew within 21,400 kilometers (13,300 miles) of that planet on September 1. The spacecraft flew over and under Saturn's rings and returned evidence of a previously unknown 11th moon, possible 12th and 13th moons, and two rings that are invisible from Earth. The 11th moon is about 400 kilometers (250 miles) in diameter, and the 12th moon seems to be 170 kilometers (105 miles) in diameter. The 13th moon, if it exists, lies 31,000 kilometers (19,800 miles) outside of the visible rings. One of the new rings is an 8,000-kilometer (5,000-mile) extension of the F-ring, which begins 81,000 kilometers (50,220 miles) from Saturn's cloud tops, and the other new ring is about 500,000 kilometers (312,500 miles) from the clouds.

Jupiter's Rings. Two *Voyager* spacecraft investigating Jupiter discovered that it has a ring about 30 kilometers (19 miles) thick and invisible from Earth. Cameras aboard *Voyager 2,* launched on Aug. 20,

1977, photographed the ring in July 1979. The pictures also revealed a previously unknown moon, about 35 kilometers (22 miles) in diameter, orbiting 57,800 kilometers (36,000 miles) from Jupiter. It is the 14th Jovian moon to be discovered, and astronomers gave it the temporary name 1979J1. *Voyager 1,* launched in September 1977, took a shorter route and made its closest approach to the planet in March. Its cameras gave the world its first close look at Io, Jupiter's third largest moon. The photographs showed glowing red debris and white-hot gas spraying out of volcanoes – the first record of active volcanism beyond Earth. The *Voyagers* took more than 32,000 photographs and made millions of measurements of Jupiter and its moons, then flew on to planned encounters with Saturn in 1980 and 1981. See Special Reports section, THE RICHES OF JUPITER'S REALM.

Longest Space Flight. Russian cosmonauts Vladimir Lyakhov, an air force officer, and Valery Ryumin, a civilian engineer, landed in Asian Russia on August 19, after spending 175 days in space. They broke the 139-day record established by Vladimir Kovalenok and Aleksander S. Ivanchenko in 1978. Both crews lived and worked aboard the *Salyut 6* space station, launched on Sept. 29, 1977.

Skylab, the first U.S. space station, abandoned since February 1974, fell to Earth as a blazing

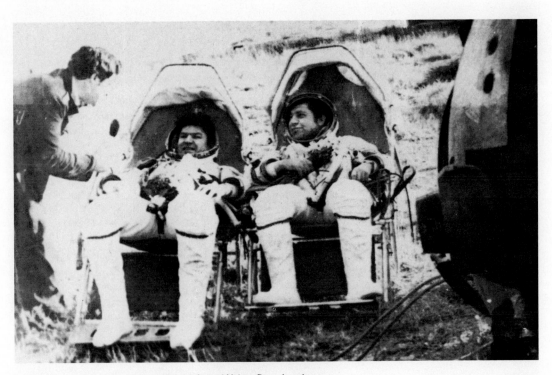

Russian Cosmonauts Vladimir Lyakhov, left, and Valery Ryumin relax on Earth after completing a record-breaking 175 days in space in August.

A Fear
Of Falling

The fall of the United States space station *Skylab* on July 11, 1979, caused more excitement throughout the world than did its launching on May 14, 1973. This space behemoth, nine stories tall and weighing 77.5 short tons (70 metric tons), housed astronauts who conducted scientific experiments and proved that human beings could live and work in space for weeks at a time. But *Skylab* had been unoccupied since 1974 and had gradually sunk closer to Earth.

The National Aeronautics and Space Administration (NASA) installs power systems to control reentry on all manned spacecraft. But NASA had always intended that *Skylab* would be unmanned when it returned to Earth. So NASA flight controllers in Houston had only the craft's small thruster rockets to maneuver the space giant, and they did not know how useful these rockets would be.

The scenario for *Skylab*'s plunge was grim. When the space station entered Earth's atmosphere, friction with air molecules would burn it and break it into hundreds of pieces. The tremendous heat would consume most of the pieces, but some bigger pieces would plunge to Earth, scattering over a path about 4,000 miles (6,400 kilometers) long. Scientists could not predict exactly where such debris would hit, but *Skylab*'s orbital limits – 50° north latitude and 50° south latitude – included all major population centers except those in the northern parts of Europe, Canada, and Siberia, Russia.

Skylab in orbit

The suspense grew steadily until *Skylab* roared down through the southern sky. Some 500 pieces of debris struck Earth along a 5,000-mile (8,000-kilometer) path in the Indian Ocean and Australia, but hit nobody.

The danger had been real enough. At least one huge piece hit land. A 1-short-ton (0.9-metric-ton) cylinder that measured 6 by 3 feet (180 by 90 centimeters) – shook the Australian countryside when it landed. Small pieces hit rooftops in Perth, Australia, a city of 731,275 population.

This was the most spectacular reentry of an unmanned artificial object, but such re-entries are literally

an everyday occurrence. Since Russia launched *Sputnik 1,* the first artificial satellite, in 1957, about 2,500 payloads – satellites, space capsules, and space probes – have been shot into orbit. These launches have also generated about 9,000 pieces of orbiting debris – rockets and pieces of rockets and payloads. The North American Air Defense Command (NORAD), which monitors their orbits, reported in August 1979 that 6,879 artificial objects – 1,334 payloads and 5,545 pieces of debris – had re-entered Earth's atmosphere or hit other planets. About one object re-enters the atmosphere per day, and half of those that re-enter reach Earth's surface.

However, there is little chance that such an object will hit a human being. Only about 30 per cent of Earth's surface is land, and our bodies occupy little of the land, even in crowded parts of China, Egypt, India, and Indonesia where there are 1,000 persons per square mile (2.6 square kilometers).

For much the same reason, artificial objects orbiting Earth do not pose a danger to rocket launches. NORAD reported that there were 4,614 artificial objects in space – 1,040 satellites, 61 probes in deep space (beyond 3,000 miles [4,800 kilometers]), and 3,513 pieces of debris. If these objects were uniformly spaced in a low orbit, such as 200 miles (320 kilometers) above the equator, a rocket launched in the equatorial plane would probably not hit any of them, because there would be 5.67 miles (9.13 kilometers) between objects.

Meteoroids – chunks of metallic or stony matter that orbit the sun – are a greater danger to people on earth. NASA estimates that 7,600 meteoroids weighing more than 1 pound (0.45 kilogram) strike Earth each year just within *Skylab*'s orbital limits of 50° north latitude and 50 ° south latitude. This meteoric shower is more than 40 times as intense as the steady dropping of artificial objects, yet no heavy meteoroid has ever hit a human.

How safe should this comparison make us feel? Just as safe as if there had never been a space program – now that *Skylab* is down.   Jay Myers

shower of burning metal on July 11. Most fragments landed in remote areas of Western Australia and nobody was injured by the debris. However, the National Aeronautics and Space Administration (NASA) was criticized for minimizing the danger of the uncontrolled landing. NASA had hoped to keep *Skylab* aloft long enough to send up astronauts in a space shuttle to attach booster rockets to it. The rockets would have increased *Skylab*'s orbit or guided the craft down to a less hazardous landing. However, conditions in space that increased the drag on *Skylab* and repeated delays in launching the shuttle prevented such a rescue. See Close-Up.

The Space Shuttle *Columbia,* a reusable spacecraft that takes off like a rocket and lands like an airplane, was scheduled to make its first orbital flight in 1979, but problems with the main rocket engines and the heat-insulation tiles postponed the launch until 1980. NASA feared that heavy vibration and air friction during the shuttle's eight minutes of powered flight through the atmosphere might loosen some tiles. Loss of even a small number of tiles could expose the shuttle to critical heating and aerodynamic stresses when it re-entered the atmosphere. In March, NASA had begun to prepare the shuttle for launch from the John F. Kennedy Space Center in Cape Canaveral, Florida. Astronauts John W. Young and Robert L. Crippen were assigned to pilot *Columbia* on its first space flight. In addition to the engineering problems, a staff of experts found "significant management deficiencies" in the shuttle program and, in August, concluded that "there remains significant potential for additional unanticipated problems and cost growth until these deficiencies are corrected." On November 29, NASA postponed the flight of two Galileo spaceships to Jupiter from 1982 to 1984 because of shuttle delays. The shuttle would carry the spaceships aloft.

The European Space Agency (ESA) completed ground tests of its three-stage *Ariane* rocket on September 13 and scheduled its first launch for December 15. But the attempt failed on the launching pad. Shortly after ignition, a first-stage engine registered abnormally low pressure, which shut down the rocket automatically. ESA developed the Ariane program, and France builds and controls the rockets. *Ariane* can place into orbit one or two satellites that have a combined weight of 1,700 kilograms (3,700 pounds), but it can be used only once.

International Cooperation. Launchings of scientific, weather, environmental, communications, and military satellites continued in 1979. These included the September 20 launch of the third High Energy Astronomy Observatory satellite (HEAO-3), the last of the series. The *Cosmos 1129* unmanned Russian spacecraft carried 13 U.S. experiments on a 19-day flight ending October 14.   William J. Cromie

In WORLD BOOK, see SPACE TRAVEL.

SPAIN struggled through 1979 with a shaky economy, widespread strikes, and continuing terrorism by Basque separatists. Gunmen of the Basque Homeland and Liberty organization (ETA) assassinated the military governor of Madrid on January 3. Violence continued through the spring and threatened the tourist industry in the summer when the ETA set off bombs on vacation beaches. The military governor of the Basque province of Guipúzcoa, shot dead on September 23, became the 12th high-ranking army officer murdered by the ETA in 1979.

The main Basque political party and the national government drafted a home-rule bill on July 17 that would give limited autonomy to the three main Basque provinces, which have a population of 1.5 million. Voters in those provinces approved the bill in an October 25 referendum. The bill did not consider the status of a fourth province, Navarre, which is half Basque, because the negotiators feared that a Navarre clause would jeopardize approval of the measure.

Suarez Re-elected. Prime Minister Adolfo Suarez Gonzalez won in the March 1 general election. His Union of the Democratic Center won 35 per cent of the popular vote and 168 of the 350 seats in parliament's lower house. The Socialists took 29 per cent of the vote and 121 seats, and the Communists, 10 per cent and 23 seats. The Socialists and Communists opposed Suarez in a March 30 confidence vote on his plan to form a minority government. But Suarez won, 183-149, and named a new Cabinet on April 5.

Wave of Strikes. The government set a 14 per cent ceiling on wage hikes in January, and labor responded by disrupting services. The government ended a railroad strike in Barcelona on March 8 by threatening to draft all employees into the army. On August 3, however, the government agreed to an extra 1.7 per cent increase in wages from June through December to offset price increases. Strikes added to the troubles of the tourist trade, which served 1.15 million fewer guests in July 1979 than in July 1978. Hotel operators also blamed higher rates and ETA violence for the decline. Tourism had brought $4.91 billion to Spain in 1978, more than wiping out the trade deficit. Local-government employees throughout Spain struck for four days on November 26, demanding higher pay.

Economic Program. A long-awaited economic plan, unveiled on August 14, projected that a tight monetary policy would hold the annual inflation rate at 16 per cent. The plan cut public spending 2.6 per cent and pruned social services, but it pumped large sums into the big cities to save them from bankruptcy. The plan's growth target was 2.7 per cent, compared with the previous goal of 4 to 5 per cent.   Kenneth Brown

See also EUROPE (Facts in Brief Table). In WORLD BOOK, see BASQUE; SPAIN.

SPORTS

SPORTS attendance was at or near record levels in the United States in 1979, but television sports interest seemed to wane. There were exceptions. The Super Bowl football game was seen in more than 35 million homes, the most ever for a sports event, and its television audience was estimated at 96 million to 104 million. The seventh game of the World Series attracted a record 80 million viewers.

However, fewer viewers watched regular-season baseball games, and World Series overall nighttime audiences dropped 20 per cent. The audience was down 26 per cent for National Basketball Association (NBA) games. Televised golf, which traditionally did best in the winter, suffered such audience losses as 45 per cent for the Hawaiian Open, 42 per cent for the Los Angeles Open, and 37 per cent for the Tournament of Champions. North American Soccer League (NASL) games drew poor ratings. The National Hockey League (NHL) could not sell its games to a major network. Tennis interest decreased. The National Football League (NFL) was barely staying even with the previous years.

In almost every sport, different factors contributed to the drop in television audiences. For example, tennis had so many syndicated series that viewers became confused when they saw one player on different channels against different opponents at the same time.

Long seasons might have contributed, too, as sports overlapped more and more. Professional football's regular season ran from September 1, its earliest opening, to Jan. 20, 1980. Major-league baseball started the regular season on April 4, when it was cold in most of the North, and the World Series ended on October 17 after a week of cold and rain. The professional basketball season extended from mid-October to June 1, the hockey season from mid-October to May 21. Tournament tennis was played year-round, tournament golf from January to November.

Other reasons for the decline might have been a general decrease in television viewing and the growth of cable television, which brought in channels from distant cities. Many cable systems carried extensive sports coverage, and some of them carried only sports. The national viewing surveys studied commercial stations and networks, but not cable systems.

In-person sports viewing remained strong. Major-league baseball attracted a record 43 million spectators during the regular season. College football attracted 35 million; college basketball, 30 million; the NFL, 12 million; the NBA, 10 million; the NHL, 9 million; and the NASL, 5 million.

Among the Winners in 1979 were:

Fencing. Russia won six of the eight titles, including all four team events, in the world championships in August in Melbourne, Australia. It captured the overall title for the 17th straight year. The United States failed to score.

Gymnastics. U.S. men made their best showing ever in

Hot-air balloons of varied designs float over the New Jersey countryside during a race staged to raise funds for students with cerebral palsy.

the world championships, winning eight of the 25 medals in December in Fort Worth, Tex. Kurt Thomas of Tempe, Ariz., finished second in all-around and won two gold and two silver medals in the six individual finals. Russian men and Romanian women took the team titles, with the American men second and American women sixth. Americans won none of the 19 women's medals.

Rowing. East Germans captured six of the eight heavyweight titles for men and three of the six for women in the world championships in August and September in Bled, Yugoslavia. The only American winner was Bill Belden of Paoli, Pa., in lightweight single sculls.

Shooting. Lieutenant Colonel Lones Wigger of Fort Benning, Ga., was America's outstanding rifleman. He won the United States small-bore three-position title for the 12th time in 17 years and gained that championship and the English match title in the Pan American Games.

Weight Lifting. Russia won 16 of the 30 gold medals in the world championships in November in Salonika, Greece. Next were Poland and Bulgaria with four each. Sultan Rachmanov of Russia swept the super-heavyweight competition with a snatch of 192.5 kilograms (424$\frac{1}{4}$ pounds), a clean and jerk of 237.5 kilograms (523$\frac{1}{2}$ pounds), and a total of 430 kilograms (948 pounds).

Wrestling. Leroy Kemp of Canton, Ohio, retained the 163-pound free-style title in the world championships in August in San Diego. Russia took both team titles, with the U.S. second in free-style and a surprising fourth in Greco-Roman.

Other Champions. *Archery,* world champions: men, Darrell Pace, Cincinnati, Ohio; women, Jin Jo Ki, South Korea. *Badminton,* world champions: men, Liem Swie King, Indonesia; women, Lene Koppen, Denmark. *Biathlon,* world champions: 10-kilometer, Frank Ullrich, East Germany; 20-kilometer, Klaus Siebert, East Germany. *Billiards,* world pocket champion: Mike Sigel, Towson, Md. *Bobsledding,* world champions: four-man, Stephan Gaisreiter, West Germany; two-man, Erich Scharer, Switzerland. *Canoeing,* U.S. 500-meter champions: canoe, Roland Muhlen, Cincinnati; men's kayak, Terry White, Manchester, Vt.; women's kayak, Linda Dragon, Washington, D.C. *Casting,* U.S. all-around champions: Steve Rajeff, San Francisco, and Chris Korich, Oakland, Calif., (tie). *Court tennis,* world champion: Howard Angus, England. *Cricket,* World Cup: West Indies. *Croquet,* U.S. champion: Richard Pearman, Bermuda. *Cross-country,* world champions: men, John Treacy, Ireland; women, Grete Waitz, Norway. *Curling,* men's champions: world, Norway; U.S., Bemidji, Minn. *Cycling,* world champions: men's amateur road, Gianni Giacomini, Italy; women's road, Petra de Bruin, the Netherlands; men's amateur sprint, Lutz Hesslich, East Germany; women's sprint, Galina Zareva, Russia. U.S. motocross champion, Stu Thomsen, Whittier, Calif. *Darts,* U.S. champion: Jake Breskowski, Nuremberg, Pa. *Equestrian events,* World Cup champion: Hugo Simon, Austria. *Field hockey,* world champions: men, Pakistan; women, the Netherlands. *Handball,* USHA four-wall champion: Naty Alvarado, Pomona, Calif. *Hang gliding,* world champion: Malcolm Jones, Tampa, Fla. *Horseshoe pitching,* world champions: men, Mark Seibold, Huntington, Ind.; women, Phyllis Negaard, St. Joseph, Minn. *Judo,* U.S. open champions: men, Shawn Gibbons, St. Petersburg, Fla.; women, Barbara Fest, Boston. *Karate,* U.S. advanced champions: men, Albert Pena, Haverstraw, N.Y.; women, Vicki Johnson, Dunlap, Ill. *Lacrosse,* U.S. champions: college, Johns Hopkins; club, Mount Washington, Baltimore. *Lawn bowling,* U.S. champions: men, Bert MacWilliams, Euclid, Ohio; women, Marie Gorman, East Meadow, N.Y. *Luge,* world champions: men, Dettlef Guenther, East Germany; women, Melitta Sollmann, East Germany. *Modern pentathlon,* world champion: Robert Nieman, Hinsdale, Ill. *Motorcycling,* U.S. Grand National champion: Steve

Eklund, San Jose, Calif. *Parachute jumping,* U.S. overall champions: men, Cliff Jones, Fort Bragg, N.C.; women, Cheryl Stearns, Scottsdale, Ariz. *Polo,* U.S. open champion: Retama, San Antonio, Tex. *Racquetball,* U.S. champions: men, Marty Hogan, St. Louis; women, Karin Walton, San Clemente, Calif. *Racquets,* U.S. champion: William Surtees, New York City. *Rodeo,* U.S. all-around champion: Tom Ferguson, Miami, Okla. *Roller skating,* U.S. champions: men, Michael Glatz, San Diego; women, Moana Pitcher, San Diego. *Roque,* U.S. champion: Jack Green, Long Beach, Calif. *Rugby,* U.S. champion: Old Blue, Oakland, Calif. *Sambo,* U.S. heavyweight champion: Mark Sanchez, LaPuente, Calif. *Shuffleboard,* U.S. summer champions: men, Lary Faris, Cincinnati; women, June Angeroth, Council Bluffs, Iowa. *Sled-dog racing,* world champion: Debbie Molburg, Center Harbor, N.H. *Softball,* U.S. fast-pitch champions: men, Midland, Mich.; women, Sun City, Ariz. *Squash racquets,* U.S. champions: men, Mario Sanchez, Mexico; women, Heather McKay, Australia. *Squash tennis,* U.S. champion: Pedro Bacallao, New York City. *Synchronized swimming,* World Cup champion: Helen Vandenburg, Calgary, Canada. *Table tennis,* world champions: men, Seiji Ono, Japan; women, Ge Xinia, China. *Tae kwon do,* U.S. heavyweight champions: men, Thomas Seabourne, Allentown, Pa.; women, Lynnette Love, Detroit. *Team handball,* U.S. champions: men, West Coast, Los Angeles; women, Northeastern, New York City. *Trampoline,* U.S. champions: men, Stuart Ransom, Memphis, Tenn.; women, Karen Kernan, Lafayette, La. *Volleyball,* AAU champions: men, Vessel's Quartermaster, Los Angeles; women, Los Angeles Mavericks. *Water polo,* World Cup champion: Hungary. *Water skiing,* world champions: men, Joel McClintock, Streetsville, Canada; women, Cindy Todd, Pierson, Fla.   Frank Litsky

See also articles on the various sports. In WORLD BOOK, see articles on the various sports.

SRI LANKA remained one of the poorer Asian states in 1979, with the gross national product (GNP) per capita put at $200. But it was still one of the most socially advanced nations in Asia, with a welfare program ranging from subsidies for low-income groups to free school textbooks. After many years of leftist governments, the voters continued to support the conservative United National Party (UNP) of President Junius Richard Jayewardene, elected in 1977. In the local elections held in May 1979, the UNP cut further into leftist strength. However, economic distress and Tamil separatism in the north of the island continued to fuel political unrest.

Tamil Separatists. After the 15th police officer was murdered in the Tamil stronghold of Jaffna, the government declared a state of emergency and enacted an antiterrorism law on July 19. Stiff penalties were provided, including up to 20 years in prison for buying arms or causing unrest, and life in prison for killing police officers, soldiers, officers of the court, or legislators. Also, the Constitution was to be amended to ban separatism.

The killing of police and many police informers was pinned on the Liberation Tigers, a secret and violent youth band numbering at least several hundred. The Tigers broke away from the more moderate Tamil United Liberation Front (TULF), which campaigned for a separate Tamil state in the 1977 election. The government instructed the new security commander in the region to eliminate "the menace of terrorism in all its forms" by the year's end. At the same time, Jayewardene moved to ensure Tamils freer admission to universities and civil service jobs – areas in which the Sinhalese majority had discriminated against them. Tamils make up about 20 per cent of Sri Lanka's population.

Supports Cut. Under pressure from the World Bank, the government removed price subsidies on such items as bread, wheat flour, and condensed milk to save $155 million a year. However, workers earning under $20 per month were given food stamps, and those earning less than $65 a month received a raise of about $3.50. The budget, announced on November 14, included a deficit of about $590 million.

Inflation finally fell below an annual rate of 20 per cent. During the year, Sri Lanka signed an agreement with Japan to provide a television network.

The major development in progress was the Mahawell Ganga project, which will provide power and irrigation reservoirs and canals. By the end of 1980, three of the five dams in the first phase of the plan were to be completed, at a cost of $1 billion – financed by foreign sources. As a result, 292,000 acres (118,000 hectares) of land will be irrigated for crops.   Mark Gayn

See also ASIA (Facts in Brief Table). In WORLD BOOK, see SRI LANKA.

A Stanley Gibbons International of London official proudly displays part of the stamp collection the firm bought for a record-breaking $10 million.

STAMP COLLECTING. A stamp and letter collection was sold for more than $10 million in August 1979, apparently setting a record for a negotiated philatelic sale. The collection belonged to Marc Haas, a 71-year-old New York City financier, who started collecting stamps when he was 5 years old. Buyer of the collection was Stanley Gibbons International of London, a stamp dealer. The collection consisted of about 3,000 items, including memorabilia signed by Presidents George Washington and Thomas Jefferson and envelopes signed by President Abraham Lincoln and Robert E. Lee, who were allowed to mail letters free by putting their signatures where a stamp would be placed ordinarily. Another prized item was a letter marked "through the lines" that was mailed from Philadelphia to Demopolis, Ala., during the Civil War.

Howard O. Fraser, chairman of the Gibbons firm, who arranged the sale of the Haas collection, said, "It was assembled with a great deal of taste, a great deal of knowledge, and a great deal of money." Fraser said that because it "represents a tremendous slice of American history," he wanted to sell the items from the collection in the United States. The previous record for a negotiated stamp sale was $4.7-million, set in 1969.

Inverted Airmail Stamps. Another record price was set in the sale on July 16 to George Manter of Coral Springs, Fla., and five members of his family

of a block of four of the celebrated U.S. 1918 inverted airmail stamps for $500,000 by an unidentified seller. Three years previously the block had sold for $170,000.

The Rarities of the World sale conducted on April 4 in New York City by the Robert A. Siegel Auction Gallery realized $2 million from 323 lots of stamps, a record sale for a single session. A single 1918 airmail invert went for $130,000, the highest price ever paid for a U.S. stamp.

Special Themes. The year was marked by a variety of omnibus issues – stamps on the same theme issued by several countries. Probably foremost among them were stamps commemorating the International Year of the Child, sponsored by the United Nations (UN) in 1979. Other omnibus themes included the 1980 Olympic Games in Moscow and the 100th anniversary of the death of Sir Rowland Hill of Great Britain, who introduced the world's first adhesive postage stamp.

The International Year of the Child was observed to arouse concern for the health and welfare of children everywhere. The UN, the United States, and Great Britain were among those issuing stamps devoted to the theme. One of the most interesting of the many issues was a vertical quartet issued by Great Britain bearing characters from four famous children's books: *The Tale of Peter Rabbit, The Wind in the Willows, Winnie-the-Pooh,* and *Alice's Adven-*

tures in Wonderland. Virtually all of Great Britain's 1979 issues were quartets depicting such subjects as dogs, wild flowers, and race horses.

The U.S. Postal Service on September 5 began issuing 15 commemorative postal items calling attention to the 1980 Olympic Games. The items included 10 adhesive stamps, three postal cards, an embossed envelope, and an air letter. It was the first time that the Postal Service had devoted a range of stamps and stamped objects to a single subject.

Stamp Sales. The Postal Service reported an unusually heavy first-day-of-sale demand for 1979 stamps commemorating Martin Luther King, Jr. (January 13), the International Year of the Child (February 15), and novelist John Steinbeck (February 27). The Steinbeck stamp was the first in a series devoted to the literary arts.

Other U.S. issues for 1979 included the 15-cent Albert Einstein stamp (March 4), which honored the great physicist on the 100th anniversary of his birth; the 15-cent Special Olympics stamp (August 9), honoring the mentally retarded children who take part in the games; and a new $1 stamp (July 2) bearing the legend, "America's light fueled by truth and reason."

The UN issued four new definitive stamps in January, all emphasizing the theme of peace. Three were designed by students.   Theodore M. O'Leary

In WORLD BOOK, see STAMP COLLECTING.

STATE GOVERNMENT. The accident at the Three Mile Island nuclear power plant near Harrisburg, Pa., on March 28, 1979, made state governments more aware of the dangers of radioactive materials. The crisis led to a series of legislative and executive acts to control waste disposal. See ENERGY (Close-Up).

New Mexico's legislature created a board to take part in negotiations on disposal of low-level nuclear waste in that state. The federal Nuclear Regulatory Commission (NRC) may authorize such state boards to license independent contractors to store low-level radioactive waste. By the end of 1979, 25 state boards had received this NRC authorization, but storage of high-level radioactive waste remained under direct NRC control.

New Mexico and South Dakota passed laws that regulate nuclear waste transportation. The New York and North Dakota legislatures passed bills that require state approval of nuclear burial sites. Illinois reacted with a law that requires 24-hour monitoring of nuclear power plants. Oregon established a 16-month moratorium on nuclear power-plant construction.

At the beginning of 1979, only Nevada, South Carolina, and Washington had disposal sites that the NRC had licensed to receive low-level radioactive wastes for long-term storage. Sites in Illinois, Kentucky, and New York had been closed to new deliveries for years because of leakage, but a great deal of radioactive material remains in these dumps. Nevada's Governor Robert F. List and Washington's Governor Dixy Lee Ray closed the sites in their states in October. Improperly packaged waste had been found in trucks bound for the Washington site, and five barrels of waste had been found buried outside the fence at the Nevada site. The shutdowns threatened much of the nation's cancer research as radioactive wastes, some of which must remain hermetically sealed for thousands of years, began to fill all the available approved storage areas in hospitals, medical centers, and laboratories throughout the United States. The two governors finally authorized the operators of the disposal sites to resume business in December.

Governor Richard W. Riley of South Carolina on October 31 announced a 50 per cent decrease in the amount of radioactive waste material that would be stored in the dumping ground in his state.

Arizona's Governor Bruce E. Babbitt on September 25 ordered the National Guard to seize the Tucson plant of a company that illuminated signs and watch faces with radioactive material. The company's process used tritium gas, a radioactive form of hydrogen. Leaking tritium had contaminated an elementary school's food supplies stored in an adjacent building. The troops sealed the tritium in

Missouri's Governor Joseph P. Teasdale calls for belt tightening in most state departments as he delivers his budget message in January.

California Governor Edmund G. Brown, Jr., signs an order that begins
gasoline rationing in May. Sign shows flags that gas stations must use.

55-gallon (208-liter) drums and stored it temporarily on National Guard property.

A dozen legislatures considered bills that would regulate the storage of hazardous industrial wastes. Iowa, Kansas, Michigan, and Mississippi enacted strong, comprehensive laws. New Hampshire joined a long list of states that require not only the licensing, but also the monitoring of transportation of hazardous wastes.

Gasoline Shortage. Already plagued by problems surrounding nuclear power, states faced a different sort of energy crisis in May and June when an oil shortage caused long lines at gasoline service stations. Some governors used state and federal emergency powers to order gasoline rationing, set minimum gasoline purchases that prevented tank topping, and institute flag systems that indicated gasoline availability. Such plans were used in affected urban areas in California, Connecticut, Delaware, Florida, Maryland, New Jersey, New York, Pennsylvania, Rhode Island, Texas, Virginia, and the District of Columbia.

At least 14 states worked with gasoline stations to provide staggered hours so that some stations in an area were open on weekends or in the evenings. California and Connecticut banned low maximum limits for gasoline purchases. California, Texas, and a few other states set a 20-gallon (76-liter) limit on gasoline purchases to prevent hoarding. In two rare

moves, Nevada's legislature authorized the state to buy and sell fuel to stimulate its sagging tourism industry, and Louisiana's legislature authorized the state to take oil instead of cash royalties as its share of oil pumped from state lands. The state was permitted to receive 32,000 barrels of oil per day to sell to local, small refineries that would produce 832,000 gallons (3.15 million liters) of gasoline daily – about one-sixth of the state's daily consumption.

The shortage caused a decline in gasoline consumption because people used their automobiles less and bought new automobiles that burned fuel more efficiently. The decrease in consumption reduced severely the gasoline tax revenues that states needed to build, replace, and maintain highways and bridges. A survey that was made in November of governors and legislative leaders revealed that at least a dozen states would be faced with severe shortages of road revenue funds in 1980.

Bills that raised gasoline taxes to compensate for shortfalls passed in Arkansas, Georgia, Montana, Nebraska, New Hampshire, Pennsylvania, South Carolina, South Dakota, and Washington. Outgoing Kentucky Governor Julian M. Carroll announced that his state would face a highway fund shortfall of almost $2 million.

Gasohol. At least 15 states considered bills to remove their sales or gasoline taxes on *gasohol* (a mixture of 9 parts gasoline to 1 part grain alcohol).

Selected Statistics on State Governments

State	Resident population(a)	Governor	Legislature (b) House (D)	(R)	Senate (D)	(R)	State tax revenue(c)	Tax revenue per capita(d)	Public school enrollment 1978-79(e)	Public school expenditures per pupil in average daily attendance 1978-79(f)
Alabama	3,714	Forrest H. James, Jr. (D)	101	4	35	0	$ 1,747	464	762	$ 1,548
Alaska	392	Jay S. Hammond (R)	24	15(g)	9	11	817	2,012	91	n/a
Arizona	2,489	Bruce E. Babbitt (D)	18	42	14	16	1,516	619	510	1,635
Arkansas	2,193	Bill Clinton (D)	94	6	35	0	995	456	457	1,219
California	22,538	Edmund G. Brown, Jr. (D)	50	30	26	14	16,352	720	4,188	n/a
Colorado	2,765	Richard D. Lamm (D)	27	38	13	22	1,441	520	558	2,129
Connecticut	3,206	Ella T. Grasso (D)	104	47	26	10	1,718	552	594	2,162
Delaware	611	Pierre S. du Pont IV (R)	20	21	13	9	492	845	111	2,080
Florida	9,301	Robert Graham (D)	88	32	27	13	4,291	484	1,514	n/a
Georgia	5,262	George Busbee (D)	159	21	52	4	2,448	478	n/a	n/a
Hawaii	931	George R. Ariyoshi (D)	42	9	18	7	876	957	171	1,616
Idaho	866	John V. Evans (D)	20	50	16	19	466	515	203	1,345
Illinois	11,376	James R. Thompson (R)	89	88	32	27	6,323	563	3,100	n/a
Indiana	5,438	Otis R. Bowen (R)	46	54	21	29	2,669	494	1,113	1,455
Iowa	2,879	Robert D. Ray (R)	44	56	23	27	1,569	541	569	2,139
Kansas	2,313	John Carlin (D)	56	69	19	21	1,188	501	434	2,075
Kentucky	3,500	John Y. Brown, Jr. (D)	75	25	29	9	2,076	589	693	1,120
Louisiana	3,930	David C. Treen (R)	95	10	39	0	2,240	556	817	1,576
Maine	1,094	Joseph E. Brennan (D)	77	73	13	19	554	505	240	1,477
Maryland	4,397	Harry Hughes (D)	125	16	40	7	2,647	638	810	1,986
Massachusetts	5,968	Edward J. King (D)	130	30	37	7	3,616	627	1,081	2,496
Michigan	9,433	William G. Milliken (R)	70	40	24	14	6,018	654	1,911	1,990
Minnesota	4,040	Albert Quie (R)	68	66	48	19	3,134	772	808	1,947
Mississippi	2,396	William F. Winter (D)	116	4(h)	48	4	1,196	497	494	1,189
Missouri	4,882	Joseph P. Teasdale (D)	117	46	23	11	2,170	446	900	1,673
Montana	766	Thomas L. Judge (D)	64	36	24	26	401	510	164	2,202
Nebraska	1,577	Charles Thone (R)	49(i) (unicameral)				743	472	298	1,746
Nevada	649	Robert F. List (R)	26	14	15	5	463	659	146	1,682
New Hampshire	870	Hugh J. Gallen (D)	169	231	11	13	264	298	172	1,635
New Jersey	7,603	Brendan T. Byrne (D)	44	36	27	13	3,729	509	1,337	2,576
New Mexico	1,198	Bruce King (D)	41	29	33	9	845	681	279	1,714
New York	18,086	Hugh L. Carey (D)	87	63	25	35	11,688	662	3,094	2,759
North Carolina	5,712	James B. Hunt, Jr. (D)	106	14	45	5	2,915	520	1,163	1,507
North Dakota	630	Arthur A. Link (D)	29	71	14	36	325	494	122	1,607
Ohio	10,933	James A. Rhodes (R)	62	37	18	15	4,620	431	2,102	1,777
Oklahoma	2,834	George Nigh (D)	75	26	38	9	1,516	524	589	1,520
Oregon	2,437	Victor Atiyeh (R)	34	26	23	7	1,384	548	471	1,990
Pennsylvania	11,913	Richard L. Thornburgh (R)	100	102	27	23	6,782	578	2,047	2,315
Rhode Island	961	J. Joseph Garrahy (D)	84	14	43	4	538	579	161	2,067
South Carolina	2,978	Richard W. Riley (D)	108	16	43	2	1,523	519	625	1,274
South Dakota	674	William J. Janklow (R)	24	48	11	24	246	356	138	1,662
Tennessee	4,345	Lamar Alexander (R)	60	38	20	12	1,844	421	873	1,172
Texas	13,098	William Clements (R)	131	19	27	4	5,738	429	2,867	1,490
Utah	1,296	Scott M. Matheson (D)	25	50	10	19	695	508	325	1,494
Vermont	497	Richard A. Snelling (R)	68	80	10	20	267	543	101	1,651
Virginia	5,261	John N. Dalton (R)	74	25(g)	31	9	2,564	493	1,055	1,791
Washington	3,784	Dixy Lee Ray (D)	49	49	29	20	2,718	692	769	2,079
West Virginia	1,809	John D. Rockefeller IV (D)	74	26	26	8	1,150	612	396	1,593
Wisconsin	4,740	Lee S. Dreyfus (R)	60	39	21	12	3,260	691	886	n/a
Wyoming	390	Ed Herschler (D)	20	42	11	19	343	762	94	2,133

(a) Number in thousands, projections as of July 1, 1980 (Bureau of the Census)
(b) As of December 31, 1979
(c) 1979 preliminary figures in millions (Bureau of the Census)
(d) 1979 preliminary figures in dollars (Bureau of the Census)
(e) Numbers in thousands, fall, 1978 (U.S. Office of Education)

(f) Number in dollars, 1978–1979 (U.S. Office of Education)
(g) 1 Independent
(h) 2 Independents
(i) Nonpartisan

These bills would make an alternative fuel available at a competitive price and would stimulate local business, because the alcohol could be produced from domestic farm products. At least eight states had provided such an exemption by June.

Tax Relief. With the message of California's Proposition 13 still ringing in their ears, 35 state governments teamed up in 1979 to provide the biggest series of tax breaks in U.S. history – almost $4.5 billion. The tax relief measures covered the gamut of taxes ranging from sales and income to property. Among the highest were Wisconsin with $940 million in tax cuts, Minnesota with $719.4-million, Oregon with $705 million, and Florida with $373 million. Texas implemented a $500-million property-tax relief measure that voters had approved in November 1978. Colorado reduced taxes by $100 million, Iowa by $110 million, Kansas by $65.5 million, Maryland by $79 million, Mississippi by $83.3 million, New York by $190 million, North Carolina by $78.2 million, and Utah by $74.5-million.

Another restraint on state revenues emerged in 1979 – the government spending cap. Only half a dozen states had such expenditure caps in earlier years. But in 1979, Florida, Kentucky, Massachusetts, and New Mexico limited increases in property-tax revenues. In November, California and Washington voters approved lids on government spending growth. Oklahoma voters defeated a referendum measure that would have limited personal income taxes, opting instead to keep tax cuts that the legislature had enacted in 1979.

The Elections. The few off-year state elections provided more than their share of surprises. John Y. Brown, Jr., a millionaire who made his fortune in the Kentucky Fried Chicken franchise business, became a late entry in the Kentucky Democratic primary in May and defeated six other well-known state politicians, including Lieutenant Governor Thelma Stovall. Brown, recently married to television sportscaster and former Miss America Phyllis George, went on in November to defeat former Republican Governor Louie B. Nunn by 177,000 votes to become governor. In December, U.S. Representative David C. Treen was elected the first Republican governor of Louisiana since Reconstruction. Treen defeated Democrat Louis Lambert, chairman of the Public Service Commission, by a slim 10,000 votes. In Mississippi, former Lieutenant Governor William F. Winter defeated Republican Gil Carmichael.

Death Penalty. On May 25, John A. Spenkelink lost his six-year legal battle to remain alive and was executed by the state of Florida for the 1973 murder of a fellow drifter. Spenkelink became the first person to be executed involuntarily in the United States since 1967. A Utah firing squad had executed Gary Gilmore in 1977, but he had not used the appeals process in his case and had expressed his desire to be executed. Death-penalty opponents had feared that the Spenkelink execution would quickly open the floodgates for execution of the other 550 persons under death sentence throughout the United States. However, only one other execution was carried out in 1979. Jesse Bishop died in Nevada's gas chamber on October 22. But he, too, had declined to exhaust all possible appeals.

Florida had issued death warrants on five persons by mid-December, but all had received stays of execution. One person in Alabama and another in South Carolina were scheduled to be executed on December 14, but appeals had been filed. Alabama's death-penalty law was upheld on June 12, when Justice William H. Rehnquist of the Supreme Court of the United States lifted the stay of execution on John Louis Evans III. Massachusetts Governor Edward J. King signed new death-penalty legislation in 1979, but New York's Governor Hugh L. Carey vetoed a death-penalty law.

On March 13, Maine's Governor Joseph E. Brennan vetoed a bill that would have prohibited smoking at all public meetings. Massachusetts raised the legal drinking age from 18 to 20 on April 16. And on August 11, Massachusetts became the 50th state to allow motorists to make right-hand turns after stopping at red lights.   Ralph Wayne Derickson

In WORLD BOOK, see STATE GOVERNMENT and articles on the individual states.

STEEL INDUSTRY. A world steel shortage beginning in the mid-1980s, with consequent higher prices for steel, was predicted by executives attending the annual meeting of the American Iron and Steel Institute (AISI) held in May 1979 in New York City. George A. Stimson, chairman of the board of the National Steel Corporation, third largest steel company in the United States, told the group that none of the major steel companies have the money to build the large plants needed to help supply the 992 million short tons (900 million metric tons) that will be needed annually by 1985.

In February, *The New York Times International Economic Survey* reported a 15 per cent decline in steel production by the European Community (Common Market) since 1974. The survey also showed that while world production of steel in 1977 reached an unprecedented 785 million short tons (712 million metric tons), Third World producers, such as Brazil and China, made the greatest gains.

U.S. Output. At the end of September, U.S. production was estimated at 106.8 million short tons (99 million metric tons), up 3.7 per cent from the previous year's 103 million short tons (93 million metric tons). Production was at 89.2 per cent of capacity, compared with 85.5 per cent a year earlier.

Steel imports rose almost 11 per cent to 1.5 million short tons (1.4 million metric tons) in July, a boost an AISI official called "discouraging," despite the fact that import figures were running below the 1978 level. For the year through July, imports reached 9.3 million short tons (8.5 million metric tons), 26 per cent less than in the same period in 1978.

A highly simplified and advanced method of making steel went into operation at a new steel plant in March near Puebla, Mexico. In two relatively simple steps, called *direct reduction*, iron ore is converted into steel. The method requires no coke, pig iron, or blast furnace and uses only natural gas and a fraction of the highly expensive equipment required for regular steel plants.

Clean Air. The U.S. Steel Corporation, America's largest steel company, announced in May that it would spend $400 million to upgrade nine of its facilities in western Pennsylvania to meet federal air and water quality regulations. In late November, the giant steel firm announced that it would close more than a dozen plants and reduce operations in other factories. The program, designed to increase profitability, would affect 13,000 of the corporation's 165,000 employees.

On January 18, independent steel haulers voted to return to the road after a nine-week strike that threatened to paralyze U.S. steel shipments. In April, the International Brotherhood of Teamsters formally sanctioned another wildcat strike by steel haulers that lasted three weeks.   Mary E. Jessup

In WORLD BOOK, see IRON AND STEEL.

STOCKS AND BONDS. Rising stock and bond prices failed to match high and rising interest rates and inflation in the United States in 1979. Although up on the average, corporate profits throughout the 1970s failed to keep pace with inflation, partly because of inflation-induced tax increases. Shareholdings in corporations were thus less attractive to many investors than investments in real estate, where values had risen somewhat faster than the general level of prices. And the market values of bonds that have fixed interest payments fell to historic lows as inflation pushed interest rates to record levels.

Consumer spending grew in the 1970s at the expense of savings, a factor that increased interest rates and limited investment in machinery, factories, and working capital, and thereby in the growth potential of the economy. Savings rates in fast-growing countries such as Japan were much higher than those in the United States and Great Britain.

The Stock Market. Standard and Poor's index of 500 common stocks climbed through the first nine months of 1979, particularly after midyear, to a midday peak of 109.32 on October 5. But it then dropped back sharply, brought to heel by the Federal Reserve System's proposed anti-inflationary tight-money policies to curb excessive growth in money, credit, and the demand for goods and services. The policy, endorsed by President Jimmy

Carter, was announced by Paul A. Volcker, new chairman of the Board of Governors of the Federal Reserve System, on October 6. See ECONOMICS.

After the new monetary-policy announcement was digested by investors for a few days, the Dow Jones average of 30 blue-chip industrial stocks (DJI) skidded 26.45 points on October 9 on a volume of 56 million shares, more than double the 1979 daily average. It was the worst day for the New York Stock Exchange (NYSE) in five years. A one-day volume record was also set on October 9 in over-the-counter trading on volume of 22 million shares, while American Stock Exchange (Amex) volume soared to 9 million shares even as the average price of an Amex share fell more than 5 per cent, a new one-day record.

For the year, the Dow Jones industrials fell from a peak closing of just under 900 to a low of just over 800 in October – a 50th-anniversary reminder of the stock market crash of October 1929. The average closed the year at 838.74, up 33.73 points from its year earlier level.

Stock Volume. More than 8.1 billion shares were traded on the NYSE in 1979, more than on all other exchanges combined but down 2 million shares from the previous year. On Amex, 1.1 billion shares were traded. Trading volume allowed brokers to have a good profit year, though they tend only

Stocks Hold the Line in 1979
Dow Jones industrial averages

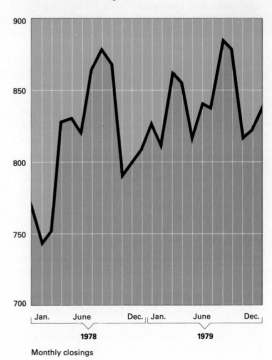

Monthly closings

A new trading post opened on the New York Stock Exchange. The electronic facility is only the first of 18 that are to be installed on the trading floor.

to break even on large transactions where commissions are highly competitive.

Interest and Dividend Yields on equities made securities investments look profitable compared with 10 years earlier, but this was something of an illusion. Among the major industrial countries, only Japan had gains in average stock prices that more than matched the inflation rate over the decade. The U.S. dollar, which depreciated at an average 7 per cent per year in the 1970s, was a worse holding, in general, than stocks, which appreciated at less than 1 per cent per year. The inflation rate, which averaged 7 per cent per year in the 1970s, reached about 13 per cent in 1979.

Long-term government bond yields exceeded 10 per cent in the United States and Canada in 1979, but were 2 or 3 percentage points lower in Japan, the Netherlands, Switzerland, and West Germany, where inflation rates – though higher in 1979 than a year earlier – were half or less that of the U.S.

The success story of the year was the money market mutual fund, which invested shareholders' money in short-term, highly liquid, high-interest securities. Investors, anxious to minimize inflation's damage, rushed to these funds, which tripled in value to $40 billion during the first 10 months of 1979. See BANKS AND BANKING.   William G. Dewald

In WORLD BOOK, see BOND; INVESTMENT; STOCK, CAPITAL; STOCK EXCHANGE.

SUDAN. A combination of economic difficulties and isolation from other Arab states posed a severe challenge to President and Prime Minister Gaafar Muhammed Nimeiri in 1979, his 10th year in power. Nimeiri's support for the peace initiatives of Egyptian President Anwar al-Sadat toward Israel – Sultan Qaboos Bin Said of Oman was the only other Arab leader to back Sadat – undercut relations with Saudi Arabia, Kuwait, and Iraq, Sudan's main suppliers of oil. By early December, Sudan, under heavy pressure from its Arab neighbors, appeared to be hedging on its support of Egypt.

Nimeiri's Egyptian policy also affected the long-sought reconciliation with his chief political opponents. Sadik al-Mahdi, leader of the Umma Party, who returned to Sudan in 1978 and rejoined Nimeiri's Sudanese Socialist Union, broke with Nimeiri and again went into exile. Former Finance Minister Sharif Hussein al-Hindi set up a new anti-government group, the Sudan Progressive Front, in Beirut, Lebanon, and called on Nimeiri to resign "in the national interest."

Streamlined Government. But the embattled Nimeiri hung on. In February, he modified his Cabinet, transferring the responsibility for such areas as education, youth and sports, and social and religious affairs to provincial councils. Autonomy for southern Sudan progressed in June with the establishment of separate legislatures for the southern provinces. The central government retained authority over only national defense, foreign affairs, communications, public services, and national resources as Nimeiri sought to broaden his political support.

Economic Troubles. The regime's ultimate success, however, depended on its ability to solve critical economic problems. Sudan's total dependence on foreign oil was an increasing drain on its limited foreign exchange, though oil found in western Sudan in July promised some relief. Shortages of gasoline and other items delayed agricultural projects designed to tap Sudan's vast potential as a food producer.

In August, taxes and price increases on basic foods and services resulted in massive protests. Students, teachers, public service workers, and the 200,000-member railway union all went on strike. Declaring a national political emergency, Nimeiri fired nine of the 17 members of the Sudanese Socialist Union Central Committee, including the secretary general, Abdel Kassim Mohammed Ibrahim, and took over the job himself. He also sacked Ibrahim as vice-president and appointed a new Cabinet, made up of his own supporters, most of whom were military officers. The reorganization and the price increases met International Monetary Fund conditions for a standby loan of $260 million.   William Spencer

See also AFRICA (Facts in Brief Table). In WORLD BOOK, see SUDAN.

SUPREME COURT OF THE UNITED STATES

made as many headlines for its off-the-bench activities as for its judicial decisions during 1979. The court's term was marked by an increasingly apparent trend away from both ideological decision making and political voting blocs.

With two hardline conservatives, Warren E. Burger and William H. Rehnquist, and two liberal holdovers from the court of Chief Justice Earl Warren – William J. Brennan, Jr., and Thurgood Marshall – the remaining five justices held a balance of power that defied categorization along stereotyped lines. The court's resulting cautious path was lauded by some observers as an honest attempt to grapple with issues without political preconceptions, but others criticized the court as rudderless and failing to supply judicial leadership. In December, two *Washington Post* reporters, Bob Woodward and Scott Armstrong, published *The Brethren,* a controversial book about the inside workings of the Burger court. The book revealed unprecedented detail about backcourt maneuvering.

No Landmark Decisions were announced during the 1978-1979 term. But in a major "reverse discrimination" ruling, the court rejected a challenge to a company's voluntary affirmative action plan. The case was *United Steelworkers of America v. Weber,* which actually was one of three cases consolidated for judgment. It was brought by Brian F. Weber, a

white worker who was left out of a craft training program run by Kaiser Aluminum and Chemical Corporation at its Gramercy, La., plant. Because Kaiser voluntarily allotted 50 per cent of the trainee openings to members of minority groups, two blacks with less seniority than Weber had been selected for the program. In a 5 to 2 decision announced on June 27, the Supreme Court rejected Weber's arguments that Congress had intended, in Title VII of the 1964 Civil Rights Act, to prohibit all racial discrimination in employment. Such an interpretation would "bring about an end completely at variance with the purpose of the statute," wrote Brennan.

The News Media. Two 1979 decisions raised howls of protest from the U.S. press. In *Herbert v. Lando,* decided by a 6 to 3 vote on April 18, the court reversed a lower court decision recognizing an "editorial privilege" against inquiry into the state of mind of news-media defendants being sued for libel by public figures. The case arose from a report on a former United States Army officer and his claim that his superiors covered up Vietnam atrocities. Even though the officer was a public figure, the court ruled he was entitled to all evidence that might help prove *actual malice* (foreknowledge that the report was false or recklessly disregarded truth) in proving his claim.

In *Gannett Co. v. DePasquale,* a 5 to 4 majority on July 2 upheld a trial judge's decision to bar reporters and the public from a pretrial hearing in a murder case. The defense had requested the move, the prosecutor had not objected, and the Sixth Amendment demands that a trial judge "minimize the effects of prejudicial pretrial publicity," Justice Lewis F. Powell noted. In the summer months following the decision, confusion arose over whether the press ban could be extended to actual trials. In a rare display of public disharmony, five justices made contradictory statements about the case's meaning.

The Business Community figured in two significant cases that were decided by unanimous court rulings. In *Teamsters v. Daniel,* the court declared on January 16 that a noncontributory, compulsory pension plan is not a legal "security," and that the Securities and Exchange Commission could not take regulatory jurisdiction over pensions.

In *Chrysler Corp. v. Brown,* the court held unanimously on April 18 that a corporation could not block the government's disclosure (to a requester under the Freedom of Information Act) of affirmative action and work-force records submitted to the U.S. Department of Labor. The court held that Chrysler might be able to stop the release under the Trade Secrets Act, however, and ordered a lower court to explore that possibility.

The court surprised some observers by curbing the detention and arrest powers of police. On March 27, the court ruled 8 to 1 that law-enforcement officers could not stop vehicles at random to check drivers' licenses and registration. And in a 6 to 2 decision issued on June 5, the court ruled that the Fourth Amendment was violated when police detained and questioned a suspect, unless they had the "probable cause" required to justify an arrest.

Other Key Decisions included:

■ A 6 to 3 ruling, on March 5, holding unconstitutional an Alabama law that allowed wives – but not husbands – to be eligible for alimony.

■ A 6 to 3 ruling, on April 17, voiding a Louisiana law that permitted a criminal defendant to be convicted by a six-member jury's nonunanimous verdict.

■ A 7 to 2 ruling, on June 5, upholding a Massachusetts veterans' preference employment law against charges that it discriminates against women.

Off the Bench. Justice Brennan, 73, suffered a mild stroke on September 4, but later announced that he would return for the 1980 term. Chief Justice Burger on April 20 ordered the dismissal of a court printshop employee suspected of leaking advance word of court decisions to a television reporter. Complying with a new federal law, all of the justices revealed their financial holdings.   David C. Beckwith

See also COURTS AND LAWS. In WORLD BOOK, see SUPREME COURT OF THE UNITED STATES.

SURGERY. See MEDICINE.

SURINAM. See LATIN AMERICA.

SWAZILAND. See AFRICA.

SWEDEN. Thorbjorn Falldin, leader of the Center Party, returned to power as prime minister on Oct. 9, 1979, after a close general election on September 16. The outcome was in doubt until absentee ballots were tallied on September 19. The non-Socialist Center, Moderate, and Liberal parties won 175 seats in the *Riksdag* (parliament) to 174 for the Social Democrats and Communists. Out of more than 5 million votes cast, the non-Socialists had an edge of only 8,400. Liberal Prime Minister Ola Ullsten resigned on September 20 to facilitate creation of a new coalition.

Falldin's selection was a surprise because the Center Party lost 22 seats in the election and was replaced by the Moderate Party as the leading non-Socialist party. But Moderate leader Gosta Bohman was considered too conservative.

Nuclear Referendum. Falldin had resigned as prime minister in October 1978 because he could not persuade the Moderates and Liberals to put the nuclear power issue to a referendum. But the Ullsten government scheduled a referendum for March 1980. The Liberals, Social Democrats, and Moderates wanted to complete 12 of the 13 nuclear power stations projected in a 1975 program and then halt construction. The Center Party and Communists wanted to stop all construction and close Sweden's six operating plants during the next 10 years. A geologist's report on March 13 rejected the power

companies' claim that waste nuclear fuel could be stored safely in a rock formation at Sternoe. This report and the March 28 accident at the Three Mile Island plant near Harrisburg, Pa., fueled the powerful antinuclear lobby. Sweden met its immediate needs by increasing gasoline and oil imports.

The Economy. The government presented a $39.8-billion budget for the 1979-1980 fiscal year on January 11. Its record deficit of $10.5 billion would be financed largely through public borrowing. Sweden's trade balance was $1 billion, and its inflation rate was only slightly above 7 per cent. The Organization for Economic Cooperation and Development forecast "a resumption of sustainable economic growth and real income" for Sweden. But a strong lobby favored closer cooperation with the European Community (Common Market).

In January, small shareholders in AB Volvo, Sweden's largest automobile company, prevented Norway from buying 40 per cent of the company for $220 million. The company's board of directors failed to obtain the approval of the necessary two-thirds of the stockholders.

The State Railways (SJ) cut passenger fares 50 per cent at vacation time, and traffic increased immediately by 14 per cent. But SJ needed a larger increase in traffic to compensate for the cuts.   Kenneth Brown

See also EUROPE (Facts in Brief Table). In WORLD BOOK, see SWEDEN.

SWIMMING. Teen-agers Cynthia (Sippy) Woodhead of Riverside, Calif., Mary T. Meagher of Louisville, Ky., and Kim Linehan of Austin, Tex., helped American women maintain world swimming supremacy in 1979. The American men remained the best, even though Russians broke world records at three of the five free-style distances.

The first World Cup competition from September 1 to 3 in Tokyo lost much of its glamour when Russia sent second-string swimmers and East Germany sent no one. The United States, with all of its women stars but minus Jesse Vassallo, Brian Goodell, and Ambrose (Rowdy) Gaines IV, won 17 of the 29 events.

The Winners. Woodhead, a 15-year-old high school sophomore, swept the 100-, 200-, and 400-meter free-styles in the World Cup; the Pan American Games in July in San Juan, Puerto Rico; and the Amateur Athletic Union (AAU) national long-course championships in August in Fort Lauderdale, Fla. She lowered her 200-meter women's world record to 1 minute 58.43 seconds in the Pan American Games and 1:58.23 in the World Cup.

Meagher was too slow to qualify for the 200-meter butterfly in the 1978 AAU long-course championships. But in 1979, the 14-year-old high school freshman broke the women's world record three times, finally lowering it to 2.701.

Linehan, a 16-year-old high school junior, moved from Sarasota, Fla., to Austin to be coached by Paul

Swimmer Tracy Caulkins accepts one of the four gold and two silver medals she won in the Pan American Games in Puerto Rico in July.

Bergen. She won three AAU titles (two long course, one short course), setting a women's world record of 16 minutes 6.63 seconds for the 1,500-meter free-style and breaking U.S. records with the other two.

Meagher, Linehan, and Tracy Caulkins of Nashville, Tenn., in individual medley and Linda Jezek of Los Altos, Calif., in backstroke won AAU, Pan American Games, and World Cup titles. All became favorites for 1980 Olympic Games titles. See CAULKINS, TRACY.

Other world leaders included the 20-year-old Goodell and the 17-year-old Vassallo, teammates at Mission Viejo, Calif., and the 20-year-old Gaines of Winter Haven, Fla.

In the European Cup championships, the Russian men and East German women won easily. The Russian men improved in all strokes, especially free-style. Their world record breakers were Sergei Kopliakov at 200 meters (1:49.83) and Vladimir Salmikov at 400 (3:51.40) and 800 meters (7:56.43).

The only other men's world record was Vassallo's 2:03.20 for the 200-meter individual medley. In all, world records fell in four of the 16 events for men and four of the 15 for women.

In diving, Greg Louganis of El Cajon, Calif., and Irina Kalinina of Russia won the World Cup platform titles. The 19-year-old Louganis also won five of the six AAU national titles.   Frank Litsky

In WORLD BOOK, see SWIMMING.

SWITZERLAND voted in three referendums, its traditional way of making decisions, in 1979. On February 18, the Swiss narrowly rejected stricter licensing procedures and local approval for new nuclear power stations by 965,271 votes to 919,271. The measure would have shut down the country's four stations and prevented new ones from being built. Four new nuclear power stations are planned for the 1980s. On May 20, the voters approved a government proposal to amend the 1959 Nuclear Act so that future construction and operation of nuclear power stations and waste dumps would require parliamentary approval. They defeated, for the second time in two years, an 8 per cent value-added tax that would have produced $750 million in revenues per year by 1981.

Switzerland has no coal, gas, or oil reserves, and the percentage of its electrical energy coming from nuclear plants is among the world's highest. The country plans to raise this proportion from 17 per cent in 1979 to 30 per cent in 1980.

The Organization for Economic Cooperation and Development (OECD) criticized Switzerland for maintaining a $15-billion cash surplus since 1974.

The Cabinet instructed the foreign ministry on March 28 to recommend to Parliament that Switzerland join the United Nations.   Kenneth Brown

See also EUROPE (Facts in Brief Table). In WORLD BOOK, see SWITZERLAND.

SYRIA. The movement toward full unity with Iraq that began in October 1978 advanced only slightly in 1979 in resolving fundamental differences between rival Syrian and Iraq Baath Party regimes. One small step was the resumption, in February, of Iraqi crude oil shipments across Syrian territory to the Baniyas refinery for refining and export. Iraq also supplied 3 million metric tons (3.3 million short tons) of oil and contributed 2,000 metric tons (2,200 short tons) of liquefied natural gas per month to help meet Syria's growing needs. The two countries formed a joint political command and established a mutual defense pact after the June 16 to 19 summit meeting of their presidents in Baghdad.

Internal Unrest. Continued political instability figured prominently in the Syrian reluctance to proceed with unification. There were a number of murders and attempted murders of prominent figures, most of them members of the Alawi minority sect to which President Hafiz al-Assad belongs. The victims included the attorney general of the state security court, Adel Mini, and several members of the secret police.

On June 16, political unrest accelerated sharply with an attack by terrorists on a military academy in Aleppo in which some 50 cadets were killed and many others wounded, most of them Alawis. The government blamed the right wing Muslim Brotherhood for the attack, and a wave of arrests followed,

TAIWAN

with 15 of the group's members sentenced and executed for complicity. Street battles between Alawi and majority Sunni Muslim factions in August in the port of Latakia caused at least 40 deaths before the army was called in to restore order.

In September, Assad began restructuring the government to give more representation to the Sunni majority, though his Syrian Baath Party retained tight control. New Sunni governors were appointed for Hama, Aleppo, and Latakia districts, where public criticism and unrest had been greatest. Assad also promised to purge corrupt civil service officials and take steps to improve the economy and maintain adequate supplies of basic staples.

Economy Up. The Syrian economy rebounded strongly in 1979 from the decline in previous years caused by sudden growth and the burden of the peacekeeping force in Lebanon. A $5.6-billion budget was approved by the People's Council in January. Defense expenditures were set at $2 billion, and the remainder was equally divided among education, food subsidies, and public works.

With all eight turbines in operation at the Tabka Dam on the Euphrates River, Syria became self-sufficient in electricity and a net exporter of electric power to Turkey and other neighbors. The dam generates 850 megawatts daily.   William Spencer

See also MIDDLE EAST (Facts in Brief Table). In WORLD BOOK, see SYRIA.

The end of United States-Taiwan official relations is symbolized by the final trip of a diplomat's car through the U.S. Embassy gates in Taipei.

TAIWAN adjusted during 1979 to the loss of diplomatic relations with its chief ally, the United States. As of Jan. 1, 1979, the United States recognized the People's Republic of China as the sole government of China, established diplomatic relations with that government, and broke off such relations with the Nationalist regime on Taiwan.

President Chiang Ching-kuo said on January 1 that Taiwan would continue to be responsible for liberating the mainland from Communism. Responding to a proposal by Peking (Beijing in the phonetic Pinyin alphabet China adopted on January 1) for talks to establish trade and other ties, a Taiwan official said that "under no circumstances will we enter into any kind of talks with the Chinese Communists." Premier Sun Yun-hsuan added on January 11 that Peking was trying to "induce us to surrender" and using "lies and tricks . . . to confuse the American people."

Relations Continued unofficially between Taiwan and the United States. In announcing formation of the Coordination Council for North American Affairs, Chiang said on February 15 that "reality requires that we have to swallow the bitter pill and to handle the current changed situation with all the fortitude at our command." President Jimmy Carter signed legislation on April 10 establishing the American Institute in Taiwan, to maintain contacts. The legislation said that all cultural, trade, and transport links would continue and that the United States would take action — which was unspecified — if Taiwan were attacked.

After a halt on new military orders during 1979, the United States agreed to sell Taiwan limited types of armaments beginning in 1980. The last uniformed U.S. servicemen left Taiwan on April 30, ending 28 years of U.S. military presence there. But some Americans remained to continue monitoring mainland activities. By the end of 1979, the U.S. break seemed to have little significance.

The Economy. Taiwan continued to prosper. The 1979 economic growth rate was expected to be at least 8.5 per cent, one of the world's highest, though inflation caused the government to restrict credit and thus slow industrial activity. Foreign investments rose 80 per cent to $250 million during the first nine months, compared with the same period in 1978. Foreign trade was up 32 per cent for the same period, heading for an annual rate of $30 billion.

The government announced on February 1 that the Taiwan dollar, which had been based on the value of the U.S. dollar, would float against a group of foreign currencies.

Taiwan refused to accept ethnic Chinese refugees who fled from Vietnam, despite appeals from other countries. See ASIA (Close-Up).   Henry S. Bradsher

See also ASIA (Facts in Brief Table). In WORLD BOOK, see TAIWAN.

TANZANIA in 1979 committed 45,000 troops and more than $200 million to destroying Idi Amin Dada's military regime in neighboring Uganda and to supporting the new civilian government that replaced Amin's. The war between Tanzania and Uganda broke out on Oct. 30, 1978, when Ugandan forces invaded territory in northwest Tanzania between Lake Victoria and the Rwanda border.

The Tanzanian army counterattacked, repulsed Amin's forces, and joined anti-Amin Ugandans in invading southern Uganda. By the end of May 1979, Amin had lost control of all of Uganda's major cities. Approximately 20,000 Tanzanian troops stayed in Uganda for the rest of the year to help maintain order. See UGANDA.

Tanzania had to divert funds from essential economic-development projects to the war effort. President Julius K. Nyerere appealed to the United States and eight other Western nations in July for $375 million in grants to Tanzania's economy. The response was limited. Western governments were reluctant to help one African government finance a war against another. However, normal economic assistance continued. The European Community (Common Market) granted $325 million for industrial and agricultural projects.   John D. Esseks

See also AFRICA (Facts in Brief Table). In WORLD BOOK, see TANZANIA.

TAPE RECORDER. See RECORDINGS.

TAXATION controversy took a back seat to spiraling inflation in the United States in 1979, and taxpayer resentment of the rising tax burden – so strong the previous year – was muted. In May, President Jimmy Carter told a news conference that he doubted "very seriously that we will have any tax cut in 1980" because of the possibility that a cut would further fuel inflation. At year's end, the inflation rate was more than 13 per cent.

In Congress and out, more attention was focused on the need to pare down federal spending and balance the budget. For example, in December a unified bloc of Republicans and some Democrats in the Senate mustered 44 votes for an amendment tacked onto the Senate version of an oil windfall-profits tax bill that would have set a ceiling on federal tax revenue. The measure, defeated by only five votes, would have set tax revenue as a fixed percentage of the gross national product (GNP) for 1981 and thereafter.

President Carter whittled down the Administration's spending plans for fiscal 1980 (Oct. 1, 1979, to Sept. 30, 1980). His "lean and austere" budget, presented in January, proposed a cut to aid in agriculture and very small increases in spending – which, in view of rapid inflation, actually constituted decreases – for social services, education, pollution control, and general revenue sharing. But the projected 3 per cent rise in military spending – after

an adjustment for inflation – made it difficult to hold down the federal budget.

Inflated wages pushed many taxpayers into higher tax brackets in 1979, and Social Security payroll taxes increased – by percentage rate and by taxable wage base – in January. The increase was one of an incremental series mandated in 1977. Tax relief, including a temporary suspension of the mandated 1981 rise in Social Security payroll taxes, was considered but not acted upon by Congress.

Federal Tax Receipts. In the fiscal year ending Sept. 30, 1979, federal tax collections totaled $460.4-billion. Individual income and employment tax receipts totaled $364.4 billion; corporation taxes, $71.4 billion; estate and gift taxes, $5.5 billion; and excise taxes, $19.05 billion.

The Internal Revenue Service (IRS) reported that the simplified short form 1040A was filed by 35.6 million taxpayers in 1979 – a 5.3 per cent rise in use of the short form, probably because of simplifications in tax law. About 87.5 million tax returns for 1978 income were filed by May 18, 1979.

Simplifying Forms. In a two-year program that cost $1.2 million, the IRS commissioned firms in four fields – accounting, public opinion polling, computer programming, and "language simplification" – to recommend changes in tax forms. The IRS wants to have its forms understood by ninth graders. Current forms supposedly can be read by 11th graders.

The Underground Economy, illegal and untaxed, appeared to be growing. According to the tax code of 1978 as amended, single wage earners with an income of at least $3,300 and married wage earners with a combined income of at least $5,400 were required to file a tax return.

But in April, tax specialist Joseph A. Pechman of the Brookings Institution in Washington, D.C., estimated that untaxed earnings totaled some $220-billion in 1978, more than 10 per cent of the GNP. Most of the underground income was paid to low-income workers – especially domestic workers, most of whom are paid by their employers in cash, with no withholding for income tax or deductions for Social Security, unemployment, or other benefits. Other nonfilers in the underground economy include retailers, plumbers, builders, and garage mechanics – as well as gangsters, racketeers, drug peddlers, and prostitutes.

In the government's first study of the underground economy, published on July 10, the General Accounting Office (GAO) estimated that about 8 per cent of all Americans who should file tax returns – about 6 million persons – had failed to file in 1978. Some 52 per cent of the nonfilers had incomes of $5,000 or less and probably owed less than $100.

The IRS reported on August 31 that it failed to collect about 10 per cent of the income taxes that were owed in 1976 because some individuals were dishonest. It estimated its losses at between $19-billion and $26 billion.

The GAO urged the IRS to improve its detection system and to watch more carefully for low-income nonfilers. But the IRS maintained that investigation of self-employed, high-income earners like physicians and attorneys was more profitable to the government, and it urged more in-depth audits of upper-bracket taxpayers.

A Windfall-Profits Tax on the earnings of oil companies profiting from decontrolled oil prices was finally passed by the 96th Congress on December 20, but it delayed apportioning the tax. Under pressure from special-interest groups, Congress had emasculated the Administration's windfall-tax proposal. See CONGRESS OF THE UNITED STATES.

State and Local Taxes. Eight states collected almost half of all state revenue in fiscal 1979. California again headed the list, collecting $16.4-billion; the next seven, in order, were New York, with $11.7 billion, followed by Pennsylvania, Illinois, Michigan, Texas, Ohio, and Florida.

Total state tax collections for fiscal 1979 came to $125.1 billion, a rise of 10.5 per cent over fiscal 1978. Sales and gross receipts taxes, collected by all 50 states, were the largest sources of state tax revenue. Forty-four states also collected individual income taxes, for a total of $32.8 billion.   Carol L. Thompson

In WORLD BOOK, see TAXATION.

TELEVISION. "Roots," the phenomenon known as Alex Haley's comet, returned in the sequel "Roots: The Next Generations" in February 1979. In spite of formidable competition from such feature films as *Marathon Man, American Graffiti,* and *The Sound of Music,* the rating impact of "Roots 2" was spectacular. During its seven-night run, the 14-hour, $18-million miniseries was seen by an estimated 110 million persons, compared with 130 million for the original "Roots" in 1977, the largest audience in television history.

The black performer gained wider exposure in weekly television in 1979. At the beginning of the fall season, three award-winning black actors were starring in new series. Louis Gossett, Jr., played a hospital chief of staff in "The Lazarus Syndrome," which was canceled early in the season; James Earl Jones, who played Alex Haley in "Roots 2," was a captain of detectives in "Paris"; and Robert Guillaume was the sardonic butler in "Benson," a spin-off of "Soap." Other shows starring blacks were "The Jeffersons" and "Diff'rent Strokes."

Black broadcasters finally cracked the TV-station ownership market in 1979. In June, WAEO-TV in Rhinelander, Wis., became the first black-owned VHF outlet, followed closely by WHEC-TV in Rochester, N.Y. By October, there were two more black-owned TV outlets – WGPR-TV in Detroit, and WGRB-TV in Willingboro, N.J.

Television Viewing reached an all-time high during the first half of 1979 – a daily average of 6 hours 34 minutes for each U.S. household. In January, when temperatures dropped to new lows in many viewing areas, average daily TV consumption climbed to 7 hours 20 minutes.

Competition for audiences was so fierce that in the spring the three networks dropped some 70 regular weekly series in an effort to present more-popular programs. The National Broadcasting Company (NBC) dropped 29; the Columbia Broadcasting System (CBS), 22; and the American Broadcasting Companies, Incorporated (ABC), 19.

Cancellations included "The Paper Chase"; "Starsky and Hutch"; "Welcome Back Kotter"; the "Mary Tyler Moore Show"; and "Kaz." The most expensive dropouts were "Battlestar Galactica" and "Supertrain," a midseason replacement.

Early fall ratings indicated that "Trapper John, M.D." (a spin-off from "M*A*S*H") and "Benson" were the most-watched new shows. The top-rated fall series, though, were such oldies as "Three's Company"; "Alice"; "Eight Is Enough"; "M*A*S*H"; "One Day at a Time"; "The Jeffersons"; "Archie Bunker's Place," a revision of "All in the Family"; and "Dallas"; along with the newer "WKRP in Cincinnati" and "The White Shadow." "Laverne and Shirley," "Happy Days," "Mork and

Robert Guillaume portrayed the title character, a sardonic butler, in "Benson," a spin-off of "Soap" and one of the few new hits of the fall TV season.

The "Real People" show's hosts, from left, Byron Allen, Skip Stephenson, Sarah Purcell, and John Barbour, share a laugh between program segments.

Mindy," "Angie," and "Taxi" – all riding high in the spring – were still popular but out of the top 10 by fall. The news-magazine series "60 Minutes" was in the top 10 all year.

The escalating costs of films made for movie theaters – as high as $4 million per showing – prompted a sharp increase in the production of made-for-TV movies, which usually cost under $2 million. A record number – more than 100 – were scheduled for the 1979-1980 season.

Film Biographies were particularly successful. *Elvis!*, with Kurt Russell as Elvis Presley, outrated *Gone with the Wind* and *One Flew Over the Cuckoo's Nest* on February 11. Other impressive biographical TV movies were *The Miracle Worker; Silent Victory: the Kitty O'Neil Story; I Know Why the Caged Bird Sings;* and *Friendly Fire.*

Biographies also developed into some outstanding miniseries in 1979, including "Backstairs at the White House," "Ike," and "Blind Ambition."

The Public Broadcasting Service's (PBS) "Masterpiece Theatre" provided two quality biographical British miniseries. Anthony Hopkins portrayed Jean-Paul Sartre's "Kean," and Francesca Annis was a luminous Lillie Langtry in "Lillie."

Other Specials included *The Jericho Mile; All Quiet on the Western Front; The Pilgrims' Adventure* starring Anthony Hopkins as the *Mayflower*'s captain; *The Corn Is Green* with the legendary Katha-

rine Hepburn; *Strangers: The Story of a Mother and Daughter*, with Bette Davis; "Beggarman, Thief"; and "From Here to Eternity." In spite of such star power, however, the top-rated TV movie of the season was *The Dallas Cowboy Cheerleaders.*

On November 4, some 80 million people tuned in *Jaws*, making it the most-watched theatrical movie in 1979. The great white shark thriller received the second highest rating of any film shown on TV, outranked only by *Gone with the Wind.*

One of the most talked-about documentaries of the year was *The Shooting of Big Man: Anatomy of a Criminal Case.* Edited from more than 100 hours of tape, the two-hour documentary followed a court case from the defendant's first meeting with his lawyer to the jury's verdict. Other standout documentary specials included *The Body Human,* about eye surgery; *Operation: Lifeline,* the profile of a compassionate San Francisco surgeon; *Infinite Horizons: Space Beyond Apollo,* hosted by Ray Bradbury; and *Blacks in America: With All Deliberate Speed.*

TV Sports. The highest rated sports show in 1979 was Super Bowl XIII, pitting the Pittsburgh Steelers against the Dallas Cowboys on January 21. That game drew 70 per cent of the TV audience – an estimated 96 million to 104 million viewers. The final World Series game between the Pittsburgh Pirates and Baltimore Orioles was second with 80 million viewers.

Public Broadcasting. In June, member stations of the Public Broadcasting Service (PBS) approved a plan dividing PBS into three programming "networks" – national prime time, regional, and educational. The three programs would be transmitted simultaneously via satellite.

Most PBS stations carried the same prime-time shows from Sunday through Wednesday for the first time in 1979. The national schedule opened on September 30 with a history of technology, "Connections," from the British Broadcasting Corporation (BBC).

In February, PBS launched the BBC's ambitious six-year cycle of William Shakespeare's plays – all 37. The first play in the series was *Julius Caesar*. Other PBS programming highlights in 1979 were a four-part adaptation of Nathaniel Hawthorne's *The Scarlet Letter*; "The Stanton Project," a series on great American women; and two programs honoring Albert Einstein's centenary.

PBS's 1979 musical programs included divas Joan Sutherland and Marilyn Horne in joint concert, *Segovia at the White House*, and *Ormandy at 80*. In April, PBS celebrated Arthur Fiedler's 50th anniversary with the Boston Pops with a lavish special. The famed conductor died on July 10 (see MUSIC, CLASSICAL [Close-Up]).

Syndicated Hits. Phil Donahue was the TV talk-show host of 1979. His syndicated Chicago-based program reached 97 per cent of the United States and was seen in 6 million homes, more than NBC's "Today" show.

Scared Straight, an Oscar-winning documentary featuring dialogue between hardened convicts and juvenile offenders, also outrated the networks in some cities when it was syndicated in March. Some affiliates pre-empted prime-time network shows early in 1979 to run the syndicated 13-week series "Edward the King." The syndicated "Muppet Show" was the most widely viewed program in the world.

Cable-TV reached 14.5 million households, about 20 per cent of all U.S. viewers in 1979. Pay cable-TV subscribers totaled 4.5 million, up from 1.6 million in 1978. In the first major study of cable-TV viewers, the A. C. Nielsen Company reported in February that "some of the most popular movies on pay cable drew up to 44 per cent of the total audience" during commercial network prime time.

Cable-TV offered the only gavel-to-gavel coverage of the U.S. House of Representatives' floor proceedings. The telecasts, which began on February 19, were carried via satellite to approximately 5 million households in all 50 states by the Cable Satellite Public Affairs Network, a nonprofit cooperative.   June Bundy Csida

See also AWARDS AND PRIZES. In WORLD BOOK, see TELEVISION.

TENNESSEE. See STATE GOVERNMENT.

TENNIS. Bjorn Borg and Martina Navratilova won the 1979 Wimbledon championships and were generally considered the world's best tennis players. John McEnroe and Tracy Austin, two young Americans, won the United States Open titles and seemed headed for further stardom. Jimmy Connors and Chris Evert Lloyd slipped a bit.

The men's Grand Prix tour encompassed 90 tournaments in 20 nations, with prize money of $11-million plus a $2 million year-end bonus pool. The women had 80 tournaments worth $7.5 million.

The leading money winners among the men were Borg with $909,345, McEnroe with $945,238, and Connors with $671,341. The women's leaders were Navratilova with $747,548, Austin with $541,676, and Lloyd with $564,398. Austin might have earned more, but after she had become the youngest woman – 16 years 8 months – to win the United States Open title, she returned to classes in her junior year at Rolling Hills (Calif.) High School.

The Men. Borg, a 23-year-old Swede, won at Wimbledon on July 7 for the fourth consecutive year, a feat never before accomplished in modern times. In the final, he beat Roscoe Tanner of Lookout Mountain, Tenn., 6-7, 6-1, 3-6, 6-3, 6-4, despite Tanner's 15 service aces. Tanner gained some revenge by eliminating Borg in the United States Open quarterfinals. Borg also won the

Tracy Austin leaps happily after beating Chris Evert Lloyd to win the U.S. Open in September. She is the youngest woman to win the title.

John McEnroe celebrates his semifinal victory over Jimmy Connors on his way to the U.S. Open title. McEnroe won more than $900,000 during the year.

French, European, and Canadian opens and the $150,000 first prize in the Grand Slam tournament.

McEnroe, a 20-year-old left-hander from Douglaston, N.Y., defeated Vitas Gerulaitis of Kings Point, N.Y., 7-5, 6-3, 6-3, in the U.S. Open final on September 9 at Flushing Meadows, N.Y.

McEnroe also won the World Championship Tennis final in Dallas in May, and he and Gerulaitis led the U.S. to victory in the Davis Cup final against Italy. McEnroe played a strong, rounded game, but he alienated spectators with frequent scowls and complaints.

McEnroe defeated Ilie Nastase of Romania, 6-4, 4-6, 6-3, 6-2, on August 3 in the U.S. Open under circumstances that will be remembered long after the result is forgotten. When Nastase constantly stalled, umpire Frank Hammond awarded a penalty point to McEnroe. Later, he penalized Nastase a full game. When Nastase ignored a warning to serve within 30 seconds, Hammond awarded game, set, and match to McEnroe. Although the rules permitted such penalties, referee Mike Blanchard replaced Hammond as umpire, and the match resumed.

The 26-year-old Connors, from Belleville, Ill., won the U.S. clay-court open for the fourth time in six years. He lost in key semifinals — to Borg at Wimbledon, to McEnroe in the U.S. Open, and to Victor Pecci of Paraguay in the French Open.

Arthur Ashe won the Grand Prix Masters final from McEnroe in January and lost the U.S. professional indoor final to Connors. Ashe, 36, underwent triple by-pass heart surgery in December.

The Women. Navratilova, a 22-year-old left-hander from Dallas, subdued Lloyd in the Wimbledon final for the second straight year, 6-4, 6-4. The spectators included Navratilova's mother, who had not seen her daughter since Martina defected from Czechoslovakia four years earlier.

In the United States Open, Austin defeated Navratilova, 7-5, 7-5, in the semifinals and Lloyd, 6-4, 6-3, in the final. Austin also won the Italian Open and the Family Circle Cup.

The 24-year-old Lloyd, from Fort Lauderdale, Fla., won the French Open and her fifth straight U.S. clay-court title. But she failed to win a fifth straight Wimbledon, and her streak of 125 clay-court victories ended in May when she lost to Austin in the Italian semifinals. She married John Lloyd, an English player, on April 17, and her priorities seemed to change.

At age 35, Billie Jean King of New York won the Wimbledon women's doubles with Navratilova for her 20th Wimbledon title, a record. King shared the previous record with Elizabeth Ryan of England. The day before King's victory, the 87-year-old Ryan collapsed on the Wimbledon grounds and died en route to a hospital.   Frank Litsky

In WORLD BOOK, see TENNIS.

TEXAS. See HOUSTON; STATE GOVERNMENT.

THAILAND felt threatened in 1979 by the Vietnamese invasion of Cambodia, which began in December 1978 and brought a strong army to Thailand's border for the first time in modern history. Alarmed, Prime Minister Kriangsak Chamanan visited the United States in February to meet with President Jimmy Carter. He said Carter assured him that the United States "will take definite action" to uphold Thai security if the nation is threatened.

The United States agreed to speed up delivery of U.S. fighter planes, tanks, small arms, and other military equipment to Thailand. In the U.S. fiscal year ending September 30, Thailand bought $400-million worth of American weapons.

The Thai Army increased its strength on the Cambodian border and fought border skirmishes with both Vietnamese and Cambodian Communist forces. Thailand also tried to control the flow of refugees from Cambodia. In June, Thailand forced at least 30,000 Cambodian refugees back across the border, many to their deaths – allegedly because Thailand could not care for them. But as war and famine in Cambodia continued, Kriangsak reversed his policy and began letting in refugees.

The new arrivals added to an estimated 215,000 Indochinese refugees already in Thailand, the largest number in any Southeast Asian nation. They included refugees from Laos and a small number of "boat people" who reached Thailand despite robbery, rape, and murder by Thai pirates that the government did virtually nothing to prevent. See ASIA (Close-Up).

Elections Indecisive. The lower house of parliament was elected April 22 after a campaign in which two candidates and at least 13 political workers were killed. No party won a majority, but the Social Action Party of former Prime Minister Kukrit Pramoj had the largest bloc, 82 out of 301 seats. The Constitution allowed Kriangsak to appoint the upper house; both houses elect the prime minister, so he retained the post. He named a new Cabinet May 25, retaining half the previous Cabinet members.

Prime Minister Kayson Phomvihan of Laos visited Bangkok and signed an agreement with Kriangsak on April 4. They agreed on a friendly border and said guerrilla bases would not be allowed on the frontier. But border tension continued along both the Laotian and Cambodian borders.

Kriangsak proclaimed 1979 "the year of the farmer," to focus attention on efforts to improve rural economic conditions. But security worries eclipsed economic efforts, and money was diverted to strengthen the armed forces. A United Nations study said that more than 11 million Thais were living in poverty.   Henry S. Bradsher

See also ASIA (Facts in Brief Table). In WORLD BOOK, see THAILAND.

The healthiest Cambodian refugees in Thailand pass through a food line. Others, in advanced stages of starvation, are fed intravenously.

THATCHER, MARGARET HILDA (1925-   ), shattered years of British parliamentary history on May 4, 1979, when she became Great Britain's first woman prime minister. She pledged that her Conservative government would reverse the country's economic slide by reducing income taxes, cutting back on social services, and lessening the government's role in life. See GREAT BRITAIN (Close-Up).

Margaret Hilda Roberts was born on Oct. 13, 1925, in Grantham, a small town north of London. Her father, a grocer, was active in local politics. After elementary school, she won a scholarship to Kesteven and Grantham Girls School. In 1947, she earned a B.S. degree in natural science from Somerville College at Oxford University. She also holds an M.A. from Oxford. After working as a research chemist from 1947 to 1951, Thatcher studied law and qualified as a barrister in 1953, specializing in tax law. Always active in politics, she was elected to the House of Commons in 1959.

In 1970, Prime Minister Edward Heath named her secretary of state for education and science. She also was appointed privy councillor and became co-chairman of the Women's National Commission. Thatcher defeated Heath for leadership of the Conservative Party in 1975.

The new prime minister and her husband, Denis Thatcher, an oil company executive she married in 1951, have a son and a daughter. Marsha F. Goldsmith

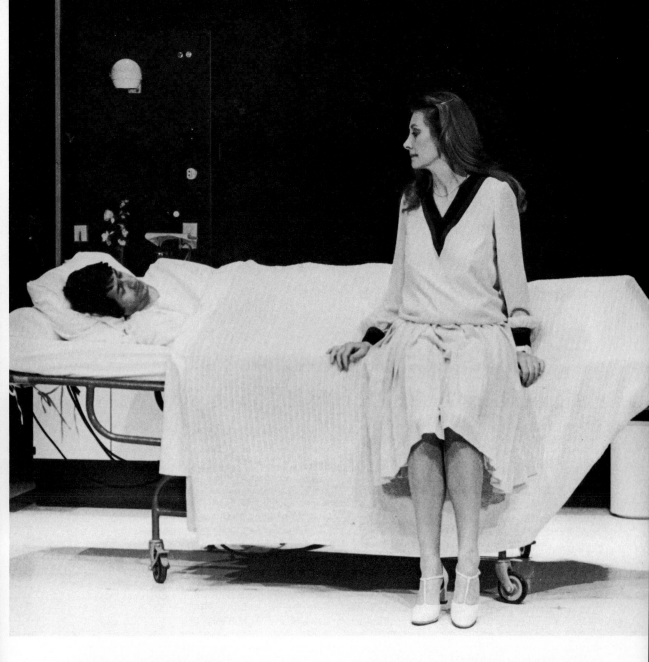

THEATER

Regional theater in the United States became truly "tributary" in 1979 and contributed importantly to the mainstream of American theater. Broadway represents a goal or pinnacle for new plays, and a record number of the year's outstanding productions there had their roots in regional theater. Broadway plays that began elsewhere included *The Elephant Man,* from St. Peter's Church theater in New York City; *Wings,* from Yale University in New Haven, Conn.; *Lone Star* and *Pvt. Wars,* from The Actors

Theater in Louisville, Ky., which also sent *Getting Out* to off-Broadway; and *Whoopee!* from the Goodspeed Opera House in East Haddam, Mass.

Serious Dramas on and off Broadway were richly varied. Bernard Pomerance's *The Elephant Man,* which moved to Broadway from the intimate theater of St. Peter's Church, is based on actual events in the 1880s. Abandoned by a traveling freak show, monstrously deformed John Merrick, "the elephant man," is brought to London Hospital and treated by

501

Composer-lyricist Stephen Sondheim served up a meaty repast of horror and musical melodrama in *Sweeney Todd, the Demon Barber of Fleet Street.*

a humanitarian doctor. Under the imaginative direction of Jack Hofsiss, actor Philip Anglim superbly suggested Merrick's deformity by twisting his body and modifying his speech. Although Merrick is repellent externally, his clarity of vision and purity of motive provide an illuminating contrast to the society that exploits, lionizes, and finally fails him.

The plight of a person whose difference sets her apart from society is also the subject of Arthur Kopit's *Wings.* In this drama, first produced at Yale, the audience enters the bewildering world of a stroke victim who is suffering from *aphasia* (loss of ability to use or understand words). Impressively played by Constance Cummings, Emily Stilson searches in a lonely and unfamiliar world for the combinations of words needed to communicate. A former aviator and wing-walker, Stilson draws hope from the fact that she survived previous airplane accidents. *Wings* is scheduled for production in the 1979-1980 season by at least four regional theaters – the South Coast Repertory Theater in Mesa, Calif.; Cleveland Play House; Cricket Theater in Minneapolis, Minn.; and Wisdom Bridge Theater in Chicago.

The aggressive heroine of Marsha Norman's *Getting Out* at the Theater deLys off-Broadway is different from almost everyone else because from the age of 12 she has been in correctional institutions. Norman's moving drama, set in two time sequences, involves both the younger and older heroine. The

play originated at the Louisville Actors Theater, which also sent two one-act comedies to Broadway, James McClure's *Pvt. Wars* and *Lone Star.* Self-centeredness in men and women is a theme of McClure's.

From England came Tom Stoppard's *Dogg's Hamlet* and *Cahoot's Macbeth,* on a U.S. tour. The new British-American Repertory Company, a group of British and American actors, directed by Ed Berman, presented both works with great imagination. The first one-acter is based on the premise of Lewis Carroll's Humpty Dumpty in *Through the Looking-Glass* that words can mean exactly what you choose them to mean. In a boys' school where the language is "Dogg" – composed mainly of monosyllabic English words that mean something other than their usual meaning – the students laboriously and hilariously stage an abbreviated *Hamlet* whose lines are to them a foreign language.

Cahoot's Macbeth is based on Czechoslovak playwright Pavel Kohout and his friends, who were prohibited by their government from working in the theater. Instead, they staged *Macbeth* in living rooms, and it is such an event that Stoppard dramatizes. However, in typical Stoppard topsy-turvy fashion, the government agent who comes to stop the play and speaks in the platitudes of drama critics is himself thwarted by a refugee from the first play, a bumbling mover of theatrical properties, now speaking fluent Dogg, which he claims to have "caught." The real Kohout was informed during the run of the play that he could not return to his homeland.

Also from England, *Whose Life Is It Anyway?* by Brian Clark starred Tom Conti as a witty and sardonic hospital patient, paralyzed from the neck down as the result of an auto accident, and battling to be allowed to die. "It's a play about freedom," says Clark. "It has the classical existential themes of freedom and choice. The element of death gives it an emotional charge, but it's really an escape story."

American Comedies that were successful on Broadway were in shorter supply, but *They're Playing Our Song* and *Romantic Comedy* became hits. Both dealt with theatrical collaborations and were written by master writers of comedy. The former, by Neil Simon, starred Lucie Arnaz and Robert Klein as neurotic lyricist and composer, respectively. According to the program it was "loosely based" on the affair between the show's composer, Marvin Hamlisch, and Carole Bayer Sager. Bernard Slade's witty *Romantic Comedy* was about a successful, self-centered playwright, Anthony Perkins, and his prim literary co-worker, Mia Farrow. Although their theatrical partnership prospers, it is 12 years before they realize they are meant for each other.

The Musical Highlight of the year was the operatic melodrama *Sweeney Todd, the Demon Barber of Fleet Street* written by Hugh Wheeler with music and lyrics by Stephen Sondheim. Sweeney Todd is a 19th-century barber unjustly sent to Australia by a judge who covets the barber's wife. When he escapes from jail, Sweeney Todd, played by Len Cariou, returns to exact revenge by cutting the throats of the judge and other unfortunates who mount the barber's chair. The victims are baked into meat pies by his friend, Mrs. Lovett, played by Angela Lansbury. See LANSBURY, ANGELA.

Sugar Babies starred old-timers Mickey Rooney and Ann Miller in a fast-moving entertainment combining vaudeville and burlesque. Musical numbers featured a chorus line kicking high or swinging on garden swings, and bawdy burlesque sketches ending with punch lines and blackouts.

Another nostalgic trip down memory lane was *The 1940s Radio Hour,* which presented a 1940-style broadcast, complete with swing band, a giveaway contest, and, of course, commercials, plus many well-known musical hits of that decade.

Evita by Tim Rice and Andrew Lloyd Webber, a smash hit in London, got a somewhat milder reception in New York City. It is a musical about Eva Perón's rise to power in Argentina.   Alice Griffin

See also AWARDS AND PRIZES (Arts Awards). In WORLD BOOK, see DRAMA; THEATER.

TIMOR. See ASIA.

TOGO. See AFRICA.

TORNADO. See DISASTERS; WEATHER.

TOYS. See GAMES, MODELS, AND TOYS.

TRACK AND FIELD. Sebastian Coe, a 22-year-old Englishman, broke the world records for three popular distances – 800 meters, 1,500 meters, and 1 mile – within 42 days in 1979. In the process, he bettered marks of such distinguished recordholders as Alberto Juantorena of Cuba, Filbert Bayi of Tanzania, and John Walker of New Zealand.

On July 5, Coe ran 800 meters in 1 minute 42.4 seconds in Oslo, Norway. On July 17, he won the mile there in 3:49.0. On August 15, he ran 1,500 meters in 3:32.1 in Zurich, Switzerland. He ended his competitive season without a race against Steve Ovett, the more celebrated English miler. A week before Coe's record mile, Ovett said, "It will be a hollow victory for the winner. It's high time the runners come to meet me where I will run."

A Memorable Race. Steve Scott of Irvine, Calif., the American champion, finished second in the record mile, 50 feet (15 meters) behind Coe, in a time rounded off to 3:51.2. His actual time of 3:51.11 missed Jim Ryun's 1967 U.S. record (then the world record) by only 1 one-hundredth of a second. Walker, whose world record of 3:49.4 was broken by Coe, ran sixth in 3:52.9.

Coe, who had just received his college degree in economics, stood 5 feet 9¼ inches (176 centimeters) and weighed only 129 pounds (58 kilograms). At the same height and weight, Miranda Coe, his 20-year-

Sebastian Coe of England streaks down the stretch as he sets a new mile record of 3 minutes 49 seconds on July 17 in a race in Oslo, Norway.

World Track and Field Records Established in 1979

Event	Holder	Country	Where made	Date	Record
Men					
200 meters	Pietro Mennea	Italy	Mexico City, Mexico	September 12	:19.72
*300 meters	Pietro Mennea	Italy	Rieti, Italy	July 21	:32.23
800 meters	Sebastian Coe	England	Oslo, Norway	July 5	1:42.4
1,500 meters	Sebastian Coe	England	Zurich, Switzerland	August 15	3:32.1
1 mile	Sebastian Coe	England	Oslo, Norway	July 17	3:49.0
25 kilometers	Bill Rodgers	U.S.A.	Saratoga, Calif.	February 21	1:14:12
110-meter hurdles	Renaldo Nehemiah	U.S.A.	Westwood, Calif.	May 6	:13.00
20-kilometer walk	Daniel Bautista	Mexico	Montreal, Canada	October 17	1:20:06.8
50-kilometer walk	Raul Gonzales	Mexico	Bergen, Norway	May 25	3:41:39
Women					
200 meters	Marita Koch	East Germany	Karl Marx-Stadt, E.Ger.	June 10	:21.71
400 meters	Marita Koch	East Germany	Turin, Italy	August 4	:48.60
1 mile	Natalia Maracescu	Romania	Auckland, New Zealand	January 27	4:22.1
*2,000 meters	Maricica Puica	Romania	Bucharest, Romania	May 19	5:35:5
100-meter hurdles	Grazyna Rabsztyn	Poland	Warsaw, Poland	June 18	†:12.48
400-meter hurdles	Marina Makeyeva	Russia	Moscow	July 27	:54.78
*Marathon	Grete Waitz	Norway	New York City	October 21	2:27.33
Javelin throw	Ruth Fuchs	East Germany	Dresden, E. Ger.	June 13	228 ft. 1 in. (69.52 meters)
400-meter relay	Koch, Schneider, Auerswald, Goehr	East Germany	East Berlin	June 10	:42.09
	Brehmer, Schneider, Auerswald, Goehr	East Germany	Turin, Italy	August 5	†:42.09
800-meter relay	Makhova, Zuskina, Prorochenko, Kulchunova	Russia-Ukraine	Moscow	July 29	1:30.8

*No official world record at this distance.   †Equals record.

old sister, was dancing in the Lido de Paris nightclub show in Las Vegas, Nev. Sebastian and Miranda were named by their mother, a former actress, for characters in William Shakespeare's *The Tempest.* Coe was coached by his father, Peter, an engineer and production supervisor for a silversmith in Sheffield, England.

Coe found appreciative audiences. After his record 1,500, he took two victory laps. After his record mile, he took three. When he walked into the athletes' reception room after the mile, Walker, Edwin Moses, Don Quarrie, Rod Dixon, and other competitors burst into applause. "That really made what I did sink in for the first time," said Coe.

He said he would try an 800-1,500 double in the 1980 Olympic Games in Moscow, but he tried to keep his new success in perspective.

"It's easy to take it much too seriously," he said. "I'm totally committed to my performance and training, but there has to be something else in life. I won't be making a profession out of athletics. I don't want to get involved in all that razzmatazz."

Cubans Beaten. It was a disappointing year for Juantorena and Alejandro Casanas, world record-holders from Cuba. In addition to losing the 800-meter record to Coe, Juantorena was beaten in the Pan American Games in July in Puerto Rico by Tony Darden of Norristown, Pa., at 400 meters and James Robinson of Oakland, Calif., at 800 meters.

Casanas lost his world record of 13.21 seconds in the 110-meter hurdles. Renaldo Nehemiah of Scotch Plains, N.J., lowered it to 13.16 seconds on April 14 in San Jose, Calif., and 13.00 seconds on May 6 in Westwood, Calif. The 20-year-old Nehemiah lost only one race all year – to Dede Cooper of San Jose – and became one of two American men who would be heavy favorites in the Olympics. The other was Moses, the 400-meter hurdler from Pomona, Calif. Moses had lost only once since his 1976 Olympic victory, and his winning streak was nearing 40 races.

Coe passed up the World Cup competition in August in Montreal, Canada. Nehemiah and Moses won there. So did Evelyn Ashford of Hollywood, Calif., the best U.S. woman sprinter in a decade.

Ashford won both World Cup sprints. She beat Marlies Goehr by 1 meter at 100 meters in 11.06 seconds, and Marita Koch by 2 meters at 200 meters in 21.83 seconds. Both losers were East German world recordholders. "I think I'm still in shock," said Ashford a day later. So was Koch, who set two world records in the 200 and two at 400 meters during the year.

In road racing, Bill Rodgers of Melrose, Mass., won his second straight Boston Marathon on April 16 and his fourth straight New York City marathon on October 21.   Frank Litsky

In WORLD BOOK, see TRACK AND FIELD.

TRANSIT systems in United States cities benefited from the 1979 gasoline shortage as commuters left their cars to ride buses and subways. Systems were hard pressed to meet the surge in patronage that occurred in the spring and early summer. Even after the shortage eased, fuel prices kept rising, and transit held its gains. The American Public Transit Association (APTA) said that October 1979 ridership was 11.4 per cent higher than that of October 1978.

Urban mass-transit systems carried 6.79 billion passengers in the first 10 months of 1979, up 7 per cent from the same period in 1978, and were headed for their seventh straight annual increase. Ridership increased 3.9 per cent in New York City, 4.9 per cent in Chicago, 4.7 per cent in Philadelphia, 7.7 per cent in Pittsburgh, and 15.7 per cent in Seattle. Los Angeles motorists were hit hard by the gasoline shortage in the spring, and transit ridership rose 3.5 per cent during the first 10 months.

The APTA said that the nationwide transit operating deficit may have leveled off in 1979, because systems carried more passengers without adding much equipment. The 1978 loss was about $2.26-billion. The federal government covers about 30 per cent of the transit deficit.

Cities helped boost ridership by replacing old buses and expanding fleets. A no-fare plan during non-rush hours from Feb. 1, 1978, through Jan. 31, 1979, sharply boosted Denver transit ridership; patronage stayed high when the free rides ended.

New Atlanta System. The Rapid Transit Authority of metropolitan Atlanta, Ga., opened its new rapid-transit system's first leg, a 6.7-mile (10.8-kilometer) segment, on June 30. Another 5.1-mile (8.2-kilometer) segment opened on December 22. Washington's Metro system opened a 3-mile (4.8-kilometer) extension of its Orange Line on December 1, boosting its completed length to 33.7 miles (54 kilometers). In October, the federal government agreed to pay off 67 per cent of $977 million in Metro revenue bonds to help build the planned 100-mile (160-kilometer) system.

The Department of Transportation (DOT) granted $100.3 million on June 7 to help build a rapid-rail system in Miami, Fla., and $54.4 million on January 26 for Baltimore's new rail-transit system and for commuter buses.

Taxing Oil for Transit. President Jimmy Carter said in a July 15 television speech that improvements in public transportation were part of his energy plan. Vice-President Walter F. Mondale announced in a Hoboken, N.J., train station on August 22 that the Administration would spend an additional $13 billion by 1990 for transit, if the federal outlays were financed by the proposed tax on windfall profits from high oil prices.

Cracked undercarriages from a fleet of 754 subway cars crowd a New York City maintenance shop. The city decided in September to replace them.

Troubled Transbus. The federal program to require all transit systems to buy the low-floor Transbus – a bus that the government designed to accommodate the handicapped – failed in 1979 because the two U.S. bus manufacturers refused to bid to build the vehicle. Grumman Corporation said on March 12 that it would not bid on a proposed Transbus package for three transit systems, and General Motors Corporation announced a similar decision on April 27. The two suppliers blamed government specifications and procurement procedures. A National Research Council study commissioned by DOT concluded that the two manufacturers correctly refused to bid on an unrealistic program. On August 3, DOT postponed indefinitely the deadline requiring new transit buses to meet Transbus specifications.

The DOT said on April 3 that it would compromise on its proposal to force cities to install elevators and other facilities in existing subway stations to accommodate the disabled. It said that only key stations would have to be revamped. But APTA and 12 mass-transit systems said that even the compromise would be too costly, and they filed suit on June 29 to prevent its enforcement.   Albert R. Karr

See also TRANSPORTATION. In WORLD BOOK, see TRANSPORTATION.

TRANSKEI. See AFRICA.

TRANSPORTATION industries in the United States began 1979 well, but soaring fuel costs and slowing business took their toll on profits by year's end. Airlines prospered under deregulation until rising expenses and a leveling-off of traffic forced them to boost fares sharply and cut service. Railroads gained, but their earnings increases began to ease in the second half; the industry's push for deregulation also bogged down. Truckers suffered from easing demand and falling net income by midyear, but managed to blunt the deregulation drive that they opposed.

The Transportation Association of America estimated United States transportation revenues at $498 billion for 1979, up 9 per cent. Mainland intercity freight increased 5.2 per cent, with air and truck freight up 5 per cent; railroads, 6 per cent; rivers, canals, and Great Lakes traffic, 7 per cent; and pipelines, 3 per cent.

Intercity passenger traffic held steady, with air travel up 12 per cent and automobile travel down 2 per cent. Railroad passenger traffic increased 5 per cent, and bus travel was up 6 per cent.

Highway Driving Decline. A gasoline shortage drove people from their cars. Starting in May, highway travel at points monitored by state agencies fell below 1978 levels, according to the Federal Highway Administration. Road traffic at those

Passengers rush to board a train going from Los Angeles to San Diego, rather than risk driving during the May gasoline shortage.

points was down 1.2 per cent for the first nine months, compared with the same period in 1978, and off as much as 6.3 per cent in July.

President Jimmy Carter advocated greater use of mass transit and Amtrak (National Railroad Passenger Corporation) trains because of new energy worries. He pledged to use some of the money from his proposed windfall-profits tax on the oil industry to increase transit spending. His Administration on June 19 announced a program to boost transportation in rural areas.

Urge Deregulation. The Administration and Interstate Commerce Commission (ICC) advocated railroad and truck deregulation, and the ICC in July moved to allow intercity bus companies more freedom from ICC regulation. The ICC said on April 20 that it would permit railroads, truckers, and barge lines to increase freight rates quickly to make up for rising fuel expenses. It permitted these carriers several rate boosts during the year and allowed bus firms to increase fares about 22 per cent between February and October.

Chairman A. Daniel O'Neal of the ICC said on October 4 that he would leave the agency at the end of 1979, and Carter named economist Darius W. Gaskins, Jr., to replace him. Transportation experts viewed Gaskins as an even more ardent deregulationist than O'Neal. Secretary of Transportation Brock Adams left the Administration on July 20, and Carter named Neil E. Goldschmidt, mayor of Portland, Ore., to succeed him on July 27. On November 29, the new secretary killed a proposal to build a 13.5-mile (21.7-kilometer) addition to an interstate highway near Dayton, Ohio, because the new road would have endangered the city's economy. See GOLDSCHMIDT, NEIL E.

Fuel Efficiency. Adams had wanted to prod automakers into producing automobiles that provided a fleet average of 40 to 50 miles per gallon (mpg) – or 17 to 21 kilometers per liter (kpl) – by the year 2000, and had wanted the government to pay some of their expenses. Auto executives and the Administration agreed on May 18 to a modest joint research program to help make cars more efficient. The Department of Transportation (DOT) said on June 20 that it would not change its requirement of a 27-mpg (11.5-kpl) average in 1984.

The House of Representatives on September 18 expressed disapproval of DOT's regulation that requires *passive restraints* (airbags or automatic safety belts) in all new cars by 1984. General Motors Corporation said on October 1 that it would delay putting the airbags on some 1981-model cars, but the company announced on December 7 that they would be available as an option on its large 1982 models.   Albert R. Karr

See also AUTOMOBILE; AVIATION; RAILROAD; SHIP AND SHIPPING; TRANSIT; TRUCK AND TRUCKING. In WORLD BOOK, see TRANSPORTATION.

TRAVEL. For automobile travelers, especially those in the United States, 1979 was the year people stayed home, or close to it. From the rocky coast of Maine to the sunny beaches of California, many drove no farther than a full tank of gas could take them. Attendance at parks, fairs, and other attractions, bookings at motels and hotels, and meals at restaurants were off 10 to 20 per cent in most parts of the country. Highway travel, which totaled about 1.45 trillion vehicle-miles (2.33 trillion vehicle-kilometers) in 1978, fell 12.5 per cent in the first six months of 1979. But train and bus travel surged.

Amtrak, the U.S. National Railroad Passenger Corporation, finally obtained sufficient funds to modernize and replace the antique rolling stock it inherited from privately owned railroads. In mid-November, Congress authorized $873.4 million to be spent over a three-year period. Meanwhile, Amtrak ridership, reflecting the gasoline shortage and gas price increases, rose 10 per cent. June was the first month in Amtrak's history that it carried more than 2 million passengers.

It was "standing room only" on many trains. Ridership during May on the six daily round-trip trains between Los Angeles and San Diego, for example, was up 69 per cent over May 1978, breaking a record set during World War II. Despite such gains, Amtrak won permission in October to drop passenger trains from Chicago to Houston, Seattle, and Miami, Fla. After a slow start, the two major intercontinental bus companies, Greyhound Bus Lines and Continental Trailways Bus Lines, reported an overall 1979 gain of 25 per cent.

Tourist Trade. There were 282 million international arrivals throughout the world in 1979, exclusive of Canada and Mexico, an increase of 6 per cent. They spent $92 billion, a 16 per cent increase. About 12 million U.S. citizens visited Canada, and an estimated 2.1 million visited Mexico.

Continuing erosion of the U.S. dollar, escalating prices in other countries, and promotional airfares and package tours all contributed to the record number of foreign arrivals – some 20.5 million, a gain of 3.3 per cent – to the United States in 1979. They spent close to $54 billion, including transportation. About 11.2 million Canadians visited the U.S., a decrease of 6 to 8 per cent. The number of visitors from Mexico increased 16 per cent to an estimated 2.5 million. There were 575,000 West Germans and 310,000 French, both up 19 per cent. A million Japanese and a million British visited the United States, as did 220,000 Australians, a record gain of 22 per cent.

Cruise Passengers. About 90 per cent of the 1.5 million vacationers who took cruises were American citizens. They generated an estimated $1.5 billion in revenue. The hundreds of tours ranged from three-day excursions between Florida and the Bahamas to three-month, round-the-world voyages.

Travelers are piped aboard the Central Kingdom Express for a 40-day, 9,300-mile (15,000-kilometer) railway trip from London to Hong Kong.

In the United States, 137,400 hotel and motel rooms were built in 1979, some 4,000 were done away with, and 168,900 were renovated. In New York City alone, four major hotels were being built, three were being completely rehabilitated, and six were undergoing major renovation. The work will give the city 5,000 more hotel rooms.

China Tours. On September 17, the Civil Aeronautics Board (CAB) approved an agreement between Pan American World Airways (PanAm) and the People's Republic of China national airline to operate the first direct commercial flights between the United States and China since the Communist takeover there in 1949. Trial service started on December 3. Two scheduled flights were to be made by PanAm and two by the Chinese airline, using a Boeing 747. The Chinese flights will be flown by an American crew. A tour package includes two weeks in China.

Japan Air Lines was allocated 1,824 tourist visas for China in August and PanAm, 5,000. The tourists spent 12 to 15 days in China, 3 days in Tokyo, and 2 days in Hong Kong. Most tours included Peking (Beijing in the Pinyin system of transcription China adopted on January 1) and three or four other Chinese cities. New hotels are planned for China, which has a shortage of tourist accommodations.

Travel Costs. According to a 1979 U.S. Department of State survey, the cost of living for tourists in Tokyo and the Belgian cities of Antwerp and Brussels was $130 per day, making these cities the most expensive to visit in the world. As a result, more American travelers to Japan, for example, stayed in *ryokans,* small inns where guests sleep on straw mats and thick quilts. Many tourists also ate traditional Japanese food and took their laundry to a *coin oppu* (laundromat) to cut expenses.

Costs were also high in other cities. In Paris, coffee with a thimbleful of brandy cost $7. A decent lunch for two with a modest bottle of wine could cost more than $50 in London, and a special businessman's lunch in Nice, France, was advertised at $25.

Traditional Tourist Attractions reported record crowds. A spokesman for San Francisco's Visitors' Bureau reported that, "The hotels are 100 per cent booked." And 1979 was New York City's biggest tourist year. More than 17 million visitors and convention delegates spent $1.8 billion there. During the 103-day exhibition of the treasures of King Tutankhamon at the Metropolitan Museum of Art, more than $1 million per day was pumped into the city's economy by visitors who came to the exhibit and spent $111 million on hotels, restaurants, and entertainment. A total of 1.2 million visitors viewed the exhibit in New York City.   Lynn Beaumont

In WORLD BOOK, see TRANSPORTATION.

TRINIDAD AND TOBAGO. See LATIN AMERICA (Facts in Brief Table).

TRUCK AND TRUCKING. The Interstate Commerce Commission (ICC) continued to deregulate the United States trucking industry in 1979. Fuel prices and fuel shortages caused trucker unrest, and the industry signed a wage contract barely within the inflation guidelines set by President Jimmy Carter. The American Trucking Associations, Incorporated (ATA), estimated that freight hauled increased 2.5 per cent to 1 billion short tons (0.9 billion metric tons) and motor-carrier revenues rose 13 per cent to $41.2 billion. But earnings fell 25 per cent from the 1978 profit of $1.08 billion, as business lagged late in the year, fuel costs climbed, and the ICC held freight-rate increases below the amounts that were sought.

The ICC did approve rate hikes of 5.5 to 5.7 per cent on April 11 and 2.8 per cent on October 1, to cover higher wages. On June 15, the agency told truck companies that hire independent owner-operators to collect a 5.6 per cent fuel surcharge and pass it on to the independent truckers. The surcharge was raised to 10 per cent on November 16. Regulated truck firms that did not use owner-operators were given a 2.7 per cent fuel surcharge, later cut to 1.6 per cent.

Independent Truckers protested against higher fuel prices and the fuel shortage, blockading truck stops and holding back deliveries for about a month beginning on June 7. The Carter Administration responded by releasing some diesel fuel and urging 10 states to boost their load limits to the 80,000-pound (36,000-kilogram) federal limit. The drivers ended their action on July 9.

The Administration tried to keep a Teamsters Union settlement with the trucking industry within its anti-inflation guideline of 7 per cent per year. An 11-day strike and industry lockout ended on April 12 with a new contract that provided gains of about 9 per cent per year. But the Administration said its guidelines technically were not violated.

Deregulation Stalls. The ICC limited the power of regional industry groups to set rates on February 28. On September 5, the commission proposed to remove most rate and market-entry controls over 12 specialized parts of the industry. The ICC decided on October 17 to emphasize more competition and less protection for established truckers when it considered bids for new truck-operating rights.

But the ICC was stopped short on October 22, when Senator Howard W. Cannon (D., Nev.), chairman of the Senate Committee on Commerce, Science, and Transportation, warned the ICC against changing truck regulations before Congress decided on deregulation bills.   Albert R. Karr

See also TRANSPORTATION. In WORLD BOOK, see TRUCK AND TRUCKING.

Alabama National Guardsmen protect tank trucks that state troopers will lead past independent truckers during June protests over fuel supplies.

509

TRUDEAU, PIERRE ELLIOTT (1919-   ), regained the leadership of Canada's Liberal Party on Dec. 18, 1979, less than a month after he resigned. On November 21, six months after he lost his post as prime minister to 40-year-old Progressive Conservative leader Joe Clark, Trudeau stepped down, urging that a leadership convention be held in March 1980 to choose his successor. See CANADA.

But after Clark lost a parliamentary vote of confidence on December 13 and a federal election was set for Feb. 18, 1980, Liberal Party leaders requested that Trudeau again take over and attempt to recapture the seat he held from April 20, 1968, until May 22, 1979. Trudeau accepted, saying, "My duty is to accept the draft of my party."

Throughout his career, Trudeau worked to achieve equality for French Canadians. He opposed separate status for Quebec and believed that the establishment of nationwide bilingualism would enable all Canada's citizens to feel at home in any province.

One area in which Trudeau succeeded was foreign policy. He enlarged Canada's contacts with countries outside the North Atlantic area, strengthening ties with nations of Western Europe and the Pacific, and recognizing the People's Republic of China in 1970. A dynamic leader on the world stage, Trudeau hoped to serve Canada again after the 1980 election.   Marsha F. Goldsmith

TUCHMAN, BARBARA (1912-   ), an American writer, was elected president of the American Academy and Institute of Arts and Letters on Jan. 24, 1979, the first woman so honored. She received the group's Gold Medal for History in 1978.

Barbara Wertheim was born on Jan. 30, 1912, in New York City. Her father, Maurice, was an international banker and philanthropist, and her mother Alma's family, the Morgenthaus, included several distinguished statesmen and diplomats. Tuchman attended the Walden School in New York City and was graduated from Radcliffe College in Cambridge, Mass., in 1933.

Her career began in 1934 in Tokyo as a researcher for the Institute of Pacific Relations. From 1935 to 1937 she was on the staff of *The Nation* magazine, and reported from Madrid on the Spanish Civil War. During World War II, she served on the Far Eastern desk of the Office of War Information.

Tuchman began turning history into literature in 1938 with *The Lost British Policy*. She went on to earn two Pulitzer Prizes – for *The Guns of August* in 1962 and *Stilwell and the American Experience in China* in 1971. Her other books include *Bible and Sword* (1956), *The Zimmerman Telegram* (1958), *The Proud Tower* (1966), *Notes from China* (1972), and *A Distant Mirror* (1978). Tuchman is divorced from Lester R. Tuchman, a physician. She has three daughters.   Marsha F. Goldsmith

TUNISIA. Labor unrest continued throughout the country in 1979, though the first anniversary of the "Black Thursday" general strike and riots passed without incident on January 26. But in March and April alone there were 39 separate strikes by various labor groups. The government used a 1978 law to conscript unemployed Tunisians for service in areas of labor shortage, and police raided cafes at the slightest provocation, gathering up hundreds of unemployed persons.

The "January 26 Collective," a Paris-based group of exiles opposed to the ruling Destour Socialist Party, charged in June that more than 100 political prisoners were being detained without trial in Tunisian jails.

With both economic development and political stability threatened by the authoritarianism of Prime Minister Hedi Nouira's government, President Habib Bourguiba returned from medical treatment in Europe to take command. In May, Bourguiba pardoned 263 persons sentenced to prison terms for their part in Black Thursday. On August 3, he approved a pardon for Habib Achour, former secretary general of the General Union of Tunisian Workers and the key figure in the trade-union movement, who had been sentenced to 10 years at hard labor despite poor health.

Another Bone of contention between the two factions was removed in May when the government approved wage increases that had been originally negotiated under the "social contract" of 1977. Guaranteed minimum wages for farmworkers went up 8 per cent to $3.49 per day, while professional wages were increased to one dinar (56 cents) per hour. The increases partially offset a 25 per cent rise in food prices.

The World Bank made four loans to Tunisia in 1979: $19 million for urban housing; $28.5 million for fisheries and port facilities; $26.5 million for urban sewerage; and $25 million for long-term water-supply development. The Abu Zaby Fund for Arab Economic Development agreed to invest $168-million in the Tunisian national fertilizer organization on condition that the organization add the word "Arab" to its title.

The Arab League transferred its headquarters from Cairo to Tunis in March after members broke ties with Egypt over its peace with Israel. A Tunisian, Information Minister Chedli Klibi, was appointed secretary general of the league on June 28. The choice of Tunis was a compromise between the radical and conservative Arab countries. It was also an ironic one, because Bourguiba fought bitterly with other league members in the 1960s when he proposed a compromise peace between Israel and the Palestinians.   William Spencer

See also AFRICA (Facts in Brief Table). In WORLD BOOK, see TUNISIA.

TUNNEL. See BUILDING AND CONSTRUCTION.

TURKEY. Prime Minister Bulent Ecevit's two years as head of the government ended abruptly on Oct. 16, 1979. Ecevit resigned when his majority Republican People's Party (RPP) was defeated in parliamentary elections. The RPP lost all five Assembly seats and 32 of 50 Senate seats up for election to opposition Justice Party candidates. The defeat — essentially a voter protest against political violence, catastrophic inflation, and consumer goods shortages — left Ecevit with a minority in both houses. The RPP fared even worse in the popular vote, receiving 29 per cent, compared with 47 per cent for the Justice Party.

Ecevit was succeeded by Justice Party leader Suleyman Demirel, whom he had ousted under similar circumstances late in 1977. The task facing Demirel's new government was an unenviable one.

Vexing Violence. To its credit, the Ecevit government made a serious effort to deal with Turkey's pressing political and economic problems, even at the expense of its popularity. Political violence was a continuing problem. Martial law, already in effect in 13 of the 67 provinces, was extended in April to six eastern provinces because of political violence.

Although schools and universities remained open, the death toll from political terrorism averaged four persons a day and included more prominent persons than in previous years, including Abdi Ipeki, the moderate editor of Turkey's leading newspaper, *Milliyet,* who was shot in February.

Perhaps because of rising internal violence, a Turkish military court sentenced four Palestinian guerrillas to death on October 25 for killing two Turkish guards during a July raid on the Egyptian Embassy in Ankara. The sentences had been expected to be more lenient, because of Turkey's sympathy for the Palestinian cause.

Economic Problems were as difficult as the political ones. More than $1.4 billion in foreign aid, needed to pay off foreign debts and save the economy from total collapse, was offered by donor countries on the condition that a strict austerity program, approved by the International Monetary Fund, be put in effect. As a result, the government introduced measures in March that would ration essential consumer goods, increase prices on some products, limit the number of government jobs, and require Turkish workers in other countries to remit their wages through the Central Bank. It also devalued the Turkish lira in June to a record low of 47 to the United States dollar, and the 24-member Organization for Economic Cooperation and Development responded with a pledge of $906 million in grants and credits.   William Spencer

See also MIDDLE EAST (Facts in Brief Table). In WORLD BOOK, see TURKEY.

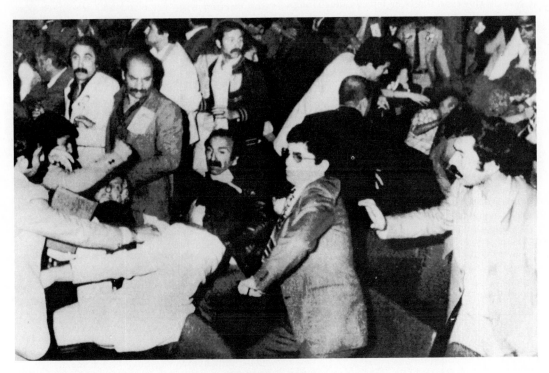

Moderate and leftist Turks break into a fist fight in Ankara as members of a Republican People's Party youth group meet for a party election.

UGANDA. Idi Amin Dada's eight-year reign of terror came to an end in April 1979 when his government was overthrown by forces from neighboring Tanzania aided by rebel Ugandan troop units. Known for its violent persecution of dissenters, Amin's government may have been responsible for the deaths of as many as 300,000 Ugandans. The conflict began in October 1978, when Amin seized part of northwestern Tanzania. Tanzania mounted a counteroffensive with regular troops and more than 1,000 Ugandan exiles.

Amin, a Muslim, sought military assistance from predominantly Muslim countries. By March 8, about 2,000 Libyan troops had been airlifted to Uganda. However, the Tanzanian forces and Ugandan exiles seized control of Uganda's capital, Kampala, on April 11, and captured the nation's second largest city, Jinja, on April 22. Forces loyal to Amin tried to retain control of Muslim areas in northern Uganda, but the last of the three northern provincial capitals they held, Arua, fell on May 29.

New Leadership. Amin fled the country when Kampala fell and was reported to be living in Libya. Yusufu K. Lule, a former head of Makerere University in Kampala, was sworn in as Uganda's new president on April 13. He was selected by the 30-member National Consultative Council (NCC) of the Uganda National Liberation Front, a coalition of 28 Ugandan exile groups formed in Tanzania in March. However, the NCC forced Lule to resign on June 20, after he created four new ministries, each headed by a member of his own Baganda tribal group, the largest in Uganda.

Lule was succeeded by Godfrey Lukogwa Binaisa, also a Baganda. However, many Baganda supported Lule and demonstrated against Binaisa during his first days in office by closing their shops and barricading Kampala's streets, because Binaisa had served as attorney general under Amin's predecessor, Apollo Milton Obote, who was considered hostile to the Baganda. See BINAISA, GODFREY L.

Disorder Widespread. About 22,000 Tanzanian troops were still in Uganda late in the year, helping the Binaisa government maintain order and guard against Amin's former soldiers who were operating in eastern and northwestern sections of the country. Although Kampala had an 8 P.M. to 6 A.M. curfew, robberies and killings were frequent.

The civil disorder hampered efforts to obtain the foreign aid and investment necessary to revive Uganda's faltering economy. Inflation was at an annual rate of almost 200 per cent.   John D. Esseks

See also AFRICA (Facts in Brief Table); TANZANIA. In WORLD BOOK, see UGANDA.

UNEMPLOYMENT. See ECONOMICS; LABOR.

UNION OF SOVIET SOCIALIST REPUBLICS (U.S.S.R.). See RUSSIA.

UNITED ARAB EMIRATES (UAE). See MIDDLE EAST.

UNITED NATIONS (UN). Andrew J. Young, Jr., the first black to serve as United States ambassador to the UN, resigned on Aug. 15, 1979, because his outspoken, freewheeling style got him into serious trouble. Young's successor was another black, Donald F. McHenry, Young's chief deputy.

Young's troubles began on July 26 at the New York City house of Kuwait's Ambassador Abdalla Yaccoub Bishara. There, Young asked Zehdi Labib Terzi, UN observer for the Palestine Liberation Organization (PLO), to help in postponing a Security Council meeting scheduled for July 31. At that meeting, Young would have had to veto a resolution backed by Third World nations advocating the creation of a Palestinian "independent state." The meeting was postponed.

The United States had promised Israel that it would not negotiate with the PLO until that organization accepted the Security Council's 1967 Resolution 242, which states that Israel has a right to exist. But Young did not consult with the U.S. Department of State about whether he should meet Terzi. And he did not tell that department about the meeting until August 11, when he was asked about a *Newsweek* magazine story on it. He then told the State Department that it was a chance social meeting with no negotiating.

Two days later, however, he told Israel's UN Ambassador Yehuda Z. Blum that he had arranged the meeting with Terzi and had negotiated postponement of the Security Council's meeting. Blum told his government, which protested publicly to the United States on August 14. U.S. Secretary of State Cyrus R. Vance then expressed "displeasure" at Young's action, and Young handed President Jimmy Carter a letter of resignation on August 15 "to avoid any further complications." Young said, "My actions, however well intentioned, have hampered the peace process," then centered on U.S.-Israeli-Egyptian talks on Palestinian autonomy.

At a news conference, Young said that he had "no regrets." He explained that he had met Terzi to head off a veto that would have caused the United States "serious consequences" in the Arab world and that he had told Blum about the meeting in order to "avoid any backlash." Young charged that Israel "decided to make this a public issue."

The Backlash began as Young expected. Some U.S. blacks turned toward the PLO, alarming many U.S. Jews who were concerned about Israel. On August 20, black ministers heading the Southern Christian Leadership Conference, the civil rights group Young headed from 1964 to 1970, lunched with Terzi in New York City and expressed support for a Palestinian homeland. They met later with PLO leader Yasir Arafat in Lebanon and sang the civil-rights hymn "We Shall Overcome."

McHenry, 42, was appointed on August 31. He told reporters he would "build upon" what Young had accomplished but do it in his own way. See McHenry, Donald F.

Meanwhile, Young had to deal with two Middle East issues as Security Council president during August. On August 24, Senegal's Ambassador Médoune Fall introduced a resolution that said the Palestinians had rights to "self-determination, national independence, and sovereignty in Palestine." But Third World delegates agreed not to bring the proposal to a vote. Bishara told the Council that Arafat had sent word from Beirut, Lebanon, that the "great man, Andrew Young," should not be embarrassed by being forced to veto the proposal. In a personal farewell statement to the Council, Young said then that it was ridiculous for the United States and Israel not to talk to the PLO and "ridiculous for many of you around this table not to have good relations" with Israel.

But, unexpectedly, he had to preside over meetings on August 29 and 30 because Lebanon asked the Council to "help consolidate" a cease-fire between Israeli troops and their Lebanese Christian allies and PLO forces on Lebanese soil. UN officials had arranged the cease-fire on August 26. Young ended his last UN debate by urging all concerned "to make permanent the cessation of hostilities."

UN Troops. Two UN military detachments remained in the Middle East in 1979, but a third was

Andrew Young, who resigned as U.S. ambassador to the United Nations, serves as the Security Council president during August, his final month.

withdrawn. The UN Interim Force in Lebanon continued to guard the troubled south of that country, and the UN Disengagement Observer Force remained between Syrian and Israeli troops in the Golan Heights. But the UN Emergency Force sent to keep Egyptian and Israeli troops apart after the 1973 Arab-Israeli war, was disbanded in July. Russia opposed using the UN Emergency Force to monitor the gradual Israeli withdrawal that was about to begin under the Egyptian-Israeli peace treaty of March 1979, and it would have vetoed a resolution to extend its mandate. The mandate expired at midnight on July 24 and, in private talks within the Security Council, Russia accepted replacing it with the 31-year-old UN Truce Supervision Organization, which consists entirely of officers.

Arab delegations caused the UN to act against Israel for arresting Mayor Bassam al-Shaka of Nablus, a Palestinian town on the occupied West Bank of the Jordan River, on November 11 and ordering him deported. On November 14, the Security Council expressed regret that Israel had arrested Shaka. The General Assembly voted 138-1 on November 16 – with Israel opposed and Papua New Guinea abstaining – to ask Israel to rescind the deportation order. Israel said that the UN actions were improper because the deportation order, which accused Shaka of showing sympathy for Palestinian terrorism, was still pending before its Supreme Court. But Israel released him and rescinded the order on December 5.

Cyprus Talks. UN Secretary-General Kurt Waldheim, in Nicosia, Cyprus, on May 19, obtained an agreement from Cyprus' President Spyros Kyprianou, a Greek Cypriot, and Turkish Cypriot leader Rauf Denktash to resume talks on Cyprus' political future. The talks had been suspended since April 1977. The Security Council renewed the mandate of the 15-year-old UN Peacekeeping Force in Cyprus on June 15 for another six months by a 14-0 vote, with China not participating. The new talks broke off after five days, however. On November 26, the Assembly adopted a resolution that called for establishing a seven-nation committee to help Waldheim solve the Cyprus problem if there was no progress toward a solution by March 31, 1980. Turkey voted against the resolution, which carried 99-5 with 35 abstentions.

Africa Troubles. South Africa had stayed away from the Assembly since it was expelled in 1974 because of its racial and colonial policies. Its delegates returned on May 23 at the start of a session on Namibia (South West Africa). But on an African proposal, and over almost solid Western opposition, the Assembly voted 96-19 on May 24 to reject South Africa's credentials as invalid. Before adjourning on May 31, the Assembly voted 118-0 with 16 abstentions to accuse South Africa of deceit in Namibian independence negotiations.

UNITED NATIONS (UN)

The Security Council on December 21 lifted the economic embargo it imposed on Rhodesia in 1966 to punish a white-minority rebellion against British rule. The vote, 13 to 0 with Czechoslovakia and Russia abstaining, came after Rhodesian factions signed an agreement for a British-conducted election in the colony to bring it to internationally recognized independence under black rule.

Indochina got UN attention much of the year. Vietnamese troops drove Cambodia's Prime Minister Pol Pot from Phnom Penh, the capital, on January 7, and installed Heng Samrin in his place. Pol Pot's faction sent the country's former ruler, Prince Norodom Sihanouk, to protest the Vietnamese aggression in a Security Council debate held between January 11 and 15. Sihanouk said Cambodia was "in full economic upswing" when Vietnam waged a "German-style blitzkrieg" to install Heng Samrin. Sihanouk then conceded that President Carter was right in calling the Pol Pot regime "the worst violator of human rights in the world."

Seven Third World countries sponsored a resolution on January 15 calling for withdrawal of "all foreign forces" from Cambodia. It received 13 votes, but Czechoslovakia voted against it and Russia vetoed it.

China invaded Vietnam on February 17, and on February 22, Great Britain, Norway, Portugal, and the United States requested a Council meeting on the situation in Southeast Asia. The debate began the next day and ended on March 16. Indonesia, Malaysia, the Philippines, Singapore, and Thailand submitted a resolution calling on "all parties to the conflicts" to cease fire and "withdraw their forces to their own countries." Again, the vote was 13-2 with Czechoslovakia and Russia against, and the resolution was killed by Russia's veto. On March 22, Waldheim accepted the Pol Pot faction's Thiounn Prasith as Cambodia's permanent ambassador. That faction's General Assembly delegation kept its seat through the May session on Namibia.

The Regular Session of the Assembly began on September 18 with the election of Tanzanian Ambassador Salim Ahmed Salim as Assembly president and the admission of Saint Lucia as the 152nd member. Pol Pot's support held firm, bolstered by the fear of Vietnamese expansion openly expressed by some neighboring countries. Indonesia, Malaysia, the Philippines, Singapore, and Thailand put the Cambodian question on the Assembly's agenda. The Assembly debated the question from November 12 to 14, and then approved a resolution that called for a cease-fire in Cambodia, withdrawal of all foreign forces, and noninterference in Cambodia's internal affairs so that the Cambodian people could choose their own government democratically. The vote was 91-21 with 29 abstentions. Cuba, Guyana, and the new Nicaraguan junta voted "no" with Russia and its Eastern Hemisphere allies.

Donald F. McHenry, right, named United States ambassador to the United Nations on August 31, chats with other members of the U.S. delegation.

At a UN conference of 65 countries in Geneva, Switzerland, on July 20 and 21, $190 million was reported pledged for relief of Indochinese refugees, most of them Vietnamese "boat people." Governments agreed to take as permanent settlers 135,000 of those in temporary asylum in Southeast Asia. And more than 70 countries pledged about $210 million at a November 5 conference in New York City to help up to 300,000 needy Cambodians in their own country and neighboring Thailand.

Pope John Paul II told the General Assembly on October 2 that he hoped for progress toward solution of "the Middle East crises." He called for "just settlement of the Palestinian question" and, alluding to the Egyptian-Israeli peace treaty, said that no single step would have value "if it did not truly represent the 'first stone' of a general overall peace in the area."

Cuba's President Fidel Castro addressed the Assembly on October 12 as chairman of the nonaligned movement. He avoided sharp attack on the United States, presented nonaligned positions, and called for rich countries to assemble a $300-billion fund for development loans and grants to poorer countries.

Crisis in Iran. The Security Council was drawn into efforts to meet the crisis that arose when about 500 Iranians seized American hostages at the U.S. Embassy in Teheran on November 4 and demanded the return of deposed Shah Mohammad Reza Pahlavi. The United States asked the Council to hold private talks, and the Council issued a plea on November 9, asking Iran to free "the diplomatic personnel being held."

Iran on November 13 asked for a Council meeting on proposals that the United States accept an "examination" of the shah's "guilt" and send Iran any of his property and funds in its jurisdiction. But Security Council President Sergio Palacios de Vizzio of Bolivia told Iran that the Council could hold no such meeting until the hostages were freed. On November 25, Waldheim asked for a meeting, using his power to bring to the Council's attention any situation he thought might threaten international peace. He called the U.S.-Iran confrontation the most dangerous since the 1962 Cuban missile crisis. The Security Council held its first session on the crisis on December 1, and it called unanimously on December 4 for the release of the hostages.

On December 10, the United States asked the International Court of Justice, an arm of the UN at The Hague, the Netherlands, to take "the quickest possible action" to ensure the release of the hostages. The court on December 15 ordered Iran to release the hostages. But Iran claimed that the court had no jurisdiction. On December 17, the General Assembly unanimously adopted a treaty against hostage taking, in the works since 1976.   William N. Oatis

In WORLD BOOK, see UNITED NATIONS.

UNITED STATES, GOVERNMENT OF THE. The
United States seemed determined to set records in 1979. Banks charged record high interest rates, gold soared to a record price of more than $525 a troy ounce (31 grams) while the value of the dollar sank to record lows, and gasoline prices jumped to well over $1 a gallon (3.8 liters).

The year was also one of diplomatic uncertainties. The United States was at peace. China and the U.S. established full diplomatic relations; President Jimmy Carter and Russia's Presidium Chairman Leonid I. Brezhnev signed the Strategic Arms Limitation Treaty (SALT II); the Panama Canal Treaty became effective; and Congress approved a trade agreement with China. Yet the United States was challenged and its prestige threatened when Iranian students seized the American Embassy in Teheran and held Americans hostage. See IRAN.

The Executive Branch. In an unprecedented move, President Carter asked for and received the resignation of every member of his Cabinet and his White House staff on July 17. Within the next week he had accepted the resignations of five Cabinet secretaries and 34 staff members. See CABINET, UNITED STATES.

President Carter on July 25 named Paul A. Volcker to replace G. William Miller as chairman of the Federal Reserve Board and, on August 31, named Donald F. McHenry to replace Andrew J. Young,

Jr., as the chief United States delegate to the United Nations (UN). Young resigned on August 15 after his unauthorized meeting with the U.N. observer from the Palestine Liberation Organization in violation of U.S. policy. Israel protested the meeting as a breach of a United States-Israeli agreement. See UNITED NATIONS (UN).

Federal Agencies. Transportation Secretary Brock Adams announced on January 31 a 12,000-mile (19,200-kilometer) reduction in National Railroad Passenger Corporation (Amtrak) rail service, effective October 1. But only a partial cut in Amtrak services of about 4,000 miles (6,400 kilometers), which President Carter signed on September 29, became effective on October 1 (see RAILROAD). In February, Adams announced a new $200-million mass transit program to be administered by the Urban Mass Transit Administration (see TRANSIT).

Nuclear Regulatory Commission (NRC) standards and competence were widely questioned in the aftermath of the March 28 nuclear accident at the Three Mile Island nuclear power plant near Harrisburg, Pa. On April 11, the President ordered an 11-member commission to investigate the accident. The commission reported to President Carter on October 30 that the risks of nuclear power can be kept "within tolerable limits" only if fundamental changes are made in the construction and operation of nuclear reactors. NRC Chairman Joseph M. Hendrie told the House Energy and Power subcommittee on November 5 that the NRC would not allow construction or operation of new nuclear power facilities for at least six months and possibly two years. In December, Carter named John F. Ahearne to replace Hendrie as NRC chairman. See ENERGY.

The Federal Aviation Administration (FAA) grounded all DC-10 airplanes on May 29 for inspection after a DC-10 crashed on May 25 in Chicago, killing 274 persons in the worst disaster in American aviation history. Engine-mount problems were responsible for the accident. The DC-10's were released one by one after inspection, grounded again on June 6, then released on July 13. See AVIATION.

Postmaster General William F. Bolger announced on November 27 that the U.S. Postal Service had a surplus – the first since 1945 – of more than $470-million for fiscal 1979. See POSTAL SERVICE, U.S.

FBI Under Fire. The Federal Bureau of Investigation (FBI) came under criticism in 1979 as details of the agency's allegedly illegal activities in earlier years came to light. In January, retired investigator M. Wesley Swearingen charged the FBI with fabricating evidence, conducting burglaries, and internal corruption. The FBI admitted on September 14 that it waged a slander campaign in 1970 to discredit actress Jean Seberg, who supported the black nationalist movement in the 1960s. Seberg committed suicide in Paris earlier in September.

UNITED STATES, GOVERNMENT OF THE

President Carter on July 31 proposed an FBI governing charter that would specify the powers and duties of the bureau and establish precise standards and procedures for investigations. FBI director William H. Webster shuffled the FBI's top management on August 7, appointing Lee Colwell, Homer H. Boynton, Jr., and Donald W. Moore, Jr., as assistant directors. None of the three had served under former Director J. Edgar Hoover, who headed the agency during the time of the alleged abuses. It was the first time since 1924 that no one closely associated with Hoover held a top FBI position.

Rear Admiral Rowland Freeman III was appointed in March to head another embattled agency, the General Services Administration (GSA). Freeman vowed to eliminate waste and corruption in the GSA.

Legislative Branch. The Democratic-controlled 96th Congress and Democratic President Jimmy Carter seldom agreed on foreign or domestic issues in 1979. The energy program, a top priority for the Carter Administration, was criticized and debated piecemeal throughout the session with some provisions surviving intact.

The Congress approved two Administration-sponsored measures—the President's plan to establish an independent Department of Education and to reorganize the Department of Health, Education, and Welfare as the Department of Health and Human Services; and the Energy and Water Development Act of 1980, with an amendment to allow the Tennessee Valley Authority to finish the Tellico Dam on the Little Tennessee River. Work on the dam was halted earlier because the dam endangered the survival of the tiny snail darter fish.

Foreign Relations. Congress approved enabling legislation to make the Panama Canal Treaty effective and the Trade Liberalization Act to make the trade agreements reached at Geneva, Switzerland, by 99 nations effective. It rebuked the President for trying to abrogate the United States mutual defense treaty with Taiwan without Senate approval; asked the President to lift the embargo against Rhodesia; and began discussion of the controversial Strategic Arms Limitation Treaty (SALT II). See CONGRESS OF THE UNITED STATES.

The Supreme Court. Acting to prevent premature disclosure of its decisions, the Supreme Court on May 18 announced new restrictions on reporter access to the Supreme Court Building. The press was also the subject of a major court decision on April 18, when the court ruled, 6 to 3, that in a libel suit a defending journalist may be required to reveal his opinions and his reasons for writing a specific news story. In another ruling on libel, on June 26, the court decided, 8 to 1, that the persons suing the *Reader's Digest* and Senator William Proxmire (D., Wis.) for libel were not public figures and need not prove "actual malice" to bring suit.

Major Agencies and Bureaus of the U.S. Government*

Executive Office of the President
President, Jimmy Carter

Vice-President, Walter F. Mondale
White House Chief of Staff, Hamilton Jordan
Presidential Press Secretary, Jody Powell
Central Intelligence Agency–Stansfield Turner, Director
Council of Economic Advisers–Charles L. Schultze, Chairman
Council on Environmental Quality–Gustave Speth, Chairman
Council on Wage and Price Stability–R. Robert Russell, Director
Domestic Policy Staff–Stuart E. Eizenstat, Executive Director
Office of Management and Budget–James T. McIntyre, Jr., Director
Office of Science and Technology Policy–Frank Press, Director

The Supreme Court of the United States
Chief Justice of the United States, Warren E. Burger

Associate Justices:
William J. Brennan, Jr.	Harry A. Blackmun
Potter Stewart	Lewis F. Powell, Jr.
Byron R. White	William H. Rehnquist
Thurgood Marshall	John Paul Stevens

State Department
Secretary of State, Cyrus R. Vance

Agency for International Development–Douglas J. Bennet, Jr., Administrator
U.S. Representative to the United Nations–Donald F. McHenry

Department of the Treasury
Secretary of the Treasury, G. William Miller

Bureau of Alcohol, Tobacco, and Firearms–G. R. Dickerson, Director
Bureau of Engraving and Printing–Harry R. Clements, Director
Bureau of the Mint–Stella B. Hackel, Director
Comptroller of the Currency–John G. Heimann
Internal Revenue Service–Jerome Kurtz, Commissioner
Treasurer of the United States–Azie T. Morton
U.S. Customs Service–Robert E. Chasen, Commissioner
U.S. Secret Service–H. Stuart Knight, Director

Department of Defense
Secretary of Defense, Harold Brown

Joint Chiefs of Staff–General David C. Jones, Chairman
Secretary of the Air Force–Hans Michael Mark
Secretary of the Army–Clifford L. Alexander, Jr.
Secretary of the Navy–Edward Hidalgo

Department of Justice
Attorney General, Benjamin R. Civiletti

Bureau of Prisons–Norman A. Carlson, Director
Drug Enforcement Administration–Peter Bensinger, Administrator
Federal Bureau of Investigation–William H. Webster, Director
Immigration and Naturalization Service–David Crosland, Acting Commissioner
Law Enforcement Assistance Administration–Henry S. Dogin, Administrator
Solicitor General–Wade H. McCree, Jr.

Department of the Interior
Secretary of the Interior, Cecil D. Andrus

Bureau of Indian Affairs–William E. Hallett, Commissioner
Bureau of Land Management–Frank Gregg, Director
Bureau of Mines–(vacant)
Geological Survey–H. William Menard, Director
National Park Service–William J. Whalen, Director
Office of Territorial Affairs–Ruth Van Cleve, Director
U.S. Fish and Wildlife Service–Lynn A. Greenwalt, Director
Water and Power Resources Service–R. Keith Higginson, Commissioner

Department of Agriculture
Secretary of Agriculture, Bob Bergland

Agricultural Economics–Howard W. Hjort, Director
Agricultural Marketing Service–Barbara Lindemann Schlei, Administrator

*As of Jan. 1, 1980. † nominated but not yet confirmed.

Agricultural Stabilization and Conservation Service–Ray V. Fitzgerald, Administrator
Farmers Home Administration–Gordon Cavanaugh, Administrator
Federal Crop Insurance Corporation–James D. Deal, Manager
Food and Consumer Services–Carol Tucker Foreman, Administrator
Forest Service–John R. McGuire, Chief
Rural Electrification Administration–Robert W. Feragen, Administrator
Soil Conservation Service–Ronello M. Davis, Administrator

Department of Commerce
Secretary of Commerce, Philip M. Klutznick

Bureau of the Census–Vincent P. Barabba, Director
Economic Development Administration–Robert T. Hall, Administrator
Industry and Trade Administration–Stanley J. Marcuss, Acting Administrator
National Bureau of Standards–Ernest Ambler, Director
National Oceanic and Atmospheric Administration–Richard A. Frank, Administrator
Office of Minority Business Enterprise–Daniel P. Henson III, Director
Patent and Trademark Office–Sidney A. Diamond†, Commissioner

Department of Labor
Secretary of Labor, F. Ray Marshall

Bureau of Labor Statistics–Janet L. Norwood, Commissioner
Employment and Training Administration–Ernest G. Green, Administrator
Employment Standards Administration–Donald E. Elisburg, Administrator
Labor-Management Services Administration–William P. Hobgood, Administrator
Mine Safety and Health Administration–Robert B. Lagather, Administrator
Occupational Safety and Health Administration–Eula Bingham, Administrator
Women's Bureau–Alexis M. Herman, Director

Department of Health, Education, and Welfare
Secretary of Health, Education, and Welfare, Patricia Roberts Harris

Administration on Aging–Robert C. Benedict, Commissioner
Alcohol, Drug Abuse, and Mental Health Administration–Gerald L. Klerman, Administrator
Center for Disease Control–William H. Foege, Director
Food and Drug Administration–Jere E. Goyan, Commissioner
Health Care Financing Administration–Leonard D. Schaeffer, Administrator
Health Resources Administration–Henry A. Foley, Administrator
Health Services Administration–George Lythcott, Administrator
National Institute of Education–(vacant)
National Institutes of Health–Donald S. Fredrickson, Director
Office of Consumer Affairs–Esther Peterson, Director
Office of Education–William Lee Smith, Commissioner
Public Health Service–Julius B. Richmond, Administrator
Rehabilitation Services Administration–Robert R. Humphreys, Commissioner
Social Security Administration–(vacant)

Department of Housing and Urban Development
Secretary of Housing and Urban Development, Moon Landrieu

Community Planning and Development–Robert C. Embry, Administrator
Federal Housing Commissioner–Lawrence B. Simons
Government National Mortgage Association–Ronald P. Laurent, President

Department of Transportation
Secretary of Transportation, Neil E. Goldschmidt

Federal Aviation Administration–Langhorne M. Bond, Administrator
Federal Highway Administration–Karl S. Bowers, Administrator
Federal Railroad Administration–John M. Sullivan, Administrator
National Highway Traffic Safety Administration–Joan B. Claybrook, Administrator
U.S. Coast Guard–Admiral John B. Hayes, Commandant
Urban Mass Transportation Administration–Theodore C. Lutz, Administrator

Department of Energy
Secretary of Energy, Charles W. Duncan, Jr.

Economic Regulatory Administration–Hazel Reid Rollins†, Administrator
Energy Information Administration–Lincoln E. Moses, Administrator
Federal Energy Regulatory Commission–Charles B. Curtis, Chairman
Office of Energy Research–Edward A. Frieman†, Director

Congressional Officials
President of the Senate pro tempore–Warren G. Magnuson

Speaker of the House–Thomas P. O'Neill, Jr.
Architect of the Capitol–George M. White
Comptroller General of the U.S.–Elmer B. Staats
Congressional Budget Office–Alice M. Rivlin, Director
Librarian of Congress–Daniel J. Boorstin
Office of Technology Assessment–John H. Gibbons, Director
Public Printer of the U.S.–John J. Boyle

Independent Agencies
ACTION–Samuel W. Brown, Jr., Director
Civil Aeronautics Board–Marvin S. Cohen, Chairman
Commodity Futures Trading Commission–James M. Stone, Chairman
Community Services Administration–Graciela Olivarez, Director
Consumer Product Safety Commission–Susan B. King, Chairman
Environmental Protection Agency–Douglas M. Costle, Administrator
Equal Employment Opportunity Commission–Eleanor Holmes Norton, Chair
Export-Import Bank–John L. Moore, President
Farm Credit Administration–Donald E. Wilkinson, Governor
Federal Communications Commission–Charles D. Ferris, Chairman
Federal Deposit Insurance Corporation–Irvine Sprague, Chairman
Federal Election Commission–Robert O. Tiernan, Chairman
Federal Emergency Management Agency–John W. Macy, Jr., Director
Federal Home Loan Bank Board–Jay Janis, Chairman
Federal Maritime Commission–Richard J. Daschbach, Chairman
Federal Mediation and Conciliation Service–Wayne L. Horvitz, Director
Federal Reserve System–Paul A. Volcker, Board of Governors Chairman
Federal Trade Commission–Michael Pertschuk, Chairman
General Services Administration–Rowland G. Freeman III, Administrator
International Communication Agency–John E. Reinhardt, Director
Interstate Commerce Commission–Darius Gaskins, Jr., Chairman
National Aeronautics and Space Administration–Robert A. Frosch, Administrator
National Credit Union Administration–Lawrence Connell, Jr., Administrator
National Endowment for the Arts–Livingston L. Biddle, Chairman
National Endowment for the Humanities–Joseph D. Duffey, Chairman
National Labor Relations Board–John H. Fanning, Chairman
National Mediation Board–David H. Stowe, Chairman
National Railroad Passenger Corporation (AMTRAK)–Alan S. Boyd, President
National Science Foundation–Richard C. Atkinson, Director
National Transportation Safety Board–James B. King, Chairman
Nuclear Regulatory Commission–John F. Ahearne, Acting Chairman
Occupational Safety and Health Review Commission–Timothy F. Cleary, Chairman
Office of Personnel Management–Alan K. Campbell, Director
Overseas Private Investment Corporation–J. Bruce Llewellyn, President
Panama Canal Commission–Dennis P. McAuliffe, Administrator
Securities and Exchange Commission–Harold M. Williams, Chairman
Small Business Administration–A. Vernon Weaver, Jr., Administrator
Smithsonian Institution–S. Dillon Ripley, Secretary
Tennessee Valley Authority–S. David Freeman, Chairman
U.S. Arms Control and Disarmament Agency–George M. Seignious, Director
U.S. Commission on Civil Rights–Arthur S. Flemming, Chairman
U.S. International Trade Commission–Catherine Bedell, Chairman
U.S. Metric Board–Louis F. Polk, Chairman
U.S. Postal Service–William F. Bolger, Postmaster General
Veterans Administration–Max Cleland, Administrator

517

Federal Spending and Revenue Receipts

Estimated U.S. Budget for Fiscal 1980*

	Billions of dollars
National defense	125.8
International affairs†	8.2
Science and space research	5.5
Natural resources, environment, energy	19.4
Agriculture	4.3
Commerce and transportation	21.0
Community and regional development	7.3
Education, employment, social services	30.2
Health	53.4
Income security	179.1
Veterans benefits and services	20.5
Law enforcement and justice	4.4
General government	4.4
Revenue sharing and federal aid	8.8
Interest	57.0
Allowances	1.4
Undistributed funds	−19.0
Total	531.6

*Oct. 1, 1979, to Sept. 30, 1980;
1975 and 1976, July 1 to June 30

†Includes foreign aid

U.S. Income and Outlays

Billions of dollars

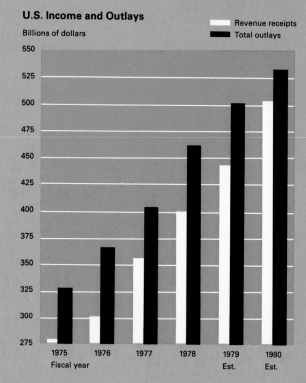

Source: U.S. Office of Management and Budget.

The court made two major rulings on sex discrimination in 1979. In a March 5 decision it ruled, 6 to 3, that an Alabama law requiring a divorced husband – but not a divorced wife – to pay alimony was unconstitutional sex discrimination. The court on June 25 affirmed a lower court ruling that, under the program of Aid to Families with Dependent Children with Unemployed Fathers, the HEW must also pay benefits to needy families with unemployed mothers. A court ruling on April 17 stated that a town and its residents can sue a realtor if they believe that he or she is illegally disturbing the racial balance of an integrated neighborhood.

In a far-reaching unanimous ruling on April 30, the court declared that unless there is "clear and convincing evidence" that a person is mentally ill and likely to be dangerous, he cannot be committed to a mental institution against his will. In another decision affecting the mentally ill, the court ruled, 6 to 3, on June 20 that state laws allowing parents to commit minor children to state mental hospitals without "rigorous impartial review" are constitutional. See Civil Rights; Supreme Court of the United States. Carol L. Thompson

In World Book, see United States, Government of the.

UNITED STATES CONSTITUTION. See Constitution of the United States.

UPPER VOLTA. See Africa.

URUGUAY. The military regime of President Aparicio Mendez Manfredini eased its harsh rule but still refused to permit dissent in 1979. It remained publicly committed to a plebiscite in 1980 to adopt a new constitution, and it also promised a presidential election in 1981. But it banned as a candidate anyone who gained office or ran for office in elections held in 1966 and 1971. In effect, none of the present leaders of the Colorado and Blanco parties, the two principal political parties, could seek office. Reportedly, the proposed constitution also provided for a National Security Council that would rule on internal security questions and a Court of the Nation that would have the authority to impeach officials, including the president.

The Mendez regime continued to exert strict control over the press, which was banned from discussing political topics or commenting on acts of the government. But it also appeared to be easing up on its security system's more violent excesses.

OAS Criticism. Federico Silva, president of the supreme military tribunal, responded on November 20 to sharp criticism by the Organization of American States (OAS), saying that the number of Uruguay's political prisoners had declined from 5,700 in 1978 to 1,529 in 1979. Silva also declared that foreign diplomats had been allowed to visit the main prison and had made only "insignificant" suggestions on how to improve it. He said the OAS General

Assembly had taken "isolated incidents, deformed them, and tried to take advantage of them."

The governor of the Brazilian state of Rio Grande do Sul disclosed in January that Brazilian police had participated in the kidnapping of four Uruguayans – a man, a woman, and two children – in November 1978, and turned them over to Uruguayan police. The adults were suspected subversives and reportedly were being held in prison. On November 22, President Mendez prohibited the proposed visit of an investigative commission of the Socialist International headed by Spanish socialist Felipe Gonzalez. Mendez said the visit would affect "the nation's sovereignty" in that the commission would try to meet with local politicians in violation of the ban on political activity.

The Economy. Economy Minister Valentin Arismendi declared on August 22 that rising international oil prices and the flood of Argentine tourists eager to shop in a country where goods are cheaper were responsible for the rapid rise in prices that was expected to reach 60 per cent by the end of the year. That was an increase of 15 percentage points over 1978's inflation rate. Everett G. Martin

See also LATIN AMERICA (Facts in Brief Table). In WORLD BOOK, see URUGUAY.

UTAH. See STATE GOVERNMENT.

UTILITIES. See COMMUNICATIONS; ENERGY; PETROLEUM AND GAS.

VEIL, SIMONE (1927-   ), a French lawyer and government official, was elected president of the European Parliament – the legislative branch of the European Community (EC or Common Market) – on July 17, 1979. She had won a seat in Parliament's first popular election on June 10. Before that election, the EC nations' legislatures selected the members. See EUROPE.

As French Minister of Health and Family Affairs since 1974, Veil steered liberal legislation on abortion, contraception, and family planning through the French Parliament. She also worked to improve hospitals and prisons and to decrease smoking and alcoholism. She regularly led polls as France's most popular public official.

Simone Jacob was born in Nice on July 13, 1927. The day after her graduation from high school in 1944, she was deported with her family to the German concentration camp in Auschwitz, Poland, and was later sent to Bergen-Belsen, a camp near Hamburg, Germany.

After World War II, she studied law and did paralegal work. She joined the Ministry of Justice in 1957 as a member of the Committee of Penitentiary Administration and became a technical adviser to the minister of justice in 1969. From 1970 to 1974, Veil was secretary-general of a body that helped the president of France select magistrates. She and her husband, Antoine, have three sons. Jay Myers

VENDA became independent from South Africa on Sept. 13, 1979. One of 10 "homelands" assigned to black population groups under South Africa's system of *apartheid* (separate racial development), it was the third to receive independence. Transkei became independent in October 1976 and Bophuthatswana in December 1977. The 10 homelands cover about 13 per cent of South Africa.

Venda has a population of 320,000 and a land area of 2,410 square miles (6,220 square kilometers) divided into two separate blocks. It is the smallest of the homelands. President Patrick Mphephu said in Independence Day ceremonies that his people needed more land, particularly to join the two blocks into one continuous territory. South Africa's government agreed to consider this and other requests for realignment and enlargement of the homeland's boundaries.

An estimated 70 per cent of the male work force is employed in urban areas of South Africa. However, with Venda's independence, these workers lost their rights as South African citizens.

On September 21, the United Nations Security Council unanimously condemned the establishment of Venda, saying South Africa intended "to divide and dispossess the African people." John D. Esseks

See also AFRICA (Facts in Brief Table); SOUTH AFRICA. In WORLD BOOK, see SOUTH AFRICA.

Freedom for Venda

★ National capital

▢ Other homelands

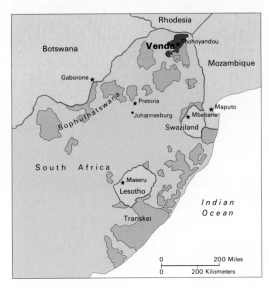

VENEZUELA. Luis Herrera Campins was sworn in as president on March 12, 1979. He became the fifth consecutive president elected since democracy was restored in Venezuela in 1958. Herrera, head of the Christian Social Party, was elected on Dec. 3, 1978.

Austerity Program. On May 28, the government announced the details of a new austerity program. Although Venezuela's income from oil exports had tripled to $10 billion a year in 1974, the outgoing administration of Carlos Andres Perez had launched so many ambitious programs that Herrera inherited a $16.2-billion public debt, a budget deficit, and a deficit in the nation's current account (international commerce plus services) of more than $5 billion. Under the new program, the administration ended long-standing price controls on 175 consumer items that were costing the government heavily in subsidies and distorting the nation's pricing picture. The adjustment raised the inflation rate to more than 20 per cent, however, and the Democratic Action Party (AD) joined with the left in the National Congress to force through a bill signed into law on December 2 granting 30 per cent salary increases to the 4 million members of the labor force. Businessmen and labor leaders later joined with the AD to oppose the government's attempt to lower high tariff barriers, which, Herrera hoped, would promote efficiency in manufacturing by introducing foreign competition.

Herrera had better luck in dealing with the problem of Venezuela's dwindling oil reserves. Total proven reserves were good for about 20 more years of production, but most of these were heavy crude oils that required special refining techniques. Reserves of lighter crudes could run out in five to seven years. On November 23, the state-owned oil company announced the discovery of new oil reservoirs in Lake Maracaibo that might contain as much as 500 million barrels of light crude. Two days later, a wildcat well in a nearby area began producing 3,500 barrels of light crude per day, kindling more hopes.

Hostage Rescued. The longest kidnapping in Latin American history ended happily on June 30 with the rescue of William F. Niehous, a United States citizen who was general manager of the U.S.-owned Owens-Illinois Glass Company in Venezuela. Niehous was abducted from his Caracas home on Feb. 27, 1976. Police stumbled by chance on the guerrilla hideout where he was being held in a remote jungle area near the Orinoco River. Niehous said he had been moved often during his captivity and had been well treated. Everett G. Martin

See also LATIN AMERICA (Facts in Brief Table). In WORLD BOOK, see VENEZUELA.

VERMONT. See STATE GOVERNMENT.

VETERANS. See COMMUNITY ORGANIZATIONS.

VICE-PRESIDENT OF THE UNITED STATES. See MONDALE, WALTER F.

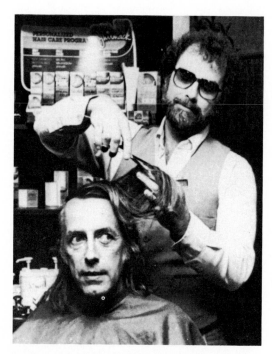

U.S. businessman William F. Niehous, kidnapped by Venezuelan guerrillas in February 1976, enjoys a haircut after his safe return home in July 1979.

VIETNAM fought wars on two broad fronts during 1979. Its invasion of Cambodia in December 1978 turned into a long, costly struggle against guerrilla forces. Vietnamese troops also remained in Laos, trying to subdue resistance there. In retaliation for the Cambodian invasion, China attacked Vietnam on February 17. Although China announced on March 15 that its troops had been withdrawn, Vietnam disputed this.

The Heng Samrin regime that Vietnam installed in Cambodia required the support of an estimated 200,000 Vietnamese soldiers. They were reported to be looting Cambodia, even taking relief food supplies. Some reports said Vietnamese settlers had begun to move into Cambodia, taking over land left unclaimed after the death of hundreds of thousands of Cambodians. The Vietnamese Communist Party leadership seemed determined to control Cambodia and Laos militarily and through local front groups, thus having power over all of what was once French Indochina. See CAMBODIA.

The Chinese Attack along Vietnam's northern border by an estimated 250,000 troops met fierce resistance. Vietnam withheld its regular army and fought back primarily with border troops and local militia, apparently trying to avoid giving China a target for a major military victory. The invasion was contained near the border, but the area suffered extensive destruction.

Vietnamese delegates to a United Nations conference on Indochina refugees—in Geneva, Switzerland, in July—ask other nations to step up their aid.

Diplomats from Vietnam and China met in Hanoi on April 18 in an effort to arrange peace. Talks continued sporadically through the year in Vietnam and China without making progress. China insisted that Vietnam withdraw its troops from Cambodia, but Vietnam refused to comply.

Russia and its allies gave Vietnam military equipment, economic aid, and diplomatic backing. Vietnam's economy, disrupted by continual warfare, economic mismanagement, and the departure of ethnic Chinese residents and other skilled personnel as refugees, became more dependent on Soviet aid.

"Boat People" fled Vietnam in small crafts in huge numbers. The refugees, many of them ethnic Chinese, were driven out by the government. An estimated 30,000 per month arrived in neighboring nations, but many others drowned at sea. The boat people became an urgent world problem when they encountered hostility from neighboring nations. Pirates attacked the boats, and the wanderers endured appalling conditions in refugee camps. See ASIA (Close-Up).

A United Nations international conference in Geneva, Switzerland, in July obtained Vietnam's promise to stop driving out refugees, but some continued to escape. Henry S. Bradsher

See also ASIA (Facts in Brief Table). In WORLD BOOK, see INDOCHINA; VIETNAM.

VIRGINIA. See STATE GOVERNMENT.

VISUAL ARTS. Exhibitions devoted to the old masters dominated museum calendars in the United States in 1979. Both the Cleveland Museum of Art and the Boston Museum of Fine Arts hosted and helped to organize the somber yet enthralling "Chardin" exhibition of paintings that had been seen previously in Paris.

Selections from one of the world's great private collections, that of the Swiss industrialist Baron Hans Thyssen-Bornemisza, began a nine-city tour at the National Gallery of Art in Washington, D.C., which also premièred the United States tour of "From Leonardo to Titian: Italian Renaissance Paintings from the Hermitage." The Los Angeles County Museum of Art presented "The Golden Age of Venetian Painting" – the first Venetian exhibition ever organized by an American museum. And two important shows of older European drawings were "Michelangelo and his World," 41 drawings from the British Museum, at the Pierpont Morgan Library in New York City; and "Roman Drawings from the 16th Century from the Louvre," presented by the Art Institute of Chicago.

Two exhibitions marked the first time that ancient and medieval works of national import were sent abroad. "Cycladic Art: Ancient Sculpture and Ceramics, from the N.P. Goulandris Collection" in Greece was shown at the National Gallery of Art, while New York City's Metropolitan Museum of Art presented "Treasures from the Kremlin" on loan from Russia.

Important Shows of 19th-century art included "Toulouse-Lautrec" at the Art Institute of Chicago, part of the institute's 100th anniversary celebration. Many of the paintings, seen for the first time in the United States, were from the Musée Toulouse-Lautrec in Albi, France, the artist's birthplace. A little-known American romantic painter was featured by the Boston Museum of Fine Arts as "A Man of Genius: The Art of Washington Allston." The Brooklyn Museum of Art in New York explored "The American Renaissance 1876-1917," while the Detroit Institute of Art, together with several British museums, assembled the first show dealing with "John Singer Sargent and the Edwardian Age."

The 100th anniversary of French lithographer Honoré Daumier's death was marked by a display of the Armand Hammer Daumier Collection founded by George Longstreet – the world's largest collection of Daumier's caricatures – at the Los Angeles County Museum of Art. The works were to become part of that museum's permanent collection. Two large exhibitions stressed the role of business firms as patrons of art. "'Art Inc.' American Paintings from Corporate Collections" was presented by the Montgomery (Ala.) Museum of Fine Arts, while the Albright-Knox Art Gallery in Buffalo, N.Y., showed "Constructivism and the Geometric Tradition: Selections from the McCrory Corporation Collection."

VISUAL ARTS

As always, exhibitions mounted by the major university museums of the United States were of a high order. For example, the Yale Center for British Art in New Haven, Conn., presented "The Fuseli Circle in Rome: Early Romantic Art of the 1770's," and the Smith College Museum of Art in Northampton, Mass., celebrated its 100th anniversary by exhibiting its wide-ranging collections to the public.

Major Gifts to museums included the bequests of Nelson A. Rockefeller. The Metropolitan Museum of Art received 1,160 primitive works, valued at more than $5 million, to augment the $20 million worth of such art that he had given the museum in 1969. And the Museum of Modern Art in New York City received 23 important paintings and four sculptures, all 20th century works, worth about $8.5-million.

The largest public collection of the paintings of Andrew Wyeth was established at the Greenville County (S.C.) Art Museum. The 26 works, purchased by the Magill family, were valued at about $4.5 million. In Sante Fe, N. Mex., the Museum of International Folk Art was planning to build a new wing to house more than 100,000 items donated by the Alexander Girard Collection. Abby Aldrich and John D. Rockefeller presented Colonial Williamsburg in Virginia with an 18th-century manor house, 500 art objects, and an estate adjacent to the historic area. The National Gallery of Art received the only surviving set of Gilbert Stuart portraits of the first five U.S. Presidents, the Gibbs-Coolidge collection, from the Coolidge family of Boston.

20th-Century European Art starred in two enormous exhibitions in 1979. "Paris-Moscow 1900-1930" at the Georges Pompidou National Center for Art and Culture in Paris showed thousands of works to affirm the close ties between the two cities. The 800 works by Pablo Picasso on display at the Grand Palais in Paris were but a small part of the 1,800 paintings, 11,000 drawings, and 1,300 sculptures and other works that made up the personal collection of the artist, which was given to the French nation by Picasso's heirs in lieu of inheritance taxes. Eventually, the entire body of work will be shown in a French national museum devoted solely to Picasso.

Other aspects of 20th-century art were displayed in "The Age of Surrealism" at the Cleveland Museum of Art. Mexico's foremost living artist was given a major retrospective by the Whitney Museum of American Art in New York City. The show was called "Rufino Tamayo: Myth and Magic."

The trend toward Post Modernist art seen in the past 20 years appears to have waned. Yet many younger artists in the United States continued to exhibit such nontraditional approaches as "performance art," "concept art," "diary art," and "minimal art." Such museum exhibitions as the one featuring the work of Joseph Beuys at the Guggenheim Museum in New York City and that of Richard

Bostonians fought hard to keep two Washington portraits by Gilbert Stuart, sought by the National Portrait Gallery, in their Museum of Fine Arts.

WASHINGTON

Artschwager at the Albright-Knox Art Gallery documented this approach in 1979.

Photography Exhibitions continued to proliferate across the United States, indicating the enhanced status of the medium and, perhaps, the lessening status of the traditional fine arts. History was the focus of such shows as "Lewis W. Hine 1874-1940: Photographer of the Human Condition," at the Brooklyn Museum of Art, while photography as art rather than as documentary was the goal of "Photography Rediscovered: 1900-1930," at the Whitney Museum. More recent photographers were accorded large exhibitions, as in "Ansel Adams and the West" at the Museum of Modern Art.

Non-Western Art was featured in two large exhibitions. "The Art of the Pacific Islands" was presented by the National Gallery of Art and a seven-museum tour of "Four Thousand Years of Korean Art" began at San Francisco's Asian Art Museum.

Sculpture Exhibitions featured works ranging from medieval to modern. They included "European Terracottas, from the 15th to the 20th century, from the Sackler Collection," presented by the National Gallery of Art; "Modern European Sculpture, 1918-1945: Unknown Beings and Other Realities," at the Albright-Knox Art Gallery; the George Segal retrospective, organized by the Walker Art Center in Minneapolis, Minn.; and the kinetic art works of George Rickey at New York City's Guggenheim Museum.

Auction Action in both Europe and America exceeded all expectations. In an era marked by increasing inflation and an intensified search for secure investments, individual works of art sold for remarkable prices, and records were set for collections. For example, a Swiss collection of 26 impressionist works, sold in London for $5.5 million, included the record high of $770,000 paid for a painting by Henri de Toulouse-Lautrec and the $619,000 paid for a work by Swiss painter Ferdinand Hodler. *The Young Sailor* by Henri Matisse set a world auction price record for an impressionist painting of $1,576,800.

The highest number of bidders ever for one auction – more than 30,000 – sent bids or attended the Benjamin Sonnenberg sale in New York City in June. A total of 1,762 lots, the result of a lifetime of acquisition, brought $4.9 million at auction. Other records were set in New York City for 19th-century American paintings. *Washington Crossing the Delaware* by Eastman Johnson sold for $370,000, and $300,000 was paid for *Still Life with Violin* by William Michael Harnett. The highest price given for one painting in 1979 was the $2.5 million paid on October 25 for the landscape *Icebergs* by Frederic Edwin Church. Joshua B. Kind

In WORLD BOOK, see ART AND THE ARTS; PAINTING; SCULPTURE.

VITAL STATISTICS. See CENSUS; POPULATION.

VOIGHT, JON (1938-), won the Academy of Motion Picture Arts and Sciences Oscar for best actor in 1979. He was honored for his role in *Coming Home,* a drama depicting problems of Vietnam veterans after their return to the United States.

Voight was born on Dec. 29, 1938, in Yonkers, N.Y. His father was a golf pro in Westchester County, New York. In one of his earliest roles, Jon played an 80-year-old German lady's man in a high school play. He studied drama at Catholic University in Washington, D.C., and graduated in 1960. That year he began studying acting at the Neighborhood Playhouse in New York City.

For his first role on Broadway, Voight played Rolf for a time in the long-running hit musical *The Sound of Music.* His first major role in New York City came in 1965, in the Arthur Miller play *A View from the Bridge.* Voight also did summer stock and some television acting in the 1960s.

As a result, Voight, like many other performers, had many credits to his name before he gained "instant stardom" with his role as Joe Buck in the movie *Midnight Cowboy* (1969). He received an Oscar nomination for that role. His film credits also include *Catch-22* (1970), *Deliverance* (1972), and *The Odessa File* (1974).

Voight married his second wife, Marcheline Bertrand, in 1971. They have one son and live in Los Angeles. Patricia Dragisic

VOLCKER, PAUL ADOLPH (1927-), was named chairman of the United States Federal Reserve Board on July 25, 1979, succeeding G. William Miller, who became the secretary of the Treasury. Volcker had served since 1975 as president of the New York Federal Reserve Bank.

Volcker was born on Sept. 5, 1927, in Cape May, N.J., and graduated with honors from Princeton University in 1949. He earned a master's degree in political economy and government in 1951 from the Harvard University Graduate School of Public Administration, then spent a year at the London School of Economics.

Volcker's varied career began in 1952 as an economist in the New York Federal Reserve Bank's research department. From 1957 to 1962, he was a financial economist at Chase Manhattan Bank. Volcker then became director of the U.S. Treasury's Office of Financial Analysis. In 1965, he rejoined Chase Manhattan as vice-president and director of forward planning, and from 1969 to 1974 he was undersecretary of the Treasury for monetary affairs. In 1974 and 1975, Volcker was senior fellow at the Woodrow Wilson School of Public and International Affairs at Princeton University.

Volcker married Barbara M. Bahnson in 1954. They have two children. Marsha F. Goldsmith

WALES. See GREAT BRITAIN.

WASHINGTON. See STATE GOVERNMENT.

WASHINGTON, D. C. Plans conceived in the 1960s to renovate the stretch of Pennsylvania Avenue connecting the Capitol with the U.S. Department of the Treasury Building came closer to realization in 1979. The General Services Administration announced on January 8 that the Harry Weese & Associates architectural firm would develop a master plan for renovating the area surrounding the Old Post Office Building on Pennsylvania Avenue. The plan includes plazas and arcades for outdoor ceremonies, with shops and restaurants on lower levels.

Private Development projects directed by the Pennsylvania Avenue Development Corporation, an organization created by Congress to channel federal funds, were also underway in 1979. They included a $110-million complex of offices, shops, restaurants, and a hotel on the former site of the National Theater, and a remodeling of the Willard Hotel.

The Federal City Council, an organization of business, professional, and civic leaders, reported in July that Metro, the City's rapid-transit system, has attracted almost $1 billion in private development funds into the area since 1976. The group predicted that private investment would exceed $6 billion by the scheduled completion of the 100-mile (160-kilometer) system in 1990.

Strikes and Protests. More than half of the city's teachers walked out in a 23-day contract dispute that ended on March 29. Although schools remained open during the strike, attendance declined sharply.

Hundreds of taxi drivers staged a two-day strike in July, demanding higher fares. The city's Public Service Commission had granted an interim increase of 10 cents per passenger per trip, while drivers sought an overall fare increase of 10 per cent.

Demanding higher farm price subsidies, an estimated 3,500 members of the American Agriculture Movement drove heavy farm vehicles into Washington on February 5, disrupting rush-hour traffic. The farmers massed on the Mall between the Capitol and the Washington Monument, where they were cordoned off by police. The group stayed in the city until March 1 to lobby for price supports.

More than 65,000 persons marched from the Capitol to the White House on May 6 protesting the use of nuclear power. An estimated 50,000 homosexuals demanded increased civil rights on October 14.

The worst snowstorm to hit Washington since 1922 struck on February 18, dumping almost 19 inches (48 centimeters) of snow on the city and closing airports, schools, and government offices and shutting down public transportation. Lobbying farmers came to the aid of the city, using their tractors to clear the streets and to transport emergency supplies and personnel.   James M. Banovetz

See also CITY. In WORLD BOOK, see WASHINGTON, D. C.

Pollutants from the Capitol power plant contribute to the "deterioration of public health," according to a clean-air suit filed against Congress in 1979.

WATER. President Jimmy Carter's Administration and environmental groups waged an intense battle in 1979 against legislation that would revise the Reclamation Act of 1902. The act helped settle the West by authorizing the federal government to build irrigation projects that were subsidized by the taxpayers to sell the irrigation water to settlers at bargain rates. It entitled one person to buy cheap water to irrigate 160 acres (65 hectares) and a man and wife to buy cheap water for 320 acres (130 hectares). The Senate approved a bill on September 14 that opponents charged would virtually destroy the aim of the act to make the federal water available only to family-sized farms.

The bill would increase the acreage limit for receiving water subsidies to 1,280 acres (520 hectares) per family, repeal the requirement that farmers live on or within 50 miles (80 kilometers) of the land, and exempt owners of land in California's Imperial Valley from acreage limits.

Secretary of the Interior Cecil D. Andrus said the bill's disregard for the basic social purposes of the Reclamation Act made it unacceptable. Representative George Miller (D., Calif.) called the Senate bill a "Western stagecoach robbery" that would cost the public "billions in tax dollars." The limitation on the size of a farm entitled to the cheap-water subsidy was loosely enforced by the Department of the Interior for many years.

National Land for People, a California group, won a federal court decision in 1976 that ordered the Interior Department to enforce the acreage limitation by moving excess land holdings into other hands, unless Congress revised the law. Large landowners began a national campaign pressuring Congress to liberalize the law to protect their subsidies.

Supporters of the bill said they would win what they called Carter's "war on the West" because of the President's interest in winning Western votes in 1980. The House of Representatives was expected to produce a bill that is tougher on large landowners. It began hearings on November 8, but final congressional action was not expected until 1980 because the issue was so complex.

Share the Cost. President Carter sent Congress legislation on May 16 that would require the states to pay 10 per cent of the costs of revenue-generating water projects that the federal government traditionally has paid. The state share would be 5 per cent for projects that do not return revenue, such as flood control. Andrus said the proposal, a key element of the Administration's reform of water policy announced in 1978, could cut down on wasteful *pork-barrel* projects – those that do not fulfill a real need – by forcing states to "put their money where their mouth is." Senators Pete V. Domenici (R., N.Mex.) and Daniel P. Moynihan (D., N.Y.) backed a proposal to grant money to the states, which would then decide themselves which projects to build.

Trouble out West. Conflicts over water in largely arid areas of the West seemed to intensify as farmers, energy companies, Indians, and municipalities sought larger shares of a limited resource. The General Accounting Office warned on May 21 that the seven states within the Colorado River Basin will face critical water shortages in 25 years. Farmers, who consume 85 per cent of the water used in the West, are fighting to maintain their share against the increasing demand.

Another critical new element in the Western water picture is the growing insistence of Indian tribes on protection and use of their water rights. Under the Winters Doctrine, established by the Supreme Court of the United States in 1908, Indian reservations have the right to "future use" of water from streams that flow through their reservations. Just how much water this amounts to has never been determined.

On August 8, the Interior Department and the 600,000-acre (240,000-hectare) Westlands Water District in California's San Joaquin Valley settled the long and bitter dispute over the cost of the federal water provided to the nation's most heavily subsidized irrigation district. Environmentalists said that the contract cost the federal treasury at least $70 million in lost revenues and was a retreat from the Administration's water policy.   Andrew L. Newman

In WORLD BOOK, see WATER.

WEATHER. The third severe winter in a row to batter the eastern half of the United States came to an end in March 1979. This was the first time that three significantly below-normal winters have been recorded consecutively since record-keeping began in the early 1820s. This third winter had yet another distinction – the temperatures were below normal from the Atlantic Coast to the Pacific Coast, rather than only in the East. A total of 98 per cent of the country suffered below-normal temperatures. Although the period through February was cold, 95 per cent of the country experienced a rebound to above-normal temperatures in March.

During the winter, many parts of the Midwest experienced record snowfall. Chicago recorded the largest seasonal snowfall in its history, about 90 inches (230 centimeters), breaking the record set the previous year. As a result, the warming in March caused rapid melting, leading to ice jams and floods.

An Atmospheric Study that analyzed data collected from 1958 through 1978 indicates an increase in carbon dioxide in the world's atmosphere. The data was gathered by the National Oceanic and Atmospheric Administration (NOAA) climate monitoring systems, according to NOAA Administrator Richard A. Frank. The effects of the carbon dioxide increase are not definitely known. However, scientists know that carbon dioxide allows short-wave solar radiation into the lower atmosphere while trapping a portion of the long-wave (heat) radiation. The result is a potential "greenhouse effect," heating the lower atmosphere. Current estimates indicate that the warming could produce serious changes between 2025 and 2075. The warming trend could change the global weather pattern, melt part of the polar ice cap, and alter the agricultural growing areas and perhaps the growing season.

Pollution and Precipitation. Meteorologists have long thought that air pollution over cities diminishes local precipitation. They reasoned that the pollution causes many small cloud droplets to form, rather than drops large enough to reach the earth when they fall. But a NOAA study funded by the Environmental Protection Agency in an area of Los Angeles polluted by oil refineries did not show this effect. As in unpolluted areas, the drops formed by pollution were large enough to fall to the ground.

Naming Hurricanes. In 1979, meteorologists stopped using only women's names to identify hurricanes and began using men's names for Atlantic Ocean, Gulf of Mexico, and Caribbean hurricanes. An international agreement was required for the Atlantic. The 1979 list for the Atlantic had a woman's name first and then alternated with men's names through the alphabet. For 1980, the list begins with a man's name. Five lists were made up and will be used again, starting in 1984. All the letters of the alphabet are used each year, with the exception of Q,U,X,Y, and Z. The names were

Record snows hit Chicago during the winter of 1978-1979. More than 20 inches (51 centimeters) of snow one January weekend produced this scene.

agreed on by participating countries in the World Meteorological Organization. The use of female names only was originally adopted in the United States in 1953.

Unfortunately, the public became well acquainted with at least two of the new names. Hurricane David, which began in August, ravaged the Caribbean and caused heavy loss of life. Hurricane Frederic struck the United States Gulf Coast in September, causing an estimated $900 million in damage.

Rain Tomorrow? After years of preparation, the Prototype Regional Observing and Forecasting Service (PROFS) came into being in October at NOAA in Boulder, Colo. The goal of PROFS is to provide improved local weather service, rather than a generalized weather forecast. All facets of observation, forecasting, communications, and dissemination were being studied. The full program will be gradually developed over three to five years.

The PROFS forecasts will be for specific sites and will be short range and timely. Relatively small-scale events cause most of the property damage, loss of life, and general inconvenience attributed to the weather, so this program will try to determine the value of localized forecasts. Private weather forecasters have been called upon to add data to the program. If the experimental phase is successful, PROFS-like systems may be developed around several metropolitan areas.

Predicting Floods. Private and government meteorologists joined forces for the first time on April 15, 1979, in an attempt to forecast flash floods on a local scale. Flash floods, by nature, have devastating effects on life and property. The Flash Flood Potential Program was funded by the Urban Drainage and Flood Control District in Denver, Colo., to provide forecasts for a six-county area surrounding and including Denver. The joint venture is aided by two color radar monitors provided by the district. One is located at the National Weather Service (NWS) at Denver's Stapleton International Airport and the other at a regional weather center in nearby Lakewood, Colo. These monitors provided continuous radar observations from the NWS radars located at Limon, Colo., and Cheyenne, Wyo.

The first year's efforts continued through the local flash flood season until September 15. The results were termed promising, even though no major flash floods occurred. Several advisories for potential flash flooding were issued, and several minor floods were experienced. The six counties all added information to improve future programs. If and when a flash flood occurs in the region, police, sheriffs, and civil defense units are well versed on the program, including protective measures for their communities.

A Cooperative Agreement between the United States and the People's Republic of China was signed in May by U.S. Commerce Secretary Juanita

M. Kreps during an official visit to China. The two nations hope to improve their weather research and forecasting efforts. They want to enhance their knowledge of severe storms and large-scale weather patterns, to improve the use of satellite data as a weather tool, and to augment computer modeling and forecasting in general.

A separate agreement was signed to develop a new weather station in China that will obtain upper air information through the use of *rawinsondes,* radio-operated instruments carried by balloon. The added data will improve weather forecasting and basic service to aviation. Asian weather information has been available only rarely to American scientists. Since most major weather features move from west to east, Asian weather patterns often move to the Pacific Ocean and the western United States. Thus, the data will help scientists understand and forecast these previously uncharted weather patterns.

Teams of experts will travel between China and the United States in the joint venture. The U.S. team will computerize China's weather prediction network, and NOAA will provide the rawinsonde equipment. The Chinese will visit the United States to study the technology used at the National Environmental Satellite Service in Washington, D.C., and the University of Wisconsin.　　Edward W. Pearl

In WORLD BOOK, see METEOROLOGY; WEATHER.

WEIGHT LIFTING. See SPORTS.

WELFARE. President Jimmy Carter on May 23, 1979, sent Congress a scaled-down welfare reform plan that would cost $5.7 billion annually. His comprehensive plan for structural reform had died in Congress in 1978, primarily because of its $20-billion price tag.

The new White House plan, which would take effect in October 1981, guaranteed that every family getting public assistance would receive at least 65 per cent of the poverty level. The minimum benefit would be $4,654 for a family of four. Thirteen states currently pay less than that. All states would be required to aid needy two-parent families whose principal wage earners are out of work; 24 states now give such coverage only if the family is headed by the mother. State and local governments that share welfare costs would receive $940 million in additional federal assistance.

Carter's proposal also dealt with jobs. He asked that 400,000 new Comprehensive Employment and Training Act positions be created, and 220,000 existing jobs be set aside for welfare recipients.

Senator Daniel P. Moynihan (D., N.Y.), a long-time proponent of welfare reform, criticized the President's proposal because it would give more money to Southern and Western states with lower welfare benefits, while Northern and Eastern states with higher benefits would receive a smaller increase. He suggested the proportions be reversed.

Other Proposals. Congress had two other welfare bills under consideration. A $1.8-billion bill sponsored by Representative Charles B. Rangel (D., N.Y.) in the House and Senator Jacob K. Javits (R., N.Y.) in the Senate would set the national minimum benefit at $5,047 for a family of four. The bill requires that the Department of Health, Education, and Welfare (HEW) report to Congress within one year of enactment on what it would cost to raise the national minimum benefit to 100 per cent of the poverty level.

Representative John H. Rousselot (R., Calif.) and Senator Russell B. Long (D., La.) offered a different approach in their bill, which would replace the current open-ended federal matching of state costs for Aid to Families with Dependent Children with a federal block-grant system. This would leave considerable discretion to the states in determining their commitment to welfare programs.

Negative Income Tax. A federally funded test study of the negative income tax – a minimum income program – concluded in February that about 4,800 low-income workers receiving a salary supplement substantially reduced the number of hours they worked. Some of those tested – in Denver, Colo., and Seattle, Wash. – used the increased free time for education or to look for a better job. The study also found that a guaranteed annual

By permission of Bill Mauldin and Wil-Jo Associates, Inc. © 1979

Soft Shoulder

income for the poor had a surprising effect on some marriages. Some incompatible couples separated when the financial dependence forcing them to remain together was reduced.

Food Stamps. Government food stamps helped feed 1 out of 14 Americans in 1979. A major change in the way the stamps are used began on January 1. Recipients no longer had to pay cash for the stamps. Instead, the program merely distributed free coupons, which could be used in retail food stores.

Eligibility requirements were also changed. The net annual income for eligibility was lowered from $7,680 to $6,540, and limits were placed on deductions for housing, child care, and medical care. Officials expected these changes to cut 1 million recipients from the food-stamp rolls while adding 3 million needier persons, for a net gain of 2 million. But by midyear, there were 3 million new recipients. Many applied because they no longer had to pay cash for any part of their monthly allotment of stamps. Other factors were the increase in food costs and a temporary rise in unemployment because of severe winter weather.

In August, President Carter signed a bill that raised the limit of $6.1 billion for fiscal 1979 and added $620 million in supplemental funds, so that the program could continue.   Virginia E. Anderson

In WORLD BOOK, see FOOD STAMP PROGRAM; POVERTY; WELFARE.

WEST INDIES. St. Lucia on Feb. 22, 1979, joined the growing list of independent nations created out of Great Britain's former Caribbean colonies. The new nation, a part of the Windward Islands chain, had been an associated state affiliated with Great Britain since 1967. Princess Alexandra represented Queen Elizabeth II at the ceremonies marking the end of 177 years of British rule.

The festivities were marred by a civil servants' strike, a Labor Party boycott of the ceremonies, and the burning of St. Lucia's ancient Royal Gaol (jail) in Castries. The strikers, who included school teachers, were demanding that recently granted pay increases be made retroactive to January 1976. The laborites, a coalition of conservatives and radicals headed by George Odlum, had strongly opposed the government's decision not to hold a referendum on independence. They also held that the government, headed by Prime Minister John Compton and members of his United Workers Party, was responsible for high unemployment and soaring inflation.

On July 2, St. Lucia held its first parliamentary election as an independent nation. The Labor Party, in a landslide victory, captured 12 of the 17 seats in the House of Assembly. Allan Louisy, a 52-year-old retired high court judge, became prime minister, and George Odlum became deputy prime minister. On September 18, St. Lucia was admitted to the United Nations as its 152nd member.

Rebel troops man a roadblock in Grenada during a pre-dawn coup d'état that overthrew the government of Prime Minister Sir Eric M. Gairy.

Grenada Coup. The government of Grenada's Prime Minister Sir Eric M. Gairy was ousted in a pre-dawn coup d'état on March 13 by 33-year-old Maurice Bishop, head of the opposition New Jewel Movement. Gairy, prime minister since the nation gained independence from Great Britain in 1974, was attending a meeting in New York City at the time of the coup.

Bishop immediately instituted an 8 P.M. to 6 A.M. curfew, suspended the Constitution, and declared himself prime minister. He indicated, however, that he would lift the curfew, suspend the emergency arrest powers granted the army, and schedule parliamentary elections as soon as feasible. He also pledged that Grenada would remain in the Commonwealth.

Jamaican Riots. Violence erupted in Jamaica shortly after the government of Prime Minister Michael Manley announced on January 8 that gasoline prices would rise from $1.86 to $1.99 a gallon (3.8 liters). Seven persons were killed and dozens injured in street battles between police and demonstrators. The bauxite mining industry was also affected as workers demonstrated in support of the rioters. Jamaica's first successful tourism season in three years was also seriously disrupted when would-be tourists canceled their proposed visits.

The situation was brought under control on January 10, the day the price increase was to take effect.

Manley maintained the increase had been levied because of price hikes by the Organization of Petroleum Exporting Countries and because of an agreement with the International Monetary Fund.

On October 27, St. Lucia was joined by St. Vincent and the Grenadines, a cluster of islands with only 150 square miles (390 square kilometers) of land and 100,000 residents, as the latest independent Caribbean nation. The Duke of Gloucester represented Queen Elizabeth II at the ceremonies. In general parliamentary elections on December 5, the governing Labor Party won 11 of the 13 seats.

The Dominican Republic was devastated by Hurricane David, which struck the island on August 31. See DISASTERS (Hurricanes).   Paul C. Tullier

See also LATIN AMERICA (Facts in Brief Table). In the WORLD BOOK SUPPLEMENT section, see SAINT LUCIA. In WORLD BOOK, see WEST INDIES; WEST INDIES ASSOCIATED STATES; WEST INDIES FEDERATION.

WEST VIRGINIA. See STATE GOVERNMENT.

WISCONSIN. See STATE GOVERNMENT.

WYOMING. See STATE GOVERNMENT.

YEMEN (ADEN). See MIDDLE EAST.

YEMEN (SANA). See MIDDLE EAST.

YOUNG MEN'S CHRISTIAN ASSOCIATION (YMCA). See COMMUNITY ORGANIZATIONS.

YOUNG WOMEN'S CHRISTIAN ASSOCIATION (YWCA). See COMMUNITY ORGANIZATIONS.

YOUTH ORGANIZATIONS. In celebration of the United Nations International Year of the Child, United States youth organizations increased their efforts in 1979 to improve the general quality of life for America's young people.

Boy Scouts of America (BSA) celebrated its 69th anniversary in 1979 by expanding scouting opportunities for the severely handicapped. Scouts with severe and permanent physical, mental, or emotional handicaps may now work toward the Eagle award, Scouting's highest, under new guidelines that permit substitutions for required merit badges when the Scouts cannot meet all the requirements.

James L. Tarr, a veteran professional scouter from Dallas, became chief executive of the BSA on April 1, succeeding Harvey L. Price. After 25 years in North Brunswick, N.J., the national office moved to Irving, Tex., so that BSA could better serve its membership from a more central location.

The ninth edition of *The Official Boy Scout Handbook*, illustrated with many of Norman Rockwell's famous Scout paintings, was published in 1979. It emphasizes fundamental outdoor and craft skills. Since its first printing in 1910, more than 29 million copies of the handbook have been sold.

Boys' Clubs of America (BCA). Some 500 members attended BCA's 12th annual National Keystone Club Conference in San Diego in March. President Jimmy Carter installed Danny Rolett, a 16-year-old

member of the North Little Rock, Ark., Boys' Club, as BCA's National Boy of the Year on September 19. Former President Gerald R. Ford and Metropolitan Life Insurance Company President Richard R. Shinn received BCA's highest honor, the Herbert Hoover Humanitarian Award, for leadership efforts in support of youth development.

Camp Fire. A major financial drive culminated in 1979 with a $711,918 gift from the Max C. Fleischman Foundation of Reno, Nev. The money was applied toward the purchase of a national headquarters building in Kansas City, Mo. A National Resource Center and a meeting room complex is currently being built in Kansas City. The center, which will provide research tools and library facilities for Camp Fire and other agencies, was begun in 1978 by a grant from the J.E. and L.E. Mahee Foundation of Tulsa, Okla.

Amy Louise Barker, a 16-year-old Camp Fire member from Ellensburg, Wash., was one of 25 youths from across the nation to be appointed to the Children's Advisory Panel of the U.S. National Commission on the International Year of the Child, 1979. The panel was to provide the commissioners with young people's perceptions of the needs and problems of their peers.

4-H Clubs reached nearly 5.3 million young rural and urban Americans from every cultural, economic, and social background under the guidance of 580,000 4-H adult and teen-age volunteer leaders.

Programs are conducted in 3,150 counties in the United States as well as in the District of Columbia, Puerto Rico, the Virgin Islands, and Guam. They contributed during 1979 to energy conservation, environmental improvement, community service, and food production. Members participated in programs that aid health, nutrition, youth employment and career decisions, and family relationships.

The Future Farmers of America (FFA) broke a record in 1979 when it received $1 million in donations from industry and individuals for its programs. Byron F. Rawls of Pleasant Home, Ala., was named national FFA adviser in May, following the retirement of H. N. Hunsicker of Millwood, Va., who had been national adviser since 1965.

At its 52nd annual convention, held in November in Kansas City, Mo., the FFA honored more than 1,500 members, individuals, and companies with awards and recognition. Kevin Holtzinger of Windsor, Pa., was named Star Farmer of America and Robert W. Lovelace of Elsberry, Mo., was designated Star Agribusinessman of America.

Girl Scouts of the United States of America (GSUSA). Jane C. Freeman of Ardsley, N.Y., elected president of GSUSA in October 1978, was appointed by President Jimmy Carter to the National Commission of the International Year of the Child.

New programs for younger girls included "Careers to Explore: For Brownie and Junior Girl

Former Scoutmaster Jimmy Carter receives the first copy of a new edition of *The Official Boy Scout Handbook* from Cub and Boy Scout representatives.

Scouts" featuring interviews with women in traditional and nontraditional jobs, and activities to stimulate exploration in the world of work. For girls from 12 to 17, "Let's Make It Happen" provided a collection of 22 special-interest projects on subjects such as auto mechanics and money management.

Girls Clubs of America (GCA) staged conferences in 1979 to educate communities on such issues as juvenile justice, human sexuality, employment, and education. The conferences were held in such cities as New York City; Dallas; Tampa, Fla.; and Pasadena, Calif. The GCA also established a National Task Force of organizations and individuals to assist in its work. Among the organizations are the National Council of Negro Women, the National Association of Junior Leagues, United Way of America, and the Johnson Foundation. Individuals include psychiatrist Karl A. Menninger, author Gail Sheehy, and sex educator Mary S. Calderone.

Junior Achievement (JA) was introduced to the Bahamas in 1979. Ten countries other than the United States now use JA methods and materials to teach young people how business systems operate. In the United States, JA continued to work with more than 300,000 young people in all 50 states. These extracurricular programs in high schools were conducted by adult volunteers.   Virginia E. Anderson

In WORLD BOOK, see entries on the individual organizations.

YUGOSLAVIA was active in foreign affairs in 1979, especially among the nonaligned nations. But economic conditions deteriorated amid many changes in the government and the Communist Party.

The main thrust of Yugoslavia's foreign diplomatic activity was aimed at neutralizing Cuba's growing role in the nonaligned movement, especially at the nonaligned summit meeting hosted by Cuba in September. President Josip Broz Tito traveled to Kuwait, Iraq, Syria, and Jordan in February and to Algeria, Libya, and Malta in May and June.

Tito also visited Moscow in May, but he failed to end disagreements between Yugoslavia and Russia over Vietnam's invasion of Cambodia. Yugoslavia condemned the invasion, but made only an impartial demand for a withdrawal of all foreign troops when China invaded Vietnam.

Controversy continued with Bulgaria over memoirs by veteran Bulgarian Communist Party Politburo member Tsola Dragoicheva, particularly his references to Macedonia, a region that extends into both Bulgaria and Yugoslavia. However, a Yugoslav Macedonian exhibition was held in Sofia, Bulgaria, in July and a Bulgarian one was held in Skopje, capital of the Yugoslav Republic (state) of Macedonia, in September.

New Officials. Edvard Kardelj, highest-ranking Communist after Tito, died on February 10 and was replaced in the Presidium by another Slovene leader,

Sergej Krajger. Tito initiated a constitutional change on October 17 to require annual rotation of all senior elective positions. In June, the influential post of secretary-general of the collective state presidency went to General Ivan Dolnicar, former undersecretary in the Ministry of Defense.

Price Hikes. Bread, cigarette, and gasoline prices rose sharply on July 25. The government froze prices temporarily to slow down Yugoslavia's 21 per cent inflation on August 3, but then raised the price of electricity, diesel fuel, heating oil, and paraffin, as well as charges for meals in schools, canteens, and restaurants on September 30.

Industrial production in the first nine months of 1979 was 9 per cent higher than in the first nine months of 1978. Exports were up 14 per cent, and imports rose 31 per cent. The grain harvest was 4.5 million metric tons (5 million short tons), 885,000 metric tons (974,000 short tons) less than in 1978 and 1.8 million metric tons (2 million short tons) less than the record 1974 harvest. The International Monetary Fund granted Yugoslavia a $340-million loan in May, and Barclays Bank International of Great Britain organized a $305-million loan in July. The International Monetary Fund and the World Bank met in Yugoslavia in October, their first meeting held in a Communist country.   Chris Cviic

See also EUROPE (Facts in Brief Table). In WORLD BOOK, see MACEDONIA; YUGOSLAVIA.

YUKON TERRITORY moved closer to provincial status in 1979. On February 5, federally appointed Commissioner Ione C. Christensen was instructed to follow the advice of the 16-member elected council on such territorial matters as local taxation, nonnative education, public works, and social services. The federal government retained control over Indian affairs, native land claims, and mining. The commissioner was no longer to sit on the executive committee, which became a Cabinet drawn from elected council members. Christensen, who was appointed Dec. 21, 1978, resigned on October 10. The former mayor of Whitehorse said she could not occupy the top position under the new constraints.

Negotiations over native land claims, underway since 1973, were spurred by the promise of provincial status and by United States determination to build the $10-billion Alaska Highway natural gas pipeline "without further delay." The Council for Yukon Indians made it clear that a satisfactory claims settlement had to be reached before construction could begin. In the meantime, the pipeline project was slowed by unresolved differences with the United States on regulatory procedures and by difficulties in obtaining private financing. It was estimated the delays were increasing the cost of the project by $3 million per day.   David M.L. Farr

See also CANADA. In WORLD BOOK, see YUKON TERRITORY.

ZAIRE. A five-nation African security force left Shaba Province in August 1979 after a year of peacekeeping in the mineral-rich region. The force, composed of about 1,500 Moroccans, 600 Senegalese, and units from Gabon, the Ivory Coast, and Togo, had been stationed in Shaba since the May 1978 invasion by Zairian exiles who opposed the government controlled by President Mobutu Sese Seko.

The security force was installed to protect Shaba's strategic copper and cobalt mines. Zaire derives nearly 70 per cent of its foreign-exchange earnings from these mines, the most important of which are located near the city of Kolwezi. Virtually all the 250 to 300 foreign technicians needed to operate the mines left the area after the invasion, and only 180 of them had returned as of September.

Belgium and France agreed in April to train two special brigades of 3,000 Zairian troops to replace the African forces. European officers were assigned to each brigade to help strengthen discipline and give assurance to foreign technicians. The first brigade was deployed in early August.

As an anti-inflation measure, Mobutu on December 24 imposed a six-day freeze on financial transactions and devalued the currency.   John D. Esseks

See also AFRICA (Facts in Brief Table). In WORLD BOOK, see ZAIRE.

ZAMBIA. See AFRICA.

ZIMBABWE RHODESIA once again became a colony of Great Britain on Dec. 12, 1979, temporarily ending 14 years of independence. On that day a British parliamentary leader, Lord Soames, was installed as interim governor and the colony reverted to its original name, Rhodesia.

The Soames government became the third to rule Rhodesia during the year. With the installation of a biracial government headed by Prime Minister Abel T. Muzorewa on June 1, Rhodesia became Zimbabwe Rhodesia. Muzorewa became the nation's first black leader, following elections held from April 17 to 21 in which his party, the United African National Council, won 51 of the 72 parliamentary seats assigned to be filled by blacks. The Rhodesian Front party headed by former Prime Minister Ian D. Smith won all of the 28 seats reserved for whites under the new Constitution adopted on January 30. The victory gave Smith's party six positions in the new 20-member Cabinet, and veto power over constitutional amendments threatening certain white interests.

Black Opposition. Leaders of the black nationalist Patriotic Front, Robert Mugabe and Joshua Nkomo, urged their followers to boycott the April elections and to reject the government formed as a result. Consequently, more than 33 per cent of the eligible voters did not participate. The Front objected to the Constitution's special privileges for whites, who comprise only 4 per cent of the population.

Black nationalist guerrillas had fought Ian Smith's white government since 1972. The Patriotic Front's forces, numbering about 15,000 guerrillas as of September, also fought against Muzorewa's government. By the end of 1979, the civil war had cost the nation an estimated 20,000 lives.

Peace Talks. Great Britain invited representatives of the government and the guerrilla forces to a peace conference in London on September 10. Both sides had agreed by November 15 to replace Muzorewa's government with a British governor and up to 300 British administrators, to organize new national elections and run the country until an elected government was ready to take over.

Soames ordered an end to Rhodesian raids upon guerrilla camps in neighboring black nations on December 13. A cease-fire agreement signed on December 21 took effect on December 28.

Great Britain, the United States, and five neighboring African nations had lifted sanctions against Rhodesia by year-end. Britain had restricted trade, currency, and other economic transactions with Rhodesia after the colony unilaterally declared its independence in 1965, and the United States and other countries had followed Britain's example (see AFRICA [Close-Up]).   John D. Esseks

See also AFRICA (Facts in Brief Table). In WORLD BOOK, see RHODESIA.

ZOOLOGY. New research shed light in 1979 on the family patterns of the jackal, one of the few species of mammals to pair and remain paired with the mate for long periods. Scientists have previously noted that other adult jackals sometimes assist the parents in raising young jackals. Zoologist Patricia D. Moehlman of the University of Wisconsin, Madison, observed 15 litters of jackals for 28 months over 3½ years at Lake Ndutu in Tanzania, and concluded that more offspring survive in jackal families with helpers than in families without helpers. In some of the families studied, the helpers were known to be jackals from a previous litter that had remained with their parents. The helpers regurgitated food for the nursing mothers and the young pups and guarded the infants when the parents were absent.

Moehlman's study showed that pup survival is closely related to the number of adults in the family. In four families with only two adults, a maximum of two pups survived. However, in families with three to five adults, an average of 3.5 pups survived. The survival of pups apparently was related not to the availability of food, but to the number of adults available to capture prey and feed the young.

Birdsong. Grouse are known for their remarkable songs, which the males use to attract hens for mating. The Scottish grouse capercaillie is noted for its very quiet song. However, Scottish scientists R. Moss and I. Lockie discovered that these grouse are

not so quiet after all. Much of their song is below 40 hertz, too low-pitched for many human ears to hear. The researchers think that the capercaillies probably can hear the low-frequency sounds that they produce. But the carrying power of such low-frequency sounds has not been determined.

Animal Magnets. How animals perform their seemingly miraculous feats of migration continues to be a subject of much research. Biologists Charles Walcott of the State University of New York in Stony Brook and James L. Gould of Princeton University, and geologist Joseph L. Kirschvink of Princeton, reported in September that they have discovered a tiny mass of magnetic tissue between the eye and the brain of the pigeon. The tissue seems to contain magnetite, as well as nerve endings. The researchers think that this mass of magnetic tissue aids the birds in their navigation. They plan to sever the nerve connections between the tissue and the brain in order to observe how well pigeons can navigate without this connection.

Previous experiments with animal migration have shown that pigeons navigate using landmark recognition, smells, the position of the sun, and the magnetic field of the earth. But, although the pigeons' magnetite seems to be connected with their use of the earth's magnetic field, the link has yet to be proved conclusively. See BIOLOGY.   Barbara N. Benson

In WORLD BOOK, see ZOOLOGY.

ZOOS AND AQUARIUMS. The future of zoos and the conservation of animal species were strongly linked in 1979. At international meetings in Copenhagen, Denmark, and San Diego, zoo scientists and managers, geneticists, conservationists, and wildlife biologists considered the prospects for preserving rare and endangered species. Any species with a small population faces possible extinction because of the negative effects of inbreeding and chance combinations of defective genes–technically known as *inbreeding depression* and *genetic drift*. Many more species will face the threat of extinction in the next few years, as habitats are destroyed and wild populations shrink.

Small populations in zoos also show evidence of these problems. For example, a team of researchers at the National Zoological Park in Washington, D.C., headed by biologist Katherine Ralls, reported in November that the mortality rate for young born to closely related parents was about 25 per cent higher than that for the young of unrelated parents. The National Zoo team studied 16 species of hoofed animals. In two species–Eld's deer and scimitar-horned oryx–none of the inbred young survived to the age of 6 months.

Maintaining Diversity. The general solution to such population problems is the maintenance of genetic diversity with large numbers of each species. But few zoos or aquariums can keep several

Newborn pygmy monkeys cling to the fingers of Stockholm, Sweden, zookeeper Jonas Wahlstrom. They were born in a cage in Wahlstrom's home in June.

hundred members of each species, so exchanges of animals–or their eggs and sperm–will probably become even more commonplace than they are currently. A management plan and worldwide cooperation will be needed for each species. Such national and international efforts were underway for Père David's deer, Przewalski's horse, orang-utan, gorilla, okapi, tiger, and several species of cranes. An urgent note was provided by the immediate plight of such species as the California condor and the Japanese crested ibis.

Advances in Reproduction continued in zoos. Colo, the first gorilla born in captivity, became a grandmother in April, giving the Columbus (Ohio) Zoo a record-breaking three generations. The Los Angeles Zoo announced the birth of a second-generation marbled cat, a very rare feline from tropical Asia.

A goal in some captive-breeding programs is restocking the wild population. In one such program, the Ohio Department of Natural Resources successfully released a young bald eagle in the summer of 1979. Its parents were from the Cincinnati (Ohio) and Brookfield (Ill.) zoos.

Artificial insemination helped produce a Speke's gazelle at the St. Louis Zoo in April. The technique is widely used for domesticated animals, but this was the first time it was used with a wild species of hoofed animal.

Three Chinese alligators were successfully hatched at the Rockefeller Wildlife Refuge in Louisiana, the first captive breeding recorded for this rare species. The adults were from the New York Zoological Park, the National Zoo, and zoos in Munich and Stuttgart, West Germany. The Cuban crocodile joined the first-captive-breeding list when several of these animals were hatched at the California Alligator Farm in Buena Park.

Major Exhibits completed in 1979 include a completely remodeled birdhouse at the St. Louis Zoo. Unobtrusive harp wire was used throughout the building to separate birds from the visitors. Also, a new small mammal building was finished at the Toledo (Ohio) Zoo.

The Robert LaFortune North American Living Museum building was in full operation at Tulsa (Okla.) Zoo. As the name implies, the building uses a combination of zoo- and museum-exhibition techniques to display desert animals effectively.

An unusual "swimthrough" aquarium opened at the Hanna-Barbera marineland in Ranchos Palos Verdes, Calif., in May. It simulates a reef in Baja California, utilizing kelp beds, corals, and about 2,500 coastal fish. Visitors don wet suits, snorkels, and face masks for their tours.   George B. Rabb

See also CONSERVATION. In the Special Reports section, see DO YOU MAKE CAGE CALLS, DOCTOR? In WORLD BOOK, see AQUARIUM; ZOO.

World Book Supplement

1974
1976
1977
1978
1979

To help WORLD BOOK owners keep their
encyclopedia up to date, the following new
or revised articles are reprinted from the 1980
edition of the encyclopedia.

See "Dinosaur," page 536.

Dinosaurs of the Jurassic Period (180 million to 130 million years ago) included the longest known dinosaur, the 90-foot (27-meter) diplodocus, *above right*. Other dinosaurs included the plated stegosaurus, *upper left*, the allosaurus, *center*, and the camptosaurus, *lower right*.

DINOSAUR

DINOSAUR was a reptile that lived millions of years ago. The word *dinosaur* comes from two Greek words meaning *terrible lizard*. Dinosaurs were not lizards. But the size of some dinosaurs was terrifying. The biggest ones were the largest animals ever to live on land. They weighed more than 10 times as much as a full-grown elephant. Only a few kinds of whales grow to be larger than these dinosaurs.

The first dinosaurs appeared on the earth more than 200 million years ago. For nearly 140 million years, they ruled the land. They lived in most parts of the world and in a variety of surroundings, from swamps to open plains. Then about 65 million years ago, dinosaurs died out rather suddenly.

Dinosaurs varied greatly in size, appearance, and habits. But the most famous kinds include such giants

Peter Dodson, the contributor of this article, is Assistant Professor of Anatomy at the School of Veterinary Medicine of the University of Pennsylvania. The paintings and diagrams were prepared for WORLD BOOK *by Alex Ebel.*

as the apatosaurus, diplodocus, and tyrannosaurus rex. Apatosaurs, also called brontosaurs, grew about 80 feet (24 meters) long. The diplodocus grew even longer—to about 90 feet (27 meters). Both the apatosaurus and the diplodocus were plant-eaters. They had a tiny head and an extremely long neck and tail. Tyrannosaurs were fierce meat-eaters. They stood almost 10 feet (3 meters) tall at the hips and had an enormous head and long, pointed teeth. But not all dinosaurs were giants. The smallest kind was about the size of a chicken.

In some ways, dinosaurs were like most present-day reptiles. For example, some had teeth, bones, and skin like those of crocodiles and other reptiles living today. Many probably were also about as intelligent as crocodiles. But dinosaurs differed from present-day reptiles in other ways. For example, no modern reptiles grow as large as large dinosaurs. Another important difference is in posture. The legs of lizards, turtles, and most other reptiles are pushed out to the sides of the body. The structure of the legs gives the animals a sprawling posture. But a dinosaur's legs were under the body like the legs of a horse. This leg structure lifted the dinosaur's body off the ground and enabled some kinds to walk on their hind legs.

Dinosaurs of the Cretaceous Period (130 million to 65 million years ago) included the tyrannosaurus rex, *upper left*, and the horned triceratops. Two anatosauruses stand in the foreground. Flowering plants appeared during this period, and opossums, snakes, and lizards were common.

Dinosaurs lived during a time in the earth's history called the *Mesozoic Era.* This era lasted from about 225 million to 65 million years ago. The Mesozoic Era is also called the *Age of Reptiles* because reptiles ruled the land, sea, and sky during that time. The most important reptiles belonged to a group of animals called *archosaurs* (ruling reptiles). In addition to dinosaurs, this group included *thecodonts,* the ancestors of the dinosaurs; crocodiles; and flying reptiles. By the close of the Mesozoic Era, all archosaurs except crocodiles had died out, and the Age of Reptiles ended.

Scientists do not know why dinosaurs disappeared. For many years, they thought that dinosaurs had left no *descendants* (offspring). But scientists now believe that certain small meat-eating dinosaurs were the ancestors of birds.

Scientists learn about dinosaurs by studying dinosaur *fossils*—that is, the preserved bones, teeth, eggs, and tracks of dinosaurs. They also study living reptiles and other animals that resemble dinosaurs in some ways.

The World of the Dinosaurs

When dinosaurs lived, the earth was much different from the way it is today. For example, the Alps, the Himalaya, and many other surface features had not yet been formed. The first flowering plants did not appear until late in the Mesozoic Era. The mammals of the Mesozoic Era were extremely small, and many of the plants and animals that were common then are now rare or extinct.

The Land and Climate. Scientists believe that the continents once formed a single land mass surrounded by an enormous sea. During the Mesozoic Era, this land mass began to break up into continents. The continents slowly drifted apart toward their present locations (see CONTINENTAL DRIFT). But for many centuries, dinosaurs could wander freely over the land connections between continents.

As the continents moved apart, their surface features and climate changed. For a time, shallow seas covered much of North America, Europe, and southern Asia. Thick forests bordered drier plains, and swamps and deltas lined the seacoasts. Later in the Mesozoic Era, the Rocky Mountains began to form, and the seas drained from North America.

Throughout much of the Mesozoic Era, dinosaurs probably lived in an almost tropical climate. Areas near the seas may have had mild, moist weather all year.

DINOSAUR

Inland regions probably had an annual dry season. Toward the end of the Mesozoic Era, the climate grew cooler and drier.

Plant and Animal Life also changed during the Mesozoic Era. During the first half of the era, cone-bearing trees were the most common plants. Other plant life consisted mainly of cycads, ferns, mosses, and tree ferns. Land animals, in addition to dinosaurs, included crocodiles, frogs, insects, lizards, and a few kinds of small mammals. Reptiles called *ichthyosaurs* and *plesiosaurs* lived in the seas, along with such animals as clams, corals, jellyfish, snails, sponges, squids, starfish, and sharks and other fish. Winged reptiles called *pterosaurs* flew on batlike wings.

By the end of the Age of Reptiles, flowering plants had become common. Trees of the forests included cypresses, ginkgoes, maples, oaks, palms, poplars, and redwoods. Birds had developed, and the first snakes appeared. Sea animals included modern fish, plus 12-foot (3.7-meter) sardines, huge turtles, and gigantic lizards called *mosasaurs*.

Kinds of Dinosaurs

Scientists divide the dinosaurs into two major groups: (1) saurischians and (2) ornithischians. The two groups differed in the structure of the hips. Saurischians, whose name means *lizard hipped*, had a hip structure much like that of lizards. Ornithischians, whose name means *bird hipped*, had a birdlike hip structure. Each of the two groups consisted of several basic kinds of dinosaurs.

Some kinds of dinosaurs lived throughout the Mesozoic Era. Other kinds lived during only one or two of the three *periods* into which the era is divided. The three periods are the *Triassic*, the *Jurassic*, and the *Cretaceous*. The Triassic Period lasted from about 225 million to 180 million years ago. The Jurassic Period lasted from about 180 million to 130 million years ago. The Cretaceous Period lasted from about 130 million to 65 million years ago.

Saurischians included the largest and fiercest dinosaurs. There were three basic kinds of saurischians: (1) prosauropods, (2) sauropods, and (3) theropods. Each of these groups included many variations.

Prosauropods, such as the plateosaurus, grew about 20 feet (6 meters) long and had a long neck and a small head. Prosauropods walked on their two hind legs sometimes and on all four legs at other times. They were the first common plant-eating dinosaurs. They appeared about 200 million years ago and apparently died out early in the Jurassic Period.

Sauropods were the giants of the dinosaur world. They averaged about 70 feet (21 meters) long and stood 12 to 15 feet (3.7 to 4.8 meters) tall at the hips. Most adults weighed from 10 to 30 short tons (9 to 27 metric tons). Sauropods walked on four heavy legs like those of an elephant. A typical sauropod had a long neck, a small head, a long tail, and a huge, deep chest. Sauropods were the main plant-eaters of the Jurassic Period. During the Cretaceous Period, other plant-eaters became more important.

One of the best-known sauropods is the apatosaurus, or brontosaurus. For many people, the word *dinosaur* brings to mind the image of an apatosaurus. The animal's front legs were shorter than its hind legs, and its back sloped down toward the base of the neck. The diplodocus, the longest dinosaur known, looked much like an apatosaurus but was slimmer and lighter. The diplodocus grew as long as 90 feet (27 meters). Both the apatosaurus and the diplodocus lived during the Jurassic Period in what is now North America.

The largest known dinosaur was the brachiosaurus, which lived in many parts of the world during the Jurassic Period. Brachiosaurs stood about 40 feet (12 meters) tall and weighed up to 85 short tons (77 metric

Kinds of Dinosaurs Scientists divide dinosaurs into two major groups—*saurischians* and *ornithischians*—according to the structure of the hips. Saurischians, such as the allosaurus, had a hip structure much like that of lizards. Ornithischians, such as the corythosaurus, had a birdlike hip structure.

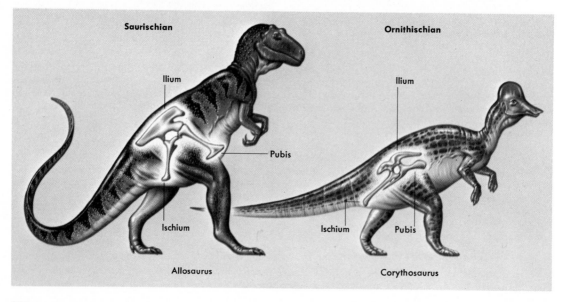

Saurischian

Ilium

Pubis

Ischium

Allosaurus

Ornithischian

Ilium

Ischium

Pubis

Corythosaurus

tons). Their front legs were longer than the back ones. The animals stood like giraffes, with the back sloping down toward the tail.

Theropods were the only meat-eating dinosaurs. The animals walked upright on two hind legs. Typical theropods had a long, muscular tail, which they carried straight out behind them for balance. Their forelimbs were slender. Large theropods had a short neck and a large, long head. Small theropods had a long neck and a smaller head. Theropods had powerful jaws and blade-like teeth. They lived throughout the Mesozoic Era.

The fierce tyrannosaurus rex is the best-known thero-pod. The name *tyrannosaurus rex* means *tyrant-lizard king*, and the tyrannosaurus was the most feared meat-eater of its time. Tyrannosaurs stood nearly 10 feet (3 meters) high at the hips and grew about 40 feet (12 meters) long. Their head measured up to 4 feet (1.2 meters) in length, and their teeth were about 6 inches (15 centimeters) long. The animals had very short fore-limbs, which probably were almost useless. Each fore-limb had two fingers. Tyrannosaurs ruled the land near the end of the Age of Reptiles. A few tyrannosaurus fossils have been discovered in North America.

About 140 million years ago, long before tyranno-saurs appeared, allosaurs were the main meat-eating dinosaurs. They resembled tyrannosaurs but were not quite as large. Allosaurs also had longer forelimbs with three fingers on each. Smaller theropods included the deinonychus and the ornithomimus. The deinonychus was about 3 feet (0.9 meter) tall. On each foot, it had a large curved claw, which probably was used to slash at prey. The ornithomimus looked much like a featherless ostrich and was about the size of an ostrich. Theropods also included the smallest known dinosaur, the comp-sognathus. It was about the size of a chicken.

Ornithischians were plant-eaters. They had a beak-like bone in front of their teeth, and many had bony plates in their skin. During the Cretaceous Period, ornithischians became the most important plant-eating dinosaurs. There were four basic kinds of ornithischians. They were, in order of their appearance on the earth: (1) ornithopods, (2) stegosaurs, (3) ankylosaurs, and (4) ceratopsians. Each group of ornithischians included numerous variations.

Ornithopods walked on two hind legs. The first dino-saur fossil discovered was that of an iguanodon, a kind of ornithopod. Iguanodons measured about 30 feet (9 meters) long. The animals had a bony spike on the thumb of each forelimb. Ornithopods lived throughout the Age of Reptiles.

Ornithopods reached their greatest development in duckbilled dinosaurs, or hadrosaurs. Duckbills were the most numerous dinosaurs of the Cretaceous Period. They lived in what are now Asia and North America. They had a flat, toothless beak like the bill of a duck, strong hind legs, and long, slender front legs with webbed toes. Duckbills grew up to 9 feet (2.7 meters) tall at the hips and more than 30 feet (9 meters) long.

Some kinds of duckbills, such as the anatosaurus, had a low, flat skull. Other kinds, such as the corythosaurus, had a showy, bony *crest* (growth) on the top of the head. Air passages from the animal's nose traveled through the crest. Some scientists believe that the crested duck-bills may have made honking sounds by using the air passages much like a trumpet.

When Dinosaurs Lived

Dinosaurs lived during the Mesozoic Era, which lasted from about 225 million to 65 million years ago. The era is divided into three periods—the Triassic, the Jurassic, and the Cretaceous. Some kinds of dinosaurs lived throughout the Mesozoic Era. Others lived during only one or two periods.

| Corals and mollusks were common. Fish appeared. Land was bare. | Algae were plentiful. | Spore-bearing plants appeared on land. | Forests developed, and insects and amphibians appeared. | Mosses developed. Reptiles appeared. |

Paleozoic Era (600 million to 225 million years ago)

Triassic Period
(225 million to 180 million years ago)

Scelidosaurus
12 feet (3.7 meters) long

Jurassic Period
(180 million to 130 million years ago)

Stegosaurus
20 feet (6 meters) long

Plateosaurus
20 feet
(6 meters) long

Apatosaurus
80 feet (24 meters) long

Ornitholestes
6 feet
(1.8 meters) long

Heterodontosaurus
3½ feet
(1.1 meters) long

Procompsognathus
3 feet
(0.9 meter) long

Brachiosaurus
80 feet
(24 meters) long

6 feet
(1.8 meters)

Seed plants developed.	Dinosaurs and mammals appeared.	Birds appeared.	Flowering plants developed.	Dinosaurs died out.	Fruits, grains, and grasses developed.	Early human beings appeared.

Mesozoic Era (225 million to 65 million years ago)	Cenozoic Era (65 million years ago to the present)

Cretaceous Period
(130 million to 65 million years ago)

Corythosaurus
30 feet (9 meters) long

Iguanodon
30 feet
(9 meters) long

Camptosaurus
15 feet (4.8 meters) long

Torosaurus
30 feet
(9 meters) long

Compsognathus
2½ feet
(0.8 meter) long

Allosaurus
30 feet
(9 meters) long

Deinonychus
9 feet (2.7 meters) long

Ankylosaurus
15 feet (4.8 meters) long

Tyrannosaurus rex
40 feet (12 meters) long

Ornithomimus
14 feet (4.3 meters) long

541

For example, a lizard's body temperature rises as the air becomes warmer. If the air cools, the lizard loses body heat. Endothermic animals have a constant, fairly warm body temperature. Such animals tend to be more active than those whose temperature varies.

Scientists disagree on whether dinosaurs were ectothermic or endothermic. Traditionally, dinosaurs were considered to be ectothermic. But many scientists now believe that they must have been endothermic to keep up their level of activity. Other experts point out, however, that large animals lose body heat very slowly. Dinosaurs could therefore have had a warm, constant body temperature and been fairly active even if they were ectothermic.

Reproduction and Growth. Scientists do not know how all dinosaur species reproduced. However, fossil dinosaur eggs have been discovered. Therefore, at least some kinds of dinosaurs laid eggs, as do most other reptiles. The female may have scratched a nest in the soil and deposited several eggs in it. Some dinosaurs may have cared for their young after they hatched. Others probably left them to survive as best they could.

Scientists can only guess how old dinosaurs lived to be. They can estimate the time it took for dinosaurs to grow to adult size. But they do not know how long the animals lived after reaching that size. The growth rate depends on whether dinosaurs were endothermic or ectothermic. Endothermic animals grow more rapidly than do ectothermic ones. If apatosaurs were endothermic, for example, it probably took them about 50 years to reach their adult weight of about 30 short tons (27 metric tons). If the animals were ectothermic, however, it may have taken them 200 years or longer to grow that large.

Group Life. Fossil evidence shows that more than 20 kinds of dinosaurs may have occupied a particular area at the same time. Many kinds, including ceratopsians, duckbills, and stegosaurs, lived in herds. Other kinds, such as apatosaurs and tyrannosaurs, probably spent most of their life alone.

Some experts think that dinosaurs, like many modern birds and reptiles, were colorful animals. Some kinds of dinosaurs perhaps attracted mates by displaying brightly colored body parts. For example, a duckbill's head crest and a ceratopsian's neck frill may have been vividly colored and so served to attract mates.

Getting Food. Sauropods may have waded into shallow lakes and swamps to eat water plants. Or they may have eaten tree leaves, as did duckbills. Ankylosaurs, ceratopsians, and stegosaurs fed on low plants that grew along shorelines or on open plains.

Allosaurs, tyrannosaurs, and other large theropods may have been hunters that preyed mainly on the huge plant-eating dinosaurs. Or these giant meat-eaters, like some other theropods, might have been *scavengers* and picked meat from dead animals they found. Some small theropods ate insects or eggs. Others hunted mammals or small dinosaurs and other reptiles. These small theropods were probably very active and could run quickly. Some of them, including the fierce deinonychus, may have hunted in packs as wolves do today.

Protection Against Enemies. Plant-eating dinosaurs had many forms of protection against theropods. The huge size of sauropods probably protected them from most predators. Ankylosaurs had bony plates for protection, and ceratopsians and stegosaurs probably used their horns and spikes to fight off enemies. Duckbills could swim into deep water to avoid attack.

Why Dinosaurs Died Out

For almost 140 million years, dinosaurs ruled the land, and other large reptiles ruled the sky and sea. Then about 65 million years ago, these huge reptiles died out and mammals took over the earth.

Scientists have developed many theories to explain the disappearance of dinosaurs and the other great reptiles. Probably the most widely accepted theory involves a change in the earth's climate. Toward the end of the Cretaceous Period, the climate cooled and may have become too cold for the dinosaurs. Dinosaurs were too large to hibernate in dens, and they had no fur or feathers for protection against the cold. Smaller animals could hibernate during cold periods. Mammals and birds had fur or feathers for protection, and some could migrate to warmer places to avoid the cold weather. In these ways, such animals could survive the cold that may eventually have killed off the dinosaurs.

Another theory also involves changes in the climate. Some scientists believe that the explosion of a nearby star gave off dangerous radiation and caused cold, unfavorable weather on the earth for thousands of years. Dinosaurs could not avoid the radiation and the cold and probably were killed off by them.

Some experts believe that plant-eating dinosaurs could not eat the new kinds of plants that developed during the Cretaceous Period and thus starved. As they died off, so did the meat-eaters that preyed on them. Other experts think that the dinosaurs could not compete successfully with mammals for food and so lost the struggle for existence.

No one theory completely explains why dinosaurs died out. It seems that dinosaurs simply could not keep up with the changes that were occurring on the earth toward the end of the Cretaceous Period. Thus, a combination of causes may have contributed to the end of the Age of Reptiles.

Learning About Dinosaurs

Scientists have many ways of learning about dinosaurs. One important way is by studying dinosaur fossils. For example, a dinosaur tooth can tell an expert whether the animal ate plants or meat. Scientists who study fossils are called *paleontologists*. Scientists also learn about dinosaurs by observing animals that have traits similar to those of dinosaurs. For example, they might study elephants and hippopotamuses in the wild to learn about the lives of large land animals.

Dinosaur Discoveries. Before the 1800's, no one knew that dinosaurs had ever existed. People who found a dinosaur tooth or bone did not realize what it was. Then in 1822, the wife of an English physician named Gideon Mantell found a large tooth partly buried in a rock. She showed the tooth to her husband, who collected fossils. Mantell learned that the tooth resembled that of a South American lizard called an *iguana*. He suggested that the tooth came from a huge, iguanalike reptile, which he named *iguanodon* (iguana tooth).

Within a few years, the remains of several other kinds

Field Museum of Natural History (WORLD BOOK photo)

University of Nebraska State Museum

Dinosaur Fossils include the preserved bones, teeth, and eggs of dinosaurs. Dinosaur bones and teeth can be fitted together to form a skeleton, such as the one of the apatosaurus at the left. The eggs shown above were laid about 80 million years ago by a protoceratops. They measure about 6 inches (15 centimeters) long.

of large, extinct reptiles had been discovered. In 1841, Sir Richard Owen, an English scientist, suggested that these reptiles belonged to a group of reptiles that were unlike any living animals. Owen called the group *Dinosauria*, and members of the group came to be known as dinosaurs.

During the late 1800's and early 1900's, large deposits of dinosaur remains were discovered in western North America, Europe, Asia, and Africa. One of these deposits lies in the Morrison Formation, a series of rock layers that extends across part of Colorado, Utah, and Wyoming. Perhaps the world's richest deposit is in the Red Deer River Valley of southern Alberta. Dinosaur deposits also lie in Belgium, Mongolia, Tanzania, West Germany, and many other parts of the world.

Working with Dinosaur Fossils. Museums and other educational institutions sponsor scientists who search for and study dinosaur fossils. Paleontologists look for fossils in areas where wind and water have worn away the land and exposed deep, fossil-bearing layers of rock. After they locate a skeleton, paleontologists remove the rock above it. In many cases, they dig out the portion of rock that contains the fossil. Then they cover the rock and fossil with cloth and plaster of Paris. The plaster dries into a hard, protective coating, and the fossil is shipped to a laboratory.

At the laboratory, workers clean the bones and teeth and repair broken ones. Specialists may then rebuild the skeleton by putting the bones together on a metal frame. In some cases, missing bones may be replaced with pieces made from fiberglass, plaster, or plastic. Scientists rarely discover all the bones of a large dinosaur, and so they estimate the animal's length based on the bones that have been found.

Some museums make models of dinosaurs for display. Experts study the skeleton and try to imagine how it looked covered with muscles and skin. They then build a metal frame that resembles the skeleton and mold wire and screen around it to shape the dinosaur's body.

Finally, they cover the model with "skin" and paint it to look realistic. PETER DODSON

Related Articles. For additional information and pictures of dinosaurs, see PREHISTORIC ANIMAL. Other related articles in WORLD BOOK include:

American Museum of
  Natural History
Andrews, Roy Chapman
Dinosaur National
  Monument

Earth
Fossil
Paleontology
Pterodactyl
Reptile

Outline

I. **The World of the Dinosaurs**
  A. The Land and Climate
  B. Plant and Animal Life
II. **Kinds of Dinosaurs**
  A. Saurischians
  B. Ornithischians
III. **How Dinosaurs Lived**
  A. Reproduction and Growth
  B. Group Life
  C. Getting Food
  D. Protection Against Enemies
IV. **Why Dinosaurs Died Out**
V. **Learning About Dinosaurs**
  A. Dinosaur Discoveries
  B. Working with Dinosaur Fossils

Questions

How did sauropods get food?

What are some theories that scientists have developed to explain why dinosaurs died out?

What were some kinds of dinosaurs that probably lived in herds?

In what kind of area do paleontologists look for dinosaur fossils?

What were the two major groups of dinosaurs? How did they differ?

Which dinosaurs were meat-eaters?

Which was the largest known dinosaur?

Why is the Mesozoic Era also called the *Age of Reptiles?*

Where have some of the most important dinosaur fossil deposits been discovered?

What kinds of animals besides dinosaurs lived during the Age of Reptiles?

Scenic Limestone Hills near the city of Kuei-lin in southern China are among the most unusual features of China's vast and varied countryside. Only Russia and Canada have more land than China.

CHINA

CHINA is a huge country in eastern Asia. It is the world's largest country in population and the third largest in area. About a fifth of all the people in the world live in China. The country covers more than a fifth of Asia. Only Russia and Canada have more territory. China's vast land area includes some of the world's driest deserts, highest mountains, and richest farmland.

The Chinese call their country *Chung-kuo*, which means *Middle Country*. This name may have come into being because the ancient Chinese thought of their country as both the geographical center of the world and the only truly cultured civilization. The name *China* was given to the country by foreigners. It may have come from *Ch'in*, the name of an early Chinese *dynasty* (series of rulers from the same family).

Most of the Chinese people live crowded together in the eastern third of the country. This region has most of China's major cities and nearly all the land suitable for farming. Agriculture has always been the chief economic activity in China. About 85 per cent of the people live in rural villages, and about three-fourths of all workers are farmers. Although only a small percentage

The seven contributors of this article are all members of the staff of the Center for Chinese Studies at the University of Michigan. The contributors are Robert F. Dernberger, Professor of Economics; Norma Diamond, Professor of Anthropology; Richard Edwards, Professor of Chinese Art; Albert Feuerwerker, Professor of History; Donald J. Munro, Professor of Philosophy; Rhoads Murphey, Professor of Geography; and William Pang-yu Ting, Assistant Professor of Political Science.

of the people live in urban areas, China has several of the largest cities in the world. They include Shanghai, with more than 10 million persons; and Peking, China's capital, with over 7 million persons.

China has the world's oldest living civilization. Its written history goes back about 3,500 years. The Chinese people take great pride in their nation, its long history, and its influence on other countries. The Chi-

---
FACTS IN BRIEF

Capital: Peking.

Official Language: Chinese (Northern dialect).

Form of Government: Communist dictatorship.

Area: 3,678,470 sq. mi. (9,527,200 km²). *Greatest Distances* —north-south, 2,500 mi. (4,023 km); east-west, 3,000 mi. (4,828 km). *Coastline*—4,019 mi. (6,468 km), including 458 mi. (737 km) for Hai-nan Island.

Elevation: *Highest*—Mount Everest, 29,028 ft. (8,848 m); *Lowest*—Turfan Depression, 505 ft. (154 m) below sea level.

Population: *Estimated 1980 Population*—893,873,000 (based on UN data); distribution, 85 per cent rural, 15 per cent urban; density, 243 persons per sq. mi. (94 per km²). *1953 Census*—582,603,417. *Chinese Government Estimate for 1978*—958,000,000. *Estimated 1985 Population*—972,200,000 (based on UN data).

Chief Products: *Agriculture*—rice, wheat, cotton, corn, tea, tobacco, sorghum, hogs, barley, millet, peanuts, potatoes, sheep, soybeans, sweet potatoes. *Manufacturing*—iron and steel, machinery, textiles, chemicals. *Mining*—coal, iron ore, petroleum, tungsten, antimony, tin, lead, manganese, and salt.

National Anthem: "March of the Volunteers."

Money: *Basic Unit*—yuan. For its price in U.S. dollars, see MONEY (table: Exchange Rates). See also YUAN.

544

Björn Klingwall

Crowded Street Scenes like this one in Shanghai are common sights in China, which has more people than any other country.

Shostal

Farming is the leading economic activity in China. About three-fourths of all Chinese workers are farmers.

Henry Weaver, Lensman

China's Artistic Heritage goes back many centuries. This superb sculpture stands outside the old imperial palace in Peking.

nese were the first people to develop the compass, gunpowder, paper, porcelain, and silk cloth. Over the centuries, Japan, Korea, Vietnam, and other Asian lands have borrowed from Chinese art, language, literature, religion, and technology.

In early times, the Chinese people were divided into many small states. In 221 B.C., the Ch'in dynasty established an empire with a strong central government. This empire lasted in some form for more than 2,000 years. During those years, Chinese society survived wars, rebellions, and the rise and fall of numerous dynasties. The Chinese developed an increasingly powerful and efficient system of government, built great cities, and created magnificent works of literature and art. From time to time, nomadic invaders conquered all or part of China. However, these invaders had little effect on Chinese civilization.

During the 1800's, the Chinese empire began to weaken. In 1911, revolutionaries overthrew the empire. The next year, China became a republic. But the *Kuomintang* (Nationalist Party), which ruled the republic, never established an effective government. In 1949, the Chinese Communist Party, led by Mao Tse-tung, defeated the Nationalists and set up China's present government. The Communists gave the nation the official name *Chung-hua Jen-min Kung-ho-kuo* (People's Republic of China). The Nationalists fled to the island of Taiwan, where they reestablished their own government. This article discusses only the People's Republic of China. For information about the Republic of China, which is ruled by the Nationalists on Taiwan, see the article TAIWAN.

China has gone through many major changes under the Communists. Industry has been placed under state ownership and direction. The government also controls trade and finance. Agricultural land is owned and farmed by large groups of peasants rather than by individual families as in the past. The Communists have dramatically increased industrial production and have expanded and improved education and medical care. The supply of food for China's people is generally sufficient though not plentiful. Nevertheless, China remains a poor country by world standards. The Communist Party and the government are making major efforts to overcome that poverty and modernize China by the year 2000.

WORLD BOOK map

China lies in eastern Asia. It covers more than a fifth of Asia and borders 11 other countries and the North Pacific Ocean.

545

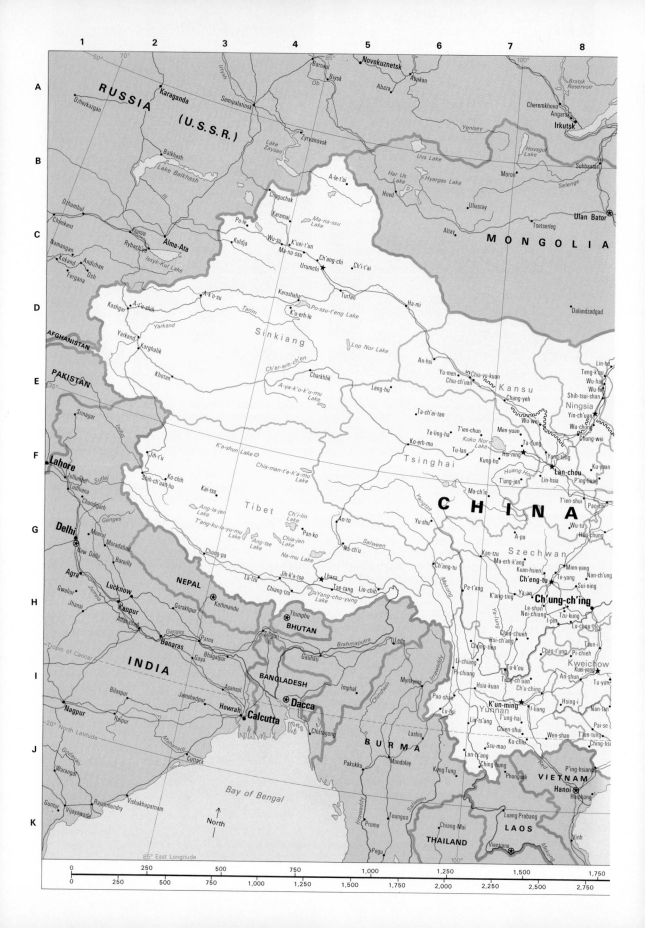

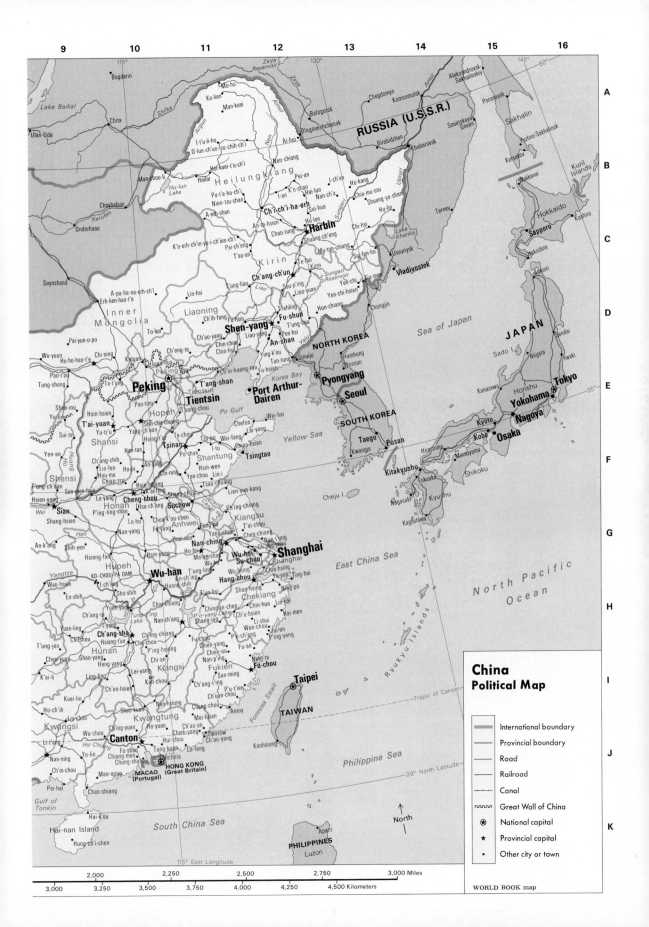

China
Political Map

▬▬▬	International boundary
▬▬	Provincial boundary
—	Road
—	Railroad
┼┼┼	Canal
∿∿∿	Great Wall of China
⊛	National capital
★	Provincial capital
•	Other city or town

WORLD BOOK map

China Map Index

Provinces

Map Name Key	Population	Area in sq. mi.	in km²	Capital
G 11 Anhwei	45,000,000	54,016	139,900	Ho-fei
H 12 Chekiang	36,000,000	39,305	101,800	Hang-chou
I 11 Fukien	24,000,000	47,529	123,100	Fu-chou
B 12 Heilung-kiang	32,000,000	274,000	710,000	Harbin
G 10 Honan	60,000,000	64,480	167,000	Cheng-chou
E 10 Hopeh	40,000,000	73,750	191,000	Shih-chia-chuang
I 9 Hunan	50,000,000	81,275	210,500	Ch'ang-sha
G 10 Hupeh	45,000,000	72,394	187,500	Wu-han
E 7 Kansu	18,000,000	205,000	530,000	Lan-chou
I 10 Kiangsi	28,000,000	63,630	164,800	Nan-ch'ang
G 11 Kiangsu	55,000,000	39,460	102,200	Nan-ching
C 12 Kirin	23,000,000	112,000	290,000	Ch'ang-ch'un
J 10 Kwangtung	50,000,000	84,900	220,000	Canton
I 8 Kweichow	25,000,000	67,180	174,000	Kuei-yang
D 11 Liaoning	36,000,000	88,800	230,000	Shen-yang
F 10 Shansi	23,000,000	60,657	157,100	T'ai-yuan
F 11 Shantung	72,000,000	59,189	153,300	Tsinan
F 9 Shensi	27,000,000	75,599	195,800	Sian
G 7 Szechwan	90,000,000	219,700	569,000	Ch'eng-tu
F 6 Tsinghai	3,000,000	278,400	721,000	Hsi-ning
I 7 Yunnan	30,000,000	168,420	436,200	K'un-ming

Autonomous Regions

Map Name Key	Population	Area in sq. mi.	in km²	Capital
D 10 Inner Mongolia	8,000,000	174,000	450,000	Hu-ho-hao-t'e
J 9 Kwangsi	32,000,000	88,800	230,000	Nan-ning
E 8 Ningsia	3,000,000	65,600	170,000	Yin-ch'uan
D 4 Sinkiang	11,000,000	635,833	1,646,800	Urumchi
G 4 Tibet	2,000,000	471,662	1,221,600	Lhasa

Special Municipalities

Map Name Key	Population	Area in sq. mi.	in km²
E 10 Peking	7,570,000	6,873	17,800
G 12 Shanghai	10,820,000	2,240	5,800
E 11 Tientsin	4,280,000	4,250	11,000

Population*

Year	Population
1985	972,200,000
1980	893,873,000
1975	830,491,000
1970	759,620,000
1965	695,000,000
1960	635,950,000
1955	582,340,000
1953	582,603,417
1950	532,870,000
1945	453,615,000
1912	353,260,000
1851	431,896,000
1776	268,238,000
1578	60,693,000
1491	53,281,000
1391	56,875,000
742	51,500,000
140	49,150,000
A.D. 2	57,671,000

Cities and Towns

Amoy . . . . . 100,000-300,000 . . I 11
An-ch'ing . 100,000-300,000 . . H 11
An-shan . . 300,000-1,000,000 . . D 12
An-shun . . . 50,000-100,000 . . I 8
An-yang . . 100,000-300,000 . . F 10
Canton . . 1,840,000 . . J 10
Chan-chiang 100,000-300,000 . . J 9
Chang-chou 100,000-300,000 . . I 11
Ch'ang-chou 100,000-300,000 . . G 12
Ch'ang-ch'un 1,000,000- . . C 12
Ch'ang-sha 300,000-1,000,000 . . H 10
Ch'ang-te . 100,000-300,000 . . H 9

Chao-tung . 50,000-100,000 . . C 12
Ch'ao-yang 100,000-300,000 . . D 11
Chefoo . . . . 100,000-300,000 . . E 12
Chen-chiang 300,000-1,000,000 . . G 11
Cheng-chou 300,000-1,000,000 . . F 10
Ch'eng-te . 50,000-100,000 . . E 11
Ch'eng-tu 1,107,000 . . H 8
Chia-hsing . 50,000-100,000 . . G 12
Chia-mu-ssu 100,000-300,000 . . B 13
Chi-an . . . 100,000-300,000 . . I 10
Chiang-men 100,000-300,000 . . J 10
Chiao-tso . 100,000-300,000 . . F 10
Ch'i-ch'i-ha-erh 300,000-1,000,000 . . C 12
Ch'ih-feng . 50,000-100,000 . . D 11
Chi-hsi . . 100,000-300,000 . . C 13
Chin-chou . 300,000-1,000,000 . . D 11
Ch'ing-chiang 100,000-300,000 . . G 11
Ching-te-chen 100,000-300,000 . . H 11
Chin-hsi . . 50,000-100,000 . . E 11
Ch'in-huang-tao 100,000-300,000 . . E 11
Chi-ning . . 100,000-300,000 . . F 11
Chi-ning . . 50,000-100,000 . . E 10

Chiu-chiang 100,000-300,000 . . H 11
Ch'uan-chou 100,000-300,000 . . I 11
Chu-chou . 100,000-300,000 H 10
Ch'ung-ch'ing 2,121,000 . . H 8
Dairen, see Port Arthur-Dairen
Foochow, see Fu-chou
Fo-shan . . 100,000- . . J 10
Fu-chou (Foochow) 1,000,000- . . I 12
Fu-hsien . . 100,000-300,000 . . E 12
Fu-hsin . . 300,000-1,000,000 . . D 12
Fu-shun . . 300,000-1,000,000 . . D 12
Fu-yang . . 50,000-100,000 . . G 10
Hai-k'ou . . 100,000-300,000 . . K 9
Hailar . . . . 100,000-300,000 . . B 11
Ha-mi . . . . 50,000-100,000 . . D 6
Han-chung . 50,000-100,000 . . G 8
Hang-chou 300,000-1,000,000 . . H 12
Han-tan . . 300,000-1,000,000 . . F 10
Harbin 1,552,000 . . C 12
Heng-yang 300,000-1,000,000 . . I 10
Ho-fei . . . 300,000-1,000,000 . . G 11
Ho-kang . . 100,000-300,000 . . B 13
Ho-pi . . . . 100,000-300,000 . . F 10
Hsiang-fan 100,000-300,000 . . G 10
Hsiang-t'an 300,000-1,000,000 . . H 10
Hsien-yang 100,000-300,000 . . G 9
Hsing-t'ai 100,000-300,000 . . F 10
Hsin-hsiang 100,000-300,000 . . F 10
Hsi-ning . . 100,000-300,000 . . F 7
Hsin-wen . . 50,000-100,000 . . F 11
Hsin-yang 100,000-300,000 . . G 10
Hsuan-hua 100,000-300,000 . . E 10
Hsu-ch'ang 100,000-300,000 . . G 10
Huai-nan . 300,000-1,000,000 . . G 11
Huang-shih 100,000-300,000 . . H 10
Hu-ho-hao-t'e 300,000-1,000,000 . . E 9
Hu-lan . . . 50,000-100,000 . . C 12
Hun-chiang 50,000-100,000 . . D 12
I-ch'ang . . 100,000-300,000 . . H 9
I-ch'un . . . 50,000-100,000 . . B 13
I-pin . . . . 100,000-300,000 . . H 8
I-tu . . . . . 50,000-100,000 . . F 11
I-yang . . . 100,000-300,000 . . H 10
K'ai-feng . 300,000-1,000,000 . . F 10
Kalgan . . 100,000-300,000 . . F 10
Kan-chou . 100,000-300,000 . . I 10
Karamai . . 50,000-100,000 . . C 4
Kashgar . . 50,000-100,000 . . D 2
Kirin . . . . 300,000-1,000,000 . . C 12

Ko-chiu . . 50,000-100,000 . . J 7
K'o-erh-ch'in-yu-i-ch'ien-ch'i . . . . . . 50,000-100,000 . . C 11
Kuei-lin . . 100,000-300,000 . . I 9
Kuei-yang 1,000,000- . . I 8
Kuldja . . . 50,000-100,000 . . C 3
K'un-ming 300,000-1,000,000 . . I 7
Lan-chou . 1,000,000- . . F 8
Le-shan . . 50,000-100,000 . . H 8
Lhasa . . . . 50,000-100,000 . . H 4
Liao-yang 100,000-300,000 . . D 12
Liao-yuan 300,000-1,000,000 . . D 12
Lien-yun-kang 100,000-300,000 . . F 11
Lin-hsia . . 50,000-100,000 . . F 7
Liu-chou . 300,000-1,000,000 . . J 9
Lo-yang . . 300,000-1,000,000 . . F 10
Lu-chou . . 100,000-300,000 . . H 8
Ma-an-shan 100,000-300,000 . . G 11
Mao-ming . 100,000-300,000 . . J 9
Mien-yang 50,000-100,000 . . G 8
Mukden, see Shen-yang
Mu-tan-chiang 300,000-1,000,000 . . C 13
Nan-ch'a . 50,000-100,000 . . B 13
Nan-ch'ang 300,000-1,000,000 . . H 11
Nan-ching (Nanking) 1,419,000 . . G 11
Nan-ch'ung 100,000-300,000 . . H 8
Nanking, see Nan-ching
Nan-ning . 300,000-1,000,000 . . J 9
Nan-t'ung 100,000-300,000 . . G 12
Nan-yang . 100,000-300,000 . . G 10
Nei-chiang 300,000-1,000,000 . . H 8
Nen-chiang 50,000-100,000 . . B 12
Ning-po . . 100,000-300,000 . . H 12
Pai-ch'eng 100,000-300,000 . . C 12
Pao-chi . . 100,000-300,000 . . G 8
Pao-ting . . 300,000-1,000,000 . . E 10
Pao-t'ou . . 300,000-1,000,000 . . E 9
Pei-an . . . 50,000-100,000 . . B 12
Pei-hai . . . 50,000-100,000 . . J 9
Peking . 7,570,000 . . E 10
Peng-pu . . 300,000-1,000,000 . . G 11
Pen-hsi . . 300,000-1,000,000 . . D 12
P'ing-hsiang 100,000-300,000 . . I 10
P'ing-ting-shan 100,000-300,000 . . G 10
Port Arthur-Dairen 1,508,000 . . E 12
Shanghai 10,820,000 . . G 12
Shao-hsing 100,000-300,000 . . H 12
Shao-kuan 100,000-300,000 . . I 10
Shao-yang 100,000-300,000 . . I 9
Sha-shih . . 100,000-300,000 . . H 10

Shen-yang (Mukden) 2,411,000 . . D 12
Shih-chia-chuang 300,000-1,000,000 . . E 10
Shuang-ya-shan 100,000-300,000 . . B 13
Sian . . . . 1,310,000 . . G 9
Soochow, see Su-chou
Ssu-p'ing . 100,000-300,000 . . D 12
Su-chou (Soochow) 300,000-1,000,000 . . G 12
Suchow . . 300,000-1,000,000 . . G 11
Sui-hua . . 50,000-100,000 . . C 12
Sui-ning . . 50,000-100,000 . . H 8
Swatow . . 300,000-1,000,000 . . J 11
T'ai-chou . 100,000-300,000 . . G 11
T'ai-yuan . 300,000-1,000,000 . . F 10
Tan-tung . 100,000-300,000 . . E 12
Ta-t'ung . . 300,000-1,000,000 . . E 10
Te-chou . . 50,000-100,000 . . F 10
Te-yang . . 50,000-100,000 . . H 8
T'ieh-ling . 50,000-100,000 . . D 12
T'ien-shui . 100,000-300,000 . . G 8
Tientsin 4,280,000 . . E 11
Ts'ang-chou 100,000-300,000 . . E 11
Tsinan 1,000,000- . . F 11
Tsingtao 1,121,000 . . F 11
Tsun-i . . . 100,000-300,000 . . I 8
Tu-k'ou . . 100,000-300,000 . . I 7
T'ung-ch'uan 50,000-100,000 . . F 9
T'ung-hua 300,000-1,000,000 . . D 12
T'ung-liao 50,000-100,000 . . D 12
T'ung-ling 100,000-300,000 . . G 11
T'un-hsi . . 50,000-100,000 . . H 11
Tu-yun . . . 50,000-100,000 . . I 8
Tzu-kung 300,000-1,000,000 . . H 8
Tzu-po . . . 50,000-100,000 . . F 11
Urumchi 1,000,000- . . C 4
Wan-hsien 100,000-300,000 . . H 9
Wei-fang . 100,000-300,000 . . F 11
Wen-chou (Yungkia) 300,000-1,000,000 . . H 12
Wu-chou . . 100,000-300,000 . . J 9
Wu-han . 2,146,000 . . H 10
Wu-hsi . . 300,000-1,000,000 . . G 12
Wu-hu . . . 300,000-1,000,000 . . G 11
Yang-chou 300,000-1,000,000 . . G 11
Yang-ch'uan 100,000-300,000 . . F 10
Yen-chi . . . 50,000-100,000 . . D 13
Yin-ch'uan 100,000-300,000 . . E 8
Ying-k'ou . 100,000-300,000 . . E 12
Yu-men . . 100,000-300,000 . . E 6
Yungkia, see Wen-chou
Yu-tz'u . . . 50,000-100,000 . . F 10

*Estimates, except 1953 census.
Sources: Total China populations from United Nations and John D. Durand, "The Population Statistics of China, A.D. 2-1953" from "Population Studies," March 1960; province populations from Chinese news services, 1975-1978; province areas from "Atlas of China," Map Publishing House, Peking, 1976, and "Handbook on Administrative Divisions of the People's Republic of China," Legal Publishing House, Peking, 1957; 1970 estimates for Peking, Shanghai, and Tientsin from "World Atlas," China Cartographic Institute, Peking, 1972; 1957 estimates for other large cities from State Statistical Bureau, Peking; population ranges for other places from "Atlas of the Provinces of the People's Republic of China," Map Publishing House, Peking, 1977.

CHINA/Government

China's Capitol is the Great
Hall of the People in Peking.
The National People's Congress
and other governmental bodies
meet in its huge chambers.

WORLD BOOK photo by Robert Borja

The Chinese government is dominated by three organizations. They are the Chinese Communist Party,
the military, and a branch of the government known as
the State Council. Almost all the leaders in the military
and the State Council also hold high positions in the
Communist Party. Thus, the party strictly controls the
political system. All persons who hold a middle-level or
lower-level position in the party or the government are
called *cadres.*

China adopted its present constitution in 1978. It
calls for the Chinese people to concentrate on modernizing agriculture, industry, the military, and science and
technology.

The Communist Party. China has the largest Communist Party in the world. About 35 million Chinese belong to the party. However, they make up only about
4 per cent of the country's total population. China also
has a number of minor political parties, but they have
little or no power.

The Communist Party's constitution states that the
National Party Congress is the organization's highest
decision-making body. The congress has about 2,000
representatives, selected by party members throughout
the nation. The congress actually has little power. In
general, it automatically approves national policies set
by the party's Central Committee and the *Politburo*
(Political Bureau).

The Central Committee consists of about 200 leading
party members. The Politburo is made up of about 25

China's Flag was adopted in
1949. The large star and four
small stars stand for the Communist Party and its members.

The State Emblem of China
is framed by wheat and rice,
the nation's leading agricultural products.

party leaders. The Politburo has a standing committee
consisting of the 5 or 6 highest party members. In
practice, this committee is the most powerful decision-
making body of the Communist Party. The chairman
of the party also serves as chairman of both the Politburo
and the Central Committee.

National Government. China's constitution estab-
lishes the National People's Congress as the highest
government authority. The Communist Party nominates all the candidates for membership in the congress.
The people elect representatives who choose the members from the party's list of candidates. The members
serve a five-year term. The congress carries out various
legislative duties. But in practice, it has no real power.
Its chief function is to transmit policies of the national
government and of the party to lower levels of govern-

Xinhua News Agency

The National People's
Congress performs legislative duties and transmits national government policies to
lower levels of government.
The Communist Party com-
pletely controls the congress.

ment. A standing committee handles the work of the congress when it is not in session.

The State Council carries on the day-to-day affairs of the government. The council is led by the premier, China's head of government. The National People's Congress approves the selection of the premier, who is nominated by the Central Committee of the Communist Party. About a dozen vice-premiers and approximately 30 ministers assist the premier. The ministers head the various government departments, including the defense ministry and the ministries responsible for economic planning.

Political Divisions. China has 29 major political divisions. They consist of 21 provinces; 5 *autonomous* (self-governing) regions; and 3 special municipalities. The autonomous regions are Inner Mongolia, Kwangsi, Ningsia, Sinkiang, and Tibet. These regions have many people who belong to non-Chinese ethnic groups. Although the regions are called autonomous, they are actually governed much like the rest of the nation. Local governments in these regions do have some powers to safeguard the culture and interests of the minority peoples. The special municipalities—Peking, Shanghai, and Tientsin—are huge metropolitan areas administered by the national government. Each consists of an urban center and a rural area.

China has three levels of local government. The 29 major political units are divided into about 2,300 counties. These counties are subdivided into more than 50,000 *communes* (rural areas) and towns. Each county, commune, and town has a people's congress and an executive body patterned after the State Council.

Courts in China do not function as an independent branch of government as they do in the United States and many other Western nations. Instead, the courts base their decisions on the policies of the Communist Party. But in the late 1970's, Chinese leaders began to draw up plans for a formal code of laws and an independent judicial system.

The highest court in China is the Supreme People's Court. It hears cases that involve national security or violations by high officials. It also supervises people's courts in the provinces and counties. The Supreme People's Procuratorate sees that the national constitution and the State Council's regulations are observed.

The Armed Forces of China are commanded by the Military Affairs Council of the Communist Party. China has an army, navy, and air force, which together make up the People's Liberation Army (PLA). The PLA has more than 4 million members—about $3\frac{1}{2}$ million in the army, 300,000 in the navy, and 400,000 in the air force. Over 5 million men and women serve in China's *militia* (citizens' army). Men may be drafted for military service after they reach the age of 18. The period of service is three years in the army, four years in the air force, and five years in the navy.

The armed forces have held enormous political power in the People's Republic of China since its birth in 1949. On the average, military officers make up about a third of the members on the Communist Party's Central Committee. Besides its military duties, the PLA helps carry out party policies and programs among the people.

Population. China has more people than any other country. About a fifth of all the people on the earth live in China. However, no one knows the exact population of the country. China's only modern census, taken in 1953, reported that the country had about 583 million persons. In 1979, the Chinese government estimated that China had a population of about 958 million at the end of 1978.

Experts outside China have attempted to estimate the country's population. Their estimates range up to 1 billion. The estimates given in WORLD BOOK of 893,-873,000 for 1980 and 972,200,000 for 1985 are based on a United Nations (UN) estimate of 852,113,000 for mid-1976. The UN figure is only one of many estimates, and many population experts believe that it is too low.

More than 10 million persons live in Shanghai, China's largest city. Peking, the capital, has over 7 million residents. China has at least 13 other cities with a population of 1 million or more. However, about 85 per cent of China's people live in rural villages and small towns. Most Chinese live in densely populated areas in eastern China. The vast territories of western China make up half the land area but have only about 5 per cent of the population.

The Chinese government is concerned about the nation's high birth rate and seeks to limit population growth. The government encourages people to postpone marriage until their late 20's and to have no more than two or three children.

Nationalities. About 94 per cent of the Chinese people belong to the *Han* nationality, which has been the largest nationality in China for centuries. The rest of the population consists of about 50 minority groups, including Kazakhs, Mongols, Tibetans, and Uigurs.

Steve Vidler, De Wys, Inc.

The Han Ethnic Group makes up about 94 per cent of China's people. These Han people are buying bread in Sian.

China
Population Density and
Major Ethnic Groups

About 94 per cent of the Chinese people belong to the Han ethnic group and live crowded together in eastern China. The rest of the population consists of about 50 minority groups. They live chiefly in the border areas and in western China.

Major Urban Areas

● More than 5 million inhabitants

• 2 million to 5 million inhabitants

○ 1 million to 2 million inhabitants

Persons per sq. mi.	Persons per km²
More than 2,000	More than 772
1,000 to 2,000	386 to 772
250 to 1,000	97 to 386
25 to 250	10 to 97
5 to 25	2 to 10
Less than 5	Less than 2

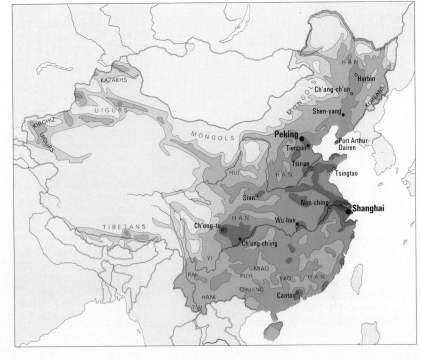

WORLD BOOK map

Almost all the peoples of China belong to the Asian geographical race (see RACES, HUMAN). The various nationalities are distinguished chiefly by their language and culture.

Most of China's minority peoples live in the border regions and the far western parts of the country. Some groups, such as the Mongols in the north and the Kazakhs in the northwest, herd sheep and goats. These people move from place to place during the year to feed their herds on fresh pastures. The Uigurs raise livestock and grow a wide variety of crops on oases in the deserts of northwestern China. The Tibetan people

Henry Herr Gill

Bicycles are a common means of transportation in China's cities. Millions of people live in the cities of eastern China, where the overcrowding has created a severe housing shortage.

Photri

Colorful Folk Dances are part of the cultural heritage of China's minority peoples, such as the Mongols, above. Many Mongols still follow their old way of life as nomadic herders.

practice simple forms of agriculture in China's southwestern highlands.

Languages. The Han people speak Chinese. Spoken Chinese has many dialects, which differ enough in pronunciation to be considered separate languages. To bring about better communication among the people of China, the government has made the Northern Chinese dialect the official language. Many non-Chinese call the official language Mandarin, but the Chinese prefer the term *p'u-t'ung hua* (common language). Northern Chinese is spoken by about 70 per cent of the nation's people, and it is now taught in all schools throughout the country. Other varieties of Chinese include Min, Wu, and Yueh (Cantonese), each of which has many local dialects. For a more detailed discussion of Chinese, see CHINESE LANGUAGE.

Although each dialect of Chinese has its own pronunciation, all speakers of Chinese write the language in the same way. The Chinese writing system uses *characters* instead of an alphabet. Each character is a symbol that represents a complete word or syllable.

Scholars have developed several systems of writing the Chinese language in the Roman alphabet. The spellings of Chinese personal and place names in this article are based on the Wade-Giles system. This system was developed during the 1800's by two English scholars, Sir Thomas Wade and Herbert A. Giles. In 1979, China began using the Pinyin system in all news reports sent abroad and in all communications with other nations. Many Chinese names are spelled somewhat differently in the two systems. For example, the names of the Chinese leaders Mao Tse-tung and Teng Hsiao-p'ing are spelled Mao Zedong and Deng Xiaoping in the Pinyin system. The province of Kwangtung is spelled Guangdong.

The minority peoples of China speak many languages, including Korean, Mongolian, and Uigur. Each group uses its own language in its schools and publications. Most members of China's minority groups learn Chinese as a second language.

Family Life has always been extremely important in Chinese culture. Before 1949, some Chinese lived in large family units. As many as 100 or more relatives lived together under the rule of the oldest male. The ideal was "five generations under one roof." However, those who lived this way were mainly the families of rich rural landowners, wealthy merchants, and government officials. Among the common people, most households consisted of only parents and children, but some also included grandparents and uncles. Today, the Chinese live in these smaller types of family units.

In the past, only men were expected to work outside the home. But today, almost all adults have a job. In many families, a grandparent looks after the house and children during the day. More and more children attend nursery school and kindergarten so that mothers can be free to work.

Relationships within Chinese families have become less formal and more democratic. Parents no longer expect their children to show unquestioning obedience. In the past, a father could legally kill his children if they disobeyed him. Young people today generally choose their own marriage partners on the basis of shared interests and mutual attraction. However, parents still play a role in arranging some marriages, especially in rural areas. Any couple would at least consult their parents about such a major decision.

Chinese families traditionally valued sons far more than daughters. A husband could divorce his wife if she failed to give birth to sons. In some cases, daughters were killed at birth because girls were considered useless. Today, girls as well as boys are valued. This change came about partly because the Communist government strongly supports the idea that women should contribute to the family income and participate in social and political activities. Women do many kinds of work outside the home. Many young husbands share in the shopping, housecleaning, cooking, and caring for the children to show that they believe the sexes are equal. However, equality between the sexes is more widely accepted in the cities than in the countryside.

Björn Klingwall

Family Life has been an important part of Chinese culture throughout the country's history. This playground in a Shanghai neighborhood is a favorite spot for family outings.

K. Scholz, Shostal

Typical Chinese Farmhouses are built of mud or clay bricks and have a tile or straw roof. The peasants farm the land co-operatively. But most families have a small plot for their own use.

Rural Life. Traditionally, most Chinese lived in villages of 100 to 200 households. Many families owned their land, though in numerous cases it was not large enough to support them. Many other families owned no land. The members of these families worked as tenants or laborers for big landowners and rich peasants. The tenant farmers had to pay extremely high rents—30 to 60 per cent of the harvest. In some cases, peasant families were so poor that they became beggars or bandits or sold their children as servants or slaves to rich families.

Under the Communist system, peasants belong to agricultural *collectives* (groups). The collectives are organized on three levels. The highest level is the *commune*, which combines political and economic administration for 20 or more villages. The commune supervises large projects, such as reforestation and the building of dams and roads. Each commune is divided into smaller units called *brigades*. A brigade may consist of one large village or several small ones. Within a brigade, neighborhoods or villages of 20 to 30 families make up units called *production teams*.

Brigades and production teams own land, tools, work animals, and small workshops in common. During the year, families receive a share of the crops they have worked together to grow. They also share in the profits from the sale of surplus crops and of goods produced in the workshops. In addition, each family owns its house and a plot on which it can grow vegetables and raise chickens or a pig for its own use.

The standard of living in rural China has risen slowly but steadily. However, it is higher in some areas than in others because some areas have better farmland and weather than other regions. The average income in rural areas is low, but most families have enough to eat and money to buy clothing. Some families also have a few luxuries, such as a bicycle, radio, sewing machine, and watch.

Most rural families live in two- or three-room houses. Older houses are made of mud bricks and have a tile or straw roof. Newer houses are made of clay bricks or stone and have a tile roof. Some of the more prosperous villages are constructing apartment buildings. The people contribute the labor, and the brigade or team pays for the building materials. Except in remote areas, most houses have electricity.

Rural people work many hours a day, especially at planting and harvesting time. They must go to team and brigade meetings to help decide how to divide the work and profits. They also attend political meetings and night classes, where they learn how to read and write or how to use scientific farming methods. Even so, the people have time for recreation. Many brigades own a television set and show motion pictures once a week. They also have a small library and equipment for such

K. Scholz, Shostal

Bridge Construction, *left,* and other major projects in rural China are carried out by *communes.* Communes are the largest units in China's system of collectivized agriculture. Each commune combines political and economic administration for 20 or more villages.

Steve Vidler, De Wys, Inc.

WORLD BOOK photo by Robert Borja

The Housing in China's Cities is a mixture of new and old, as shown by these two photographs taken in the city of Kuei-lin. Some city residents live in modern apartment complexes, *left.* Others live in older neighborhoods where the houses resemble those in rural areas, *right.*

sports as basketball and table tennis. Some brigades have a small choral group, orchestra, or theater group.

City Life. Many city residents live in older neighborhoods where the houses resemble those in the countryside. Many other city dwellers live in big apartment complexes. City governments construct some apartment buildings, and large factories build others.

Families are assigned an apartment by the factory or other unit for which they work. Most apartments have plumbing and heating, but many have less space than rural houses have. China's cities are overcrowded, and new housing is in great demand. In some cases, two families must share an apartment.

Each city neighborhood or apartment complex has an elected residents' committee. The committee supervises various neighborhood facilities and programs,

such as day-care centers, evening classes, and after-school activities for children. When fights, petty crimes, or acts of juvenile delinquency occur in the neighborhoods, committee members talk with the people involved and try to help them solve the problem. These neighborhood organizations seek to keep crime from being a serious problem in spite of the overcrowding in China's cities.

People in the cities are better paid than most people in the countryside. Factory workers earn about $30 to $40 a month, and highly skilled people can make $60 to $70 monthly. Most households have at least two wage earners. Rents are only a few dollars a month, and a family of five needs no more than $30 a month for food. Medical care, child care, and recreational activity cost little. As a result, most city people gener-

Steve Vidler, De Wys, Inc.

Small Food Shops like this one are common in the cities of China. Most cities also have at least one government-owned department store as well as many small specialty shops.

Milt and Joan Mann

Dining in a Restaurant is a popular activity in China just as it is in Western countries. People in different parts of China eat different foods, but grain is the basic food in all areas.

Ancient Chinese Exercises called *tai chi chuan* are performed by many Chinese first thing every morning. Tai chi chuan emphasizes relaxation, balance, and proper techniques of breathing.

ally have some spare money. Many families have saved this money because the consumer goods they would like to buy have not been available.

For many years, the Chinese government has tried to eliminate the gap between living standards in the city and in the countryside. However, city people still have an easier life and more cultural advantages. Like rural people, city residents attend classes and meetings. On their days off, they enjoy browsing in stores; dining at a restaurant; or going to a park, museum, theater, or sporting event.

Food. Grain is the main food in China. Most working adults eat more than 1 pound (0.5 kilogram) of grain a day. Rice is the favorite grain among people in the south. In the north, people prefer wheat, which they make into bread and noodles. Northerners also eat corn, *kaoliang* (sorghum), and millet. The Chinese vary their diet with many kinds of vegetables, especially cabbage, cucumbers, eggplant, radishes, tomatoes, and turnips. Every area has its fruit specialties, such as bananas and oranges in the south and apples and peaches in the north.

Meat makes up only a small part of the Chinese diet. Many families eat meat only on special occasions. Pork is the favorite meat, but it is rationed so that everyone gets a share. The people also like such high-protein foods as eggs, fish, and poultry, which are becoming increasingly available. Soybeans provide an additional source of protein. Tea has long been the favorite beverage in China.

Clothing. Most Chinese make their own clothes, chiefly of cotton or synthetic materials. The government rations cotton cloth, which is in short supply. However, fabrics made of synthetic fibers are becoming increasingly available as China's petroleum and chemical industries develop.

The Chinese dress for comfort and practicality rather than for style. Some women, especially in the cities, wear skirts or dresses. But throughout China, both men and women generally wear Western-style shirts and

loose-fitting trousers. They dress in dull blues, greens, or dark colors. Only children and young women wear bright colors and patterns. Men wear their hair short. Women also wear their hair in short simple styles. Most girls and young women wear their hair in braids.

Government officials and technicians may buy better-quality clothing at special stores. Such clothing includes high-collared suits, which are worn for formal occasions. But most of the time, it is difficult to tell from a person's clothing whether that person is an ordinary worker, a government official, or a technician. In earlier times, however, the kinds of clothes that people wore indicated their place in Chinese society. For example, scholars traditionally dressed in long blue gowns. Women of the upper classes wore elaborate hairdos, long fingernails, and colorful robes. In contrast, peasants wore patched and faded jackets and trousers.

Health Care in China combines traditional Chinese medicine and modern Western medicine. Traditional

Baseball is a favorite pastime in China, where everyone is encouraged to participate in at least one sport. Other popular sports in China include basketball, soccer, and volleyball.

medicine is based on the use of herbs, attention to diet, and *acupuncture*. Acupuncture is a technique in which thin needles are inserted into the body at certain points to relieve pain or treat disease (see ACUPUNCTURE). From Western medicine, the Chinese have adopted many drugs and surgical methods.

All Chinese cities and towns and most communes have hospitals. Medical teams from the hospitals visit the villages periodically. Villages also have small clinics staffed by part-time medical workers called *barefoot doctors*. The term indicates that these workers share the simple life of the peasants they serve. It does not mean that they are actually barefoot. Barefoot doctors, many of whom are women, receive a year or two of training at a nearby hospital. They can treat simple illnesses, assist at childbirth, prepare medicines made of herbs, and issue prescriptions.

Barefoot doctors organize public health programs in their communities. They check the purity of drinking water, vaccinate people against diseases, and make sure that garbage is disposed of. They also supervise the extermination of harmful insects and rodents. In addition, the barefoot doctors encourage people to practice birth control, and they give advice on infant care and nutrition. All these programs have made the people much healthier than they were in the 1950's. The Chinese have almost wiped out malaria, tuberculosis, and other terrible diseases that once killed millions of them each year.

Religion is discouraged by the Communist government of China. However, it played an important part in traditional Chinese life. Confucianism, Taoism, and Buddhism were the major religions throughout most of China's history. The religious beliefs of many Chinese included elements of all three religions.

Confucianism is based on the ideas of Confucius, a Chinese philosopher who was born about 550 B.C. It stresses the importance of moral standards and of a well-ordered society in which parents rule their children, men rule women, and the educated rule the common people. In addition, Confucianism strongly emphasizes

Björn Klingwall

Chinese Physicians practice a combination of traditional Chinese medicine and modern Western medicine. The doctors pictured above are examining patients in a clinic in Shanghai.

deep respect for one's ancestors and for the past. See CONFUCIANISM.

Taoism is also a native Chinese religion. It teaches that a person should withdraw from everyday life and live in harmony with nature. Taoism began during the 300's B.C. and is based largely on a book called the *Tao Te Ching* (*The Classic of the Way and the Virtue*). Taoism came to include many elements of Chinese folk religion and so became a religion with many protective gods. See TAOISM.

Buddhism reached China from India before A.D. 100 and became well established throughout the country during the 300's. Under the influence of Confucianism and Taoism, Chinese varieties of Buddhism developed. They taught strict moral standards and the ideas of rebirth and life after death. The Chinese Buddhists worshiped many gods and appealed to them for help in times of troubles. See BUDDHISM.

The Chinese government regards religion as superstition. It encourages the people to study science and political writings to solve their problems. The Communists especially oppose Confucianism because it emphasizes the past and justifies inequality in society. They have tried to remove all Confucian influences from family life, education, and politics. The Communists have also turned Taoist and Buddhist temples into museums, schools, and meeting halls.

Among China's minority peoples, about 25 million persons are Muslims. The government permits them to follow their religion, but it does not encourage them to do so. Christian missionaries worked in China for many years. A few churches remain open in the larger cities, but no one knows how many Chinese still believe in Christianity.

Education. The Chinese have always prized education and respected scholars. Before the Communists came to power in 1949, there were two major reasons for this high regard for education. (1) The Confucians believed that people could perfect themselves through study. The Confucians made no sharp distinction between academic education and moral education. They believed that the function of all study was to build character. (2) The ability to read and write and a knowledge of Confucian sacred writings paved the way to financial security and social position. Candidates for government jobs had to pass an examination based on the Confucian works.

Education continues to play a central role in Chinese society. The Communists regard it as a key to reaching their political, social, and economic goals. Since their rule began, they have conducted adult education programs in an effort to teach all Chinese to read and write. As a result, more than 90 per cent of Chinese adults can now read and write. China's formal education system stresses scientific and technical training. This training is intended to give students the skills needed to modernize China's economy and improve the standard of living.

Moral education also remains important in China, but it teaches morality as defined in a Communist sense. The Chinese say that students should be both politically committed to Communist ideas and tech-

Foreign Language Classes are an important part of every Chinese student's education. These youngsters are learning English, the most widely studied foreign language in China.

WORLD BOOK photo by Robert Borja

nically skilled. Courses combine the teaching of academic facts and political values. For example, a geography text might provide information not only about China's physical features but also about the desirability of having patriotic feelings toward the land. Special courses teach the ideas of such Communist thinkers as Karl Marx, V. I. Lenin, and Mao Tse-tung. Most classrooms have posters describing the deeds of model citizens as moral examples for the students.

An important issue in Chinese education involves the conflict between basic Communist principles and the desire to modernize China's economy rapidly. Rapid modernization requires high-quality education with special opportunities and facilities for talented students. However, a Communist principle stresses equality in education. Supporters of this principle would like to increase the educational opportunities of peasants and workers at the expense of more privileged groups, such as scientists and government officials. Since 1949, the Communists have alternately stressed equality in education and high-quality education for modernization. At present, supporters of rapid modernization control the educational system.

Students who show outstanding ability on nation-wide examinations go to *key schools*, which have the best faculties and facilities. The key schools exist at the elementary, secondary, and college levels.

Elementary and Secondary Schools. The Chinese have made great progress in providing elementary school education for their children. The law does not require children to go to school. However, about 95 per cent of Chinese children attend elementary school. Youngsters enter elementary school at the age of 6 or 7 and stay for 5 years. They study the Chinese language, mathematics, music, natural science, painting, physical education, and political education. In the third grade, they also begin to study English, Russian, or some other foreign language.

After completing elementary school, many Chinese students enter secondary schools called *middle schools.*

The Ministry of Education in Peking selects the courses and textbooks for all middle schools throughout China. The middle school courses include many of the subjects studied in elementary school plus history, hygiene, literature, and physiology. China has about 123,000 middle schools. More than 58 million students attend these schools, nearly four times the number enrolled in 1966.

Rural areas of China lag behind the cities in educational progress. For example, the goal for 1985 is for most city students to attend middle school for five years. But the most the government expects for rural students by 1985 is that they attend middle school for three years.

Higher Education. Young people who wish to attend an institution of higher learning must pass an entrance examination. Some students who pass the examination enter a university. The chief university subjects include languages, mathematics, and natural sciences. Others who pass the examination enter a technical college. Each technical college specializes in one particular field, such as agriculture, forestry, medicine, mining, or teacher training. Many technical schools are administered by the government ministry specifically concerned with the subject that is taught. This system enables government leaders to plan the number of graduates who will have the special skills needed to run China's farms and factories.

China has about 460 institutions of higher learning, including both universities and technical colleges. Altogether, they have about 860,000 students, and enrollments are gradually increasing. Nevertheless, only a small percentage of the students who wish to attend college can do so because of a shortage of faculties and facilities. Unsuccessful candidates can continue their education at "workers' universities" run by factories. These schools offer short-term courses. Youths who dropped out of middle school can resume their studies at spare-time schools or through television and correspondence courses.

Detail of a painting on clay tile (A.D. 1-99) by
an unknown Chinese artist; Museum of Fine
Arts, Boston, Denman Waldo Rose Collection

Paintings on the Tiles of Tombs during the Han dynasty
were done in a graceful, lively style. This tomb tile shows two officials of the Chinese emperor's court.

China's visual arts date from at least the 4000's
B.C. Many extraordinary ancient works have been discovered, chiefly in tombs. Chinese visual arts in general
reached their highest development during four dynasties. These dynasties were the Han (202 B.C. to A.D.
220); the T'ang (618-907); the Sung (960-1279); and the
Ming (1368-1644). The masterpieces of these dynasties
include not only paintings and sculptures but also such
objects as pottery, ivory and jade carvings, furniture,
and lacquer ware. See BRONZE; FURNITURE (China);
IVORY; JADE; LACQUER WARE; PORCELAIN.

In present-day China, artists receive support from
the government or work as amateurs in addition to their
regular jobs. The Communists teach that the arts originate from the people—that is, the farmers, workers,
and soldiers. The Communists also stress that all art
should express the aims of their new society. As a result, much Chinese art today deals with events from
the Communist revolution or from the daily life of
workers and peasants. In addition, the Communists
promote the preservation of folk dances and other traditional arts of China's minority peoples.

Literature. China has one of the oldest and greatest
literatures in the world. The first significant work of
Chinese literature was a collection of poems called the
Classic of Songs. Some of these poems probably date
from the 1100's B.C. For more information on China's
rich literary heritage, see CHINESE LITERATURE.

Painting has been an established art in China since
at least the 300's B.C. Most early paintings were of
people, but landscapes became the chief subject of
Chinese painting by the A.D. 900's. During the Sung
dynasty, many artists painted landscapes called *shan-*

shui (mountain-water), which showed towering mountains and vast expanses of water. In these paintings,
the artist tried to suggest a harmony between nature
and the human spirit.

Chinese painting was closely linked with the arts of
poetry and *calligraphy* (fine handwriting). The Chinese
traditionally considered calligraphy a branch of painting. During the 1200's, Chinese painters began to combine shan-shui with written inscriptions that formed an
important part of the overall design of their works. In
many cases, these inscriptions consisted of a poem plus
a description of the circumstances under which the
painting was created.

Buddhist Temple Amid Clearing Mountain Peaks (A.D. 967),
an ink painting on silk attributed to Li Ch'eng; Nelson
Gallery-Akins Museum, Kansas City, Mo., Nelson Fund

Landscapes became the chief subject of Chinese painting by
the A.D. 900's. The work above is a fine example of the *shan-shui*
(mountain-water) style developed during the Sung dynasty.

Chinese artists used the same brush for painting and calligraphy. It consisted of a wooden or bamboo handle with bristles of animal hair arranged to form an extremely fine point. The artist could paint many kinds of lines by adjusting the angle of the brush and the pressure on it. Chinese artists painted chiefly with black ink made of pine soot and glue. They sometimes used vegetable or mineral pigments to add color to their paintings. Chinese painters created many works on silk scrolls, which could be rolled up for storage and safekeeping. Other paintings were done on plaster walls and on paper. See PAINTING (Chinese Painting).

Sculpture and Pottery. The earliest Chinese sculptures were small figures placed in tombs. From the Shang dynasty (1766?-1122 B.C.) through the Chou dynasty (1122-256 B.C.), sculptors created chiefly bronze and jade works. Shang and Chou artists used bronze to make elaborate sacrificial vessels used in ceremonies for the dead. These works were cast in molds, and most had complicated designs based on animal forms.

In 1974, thousands of clay figures of people and horses were discovered in burial pits near the tomb of China's first emperor. These figures, which are the earliest known life-sized Chinese sculptures, date from the 200's B.C.

Buddhism reached China from India during the Han period. Sculptors then began to turn their skills to the service of this new religion. Temples were built in or near cities. In rural areas, cliffsides were hollowed out to form elaborate chapels. Sculptors decorated the chapels with figures of Buddha and his attendants. Some sculptures were carved from local stone. Others were molded of clay and painted. Still other sculptures were cast of bronze and coated with gold. As artistic expressions of religious faith, these works rival the finest sculptures in the monasteries and cathedrals of Europe. See SCULPTURE (China).

Ink painting on silk (1279-1368) by an unknown Chinese artist; National Museum, Taipei, Taiwan (Wan-go H. C. Weng)

Fine Handwriting called *calligraphy* forms an essential part of many Chinese paintings. Artists of the Yuan period often combined calligraphy with paintings of bamboo, as on the fan above.

The Chinese have made pottery since prehistoric times. They began to use the potter's wheel before 2000 B.C. and produced glazed pottery as early as the 1300's B.C. During the T'ang dynasty, the Chinese developed the world's first porcelain. Porcelain dishes and vases produced during the T'ang, Sung, Ming, and early Ch'ing periods are among the greatest treasures of Chinese art.

Jade disk (400-200 B.C.) by an unknown Chinese artist; Nelson Gallery-Akins Museum, Kansas City, Mo., Nelson Fund

Bronze vessel (1100's B.C.) by an unknown Chinese artist; Freer Gallery of Art, Smithsonian Institution, Washington, D.C.

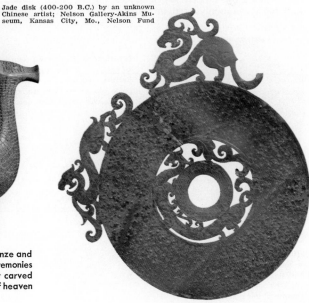

Chinese Ceremonial Art included works created in bronze and jade. Bronze vessels like the one above were used in ceremonies for the dead during the Shang dynasty. The elaborately carved jade disk on the right, called a *pi*, was used as a symbol of heaven in religious ceremonies. It dates from the Chou dynasty.

Gilded bronze statue by an unknown Chinese sculptor; Asian Art Museum of San Francisco, Avery Brundage Collection

Steve Vidler, De Wys, Inc.

Chinese Sculpture was greatly influenced by Buddhism. The oldest known Chinese Buddhist sculpture is a seated Buddha, *left*, which dates from A.D. 338. Sculptors also created huge figures of Buddha and his attendants for cliffside chapels, such as the Feng-hsien cave in Honan province, *right*.

Architecture. Traditionally, most of the public buildings in China were constructed of wood on a stone foundation. The most outstanding feature of Chinese architecture was a large tile roof with extending edges that curved gracefully upward. These roofs were supported by wooden columns connected to the ceiling beams by wooden brackets. Walls did not support the roof but merely provided privacy. Most buildings had only one story, but the Chinese also built many-storied towers called *pagodas* (see PAGODA). Chinese architects no longer use the traditional styles, and new buildings in Chinese cities look much like those in Western cities.

Music. Chinese music sounds much different from Western music because it uses a different scale. The scales most commonly used in Western music have eight tones, but the Chinese scale has five tones. Melody is the most important element in Chinese music. Instruments and voices follow the same melodic line instead of blending in harmony.

Chinese musical instruments also differ from those played by Western musicians. Chinese instruments include the *ch'in*, a seven-stringed instrument, and the *sheng*, a mouth organ made of seven bamboo pipes. The Chinese also have a lutelike instrument called the *p'i-p'a* and two kinds of flutes, the *hsiao* and the *ti*. Today, Chinese musicians also play Western instruments and perform the music of many of the great European composers.

Theater. Formal Chinese drama began during the Yuan dynasty (1279-1368). Since the 1800's, the most popular form has been *Peking opera*. This type of drama

Multicolor Ceramics were developed in the T'ang era. Potters combined different color glazes to form patterns like the one on the vase below.

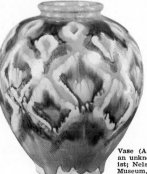

Bowl (late 1400's); Freer Gallery of Art, Smithsonian Institution, Washington, D.C.

Unglazed clay jar (about 1200 B.C.); Freer Gallery of Art, Smithsonian Institution, Washington, D.C.

White Pottery made during the Shang dynasty had a polished surface with carved designs. The jar above is a fine example of this pottery.

Vase (A.D. 618-907) by an unknown Chinese artist; Nelson Gallery-Akins Museum, Kansas City, Mo., Nelson Fund

Fine White Porcelain was produced during the Ming dynasty. Like much Ming porcelain, the bowl above is decorated with a blue underglaze.

WORLD BOOK photo by Robert Borja

Chinese Musicians play both Western and Chinese instruments. In the group shown above, the girl on the left is playing a cello, and her friends are playing traditional Chinese instruments.

combines spoken dialogue and songs with dance and symbolic gestures. Peking opera features colorful and elaborate costumes. The plays are based on traditional Chinese stories, history, and folklore. During the 1950's, the Chinese began to develop a dance form called *revolutionary ballet*. Revolutionary ballet uses Western ballet forms to present stories about the struggle that led to Communist rule in China.

Steve Vidler, De Wys, Inc.

Peking Opera, the most popular form of drama in China, combines dialogue and songs with dance and symbolic gestures. The plays are based on stories from Chinese history and folklore.

China is the world's third largest country. Only Russia and Canada are larger. China's land is as varied as it is vast. It ranges from subarctic regions in the north to tropical lowlands in the south and from fertile plains in the east to deserts in the west.

Several regions of China have traditionally been known by certain names. Northeastern China is called *Manchuria. Sinkiang* covers the far northwest, and *Tibet* covers the far southwest. *Inner Mongolia* lies in the north. The eastern third of China, south of Manchuria and Inner Mongolia, is commonly called *China Proper*. It has always had most of China's people.

China can be divided into eight major land regions. They are (1) the Tibetan Highlands, (2) the Sinkiang-Mongolian Uplands, (3) the Mongolian Border Uplands, (4) the Eastern Highlands, (5) the Eastern Lowlands, (6) the Central Uplands, (7) the Szechwan Basin, and (8) the Southern Uplands.

The Tibetan Highlands lie in southwestern China. The region consists of a vast plateau bordered by towering mountains—the Himalaya on the south, the Pamirs on the west, and the Kunlun on the north. The world's highest mountain, Mount Everest, rises 29,028 feet (8,848 meters) above sea level in the Himalaya in southern Tibet. Two of the world's longest rivers, the Huang Ho and Yangtze, begin in the highlands and flow eastward across China to the sea.

Tibet suffers from both drought and extreme cold. Most of the region is a wasteland of rock, gravel, snow, and ice. A few areas provide limited grazing for hardy yaks—woolly oxen that furnish food, clothing, and transportation for the Tibetans. Crops can be grown only in a few lower-lying areas. See TIBET.

The Sinkiang-Mongolian Uplands occupy the vast desert areas of northwestern China. The region has plentiful mineral resources. However, it is thinly populated because of its remoteness and harsh climate.

The eastern part of the Sinkiang-Mongolian Uplands consists of the Ordos Desert and a portion of the Gobi Desert. The western part of the region is divided into two areas by the Tien Shan range, which has peaks more than 20,000 feet (6,096 meters) above sea level. South of the mountains lies one of the world's driest deserts, the Takla Makan. The Turfan Depression, an oasis near the northern edge of the Takla Makan, is the lowest point in China. It lies 505 feet (154 meters) below sea level. To the north of the Tien Shan, the Dzungarian Basin stretches northward to the Altai Mountains along the Mongolian border.

The Mongolian Border Uplands lie between the Gobi Desert and the Eastern Lowlands. The Greater Khingan Mountains form the northern part of the region. The terrain there is rugged, and little agriculture is practiced. The southern part of the region is thickly covered with *loess,* a fertile, yellowish soil deposited by the wind. Loess consists of tiny mineral particles and is easily worn away. The Huang Ho and its tributaries have carved out hills and steep-sided valleys in this soft soil. The name *Huang Ho* means *Yellow River* and comes from the large amounts of loess carried by the river.

The Eastern Highlands consist of the Shantung Peninsula and eastern Manchuria. The Shantung Peninsula

561

The Sinkiang-Mongolian Uplands are a vast area of deserts and rugged mountains in northwestern China. This photograph shows the edge of the Gobi Desert in the eastern part of the region.

Jean DeLord, De Wys, Inc.

is a hilly region with excellent harbors and rich deposits of coal. The hills of eastern Manchuria have China's best forests, and timber is a major product of the region. The highest hills are the Ch'ang Pai Mountains (Long White Mountains) along the Korean border. To the north, the Amur River forms the border with Russia. Just south of the river are the Lesser Khingan Hills.

The Eastern Lowlands lie between the Mongolian Border Uplands and the Eastern Highlands and extend south to the Southern Uplands. From north to south, the region consists of the Manchurian Plain, the North China Plain, and the valley of the Yangtze River. The Eastern Lowlands have China's best farmland and many of the country's largest cities.

The Manchurian Plain has fertile soils and large deposits of coal and iron ore. Most of Manchuria's

people live on the southern part of the plain near the Liao River. To the south lies the wide, flat North China Plain in the valley of the Huang Ho. Wheat is the main crop in this highly productive agricultural area. Major flooding of the Huang Ho occurs about every 5 years, with disastrous floods at least every 25 years. These frequent and destructive floods have earned the river the nickname "China's Sorrow."

The Yangtze Valley has the best combination of level land, fertile soil, and sufficient rainfall anywhere in China. In the so-called Fertile Triangle between Nan-ching, Shanghai, and Hang-chou, the rural population exceeds 5,000 persons per square mile (1,900 per square kilometer). The Yangtze River and its many tributaries have long formed China's most important trade route.

Photri

The Eastern Lowlands have China's most productive farmland. These farmers are planting rice seedlings in a flooded field in the Yangtze Valley, which forms the southern part of the Eastern Lowlands. Wheat is the main crop in northern parts of the region.

The Central Uplands are an area of hills and mountains between the Eastern Lowlands and the Tibetan Highlands. The Tsinling Mountains are the chief physical feature of the region. Peaks in the range rise more than 12,000 feet (3,658 meters) above sea level near the city of Sian. The Tsinling cross the region from east to west. They form a natural barricade against seasonal winds that carry rain from the south and dust from the north. For this reason, the Tsinling Mountains are China's most significant geographic boundary. To the north of the mountains are dry wheat-growing areas.

To the south lie warm, humid areas where rice is the major crop.

The Szechwan Basin lies south of the Central Uplands. It is a region of hills and valleys surrounded by high mountains. A mild climate and a long growing season make the Szechwan Basin one of China's main agricultural regions. Most crops are grown on *terraced fields*—that is, on level strips of land cut out of the hillsides. The name *Szechwan* means *Four Rivers* and refers to the four streams that flow into the Yangtze in the region. The rivers have carved out deep gorges in the

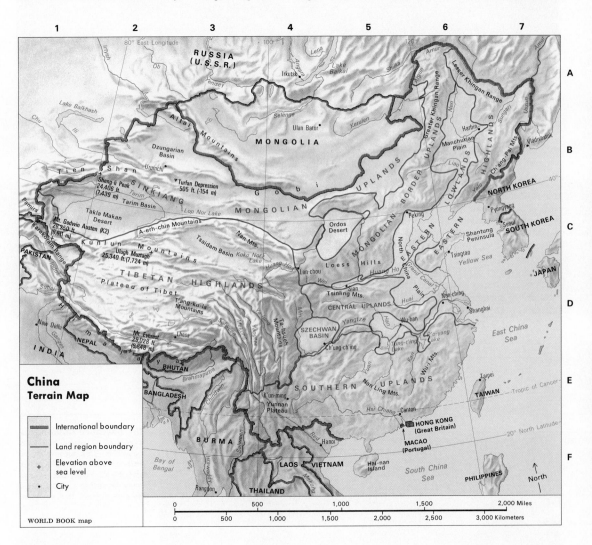

China
Terrain Map

International boundary

Land region boundary

+ Elevation above sea level

• City

WORLD BOOK map

Physical Features

Shostal

The Central Uplands include dry wheat-growing areas like this one near the city of Sian. To the south of this area, the Tsinling Mountains cross the Central Uplands from west to east.

red sandstone of the region and so made land travel difficult. Ships can travel on the Yangtze into western Szechwan, but only small craft can navigate the river's swift-flowing tributaries.

The Southern Uplands cover southeastern China, including the island of Hai-nan. The Southern Uplands are a region of green hills and mountains. The only level area is the delta of the Hsi Chiang (West River). The Hsi Chiang and its tributaries form the main transportation route for southern China. Canton (Kuang-chou), southern China's only major city, lies near the mouth of the Hsi Chiang. Deep, rich soils and a tropical climate help make the delta area an extremely productive agricultural region.

The rest of the Southern Uplands is so hilly and mountainous that little land can be cultivated, even by terracing. The central part of the region, near the city of Kuei-lin, is one of the most beautiful areas in China. It has many isolated limestone hills that rise 100 to 600 feet (30 to 182 meters) almost straight up.

Henry Herr Gill

The Southern Uplands are a region of green hills and mountains. This picture shows part of the city of Kuei-lin and the Li River, one of the many important waterways in the central part of the region.

China has an extremely wide range of climates because it is such a large country and has such a variety of natural features. The most severe climatic conditions occur in the Takla Makan and Gobi deserts. Daytime temperatures in these deserts may exceed 100° F. (38° C) in summer, but nighttime lows may fall to −30° F. (−34° C) in winter. Both Tibet and northern Manchuria have long, bitterly cold winters. In contrast, coastal areas of southeastern China have a tropical climate.

Seasonal winds called *monsoons* greatly affect China's climate. In winter, monsoons carry cold, dry air from central Asia across China toward the sea. These high winds often create dust storms in the north. From late spring to early fall, the monsoons blow from the opposite direction and spread warm, moist air inland from the sea. Because of the monsoons, more rain falls in summer than in winter throughout China. Most parts of the country actually receive more than 80 per cent of their rainfall between May and October.

Summers tend to be hot and humid in the eastern half of China Proper and in southern Manchuria. In fact, summer temperatures average about 80° F. (27° C) throughout much of China. However, northern China has longer and much colder winters than the south has. In January, daily low temperatures average about −13° F. (−25° C) in northern Manchuria and about 20° F. (−7° C) throughout much of northern China Proper. In contrast, Canton has an average January temperature of 57° F. (14° C). Southern China and the Yangtze Valley west of Wu-han are shielded from the cold winter winds by mountains. The Szechwan Basin is especially well protected, and frost rarely occurs there.

The amount of precipitation varies greatly from region to region in China. The deserts of Sinkiang and Inner Mongolia receive less than 4 inches (10 centimeters) of rain yearly. More than 40 inches (100 centimeters) of rain falls each year in many parts of southern China Proper. Some areas of southeastern China receive up to 80 inches (200 centimeters) annually. In northern China the amount of precipitation varies widely from year to year. However, most areas receive less than 40 inches (100 centimeters) yearly. For example, annual precipitation averages about 25 inches (63 centimeters) in Peking and 28 inches (70 centimeters) in Shen-yang (Mukden). Snowfalls occur only in the north. But even there, they are infrequent and usually light.

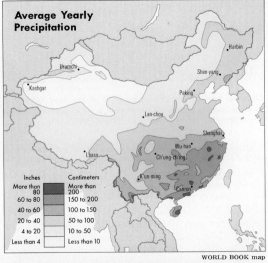

Average Yearly Precipitation

Inches	Centimeters
More than 80	More than 200
60 to 80	150 to 200
40 to 60	100 to 150
20 to 40	50 to 100
4 to 20	10 to 50
Less than 4	Less than 10

WORLD BOOK map

Rainfall in China is heaviest in the southeast, where it averages from 40 to 80 inches (100 to 200 centimeters) yearly. In the north, the amount of precipitation varies widely from year to year.

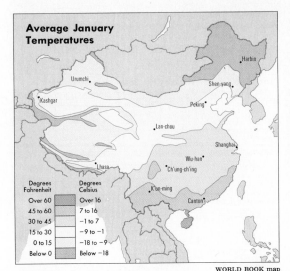

Average January Temperatures

Degrees Fahrenheit	Degrees Celsius
Over 60	Over 16
45 to 60	7 to 16
30 to 45	−1 to 7
15 to 30	−9 to −1
0 to 15	−18 to −9
Below 0	Below −18

WORLD BOOK map

Northern and western China have far colder winters than the south. January temperatures average below 0°F. (−18°C) in Manchuria and Tibet but over 60°F. (16°C) on the south coast.

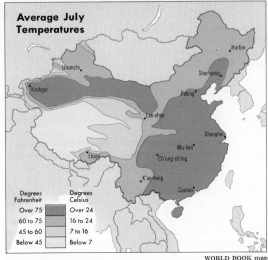

Average July Temperatures

Degrees Fahrenheit	Degrees Celsius
Over 75	Over 24
60 to 75	16 to 24
45 to 60	7 to 16
Below 45	Below 7

WORLD BOOK map

Temperatures in July average above 75°F. (24°C) throughout China Proper and in southern Manchuria. Daytime temperatures may exceed 100°F. (38°C) in the deserts of northwestern China.

Chinese Agriculture produces nearly all the food needed to feed the nation's people. These women are picking tea, which is one of the main crops grown in southern China.

China has one of the world's largest economies in terms of its *gross national product* (GNP). The GNP is the value of all goods and services produced in a country yearly. Only the United States, Russia, Japan, West Germany, and France—in that order—have a higher GNP than China has. However, China ranks below more than 100 other countries in *per capita* (per person) GNP, which is determined by dividing the GNP by the nation's population. Economists consider China a developing country because it has such a low per capita GNP and because only about 10 per cent of all workers are employed in industry.

The national government has tremendous control over China's economy. It owns and operates all important industrial plants and directly controls most nonagricultural employment and wages. The government also controls and operates the banking system, all long-distance transportation, and foreign trade. It rations food, clothing, and other necessities and sets the prices of most goods and services. The government receives most of its income from the profits of state-owned businesses. Government planners have used these profits to invest heavily in the development of China's manufacturing industries.

The Communist government has achieved an impressive record of economic growth. The Communists have provided widespread employment opportunities, job security, and a more even distribution of income among the people. The prospects for China's economy to continue growing remain favorable. The country has enough mineral and fuel resources to become one of the world's developed nations. Another extremely important resource is China's hard-working and skillful people.

In 1978, China's leaders announced an ambitious economic plan for the period from 1978 to 1985. This plan calls for an annual rate of growth of 4 to 5 per cent

in agricultural production and 10 per cent in industrial production.

Agriculture is the backbone of China's economy. About three-fourths of all workers are farmers. In southern China, rice and tea are the major crops. Wheat is the chief crop in the north, followed by corn and *kaoliang* (sorghum). China produces more rice, tobacco, and vegetables than any other country. In addition, it is a leading producer of barley, corn, cotton, oats, sugar cane, tea, and wheat. Chinese farmers also raise a wide variety of other crops, including millet, peanuts, and soybeans. Farmers on Hai-nan Island grow tropical crops, such as bananas, coconuts, and coffee.

Only about 13 per cent of China's land area can be cultivated. Thus, farmers have extremely little cropland to support themselves and the rest of the huge population. However, they manage to provide almost enough food for all the people. Only small supplies must be imported. This accomplishment is made possible partly by the long growing season in southern China. Farmers there can grow two or more crops on the same land each year. Chinese farmers must do most

China's Gross National Product

Total gross national product in 1975—$323,000,000,000

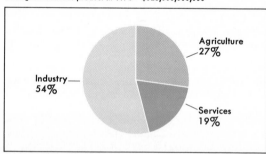

The gross national product (GNP) is the total value of goods and services produced by a country in a year. The GNP measures a nation's total annual economic performance. It can also be used to compare the economic output and growth of countries.

Production and Workers by Economic Activities

Economic Activities	Per Cent of GNP Produced	Employed Workers	
		Number of Persons	Per Cent of Total
Industry	54	40,700,000	9
Agriculture & Fishing	27	330,000,000	77
Trade & Finance	19	18,000,000	4
Construction	(*)	6,500,000	2
Government & Defense	(†)	9,700,000	2
Health, Education, & Culture	(†)	14,200,000	3
Other Services	(†)	1,100,000	1
Transportation & Communication	(†)	8,900,000	2
Total	100	429,100,000	100

*Included in Industry.
†Included in Trade & Finance.
Sources: *Chinese Economy Post-Mao*, Joint Economic Committee, Congress of the U.S., November 1978; *Economic Growth and Employment in China*, Thomas G. Rawski, Oxford for the World Bank, 1979.

of their work by hand with simple tools. They make extensive use of irrigation and organic fertilizers and practice soil conservation.

During the 1950's, the Communists *collectivized* China's agriculture. They organized the peasants into groups to farm the land cooperatively. The basic unit in the collectivized system is the production team, which on the average consists of about 30 households. Each production team pays an agricultural tax and agrees to sell a certain portion of its output to the state. However, the team decides what crops to grow and how to use its workers. It also decides how to distribute the output that remains after the tax has been paid and the required sale to the state has been made.

Collectivization has expanded China's farm output by increasing both the size of the labor force and the amount of cultivated land. However, unfavorable terrain and climate have limited the annual rate of growth in productivity to 2 to 3 per cent since the 1950's. Faster growth will require the introduction of higher-yielding seeds, increased use of machinery, expanded irrigation, and wider use of chemical fertilizers.

Livestock production has increased significantly in China since the 1950's. In rural areas, many families raise chickens and ducks, and nearly every household has a pig. Pigs provide both meat and fertilizer. The Chinese use so much pig manure to fertilize the soil that the pig is called the "Chinese fertilizer factory." China has over 250 million hogs, more than a third of the world's total. China also has large numbers of cattle, goats, horses, and sheep.

Manufacturing in China is concentrated in and around large cities near the coast. A shortage of modern

Henry Weaver, Lensman

Raising Hogs is a major agricultural activity in China. Hogs are the main source of meat for the Chinese, and Chinese farmers use huge quantities of hog manure to fertilize the soil.

transportation has hampered attempts to build factories in other areas. Shanghai is China's biggest industrial center. Peking and Tientsin also have many large manufacturing plants. In Manchuria, the Chinese have developed a major center of heavy industry in the Shen-yang area, with smaller centers at An-shan, Ch'ang-ch'un, Fu-shun, and Pen-ch'i.

After the Communists came to power, they began to rebuild China's factories in an effort to make the nation an industrial power. They concentrated on the development of heavy industries, such as the produc-

China
Land Use

This map shows the major uses of land in China. Nearly all of China's cropland is in the eastern half of the country. Extremely dry conditions in western China make much of the land there unproductive.

Intensively cultivated land

Other cultivated land

Grazing land

Forest land

Generally unproductive land

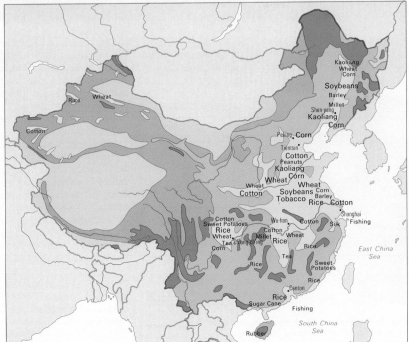

WORLD BOOK map

tion of metals and machinery. Since 1949, China's industrial production has grown at an average annual rate of more than 12 per cent. Today, China has one of the world's largest steel industries. It produces about 30 million short tons (27.2 million metric tons) of steel annually. The machine-building industry provides metalworking tools and other machines for new factories. Other major manufactured products include fertilizer and other chemicals, irrigation equipment, locomotives, military equipment, ships, tractors, and trucks.

China's consumer goods industries have not grown as quickly as heavy industries. The largest consumer goods industries are the textile industry and the food-processing industry. As the standard of living in China improves, demand is growing for such consumer goods as bicycles, radios, sewing machines, and watches. As a result, the Chinese are increasing their production of these items.

The continuation of China's rapid pace of industrial development faces some major obstacles. The greatest problem is China's outdated technology and a shortage of highly trained engineers and technicians. To help solve this problem, China's leaders have made contracts with foreign companies to modernize the country's factories and to build new ones. They have also begun to improve and expand scientific and technical education in China and to send students abroad for training. Waste and inefficiency in industry are also problems. Steps to combat these problems include greater government control over factories and the introduction of wage and bonus systems that give workers more pay for more production.

Mining. China is one of the world's largest producers of coal. Coal deposits occur in many parts of China, but the best fields are in the north.

During the early 1950's, more than 90 per cent of China's energy came from coal. Since that time, however, the Chinese have discovered and rapidly made use of large deposits of petroleum. Today, oil provides

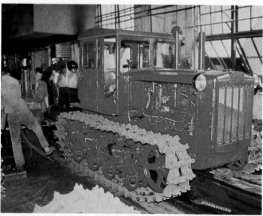

Björn Klingwall

The Production of Machinery plays a vital role in the development of China's economy. This factory manufactures tractors, which will help modernize agriculture in China.

about 20 per cent of China's energy, and natural gas supplies about 10 per cent. China's largest oil field is at Ta-ch'ing in northern Manchuria. Other major Chinese oil fields include those at Sheng-li on the Shantung Peninsula; at Takang, near Tientsin; and at Karamai in Sinkiang.

The Chinese have greatly increased the mining of iron ore to meet the needs of their growing iron and steel industry. Today, China is a leading producer of iron ore. Most of the country's iron ore comes from large, low-grade deposits in the northeastern provinces. Some mines in central and northern China yield rich iron ore.

China outranks all other countries in the production of tungsten, and it is a leading producer of antimony and tin. China also mines bauxite, lead, manganese, salt, uranium, and zinc.

Fishing Industry. China has one of the world's largest fishing industries. The Chinese catch about $7\frac{1}{2}$ million short tons (6.9 million metric tons) of fish and shellfish annually. About two-thirds of the catch comes from freshwater fisheries, and the rest comes from the sea. Fish farming is growing in importance in China. Fish farmers raise fish in ponds both for food and for use in fertilizer.

Trade is vital to China's economic development. During the 1950's, the Chinese imported from Russia most of the machinery needed to build their industries. However, friendly relations between China and Russia broke down in the early 1960's. The Chinese then began to follow a policy of economic self-reliance and sought to limit imports. But China's present leaders have largely abandoned the principle of self-reliance. They are importing the machinery and other technology needed to modernize China's economy. In addition, the Chinese are even seeking foreign loans to finance these imports.

China's chief imports are metals and machinery. Other leading imports include grain, cotton, and fertilizers. The country's main exports consist of textiles, tea, and such foods as fruits, grain, pork, and vegetables. During the 1970's, the Chinese began to export large quantities of petroleum. They hope to export more and more petroleum to help pay for their imports. Japan is China's largest trading partner, followed by Hong Kong, West Germany, and France.

Transportation. The Chinese rely mainly on simple, traditional means for transportation over short distances. The people carry heavy loads fastened to their back or hanging from poles carried across their shoulders. Carts and wagons are pulled either by people or by donkeys, horses, or mules. Boats are pulled along canals and rivers by animals on the bank.

Railroads make up by far the most important part of China's modern transportation system. The country has about 30,000 miles (48,000 kilometers) of railroad tracks. Rail lines link all the major cities and manufacturing centers. The railroads transport over 60 per cent of the freight hauled by modern means. They also carry much of China's passenger traffic.

China has about 500,000 miles (800,000 kilometers) of highways, of which only about an eighth are paved.

Dockworkers load agricultural products on to barges and small boats, which transport the goods over China's inland waterways. For most transportation over short distances, the Chinese use simple, traditional means. For example, they carry heavy loads on their back or hanging from a pole that rests across the shoulders.

Henry Weaver, Lensman

In contrast, the United States has more than 3,200,000 miles (5,150,000 kilometers) of highways, of which more than three-fourths are paved. Highway traffic in China consists chiefly of trucks and buses. China has very few automobiles.

About a fourth of China's more than 100,000 miles (160,000 kilometers) of inland waterways can be used by passenger steamers and freighters. The Grand Canal, the world's longest artificially created waterway, extends more than 1,000 miles (1,600 kilometers) from Hang-chou in the south to Peking in the north.

China's major ports include Canton, Dairen, Shanghai, and Tsingtao. The chief airports are at Peking, Shanghai, and Canton. The Civil Aviation Administration of China (CAAC) operates flights that link over 70 cities within the country. The CAAC and several foreign airlines fly planes between China and a number of cities in Asia and Europe.

Communication in China comes under strict government control. China's rulers decide what people read in newspapers and magazines, what they hear on radio, and what they see on television.

The government and the Chinese Communist Party publish hundreds of daily newspapers and many weeklies. China's leading newspaper is *Jen Min Jih Pao* (People's Daily) of Peking, the official paper of the Communist Party. In addition to printed newspapers, China has countless mimeographed and handwritten newssheets that are posted on walls and bulletin boards. China's constitution guarantees the people the right to express their political opinions on so-called big-character posters. People place these posters on walls in Peking and other major cities. However, the authorities quickly remove any posters that express what they consider unacceptable opinions.

China has about 150 radio stations and about 40 television stations. Many Chinese families own a radio. Radio programs are also broadcast over loudspeakers in many public areas. Few Chinese families can afford a television set, and so most sets are owned by groups. The Chinese use their telephone and telegraph systems mainly for official purposes or in emergencies. The people depend chiefly on the postal system for personal communication.

Steve Vidler, De Wys, Inc.

Wall Posters serve as an important means of communication in China. The people use posters to express their opinions on national or local issues. They place the posters on walls in parks and other public areas.

WORLD BOOK photo by Robert Borja

The Great Wall of China was constructed by the ancient Chinese to keep out invaders from central Asia. It extends more than 1,500 miles (2,410 kilometers) across northern China.

────── **IMPORTANT DATES IN CHINA** ──────

1766?-1122 B.C. China's first dynasty, the Shang, ruled the nation.

1122 B.C. The Chou people of western China overthrew the Shang and set up a new dynasty that ruled until 256 B.C.

221-206 B.C. The Ch'in dynasty established China's first strong central government.

202 B.C.-A.D. 220 China became a powerful empire under the Han dynasty. Chinese culture flourished.

581-618 The Sui dynasty reunified China after almost 400 years of division.

618-907 The T'ang dynasty ruled China during a period of prosperity and great cultural accomplishment.

960-1279 The Sung dynasty ruled the empire and made Neo-Confucianism the official state philosophy.

1275-1292 Marco Polo visited China.

1279 The Mongols gained control of all China.

1368-1644 The Ming dynasty governed China.

1644-1912 The Manchus ruled China as the Ch'ing dynasty.

1842 The Treaty of Nanking gave Hong Kong to Great Britain and opened five Chinese ports to British trade.

1851-1864 Millions of Chinese died in bloody warfare during the Taiping Rebellion.

1900 Secret societies attacked and killed Westerners and Chinese Christians during the Boxer Rebellion.

1912 The Republic of China was established.

1928 The Nationalists, led by Chiang Kai-shek, united China under one government.

1931 The Japanese seized Manchuria.

1934-1935 Mao Tse-tung led the Chinese Communists on their Long March to Shensi.

1937-1945 War with Japan shattered China.

1949 The Chinese Communists defeated the Nationalists and established the People's Republic of China.

1953 China began its First Five-Year Plan for economic development.

1958 The Communists launched the Great Leap Forward, which severely weakened China's economy.

1962 Chinese troops fought a border war with India.

1963 Friendly relations between China and Russia ended.

1966-1969 The Cultural Revolution disrupted education, the government, and daily life in China.

1971 China was admitted to the United Nations (UN).

1972 U.S. President Richard M. Nixon visited China.

1976 Communist Party Chairman Mao Tse-tung and Premier Chou En-lai died.

1979 China and the United States established normal diplomatic relations.

The oldest written records of Chinese history date from the Shang dynasty (1766?-1122 B.C.). These records consist of inscriptions inside bronze vessels and notations scratched on thousands of turtle shells and animal bones. About 100 B.C., a Chinese historian named Ssuma Ch'ien wrote the first major history of China. Through the centuries, the Chinese have always appreciated the importance of history and so have kept detailed records of the events of their times.

Beginnings of Chinese Civilization

People have lived in what is now China since long before the beginning of written history. A type of prehistoric human being called *Peking man* lived about 375,000 years ago in what is now northern China. By about 10,000 B.C., a number of New Stone Age cultures had developed in this area. From two of these cultures— the Yang-shao and the Lung-shan—a distinctly Chinese civilization gradually emerged.

The Yang-shao culture reached the peak of its development about 3000 B.C. The culture extended from the central valley of the Huang Ho to the present-day province of Kansu. In time, the Yang-shao culture was displaced by the Lung-shan, which spread over most of China Proper. The Lung-shan people lived in walled communities, cultivated millet and rice, and raised cattle and sheep.

China's first dynasty, the Shang dynasty, arose from the Lung-shan culture during the 1700's B.C. The Shang kingdom was centered in the Huang Ho Valley. It became a highly developed society governed by a hereditary class of aristocrats. The dynasty's outstanding accomplishments included the creation of magnificent bronze vessels, the development of horse-drawn war chariots, and the establishment of a Chinese system of writing.

In 1122 B.C., the Chou people of western China overthrew the Shang and established their own dynasty. The Chou dynasty ruled China until 256 B.C. From its

beginning, the dynasty directly controlled only part of northern China. In the east, the Chou gave authority to certain followers, who became lords of semi-independent states. As time passed, these lords grew increasingly independent of the royal court and so weakened its power. Battles over the years between the Chou rulers and non-Chinese invaders further weakened the dynasty. In 771 B.C., the Chou were forced to abandon their capital, near what is now Sian, and move eastward to Loyang.

During the later Chou period, the rulers of the eastern states fought one another for the control of all China. The fighting reached a peak between 403 and 221 B.C. Efforts to find a way to restore order to Chinese society

WORLD BOOK maps

China's First Dynasty, the Shang, arose in the Huang Ho Valley during the 1700's B.C. It ruled China until 1122 B.C.

The Ch'in Dynasty, in 221 B.C., established China's first empire controlled by a strong central government.

The Han Dynasty gained control of China in 202 B.C. Han rulers expanded the Chinese empire into central Asia.

helped produce a flowering of Chinese thought during this period. The great philosopher Confucius proposed new moral standards to replace the magical and religious standards of his time. This development in Chinese thought compared in many ways to the shift from religion to philosophy that occurred among the people of Greece at about the same time.

In 221 B.C., the Ch'in state defeated all its rivals and established China's first empire controlled by a strong central government. The Ch'in believed in a philosophy called *Legalism,* and their victory resulted partly from following Legalistic ideas. Legalism emphasized the importance of authority, efficient administration, and strict laws. A combination of Legalistic administrative practices and Confucian moral values helped the Chinese empire endure for more than 2,000 years.

The Age of Empire

The Early Empire. The Ch'in dynasty lasted only until 206 B.C. However, it brought great changes that influenced the entire age of empire in China. The first Ch'in emperor, Shih Huang Ti, abolished the local states and set up a strong central government. His government standardized weights and measures, the currency, and the Chinese writing system. To keep out invaders, Shih Huang Ti ordered the construction of the Great Wall of China. Laborers built the wall by joining shorter walls constructed during the Chou dynasty. The Great Wall stretches about 1,500 miles (2,410 kilometers) from the coast to the province of Kansu in north-central China.

Shih Huang Ti taxed the Chinese people heavily to support his military campaigns and his vast building projects. These taxes and the harsh enforcement of laws led to civil war soon after his death in 210 B.C. The Ch'in dynasty quickly collapsed. The Han dynasty then gained control of China. It ruled from 202 B.C. to A.D. 220.

During the Han period, Confucianism became the philosophical basis of government. Aristocrats held most of the important state offices. However, a person's qualifications began to play a role in the selection and placement of officials. Chinese influence spread into neighboring countries, and overland trade routes linked China with Europe for the first time.

In A.D. 8, a Han official named Wang Mang seized the throne and set up the Hsin dynasty. However, the Han dynasty regained control of China by A.D. 25. Art, education, and science thrived during this later Han period. Writers produced histories and dictionaries. They also collected classics of literature from earlier times. In A.D. 105, the Chinese invented paper. During the late Han period, Buddhism was introduced into China from India.

Political struggles at the royal court and administrative dishonesty plagued the last century of Han rule. In addition, powerful regional officials began to ignore the central government. Large-scale rebellion finally broke out, and the Han fell in 220. China then split into three competing kingdoms. Soon afterward, nomadic groups invaded northern China. A series of short-lived non-Chinese dynasties ruled all or part of the north from 304 to 581. In the south, the so-called Six Dynasties followed one another from 317 to 589. During these centuries of division, Buddhism spread across China and influenced all aspects of life.

The brief Sui dynasty (581-618) reunified China. By 605, the Grand Canal linked the Yangtze Valley with northern China. The canal made the grain and other products of the south more easily available to support the political and military needs of the north.

The T'ang Dynasty replaced the Sui in 618 and ruled China for nearly 300 years. The T'ang period was an age of prosperity and great cultural accomplishment. The T'ang capital at Ch'ang-an (now Sian) had more than a million persons, making it the largest city in the world. It attracted diplomats, traders, poets, and scholars from throughout Asia and the Mediterranean area. Some of China's greatest poets, including Li Po and Tu Fu, wrote during the T'ang period. Buddhism remained an enormous cultural influence, but followers adapted it to Chinese ways. Distinctly Chinese schools of Buddhism developed, including *Ch'an* (Zen) and *Ching-t'u* (Pure Land). During the 800's, however, a revival of Confucianism began.

In 755, a rebellion led by a northern general named An Lu-shan touched off a gradual decline in T'ang power. From 875 to 884, another great rebellion further weakened the T'ang empire, which finally ended in 907. During the period that followed, a succession of

"Five Dynasties and Ten Kingdoms" struggled for control of the shattered empire. In 960, the Sung dynasty reunified China.

The Sung Dynasty brought two major changes that affected the Chinese empire throughout the rest of its existence. First, the Sung rulers firmly established a system of civil service examinations that had begun during the T'ang period. They thus completed the shift of social and political power from aristocratic families to officials selected on the basis of talent. The second significant change was the development of *Neo-Confucianism*, which combined the moral standards of traditional Confucianism with elements of Buddhism and Taoism. The philosopher Chu Hsi was largely responsible for this new Confucianism. The Sung dynasty established Neo-Confucianism as the official state philosophy, and all later Chinese dynasties continued to support it.

During the Sung period, the introduction of early-ripening rice made it possible to grow two or three crops a year in the south. The increased rice production helped support the population, which for the first time exceeded 100 million. Chinese inventions during this period included gunpowder, the magnetic compass, and movable type for printing. Literature, philosophy, and history flourished as more and more people learned how to read and write. In the fine arts, the great Sung achievements were hard-glazed porcelains and magnificent landscape paintings.

The Sung dynasty never had great military strength. In 1126, it lost northern China to invaders from Manchuria. The Sung then moved their capital from K'aifeng to Hang-chou on the wealthy lower Yangtze Delta, and the dynasty became known as the Southern Sung.

Mongol Rule. During the 1200's, Mongol warriors swept into China from the north. The Mongol leader Kublai Khan established the Yuan dynasty. It controlled China from 1279 to 1368, the first time that all China had come under foreign rule. During the Yuan period, Europeans became aware of China through the reports of travelers and traders. The most enthusiastic reports came from Marco Polo, a trader from Venice. After traveling widely in China from 1275 to 1292, Polo returned home with glowing accounts of the highly civilized country he called *Cathay*.

The Mongols ruled China harshly. During the mid-1300's, rebellions drove the Mongols out of China and led to the establishment of the Ming dynasty.

The Ming Dynasty ruled from 1368 to 1644, a period of stability, prosperity, and revived Chinese influence in eastern Asia. Literature and art flourished again. In reaction to Mongol rule, the Ming emperors looked down on all things foreign. When European traders visited China during the 1500's and 1600's, the Ming rulers treated them as inferiors. In addition, the Chinese considered the Europeans' trade activities to be smuggling and piracy. The low opinion the Chinese had of European traders hampered Roman Catholic missionaries who began to reach China about 1600.

The Early Rule of the Manchus. In 1644, the Manchu people of Manchuria invaded China and established the Ch'ing dynasty. The Manchus ruled China until

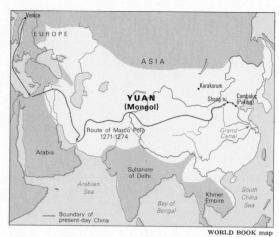

WORLD BOOK map

The Yuan (Mongol) Dynasty ruled China from 1279 to 1368. During this period, China was part of the vast Mongol Empire. Marco Polo, a trader from Venice, visited China during the Yuan period and carried home reports of a highly civilized country.

1912. Like the Mongols, the Manchus were foreigners. But unlike the Mongols, the Manchus had adopted many elements of Chinese culture before they gained control of the empire. The Manchus strongly supported Neo-Confucianism and modeled their political system after that of the Ming.

From 1661 to 1799, the Ch'ing empire enjoyed stability and prosperity. Chinese influence extended into Mongolia, Tibet, and central Asia. Commerce and the output of agriculture and the handicraft industry increased remarkably. China's population expanded rapidly. It rose from about 150 million in 1700 to more than 400 million by 1850.

By the late 1700's, the standard of living in China began to decline as the population grew faster than agricultural production. After the 1760's, political dishonesty plagued the Ch'ing administration. In 1796, the worsening economic and political conditions touched off a rebellion, which was led by anti-Manchu secret societies. The rebellion lasted until 1804 and greatly weakened the Ch'ing dynasty.

Clash with the Western Powers. European merchants had little effect on China before the 1800's. The Chinese government restricted foreign trade to the port of Canton and severely limited contact between foreigners and Chinese. China exported large quantities of tea and silk to the West but purchased few goods in return. To balance their trade, European merchants began to bring opium to China during the early 1800's. The Chinese had outlawed the importation of opium, and so the Europeans were smuggling the drug.

Opium smuggling created much local disorder in China, and the large outflow of silver to pay for the opium seriously disturbed the economy. In March 1839, Chinese officials tried to stop the illegal trade by seizing 20,000 chests of opium from British merchants in Canton. The Opium War then broke out between China and Great Britain. Britain easily won the war, which ended with the Treaty of Nanking in 1842.

The Treaty of Nanking was the first of what the Chinese called the *unequal treaties*. It gave the Chinese island of Hong Kong to Great Britain and opened five Chinese ports to British residence and trade. The Treaty of Nanking also granted British officials the right to deal on equal terms with Chinese officials and to try criminal cases involving British citizens. China signed similar treaties with France and the United States in 1844 and with several other European nations by 1851. These treaties stated that any rights granted to one foreign power must also be given to the other nations. The Western nations thus acquired a common interest in maintaining their special privileges in China.

From 1858 to 1860, China and the foreign powers signed more treaties. These treaties opened additional ports to trade, permitted foreign shipping on the Yangtze, and allowed missionaries to live and own property in the interior of China. The treaties also called for the Western nations to establish permanent diplomatic offices in Peking. Great Britain added the Kowloon Peninsula to its Hong Kong colony, and Russia received all Chinese territory north of the Amur River and east of the Ussuri River.

The Taiping Rebellion. A series of uprisings during the mid-1800's posed a serious threat to the survival of the Ch'ing dynasty. The most important uprising was the Taiping Rebellion. It lasted from 1851 to 1864 and caused the loss of millions of lives. The Taipings were a semireligious group that combined Christian beliefs with ancient Chinese ideas for perfecting society. They challenged both the Ch'ing dynasty and Confucianism with a program to divide the land equally among the people. After 14 years of bloody civil war, local Chinese officials organized new armies, which defeated the Taipings. The Ch'ing received some military aid from the foreign powers. These nations wanted the dynasty to survive so that the terms of the unequal treaties could remain in effect.

The Fall of the Manchus. A disastrous war with Japan in 1894 and 1895 forced the Chinese to recognize Japan's control over Korea. China also had to give the Japanese the island of Taiwan, which China had controlled since 1683. France, Germany, Great Britain, and Russia then forced the crumbling Chinese empire to grant them more trading rights and territory. The

division of China into a number of European colonies appeared likely. But the Chinese people had begun to develop strong feelings of belonging together as a nation. This growth of nationalism helped prevent the division of the country. In addition, the United States wanted China to remain independent. In 1899, the United States persuaded the other Western powers to accept the *Open-Door Policy*, which guaranteed the rights of all nations to trade with China on an equal basis.

By the 1890's, some Chinese violently opposed the spread of Western and Christian influences in China. Chinese rebels formed secret societies to fight these influences. The best-known society was called the *Boxers* by Westerners because its members practiced Chinese ceremonial exercises that resembled shadowboxing. In the Boxer Rebellion of 1900, the Boxers and other secret societies attacked and killed Westerners and Chinese Christians. Even the Manchu court supported this campaign of terror. A rescue force from eight nations crushed the rebellion.

In the years following the Boxer Rebellion, the Manchus set out to reform the Chinese government and economy. They abolished the Confucian civil service examinations, established modern schools, and sent students abroad to study. They also organized and equipped a Western-style army. In addition, the Ch'ing court reorganized the central government, promised to adopt a constitution, and permitted the provinces to elect their own legislatures.

The Manchu reforms came too late to save the dynasty. A movement to set up a republic had been growing since the Japanese defeat of China in 1895. In 1905, several revolutionary republican organizations combined to form the United League. They chose as their leader Sun Yat-sen, a Western-educated physician.

From 1905 to 1911, the rebels staged a series of unsuccessful armed attacks against the Manchus. Finally, on Oct. 10, 1911, army troops loosely associated with the United League revolted at Wu-ch'ang. By the year's end, all the southern and central provinces had declared their independence from Manchu rule.

Modern China

The Early Republic. In December 1911, the leaders of the revolution met in Nan-ching to establish the Re-

WORLD BOOK maps

The Ch'ing Dynasty, an empire established by the Manchu people of Manchuria, ruled China from 1644 to 1912.

In 1934, the Nationalists forced the Communists to flee their bases in southern China and begin their famous Long March.

Japanese Expansion into China reached its greatest extent in 1944, when the Japanese controlled much of eastern China.

Photoworld

Troops from Eight Nations crushed the Boxer Rebellion of 1900—an anti-Western campaign waged by Chinese secret societies. Victorious foreign troops paraded in Peking, above.

May 4, 1919, students in Peking demonstrated against the Versailles Peace Conference. The conference permitted Japan to keep control of the German holdings it had seized in China during World War I (1914-1918). The student demonstrations helped spread the ideas presented by *New Youth* and other journals. This revolution in thought became known as the *May Fourth Movement*. It contributed greatly to the growth of Chinese nationalism and so strengthened the drive for political revolution.

In 1919, Sun began to reorganize the Nationalist Party and to recruit supporters from among students. At almost the same time, the first Communist student groups appeared in Peking and Shanghai. In 1923, Russia sent advisers to China to help the Nationalists. The Russians also persuaded the Chinese Communists to join the Nationalist Party and help it carry out the revolution. The party began to develop its own army and to organize workers and peasants to prepare for an attack on the northern warlords.

Sun Yat-sen died in 1925, and leadership of the Nationalist Party gradually passed to its military commander, Chiang Kai-shek. In 1926, the Nationalists began a campaign to defeat the northern warlords and soon won some major victories. In 1927, Chiang and his troops turned against the Communists and destroyed the Communist-backed labor unions in Shanghai. Most Communist leaders fled to the hills in the province of Kiangsi in southern China. In 1928, the Nationalists captured Peking and united China under one government for the first time since 1916.

Nationalist Rule. The Nationalist government was a one-party dictatorship that never gained full control of China. Communist opposition and Japanese aggression severely limited the Nationalist government's power and accomplishments.

By 1931, the Communists had established 15 rural bases and set up a rival government in southern and central China. In 1934, Chiang Kai-shek's armies forced the Communists to evacuate their bases and begin their famous *Long March*. By the end of 1935, the Communists had marched more than 6,000 miles (9,700 kilometers) over a winding route to the province of Shensi in northern China. Of the approximately 100,000 Communists who began the march, only a few thousand survived to reach Shensi. During the Long March, Mao Tse-tung became the leader of the Chinese Communist Party.

While Chiang was fighting the Communists, the Japanese were seizing more and more Chinese territory. In 1931, the Japanese occupied Manchuria and made it a puppet state called *Manchukuo*. They then extended their military influence into Inner Mongolia and other parts of northern China. Chiang agreed to a series of Japanese demands because he felt unprepared to fight the Japanese until he had defeated the Communists.

Many students and intellectuals opposed Chiang's giving in to Japan. They organized demonstrations and anti-Japanese associations. Dissatisfaction with Chiang's policies spread to Manchurian troops who were blockading the Communist-held areas in the northwest. In 1936, the Manchurian forces kidnapped

public of China. They named Sun Yat-sen temporary president of the republic. The desperate Manchus then called upon a retired military official named Yuan Shih-k'ai to try to defeat the republicans. However, Yuan secretly arranged a settlement with Sun and his followers. The last Manchu emperor, a 6-year-old boy, gave up the throne on Feb. 12, 1912. On March 10, Yuan became president in place of Sun, who had agreed to step down.

Yuan quickly moved to expand his personal power and ignored the wishes of the republicans. In 1913, the former revolutionaries established the *Kuomintang* (Nationalist Party) and organized a revolt against Yuan. The revolt failed, and the Nationalist leaders fled to Japan. Yuan's presidency became a dictatorship, and he took steps to establish himself as emperor. But even Yuan's own followers opposed the reestablishment of the empire. A rebellion by military leaders in the provinces forced him to abandon his plans.

The Warlord Period. Yuan Shih-k'ai died in 1916, and the power of the central government quickly crumbled. Presidents continued to hold office in Peking, but the real power in northern China lay in the hands of *warlords* (local military leaders). With the support of southern warlords, Sun Yat-sen set up a rival government in Canton in 1917. By 1922, the republic had failed hopelessly and civil war was widespread.

Meanwhile, great changes were occurring in Chinese culture and society. For example, a magazine called *New Youth* attacked Confucianism and presented a wide range of new philosophies and social theories. On

Chiang in Sian. He was released only after agreeing to end the civil war and form a united front with the Communists against the Japanese.

War with Japan. The Japanese army launched a major attack against China in 1937. The Chinese resisted courageously, but Japanese armies controlled most of eastern China by the end of 1938. The Nationalist forces withdrew to the province of Szechwan, where they made Ch'ung-ch'ing the wartime capital.

China joined the Allies in World War II on Dec. 8, 1941, one day after the Japanese attacked the United States at Pearl Harbor, Hawaii. The Allies provided China with aid, but constant warfare against the Japanese exhausted China's resources and strength. The cost of the war caused severe inflation, which demoralized the Chinese people and weakened support for the Nationalists.

For the Communists, the war against Japan provided an opportunity for political and military expansion. In northern China, they gained control of large areas that the Japanese army had overrun but lacked the forces to defend. The Communists enlarged their army and organized the people to provide food and shelter for their soldiers. They also began a social revolution in the countryside, which included redistributing land to the peasants in Communist-controlled areas. When the war against Japan ended in August 1945, the Communists held an area in northern China with a population of about 100 million. In addition, they claimed to have an army of more than 900,000 soldiers.

Civil War. In 1946, the United States sent General George C. Marshall to China to attempt to arrange a political settlement between the Nationalists and the Communists. However, neither the Nationalists nor the Communists believed that they could achieve their goals by coming to terms with the other side. In mid-1946, full-scale fighting began.

The superior military tactics of the Communists and the social revolution they conducted in the countryside

Eastfoto

Chinese Communists, led by Mao Tse-tung, defeated the Nationalist government in a war from 1946 to 1949. Mao is shown here on horseback, moving with his soldiers across Shensi in 1947.

gradually turned the tide against the Nationalists. After capturing Tientsin and Peking in January 1949, Mao Tse-tung's armies crossed the Yangtze River and drove the Nationalists toward southern China. On Oct. 1, 1949, Mao proclaimed the establishment in Peking of the People's Republic of China. In December of that year, Chiang Kai-shek and his followers fled to the island of Taiwan.

The Beginning of Communist Rule took place under the direction of Mao Tse-tung, who served as both head of state and chairman of the Communist Party. Premier Chou En-lai directed all government departments and ministries. Military and economic aid from Russia helped support the new government. From 1949 to 1952, the new government firmly established its control over China and promoted the recovery of the nation's economy. They seized farmland from landlords and redistributed the land among the peasants. This process of land redistribution was a bloody one. Estimates of the number of landlords killed range from 50,000 to several million.

In 1953, China began its First Five-Year Plan for economic development. During the period from 1953 to 1957, industry grew at the rapid rate of about 15 per cent a year. By 1957, the Communists had brought all industry under government control. In addition, peasants were forced or persuaded to combine their landholdings into agricultural cooperatives. But agricultural production increased much more slowly than industrial output.

The Great Leap Forward was the name given to China's Second Five-Year Plan. Launched in 1958, the Great Leap Forward was a campaign to accelerate dramatically China's economic development. It was based on Mao's firm belief that human willpower and effort could overcome all obstacles. Thus, the government tried to speed development by greatly increasing the number of workers and their hours while ignoring China's lack of capital and modern technology. The government combined the agricultural cooperatives into huge communes to improve the efficiency of farmworkers. In industry, laborers worked extra shifts. Machinery was operated continuously, without being stopped even for maintenance.

The Great Leap Forward shattered China's economy. From 1959 to 1961, China experienced economic depression, food shortages, and a decline in industrial output. By 1962, the economy began to recover. However, the Chinese had not solved the problem of achieving economic growth while maintaining revolutionary values. Disagreement over this issue began to produce a major split within the Communist Party between *radicals* and *moderates*. The radicals called for China to strive for a classless society in which everyone would work selflessly for the common good. The moderates, however, stressed the importance of economic development. They believed that the policies of the radicals were unrealistic and hampered the modernization of China.

Break with Russia. Friendly relations between China and Russia ended in the early 1960's. China had criticized the Russians as early as 1956 for their policy of "peaceful coexistence" with the West. Unlike the Russians, the Chinese at that time believed that war with the West was inevitable. They also accused Russia of betraying the aims of Communism. In 1960, Russia stopped its technical assistance to China. In 1962, the Russians refused to support China in its border war with India. Russia signed a nuclear test ban treaty with the United States and Great Britain in 1963. The Chinese then broke with the Russians, whom they accused of joining an anti-Chinese plot.

The Cultural Revolution. In 1966, Mao Tse-tung gave his support to the radicals in the Communist Party. Mao thus began what he called the *Cultural Revolution.* The radicals accused many top party and government officials of failing to follow Communist principles and removed them from their positions. These officials included Liu Shao-chi, who had replaced Mao as head of state in 1959. Students and other young people formed semimilitary organizations called the *Red Guards.* They marched and demonstrated in the major cities against those whom they called counterrevolutionaries and anti-Maoists. The universities were closed from 1966 to 1970, and the entire educational system was disrupted. Radicals seized control of many provincial and city governments. Violence frequently broke out as competing radical groups struggled for power.

Mao's attempt to put China back on a revolutionary path wrecked the government and economy so severely that he had to call out the army in 1967 to restore order. In 1969, the Communist Party, the government, and the educational system gradually began to resume their normal activities. But the conflict between radicals and moderates within the party continued.

Improved Relations with the West. During the early 1970's, Canada and several other Western nations established diplomatic relations with the People's Re-

Dirck Halstead, Black Star

Vice-Premier Teng Hsiao-p'ing visited the United States early in 1979. At a White House ceremony, above, he and President Jimmy Carter signed agreements on trade and other matters.

public of China. The United States continued to recognize the Nationalist government on Taiwan. But in 1971, the United States ended its long-standing opposition to United Nations (UN) membership for the People's Republic. Instead, it favored UN membership for both the People's Republic and Taiwan. In October 1971, the UN voted to admit the People's Republic in place of Taiwan.

In 1972, U.S. President Richard M. Nixon traveled to China and met with Premier Chou En-lai and Communist Party chairman Mao Tse-tung. During Nixon's visit, the United States and China signed the Shanghai Communiqué, which looked forward to the establishment of normal relations. The two nations opened diplomatic offices in each other's country in 1973. President Gerald R. Ford visited China in 1975.

China After Mao. Both Chou En-lai and Mao Tse-tung died in 1976. A power struggle then developed between a group of moderates led by Hua Kuo-feng and a radical group led by Mao's widow, Chiang Ch'ing. Hua's group won the struggle, and he succeeded Chou as premier and Mao as chairman of the Communist Party. Hua's group arrested Chiang Ch'ing and three of her followers—the so-called Gang of Four. The Gang of Four was publicly blamed for harming China's development since the mid-1960's.

Many changes have occurred in China since 1976. For example, the people have greater political freedom, and trade and cultural contacts with foreign countries have increased. In 1977, Teng Hsiao-p'ing became vice-premier and began to exercise considerable power in the government. Under the new leadership of Hua and Teng, the government's goal is to achieve full modernization of China by the year 2000. On Jan. 1, 1979, the United States and the People's Republic officially established normal diplomatic relations.

ROBERT F. DERNBERGER, NORMA DIAMOND,
RICHARD EDWARDS, ALBERT FEUERWERKER, DONALD J. MUNRO,
RHOADS MURPHEY, and WILLIAM PANG-YU TING

Eastfoto

The Red Guards demonstrated in China's cities during the Cultural Revolution (1966-1969). The Cultural Revolution was Mao Tse-tung's attempt to return China to a revolutionary course.

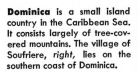

Dominica is a small island country in the Caribbean Sea. It consists largely of tree-covered mountains. The village of Soufriere, *right,* lies on the southern coast of Dominica.

© Fritz Henle, Photo Researchers, Inc.

DOMINICA is a small island country in the Caribbean Sea. It consists of a single island that lies 320 miles (515 kilometers) north of the Venezuelan coast. For location, see WEST INDIES (map). Dominica has an area of 290 square miles (751 square kilometers) and a population of about 79,000.

Dominica became independent in 1978 after being ruled by Great Britain since the 1700's. Its official name is Commonwealth of Dominica. Roseau is the capital and largest city. Dominica's basic unit of money is the East Caribbean dollar.

Government. Dominica is a republic headed by a prime minister. The prime minister is a member of an eight-member Cabinet, which conducts the operations of the government. A legislature called the House of Assembly makes the nation's laws and elects the prime minister from among its members. It consists of 21 members elected by the people and 3 appointed by the government.

People. Most Dominicans have African or mixed African, British, and French ancestry. A small percentage have mostly Carib Indian ancestry. About two-thirds of the people live in rural villages, and the rest live in urban areas. Most of the people live in Western-style houses or thatch-roofed huts. They wear Western-style clothing. Their main foods include bananas, crabs, crayfish, frog legs, lobsters, and sweet potatoes.

The majority of Dominicans who live in cities speak English, the nation's official language. The villagers speak chiefly a kind of language called *French patois,* which is a mixture of African languages and French. About 80 per cent of the people are Roman Catholics, and almost all the rest are Protestants. Dominica has about 55 elementary schools and 7 high schools.

Land and Climate. Dominica is a mountainous, tree-covered island that was formed by volcanic eruptions. Some mountains in the north and south rise more than 4,000 feet (1,200 meters). Flat land lies along parts of the coast. The country has many rivers, but most are too rough to be used by boats other than canoes.

Temperatures in Dominica seldom rise above 90° F. (32° C) or fall below 65° F. (18° C). The annual rainfall ranges from 79 inches (201 centimeters) in Roseau, on the southwest coast, to 400 inches (1,000 centimeters) in the mountainous areas.

Economy of Dominica is based on agriculture. More than 60 per cent of the people work on farms, and most of the rest are employed in processing agricultural products. Bananas are the country's chief product and export. Other products and exports include coconuts and coconut by-products. Manufacturing, mining, retail trade, and tourism are minor economic activities in Dominica.

History. The first inhabitants of Dominica were the Arawak Indians. They settled on the island about 2,000 years ago. The Carib Indians took it from the Arawaks about 1,000 years later. On Nov. 3, 1493—a Sunday—Christopher Columbus became the first European to sight the island. He named it *Dominica,* the Latin word for *Sunday.*

French and British settlers started to arrive in Dominica during the 1600's. For many years, the Carib, British, and French fought for control of the island. The British gained possession of it in 1763 and shipped African slaves to Dominica as farm workers. Britain freed the slaves in 1834. From the 1930's to the 1970's, Britain gradually increased Dominica's control over its own affairs. Dominica gained independence on Nov. 3, 1978.　　GUSTAVO A. ANTONINI and DIANNE E. ROCHELEAU

ROSEAU, *roh ZOH* (pop. 12,000), is the capital and largest city of Dominica, an island country in the Caribbean Sea. The city lies on the southwestern coast of the island, at the mouth of the Roseau River.

Roseau has a busy port whose import and export activities are the basis of the city's economy. The community includes modern office buildings as well as large stone structures that date from the 1700's. Many of Roseau's people live in small wooden houses.

Roseau was founded in the mid-1700's by French settlers. They named the site *Roseau,* which means *reed* in French, because reeds grew there. From the 1600's to 1759, France and Great Britain struggled for control of Dominica. Britain ruled the country from 1759 to 1978, when Dominica became an independent country.　　GUSTAVO A. ANTONINI and DIANNE E. ROCHELEAU

SAINT LUCIA

© Nicholas DeVore III, Bruce Coleman Inc.

St. Lucia, a country in the Caribbean Sea, consists of one small island. It has a tropical climate. Palm trees grow along the shore at a small fishing village on the west coast, *above*.

SAINT LUCIA is a small island country in the West Indies. It consists of a single island—also called St. Lucia—in the Caribbean Sea about 240 miles (386 kilometers) north of Venezuela. For location, see WEST INDIES (map). St. Lucia has an area of 238 square miles (616 square kilometers) and a population of about 115,-000.

St. Lucia became independent in 1979 after being ruled by Great Britain since 1814. Castries, on the northwest coast, is the capital and largest city. "Sons and Daughters of Saint Lucia" is the country's national anthem. The East Caribbean dollar is the basic unit of currency.

Government. St. Lucia is a constitutional monarchy and a member of the Commonwealth of Nations (see COMMONWEALTH OF NATIONS). A prime minister heads the country's government. He or she governs with the aid of a Cabinet of 10 members. A 20-member House of Assembly and an 8-member Senate pass the nation's laws. The members of the House, who are elected by the people, choose the prime minister. The *governor general*, a symbolic official appointed by the British monarch, appoints the members of the Senate.

People. About 90 per cent of the people of St. Lucia are descendants of black African slaves. Early British and French settlers brought the slaves to the island. Whites make up most of the rest of the population. They include many descendants of the British and French. More than 90 per cent of the islanders are Roman Catholics.

About 85 per cent of the islanders live in rural areas, and about 15 per cent live in urban areas. English, the nation's official language, is widely used, but many islanders speak a French dialect. St. Lucians wear Western-style clothing. Large numbers of them live in pastel-colored wooden houses.

Land and Climate. St. Lucia is mountainous and has little flat land. Tropical vegetation covers the country. Mount Gimie, St. Lucia's highest peak, rises 3,145 feet (959 meters) near the center of the island. Gros Piton and Petit Piton, twin peaks in the southwest area, are famous for their sugarloaf shapes. St. Lucia has an average of about 100 inches (254 centimeters) of rain annually. Temperatures range from about 70° to 95° F. (21° to 35° C).

Economy of St. Lucia is based on agriculture. The islanders use most of the produce that they grow, and few crops except bananas and coconuts are exported. St. Lucian factories manufacture clothing, electrical parts, paper products, and textiles. However, industry plays a minor role in the economy.

A paved road encircles the island and connects all the main towns with Castries. The country has two airports, and planes from the islands of Barbados and Trinidad make daily flights to St. Lucia.

History. The Arawak Indians were the original inhabitants of St. Lucia. They were conquered by the Carib Indians of South America about 1300. During the early 1600's, the Caribs fought the French and British and prevented them from settling on the island. French settlers finally established a permanent colony there in the mid-1600's. The French, and also the British, later began other settlements in St. Lucia.

Control of St. Lucia alternated between Britain and France seven times until Britain took over the island in 1814. Through the years, both the British and French brought slaves from Africa to work on their plantations. In 1834, Britain banned slavery throughout its empire. The British gradually gave St. Lucia more control over its affairs, and the country became independent on Feb. 22, 1979.   THOMAS G. MATHEWS

SOLOMON ISLANDS is an island country in the South Pacific Ocean. Its largest islands are Choiseul, Guadalcanal, Malaita, New Georgia, San Cristobal, and Santa Isabel. Its many other islands include Bellona, Rennell, and the Santa Cruz Islands.

The country's largest islands are part of an island chain that is also called the Solomon Islands. However, not all the islands in the chain belong to the country of the Solomon Islands. Bougainville, Buka, and a few smaller islands in the northern part of the chain are part of Papua New Guinea.

The Solomon Islands lies about 1,000 miles (1,610 kilometers) northeast of Australia. It has a land area of 11,500 square miles (29,785 square kilometers). The country spreads over about 230,000 square miles (600,000 square kilometers) of ocean. About 230,000 persons live in the Solomon Islands.

Great Britain ruled the Solomons from 1893 to 1978, when the islands became independent. Honiara, on Guadalcanal, is the capital. The Solomon Islands dollar is the country's basic unit of currency. "God Save Our Solomon Islands" is the national anthem.

Government. The Solomon Islands is a constitutional monarchy and a member of the Commonwealth of Nations (see COMMONWEALTH OF NATIONS). A prime minister, who is the leader of the political party with the most seats in Parliament, heads the government. An eight-member Cabinet helps the prime minister run the government. Cabinet members are appointed by the

National capital
Town or village
Elevation above sea level
International boundary
Road

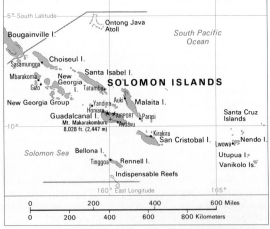

WORLD BOOK map

prime minister. A 38-member Parliament makes the country's laws. The people elect the members of Parliament to four-year terms. A governor general represents the British monarch in the Solomon Islands.

The Solomon Islands is divided into four districts for purposes of local government. Elected local councils govern the districts.

People. Most Solomon Islanders are dark-skinned people called Melanesians, and more than 90 per cent of them live in rural villages. Many of the people build houses on stilts to keep the dwellings cool. The main foods include chicken, fish, pork, coconuts, and *taro*, a tropical plant with one or more edible rootlike stems.

Although English is the official language of the Solomon Islands, about 90 languages are spoken among the Melanesians. The islanders also speak *Pidgin English*, which helps them cross language barriers (see PIDGIN ENGLISH). About 80 per cent of the people are Protes-

tants. The other islanders are Roman Catholics or follow local traditional beliefs. The nation has about 350 elementary schools, about 10 high schools, and a technical school. About 200 islanders go to universities in Papua New Guinea and Fiji.

Land and Climate. The country's main islands were formed by volcanoes. They are rugged, mountainous, and covered with tropical plants. The islands range from 90 to 120 miles (140 to 190 kilometers) long and from 20 to 30 miles (32 to 48 kilometers) wide. Each island has a central spine that has mountains up to about 7,000 feet (2,100 meters) high. The land drops sharply to the sea on one side of the island and gently to a narrow coastal strip on the other. Some of the outlying islands are *atolls* (ring-shaped coral reefs).

Rainfall in the Solomon Islands varies from 60 to 200 inches (150 to 500 centimeters) annually. Temperatures range from 70° to 90° F. (21° to 32° C).

Economy. Fish, timber, and *copra* (dried coconut meat) are the main products of the Solomon Islands. Japan buys almost all the fish and timber exported by the country. Food, machinery, manufactured goods, and gasoline are imported from Australia, Great Britain, Japan, Malaysia, and Singapore. The country has good shipping services, but most of its roads are poor. Air routes connect the Solomon Islands with Australia and other neighboring islands. The government publishes a weekly newspaper and broadcasts radio programs in both English and Pidgin English.

History. Scholars believe the Solomon Islands were first settled about 3,000 years ago by people from New Guinea. In 1568, a Spanish explorer named Álvaro de Mendaña became the first European to reach the islands. Few other Europeans went there until the 1700's. From 1870 to 1911, Europeans recruited nearly 30,000 islanders to work on plantations in Fiji and in Queensland, Australia. Some of the islanders were recruited by force and treated harshly. As a result, Great Britain took control of the Solomons in 1893 and made them a protectorate.

Guadalcanal and other islands in the Solomons were the scene of fierce fighting between Allied and Japanese forces in 1942 and 1943, during World War II. The Solomon Islands gained independence from Great Britain on July 7, 1978.   ROBERT LANGDON

Janet Young

A Village School in the Solomon Islands has several huts, each housing one grade. About two-thirds of the children in the country attend elementary and high school.

TUVALU

TUVALU, *too VAH loo* or *TOO vuh LOO*, is a small island country in the South Pacific Ocean. It has a population of only 8,000 and a land area of only 10 square miles (26 square kilometers). Tuvalu ranks second to Vatican City as the world's smallest nation in population. It is the fourth smallest in area, after Vatican City, Monaco, and Nauru.

Tuvalu lies about 2,000 miles (3,200 kilometers) northeast of Australia. For location, see PACIFIC ISLANDS (map). It consists of nine islands that are spread over about 360 miles (579 kilometers).

Tuvalu, formerly called the Ellice Islands, was ruled by Great Britain from the 1890's to 1978. It became independent in 1978.

Funafuti, a village of about 900 people, is the capital of Tuvalu. The country's basic unit of money is the tala.

Government. Tuvalu is a constitutional monarchy and a member of the Commonwealth of Nations (see COMMONWEALTH OF NATIONS). A prime minister, chosen by a legislature of 12 members elected by the people, heads the government. Each island is administered by a council of 6 members. Island courts handle most trials. The High Court of Tuvalu hears appeals.

People. Most of the people of Tuvalu are Polynesians. They live in villages, most of which cluster around a church and a meeting house. Tuvaluan houses have raised foundations, open sides, and thatched roofs. The main foods of the people are bananas, coconuts, fish, and *taro*, a tropical plant with one or more edible rootlike stems. The islanders raise pigs and chickens to eat at feasts. Tuvaluans usually wear light, bright-colored cotton clothing.

The people speak the Tuvaluan language, and many also know English. Both languages are used in official government business. All the islands except one have an elementary school supported by the government. A few Tuvaluans attend a university in Fiji, an island country to the south.

Land and Climate. The nine islands of Tuvalu are, from north to south, Nanumea, Niutao, Nanumanga, Nui, Vaitupu, Nukufetau, Funafuti, Nukulaelae, and Niulakita. Most of the islands are *atolls* (ring-shaped coral reefs) that surround lagoons. The principal trees of Tuvalu are coconut palms and pandanus palms.

Tuvalu has a tropical climate, with daytime temperatures of about 80° F. (27° C). The southern islands receive about 140 inches (356 centimeters) of rain a year. The northern islands are drier.

Economy. Tuvalu has poor soil, few natural resources, almost no manufacturing, and no mining. Coconut palm trees cover much of the country, and the islanders use the coconuts to produce *copra* (dried coconut meat), their chief export (see COPRA). The people grow such crops as bananas and taro for their own use. They also weave baskets and mats for export. Many young islanders work on ocean ships because of a lack of opportunities at home. Tuvalu receives aid from some other countries, including Australia and Great Britain.

History. The first inhabitants of Tuvalu probably came from Samoa hundreds of years ago. In 1568, Álvaro de Mendaña, a Spanish explorer, became the first European to see part of Tuvalu. But the islands remained largely unknown to Europeans until the early 1800's. Europeans called them the Ellice Islands. Great Britain took control of the islands in the 1890's. In 1916, Britain combined the islands with the Gilbert Islands to the north to form the Gilbert and Ellice Islands Colony. In 1975, the two island groups were separated. The Ellice Islands were renamed Tuvalu. Great Britain granted Tuvalu independence on Oct. 1, 1978. ROBERT LANGDON

FUNAFUTI, *FOO nah FOO tih* (pop. 900), is the capital of Tuvalu, a small island country in the South Pacific Ocean. Funafuti is one of the world's smallest and most unusual national capitals. It is the largest islet of an *atoll* that is also called Funafuti. An atoll is a ring-shaped coral reef that surrounds a lagoon. The Funafuti atoll consists of 30 islets that have a total area of 689 acres (279 hectares).

All the people of the atoll live in Fongafale village on the islet of Funafuti. The main government offices of Tuvalu, and a hospital, a hotel, and a jail, are on the islet. A wharf and an airport are nearby. Funafuti was the site of a United States military base during World War II (1939-1945). ROBERT LANGDON

Schoolchildren in Funafuti, the capital of Tuvalu, play a game near their school. All except one of the islands of Tuvalu have a government-sponsored elementary school.

1975
1976
1977
1978
1979

Dictionary Supplement

This section lists important words from the 1980 edition of THE WORLD BOOK DICTIONARY. This dictionary, first published in 1963, keeps abreast of our living language with a program of continuous editorial revision. The following supplement has been prepared under the direction of the editors of THE WORLD BOOK ENCYCLOPEDIA and Clarence L. Barnhart, editor in chief of THE WORLD BOOK DICTIONARY. It is presented as a service to owners of the dictionary and as an informative feature to subscribers to THE WORLD BOOK YEAR BOOK.

A a

age|ist (āʹjist), *adj.* discriminating against old or elderly people; practicing ageism: *Our ageist society usually lumps all old people into one great, gray mass without differentiating them* (Maggie Kuhn).

an|ti|feed|ant (anʹtē fēʹdənt), *n.* a chemical substance, such as an alkaloid, coumarin, or terpene, that repels plant-eating insects: *New approaches to pest control . . . exploit the use of juvenile hormone analogues, "antifeedants," and chemosterilants* (Nature). *If crops were sprayed with efficient, synthetic antifeedants, the pests might turn from crops to weeds* (G. B. Kauffman).

ar|a-A (arʹə āʹ), *n.* a drug used to control viral infections. It is made from a sugar derived from gum arabic and a substance present in nucleic acid. Ara-A is effective against encephalitis, hepatitis, and influenza. *Hailed as the most significant advance since the first clinical use of penicillin in 1941, ara-A is derived from a type of sponge found in the Caribbean Sea* (Dianne Rafalik). [< *ara*(binose)-*A*(denine), constituents of the drug]

assertiveness training, a method of training submissive individuals to behave with confidence, usually by adopting an aggressive attitude: *Cosmetic treatments, charm schools, assertiveness training—nothing helped make her anything except more . . . self-conscious* (TV Guide).

a|ya|tol|lah (ä''yə tōlʹə), *n.* the title of a Shiite Moslem religious teacher of the highest rank, especially in Iran: *The prime force was the bitterness of the mullahs and of their leaders—the ayatollahs—against the Shah's industrializing and modernizing campaign* (Max Lerner). [< Arabic *āyatollāh* (literally) sign of God]

B b

bar-code (bärʹkōd'), *v.,* **-cod|ed, -cod|ing.** = bar code (def. 2).

bar code, 1 a code of lines and numbers for identifying a product in a computerized system of checkout and inventory. The Universal Product Code is a bar code. **2** to furnish with such a code: *The Council of Periodical Distributors Associations has asked mass market publishers to "bar code" their books* (Publishers Weekly).

beau|til|i|ty (byü tilʹə tē), *n.* the qualities of beauty and usefulness or purpose combined in the design of a building, a piece of furniture, or some other object or structure: *The best new word that fills a gap in the language was minted by architectural writer Ada Louise Huxtable to describe a happy marriage of form and function: "beautility"* (William Safire). [blend of *beauty* and *utility*]

bi|o|a|vail|a|bil|i|ty (bīʹō ə vāʹlə bilʹə tē), *n.* the efficacy of a drug at the site of disease or malfunction in the body: *Researchers have been giving a lot of attention lately to what they call bioavailability—how much of the original drug administered is delivered undiminished or unchanged to the site of the body where it is needed* (Sunday Times).

blow dryer, a portable electric blower for drying and styling the hair: *Using a blow dryer has become a unisex morning ritual. The results are natural and uncontrived—though not unstyled* (Consumer Reports).

blue box, an electronic device that generates telephone dialing tones, used fraudulently to make direct long-distance calls undetected by the telephone billing apparatus: *[He] was convicted by a federal jury here on felony charges of cheating a telephone company by using "blue boxes" to make illegal overseas calls* (Wall Street Journal).

bong² (bông, bong), *n.* a water pipe for smoking marijuana: *A bong is a long, vertical pipe with a large smoke chamber and a hole that creates a carburetor effect* (New York Times Magazine). [origin unknown]

bur|ri|to (bér rēʹtō, bù-), *n., pl.* **-tos.** a thick tortilla rolled up with a filling of meat and often cheese: *The drive-in Dairy Queen offers tacos, enchiladas, and burritos along with its standard shakes, burgers, and fries* (New Yorker). [< Mexican Spanish *burrito* (literally) little burro]

C c

China syndrome, a condition in which the radioactive fuel of a nuclear reactor overheats to such a high temperature that the core burns through its protective shield and deep into the earth: *In nuclear slang, "the China syndrome" could theoretically occur if the radioactive core of a nuclear plant were uncovered, allowing the searing heat of the core to melt through the steel pressure vessel, through the concrete bottom of the building, through the earth and "into China"* (New York Times).

chy|mo|pa|pa|in (kīʹmə pə pāʹən, -pīʹən), *n.* any one of various enzymes that break down proteins into simpler compounds; papain. Chymopapains are obtained from the papaya fruit and leaves. *In numerous orthopedic clinics, . . . chymopapain (sold in grocery stores as a meat tenderizer), has been injected directly into prolapsed intervertebral discs. By partially digesting the disc material, the enzyme reduces pressure on nerve roots and thus eliminates pain* (Frank F. Mathews). [< *chyme* + *papain*]

cuisine min|ceur (maN sœr'), a style of French cooking that restricts the use of ingredients having high caloric content. [< French *cuisine minceur* cuisine of slimness]

D d

de|law|yer (dē lôʹyər), *v.t.* to remove the need for legal action or the use of lawyers in (some settlement or legal process): *In other areas, procedural reforms such as no-fault insurance offer ways to "delawyer" particular problems* (Thomas Ehrlich). *Several states have enthusiastically embraced "delawyering" proposals* (David C. Beckwith).

Dergue or **Dirgue** (dèrg, dirg), *n.* the ruling military council of Ethiopia, established after the deposition of Emperor Haile Selassie: *The military administration, the Dergue, has . . . announced a jargon-heavy political programme which included the rights to form political parties* (Manchester Guardian Weekly). [< Amharic *dergue, dirgue* (literally) committee]

die|so|hol (dēʹzə hôl, -hol), *n.* a mixture of diesel oil and ethyl alcohol, used as a fuel in diesel engines: *As prices for petroleum products rise the economics should become favorable for gasohol and for the diesel fuel-ethanol combination, called diesohol* (John Patrick Jordan). [< *dies*(el) + (alc)*ohol*]

dis|co (disʹkō), *n., pl.* **-cos,** *v.,* **-coed, -co|ing. — v.i.** U.S. to dance to disco music: *You can disco to your heart's content at Clark Center* (New York Post).

Dji|bou|ti|an (jə büʹtē ən), *adj., n. — adj.* of or belonging to Djibouti, a country in eastern Africa (formerly the French Territory of Afars and Issas), independent since 1977. — *n.* a native or inhabitant of Djibouti.

down|link (dounʹlingk'), *n.* the communications connection for the transmission of signals from a spacecraft or satellite to a ground station: *Italy achieved its first experimental geostationary communications capability, and went directly to the higher frequencies of 18 and 12 G Hz . . . The apparently reversed numerical sequence is due to the convention of giving the uplink frequency ahead of the downlink* (John F. Clark).

down|size (dounʹsīz'), *v.t.,* **-sized, -siz|ing.** to reduce in size; scale down: *For the 1978 model year, GM downsized its four intermediate cars . . . trimming their length by about 8 inches and their weight by up to 825 pounds* (David L. Lewis).

E e

e|co|fal|low (ēʹkə falʹō, ekʹə-), *n.* a system that combines crop rotation and reduced tillage to control the growth of weeds and conserve soil moisture: *Ecofallow markedly increased the grain yields of wheat and sorghum* (M. G. Boosalis). [< *eco-* + *fallow*]

en|cap|si|date (en kapʹsə dāt), *v.t.,* **-dat|ed, -dat|ing.** to enclose in the protein coat of a virus particle: *Once assembly begins the virion RNA will be sequestered . . . But since neither (-) strands nor coat protein mRNA are encapsidated . . . the production of virions can continue* (Nature). **—en|cap'si|da'tion,** *n.*

enhanced radiation weapon, a nuclear weapon designed to release large amounts of high-energy neutron radiation with lesser blast effects; neutron bomb: *Regular tactical nuclear weapons create more thermal and blast damage, and leave greater amounts of residual radiation, and thus such weapons are claimed to be inferior by proponents of enhanced radiation weapons . . . . Some of those in opposition to the enhanced radiation weapons suggested that it is immoral to design a weapon to kill persons but to spare property* (Robert M. Lawrence).

ERW (no periods), enhanced radiation weapon.

external fertilization, the fertilization of an egg, especially a human ovum, outside the body, usually by the introduction of sperm into an egg cell surgically removed from an ovary: *The so-called test-tube babies were of course not monsters but simply ordinary babies produced by external fertilization* (John Newell). *Some clergymen saw no ethical problems in external fertilization: others called it interference with nature* (Albin Krebs).

F f

fac|tion² (fak'shən), *n.* a story, description or other narrative based on facts but written as fiction; writing that combines fact and fiction: [*Alex*] *Haley maintained that he had created a work of "faction," historical material made readable by fictional embellishment* (Philip Kopper). [blend of *fact* and *fiction*]

fe|to|scope (fē'tə skōp), *n.* an instrument that permits direct visual observation of a fetus inside the womb: *Looking through a fetoscope, Yale's Dr. John Hobbins guides a hairlike needle into a blood vessel on a pregnant woman's placenta* (New York Times Magazine). [< *feto-* (< Latin *fētus* fetus) + English *-scope*]

flash|er (flash'ər), *n.* **2** *U.S. Slang.* a person who exposes himself indecently in public: *a compulsive flasher.*

fu|sion (fyü'zhən), *n.* **5** a blend of jazz and other popular musical styles; crossover: *Fusion enjoys a crucial advantage over mainstream and avant-garde jazz: it "crosses over" a wide range of formats* (Rolling Stone). [< Latin *fūsiō, -ōnis* < *fundere* pour, melt] **—fu'sion|a|ble,** *adj.*

G g

gas|o|hol (gas'ə hôl, -hol), *n.* **1** a mixture of gasoline and ethyl alcohol, used as a fuel in gasoline engines: *They say that widespread use of gasohol ... would do a lot to ease the energy crisis and cut pollution levels* (Tom Ferrel and Virginia Adams). **2 Gasohol,** a trademark for such a mixture. [< *gas²* + (alc)*ohol*]

gen|tri|fi|ca|tion (jen'trə fə kā'shən), *n.* the act or process of increasing the value of real estate in a neighborhood or other area by selling its houses to buyers of greater means than the present owners or tenants: *In Grimsby or Stoke-on-Trent, where the typical landlord owns only a house or two ... "gentrification" does not arise* (Manchester Guardian Weekly).

gen|tri|fy (jen'trə fī), *v.t.* **-fied, -fy|ing.** to increase the value of real estate in (a neighborhood or area) by gentrification: *It was useless to buy up substandard housing, when councils put most of their improvement budget into gentrifying their own older estates* (London Sunday Times).

gray|wat|er (grā'wôt'ər, -wot'-), *n.* wastewater, such as that from a sink, bathtub, or washing machine, that does not drain from a toilet or other heavily contaminating source of pollution: *In most countries, graywater simply goes into the backyard. Open ditches direct the water to trees or crops that need watering* (Peter Warshall).

green belt, trees and shrubs planted around an area of little rainfall to protect it from becoming desert land: *These projects include establishment of green belts in the northern and southern fringes of the Sahara, to ... allow regeneration of some of the region's lost farming land* (Science News).

H h

ha|vu|rah (нä vü'rä), *n., pl.* **ha|vu|rot** (нä vü rōt'). any one of a number of small groups of American Jews that meet informally for prayer sessions, meals, and classes or discussions on Judaism: *While havurah members do not necessarily live together or pool their finances, they share an intense commitment to making religion part of everyday living* (Time). [< Hebrew *hābhurāh* fellowship < *hābhēr* friend, comrade]

hes|i|fla|tion (hez'ə flā'shən), *n.* a condition in which continuous inflation is combined with a wavering rate of business and industrial growth. [blend of *hesitation* and *inflation*]

hu|mung|ous (hyü mung'gəs), *adj.* unusually large or great in any way; impossible to measure by ordinary standards; colossal; gigantic.

hy|phen|ate (hī'fə nāt), *v.,* **-at|ed, -at|ing,** *adj., n.* **2** *Informal.* a person who has more than one job or fills more than one position, especially in the creative arts: *He [Robert Redford] is the most recent and successful example of a burgeoning new Hollywood hyphenate, the actor-producer* (Mel Gussow).

I i

ink-jet (ingk'jet'), *adj.* of or having to do with a high-speed printing process using jets of ink broken up into electrically charged droplets that form letters and pictures on paper in a magnetic field regulated by a computer: *Ink-jet printers have to be used in conjunction with a computer* (New Scientist). *The ink-jet machines are appearing where high speed or automated typing is required* (Richard K. Pefley).

I.R.A. or **IRA³** (no periods), Individual Retirement Account (a pension fund, established by an individual not enrolled in a company or union pension plan, into which a person deposits wages and defers paying tax on them until withdrawals begin): *With an I.R.A., a person can put 15 percent of his earnings each year up to a [specified] maximum in a special account and build up an untaxed nest egg until normal retirement age* (New York Times).

K k

Kam|pu|che|an (kam'pú chē'ən), *adj.* of or having to do with Kampuchea, the official name of Cambodia.

killer bee, 1 a black honeybee of Africa, noted for its sensitivity and aggressive reaction to disturbances of its hive. It was imported to Brazil in 1956 and accidentally released to migrate and breed with native bees. *The "killer bee" ... is also a hard worker and an excellent producer of honey* (George Alexander). **2** any one of numerous hybrid varieties of honeybee, developed from the African killer bee and native South American bees; Brazilian bee. Some varieties are noted for their aggressive behavior.

knee|cap|ping (nē'kap'ing), *n.* the act or practice of shooting a person in the knee or leg as a form of punishment or terrorism: *The execution or kneecapping of informers ... has evolved from the old Irish custom of cattle houghing* (Maclean's).

L l

lifeboat ethic, a principle of conduct which asserts that in a situation of peril priorities should be assigned according to urgency or expediency: *The Age of Scarcity and accompanying new 'lifeboat ethic' threatens some basic American beliefs ... and heightens the conflict between rich and poor* (Richard J. Barnet).

link|age (ling'kij), *n.* **4** the policy or practice of having some aspect of the relations between two countries dependent upon the success or failure of another aspect of their relations.

liquid protein, a preparation of concentrated protein processed mainly from gelatin, as in cowhide, and once recommended as a food substitute to reduce weight: *Analyses of liquid protein products ... suggest a deficiency of essential minerals and nutrients would occur if the products were consumed in place of natural foods* (Julie Ann Miller).

love-bomb|ing (luv'bom'ing), *n.* the practice of overwhelming potential recruits into a cult with a show of warm fellowship, concern, and affection: *The attractant consists of deception in the form of love-bombing and a contrived appeal to the subject's idealistic and altruistic impulses* (Melvin S. Finstein).

low|rid|er (lō'rī'dər), *n.* a person who takes part in lowriding.

low|rid|ing (lō'ri'ding), *n.* a practice of lowering the clearance of a car to within a few inches of the ground. The style is to cruise slowly and exhibit a lavishly decorated automobile.

M m

MAD (mad), *n.* mutual assured destruction: *Called MAD ... the doctrine holds that peace is best maintained by threatening to obliterate an entire enemy society in retaliation for a nuclear attack* (Time).

min|i|se|ries (min'ē sir'ēz), *n., pl.* **-ries.** a short serial, especially on television: *Miniseries—a series of programs that would end after six, eight, 10 or whatever number [of programs] the writers feel necessary ... to tell one complete story* (TV Guide).

mi|rac|u|lin (mə rak'yə lin), *n.* the taste-modifying protein of the miracle fruit, isolated for use as a sweetener and for research into the mechanism of taste: *A glycoprotein of comparatively small molecular size, ... miraculin possesses no taste itself. If, however, a person ingests miraculin and then sometime later eats a sour, acid food, that food will taste sweet* (Magnus Pyke). [< *miracul*(ous) + *-in²*]

mo|nen|sin (mō nen'sən), *n.* a product of fermentation resulting from the action of a species of streptomyces. Monensin

---

Pronunciation Key: hat, āge, cãre, fär; let, ēqual, tėrm; it, īce; hot, ōpen, ôrder; oil, out; cup, put, rüle; child; long; thin; ᴛHen; zh, measure; ə represents **a** in about, **e** in taken, **i** in pencil, **o** in lemon, **u** in circus.

is used as an additive to feed for beef cattle to inhibit the formation of certain gases which promotes the absorption of energy from feed. It is also noted for its ability to carry ions across lipid barriers. *Monensin and DES can reduce total feed requirements by as much as 25 percent* (Science). [< (*Streptomyces cinna*) *monensis,* the species of streptomyces + -in²]

N n

nu|cle|o|som|al (nü′klē ə sō′məl, nyü′-), *adj.* of or having to do with a nucleosome or nucleosomes.

nu|cle|o|some (nü′klē ə sōm, nyü′-), *n.* the basic structural unit of chromatin: *Each nucleosome is roughly spherical, about 100 A (10 nm) in diameter, and consists of 8 histone molecules and about 200 pairs of DNA* (Bruce A. J. Ponder). *The discovery of the nucleosome was a great advance in understanding chromosome structure* (Eugene R. Katz). [< *nucleo-* + *-some³*]

number (num′bər) *n., v.* **do a number on,** *U.S. Slang.* **a** to make fun of; kid: *Fearless Johnny Carson . . . did a number on his new boss, NBC president Fred Silverman . . . with this line: "Freddy Silverman has just canceled his mother"* (New York Post). **b** to mislead; deceive: *The wife was shaken. "If I'm doing a number on the kid, I want to know about it,"* Mrs. Braun said (Janet Malcolm).

O o

o|pi|oid (ō′pē oid), *n.* any synthetic drug that resembles an opiate in its effects: *It [methadone] is a narcotic—an "opioid"—for in action it is fundamentally similar to morphine or heroin, and it is fully as addictive* (Horace Freeland Judson). [< *opi*(ate) + *-oid*]

or|thot|ic (ôr thot′ik), *adj., n.* —*n.* a device providing artificial support for an impaired joint or muscle of the leg or foot.

P p

particle beam, **1** a concentrated flow of charged nuclear particles: *Particle beams have been essential research tools for [studying] the structure of the atom and its constituent particles* (New York Times). **2** a directed, high-energy stream of such particles, used as a weapon; death ray: *Particle beams fired from the ground or space at close to the speed of light . . . have been suggested as a means of stopping enemy nuclear missiles* (New York Post).

passive smoking, the inhaling of smoke from other people's cigarettes, cigars, and pipes: *Passive smoking can injure the health of . . . people with chronic heart and lung diseases and allergies to tobacco smoke* (Jane E. Brody).

phal|lo|crat (fal′ə krat), *n.* a believer in the superiority of the male sex; male chauvinist. [< French *phallocrate*] —**phal|lo|crat′ic,** *adj.*

pri|or|i|tize (prī ôr′ə tīz, -or′-), *v.t.,* **-tized, -tiz|ing.** to arrange in order of importance: *The persons attending the Quarterly Parish meeting Wednesday night all prioritized these goals* (Elizabeth Kent). [< *priority* + *-ize*]

proximity talks, negotiations between belligerent countries or other disputing parties who occupy separate quarters in some confined area, such as a building, while a third party moves between them acting as a mediator: *He [Hafez al-Assad] again sank a U.S. proposal for Arab-Israeli "proximity" talks during the September UN General Assembly meeting* (F. Nicholas Willard).

psychic healing, the alleviation or healing of disease or its symptoms by belief in the effects of the laying on of hands: *Of all the parapsychological arts, psychic healing is the one that has the greatest impact on the lives of the general public* (Peter Gwynne).

R r

recreational vehicle, a vehicle used for recreational activities, such as a camper, trailer, or dune buggy.

rec|vee (rek′vē′), *n. U.S. Informal.* a vehicle used for recreational activities, such as a camper or trailer; recreational vehicle: *The travel trailer is the most popular of all the recvees* (Norman Strung).

ret|ro² (ret′rō), *n., adj.* — *n.* a revival, as of the fashion, music, or plays, of earlier decades, especially in France: *The Group TSE's productions . . . have been in the vanguard of the French vogue for "retro"* (Manchester Guardian Weekly). —*adj.* characteristic of or belonging to such a revival. [< French *rétro* < Latin *retrō* backward]

role model, a person whose behavior, especially that exhibited in a particular capacity, serves as a model or standard for another person to follow: *I am unclear what a "role model" is, but those who used the term seemed to be saying that teachers are people children tend to emulate* (Russell Baker).

S s

San|di|nis|ta (san′də nēs′tə), *n.* a member of a guerrilla organization of Nicaragua: *In October the Sandinistas . . . launched a major offensive with the declared intention of overthrowing the Somoza regime and establishing a broadly based democracy* (Henry Webb, Jr.). [< Spanish *Sandinista* < Augusto César *Sandino,* Nicaraguan nationalist leader murdered in 1933 + *-ista* -ist]

SOMPA (som′pə), *n.* System of Multicultural Pluralistic Assessment (an intelligence test that compares individual scores with the scores of others from similar cultural backgrounds to compensate for the cultural bias of standard IQ tests): *The SOMPA technique would remove the "retarded" stigma from many children but leaves them in a position where they still need special educational attention* (Edward B. Fiske).

spe|cies|ism (spē′shēz iz əm), *n.* discrimination in favor of one species of animal over another, especially in regard to the misuse or exploitation of various animals by human beings.

super slurper, a material that absorbs several thousand times its weight in water or some solution of water. Super slurpers are made by combining starch molecules with synthetic polymers. *The U.S. Department of Agriculture (USDA) increased the*

absorbability of its super slurper almost threefold. The newest modified version of this substance soaks up 5,000 times its weight of water (Frederick C. Price).

syn|gas (sin′gas′), *n.* synthetic gas made especially from low-grade coal: *Becoming a feedstock for "syngas" would open a major new potential for coal, especially the now stymied high-sulfur varieties* (Time). [< *syn*(thetic) + *gas¹*]

T t

tail|gate (tāl′gāt′), *n., v.,* **2** *U.S.* to serve or eat a meal or refreshments on the tailgate of a station wagon: *Tailgating started . . . at Ivy League games, where alumni would serve genteel picnics from the backs of their station wagons* (Time).

test-tube baby, **1** (formerly) a baby that is conceived and develops outside the womb. **2** a baby conceived outside the womb that develops as a fetus after implantation in the womb: *The world's first test-tube baby, a girl, was born by Caesarean section to Lesley Brown just before midnight, on July 25 [1978], at Oldham and District General Hospital, Greater Manchester [England]. She weighed 5 pounds, 12 ounces* (T. J. O. Hickey). **3** a baby conceived through test-tube means.

tur|bo|pause (tėr′bō pôz′), *n.* an area in which atmospheric turbulence ceases, especially such an area at the base of the thermosphere: *At the so-called turbopause this mixing [of gases] effectively ceases and the helium is released. Thus, if the turbopause falls in altitude, more helium rises to the upper atmosphere* (New Scientist). *Important to an understanding of the [Venusian] atmosphere is the turbopause, apparently about 144 km above the surface* (Science News).

U u

urban homesteading, a program of the U.S. government to restore run-down urban areas by offering ownership of abandoned or neglected housing in return for repairing a building to suitable condition and living in it for a specified length of time: *Urban homesteading offers abandoned or foreclosed housing, free or at nominal cost, to those agreeing to rehabilitate and occupy it over a given period* (Joseph P. Fried).

V v

vis|u|o|spa|tial (vizh′ú ō spā′shəl), *adj.* of the field of vision, especially as it involves the relationships of space and configuration of the objects seen: *Psychological testing has repeatedly shown that girls are in general better at verbal skills, whereas boys are better at visuospatial skills (such as jigsaw puzzles)* (London Times).

W w

weath|er|ize (weᴛн′ə rīz), *v.t.,* **-ized, -iz|ing.** *U.S.* to insulate against cold weather, especially in order to conserve fuel: *Operation Open City helps the poor weatherize their homes and apartments and prevent wasting of fuel* (New York Times). —**weath′er|i|za′tion,** *n.*

Index

A

Abdul Aziz ibn Saud, *79*–88
Abdul-Jabbar, Kareem, *79*–219, *78*–218
Abel, I.W., *78*–374
Aborigines, *79*–203; mines, *79*–404
Abortion: civil rights, *79*–258; Congress, *78*–263; Italy, *79*–363; Roman Catholic, *79*–468, *78*–465; state government, *79*–489, *78*–487; Supreme Court, *78*–491
Abruzzo, Ben, *79*–439
Abu Zaby, *78*–515
Academy of Motion Picture Arts and Sciences, *80*–207, *79*–210, *78*–208
Accidents. See **DISASTERS; SAFETY.**
Acheampong, Ignatius Kutu, *80*–338, *79*–337
Acid rain: Canada, *80*–235; coal, *80*–256; environment, *80*–313
Acidophilus milk, *78*–326
Acne: medicine, *80*–398
Acoustic microscope, *80*–220
Acrodermatitis enteropathica: nutrition, *79*–429
Acrylonitrile, *79*–247
ACTH: biochemistry, *78*–221
Acupuncture: *il.*, *79*–69
Adair, Paul (Red), *78*–432
Adamek, Donna, *80*–223, *78*–227
ADAMS, BROCK, *78*–174; Cabinet, *80*–229; *il.*, *80*–459, *79*–509; transportation, *78*–510
Additives, food: food, *79*–328, *78*–326; nutrition, *79*–428
Addonizio, Hugh J., *78*–417
Adélie penguin: *il.*, *78*–90
Aden. See **YEMEN (ADEN).**
Adenine arabinoside, *78*–394
Admissions policy: college costs, *Special Report*, *79*–84; education, *80*–302, *Focus*, *79*–43; Supreme Court, *Close-Up*, *79*–495
ADOLESCENT, *WBE*, *79*–548
Adoption, *79*–250, *78*–250
Adoula, Cyrille, *79*–285
Adrenocorticotropic hormone, *78*–221
Adrian, Lord Edgar Douglas, *78*–281
Adult education, *78*–147
Advanced Communications Service, *79*–263
ADVERTISING, *80*–176, *79*–176, *78*–174; architecture, *79*–191, *78*–190; courts, *78*–274; dentistry, *80*–287; food, *79*–328; magazine, *78*–39C; Supreme Court, *78*–492
Aegean Sea: courts, *79*–276
Aeppli, Oswald: *il.*, *78*–213
Aerosol spray: chemical industry, *79*–246; environment, *78*–313; Sweden, *79*–496
Aerospace industry. See **AVIATION; SPACE EXPLORATION.**
Afars and Issas, Territory of. See **DJIBOUTI.**
Affirmative action: civil rights, *79*–257; Detroit, *79*–294; education, *79*–305, *78*–303; *Focus*, *79*–43; Supreme Court, *80*–491, *78*–491, *Close-Up*, *79*–495
Affirmed, *80*–350, *79*–347
AFGHANISTAN, *80*–177, *79*–177, *78*–175; Asia, *80*–196, *79*–199, *78*–197; Middle East, *80*–400
AFRICA, *80*–178, *79*–179, *78*–177; civil rights, *78*–256; *Close-Up*, *80*–183; mining, *80*–404; Russia, *79*–470, *78*–468; United Nations, *79*–514, *78*–515. See also entries for specific countries.
African elephant: conservation, *79*–273
African Methodist Episcopal Church, *80*–461, *79*–462, *78*–460
African Methodist Episcopal Zion Church, *80*–461, *79*–462, *78*–460
Afrifa, Akwasi A.: Ghana, *80*–338
Age discrimination, *79*–430
Age Discrimination in Employment Act, *78*–425; Congress, *79*–265; labor, *79*–373
Agent Orange, *80*–259
AGRICULTURE, *79*–183, *78*–181; archaeology, *79*–191; Asia, *79*–198; *Close-Up*, *79*–186; Congress, *78*–264; economics, *78*–299; Europe, *79*–321, *78*–320; Greece, *78*–341; Russia, *79*–471; St. Louis, *78*–470; water, *79*–526, *78*–527. See also **FARM AND FARMING.**
Agriculture, U. S. Department of: forest, *79*–332
Aid to Families with Dependent Children, *79*–481
Ain't Misbehavin': theater, *79*–504
Air Force, U.S., *80*–193, *79*–195, *78*–192
Air pollution: botany, *80*–222; Canada, *80*–235; chemical industry, *80*–242; coal, *80*–256; energy, *79*–313; environment, *80*–313, *79*–315, *78*–313; weather, *80*–525, *78*–530
Airbag: automobile, *80*–204; safety, *78*–469; transportation, *78*–510
Airlines. See **AVIATION.**
Airport: Boston, *78*–226; Chicago, *78*–249; St. Louis, *78*–470

Akiyoshi, Toshiko, *78*–413
Akron: building, *80*–226
AKUFFO, FREDERICK WILLIAM KWASI, *79*–187; Ghana, *80*–338, *79*–337
Alabama, *80*–487, *79*–490, *78*–488
Alaska: conservation, *80*–267, *79*–272, *78*–269; hunting, *80*–355, *79*–351; mining, *80*–404; state government, *80*–487, *79*–490, *78*–488
Alaska Highway: Canada, *78*–241; Yukon, *78*–535
Alaska pipeline: petroleum, *78*–436
ALBANIA, *80*–185, *79*–187, *78*–184; China, *79*–253, *78*–253; Europe, *80*–317, *79*–320, *78*–317
ALBERTA, *80*–185, *79*–188, *78*–185
Albuquerque, *80*–252
Alcan pipeline: Canada, *78*–241; Yukon, *79*–531, *78*–535
Alcoholic beverages: health, *80*–347; mental health, *79*–397; psychology, *80*–455; public health, *79*–457
Alcorta, Alfredo, *78*–431
Aleixandre, Vicente, *78*–420
Alemán, Juan: Argentina, *79*–193
Algae: botany, *80*–222
ALGERIA, *80*–185, *79*–188, *78*–185; Africa, *80*–180, *79*–180, *78*–178
al-Huss, Salim Ahmad: Lebanon, *80*–383, *79*–378
Ali, Muhammad, *80*–223, *79*–228, *78*–228
Alia, Queen: *il.*, *78*–282; Jordan, *78*–368
Alien. See **IMMIGRATION.**
All-African Conference of Churches, *79*–455
Allen, Bryan: *il.*, *78*–207; personalities, *80*–434; science, *80*–474
Allen, Clifford R., *79*–285
Allen, James B., *79*–285
ALLEN, WOODY, *79*–188; humor, *Special Report*, *79*–124; *il.*, *80*–66
Almirante Brown Station: *il.*, *78*–84
Alonso, Alicia: *il.*, *79*–284
Alpert, Herb, *80*–414
Altered state of consciousness: hypnosis, *Special Report*, *80*–70
Alvarez, Gregorio: Uruguay, *79*–521
Alves, Nito: Angola, *78*–186
Alvin: *il.*, *80*–138
Amazon Pact: Latin America, *79*–377; water, *79*–526
American Agriculture Movement, *78*–181
American Ballet Theatre, *80*–276, *79*–283, *78*–278
American Baptist Association, *80*–461, *79*–462, *78*–460
American Baptist Churches in the U.S.A., *80*–461, *79*–462, *78*–460
American Bar Association: advertising, *80*–175; courts, *80*–272, *79*–276, *78*–274
American Express Co.: publishing, *80*–456
American Federation of Teachers, *80*–301, *79*–307, *78*–305
American Hospital Association, *78*–175
American Indian. See **INDIAN, AMERICAN.**
American Indian Movement, *79*–353
American Institute of Architects: architecture, *80*–189, *79*–191, *78*–189
American Kennel Club, *80*–291, *79*–297, *78*–435
American Legion, *79*–264, *78*–262
AMERICAN LIBRARY ASSOCIATION, *80*–186, *79*–189, *78*–185; awards, *79*–211; literature for children, *79*–387, *78*–389
American Lutheran Church, The, *80*–461, *79*–462, *78*–460
American Medical Association, *78*–175
American Telephone and Telegraph Company: building, *79*–232; communications, *79*–263
Amin, Hafizullah: Afghanistan, *80*–177; Middle East, *80*–400
Amin Dada, Idi: Africa, *80*–179, *78*–177; civil rights, *78*–256; Tanzania, *79*–498; Uganda, *80*–512, *78*–514
Amino acids: biochemistry, *78*–221; chemistry, *80*–243
Amish: *il.*, *80*–455
Amnesty International: courts, *80*–271; Nobel Prizes, *78*–420
Amoco Cadiz: *il.*, *79*–315
AMOUZEGAR, JAMSHID, *78*–186; Iran, *78*–361
Amsterdam: *il.*, *78*–256
Amtrak: railroad, *80*–459, *78*–456; travel, *80*–507, *79*–511, *78*–512
Anchovy: *Special Report*, *80*–132; fishing industry, *79*–326
Andean Common Market, *78*–380
Andean Group, *80*–381
Anderson, Charles (Chic), *80*–279
Anderson, Eddie (Rochester), *78*–281
ANDERSON, JOHN B., *80*–186; Republican Party, *80*–464
Anderson, Marian: *il.*, *78*–433; music, classical, *78*–412

Anderson, Maxie, *79*–439
Anderson, Philip W., *78*–420
Andorra, *80*–317, *79*–320, *78*–317
Andras, Robert K., *79*–237
Andreotti, Giulio, *80*–366, *79*–362, *78*–364,
Andretti, Mario, *79*–207, *78*–204
ANDRUS, CECIL DALE, *78*–186; conservation, *80*–267, *79*–272, *78*–269; water, *78*–528
Anesthetics: dentistry, *80*–287; hypnosis, *Special Report*, *80*–79; zoo medicine, *Special Report*, *80*–100
Angel dust: drugs, *79*–298
Anglicans: Eastern Orthodox, *78*–296; Protestantism, *79*–455, *78*–451; Roman Catholic, *80*–468, *78*–466
ANGOLA, *79*–189, *78*–186; Africa, *80*–180, *79*–180, *78*–178; Russia, *79*–471; Zaire, *80*–531, *79*–531, *78*–535
Anguilla, *78*–531
Animal. See **AGRICULTURE; CAT; CONSERVATION; DOG; FARM AND FARMING; PET; WILDLIFE; ZOOLOGY; ZOOS AND AQUARIUMS.**
Annealer: electronics, *80*–307
Annie: *il.*, *78*–504
Annie Hall, *78*–188
ANTARCTICA, *79*–189, *78*–187; environment, *78*–312; New Zealand, *80*–420; *Special Report*, *78*–80
Anthony, Earl, *80*–222, *79*–228, *78*–227
ANTHROPOLOGY, *80*–187, *79*–190, *78*–188. See also **ARCHAEOLOGY.**
Anticancer drugs: *Close-Up*, *79*–395
Antidepressant drug, *80*–399
Antiochian Orthodox Christian Archdiocese of North America, The, *80*–461, *79*–462, *78*–460
Antitrust laws: publishing, *79*–457
Antivirus drug: medicine, *78*–394
Anturane: medicine, *79*–396
Apartheid: Roman Catholic, *78*–464; South Africa, *79*–482; United Nations, *78*–515; Venda, *80*–519
Ape: zoology, *79*–532
Apocalypse Now: *il.*, *80*–406
Appalachians: geology, *80*–336
Aquaculture, *79*–326
Aquariums. See **ZOOS AND AQUARIUMS.**
Aquino, Benigno S., Jr., *80*–441, *78*–439
Ara-A: medicine, *78*–394
Arab Economic Unity Council, *79*–404
Arabia. See **MIDDLE EAST; SAUDI ARABIA; YEMEN (ADEN; SANA).**
Arabian oryx, *79*–534
Arabs: Egypt, *80*–303, *79*–306; Iraq, *79*–360; Israel, *80*–364, *79*–361, *78*–362; Jordan, *80*–369, *79*–366, *78*–368; Lebanon, *78*–380; Libya, *78*–382; Middle East, *80*–400, *79*–400, *78*–400; religion, *79*–462; Russia, *80*–470; Saudi Arabia, *80*–472, *79*–474, *Special Report*, *78*–87; Sudan, *80*–490, *78*–491; Syria, *79*–497, *78*–495; Tunisia, *80*–510, *78*–516; United Nations, *80*–513, *78*–516; Yemen (Aden), *78*–531
Arafat, Yasir, *80*–369, *78*–368; Austria, *80*–202
Arber, Werner, *79*–425
Archaebacteria: biology, *79*–222, *78*–222
Archaeological Conservation Act, *80*–474
ARCHAEOLOGY, *80*–188, *79*–191, *78*–189; museum, *79*–410. See also **ANTHROPOLOGY.**
Archery: sports, *80*–483, *79*–485, *78*–484
ARCHITECTURE, *80*–189, *79*–191, *78*–190; awards, *80*–207, *79*–210. See also **BUILDING AND CONSTRUCTION.**
ARGENTINA, *80*–191, *79*–193, *78*–191; Canada, *80*–236; courts, *79*–276; Latin America, *80*–380, *79*–377, *78*–378; soccer, *79*–479
Ariane: space exploration, *80*–481
Arias, Arnulfo: Panama, *79*–434
Arizona, *80*–487, *79*–490, *78*–488; hospital, *79*–348
Arizona State University: football, *80*–330
Arkansas, *80*–487, *79*–490, *78*–488
Arlington Heights, Ill.: housing, *78*–349
ARMED FORCES, *80*–191, *79*–194, *78*–192; Europe, *80*–318, *79*–321, *78*–320; Latin America, *78*–380; President of the U.S., *79*–452. See also entries for specific continents and countries.
Armenian Church of America, Diocese of the, *80*–461, *79*–462, *78*–460
Army, U.S., *80*–193, *79*–195, *78*–193
Army Corps of Engineers, *78*–314
Aromaticity: chemistry, *79*–247
Arrington, Richard: *il.*, *80*–306
Arson: Boston, *78*–226; insurance, *80*–359
Artificial gene: biochemistry, *78*–220
Artificial insemination: zoo medicine, *Special Report*, *80*–113
Artificial sweetener, *80*–327, *79*–298, *78*–290
Arts: awards, *80*–207, *79*–210, *78*–208; crime, *80*–273; *Focus*, *79*–49, *78*–49; Perspective, *80*–169, *78*–171; photography, *79*–444, *78*–439; Saint Louis, *79*–473; San Francisco, *79*–

F

G

H

Acknowledgments

The publishers acknowledge the following sources for illustrations. Credits read from top to bottom, left to right, on their respective pages. An asterisk (*) denotes illustrations created exclusively for THE YEAR BOOK. All maps, charts, and diagrams were prepared by THE YEAR BOOK staff unless otherwise noted.

3	Steve Hale*
9	© 1979 Ledru, Sygma
10	© 1979 Alon Reininger, Contact; © 1979 J. Andanson, Sygma
11	© 1979 Martin A. Levick, Black Star; © 1979 Alain Dejean, Sygma; © 1979 Arthur Grace, Sygma
12	© 1979 Sygma
13	© 1979 Arthur Grace, Sygma; © Sipa Press from Black Star; © 1979 Ira Wyman, Sygma; © 1979 F. Darquennes, Sygma
14	© 1979 Alain Nogues, Sygma; © 1979 Peter Marlow, Sygma; © 1979 Arnold Zann, Black Star
15	© 1979 Alain Nogues, Sygma; © 1979 C. Simonpietri, Sygma
16	© 1979 Sipa Press from Black Star; © 1979 Dennis Brack, Black Star; © 1979 Giannini, Sygma
17	© 1979 Michael A. Norcia, Sygma; © 1979 Sipa Press from Black Star; © 1979 P. Breeze, Liaison
18	© 1979 Ken Hawkins, Sygma; © 1979 Sipa Press from Black Star; © 1979 Sipa Press from Black Star
19	© 1979 John Troha, Black Star; © 1979 Frank Alexander, Lensman
20	© 1979 Ledru, Sygma; © 1979 Stan Barouh, Lensman
21	© 1979 Dirck Halstead, Liaison
23	Steve Hale*
24	Steve Hale*; Steve Hale*; Steve Hale*; Steve Hale*; Arthur Grace, Sygma
25	Steve Hale*; Steve Hale*; Steve Hale*; Arthur Grace, Sygma
29	© 1979 Sepp Seitz, Woodfin Camp, Inc.; BBC Hulton Picture Library; Steve Hale*
31	© James R. Holland, Stock, Boston
33	© Owen Franken, Stock, Boston
34	Steve Hale*
35	© Bill Gillette, Stock, Boston
36	Martin A. Levick, Black Star
37	Steve Hale*, Martin A. Levick, Black Star
38-39	Steve Hale*
40	© 1979 Olivier Rebbot, Woodfin Camp, Inc.
42	Steve Hale*
43	Steve Hale*; © Arthur Grace, Stock, Boston
44	Steve Hale*
45	Dan Morrill*
46	© 1979 Annie Hagman, Contact; Steve Hale*
51	Polly McCann
52-53	Copyright © 1977 Twentieth Century-Fox Film Corporation. All rights reserved.
54	Culver; Copyright © 1950 Eagle Lion Films from Culver
55	Copyright © 1968 Metro-Goldwyn-Mayer Inc. from Jeff Rovin for SFXperts
56	Photo from WHEN WORLDS COLLIDE: Copyright © MCMLI by Paramount Picture Corporation. All Rights Reserved. From Culver; Copyright © 1961 American International Pictures from Jeff Rovin for SFXperts; Copyright © 1950 Eagle Lion Films from The Granger Collection; Copyright © 1964 American International Pictures from Jeff Rovin for SFXperts; Copyright © 1964 New Realm from Jeff Rovin for SFXperts
57	Copyright © 1966 Twentieth Century-Fox Film Corporation. All rights reserved. From Cinemabilia; Copyright © 1977 Twentieth Century-Fox Film Corporation. All rights reserved.
58	BBC Hulton Picture Library; Copyright © 1977 Twentieth Century-Fox Film Corporation. All rights reserved; Copyright © 1956 Loew's Incorporated from Photo Trends; Copyright © 1973 Metro Goldwyn-Mayer Inc.; Copyright © 1972 Universal City Studios from Jeff Rovin for SFXperts; Copyright © 1971 Warner Bros. Inc.
60	Copyright © 1960 Loew's Incorporated and Galaxy Films, Inc.
61	Copyright © 1979 Universal Studio Tours. All rights reserved.
63	Jeff Rovin for SFXperts; © Chris Springmann, Black Star; © Chris Springmann, Black Star
64	© King Features Syndicate/1935 Universal City Studios from The Granger Collection; Copyright © 1936 United Artists Corporation from Culver; Copyright © 1951 Twentieth Century-Fox Film Corporation. All rights reserved. From Culver; Copyright © 1936 United Artists Corporation from Jeff Rovin for SFXperts; Photograph from STAR TREK—The Motion Picture; Copyright © MCMLXXIX by Paramount Pictures Corporation. All Rights Reserved, the trade mark owner.
65	Copyright © 1977 Twentieth Century-Fox Film Corporation. All rights reserved.
66	Copyright © 1973 United Artists Corporation from John R. Hamilton, Globe Photos.
68	Copyright © 1930 Fox from Jeff Rovin for SFXperts; Copyright © 1936 United Artists Corporation from Bettmann Archive; Copyright © 1976 Metro-Goldwyn-Mayer Inc.
70-71	Gerry Contreras*
72-73	Steve Hale*
74	Bettmann Archive; Steve Hale*; Steve Hale*; Bettmann Archive
75	Steve Hale*; Bettmann Archive; Culver Pictures
76	Gerry Contreras*
78	Steve Hale*
81	Brent Jones*
83	Gerry Contreras*
84	James B. Maas from Deeper Into Hypnosis
86-97	Jet Propulsion Laboratory
98	San Diego Zoo
101	Bettmann Archive; San Diego Zoo
103	San Diego Zoo
104-105	Polly McCann
106	Gladys Porter Zoo
107	San Diego Zoo
109	Lincoln Park Zoo (Steve Hale*)
110	Gladys Porter Zoo; San Diego Zoo; San Diego Zoo
111	San Diego Zoo
113	Minnesota Zoological Garden
114	China Pictorial
116	Steve Hale*; Peter Bradt, ICON; Office of Representative John B. Anderson; Penelope Breese, Liaison; Jim Pickerell, Lensman; Steve Hale*; Steve Hale*; Office of Senator Robert J. Dole; Peter Bradt, ICON; The White House; The White House; David Burnett, Contact; Jack R. McKenney; Office of John B. Connally
119	United Press Int.
120	Karsh, Ottawa; Office of Senator Barry M. Goldwater; The White House; Historical Pictures Service
121	The White House; Office of Senator George S. McGovern; William Fitz-Patrick, The White House; The White House
122-123	Steve Hale*
124	Karl Schumacher, The White House; CBS News; Steve Hale*
128-129	© Ron Dorman, Bruce Coleman Inc.
131	William J. Cromie
132	Jean Helmer*
133	© Georg Gerster, Photo Researchers, Inc.
135	Woods Hole Oceanographic Institution; Charles K. Ross, Bedford Institute of Oceanography, Nova Scotia
136	© Herman J. Kokojan, Black Star
138-139	Woods Hole Oceanographic Institution; John M. Edmond, Massachusetts Institute of Technology
140-141	Jean Helmer*
142	© Van Bucher, Photo Researchers, Inc.
144-156	Gary Soszynski*
159	The Newberry Library, Chicago
161-171	George Suyeoka*; The Newberry Library, Chicago
175	U.S. Navy
176	The Advertising Council
177	Wildenberg, Sipa Press from Black Star
178-179	H. Villalobos, Gamma from Liaison
183	United Press Int.; Peter Jordan, Liaison
184-185	Wide World
187	© Larry Nighswander; Barney Taxel, NYT Pictures
188	© 1979 Kit Sagendorf, by permission of Saturday Review
190-193	Wide World
195	U.S. Navy
197	United Press Int.
198	Alain Dejean, Sygma
199	Ted Offret, University of Arizona
201	Australian Information Service
202-206	Wide World
211	Copyright 1979 by Herblock in The Washington Post
212-215	Wide World
217	United Press Int.
219	Wide World
222-224	United Press Int.
226	Keystone

A Preview of 1980

January

```
          1  2  3  4  5
 6  7  8  9 10 11 12
13 14 15 16 17 18 19
20 21 22 23 24 25 26
27 28 29 30 31
```

1 **New Year's Day.**
  St. Basil's Day, Eastern Orthodox feast day.
3 **96th Congress** convenes for second session.
6 **Epiphany,** 12th day of Christmas, celebrates visit of the Three Wise Men.
15 **Martin Luther King, Jr.'s Birthday,** celebrated in 15 states to honor the slain civil rights leader.
28 **Australia Day** commemorates Captain Arthur Phillip's landing in 1788 at site where Sydney now stands.

February

```
                1  2
 3  4  5  6  7  8  9
10 11 12 13 14 15 16
17 18 19 20 21 22 23
24 25 26 27 28 29
```

2 **Ground-Hog Day.** Legend says six weeks of winter weather will follow if ground hog sees its shadow.
8 **Boy Scouts of America Birthday Anniversary.**
12 **Abraham Lincoln's Birthday,** observed in 26 states.
13 **Olympic Winter Games** in Lake Placid, N.Y., through February 24.
14 **Saint Valentine's Day,** festival of romance and affection.
15 **Susan B. Anthony Day,** commemorates the birth of the suffragist leader.
16 **Chinese New Year,** begins year 4678 of ancient Chinese calendar, the Year of the Monkey.
18 **George Washington's Birthday,** according to law, is now legally celebrated by federal employees, the District of Columbia, and all 50 states on the third Monday in February. The actual anniversary is the 22nd.
19 **Mardi Gras,** last celebration before Lent, the penitential period that precedes Easter, observed in New Orleans and in many Roman Catholic countries.
20 **Ash Wednesday,** first day of Lent.
29 **Leap-Year Day** occurs every four years.

March

```
                      1
 2  3  4  5  6  7  8
 9 10 11 12 13 14 15
16 17 18 19 20 21 22
23 24 25 26 27 28 29
30 31
```

1 **Easter Seal Campaign** through April 6.
  Red Cross Month through March 31.
2 **Purim** commemorates the saving of Jews through the death of the ancient Persian despot Haman.
9 **Girl Scout Week,** through March 15, marks the organization's 68th birthday.
16 **Camp Fire Girls Birthday Week,** to March 22, marks 70th birthday of the organization.
17 **St. Patrick's Day,** honoring the patron saint of Ireland.
20 **First day of Spring,** 6:10 A.M., E.S.T.

April

```
       1  2  3  4  5
 6  7  8  9 10 11 12
13 14 15 16 17 18 19
20 21 22 23 24 25 26
27 28 29 30
```

1 **April Fool's Day.**
  Cancer Crusade lasts through April 30.
  Passover, or Pesah, first day, starting the 15th day of the Hebrew month of Nisan. The eight-day festival celebrates the deliverance of the ancient Jews from bondage in Egypt.
3 **Maundy Thursday,** celebrates Christ's injunction to love one another.
4 **Good Friday,** marks the death of Jesus on the cross. It is observed as a public holiday in 17 states.
6 **Easter Sunday,** commemorating the Resurrection of Jesus Christ.
13 **National Boys' Club Week** through April 19.
  National Library Week through April 19.
30 **Walpurgis Night,** according to legend, the night of the witches' Sabbath gathering in Germany's Harz Mountains.

May

```
                1  2  3
 4  5  6  7  8  9 10
11 12 13 14 15 16 17
18 19 20 21 22 23 24
25 26 27 28 29 30 31
```

1 **May Day,** observed as a festival of spring in many countries.
  Law Day, U.S.A.
3 **Kentucky Derby** at Churchill Downs, Louisville, Ky.
4 **National Family Week** through May 11.
  National Music Week through May 11.
11 **Mother's Day.**
15 **Ascension Day,** or Holy Thursday, 40 days after Easter Sunday, commemorating the ascent of Jesus into heaven.
21 **Shabuot,** Jewish Feast of Weeks, marks the revealing of the Ten Commandments to Moses on Mount Sinai.
25 **Whitsunday,** or Pentecost, the seventh Sunday after Easter, commemorates the descent of the Holy Spirit upon Jesus' 12 apostles.
26 **Memorial Day,** by law, is the last Monday in May.

June

```
 1  2  3  4  5  6  7
 8  9 10 11 12 13 14
15 16 17 18 19 20 21
22 23 24 25 26 27 28
29 30
```

2 **Stratford Festival,** drama and music, Ontario, Canada, through November 8.
6 **D-Day,** commemorates the day the Allies landed to assault the German-held continent of Europe in 1944.
8 **National Flag Week** through June 14.
14 **Queen's Official Birthday,** marked by trooping of the colors in London.
15 **Father's Day.**
21 **First day of Summer,** 12:47 A.M., E.S.T.
29 **Freedom Festival** through July 4.

July

		1	2	3	4	5
6	7	8	9	10	11	12
13	14	15	16	17	18	19
20	21	22	23	24	25	26
27	28	29	30	31		

1 **Dominion Day** (Canada) celebrates the confederation of the provinces in 1867.

4 **Independence Day,** marks Continental Congress' adoption of Declaration of Independence in 1776.

14 **Bastille Day** (France) commemorates popular uprising against Louis XVI in 1789 and seizure of the Bastille, the infamous French prison.
Ramadan, the ninth month of the Muslim calendar, begins, observed by fasting.

15 **Saint Swithin's Day.** According to legend, if it rains on this day, it will rain for 40 days.

19 **Olympic Summer Games** through August 3 in Moscow.

20 **Moon Day,** the anniversary of man's first landing on the moon in 1969.

22 **Tishah B'ab,** Jewish fast day, on ninth day of Hebrew month of Ab, marking Babylonians' destruction of the First Temple in Jerusalem in 587 B.C.; Roman destruction of the Second Temple in A.D. 70; and Roman suppression of Jewish revolt in A.D. 135.

25 **National Farm Safety Week** through July 31.

August

					1	2
3	4	5	6	7	8	9
10	11	12	13	14	15	16
17	18	19	20	21	22	23
24	25	26	27	28	29	30
31						

14 **V-J Day** (original) marks Allied victory over Japan in 1945.

15 **Feast of the Assumption,** Roman Catholic and Eastern Orthodox holy day, celebrates the ascent of the Virgin Mary into heaven.

17 **Edinburgh International Festival,** music, drama, and film, through September 6 in Scotland.

19 **National Aviation Day** commemorates the birthday of pioneer pilot Orville Wright.

26 **Women's Equality Day,** commemorating the ratification of the 19th Amendment giving women the vote.

September

	1	2	3	4	5	6
7	8	9	10	11	12	13
14	15	16	17	18	19	20
21	22	23	24	25	26	27
28	29	30				

1 **Labor Day** in the United States and Canada.

11 **Rosh Hashanah,** or Jewish New Year, the year 5741 beginning at sunset. It falls on the first day of the Hebrew month of Tishri, and lasts for two days.

20 **Yom Kippur,** or Day of Atonement, most solemn day in the Jewish calendar, marking the end of the period of penitence.

22 **First day of Autumn,** 4:09 P.M., E.S.T.

24 **Harvest Moon,** the full moon nearest the autumnal equinox of the sun, shines with special brilliance for several days and helps farmers in the Northern Hemisphere to get more field work done after sunset.

25 **Sukkot,** or Feast of Tabernacles, begins the nine-day Jewish observance, which originally celebrated the end of harvest season.

October

		1	2	3	4
5	6	7	8	9	10	11
12	13	14	15	16	17	18
19	20	21	22	23	24	25
26	27	28	29	30	31	

1 **Anniversary of the 1949 Chinese Communist Revolution,** China's national holiday.

5 **Fire Prevention Week** through October 11.
National 4-H Week through October 11.

9 **Leif Ericson Day,** honoring early Norse explorer of North America.

12 **National Handicapped Awareness Week** through October 18.
National Y-Teen Week through October 18.

13 **Columbus Day,** commemorates Columbus' discovery of America in 1492. Originally celebrated on October 12.
Thanksgiving Day, Canada.

19 **National Cleaner Air Week** through October 25.

31 **Halloween,** or All Hallows' Eve.
Reformation Day, celebrated by Protestants, marks the day in 1517 when Martin Luther nailed his Ninety-Five Theses of protest to to the door of a church in Wittenberg, Germany.
United Nations Children's Fund (UNICEF) Day.

November

							1
2	3	4	5	6	7	8
9	10	11	12	13	14	15
16	17	18	19	20	21	22
23	24	25	26	27	28	29
30						

1 **All Saints' Day,** observed by the Roman Catholic Church.

4 **Election Day,** United States.

5 **Guy Fawkes Day** (Great Britain), marks the failure of a plot to blow up King James I and Parliament in 1605 with ceremonial burning of Guy Fawkes in effigy.

11 **Veterans Day.**

16 **American Education Week** through November 22.

27 **Thanksgiving Day,** United States.

30 **Advent** begins; first of the four Sundays in the season before Christmas.

December

	1	2	3	4	5	6
7	8	9	10	11	12	13
14	15	16	17	18	19	20
21	22	23	24	25	26	27
28	29	30	31			

3 **Hanukkah,** or Feast of Lights, eight-day Jewish holiday beginning on the 25th day of the Hebrew month of Kislev that celebrates the Jewish defeat of the Syrian tyrant Antiochus IV in 165 B.C. and the rededication of the Temple in Jerusalem.

6 **Saint Nicholas Day,** when children in parts of Europe receive gifts.

10 **Nobel Prize Ceremony,** in Stockholm, Sweden, and Oslo, Norway.

15 **Bill of Rights Day,** marks the ratification of that document in 1791.

21 **First day of Winter,** 11:56 A.M., E.S.T.

25 **Christmas.**

26 **Boxing Day** in Canada and Great Britain.

31 **New Year's Eve.**

Cyclo-teacher® The easy-to-use learning system

Features hundreds of cycles from seven valuable learning areas

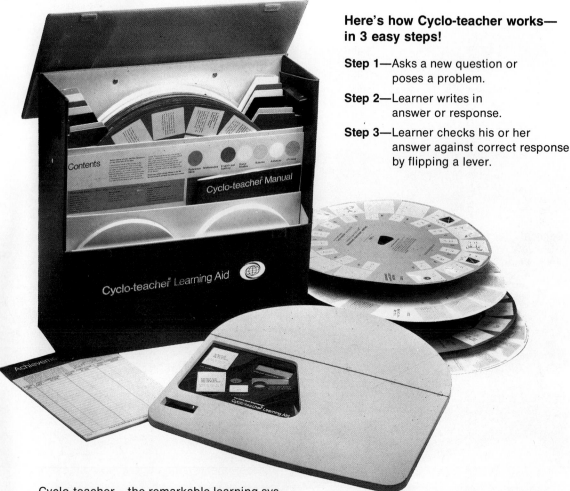

Here's how Cyclo-teacher works— in 3 easy steps!

Step 1—Asks a new question or poses a problem.

Step 2—Learner writes in answer or response.

Step 3—Learner checks his or her answer against correct response by flipping a lever.

Cyclo-teacher —the remarkable learning system based on the techniques of programmed instruction —comes right into your home to help stimulate and accelerate the learning of basic skills, concepts, and information. Housed in a specially designed file box are the Cyclo-teacher machine, Study Wheels, Answer Wheels, a Manual, a Contents and Instruction Card, and Achievement Record sheets.

Your child will find Cyclo-teacher to be a new and fascinating way to learn —much like playing a game. Only, Cyclo-teacher is much more than a game —it teaches new things

. . . reinforces learning . . . and challenges a youngster to go beyond!

Features hundreds of study cycles to meet the individual needs of students —your entire family —just as *Year Book* is a valuable learning aid. And, best of all, lets you track your own progress —advance at your own pace! Cyclo-teacher is available by writing us at the address below:

The World Book Year Book
Post Office Box 3564
Chicago, IL 60654

These beautiful bookstands-

specially designed to hold your entire program, including your editions of *Year Book*.

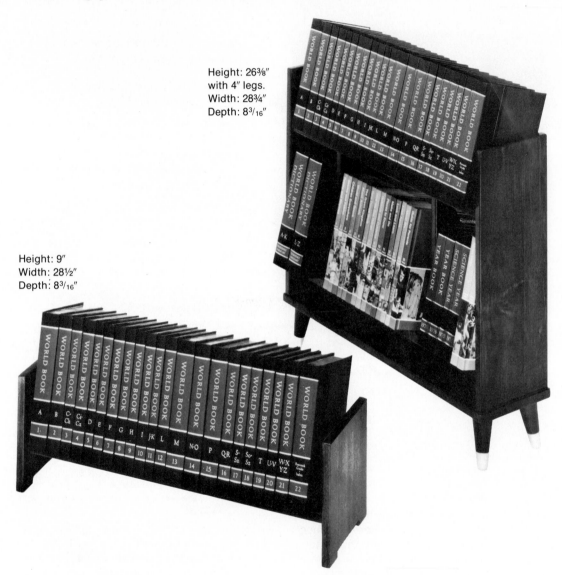

Height: 26⅜"
with 4" legs.
Width: 28¾"
Depth: 8³/₁₆"

Height: 9"
Width: 28½"
Depth: 8³/₁₆"

Most parents like having a convenient place to house their *Year Book* editions and their *World Book Encyclopedia*. A beautiful floor-model bookstand —constructed of solid hardwood —is available in either walnut or fruitwood finish.

You might prefer the attractive hardwood table racks, also available in either walnut or fruitwood finish. Let us know by writing us at the following address:

The World Book Year Book
Post Office Box 3564
Chicago, IL 60654